Scandinavia

written and researched by

Phil Lee, Lone Mouritsen,
James Procter and Neil Roland

with additional contributions by

Jules Brown, Mick Sinclair

and S. Andrew Spooner

ROUGH
GUIDES

www.roughguides.co

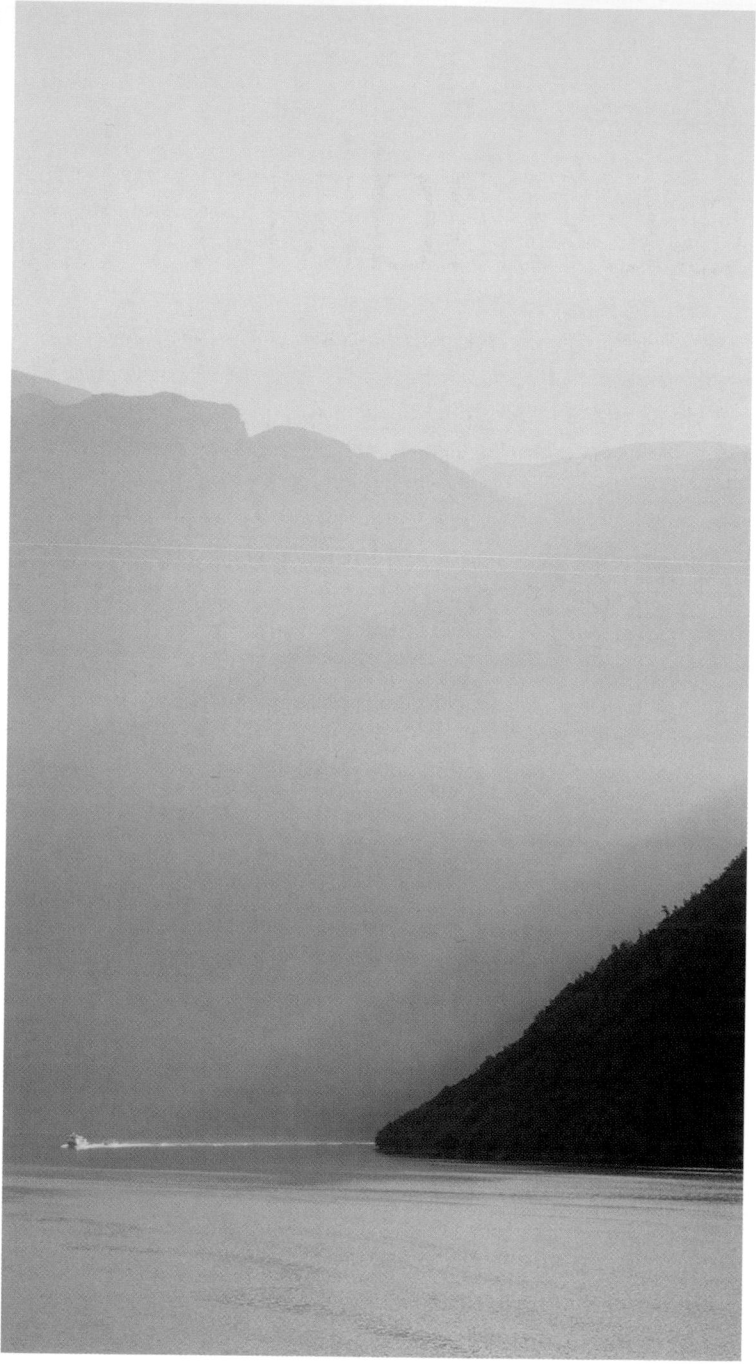

Introduction to
Scandinavia

Scandinavia – Denmark, Norway, Sweden and Finland – conjures up resonant images: wild, untamed lands, fjords, reindeer and the Midnight Sun; and wealthy, healthy, blue-eyed blondes enjoying life in a benevolent welfare state. The region holds some of Europe's most unspoilt terrain, and is certainly affluent by Western European standards, with a high quality of life and little poverty. But it's by no means paradise: there's a social conformity that can be stifling, and the problems of other industrialized countries – drug addiction, racism, street violence – are beginning to make themselves felt. Nonetheless, Scandinavia is an enthralling and rewarding region to explore. The larger part of the population clusters in the south, where there's all the culture, nightlife and action you'd expect, but with the exception of Denmark, these are large, often physically inhospitable countries. Rural traditions remain strong, not least in the great tracts of land above the Arctic Circle, where the Sámi peoples survive as they have done for thousands of years – by reindeer herding, hunting and fishing.

Historically, the Scandinavian countries have been closely entwined, though in spite of this they remain strikingly individual. Easy to reach and the best known of the Scandinavian countries, **Denmark** is the geographical and social bridge between Europe and Scandinavia. The Danes are much the most gregarious of the Nordic peoples, something manifest in the region's most relaxed and appealing capital, Copenhagen, and the decidedly more permissive attitude to alcohol.

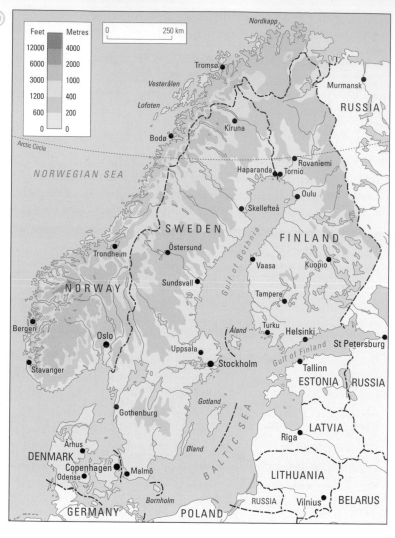

With great mountains, a remote and bluff northern coast and the mighty western fjords, **Norway**'s raw, often inaccessible landscapes can demand long, hard travel. Even by Scandinavian standards the country is sparsely populated, and people live in small communities along a coastline which stretches from the lower reaches of the North Sea right up to the Russian border.

The most "Scandinavian" country in the world's eyes, **Sweden** is afflu-ent and boasts a social system and consensus politics that are considered an enlightened model – though confidence in the country's institutions was shaken in the late 1990s by a short-lived economic slowdown combined with the fragmentation of old alliances. Travelling is simple enough, although Sweden has Scandinavia's least varied landscape – away from the southern cities and coastal regions an almost

> **Historically, the Scandinavian countries have been closely entwined, but in spite of this they remain strikingly individual**

unbroken swath of lakes, forests and hills, in which most Swedes have a second, peaceful, weekend home.

Perhaps the least known of the mainland Scandinavian countries, **Finland** was ruled for hundreds of years by the Swedes and then the Russians – the country became independent only at the beginning of the twentieth century and has grown into a vibrant, confident nation. Its vast coniferous

The sky at night

Weather permitting, Scandinavia's best free entertainment can be enjoyed by simply looking up to the heavens. From late May to mid-July, the Midnight Sun provides 24 hours of daylight – but to see the full effect, where the whole sun is visible at midnight, you'll need to be above the Arctic Circle, the imaginary line drawn at 66° 33' latitude which stretches across Norway, Sweden and Finland. Conversely, in winter, when there's often 24 hours of darkness, the aurora borealis, or northern lights, illuminate the Arctic sky. Caused by electronically charged particle streams from the sun hitting the earth's atmosphere, these spectacular arcs and waves of shimmering green-blue light are stronger the further north you go.

forests and great lake systems have produced a strong empathy between the Finns and the natural environment which is hard to ignore. Also, though Finland is undeniably Scandinavian and looks to the West for its lifestyle, there are, historically and culturally, a number of similarities with Eastern Europe.

Travelling in Scandinavia is easy. Public transport is efficient and well coordinated, there is a minimum of border formalities between the countries and excellent connections between all the main towns and cities: indeed, it's perfectly feasible to visit several, if not all, of the mainland countries on one trip. From Western Europe it's simplest to enter Denmark,

The Finnish sauna

One of the few Finnish words understood worldwide, sauna originated in the countryside. After toiling in the fields, workers would cleanse themselves by sweating profusely in a wooden hut heated by steam, generated by water thrown on hot stones. Today, saunas are an integral part of national culture and Finns of all ages can't get enough of them. A Finnish sauna is usually single-sex, nudity is pretty much compulsory and bathers must sit on sheets of paper or a board provided at the door to prevent sweat soaking into the benches. The end to a perfect sauna is a dip in a nearby lake, or, in winter, a refreshing roll in the snow.

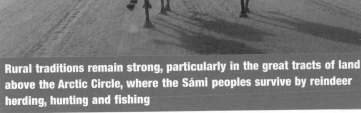

Rural traditions remain strong, particularly in the great tracts of land above the Arctic Circle, where the Sámi peoples survive by reindeer herding, hunting and fishing

from where you can continue northwards into Norway (by boat) or Sweden (by boat or train), the two countries separated by a long north–south border. From Sweden's east coast there are ferries across to Finland, as well as a land border between the two in the far north.

As for **costs**, the Scandinavian countries are expensive by north European standards, but not excessively so. Their reputation for high prices is largely based on the cost of consumables – from books to meals and beer – rather than more substantial items, particularly accommodation, where first-rate budget opportunities are ubiquitous.

When to go

Deciding **when to go** isn't easy since, except for Denmark, Scandinavia experiences intense seasonal changes. The short summers (roughly mid-June to mid-August) can be as hot as in any southern European resort, with high temperatures regularly recorded in Denmark, southern Norway and Sweden, and the Baltic islands. Even the northern areas of each country are temperate, and the whole of the Norwegian west coast, for example, is warmed by the Gulf Stream. Rain, though, is regular, and in the far north of Norway especially – and to a lesser extent in Sweden and Finland – summer temperatures can plunge extremely low at night, so campers need decent equipment for extended spells of sleeping out. One bonus this far north, though not exactly a boon to sleep, is the almost constant daylight provided by the Midnight Sun.

The **summer** is celebrated everywhere with a host of outdoor events and festivities, and is the time when all the facilities for travellers (tourist offices, hotel and transport discounts, summer timetables) are functioning. However, it's also the most crowded time to visit, as the Scandinavians are all on holiday, too: go either side of summer (late May/early June or September), when the weather is still reasonable, and you'll benefit from more

peace and space. Autumn, especially, is a beautiful time to travel, with the trees and hillsides turning golden brown in a matter of days.

In **winter**, from November to around late May, only Denmark retains a semblance of Western European weather, while the other countries suffer long, dark and extremely cold days. The cold may be severe, but it's crisp and sharp, never damp, and if you're well wrapped up the cities at least needn't be off limits – though, unless you're exceptionally hardy, the far north is best left to its own gloomy devices. You'll find broad climatic details in the introductions to each country; for mean temperatures all year round, check the **temperature chart** below.

Average temperatures °F

	Jan	Feb	Mar	Apr	May	June	July	Aug	Sept	Oot	Nov	Dec
Denmark												
Copenhagen	32	32	35	44	53	60	64	63	57	49	42	36
Norway												
Oslo	23	25	30	41	52	59	63	61	52	43	34	28
Bergen	35	35	37	43	50	55	59	59	54	46	41	37
Tromsø	26	25	28	32	38	48	54	54	45	37	32	28
Sweden												
Stockholm	27	30	30	39	53	57	64	62	51	45	40	34
Östersund	18	26	22	33	50	52	59	54	44	39	30	27
Haparanda	14	21	15	30	48	56	61	55	44	36	25	22
Finland												
Helsinki	22	21	26	37	48	58	63	61	53	43	35	28
Tampere	17	17	23	35	47	56	61	59	50	40	32	25
Ivalo	8	8	16	27	39	49	56	52	42	31	21	14

Note that these are *average temperatures*. The Gulf Stream can produce some very temperate year-round weather and, in summer, southern Scandinavia can be blisteringly hot. In winter, on the other hand, temperatures of -40°F are not unknown in the far north.

Sweden's fab four: ABBA

Having captured the world's attention by trouncing their Eurovision opponents with *Waterloo* in 1974, ABBA – lycra devotees Anni-Frid Lyngstad, Benny Andersson, Björn Ulvæus and Agnetha Fältskog – went on to become the biggest-selling group in the world, second only to Volvo as Sweden's largest export earner and topping the charts for a decade with hits such as *Mama Mia*, *Money Money Money* and *Dancing Queen* (the latter performed to celebrate the 1976 marriage of Swedish King Carl Gustaf). Though the group split some twenty years ago following the divorces of the two band-member couples, ABBA's phenomenal kitsch appeal has endured, spawning a host of tribute bands and a successful London-based musical, and ensuring that record sales remain remarkably healthy.

What to take

t's as well to give some thought as to **what to take** – and worth packing that bit more to stave off hardship later. Expect occasional rain throughout the summer and take a waterproof jacket and a spare sweater. A small, foldaway umbrella is useful, too. If camping, a warm sleeping bag and good walking shoes are vital (and useful, too, in sprawling cities and the flat southern lands). Mosquitoes are a pest in summer, especially further north and in lake regions, and some form of protective cream is essential. For winter travel, take as many layers as you can pack. Gloves, a hat or scarf that covers your face, thick socks and thermal underwear are all obligatory.

32

things not to miss

It's not possible to see everything that Scandinavia has to offer in one trip – and we don't suggest you try. What follows is a selective taste of the country's highlights: magnificent fjords, imposing castles, absorbing galleries and pristine medieval towns. It's arranged in five colour-coded categories, so that you can browse through to find the very best things to see, do and experience. All highlights have a page reference to take you into the guide, where you can find out more.

01 **Skagen, Denmark** Page **181** • Heather-topped sand dunes and yellow-painted houses play second fiddle to a slew of galleries displaying works from artists attracted here by the wonderful light.

03 The Munch Museum, Norway Page 246 • A huge wedge of work from the country's finest artist, including several versions of *The Scream*.

02 Holmenkollen ski jump, Norway Page 41 • From cross-country snowboarding to ski-jumping in Oslo, winter sports are a Norwegian national passion.

04 Skåne, Sweden Page 510 • The brilliantly hued southern countryside is a wonderfully scenic backdrop for a gentle summertime drive.

05 **Savonlinna Castle, Finland** Page **745** • Perched atop an island, this is the best preserved medieval castle in Scandinavia.

06 **Sauna, Finland** Page **756** • The traditional way to cleanse body and mind, saunas are best followed with an ice-cold dip in a lake or a roll in the snow.

07 Viking Ships Museum, Norway Page **244** • An excellent place to view Viking longships at close hand.

08 Danish pastry, Denmark Page **63** • These ubiquitous buns are known as "Viennese bread" in their home territory – buy them fresh from bakeries in any town or city.

09 Icehotel, Sweden Page **646** • Experience a night in one of the most famous hotels in the world – at a chilly -5ºC.

10 Fürstenburg Gallery, Sweden Page **488** • These gloriously evocative paintings by Sweden's finest nineteenth-century artists are the highlight of Gothenburg Art Museum.

11 Århus old town, Denmark Page **162** • Holding several worthwhile churches and museums, the tight cluster of narrow medieval streets is an atmospheric place for a wander.

12 Mandal beach, Norway Page **283** • Enclosed by rocky headlands and bordered with pine trees, this is the country's best place for an ocean swim.

13 **Husky safari, Finland** Page **781** • Sleigh through Lapland's silent snow-covered forests and across frozen lakes, and overnight in a wilderness cabin.

14 **Nimis, Sweden** Page **520** • Made entirely of driftwood, this extraordinary stairway-and-tower sculpture teeters toward the waters of the Kullen Peninsula.

15 **Århus nightlife, Denmark** Page **166** • With a host of excellent venues, Denmark's cultural capital is the best place in the country for a night out.

16 **Jotunheimen National Park, Norway** Page **268** • This craggy and severe mountain range is the most sumptuously beautiful example of Norway's wild mountain scenery.

17 **Nyhavn, Denmark** Page **95** • Best experienced at night, when the canalside restaurants and bars come into their own.

18 **Santa Claus Village, Finland** Page **773** • Log cabins, reindeer and copious amounts of snow make this *the* place to meet Mr Claus.

19 **Flåmsbana railway, Norway** Page **316** • Zigzagging down a mountainside and inching through hairpin tunnels, this precipitous ride is a thrilling experience.

20 **Grenen, Denmark** Page **182** • The meeting of the Skaggerak and Kattegat seas here makes suitably dramatic viewing.

21 **Pickled herring and a beer, Denmark** Page **62** • The ultimate Danish delicacies.

22 **Svalbard, Norway** Page **396** • Offering everything from glacier walks to snowmobile excursions, this archipelago in the Arctic Ocean is an impressively remote adventure tourism centre.

23 **Aurora borealis, Norway, Sweden and Finland** If conditions are right, these amazing technicolour displays are an unforgettable sight.

24 **Tivoli Gardens midnight fireworks, Denmark** Page **101** • These glorious pyrotechnics are the time-honoured way to wind up a day in Copenhagen.

25 **Nordkapp, Norway** Page **393** • This greyish-black hunk of slate, stuck at the end of a bare, wind-battered promontory, is mainland Europe's northernmost point – almost.

26 Kalmar Castle, Sweden Page **558** • Beautifully remodelled into a Renaissance Palace, this sensational twelfth-century stronghold lends a fairytale aspect to the Småland coast.

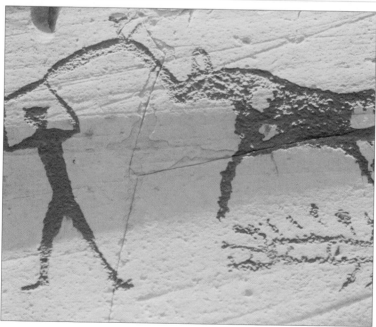

27 Alta rock carvings, Norway Page **383** • These prehistoric drawings provide an extraordinary reminder of north Norway's earliest peoples.

28 Vigelandsparken, Norway
Page **248** • Whatever you do, don't miss this phantasmagorical open-air sculpture park.

29 Gamla Stan, Sweden
Page **444** • A maze of medieval lanes and alleys that form the heart of the Swedish capital.

30 Inlandsbanan Railway, Sweden
Page **627** • A chance to experience the raw beauty of virgin forests and crystal-clear mountain streams close up.

31 **Whale-watching, Norway** Page **366** • Between late May and mid-September, safaris from remote Andenes can pretty much guarantee sightings.

32 **Louisiana Museum of Modern Art, Denmark** Page **114** • An outstanding collection housed in an equally arresting nineteenth-century villa overlooking the Øresund.

Contents

Using this Rough Guide

We've tried to make this Rough Guide a good read and easy to use. The book is divided into four main sections, and you should be able to find whatever you want in one of them.

Colour section

The front colour section offers a quick survey of Scandinavia. The **introduction** aims to give you a feel for the place, with suggestions on when to go and what to take. Next, our authors round up their favourite aspects of Scandinavia in the **things not to miss** section – whether it's great food, amazing sights or a spectacular festival. Right after this comes a full contents list.

Basics

The Basics section covers all the **pre-departure** nitty-gritty to help you plan your trip. This is where to find out which airlines fly to Scandinavia, what to do about money and insurance, Internet access, food, public transport, car rental and overland travel – in fact just about every piece of **general practical information** you might need.

Guide

This is the heart of the Rough Guide, divided into user-friendly chapters, each of which covers a specific country. Every chapter starts with a list of **highlights** and an **introduction** that helps you to decide where to go, depending on your time and budget. The introduction prefaces the **minibasics** section, which is full of specific practicalities. This is followed by a brief **history**, plus a language section and a list of books for further reading. Chapters then move on to **detailed coverage** of your destination. Introductions to the various towns and smaller regions within each chapter should help you plan your itinerary. We start most **town accounts** with information on arrival and accommodation, followed by a tour of the sights, and finally reviews of places to eat and drink, and details of nightlife. Longer accounts also have a directory of practical listings. Each chapter concludes with **public transport** details.

Index + small print

Apart from a **full index**, which includes maps as well as places, this section covers publishing information, credits and acknowledgements, and also has our contact details in case you want to send in updates and corrections to the book – or suggestions as to how we might improve it.

Map and chapter list

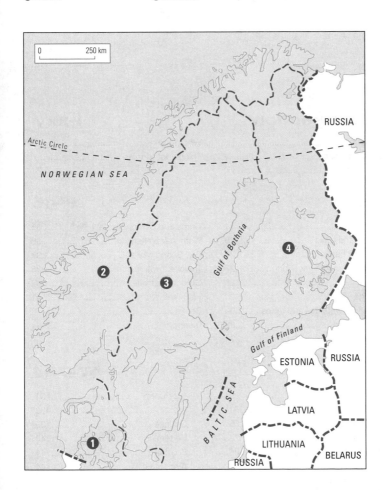

Contents

Index and small print

785–796

Map symbols

maps are listed in the full index using coloured text

Motorway		] [	Tunnel/bridge
Major road		∴	Ruin
Minor road		♦	General point of interest
Pedestrianized street		🅿	Fuel station
Steps		🛐	Monastery/convent
Path		⊙	Statue/memorial
Railway		ⓘ	Tourist office
Wall		⊠	Post office
Ferry route		☏	Telephone
Waterway		@	Internet access
Canal		P	Parking
Chapter division boundary		🏊	Swimming pool
International boundary		✡	Synagogue
Provincial/regional boundary		★	Bus stop
▲ Mountain peak		⊞	Hospital
✈ Airport		◉	Accommodation
♜ Castle		▣	Restaurant/café/bar
🏛 Stately home		▬	Building
⚲ Church		⊞	Church (town maps)
♟ Museum		⊞	Cemetery
Lighthouse			Park/National Park
Ski trails			Forest
Campsite			Sand/beach
Viewpoint			Glacier

7

Basics

Basics

Getting there

From the UK and Ireland, the most convenient way of getting to Scandinavia is to fly – there's a good selection of flights and the cheapest fares are often less expensive than the long and arduous journey by train or coach. There are a few ferry services from Britain to Denmark, Norway and Sweden, though these can be pretty costly in high season and are really only worth considering if you're taking your car. From North America, a handful of airlines fly direct to the Scandinavian capitals, though it may be cheaper to route via London, picking up a budget flight onwards from there. There are no direct flights from Canada, Australia or New Zealand.

Airfares depend on the **season**, with the highest from (roughly) early June to mid-September, when the weather is best; fares drop during the "shoulder" seasons – mid-September to early November and mid-April to early June – and you'll get the best prices during the low season, November through to April (excluding Christmas and New Year, when prices are hiked up and seats are at a premium). Bear in mind, though, that ticket prices from the UK are not subject to seasonal changes to the extent that they are in North America. Note also that flying on weekends is generally more expensive; price ranges quoted below assume midweek travel.

You can often cut costs by going through a **specialist flight agent** – either a consolidator, who buys up blocks of tickets from the airlines and sells them at a discount, or a **discount agent**, who in addition to dealing with discounted flights may also offer special student and youth fares and a range of other travel-related services such as insurance, rail passes, car rentals, tours and the like. Bear in mind, though, that penalties for changing your plans on discounted tickets can be stiff. Some agents specialize in **charter flights**, which may be cheaper than scheduled services, but again departure dates are fixed and withdrawal penalties are high. Don't automatically assume that tickets purchased through a travel specialist will be cheapest – once you get a quote, check with the airlines and you may turn up an even better deal.

Students might be able to find cheaper flights through the major student travel agencies, such as Council Travel, STA Travel or, for Canadian students, Travel CUTS (see relevant sections for details).

If you are travelling to Scandinavia as part of a longer trip, consider buying a **Round-the-World** (RTW) ticket, although since Scandinavia is not one of the more obvious destinations for round-the-world travellers, you'll probably have to have a custom-designed RTW ticket assembled for you by a travel agent, which is more expensive than an off-the-shelf RTW ticket.

Air passes in Scandinavia

Visit Scandinavia The SAS Visit Scandinavia Air Pass comes in the form of discount coupons for air travel within Norway, Sweden, Denmark and Finland. It can only be purchased in conjunction with an international flight on SAS in your home country. The coupons are valid for three months from arrival and cost £50–80 depending on the distance and route.

Nordic Pass Operated by Finnair (summer only) and only available once you are in Finland (call Finnair reservations on ☎02/0314 0160 for more information), this is valid for travel in Finland, Norway, Denmark and Sweden. Coupons are around £60 each.

Booking flights online

Many airlines and discount travel websites offer you the opportunity to **book tickets online**, cutting out the costs of agents and middlemen. Good deals can often be found through discount or auction sites, as well as through the airlines' own websites.

Online booking agents and general travel sites

ⓦ **www.cheapflights.com** Bookings from the UK and Ireland only. Flight deals, travel agents, plus links to other travel sites.

ⓦ **www.cheaptickets.com** Discount flight specialists.

ⓦ **www.etn.nl/discount.htm** A hub of consolidator and discount agent Web links, maintained by the nonprofit European Travel Network.

ⓦ **www.expedia.com** Discount airfares, all-airline search engine and daily deals.

ⓦ **www.flyaow.com** Online air travel info and reservations site.

ⓦ **www.gaytravel.com** Gay online travel agent, concentrating mostly on accommodation.

ⓦ **www.geocities.com/thavery2000** Has an extensive list of airline toll-free numbers (US only) and websites.

ⓦ **www.hotwire.com** Bookings from the US only. Last-minute savings of up to forty percent on regular published fares. Travellers must be at least 18 and there are no refunds, transfers or changes allowed. Log-in required.

ⓦ **www.lastminute.com** Offers good last-minute holiday package and flight-only deals.

ⓦ **www.priceline.com** Name-your-own-price website that has deals at around forty percent off standard fares. You cannot specify flight times (although you do specify dates) and the tickets are non-refundable, non-transferable and non-changeable.

ⓦ **www.skyauction.com** Bookings from the US only. Auctions tickets and travel packages using a "second bid" scheme. The best strategy is to bid the maximum you're willing to pay, since if you win you'll pay just enough to beat the runner-up regardless of your maximum bid.

ⓦ **www.skydeals.co.uk**. Discount flight-only specialists for worldwide destinations.

ⓦ **www.smilinjack.com/airlines.htm** Lists an up-to-date compilation of airline website addresses.

ⓦ **www.travelocity.com** Destination guides, hot Web fares and best deals for car hire, accommodation and lodging as well as fares. Provides access to the travel agent system SABRE, the most comprehensive central reservations system in the US.

ⓦ **www.travelshop.com.au** Australian website offering discounted flights, packages, insurance, online bookings.

ⓦ **travel.yahoo.com** Incorporates a lot of Rough Guide material in its coverage of destination countries and cities across the world, with information about places to eat and sleep etc.

Flights from Britain

Airfares from the UK to Scandinavia continue to drop as new operators join the fray. The best starting point for cheap deals is often the **classified sections** in the Sunday newspapers (*The Sunday Times* especially) or, if you live in London, *Time Out* magazine or the *Evening Standard*. Special offers are often advertised in many newspapers' weekend travel supplements, or, if you can travel at short notice, Ceefax lists a large number of travel agents touting last-minute discounted tickets. Better still, all major airlines have **websites** giving up-to-the-minute information about timetables, fares and special offers, while various other travel sites will signpost you to the booking agent or airline offering the lowest current prices. Failing that, go straight to a **discount flight agent** like STA Travel (see p.14); they specialize in youth flights, and generally have good deals if you're under 26 or a student, as well as ordinary discounted tickets if you're not. It's worth checking their websites for special offers too.

It's also worth contacting the major **airlines** – British Airways, SAS (the airline of Denmark, Norway and Sweden), Maersk (the Danish airline) or Finnair – directly. All offer various discounts and special deals, such as SAS's "Rock Bottom" and (slightly more expensive) "Super Saver" tickets, plus discounted fares for under-26s and over-65s, though the latter is only available on certain destinations. Discount tickets do, however, tend to carry restrictions: they must often be booked at least seven days in advance, you must stay abroad at least one Saturday night, and you can't usually change your return flight date.

Special offers and discounted tickets apart, the **scheduled fares** of the major airlines are pretty well matched; the cheaper seats tend to be found on smaller carriers such as Maersk and British Midland. Low-cost carriers such as Go (Copenhagen only) and Ryanair (several Scandinavian destinations) offer the best deals. It's worth noting though that the cheapest airlines often don't fly to a city's main airport, which can in some cases mean a two-hour bus ride to the city centre – Ryanair flights to Stockholm, for example, land at Skavsta airport, about 100km from the capital. When no direct flights are available, airlines can usually offer you **connections** to Scandinavian airports via a Scandinavian partner (British Midland with SAS, or British Airways with Sun Air, for example).

You might also consider buying an **air pass**, usually sold only in conjunction with tickets from Britain, which can be useful for getting around the vast expanses of Scandinavia. Contact the relevant airline or a travel agent for more information.

To Denmark

The Scandinavian country closest to Britain, Denmark also has the greatest number of flights, with daily services from London to Copenhagen (1hr 45min) with SAS, British Airways, British Midland, Go and Maersk Air and regular flights with a number of airlines (see p.14 for a full list) to other destinations like Billund, Århus and Esbjerg. Denmark is also well served by **regional airports** in the UK, including services from **Aberdeen** to Esbjerg (with British Midland), **Birmingham** to Copenhagen (SAS and Maersk Air Ltd), **Glasgow** to Copenhagen (British Midland), **Manchester** to Copenhagen (SAS), and **Newcastle** to Copenhagen (British Airways). All these carriers operate at least one flight a day, though services may be reduced at weekends.

The lowest regular **fares** to Copenhagen at the time of writing were with Go and Maersk Air at around £100 return, though Go will often have limited seats at discount fares of around £70. Ryanair often has special offers for around £70 or lower on its flights to Århus and Esbjerg; alternatively you could get a good deal on a Ryanair flight to

Malmö (Sturup) in Sweden, from where it's only an hour or so to Copenhagen via the Øresunds Link (see p.84). Otherwise, expect to pay in the region of £125, including tax, for a discounted return ticket from Britain to Denmark bought directly from SAS, British Midland or British Airways (though watch out for occasional offers that bring fares down below £100 return).

To Norway

There's a good choice of direct flights **from London** to **Oslo** with SAS, British Airways and British Midland, while Ryanair flies twice daily to Oslo (Torp). SAS also flies from Heathrow to **Stavanger** and **Bergen**. The other Norwegian destination connected to London is **Kristiansand**, with six Maersk Air flights a week from Gatwick via Copenhagen.

There's a reasonably good choice of flights from **regional airports** too. Ryanair flies from **Glasgow** to Oslo, and SAS flies to Stavanger from **Aberdeen** and **Newcastle**. British Airways operates daily direct flights from Manchester to Oslo, and SAS flies between **Manchester** and Oslo via Copenhagen.

The cheapest **fares** at present are to Oslo with Ryanair (from as low as £70 return). Expect to spend around £130 inclusive of taxes to Oslo on most other carriers, and to pay more if flying from regional airports. As ever, you'll need to book well in advance and have flexible arrangements to take advantage of the cheapest fares.

To Sweden

Flying to Sweden, the choice of routes is not as wide as you might expect, though routes **from London** to Stockholm and Gothenburg are well served. There are ample flights **to Stockholm** with SAS, Finnair, British Midland and British Airways, while Ryanair has several daily services to Stockholm (either Västerås or Skavsta, both around 100km from the centre) from Stansted. Ryanair also flies daily to **Malmö** and **Gothenburg**, while SAS operates daily flights from Heathrow to Gothenburg. Apart from London, **Manchester** has direct flights to Stockholm with Finnair, British Airways and SAS; and to Gothenburg with British Airways. From **Birmingham**, Maersk Air Ltd offers direct flights to Stockholm and Gothenburg.

The cheapest **fares** are currently with Ryanair (from £70 return to Malmö and from £100 return to Stockholm). Otherwise, expect to pay upwards of £130 return.

To Finland

Finnair offers a good choice of flights to Finland, with several services daily **from London to Helsinki**. British Airways also fly to Helsinki (five daily from Heathrow; two daily from Gatwick). From **Manchester** there are daily services to Helsinki on Finnair and British Airways. No other British airports have direct flights to Finland, though you can arrange connecting flights through SAS, Maersk, British Midland and British Airways, among others.

Discount fares go for around £205 return, though special offers may bring this figure down to as low as £140 at certain times of the year (usually Jan–March). There are also charter flights to Lapland during the winter, particularly around Christmas – check with the specialist tour operators listed on p.15.

Airlines in Britain

Braathens SAFE c/o KLM and SAS (see below for details) ⓦ www.braathens.no. Newcastle to Stavanger.
British Airways ☎ 0845/773 3377, ⓦ www.ba.com. London Heathrow and Gatwick to Billund, Copenhagen, Oslo, Stavanger, Stockholm, Gothenburg and Helsinki; Manchester to Helsinki, Oslo and Stockholm; Newcastle to Copenhagen.
British Midland ☎ 0870/607 0555, ⓦ www.flybmi.com. London to Oslo, Stavanger, Gothenburg, Stockholm and Copenhagen. Aberdeen to Esbjerg and Glasgow to Copenhagen.
Finnair ☎ 020/7408 1222, ⓦ www.finnair.com. London Heathrow and Manchester to Helsinki and Stockholm.
Go ☎ 0870/607 6543, ⓦ www.go-fly.com. Online and telephone booking only. Two to three flights daily from London Stansted to Copenhagen.
KLM ☎ 0870/507 4074, ⓦ www.klmuk.com. London Heathrow, London City or Aberdeen to Copenhagen, Billund, Helsinki, Stockholm and Oslo, all via Amsterdam.
Maersk Air ☎ 020/7333 0066, ⓦ www.maersk-air.com. London Gatwick to Copenhagen and Billund,

and Kristiansand (via Copenhagen). The sister company, **Maersk Air Ltd** (☎ 0121/743 9090), flies from Birmingham to Copenhagen, Stockholm and Gothenburg.
Ryanair ☎ 0871/246 0000, ⓦ www.ryanair.com. Daily flights from London Stansted to Stockholm (Västerås and Skavsta), Oslo (Torp), Gothenburg City, Århus, Esbjerg and Malmö (Sturup). Also Glasgow to Oslo.
SAS Scandinavian Airlines ☎ 0845/607 2772, ⓦ www.scandinavian.net. London Heathrow direct to Copenhagen, Oslo, Stavanger, Stockholm, Gothenburg and Bergen with connections on to several other Scandinavian cities. Also Manchester to Copenhagen, Stockholm and Oslo (the latter via Copenhagen); Birmingham to Copenhagen; Aberdeen to Stavanger; Newcastle to Stavanger.

Flight and travel agents

Bridge the World ☎ 0870/444 7474, ⓦ www.bridgetheworld.com. Specializing in round-the-world tickets, with good deals aimed at the backpacker market.
Destination Group ☎ 020/7400 7045, ⓦ www.destination-group.com. Good discount airfares.
Flightbookers ☎ 0870/010 7000, ⓦ www.ebookers.com. Low fares on an extensive selection of scheduled flights.
North South Travel ☎ 01245/608 291, ⓦ www.northsouthtravel.co.uk. Friendly, competitive travel agency, offering discounted fares worldwide – profits are used to support projects in the developing world, especially the promotion of sustainable tourism.
STA Travel ☎ 0870/1600 599, ⓦ www.statravel.co.uk. Worldwide specialists in low-cost flights and tours for students and under-26s, though other customers welcome.
Top Deck ☎ 020/7244 8000, ⓦ www.topdecktravel.co.uk. Long-established agent dealing in discount flights.
Trailfinders ☎ 020/7628 7628, ⓦ www.trailfinders.com. One of the best-informed and most efficient agents for independent travellers.
Travel Cuts ☎ 020/7255 2082 or 7255 1944, ⓦ www.travelcuts.co.uk. Canadian company specializing in budget, student and youth travel and round-the-world tickets.

Organized tours

Don't be put off by the idea of an **inclusive package**. In such an expensive part of Europe, it can be the cheapest way to do things, and may also be the only way to reach remote parts of the region at inhospitable times of year. If you just want to see one city and its environs, then **city breaks** invariably work out cheaper than arranging the same trip independently. Prices include return travel, usually by plane, and accommodation (with breakfast), with most operators offering a range from hostel to luxury-class hotel. As a broad guide, two-night hotel stays in one of the Scandinavian capital cities will cost £250–300 per person out of season. If you stay for a week, rates per night fall considerably.

There are also an increasing number of operators offering **special-interest holidays** to Scandinavia, from camping tours to Arctic cruises (see p.18). Prices for these are a good deal higher, but are generally excellent value for money.

Specialist tour operators

Aeroscope ☎01608/650 103. One- and two-centre city breaks.
Anglers' World Holidays ☎01246/221 717, ⊛www.anglers-world.co.uk. Angling holidays in Denmark and Sweden.
Arctic Experience/Discover the World ☎01737/218 800, ⊛www.discover-the-world .co.uk. Specialist adventure tours including whale-watching in Norway and dog-sledging in Lapland.
Ashley Tours ☎01886/888 335. Specializing in jazz tours with group tours to the Gothenburg Jazz Festival.
Crystal Holidays ☎08701/606 040, ⊛www.crystalholidays.co.uk. City breaks, country tours and Norwegian skiing holidays.
DA Study Tours ☎01383/882 200. Coach tours for culture vultures in Denmark, Norway and Sweden.
DFDS Seaways ☎0870 5333 000, ⊛www.dfdsseaways.co.uk. Breaks in Denmark and Sweden, including two nights on board ship and two or three nights abroad – good deals out of season.
Emagine ☎01942/262 662, ⊛www.emagine-travel.co.uk. Tailor-made Finnish and Swedish holidays, Helsinki city breaks, cruises and winter trips to Lapland.
Inntravel ☎01653/629 010, ⊛www.inntravel.co.uk. Outdoor holidays in Norway including skiing, walking, fjord cruises, and whale- and reindeer-watching.
Insight ☎0990/143 433, ⊛www.insighttours.com. City tours and "Spectacular Scandinavia and its fjords" – a 15-day trip for £1390.
King's Angling Holidays ☎01708/453 043, ⊛www.kingsanglingholidays.co.uk. Angling in Denmark and Sweden.

ScanMeridian ☎020/7431 5322, ⊛www.scanmeridian.co.uk. Scandinavia specialists offering city breaks, fly-drive, cottage holidays, cruises and tailor-made trips.
Scantours ☎020/7839 2927, ⊛www.scantoursuk.com. Scandinavia specialists with a huge range of packages and tailor-made holidays.
Specialised Tours ☎01342/712 785, ⊛www.specialisedtours.com. Specialists in Scandinavia offering independent, tailor-made or group city breaks and holidays.
Taber Holidays/Norway Only ☎01274/594 642, ⊛www.taberhols.co.uk. Norwegian specialists with dozens of options, including self-catering holidays, fjord cruises, motoring tours and guided coach trips.

From Ireland

The easiest route to Scandinavia from Ireland is on one of the twice daily SAS flights **from Dublin to Copenhagen** or **Stockholm**, from where you can connect to virtually anywhere in the region. You can also fly with Aer Lingus to Stockholm, Helsinki and Copenhagen (about five weekly in summer; fewer in winter), via London Heathrow, while Finnair flies direct from Dublin to Helsinki (four weekly).

Official **fares** to Copenhagen start at around €228 plus tax for a midweek rock-bottom economy fare, although special offers are sometimes available, and a discount agent (see p.12) may have youth, student or discounted tickets for even less. To really do it on the cheap you could find one of the numerous special deals to London with a carrier like Ryanair and then take advantage of the more competitive airfares available from there (see opposite). SAS passengers flying from the Republic can also purchase the Visit Scandinavia Air Pass (see box on p.11).

From Belfast, there are no direct flights to Scandinavia, and your best bet is probably to fly via London or Dublin with British Midland or SAS. **Fares** to Copenhagen, Stockholm or Oslo usually start at about €250 for an economy return, €300 to Helsinki, but special offers can take these as low as €190 return to Copenhagen, and just over €250 to other Scandinavian capitals. Failing that, you should be able to get a reasonable deal through a discount agent, either in Northern Ireland or in mainland Britain.

If you are planning to travel from Ireland **by train**, the best option by far is to buy an InterRail pass (see p.22). Getting to Scandinavia **by coach** involves going to London and picking up a connection there. For motorists, combined **ferry** fares covering Celtic Sea and North Sea crossings are generally available through the contacts below.

Airlines in Ireland

Aer Lingus UK ☎0845/084 4444, Republic of Ireland ☎0818/365 000, ⊛www.aerlingus.ie. Dublin to Copenhagen, Helsinki and Stockholm via London Heathrow.

British Airways UK ☎0845/773 3377, Republic of Ireland ☎1800/626 747, ⊛www.ba.com. Flights from Dublin and Cork to London for onward connections.

British Midland UK ☎0870/607 0555, Republic of Ireland ☎01/407 3036, ⊛www.flybmi.com. Dublin to London for onward connections to Stockholm; or Dublin to Manchester for onward connections to Copenhagen.

Finnair ☎020/7408 1222, Republic of Ireland ☎01/844 6565, ⊛www.finnair.com. Direct flights from Dublin to Helsinki four times weekly.

Ryanair UK ☎0871/246 0000, Republic of Ireland ☎01/609 7800, ⊛www.ryanair.com. Flights from Dublin to London Stansted from where Ryanair flies to Stockholm, Oslo, Århus, Esbjerg, Malmö and Gothenburg.

SAS Scandinavian Airlines UK ☎0845/607 2772, Republic of Ireland ☎01/844 5440, ⊛www.scandinavian.net. Direct flights from Dublin to Copenhagen and Stockholm.

Organized tours

Not many operators run **package tours** to Scandinavia from Ireland, although where available these may be the cheapest way to travel, and sometimes the only way to reach remote parts of the region at inhospitable times of year. Likewise, city-break packages may well work out cheaper than arranging the same trip independently. British operators are listed on p.15, those based in Ireland are included in the list on below.

Flight, travel agents and tour operators in Ireland

Aran Travel International Galway ☎091/562 595, ⊛homepages.iol.ie/~arantvl/aranmain.htm. Good-value flights to all parts of the world.

CIE Tours International Dublin ☎01/703 1888, ⊛www.cietours.ie. General flight and tour agent.

Co-op Travel Care Belfast ☎0870/902 0033, ⊛www.travelcareonline.com. Flights and holidays around the world.

Crystal Holidays ☎01/433 1080. City breaks and skiing holidays.

Go Holidays Dublin ☎01/874 4126, ⊛www.goholidays.ie. Package tour specialists with one- or two-centre city-breaks to Copenhagen, Helsinki and Stockholm.

Joe Walsh Tours Dublin ☎01/676 0991, ⊛www.joewalshtours.ie. General budget fares agent.

McCarthy's Travel Cork ☎021/427 0127, ⊛www.mccarthystravel.ie. General flight agent.

Neenan Travel Dublin ☎01/607 9900, ⊛www.neenantrav.ie. Specialists in European city breaks.

Premier Travel Derry ☎028/7126 3333, ⊛www.premiertravel.uk.com. Discount flight specialists.

Rosetta Travel Belfast ☎028/9064 4996, ⊛www.rosettatravel.com. Flight and holiday agent.

Student & Group Travel Dublin ☎01/677 7834. Student and group specialists, mostly to Europe.

Trailfinders Dublin ☎01/677 7888, ⊛www.trailfinders.ie. One of the best-informed and most efficient agents for independent travellers; produces a very useful quarterly magazine worth scrutinizing for round-the-world routes.

Ferry contacts

Irish Ferries UK ☎0870/517 1717, Northern Ireland ☎0800/0182 211, Republic of Ireland ☎1890/313 131, ⊛www.irishferries.com. Dublin to Holyhead; Rosslare to Pembroke, Cherbourg and Roscoff. Continental services March to end Sept. Irish Agents for DFDS Seaways.

Norse Merchant Ferries UK ☎0870/600 4321, Republic of Ireland ☎01/819 2999, ⊛www.norsemerchant.com. Belfast and Dublin to Liverpool.

P&O Irish Sea UK ☎0870/242 4777, Republic of Ireland ☎1800/409 049, ⊛www.poirishsea.com. Larne to Cairnryan and to Fleetwood; Dublin to Liverpool.

Sea Cat UK ☎0870/5523 523, Republic of Ireland ☎1800/551 743, ⊛www.seacat.co.uk. Belfast to Stranraer, to Heysham, to Troon, and to Isle of Man; Dublin to Liverpool and to Isle of Man.

Flights from the US and Canada

From **North America**, Scandinavia is well served by numerous American and European airlines, though only SAS, American, Delta and Finnair provide direct flights. If you are visiting more than one country, an air pass might be your best bet.

The majority of flights to Scandinavia from North America involve **changing planes** in London, Reykjavik, Brussels, Amsterdam, Paris, Frankfurt or Zurich – and if you don't live in one of the gateway cities for flights in North America, you might have to change planes more than once. **Direct flights** are obviously preferable, and if you can be fairly flexible with your departure dates you should be able to take advantage of the special promotional fares offered regularly by the airlines. **Fares** to Copenhagen, Oslo and Stockholm are fairly similar, whichever carrier you choose, though it's still worth shopping around. Flights to Helsinki tend to be more expensive, unless you fly with Finnair, in which case the difference is minimal.

From New York you can fly direct to Copenhagen, Stockholm and Oslo on SAS, to Helsinki on Finnair, and to Stockholm on Delta (journey time from 7hr 30min to over 10hr on an indirect flight); SAS also flies from **Washington DC** to Copenhagen. Fares from the east coast are US$900–1000 round-trip in high season, US$450–550 in low season. **From Chicago**, American Airlines fly direct to Stockholm (journey time from 8hr 30min to at least 11hr on an indirect flight), while SAS flies direct to both Stockholm and Copenhagen. Round-trip fares are US$950–1100 in high season, US$450–500 in low. **From Seattle**, SAS flies direct to Copenhagen; fares are around US$1100–1300 (high season), US$550–600 (low). Fares are similar **from Los Angeles and San Francisco**, though there are no direct flights from here to Scandinavia.

You'll also need to change planes if travelling **from Canada**, from where flying time can vary between 9–13hr from Toronto, and 13–18hr from Vancouver, depending on connections. You might consider taking a cheap flight to New York or Chicago and continuing from there. Fares from Toronto or Montréal are Can$1500–1650 (high season), Can$900–1200 (low). From Vancouver, fares are around Can$1950 (high season), Can$1250 (low). It's worth considering the direct SAS flight from Seattle to Copenhagen (see p.18). If you're thinking about getting

around Scandinavia by air, check out the **Visit Scandinavia Air Pass** offered by SAS (see box on p.11). If fares to Scandinavia seem high, you might want to consider flying to **London**, one of the cheapest European cities to get to, and taking a flight, train or ferry on to Scandinavia (see p.12).

Airlines

Air Canada ☎1-888/247-2262, ⊛www.aircanada.ca. Daily from Toronto (with connections from Vancouver) to Frankfurt and Zurich, and five to seven weekly to Paris, with onward connections to major Scandinavian cities.

Air France US ☎1-800/237-2747, ⊛www.airfrance.com, Canada ☎1-800/667-2747, ⊛www.airfrance.ca. Daily from many North American cities to Paris, with connecting flights to major Scandinavian cities.

American Airlines ☎1-800/433-7300, ⊛www.aa.com. Daily from Chicago direct to Stockholm.

British Airways ☎1-800/247-9297, ⊛www.british-airways.com. Daily flights from 22 North American cities to London, with onward connections to major Scandinavian cities.

British Midland ☎1-800/788-0555, ⊛www.flybmi.com. Flights to London with onward connections to destinations in Scandinavia.

Continental Airlines domestic ☎1-800/523-3273, international ☎1-800/231-0856, ⊛www.continental.com. Daily flights between various major North American cities and European cities with connections to Scandinavia.

Delta Air Lines domestic ☎1-800/221-1212, international ☎1-800/241-4141, ⊛www.delta.com. Daily direct flights from New York (JFK) to Stockholm.

Finnair ☎1-800/950-5000, ⊛www.finnair.com. Direct flights to Helsinki from New York; frequency varies with the season.

Icelandair ☎1-800/223-5500, ⊛www.icelandair.com. Daily direct flights to Reykjavik from New York, Baltimore, Boston and Minneapolis plus two weekly from Orlando and Halifax, with onward connections to Oslo, Stockholm and Helsinki. Some flights allow a three-night stopover in Reykjavik.

Lufthansa US ☎1-800/645-3880, Canada ☎1-800/563-5954, ⊛www.lufthansa-usa.com. Daily flights from major North American cities via Frankfurt to Scandinavia.

Northwest/KLM Airlines domestic ☎1-800/225-2525, international ☎1-800/447-4747, ⊛www.nwa.com, ⊛www.klm.com. Flights from major North American cities to Scandinavia via Amsterdam.

SAS (Scandinavian Airlines) ☎1-800/221-2350, ⊛www.scandinavian.net. Daily direct flights to Copenhagen, Stockholm and Oslo from New York (Newark); to Stockholm and Copenhagen from Chicago; to Copenhagen from Seattle and Washington DC.
Swiss ☎1-877/359-7947, ⊛www.swiss.com. Daily to Zurich from Atlanta, Boston, Chicago, Cincinnati, Los Angeles, Miami, Newark, New York (JFK) and Montréal, with connections to Scandinavia.
Virgin Atlantic Airways ☎1-800/862-8621, ⊛www.virgin-atlantic.com. Daily from various US cities to London, with onward connections to Scandinavia.

Discount travel companies in North America

Airtech ☎212/219-7000, ⊛www.airtech.com. Standby seat broker; also deals in consolidator fares.
Airtreks.com ☎1-877-AIRTREKS or 415/912-5600, ⊛www.airtreks.com. Round-the-world and Circle Pacific tickets. The website features an interactive database that lets you build and price your own round-the-world itinerary.
Council Travel ☎1-800/2COUNCIL, ⊛www.counciltravel.com. Nationwide organization that mostly specializes in student/budget travel. Flights from the US only. Owned by STA Travel.
Educational Travel Center ☎1-800/747-5551 or 608/256-5551, ⊛www.edtrav.com. Student/youth discount agent.
New Frontiers ☎1-800/677-0720 or 310/670-7318, ⊛www.newfrontiers.com. French discount-travel firm based in New York City. Other branches in Los Angeles, San Francisco and Québec City.
Skylink US ☎1-800/247-6659 or 212/573-8980, Canada ☎1-800/759-5465, ⊛www.skylinkus.com. Consolidator.
STA Travel ☎1-800/781-4040, ⊛www.sta-travel.com. Worldwide specialists in independent travel; also student IDs, travel insurance, car rental, rail passes, etc.
Student Flights ☎1-800/255-8000 or 480/951-1177, ⊛www.isecard.com. Student/youth fares, student IDs.
TFI Tours ☎1-800/745-8000 or 212/736-1140, ⊛www.lowestairprice.com. Consolidator.
Travac ☎1-800/TRAV-800, ⊛www.thetravelsite.com. Consolidator and charter broker with offices in New York and Orlando.
Travelers Advantage ☎1-877/259-2691, ⊛www.travelersadvantage.com. Discount travel club; annual membership fee required (currently $1 for 3 months' trial).

Travel Avenue ☎1-800/333-3335, ⊛www.travelavenue.com. Full-service travel agent that offers discounts in the form of rebates.
Travel Cuts Canada ☎1-800/667-2887, US ☎1-866/246-9762, ⊛www.travelcuts.com. Canadian student-travel organization.
Worldtek Travel ☎1-800/243-1723, ⊛www.worldtek.com. Discount travel agency for worldwide travel.

Packages and organized tours

There are a good number of companies operating **organized tours** around Scandinavia, ranging from city breaks to deluxe cruises or cycling holidays. Group tours can be very expensive, and occasionally don't include the airfare, so check what you're getting. If your visit is centred on cities you could simply book a hotel-plus-flight package (which can work out cheaper than booking the two separately). Scanam and Passage Tours offer very reasonable weekend deals in the low season (see opposite). Tour reservations can often be made through your local travel agent.

Tour operators

Abercrombie and Kent ☎1-800/323-7308, ⊛www.abercrombiekent.com. Upmarket company offering tailor-made Scandinavian and Baltic coach tours and cruises.
Adventure Center ☎1-800/228 4747, ⊛www.adventurecenter.com. Fifteen-day camping tour of Norway, Sweden and Finland from US$800.
Adventures Abroad ☎1-800/665-3998, ⊛www.adventures-abroad.com. Offer a variety of Scandinavian packages, specializing in small group tours.
American Express Vacations ☎1-800/241-1700, ⊛www.americanexpress.com. Flight-plus-hotel packages to major Scandinavian cities.
Backroads ☎1-800/462-2848, ⊛www.backroads.com. Specializing in activity holidays, including a six-day cycle tour of Denmark and a six-day hiking tour of the Norwegian mountains, glaciers and fjords.
BCT Scenic Walking ☎1-800/473-1210, ⊛www.bctwalk.com. Walking tours in Norway.
Borton Overseas ☎1-800/843-0602, ⊛www.bortonoverseas.com. Adventure-vacation specialists with a large selection of biking, hiking, rafting, birdwatching, dog-sledging and cross-country skiing tours, plus farm and cabin stays and city packages.

Brekke Tours ☎1-800/437-5302,
ⓦ www.brekketours.com. A well-established
company specializing in tours to Scandinavia with a
host of sightseeing and cultural tours.
Contiki Tours ☎888 CONTIKI, ⓦ www.contiki.com.
Tours of Scandinavia for 18- to 35-year-olds for
around US$1419 for 24 days. Campsite/cabin
accommodation.
Euro-Bike & Walking Tours ☎1-800/321-6060,
ⓦ www.eurobike.com. Summer cycling and walking
tours of Denmark.
EuroCruises ☎1-800/688-3876,
ⓦ www.eurocruises.com. Cruises of the Baltic Sea,
the fjords of Norway and the canals of Sweden.
Euroseven ☎1-800/890-3876,
ⓦ www.euroseven.com. Hotel-plus-flight packages
from New York, Baltimore or Boston to Scandinavia.
Loma Travel ☎1-888/665-9899. Canadian tour
operator offering cheap flights, tours and cruises.
Nordic Saga Tours ☎1-800/848 6449,
ⓦ www.nordicsaga.com. Packages, flights and
information on air passes within Scandinavia.
Nordique Tours/Norvista ☎1-800/995-7997,
ⓦ www.nordiquetours.com. A wide range of
Scandinavian packages including "Scandinavian
capitals", Lapland and the Norwegian fjords.
**Norwegian Coastal Voyage – Bergen Line
Services** ☎1-800/323-7436,
ⓦ www.coastalvoyage.com. A mixture of escorted
and independent cruises along the Norwegian
coastline and on Swedish canals.
Passage Tours ☎1-800/548-5960,
ⓦ www.passagetours.com. Scandinavian specialist
offering tours like "The Northern Lights" and dog-
sledging, ski packages and cheap weekend breaks.
Saga Holiday ☎1-800/343-0273,
ⓦ www.sagaholidays.com. Specialists in group
travel for seniors, offering a cruise and coach tour of
Sweden, Norway and Finland.
Scanam World Tours ☎1-800/545-2204,
ⓦ www.scanamtours.com. Scandinavian specialist
with group and individual tours and cruises, plus
cheap weekend breaks.
Scand-America Tours ☎1-800/886-8428 or
727/939-1505, ⓦ www.scandamerica.com. Offers
a wide variety of packages – everything from dog-
sledging to garden tours – throughout Scandinavia.
Scanditours ☎1-800/432-4176,
ⓦ www.scanditours.com. Canadian Scandinavia
specialist with wide range of travel options. Offices in
Toronto and Vancouver.
Scantours ☎1-800/223-7226,
ⓦ www.scantours.com. Major Scandinavian holiday
specialists offering vacation packages and
customized itineraries, including cruises and city
sightseeing tours.

Vantage Deluxe World Travel ☎1-800/322-
6677, ⓦ www.vantagetravel.com. Deluxe group
tours and cruises in Scandinavia.

Flights from Australia and New Zealand

There are **no direct flights** from Australia or
New Zealand to Scandinavia; instead you'll
have to fly to either a European or Asian
gateway city, from where you can get a connecting flight or other onward transport.
Fares are pretty steep, so if you're on a tight
budget it's worth flying to London (see
"Airlines in Britain", p.14), Amsterdam or
Frankfurt first, and picking up a cheap flight
from there. If you intend to take in a number
of other European countries on your trip, it
might be worth buying a Eurail pass before
you go (see p.22).

Airfares to Europe vary significantly with the
season: low season runs from mid-January
to the end of February and during October
and November; high season runs from mid-
May to the end of August and from
December to mid-January; the rest of the
year is counted as shoulder season. Tickets
purchased direct from the **airlines** tend to be
expensive, with published fares ranging from
A$2000/NZ$2500 (low season) to A$2500–
3000/NZ$3000–3600 (high). Travel agents
offer better deals on fares and have the latest
information on special deals, such as free
stopovers en route and fly-drive-accommo-
dation packages. STA (see opposite for
details) generally offer the best discounts,
especially for students and those under 26.
For a discounted ticket to Scandinavia from
Sydney, **Melbourne** or **Auckland**, expect to
pay A$1600–2500/NZ$2000–2700. Fares
from **Perth** and **Darwin** are slightly cheaper
via Asia, rather more expensive via Canada
and the US. Fares from **Christchurch** and
Wellington are around NZ$150–300 more
than those from Auckland.

Airlines flying out of Australia and New
Zealand often use SAS and Finnair for connecting services on to cities in Sweden,
Norway, Denmark and Finland. For flights
to other **European cities**, the lowest fares
are with Britannia to London, during its
limited charter season (Nov–March), when
you can expect to pay A$1000–1600/
NZ$1200–1900. For a scheduled flight, count

on paying A\$1500–2260/NZ\$1900–2800 on Alitalia or KLM; A\$1900–2500/NZ\$2280–3000 on SAS, Thai Airways and Lufthansa; A\$2400–2850/NZ\$2700–3400 on British Airways, Qantas, Singapore Airlines, Air New Zealand and Canadian Airways depending on the season. See below for a full rundown of airlines and routes.

Air passes which allow for discounted flights within Europe and Scandinavia, such as the SAS "Visit Scandinavia Pass" (see box on p.11) and British Airways–Qantas "One World Explorer", are available in conjunction with a flight to Scandinavia, and must be bought at the same time. Expect to pay A\$2400–2850/NZ\$2600–3000. For extended trips, **Round-the-World** tickets can be good value. Tickets that take in Scandinavia include the Star Alliance package (bookable through Ansett and Air New Zealand; around A\$2800/NZ\$3350) based on miles travelled (open-jaw travel and backtracking permitted), and the One World Alliance "Global Explorer" (bookable through Qantas; A\$2400–2900/NZ\$2900–3400).

There are very few **package holidays** to Scandinavia. Your best bet is Bentours (see opposite for details), which can put together a package for you, and are about the only agents who offer skiing holidays. Alternatively, wait until you get to Europe, where there's a greater choice of holidays and prices (see p.14).

If you're planning to travel a lot **by train**, or use trains to get to Scandinavia from another European country, it's worth considering a train pass. **Eurail passes**, which come in numerous versions (see p.22 for a rundown) are available from most travel agents, or from branches of CIT (see opposite) or Bentours (see opposite There's also a specific pass for Scandinavia, the **ScanRail** pass, which is sold by Bentours – further details on p.32.

Airlines

Air New Zealand Australia ☎13 24 76, New Zealand ☎0800/737 000, ⊛www.airnz.com. Daily flights from Auckland to London or Frankfurt via Los Angeles, then onward connections with SAS to Scandinavia.

Alitalia Australia ☎02/9244 2445, New Zealand ☎09/308 3357, ⊛www.alitalia.com. Six flights weekly from Sydney (with Ansett connections from

other state capitals) to major Scandinavian cities via Amsterdam or Milan.

British Airways Australia ☎02/8904 8800, New Zealand ☎0800/274 847 or 09/357 8950, ⊛www.britishairways.com. Daily to London from Sydney, Perth or Brisbane with onward connections to Scandinavian cities.

Cathay Pacific Australia ☎13 17 47 or 1300/653 077, New Zealand ☎09/379 0861 or 0508/800 454, ⊛www.cathaypacific.com. Several flights weekly from Australia and New Zealand to Hong Kong, with onward connections to Scandinavia.

Finnair Australia ☎02/9244 2299, ⊛www.finnair.com.

Lufthansa Australia ☎1300/655 727, ⊛www.lufthansa-australia.com, New Zealand ☎09/303 1529, ⊛www.lufthansa.com/index_en .html. Daily flights from major cities via Bangkok or Singapore and Frankfurt.

Qantas Australia ☎13 13 13, ⊛www.qantas.com .au, New Zealand ☎09/357 8900, ⊛www.qantas.co.nz. Daily flights from state capitals via Asia or Europe to Scandinavia.

Scandinavian Airlines (SAS) Australia ☎1300/727 707, New Zealand agent: Air New Zealand ☎09/357 3000, ⊛www.scandinavian.net. No flights from Australia or New Zealand, but can organize connections to Scandinavia via Bangkok, Beijing, Singapore or Tokyo.

Singapore Airlines Australia ☎13 10 11, New Zealand ☎09/303 2129, ⊛www.singaporeair.com. Daily service from major Australian and New Zealand cities to Scandinavia via Singapore.

Thai Airways Australia ☎1300/651 960, New Zealand ☎09/377 0268, ⊛www.thaiair.com. Three flights weekly to Stockholm from Auckland and Sydney via Bangkok.

Flight and travel agents

Budget Travel New Zealand ☎0800/808 480, ⊛www.budgettravel.co.nz. Discount flight specialist.
Flight Centre Australia ☎13 31 33 or ☎02/9235 3522, ⊛www.flightcentre.com.au; New Zealand ☎0800 243 544 or ☎09/358 4310, ⊛www.flightcentre.co.nz. One of the best discount flight specialists.
STA Travel Australia ☎1300/733 035, ⊛www.statravel.com.au; New Zealand ☎0508/782 872, ⊛www.statravel.co.nz. Worldwide specialists in low-cost flights and tours for students and under-26s, though other customers welcome. Also do rail passes.
Student Uni Travel Australia ☎02/9232 8444; New Zealand ☎09/300 8266; ⊛www.sut.com.au. Specializing in low-cost flights for students.

Thomas Cook Branches throughout Australia (call ☎13/1771 for nearest branch, ☎1800/801002 for direct telesales); New Zealand ☎09/379 3920; ⓦ www.thomascook.com.au. Flight deals and package holidays.

Trailfinders Australia ☎02/9247 7666, ⓦ www.trailfinders.com.au. One of the best-informed and most efficient agents for independent travellers, offering flight and accommodation advice.

Usit Beyond New Zealand ☎0800/788336, ⓦ www.usitbeyond.co.nz. Student and youth flight specialists.

Specialist agents and tour operators

Adventures Abroad New Zealand ☎0800/800 434, ⓦ www.adventures-abroad.com. Wide range of Scandinavian packages from one to three weeks.

Bentours Australia ☎02/9241 1353, ⓦ www.bentours.com.au. Ferry, rail, bus and hotel passes and a host of scenic tours throughout Scandinavia including fjord-travel and cycling in Denmark.

CIT Australia ☎02/9267 1255, ⓦ www.cittravel .com.au. Europe-wide rail passes.

Contiki Australia ☎02/9511 2200, New Zealand ☎09/309 8824, ⓦ www.contiki.com. Frenetic tours for 18–35 year-old party animals including a 22 day tour of Scandinavia.

Explore Holidays Australia ☎02/9857 6200 or 1300/731 000, ⓦ www.exploreholidays.com.au. Stockholm mini-stays and 21-day adventure tour through central and northern Sweden and coastal Norway.

ⓦ **travel.com.au** Australia ☎1300/130 482 or 02/9249 5444, ☏02/9262 3525, New Zealand ☎0800/468 332, ⓦ www.travel.co.nz. Comprehensive online travel company.

Travel Plan Australia ☎02/9958 1888 or 1300/130 754, ⓦ www.travelplan.com.au. Skiing specialist with some packages to Scandinavia.

Viatour Australia ☎02/8219 5400, ⓦ www.viator.com. Bookings for hundreds of travel suppliers worldwide, including Europe.

By rail from the UK and Ireland

Taking a **train** can be a relaxed way of getting to Scandinavia, though it's likely to work out considerably more expensive than flying, especially if you're over 26. A number of deals involving rail passes (see below) make it possible to cut **costs**, however, and there's the added advantage of being able to break your journey – travelling to Oslo, for instance,

you could stop off at Brussels, Hamburg, Copenhagen and Gothenburg.

With the **Channel Tunnel** you have the choice between crossing over to the continent by boat or taking the Eurostar from Waterloo International in London. Almost all ticketing for train travel within Europe is now handled by **Rail Europe** (see below) who provide the fastest and most convenient routings via the Eurostar to Paris or Brussels and then on to Scandinavia. Rail Europe can sell you through-tickets from most UK starting points, and, as always, check for special offers. Through-tickets for the train/cross-channel ferry option are only available from a few agents and main Connex stations. You could, with careful planning, organize your own train and ferry tickets, although this is obviously a complicated, if potentially money-saving process (for ferry operators, see p.24).

To get the cheapest fares on Rail Europe you'll need to book a round-trip fourteen days in advance with one Saturday night away. With this type of ticket, the fare to Copenhagen is currently £234, and the journey takes around 20 hours, via Brussels and Hamburg. Getting **to Norway, Sweden or Finland** by train from Britain involves first travelling to Copenhagen, as described above, and then taking one of the daily services onward. The onward fare to Oslo is £96 one way; to Stockholm £88.

No through-ticketing is available to **Finland** from the UK, though it's possible to connect with the Silja line ferry to Helsinki in Stockholm.

Rail passes

Rail passes can reduce the cost of train travel significantly, especially if you plan to travel extensively around Scandinavia or visit as part of a wider tour of Europe. There's a huge array of passes available, covering regions as well as individual countries. Some have to be bought before leaving home, while others can only be purchased in the country itself. Rail Europe is the umbrella company for all national and international rail tickets, and its comprehensive website (ⓦ www.raileurope.co.uk/ⓦ www.raileurope .com) is the most useful source of information on which rail passes are available; it also gives all current prices. For details of rail passes for use specifically within Scandinavia, such as ScanRail, see "Getting Around" p.32; for information on individual country passes see the "Getting Around" section of the relevant country.

Inter-Rail pass

If you have no clear itinerary, the **Inter-Rail pass** might be your best bet. These are only available to European residents, and you will be asked to provide proof of residency before being allowed to purchase one. They come in over-26 and (cheaper) under-26 versions, and cover 28 European countries (including Turkey and Morocco) grouped together in **zones**: **A** (Republic of Ireland/Britain); **B** (Norway, Sweden, Finland); **C** (Germany, Austria, Switzerland, Denmark); **D** (Czech & Slovak Republics, Poland, Hungary, Croatia); **E** (France, Belgium, Netherlands, Luxembourg); **F** (Spain, Portugal, Morocco); **G** (Italy, Greece, Turkey and Slovenia, plus some ferry services between Italy and Greece); and **H** (Bulgaria, Romania, Yugoslavia, Macedonia). The passes are available for 22 days (one zone only) or one month, and you can purchase up to three zones or a global pass covering all zones. You can save £5 by **booking** via the Inter-Rail website (ⓦwww.inter-rail .co.uk). Inter-Rail passes do not include travel between Britain and the continent, although holders are eligible for discounts on rail travel in Britain and Northern Ireland and cross-Channel ferries. The pass also gives discounts on the London–Paris Eurostar service and several ferry routes, including the Harwich to Esbjerg, as well as several

ferries in Scandinavia and between Scandinavia and Germany – some of the very short ones are free.

Eurail Pass

The **Eurail Pass** (only available to non-Europeans) is not likely to pay for itself if you're planning to stick to one country. The pass, which must be purchased before arrival in Europe, allows unlimited free first-class train travel in seventeen European countries, including all four covered in this book, and is available in increments of fifteen days, 21 days, one month, two months and three months. If you're under 26, you can save money with a **Eurail Youthpass**, which is valid for second-class travel or, if you're travelling with between one and four companions, a joint **Eurail Saverpass**; both of these are available in the same increments as the Eurail Pass. You stand a better chance of getting your money's worth out of a **Eurail Flexipass**, which is good for ten or fifteen days' travel within a two-month period. This, too, comes in first-class, under-26/second-class (**Eurorail Youth Flexipass**) and group (**Eurail Saver Flexipass**) versions.

Details of prices for all these passes can be found on ⓦwww.raileurope.com, and the passes can be purchased from one of the agents listed below.

Rail contacts

In North America

CIT Rail US ☎1-800/223-7987 or 212/730-2400, Canada ☎1-800/361-7799, ⓦwww.cit-rail.com. Eurail, Europass, German and Italian passes.

Useful timetable publications

The red-covered **Thomas Cook European Timetables** details schedules of over 50,000 trains in Europe, as well as timings of over 200 ferry routes and rail-connecting bus services. It's updated and issued every month; main changes are in the June edition (published end of May), which has details of the summer European schedules, and the October one, (published end of September), which includes winter schedules; some have advance summer/winter timings also. The book can be purchased online (which gets you a ten percent discount) at ⓦwww.thomascookpublishing.com or from branches of Thomas Cook (see ⓦwww.thomascook.co.uk for your nearest branch), and costs £9.50. Their useful *Rail Map of Europe* can also be purchased online for £6.95.

DER Travel US ☎1-888/337-7350,
🖳www.dertravel.com/rail. Eurail, Europass and
many individual country passes.
Europrail International Canada ☎1-888/667-
9734, 🖳www.europrail.net. Eurail, Europass and
many individual country passes.
Rail Europe US ☎1-800/438-7245, Canada ☎1-
800/361-7245, 🖳www.raileurope.com/us. Official
North American Eurail Pass agent; also sells
Europass, multinational passes and most single-
country passes.
ScanTours US ☎1-800/223-7226 or 310/636-
4656, 🖳www.scantours.com. Eurail and many
other European country passes.

In the UK and Ireland

Eurostar ☎0870/1606600, 🖳www.eurostar.co.uk.
Rail Europe (SNCF French Railways) UK
☎0870/5848 848, 🖳www.raileurope.co.uk.
Discounted rail fares for under-26s on a variety of
European routes; also agents for Inter-Rail, and
Eurostar, and sells rail passes for Scandinavia.

In Australia and New Zealand

Rail Plus Australia ☎1300/555 003 or 03/9642
8644, 🖳www.railplus.com.au. Eurail, Europass and
Britrail.
Bentours Australia ☎02/9241 1353,
🖳www.bentours.com.au. Scandinavian rail and bus
passes.
CIT World Travel Australia ☎02/9267 1255 or
03/9650 5510, 🖳www.cittravel.com.au. Eurail and
Europasses.
Trailfinders Australia ☎02/9247 7666,
🖳www.trailfinder.com.au. All Europe passes.

By coach from Britain

A **coach journey** to Scandinavia can be an
endurance test, and with airfares falling it
can actually prove more expensive than flying. It's only worth taking the bus if time is no
object and price all-important, or if you
specifically do not want to fly.

The major UK operator of international
coach routes is **Eurolines** (UK ☎0870/514
3219, Republic of Ireland ☎01/836 6111);
tickets are bookable on the Internet at
🖳www.eurolines.co.uk, through most major
travel agents (see p.14), and through any
Eurolines or National Express agent (☎0870/
580 8080, 🖳www.nationalexpress.co.uk or
🖳www.gobycoach.com).

Eurolines run eight services weekly to
Copenhagen either via Brussels (20hr) or

Amsterdam (26hr). From Copenhagen there
are connections on to **Gothenburg** (five
weekly; 25hr 45min), **Stockholm** (three
weekly; 30hr 30min) and **Oslo** (five weekly;
30hr 35min). Buses also run five times
weekly from London to **Århus** via Brussels
(20hr) or Amsterdam (25hr), continuing on to
Aalborg and Hirtshals. There are no through-
ticketed coach arrangements between
Britain and Finland. **Fares** to Danish destinations start at £102 return, though the Euro-
Apex fare (must be booked seven days in
advance; return within one month) reduces
this to £69. Euro-Apex fares to Oslo are
£189 return; Stockholm £152. If you're
under 26, expect to save between £5 to
£20 on each fare. Note that in the peak
summer months, all fares increase slightly.

Another option is the **Euroline Pass**,
which offers unlimited coach travel throughout much of Europe, including Denmark and
Sweden but excluding Norway and Finland.
The pass is valid either for fifteen days
(under 26/over 26 £99/£117); thirty days
(£136/£167) or sixty days (£167/£211);
expect to pay up to 25 percent more in
summer.

There are no through services from anywhere in Britain outside London, though
National Express connect with Eurolines
buses in London from all over the British
Isles.

By car and ferry from Britain

Ferry connections out of Harwich and
Newcastle link Britain with Denmark, western
Sweden and southern Norway. Fares aren't
cheap – prices vary enormously according to
the season, number of passengers and type
of cabin accommodation – but discounts
and special deals, such as DFDS Seaways'
"All in one car" midweek return fares, can cut
costs greatly. Not surprisingly, fares are usually at their lowest during the winter months.

An alternative to sailing directly to
Scandinavia is to take a ferry **to Germany** or
Holland (or even Belgium or France), and
drive from there. DFDS Seaways' crossings
from Harwich to Hamburg and Stena Line's
from Harwich to the Hook of Holland are
probably the most convenient options if
you're heading straight for Scandinavia.

To Scandinavia from Britain

From the UK **to Denmark**, DFDS Seaways sail from **Harwich to Esbjerg** three times a week, a trip of nearly twenty hours. Fares in low season start at £49 one-way/£79 return, plus £35 each way for a car (£274 for an "All in one car" fare covering 1 car and 3–4 people), rising to £98/166 plus £65 each way for a car (£620 "All in one car") in high season; for unreserved weekend fares a £10 supplement is payable. All prices above include a berth in a sleeping cabin.

For most of the year, the only services from Britain to **Norway** are the two or three sailings each week with Fjord Line from **Newcastle to Stavanger** (20hr), **Haugesund** (23hr) and **Bergen** (27hr). Tickets cost the same to all three ports, with a minimum fare in winter of £62 each way (including a cabin berth), plus £60 each way for a car, rising in summer to £96 each way and £70 per car. During the summer months reclining seats are available instead of a cabin for £42. Motorbikes are carried for £30 each way, bicycles £10. From May to September, Northlink Ferries operate from **Aberdeen** to **Lerwick** in Shetland, from where Smyril Line run a service to **Bergen**, but there's currently no through-ticketing. The Aberdeen to Shetland fares start at £26.50 one-way (£60 extra for a cabin berth); £120 one-way with a car. Shetland to Bergen fares start at £52 one-way, £42 each way for a car. The journey from Aberdeen to Bergen takes about three days in all and involves a stopover in Lerwick.

To Sweden, DFDS Seaways operate a twice-weekly service from **Newcastle to Gothenburg** (26hr) which stops in Norway at **Kristiansand** (18hr) en route. Prices to both destinations are the same and start at £64 one-way in low season, £104 return. The "All in one car" fare is £374 return. Expect to pay more in the spring and summer months, and supplements at weekends. All fares include a cabin berth.

There are no direct passenger ferries from Britain to **Finland**.

To Scandinavia from other countries

There are numerous ferry links to Scandinavia from **other European countries**.

The main routes are given below – note that there are also minor connections to the Danish islands. More details can be obtained from ferry companies and travel agents, and in the relevant "Travel Details" sections of the guide.

From **Germany**, the most useful route is the hour-long crossing from Puttgarten to Rødby, on the way to Copenhagen. Ferries run half-hourly round the clock all year. Other routes include Rostock to Gedser (9–11 daily; 2hr), Kiel to Oslo (1 daily; 19hr 30min), Kiel to Gothenburg (1 daily; 14hr), Rostock to Trelleborg (ferry: 4–5 daily; 5hr 30min–7hr; catamaran: 2–3 daily; 2hr 45min) and Sassnitz to Trelleborg (4–5 daily; 3hr 30min). From Travemünde, you can get ferries to Rødby (1 daily; 2hr 30min), Malmö (2 daily; 9hr) and Trelleborg (2–6 daily; 7–8hr), and there are also services from Travemünde and Lübeck to Helsinki (1–3 weekly; 22hr and 36hr respectively).

From **Poland**, ferries run from Swinoujscie to Copenhagen (5 weekly; 9hr 15min), Malmö (1–2 daily; 9hr) and Ystad (1 daily; 6hr 45min), Gdansk to Oxelosund (3–6 weekly; 18hr 30min), and Gdynia to Karlskrona (6 weekly; 10hr 30min). They also run from Tallinn, the capital of **Estonia**, to Helsinki (ferry: 6 daily; 3hr 30min–6hr 45min; hydrofoil: 4–6 daily; 1hr 30min; catamaran: 2–3 daily; 1hr 45min) and Stockholm (1 daily; 15hr).

Ferry contacts

DFDS Seaways UK ☎0870/5333 000, ⊛www.dfdsseaways.co.uk. Harwich to Esbjerg and Hamburg; Newcastle to Gothenburg and Kristiansand.
Fjord Line UK ☎0191/296 1313, ⊛www.fjordline.com. Newcastle to Norway: principally Stavanger, Bergen and Haugesund.
Hoverspeed UK ☎0870/240 8070, ⊛www.hoverspeed.co.uk. Twenty-four daily departures. Dover to Calais and Ostend; Newhaven to Dieppe.
P&O Stena Line UK ☎0870/600 0600 or 01304/864 003, ⊛www.posl.com. Dover to Calais.
P&O North Sea Ferries UK ☎0870/129 6002, ⊛www.ponsf.com. Hull to Rotterdam and Zeebrugge.
P&O Portsmouth UK ☎0870/242 4999, ⊛www.poportsmouth.com. Portsmouth to Cherbourg, Le Havre and Bilbao.

Northlink Ferries UK ☎0845/600 0449. Aberdeen to Lerwick (Shetland) for connection onwards with Smyril line to Bergen.
Sea France ☎0870/571 1711, ⊛www.seafrance.com. Dover to Calais.
Sea Cat UK ☎0870/5523 523, Republic of Ireland ☎1800/551 743, ⊛www.seacat.co.uk. Belfast to Stranraer, to Heysham, to Troon, and to Isle of Man; Dublin to Liverpool and to Isle of Man.

Smyril Line ☎01595/690 845. Services from Lerwick (Shetlands) to Bergen.
Stena Line UK ☎0870/570 70 70, Northern Ireland ☎028/9074 7747, Republic of Ireland ☎01/204 7777, ⊛www.stenaline.co.uk. Harwich to the Hook of Holland; Fishguard to Rosslare; Holyhead to Dun Laoghaire and Dublin; Stranraer to Belfast.

Red tape and visas

European Union, US, Canadian, Australian and New Zealand citizens need only a valid passport to enter Denmark, Norway, Sweden or Finland for up to three months. All other nationals should consult the relevant embassy about visa requirements.

For **longer stays**, EU nationals can apply for a residence permit while in the country, which, if it's granted, may be valid for up to five years. Non-EU nationals can only apply for residence permits before leaving home, and must be able to prove they can support themselves without working. Contact the relevant embassy in your country of origin.

In spite of the lack of restrictions, **checks** are frequently made on travellers at the major points of entry. If you're young and are carrying a rucksack, be prepared to prove that you have enough money to support yourself during your stay. You may also be asked how long you intend to stay and why. Be polite. It's the only check that will be made, since once you get into Scandinavia there are few passport controls between the individual countries.

Scandinavian embassies and consulates

The addresses given are for the main embassy or consulate in that country. To find out if there is a consulate in a major city nearer to your home, contact the main embassy.

Australia

Denmark 15 Hunter St, Yarralumla, Canberra ACT 2600 ☎02/6273 2195 or 6273 2196; **Finland** 12 Darwin Ave, Yarralumla, Canberra ACT 2600 ☎02/6273 3800; **Norway** 17 Hunter St, Yarralumla, Canberra 2600 ☎02/6273 3444; **Sweden** 5 Turrana St, Yarralumla, Canberra ACT 2600 ☎02/6270 2700.

Canada

Denmark 47 Clarence St, Suite 450, Ottawa, ON, K1N 9K1 ☎613/562-1811; **Finland** 55 Metcalfe St, Suite 850, Ottawa, ON K1P 6L5 ☎613/236-2389; **Norway** 90 Sparks St, Suite 532, Ottawa, ON, K1P 5B4 ☎613/238-6571; **Sweden** Mercury Ct, 377 Dalhousie St, Ottawa, ON K1N 9N8 ☎613/241-8553.

Ireland

Denmark 121 St Stephen's Green, Dublin 2 ☎01/475 6404; **Finland** Russell House, Stokes Place, St Stephen's Green, Dublin 2 ☎01/478 1344; **Norway** 34 Molesworth St, Dublin 2 ☎01/662 1800; **Sweden** 13–17 Dawson St, Dublin 2 ☎01/671 5822.

New Zealand

Denmark Level 1, 45 Johnston St, Wellington ☎04/471 0520; **Finland** 42–52 The Terrace, PO Box 2402, Wellington ☎04/499 4599; **Norway** 61 Molesworth St, Wellington ☎04/471 2503; **Sweden** 13th Floor, Vogel Building, Aitken St, Thorndon, Wellington ☎04/499 9895.

UK

Denmark 55 Sloane St, London SW1X 9SR ☎020/7333 0200; **Finland** 38 Chesham Place, London SW1X 8HW ☎020/7838 6200; **Norway** 25 Belgrave Square, London SW1X 8QD ☎020/7591 5500; **Sweden** 11 Montagu Place, London W1H 2AL ☎020/7917 6400.

US

Denmark 3200 Whitehaven St NW, Washington, DC 20008 3683 ☎202/234-4300; **Finland** 3301 Massachusetts Ave NW, Washington, DC 20008 ☎202/298-5800; **Norway** 2720 34th St NW, Washington, DC 20008 ☎202/333-6000; **Sweden** 1501 M St NW, Washington, DC 20005 ☎202/467-2600.

Money and banks

Of the three Scandinavian countries in the European Union (EU) – Denmark, Finland and Sweden – only Finland has joined the single European currency and converted to the euro. As a result you'll need a mixture of currencies if you're visiting more than one of the Scandinavian countries.

Denmark and Norway use **kroner**, Sweden **kronor** – abbreviated respectively as Dkr, Nkr and Skr, or as DKK, NOK and SEK. In this guide, we've abbreviated each as "kr", except where it's not clear to which country's money we're referring, in which case we've prefixed it with an "S" (Swedish), "D" (Danish) or "N" (Norwegian). Though they share a broadly similar exchange rate (currently around 11.8 to £1, 7.6 to US$1 for the Dkr and Nkr; 14.5 to £1, 9.4 to US$1 for the Skr), the currencies are not interchangeable. Finland changed over to the **euro** (€) in 2002 (currently 1.6 to the £, 1 to the US$1); its former currency, the markka, is no longer accepted. See the individual country basics for further details of the denominations of each currency and average daily costs.

Traveller's Cheques

It's easiest and safest to carry money as **traveller's cheques**, in either dollars, euros or pounds sterling. They're available from any bank and some building societies. The usual fee for traveller's cheque sales is one or two percent, though this may be waived if you buy the cheques through a bank where you have an account. It pays to get a selection of denominations. Make sure to keep the purchase agreement and a record of cheque serial numbers safe and separate from the cheques themselves. In the event

that cheques are lost or stolen, the issuing company will expect you to report the loss forthwith to their local office; most companies claim to replace lost or stolen cheques within 24 hours. In all likelihood you'll be issued with American Express, Visa or Thomas Cook cheques, all of which are widely accepted in Scandinavia.

Credit, charge and debit cards

The major **credit and charge cards** – Visa, MasterCard, American Express and Diners Club – are accepted almost everywhere in Scandinavia. You can also use your credit card to withdraw local currency from cashpoint machines (**ATMs**), though remember that all cash advances on credit cards are treated as loans, with interest accruing daily from the date of withdrawal; there may be a transaction fee on top of this. Most major **debit cards** can also be used to withdraw cash from an ATM (check with your bank) for which you'll pay a flat transaction fee (usually quite small) – your bank will able to advise on this. See the individual country "Basics" section for more specific details.

Exchanging Money

Exchanging money is easy but usually expensive. Banks have standard exchange rates, but commissions can vary enormously and it's always worth shopping around. Post offices often provide good exchange rates too. Some places charge per transaction, others per cheque, so it makes sense to carry large denomination cheques, or to try to change several people's money at once.

Banking hours vary from country to country – check each country "Basics" section under "Costs, Money and Banks". Outside those times, and especially in more remote areas, you'll often find that you can change money at hostels, hotels, campsites, tourist offices, airports and ferry terminals – though usually at worse rates than at the bank.

Mail and telecommunications

Post office opening hours and more specific information on how to use the mail and telephone systems is given under each individual country's section on "Mail and telecommunications".

Mail

You can have letters sent **poste restante** to any post office in Scandinavia by addressing them "Poste Restante", followed by the name of the town and country. When picking mail up you'll need to take your passport; make sure to check under middle names and initials, as letters often get misfiled.

Telephones

Phone boxes are plentiful, and almost always work; English instructions are normally posted inside. To make a collect call, dial the operator, who will speak English. To make a **direct call** to Britain or North America, dial the international access and country code, wait for the tone, then dial the area code (omitting the first 0 if there is one) and then the subscriber number.

Mobile phones

If you want to use your **mobile phone** abroad, you'll need to check with your service provider whether it will work, and what the call charges are. Unless you have a triband phone, it's unlikely that a mobile bought for use in the US will work elsewhere. Most mobiles in Australia and New Zealand use GSM, which works well in Europe; again check with your provider.

Most UK mobiles also use GSM. In the UK, for all but the very top-of-the-range

packages, you'll have to inform your phone provider before going abroad to get international access switched on. You may get charged extra for this depending on your existing package and where you are travelling to. You are also likely to be charged extra for incoming calls when abroad, as the people calling you will be paying the usual rate. If you want to retrieve messages while you're away, you'll have to ask your provider for a new access code, as your home one is unlikely to work abroad. For further information about using your phone abroad, check out ⓦ www.telecomsadvice.org.uk/features/using_your_mobile_abroad.htm.

International dialling codes

To Scandinavia:

Dial your country's international access code, then:
Denmark ☎ 45
Finland ☎ 358
Norway ☎ 47
Sweden ☎ 46

From Denmark, Norway or Finland to:

Australia ☎ 00-61
Britain ☎ 00-44
Ireland ☎ 00-353
New Zealand ☎ 00-64
US & Canada ☎ 00-1

From Sweden to:

Australia ☎ 009-61

Britain ☎009-44
Ireland ☎009-353
New Zealand ☎009-64
US & Canada ☎009-1

Email

One of the best ways to keep in touch while travelling is to sign up for a free **Internet email address** that can be accessed from anywhere, for example YahooMail or Hotmail – accessible through ⓦwww.yahoo.com and ⓦwww.hotmail.com. Once you've set up an account, you can use these sites to pick up and send mail from any Internet café or hotel with Internet access. There's no shortage of places in Scandinavia to send and receive email, with cybercafés in most of the region's cities, as well as plentiful online access in public libraries, often free.

 # Health

The health risks while travelling in Scandinavia are minimal and health care is excellent and widely available. Language is rarely a problem and the nearest tourist office will be able to recommend local doctors and hospitals.

EU nationals can take advantage of health services in Denmark, Sweden, Finland and Norway under the same terms as residents of the country. To do this you need to get form **E111** before you leave; they're available free from post offices and travel agents. The E111 entitles you to free emergency treatment and a reduction on non-hospital treatment. As you may still end up having to pay out something, it also pays to have travel insurance to cover any non-emergency treatments.

North American visitors will find that medical treatment is far less expensive than they're accustomed to in the United States, but even so it's essential to take out travel insurance (see opposite). In the case of an emergency, you should go to a hospital, since this will prove less expensive than a doctor's visit.

Medical services

In **Denmark**, tourist offices and health offices (*Kommunes Social og Sundhedforvaltning*) have lists of doctors. If the doctor decides you need hospital treatment, it'll be arranged for free, but always take your E111 with you. For doctors' consultations and prescriptions (available from an *apotek*, or pharmacy) you'll have to pay the full cost in cash on the spot, but keep a receipt and take this together with your E111 and passport to the local Danish health office for a refund – sometimes a long and frustrating process. Emergency health care in Denmark is free for American visitors, provided it doesn't look like you've come to the country with the intention of having a serious illness treated for free.

In **Norway**, most good hotels, pharmacies and tourist offices have lists of local doctors and dentists, and there'll usually be an emergency department you can go to outside surgery hours. You'll pay upwards of 120kr for an appointment, but EU citizens will be reimbursed for part of the cost of any treatment. Get a receipt (*legeregning*) at the time of payment, and take this, your E111 and passport to the social insurance office (*trygdekasse*) of the district where treatment was obtained. For prescription drugs, go to a pharmacy (*apotek*); late-opening ones in the main cities are detailed in the listings sections of the Guide.

In **Sweden** there is no local doctor system: go to the nearest hospital or clinic with your passport and E111 if appropriate and they'll treat you for a fee of up to 240kr. If you need medicine you'll get a prescription to take to a pharmacy (*apotek*), for which the maximum charge is normally around 100kr. Hospital stays cost 90kr per day; the emergency department is called the *akut-mottagning*.

In **Finland**, if you're insured, you'll save time by seeing a doctor at a private health centre (*lääkäriasema*) rather than queuing at a national health centre (*terveyskeskus*), although they are free. Medicines have to be paid for at a pharmacy (*apteekki*) – although, provided you have your passport, you won't be charged any more than Finns. Hospitals levy charges whether you stay in a bed or are treated as an outpatient.

Insurance

Most people will want to take out some kind of comprehensive travel insurance. A typical policy usually provides cover for the loss of baggage, tickets and – up to a certain limit – cash or cheques as well as cancellation or curtailment of your journey.

Before paying for a new policy, however, it's worth checking whether you are already covered. Some all-risks home insurance policies may cover your possessions when overseas, and many private medical schemes include cover when abroad. In Canada, provincial health plans usually provide partial cover for medical mishaps overseas, while holders of official student/teacher/youth cards in Canada and the US are entitled to meagre accident coverage and hospital in-patient benefits. Students will often find that their student health coverage extends during the vacations and for one term beyond the date of last enrolment.

After exhausting the possibilities above, you might want to contact a specialist travel insurance company, or consider the travel insurance deal we offer (see box below). Most of them exclude so-called dangerous sports unless an extra premium is paid: in Scandinavia this can mean **hiking and skiing** though probably not kayaking. Check carefully that any insurance policy you are considering will cover all of the activities you'll be doing. Many policies can be chopped and changed to exclude coverage you don't need – for example, sickness and accident benefits can often be excluded or included at will. If you do take medical coverage, ascertain whether benefits will be paid as treatment proceeds or only after

Rough Guides travel insurance

Rough Guides offers its own travel insurance, customized for our readers by a leading UK broker and backed by a Lloyd's underwriter. It's available for anyone, of any nationality and any age, travelling anywhere in the world.

There are two main Rough Guide insurance plans: **Essential**, for basic, no-frills cover; and **Premier** – with more generous and extensive benefits. Alternatively, you can take out **annual multi-trip insurance**, which covers you for any number of trips throughout the year (with a maximum of 60 days for any one trip). Unlike many policies, the Rough Guides schemes are calculated by the day, so if you're travelling for 27 days rather than a month, that's all you pay for. If you intend to be away for the whole year, the Adventurer policy will cover you for 365 days. All can be supplemented with a "Hazardous Activities Premium" if you plan to indulge in sports considered dangerous, such as skiing, scuba-diving or trekking.

For a policy quote, call the Rough Guide Insurance Line on UK freefone ☎0800/015 0906; US toll-free ☎1-866/220 5588, or, if you're calling from elsewhere ☎+44 1243/621 046. Alternatively, get an online quote or buy online at ⊛www.roughguidesinsurance.com.

return home, and whether there is a 24-hour medical emergency number. When securing baggage cover, make sure that the per-article limit – typically under £500 – will cover your most valuable possession. If you need to make a **claim**, you should keep receipts for medicines and medical treatment, and in the event you have anything stolen, you must obtain an official statement from the local police.

Information and maps

Before you leave, it's worth contacting national tourist boards for free maps, timetables, accommodation listings and brochures – though don't go mad, since much of what you'll need can easily be obtained once you arrive. There's also a wealth of information available online; we've included a selection of general sites below, but country-specific lists are given in the relevant "Basics" sections of the Guide.

Almost every Scandinavian town (and even some villages) has a **tourist office**, where you can pick up free town plans and information, brochures and other bumph. Many book private rooms (sometimes youth hostel beds), rent bikes, sell local discount cards and change money. During summer, they're open daily until late evening; out of high season, shop hours are more usual, and in winter they're sometimes closed at weekends. You'll find full details of individual offices throughout the text.

National tourist board offices

Australia

Denmark Level 4, 81 York Street, Sydney, New South Wales 2000 ☎02/9262 5832, ☏www.scandinavia.com.au.
For Sweden, Norway and Finland contact the embassies (see p.25).

Britain

Denmark 55 Sloane St, London SW1 ☎020/7259 5959, ☏www.visitdenmark.com.
Finland 3rd floor, 30–35 Pall Mall, London SW1 ☎020/7365 2512, ☏www.finland-tourism.com.
Norway 5th floor, Charles House, 5 Lower Regent St, London SW1 ☎020/7839 2650, ☏www.visitnorway.com. No walk-in service, correspondence only.
Sweden 11 Montagu Place, London W1 ☎00800/ 3080 3080 (free), ☏www.visitsweden.com.

Canada

Denmark Box 115, Station N, Toronto, ON M8V 3S4 ☎416/823-9620.
For Sweden, Norway and Finland contact the embassies (see p.25).

Ireland

No tourist board offices, but the embassies (see p.25) handle tourist information.

New Zealand

Again, the embassies (see p.25) supply tourist information.

US

Scandinavian Tourist Board, 655 3rd Ave, Suite 1810, New York, NY 10017 ☎212/885-9700, ☏www.goscandinavia.com.

Scandinavia online

☏ **www.goscandinavia.com** The official website of the Scandinavian Tourist Board in North America, offering a general introduction to Scandinavia, latest travel deals and links to tourist board sites of each country.
☏ **www.yahoo.com/regional_information/ countries** Over ten thousand links, clearly labelled, to Scandinavian sites.
☏ **www.itv.se/boreale/samieng.htm** Comprehensive introduction to the Sami people and their culture, with features on history, music, art and reindeer.
☏ **www.sametinget.se** Focusing on Sami political issues and the Sami parliament.

ⓦ www.santaclausoffice.fi Email Santa directly at his office in Finnish Lapland.

ⓦ www.scandinavia.com.au Excellent source of info with useful sections on current events and exhibitions, plus helpful advice on where to go for best flight deals.

Maps

The **maps** in this book should be adequate for most purposes, but drivers, cyclists and hikers will require something more detailed. Tourist offices often give out reasonable road maps and town plans, but anything better you'll have to buy.

For **Scandinavia** as a whole, Kümmerley & Frey produce a road map on a scale of 1:1,000,000; while Rand McNally publish a good road atlas of Scandinavia. For really detailed plans of the **capital cities**, the fold-out Falk maps are excellent and easy to use.

For individual countries, maps of **Denmark** are produced by Kümmerley & Frey (1:300,000), Ravenstein (1:500,000) and Baedeker (1:400,000); **Finland** is covered by Kümmerley & Frey (1:1,000,000). For **Norway**, you're best off with the Kümmerley & Frey (1:1,000,000) or the Roger Lascelles 1:800,000 map, which also has a place-name index. For **Sweden** as a whole, the best maps are produced by Terrac and Hallwag.

If you're staying in one area for a long time, or are **hiking**, you'll need something even more detailed – a minimum scale of 1:400,000; much larger (1:50,000) if you're doing any serious trekking. The larger tourist offices also sometimes have decent hiking maps of the local area. For **Norway**, the 1:400,000 Kümmerley & Frey regional maps are very good, while the government agency, Statens Kartverk, produces a series of high-quality 1:50,000 maps covering the entire country; these are widely available from tourist offices and bookshops, and also from the national hiking organization, DNT. For **Sweden** there's the 1:300,000 Esselte Kartor series and the 1:400,000 Kartförlaget series; these and others are available from Sweden's hiking organization, STF. In **Finland**, Kümmerley & Frey produce a number of regional maps of Finland at a scale of 1:400,000; the best source of hiking maps is Aleksi, Unioninkatu 32, Helsinki. The

provinces of **Denmark** are covered by the 1:200,000 Kort og Matrykelstyren series.

Map outlets

In the UK and Ireland

Blackwell's Map and Travel Shop 50 Broad St, Oxford OX1 3BQ ☎01865/793 550, ⓦmaps.blackwell.co.uk.

Easons Bookshop 40 O'Connell St, Dublin 1 ☎01/858 3881, ⓦwww.eason.ie.

Heffers Map and Travel 20 Trinity St, Cambridge CB2 1TJ ☎01865/333 536, ⓦwww.heffers.co.uk.

Hodges Figgis Bookshop 56–58 Dawson St, Dublin 2 ☎01/677 4754, ⓦwww.hodgesfiggis.com.

John Smith and Sons 26 Colquhoun Ave, Glasgow, G52 4PJ ☎0141/221 7472.

The Map Shop 30a Belvoir St, Leicester LE1 6QH ☎0116/247 1400, ⓦwww.mapshopleicester.co.uk.

National Map Centre 22–24 Caxton St, London SW1H 0QU ☎020/7222 2466, ⓦwww.mapsnmc.co.uk.

Newcastle Map Centre 55 Grey St, Newcastle-upon-Tyne, NE1 6EF ☎0191/261 5622.

Stanfords 12–14 Long Acre, London WC2E 9LP ☎020/7836 1321, ⓦwww.stanfords.co.uk.

The Travel Bookshop 13–15 Blenheim Crescent, W11 2EE ☎020/7229 5260, ⓦwww.thetravelbookshop.co.uk.

US and Canada

Adventurous Traveler.com US ☎1-800/282-3963, ⓦadventuroustraveler.com.

Book Passage 51 Tamal Vista Blvd, Corte Madera, CA 94925 ☎1-800/999-7909, ⓦwww.bookpassage.com.

Distant Lands 56 South Raymond Ave, Pasadena, CA 91105 ☎1-800/310-3220, ⓦwww.distantlands.com.

Elliot Bay Book Company 101 South Main St, Seattle, WA 98104 ☎1-800/962-5311, ⓦwww.elliotbaybook.com.

Globe Corner Bookstore 28 Church St, Cambridge, MA 02138 ☎1-800/358-6013, ⓦwww.globecorner.com.

Map Link 30 South La Patera Lane, Unit 5, Santa Barbara, CA 93117 ☎1-800/962-1394, ⓦwww.maplink.com.

Rand McNally US ☎1-800/333-0136, ⓦwww.randmcnally.com. Around thirty stores across the US; dial ext 2111 or check the website for the nearest location.

The Travel Bug Bookstore 2667 West Broadway, Vancouver V6K 2G2 ☎604/737-1122, ⓦwww.swifty.com/tbug.
World of Maps 1235 Wellington St, Ottawa, Ontario K1Y 3A3 ☎1-800/214-8524, ⓦwww.worldofmaps.com.

In Australia and New Zealand

The Map Shop 6–10 Peel St, Adelaide, SA 5000 ☎08/8231 2033, ⓦwww.mapshop.net.au.

Specialty Maps 46 Albert St, Auckland 1001 ☎09/307 2217, ⓦwww.ubdonline.co.nz/maps.
MapWorld 173 Gloucester St, Christchurch ☎0800/627 967 or 03/374 5399, ⓦwww.mapworld.co.nz.
Mapland 372 Little Bourke St, Melbourne, Victoria 3000 ☎03/9670 4383, ⓦwww.mapland.com.au.
Perth Map Centre 1/884 Hay St, Perth, WA 6000 ☎08/9322 5733, ⓦwww.perthmap.com.au.

Getting around

Public transport systems are good throughout Scandinavia. Denmark, Norway, Sweden and Finland have a fairly comprehensive rail network which runs as far north as it dares before plentiful buses take over. Fjords and inordinate amounts of water – lakes, rivers and open sea – make ferries a major form of transport too.

For further information see each country's individual "Getting Around" section, and the "Travel Details" at the end of every chapter.

By rail

Travel by train in Scandinavia isn't cheap, but a number of **passes** can ease the burden. If you're travelling to and around the region by train, the InterRail or Eurail passes (see "Getting there", p.22) can cut costs. If you're planning to travel by train only within Scandinavia itself, it's well worth considering a **ScanRail** pass (ⓦwww.scanrail.com), which covers all four countries and is available to all, although you'll have to buy it before you leave home (for details of outlets see p.23). The regular ScanRail pass is available for travel on any five days in a two-month period (adult £139/US$214; under-26s £105/US$161), any ten days in two months (adult £187/US$288; under-26s £140/US$216) and 21 consecutive days (adult £216/US$332; under-26s £162/US$249). Over-60s get a discount of about fifteen percent on the full price of the pass. There's also an eight-day **ScanRail Drive Pass**, which allows five days of train travel and two days of car rental, with the option of adding additional car days. Note that a small

supplement is charged for certain inter-city express trains.

ScanRail passes also give a fifty percent discount on a number of ferry routes and a twenty percent discount on an Oslo card (see p.231).

Another possibility is the **EuroDomino Pass** (only available to those who have been resident in Europe for six months), valid for between three and eight days, which offers unlimited train travel within any one of 25 European countries including Sweden, Denmark, Finland and Norway over a one month period. Like the ScanRail pass, you must purchase it before you leave home, and you'll have to buy a separate pass for each country, which comes in under-26 standard-class, over-26 standard-class and first-class versions, with varying prices for different countries. Denmark is the cheapest, with three days' travel within a month costing £41/80 (under-26/over-26), eight days £82/158. Sweden is the most expensive, with three days costing £85/139, eight days £136/173. The prices for Finland and Norway fall somewhere between (for details of outlets, see individual "Basics" sections).

By air

Internal **flights** can be a surprisingly good bargain in Scandinavia and, particularly if you're heading for the far-northern reaches, may save a great deal of time. During the summer – usually July and the early part of August – SAS usually has cheap set-price tickets to anywhere in mainland Scandinavia except Finland, plus other discounts for families and young people. Contact SAS offices in Denmark, Norway and Sweden for the latest deals – they're detailed under "Listings" in the accounts of the capital cities. Also, check out the **air passes** on offer before leaving home (see box on p.11); the relevant airlines can give you more information and current prices.

By car

Car rental is pricey, although some tourist offices do arrange summer deals which can bring the cost down a little. On the whole, expect to pay upwards of £350/US$480 a week for a small car plus fuel; see each country's "Getting Around" section for specific prices and details of rules of the road and documentation.

You may well find it cheaper, especially if you're travelling from North America, to arrange car hire before you go; airlines sometimes have special deals with rental companies if you book your flight and car through them. Alternatively, if you don't want to be tied down, try an agency such as Holiday Autos, who will arrange advance booking through a local agent and can usually undercut the big companies considerably (see the list below for phone numbers). For addresses of car rental firms in Scandinavia, see the "Listings" sections of major cities.

Car rental agencies

In the UK

Avis ☎0870/606 0100, ⓦwww.avisworld.com.
Budget ☎0800/181 181, ⓦwww.budget.co.uk.
Europcar ☎0845/722 2525,
ⓦwww.europcar.co.uk.
National ☎0870/536 5365,
ⓦwww.nationalcar.com.

Hertz ☎0870/844 8844, ⓦwww.hertz.co.uk.
Holiday Autos ☎0870/400 0099,
ⓦwww.holidayautos.co.uk.
Thrifty ☎01494/751 600, ⓦwww.thrifty.co.uk.

In Ireland

Avis Northern Ireland ☎028/9024 0404, Republic of Ireland ☎01/605 7500, ⓦwww.avis.ie.
Budget Republic of Ireland ☎01/9032 7711,
ⓦwww.budgetcarrental.ie.
Cosmo Thrifty Northern Ireland ☎028/9445 2565, ⓦwww.thrifty.ie.
Europcar Northern Ireland ☎028/9442 3444, Republic of Ireland ☎01/614 2800,
ⓦwww.europcar.ie.
Hertz Republic of Ireland ☎01/660 2255,
ⓦwww.hertz.ie.
Holiday Autos Republic of Ireland ☎01/872 9366, ⓦwww.holidayautos.ie.

In North America

Auto Europe US ☎1-800/223-5555, Canada ☎1-888/223-5555, ⓦwww.autoeurope.com.
Avis US ☎1-800/331-1084, Canada ☎1-800/272-5871, ⓦwww.avis.com.
Budget US ☎1-800/527-0700,
ⓦwww.budgetrentacar.com.
Europe by Car US ☎1-800/223-1516,
ⓦwww.europebycar.com.
Hertz US ☎1-800/654-3001, Canada ☎1-800/263-0600, ⓦwww.hertz.com.
National ☎1-800/227-7368,
ⓦwww.nationalcar.com.
Thrifty US ☎1-800/367-2277, ⓦwww.thrifty.com.

In Australia

Avis ☎13 63 33, ⓦwww.avis.com.au.
Budget ☎1300/362 848, ⓦwww.budget.com.au.
Dollar ☎02/9223 1444, ⓦwww.dollarcar.com.au.
Hertz ☎13 30 39, ⓦwww.hertz.com.au.
National ☎13 10 45, ⓦwww.nationalcar.com.au.
Thrifty ☎1300/367 227, ⓦwww.thrifty.com.au.

In New Zealand

Apex ☎0800/93 95 97 or 03/379 2647,
ⓦwww.apexrentals.co.nz.
Avis ☎09/526 2847, ⓦwww.avis.co.nz.
Budget ☎09/976 2222, ⓦwww.budget.co.nz.
Hertz ☎0800/654 321, ⓦwww.hertz.co.nz.
National ☎0800/800 115 or 03/366 5574,
ⓦwww.nationalcar.co.nz.
Thrifty ☎09/309 0111, ⓦwww.thrifty.co.nz.

Accommodation

Accommodation is going to be your major daily expense in Scandinavia. If you plan ahead, however, there are a number of ways to avoid paying over the (already high) odds. Youth hostels, campsites and cabins are the obvious budget options, and not just for tourists – they're popular with Scandinavians, too. There's also a series of discount passes available, for use in hotel chains all over Scandinavia.

Hotels

Scandinavian **hotels** aren't as expensive as you might think; certainly not if you compare them with equivalent accommodation in, say, London or New York. Lots of Scandinavian hotels, usually dependent on business travellers, drop their prices drastically at weekends and during the summer holiday period, so it's always worth enquiring in the tourist office about special local deals. The major cities also feature cheap "packages", usually involving a night's hotel accommodation and a free city discount card. More details, and a guide to prices, are given under each country's "Accommodation" section, as well as under the specific town and city accounts.

In addition, some Scandinavia-wide hotel chains operate a discount or **hotel cheque system** which you can organize before you leave. You either purchase cheques in advance, redeemable against a night's accommodation in any hotel belonging to the particular chain, or you buy a **hotel pass** which entitles you to a hefty discount on normal room rates. There are a bewildering number of schemes available, but most only operate from June to September and all offer basically the same deal: consult your travel agent, or one of the national tourist boards.

Hostels

Joining the **Hostelling International** (HI) association gives you access to what is sometimes the only budget accommodation available in Scandinavia. Non-members can use most HI hostels but will pay slightly more – the difference may add up to a sizeable sum over a couple of weeks, considering the low cost of annual membership. You'll also need a **sheet sleeping bag**, the only kind

allowed in HI hostels. They can either be rented at the hostels or bought at camping shops; alternatively, you can simply stitch a couple of old sheets together and take a pillowcase. If you're planning to cook for yourself using youth hostel kitchens, bear in mind that many don't provide pots, pans and utensils – take at least the basic equipment with you.

You can join Hostelling International either at home (for addresses, see below or in Scandinavia itself (the addresses of the relevant national hostelling organizations are given in each country's "Accommodation" section). For a complete listing of Scandinavian hostels, consult the annually-produced *Hostelling International Guide*, available from hostel associations and online via their websites.

Youth hostel associations

In the US

Hostelling International-American Youth Hostels ☎202/783-6161, ⊛www.hiayh.org. Annual membership for adults (18–55) is $25; $15 for seniors (55 or over), and free for under-18s and groups of ten or more. Lifetime memberships are $250.

In Canada

Hostelling International Canada ☎1-800/663 5777 or 613/237 7884, ⊛www.hostellingintl.ca. Rather than sell the traditional one- or two-year memberships, the association now sells one Individual adult membership with a 16- to 28-month term. The length of the term depends on when the membership is sold, but members can receive up to 28 months of membership for just $35. Membership is free for under-18s and you can become a lifetime member for $175.

In England and Wales

Youth Hostel Association (YHA) ☎0870/770
8868, @www.yha.org.uk or @www.iyhf.org.
Annual membership £13; under-18s £6.50; lifetime
£190 (or five annual payments of £40).

In Scotland

Scottish Youth Hostel Association ☎0870/155
3255, @www.syha.org.uk. Annual membership £6,
for under-18s £2.50.

In Ireland

Irish Youth Hostel Association ☎01/830 4555,
@www.irelandyha.org. Annual membership €15;
under-18s €7.50; family €31.50; lifetime €75.
Hostelling International Northern Ireland
☎028/9032 4733, @www.hini.org.uk. Adult
membership £10; under-18s £6; family £20; lifetime
£75.

In Australia

Australia Youth Hostels Association
☎02/9261 1111, @www.yha.com.au. Adult
membership rate A$52 (under-18s, A$16) for the
first twelve months and then A$32 each year after.

In New Zealand

Youth Hostelling Association New Zealand
☎0800/278 299 or 03/379 9970, @www.yha.co.nz.
Adult membership NZ$40 for one year, NZ$60 for
two and NZ$80 for three; under-18s free; lifetime
NZ$300.

Camping

Camping is hugely popular in Scandinavia. If
you're planning to camp a lot, an **international camping carnet** (CCI) is a good
investment. The carnet gives discounts at
member sites, serves as useful identification,
and is obligatory on some sites in
Scandinavia (you can buy one at the first site
you visit). Many campsites will take it instead
of making you surrender your passport during your stay, and it covers you for third-
party insurance when camping. Note, however, that the carnet is not recognized in
Sweden, where you may have to join their
own carnet scheme. In the **US and
Canada**, the carnet is available from home
motoring organizations, or from **Family
Campers and RVers** (FCRV; ☎1-800/245-
9755, @www.fcrv.org). FCRV annual membership costs $25, and the carnet an addi-
tional $10. In the **UK and Ireland**, the carnet
costs £4.50, and is available to members of
the AA or the RAC, or for members only
from either of the following: the **Camping
and Caravanning Club** (☎024/7669 4995,
@www.campingandcaravanningclub.co.uk),
or the foreign touring arm of the same
company, the **Carefree Travel Service**
(☎024/7642 2024), which provides the CCI
free if you take out insurance with them; they
also book ferry crossings and inspect camping sites in Europe.

Further details on camping are given in
each country's "Accommodation" section,
but one general point to note is that most
campsites in Scandinavia have furnished
cabins; if you intend to use these take a
sleeping bag as bedding is not usually
provided.

Crime and personal safety

**Scandinavia is one of the most peaceful corners of Europe. You will find that
most public places are well lit and secure, most people genuinely friendly and
helpful, and street crime and hassle relatively rare.**

It would be foolish, however, to assume
that problems don't exist. The capital cities
have their share of **petty crime**, fuelled by a
growing number of drug addicts and alco-
holics after easy money. Keep tabs on your
cash and passport (and don't leave anything
visible in your car when you leave it) and you
should have little reason to visit the **police**. If
you do, you'll find them courteous, concerned, and, most importantly, usually able

to speak English. If you have something stolen, make sure you get a **police report** – essential if you are to make an insurance claim.

As for **offences** you might commit, **nude sunbathing** is universally accepted in all the major resorts (elsewhere there'll be no one around to care); and **camping rough** is a tradition enshrined in law in Norway and Sweden, and tolerated in Finland, though in Denmark it's more difficult. Being **drunk** on the streets can get you arrested, and **drinking and driving** is treated especially rigorously. **Drug** offences, too, meet with the same harsh attitude that prevails throughout the rest of Europe.

Women travellers

In general, the social and economic position of women in Scandinavia is more advanced than in almost all other European countries – something which becomes obvious after a short time there. Many women are in traditionally male occupations, and sexual harassment is less of a problem than elsewhere in Europe.

You can walk almost everywhere in comparative comfort and safety, and although in the capital cities you can expect to receive occasional unwelcome attentions, it's very rarely with any kind of violent intent. Needless to say, travelling alone on the underground systems in Copenhagen, Oslo, Stockholm and Helsinki late at night is unwise. If you do have any problems, the fact that almost everyone understands English makes it easy to get across an unambiguous response.

Women's organizations

Denmark's women's movement is in a state of flux: the once prominent *Rødstrømper* (Red Stockings) – the Radical Feminists – are now less active. But there are lots of feminist groups around the country, and in Copenhagen a couple of active women's centres: Kvindehuset, Gothersgade 37 (☎33 14 28 04) and KVINFO (☎33 13 50 88, 🖲www.kvinfo.dk), Christians Brygge 3, which has a library and information centre.

Norway's women's movement is highly developed, assisted by progressive government and a 1986–89 Labour administration led by a woman, Dr Gro Harlem Brundtland, which endeavoured to even out parliamentary representation by promoting women into the cabinet. Contacts in Oslo can be made through the Norsk Kvinnessaksforening, Majorstuveien 39 (☎22 60 42 27, 🖲www.kvinnesak.no).

In **Sweden**, You'll find women's centres in most major towns; contact the organization Frederika Bremer, Östermalmsgatan 33, Stockholm, (☎08/644 3260) for further details.

The women's movement in **Finland** is lagging behind the rest of Scandinavia, and there have been fewer reforms to benefit the lot of women over the years. The major feminist organization, Unioni, first established in 1892 in Helsinki, is the best place for up-to-date information (Bulevardi 11A; ☎09 64 31 58, 🖲www.naisunioni.fi; closed mid-June to July).

Gay Scandinavia

Scandinavia comprises some of the most liberated and tolerant countries in Europe. Gays are rarely discriminated against in law, and the age of consent is almost uniformly the same as for heterosexuals – usually fifteen or sixteen. However, in all four mainland countries you'll not find much of a scene outside the capitals; the websites of the national associations are all a useful starting point for further information and listings.

Attitudes and the law

Denmark used to have a reputation for being the gay pornography capital of the world, and although this is no longer so, there is a very good gay scene in Copenhagen. As far as the law goes, in 1989 the Danish parliament voted to make a form of homosexual marriage legal, and it has continued to investigate other ways of eliminating discrimination against gays. For more information contact the Danish National Association for Gays and Lesbians (*Landsforeningen for Bøsser og Lesbiske*; ⓦwww.lbl.dk) in Copenhagen at Teglgårdsstræde 13 (☎33 13 19 48), Århus at Jægergårdsgade 42 (☎86 13 19 48) or Aalborg at Toldbodgade 27 (☎98 16 45 07).

Norway was one of the first countries in the world – in 1981 – to pass a law making discrimination against homosexuals illegal, and Norwegian society is reasonably tolerant of homosexuality. There is a strong and effective gay and lesbian organization, LLH (*Landsforeningen for lesbisk og homofil frigjøring*), with a national HQ in Oslo at Nordahl Brunsgate 22 (☎23 32 73 73). The website, ⓦwww.llh.oslo.no, is Norwegian-only, but you can send mail or faxes to PO Box 6838, St Olavsplass 2. There are also LLH branches throughout the country.

In **Sweden** gay marriage is now legal. However, there are few gay bars, and gay saunas and video shops with cubicles have been outlawed since mid-1987. The national organization, the RFSL, can be contacted at Sveavägen 57–59, 10126 Stockholm (☎08/457 13 22, ⓦwww.rfsl.se).

From a legal point of view, there is some discrimination against gays in **Finland**. The country's penal code forbids the public encouragement of homosexuality, although nobody has ever been convicted for breaking the anti-gay laws. SETA (Organization for Sexual Equality in Finland), at Hietalahdenkatu 2 B 16, 3rd floor, Helsinki (☎09/681 2580, ⓦwww.seta.fi), can provide further information – on Helsinki and elsewhere – and publishes a bimonthly nationwide magazine; during the summer they also print useful pages of information in English for foreign visitors to Helsinki.

Contacts for gay and lesbian travellers

In the US and Canada

Damron ☎1-800/462-6654 or 415/255-0404, ⓦwww.damron.com. Publisher of the *Men's Travel Guide*, a pocket-sized yearbook full of hotel, bar and club listings and resources for gay men; the *Women's Traveler*, which provides similar listings for lesbians; and *Damron Accommodations*, which provides detailed listings of over 1000 accommodations for gays and lesbians worldwide. All of these titles are offered at a discount on the website, where a search facility gives gay-friendly hotels and listings for major Scandinavian cities.
Gaytravel.com ☎1-800/429-8728, ⓦwww.gaytravel.com. The premier site for trip planning, bookings and general information about international gay and lesbian travel – including city breaks to Copenhagen and Stockholm.
International Gay & Lesbian Travel Association ☎1-800/448-8550 or 954/776-2626, ⓦwww.iglta.org. Trade group that can provide a list of gay- and lesbian-owned or -friendly travel agents, accommodation and other travel businesses.

In the UK

ⓦwww.gaytravel.co.uk Online gay and lesbian travel agent, offering good deals on all types of holiday. Also lists gay- and lesbian-friendly hotels around the world.

Also check out **adverts** in the weekly papers *Boyz* and *Pink Paper*, handed out free in gay venues.

In Australia and New Zealand

Gay and Lesbian Tourism Australia
ⓦ www.galta.com.au. Directory and links for gay and lesbian travel in Australia and worldwide.
Parkside Travel ☎ 08/8274 1222,

ⓔ parkside@herveyworld.com.au. Gay travel agent associated with local branch of Hervey World Travel; all aspects of gay and lesbian travel worldwide.
Silke's Travel ☎ 1800/807 860 or 02/8347 2000, ⓦ www.silkes.com.au. Long-established gay and lesbian specialist, with the emphasis on women's travel.
Tearaway Travel ☎ 03/9510 6644, ⓦ www.tearaway.com. Gay-specific business dealing with international and domestic travel.

Travellers with disabilities

Scandinavia is, in many ways, a model of awareness for the disabled traveller: wheelchair access, other facilities and help are generally available at hotels, hostels, museums and public places. Getting there, too, is becoming easier: DFDS ferries have specially adapted cabins, and Silja Line offer discounts for disabled passengers.

Planning a holiday

There are **organized tours and holidays** specifically for people with disabilities – the contacts listed below will be able to put you in touch with specialists for trips to Scandinavia. The tourist board websites of the Scandinavian countries also provide some information on provisions for disabled travellers in the relevant country. It's important to know where you may expect help and where you must be self-reliant, especially regarding transportation and accommodation. It's also vital to be honest with travel agencies, insurance companies and travel companions. It's worth thinking about your limitations and making sure others know them, too. If you don't use a wheelchair all the time but your walking capabilities are limited, remember that you are likely to need to cover greater distances while travelling (sometimes over rougher terrain and in hotter/colder temperatures than you are used to). If you use a wheelchair, it's always wise to have it serviced before you go and carry a repair kit.

People with a pre-existing medical condition are sometimes excluded from travel **insurance policies**, so read the small print

carefully. To make your journey simpler, ask your travel agent to notify airlines or bus companies, who can cope better if they are expecting you. A **medical certificate** of your fitness to travel, provided by your doctor, is also extremely useful; some airlines or insurance companies may insist on it. Make sure that you have extra supplies of drugs – carried with you if you fly – and a prescription including the generic name in case of emergency. Carry spares of any clothing or equipment that might be hard to find; if there's an association representing people with your disability, contact them early in the planning process.

Facilities in Scandinavia

In **Denmark**, facilities are generally outstanding. The Danish Tourist Board (see p.30 for addresses) publishes the comprehensive 100-page *Access in Denmark – a Travel Guide for the Disabled*, which covers everything from airports to zoos.

The **Norwegian** Tourist Board uses the wheelchair symbol throughout its publications to denote accessibility. Transport is not too much of a problem: Norwegian State Railways have special carriages on most main routes with wheelchair space, hydraulic lifts and a disabled toilet; new ships on the Hurtigrute Coastal Express route have lifts and cabins for disabled people; and new fjord ferries also have lifts from the car deck to the lounge and toilets. According to Norwegian law, all new public buildings must be accessible to disabled people. For further information, contact the Norwegian Association of the Disabled, PO Box 9217, Grønland, N-0134 Oslo (☏24 10 24 00, ⓦwww.nhf.no); their website is an excellent starting point.

In **Sweden**, many hotels are provided with specially adapted rooms, and camping-cabin holidays are not beyond wheelchair users either, as some chalet-villages have cabins with wheelchair access. The Stockholm T-bana system has elevators at most stations, and there are specially converted minivans and taxis for hire. A useful holiday guide with more information is available from Swedish tourist offices, or contact the Swedish Federation of Disabled Persons (DHR), Katrinebergsvägen 6, S-117 43 Stockholm (☏86 85 80 00, ⓦwww.dhr.se).

Finland is as welcoming to the disabled traveller as the other Scandinavian countries. The Finnish Tourist Board issues a free leaflet, *Tourist Services for the Disabled*, giving a brief overview of facilities; further information can be obtained from Mr Jens Gellin, Rullaten ry, Vartiokyläntie 9, 00950 Helsinki (☏09/322 069) or the Finnish Association of People with Mobility Disabilities, Kumpulantie 1A, 00520 Helsinki (☏09/613 191, ⓦwww.invalidiliitto.fi).

Contacts for travellers with disabilities

In the UK and Ireland

Access Travel 6 The Hillock, Astley, Lancashire M29 7GW ☏01942/888 844, ⓦwww.access-travel.co.uk. Tour operator that can arrange flights, transfer and accommodation.
Holiday Care 2nd floor, Imperial Building, Victoria Rd, Horley, Surrey RH6 7PZ ☏01293/774 535, Minicom ☏01293/776 943,

ⓦwww.holidaycare.org.uk. Provides free lists of accessible accommodation, and information on financial help for holidays.
Irish Wheelchair Association Blackheath Drive, Clontarf, Dublin 3 ☏01/818 6400, ⓦwww.iwa.ie. Useful information on travelling abroad with a wheelchair.
Tripscope Alexandra House, Albany Rd, Brentford, Middlesex TW8 0NE ☏0845/758 5641, ⓦwww.justmobility.co.uk/tripscope. Registered charity that provides a national telephone information service offering free advice on UK and international transport for people with mobility problems.

In the US and Canada

Access-Able ⓦwww.access-able.com. Online resource for travellers with disabilities.
Directions Unlimited 123 Green Lane, Bedford Hills, NY 10507 ☏1-800/533-5343 or 914/241-1700. Travel agency specializing in bookings for people with disabilities.
Mobility International USA 451 Broadway, Eugene, OR 97401 ☏541/343-1284, ⓦwww.miusa.org. Information and referral services, access guides, tours and exchange programmes. Annual membership $35 (includes quarterly newsletter).
Society for the Advancement of Travelers with Handicaps (SATH) 347 5th Ave, New York, NY 10016 ☏212/447-7284, ⓦwww.sath.org. Non-profit educational organization that has actively represented travellers with disabilities since 1976.
Wheels Up! ☏1-888/389-4335, ⓦwww.wheelsup.com. Provides discounted airfare, tour and cruise prices for disabled travellers, also publishes a free monthly newsletter and has a comprehensive website.

In Australia and New Zealand

ACROD (Australian Council for Rehabilitation of the Disabled) PO Box 60, Curtin ACT 2605; Suite 103, 1st floor, 1–5 Commercial Rd, Kings Grove 2208; ☏02/6282 4333, TTY ☏02/6282 4333, ⓦwww.acrod.org.au. Provides lists of travel agencies and tour operators for people with disabilities.
Disabled Persons Assembly 4/173–175 Victoria St, Wellington, New Zealand ☏04/801 9100 (also TTY), ⓦwww.dpa.org.nz, ⓔgen@dpa.org.nz. Resource centre with lists of travel agencies and tour operators for people with disabilities.

BASICS | Travellers with disabilities

Outdoor activities

Scandinavia is a wonderful place if you love the great outdoors, with marvellous hiking, fishing and, of course, skiing opportunities. Best of all, you won't find the countryside overcrowded – there's plenty of space to get away from it all, especially in the north. As you might expect, any kind of hunting is forbidden without a permit, and fishing usually requires a special licence, available from local tourist offices.

Hiking

Scandinavia offers the ultimate in **hiking** experiences – a landscape of rugged mountains, icy glaciers and deep green fjords, much of it far from the nearest road. Many of the best hiking areas have been set aside as **national parks**, with information centres, lodges and huts dotted along well-marked trails. Huts are usually run by national or local hiking organizations, and you will have to become a member to be able to use them. See "Information and Maps " (p.30) for map suppliers, and note also that **tourist offices** in the hiking areas supply maps and leaflets describing local routes. (Where hiking routes are covered in the Guide we've listed the best source of local information.) It's essential to **plan your route** thoroughly before setting out, taking weather conditions into account, and not to overestimate what you can manage in the time. In many areas, solo hiking is strongly advised against.

As far as **equipment** goes, for day walking you'll need warm clothing and gloves, waterproofs, and sun and mosquito protection; on all but the easiest and shortest hikes, a compass is a good idea – as long as you know how to use it. For long-distance treks you'll also need a sleeping bag, medical kit and a torch, plus a pair of sturdy, comfortable boots. Note that Camping Gaz is only available from selected outlets in Scandinavia – details from national tourist boards – so take your own supply. For hiking campers, a plastic survival bag keeps you and your pack dry. And take a torch.

If you're planning to camp, you should be aware of some specific **ground rules**. The landscape is there for everyone's use and camping rough is legal much of the time –

but the Scandinavians are concerned to protect the environment both from the damage caused by excessive tourism and the potential disasters that can result from ignorance or thoughtlessness.

Don't **light fires** anywhere other than at designated spots – and even these shouldn't be used in times of drought. **Tents** may only be placed on marked sites or, on some hikes, in other designated areas. When camping, do not break tree branches or leave **rubbish**; and try not to disturb nesting **birds**, especially in the spring.

In the northern reaches of Scandinavia, be wary of frightening **reindeer herds**, since if they scatter it can mean several extra days' work for the herder; also, avoid tramping over moss-covered stretches of moorland – the reindeer's staple diet. **Picking flowers, berries and mushrooms** is also usually prohibited in the north. If you are going to pick and eat anything, however, it's a wise idea, post-Chernobyl, to check on the latest advice from the authorities – tourist offices should know the score.

Glaciers are slow-moving masses of ice in constant, if normally imperceptible, motion, and are therefore potentially dangerous. Never climb a glacier without a guide, never walk under one and always heed the instructions at the site. Guided crossings can be terrific; local tourist offices and hiking organizations have details – see the relevant accounts in the Guide.

Cycling, golf and canoeing

Several package tour operators (see p.15 and p.18) offer **cycling tours** within Scandinavia – Denmark in particular is ideal for a cycling holiday given its largely flat landscape and excellent provision of cycle lanes covering more than 10,000km, all of them marked on detailed cycling maps. **Golf** enthusiasts won't be disappointed either – Denmark and Sweden in particular have excellent golf facilities: over 500 courses between them in a variety of stunning natural landscapes and with some of the lowest green fees in Europe.

Scandinavia's inland waterways and endless miles of coastline afford ample opportunity for **canoeing** or **sea-kayaking**. Sweden is criss-crossed with canoeing routes, with numerous places to stop and camp along the way and all grades of difficulty from gentle paddling along winding rivers to whitewater thrills.

Winter sports

Aside from the cities, which maintain their usual roster of activities and attractions, though sometimes with reduced opening hours, the big incentive for coming to Scandinavia in winter is the range of winter sports available: skiing, snowboarding, dog-sledding, tobogganing, ice-skating, scooter safaris and ice fishing, to name a few. All can be easily fixed up once in Scandinavia; enquire at local tourist offices.

Skiing

Scandinavia is an excellent place to ski, though **skiing** packages here will be more expensive than other European destinations. Even if you can't afford a package it's always easy to arrange a few days' cross-country skiing wherever you are. There are even ski runs within the city boundaries of Oslo and Stockholm, and plenty of places to rent equipment. Norway is particularly well equipped for **cross-country skiing**, with a large network of special trails (many floodlit after dark) of varying lengths, which often have cabins along the route in which to overnight. Check out the tourist board websites for each country (see p.30) for more information and details on the various skiing associations who will be able to recommend routes and destinations according to your trip.

Work and study

Norway, Sweden and Finland in particular are extremely suspicious of potential non-EU foreign workers, and you may have to prove on entry that you are not there to seek work (by showing return tickets and sufficient cash, for instance). The chances of finding casual work are, in any case, decidedly slim.

Paperwork

If you're serious about **working**, and are an EU citizen, **Denmark** and **Sweden** are the best options, though for other than relatively low-paid bar/restaurant/hotel work you really need to speak the language. You can stay for up to three months while you look for work, and, if you find it, a residence permit should be granted. Fast-food restaurants and larger hotels have a fairly high turnover of foreign staff, and private employment agencies can sometimes place unskilled foreign workers. Non-EU citizens are not allowed to look for work after arriving and need to set up employment before leaving home. **Australians** between the ages of 18 and 30 can take advantage of the **Working Holiday Maker** (WHM) scheme, which allows you to work legally for twelve months in a number of European countries including Denmark, Sweden and Norway. A special WHM visa must be obtained from the relevant embassy before leaving home.

Other options

The best-paid opportunity to live and work in Scandinavia for a short period is by **working on a farm**: you live with a farming family, work incredibly hard and receive board and lodging and pocket money in return. Vacancies are usually for the spring and summer, although some jobs stay open for a full year. Serious vacancies (ie for young farmers and/or people with experience) are dealt with by HOPS, the International Farm Experience Programme, YFC Centre, National Agricultural Centre, Kenilworth, Warwickshire CV8 2LG (☎02476/857 200, ⓦwww.nfyfc.org.uk). For summer farm work (no experience necessary), 18- to 30-year-olds should contact the Norwegian Youth Council (*Landsradet for Norske Ungdomsorganisasjoner*), Working Guest Programme, Rolf Hofmosgate 18, Oslo 6, Norway (apply by April 15).

If you would like to do **voluntary work** in mainland Scandinavia, contact one of the organizations listed below.

Useful publications, websites and contacts

For more information about working in Scandinavia – paid or voluntary – consult the series of **books** published in Britain by Vacation Work (☎01865/241 978, ⓦwww.vacationwork.co.uk): *Live and Work in Scandinavia*; *The International Directory of Voluntary Work*; *Summer Jobs Abroad* and *Work Your Way Around the World*.

Another pre-planning strategy for working abroad is to get hold of *Overseas Jobs Express* (☎01273/699 611, ⓦwww.overseasjobs.com), a fortnightly publication with a range of job vacancies, available by subscription only. Travel magazines like the reliable Wanderlust (every two months; £2.80) have a section which often advertises job opportunities with tour companies. The useful **website** ⓦwww.studyabroad.com has listings and links to study and work programmes in Scandinavia.

Study and volunteer programmes

ASSE International, 228 North Coast Highway, Laguna Beach, CA 92651 ☎714/494 4100; 7 Rue De La Commune Quest, Suite 204, Montréal, PQ H2Y 2C5 ☎514/287 1814; PO Box 20, Harwich, Essex, CO12 4DQ ☎01255/506 347; c/o Southern Cross Cultural Exchange, Locked Bag 1200, Mt Eliza, VIC 3930 ☎03/9776 4711; PO Box 340, Te Puke, New Zealand ☎07/573 5717; ⓦwww.asse.com. International student exchanges to Scandinavia.

Australians Studying Abroad ☎03/9509 1955, ⓦwww.asatravinfo.com.au. Study tours focusing on art and culture. Tours vary from year to year so there may not always be a Scandinavia option.

Council on International Educational Exchange (CIEE), 633 3rd Avenue, 20th floor, New York NY 10017 ☎1-800-407-8839, ⓦwww.ciee.org; 52 Poland St, London W1V 4JQ ☎020/7478 2000; Level 3, 91 York St, Sydney, NSW 2000 ☎02/8235 7000, ⓦwww.ciee.org.au. International organization offering advice on studying, working and volunteering in Europe. Runs summer and one-year study programmes and volunteer projects in Denmark and Sweden.

Erasmus EU-run student exchange programme enabling students at participating universities in Britain and Ireland to study in one of 26 European countries. Mobility grants available for three months to a full academic year. Anyone interested should contact their university's international relations office, or check the Erasmus website ⓦeuropa.eu.int/comm/education/erasmus.html

Field Studies Council Overseas Montford Bridge, Shrewsbury, Shropshire SY4 1HW ☎01743/852 150, ⓦwww.fscoverseas.org.uk. Respected educational charity with over twenty years' experience of organizing specialized holidays with study tours visits worldwide. Group size is generally limited to ten to fifteen. *Overseas Experiences* brochure available.

SCI International Voluntary Service 499 Elizabeth St, Surry Hills, NSW 2010 Australia ☎02/9699 1129; 110 George Street South, Unit 909, Toronto, Ontario M5A 4P9 ☎416/216-0914; 30 Mountjoy Square, Dublin 1, Ireland ☎01/8551011; Old Hall, East Bergholt, Colchester CO7 6TQ, UK ☎01206/298215; 3213 West Wheeler St, Seattle, WA 98199, US ☎206/3506585; ⓦwww.sci-ivs.org. A wide range of short two- to three-week summer camps and longer three- to six-month postings on various cultural and community projects in Scandinavia.

Books

There are surprisingly few books on Scandinavia in English: hardly any travellers have written well (or indeed at all) about the region, and historical or political works tend to concentrate almost exclusively on the Vikings, who have a burgeoning literature.

However, more and more Scandinavian literature is appearing in translation – notably the Icelandic Sagas and selected modern novelists – and it's always worth looking out for a c.1900 *Baedeker's Norway and Sweden*, if only for the phrasebook, from which you can learn the Swedish and Norwegian for "We must tie ourselves together with rope to cross this glacier."

Of the publishers, Peter Owen (@www.peterowen.com) and Forest Books regularly produce fine new translations of modern Scandinavian novels. Norvik Press (@www.uea.ac.uk/llt/norvik_press), too, is a good source of new translations of old and new Scandinavian writing. Finally, *The Babel Guide to Scandinavian Fiction in Translation* by Paul Binding reviews books available in English by leading Scandinavian writers – both classic and modern.

Titles go in and out of print regularly (in our list o/p denotes out of print); if your library doesn't have copies, your local bookshop may be able to order them for you, or try online booksellers such as @www.amazon.com. For books by specific Scandinavian authors or titles related to specific countries see the relevant "Books" section for each country.

Travel and general

Jeremy Cherfas *The Hunting of Whale*. Subtitled "A tragedy that must end", this is a convincing condemnation of whaling and all those – like Norway – involved in it.

Tom Cunliffe *Topsail and Battleaxe*. The intertwined stories of the tenth-century Vikings who sailed from Norway, past the Faroes and Iceland to North America, and the author's parallel trip in 1983 – made in a 75-year-old pilot cutter. Enthusiastically written, with good photos.

Christer Elfving & Petra de Hamer *New Scandinavian Cooking*. A cook's tour through Scandinavia's capital cities mixing history, culinary trends and tips on the hottest chefs and restaurants with delicious modern recipes.

Tony Griffiths *Scandinavia*. A wide-ranging look at the cultural, artistic and political developments and exchanges of the last two centuries that have helped shape the Scandinavian psyche.

John McCormick *Acid Earth*. Good for background on the burning issue of acid rain, of which the Scandinavian countries are net recipients – especially from Britain.

Ben Nimmo *In Forkbeard's Wake: Coasting Around Scandinavia*. Light and lively account of the author's sailing trip around Scandinavia, brimming with sailing mishaps and encounters with Nordic types – divers, fishermen, archeologists and a drunk Swedish dentist. An all too rare modern travel book on the area.

Christoph Ransmayr *The Terrors of Ice and Darkness*. Clever mingling of fact and fiction as the book's main character follows the route of the 1873 Austro-Hungarian expedition to the Arctic. A story of obsession and, ultimately, madness.

Mary Wollstonecraft *A Short Residence in Sweden, Norway and Denmark*. A searching account of Wollstonecraft's three-month solo journey through southern Scandinavia in 1795.

History

If you're interested in the **Vikings** you'll be spoilt for choice, but there's also a good selection of books on Norse mythology, though disappointingly little on modern Scandinavia.

General

T.K. Derry *A History of Scandinavia*. Authoritative history from the Stone Age to the 1990s. Rather dense and scholarly, but one of the only recent works on the topic in paperback.

Knut Helle et al *The Cambridge History of Scandinavia*. Comprehensive new tome for history buffs, covering the period from the Stone Age to the Middle Ages.

John van der Kiste *Northern Crowns: The Kings of Modern Scandinavia.* All you ever wanted to know about the Scandinavian monarchies, from the nineteenth century to the present day.

Chris Mann *Hitler's Arctic War.* A new account of one of the most critical – yet most often overlooked – campaigns of World War II, chronicling the failure of German forces in the inhospitable landscape of the Arctic that played a crucial role in the Allied victory.

P.V. Glob *The Bog People.* A fascinating study of the various Iron Age bodies discovered fully preserved in northwestern European peat bogs, most of them in Denmark. Excellent, if ghoulish, photographs.

Geoffrey Parker *The Thirty Years' War.* One of the more recent accounts of this turbulent period, this is an authoritative, if dry, read.

The Vikings

Johannes Brøndsted *The Vikings* (o/p). Classic and immensely readable account of the Viking period, with valuable sections on social and cultural life, art, religious beliefs and customs.

Paddy Griffith *The Viking Art of War.* A critical and controversial re-examination of the sources that questions the superlative warrior status of the Vikings and examines their tactics from the viewpoint of modern military thinking.

Gwyn Jones *A History of the Vikings.* Probably the best book on the subject: a superb, thoughtful and thoroughly researched account of the Viking period.

F. Donald Logan *The Vikings in History.* Scholarly – and radical – re-examination of the Vikings' impact on medieval Europe, indispensable for the Viking fan.

Magnus Magnusson *The Vikings.* The veteran TV broadcaster and amateur historian is the latest to add his take on the topic, with this illustrated and well written exploration of the contradictions that characterized the rampaging yet culturally enlightened Norsemen.

Else Roesdahl *The Vikings.* A lucid account of the 300-year reign of Scandinavia's most famous (and most misunderstood) cultural ambassadors, and the traces that they've left throughout northern Europe.

Mythology

George Webb Dasent *Popular Tales from Norse Mythology.* Riveting re-telling of over forty of the authentic folk tales of gods, mighty warriors, princesses and giants that help make up the folkloric heritage of Western civilization, including favourites like *The Goatherd* (the origin of the Sleepy Hollow legend).

H.R. Ellis Davidson *The Gods and Myths of Northern Europe.* A handy Saga companion, this is a *Who's Who* of Norse mythology, including some useful reviews of the more obscure gods. Displaces the classical deities and their world as the most relevant mythological framework for northern and western European culture.

Andrew Orchard *Cassell's Dictionary of Norse Myth and Legend.* Brand new guide to the complete cast of Scandinavian gods, trolls, heroes and monsters, complete with the social and historical background to the myths and coverage of topics such as burial rites, sacrificial practices and runes.

Directory

Addresses In Scandinavia addresses are always written with the number after the street name. In multi-floored buildings the ground floor is always counted as the first floor, the first the second, and so on.

Alcohol Except in Denmark, alcohol is very expensive throughout Scandinavia. For spirits especially, you'll find it cheaper to exceed your duty-free limit and pay the duty than buy when you get there.

Books You'll find English-language books in almost every bookshop, though at about twice the price you'd pay at home.

Bring An alarm clock is useful for early-morning buses and ferries, mosquito repellent and antiseptic cream handy (vital in the far north), and a raincoat or foldaway umbrella more or less essential.

Left luggage There are luggage lockers in

most train stations, ferry terminals and long-distance bus stations.

Museums and galleries As often as not there's a charge to get in, though other than for the really major collections it's rarely very much; ISIC cards are valid for reductions at most. Opening times vary greatly: in winter they are always reduced; the likely closing day is Monday.

Newspapers You'll find British newspapers on sale in every capital city – often on the day of issue – as well as in many other large towns. Your only other choices are likely to be the *International Herald Tribune* and *USA Today*.

Time Denmark, Sweden and Norway are one hour ahead of the UK; Finland is two hours ahead. Denmark, Sweden and Norway are six to nine hours ahead of the eastern US; Finland is seven to ten hours ahead.

World Service You can keep in touch with British and world events by listening to the BBC World Service, which is broadcast to all of mainland Scandinavia. Frequencies vary according to area and usually change every few months. For the latest details, visit ⓦ www.bbc.co.uk/worldservice, or write for the free *Programme Guide* to BBC External Services Publicity, Bush House, PO Box 76, Strand, London WC2.

Guide

Guide

Denmark

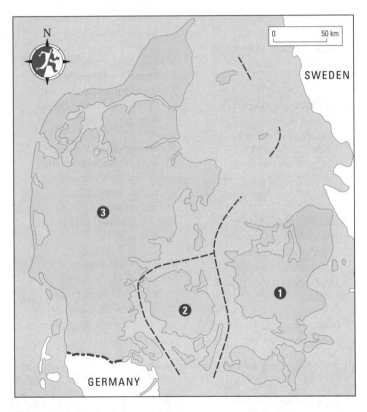

Denmark highlights

* **Smørrebrød** Rye bread loaded with Danish delicacies, these traditional open sandwiches are simply mouthwatering. **See p.62**

* **Christiania** Declared a "free city" In 1971, Christiania is a fascinating place for a wander. **See p.101**

* **Ny Carlsberg Glyptotek** Greek, Roman and Egyptian art and artefacts, and one of the biggest (and best) collections of Etruscan art outside Italy. **See p.102**

* **Louisiana Museum of Modern Art** A marvellous collection set in an unusual building overlooking the sculpture park and Øresund. **See p.114**

* **Island-hopping, Funen** Quaint villages and beautiful sandy beaches are the main draws of southern Funen's archipelago. **See p.141**

* **Hindsholm Peninsula** This remote and beautiful area is best explored by bike. **See p.141**

* **Moesgård Prehistoric Museum, Århus** Get the lowdown on Danish civilizations since the Stone Age. **See p.164**

* **Århus nightlife** From clubs to up-and-coming Danish and international bands and jazz, rock or techno acts, Århus's scene is hard to beat. **See p.166**

* **Djursland beaches** The white-sand beaches around Ebeltoft, Grenå and Fjellerup are some of Denmark's finest. **See p.169**

Introduction and Basics

Delicately balanced between Scandinavia proper and mainland Europe, Denmark is a difficult country to pin down. In many ways it shares the characteristics of both regions: it's an EU member, and has prices and drinking laws that are broadly in line with the rest of Europe. But Danish social policies and style of government are distinctly Scandinavian: social benefits and the standard of living are high, and its politics are very much that of the consensus.

It may seem hard to believe, but it wasn't so long ago that tiny Denmark ruled a good chunk of northern Europe. Since imperialist times, however, the country's energies have been turned inwards, towards the development of a well-organized but rarely over-bureaucratic society that does much to foster a pride in Danish arts and culture and uphold the freedoms of the individual. Indeed, once here, it becomes easy to share the Danes' puzzlement as to why other small, formerly Empire-owning nations haven't followed their example.

Where to go

While Denmark is the easiest Scandinavian country in which to travel – both in terms of cost and distance – the landscape itself is the region's least dramatic: largely green, flat and rural farmland punctuated by innumerable fairytale half-timbered villages, with surprisingly few urban settlements. Apart from a scattering of small islands, the country is made up of three main **landmasses** – the islands of Zealand and Funen and the peninsula of Jutland, which extends northwards from Germany.

The vast majority of visitors make for **Zealand** (*Sjælland*) and, more specifically, **Copenhagen**, the country's one truly large city and an atmospheric and exciting focal point. The compact capital has everything: a beautiful old centre, a good array of museums – both national collections and smaller oddball establishments – and a boisterous nightlife. But Copenhagen has little in common with the rest of Zealand, which is largely quiet and rural – much like the country as a whole. Zealand's smaller neighbour, **Funen** (*Fyn*), has only one urban draw in **Odense**, and is otherwise sedate, renowned for the cuteness of its villages, the sandy beaches of its southern coast – a major holiday destination – and numerous explorable small islands.

Only **Jutland** (*Jylland*) is far enough away from Copenhagen to enjoy a truly individual flavour, as well as Denmark's most varied

---

Denmark on the net

ⓦ **www.visitdenmark.com** Official Danish Tourist Board website with links to all regional sites.

ⓦ **www.useit.dk** Loads of useful, practical info, from cheap accommodation to nightlife and events listings. Primarily aimed at budget travellers in the Copenhagen area.

ⓦ **www.woco.dk** The stylish site of the Wonderful Copenhagen office, packed with the latest in restaurants, bars, nightlife and events.

ⓦ **www.aok.dk** Extensive English-language site with the latest listings for Copenhagen.

ⓦ **www.rejseplanen.dk** Door-to-door public transport journey planner.

ⓦ **www.net-bb.dk** Nationwide farm holiday and private accommodation booking.

ⓦ **www.dmol.dk** Museum website with virtual tours of the best places.

ⓦ **www.kulturnet.dk** Directory of cultural exhibits and events. Click on the English-language icon.

ⓦ **www.lego.com** Lots of games, virtual plastic bricks and information about the original Legoland at Billund, Denmark.

scenery, ranging from soft green hills to desolate heathlands. In **Århus**, Jutland also has the most lively and enjoyable city outside the capital.

When to go

Copenhagen attracts visitors all year round, but the intake peaks during July and August – which means **May**, **early June** and **September** are probably the most pleasant times to be there, although there's plenty happening in the city throughout the year. Anywhere else is enjoyably crowd-free all year round except for **July**, the Danish vacation month, when the population heads en

masse for the countryside and the coastal strips – though, even then, only the most popular areas are uncomfortably crowded. Many **outdoor events** – from big rock festivals to local folk dance displays – take place between mid-June and mid-August, when all tourist facilities and transport services (including the more minor ferry links) are operating in full. In more isolated areas things begin to slacken off in September.

Denmark has the least extreme **climate** of the Scandinavian countries, but due to the proximity of the sea the weather can fluctuate rapidly. A wet day will as likely be followed by a sunny one and vice versa, and stiff breezes are common, especially along Jutland's west coast, where they can be

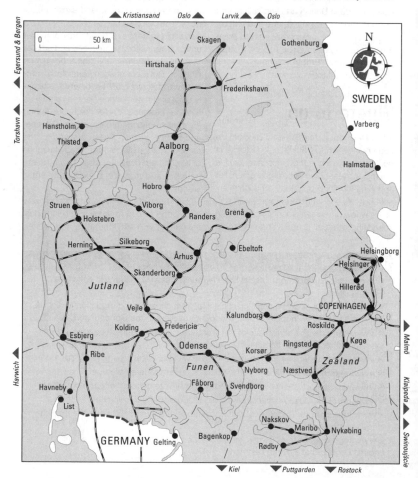

particularly strong. **Summer** is on the whole sunny and clear: throughout July the temperature averages 20°C (68°F), often reaching 26°C (78°F). **Winter** conditions are cold but not severe: there's usually a snow covering from December to early February, and the temperature can at times drop as low as minus 15°C (5°F), but generally it hovers around or just below freezing point.

Getting there from the rest of Scandinavia

One look at a map will show you there'll be few problems **getting to Denmark** from the other Scandinavian countries. Links by **rail**, **sea** and **air** are fast and frequent all year round and, generally speaking, the journey to Denmark can be a rewarding part of your trip rather than a chore.

By train

Copenhagen is a major junction for **trains** between Europe and the rest of Scandinavia, and the new **Øresunds Link** – a part-tunnel, part-bridge connection between Copenhagen and Malmö in Sweden – has improved services immensely. Trains depart every twenty minutes and the journey from Malmö takes only 35 minutes. There are also several daily services to Copenhagen from the major Scandinavian cities – Stockholm, Gothenburg, Oslo, Bergen, Turku and Helsinki – and less frequent links (usually one a day in summer) with remoter spots in the far north, such as Narvik (in Norway) and Kiruna (in Sweden). InterRail, Scanrail and Eurail **passes** are valid on all the international routes into Denmark (see Basics, p.32).

By bus

There are several direct **bus** links between the major Danish cities and the rest of Scandinavia, using either the Øresunds Link or the ferry routes outlined below. From Sweden to Copenhagen, there are usually two buses a day from Stockholm and seven a day from Gothenburg and Olso (Norway). For long-distance enthusiasts, there's also a bus to Helsinki eight times a week in summer, travelling from Copenhagen via Stockholm.

By ferry

Since timetables and prices fluctuate constantly, ferry companies' websites or latest brochures are the best way to check precise details of the numerous **ferries** into Zealand and Jutland from Norway and Sweden; you can also contact any tourist office. There are sometimes reductions for railcard holders (see Basics, p.32), and **fares** are usually a lot cheaper outside the peak period, roughly from the end of June to early August – though bear in mind that services are likely to be less frequent out of season, and possibly non-existent in winter. Even if you're heading for Copenhagen, don't disregard the possibility of a quicker, and cheaper, crossing into north Jutland – an interesting part of Denmark, with easy rail and bus links to the capital; or, from Sweden, reaching Denmark by way of the pretty island of Bornholm.

From Sweden

The cheapest is the Scandlines crossing **from Helsingborg** to Helsingør (@www.scandlines.dk; 20min; one-way tickets 20Skr for foot passengers, 275Skr for cars), which runs around the clock; you can walk, cycle or drive straight on board. Gothenburg–Copenhagen trains used to use this ferry, but are now routed via the new Øresunds Link **from Malmö** to Copenhagen, thus reducing the crossing time from fifty to twenty minutes. Two other operators make the same crossing – see the Helsingør section (p.115) for details.

Stena Line (@www.stenaline.dk) has luxury boats sailing several times a day in summer **from Gothenburg** to Frederikshavn in Jutland (3hr 15min; one-way fares from 100Skr for foot passengers, or from 695Skr for cars; ScanRail holders half price). They also run a hydrofoil Express on the same route, which takes just two hours and costs, one-way, from 140Skr (cars from 795Skr). There's also a twice-daily Stena Line ferry (4hr) from Varberg to Grenå (for Århus) for a basic fare from 100Skr one-way (cars from 695Skr). All Stena Line car fares include five passengers.

With time to spare, you could reach Denmark proper by way of **Bornholm**, a sizeable Danish island in the Baltic that's actually nearer to Sweden's south coast; Bornholm Ferries (⊚ www.bornholmferries.dk) run a service several times daily between Ystad in Sweden and Rønne on Bornholm (1hr 20min; 140Skr). From Rønne, you can take the twice-daily (once in winter) Bornholm Ferries service to Copenhagen, but it's quicker to use the new bus route (*Bornholmerbussen*: ⊚ www.graahundbus.dk; 3hr; 195Skr one-way) via Ystad, which uses the Øresunds Link and is cheaper, too.

From Norway

The only direct connection from Norway to Copenhagen is on the DFDS (⊚ www.dfdsseaways.dk) crossing **from Oslo** (one-way fares from 665Nkr for foot passengers, 930Nkr for cars), though you'll save a lot of money by taking one of the numerous routes to either Hanstholm, Frederikshavn or Hirtshals in Jutland. From Oslo to Frederikshavn, there are four to seven crossings a week with Stena (8hr 30min; from 160–340Nkr one-way), and a similar number to Hirtshals with Color Line (⊚ www.colorline .dk; 8hr 30min; 180–430Nkr). There are also connections **from Bergen via Egersund** to Hanstholm with Fjord Line (⊚ www.fjordline .com; from Bergen 16hr 30min, 720Nkr; from Egersund: 7hr, 420Nkr) and with Color Line **from Larvik** to Frederikshavn (6hr 15min; 180–430Nkr) and Kristiansand to Hirtshals (4hr 30min; same fare). Any of these routes should be cheaper than the fare from Oslo – except perhaps on a summer weekend, when all the lines are at their most expensive.

By plane

SAS (⊚ www.scandinavian.net) operate around twenty direct **flights** daily into Copenhagen **from Oslo and Stockholm**, and eight daily from Helsinki (all 1hr 10min flight time); Finnair (⊚ www.finnair.com) fly several times daily to Copenhagen from Helsinki (2hr 40min). Check the websites or contact a tourist office or travel agent to find out about special reduced fare deals between the Scandinavian capitals – there are usually several each summer.

Copenhagen is very much the Danish hub of the SAS network (Århus is a poor second) and international arrivals often dovetail with domestic flights to other Danish cities, which cost little extra on top of the international fare. The smaller **Maersk Air** (⊚ www.maersk -air.dk) and **Cimber Air** (⊚ www.cimber.dk) link Copenhagen with smaller Danish cities and islands.

British Airways (⊚ www.britishairways .com) run daily flights from Oslo, Stockholm and Gothenburg to Århus, and also three daily flights between Olso and Billund. Maersk Air has three daily connections between Stockholm and Billund, and Kristiansand and Copenhagen, while Danish Air Transport (⊚ www.dat.dk) connects Bergen and Stavanger with Billund and Esbjerg once a day.

Fares for the services listed above vary; one-way fares are upwards of 1500Dkr, but under-26s can enjoy substantial discounts – sometimes paying as little as 500Dkr. Again, check with a travel agent or visit the websites. For flights between Denmark and Finland check with SAS or Finnair.

Costs, money and banks

Costs for virtually everything – eating, sleeping, travelling and entertainment – are **lower** in Denmark than in any other Scandinavian country.

If you come for just a few days, stay in youth hostels or on campsites and don't eat out, it's possible to survive on £20/US$30 a day. Otherwise, moving around the country, combining campsites or hostels with cheap hotel accommodation, visiting museums, eating in a restaurant each day as well as buying a few snacks and going for a drink in the evening, you can expect to spend a minimum of £30–40/US$45–60 per day.

Danish currency is the **krone** (plural kroner), made up of 100 øre, and comes in notes of 1000kr, 500kr, 200kr, 100kr, 50kr, and coins of 20kr, 10kr, 5kr, 2kr, 1kr, 50øre and 25øre.

Banks are the best places to change traveller's cheques and foreign cash; there's a uniform commission of 25kr per transaction

– so change as much as is feasible in one go. Den Danske Bank service American Express card holders free of charge. Banking hours are Mon–Wed & Fri 10am–4pm, Thurs 10am–6pm. Most international airports, train stations and ferry ports have late-opening exchange facilities which charge a similar amount of commission. Alternatively, the red Kontanten high-street **cash machines** (ATMs) give cash advances on credit cards and, if you've a link symbol on your ATM card, will allow you to withdraw funds from your home account in local currency (check with your home bank), which can work out cheaper than changing cash or traveller's cheques.

Mail and communications

Like most other public bodies in the country, the Danish **post office** runs an exceedingly tight ship – within Denmark, anything you post is almost certain to arrive within two days. You can buy **stamps** from most newsagents, and from post offices, most of which are open Mon–Fri 9.30am–5pm, Sat 9.30am–1pm, with reduced hours in smaller communities. Mail under 20g costs 5kr to other parts of Europe, and 6kr to the rest of the world. **Poste restante** is available at any post office, and many hotels, youth hostels and campsites will hold mail ahead of your arrival.

Danish **public telephones** come in two forms. Coin-operated ones are white and require a minimum of 2kr (either one 2kr coin or two 1kr coins) for a local call (the machines irritatingly swallow your money if the number is engaged), and 5kr to go international; cards for the blue cardphones come in denominations of 30kr, 50kr and 100kr and work out a little cheaper; they're sold in newsagents and post offices. Most hotel rooms have a phone but it's much cheaper to make calls from the public phone at reception. Youth hostels and campsites generally have public phones; if not, the warden will probably let you use the house one for a payphone fee. You can use your **mobile phone** in Denmark if it's been connected via the GSM or DCS1800 systems.

In an **emergency**, dial ☎112 from any phone box for a fast free connection to the emergency services.

Calling Denmark from abroad, the **international code** is ☎45; codes for international calls from Denmark are given on p.27. To make a **collect international call**, dial ☎141 for the operator and ask to be connected to the operator in your own country, who will then put through the collect call – full instructions for this "Country Direct" system are displayed in phone booths, and you can dial ☎80 60 40 50 for free assistance. Be warned that **directory enquiries** (international ☎113, domestic ☎118) are expensive, with a minimum charge of 5kr per call, plus a 7kr per-minute accumulating charge that climbs ridiculously high whilst the operator puzzles out your request. Almost all operators speak English. To save money try a phone book (there should be one in all public phone booths), the national phone company's website, ⊛www.teledanmark.dk, or the online (Danish-language) yellow pages, ⊛www.degulesider.dk.

Internet access is available for free at most libraries and some tourist offices. Alternatively hotels, hostels and some sleep-ins will offer access for 20–30kr per hour, and Internet cafés can be found in most towns; we've detailed the most accessible in the Guide.

The media

For a country of its size, Denmark has an impressive number of newspapers and freesheets. By the lowest-common-denominator standards of the modern global media, the Danish press, with its predominantly serious and in-depth coverage of worthy issues, can't help but seem a little anachronistic.

If you can read Danish, your choices among the main daily **newspapers** (each costing 13–18kr) are *Politiken*, a reasonably impartial broadsheet with strong arts features; the conservative/centrist *Berlingske Tidende*; *Kristeligt Dagblad*, a Christian paper; *Jyllands-Posten*, a well-respected right-wing paper; and *Information*, left-wing and intellectual. The weekly *Weekendavisen*, published on Thursdays, has excellent background features. The best sports coverage can be found in the two tabloids – *BT*, which has a conservative bias, and *Ekstra Bladet*. You'll find excellent **entertainment listings** in both *Jyllands-Posten* and *Politiken*, and every Thursday *Information* has a section devoted to listings too. The free Danish **rock music** paper, the monthly *Gaffa*, lists most of the bigger rock shows, and innumerable similar regional papers do the same for their areas – find them in cafés, record shops and the like. The **English-language newspaper** *Copenhagen Post* covers domestic issues and has an in-depth listings section; it comes out every Friday and costs 15kr. **Overseas newspapers** are sold in all the main towns: most UK weekday titles cost 15–24kr and are available the day after publication from train stations and the bigger newsagents, which are also likely to stock recent issues of *USA Today*. There's also a very short *News In English* programme weekdays at 8.40am, 11am, 5.10pm and 10pm on Radio Denmark International (1062MHz).

After a slow start, **Danish television** has expanded rapidly. Ten years ago there was only one national station; today, there are four national and four cable channels. The four nationals are the non-commercial DR1 and DR2, and the commercial channels TV2 and TV2 Zulu – though, apart from the advertising, you'll probably struggle to spot the difference between them. The cable channels, some of which are shared with Sweden and Norway, are all commercial and prolific in American sitcoms and soaps (usually with Danish subtitles). If you're staying in a hotel, or a youth hostel with a TV room, you may also have the option of German and Swedish channels – plus a dozen cable and satellite stations.

Getting around

Despite being made up largely of islands, Denmark is a swift and easy country in which to travel. All types of **public transport** – trains, buses and the essential ferries – are punctual and efficient, and where you need to switch from one type to another,

you'll find the timetables impressively well integrated.

And with Denmark being such a small country, you can get from one end to the other in half a day; even if, as is more likely, you're planning to see it all at leisure, you'll rarely need to do more than an hour's daily travelling. Besides being small, Denmark is also very flat, with scores of villages linked by country roads – ideal for effortless cycling.

Trains

Trains are easily the most efficient and convenient way to get about. Danske Statsbaner (DSB) – Danish State Railways – run an exhaustive and reliable network. InterRail, Eurail and ScanRail **passes** are valid on all routes except the few private lines that operate in some rural areas. There are just a few out-of-the-way regions that trains fail to penetrate, though these can be easily crossed by buses, which often run in conjunction with local train connections. Some of these buses are operated privately, but on those run by DSB, train passes are valid (for more on buses, see opposite).

Trains range from **inter-city expresses** (**ICLyn**), with a buffet service, to smaller **local trains** (**regionaltog**). Departure times are listed on notices both on station concourses and the platforms (departures in yellow, arrivals in white), and announced over the loudspeaker. On the train, each station is usually called a few minutes before you arrive. Watch out for *stillekupé* – special quiet compartments where children, pets and mobile phones are prohibited.

Tickets should be bought in advance from train stations, either from ticket booths or automated machines, which take all major credit cards but no cash. On international services and ICLyn trains using the new bridge over the Store Bælt between Zealand and Funen, you must also purchase a seat reservation (20kr); other trains don't require advance reservations, but then there's no guarantee that you'll get a seat. There's an extra charge of 25kr if you buy tickets on board the train. All trains have an inspector who checks tickets: he/she is almost certain to speak English and will normally be able to answer questions about routes and times.

Fares are calculated on a zonal system. Copenhagen–Odense, for example, costs 202kr one-way, Copenhagen–Århus, 287kr. Both these fares include the cost of a seat reservation, and your train ticket will also get you around on the local buses (and S-trains in Copenhagen) in the departure and arrival town of your journey on the day the ticket is valid. The price of a return ticket is no cheaper than two one-ways. If you're between 16 and 25 and plan to do lots of train travel, it may be worthwhile buying a DSB Wildcard (175kr), which gives you a 25 percent discount on normal tickets and 50 percent discount if you avoid travelling on Friday or Sunday from 4am until 4am the next day. There are no student discounts, but people over 65 qualify for the same discounts as Wildcard holders. Travelling in a group of eight or more also entitles you to a 25–30 percent discount – get details from any Danish tourist office.

As for timings, DSB's Køreplan (30kr from any newsagent) details all DSB train, bus and ferry services inside (and long-distance routes outside) the country, including the local Copenhagen S-train system and all private services, and is a sound investment if you're planning to do a lot of travelling within the country. If you're not, smaller timetables detailing specific routes can be picked up for free at tourist offices and station ticket offices.

Buses

There are only a handful of long-distance bus services in Denmark. Abildskous Rutebiler (☎70 21 08 00, ❀www.abildskou .dk) run a swift Århus–Copenhagen service five to seven times a day, some routed via Ebeltoft, at 210kr one-way (students pay 110kr at specified times). The Aalborg–Copenhagen route is serviced by Thinggard (☎70 10 00 10, ❀www.thinggaard-bus.dk; 220kr one-way), which also runs a Frederikshavn–Esbjerg service (240kr) that stops in Aalborg, Viborg, Herning and Grinsted. Søndergaards Busser (☎70 10 00 33, ❀www.sondergaards-busser.dk; 260kr one-way) run a service between Fjerritslev and Copenhagen three to four times a day, with stops in Løgstør, Hobro, Randers and Grenå, while Bornholmerbussen (☎44 68 44

00, ❀www.graahundbus.dk) run a service three to five times a day (200kr one-way) between Copenhagen and Bornholm, via the new Øresunds Link and Ystad in Sweden. These fares represent quite a saving over full train fares but, while just as efficient, long-distance buses are much less comfortable than trains. However, buses really come into their own in the few areas where trains are scarce or connections complicated – much of Funen and northeast Jutland, for example – and if you're travelling from Esbjerg to Frederikshavn or Aalborg you save several hours, and a lot of timetable reading, by taking the bus. Around Jutland, the government-run X-busser express buses (☎98 90 09 00, ❀www .xbus.dk) are especially worth checking out. Buses are also often the best way of getting to smaller outlying towns; head for the local tourist office or bus station for information.

Ferries

Ferries connect all the Danish islands, and vary in size and speed from the state-of-the-art catamaran linking Zealand and Jutland to raft-like affairs serving tiny, isolated settlements a few minutes off the (so-called) mainland. Where applicable, train and bus fares include the cost of ferry crossings (although you can also pay at the terminal and walk on), while the smaller ferries charge 10–50kr for foot passengers. Contact the nearest tourist office for full details.

Planes

Domestic flights are hardly essential in somewhere of Denmark's size, but can be handy if you're in a rush: from Copenhagen it's less than an hour's flying time to anywhere in the country. Three airlines connect the country: SAS (☎60 72 77 27, ❀www .scandinavian.net), Maersk Air (☎73 33 00 66, ❀www.maersk-air.com) and Cimber Air (☎74 42 22 23, ❀www.cimber.dk). They often run routes in partnership, so you may well find yourself on an SAS plane with a Cimber Air ticket. Fares vary only slightly between the three companies, although it can be worthwhile to check for special offers. The longer in advance you book, the cheaper the flight, and if you're under 25 you always get good deals, such as 400kr one-way from Copenhagen to Århus. Weekend tickets are generally cheaper than weekdays, from 880kr return between Copenhagen and Århus if you book 21 days in advance; get details from an SAS desk or tourist office.

Driving and hitching

Given the excellent public transport system, the size of the country, and the comparatively high price of petrol, **driving** isn't really economical unless you're in a group. **Car rental** is expensive, though it's worth checking the cut-price deals offered by some airlines. You'll need an international driving licence and must be aged at least 20 to take to the roads, although many firms won't rent vehicles to anyone under 25. Costs start at around 2850kr a week for a small hatchback with unlimited mileage, Rent a Wreck (*Lej et lig*; ⊕www.lejetlig.dk, ☎39 29 85 05) offers the best deal for limited mileage (100km per day) at 2100kr for a week – the cars aren't really wrecks, they're just not new. Danes drive on the right, and there's a speed limit in towns of 50kph, 80kph in open country and 110kph on motorways. As in Sweden and Finland, headlights need to be used at all times. There are random breath tests for suspected drunken drivers, and the penalties are severe. When parked in a town, not on a meter, a parking-time disc must be displayed; get one from a tourist office, police station or bank. You set the time when you've parked on the hands of the clock, then return before your allotted time (indicated by signs) is up. The national motoring organization, Forenede Danske Motorejere, operates a 24-hour **breakdown service** (☎45 88 00 25) for AA members; if you're not an AA member, Dansk Autohjælp (☎70 10 80 90) and Falck (☎70 10 20 30) can be summoned from callboxes by the road. A standard call-out fee will be charged – Dansk Autohjælp is the cheapest at 547kr per hour.

Hitching is illegal on motorways, but otherwise it's a fairly easy and reasonably safe way to get around.

Cycling

Cycling is the ideal way to appreciate Denmark's pastoral, and mostly flat, landscape, as well as being a good method of getting around the towns. Traffic is sparse on most country roads and all large towns have cycle tracks – though watch out for sometimes less-than-careful drivers on main roads. Bikes can be **rented** at nearly all youth hostels and tourist offices, at most bike shops and at some train stations for around 40–50kr per day or 225kr per week; there's often a 200kr refundable deposit, too. For long-distance cycling, take the frequent westerly winds into account when **planning your route** – pedalling is easier facing east than west. The Danish cyclist organization Dansk Cyklistforbund (☎33 32 31 21, ⊕www.dcf.dk) offers cycling advice.

If the wind gets too strong, or your legs get too tired, you can take your bike on all types of public transport except city buses. On trains, you'll have to pay according to the zonal system used to calculate passenger tickets – for example, 50kr to take your bike from Copenhagen to Århus, with 20kr on top if you want to reserve a place in advance. The brochure *Cyckle i Tog* (free from train stations) lists rates and rules in full. For a similar fee, long-distance buses have limited cycle space, while ferries let bikes on free or for a few kroner. Domestic flights charge around 200kr for airlifting your bike.

Accommodation

While less costly in Denmark than in other Nordic countries, **accommodation** is still going to be your major daily expense, and you should plan it carefully. **Hotels** are by no means off-limits if you seek out the better offers, and both **youth hostels**, **sleep-ins** and **campsites** are plentiful – and of a uniformly high standard.

Hotels, inns and private rooms

Coming to Denmark on a standard package trip (see Basics, p.15) is one way to stay in a **hotel** without spending a fortune. Another is simply to be selective. Most Danish hotel rooms include phone, TV and bathroom, for which you'll pay from around 700kr for a double (singles from around 450kr); going without the luxuries can result in big savings,

The hotels and guesthouses listed in the Danish chapters of this Guide have been graded according to the following price bands, based on the cost of the **least expensive double room in summer.**

- ❶ Under 300kr
- ❷ 300–400kr
- ❸ 400–500kr
- ❹ 500–650kr
- ❺ 650–900kr
- ❻ 900–1300kr
- ❼ Over 1300kr

and in most large towns you'll find hotels offering rooms with access to a shared bathroom for as little as 500kr for a double (350kr a single). Some **inns** (called *kro*) in country areas match this price – sometimes for rooms with full facilities. Other advantages of staying in a hotel or inn are the lack of a curfew (common in hostels in big cities) and the inclusion of an all-you-can-eat breakfast – so large you won't need to buy lunch.

Danish tourist offices overseas (see p.30) can provide a free list of hotels throughout the country, though much more accurate and extensive information can be found at local tourist offices. It's a good idea to **book in advance**, especially in peak season, which is most easily done via the tourist office or hotel website (listed in relevant places throughout the Guide chapters); booking directly on the net yourself can result in discounts of up to 35 percent. Tourist offices can also supply details of **private rooms** in someone's home, vaguely akin to British-style bed-and-breakfasts (often without breakfast). These vary greatly in price and standard, but reckon on paying 400–500kr for a double. Alternatively, staying on **farms** (*Bondegårdsferi*) is becoming increasingly popular in Denmark; as well as your room, there's the opportunity to watch a farm at work. Information and catalogues can be obtained from Ferie på Landet, Ceresvej 2, 8410 Rønde (☎86 37 39 00, ⓦwww.bondegaardsferie.dk).

Youth hostels and sleep-ins

Youth hostels (*vandrerhjem*) are Denmark's cheapest option under a roof. Every town has one, they're much less pricey than hotels, and they have a high degree of comfort. Most offer a choice of various sizes of private room (we've given price codes for

these in the Guide chapters), often with toilets and showers, and all have dormitory accommodation; nearly all have cooking facilities, too. **Rates** are around 100kr for a dormitory bed to 200–400kr for a private room. Other than those in major towns or ferry ports, it's rare for hostels to be full, but during the summer it's always wise to phone ahead to make a reservation, and to check on location – some hostels are several kilometres outside the town centre.

As with all Scandinavian hostels, sleeping bags are not allowed, so you need to bring either a sheet sleeping bag or rent hostel linen – which can become expensive over a long stay. It's a good idea, too, to get an **HI card**, since without one you'll be hit with the cost of either an overnight card (30kr) or a year-long Danish membership card (1600kr). If you're planning on doing a lot of hostelling, it's worth contacting Danhostel Danmarks Vandrerhjem, Vesterbrogade 39, DK-1620, Copenhagen V (☎33 31 36 12, ⓦwww.danhostel.dk) to get a copy of their free guide to Danish hostels, *Danmarks Vandrerhjem*, which is published in several languages including English, and for their very informative hostel/campsite map of Denmark.

Sleep-ins are a similarly cheap option if you're on a budget but don't want to camp. Originally run by the local authorities, sleep-ins are now just a more traveller-oriented version of a hostel – privately run and generally always packed with young backpackers. Some open between May and August only, but most now open year-round. For bed, shower and breakfast, expect to pay around 100kr; bear in mind that you'll need your own sleeping bag, that only one night's stay is permitted in some cases, and that there may be an age restriction (typically 16- to 24-year-olds only, although this may not be strictly enforced). Sleep-ins come and go, so check the current situation at a local tourist office, or with Use-It in Copenhagen (see p.85).

Camping

If you don't already have an International Camping Card from a camping organization in your own country, you'll need a Camping Card Scandinavia to **camp** in Denmark, which costs 80kr for both individuals and families, can be bought from any campsite and is valid on all official sites in Scandinavia until the end of the year in which it was bought. A Transit Pass can be used for a single overnight stay and costs 20kr per person. **Camping rough** without the landowner's permission is illegal, but possible if you stay out of sight; a dim view is taken of camping on beaches and an on-the-spot fine may well be imposed. In a few rural spots, the local tourist office will be able to inform you about a corner of a nearby field that's been assigned for rough camping.

Campsites (*camping plads*) can, in any case, be found virtually everywhere. All are open in June, July and August, many are open from April through to September, and a few operate all year round. There's a rigid **grading system**: one-star sites have drinking water and toilets, two-star sites have, in addition, kitchen, showers, laundry and a food shop within a kilometre, while three-star sites (by far the majority) have all the above plus a TV room, on-site shop, cafeteria, and perhaps other facilities such as a swimming pool. **Prices** vary only slightly, three-star sites charging 45–60kr per person, the others a few kroner less, though you may pay more at city sites or those in other particularly popular locations. Many campsites also have **cabin accommodation**, usually with cooking facilities, which at 2000–4000kr for a six-berth affair for a week may represent a saving for several people sharing, although on busy sites cabins are often booked up throughout the summer. Any Danish tourist office can give you a free leaflet listing all the country's sites and the basic camping rules, or there's an official guide, *Camping Danmark*, available from kiosks, bookshops and tourist offices (95kr). For further information, contact the Campingrådet, Hesseløgade 16, DK-2100 København Ø (☎39 27 88 44, ⓦwww.campingraadet.dk).

Food and drink

Although good **food** can cost a lot, there are plenty of ways to eat affordably and healthily in Denmark, and with plenty of variety, too. Much the same applies to **drink**: the only Scandinavian country free of social drinking taboos, Denmark is an imbiber's delight – both for its huge choice of tipples, and for the number of places where they can be sampled.

Food

Traditional **Danish food** is centred on meat and fish: beef, veal, chicken and pork are frequent menu items – though rarely bacon, which is mainly exported – along with various forms of salmon, herring, eel, plaice and cod. Combinations of these are served with potatoes and another, usually boiled, vegetable. Ordinary **restaurant** meals can be expensive, especially in the evening, and are often no-go areas for vegetarians – but there are other ways to eat Danish food that won't ruin your budget or your diet.

Breakfast

Breakfast (*morgenmad*) can be the tastiest and is certainly the healthiest (and most meat-free) Danish meal. Almost all hotels offer a sumptuous breakfast as a matter of course, as do youth hostels. You can often attack a buffet table laden with cereals, bread, cheese, boiled eggs, fruit juice, milk, coffee and tea for around 40kr. Breakfast elsewhere will be far less substantial: many cafés offer a very basic one for around 30kr, but you're well advised to hold out until 10am and go for **brunch** instead. Served until mid-afternoon, brunch is a filling option for late starters consisting of variations of international-style breakfasts (American, English etc) for 40–90kr depending on your craving. Later in the day, a tight budget may leave you dependent on self-catering.

Lunch and snacks

You can track down an excellent-value **lunch** (*frokost*) simply by walking around and reading the signs chalked up outside any café, restaurant or *bodega* (a kind of bar that also sells no-frills food). On these

Glossary of Danish food and drink terms

Basics

Brød	Bread
Bøfsandwich	Hamburger
Chokolade (varm)	Chocolate (hot)
Det kolde bord	Help-yourself cold buffet
Is	Ice cream
Kaffe (med fløde)	Coffee (with cream)
Letmælk	Semi-skimmed milk
Mælk	Milk
Kiks	Biscuits
Ostebord	Cheese board
Pølser	Frankfurters/ sausages
Sildebord	A selection of spiced and pickled herring
Skummetmælk	Skimmed milk
Smør	Butter
Smørrebrød	Open sandwiches
Sødmælk	Full-fat milk
Sukker	Sugar
Te	Tea
Wienerbrød	"Danish" pastry

Egg (æg) dishes

Kogt æg	Boiled egg
Omelet	Omelette
Røræg	Scrambled eggs
Spejlæg	Fried eggs

Fish (Fisk)

Ål	Eel
Forel	Trout
Gedde	Pike
Helleflynder	Halibut
Hummer	Lobster
Karpe	Carp
Klipfisk	Salt cod
Krabbe	Crab
Krebs	Crayfish
Laks	Salmon
Makrel	Mackerel
Rejer	Shrimp
Rogn	Roe
Rødspætte	Plaice
Røget Sild	Kipper
Sardiner	Sardines
Sild	Herring
Søtunge	Sole
Stør	Sturgeon
Store rejer	Prawns
Torsk	Cod

Meat (Kød)

And(ung)	Duck(ling)
Oksekød	Beef
Dyresteg	Venison
Fasan	Pheasant
Gås	Goose
Hare	Hare
Kalkun	Turkey
Kanin	Rabbit
Kylling	Chicken
Lam	Lamb
Lever	Liver
Rensdyr	Reindeer
Skinke	Ham
Svinekød	Pork

Vegetables (Grøntsager)

Artiskokker	Artichokes
Asparges	Asparagus
Blomkål	Cauliflower
Champignons	Mushrooms
Grønne bønner	Runner beans
Gulerødder	Carrots
Brune bønner	Kidney beans
Hvidløg	Garlic
Julesalat	Chicory
Kartofler	Potatoes
Linser	Lentils
Løg	Onions
Majs	Sweetcorn
Majskolbe	Corn on the cob
Nudler	Noodles
Peberfrugt	Peppers
Persille	Parsley
Porrer	Leeks
Ris	Rice
Rødbeder	Beetroot
Rødkål	Red cabbage
Rosenkål	Brussels sprouts
Salat	Lettuce, salad
Salatgurk	Cucumber
Selleri	Celery
Spinat	Spinach
Turnips	Turnips

Fruit (Frugt)

Æbler	Apples
Abrikoser	Apricots
Ananas	Pineapple
Appelsiner	Oranges
Bananer	Bananas
Blommer	Plums
Blåbær	Blueberries

continued overleaf ↘

Brombær	Blackberries	**Drink (Drikke)**	
Citron	Lemon	Æblemost	Apple juice
Ferskner	Peaches	Appelsinvand	Orangeade
Grapefrugt	Grapefruit	Citronvand	Lemonade
Hindbær	Raspberries	Eksport-Øl	Export beer (very
Jordbær	Strawberries		strong lager)
Kirsebær	Cherries	Fadøl	Draught beer
Mandariner	Tangerines	Guldøl	Strong beer
Melon	Melon	Husets vin	House wine
Pærer	Pears	Hvidvin	White wine
Rabarber	Rhubarb	Kærnemælk	Buttermilk
Rosiner	Raisins	Mineralvand	Soda water
Solbær	Blackcurrants	Øl	Beer
Stikkelsbær	Gooseberries	Rødvin	Red wine
Svesker	Prunes	Tomatjuice	Tomato juice
Vindruer	Grapes	Vin	Wine

Danish specialities

Æbleflæsk	Smoked bacon with onions and sautéed apple rings
Æggekage	Scrambled eggs with onions, chives, potatoes and bacon pieces
Ålesuppe	Sweet and sour eel soup
Boller i karry	Meatballs in curry sauce served with rice
Flæskesteg	A hunk of pork with red cabbage, potatoes and brown sauce
Frikadeller	Pork rissoles
Grillstegt kylling	Grilled chicken
Hakkebøf	Thick minced-beef burgers fried with onions
Kalvebryst i frikasseé	Veal boiled with vegetables and served in a white sauce with peas and carrots
Kogt torsk	Poached cod in mustard sauce with boiled potatoes
Medisterpølse	A spiced pork sausage, usually served with boiled potatoes or stewed vegetables
Røget sild	Smoked herring on rye bread garnished with a raw egg yolk, radishes and chives
Sild i karry	Herring in curry sauce
Skidne æg	Poached or hard-boiled eggs in a cream sauce, spiced with fish mustard and served with rye bread, garnished with sliced bacon and chives
Skipper labskovs	Danish stew: small squares of beef boiled with potatoes, peppercorns and bay leaves
Stegt ål med stuvede kartofler	Fried eel with diced potatoes and white sauce

notices, put out between 11.30am and 2.30pm, you'll often see the word **tilbud**, which refers to the "special" priced dish, or **dagens ret**, meaning "dish of the day" – a plate of chilli con carne or lasagne for around 40kr, or a two-course set lunch for about 60kr. Some restaurants carry a fixed-price (70–90kr) three-course lunch where you can pick from a selection of dishes. A variation on this idea is a choice of **smørre-brød**, or open sandwiches: slices of rye bread heaped with meat (commonly either ham, beef or liver pâté), fish (salmon, eel, caviar, cod roe, shrimp or herring) or cheese, and generously piled with assorted trimmings (mushrooms, cucumber, pickles or slices of lemon). A selection of three or four of these costs about 75kr. You can buy smørrebrød to go for 9–25kr from the special shops you'll see in every fairly sizeable town; one of them usually opens late, too, until 10pm. At cafés you'll always be able to find a bulky sandwich (30–50kr) or a filling portion of salad (usually served with fresh bread) for 50–70kr. Otherwise, the American **burger** franchises are as commonplace and as popular as you'd expect, as are **pizzerias**, which are dependable and affordable at any time of day, with many offering special deals such as all-you-can-eat-salad with a basic pizza for about 50kr, or a more exotic dish or pizza topping for 50–70kr. **Shawarmas** (kebabs) and **China Boxes** (your selection of Chinese dishes from a buffet served in a takeaway box) are also easy to find in most larger towns; both cost around 25kr. You can also get a very ordinary self-service meat, fish or omelette lunch in a **supermarket cafeteria** for 50–90kr.

Most Danes buy **snacks** from the very popular fast-food stands (*pølsevogn*) found on all main streets and at train stations. These serve various types of **sausage** (*pølser*) for 16–24kr: the hotdog with trimmings such as roasted onion, remoulade and pickled cucumber, the long thin *wiener*, the fatter *frankfurter*, or the *franske hotdog*, a sausage inside a cylindrical piece of bread. Alternatives include a **toasted ham and cheese sandwich** (*parisertoast*) for 12–15kr – vegetarians can ask for the ham to be left out – and **chips** (*pommes frites*), which come in big (*store*) and small (*lille*) forms. All of the above come with various types of ketchup and mustard to order.

If you just want a cup of **coffee** (all Italian or French versions are widely available, as is freshly made filter coffee) or **tea** (usually a fairly exotic teabag brew), drop into the nearest café, where either will cost 12–35kr. You help it down with a **Danish pastry** (*wienerbrød*), tastier and much less sweet than the imitations sold abroad under the same name.

Dinner

Dinner (*aftensmad*) in Denmark presents as much choice as lunch, but the cost can be a lot higher. Pizzerias and similar places keep their prices unchanged from lunchtime, and many youth hostels serve simple but filling evening meals for up to 65kr, though you have to order in advance. The most cost-effective dinners (70–90kr), however, are usually found in **ethnic restaurants** (most commonly Chinese or Middle Eastern, with a smaller number of Indian, Indonesian and Thai), which, besides à la carte dishes, often have a buffet table – ideal for gluttonous over-indulgence – and you usually get soup and a dessert thrown in as well. The **Danish restaurants** that are promising for lunch often turn into expense-account affairs at night, offering an atmospheric, candle-lit setting for the slow devouring of immaculately prepared meat or fish; you'll be hard-pushed to spend less than 200kr per person.

Shops and markets

An especially tight budget may well leave you dependent on **shopping for food**. Brugsen, Føtex and Irma are the most commonly found **supermarkets** (usually open Mon–Fri 9am–5.30pm, later on Thurs & Fri, Sat 9am–5pm), and there's little difference in price between them. You'll also come across Aldi, Netto and Fakta, which are cheaper but also more chaotic and with less choice. Smaller supermarkets may be open shorter hours, especially on Saturdays, when they tend to close at 1pm or 2pm except on the first Saturday of the month. Late-night shopping is generally impossible, although in bigger towns, the DSB supermarket at the train station is likely to be open until midnight. The best spots for fresh fruit and veg are the Saturday and (sometimes) Wednesday **markets** held in most towns.

Drink

If you've arrived from near-teetotal Norway or Sweden, you're in for a shock. Not only is alcoholic **drink** entirely accepted in Denmark, it's quite common to see people strolling along the pedestrianized streets swigging from a bottle of beer, and although extreme drunkenness is frowned upon, alcohol is widely consumed throughout the day by most types of people.

Although you can buy booze more cheaply from supermarkets, the most sociable **places to drink** are pubs and cafés, where the emphasis is on beer – although you can also get spirits and wine (or tea and coffee). There are also bars and *bodegas* (see p.60), in which, as a very general rule, the mood tends to favour wines and spirits, and the customers are a bit older than those found in cafés.

The cheapest type of beer is **bottled beer**, which costs 18–25kr for a third of a litre, and is less potent than so-called **gold beer** (*Guldøl* or *Elefantøl*), also in bottles and costing 20–30kr per bottle. **Draught beer** (*fadøl*) is more expensive, with a quarter of a litre costing 15–30kr, half a litre 30–45kr. It's a touch weaker than both types of bottled beer, but tastes fresher and is increasingly popular. All Danish beer is lager-style, the most common brands being Carlsberg and Tuborg, and although a number of towns have their own locally brewed rivals, you'll need a finely tuned palate to spot much difference between them. One you will notice the taste of is Lys Pilsner, a very low-alcohol lager.

Most international **wines and spirits** are widely available, a shot of the hard stuff costing 15–35kr in a bar, a glass of wine upwards of 25kr. While in the country, you should investigate the many varieties of the schnapps-like **Akvavit**, which Danes consume as eagerly as beer, especially with meals; more than two or three turn most non-Danes pale. A tasty relative is the gloriously hot and strong Gammel Dansk Bitter Dram – Akvavit-based but made with bitters – only ever drunk with food at breakfast time.

Directory

Emergencies ☎112. Ask for fire, police or ambulance.

Fishing Well stocked with bream, dace, roach, pike, trout, zander and much more, Denmark's lakes and rivers are a fishing enthusiast's dream. The only problem is bringing enough bait (more expensive than you might expect) to cope with the inevitably large catch. The time to come is in early or late summer, and the prime areas are in central Jutland, around Randers and Viborg, and slightly further north around Silkeborg and Skanderborg. For specialist angling trips, see the "Getting There" sections in Basics, p.15.

Public holidays On the following days, all shops and banks are closed, while public transport and many museums run to Sunday schedules: January 1, Maundy Thursday, Good Friday, Easter Monday, Common Prayers Day (fourth Friday after Easter), Ascension Day (fortieth day after Easter), Whit Monday (eighth Monday after Easter), Labour Day (the afternoon of May 1 – unofficial, but observed by most work places), Constitution Day (June 5), Christmas Eve (afternoon only), Christmas Day and Boxing Day.

Sales tax A tax of 25 percent is added to almost everything you'll buy – but it's always included in the marked price.

Shops Opening hours are Mon–Thurs 10am–5.30pm, Fri 10am–6pm or 7pm, Sat 9am–1pm or 2pm, Sun closed. Supermarkets in larger towns open a bit later. On the first Saturday of the month shops stay open until 5pm.

Tipping Unless you need porters to help carry your luggage, you'll never be expected to tip – restaurant bills include a 15 percent service charge.

History

Spending much time in Denmark soon makes you realize that its history is entirely disproportionate to its size. Nowadays a small – and often overlooked – nation, Denmark has nonetheless played an important role in key periods of European history, firstly as home-base of the Vikings, and later as a medieval superpower. Markers to the past, from prehistory to the wartime resistance movement, are never hard to find. Equally easy to spot are the benefits stemming from one of the earliest welfare state systems and some of western Europe's most liberal social policies.

Early settlements

Traces of human habitation, such as deer bones prized open for marrow, have been found in central Jutland and dated at 50,000 BC, but it's unlikely that any settlements of this time were permanent, as much of the land was still covered by ice. From 14,000 BC, tribes from more southerly parts of Europe arrived during the summer to hunt reindeer for their meat, and antlers which provided raw material for axes and other tools. The melting ice caused the shape of the land to change and the warmer climate enabled vast forests to grow in Jutland. From about 4000 BC, settlers with agricultural knowledge arrived: they lived in villages, grew wheat and barley and kept animals, and buried their dead in **dolmens** or megalithic graves.

The earliest metal and bronze finds are from 1800 BC, the result of trade with southern Europe. (The richness of some pieces indicates an awareness of the cultures of Crete and Mycenae.) By this time the country was widely cultivated and densely populated. Battles for control over individual areas saw the emergence of a ruling warrior class, and, around 500 AD, a tribe from Sweden calling themselves **Danes** migrated southwards and took control of what became known as **Danmark**.

The Viking era

Around 800 AD, under **King Godfred**, the Danish boundaries were marked out. However, following Charlemagne's conquest of the Saxons in Germany, the Franks began to threaten the Danes' territory, and they had to prepare an opposing force. The Danes built fast, seaworthy vessels and defeated Charlemagne easily. Then, with the Norwegians, they attacked Spanish ports and eventually invaded Britain. By 1033, the Danes controlled the whole of England and Normandy and dominated trade in the Baltic.

In Denmark itself, which then included much of what is now southern Sweden, the majority of people were farmers: the less wealthy paid taxes to the king and those who owned large tracts of land provided the monarch with military forces. In time, a **noble class** emerged, expecting and receiving privileges from the king in return for their support. Law-making was the responsibility of the *ting*, a type of council consisting of district noblemen. Above the district *ting* there was a provincial *ting*, charged with the election of the king. The successful candidate could be any member of the royal family, which led to a high level of feuding and bloodshed.

In 960, with the baptism of King **Harald** ("**Bluetooth**"), Denmark became officially Christian – principally, it's thought, to stave off imminent invasion by the German emperor. Nonetheless, Harald gave permission to a Frankish monk, **Ansgar**, to build the **first Danish church**, and Ansgar went on to take control of missionary activity throughout Scandinavia. Harald was succeeded by his son **Sweyn I** ("**Forkbeard**"). Though he was a pagan, Sweyn tolerated Christianity, despite suspecting the missionaries of bringing a German influence to bear in Danish affairs. In 990 he joined with the Norwegians in attacking Britain, whose king was the well-named Ethelred "the Unready". Sweyn's son, **Knud I** ("**the Great**") – King Canute of England – married Ethelred's widow, took the British throne and soon controlled a sizeable empire around the North Sea – the zenith of Viking power.

The rise of the Church

During the eleventh and twelfth centuries, Denmark was weakened by violent **internal struggles**, not only between different would-be rulers but also among the Church, nobility and monarchy. Following the death of Sweyn II in 1074, two of his four sons, Knud and Harald, fought for the throne, with Harald (supported by the peasantry and the Church) emerging victorious. A mild and introspective individual, Harald was nonetheless a competent monarch, and introduced the first real Danish currency. He was constantly derided by Knud and his allies, however, and after his death in 1080 his brother became Knud II. He made generous donations to the Church, but his introduction of higher taxes and the absorption of all unclaimed land into the realm enraged the nobility. The farmers of north Jutland revolted in 1086, forcing Knud to flee to Odense, where he was slain on the high altar of Skt Alban's Kirke. The ten-year period of poor harvests that ensued was taken by many to be divine wrath, and there were reports of miracles occurring in Knud's tomb, leading to the murdered king's canonization in 1101.

The battles for power continued, and eventually, in 1131, a **civil war** broke out that was to simmer for two decades, with various claimants to the throne and their offspring slugging it out with the support of either the Church or nobility. During this time the power of the clergy escalated dramatically thanks to **Bishop Eskil**, who enjoyed a persuasive influence on the eventual successor, Erik III. Following Erik's death in 1143, the disputes went on, leading to the division of the kingdom between two potential rulers, Sweyn and Knud. Sweyn's repeated acts of tyranny resulted in the death of Knud in Roskilde, but Knud's wounded aide, Valdemar, managed to escape and raise the Jutlanders in revolt at the **battle of Grathe Heath**, south of Viborg.

The Valdemar era

Valdemar I ("**the Great**") assumed the throne in 1157, strengthening the crown by ending the elective function of the *ting*, and shifting the power of choosing the monarch to the Church. Technically the *ting* still influenced the choice of king, but in practice hereditary succession became the rule.

After Bishop Eskil's retirement, **Absalon** became Archbishop of Denmark, erecting a fortress at the fishing village of **Havn** (later to become København – Copenhagen). Besides being a zealous churchman, Absalon possessed a sharp military mind and came to dominate Valdemar I and his successor, Knud IV. During this period, Denmark saw some of its best years, expanding to the south and east, and taking advantage of internal strife within Germany. In time, after Absalon's death and the succession of **Valdemar II**, Denmark controlled all trade along the south coast of the Baltic and in the North Sea east of the Ejder. Valdemar II was also responsible for subjugating Norway, and in 1219 he set out to conquer Estonia and take charge of Russian trade routes through the Gulf of Finland. According to Danish legend, the national flag, the Dannebrog, fell down from heaven during a battle in Estonia in 1219.

However, in 1223 Valdemar II was kidnapped by Count Henry of Schwerin (a Danish vassal) and forced to give up many Danish possessions.

There was also a redrawing of the southern boundary of Jutland, which caused the Danish population of the region to be joined by a large number of Saxons from Holstein.

Within Denmark, the years of expansion had brought great prosperity. The rules of the *ting* were written down as the **Jutlandic Code**, thus unifying laws all over the country – an act which had the effect of concentrating powers of justice in the person of the monarch, rather than the *ting*. The increasingly affluent nobles, however, demanded greater rights if they were to be counted on to support the new king. The Church was envious of their growing power and much bickering ensued in the following years, resulting in the eventual installation of Valdemar II's son, Christoffer I, as monarch.

Christoffer died suddenly in Ribe when his only son Erik was two years old; Queen Margrethe took the role of regent until **Erik V** came of age. Erik's overbearing manner and penchant for German bodyguards annoyed the nobles, and they forced him to a meeting at Nyborg in 1282 where his powers were limited by a *håndfæstning*, or charter, that included an undertaking for annual consultation with a Danehof, or forum of nobles. In 1319 **Christoffer II** became king, after agreeing to an even sterner charter, which allowed for daily consultations with a *råd* – a council of nobles. In 1326, in lieu of a debt which Christoffer had no hope of repaying, **Count Gerd of Holstein** occupied a large portion of Jutland. Christoffer fled to Mecklenburg and Gerd installed the twelve-year-old Valdemar, Duke of Schleswig, as a puppet king.

As they proceeded to divide the country among themselves, the Danish nobles became increasingly unpopular with both the Church and the peasantry. Christoffer attempted to take advantage of the internal discord to regain the crown in 1329 but was defeated in battle by Gerd. Under the peace terms, Gerd was given Jutland and Funen, while his cousin, Count Johan of Plön, was granted Zealand, Skåne, Lolland and Falster. In 1332 Skåne, the richest Danish province, inflicted a final insult on Christoffer when its inhabitants revolted against Johan and transferred their allegiance to the Swedish king, Magnus.

Gerd was murdered in 1340. The years of turmoil had taken their toll on all sections of Danish society: from Christoffer's death in 1332, the country had been without a monarch and it was felt that a re-establishment of the crown was essential to restoring stability. The throne was given to **Valdemar IV** and the monarchy strengthened by the taking back of former crown lands that had been given to nobles. Within twenty years Denmark had regained its former territory, with German forces driven back across the Ejder. The only loss was Estonia, a Danish possession since 1219, which was sold to the Order of Teutonic Knights.

In 1361, the buoyant king attacked and conquered Gotland, much to the annoyance of the Hanseatic League, a powerful Lübeck-based group of tradesmen who were using it as a Baltic trading base. A number of anti-Danish alliances sprang up and the country was slowly plundered until peace was agreed in 1370 under the **Treaty of Stralsund**. This guaranteed trade for the Hanseatic partners by granting them control of castles along the west coast of Skåne for fifteen years. It also laid down that the election of the Danish monarch had to be approved by the Hanseatic League – the peak of their power.

The Kalmar Union

Valdemar's daughter Margrethe forced the election of her five-year-old son, Olav, as king in 1380, installing herself as regent. Following his untimely death after only a seven-year reign, Margrethe became Queen of Denmark and Norway, and later of Sweden as well – the first ruler of a united Scandinavia. In 1397, a formal document, the **Kalmar Union**, set out the rules of the union of the countries, which allowed for a Scandinavian federation sharing the same monarch and foreign policy, whilst each country had its own internal legislation. It became evident that Denmark was to be the dominant partner within the union when Margrethe placed Danish nobles in civic positions in Norway and Sweden but failed to reciprocate with Swedes and Norwegians in Denmark.

Erik VII ("of Pomerania") became king in 1396, and was determined to remove the Counts of Holstein who had taken possession of Schleswig in northern Germany. In 1413, he persuaded a meeting of the Danehof to declare the whole of Schleswig to be crown property, and three years later war broke out with the German-influenced nobility of the region. Unhappy with the Holstein privateers who were interfering with their trade, the Hanseatic League initially supported the king. But Erik also introduced important economic reforms within Denmark, ensuring that foreign goods reached Danish people through Danish merchants instead of coming directly from Hanseatic traders. This led to a war with the League, after which, in 1429, Erik imposed the **Sound Toll** (*Øresundstolden*) on shipping passing through the narrow strip of sea off the coast of Helsingør.

The conflicts with the Holsteiners and the Hanseatic League had, however, badly drained financial resources. Denmark still relied on hired armies to do its fighting, and the burden of taxation had caused widespread dissatisfaction, particularly in Sweden. With the Holstein forces gaining ground in Jutland, Erik fled to Gotland, and in 1439 Swedish and Danish nobles elected in his place **Christoffer III**, who acquiesced to the nobles' demands and ensured peace with the Hanseatic League by granting them exemption from the Sound Toll.

His sudden death in 1448 left – after internal struggle – **Christian I** to take the Danish throne. Following the death

of his uncle and ally, the Count of Holstein, he united Schleswig and Holstein at Ribe in 1460 and became Count of Holstein and Duke of Schleswig. In Denmark itself he also instigated the *stændermøde*: a council of merchants, clergy, freehold peasants and nobility, forging a powerful position for the crown – a policy that was continued by his successor, Hans.

Hans died in 1513 and **Christian II** came to the throne, seeking to re-establish the power of the Kalmar Union and reduce the trading dominance of the Hanseatic League. He invaded Sweden in 1520 under the guise of protecting the Church, but soon crowned himself King of Sweden at a ceremony attended by the cream of the Swedish nobility, clergy and the merchant class – an amnesty being granted to those who had opposed him. It was, however, a trick. Once inside the castle, 82 of the "guests" were arrested on charges of heresy, sentenced to death, and executed – an event that became known as the **Stockholm Bloodbath**. This was supposed to subdue Swedish hostility to the Danish monarch but in fact had the opposite effect. Gustavus Vasa, previously one of six Swedish hostages held by Christian in Denmark, became the leader of a revolt that ended Christian's reign in Sweden and finished the Kalmar Union.

Internally, too, Christian faced a revolt, to which he responded with more brutality. At the end of 1522, a group of Jutish nobles banded together with the intention of overthrowing him, joining up with Duke Frederik of Holstein-Gottorp (heir to half of Schleswig-Holstein), who also regarded the Danish king with disfavour. The following January, the nobles renounced their royal oaths and, with the support of forces from Holstein, gained control of all of Jutland and Funen. As they prepared to invade Zealand, Christian fled to Holland, hoping to assemble an army and return. In his absence, Frederik of Holstein-Gottorp became **Frederik I**.

The Reformation

At the time of Frederik's acquisition of the crown there was a growing unease with the role of the Church in Denmark, especially with the power – and wealth – of the bishops. Frederik was a Catholic but refused to take sides in religious disputes and did nothing to prevent the destruction of churches, being well aware of the groundswell of peasant support for Lutheranism. Frederik I died in 1533 and the fate of the Reformation hinged on which of his two sons would succeed him. The elder and more obvious choice was Christian, but his open support for Lutheranism set the bishops and nobles against him. The younger son, Hans, was just 12 years old, but was favoured by the Church and the nobility. The civil war that ensued became known as the **Counts' War**, and ended in 1536 with Christian III on the throne and the establishment of the new Danish Lutheran Church, with a constitution placing the king at its head.

Danish–Swedish conflicts

New trading routes across the Atlantic had reduced the power of the Hanseatic League, and Christian's young and ambitious successor, **Frederik II**, saw this as a chance for expansion. Sweden, however, had its own expansionist designs, and the resulting **Seven Years' War** (1563–1570) between the two countries caused widespread devastation and plunged the Danish economy into crisis.

The crisis turned out to be short-lived: price rises in the south of Europe led to increasing Danish affluence, reflected in the building of the elaborate castle of Kronborg in Helsingør. By the time **Christian IV** came to the throne in 1596, Denmark was a solvent and powerful nation. Christian's reign was to be characterized by bold new town layouts and great architectural works. Copenhagen became a major

European capital, acquiring many of the buildings which still grace the city today, including Rosenborg, Børsen and Rundetårnet.

To stem the rise of Swedish power after the Seven Years War, Christian IV took Denmark into the abortive **Thirty Years' War** in 1625, in which Danish defeat was total, and the king was widely condemned for his lack of foresight. The war led to increased taxes, inflation became rampant, and a number of merchants displayed their anger by petitioning the king over tax exemptions and other privileges enjoyed by nobles.

In 1657 Sweden occupied Jutland, and soon after marched across the frozen sea to Funen with the intention of continuing to Zealand. Hostilities ceased with the signing of the **Treaty of Roskilde**, under which Denmark finally lost all Swedish provinces. Sweden, however, was still suspicious of possible Danish involvement in Germany, and broke the terms of the treaty, commencing an advance through Zealand towards Copenhagen. The Dutch, to whom the Swedes had been allied, regarded this as a precursor to total Swedish control of commercial traffic through the Sound and sent a fleet to protect Copenhagen. This, plus a number of local uprisings within Denmark and attacks by Polish and Brandenburg forces on Sweden, halted the Swedes' advance and forced them to seek peace. The **Treaty of Copenhagen**, signed in 1660, acknowledged Swedish defeat but allowed the country to retain the Sound provinces acquired under the Treaty of Roskilde, so preventing either country from monopolizing trade through the Sound.

Absolute monarchy

In Denmark, the financial power of the nobles was fading as towns became established and the new merchant class grew. The advent of firearms caused the king to become less dependent on the foot soldiers provided by the nobles, and there was a general unease about the privileges – such as exemption from taxes – that the nobles continued to enjoy. Equally, few monarchs were content with their powers being limited by *håndfæstning*.

During the Swedish siege of Copenhagen, the king had promised special concessions to the city and its people, in the hope of encouraging them to withstand the assault. Among these was the right to determine their own rate of tax. A meeting of the city's burghers decided that everyone, including the nobility, should pay taxes; the nobles had little option but to submit. Sensing their power, the citizens went on to suggest that the crown become hereditary and end the *håndfæstning* system. Frederik III accepted and, with a full-scale ceremony in Copenhagen, was declared hereditary monarch. The task of writing a new constitution was left to the king, and its publication in 1665 revealed that he had made himself absolute monarch, bound only to uphold the Lutheran faith and ensure the unity of the kingdom. The king proceeded to rule, aided by a Privy Council in which seats were drawn mainly from the top posts within the civil service. The noble influence on royal decision-making had been drastically cut.

Christian V, king from 1670, instigated a broad system of royal honours, creating a new class of landowners who enjoyed exemptions from tax, and whose lack of concern for their tenants led Danish peasants into virtual serfdom. In 1699 **Frederik IV** set about creating a Danish militia to make the country less dependent on foreign mercenaries. While Sweden turned its allegiances towards Britain and Holland, Denmark re-established relations with the French, a situation which culminated in the **Great Northern War** (1709–1720). One result of this was the emergence of Russia as a dominant force in the region, while Denmark emerged with a strong position in Schleswig, and Sweden's exemption from the Sound Toll was ended.

The two decades of peace that followed saw the arrival of **Pietism**, a form of Lutheranism which strove to renew the devotional ideal. Frederik embraced the doctrine towards the end of his life, and it was adopted in full by his son, **Christian VI**, who took the throne in 1730. He prohibited entertainment on Sunday, closed down the Royal Theatre, and made court life a sombre affair: attendance at church on Sundays became compulsory and confirmation obligatory.

The Enlightenment

Despite the beliefs of the monarch, Pietism was never widely popular, and by the 1740s its influence had waned considerably. The reign of **Frederik V**, from 1746, saw a great cultural awakening: grand buildings such as Amalienborg and Frederikskirke were erected in Copenhagen (though the latter's completion was delayed for twenty years), and there was a new flourishing of the arts. The king, perhaps as a reaction to the puritanism of his father, devoted himself to a life of pleasure and allowed control of the nation effectively to pass to the civil service. **Neutrality** was maintained and the economy benefited as a consequence.

In 1766, **Christian VII** took the crown. His mental state was unstable, his moods ranging from deep lethargy to rage and drunkenness. By 1771 he had become incapable of carrying out even the minimum of official duties. The king's council, filled by a fresh generation of ambitious young men, insisted that the king effect his own will – under guidance from them – and disregard the suggestions of his older advisers.

Decision-making became dominated by a German court physician, **Johann Friedrich Struensee**, who had accompanied the king on a tour of England and had gained much of the credit for the good behaviour of the unpredictable monarch. Struensee combined personal arrogance with a sympathy for many of the ideas then fashionable elsewhere in Europe; he spoke no Danish (German was the court language) and had no concern for Danish traditions. Through him a number of sweeping **reforms** were executed: the Privy Council was abolished, the Treasury became the supreme administrative organ, the death penalty was abolished, the moral code lost many of its legal sanctions, and the press was freed from censorship.

There was opposition from several quarters. Merchants complained about the freeing of trade, and the burghers of Copenhagen were unhappy about their city losing its autonomy. In addition, there were well-founded rumours about the relationship between Struensee and the queen. Since nothing was known outside the court of the king's mental state, it was assumed that the monarch was being held prisoner. Struensee was forced to reintroduce censorship of the press as their editorials began to mount attacks on him. The Royal Guards mutinied when their disbandment was ordered, while at the same time a coup was being plotted by Frederik V's second wife, Juliane Marie of Brunswick, and her son, Frederik. After a masked ball at the palace in 1772, Struensee was arrested and tried, and soon afterwards beheaded. The dazed king was paraded before his cheering subjects.

The court came under the control – in ascending order of influence – of Frederik, Juliane, and a minister, **Ove Høegh-Guldberg**. All those who had been appointed to office by Struensee were dismissed, and while Høegh-Guldberg eventually incurred the wrath of officials by operating in much the same arrogant fashion as Struensee had, he recognized – and exploited – the anti-German feelings that had been growing for some time. Danish became the language of command in the army and later the court language, and in 1776 it was declared that no foreigner should be given a position in royal office.

In the wider sphere, the country prospered through dealings in the Far East,

and Copenhagen consolidated its role as the new centre of Baltic trade. The outbreak of the American War of Independence provided neutral Denmark with fresh commercial opportunities. In 1780 Denmark joined the **League of Armed Neutrality** with Russia, Prussia and Sweden, which had the effect of maintaining trading links across the Atlantic until the end of the war.

Faced with the subsequent conflict between Britain and revolutionary France, Denmark joined the second armed neutrality league with Russia and Sweden, until a British naval venture into the Baltic during 1801 obliged withdrawal. British fears that Denmark would join Napoleon's continental blockade resulted in a British attack led by Admiral Nelson, which destroyed the Danish fleet in Copenhagen. The pact between France and Russia left Denmark in a difficult situation. To oppose this alliance would leave them exposed to a French invasion of Jutland. To oppose the British and join with the French would adversely affect trade. As the Danes tried to stall for time, the British lost patience, occupying Zealand and commencing a three-day bombardment of Copenhagen. Sweden had aligned with the British and was demanding the ceding of Norway if Denmark were to be defeated – which, under the **Treaty of Kiel**, was exactly what happened.

The Age of Liberalism

The Napoleonic Wars destroyed Denmark's international prestige and left the country bankrupt, and the period up until 1830 was spent in recovery. Meanwhile, in the arts, a **national romantic movement** was gaining pace. The sculptor Thorvaldsen and the writer-philosopher Kierkegaard are perhaps the best-known figures to emerge from the era, but the most influential domestically was a theologian called **N.F.S. Grundtvig**, who, in 1810, developed a new form of Christianity – one that was free of dogma and drew on the virtues espoused by the heroes of Norse mythology. In 1825 he left the intellectual circles of Copenhagen and travelled the rural areas to guide a religious revival, eventually modifying his earlier ideas in favour of a new faith in the wisdom of "the people" – something that was to colour the future liberal movement.

On the political front, there was trouble brewing in Danish-speaking **Schleswig** and German-speaking **Holstein**. The Treaty of Kiel had compelled Denmark to relinquish Holstein to the Confederation of German States – although, confusingly, the Danish king remained duke of the province. He promised to set up a consultative assembly for the region, while within Holstein a campaign sought to pressure the king into granting the duchy its own constitution. The campaign was suppressed, but the problems of the region were not resolved. Further demands called for a complete separation from Denmark, with the duchies being brought together as a single independent state. The establishment of consultative assemblies in both Holstein and Schleswig eventually came about in 1831, though they lacked any real political muscle.

Although absolutism had been far more benevolent towards the ordinary people in Denmark than elsewhere in Europe, interest was growing in the liberalism that was sweeping through the continent. In Copenhagen a group of scholars proffered the idea that Schleswig be brought closer to Danish affairs, and in pursuit of this they formed the Liberal Party and brought pressure to bear for a new liberal constitution. As the government wavered in its response, the liberal movement grew and its first newspaper, *Fædrelandet*, appeared in 1834.

In 1837, the crown agreed to the introduction of elected town councils and, four years later, to elected bodies in parishes and counties. Although the franchise was restricted, many small farmers gained political awareness

through their participation in the local councils.

In 1839, **Christian VIII** came to the throne. As Crown Prince of Norway, Christian had approved a liberal constitution in that country, but surprised Danish liberals by not agreeing to a similar constitution at home. In 1848 he was succeeded by his son **Frederik VII**. Meanwhile, the liberals had organized themselves into the **National Liberal Party**, and the king signed a **new constitution** that made Denmark the most democratic country in Europe, guaranteeing freedom of speech, freedom of religious worship, and many civil liberties. Legislation was to be put in the hands of a Rigsdag elected by popular vote and consisting of two chambers: the lower Folketing and upper Landsting. The king gave up the powers of an absolute monarch, but his signature was still required before bills approved by the Rigsdag could become law. And he could select his own ministers.

Within Schleswig-Holstein, however, there was little faith that the equality granted to them in the constitution would be upheld. A delegation from the duchies went to Copenhagen to call for Schleswig to be combined with Holstein within the German Confederation. A Danish compromise suggested a free constitution for Holstein with Schleswig remaining as part of Denmark, albeit with its own legislature and autonomy in its internal administration. The Schleswig-Holsteiners rejected this and formed a provisional government in Kiel.

The inevitable war that followed was to last for three years and, once Prussia's support was withdrawn, it ended in defeat for the duchies. The Danish prime minister, C.C. Hall, drew up a fresh constitution that excluded Holstein from Denmark. Despite widespread misgivings within the Rigsdag, the constitution was narrowly voted through. Frederik died before he could give the royal assent and it fell to **Christian IX** to put his name to the document that would almost certainly trigger another war.

It did, and under the peace terms Denmark ceded both Schleswig and Holstein to Germany, leaving the country smaller than it had been for centuries. The blame was laid firmly on the National Liberals, and the new government, appointed by the king and drawn from the country's affluent landowners, saw its initial task as replacing the constitution, drawn up to deal with the Schleswig-Holstein crisis, with one far less liberal in content. The election of 1866 resulted in a narrow majority in the Rigsdag favouring a new constitution. When this came to be implemented, it retained the procedure for election to the Folketing, but made the Landsting franchise dependent on land and money and allowed twelve of the 64 members to be selected by the king.

The landowners worked in limited cooperation with the National Liberals and the Centre Party (a less conservative version of the National Liberals). In opposition, a number of interests, encompassing everything from leftist radicals to followers of Grundtvig, were shortly combined into the **United Left**, which put forward the first political manifesto seen in Denmark. It called for equal taxation, universal suffrage in local elections, more freedom for the farmers, and contained a vague demand for closer links with the other Scandinavian countries. The United Left became the majority within the Folketing in 1872.

The ideas of **revolutionary socialism** had begun percolating through the country around 1871 via a series of pamphlets edited by Louis Pio, who attempted to organize a Danish Internationale. In April 1872, Pio led 1200 bricklayers into a strike, announcing a mass meeting on May 5. The government banned the meeting and had Pio arrested: he was sentenced to five years in prison and the Danish Internationale was banned. The workers, however, began forming trade unions and workers' associations.

The intellectual left also became active. A series of lectures delivered by Georg Brandes in Copenhagen cited Danish culture, in particular its literature, as dull and lifeless compared to that of other countries. He called for fresh works that questioned and examined society, instigating a bout of literary attacks on institutions such as marriage, chastity and the family. As a backlash, conservative groups in the government formed themselves into the **United Right** under Prime Minister **J.B.S. Estrup**.

The left did their best to obstruct the government but gradually lost influence, while the strength of the right grew. In 1889, the left issued a manifesto calling for reductions in military expenditure, a declaration of neutrality, the provision of old age pensions, sick pay, a limit to working hours, and votes for women. The elections of 1890 improved the left's position in the Folketing, and also saw the election of two **Social Democrats**. With this, the left moved further towards moderation and compromise with the right. The trade unions, whose membership escalated in proportion to the numbers employed in the new industries, grew in stature, and were united as the Association of Trade Unions in 1898. The Social Democratic Party grew stronger with the support of the industrial workers, although it had no direct connection with the trade unions.

Parliamentary democracy and World War I

By the end of the century the power of the right was in severe decline. The elections of 1901, under the new conditions of a secret ballot, saw them reduced to the smallest group within the Folketing and heralded the beginning of **parliamentary democracy**.

The government of 1901 was the first real democratic administration, assembled with the intention of balancing differing political tendencies – and it brought in a number of reforms. Income tax was introduced on a sliding scale, and free schooling beyond the primary level began. As years went by, Social Democrat support increased, while the left, such as it was, became increasingly conservative. In 1905 a breakaway group formed the **Radical Left** (*Det Radikale Venstre*), politically similar to the English Liberals, calling for the reduction of the armed forces to the status of coastal and border guards, greater social equality, and votes for women.

An alliance between the Radicals and Social Democrats enabled the two parties to gain a large majority in the Folketing in the election of 1913, and a year later conservative control of the Landsting was ended. Social advances were made, but further domestic progress was halted by international events as Europe prepared for war.

Denmark had enjoyed good trading relations with both Germany and Britain in the year preceding **World War I**, and was keen not to be seen to favour either side in the hostilities. On the announcement of the German mobilization, the now Radical-led cabinet, with the support of all the other parties, issued a **statement of neutrality** and was able to remain clear of direct involvement in the conflict.

At the conclusion of the war, attention was turned again towards Schleswig-Holstein, and under the **Treaty of Versailles** it was decided that Schleswig should be divided into two zones for a referendum. In the northern zone a return to unification with Denmark was favoured by a large percentage, while the southern zone elected to remain part of Germany. A new German–Danish border was drawn up just north of Flensburg.

High rates of unemployment and the success of the Russian Bolsheviks led to a series of strikes and demonstrations, the unrest coming to a head with the **Easter crisis** of 1920. During March of that year, a change in the electoral system towards greater proportional representation was agreed in the Folketing but the prime minister, **Carl Theodore Zahle**, whose Radicals

stood to lose support through the change, refused to implement it. The king, Christian X, responded by dismissing him and asking **Otto Liebe** to form a caretaker government to oversee the changes. The royal intervention, while technically legal, incensed the Social Democrats and the trade unions, who were already facing a national lockout by employers in response to demands for improved pay rates. Perceiving the threat of a right-wing coup, the unions began organizing a general strike to begin after the Easter holiday. There was a large republican demonstration outside Amalienborg.

On Easter Saturday, urgent negotiations between the king and the existing government concluded with an agreement that a mutually acceptable caretaker government would oversee the electoral change and a fresh election would immediately follow. Employers, fearful of the power the workers had shown, met many of the demands for higher wages.

The next government was dominated by the Radical Left. They fortified existing social policies, and increased state contributions to union unemployment funds. But a general economic depression continued, and there was widespread industrial unrest as the krone declined in value and living standards fell. A month-long **general strike** followed, and a workers' demonstration in Randers was subdued by the army.

Venstre and the Social Democrats jostled for position over the next decade, though under the new electoral system no one party could achieve enough power to undertake major reform. The economy did improve, however, and state influence spread further through Danish society than ever before. Enlightened reforms were put on the agenda, too, making a deliberately clean break with the moral standpoints of the past – notably on abortion and illegitimacy. Major public works were funded, such as the bridge between Funen and Jutland over the Lille Bælt, and the Stormstrømsbro, linking Zealand to Falster.

The Nazi occupation

While Denmark had little military significance for the Nazis, the sea off Norway was being used to transport iron ore from Sweden to Britain, and the fjords offered good shelter for a fleet engaged in a naval war in the Atlantic. To get to Norway, the Nazis planned an invasion of Denmark. At 4am on April 9, 1940, the German ambassador in Copenhagen informed Prime Minister Stauning that German troops were preparing to cross the Danish border and issued the ultimatum that unless Denmark agreed that the country could be used as a German military base – keeping control of its own affairs – Copenhagen would be bombed. To reject the demand was considered a postponement of the inevitable, and to save Danish bloodshed the government acquiesced at 6am. "They took us by telephone," said a Danish minister.

A national coalition government was formed which behaved according to protocol but gave no unnecessary concessions to the Germans. Censorship of the press and a ban on demonstrations were imposed, ostensibly intended to prevent the Nazis spreading propaganda. But these measures, like the swiftness of the initial agreement, were viewed by some Danes as capitulation and were to be a thorn in the side of the Social Democrats for years to come.

The government was reshuffled to include non-parliamentary experts, one of whom, **Erik Scavenius**, a former foreign minister, conceived an ill-fated plan to gain the confidence of the Germans. He issued a statement outlining the government's friendly attitude to the occupying power, and even praised the German military victory – which upset the Danish public and astonished the Germans, who asked whether Denmark would like to enter into commercial agreement immediately rather than wait until the end of the war. Scavenius was powerless to do anything other than agree, and a deal was signed within days. Under its terms, the krone was to be phased out and German currency made legal tender.

Public reaction was naturally hostile, and Scavenius was, not surprisingly, regarded as a traitor. Groups of Danes began a systematic display of antipathy to the Germans. Children wore red, white and blue "RAF caps", Danish customers walked out of cafés when Germans entered, and the ban on demonstrations was flouted by groups who gathered to sing patriotic songs. On September 1, 1940, an estimated 739,000 Danes around the country gathered to sing the same song simultaneously. The king demonstrated his continued presence by riding on horseback each morning through Copenhagen.

Meanwhile, the Danish government continued its balancing act, knowing that failure to co-operate at least to some degree would lead to a complete Nazi takeover. It was with this in mind that Denmark signed the Anti-Comintern Pact making Communism illegal, but insisted on the insertion of a clause that allowed only Danish police to arrest Danish Communists.

Vilhelm Buhl, who was appointed prime minister on May 3, 1942, had been an outspoken opponent of the signing of the Anti-Comintern Pact and it was thought he might end the apparent appeasement. Instead, the tension between occupiers and occupied was to climax with Hitler's anger at the curt note received from Christian X in response to the Führer's birthday telegram. Although it was the king's standard reply, Hitler took the mere "thank you" as an insult and immediately replaced his functionaries in Denmark with hardliners who demanded a new pro-German government.

Scavenius took control and, in 1943, elections were called in an attempt to show that freedom of political expression could exist under German occupation. The government asked the public to demonstrate faith in national unity by voting for any one of the four parties in the coalition, and received overwhelming support in the largest ever turnout for a Danish election.

Awareness that German defeat was becoming inevitable stimulated a wave of strikes throughout the country. Berlin declared a state of emergency in Denmark, and demanded that the Danish government comply – which it refused to do. Germany took over administration of the country, interning many politicians. The king was asked to appoint a cabinet from outside the Folketing, and Germans were free for the first time to round up Danish Jews. Resistance was organized under the leadership of the **Danish Freedom Council**. Sabotage was carefully co-ordinated, and an underground army, soon comprising over 43,000, prepared to assist in the Allied invasion. In June 1944, rising anti-Nazi violence led to a curfew being imposed in Copenhagen and assemblies of more than five people being banned, to which workers responded with a spontaneous general strike. German plans to starve the city had to be abandoned after five days.

The postwar period

After the German surrender in May 1945, a **liberation government** was created, composed equally of pre-war politicians and members of the Danish Freedom Council, with Vilhelm Buhl as prime minister. Its internal differences earned the administration the nickname "the debating club".

While the country had been spared the devastation seen elsewhere in Europe, it still found itself with massive economic problems and it soon became apparent that the liberation government could not function. In the ensuing election there was a swing to the Communists, and a minority Venstre government was formed. The immediate concern was to strengthen the economy, although the resurfacing of the southern Schleswig issue began to dominate the Rigsdag.

Domestic issues soon came to be overshadowed by the **international situation** as the Cold War began.

Denmark had unreservedly joined the United Nations in 1945, and had joined the IMF and World Bank to gain financial help in restoring its economy. In 1947, Marshall Plan aid brought further assistance. As world power became polarized between East and West, the Danish government at first tried to remain impartial, but in 1947 agreed to join NATO – a total break with the established concept of Danish neutrality (though to this day, the Danes remain opposed to nuclear weapons).

The years after the war were marked by much political manoeuvring among the Radicals, Social Democrats and Conservatives, resulting in many hastily called elections and a number of ineffectual compromise coalitions distinguished mainly by the level of their infighting. Working-class support for the Social Democrats steadily eroded, and support for the Communists was largely transferred to the new, more revisionist, **Socialist People's Party**.

Social reforms, however, continued apace, not least in the 1960s, with the abandoning of all forms of censorship and the institution of free abortion on demand. Such measures are typical of more recent social policy, though Denmark's odd position between Scandinavia and the rest of mainland Europe still remains a niggling concern. A referendum held in 1972 to determine whether Denmark should join the EC resulted in a substantial majority in favour, making Denmark the first Scandinavian member of the community – Sweden, the second, didn't join until 1995 – though public enthusiasm remained lukewarm.

The 1970s and 1980s

Perhaps the biggest change in the 1970s was the foundation – and subsequent influence – of the new **Progress Party** (*Fremskridtspartiet*), headed by Mogens Glistrup, who claimed to have an income of over a million kroner but to be paying no income tax through manipulation of the tax laws. The Progress Party stood on a ticket of immigration curbs and drastic tax cuts, and Glistrup went on to compare tax avoidance with the sabotaging of Nazi railway lines during the war. He also announced that if elected he would replace the Danish defence force with an answering machine saying "we surrender" in Russian. He was eventually imprisoned after an investigation by the Danish tax office; released in 1985, he set himself up as a tax consultant.

The success of the Progress Party pointed to dissatisfaction with both the economy and the established parties' strategies for dealing with its problems. In September 1982, **Poul Schlüter** became the country's first Conservative prime minister of the twentieth century, leading the widest-ranging coalition yet seen – including Conservatives, the Venstre, Centre Democrats and Christian People's Party. In keeping with the prevailing political climate in the rest of Europe, the prescription for Denmark's economic malaise was seen to be spending cuts, not sparing the social services, and with an extension of taxation into areas such as pension funds. These policies continued until the snap election of 1987, which resulted in a significant swing to the left. Nevertheless, Schlüter was asked to form a new government, which he did in conjunction with the Progress Party in order to gain a single-seat working majority. A further election, in May 1988, largely served to affirm the new Schlüter-led government, if only, perhaps, because of the apparent lack of any workable alternative.

Into the new millennium

In January 1993 Schlüter's government was forced to resign over a political scandal (it was revealed that asylum had been denied to Sri Lankan Tamil refugees in the late 1980s and early 1990s, in contravention of Danish law). The Social Democrats, led by **Poul Nyrup Rasmussen**, took power in 1994 and formed a four-party coalition.

For the first time in ten years Denmark was ruled by a majority government – a centre-left majority coalition which came under attack for its weak policies on tax reform, the welfare state and the thorny issue of **European union**.

Though traditionally a reluctant member of the EC, Denmark was carried into the European **Exchange Rate Mechanism** (or ERM, then viewed as the first step towards a single European currency) by Schlüter at the start of the 1990s, a move that transformed the Danish economy into one of the strongest in Europe and made its inflation rate the lowest of any EC member. The price for this, however, was soaring unemployment and further cuts in public spending.

The outcome of the **referendum on the Maastricht Treaty** (the blueprint for European political and monetary union) in June 1992, however, provided an unexpected upset to the Schlüter applecart. Despite calls for a "Yes" vote not only from the government but also from the opposition Social Democrats, over 50 percent of Danes rejected the treaty – severely embarrassing the prime minister and sending shivers down the spine of every western European government. The government and other pro-Europe parties didn't give up, however, but set to work on a revised version of the Maastricht Treaty, with the emphasis on protecting national interests – it included a pledge allowing the Danish people to reject citizenship of a United Europe.

A **second referendum** in May 1993 was a triumph for the government, with almost 57 percent of the Danish population voting in favour of the new Treaty. Anti-European feelings, already intense, reached boiling point, and the night after the referendum young left-wingers and anarchists came together in central Copenhagen to declare the area an "EU-free zone". The police moved in to break up the demonstration, battles with the demonstrators ensued, and for the first time ever the Danish police opened fire against a crowd of civilians.

Fortunately nobody died, but the incident sparked off a major investigation into the actions of the police, and while Denmark avoided the risk of economic isolation in an increasingly integrated European community, doubts among the Danish people remain, along with a continuing dissatisfaction at the way the "Yes" vote was achieved.

Rasmussen and the Social Democrats retained the largest share of the vote in subsequent elections in 1998 and, as the new millennium dawned, the country was well placed for life in a new Europe. Danes were ranked at the top of the newly created "European Future Readiness Index", which measures social costs and problems such as environmental quality, healthcare costs, poverty and unemployment, while the organization Transparency International revealed that Denmark had been chosen as the world's **least corrupt nation**: of 99 countries surveyed, only Denmark received a perfect score on its "Anti-Corruption Index". All was not absolutely well, however. In 1999, crime and poverty in Copenhagen were becoming a serious worry for the first time in many years. Things came to a head during a November **riot** in the city when police used tear gas to quell more than one hundred protesters – the first such disturbance since the 1993 anti-Maastricht demonstrations. This time vandals wielded crowbars, bricks and bombs as they broke shop windows and set fires to protest about the extradition of a Danish hoodlum from Turkey. City officials were hoping dearly that it would not be the precursor of further violence.

Denmark today

In November 2001, the political tide changed dramatically: Poul Nyrup Rasmussen and the centre-left coalition lost the election to a right-wing coalition led by Anders Fogh Rasmussen. The reasons for this radical shift have been long-debated. The global move to the political right which followed the September 11 terrorist attack in the US played a part; a feeling of growing resentment against refugees and second-generation Danes (mainly from Turkey) had already been nurtured by the right-wing zealot Pia Kærsgård, and after the World Trade Centre tragedy, people started listening. Apart from taking a hostile position toward "foreigners", the new government has also marked itself as anti-environment (by way of massive cuts in energy saving initiatives); anti-development (cuts in overseas aid) and anti-culture (the slashing of financial support to alternative types of entertainment). A recent poll has, however, shown a renewed majority in support of the centre left, and the Danish people are counting the days until the next election, due to be held in November 2005 at the latest.

Books

Though there's not a huge amount of English-language books on Denmark, we've listed some of the best titles below. Those marked with a ⬧ represent essential reads.

History and philosophy

Inga Dahlsgård *Women in Denmark, Yesterday and Today* (o/p). A refreshing presentation of Danish history from the point of view of its women.

W. Glyn Jones *Denmark: A Modern History* (o/p). A valuable account of the twentieth century (up until 1984), with a commendable outline of pre-twentieth-century Danish history.

Strong on politics, useful on history and the arts, but disappointingly brief on recent grassroots movements.

Søren Kierkegaard *Either/Or*. A new translation of Kierkegaard's most important work, packed with wry and wise musings on love, life and death in nineteenth-century Danish society; includes the (in)famous "Seducer's Diary".

Roger Poole and Henrik Stangerup (eds) *A Kierkegaard Reader* (o/p). By far the best and most accessible introduction to this notoriously difficult nineteenth-century Danish philosopher and writer, with a sparkling introductory essay.

Literature and biography

Hans Christian Andersen (ed. Naomi Lewis) *Hans Andersen's Fairy Tales*. Still the most internationally prominent figure of Danish literature, Andersen's fairy tales are so widely translated and read that the full clout of their allegorical content is often overlooked: interestingly, his first collection of such tales (published in 1835) was condemned for its "violence and questionable morals". *A Visit to Germany, Italy and Malta, 1840–1841* (o/p) is the most enduring of his travel works, while his autobiography, *The Fairy Tale of My Life*, is a fine alternative to the numerous sycophantic portraits which have appeared since.

Steen Steensen Blicher *Diary of a Parish Clerk*; *Twelve Stories*. Blicher was a keen observer of Jutish life, writing stark, realistic tales in local dialect and gathering a seminal collection of Jutish folk tales – published as *E. Bindstouw* in 1842.

Karen Blixen (Isak Dinesen) *Out of Africa*; *Letters from Africa*; *Seven Gothic Tales*. *Out of Africa*, the account of Blixen's attempts to run a coffee farm in Kenya after divorce from her husband, is a lyrical and moving tale. But it's in *Seven Gothic Tales* that Blixen's fiction was at its zenith: a flawlessly executed, weird, emotive work, full of twists in plot and strange, ambiguous characterization.

Tove Ditlevsen *Early Spring*. An autobiographical novel of growing up in the working-class Vesterbro district of Copenhagen during the 1930s. As an evocation of childhood and early adulthood, it's totally captivating.

Martin A. Hansen *The Liar*. An engaging novel, showing why Hansen was one of Denmark's most perceptive – and popular – authors during the postwar period. Set in the 1950s, the story examines the inner thoughts of a lonely schoolteacher living on a small Danish island.

Peter Høeg *Miss Smilla's Feeling for Snow*. A worldwide bestseller, this compelling thriller deals with Danish colonialism in Greenland and the issue of cultural identity.

Dea Trier Mørch *Winter's Child* (o/p). A wonderfully lucid sketch of modern Denmark as seen through the eyes of several women in the maternity ward of a Copenhagen hospital. See also *Evening Star*, which deals with the effect of old age and death on a Danish family.

Judith Thurman *Isak Dinesen: The Life of Karen Blixen*. The most penetrating biography of Blixen, elucidating details of the farm period not found in the two "Africa" books.

A brief guide to Danish

Danish in some ways is similar to German, but there are significant differences in pronunciation, Danes tending to swallow the ending of many words and leave certain letters silent. English is widely understood, as is German; young people especially often speak both fluently. And if you can speak Swedish or Norwegian then you should have little problem making yourself understood – all three languages share the same root.

In **pronunciation**, unfamiliar **vowels** include:

æ when long between air and tailor. When short like get. When next to r sounds more like hat.

å when long like saw, when short like on.

ø like fur but with the lips rounded.

e, when long, is similar to plate, when short somewhere between plate and hit; when unstressed it's as in above.

Consonants are pronounced as in English, except:

d at the end of a word after a vowel, or between a vowel and an unstressed e or i, like this. Sometimes silent at the end of a word.

g at the beginning of a word or syllable as in go. At the end of a word or long vowel, or before an unstressed e, usually like yet but sometimes like the Scottish loch. Sometimes mute after an a, e, or o.

hv like view.

hj like yet.

k as English except between vowels, when it's as in go.

p as English except between vowels, when it's as in bit.

r pronounced as in French from the back of the throat but often silent.

sj as in sheet.

t as English except between vowels, when it's as in do. Often mute when at the end of a word.

y between bee and pool.

Basics

Do you speak English? – **Taler De engelsk?**
Yes – **Ja**
No – **Nej**
I don't understand – **Jeg forstår det ikke**
I understand – **Jeg forstår**

Please – **Værså venlig**
Thank you – **Tak**
Excuse me – **Undskyld**
Good morning – **Godmorgen**
Good afternoon – **Goddag**
Goodnight – **Godnat**
Goodbye – **Farvel**
Yesterday – **I går**
Today – **I dag**
Tomorrow – **I morgen**
Day after tomorrow – **I overmorgen**
In the morning – **Om morgenen**
In the afternoon – **Om eftermiddagen**
In the evening – **Om aftenen**

Some signs

Entrance – **Indgang**
Exit – **Udgang**
Push/pull – **Skub/træk**
Danger – **Fare**
Gentlemen – **Herrer**
Ladies – **Damer**
Open – **Åben**
Closed – **Lukket**
Arrival – **Ankomst**
Departure – **Afgang**
Police – **Politi**
No smoking – **Rygning forbudt/Ikke rygere**
No entry – **Ingen adgang**
No camping – **Campering forbudt**
No trespassing – **Adgang forbudt for uvedkommende**

Questions and directions

Where is? – **Hvor er?**
When? – **Hvornår?**
What? – **Hvad?**
Why? – **Hvorfor?**
Who? – **Hvem?**
How much? – **Hvor meget?**
How much does it cost? – **Hvad koster det?**

Here - **Her**
There - **Der**
Good/bad - **God/dårlig**
Cheap/expensive - **Billig/dyr**
Hot/cold - **Varm/kold**
Better/bigger/cheaper - **Bedre/større/billigere**
Near/far - **Nær/fjern**
Left/right - **Venstre/højre**
Straight ahead - **Ligeud**
I'd like ... - **Jeg vil gerne ha ...**
Where is the youth hostel? - **Hvor er vandrerhjemmet?**
Can we camp here? - **Må vi campere her?**
It's too expensive - **Det er for dyrt**
Where are the toilets? - **Hvor er toiletterne?**
How far is it to ...? - **Hvor langt er der til ...?**
Where can I get a train/bus/ferry to ...?
- **Hvor kan jeg tage toget/bussen/færgen til ...?**
At what time does ...? - Hvornår går ...?
Ticket - Billet

Numbers

0 - **Nul**	8 - **Otte**
1 - **En**	9 - **Ni**
2 - **To**	10 - **Ti**
3 - **Tre**	11 - **Elleve**
4 - **Fire**	12 - **Tolv**
5 - **Fem**	13 - **Tretten**
6 - **Seks**	14 - **Fjorten**
7 - **Syv**	15 - **Femten**

16 - **Seksten**	70 - **Halvfjerds**
17 - **Sytten**	80 - **Firs**
18 - **Atten**	90 - **Halvfems**
19 - **Nitten**	100 - **Hundrede**
20 - **Tyve**	101 - **Hundrede og et**
21 - **Enogtyve**	151 - **Hundrede og**
30 - **Tredive**	**enoghalvtreds**
40 - **Fyrre**	200 - **To hundrede**
50 - **Halvtreds**	1000 - **Tusind**
60 - **Tres**	

Days and months

Monday - **mandag**
Tuesday - **tirsdag**
Wednesday - **onsdag**
Thursday - **torsdag**
Friday - **fredag**
Saturday - **lørdag**
Sunday - **søndag**
January - **januar**
February - **februar**
March - **marts**
April - **april**
May - **maj**
June - **juni**
July - **juli**
August - **august**
September - **september**
October - **oktober**
November - **november**
December - **december**
(Days and months are never capitalized)

Glossary of Danish terms and words

Banegård - Train station
Bakke - Hill or ridge
Domkirke - Cathedral
Gammel or Gamle - Old
Hav - Sea
Havn - Harbour
Herregård - Manor house
Jernebane - Railway
Kirke - Church
Klint - Cliff
Kloster - Monastery

Kro - Inn
Plads - Square
Rutebilstation - Coach station
Rådhus - Town hall
Skov - Wood or forest
Stue - Room
Sø - Lake
Torv - Market square
Tårn - Tower
Vand - Water

1.1

Zealand

As the largest of Denmark's islands and the home of its capital, **Zealand** (*Sjælland*) is the country's most important – and most visited – region. Copenhagen, though not an especially big city, dominates much of the island; the nearby towns, while far from being drab suburbia, tend inevitably to be dormitory territory. Only much further away, towards the west and south, does the pace become more provincial.

It would be perverse to come to Zealand and not visit **Copenhagen** – easily the most extrovert and cosmopolitan place in the country, and as lively by night as it is by day. But once there you should make at least a brief journey into the country to see how different the rest of Denmark can be. Woods and expansive parklands appear almost as soon as you leave the city – and even if you don't like what you find, the swiftness of the metropolitan transport network, which covers almost half the island, means that you can be back in the capital in easy time for an evening drink.

North of Copenhagen, the coastal road passes the outstanding modern art museum of **Louisiana** and the absorbing Karen Blixen museum at **Rungsted** before reaching **Helsingør**, site of the renowned **Kronborg Slot** (better known as Elsinore Castle), an impressive fortification that nevertheless quite unfairly steals the spotlight from **Frederiksborg Slot**, an even more eye-catching castle in nearby **Hillerød**. West of Copenhagen and on the main route to Funen is **Roskilde**, a former capital with an extravagant cathedral that's still the last resting place for Danish monarchs, and with a gorgeous location on the Roskilde fjord – from where five Viking boats were salvaged that are now restored and displayed in a specially built museum. South of Copenhagen, at the end of the urban S-train system, is **Køge**, which – beyond the industrial sites that flank it – has a well-preserved medieval centre and long, sandy beaches lining its bay.

Further out from the sway of Copenhagen, central Zealand's towns are appreciably smaller, more scattered, and far less full of either commuters or day-trippers. **Ringsted**, plumb in the heart of the island, is another one-time capital, a fact recalled by the twelfth- and thirteenth-century royal tombs in its church. Further south, **Næstved**, surrounded by lush countryside, gives access to three smaller islands just off the coast: **Lolland**, **Falster** and **Møn**. Each of these is busy during the summer, but outside high season you'll find them green and peaceful, with Lolland offering a leisurely backdoor route, via Langeland, to Funen.

Not part of Zealand, but conveniently reached (via the new Øresunds Link) from Copenhagen, is the island of **Bornholm**. A huge slab of granite in the Baltic, it houses a few small fishing communities and has some fine beaches and an unusual history, making a stimulating detour if you're heading for Sweden – it's nearer Sweden than Denmark, with regular ferry connections to both countries.

Copenhagen

As any Dane will tell you, **COPENHAGEN** is no introduction to Denmark; indeed, a greater contrast with the sleepy provincialism of the rest of the country would be hard to find. Despite that, the city completely dominates Denmark: it's the seat of all the nation's institutions – political, financial and artistic – and provides

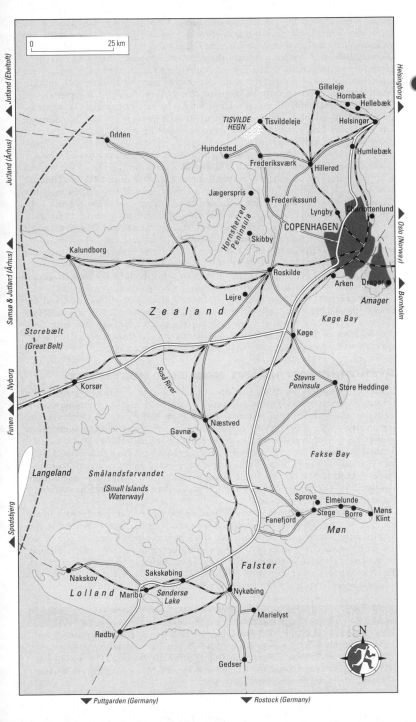

0   25 km

Gilleleje
Hornbæk
Hellebæk
TISVILDE
HEGN   Tisvileleje
Helsingør
Odden
Hundested   Humlebæk
Frederiksværk   Hillerød
Jægerspris   Frederikssund
Lyngby   Charlottenlund
COPENHAGEN
Skibby
Kalundborg   *Hornsherred Peninsula*
Roskilde
Arken   Dragør
Lejre   *Amager*
Z e a l a n d   *Køge Bay*
*Storebælt
(Great Belt)*   Køge
*Stevns
Peninsula*   Store Heddinge
Korsør
Suså River
Næstved   *Fakse Bay*
Gavnø
Langeland   *Smålandsfarvandet
(Small Islands
Waterway)*
Sprove   Elmelunde   Møns
Klint
Fanefjord   Stege   Borre
Møn
Spodsbjerg
Falster
Nakskov   Sakskøbing
Lolland   Maribo   *Søndersø
Lake*   Nykøbing
Marielyst
Rødby
Gedser

N

Jutland (Ebeltoft)
Jutland (Århus)
Samsø & Jutland (Århus)
Nyborg
Funen

Puttgarden (Germany)   Rostock (Germany)

the driving force for the country's social reforms. Copenhagen is also Scandinavia's most affordable capital, and one of Europe's most user-friendly cities: small and welcoming, it's a place where people rather than cars set the pace, as evidenced by the multitude of pavement cafés and the number of thoroughfares that have been given over to pedestrians. In summer especially, there's a varied range of lively street entertainment, while at night the multitude of cosy bars and intimate club and live music networks could hardly be bettered. The history museums and galleries of Danish and international art, as well as a worthy batch of smaller collections, shouldn't be overlooked, either. If you're intent on heading north into Scandinavia's less populated (and pricier) reaches, you'd certainly be wise to spend a few days living it up in Copenhagen first.

There was no more than a tiny fishing settlement here until the twelfth century, when Bishop Absalon oversaw the building of a castle on the site of the present Christiansborg. The settlement's prosperity grew after Erik of Pomerania granted it special privileges and imposed the Sound Toll on vessels passing through the Øresund strait between Denmark and Sweden, which was then under Danish control. The revenue from the tolls enabled a self-confident trading centre to flourish. Following the demise of the Hanseatic ports, the city became the Baltic's principal harbour, earning the name København ("merchant's port"), and in 1443 it was made the Danish capital. A century later, Christian IV began the building programme that was the basis of the modern city: up went Rosenborg Slot, Børsen, Rundetårnet, and the districts of Nyboder and Christianshavn, while in 1669 Frederik III graced the city with its first royal palace, Amalienborg, for his queen, Sophie Amalie.

These structures still exist, like much of the Copenhagen of that time, and the taller of them remain the highest points in what is a refreshingly low skyline. It's an easy city to get around: you're unlikely to need to venture far from the central section, still largely hemmed in by the medieval ramparts (now a series of parks), which is where most of the activity and sights are contained.

Arrival, information and city transport

Whatever means you use to get to Copenhagen, you'll be within easy reach of the centre when you arrive. **Trains** pull into Central Station (*Hovedbanegården*), near Vesterbrogade, while **long-distance buses** from other parts of Denmark and abroad stop only a short bus or S-train ride from the centre: services from Århus stop at Valby S-train station; buses from Aalborg and Bornholm at the Central Station, and those from and Fjerritsslev on Hans Knudsens Plads near Ryparken S-train station on line H. Buses from abroad stop either by the Central Station or Sjælør S-train station on the A & E lines, depending on where they come from. **Ferries** from Bornholm, Norway, Lithuania and Poland dock close to Nyhavn, a few minutes' walk from the city centre.

Modern **Kastrup Airport**, 8km southeast of the city on the eastern edge of the island of Amager, is the air hub of Scandinavia and your likely entry point if travelling by plane. Getting into Copenhagen from here couldn't be easier: one of the fastest airport-to-city train links in Europe runs directly to Central Station six times an hour; one an hour (26min past the hour) from midnight to 5am (13min; 21kr). There's also a slower city bus (#250S; 21kr) to the Central Station and Rådhuspladsen, only really convenient if you want to get off on the way.

Onward travel to Sweden and Norway – the Øresunds Link

Opened in July 2000, the brand new **Øresunds Link** (see p.125) offers a quick tunnel and bridge connection between Copenhagen Central Station and Kastrup Airport, to Malmö and – via fast train – Stockholm, Gothenburg and Oslo. Using this new link, the ride across the Øresund now takes 30 minutes (around half an hour quicker than the old ferry–shuttle combination) and costs 62kr.

Information

Across the road from the Central Station at Bernstorffsgade 1, the Wonderful Copenhagen **tourist office** (May–Aug Mon–Sat 9am–8pm, Sun 10am–6pm; rest of year Mon–Fri 9am–4.30pm, Sat 9am–1.30pm; telephone enquiries Mon–Fri 10am–4.30pm; ☎70 22 24 42, ⊛www.visitcopenhagen.dk) offers maps, general information and accommodation reservations for hotels and hostels (booking fee 60kr). The office also provides countrywide information and distributes the free *Copenhagen This Week*, an up-to-date monthly news and listings magazine. Far better for youth and budget-oriented help, though, is the **Use-It** information centre (mid-June to mid-Sept daily 9am–7pm; rest of year Mon–Wed 11am–4pm, Thurs 11am–6pm, Fri 11am–2pm; ☎33 73 06 20, ⊛www.useit.dk), centrally placed in the Huset complex at Rådhusstræde 13. A wide range of help for travellers is available, including poste restante and free email services, accommodation (staff fall over themselves to help find you a room in the busy summer period) and entertainment information, luggage storage facilities and an extremely useful free magazine called *Playtime*. Finally, ⊛www.aok.dk has plenty of information on Copenhagen and Zealand, with particular emphasis on restaurants, music venues and events.

If you plan to visit many museums, either in Copenhagen or in nearby towns like Helsingør, Roskilde and Køge, you might want to buy a **Copenhagen Card**, which is valid for transport on the entire metropolitan system (which includes the towns mentioned above) and gives entry to most museums in the area. Obviously its worth will depend on your itinerary, but it can certainly save money if well used – especially since it also gets you twenty to fifty percent discounts on some car hire and ferry rides, and on certain museum entry prices across the sound in southern Sweden. Three-day (495kr), 48-hour (375kr) and 24-hour cards (215kr) are available from tourist offices, hotels and travel agents in the metropolitan region, and at train stations.

City transport

The best way to see most of Copenhagen is simply to **walk**: the inner city is compact and much of the central area pedestrianized. There is, however, an integrated zonal network of buses and electric "**S-trains**" (*S-tog*) covering Copenhagen and the surrounding areas, which run about every ten to fifteen minutes between 5am and 12.30am, after which a night-bus (*Natbusserne*) system comes into operation – less frequent, but still with services once or twice an hour. Stations are marked by red hexagonal signs with a yellow "S" inside them. Ten of the twelve lines stop at the Central Station, and the two remaining lines run a circular route around the centre. Each line has a letter, from A to M (some letters are not used); lines running similar routes, but stopping at less stations, have a + symbol after the letter (eg H+); and each line is also colour-coded on route maps. It's essential to study a map before boarding an S-train or you could end up some way from your intended destination.

So long as you avoid the rush hour (7–9am and 5–6pm), **buses** can be a swifter means of getting around once you get the hang of finding the stops – marked by yellow placards on signposts. The city's bus terminal is a black building adjacent to City Hall on the big open square called Rådhuspladsen, a block from both Central Station and the Tivoli Gardens; you can pick up bus-route maps here, and get general information about the metropolitan transport system. **Night-bus** numbers always end with "N", and the stops are well marked by yellow signs on major routes into and out of the city. Another around-town option are the new city-run yellow **harbour buses**, which run along the harbourfront between Nordre Toldbod (near the Little Mermaid) and the Royal Library, and stop five times on the way (twice on the Christianshavn side).

You can use InterRail, Scanrail or Eurail cards on S-trains, buses and harbour buses, but the best option after a **Copenhagen Card** (see above) or the **24-timer**

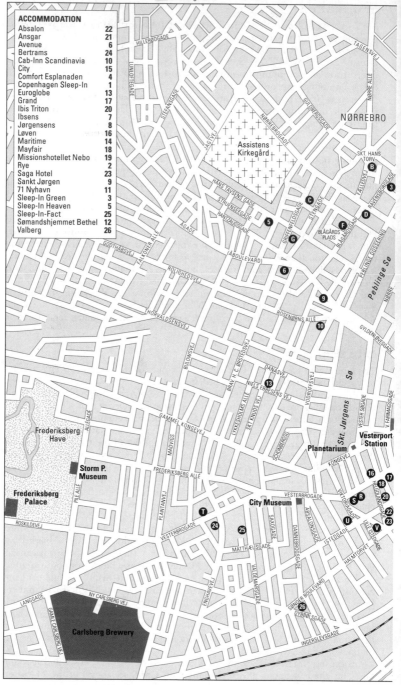

▲ Grundtvigs Kirke

ACCOMMODATION

Absalon	22
Ansgar	21
Avenue	6
Bertrams	24
Cab-Inn Scandinavia	10
City	15
Comfort Esplanaden	4
Copenhagen Sleep-In	1
Euroglobe	13
Grand	17
Ibis Triton	20
Ibsens	7
Jørgensens	8
Løven	16
Maritime	14
Mayfair	18
Missionshotellet Nebo	19
Rye	2
Saga Hotel	23
Sankt Jørgen	9
71 Nyhavn	11
Sleep-In Green	3
Sleep-In Heaven	5
Sleep-In-Fact	25
Sømandshjemmet Bethel	12
Valberg	26

NØRREBRO

Assistens
Kirkegård

Frederiksberg
Have

Storm P.
Museum

Frederiksberg
Palace

Carlsberg Brewery

Planetarium

Vesterport
Station

City Museum

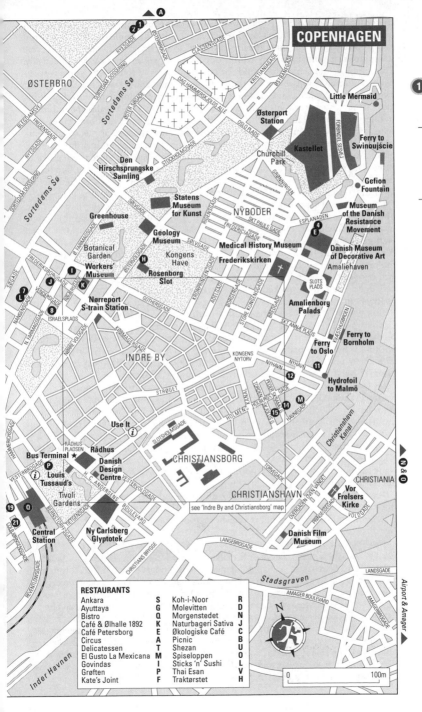

COPENHAGEN

Little Mermaid

Ferry to Swinoujście

Østerport Station

Kastellet

Churchill Park

Gefion Fountain

ØSTERBRO

Den Hirschsprungske Samling

Museum of the Danish Resistance Movement

Statens Museum for Kunst

NYBODER

Greenhouse

Geology Museum

Medical History Museum

Danish Museum of Decorative Art

Botanical Garden

Kongens Have

Frederikskirken

Amaliehaven

Workers' Museum

Rosenborg Slot

Amalienborg Palads

Nørreport S-train Station

ISRAELSPLADS

Ferry to Bornholm

Ferry to Oslo

INDRE BY

KONGENS NYTORV

STRØGET

NYHAVN

Hydrofoil to Malmö

Use It

Rådhus

CHRISTIANSBORG

Christianshavn Kanal

CHRISTIANIA

Bus Terminal

Danish Design Centre

CHRISTIANSHAVN

Vor Frelsers Kirke

Louis Tussaud's

Tivoli Gardens

see 'Indre By and Christiansborg' map

Central Station

Ny Carlsberg Glyptotek

Danish Film Museum

LANGEBROGADE

LANDSGADE

Inder Havnen

Stadsgraven

AMAGER BOULEVARD

Airport & Amager

RESTAURANTS

Ankara	S	Koh-i-Noor	R
Ayuttaya	G	Molevitten	D
Bistro	Q	Morgenstedet	N
Café & Ølhalle 1892	K	Naturbageri Sativa	J
Café Petersborg	E	Økologiske Café	C
Circus	A	Picnic	B
Delicatessen	T	Shezan	U
El Gusto La Mexicana	M	Spiseloppen	O
Govindas	I	Sticks 'n' Sushi	L
Grøften	P	Thai Esan	V
Kate's Joint	F	Traktørstet	H

N

0   100m

ticket (85kr) – which covers the same transportation area but without admission to museums – is a two- (90kr) or three-zone (120kr) **klippekort**, which has ten stamps that you cancel individually according to the length of your journey; one stamp gives unlimited transfers within one hour in two or three zones respectively. Two simultaneous stamps are good for ninety minutes in four or six zones respectively, and three stamps allow two hours in six or nine zones respectively. Note that two or more people can use tickets from the same carnet simultaneously. For a single journey of less than an hour, use a **billet** (14kr), which is valid for unlimited transfers within two zones in that time. *Billets* can be bought on board buses or at train stations, while *klippekort* and 24-timers are only available at bus or train stations and HT Kortsalg kiosks; *klippekort* should be stamped when boarding the bus or via machines on train station platforms. Except on buses, it's rare to be asked to show your ticket, but if you don't have one you face an instant fine of 500kr. Route maps can be picked up free at stations, and most free maps of the city include bus lines and a diagram of the S-train network.

The basic **taxi** fare within Copenhagen is generally a flat starting fare of 22kr, plus 10kr per kilometre travelled (11kr after 3pm and 13kr at weekends) – only usually worthwhile if several people are sharing. There's a taxi rank outside Central Station, or phone Taxamotor (℡38 10 10 10 for a cab, ℡35 39 35 35 for a minibus). Alternatively, just hail a cab in the street that's showing a green "*Fri*" sign on top. A fun new addition to the scene are Quickshaw **cycle taxis**. Carrying a maximum of two people, they operate with a zonal system (25–90kr for 1–5 zones) and can be hailed just like taxis, or picked up at key transport points.

Bikes can also be a good way to get around the city, and are handy for exploring the immediate countryside. The best places to rent one are Københavns Cyklebørs, Gothersgade 157 (℡33 14 07 17); Cykeltanken, Godthåbsvej 247 (℡31 87 14 23); or the DSB Cykelcenter, to the side of Central Station on Reventlowsgade (℡33 33 86 13, ⊛www.rentabike.dk). Bike rental normally costs 45–50kr per day or 225–250kr per week, plus a refundable 200–300kr deposit. Also bear in mind the summer-only free **City Bike scheme** (⊛www.bycyklen.dk), whereby 1500 free bikes (easily recognized by the advertisements painted onto their solid wheels) are scattered about the city at S-train stations and other busy locations; a refundable 20kr deposit unlocks one. The rules are simple: leave the bike in a rack when you've finished with it (you get your coin back automatically as you re-lock the bike), or just leave it out on a sidewalk, in which case someone else will happily return it and pocket the coin. Don't secure one with your own lock and don't take one outside the city limits (the old rampart lakes mark the border) or you risk a fine. If you want to cycle after dark, it's a good idea to get yourself some lights as you'll be fined if you're caught without.

Boat tours leave frequently from Gammel Strand and Nyhavn and sail around the canals and harbour. Cheapest is Netto-Bådene (℡32 54 41 02, ⊛www .havnerundfart.dk), which offers one-hour tours for 20kr that pass both Nyhavn

---

The Metro – underground and overdue

Copenhagen's transport system got a much-needed boost in October 2002 with the opening of the first stretch of the **Metro**, Copenhagen's new underground train system, running from Nørrebro to Christianshavn and Vestamager. Convenient stops include Kongens Nytorv (the huge square/traffic circle beside Nyhavn canal) and Bella Centret – a five-minute walk from the *Copenhagen Hostel* on Amager. Services are swift and run every couple of minutes during rush hour. By 2006, a new section of will be opened, linking central Copenhagen not just to its own suburbs but also with the new Øresunds Link to Sweden and with Kastrup Airport. The evidence of this work is obvious all over the city, disrupting views and traffic in high-visibility areas such as Christianshavn and Nørreport, but there is, at last, a light at the end of the tunnel.

and Christianshavn. DFDS Canal Tours (☎32 96 30 00, ⓦwww.canal-tours.dk) have two fifty-minute options which go to either Nyhavn or Christianshavn; however, at 50kr, you'll get more for your money with Netto-Bådene. DFDS also run two **waterbuses**, one going east to the Trekroner fort/island, one going west to the new Fisketorvet shopping complex; both stop 12–15 times on the way. A two-day unlimited-use ticket costs 40kr, and a single trip 30kr.

Accommodation

Whether it's a hostel bed or a luxury hotel suite, **accommodation** isn't always easy to come by in Copenhagen, especially if you're arriving late in the day, or during July and August (the busiest time of year) when it's essential to book in advance, if only for the first night. If you arrive without a reservation, Wonderful Copenhagen's tourist information office (see p.85) will find you a hotel room, although queues for this service can be lengthy during high season, and it costs 60kr. You can also book in advance for free using their website (ⓦwww.bookcopenhagen.dk) or phone line (☎70 22 24 42; Mon–Fri 10am–4.30pm). If you book in advance using an individual hotel's website, you can often get discounts of up to 35 percent.

Note that we list a couple of gay- and lesbian-friendly accommodation options on p.111, and that all the places listed below are in the city centre unless otherwise stated.

Hotels

You won't find a grotty **hotel** in Copenhagen, though the cheaper ones often forgo the pleasures of private bathroom, phone and TV. Prices do, however, almost always include **breakfast** (unless otherwise stated, it's included in the rates for all places listed below). Most of the budget hotels are just west of the inner centre, around Istedgade – a slightly seedy (though rarely dangerous) area on the far side of the train station. This area is also home to a number of mid-range hotels, and there are further mid-price options around Nyhavn canal, on the other side of Indre By, and out towards the quiet suburb of Frederiksberg.

Absalon Helgolandsgade 15, Vesterbro ☎33 24 22 11, ⓦwww.absalon-hotel.dk. Very large, quiet and relaxing family-run hotel near the Central Station. Vast range of rooms (some with shared bath) to suit most budgets. ❹–❺
Ansgar Colbjørnsensgade 29, Vesterbro ☎33 21 21 96, ⓦwww.ansgar-hotel.dk. Close to the Central Station, with compact and tidy rooms. ❻
Avenue Åboulevard 29, Frederiksberg ☎35 37 31 11, ⓦwww.avenuehotel.dk. Comfortable and welcoming place, on a main suburban boulevard but surprisingly close to downtown Copenhagen (take bus #11 from the Central Station or bus #2 or #11 from Rådhuspladsen). Free parking. ❻
Bertrams Vesterbrogade 107, Vesterbro ☎33 25 04 05, ☎33 25 04 02. Halfway between the Central Station and the Carlsberg Brewery (take bus #6 or #650S from the station). Cosy, good-value place with large rooms, some sharing bathroom facilities. ❺
Cab-Inn Scandinavia Vodroffsvej 57, Frederiksberg ☎35 36 11 11, ⓦwww.cab-inn.dk. Maritime-style decor (flip-up tables and tiny showers) may make you feel like a passenger on

an overnight boat, but the *Cab-Inn* is clean and safe with pleasant staff. It's set in a quiet suburb very close to the city centre; similar rooms are also available at the nearby smaller branch at Danasvej 32 (☎33 21 04 00). Breakfast (50kr) is not included. Bus #2 or #11. ❹
City Peder Skramsgade 24 ☎33 13 06 66, ⓦwww.hotelcity.dk. Three-star, environmentally friendly Best Western chain-hotel serving lush organic breakfasts. Set in the central Nyhavn area, though you pay for the location. Bus #550S from Central Station. ❻
Comfort Esplanaden Bredgade 78 ☎33 48 10 00, ⓦwww.choicehotels.dk. Very decent rooms in a nice location near Churchillparken (bus #29 from Rådhuspladsen, or #650S from Central Station). Free parking. ❻
Euroglobe Niels Ebbesens Vej 22, Frederiksberg ☎33 79 79 54, ⓦwww.hoteleuroglobe.dk. Exceptionally good-value hotel occupying an old villa. Simple rooms, sharing bathroom and kitchen facilities. Bus #29 from Rådhuspladsen. ❸
Grand Vesterbrogade 9A, Vesterbro ☎33 31 61 00, ⓦwww.grandhotelcopenhagen.dk. Very

popular with British travellers, this stylish hotel is quite close to both the Tivoli Gardens and a row of British- and American-style pubs and restaurants. ❼
Ibis Triton Helgolandsgade 7–11, Vesterbro ☎33 31 32 66, ⓦwww.accorhotel.dk. A centrally located showpiece of contemporary Danish design, well-suited to a cosy stay. Breakfast not included. ❺
Ibsens Vendersgade 23 ☎33 13 19 13, ⓦwww.ibsenshotel.dk. Quiet yet central location near the city's picturesque lakes (bus #5 from Nørreport Station or #16 from Central Station) makes this place a winner. Bounteous Danish breakfast spread. ❻
Løven Vesterbrogade 30, Vesterbro ☎33 79 67 20, ⓦwww.loeven.dk. Good value, albeit slightly noisy place two minutes' walk from Vesterport or Central Station. Rooms are basic (some have shared bath), and there's access to a guest kitchen. Some rooms (200kr per person) sleep up to six people. ❷–❸
Maritime Peder Skramsgade 19 ☎33 13 48 82, ⓦwww.hotel-maritime.dk. Comfortable rooms in a newly refurbished former seamen's home, close to Nyhavn's cafés and nightlife. Bus #550S from Central Station. ❻
Mayfair Helgolandsgade 3 ☎33 31 48 01, ⓦwww.themayfairhotel.dk. Part of the Best Western chain, offering "ye olde" English-style rooms with every modern convenience in a central location (ten minutes' walk from Central Station). ❻
Missionshotellet Nebo Istedgade 6, Vesterbro ☎33 21 12 17, ⓦwww.nebo.dk. Small, friendly and one of the best deals in this part of the city, though it's on one of the area's famously sleazy streets. Parking costs 25kr per day. ❺

Rye Ryesgade 115, Østerbro ☎35 26 52 10, ⓦwww.hotelrye.dk. New, small hotel near lively Sankt Hans Torv. The comfortable rooms share bathroom facilities. Bus #6 from Central Station and Rådhuspladsen, or #16 from Rådhuspladsen. ❺
Saga Hotel Colbjørnsensgade 18–20, Vesterbro ☎33 24 49 44, ⓦwww.sagahotel.dk. This small and friendly family-run hotel with basic rooms (some share bathroom facilities) is possibly the best deal this close to the centre. ❹
Sankt Jørgen Julius Thomsens Gade 22, Frederiksberg ☎35 37 15 11, ⓦwww.dkhotellist.dk/stjorgen. Family hotel spread over two floors of an apartment building. Large and bright rooms and shared bathrooms in the corridor. Bus #8 or #13 from Central Station. ❹
71 Nyhavn Nyhavn 71 ☎33 43 62 00, ⓦwww.71nyhavnhotelcopenhagen.dk. Nineteenth-century warehouse right on the famous canals, which also houses one of the city's best restaurants. The 84 classy rooms come at a price and breakfast is not included. Bus #650S from Central Station. ❼
Sømandshjemmet Bethel Nyhavn 22 ☎33 13 03 70, ⓕ33 15 85 70. Still a hotel for professional sailors (visiting mariners get first priority) this central hotel is perfectly located for a night on the town. The bare and basic rooms are nothing to write home about, but you're paying for the location – the view from the rooms is fantastic. ❺
Valberg Sønder Boulevard 53, Vesterbro ☎33 25 25 19, ⓦwww.valberg.dk. Fifth floor of an apartment building in the quieter part of Vesterbro. Large rooms, all with TV, sink and fridge. Bathrooms are shared. Bus #10 from the Reventlowsgade exit of Central Station. ❹

Hostels and sleep-ins

Copenhagen has a great selection of **hostels** and **sleep-ins**, which are ideal for those on a budget – a dormitory bed costs 85–120kr. Space is only likely to be a problem in the peak summer months (June–August), when you should call ahead or turn up as early as possible on the day you want to stay. For the most up-to-date information, head for Use-It (see p.85).

If you're in Copenhagen for more than a couple of weeks, sub-letting a room in a **student hall** or **shared flat**, or renting a **private room** in someone's home (generally 130–175kr per person per day – ask at Use-It), can be a money-saving option. You can also arrange private rooms through the tourist office (see p.85) for a fee of 60kr, though you can only do so by visiting the office in person on the day itself. If you want to confirm a booking before you arrive, Bed & Breakfast in Denmark (☎39 61 04 05, ⓕ39 61 05 25, ⓦwww.bbdk.dk) can make advance arrangements for you, as well as book on the day. Their rooms cost between 350kr and 500kr for a double and, despite the organization's name, breakfast is not included.

Bellahøj Vandrehjem Herbergvejen 8, Brønshøj ☎38 28 97 15, ⓦwww.danhostel.dk/bellahoej. Situated in a distant residential part of the city, this HI hostel is more homely than its rivals, offering

cheap beds in large dorms, and some 2-bed rooms (❶). Reception is open 24hr and there's no curfew, although there's a dormitory lockout from 10am–1pm. Breakfast is 40kr. Simple to reach, too: a 15min ride from the city centre on bus #2 or #11 (nightbus #82N). Open March to mid-Jan.

City Public Hostel Absalonsgade 8, Vesterbro ☎33 31 20 70, ⊛www.city-public-hostel.dk. Conveniently situated ten minutes' walk from Central Station between Vesterbrogade and Istedgade, with a noisy sixty-bed dormitory on the lower floor, less crowded dorms of 4–20 beds on other levels, and a kitchen. Easygoing, and no curfew. Bed linen is 30kr extra, and breakfast 20kr. Buses #6 and #28. Open May–Aug.

Copenhagen Hostel Vejlands Allé 200, Amager ☎32 52 29 08, ⊛www.danhostel.dk/copenhagen. HI hostel with fairly frugal 2-bed (❶) and 5-bed rooms. Bus #46 (daytime only), or take the E or A line S-train to Sjælør, then bus #100S towards Svanemøllen: a 30–40min journey in total. There's also a new Metro stop close by and it's a good twenty minutes' walk from the airport. No curfew, breakfast 40kr. Open mid-Jan to Nov.

Copenhagen Sleep-In Blegdamsvej 132, Østerbro ☎35 26 50 59, ⊛www.sleep-in.dk. A vast hall divided into four- and six-bed compartments. Nice, if busy, atmosphere, with a young and friendly staff and sporadic free gigs by local bands; no curfew. If you don't have a sleeping bag you can rent sheets for 30kr (plus 40kr deposit); breakfast is 30kr. Bus #1, #6, #14, #85N or #95N from Rådhuspladsen or Central station. Open July–Aug.

Ishøj Strand Hostel Ishøj Strandvej 13, Ishøj ☎43 53 50 15, ⊛www.danhostel.dk/ishoj. A great five-star HI hostel next to Køge beach park and the Arken modern art gallery, with a few two-person family rooms (❷). Thirty minutes from the centre on A or E line S-trains. Open all year.

Jørgensens Rømersgade 11 ☎33 13 81 86, ⊛www.hoteljoergensen.dk. A stone's throw from

Nørreport station on Israels Plads. Predominantly dormitory accommodation (6-, 9- and 12-bed rooms), plus a few basic doubles with shared bathrooms (❹). Popular with gay travellers, and an upper age limit of 35. Breakfast is included. Open all year.

Sleep-In-Fact Valdemarsgade 14 ☎33 79 67 79, ⊛www.sleep-in-fact.dk. In the heart of Vesterbro, this is a sports centre out of season and has all sorts of sport facilities for hire when serving as a sleep-in. The 80 beds are divided between two large hall-type rooms which can get very noisy at times, and you'll pay 30kr for a measly breakfast. Fifteen minutes' walk from the Central Station or take bus #6. Open mid-June to mid-Aug.

Sleep-In Green Ravnsborggade 18, Nørrebro ☎35 37 77 77, ⊛www.sleep-in-green.dk. Eco-conscious hostel right in hip Nørrebro overlooking a pretty interior courtyard. Good all-volunteer staff and bright rooms with 10, 20 and 38 beds. Extra charges for bedding (30kr) and organic breakfast (30kr), and there's a noon–4pm lockout. Bus #5, #16, #81N or #84N. Open June to mid-Oct.

Sleep-In Heaven 7th floor, Struenseegade 7, Nørrebro ☎35 35 46 48, ⊛www.sleepinheaven.com. Sizeable hostel outside the city centre with four- and eight-bed dorms, lockers and Internet access; breakfast is 35kr. Buses #8, #12 and #13 from Central Station or nightbus #92N from Rådhauspladsen. Credit cards accepted. Open all year.

YWCA Interpoint Valdemarsgade 15, Vesterbro ☎33 31 15 74. Twenty-eight cheap dorm beds in 4-, 6- and 10-bed rooms; 12.30am curfew, and a 25kr charge for breakfast. Fifteen minutes' walk from Central Station, or bus #3, #6 or #16. Open mid-June to mid-Aug; reception open daily 8.30–11.30am, 3.30–5.30pm and 8pm–12.30am.

Campsites

Only one of Copenhagen's various **campsites** is close to the city centre, but the others are fairly easily reached by public transport. There's little difference in price among them (around 60kr per person per night, plus up to 20kr per tent per night), nor in facilities: all have laundries, kitchen areas with cookers, also television rooms, playgrounds and the like.

If you arrive by campervan, there is a good new option for a cheap central stay. For 220kr per vehicle per day, *City Camp* (☎21 42 53 84, ⊛www.citycamp.dk), near the Fisketorvet shopping complex, offers safe parking and basic facilities such as showers and washing machines.

Absalon Korsdalsvej 132, Rødovre ☎36 41 06 00, ⊛www.dcu.dk. Occupying a large field next to a housing estate, about 9km to the southwest of the city. Take S-train line B to Brøndbyøster, then a fifteen-minute walk or bus #550S (nightbus #93N). Open all year.

Bellahøj Hvidkildevej Brønshøj ☎38 10 11 50. Near the *Bellahøj* youth hostel, this is the most central but least comfortable option, with long queues for the showers and cooking facilities. Buses #11 to Bellahøjvej or S-train F or M to Fuglebakken (nightbus #82N). Open June–Aug.

Charlottenlund Strandpark Strandvejen 144B, Charlottenlund ☏ 39 62 36 88, ⓦ www.campingcopenhagen.dk. Beautifully situated at Charlottenlund Fort and beach, 8km north of the city centre; take bus #6 (nightbus #85N). Open mid-May to mid-Sept.
Nærum Ravnebakken ☏ 45 80 19 57, ⓦ www.camping-naerum.dk. Around 15km from the centre, but very pleasant: take bus #150S from

the Central Station or S-train line B to Jægersborg, then private train (InterRail, Scanrail and Eurail not valid) to Nærum. Open April–Sept.
Tangloppen FDM Ishøj Havn ☏ 43 54 07 67, ⓦ www.fdm.dk. Some 17km south of the city centre, but close to some good and popular beaches. Take any train to Ishøj, then a two-minute walk or bus #128. Open May to mid-Sept.

The City

Exploring Copenhagen is supremely easy. Most of what you're likely to want to see can be found in the city's relatively small – and effortlessly walkable – centre, between the long inlet of the inner harbour (Inder Havnen) on the east and a semi-circular series of lakes on the west. Within this area the divisions are well defined. **Indre By** forms the city's inner core, an intricate maze of streets, squares and alleys whose pleasure lies as much in its general daily bustle as in specific sights. The area **northeast of Indre By**, beyond the major thoroughfare of Gothersgade, is quite different, a boldly proportioned grid-pattern of streets and avenues built to accommodate the dwellings of the Danish nobility in the seventeenth century and reaching a pinnacle of affluence with the palaces of Amalienborg and Rosenborg. The far end of this stretch is guarded, now as three hundred years ago, by the Kastellet, which lies within the fetching open spaces of Churchill Park.

Separated by a moat from Indre By, **Christiansborg** is the administrative centre for the whole country, housing the national parliament and government offices, as well as a number of museums and the ruins of Bishop Absalon's original castle. **Christianshavn**, facing Christiansborg across the inner harbour, provides further contrast, with its tightly proportioned and traditionally working-class streets and a pretty waterfront lined by Dutch-style dwellings. A few blocks to the east lies **Christiania**, the "free city" colonized by the young and homeless in the early 1970s, whose alternative society remains an enduring controversy in Danish life – and merits at least a quick look. **West of the city centre**, Vesterbrogade is the prime thoroughfare, beginning at the carefree delights of the Tivoli Gardens and running to the city fringes at Frederiksberg Have.

Indre By

The natural place from which to begin exploring Indre By (though not actually in it) is the buzzing open space of **Rådhuspladsen**. Here, the **Rådhus**, or City Hall (Mon–Fri 8am–5pm; guided tours in English Mon–Fri 3pm, Sat 10 & 11am; 30kr), has a spacious and elegant main hall that retains many of its original early twentieth-century features, not least the sculptured banisters heading up from the first floor; there's also a lift up to the **bell tower** (tours June–Sept Mon–Fri 10am, noon & 2pm, Sat noon; Oct–May Mon–Sat noon; 20kr), but the view over the city isn't particularly impressive. Note that the tower, but not the World Clock, is included in the Rådhus tour. More interesting is **Jens Olsen's World Clock** (Mon–Fri 10am–4pm, Sat 10am–1pm; 10kr), in a side room close to the entrance. What looks like a mass of inscrutable dials is an astronomical timepiece which took 27 years to perfect and contains a 570,000-year calendar plotting eclipses of the moon and sun, solar time, local time and various planetary orbits – all with incredible accuracy. At no. 57 Rådhuspladsen, and with an appeal of an entirely different kind, **Ripley's Believe It Or Not!** (June–Aug daily 9.30am–10.30pm; Sept–May Mon–Thurs & Sun 10am–6pm, Fri & Sat 10am–8pm; ⓦ www.ripleys.dk; 74kr) is a collection of oddities based on the cartoons of American Robert L. Ripley – a life-size model of

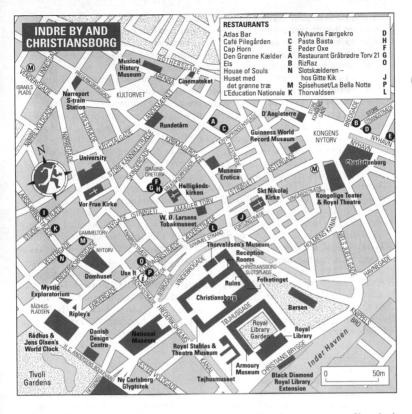

RESTAURANTS

Atlas Bar	I	Nyhavns Færgekro	D
Café Pilegården	C	Pasta Basta	H
Cap Horn	E	Peder Oxe	F
Den Grønne Kælder	A	Restaurant Gråbrødre Torv 21	G
Els	B	RizRaz	O
House of Souls	N	Slotskælderen –	
Huset med		hos Gitte Kik	J
det grønne træ	M	Spisehuset/La Bella Notte	P
L'Education Nationale	K	Thorvaldsen	L

the world's tallest man and a bicycle made from matchsticks are just two of hundreds of exhibits. Next door, also at no. 57 but to the right, **The Mystic Exploratorium** (June–Aug daily 9.30am–10.30pm; Sept–May Mon–Thurs & Sun 10am–6pm, Fri & Sat 10am–8pm; ⊛www.exploratorium.dk; 59kr, 109kr for a joint ticket with Ripley's) offers a surprisingly engaging chance to explore odd natural phenomena, such as how the weather works, and can be manipulated (at least on a small scale).

Along Strøget

Indre By proper begins with **Strøget** (literally "level measure"), the series of streets – Vesterbrogade, Frederiksberggade, Nygade, Vimmelskaftet, Amagertorv and Østergade – which run east–west across the district, lined by pricey stores and graceless fast-food dives. Very much the public face of Copenhagen, it's hard to imagine anything unpleasant ever happening here, and the strip is perfectly suited to stress-free ambling amongst the crowds of locals and street entertainers who parade along it. The most active part is usually around **Gammeltorv** and **Nytorv**, two adjacent squares ("old" and "new") flanking Strøget, where there's a morning fruit-and-vegetable market (until around noon), stalls selling handmade jewellery and bric-a-brac. It was between these squares that the fifteenth-century Rådhus stood before it was destroyed by fire in 1795. A new Rådhus was erected on Nytorv a century later, and this is now the city's **Domhuset**, or Law Courts, marked by a suitably forbidding row of Neoclassical columns.

Just east of here is the **Helligåndskirken** (daily noon–4pm), one of the oldest churches in the city, founded in the fourteenth century though largely rebuilt from 1728 onwards. While it's still in use as a place of worship, there are often art shows and other free exhibitions inside which provide a good excuse for a peek at the church's vaulted ceiling and slender granite columns. Of equally low-key appeal is the tobacco shop directly across Strøget which holds the **W.Ø. Larsens Tobaksmuseet** (Mon–Thurs 10am–6pm, Fri 10am–7pm, Sat 9am–5pm; free) and its briefly diverting clutter of vintage pipes, ornate cigar holders and every conceivable smoking accessory, plus paintings and drawings satirizing the deadly habit. Just beyond, a path leads south off Strøget, through Højbro Plads and on to the grandiose (and now deconsecrated) **Skt Nikolai Kirke** (daily 10am–5pm; ⓦwww.nikolaj-ccac.dk; 20kr); the building's upper floors are employed as one of Copenhagen's prime exhibition spaces for contemporary artists, while at ground level there's a pricey daytime café, packed with lunchers on business accounts.

The final section of Strøget is Østergade, where you'll find another international tourist pull: the **Guinness World Records Museum** (June–Aug daily 10am–10pm; Sept–May Mon–Thurs & Sun 10am–6pm, Fri & Sat 10am–8pm; ⓦwww.guinness.dk; 74kr). It's much as you'd expect, with family-oriented exhibits on the world's tallest, fastest and smallest. Beyond, Østergade flows past the swish and chic *Hotel d'Angleterre* into the biggest of the city squares, **Kongens Nytorv**. Built on what was the edge of the city in medieval times, the square has an equestrian statue of its creator, Christian V, in its centre and a couple of grandly ageing structures around two of its shallow angles. One of these, the **Kongelige Teater** or Royal Theatre, dates from 1874; the other, **Charlottenborg**, next door, was finished in 1683, at the same time as the square itself, for a son of Frederik III. It was later sold to Queen Charlotte Amalie, but since 1754 has been the home of the Royal Academy of Art, which uses some of the spacious rooms for eclectic art exhibitions (daily 10am–5pm; ⓦwww.charlottenborg-art.dk; 20kr). Drop in, if only to glimpse the elegant interior.

The Latin Quarter and around

There's more interest among the tangle of buildings and streets **north of Strøget**. Crossing Gammeltorv and following Nørregade leads to the old university area, sometimes called the **Latin Quarter** – parts of it retain an academic function, which accounts for the book-carrying students milling around. The old university building is overlooked by Copenhagen's cathedral, **Vor Frue Kirke** (Mon–Sat 8.30am–5pm, Sun noon–3pm; free). Built on the site of a twelfth-century church, the present structure dates from 1829, when it was erected amidst the devastation caused by the British bombardment in 1807. The weighty figure of Christ behind the altar and the solemn statues of the apostles, some crafted by Bertel Thorvaldsen (for more on whom, see p.100), others by his pupils, merit a quick call. From the cathedral, dodge across Skindergade into **Gråbrødretorv**, a charming cobbled square filled with good cafés and restaurants and often crowded with buskers. The square dates back to 1238, when the city's first monastery was built here; today, it's a gathering place for locals in the know, who come in good weather to dine well or just enjoy a cool beer. Just north of here is the **Rundetårn** (June–Aug Mon–Sat 10am–8pm, Sun noon–8pm; Sept–May Mon–Sat 10am–5pm, Sun noon–5pm; ⓦwww.rundetaarn.dk; 20kr), a round tower with a gradually ascending spiral ramp winding to its summit, built by Christian IV as an **observatory** – and perhaps also to provide a vantage point from which his subjects could admire his additions to the city. Today the best views are of the more immediate hive of medieval streets and the pedestrians filling them. Legend has it that Tsar Peter the Great sped to the top on horseback in 1715, pursued by the Tsarina in a six-horse carriage – a smoother technique than descending the cobbles on a skateboard, a short-lived fad in more recent times. If you're not quite up to trying that, look in on the contemporary **art gallery** part of the way up instead, which stages changing temporary exhibitions.

After leaving the Rundetårn, you could easily spend half an hour browsing the bookshops of Købmagergade, or visit the **Museum Erotica** (May–Sept daily 10am–11pm, Oct–April Sun–Thurs 11am–8pm, Fri & Sat 10am–10pm; ⊛www.museumerotica.dk; 89kr), which lurks along here at no. 24, a shrine to the erotic (and the just plain pornographic) through the ages. For something more traditional, the **Musical History Museum**, just off Kultorvet at Åbenrå 30 (May–Sept Mon–Wed & Fri–Sun 1–3.50pm; Oct–April Mon, Wed, Sat & Sun 1–3.50pm; ⊛www.musikhistoriskmuseum.dk; 30kr), has an impressive quantity of musical instruments and sound-producing devices spanning the globe and the last thousand years. Naturally the bulk come from Denmark (there are recordings to listen to), and there are some subtle insights into the social fabric of the nation to be gleaned from the yellowing photos of country dances and other get-togethers hung alongside the instruments.

Less musical sounds are provided by the cars hurtling along Nørre Voldgade, at the top of Kultorvet, which marks the edge of the pedestrianized streets of the old city. There are two reasons to queue up at the traffic lights and cross over: the first is the fruit-and-vegetable **market** – and Saturday flea market – on Israel Plads; the second is the **Workers' Museum** (*Arbejdermuseet*) at Rømersgade 22 (July–Oct daily 10am–4pm; rest of the year Tues–Sun 10am–4pm; ⊛www.arbejdermuseet.dk; 50kr), an engrossing and thoughtful guide to working-class life in Copenhagen from the 1930s to the 1950s. Entering the museum, you walk down a reconstructed Copenhagen street – complete with passing tram and a shop window hawking the consumer durables of the day – and continue, via a backyard where washing hangs drying, through a printing works subsidized by the Marshall Plan and into a coffee shop, which sells an old-fashioned coffee-and-chicory blend by the cup. Elsewhere, mock-up house interiors contain family photos, newspapers and TVs showing newsreels of the time, while the permanent displays are backed up by some outstanding temporary exhibitions from labour movements around the world. There's a lunchtime restaurant in the basement serving good traditional Danish fare.

Gothersgade, the road marking the northern perimeter of Indre By, is home to the **Cinematek** (Tues–Fri 9.30am–10pm, Sat & Sun 12.30–10pm; ⊛www.cinemateket.dk), where there's a three-screen art-house cinema (tickets cost 50kr) and a *videotek* section where free films are shown.

North of Gothersgade

There's a profound change of mood **north of Gothersgade**. The congenial medieval alleyways of the old city give way to long, broad streets and a number of proud, aristocratic structures. There's a whole group of these in the **harbour area** near Nyhavn, although perhaps the most impressive building of all is **Rosenborg Slot**, a short way to the west away from the harbour and close to several major **museums**.

From Nyhavn to Esplanaden

Running from Kongens Nytorv to the waterfront, **Nyhavn** is a wide but quite short street, its two sides divided by a slender canal, which was until recently frequented by sailors but is now in the advanced stages of gentrification. One or two of the old tattoo shops remain, now looking decidedly artificial and increasingly outnumbered by small but expensive restaurants and cafés. The canalside is picturesque, though, with yachts moored on the water and well preserved eighteenth-century houses lining the street, three of which (numbers 18, 20 and 67) were lived in at various times by Hans Christian Andersen. Nyhavn is one of the city's most attractive places, with an astounding variety of restaurants crammed into the brightly painted townhouses alongside the canal. Fishing vessels, wooden pleasure craft and the city's canal tour boats fill the water with activity during the days, and a nightly ritual brings hundreds of young city residents to sit by the canal and drink "hand beers" bought at the nearest corner shop, facing off against the well-heeled tourists and locals dining at the extravagant restaurants and bars. The far end of Nyhavn is the departure point for the boat to Rønne and, a block away at the end of Skt Annæ Plads, ferries for Oslo.

From Skt Annæ Plads, Amaliegade leads under a colonnade into the cobbled **Amalienborg Plads**. The statue of Frederik V in its centre reputedly cost more than all four of the identical Rococo palaces that flank it – thanks to French sculptor Jacques Saly, who spent thirty years in Copenhagen at the court's expense creating it. Dating from the mid-eighteenth century, this quartet of imposing palaces provides a sudden burst of welcome symmetry into the city's generally haphazard layout. Two of them now serve as royal residences and there's a changing of the guard each day at noon when Queen Margarethe II is at home – generally attended by gangs of camera-toting observers.

Between the square and the harbour are the lavish gardens of **Amaliehaven**, while in the opposite direction, on Bredgade, looms the great dome of **Frederikskirken**, also known as the "Marmorkirken", or "Marble Church" (Mon, Tues & Thurs 10am–5pm; Wed 10am–6pm, Fri–Sun noon–5pm). Modelled on – and intended to rival – St Peter's in Rome, the church was begun in 1749, but because of its enormous cost lay unfinished until a century and a half later, when its most prominent feature (one of Europe's largest domes) was completed with Danish (rather than the more expensive Norwegian) marble. If you can time your visit to coincide with the **guided tour** (mid-June to Aug daily 1pm & 3pm; rest of the year Sat & Sun 1pm & 3pm; 20kr), the reward is the chance to climb first to the whispering gallery and then out onto the rim of the dome itself. From here there's a stunning, and usually blustery, view over the sharp geometry of Amalienborg and across the sea to the factories of Malmö in Sweden.

Over the road at Bredgade 62, the former Danish Surgical Academy now holds the **Medical History Museum** (guided tours only; in English mid-July to mid-Aug Thurs 3pm & Sun at 2pm; rest of the year in Danish only Wed–Fri 11am & 1pm, Sun 1pm; ⓦwww.mhm.ku.dk; 30kr) – not a place to visit if you've spent the morning on a brewery binge, since the enthusiastically presented hour-long tour features aborted foetuses, straitjackets, syphilis treatments, amputated feet, eyeballs and a dissected head. Further along Bredgade at no. 68, the former Frederiksberg Hospital now houses the **Danish Museum of Decorative Art** (Tues–Fri 10am–4pm, Sat & Sun noon–4pm; ⓦwww.kunstindustrimuseet.dk; 35kr), a definite must if you have any interest in design. The exhibits trace the development of European – and particularly Danish – design, and examine the influence of Eastern styles on Western design. There's also an excellent café.

The Kastellet and around

A little way beyond the Museum of Decorative Art, Bredgade concludes at Esplanaden, facing the green space of **Churchill Park**. To the right, the German armoured car that was commandeered by Danes and used to bring news of the Nazi surrender marks the entrance to the **Museum of the Danish Resistance Movement** (*Frihedsmuseet*; May to mid-Sept Tues–Sat 10am–4pm, Sun 10am–5pm; mid-Sept to April Tues–Sat 11am–3pm, Sun 11am–4pm; ⓦwww.frihedsmuseet.dk; 30kr, free Wed). Initially, the Danes put up little resistance to the German invasion, but later the Nazis were given a systematically wretched time. The museum records the growth of the organized response and has a special section on the youths from Aalborg who formed themselves into the "Churchill Club". Feeling the adults weren't doing enough, this gang of 15-year-olds set about destroying German telegraph cables, blowing up cars and trains and stealing weapons. There's also a small, but inevitably moving, collection of artworks and handicrafts made by concentration camp inmates.

The road behind the museum crosses into the grounds of the **Kastellet** (daily 6am–10pm; free), a fortress built by Christian IV and expanded by his successors through the seventeenth century, after the loss of Danish possessions in Skåne had

△ Sand dunes, Danish coast

put the city within range of Swedish cannonballs. It's now occupied by the Danish army and its buildings are closed to the public. The tall arches and gateways, however, are an enjoyable setting for a stroll, as are the grassy slopes beside the moat. In a corner of the park, perched on some rocks just off the harbour bank – though you can't get there directly from the military compound, and must swing back to the road to find it – the **Little Mermaid** (*Den Lille Havfrue*) exerts an inexplicable magnetism on tourists. Since its unveiling in 1913, this bronze statue of a Hans Christian Andersen character, sculpted by Edvard Erichsen and paid for by the boss of the Carlsberg brewery, has become the best-known emblem of the city – a fact which has led to it being the victim of several subversive pranks: the original head disappeared in 1964, a cow's head was forced over the replacement in 1986, and more recently one of its arms was stolen. A hundred metres away is the far more spectacular **Gefion Fountain**, created by Anders Bundgaard and showing the goddess Gefion with her four sons, whom she's turned into oxen, having been promised in return as much land as she can plough in a single night. The legend goes that she ploughed a chunk of Sweden, then picked it up (creating Lake Vänern) and tossed it into the sea – where it became Zealand.

West from the harbour: Rosenborg Slot and the museums

Just southwest of the Kastellet lies **Nyboder**, a curious area of short, straight and narrow streets lined with rows of compact yellow dwellings. Although some of these are recently erected apartment blocks, the original houses, on which the newer constructions are modelled, were built by Christian IV to encourage his sailors to live in the city. The area at one time declined into a slum, but recent vigorous revamping has made it an increasingly sought-after district. The oldest (and prettiest) houses can be found along Skt Pauls Gade.

Across Sølvgade from Nyboder is the main entrance to **Rosenborg Slot** (May & Sept daily 11am–4pm; June–Aug daily 10am–5pm; Oct daily 11am–3pm, Nov–April Tues–Sun 11am–2pm; 60kr), a Dutch Renaissance palace and one of the most elegant buildings bequeathed by Christian IV to the city. Though intended as a country residence, Rosenborg served as the main domicile of Christian IV (he died here in 1648) and, until the end of the nineteenth century, the monarchs who succeeded him. It became a museum as early as 1830 and in the main building you can still see the rooms and furnishings used by the regal occupants. The highlights, though, are in the treasury downstairs, which displays the rich accessories worn by Christian IV (and his horse), the crown of absolute monarchs and the present crown jewels. Outside, the splendidly neat garden, Rosenborg Have, can be reached by leaving the palace itself and using the park's main entrance on the corner of Øster Voldgade and Sølvgade. On the west side of the Slot is Kongens Have, the city's oldest public park and a popular place for picnics, and, across Øster Voldgade, the **Botanical Garden** (*Botanisk Have*; daily April–Sept 8.30am–6pm; Oct–March 8.30am–4pm; free).

Opposite Rosenborg Have, and marked by a few runic stones, is the **Geology Museum** (Tues–Sun 1–4pm; ⓦwww.geologisk-museum.dk; 25kr), which has a great meteorite section but is otherwise quite missable unless you're a mineral freak. More worthwhile is the neighbouring National Gallery, the **Statens Museum for Kunst**, Sølvegade 48–50 (Tues & Thurs–Sun 10am–5pm, Wed 10am–8pm; ⓦwww.smk.dk; 50kr, free Wed to the permanent collection), a mammoth collection that's too large to take in on a short visit. While all the big cheeses have their patch – there are some minor Picassos and more major works by Matisse and Braque, Modigliani, Dürer and El Greco – it's the creations of Emil Nolde, with their bloated ravens, hunched figures and manic children, that best capture the mood of the place. In an effort to keep up with the times, the museum recently doubled in size, adding a new building for modern art (including contemporary Danish and other European work), which also has a restaurant and children's room, and affords good views of Kongens Have.

Art fans will find further rich pickings across the park behind the museum, in the fine **Den Hirschsprungske Samling** (Mon & Thurs–Sun 11am–4pm, Wed 11am–9pm; ●www.hirschsprung.dk; 25kr, free Wed) on Stockholmsgade. Heinrich Hirschsprung was a late-nineteenth-century tobacco baron who sunk some of his profits into the patronage of emerging Danish artists, including the Skagen artists (see p.181). It was Hirschsprung's wish that on his death the collection – which also features Eckersburg, Købke and lesser names from the Danish mid-nineteenth-century Golden Age – would be given to the nation, but the government of the day vetoed the plan, and Hirschsprung set up his own gallery.

Christiansborg

Connected to Indre By by several short bridges, **Christiansborg** sits on the island of Slotsholmen. It's a mundane part of the city, but administratively – and historically – an important one. It was here, in the twelfth century, that Bishop Absalon built the castle that was the origin of the city, and the drab royal palace (completed in 1916) that occupies the site is nowadays given over primarily to government offices and the state parliament or **Folketinget** (guided tours in English: July–Sept daily at 2pm; rest of the year Sun 2pm only; free). Close to the bus stop on Christiansborg Slotsplads is the entrance to Christiansborg's main courtyard; in this passageway, you'll find the **Ruins under Christiansborg** (May–Sept daily 9.30am–3.30pm; Oct–April Tues, Thurs & Sun 9.30am–3.30pm; 20kr), where a staircase leads down to the remains of Bishop Absalon's original castle. The first fortress suffered repeated mutilations by the Hanseatic League, and Erik of Pomerania had a replacement erected in 1390, into which he moved the royal court. This in turn was pulled down by Christian VI and another castle built between 1731 and 1745. The stone and brick walls that comprise the ruins, and the articles from the castles stored in an adjoining room, are surprisingly absorbing, the mood enhanced by the semi-darkness and lack of external noise. Turn left into the palace courtyard as you exit the ruins and you'll find the entrance to the **Royal Reception Rooms** (guided tours in English: May–Sept daily at 11am, 1 & 3pm, Oct–April 11am & 3pm; 40kr) on the right. They're used by the royal family to entertain important visitors, and it's worth popping in to peek at the richly decorated throne room, with delicate silk from Lyon covering the walls and a recently completed row of modern tapestries (made for the Queen's fiftieth birthday) depicting Denmark's colourful past.

There are a number of other, less captivating museums in and around Christiansborg Slotsplads, to which the ticket office for the ruins can provide directions – the confusing array of buildings makes it easy to get lost. That said, you could probably sniff your way to the **Royal Stables** (May–Sept Fri–Sun 2–4pm; Oct–April Sat & Sun 2–4pm; 20kr), dating from 1745 and one of the few remaining parts of the original Baroque Christiansborg, lavishly decorated with pillars, vaulted ceilings and walls of Tuscan marble. Apparently not even the king's own chambers were this extravagant. Nearby, the **Theatre Museum** (Wed 2–4pm, Sat & Sun noon–4pm; 20kr) is housed in what was the eighteenth-century Court Theatre and displays original costumes, set-models and the old dressing rooms and boxes. Exiting the courtyard and walking through Tøjhusgade takes you to the **Armoury Museum** (*Tøjhusmuseet*; Tues–Sun noon–4pm; 40kr, free Wed), an Eldorado for arms buffs where you can view weaponry from Christian IV's arsenal up until today, and a host of crests and coats of arms. A few strides further on, a small gateway leads into the gorgeous tree-lined grounds of the **Royal Library** – an excellent venue for a picnic. The library itself (Mon–Sat 8am–11pm) exhibits original manuscripts by Hans Christian Andersen, Karen Blixen and Søren Kierkegaard. On the waterfront at Christian's Brygge 8, the library's big black extension building – completed in 2000 and known as the "Black Diamond" – has doubled the library's capacity, and includes a concert hall, conference rooms and restaurants, as well as computers with free Internet access. Finally, adjacent to

Christiansborg Slotsplads sits the long, low form of the seventeenth-century **Børsen**, or Stock Exchange – with its spire of four entwined dragons' tails, it's one of the most distinctive buildings in the city and worth seeking out.

Thorvaldsen's Museum and the National Museum

On the far north side of Slotsholmen island, **Thorvaldsen's Museum** (Tues–Sun 10am–5pm; ®www.thorvaldsensmuseum.dk; 20kr, free Wed) is home to an enormous collection of work and memorabilia of Denmark's most famous sculptor, and also houses the remains of the man himself. Despite negligible schooling, Bertel Thorvaldsen (1770–1844) drew his way into the Danish Academy of Fine Arts before moving onto Rome, where he perfected the heroic, classical figures for which he became famous. Nowadays he's not widely known outside Denmark, although in his day he enjoyed international renown and won commissions all over Europe.

Other than a selection of early works in the **basement**, the labels of the great, hulking statues read like a roll call of the famous and infamous: Vulcan, Adonis, John Russell, Gutenberg, Pius VII and Maximilian; while the **Christ Hall** contains the huge casts of the statues of Christ and Apostles which can be seen in Vor Frue Kirke (see p.94). A prolific and gifted sculptor, Thorvaldsen was something of a wit, too. Asked by the Swedish artist J.T. Sergel how he managed to make such beautiful figures, he held up the scraper with which he was working and replied, "With this".

There's another major collection a short walk west over the Slotsholmen moat: the **National Museum** (Tues–Sun 10am–5pm; ®www.natmus.dk; 40kr, free Wed), which has an ethnographic section in a separate wing at Ny Vestergade 10, is really strongest (as you'd expect) on Danish history, and if you've any interest in the subject, you could easily spend a couple of hours here. Much of the early stuff, ranging from prehistory to the Viking days, comes from Jutland – jewellery, bones and even bodies, all remarkably well preserved; much of it was only discovered after wartime fuel shortages led to large-scale digging of the Danish peat bogs. Informative explanatory texts help clarify the **Viking section**, whose best exhibits – apart from the familiar horned helmets – are the sacrificial gifts, among them the Sun Chariot, a model horse carrying a sun disc with adornments of gold and bronze. Further floors store a massive collection of almost anything and everything that featured in Christian-era Denmark up to the nineteenth century – finely engraved wooden altarpieces, furniture, clothing and more – as well as a good section on peasant life.

Christianshavn

From Christiansborg, the Knippels Bro bridge crosses the Inder Havnen to the island of Amager and into **Christianshavn**, built by Christian IV as an autonomous new town in the early sixteenth century to provide housing for workers in the shipbuilding industry. It was given features more common to Dutch port towns of the time, even down to a small canal (Wilders Kanal), and in parts the area is more redolent of Amsterdam than Copenhagen. Although its present inhabitants are fairly well-off – as evidenced by some immaculately preserved houses along Overgaden oven Vandet – Christianshavn still has the mood of a working-class quarter, with a group of secondhand shops along the district's main street, Torvegade.

Poking skywards through the trees near Torvegade is the blue-and-gold spire of **Vor Frelsers Kirke** (April–Aug 11am–4.30pm; Sept–Oct 11am–3.30pm, Nov–March Mon–Sat 11am–3.30pm, Sun noon–3.30pm; free; access to spire April–Oct only, 20kr), on the corner of Prinsessegade and Skt Annæ Gade. The **spire**, with its helter-skelter outside staircase, was added to the otherwise plain church in the mid-eighteenth century, instantly becoming one of the more recognizable features on the city's horizon. Climbing the spire (which you can do between April and October only) is fun, but not entirely without risk – though the rumour that the builder fell off it and died is, while plausible, untrue. To get to the spire, go through the church and up to a trap door which opens onto the platform where the external steps begin: there are four hundred of them, slanted and slippery (especially after rain) and gradually becoming smaller. The reward for reaching the top is a great view of Copenhagen and beyond.

Christiania

A few streets northeast of Vor Frelsers Kirke, **Christiania** occupies an area that was for centuries used as a barracks, before the soldiers moved out in 1971 and it was colonized by young and homeless people. It was declared a **"free city"** on September 24, 1971, with the aim of operating autonomously from Copenhagen, and its continued existence has fuelled one of the longest-running debates in Danish (and Scandinavian) society. One by-product of its idealism and the freedoms assumed by its residents (and, despite recent lapses, generally tolerated by successive governments and the police) was to make Christiania a refuge for petty criminals and shady individuals from all over the city. But the problems have inevitably been overplayed by Christiania's critics, and a surprising number of Danes – of all ages and from all walks of life – do support the place, not least because Christiania has performed usefully, and altruistically, when established bodies have been found wanting. An example has been in the weaning of heroin addicts off their habits (once, a 24-hour cordon was thrown around the area to prevent dealers reaching the addicts inside: reputedly the screams – of deprived junkies and suppliers being "dealt with" – could be heard all night). And Christiania residents have stepped in to provide free shelter and food for the homeless at Christmas when the city administration declined to do so.

The population of around one thousand is swelled in summer by the curious and the sympathetic, with many heading straight for the open hash market, known as *Pusherstreet*, where cannabis smoking is tolerated by the government. Bob Marley and John Lennon blare out from the bars and the area is awash with psychedelic painting. Residents ask people not to camp here, and tourists not to point cameras at the weirder-looking inhabitants. The craft shops and restaurants are – partly because of their refusal to pay any kind of tax – fairly cheap, and nearly all are good, as are a couple of innovative music and performance art venues (see p.110). These, and the many imaginative dwellings, including some built on stilts in a small lake, make a visit worthwhile. Additionally, there are a number of alternative political and arts groups based in Christiania; for **information** on these – and on the district generally – call in to Galopperiet (Tues–Sun noon–5pm), to the right of the area's main entrance on Prinsessegade. Christiania can be quite confusing to navigate, so it's a good idea to go on one of the two-hour **guided tours** of the area, which are conducted by local residents (daily noon–3pm on the hour; 30kr; ☎32 57 96 70; ⓦwww.christiania.org); if you're in a group of four people or more, try to book at least one day in advance; otherwise, you can just turn up. Commencing with a short video presentation about Christiania's history, the tours are extremely informative, especially if you're interested in alternative ways of social organization.

Christiania is also the gateway to **Holmen**, once a forgotten naval station but now a complex of four art schools – the National School of Architecture, the National School of Theatre, the National Film School and the Rhythmical Music Conservatory – which the city plans to continue developing in coming years. Check the area for current developments – change is in the air and it's quickly becoming Europe's latest industrial zone to be taken over by artists and revellers.

Along Vesterbrogade

Hectic **Vesterbrogade** begins on the far side of Rådhuspladsen from Strøget, and its first attraction is Copenhagen's most famous after the Little Mermaid: the **Tivoli Gardens** (mid-April to mid-June & mid-Aug to late-Sept Mon, Tues & Sun 11am–11pm, Wed & Thurs 11am–midnight, Fri & Sat 11am–1am; 50kr; mid-June to mid-Aug Mon–Thurs & Sun 11am–midnight, Fri & Sat 11am–1am; 55kr;

www.tivoligardens.com). This park of many bland amusements, which first flung open its gates in 1843, was modelled on the Vauxhall Gardens in London, and in turn became the model for the Festival Gardens in London's Battersea Park. The name is now synonymous with Copenhagen at its most innocently pleasurable, and the opening of the gardens each year on May 1 is taken to mark the beginning of summer. There are fountains, over 25 fairground rides (10, 20 or 30kr each, paid with 10kr tickets bought in books from two ticket outlets; these also sell 180kr passes which cover all the rides), and fireworks displays at midnight (Wed & Sat; between April and June call ☎33 75 10 01 for timings), as well as nightly entertainment in the central arena, encompassing everything from acrobats and jugglers to the mid-Atlantic tones of various fixed-grin crooners. Naturally, it's overrated and overpriced, but an evening spent wandering among the revellers of all ages indulging in the mass consumption of ice cream is an experience worth having – once, at any rate. Close to the gardens' Vesterbrogade entrance, on the corner of Hans Christian Andersens Boulevard, is the predictable **Louis Tussaud's Wax Museum** (May–Aug 10am–10pm; rest of the year 10am–5pm; www.tussaud.dk; 69kr).

Behind the Tivoli, across Tietgensgade towards the harbour, is the dazzling **Ny Carlsberg Glyptotek**, Dantes Plads 7 (Tues–Sun 10am–4pm; www.glyptoteket .dk; 30kr, free Wed & Sun), opened in 1897 by brewer Carl Jacobsen as a venue for ordinary people to see classical art exhibited in classical style. Its centrepiece is the conservatory: "Being Danes," said Jacobsen, "we know more about flowers than art, and during the winter this greenery will make people pay a visit; and then, looking at the palms, they might find a moment for the statues." It's an idea that succeeded, and even now the gallery is well used – and not just by art lovers: there's a programme of classical music concerts every Sunday and some Wednesdays (call ☎33 41 81 41 for details), as well as a seasonal roster of other events, some free; pick up a schedule at the entrance.

As for the contents, this is by far Copenhagen's finest gallery, with a stirring array of Greek, Roman and Egyptian art and artefacts, as well as what is reckoned to be the biggest (and best) collection of Etruscan art outside Italy. There are excellent examples of nineteenth-century European art too, including a complete collection of Degas casts made from the fragile working sculptures he left at his death, Manet's *Absinthe Drinker*, and two small cases containing tiny caricatured heads by Honore Daumier. Easily missed, but actually the most startling room in the place, is an antechamber with just a few pieces – early works by Man Ray, some Chagall sketches and a Picasso pottery plate. There's also a French wing containing Impressionist art and work from Danish painting's so-called "Golden Age" (1800–1850), plus a French café on a balcony overlooking greenhouses of palm trees.

Finally, if you're at all interested in Denmark's world-class tradition of design, don't leave this area without at least looking in on the new **Danish Design Centre**, 27–29 Hans Christian Andersens Boulevard (Mon–Fri 10am–5pm, Sat & Sun 11am–4pm; www.ddc.dk; 30kr). The building, designed by Danish architect Henning Larsen, serves as an exhibit hall, research facility and showcase for all sorts of industrial design, from Bang & Olufsen stereo equipment to Børge Mogensen furniture.

Beyond the Tivoli Gardens

Just west of the train station, the streets between Vesterbrogade and **Istedgade** used to be Copenhagen's token red-light area, and the only part of the city where you might have felt unsafe. Over the years, though, the low rents attracted students and a large number of immigrant families, who are now, in turn, gradually being replaced by young middle-class families as the area undergoes the city's most extensive refurbishment programme. However, you can still walk along Istedgade and be likely to find rastas and Turks sipping tea from tulip glasses, plus a number of diverse (but well-priced) ethnic eateries.

Søren Kierkegaard

Søren Kierkegaard is inextricably linked with Copenhagen, yet his championing of individual will over social conventions and his rejection of materialism did little to endear him to his fellow Danes. Born in 1813, Kierkegaard believed himself set on an "evil destiny" – partly the fault of his father, who is best remembered for having cursed God on a Jutland heath. Kierkegaard's first book, **Either/Or**, published in 1843, was inspired by his love affair with one **Regine Olsen**; she failed to understand it, however, and married someone else. Few other people understood *Either/Or*, in fact, and Kierkegaard, though devastated by the broken romance, came to revel in the enigma he had created, becoming a "walking mystery in the streets of Copenhagen" (he lived in a house on Nytorv). He was a prolific author, sometimes publishing two books on the same day and often writing under pseudonyms. His greatest philosophical works were written by 1846 and are often claimed to have laid the foundations of **existentialism**.

At Vesterbrogade 59 is the **City Museum** (*Københavns Bymuseum*; Mon & Wed–Sun: May–Sept 10am–4pm; Oct–April 1–4pm; ⓦ www.kbhbymuseum.dk; 20kr, free Fri), which has reconstructed ramshackle house exteriors and tradesmen's signs from early Copenhagen. Looking at these, the impact of Christian IV becomes resoundingly apparent. There's a large room recording the form and cohesion that this monarch and amateur architect gave the city, even including a few of his own drawings. The rest of the city's history is told by paintings – far too many paintings, in fact. Head upstairs for the room devoted to Søren Kierkegaard, filled with bits and bobs – furniture from his home, paintings of his girlfriend Regine Olsen, jewellery, books and manuscripts – that form an intriguing footnote to the life of this nineteenth-century Danish writer and philosopher, and much the most interesting part of the museum (see box above).

A few minutes to the north of Vesterbrogade, on the corner with Vester Søgade at Gammel Kongevej 10, is the **Tycho Brahe Planetarium** (daily 10.30am–9pm; ⓦ www.tycho.dk; 25kr); the biggest in Scandinavia, it's named after the world-famous Danish astronomer who invented instruments to accurately plot the sun, planets and stars for the first time. Apart from an astronomical- and space-related section, the in-house Omnimax Theatre, with a 1000-square-metre dome screen, is the best part of the Planetarium. Films (in 3D) are shown every hour on the hour, and cost a steep 85kr to watch (includes entrance ticket to Planetarium).

West to the Carlsberg Brewery and Frederiksberg Have

Way out west along Vesterbrogade (save your legs by taking bus #6 or #18 to Valby Langgade and crossing the street), down Gammel Carlsberg Vej, you'll find the **Carlsberg Brewery**'s Visitor Centre at no. 11 (Tues–Sun 10am–4pm; free). There's a free beer once you've made your way through the surprisingly absorbing centre, which depicts the history of Danish beer brewing. Once inside the brewery proper, note the fine Elephant Gate that used to be the main entrance: four elephants carved in granite supporting the building.

Vesterbrogade finishes up opposite the **Frederiksberg Have**, which contains the Frederiksberg Palace, now used as a military academy and closed to the public. Throughout the eighteenth century, the city's top brass came here to mess about in boats along the network of canals that dissect the copious lime-tree groves, and its pleasant surrounds are now a popular weekend picnic spot for locals. While here, you might call in at the entertaining **Storm P. Museum** (May–Sept Tues–Sun 10am–4pm; Oct–April Wed, Sat & Sun 10am–4pm; 20kr), by the gate facing Frederiksberg Allé. It's packed with the satirical cartoons that made "Storm P." (Robert Storm Petersen) one of the most popular bylines in Danish newspapers from the 1920s. Even if you don't understand the Danish captions, you'll leave the museum with an insight into the national sense of humour.

Beyond the Frederiksberg Palace, at Roskildevej 32 (buses #28, #39, #100S and #550S), is Copenhagen's **Zoo** (June–Aug daily 9am–6pm; April–May Mon–Fri 9am–5pm, Sat & Sun 9am–6pm; Sept–Oct daily 9am–5pm; Nov–March daily 9am–4pm; ❀www.zoo.dk; 80kr), which has the usual array of caged lions, elephants and monkeys, plus a special children's section.

Out from the centre

Unlike many other major European cities, Copenhagen has only a few miles of drab housing estates on its periphery before the countryside begins. There are a number of things worth venturing out for, although none of them need keep you away from the main action for long.

Just northwest of the inner city, only fifteen minutes on foot from Indre By, is **Assistens Kirkegård**, a cemetery built to cope with the dead from the 1711–12 plague. More interestingly, it contains the graves of Hans Christian Andersen and Søren Kierkegaard – both well signposted, although not from the same entrance. If you get lost, look at the handy catalogue by the gate on Kapelvej. The cemetery is off Nørrebrogade in the district of Nørrebro: walk from the Nørreport station along Frederiksborggade and over the lake. Alternatively, buses #5, #16 and #18 run along the graveyard's edge. Further northwest is **Grundtvigs Kirke** (April–Oct Mon–Sat 9am–4.45pm, Sun noon–4pm; rest of the year Mon–Sat 9am–4pm, Sun noon–1pm), an astonishing yellow-brick creation whose gabled front resembles a massive church organ which rises upwards and completely dwarfs the row of terraced houses that share the street. Named after and dedicated to the founder of the Danish folk high schools, the church was designed by Jensens Klint and his son in 1913, but was not finished until 1926. From the city centre, it's a twenty-minute journey on buses #10, #16, #21 or #69. Get off in the small square of Bispetorv soon after passing the Bispebjerg Hospital; the church itself is in På Bjerget.

South

If the weather's good, take a trip south to the **Amager beaches**, about half an hour away by bus #12 or #13 along Øresundsvej (ask for Helgoland). On the other side of the airport from the beaches (take bus #30, #31, #32 or #350S) lies **DRAGØR**, an atmospheric cobbled fishing village with a couple of good local history collections in the **Dragør Museum** by the harbour (May–Sept Tues–Sun noon–4pm; ❀www.dragoer-information.dk; 20kr), and the **Amager Museum** (May–Sept Tues–Sun noon–4pm; Oct–April Wed & Sun noon–4pm; ❀www .dragoer-information.dk; 20kr), a fifteen-minute walk away down Kirkevej (or take bus #30).

Further out from the city centre, on the road to Køge, the southern suburb of **Ishøj** is home to many ethnic communities, mainly from the Middle East, and an excellent museum of modern art, **Arken** (Tues & Thurs–Sun 10am–5pm, Wed 10am–9pm; ❀www.arken.dk; 55kr). Looking very much like a ship, this sleek showcase rises from Ishøj beach and houses excellent temporary exhibitions, plus a glassed-in restaurant overlooking the bay that serves herring specialities for lunch. From central Copenhagen take the S-train line A or E to Ishøj station and then bus #128, a thirty-minute journey altogether.

North

If you're tired of history, culture and the arts, you might fancy a trip to the **Experimentarium** (Mon, Wed & Fri 9am–5pm, Tues 9am–9pm, Sat & Sun 11am–5pm; ❀www.experimentarium.dk; 89kr). Located in a former beer-bottling hall, this workshop-cum-museum attempts to raise scientific awareness through some interesting and entertaining hands-on exhibits, such as a disco which beats to your biorhythms. There's a pavilion area for young children as well, with trick mirrors, a Fairy-Tale Room, and the chance to build a house using "superlight" bricks.

The constantly changing special exhibits are generally always well-made state-of-the-art affairs, and worth checking out.

Just outside the city limits, reached by S-train line C or bus #6, **CHARLOTTENLUND** has a lovely beach, good for sunbathing – as long as you can ignore the smoke-belching chimneys in the background. Its main attraction these days is the **Danish Aquarium** (mid-Feb to mid-Oct daily 10am–6pm; rest of the year Mon–Fri 10am–4pm, Sat & Sun 10am–5pm; ⊛ www.danmarks-akvarium.dk; 65kr), with its impressive collection of tropical fish, sharks, crocodiles and turtles. Nearby **Charlottenlund Fort**, these days housing a campsite (see p.92), has a few abandoned cannons and great views over the city and out to sea. If not camping, you're better off making for **Charlottenlund Slotshave**, a former manor house with a gorgeous park (open 24hr; free) perfect for strolling and picnicking.

If you're in the mood for an amusement park but can't face (or afford) Tivoli, venture out to **Bakken** (July daily noon–midnight; late-March to June & Aug Mon–Fri 2pm–midnight, Sat 1pm–midnight, Sun noon–midnight; free, tour passes to all 35 rides 198kr), close to the Klampenborg stop at the end of line C on the S-train network. Set in a corner of Kongens Dyrehave (the Royal Deer Park), it's possibly more fun than its city counterpart – and certainly more down-to-earth – and besides the usual swings and roller-coasters offers easy walks through oak and beech woods. Strolling back towards Klampenborg along Christiansholmsvej, a left turn at the restaurant *Peter Lieps Hus* gives superb views over the Øresund.

Finally, half an hour's bus journey (#184) to the north is the village of **LYNGBY**, and its **Open-Air Museum** (*Frilandsmuseet*; late April to Sept Tues–Sun 10am–5pm; ⊛ www.natmus.dk; 40kr, free Wed), set inside a large park and comprising restored seventeenth- to mid-nineteenth-century buildings, drawn from all over Denmark and its former territories. A walk through the park leads to the Sorgenfri Palace, one-time home of Frederik V (closed to the public). Take S-train line B to Sorgenfri.

Eating

Whether you want a quick coffee and pastry, or to sit down to a five-course gourmet dinner, you'll find more choice – and lower prices – in Copenhagen than in any other Scandinavian capital. Many of the city's innumerable **cafés** offer good-value, filling brunches, sandwiches and snacks, and double up in the evening as bars. There are also plenty of places selling shawarmas, kebabs, pizzas, pitta breads with falafel and china boxes, and as a general rule they get cheaper the further away from the centre you get. Most **restaurants** are open for lunch and dinner: prices tend to be higher in the evenings, but there are generally good-value deals at lunchtime, so those on a budget needn't deprive themselves of a blowout. Note that all the places listed below are in the city centre unless otherwise stated.

If you're stocking up for a **picnic** – or a trip to Sweden or Norway – take advantage of the numerous outlets selling *smørrebrød* (open sandwiches); Domhusets Smørrebrød, on Kattesundet 18, and Københavns Smørrebrød, Vesterbrogade 6c, are two of the most central. For more general food shopping, use one of the **supermarkets**: ISO at Vesterbrogade 23, Irma at Vesterbrogade 1 and Superbrugsen by Nørreport Station are all top range. Netto and Fakta are by far the cheapest and more chaotic; you'll find Netto branches at Nørre Voldgade 94, Fiolstræde 9, Landemærket 11 and Store Kongensgade 47; and Fakta on Nørrebrogade 14–16 and on Borgergade 27.

Brunch and light snacks

Bang & Jensen Istedgade 130, Vesterbro. At the quieter end of Istedgade, a popular café with a renowned brunch daily until 4pm from 65kr. There's also a breakfast buffet until 10am at 35kr, and sandwiches start at 40kr.

Bar Bar Bar Vesterbrogade 51, Vesterbro. A relaxed place on Vesterbro Torv good for a coffee, drink or light snack.

Bastionen & Løven Voldgade 50, Christianshavn. Restaurant set in a converted windmill, with a view of the moat that once defended the city. Known for its brunch, 80kr during the week (until noon) and 120kr during weekends (until 2pm), with everything you could possibly desire.

Burgery & Bakery Godthåbsvej 109A, Frederiksberg. Out from the city centre, but highly recommended by locals. As you'd expect from the name, the menu mostly comprises burgers and pastries.

Café Amokka Dag Hammarskjolds Allé 38–40, Østerbro. Something of a coffee temple in the Østerbro area near the station, with great sweets to go with the good (and pricey) coffee, plus some eclectic food (such as tofu, sprouts and asparagus salad with miso dressing) and a special children's menu. Outdoor seating.

Café Europa Amagertorv 1. Apart from its coffee (pricey, but the best in town), the main attraction is the outdoor seating on Strøget. Also fabulous cakes, sandwiches and light meals.

Café Kunstforeningen Gammel Strand 48, near Christiansborg Palace. Salads and sandwiches (from 55kr) in a basement or at pavement tables, with museum views in good weather. Good Sunday brunches (90kr).

Café Sommersko Kronprinsensgade 6. Off the Købmagergade pedestrian street. A popular café visited both for its food and drinks – the filling Sunday brunch is especially recommended (90kr for meat-eaters, 99kr for vegetarians).

Café Sonja Saxogade 86, Vesterbro. Daily special (often Danish fare, always a vegetarian option) with salad and bread for 30kr. Dessert 10kr.

Den Sorte Gryde Istedgade 108, Vesterbro. Legendarily huge burgers (33kr for a 300gram treat) but also good for traditional Danish fare. Try the *biksemad* (diced beef and potato served with pickled beetroot and a fried egg on top) for 45kr.

Floras Kaffebar Blågårdsgade 27, Nørrebro. Cheapest main course (chilli con carne) at 55kr, plus soups and cakes, served in an easygoing atmosphere. Come back at night for cheaper-than-average beer and a game of backgammon.

Front Page Sortedams Dosseringen 21, Nørrebro. A beautiful spot overlooking one of Copenhagen's finest lakes. Perfect for a quiet coffee, a beer or a plate of filling tapas.

Hackenbusch Vesterbrogade 124, Vesterbro. Colourful café-bar with an inventive blackboard menu. Dishes (always one vegetarian) from 88kr, and Tuesdays offer bargain burgers for 25kr.

Husets Café Rådhusstræde 13, Nørrebro. Sandwich spot located in the Huset complex (sandwiches from 25kr and lunch buffet for 39kr), which doubles as *Jazzhouse Vognporten* in the evening. Open Mon–Sat.

Kaffe Salonen Peblinge Dosserling 6. Super-hip coffee house in Nørrebro with outdoor tables looking out onto a lake, and a waterside terrace on a floating dock, too; coffee, beer, ice creams and some food – try the roast beef.

Konditoriet Amagertorv 6. Upstairs tea-room of the Royal Copenhagen porcelain and silverware shop, serving coffees, cocoa and fine Danish pastries, as well as finger sandwiches.

La Galette Larsbjørnstræde 9. A bit difficult to find (you have to cross a courtyard to get to no. 9) but worth it for the authentic Breton pancakes (20–70kr), made with organic buckwheat and a whole array of fillings – sweet and savoury – from smoked salmon to chocolate and chestnut mousse.

O's American Breakfast & Barbecue Øster Farimagsgade 27. American-style Southern cooking northwest of the Botanic Gardens (bus #40). Serves big breakfasts until late afternoon, then switches to barbecue meals for dinner. A branch has also opened at Gothersgade 15, the nightlife area, where you can get breakfast from 3am during the weekend.

Pussy Galore's Flying Circus Sankt Hans Torv 30, Nørrebro. Trendy brunch spot with outdoor seating on the square. Brunch until 4pm at 45–95kr. Also popular in the evenings, when beer and wine take priority.

The Taco Shop Nørre Farimagsgade 57. The best taco spot in town, though take-away only, serving up tacos from 27kr and doritos from 42kr. Stays open much later (until 10pm nightly) than most places in the capital.

Tim's Cookies Nørrebrogade 41. Home-made American-style cookies and brownies and cheap sandwiches on tasty bread, all between 12kr and 35kr.

Restaurants

Many of the city's **Danish restaurants** knock out affordable (around 80kr) and high-quality **lunches**, either from a set menu or from an open buffet. **Dinner** will always be more expensive, although Copenhagen's growing band of **ethnic restaurants** are making it increasingly affordable – many have adopted the Scandinavian open-table idea, offering all-you-can-eat meals from around 60kr, but don't plan a night's dancing after wading through one. These are also usually the best bet for finding vegetarian food.

For late-night eating, as well as *Pasta Basta*, listed on p.108, and the late-opening cafés mentioned under "Nightlife", you might want to join the thespians munching fresh bread and rolls in *Herluf Trolle*, on Herluf Trolles Gade, just behind the Royal Theatre. Filling breakfasts can be had from 3am at *O's American Breakfast & Barbecue* (see opposite).

As a rule, Danes tend to finish dining early, if they dine out at all – most actually prefer eating at home. As a result, most restaurants in the city cater to tourists and stay open until 11pm or midnight. Roughly half the city's restaurants don't open at all on Sunday, and those that do keep shorter hours, usually opening for dinner only.

Finally, Danes are keen on **reserving tables** in advance, and while you're unlikely to have to wait long for a place, it's still a good idea to ring ahead at the city's more popular spots. We've given telephone numbers for those restaurants where reservations are advisable.

Danish restaurants

Bistro Central Station. Believe it or not, you can get a broad, comparatively low-cost introduction to Danish food right inside the station concourse. Allow a couple of hours to explore the massive cold buffet, served from 11.30am to 10pm for 149kr; there are far cheaper daily specials, too.

Café Petersborg Bredgade 76 ☎33 12 50 16. In an eighteenth-century building between Nyhavn and Kongens Nytorv, the menu centres on traditional fare such as meatballs with red cabbage, or old fashioned egg-cake (a type of scrambled eggs with bacon and chives served on rye bread), as well as lots of *smørrebrød* choices at lunchtime. Main courses from 65kr.

Café Pilegården Pilestræde 44 ☎33 15 48 80. Just off Strøget, and offering a magnificent all-you-can-eat lunchtime open-sandwich buffet for 90kr.

Café & Ølhalle 1892 Rømersgade 22, Nørreport ☎33 93 25 75. In the basement of the Workers' Museum, *Ølhalle* specializes in old-fashioned traditional Danish food that you won't find anywhere else. Try the *bidesild* (strong pickled herring) or *æbleflæsk* (stewed apple and pork), prepared just as they were 100 years ago.

Els Store Strandstræde 3 ☎33 14 13 41. Very plush, with a game-oriented menu and walls lined with elegant mid-nineteenth-century Danish art. A full meal will set you back around 300kr.

Grøften Tivoli Gardens ☎33 75 06 75. *Grøften* continues to win admirers for its good traditional Danish food, served within the walls of the famous amusement park. The prawn sandwiches are locally famous, as is the *skibberlapskovs*, a traditional Danish stew.

Huset med det grønne træ Gammeltorv 20 ☎33 12 87 86. The "House with the Green Tree" does indeed have a tree – and some of the finer Danish lunches in the downtown area. *Smørrebrød* from 35kr a piece, main courses for 80–100kr.

Nyhavns Færgekro Nyhavn 5 ☎33 15 15 88. Deservedly pricey traditional food – the scrumptious, fish-laden lunchtime buffet at 89kr is sublime. You can also try the upstairs à la carte restaurant with main courses from 165kr. Outdoor seating in summer.

Peder Oxe Gråbrødretorv 11 ☎33 11 00 77. Very popular steakhouse on a small square off Strøget. Three pieces of *smørrebrød* for 118kr, at lunchtimes only, and magnificent organic burgers for 89kr. Also has a good wine cellar.

Restaurant Gråbrødre Torv 21 Gråbrødretorv 21. One of the capital's best places for Danish fare, set on a lively small pedestrian square. *Smørrebrød* from 40kr a piece, main courses, such as calf liver with new potatoes, crispy onions and bacon, served with home-pickled rhubarb, from 115kr.

Slotskælderen – hos Gitte Kik Fortunstræde 4 ☎33 11 15 37. A great lunchtime spot, overlooking Christiansborg and the canal, serving heavily laden pieces of *smørrebrød* from 35kr. A favourite politicians' hangout (parliament is across the canal).

Spisehuset/La Bella Notte Magstræde 12–14 ☎33 11 52 70. In the winter it's *Spisehuset*, offering generous portions of basic local fare; in the summer, as *La Bella Notte*, proceedings move outside into a courtyard remnant of that old Walt Disney classic, and the pasta and pizza menu is firmly Italian. Main courses from 80kr.

Spiseloppen Christiania ☎32 57 95 58. Since winning many culinary awards, *Spiseloppen* has hiked up its prices considerably (meals cost 140–200kr). That said, it's still good, and so are the portions; try roast New Zealand lamb or steamed cod in mustard sauce. Closed Mondays.

Thorvaldsen Gammel Strand 34 ☎33 32 04 00. Across the canal from the Christiansborg Palace, *Thorvaldsen* serves a strange combination of Danish and Spanish food, but somehow it all works well enough.

Traktørstet Øster Voldgade 44 ☏ 33 15 76 20. Rather expensive place on a lawn and terrace just outside Rosenborg castle. Very good food, but you pay for the location.

Ethnic restaurants

Ankara Vesterbrogade 35, Vesterbro ☏ 33 31 92 33. Popular Turkish restaurant with an all-you-can-eat buffet costing 49kr at lunch, and 69kr for dinner. Belly dancing every Saturday.

Atlas Bar Larsbjørnstræde 18 ☏ 33 15 03 52. Eco-conscious café-restaurant serving tasty Asian and South American dishes. The portions are enormous, the salad platter costs 80kr, and the main courses start at 100kr. Closed Sunday.

Ayuttaya Griffenfeldsgade 39, Nørrebro ☏ 35 37 38 68. One of the city's top Thai restaurants, and consequently usually packed – reservations aren't a bad idea.

Circus Rosenvængets Allé 7, Østerbro ☏ 35 55 77 72. A trendy butcher-cum-hairdresser-cum-restaurant on Østerbro; keep an eye out for the preserved murals from 1900 depicting a cow's journey from the field to the butchers' shop. Popular all day (renowned for its weekend brunch) but especially busy during the evening. French-inspired main courses start at 75kr. Outdoor seating.

Delicatessen Vesterbrogade 120, Vesterbro ☏ 33 22 16 33. Up-and-coming cosy basement restaurant serving outstanding dishes from around the globe. Main courses average at 150kr and the tasty tapas cost 20kr a piece. Take-away available, and the kitchen opens until 1am.

El Gusto La Mexicana Havnegade 47 ☏ 33 11 32 16 Good-value Mexican food, with the standard array of enchiladas, tostadas, burritos and fajitas from 69kr.

House of Souls Vesterbrogade 3, Vesterbro ☏ 33 91 11 81. Cajun/American restaurant not far from the centre of town and Central Station. Try the seafood gumbo and expect things to be spicy.

Kate's Joint Blågardsgade 12, Nørrebro. Excellent, inexpensive Thai and Caribbean-influenced meals in popular, small and homely spot.

Koh-i-Noor Vesterbrogade 33, Vesterbro ☏ 33 24 64 17. A mix of Indian and Pakistani cuisines (all meat is halal), with vegetarian dishes available; the three-course set dinner costs 89kr.

L'Education Nationale Larsbjørnsstræde 12 ☏ 33 91 53 60. Authentic French meals (all ingredients are imported from France) from 150kr; try the rabbit stew in mustard sauce, or the warm goat's cheese salad.

Molevitten Nørrebrogade, Nørrebro 13 ☏ 33 39 49 00. Right on Nørrebro's main thoroughfare, serving Malay food with a modern Danish edge,

including great laksa (noodle soups) from around 60kr.

Pasta Basta Valhendorfsgade 22 ☏ 33 11 21 31. An array of fish and meat pasta dishes and pasta salads from which you can help yourself for 69kr. Open until 5am, this is a favourite final stop for late-night groovers and wildly popular with locals anytime. On a road parallel with and to the north of Strøget.

Shezan Viktoriagade 22, Vesterbro ☏ 33 24 78 88. The first Pakistani restaurant in Copenhagen and still going strong, with another branch at Havnegade 33. Main courses start at 50kr, and vegetarian dishes are available.

Sticks'n'Sushi Nansensgade 59, Nørreport ☏ 33 11 14 07. Copenhagen's best sushi restaurant, a block south of the Peblinge Sø lake. There's a take-away further down the road at no. 47.

Thai Esan Lille Istedgade 7, Vesterbro ☏ 33 24 12 69. Bargain Thai eating in this crammed but authentic restaurant, where main courses start at 54kr. There are two more branches around the corner at Halmtorvet 44 and Amagerbrogade 16.

Vegetarian and organic

Cap Horn Nyhavn 21 ☏ 33 12 85 04. Expensive, but worth splashing out on if you're wanting high-quality cooking with organic ingredients. The humungous seafood salads are legendary.

Den Grønne Kælder Pilestræde 48 ☏ 33 93 01 40. A simple tiled-floor vegetarian eatery close to Strøget, offering a very filling *grøn platte* for 75kr, and organic wines. Opens until 10pm Mon–Sat.

Govindas Nørre Farimagsgade 82, Nørreport. Krishna-run restaurant producing mediocre but affordable lacto-vegetarian meals for 35kr (45kr after 3pm).

Morgenstedet Langgade, Christiania. Tasty and mostly organic vegan and vegetarian salads, snacks and main meals at very affordable prices. Smoking and alcohol prohibited. Closed Tues.

Naturbageri Sativa Corner of Frederiksborggade and Nørre Farimagsgade, Nørreport. Good little organic bakery in the heart of Nørrebro.

Økologiske Café Griffenfeldsgade 17, Nørrebro. Gathering place for green-types, with meat and fish served on one day of every week. Closed weekends.

Picnic Fælledvej 22B, Norrebrø. Tiny, friendly sandwich and lunch place on Skt Hans Torv, that also does pre-packed picnic baskets. Very little seating.

RizRaz Kompagnistræde 20. Excellent-value Mediterranean food, with a vegetarian lunchtime buffet at 49kr, and evening buffet at 59kr. Popular with backpackers.

Drinking, nightlife and entertainment

An almost unchartable network of **cafés and bars** covers Copenhagen. You can get a **drink** – and usually a snack, too – in any of them, although some are especially noted for their congeniality and ambience, and it's these we've listed below. Almost all the better cafés and bars are in – or close to – either Indre By or the Nørrebro and Nørreport districts just to the north, and it's no hardship to sample several on the same night, though bear in mind that Fridays and Saturdays are very busy, and you'll probably need to queue before getting in anywhere.

The city also excels in **live music**. Major international names visit regularly, but it's with its small-scale shows that Copenhagen really stands out. Minor gigs early in the week in cafés and bars are often free, making it a cheap and simple business to take in several places until you find something to your liking; later in the week there may be a modest cover charge. There are also a number of medium-sized halls that host the best of Danish and overseas rock, jazz, hip-hop and funk. Things normally kick off around 10pm and, if not free, admission is 25–75kr. Throughout the summer, there are many **free concerts** in the city's parks, some featuring leading Danish bands. You can find out who's playing where by reading the latest copy of *Gaffa*, free from music and record shops, or by visiting ⊛www.aok.dk, which is also good for general entertainment **information**. New **film** releases, often in English with Danish subtitles, are shown all over the city; more esoteric fare is screened at Cinemateket on Gothersgade (☎33 74 34 12, ⊛www.dfi.dk), the Gloria, in a basement on Rådhuspladsen (☎33 12 42 92, ⊛www.gloria.dk), or Vester Vov Vov, on Vesterbrogade (☎33 24 42 99, ⊛www.vestervovvov.dk). Full listings are printed in all newspapers. For **kids' cinema**, both Palads by Vesterport station (☎70 13 12 11) and Cinemaxx on Fisketorvet (☎70 10 12 02) have a special children's section, but films will more often than not be dubbed in Danish.

With the plethora of late-opening cafés and bars, you'll never have to choose between going to a **club** and going to bed. If you do get a craving for a dancefloor fling, however, you'll find the discos, as most Danes call them, much like those in any major city, although they're generally more concerned with having a good time than defining the cutting edge of fashion. You'll be dancing alone if you turn up much before midnight; after that time, especially on Fridays and Saturdays, they fill rapidly – and stay open until 5am. Another plus is that drink prices are seldom hiked up and admission is fairly cheap at 25–55kr. For full **listings** of events and all kinds of entertainment, check out the free monthly tourist magazine *Copenhagen This Week*, and keep an eye out for notices in Use-It (see p.85) and cafés all around the city.

Note that all the places listed below are in the city centre unless otherwise stated.

Bars and cafés

Bang & Jensen Istedgade 130, Vesterbro. Former chemist's shop that's now a popular breakfast spot which turns into a late-opening bar. Saturday night is cocktail night.

Bibendum Nansengade 24, Nørreport. The city's hottest new wine bar, with over 70 different wines by the glass at any one time. Prices start at 25kr a glass, and the tapas are a treat.

Café Blågårds Apotek Blågårds Plads 20, Nørrebro. Pretty, candlelit café on a Nørrebro square with lots of wines, draught beers and occasional live music.

Café Dan Turell Store Regnegade 3. Something of an institution with the artier student crowd (it takes its name from a famous Danish writer) and a

fine central place for a sociable tipple. Packed during weekends when it's open until 4am; during the week it's open until midnight.

Café Louise Nørrebrogade 5, Nørrebro. Open until 9am during weekends and 4am during the week, this once traditional bar has become a legendary last stop after a night out. You have to ring a doorbell to get in, but sobriety is not a requirement of entry.

Café Ludvigsen Sundevedsgade 2. Vesterbro's most popular pool bar, complete with jukebox and inexpensive beer as well as the requisite green baize. Crammed at weekends.

Café Sommersko Kronprinsensgade 6. Sizeable, but crowded most nights, with Parisian-style food and drink and free live music on Sunday afternoons to soothe away hangovers. A block north of Strøget.

Charlie's Bar Pilestræde 33. Award-winning Real Ale pub with an impressive array of draught beers and lagers, and even a Somerset cider, from 38kr a pint. Generally packed with beer enthusiasts.

Drop Inn Kompagnistræde 34. Easygoing, unpretentious place near Huset with live blues or rock almost every night. Cheap beer (especially before 7pm) and late opening hours.

Foley's Irish Pub Lille Kannikestræde 3. Authentic Irish pub a few blocks north of Strøget, often the final stop for local Irish after a night of pub-crawling. Decent Irish food, too.

Globe Irish Pub Nørregade 43–45, Nørreport. Loud and flashy pub near Nørreport station with lots of televized sports, although your fellow drinkers are more likely to be tourists than ex-pat Irish.

Hard Rock Café Vesterbrogade 3, next to Tivoli Gardens. As seen on a million T-shirts, and as popular and bland as you'd expect. Occasional live music.

Hviids Vinstue Kongens Nytorv 19. Old-fashioned bar with crowded rooms patrolled by uniformed waiters. Outdoor seating in the summer.

Krasnapolsky Vestergade 10, near the Rådhus. The Danish avant-garde art hanging on the wall reflects the trendsetting reputation of this ultramodern watering hole. Come here at least once, if only to drink at the very long bar. DJs Thurs–Sat, and tasty food, too.

Krut's Karport Øster Farimagsgade 12, Østerbro. Small, slightly run-down but nonetheless very popular and well-known for its vast selection of single malt whiskies – and one of the few Copenhagen bars selling absinthe.

Kulkafeen Teglgårdsstræde 5. Cosy café that attracts a multicultural crowd; liveliest in the evenings and has bands on Saturdays.

The Moose Sværtegade 5. Tiny-looking bar that stretches back into a spacious room with pool tables. Special feature is the daily happy hour (9pm–2am) which ensures a big, lively crowd.

Peder Hvitfeldt P. Hvitfeldtsstræde 15. Spit-and-sawdust-type place on a short street one block south of Kultorvet, immensely popular with a youthful crowd. Come early if you want to sit down.

Sabines Cafeteria Teglgårdsstræde 4. A single smallish room with large windows facing the street, where the young and good-looking begin their evening's drinking.

Sebastopol Sankt Hans Torv 2, Nørrebro. Trendy spot on the square that catches the last rays of sun and large crowds in the summer. Also good brunch and café food.

Supergejl Nørrebrogade 184, Nørrebro. Busy new café-bar, especially popular among the younger crowd. Funky DJ in the basement on Fri and Sat.

Universitetscaféen Fiolstræde 2, Nørreport. A prime central location directly south of Nørreport Station. Open until 5am, and a good spot, early or late, for a leisurely beer. Outdoor seating during the summer and live blues or rock every Thursday.

Live music venues and clubs

Barcelona Fælledvej 21, Nørrebro ☎35 35 76 11. Swanky hangout that's very much the place to be seen. Renamed *Bar'Cuda* on Fri & Sat, when it becomes a sweaty club playing funk and soul, and stays open till 5am.

Barfly & Britannia Løvstræde 4 ☎33 14 89 69. A new multi-storey temple of entertainment, with music from the 70s and 80s on the lower floors, and techno and mainstream pop for a younger crowd upstairs, where there's also pool tables and pinball machines. Open Wed–Sat until 5–6am.

Copenhagen JazzHouse Niels Hemmingsensgade 10 ☎33 15 26 00, ✆www.jazzhouse.dk. Near Amagertorv, this is the country's premier jazz venue, with regular performances from international names as well as Denmark's finest. Can be pricey, but students get big discounts. Closed Sun & Mon.

Discotek IN Nørregade 1 ☎33 11 74 78. Cavernous disco just south of Nørreport Station playing mainstream hits, with a gimmicky entrance policy of free drinks once you've paid the door fee, which varies from 50kr to 150kr depending on

when you turn up, and whether you're male or female. Always crowded and raucous due to the flowing alcohol. Open Thurs until 6am and Fri & Sat until 10am the following day.

Femøren and **Tiøren** Amager (no phone). Two open-air rock concert venues on the beach hosting local and international bands from June to Aug. Get there by bus #12 or #13.

JazzHuset Vognporten Rådhusstræde 13 ☎33 15 20 02. In the same building as Use-It (see p.85) this is a bar-cum-music-venue with regular live bands: Mon–Thurs is beebop, Fri & Sat old-fashioned, danceable jazz.

Klaptræet Kultorvet 11 ☎33 13 40 38. A café-bar during the week that's transformed on Fridays and Saturdays into a favourite haunt of the Copenhagen high-school crowd, with a DJ and dancefloor out back and extended opening hours until 5am.

Level CPH Skindergade 45 ☎33 13 26 25. A short block north of, and parallel to, Strøget, this supremely funky place is decorated like an SAS airport lounge – including original airplane seats.

DJs pump out house and electronica grooves on the big dancefloor, and there's a beer cellar, too. **Loppen** Bådsmandsstræde 43, Christiania ☎32 57 84 22. On the edge of the "free city" and a suitably cool warehouse setting for both established and experimental Danish rock, jazz and performance artists, and quite a few British and American ones, too. There's a disco after the live act on Fri and Sat until 5am.

Mojo Løngangstræde 21☎33 11 64 53, ⊛www.mojo.dk. Cosy, diminutive place that's renowned for its jazz and blues evenings – live music every night. Happy hour daily 8–10pm.

Park Diskotek Østerbrogade 79, Østerbro ☎35 42 62 48, ⊛www.parkcafe.dk. Permanently jammed club with a bar, café and a music policy of disco and house. Usually draws a fun, mixed crowd who spill out onto the rooftop terrace to cool off during summer.

Pumpehuset Studiestræde 52 ☎33 93 19 60, ⊛www.pumpehuset.dk. Live music venue between Vesterport Station and Vor Frue Kirke, offering a broad sweep of middle-strata rock, hip-hop and funk from Denmark and around the world about three times a month.

Q-House of Dance Axeltorv 5 ☎33 11 19 15. You can't miss this multicoloured club, playing mostly mainstream pop. It's easily reachable (and visible) from central Copenhagen and not far from Central Station, either.

Rust Guldbergsgade 8, Nørrebro ☎35 24 52 00, ⊛www.rust.dk. Huge complex catering for all tastes: rock bands play on a main stage, and the three dancefloors offer a musical range from breakbeats to Latin jazz. Closed Mon.

Sabor Latino Vester Voldgade 85 ☎33 11 97 66. Popular Latin club with complete focus on dancing. Free Salsa lessons on Thurs, Fri & Sat 10–11pm.

Stengade 30 Stengade 18, Nørrebro ☎35 36 09 38, ⊛www.stengade30.dk. Alternative-type place with a mixed bag of live music and club nights; regular hardcore metal sessions, and techno on Thurs. Closed Mon.

Stereo Bar Linnésgade 16, Nørreport ☎33 13 61 13. *The* place for retro 1970s music, illuminated by lava lamps – they also do Latino, jazz and world-music nights.

Vega Enghavevej 40 ☎33 25 70 11, ⊛www.vega.dk. In a former union hall, this large multi-levelled musical Mecca retains its 1950s and 1960s decor – zigzag tiles and suchlike – while showcasing plenty of modern underground rock via live acts (at Store Vega) and club nights (at Lille Vega); once you've paid to get in, it's access all areas. Music ranges from house and techno to disco. Over-20s only.

Woodstock Vestergade 12 ☎33 11 20 71. Pulls a large, fun-loving crowd eager to dance to anything with a beat – though the music is predominantly 1960s. Close to the Rådhus.

Gay and Lesbian Copenhagen

As you'd expect from the capital of a country with a very liberal attitude to homosexuality (the age of consent is 15, and gay marriages are legal as long as one of the partners is Danish), Copenhagen has a lively **gay scene**, which includes a good sprinkling of bars and clubs (one with a sauna), a bookshop and a few exclusively gay **accommodation options**: *Copenhagen Rainbow*, Frederiksberggade 25C (☎33 14 10 20, ⊛www.copenhagen-rainbow.dk; ➎), *Hotel Windsor*, Frederiksborggade 30 (☎33 11 08 30, ⊛www.hotelwindsor.dk; ➎), and *Carstens Guesthouse*, Christians Brygge 28, 5th floor (☎40 50 91 07; ➍).

For **information**, visit ⊛www.copenhagen-gay-life.dk, call the **gay switchboard** (☎33 36 00 86) or contact the National Organization for Gay Men and Women (*Landsforeningen for Bøsser og Lesbiske*; ☎33 13 19 48, ⊛www.lbk.dk), based at Teglgårdsstræde 13, where there's also a bookshop/café. Alternatively, check *Pan* magazine – in Danish, but easily understood – which doesn't have listings but does have ads announcing the latest happenings, while there's also *Pan*'s English-language *Gay Guide to Copenhagen*. Both are free and available at most gay bars, where you should also be able to pick up a free map of gay Copenhagen.

Note all the places listed below are in the city centre.

Bars and clubs

Amigo Bar Schønbergsgade 4. Frequented by gay men of all ages; serves snacks too.
Café Intime Allégade 25. Not the most interesting crowd, but a piano player and live acts keep things

moving along.
Can Can Mikkel Bryggersgade 11. A favourite late-night drinking spot for gay men, one block northwest of Rådhus. Open until 5am Fri & Sat.

Centralhjornet Kattesundet 18. In the city centre, just northeast of *Can Can*, this is an ordinary and somewhat dreary place, with only history – it's Copenhagen's oldest gay bar – on its side.

Club Amigo Studiestræde 31A. One of several gay venues in Studiestræde, between Vesterport Station and Vor Frue Kirke, this enormous club offers, amongst other things, a bar, cinemas, sauna and solarium, pool room and video room. Gay men only.

Cosy Bar Studiestræde 24. Frequented by men of all ages, this popular place gets busy late, and stays open right through until morning.

Heaven Café-Bar & Restaurant Kompagnistræde 18 ☎ 33 15 19 00. A daytime café downstairs which in the evening becomes a popular bar, mostly frequented by gay men, while upstairs holds a trendy restaurant (meals from 100kr) for which you should book tables in advance.

Jailhouse CPH Studiestræde 12. New and popular gay bar on Studiestræde, with an upstairs restaurant serving traditional Danish food at reasonable prices.

Jeppes Klub Allégade 25, Frederiksberg. A lesbian club-bar open every first and last Friday of the month from 9pm to 3am.

Kvindehuset Gothersgade 37 ☎ 33 14 28 04. Lesbian bookshop and info centre with a café and, every third Friday of the month, the *Das Wunderbar* disco night.

Masken Bar Studiestræde 33, Vesterport. Great club-bar on two floors, often featuring drag shows and popular with a younger student crowd due to its affordable booze. Things don't pick up until 11pm and Fridays in particular are a bit cruisey.

Men's Bar Teglgårdsstræde 3. The city's most macho bar, popular with leather and motorbike types; monthly Sunday brunches are well attended. Strictly men only.

Oscar Bar & Café Rådhuspladsen 77. One of Copenhagen's newest gay café-bars, with an excellent information point that's well stocked with maps and guides. In the evening, the clientele are mostly young and trendy.

Pan Club Knabrostræde 3. Three-storey behemoth right in the centre of the city, just off Strøget, this is the unquestioned hub of the city's gay nightlife and is always buzzing.

Sebastian Hyskenstræde 10. A bright and popular café-restaurant with touches of culture – art, magazines, live music – as well as a pool table. One block south of Strøget.

Listings

Airlines British Airways, Rådhuspladsen 16 ☎ 80 20 80 22; Finnair, Nyropsgade 47 ☎ 33 36 45 45; SAS, Hammerichsgade 1–5 ☎ 70 10 30 00 (domestic reservations), ☎ 70 10 20 00 (overseas reservations).

Banks and exchange Den Danske Bank: Kastrup Airport (open daily 6am–10pm); Rådhuspladsen 45; Nørrebrogade 26; Halmtorvet 27; Holmens Kanal 12; and Store Kongensgade 49. To change money at bank rates out of banking hours, try Arbejdernes Landsbank, Vesterbrogade 5 (24hr), or Forex, Central Station (daily 8am–9pm).

Bookshops Most of the city's bookshops are in the area around Fiolstræde and Købmagergade; all stock guidebooks and maps for budget travellers. The Book Trader, Skindergade 23, has a varied selection of old and new books in English. For new books try GAD, at Vimmelskaftet 32 (on Strøget) and inside Central Station; Nordisk Korthandel, Studiestræde 26–30; Arnold Busck, Købmagergade 49; and Boghallen, Rådhuspladsen 37 ☎ 33 47 25 60.

Car parks Usually pay-and-display, with different rates depending on zone colour: in descending level of expense, zones are coloured red (20kr per hour), green (12kr) and blue (7kr). Downtown car parks are thin on the ground, but there's a handy one at the Statoil petrol station in Israel Plads

(15kr for 1hr, 75kr per day) and another attached to the Q8 station near Vesterport Station at Nyropsgade 42 (10kr per hour, 70kr per day).

Car rental Avis, Kampmannsgade 1 ☎ 33 73 40 99, ☻ www.avis.dk; Hertz, Ved Vesterport 3 ☎ 33 17 90 20, ☻ www.hertzdk.dk; Europcar, Østergaard, Gammel Kongevej 13 ☎ 70 20 61 61, ☻ www.europcar.dk; Budget, Helgolandsgade 2 ☎ 33 55 70 00, ☻ www.budget.dk; Lej et Lig (Rent-a-Wreck), Nyborggade 30 ☎ 39 29 85 05, ☻ www.lejetlig.dk.

Dentist Tandlægevagten, Oslo Plads 14 ☎ 35 38 02 51. Open for emergencies only nightly 8–9.30pm, Sat & Sun also 10am–noon. Turn up and be prepared to pay at least 150kr on the spot.

Doctors Call ☎ 33 15 46 00 Mon–Fri 8am–4pm or ☎ 70 13 00 41 evenings and weekends, and you'll be given the name of a doctor in your area. There's a consultation fee of 400kr–600kr, which must be paid in cash. For non-urgent treatment, get a list of doctors from the tourist office, Use-It, or a local health department (*Kommunens social og sundhedsforvaltning*).

Embassies Australia, Dampfærgevej 26 ☎ 70 26 36 76; Canada, Kristen Bernikowsgade 1 ☎ 33 48 32 00; Ireland, Østbanegade 21 ☎ 35 42 32 33; UK, Kastelsvej 40 ☎ 35 44 52 00; USA, Dag

Hammerskjolds Allé 24 ☎35 55 31 44. Note that New Zealand uses the UK office.

Emergencies ☎112 for police or ambulance.

Hitching First check the car-share notices on Use-It notice boards. If they don't deliver anything, use the following routes (and remember you're not supposed to hitch on motorways). Heading south to Germany, take S-train line A or bus #10 to Ellebjerg station, which leaves you by the ring road, near the start of motorway E20. Going north to Helsingør and Sweden, take S-train line H or F to Ryparken (or bus #1, #150S or #184 to Hans Knudsen Plads) and hitch along Lyngbyvej (for the E4). West for Funen and Jutland, take S-train line B to Tåstrup, then walk along Køgevej and hitch from Roskildevej (A1).

Hospitals There are emergency departments at Bispebjerg Hospital, Tuborgvej 7C (☎35 31 23 73) and Frederiksberg Hospital, Nordre Fasanvej 57 (☎38 16 35 13); EU and Scandinavian nationals get free treatment, though others are unlikely to have to pay.

Internet access Free access is available at Use-It, Rådhusstræde 13, and at the Royal Library, Søren Kirkegaard Plads 1, but in both cases you may have to wait. Internet cafés include Boomtown, Axeltorv 1–3 ⑳www.boomtown.net (daily 24hr; 30kr per hr); Faraos Cigarer, Skindergade 27 ⑳www.faraos.dk (Mon–Sat 10am–midnight, Sun noon–midnight; 15kr per hr); MåneBase Alpha, Elmegade 20, Nørrebro ☎35 36 34 41 (daily noon–midnight; 20kr per hr; Nethulen, Istedgade 114, Vesterbro ⑳www.nethulen.dk (Mon–Fri 9am–11pm, Sat–Sun 4–11pm; 25kr per hr).

Late-opening shops The supermarket at Central Station is open daily from 8am until midnight.

Laundry Central places to do washing include Alaska Vask & Rens, Borgergade 2; Møntvask, Istedgade 29; Maxirens, Istedgade 45; Vaskeri, Ryesgade 10; and Vasketeria, Dronningensgade 42. A load costs about 30kr.

Left luggage The DSB Garderobe office (Mon–Sat 5.30–1am, Sun 6am–1am) downstairs in Central Station stores luggage for 20kr per day per pack, and there are also small and large lockers for 25–35kr per day. Luggage storage is free for a day at Use-It, Rådhusstræde 13.

Library Hovedbiblioteket, Krystalgade 15–17 (Mon–Fri 10am–7pm, Sat 10am–2pm), is the main city library, with mostly Danish books and magazines. Use it, Rådhusstræde 13, also has a very well-stocked reading room, with international magazines and newspapers.

Lost property The police department's lost property office is at Slotherrensvej 113, Vanløse

☎38 74 88 22. Otherwise, for things lost on a bus, call ☎36 13 14 15; on trains, call the DSB office at Central Station ☎33 16 21 10 (Mon–Fri 9am–4pm); on a plane, contact the airline or Kastrup Airport ☎32 47 47 00 or ☎32 32 00 00.

Markets There's a good flea market at Israel Plads on Saturdays (May–Oct 8am–2pm; S-train to Nørreport Station or bus #5 or #16), and a Salvation Army market selling bric-a-brac and old clothes at Hørhusvej (Tues–Fri 1–5pm, Sat 9am–1pm; take bus #12 or #13 to Tingvej). Try also the various summertime markets that pop up around Christiania, and the Saturday-morning market behind Frederiksberg Rådhus (mid-April to mid-Oct 8am–2pm; bus #1 or #14) and along Assistens Kirkegårdens wall on Nørrebrogade (same hours; bus #5 or #16).

Newspapers and news in English Overseas newspapers are sold at the stall in Rådhuspladsen and some newsagents along Strøget. Radio Denmark (1062MHz in Copenhagen) broadcast news in English Mon–Fri at 8.40am, 11am, 5.10pm and 10pm.

Pharmacy Steno Apotek, Vesterbrogade 6 and Sønderbro Apotek, Amagerbrogade 158, are both open 24-hours.

Post offices Main office at Tietgensgade 39, right behind Central Station (Mon–Fri 11am–6pm, Sat 10am–1pm); there's another at Central Station (Mon–Fri 8am–9pm, Sat 9am–4pm, Sun 10am–4pm). Poste restante is available at Use-It, Rådhusstræde 13, 1466 Copenhagen K, or any named post office.

Swimming pools & saunas There are public pools and saunas at Angelgade 4, Vesterbro (☎33 22 05 00), Sanbjerggade 35, Nørrebro (☎35 85 19 55) and Helgesvej 29 (Frederiksberg), and summer-only outdoor pools at Enghavevej 90, Vesterbro (☎33 21 49 00) and Borgmester Jensens Allé 50, Østerbro (☎35 42 68 60). All generally open Mon–Fri 8am–6.30pm, Sat 8am–2pm, and cost 24kr per person. The posh new swim centre DGI-byen, at Tietgensgade 65 in Vesterbro (☎33 29 80 00), costs 47kr, and has pools of all shapes and sizes including one for diving, jacuzzis and a massage and body treatment clinic.

Travel agents Kilroy Travels, Skindergade 28 (☎33 11 00 44, ⑳www.kilroytravels.com), can give advice on travelling around Denmark, the rest of Scandinavia and Europe. They also have offices at Østerbrogade 100 and Falkoner Allé 14. STA Travel, Fiolstræde 18 (☎33 14 15 01, ⑳www.sta.com) offer youth and student tickets.

Around Zealand

It's easy to see more of Zealand by making day-trips out from the capital, although, depending on where you're heading next, it's often a better idea to pack your bags and leave Copenhagen altogether. Transport links are excellent throughout the region, making much of northern and central Zealand commuter territory for the capital; but that's hardly something you'd notice as you pass through dozens of tiny villages and large forests on the way to historic centres such as **Helsingør**, **Køge** and – an essential call if you're interested in Denmark's past – **Roskilde**. Except for the memorable vistas of the **northern coast**, and the explorable smaller **islands** off southern Zealand and **Bornholm** to the east, however, you'll find the soft green terrain varies little; and, unless you're a true nature lover, you'll soon want to push on (which is easily done) to the bigger cities in Funen and Jutland.

North Zealand

The **coast north of Copenhagen**, as far as Helsingør, rejoices under the tag of the "Danish Riviera", a label which neatly describes its line of tiny one-time fishing hamlets, now inhabited almost exclusively by the super-wealthy. It's best seen on the hour-long bus journey (#388) north to Helsingør from Klampenborg, itself the last stop on line C or F of the S-train system – the views of beckoning beaches are lovely. There's also a frequent fifty-minute train service between Copenhagen and Helsingør; it's quicker than the bus, but you won't see much unless you break the journey, since views are obscured by trees almost the entire way.

The Karen Blixen Museum, Humlebæk and Louisiana

There are two good reasons to stop before Helsingør. The **Karen Blixen Museum** (May–Sept Mon–Sat 10am–5pm; Oct–April Wed–Fri 1–4pm, Sat & Sun 11am–4pm; ✆www.isak-dinesen.dk; 35kr) is a fifteen-minute walk or a short ride on bus #388 from Rungsted Kyst train station on the *regionaltog* train line going north towards Helsingør. The museum is housed in the family home of the writer who, while long a household name in Denmark for her short stories (often written under the pen name of Isak Dinesen) and outspoken opinions, enjoyed a resurgence of international popularity during the mid-1980s when the film *Out of Africa* – based on her 1937 autobiographical account of running a coffee plantation in Kenya – was released. After returning from Africa, Blixen lived here until her death in 1962, and much of the house is maintained as it was during her final years. Texts describing Blixen's eventful life (her father committed suicide and she married the twin brother of the man she loved, among other things) line the walls, while exhibits include a collection of first editions and the tiny typewriter she used in Africa. Even if you've never read a word of Blixen, it's hard not to be impressed by accounts of her spirit and strength, which shine through the museum. After seeing the house, make for the well-tended flower garden, where Blixen's simple grave lies beneath a protective beech tree.

In Humlebæk, the next community of any size, you'll find **Louisiana** (daily 10am–5pm, Wed until 10pm; ✆www.louisiana.dk; 68kr), a modern-art museum on the northern edge of the village at Gammel Strandvej 13, a short walk from the train station. Even if you go nowhere else outside Copenhagen, it would be a shame to miss this: the setting alone is worth the journey, harmoniously combining art, architecture and landscape. The entrance is in a nineteenth-century villa, from which lead two carefully designed modern corridors containing the indoor collection, their windows giving views of the sculpture park and Øresund outside.

It seems churlish to mention individual items, but the museum's American section, in the south corridor, includes some devastating pieces by Edward Kienholz, Malcolm Morley's scintillatingly gross *Pacific Telephone Los Angeles Yellow Pages*, in which the telephone directory cover expands to monstrous proportions and coffee stains rib the city skyline like a weird metallic grid, and (in the reading room) Jim Dines' powerful series *The Desire*. You'll also find some of Giacometti's gangly figures haunting a room of their own off the north corridor, and an equally affecting handful of sculptures by Max Ernst squatting outside the windows and leering inwards. Except for some collages by Arthur Køpcke and paintings by various Danish luminaries of the CoBrA group, home-grown artists have a rather low profile, although their work is often featured in temporary exhibitions.

Helsingør

First impressions of **HELSINGØR** are none too enticing. The bus stops outside the noisy train station, outside which Havnepladsen is usually full of transit passengers loitering around fast-food stalls before making for the ferry terminal, 100m distant. Away from the hustle, though, Helsingør is a quiet and likeable town. Strategically positioned on the four-kilometre strip of water linking the North Sea and the Baltic, the town's wealth was founded on the Sound Toll of 1429, which was levied on passing ships right up until the nineteenth century. Shipbuilding subsequently restored some of Helsingør's fortunes after the toll was abolished, but today it's once again the sliver of water between Denmark and Sweden, and the ferries across it to Helsingborg, which account for most of the town's livelihood.

The Town

Helsingør's main draw, on a sandy curl of land extending seawards, is **Kronborg Slot** (May–Sept daily 10.30am–5pm; April & Oct Tues–Sun 11am–4pm; Nov–March Tues–Sun 11am–3pm; ⓦ www.kronborg.dk; 40kr, 60kr joint ticket with Maritime Museum), famous principally as the setting – under the name of Elsinore Castle – for Shakespeare's *Hamlet*. Actually, the playwright never visited Helsingør, and his hero was based on one Amleth (or Amled), a tenth-century character lost in the mists of Danish mythology who certainly predated the castle – none of which has affected Kronborg's thriving trade in Hamlet souvenirs nor the hundreds of requests asking for the whereabouts of "Hamlet's bedroom". The castle was awarded UNESCO World Heritage Site status in 2000 and, consequently, it has become markedly more visitor-friendly. **Guided tours** of the royal chambers take

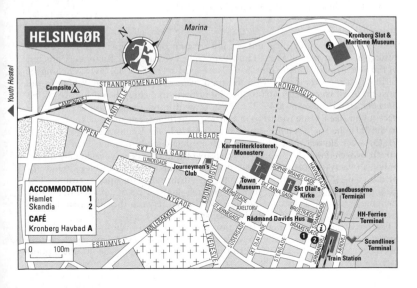

place daily at 2pm in the summer, and 1pm during winter, and well-informed attendants also hover in every room ready to answer questions.

Construction of the present castle, built on the site of Erik of Pomerania's fortress, was instigated during the sixteenth century by Frederik II. Frederik commissioned the Dutch architects Van Opbergen and Van Paaske, who took their ideas from the buildings of Antwerp. Various bits have been destroyed and rebuilt since, but it remains a grand affair, enhanced immeasurably by its setting, and with an interior, the royal chapel in particular, that is spectacularly ornate – appreciation, though, is hampered by the steady flow of tourists. Crowds are less of a problem in the labyrinthine **cellars** – the casemates – which can be seen on guided tour (daily: summer 12.30pm and 3.30pm, winter 2.30pm) departing from the cellar entrance. The body of Holger Danske, a mythical hero from the legends of Charlemagne, is said to lie beneath the castle, ready to wake again when Denmark needs him, although the tacky Viking-style statue depicting the legend detracts somewhat from the cellars' authentic aura of decay. The castle also houses the national **Maritime Museum** (same hours; ⓦwww.maritime-museum.dk; 30kr), an uninspiring collection of model ships and nautical knick-knacks.

Away from Kronborg and the harbour area, Helsingør has a well-preserved **medieval quarter**. **Stengade** is the main pedestrianized street, linked by Bjergegade to **Axeltorv**, the town's small market square and a good spot to linger over a beer – alternatively, stroll into nearby **Brostræde**, a narrow alleyway that's famous for shops selling immense ice creams made with traditional ingredients. Near the corner of Stengade and Skt Annagade the newly renovated cathedral, the spired **Skt Olai's Kirke** (May–Aug Mon–Sat 10am–4pm, Sept–April Mon–Sat 10am–2pm) contains a small but interesting exhibit on the building's history. Just beyond is the **Karmeliterklosteret Monastery** (mid-May to mid-Sept Mon–Fri 10am–3pm; rest of the year Mon–Fri 10am–2pm; 20kr, guided tours in the summer only at 2pm) which originally served as a hospital, during which time it prided itself on its brain operations. The unnerving tools of this profession are still on show next door at the **Town Museum** (daily noon–4pm; 10kr), together with diagrams of the corrective insertions made into patients' heads. For something less disturbing, seek out the oddball **Journeymen's Club** (*Naverhulen*), tucked into a nearby courtyard at Sankt Anna Gade 21 and cluttered with souvenirs of world travel, such as crab puppets and armadillo lampshades. Act interested and you might get a free guided tour; there are no set opening hours.

Practicalities

You can pick up a free map and get information on Helsingør from the **tourist office** (mid-June to July Mon–Thurs 9am–5pm, Fri 9am–6pm, Sat 10am–3pm; rest of the year Mon–Fri 9am–4pm, Sat 10am–1pm; ☎49 21 13 33, ⓦwww.helsingor-turist.dk), across Strandgade from the train station at Havnepladsen 3. Due to the high numbers of visiting tourists, the closest thing to a cheap **hotel** in town is the *Skandia*, Bramstræde 1 (☎49 21 09 02, ⓦwww.hotel-skandia.dk; ❸), which is decent and clean; some rooms have a shared bath. If you can afford it, treat yourself to the "Hamlet" or "Ophelia" suites at the *Hotel Hamlet*, Bramstræde 5 (☎49 21 05 91; ❺), a handsome white three-star with a fish and steak restaurant. There's also a **youth hostel** (☎49 21 16 40, ⓦwww.helsingorhostel.dk; Feb–Nov) literally on the beach, a twenty-minute walk to the north along the coastal road (Ndr. Strandvej), or take bus #340 from the station and get off just after the sports stadium. The *Helsingør Camping* **campsite**, at Standalleen 1 (☎49 21 58 56, ⓦwww.helsingor-camping.dk), is closer to town and also by a beach, between the main road Lappen (which begins where Skt Annagade ends) and the sea.

For **eating**, the usual pizza and fast-food outlets are two-a-penny around Stengade. A little more expensively, there's fine Danish food in the small, atmospheric *Rådmand Davids Hus*, close to the train station at Standgade 70, and a good café, the *Kronborg Havbad*, right next to Kronborg Slot. Given the proximity of the

Ferries to Sweden

Three **ferry lines** make the twenty-minute crossing from Helsingør to Helsingborg in Sweden. The main one, and probably the best option, is the **Scandlines** boat leaving every twenty minutes from 6am to 11.30pm and every thirty minutes at night from the main terminal by the train station (16kr one way, 32kr return). The alternative options are **Sundbusserne**, which operates a small craft that's often heavily buffeted by the choppy waters. It runs every twenty minutes between 6.30am and 7.30pm (less frequent during weekends), and costs 19kr one way, 32kr for a return and 16kr for a Sunday day return. HH Ferries offer the cheapest off-peak prices (8kr one way and 16kr return), but they dock a good walk from the centre of Helsingborg. Rail passes are valid on all three companies' services, and a Copenhagen Card gives a fifty percent discount. It's perfectly feasible, and on a sunny day very enjoyable, to rent a **bike** at Kongevejen 17 (80kr a day) and cross to Helsingborg for a day's cycling along the Swedish coast. But take food and especially drink with you – both tend to be more expensive in Sweden than in Denmark, alcohol exorbitantly so.

capital, nightlife of note is a rare commodity, but for an evening drink, stroll the streets on either side of Stengade, where there are several decent bars. Rowdier boozing goes on at the top end of Axeltorv, popular with Swedes taking advantage of Denmark's more liberal licensing laws.

Onwards from Helsingør: the North Zealand coast

Some of the best beaches in Zealand and several attractive fishing villages are within easy reach of Helsingør, either by bike, local buses or a network of private trains (on which the Copenhagen Card is valid, although InterRail, Eurail and Scanrail passes are not). No one particular place has the power to hold you for long, but the region as a whole is hard to beat for a few days' relaxation.

Hellebæk and Hornbæk

A string of fine beaches can be found simply by following Ndr. Strandvej from Helsingør towards the sleepy village of **HELLEBÆK**, some 5km north. At Hellebæk itself, part of the beach is a well-known, if unofficial, venue for nude bathing. Trains from Helsingør stop at Hellebæk and then continue for 7km to the moderately larger **HORNBÆK**, blessed with excellent beaches and fabulous views over the sea towards Kullen, the rocky promontory jutting out from the Swedish coast. Though fast becoming a playground for yacht-owners and their cronies, Hornbæk is a lovely spot to stay over. Staff at the **tourist office** (Mon, Tues & Thurs 2–7pm, Wed & Fri 10am–5pm, Sat 10am–2pm; ☏49 70 47 47, ⓦwww .hornbaek.dk), in the library just off the main street, can find you private rooms and summer cottages. Or, from June to August, try the inexpensive pension *Ewaldsgården*, close by the train station at Johannes Ewalds Vej 5 (☏49 70 00 82, ⓦwww.ewaldsgaarden.dk; ❸), which has single, double and family rooms. Just a few minutes' walk away is Hornbæk's **campsite** (☏49 70 02 23, ⓦwww.camping -hornbaek.dk), beautifully situated on the edge of a pine forest, and ten minutes' walk from the beach.

Gilleleje and Tisvildeleje

From Hornbæk, trains continue along the coast to **GILLELEJE**, fifteen minutes further on, another appealing fishing village that does a roaring tourist trade. It's a good place for a short stopover, though unfortunately **accommodation** tends to be booked up far in advance and the only hotel in town is the Swiss-chalet-style *Strand*, Vesterbrogade 4B (☏48 30 05 12, ☎48 30 18 59; ❺). The budget option is the all-year-round campsite, just outside the village at Bregnerødvej 21 (☏49 71 97 55). An alternative is to head west to the youth hostel in Tisvildeleje (see p.118).

While in Gilleleje, negotiate at least some of the footpath that runs along the top of the dunes, where, in 1835, **Søren Kierkegaard** took lengthy contemplative walks, later recalling: "I often stood there and reflected over my past life. The force of the sea and the struggle of the elements made me realize how unimportant I was." Ironically, so important would Kierkegaard become that a monument to him now stands on the path bearing his maxim: "Truth in life is to live for an idea." The **tourist office** on Gilleleje Hovedgade 6F (mid-June to Aug Mon–Sat 10am–6pm, May to mid-June Mon–Fri 9am–4pm, Sat 9am–3pm; rest of the year Mon–Fri 9am–4pm, Sat 9am–noon; ☎48 30 01 74) has maps of seven different routes he used to walk.

From Gilleleje, bus #363 largely follows the coast to **TISVILDELEJE** (a 30min journey), where there are yet more beaches and Tisvilde Hegn (locally called simply "Hegn"), a forest of wind-tormented trees planted here during the eighteenth century to prevent sand drifts. The **youth hostel** at Bygmarken 30 (☎48 70 98 50, ⓦwww.helene.dk) is part of a holiday complex, the *Sankt Helene Centeret*, and has forty-odd family rooms with dorm beds and some some doubles (❸).

Inland from the coast

It's hard to continue along the coast without first detouring **inland**, and in any case the effort is barely worthwhile. Trains from both Tisvildeleje and Gilleleje run to Hillerød, in the heart of North Zealand, which – thanks to its magnificent castle – is the place to make for.

Hillerød: Frederiksborg Slot

HILLERØD is forty minutes by S-train from Helsingør, and a similar distance from Copenhagen (last stop on line A and E). The town's main claim to fame is **Frederiksborg Slot** (daily: April–Oct 10am–5pm; Nov–March 11am–3pm; 50kr), a castle which easily pushes the more famous Kronborg into second place and lies decorously across three small islands within an artificial lake. Buses #701, #702 and #703 run from the train station to the castle, or it's a twenty-minute walk, following the signs (*Slottet*) through the town centre.

Frederiksborg Slot was the home of Frederik II and birthplace of his son Christian IV. At the turn of the seventeenth century, under the auspices of Christian, rebuilding began in an unorthodox Dutch Renaissance style. It's the unusual aspects of the design – a prolific use of towers and spires, Gothic arches and flowery window ornamentation – that still stand out, despite the changes wrought by fire and restoration.

You can see the exterior of the castle for free simply by walking through the main gates, across the seventeenth-century S-shaped bridge, and into the central courtyard. Since 1882, the interior has functioned as a **Museum of National History**, largely funded by the Carlsberg brewery magnate Carl Jacobsen in an attempt to create a Danish Versailles, and to heighten the nation's sense of history and cultural development. It's a good idea to buy the illustrated **guide** (40kr) to the museum, since without it the contents of the sixty-odd rooms are barely comprehensible. Many of the rooms are surprisingly free of furniture and household objects, and attention is drawn to the ranks of portraits along the walls – a motley crew of flat-faced kings and thin consorts who between them ruled and misruled Denmark for centuries, giving way in later rooms to politicians, scientists and writers.

Two rooms deserve special mention. The **chapel**, where monarchs were crowned between 1671 and 1840, is exquisite, its vaults, pillars and arches gilded and embellished, and the contrasting black marble of the gallery riddled with gold lettering. The shields, in tiered rows around the chapel, are those of the knights of the Order of the Elephant, who sat with the king in the late seventeenth century. The **Great Hall**, above the chapel, is a reconstruction, but this doesn't detract from its beauty. It's bare but for the staggering wall and ceiling decorations: tapestries, wall reliefs, portraits and a glistening black-marble fireplace. In Christian IV's day the hall was a ballroom, and the polished floor still tempts you to some fancy footwork as you slide up and down its length.

Away from the often crowded interior, the **gardens**, on the far side of the lake, have some photogenic views of the castle from their stepped terraces and are a good spot for a rest. The quickest way to them is through the narrow Mint Gate to the left of the main castle building, which adjoins a roofed-in bridge leading to the King's Wing. In summer you can also do a half-hour trip on the lake aboard the *M/F Frederiksborg* ferry, which leaves every half hour from outside the castle (mid-May to mid-Sept Mon–Sat 11am–5pm, Sun 1–5pm; 20kr).

Though Frederiksborg is the main reason to come to Hillerød, you could easily spend an absorbing half hour in the **Money Historical Museum** (Mon–Thurs 9.30am–4.30pm, Fri 9.30am–4pm; free) at Slotsgade 38. During the reigns of Frederik II and Christian IV all Danish coins were minted in Hillerød, and besides samples of these, the place displays currencies from all over the world.

If you do want to **stay**, try the three-star *Hotel Hillerød*, Milnersvej 41 (☎48 24 08 00, ⊛www.hotelhillerod.dk; ❺). The *Nordiske Lejerskole og Kursuscenter*, Lejerskolevej 4 (☎48 26 19 86, ⊛www.nordlejr.dk; ❷), is less expensive, with shared bathrooms. The only budget option is the **campsite**, 1km from the centre by the agricultural showground at Blytækkervej 18 (☎48 26 48 54, ⊛www.hillerodcamping.dk; Easter to mid-Sept). The **tourist office**, Slangerupgade 2 (☎48 24 26 26, ⊛www.hillerodturist.dk; mid-June to Aug Mon–Fri 10am–6pm, Sat 10am–3pm; rest of year Mon–Fri 10am 5pm, Sat 10am–1pm) can arrange **private rooms** for around 150kr per person (25kr booking fee). For **food**, the *Spisestedet Leonora*, in one of the castle's gatehouses, serves fantastic *smørrebrød* starting at 35kr a piece – one should suffice if you're not too famished. Otherwise the *Engelhardt's Café*, at Slotsarkaderne 112, serves good-value sandwiches and light snacks.

Fredensborg Slot

Before leaving Hillerød altogether, you might want to make a short trip to Fredensborg (on the train line toward Helsingør) and spend a few hours at another royal residence, **Fredensborg Slot** (July daily 1–4.30pm; guided tours 30kr), built by Frederik IV to commemorate the 1720 Peace Treaty with Sweden. The castle is only open in July when the Queen is away staying at her summer home, Marselisborg in Århus (see p.164), but even outside this month its grand, statue-lined gardens (open all year; free), stretching down to an expansive lake, are distinctly appealing for a wander.

West from Copenhagen: Roskilde and beyond

There's very little between Copenhagen and the West Zealand coast to see and explore except for the ancient former Danish capital of **ROSKILDE**, less than half an hour by train from the big city. There's been a community here since prehistoric times, and later the Roskilde fjord provided a route to the open sea that was used by the Vikings. But it was the arrival of Bishop Absalon in the twelfth century that made the place the base of the Danish church – and, as a consequence, the national capital for a while. Roskilde's importance waned after the Reformation, and it came to function mainly as a market for the neighbouring rural communities – much as it does today, as well as serving as dormitory territory for Copenhagen commuters. In high season, especially, it can be crammed with day-trippers seeking the dual blasts from the past supplied by its royal tombs and Viking boats, while the first week of each July sees a massive influx of visitors when it hosts the **Roskilde Festival** – northern Europe's biggest open-air rock event. Yet at any other time the ancient centre makes Roskilde one of Denmark's most appealing towns, and the surrounding countryside quiet and unspoilt.

The Town

The major pointer to the town's former status is the fabulous **Domkirke** (April–Sept Mon–Sat 9am–4.45pm, Sun 12.30–4.45pm; Oct–March Mon–Sat 10am–3.45pm, Sun 12.30–3.45pm; 15kr), founded by Bishop Absalon in 1170 on the site of a tenth-century church erected by Harald Bluetooth, and finished during the fourteenth century – although portions have been added right up to the twentieth. The result is a mishmash of architectural styles, though one that hangs together with surprising neatness. Every square inch seems adorned by some curious mark or etching, but it's the claustrophobic collection of coffins containing the regal remains of twenty kings and seventeen queens in four large **royal chapels** that really catches the eye. The most richly endowed chapel is that of Christian IV, a previously austere resting place jazzed-up – in typical early nineteenth-century Romantic style – with bronze statues, wall-length frescoes and vast paintings of scenes from his reign. A striking contrast is provided by the simple red-brick chapel just outside the cathedral, where Frederik IX was laid to rest in 1972. Try to get to the Domkirke just before the hour to see and hear the animated medieval **clock** above the main entrance: a model of St Jørgen gallops forward on his horse to wallop the dragon and the hour is marked by the creature's squeal of death.

From one end of the cathedral, a roofed passageway, the **Arch of Absalon**, feeds into the yellow **Bishop's Palace**. The incumbent bishop nowadays confines himself

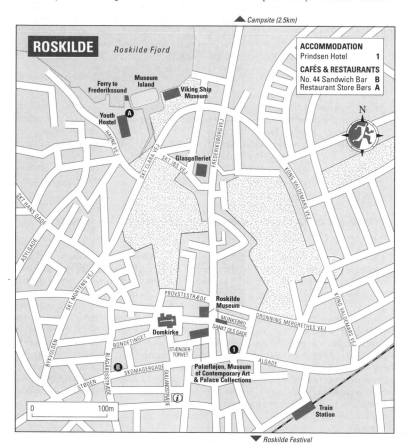

to one wing, while the others have been turned into showplaces for (predominantly) Danish art. The main building houses the **Museum for Contemporary Art** (*Museet for Samtidskunst*; Tues–Fri 11am–5pm, Sat & Sun noon–4pm; 20kr), whose diverse temporary exhibitions often reflect current trends. The theme continues in the west wing, where the **Palæfløjen** gallery (Tues–Sun noon–4pm; free), run by the local arts society, extends outdoors, turning up a collection of striking sculpture beneath the fruit trees of the bishop's garden. The less compelling **Palace Collections** (mid-May to mid-Sept daily 11am–4pm; rest of the year Sat & Sun 2–4pm; 25kr) are made up of paintings, furniture and other artefacts belonging to the wealthiest Roskilde families of the eighteenth and nineteenth centuries.

The **Roskilde Museum**, close to the cathedral at Skt Ols Gade 18 (daily 11am–4pm; 25kr), is a little more enticing, with strong sections on medieval pottery and toys. Look out for the strange photos that satirist Gustav Wied (who lived in Roskilde for many years and whose rooms are reconstructed here) took of his family. The museum extends to Ringstedgade 6, a shop kitted out in early twentieth-century style, where locals dutifully turn up to buy traditional salted herring and sugar loaves.

More absorbing, and better known, is the **Viking Ship Museum** (May–Sept daily 9am–5pm; 60kr; rest of the year 10am–4pm; 45kr; ⓦwww.vikingeskibsmuseet .dk), set in the green surrounds of Strandengen on the banks of the fjord fifteen minutes' walk north of the centre. This is one of Denmark's most interesting little museums, with five excellent specimens of Viking shipbuilding given the space they deserve: there's a deep-sea trader, a merchant ship, a man-of-war, a ferry and a long-ship, each retrieved from the fjord where they had been sunk to block invading forces. Together, they give an impressive indication of the Vikings' nautical versatility, their skills in boat-building, and their far-ranging travels to places as various as Paris, Hamburg and North America. The material here tries hard to convince you that the Vikings sailed abroad not only to rape and pillage, but also to find places where they could quietly settle down and farm. Boat-building and sail-making demonstrations also take place outdoors all year, on the museum island – the Vikings' sails were spun from a special wool produced from wild Norwegian sheep – and there's a decent gift shop as well.

From the adjacent docks, the **cruise boat** *M/F Harald Blåtand* sails twice daily up the pretty fjord to Frederikssund and back (ⓣ47 38 87 50, ⓦwww.vikingruten .dk; 80kr one way, 120kr return), a journey of a little less than two hours each way. You can also do either the outbound or return leg of the trip on the Frederikssund bus, which takes the same amount of time but costs about half as much.

Whilst in town, take a moment to inspect the **Glasgalleriet**, Skt Ibs Vej 12 (Mon–Fri 10am–5pm, Sat & Sun noon–4.30pm; free), a good little glasswork gallery in the old Roskilde Gasworks building between the harbour and the city's central green park. This park, quiet and soothing and with views of the fjord, was once the stronghold of Viking power – a spot now marked by a hard-to-find plaque and a walking path to town, but nothing else.

Practicalities

Copenhagen is less than an hour's drive northeast of Roskilde, but if you're heading towards Funen or further south in Zealand it's easiest to **stay** here for the night. This is now a cheaper proposition than it once was, thanks to the beautiful new **youth hostel**, ideally located on the harbour next to the Viking Museum at Vindeboder 7 (ⓣ46 35 21 84, ⓦwww.danhostel.dk/roskilde), which has dorms, double rooms (❷), a communal kitchen and a view of the water. If that's full, there's a **campsite** (ⓣ46 75 79 96, ⓦwww.roskildecamping.dk; mid-April to mid-Sept) on the wooded edge of the fjord about 4km north of town – an appealing setting that means it gets very crowded at peak times; it's linked to the town centre by bus #603 towards Veddelev. There's also the pricey *Prindsen* hotel at Algade 13 (ⓣ46 30 91 00, ⓦwww.hotelprindsen.dk; ❻). For general information or to arrange a private

The Roskilde Festival

Held over four days and nights during the last weekend in June, the **Roskilde Festival** (🌐 www.roskilde-festival.dk) has grown from humble beginnings into one of Europe's largest rock events, a weekend of live music that now attracts some 100,000 people annually. In the summer of 2000 the festival experienced its darkest moment when nine people died as a result of a crowd surge in front of the main stage. Since then, **safety** has been improved significantly and Roskilde is now deemed one of the world's safest festivals (pick up the leaflet about crowd safety at Use-It or from the festival organizers if you want to come prepared). There's a special free camping ground beside the festival site, to which shuttle buses run from the train station every ten minutes, and tens of thousands of tickets are sold in advance (try to buy one in advance, as they're often sold out at the gate).

room, call in at Roskilde's **tourist office** at Gullandstræde 15 (July–Aug Mon–Fri 9am–6pm, Sat 10am–2pm, April–June Mon–Fri 9am–5pm, Sat 10am–1pm, Sept–March Mon–Thurs 9am–5pm, Fri 9am–4pm, Sat 10am–1pm; ☎46 35 27 00, 🌐 www.visitroskilde.dk).

Eating isn't a problem in Roskilde, with plenty of options. On the waterfront and across the docks from the museum at Havnevej 43 you'll find *Restaurant Store Børs*, which does sandwiches and fish specials from 70kr; take your picnic to the pleasant little park at the top of the stairs behind the harbour, from where there are good views of the town. Other options include loads of mainstream restaurants, cafés and pubs lining Skomagergade, just south of the Domkirke, and the maze of streets branching off it; for a quick bite, pop into the *No. 44 Sandwich Bar* at 44 Skomagergade, where sandwiches go for around 40kr, or head for the Irma supermarket at 21 Skomagergade.

Evening **entertainment** in Roskilde amounts to visiting the sprinkling of bars around the town centre, taking in the occasional free event in the town park, or a pleasant walk along the banks of the fjord. Serious revellers head for Copenhagen.

Lejre Historical-Archeological Centre

Iron Age Denmark is kept alive and well at the **Lejre Historical–Archeological Centre**, 8km west of Roskilde, by volunteer families who spend the summer living in a reconstructed Iron Age settlement, farming and carrying out domestic chores using implements – and wearing clothes – copied from those of the period. Modern-day visitors are welcome (mid-June to mid-Aug daily 10am–5pm; rest of the year Tues–Sun 10am–5pm; 🌐 www.lejrecenter.dk; 70kr), and can try their hand at grinding corn or paddling a dugout canoe. The serious scientific purpose is to gain an understanding of family life in Denmark 2500 years ago, but the centre can be a lot of fun to visit as a day-trip. To get here, take a local train from Roskilde to the village of Lejre; from Lejre station, bus #233 covers the 4km to the historical centre's entrance.

Beyond Roskilde: western Zealand

Beyond Roskilde, western Zealand is flat and bland. You might find yourself travelling through on the way to **Kalundborg**, from where ferries depart for Århus and the island of Samsø, or to **Korsør**, the other main town on the west coast, from where a bridge connects Zealand with Funen. Apart from these, the area's only real interest lies in the **Hornsherred Peninsula**, which divides the Roskilde fjord and Isefjord. There are long, quiet beaches along the peninsula's western coast, though the lack of a railway and the paucity of local buses means the region is best toured by bike. Make for the medieval frescoes in the eleventh-century churches at **Skibby** or **Over Dråby**, or keep on northward for **Jægerspris** and its **castle** (50min guided tours only: mid-March to Oct Tues–Sun at 11am, noon, 1pm, 2pm and 3pm; 35kr), built during the fifteenth century as a royal hunting seat and last used by the eccentric Frederik VII, who lived here during the mid-1800s with his third wife. She inherited the castle after the king's death and turned it into an institution for "poor and unfortunate girls". The most convenient place to stay in the area is the small *Jægerpris Vandrerhjem* hostel (☎47 31 10 32, ⊛www.lundehuset.dk; closed Jan), which has singles, doubles (❷) and family rooms, as well as kitchen facilities. It's located at Skovnæsvej 2 near the Roskilde fjord bridge – the only bridge that crosses the fjord (as Route 53) from Frederikssund west to Jægerpris.

South from Copenhagen: Køge and around

Not too long ago, **KØGE** was best known for the pollution caused by the rubber factory and chemical works on its outskirts, and despite the town's fine sandy beaches, few ventured here to sample the waters of Køge Bay. In recent years, though, the place has been considerably cleaned up, while an extension of line E and A+ of the Copenhagen S-train network has linked the town to the capital, putting its evocatively preserved medieval centre and beaches within easy reach. It's also a good base for touring the **Stevns Peninsula**, which bulges into the sea just south of the town.

The town and beaches

Saturday is the best day to visit Køge: a variety of free entertainment sweeps through the main streets in the morning and from noon onwards the harbourside bars are at their liveliest. Walk from the **train station** along Jernbanegade and turn left into Nørregade for Torvet, which is the hub of the action. On a corner of the square is the **tourist office** (June–Aug Mon–Fri 9am–5pm, Sat 10am–2pm; rest of the year Mon–Fri 9am–5pm, Sat 10am–1pm; ☎56 67 60 01, ⊛www.visitkoege .com), while nearby, at Nørregade 4, the **Køge Museum** (June–Aug Tues–Sun 11am–5pm, Sept–May Mon–Fri 11am–5pm, Sat 11am–3pm, Sun 1–5pm; 25kr) contains remnants from Køge's bloody past, not least the local executioner's sword. If the tales are to be believed, the beheading tool was wielded frequently on Torvet, a place which, perhaps not surprisingly, is also said to have been the scene of several incidents of witchcraft and haunting. On the site of what is today a clothes shop, the Devil is said to have appeared in the forms of a clergyman, a frog, a dog and a pig, to have thrown a boy from his bed out into the yard, and caused hands to swell – among other unwholesome occurrences.

Once its market stalls are cleared away, a suitably spooky stillness falls over Torvet and the narrow cobbled streets that run off it. One of these streets, Kirkestræde, is lined with sixteenth-century half-timbered houses and leads to **Skt Nikolai Kirke** (mid-June to Aug Mon–Fri 10am–4pm, Sat 10am–noon; Sept to mid-June Mon–Fri 10am–noon), where pirates captured in Køge Bay were hung from the **tower** – it's opened up every half an hour from mid-June to July between 10am and 1.30pm. Along the nave, some of the carved angel faces on the pew ends lack noses, having been sliced off by drunken Swedish soldiers during the seventeenth century, while the font, an unattractive black-marble and pine item, replaces an earlier one defiled by a woman who performed "an unspeakable act" in it. On a more aesthetic level, the intriguing **Køge Art Museum of Sketches**, at Nørregade 29 (Tues & Thurs–Sun 10am–5pm, Wed 10am–8pm; ⊛www.skitsesamlingen.dk; 25kr), focuses on the creative process from idea to finished work. Its collection includes drawings, sculptures and models made by important Danish artists of the twentieth century, plus temporary exhibitions of works in progress by both local and international artists.

The town's **beaches**, which draw many jaded Copenhageners on weekends, stretch along the bay to the north and south of the town. To take full advantage of the sands, **stay** at one of the two campsites beside the southerly beach: *Køge Sydstrand* (☎56 65 07 69, ⓦwww.kogesydstrandcamping.dk; April–Sept) is virtually on the sand, while *Vallø* (☎56 65 28 51, ⓦwww.dk-camp.dk/vallo) is across Strandvejen, close to a pine wood. Further away, 3km from the town centre along Vamdrupvej, is Køge's **youth hostel** (☎56 65 14 74, ⓦwww.danhostel.dk/koege; April to mid-Dec) with bunks and some double rooms (❸). Take bus #210 from the train station and get off when the bus turns into Agerskovvej. Staying in the town centre isn't expensive; head for the small and comfortable *Centralhotellet* (☎56 65 06 96; ❸), next door to the tourist office at Vestergade 3.

Around Køge: Stevns Peninsula

Stevns Peninsula, easily reached from Køge, is a fairly neglected part of Zealand, mainly because the coastline here is more rugged and less suited to swimming than that immediately around Køge or in North Zealand. The town of **STORE HEDDINGE**, where you'll find a curious octagonal limestone church, is the obvious starting point for explorations; you can get there on the private train line (InterRail, Scanrail and Eurail passes not valid) from Køge in half an hour. In Store Heddinge you'll find a simple **youth hostel** at Ved Munkevænget 1 (☎56 50 20 22, ⓦwww.danhostel.dk/store-heddinge; April–Sept), which has dorms and exceptionally inexpensive doubles (❶). There are several **campsites** on the beaches to the south: the nearest to Køge is *Nordstevns*, Strandvejen 29 (☎56 67 70 03, ⓦwww.nordstevns.dk), in the woodlands around Strøby, accessible by the frequent buses #208 or #209.

Central Zealand: Ringsted and around

Though now little more than a small farming town, **RINGSTED**'s central location made it one of the most important settlements in Zealand from the end of the Viking era until the Reformation. It was the burial place of medieval Danish monarchs as well as being the site of a regional *ting*, the open-air court where prominent merchants and nobles made the administrative decisions for the province.

The three *ting* stones around which the nobles gathered remain in Ringsted's market square, but they're often concealed by the market itself, or the backsides of weary shoppers. It's the sturdy **Skt Bendts Kirke** (May to mid-Sept Mon–Fri 10am–noon & 1–5pm; mid-Sept to April Mon–Fri 1–3pm) that dominates the square, as it has done for over eight hundred years. Erected in 1170 under the direction of Valdemar I, the church was the final resting place for all Danish monarchs until 1341. Many affluent Zealanders also had themselves buried here, presumably so that their souls could spend eternity in the very best company. Four thousand people are said to have been present for the church's consecration, and although these days it receives a mere trickle of visitors compared to those flocking to the royal tombs at Roskilde, it nevertheless represents a substantial chunk of Danish history. During the seventeenth century a number of the coffins were opened and the finds are collected in the **Museum Chapel** within the church. Besides the lead slab found inside Valdemar I's coffin, there are plaster casts of the skulls of Queen Bengård and Queen Sofia, a collection of coins found in the church and a replica of the Dagmar Cross, discovered when Queen Dagmar's tomb was opened in 1697 – the original is in the National Museum in Copenhagen.

Once you've seen the church you've more or less exhausted Ringsted. The town's only other noteworthy attraction is the **Ringsted Museum & Windmill** (Tues–Thurs & Sun 11am–4pm; 25kr), on Køgevej, ten minutes' walk from the church. It's a surprisingly interesting introduction to the history of the local farming community, from the Danish land reform up until the present-day organic farming movement, and has an operating windmill from 1805 – you can buy freshly ground organic wheat flour, should you have the need.

Around Ringsted

Beyond Ringsted, the road and rail network out of Copenhagen splits into two: one line heads further south to the islands of Falster, Lolland and Møn (see pp.126 and 127) via Næstved, while the other heads westwards towards the multimillion-kroner combined **bridge and tunnel** that has carried road and rail traffic across the 18km-wide Store Bælt since it opened in 1998. There was a regular ferry between **KORSØR** on Zealand and Nyborg on Funen for more than two centuries, and archeological research on the mid-channel island of Sprogø suggests that Danes have been boating back and forth for many thousands of years. Up until recently there was no particular reason to stop in Korsør, but if you have any interest in grand engineering feats, a stop at the **Great Belt Bridge and Nature Centre** (July & Aug daily 10am–7pm; March–June and Sept–Oct Wed–Mon 10am–5pm; ⑩www.bro-natur.dk; 25kr) is a definite must. Here you'll find robotic models, videos and interactive computer simulations detailing everything you could possibly want to know about the engineering expertise behind the project, which involved, amongst other things, the construction of what was briefly the world's longest suspension bridge. It's all described in an easily graspable way, and if you haven't already, you'll quickly grow to understand the construction's magnificence – the two bridge pylons, for example, are Denmark's highest points.

Another recently completed architectural feat covered by the centre, albeit with less enthusiasm, is the **Øresunds Link** – the 4km-long tunnel linking Kastrup on Amager with the artificial island of Peberholm, and from there a 7.8km-long bridge on to the Swedish coast, just outside Malmö. There's a miniature model of the Link as well as a couple of placards discussing its effect on the sea environment in Kattegat. You'll find the centre left of the bridge toll booths.

Practicalities

For accommodation, Ringsted's **youth hostel** (☏57 61 15 26, ⑩www.amtstuegaarden.dk) is handily situated across the road from the church – with no campsites nearby, this is the only budget option, and it also has doubles (❷). Ringsted does have some pricey hotels, and the **tourist office** (mid-June to Aug Mon–Fri 9am–5pm, Sat 9am–2pm; Sept to mid-June Mon–Fri 10am–5pm, Sat 10am–1pm; ☏57 62 66 00, ⑩www.met-2000.dk), a few doors along between the hostel and Torvet, can advise on these as well as arranging private rooms (from 125kr per person). One decent hotel choice is the *Scandic* at Nørretorv 57 (☏57 61 93 00, ⑩www.scandic-hotels.dk; ❻), which has comfortable rooms, a sauna, restaurant and children's playground.

Southern Zealand and the islands

Southern Zealand is seriously rural, consisting almost solely of rich, rolling farmland and villages. South from Ringsted, most routes lead to **NÆSTVED**, by far the largest town in the region. Aside from a smartly restored medieval centre and a minor museum, however, Næstved has little to offer except its proximity to unspoilt countryside and the **River Suså**, whose lack of rapids and negligible current makes it a good base for novice **canoe trips** – although busy at weekends, it's free of crowds at other times. Canoes can be rented at Suså Kanoudlejning, Næsbyholm Allé 6, in nearby Glumsø (☏55 64 61 44, ⑩www.kanoudlejning.dk), for around 330kr a day. Off the river, time is best spent strolling amid the town's half-timbered buildings and visiting the **Næstved Museum** at Ringstedgade 4 (Tues–Sun 10am–4pm; 20kr) for its jumble of (mainly religious) oddments and a fairly ordinary selection of historical arts and crafts from the town.

The local **tourist office** (July Mon–Fri 9am–6pm, Sat 9am–2pm; June & Aug Mon–Fri 9am–5pm, Sat 9am–2pm; rest of the year Mon–Fri 10am–4pm, Sat 9am–noon; ☏55 72 11 22, ⑩www.visitnaestved.com) in the yellow house known as

Det Gule Pakkus, Havnen 1, can fill you in on practical details and offer suggestions for **staying over** in Næstved. Alternatively, there are comfortable but pricey
rooms at the *Vinhuset* (☎55 72 08 07, ⊛www.hotel-vinhuset.dk; ❺), centrally located
on the church square, Skt Peders Kirkeplads. Farther from town but similarly priced
is the nicely renovated *Menstrup Kro* (☎55 44 30 03, ⊛www.menstrupkro.dk; ❺),
which has a sauna, pool and tennis court. The only really cheap spot in town is the
youth hostel at Frejasevej 8 (☎55 72 20 91, ⊛www.danhostel.dk/naestved; mid-
March to mid-Nov), which has dorm beds and doubles (❶); from the train station
(which is about 1km from the centre on Jernbanegade), turn left into Farimagsvej
and left again along Præstøvej. There's also a basic **campsite** (also ☎55 72 20 91)
beside the hostel, with the same opening season.

If you have the opportunity, take a trip to the island of **Gavnø**, a few miles south
of Næstved at the mouth of the River Suså, to see its eponymous eighteenth-century Rococo **palace** (May–Aug daily 10am–5pm; May–June 50kr, July–Aug 40kr;
⊛www.gavnoe.dk). The imposing structure itself is enhanced by a delightful tulip
garden, which attracts hordes of visitors when in bloom (hence the higher early
summer entry price). Parts of the building are still occupied by the descendants of
the original owners, and there's a large collection of books and paintings on display, as well as a butterfly house and a museum devoted to fire protection. The
Friheden ferry (☎55 77 38 36; 80kr round-trip) runs about three times a day during
the summer between Næstved, the palace, and Karrebæksminde.

Falster, Lolland and Møn

Off the south coast of Zealand lie three sizeable islands – **Falster**, **Lolland** and
Møn. All three are connected to the mainland by road, and Falster and Lolland have
rail links too, making them relatively easy to reach, but once there you'll need your
own transport to do any serious exploration outside the larger communities, since
local buses are rare; bikes can be rented from virtually all tourist offices and campsites, however.

Falster

Falster is by far the least interesting of the trio. There are some pleasant woods on
the eastern side and some good, but very crowded, beaches, particularly around the
major resort of **MARIELYST** on the Baltic (eastern) coast. There's not much to do
in Marielyst except enjoy the beach and the bustling **nightlife**: bars, clubs and cafés
are plentiful. The two most affordable **hotels** are the neighbouring *Marielyst Strand*
(☎54 13 68 88, ⊛www.hotel-marielyst.dk; ❹) and the *Hotel Østersøens Perle* (☎54
13 62 05, ☎54 13 52 92; ❹), both near the beach. You can also ask at the **tourist
office**, just off Skovby Ringvej as you enter Marielyst from Nykøbing (☎54 13 62
98, ⊛www.marielyst.org), for a list of private rooms. Of the five **campsites** in the
area, the best are *Smedegårdens Camping* (☎54 13 66 17, ⊛www.marielyst.dk) and
Marielyst Camping (☎54 13 53 07, ⊛www.marielyst-camping.dk), both close to the
beach.

The island's main town, **NYKØBING** – usually written Nykøbing F – has a
quaint medieval centre, and is of practical use for its **tourist office** at Østergågade
7 (☎54 85 13 03, ⊛www.tinf.dk), which handles enquiries on all three islands and
can help with private accommodation (150–200kr per person per night).
Nykøbing's main attraction is the new **Medieval Centre** (May–Sept daily
10am–4pm, ⊛www.middelaldercentret.dk; 75kr), an open-air experimental museum set in a recreated village which provides a thought-provoking insight into the
hardship of medieval life. If you're here with children, don't miss the **Folkepark
Zoo** (daily: mid-April to Sept 10am–6pm; Oct to mid-Dec 9am–4pm; Feb to mid-
April 10am–4pm; 30kr), which offers the chance to come face to face with a llama
as well as some native Danish creatures. For hotel **accommodation**, try the three-
star *Falster* at Skovalleen (☎54 85 93 93, ⊛www.hotel-falster.dk; ❺). There's also the
island's only **youth hostel** (☎54 85 66 99, ⊛www.danhostel.dk/nykoebingfalster;

closed mid-Dec to mid-Jan), about 2km from the Nykøbing train station at Østre Allé 110, which has doubles (**②**) and an adjoining **campsite** (☎54 85 45 45, ⊛www.nyk-f-camp.dk; open all year).

If you're ultimately making for the port of **GEDSER**, to the south of Falster, for the ferry to Rostock in Germany, don't bother getting off the train before the ferry dock. Gedser itself doesn't have much to offer except for a decent beach to the east of town.

Lolland

Larger and less crowded than Falster, **Lolland** is otherwise much the same: wooded, with excellent beaches and lots of quiet, explorable corners. A private railway (InterRail, Scanrail and Eurail passes not valid) runs to Lolland from Nykøbing on Falster, taking in Sakskøbing, Maribo and finally Nakskov, at the western extremity of the island, near to where ferries cross to Langeland (alternatively, bus #800 goes straight from Nykøbing station onto the ferry, and continues on to Svenborg and Odense on Funen); there's also a DSB train from Nykøbing to Rødby on the south coast. Each town has a tourist office, youth hostel and campsite, but **MARIBO**, delectably positioned on the Søndersø lake, is the most scenic setting for a short stay, with a **youth hostel** with dorms and doubles (**①**) at Sdr Boulevard 82B (☎54 78 33 14, ⊛www.danhostel.dk/maribo), a **campsite** at Bangshavevej 25 (☎54 78 00 71, ⊛www.maribo-camping.dk; Easter to Oct), and a good-value two-star **hotel**, *Ebsens*, near the train station at Vestergade 32 (☎5t4 78 10 44, ℗54 75 60 44; **③**). The **tourist office** is easy to find in the old town hall on Torvet (Mon–Fri 10am–5pm, Sat 10am–1pm; ☎54 78 04 96, ⊛www.lolland-falster.dk).

After the beaches, the island's top attraction is probably **Aalholm Slot** in the southeast and its **Automobile Museum** (June–Aug daily 10am–5pm; rest of the year Sat & Sun 10am–4pm; ⊛www.aalholm.dk; 70kr), a magnificent twelfth-century castle which is sadly no longer open to the public; however, you can still walk the grounds, and the museum next door contains over two hundred antique cars, lovingly maintained by the castle's previous owner. Though Lolland is not the most obvious place to spot big game, you can see antelopes, zebra, giraffes and more at the drive-through **Knuthenborg Safari Park**, 7km north of Maribo (May–Sept 9am–5pm; ⊛www.knuthenborg.dk; 90kr). Lastly, for some of the region's most distinct cultural history, head for **Denmark's Sugar Museum** in Nakskov on the west coast (May–Dec Tues–Sun 11am–4pm, Jan–April Sun 10am–2pm; 20kr). Most of Denmark's sugar beet is grown on Lolland – something you'll quickly notice when looking over the fields, and the museum's displays detail the history of the crop and of the Polish immigrants who came here to work in the fields and the processing plant.

Møn

Since it's not connected by train, **Møn** is the most difficult of the three islands to get to from Zealand, but it's well worth the effort of getting there: take bus #62 or #64 from Vordingborg (on the rail line from Copenhagen to Nykøbing). Møn is known for its white chalk cliffs, but what really sets it apart are the **Neolithic burial places** which litter the island by the score, and its unique whitewashed churches, many of which feature fourteenth-century frescoes depicting rural life – the work, apparently, of one peasant painter. The main town, **STEGE**, is, at least for those without their own transport, the most feasible base, since it's the hub of the island's minimal bus service and has a good if pricey **hotel**, the *Præstekilde* (☎55 86 87 88, ⊛www.praestekilde.dk; **⑤**) at Klintvej 116 near the beach, and an inexpensive **campsite** on Falckvej 5 (☎55 81 53 25; May to mid-Sept). Of the four other campsites on the island, *Camping Møns Klint* at Klintvej 544 in **Borre** (☎55 81 20 25, ⊛www.campingmoensklint.dk; April–Oct), to the east, is the best, while *Ulvshale Camping* (☎55 81 53 25, ⊛www.ulvscamp.dk; April–Oct) is right on the beach at the island's northernmost point. If you'd rather sleep in a bed, check out current options with the helpful Stege **tourist office**, by the bus station at Storegade 2 (mid-June to Aug Mon–Fri 9am–5pm, Sat 9am–6pm, Sun 10am–noon; Sept to mid-June Mon–Fri 10am–5pm, Sat 9am–noon; ☎55 86 04 10, ⓦwww.moen-touristbureau.dk).

The best of the Neolithic barrows is **Kong Asker's Høj**, about 20km from Stege near **Sprove**, while the foremost frescoes can be admired at **ELMELUNDE** (daily: April–Sept 7am–5pm, Oct–March 8am–4pm; free), connected to Stege bus #52; and **FANEFJORD** (same hours as Elmelunde), reachable via the Vordingborg bus from Stege – and get out at Store Damme, then walk; the latter also has a Neolithic barrow in its churchyard. As for the **cliffs** (*Møn Klint*), they're at the eastern end of the island and stretch for about eight kilometres. Bus #52 runs between the cliffs and Stege four to five times a day depending on the season. Fifteen minutes' walk from the cliffs, at Langebjergvej 1, is a basic **youth hostel** (☎55 81 20 30, ⓦwww.danhostel.dk/moen; May–Sept), which has dorms and some private double rooms (❶).

Bornholm

Much nearer to Sweden than Denmark, **Bornholm** (shown on the map on p.511) was under Swedish rule for many years. After a long and bloody revolt, it was finally returned to Denmark in 1522 after the infamous Swedish governor was shot by a single silver bullet in the heart. Once an important Baltic trading post, its population now lives by fishing, farming and, increasingly, tourism. The coastline is blessed with great beaches in the south and some invitingly rugged coastline and hilly landscapes to the north, while the island's centre is covered in woods with good walking possibilities. It's no wonder that Scandinavian and German holidaymakers fill the island each summer, especially now that the new bridge-and-tunnel **Øresunds Link** between Copenhagen and Malmö makes travelling to Bornholm a lot quicker and easier than before. Buses now leave up to four times a day from Copenhagen, crossing over the Link to Malmö in Sweden and driving onto the ferry from Ystad to Rønne on Bornholm, a total journey time of three hours. Compared to six hours by direct ferry from Copenhagen to Rønne – which used to be the quickest route (bar flying), and is still an option – this is a vast improvement. There's also a train link to Bornholm which catches the same Ystad–Rønne ferry as the bus, and takes just as long. All three travel options cost roughly the same. Bornholm is also quite feasible as a stopover if you're heading to Germany or Poland on one of several ferry crossings (see "Travel Details", p.131).

To get the most out of Bornholm, you really need to travel around the whole coast – not difficult, since the island is only about 30km across from east to west – and spend at least three or four days doing it. **Getting around** is easy and best done by **bike**: the island is criss-crossed by some two hundred bike trails along the old rail tracks. Bikes can be rented in Rønne at Cykel-Centret, Søndergade 7 (☎56 95 06 05) or Bornholm's Cykeludlejning, Nordre Kystvej 5 (☎56 95 13 59), as well as numerous other places around the island (ask at tourist offices); for maps and suggestions visit ⓦwww.bornholminfo.dk. If this seems too energetic, you can make use of the reliable **bus** services (all buses are equipped to carry bikes; information on ☎56 95 21 21, ⓦwww.bat.dk), but it's a good idea to check the timetable beforehand as some services are quite infrequent. **Accommodation** is straightforward, too: there's a youth hostel in each of the main settlements and campsites are sprinkled fairly liberally around the coast. Tourist offices can also help with private rooms. The peak weeks of the summer are very busy, and you should phone ahead to check there's space. But at any other time of year there'll be little difficulty. The **nightlife** on the island can also be surprisingly lively, although often limited to one spot in each town – invariably the café in the main square.

The island

Ferries from Copenhagen arrive in **RØNNE**, Bornholm's main town, where the **tourist office** is right on the harbour at Ndr. Kystvej 3 (Jan–May & Sept–Oct Mon–Fri 9am–4pm, Sat 10am–1pm; June Mon–Sat 10am–4pm, Sun 10am–3pm; July & Aug Mon–Sat 9.30am–5.30pm, Sun 10am–4pm; Nov & Dec Mon–Fri 9am–4pm; ☎56 95 95 00, ⊚www.bornholminfo.dk). Staff can fill you in on accommodation and transport details, and give you a copy of *Bornholm Denne Uge*, the free weekly listings magazine – in Danish and German only, but still informative. If you've arrived on an overnight or early boat, the only place open for breakfast is *Café 66*, at the ferry terminal. Otherwise, there are plenty of places to **eat** and stock up around the main town square, Store Torv.

The triangle between Store Torv and Lille Torv (literally, "large" and "small" squares) and the ferry terminal has the most charm, its streets lined with traditional wood-beamed townhouses painted in bright colours. Otherwise, Rønne lacks the character of many of the other island settlements. However, it's well worth taking in some detail on the island's turbulent history at the **Bornholms Museum**, Sct Mortensgade 29 (April–Oct Mon–Sat 10am–5pm; Nov–March Tues–Sat 1–4pm; ⊚www.bornholmsmuseer.dk; 30kr) – look out for the large golden clothes pin found in a field early in 2002, which is one of Denmark's largest-ever archeological gold finds. If you do need to **stay over**, there are plenty of options: a youth hostel at Arsenalvej 12 (☎56 95 13 40, ☎56 95 01 32; March–Oct), which has some doubles (❷) as well as dorms; a campsite, *Galløkken Camping*, at Strandvejen 4 (☎56 95 23 20, ⊚www.gallokken.dk; mid-May to Aug); or the small *Sverres Hotel* at Skt Snellemark 2 (☎56 95 03 03, ⊚www.sverres-hotel.dk; ❸). Contact the tourist office for info on private rooms, which start at around 125kr per person per night.

If you're eager to get to the beach, head south to **DUEODDE**, where there's nothing but sand and a string of campsites. In summer Dueodde lighthouse is open to the public (May to mid-Oct 9am–dusk; 5kr), offering superb views. At the other corner of the eastern coast, surrounded by spectacular scenery of steep cliffs and affording great views, **SVANEKE** is a quiet place which until recently was favoured by Danish retirees, but is now experiencing a massive influx of **craftsmen** – mostly potters and glass-blowers – whose workshops and fantastic exhibits have come to dominate the town scene. In the mid-1970s Svaneke won a Council of Europe prize for town preservation and these days upmarket hotels and restaurants occupy some of the renovated old buildings. If you want to **stay**, first choice is the excellent *Siemsens Gaard*, Havnebryggen 9 (☎56 49 61 49, ⊚www.siemsens.dk; ❺), whose front rooms give great views. Otherwise, the youth hostel at Reberbanevej 9 (☎56 49 62 42, ⊚www.danhostel-svaneke.dk; April–Oct), near the Christiansø ferry landing, has doubles (❷) and dorms, and there are two campsites, both basic but beautifully situated near the cliffs; *Møllebakkens Familiecamping* (☎56 49 64 62, ⊚www.svaneke-camping.dk) is slightly better equipped. The **tourist office** at Storegade 24 (June–Aug Mon–Fri 10am–5pm, Sat 9am–2pm; Sept–May Mon–Wed 10am–4pm, Thurs & Fri 11am–5pm; ☎56 49 70 79) should be able to help with any queries.

Halfway along the north coast, **GUDHJEM** is pretty too, its tiny streets winding their way around the foot of a hill. The town lends its name to a traditional open sandwich combination called *Sol over Gudhjem* ("sunrise over Gudhjem") – a slice of rye bread layered with smoked herring, raw egg yoke, chopped onion and capers, sold nationally in *smørrebrød* shops. If you want to taste it at source, head for the *Røgeri* (smokehouse) on Ejner Mikkelsensvej 13, near the harbour, where sandwiches cost 25kr. **Accommodation** in Gudhjem is plentiful. Most romantic is the pricey *Janzens Hotel* (☎56 48 50 17, ⊚www.jantzenshotel.dk; ❺) close to the harbour at Brøddegade 33. Next door at 31 Brøddegade, the cheaper *Therns Hotel* (☎56 48 50 99, ⊚www.therns-hotel.dk; ❹) is also nice; some rooms have shared bath. Best value, however, is the youth hostel at Ejner Mikkelsens Vej 14 (next door to the smokehouse) with comfortable three- and four-person rooms for 400kr and

500kr respectively. Buses run the 5km or so north to the **Bornholms Kunstmuseum** (June–Aug daily 10am–5pm, May & Sept–Oct Tues–Sun 10am–5pm; Nov–April Tues & Thurs 1–5pm, Sun 10am–5pm; ⓦwww.bornholms-kunstmuseum.dk; 40kr), a gallery displaying works from the Bornholm School that thrived here in the first half of the twentieth century. Gudhjem is also a good jumping-off point for the six-kilometre trip inland to **ØSTERLARS**, site of the largest and most impressive of the island's fortified round churches, which date from the twelfth and thirteenth centuries. A similar distance further inland, right in the centre of the island, is Bornholm's largest (and Denmark's third largest) forest, **Almindingen**, criss-crossed by cycle paths, and boasting a lookout tower in the centre which affords fabulous views of the entire island. **SANDVIG**, on the island's northwest corner (12km from Gudhjem and reachable by bus #1 or #2 from Rønne and #7 from Gudhjem), is the start of another worthwhile walk, along **Hammeren**, the massive granite headland that juts out towards Sweden. Just south of Sandvig are the remains of the thirteenth-century **Hammershus**, not much in themselves but worth a visit for the views from the tall crag which the castle occupied, and noteworthy as northern Europe's largest castle ruin.

If Bornholm suddenly seems too big, and the weather's good, take one of the ferries (from Svaneke, Gudhjem or Allinge; check with any tourist office for the latest details) to the tiny island of **Christiansø**, some 25km northeast of Bornholm – a speck in the Baltic that served as a naval base during the seventeenth century, and later as a prison; these days, the minuscule population prides itself on its spiced herring. From Christiansø there's a footbridge over to the island of **Frederiksø**, a breeding ground for eider ducks. If you want to savour the peace of these little islands, you can **stay** at the *Gæstgiveriet* on Christiansø (☎56 46 20 15, ⓦwww .christiansoekro.dk; ❸), one of the few lodgings in these parts, which also runs a campsite.

Travel details

Trains

Copenhagen to: Århus (34 daily; 3hr 16min); Esbjerg (10 daily; 3hr); Helsingør (72 daily; 52min); Næstved (36 daily; 1hr); Nykøbing F (22 daily; 1hr 40min); Odense (55 daily; 1hr 30min); Ringsted (76 daily; 40min); Roskilde (115 daily; 25min).
Helsingør to: Gilleleje (33 daily; 40min); Hellebæk (35 daily; 10min); Hillerød (29 daily; 22min); Hornbæk (35 daily; 25min).
Køge to: Fakse (17 daily; 34min); Store Heddinge (17 daily; 30min).
Nykøbing F to: Nakskov (30 daily; 45min); Rødby (11 daily; 23min); Sakskøbing (29 daily; 15min).
Roskilde to: Kalundborg (22 daily, connects with ferry to Jutland; 1hr 10min).

Buses

Copenhagen to: Aalborg (2–4 daily; 4hr 45min); Århus (4–6 daily; 3hr 45min via Ebeltoft, 3hr direct); Ebeltoft (2–3 daily; 3hr); Fjerritslev via Grenå, Randers, Hobro and Løgstør (2–5 daily; 6hr 10min).

Nykøbing to: Odense via Svendborg (4–8 daily; 3hr 40min).

Ferries

Allinge to: Christiansø (May–Sept Mon–Sat 1 daily; 1hr 10min).
Copenhagen to: Rønne (1–2 daily; 6–7hr).
Gudhjem to: Christiansø (July & Aug 3 daily; May–June & Sept 1 daily; Oct–April Mon–Fri 1 daily; 55min).
Kalundborg to: Århus (3–7 daily; 2hr 30min).
Odden to: Ebeltoft (8–15 daily; 45min); Århus (5 daily; 65min).
Svaneke to: Christiansø (May–Sept Mon–Fri 1 daily; 1hr 25min).
Tårs (Langeland) to: Spodsbjerg (14–18 daily; 45min).

International trains

Copenhagen to: Bergen (2–3 daily, change in Gothenburg and Oslo; 16hr 40min); Gothenburg (6 daily; 3hr 25min); Hamburg (5 daily; 4hr 30min); Helsinki (2–3 daily, change to ferry in Stockholm;

23hr); Kiruna (2 daily in summer, change in Stockholm; 22hr 30min); Malmö (72 daily; 35min); Narvik (2 daily in summer, change in Stockholm and Boden; 25hr 15min); Oslo (2–3 daily, change in Gothenburg; 8hr 30min); Stockholm (5–8 daily, some change in Malmö; 5hr 20min); Turku (2 daily, change to ferry in Stockholm; 18hr–22hr 30min).

International ferries and catamarans

Copenhagen to: Oslo (1 daily; 16hr); Swinoujscie (5 weekly; 10hr); Klaipeda (2 weekly; 21hr).

Gedser to: Rostock, Germany (8 daily in summer; rest of year 3 daily; 2hr).

Helsingør to: Helsingborg (HH Ferries 30–40 daily; 20min; Sundbusserne 30–36 daily; 20min; Scandlines 63 daily in summer; 20min).

Neksø to: Kolobrzeg, Poland (catamaran 2–3 daily in summer; 2 hr).

Rødby to: Puttgarden (46 daily; 45min).

Rønne to: Sassnitz, Germany (1–2 daily in summer; rest of year 3–4 weekly; 3hr 30min); Ystad (catamaran 2–6 daily; 1hr 20min; ferry 1–3 daily; 2hr 30min).

1.2

Funen

Known as "the garden of Denmark" for the lawn-like neatness of its fields and for the immense amount of fruit and vegetables that come from them, **Funen** (*Fyn*) is the smaller of the two main Danish islands, and one which many visitors pass quickly through on their way between Zealand and Jutland. The island's bucolic outlook and coastline draw many, but its attractions are mainly low-profile, such as the various collections of the Funen painters and the birthplaces of writer Hans Christian Andersen and composer Carl Nielsen, who eulogized the distinctive sing-song Funen accent and claimed it inspired his music. If you are still keen, the island's best seen by cycling; otherwise, you'll be getting around on buses more often than trains, since the latter are relatively scarce.

Arriving from Zealand brings you through **Nyborg**, a town with a heavily restored twelfth-century castle, though there's little reason to linger long on the **east coast** and it's preferable to stay on the cross-country railway that continues to **Odense**, Denmark's third-largest city and an obvious base if you want to explore villages by day but would like something other than rural quiet by night. Close by, the former fishing town of **Kerteminde** retains some faded charm, and is a good base for visiting both the **Ladby Boat**, an important Viking relic, and the isolated **Hindsholm Peninsula**. To the **south**, Funen's coastal life centres on maritime **Svendborg**, possibly the top scenic draw on Funen with its good beaches and fragmented archipelago of pretty **islands**. This is vacation territory for the most part, well served by ferries and connected by train with Odense via the island's only branch rail line.

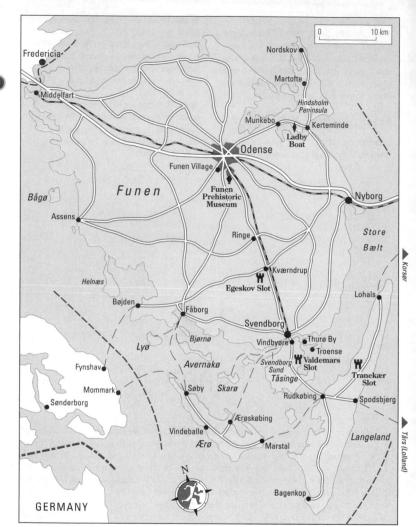

East Funen

Travelling from Zealand to Funen takes you over the **Store Bælt** ("Great Belt") on the 18-kilometre road and rail link which connects the two islands, before bringing you to **Nyborg**, Funen's easternmost town and one that few people see more of than a train station.

Unless you're in a rush to reach Odense, spare a few hours for Nyborg's strollable old streets and thirteenth-century **castle**, for two hundred years the seat of Danish political power. Otherwise, apart from countless lookalike villages, there's not much in East Funen to detain you.

Nyborg

NYBORG is small and easily navigated and you'll have no trouble finding your way to **Nyborg Slot**, built around 1200 by Valdemar the Great as part of a chain of coastal fortresses to guard against Wend piracy. For more than two hundred years, the Danehof – a summertime national assembly involving king, clergy and nobility – met here (and in 1282 drew up the first Danish constitution), which effectively made Nyborg the Danish capital until 1443, when power moved to Copenhagen. The castle bears little evidence of those years, however. Many of the surrounding fortifications have been turned into ordinary homes and all that remains on view is the narrow building holding the living quarters, its distinctive harlequin brickwork a result of 1920s restoration. Inside, the **museum** (daily: March–May & Sept–Oct 10am–3pm; July 10am–5pm; June & Aug 10am–4pm; 30kr) leads through low-beamed chambers and emerges into an expansive attic; the rooms themselves are much more evocative of the past than the odd table, chest, or suit of armour with which they are decorated.

With the bright lights of Odense just 25km away to the west, there's little temptation to spend a night in Nyborg. If you decide to do so, though, *Villa Gulle*, on Østervoldgade 44 (☎65 30 11 88, ⊛www.villa-gulle.dk; ❹), is a fair-priced hotel, while there's a beachside **campsite** (☎65 31 02 56, ⊛www.strandcamping.dk; April–Sept) at Hjejlegade 99. For further information, drop in to the **tourist office** at Torvet 9 (mid-May to Aug Mon–Fri 9am–5pm, Sat 9am–2pm; rest of the year Mon–Fri 9am–4pm, Sat 9.30am–12.30am; ☎65 31 02 80, ⊛www.nyborgturist.dk).

Odense

Funen's sole industrial centre and one of the oldest settlements in the country, **ODENSE** – named after Odin, chief of the Norse gods – gained prominence in the early nineteenth century when the opening of the Odense canal linked the city to the sea and made it the major transit point for the produce of the island's farms. Nowadays it's a pleasant provincial university town of museums and decent shopping, with a large manufacturing sector hugging the canal bank on the northern side of the city, well out of sight of the compact old centre. The **old town** houses some fine museums and – thanks to the resident students – a surprisingly vigorous nightlife. Odense is also known, throughout Denmark at least, as the birthplace of Hans Christian Andersen, and although it's all done quite discreetly, the fact is celebrated with souvenir shops and hotels catering for travellers lured by the prospect of a romantic Andersen experience – something they (almost inevitably) won't find.

Arrival, information and city transport

Long-distance **buses** terminate at the efficient **train station**, a ten-minute walk north of the city centre. In the centre you'll find the **tourist office** (mid-June to Aug Mon–Fri 9.30am–7pm, Sat 10am–5pm, Sun 10am–4pm; Sept to mid-June Mon–Fri 9.30am–4.30pm, Sat 10am–1pm; ☎66 12 75 20, ⊛www.odenseturist.dk) on the first floor of the nineteenth-century Rådhus on Vestergade. On Odense's **bus** system you pay 12kr as you enter to travel within the city limits: if you have to use more than one bus, ask the driver for a "change ticket" (*omstigning*) to use on the next bus. Better value if you're planning to see Odense's museums is the **Adventure Pass** (*Odense Eventyrpas*: one day for 100kr, two days 140kr), which gets you into all bar the train museum (though there's a discount) and allows unlimited travel on local buses, along with reductions on the *Odense Åfart* boat and the zoo (see p.138); buy it from any tourist office, most train stations, youth hostels, campsites and hotels on Funen. If you can't face the buses, you can **rent a bike** at City Cykler, Vesterbro 27 (☎66 13 97 83, ⊛www.citycykler.dk; from 99kr per day, 500kr per week) or, next to the train station on Østre Stationsvej 33, from Rolsted (☎66 17 77 36, ⊛www.rolstedodense.dk; 95kr per day, 500kr per week). For

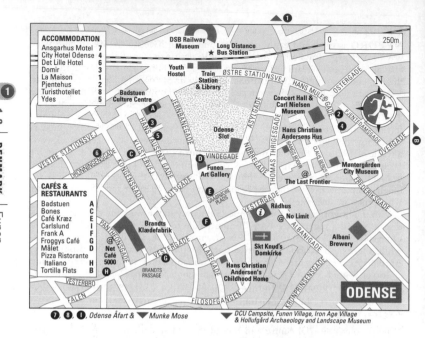

ACCOMMODATION
Ansgarhus Motel 7
City Hotel Odense 4
Det Lille Hotel 6
Domir 3
La Maison 1
Pjentehus 2
Turisthotellet 8
Ydes 5

CAFÉS & RESTAURANTS
Badstuen A
Bones C
Café Kræz E
Carlslund I
Frank A F
Froggys Café G
Målet D
Pizza Ristorante
Italiano H
Tortilla Flats B

7, **8**, **1**, *Odense Åfart &* ▼ *Munke Mose*   ▼ *DCU Campsite, Funen Village, Iron Age Village & Hollufgård Archaeology and Landscape Museum*

Internet access, head for No Limit Cyber Café, Albani Torv 5 (daily noon–midnight, weekends noon–8am; 20kr per hour) or The Last Frontier, Overgade 13 (daily noon–midnight, Sat & Sun 10am–midnight; 25kr per hour). Free access is available at the large local library inside the train station, though you must book in advance on ☎66 14 88 14, extension 4421.

Accommodation

Thanks to Hans Christian Andersen, Odense has a plethora of pricey accommodation, although there are several affordable alternatives, including two central and affordable **B&Bs**, both quite close to the Andersen museums. There are also a couple of **hostels**, as well as a campsite in the city and another on the outskirts.

Hotels

Ansgarhus Motel Kirkegård Allé 19 ☎66 12 88 00, ⊛www.ansgarhus.dk. One of Odense's cheapest options, conveniently located just outside the city centre – it's a 15min walk from the station via Jernbanegade, turning right down Vindersgade. Rooms are sparse but comfortable. ❸

City Hotel Odense Hans Mules Gade 5 ☎66 12 12 58, ⊛www.city-hotel-odense.dk. Bright and sparkling new upmarket option with a prominent yellow facade. Rooms are cosy with en-suite bathrooms. Three mins walk from the train station: continue straight along Østre Stationsvej. ❺

Det Lille Hotel Dronningensgade 5 ☎ & ℡66 12 28 21. Small hotel run by a very friendly proprietor who has done plenty of travelling himself. Rooms are adequate with shared bathrooms. ❸

Hotel Domir Hans Tausens Gade 19 ☎66 12 14 27, ⊛www.domir.dk. Bright, welcoming and of a slightly higher standard than sister hotel *Ydes* further down the street. Rooms all have private baths and come frighteningly clean. ❸

La Maison Billesgade 9 ☎66 13 00 74, ⊛www.lamaison-bb.dk. Good value, with smallish rooms and shared bathrooms; breakfast costs 30kr extra. Rooms are tight and bathrooms are shared. ❶

Pjentehus Pjentedamsgade 14 ☎66 12 15 55, ⊛www.net-bb.dk. Located in the heart of the cobbled section of Odense, this beautifully renovated old house has a garden that guests can use; rooms are adequate, if on the small side. Breakfast costs 35kr extra. ❶

Turisthotellet Gerthasminde 64 ☎66 11 26 92, ⊛www.turist-hotellet.dk. Cosy, Gothic-looking hotel – the small tower houses one of the rooms.

Other rooms aren't spacious, but the rates are reasonable. ❸

Ydes Hans Tausens Gade 11 ☏66 12 11 31, ⊛www.ydes.dk. Cheaper and more basic than sister hotel *Domir* (see above); all rooms have private bathrooms. ❸

Hostels

Odense City Hostel Østre Stationsvej 31 ☏63 11 04 25, ⊛www.cityhostel.dk. New and brightly decorated, and very convenient for to the train station. Good doubles (❷) as well as dorms.

OdenseVandrerhjem Kragsbjergvej 121 ☏66 13 04 25, ⊛www.odense-danhostel.dk. Cheaper than its urban counterpart and also much quieter. Located just outside town; take bus #61 from the train station or cathedral south towards Tornbjerg

or Fraugde and get out along Munkebjergvej at the junction with Vissenbjergvej. Open mid-Feb to Nov.

Campsites

DCU-Camping Odensevej 102 ☏66 11 47 02, ⊛www.camping-odense.dk. The only campsite actually in Odense, near Funen Village, fully equipped with excellent cooking facilities. Take bus #21, #22 or #23 from the Rådhus or train station towards Højby.

Blommenslyst Middelfartvej 494 ☏&☏65 96 76 41. Facilities are pretty basic but the location, just next to a picturesque lake, is lovely. The site is about 10km from Odense; half-hourly buses #830, #831, #832 or #833 from the train station make the journey in 20mins. Open March–Oct.

The Town

Save for three outlying museums which are a bus ride away, Odense is easily explored on foot. There's a lot to be said for simply wandering around the compact **centre** with no particular destination in mind, but you shouldn't pass up the chance to visit the **Hans Christian Andersen** museums – very much what the town is known for – or fail to take in at least one of several absorbing **art collections**. Two other **museums** provide more offbeat fare: one celebrates composer Carl Nielsen – after Andersen, Odense's most famous son – and the other eulogizes Danish railways.

The Hans Christian Andersen museums and around

Odense's showpiece museum is the **Hans Christian Andersens Hus** at Hans Jensen Stræde 37–45 (mid-June to Aug daily 9am–7pm; Sept to mid-June Tues–Sun 10am–4pm; 35kr), set in the house where the writer was born and which he described in *The Fairy Tale of My Life*. Oddly enough, Andersen was only really accepted in his own country towards the end of his life; his real admirers were abroad, which was perhaps why he travelled widely and left Odense at the first opportunity. He wrote novels and a few (best-forgotten) plays, but since his death it's his fairy tales that have gained most renown, partly autobiographical stories (not least *The Ugly Duckling*) that were influenced by *The Arabian Nights*, German folk stories, and the traditional Danish folk tales passed on by inmates of the Odense workhouse where his grandmother looked after the garden.

Few of the less-than-fairy-tale aspects of Andersen's life are touched upon in the museum, which was founded on the centenary of Andersen's birth when Odense first began to cash in on its famous ex-citizen. The son of a hard-up cobbler, Andersen's first home was a single room that doubled as a workshop in what was then one of Odense's slum quarters. It was a rough upbringing: Hans's ill-tempered mother was fifteen years older than his father, whom she married when seven months pregnant with Hans (she also had an illegitimate daughter by another man); his grandfather was insane; and descriptions of his grandmother, often given charge of the young Hans, range from "mildly eccentric" to "a pathological liar".

There's a nagging falseness about some aspects of the collection, but as Andersen was a first-rate hoarder it's stuffed with intriguing items: bits of school reports, his certificate from Copenhagen University, early notes and manuscripts of his books, chunks of furniture, his umbrella, and paraphernalia from his travels, including the piece of rope he carried to facilitate escape from hotel rooms in the event of fire. A separate gallery contains a library of Andersen's works in seventy languages, and headphones for listening to some of his best-known tales as read by the likes of Sir Laurence Olivier. Nearby is a very mixed collection of illustrations and other art inspired by his writing.

The area around the museum, all half-timbered houses and spotlessly clean, car-free cobbled streets, lacks much character; indeed, if Andersen was around he'd hardly recognize the neighbourhood, which is now one of Odense's most expensive. For more realistic local history, head to the **Møntergården City Museum** (Tues–Sun 10am–4pm; 25kr), a few streets away at Overgade 48–50, where there's an engrossing assemblage of artefacts dating from the city's earliest settlements to the Nazi occupation.

There's more, but not much more, about Andersen at Munkemøllestræde 3–5, in the tiny **Hans Christian Andersen's Childhood Home** (mid-June to Aug daily 10am–4pm; Sept to mid-June Tues–Sun 11am–3pm; 10kr), the house where Andersen lived from 1807 to 1819 before moving to Copenhagen, where he spent the rest of his life. More interesting, though, is the nearby **Skt Knud's Domkirke** (April–Oct Mon–Sat 9am–5pm, Sun noon–3pm; Nov–March Mon–Sat 10am–4pm, Sun noon–3pm; ⓦwww.odense-domkirke.dk), whose crypt holds one of the most unusual and ancient finds Denmark has to offer: the **skeleton of Knud II**. Knud was slain in 1086 – by Jutish farmers, angry at the taxes he'd imposed on them – in the original Skt Albani Kirke, the barest remains of which were found some years ago in the city park. The king was laid to rest in the original church in 1101, but the miraculous events of the following years (see "History", p.66) resulted in his canonization as Knud the Holy, and his remains were subsequently moved to the present Domkirke. Close to Knud's is another coffin, thought to hold the remains of his brother Benedict (though some claim them to be St Alban, whose body was brought to Denmark by Knud), while displayed alongside is the fading, but impressive, Byzantine-style silk tapestry sent as a shroud by Knud's widow, Edele.

The cathedral itself is noteworthy, too. Mostly late thirteenth-century, it's the only example of pure Gothic church architecture in the country, set off by a finely detailed sixteenth-century wooden altarpiece that's rightly regarded as one of the greatest works of the Lübeck master-craftsman, Claus Berg.

Odense's art museums

The **Funen Art Gallery** (*Fyns Kunstmuseum*; Tues–Sun 10am–4pm; 25kr), a few minutes' walk from the cathedral at Jernbanegade 13, gives a good idea of the region's importance to Danish art during the late nineteenth century, when a number of Funen-based painters gave up creating portraits of the rich in favour of impressionistic landscapes and studies of the lives of the peasantry. The collection also contains some stirring works by many Nordic greats, among them Vilhelm Hammershøi, P.S. Krøyer, and Michael and Anne Ancher, but most striking of all is H.A. Brendekilde's enormously emotive *Worn Out*. The modern era isn't forgotten, with selections from Asger Jorn, Richard Mortensen and Egill Jacobsen, among many others, drawn from the museum's large collection.

For more modern art, walk along Vestergade and turn down Brandst Passage to reach **Brandts Klædefabrik** (ⓦwww.brandts.dk), a large former textile factory that's now given over to a number of cultural endeavours: three museums, a gallery, an art school, a music library and a cinema, along with cafés and restaurants. The **Art Exhibition Hall** here (July & Aug daily 10am–5pm; Sept–June Tues–Sun 10am–5pm; 30kr) is an increasingly prestigious spot for displays of work by high-flying new talent in art and design; close by are the varied displays of the **Museum of Photographic Art** (same hours; 25kr), taken from the cream of modern (and some not so modern) art photography and almost always worth a look. There's also the more down-to-earth **Danish Museum of Printing** (same hours; ⓦwww.mediemuseum.dk; 25kr), with its bulky machines and devices chronicling the development of printing, bookbinding and illustrating from the Middle Ages to

△ Odense

the present. Further down Brandts Passage on the second floor of no. 27, the **Tidens Samling** ("Time Collection"; daily 10am–5pm; ⊛www.tidenssamling.dk; 25kr) gives a fascinating insight into the development of fashion and housing interiors since the turn of the last century. You can buy a combined ticket for all four exhibits for 50kr.

The Carl Nielsen and railway museums

The **Carl Nielsen Museum**, inside the concert hall at Claus Bergs Gade 11 (June–Aug Tues–Sun noon–4pm; rest of the year Thurs–Sun noon–4pm; 25kr), celebrates the life and work of Odense's second most famous son. Born in a village just outside Odense in 1865, Nielsen displayed prodigious musical gifts from an early age and joined the Odense military band as a cornet player when just 14 (wearing a specially shortened uniform). From there he went to study at the Copenhagen *conservatoire* and then on to gain worldwide acclaim as a composer, for his symphonies particularly, the musical cognoscenti in his own country regarding him as having salvaged Danish music from a period of decline. Despite his travels, and long period of residence in Copenhagen, Nielsen continually praised the inspirational qualities of Funen's nature and the island's tuneful dialect, even writing a somewhat sentimental essay romanticizing the landscape in which "even trees dream and talk in their sleep with a Funen lilt". If you've never heard of Nielsen, be assured that his music is nowhere near as half-baked as his prose: in the museum you can listen to some of his work on headphones, including excerpts from his major pieces and the polka he wrote when still a child. The actual **exhibits**, detailing Nielsen's life and achievements, are further enlivened by the accomplished sculptures of his wife, Anne Marie, many of them early studies for her equestrian statue of Christian IX that now stands outside the Royal Stables in Copenhagen.

The final museum in central Odense is hardly essential viewing unless you've been particularly impressed by the comfort and efficiency of modern Danish trains. The **DSB Railway Museum** (*Jernbanemuseum*; daily 10am–4pm; ⊛www.jernbanemuseum.dk; 40kr, with 25 percent discounts for Adventure Pass, InterRail, Scanrail and Eurail pass holders), immediately behind the station, houses some of the state railways' most treasured artefacts, which include royal and double-decker carriages and the reconstruction of an entire early twentieth-century station, as well as a feast of otherwise forgotten facts pertaining to the rise of Danish railways.

South of Odense

A couple of kilometres south of the city centre on Sejerskovvej, the open-air **Funen Village** museum (April to mid-June & mid-Aug to Oct Tues–Sun 10am–5pm; Nov–March Sun only 11am–3pm; 40kr; mid-June to mid-Aug daily 9.30am–7pm; 55kr) comprises a reconstructed nineteenth-century country village which is lent an air of authenticity by its period gardens and wandering geese. From the farmhouse to the poorhouse, all the buildings are originals from other parts of Funen, their exteriors painstakingly reassembled and interiors carefully refurbished. In summer, the old trades are revived in the former workshops and crafthouses, and there are free shows at the open-air theatre. Though often crowded, the village is well worth a visit – look out, too, for the village-brewed beer, handed out free on special occasions. Buses #21, #22 and #42 run to the village from the city centre (get out at the Den Fynske Landsby sign), or do what the locals do and get on the *Odense Åfart* boat (⊛www.aafart.dk; 32kr single, 48kr return, 25 percent discount with an Adventure Pass), which runs along the canal from Munke Mose park in the city centre and terminates at Funen Village. From June to mid-August, it sails daily on the hour from 10am to 5pm, and from May to mid-August and in September, daily at 11am, noon, 2pm and 5pm. It also stops at **Odense Zoo** (July daily 9am–7pm; May–June & Aug Mon–Fri 9am–6pm, Sat & Sun 9am–7pm; April & Sept–Oct Mon–Fri 9am–5pm, Sat & Sun 9am–6pm; Nov–March daily 9am–4pm; ⊛www.odensezoo.dk; 85kr) on the way.

Also easily reached from the town centre (bus #91 towards Allesø) is the **Funen Prehistoric Museum**, some 5km southeast of the city centre at Store Klaus 40 (July & Aug Mon–Fri & Sun 10am–4pm; Sept–June Mon–Thurs 8.30am–3.30pm, Fri 8.30am–2pm; 20kr), one of many prehistoric collections in Denmark, but one that at least makes an effort to be different. There's a simulated TV news broadcast covering events in Bronze Age Denmark, alongside displays describing how ancient symbols are used in modern times. A bit closer to the centre, and a good stop on the way back is **Hollufgård Archaeology and Landscape Museum** (Feb–March Tues–Sun 10am–4pm; May–Oct Thurs–Sun 10am–4pm; Nov–Jan Sun 10am–4pm; 25kr), devoted to the most important finds on Funen over the past 10,000 years, plus an immense coin collection – from as long ago and as far afield as England under Danelaw and Danish rule in Estonia. The museum occupies several buildings in the grounds of a sixteenth-century manor house, whose enjoyable landscaped **gardens** (open dawn–dusk; free) are decorated with sculptures with students from the Danish Academy of Fine Arts.

Eating and drinking

Most of Odense's **restaurants** and **snack bars** are squeezed into the central part of town, which means there's a lot of competition and potentially some very good bargains during the day. If the weather is right for outdoor eating, pick up a freshly made sandwich from the in-house bakery at *Den Gyldne Ovn*, across the road from the tourist office on Fisketorvet.

Badstuen Østre Stationsvej 26. A stone's throw from the station, this inexpensive café on the upper floor of the cultural centre offers some of the best meal deals in town. The dish of the day costs 35kr and is served promptly between 5pm and 7pm, while salads, sandwiches and burgers go for 15kr throughout the day.
Bones Vindegade 53. Odense's branch of the steak and spare-rib chain. A carnivorous Eldorado.
Café Kræz Gråbrødre Plads 6. Just off Jernbanegade, serving simple, tasty salad, sandwich and soup café fare. Outdoor seating.
Carlslund Fruens Bøge Skov 7 ☎65 91 11 25. Near the Funen Village, this is a typical Danish restaurant (delicious *smørrebrød*) with the bonus

of live jazz on summer Saturdays; call for info.
Frank A Jernbanegade 4. Good café fare and decent full meals a short walk from the train station. Outdoor seating during summer and busy most evenings for after-dinner drinking.
Froggys Café Vestergade 68. Pleasant spot for a cup of coffee and pie or a quick lunch platter.
Målet Jernbanegade 17. Reasonably priced Danish menu, and sports of any sort shown on a big screen.
Pizza Ristorante Italiano Vesterbro 9. Reliable pizzas and pasta at the best and oldest of the city's many pizzerias.
Tortilla Flats Frederiksgade 38. Mexican food at its best: tortillas, burritos and the whole enchilada.

Nightlife and live music

Odense has a plethora of **late-opening cafés** that have usurped the role of night-clubs as evening hangouts. A good first stop is *Café Biografen* at Brandts Klœdefabrik – enduringly fashionable and decorated with a dazzling display of movie posters; from there, move on to *Cuckoo's Nest* next door, which is one of the few spots with any life early in the week. For unpretentious drinking, *Carlsens Kvarter*, Hunderupvej 19, south of the Hans Christian Andersen Childhood Home, is the place for knocking back the Carlsberg; *Ryan's of Odense* at Fisketorvet 12, just north of the Rådhus, is a true Irish pub, with live music on weekends.

If you're in the mood for a gamble, try your luck at the **casino** (daily 7pm–4am; 50kr) in the *SAS Hotel* on Claus Bergs Gade. For details on Odense's **gay and lesbian** scene, contact the Lambda organization. Odense's **live music** scene is also worth investigating; pick up the leaflets spread out at most cafés, music shops and the tourist office for details of upcoming events. *Rytmeposten*, Østre Stationsvej 35 (☎66 13 60 20, ⊛www.rytmeposten.dk), is Funen's prime live music venue, a converted post office where you'll often find heavy rock bands performing. Another busy spot is the radical cultural centre *Badstuen*, just opposite at Østre Stationsvej 26

(☎66 13 48 66, ⊛www.badstuen.dk), which regularly hosts raucous live bands, while *Jazzhus Dexter*, Vindegade 65 (☎63 11 27 28, ⊛www.dexter.dk), offers all types of **jazz**, from swing to fusion, four or five times a week until early morning. There's bluesier fare to be found in the new *Cabarbaret*, Vintapperstræde 39 (☎63 11 01 30, ⊛www.cabarbaret.dk), also featuring the hottest **club scene** during weekends, and easier rock at *Rådhuskælderen*, Vestergade 15–17 (☎66 12 58 08).

Kerteminde and around

A half-hour bus ride (#885 and #890) northeast from Odense, past the huge cranes and construction platforms at Munkebo – until recently a tiny fishing hamlet but now the home of Denmark's biggest shipyard – lies **KERTEMINDE**, itself a place with firm maritime links, originally in fishing and now increasingly in tourism. The town is a centre for sailing and holidaymaking, and can get oppressively busy during the peak weeks of the summer. At any other time of year, though, it makes for a well-spent day, split between the town itself and the Viking-era Ladby Boat just outside.

The heart of Kerteminde, around the fifteenth-century Skt Laurentius Kirke and along Langegade and Strandgade, is a neat and prettily preserved nucleus of shops and houses. Across the road from the bus station, on Margrethes Plads 1, **Fjord & Bæltcentret** (mid-Feb to June & mid-Aug to Nov Mon–Fri 10am–4pm, Sat & Sun 10am–5pm; July to mid-Aug daily 10am–6pm; 70kr; ⊛www.gounderwater.com), a state-of-the-art aquarium with a 50m-long underwater tunnel from where you can observe seals and porpoises in their natural sea environment, is worth a visit. On Strandgade itself, the **town museum** (*Farvergården*; Tues–Sun 10am–4pm; 15kr) has five reconstructed craft workshops and a collection of local fishing equipment. On a grander note, a ten-minute stroll north around the waterfront brings you to the one-time house of the "birdman of Funen", the painter Johannes Larsen, on Møllebakken 14, which has been opened up as the **Johannes Larsen Museum** (June–Aug daily 10am–5pm; March–May, Sept & Oct Tues–Sun 10am–4pm; Nov–Feb Tues–Sun 11am–4pm; 50kr). During the late nineteenth century, Larsen produced etchings of rural landscapes and birdlife, going against the grain of prevailing art world trends in much the same way as the Skagen artists (see p.181). The house is kept as it was when Larsen lived there, with his furnishings and knick-knacks, many of his canvases and, in the dining room, his astonishing wall paintings. To the chagrin of the pious locals, the house became a haunt of the country's more bacchanalian artists and writers in its day, and the garden holds a sculpted female figure by frequent visitor Kai Nielsen. A story goes that during one particularly drunken party the piece was dropped and the legs broke off. Someone called the local *falck* (emergency services), but despite much inebriated pleading, the (sober) officer who rushed to the scene refused to take the sculpture to hospital.

Practicalities

Kerteminde's **tourist office**, opposite the Skt Laurentius Kirke across a small alleyway (mid-June to Aug Mon–Sat 9am–5pm; Sept to mid-June Mon–Fri 9am–4pm, Sat 9.30am–12.30pm; ☎65 32 11 21, ⊛www.kerteminde-turist.dk), has details on Kerteminde's **accommodation** bargains. If you want to stay over at any other time, the only low-cost option is the youth hostel (☎65 32 39 29, ⊛www.danhostel.dk/kerteminde) at Skovvej 46, a twenty-minute walk from the centre (cross the Kerteminde fjord by the road bridge, take the first major road left and then turn almost immediately right to reach it). There's also a **campsite**, *Kerteminde Camping* (☎65 32 19 71, ⊛www.dk-camp.dk; mid-April to mid-Sept), not far from the Larsen museum at Hindsholmvej 80, the main road running along the seafront – a thirty-minute walk from the centre. If you want something more upmarket, try the three-star *Tornøes Hotel*, Standgade 2 (☎65 32 16 05, ⊛www.tornoeshotel.dk; ❺).

Around Kerteminde: the Ladby Boat and Hindsholm Peninsula

About 4km southwest of Kerteminde, along the banks of the fjord at Vikingvej 123, is the **Ladby Boat** (*Ladbyskibet*; June–Aug daily 10am–5pm; March–May & Sept–Oct Tues–Sun 10am–4pm; Nov–Feb Wed–Sun 11am–3pm; 25kr), a vessel dredged up from the fjord that was found to be the burial ship of a Viking chieftain. The 22-metre craft, along with the remains of the weapons, hunting dogs and horses that accompanied the deceased on his journey to Valhalla, is kept in a tiny purpose-built museum. It's an interesting find, but you'll need only half an hour for a close inspection. Bus #482 runs to the museum several times a day from Monday to Friday, but it's more pleasant to rent a bike in town and cycle there.

Cycling is also the best way to explore the **Hindsholm Peninsula**, north of Kerteminde, since it's quite small; if this seems too energetic, the tourist office should have the latest bus schedules. There's not actually much to see, save perhaps the ancient **underground burial chamber** (*Mårhøj Jættestue*) near Martofte, 10km due north of Kerteminde, which is open to the public (though the bodies, of course, are long gone). Outside high season, however, the area becomes an unparalleled spot to pitch a tent and revel in quiet seclusion. There are two **campsites** further into the peninsula: *Bøgebjerg Strand* (☏65 34 10 52, ⊛www.bogebjerg.dk; April to mid-Sept), on the shore opposite the island of Romsø; and, on the northernmost tip just past Nordskov at Fynshovedvej 748, *Fyns Hoved Camping* (☏65 34 10 14, ⊛www.dk-camp.dk).

Southern Funen and the islands

Southern Funen is noted above all for its many miles of sandy beaches, which are packed with tourists during the peak season. In July and August, the **islands** of the southern archipelago are more enticing: connected by an efficient network of ferries, they range from larger chunks of land such as Tåsinge, Langeland and Ærø – the second two certainly worth a few nights' stay – to minute and sparsely populated places like Lyø or Avernakø, which are a pleasure to explore, if only for a few hours. From Odense, the simplest plan is to take a train to Svendborg, the main centre on the south coast, although you might also find the smaller Fåborg a good base; it's an hour's bus ride from Odense (#960, #961 or #962).

Svendborg

A favourite of the Danish yachting fraternity, with marinas clogging the coastline from here to Fåborg, 24km west, **SVENDBORG** exudes a certain gritty charm, with colourful houses lining cobbled lanes dipping down to the water. Svendborg is a pleasant place to plot your travels around the archipelago, and boasts some of the best nightlife in an otherwise very quiet region. While you're there, spend an hour or two meandering around the narrow backstreets, spattered with beautiful bronzes by one of Denmark's best-known sculptors, locally born Kai Nielsen, and head down to the harbourfront to take in the bustling shipyard, packed with beautiful old wooden boats from all over Scandinavia and the Baltic.

Before heading off to the islands, a couple of historical collections might occupy a bit of your time. The **County Museum** (*Viebæltegård*; May–Oct daily 10am–5pm; Nov–April closed Sat & Sun; ⊛www.svendborgmuseum.dk; 25kr), located in the town's old poorhouse at Grubbemøllevej 13, has the usual regional collections as well as well-preserved finds from a Franciscan monastery, while on Fruenstræde 3, the beautiful **Anne Hvides Gård** (June–Sept daily 10am–5pm; 20kr) is Svendborg's oldest secular building (dating from the sixteenth century), and now holds a museum displaying local artefacts alongside changing worldwide cultural exhibits. More entertaining is the **L. Lange & Co. Stove Museum** (10kr), Vestergade 45, an eccentric horde of cookers and burners produced by a Svendborg-based firm from 1850 to 1984. It opens on request only; contact the County Museum.

The Helge steamer

Between mid-May and October, the *Helge* steamer (built in 1924) leaves Svendborg three to five times daily for the island of **Tåsinge**, calling at Vindebyøre, Svendborg's extension just across the Svendborg Sund; Christiansminde, a beach resort next to Svendborg's exclusive marina; the thatched village of Troense, criss-crossed by quiet streets of carefully preserved houses; Grasten, on the small islands of Thurø and a few minutes' walk from a breach campsite; and the seventeenth-century Valdemar's Slot. The return sailing time is two hours, and **tickets** (65kr round-trip from the harbour; information on ☏62 21 09 80) are good for one stop-off along the way.

The *Helge*'s last stop is the best: **Valdemar's Slot** (ⓦwww.valdemarsslot.dk), an imposing pile with Baroque interiors begun by Christian IV and continued by his son, Valdemar, who died before taking up residence. Filled with three centuries of furniture, paintings and tapestries, the castle serves as a **museum** (May–Aug daily 10am–5pm; Sept Tues–Sun 10am–5pm; Oct–April Sat & Sun 10am–5pm; 55kr). Outside, the castle's two wings hold a **yachting museum** (same hours; 25kr, 75kr for a joint ticket with the castle), with a number of finely crafted wooden yachts on display, and a **Toy Museum** (*Legetøjsmuseet*; same hours; 35kr, 85kr for joint ticket with castle, 105kr for all three), with a collection that should appeal to kids and adults alike. While you're waiting for the *Helge* to carry you back to Svendborg, have a snack at the *Æblehaven Kiosk* just outside the castle, or go for a full-on meal at the exclusive *Restaurant Valdemars Slot* in the castle cellars. The restaurant's former tea pavilion, at the end of the courtyard, is no longer open, but the views out to the long, narrow island of Langeland from there are still great.

Should you want to stay over on Tåsinge, there are four **campsites** on the island; most convenient for the steamer and with access to a beautiful beach is *Vindebyøre Camping* (☏62 22 54 25, ⓦwww.vindebyoere.dk). Tåsinge also houses a couple of **hotels**: the cosy *Det Lille* (☏62 22 53 41, ⓦwww.detlillehotel.dk; ❸) and the better *Hotel Troense* (☏62 22 54 12, ⓦwww.hoteltroense.dk; ❺) – both in Troense.

Practicalities

The Lange company's former foundry, next door to the Lange museum at Vestergade 45, is now the town's **youth hostel** (☏62 21 66 99, ⓦwww.danhostel -svendborg.dk), which has dorms and doubles (❷). Otherwise, there's the pricey *Hotel Svendborg*, Centrumpladsen 1 (☏62 21 17 00, ⓦwww.hotel-svendborg.dk; ❻), or, via a five-minute bus ride from the centre along the coast (#202), the reasonably priced *Stella Maris Missionhotel* (☏62 21 38 91, ⓦwww.stellamaris.dk; ❸). The **tourist office** (mid-June to Aug Mon–Fri 9.30am–6pm, Sat 9.30am–3pm; Sept to mid-June Mon–Fri 9am–5pm, Sat 9.30–12.30am; ☏62 21 09 80, ⓦwww.svendborg .dk), next door to the *Hotel Svendborg* at Centrumpladsen 4, can provide details of other accommodation, including private rooms (from 300kr per night) and numerous local **campsites**, as well as the latest ferry timetables.

For **food**, don't miss the sublime, good-value fast food at *Jette's Diner* on Kullinggade 1, and the traditional Danish sailors' fare on offer at *Restaurant Svendborgsund*, Havnepladsen 5 – try the *stegt flæsk* (fried pork and potatoes in parsley sauce). The nightlife, such as it is, usually starts at café-bar *Under Uret*, Gerritsgade 50, and continues on to *Café Citronen*, Brogade 33, or *Standlyst*, Brogade 5, both of which have live music and all-night dancing at weekends.

Fåborg

An alternative base for the south coast, **FÅBORG** is a likeably small and sedate place, rarely as overwhelmed by holidaymakers as Svendborg and with equally good connections to the archipelago (ferries sail to Søby on Ærø, and to Lyø and Avernakø). If you've an interest in Danish art, the town's other big attraction is the **Fåborg Museum** at Grønnegade 75 (June–Aug daily 10am–5pm; April, May, Sept

& Oct daily 10am–4pm; Nov–March Tues–Sun 11am–3pm; ⓦwww.faaborgmuseum
.dk; 35kr). The museum opened in 1910 and quickly became the major showcase
for the **Funen artists**, particularly the work of Fritz Syberg and Peter Hansen,
both of whom studied under the influential Kristian Zahrtmann in Copenhagen
and typically filled their canvases with richly coloured depictions of Funen
landscapes. Apart from the chance to admire the skills of the painters, the works
demonstrate how little the Funen countryside has changed since they were painted
the best part of a century ago.

Almost next door to the museum at Grønnegade 72–73 is one of the country's
quaintest **youth hostels** (ⓣ62 61 12 03, ⓦwww.danhostel.dk/faaborg; April–Oct),
with dorm beds and eighteen inexpensive double rooms (❶). There's a **campsite** at
Odensevej 140 (ⓣ62 61 77 94), half a mile north of town, and a number of other
camping areas on the beach as well. The bare-bones *Hotel Færgegården*, Chr. d IX's
Vej 31 (ⓣ62 61 11 15, ⓦwww.hotelfg.dk; ❺) is the cheapest in town, while outside
Fåborg, in the neighbouring village of Astrup, lies the simple *Mosegaard Inn*,
Nabgyden 31 (ⓣ62 61 56 91, ⓦwww.hotelmosegaard.dk; ❹). The **tourist office** at
Banegårdspladsen 2A (May–Sept Mon–Sat 9am–5pm; Oct–April Mon–Sat
10am–5pm; ⓣ62 61 07 07, ⓦwww.visitfaaborg.dk) can help with a list of inexpen-
sive **private rooms** (❷) and local travel information.

For **food**, splash out and try the fish restaurant *Ved Brønden*, at Torvet 5, or the
traditional Danish *Restaurant Tre Kroner*, Strandgade 1. Otherwise, there's a plethora
of pizza places, and you can stock up on provisions at the Super Brugsen or Føtex
markets, which are next to each other on Mellemgade near the bus station.

Around Fåborg: Egeskov Castle and the smaller islands

In Kværndrup, just ten minutes from Fåborg by bus, is the Renaissance castle
Egeskov Slot ("Oak-forest Castle"). You're allowed in (daily: July 10am–8pm; June
& Aug 10am–6pm; May & Sept 10am–5pm; ⓦwww.egeskov.dk; 130kr), though it's
really more impressive from the outside, and the price of entry is rather steep. Far
better is to head for the adjacent **Egeskov Veteranmuseum** (same hours; 75kr),
where there are displays of around three hundred antique cars; the entry price also
gets you into the castle **gardens**, which include an intricate bamboo maze designed
by Danish designer-cum-philosopher-cum-poet Peit Heim, award-winning rose
garden and a romantic water garden surrounded by azaleas and rhododendrons.

If you're looking for some quiet, it's easy enough to visit one of the three small
islands of **Bjørnø**, **Lyø** and **Avernakø**. All are connected with Fåborg by small ferries (at least 5 daily; journey time 10–20min; information on ⓣ62 61 23 07,
ⓦwww.oe-faergen.dk). There's not much to do on the islands apart from walking
in the beautiful countryside: rolling hills and fine sandy beaches abound. If you
want to **stay** overnight, contact the tourist office in Fåborg (see above), which can
arrange stays with local families for around 150kr per person per night.

Langeland

The largest of the southern islands, long, thin and fertile **Langeland** is just off the
southeast coast of Funen, to which it's connected by road bridge (hence you don't
need to catch a ferry to reach it). Frequent buses make the half-hour journey from
Svendborg to **RUDKØBING**, the main town, from where there are ferry links to
Marstal on Ærø; there's also a ferry to Tårs on Lolland (see p.127), leaving from
Spodsbjerg, about 6km to the east. Rudkøbing in itself doesn't have a lot to offer
except for a pleasant fishing harbour and the historical collection in the
Langelands Museum at Jens Winthersvej 12 (Mon–Thurs 10am–4pm, Fri
10am–1pm; 20kr). The town's **tourist office**, at Torvet 5 (mid-June to Aug
Mon–Sat 9am–5pm; Sept to mid-June Mon–Fri 9.30am–4.30pm, Sat
9.30am–12.30pm; ⓣ62 51 35 05, ⓦwww.langeland.dk), can provide advice on
accommodation; alternatively, head for the low yellow **youth hostel** at
Engdraget 11 (ⓣ62 51 18 30, ⓦwww.danhostel.dk/rudkobing), which has dorms

and doubles (**②**); or one of the island's seven **campsites**. The two best are at Spodsbjergvej 335 (☎62 50 11 36, ⓦwww.spodsbjerg.dk) and no. 182 (☎62 50 10 06, ⓦwww.billevaenge-camping.dk). **Hotel** choices include the budget *Spodsbjergvej Badehotel* at Spodsbjergvej 317 (☎ & ☎62 50 10 64; **③**) and the better-located, if more expensive, *Rudkøbing Skudehavn*, on the harbour at Havnegade 21 (☎62 51 46 00, ⓦwww.sitecenter.dk/skudehavnen; **⑤**).

North of Rudkøbing, Langeland consists mostly of farmland and the occasional village, with just one sight to head for: the fairy-tale thirteenth-century **Tranekær Slot**, approximately 7km north of Rudkøbing and surrounded by a beautiful park dotted with sculptures made from natural materials. There's a **museum** (June to mid-Sept Mon–Fri 10am–5pm, Sat & Sun 1–5pm; 20kr) in the old water mill opposite, covering the history of Tranekær village and its castle. To find the island's best **beaches**, head 15km southwest of Rudkøbing to **Ristinge**, one of the loveliest in the country, or make for the southern coast, where there are also a couple of **bird sanctuaries**, Gulstav Mose and Tryggelev Nor. Local buses serve all the main sites on the island.

Ærø

For a more varied few days, take the ferry from Svendborg or Rudkøbing to **Ærø**, a pretty island just north of the coast of Germany. Although getting here can require the better part of a day, it's worth the effort for the island's ancient burial sites, abundant stretches of sandy beach, traditional farms and, in the principal town of **Ærøskøbing**, a peach of a medieval merchants' town.

Ærøskøbing

When passing shipping brought prosperity to Ærø in the nineteenth century, the island historically split into three divisions: fisherfolk resided on the windy western tip at Søby; the wealthy shipping magnates and captains resided in Marstal, to the east; while the local middle classes collected in the town of **ÆRØSKØBING**. The narrow streets, lined with tidy houses, are made for wandering – look out for the oldest building, dating from 1645, at Søndergade 36. If it's raining, you could drop in to see the eye-catching **Bottle Ship Collection** (April to mid-Sept daily 10am–5pm; mid-Sept to mid-Oct daily 10am–4pm; mid-Oct to March Tues–Fri 1–3pm, Sat 11am–1pm, Sun 10am–noon; 25kr) at Smedegade 22, or **Hammerichs House** at Gyden 22 (mid-June to mid-Sept daily noon–4pm; 20kr), a riot of woodcarvings, furnishings and timepieces from bygone days.

Ærøskøbing's **tourist office** (mid-June to Aug Mon–Fri 9am–5pm, Sat 9am–2pm, Sun 9.30am–12.30pm; Sept–May Mon–Fri 9am–4pm, Sat 9am–12.30pm; ☎62 52 13 00, ⓦwww.aeroe-turistbureau.dk), on Vestergade 1, can give information on the island's burial places and other secluded spots. As for **accommodation**, there's a terrific youth hostel with ocean views, friendly management and some doubles (**①**) at Smedevejen 15 (☎62 52 10 44, ⓦwww.vandrerhjem-aeroe.dk; April–Sept), about 2km west of the ferry dock on the road to Marstal. There's also *Ærøskøbing Camping* campsite at Sygehusvej 40B (☎62 52 18 54, ⓦwww.aeroe.dk; May–Sept), appealingly sited next to the beach. A local bus serves the island's main roads, but the best way to get around is by **bike**, though you'll need to pedal hard to get up some of the hills; the tourist office supplies free bike maps to help plan your route, and cycles can be rented for 50kr a day at Pilebækkens Cykelservice (☎62 52 11 10), a gas station out on Marstal road about 200m west of the main marketplace.

Eating options include *Det Lille Hotel*'s good Danish restaurant at Smedegade 33 (☎62 52 23 00) and the popular *Café Lille Claus*, a burger and fried-fish joint close by the ferry landing. There are fancier places along the main street, often stuffed with vacationing Germans. For provisions, there are two small supermarkets, Spar and Merko, in the town centre, and a good little bakery, *Ærøskøbing Bageri*, on Vestergade 62. When getting on or off the Svendborg ferry, be sure to look in on the little smoked-fish place, *Ærøskøbing Røgeri*, facing the water at Havnen 15 – the fish is outstanding.

Nightlife is pretty much limited to the *Strandskoven* bar by the water and the *Arrebo* pub at Vestergade 4, which sometimes hosts live music acts. Summertime brings the occasional open-air concert to the streets of town, too.

Marstal and beyond

If you're looking to escape the tourists, then **MARSTAL**, at the east end of the island and reached by bus from Ærøskøbing (or ferry from Rudkøbing in Langeland), is a good alternative base. Once there, don't miss the superb **Marstal Søfartsmuseum** (July daily 9am–8pm; June & Aug daily 9am–5pm; May & Sept daily 10am–4pm; Oct–April Tues–Fri 10am–4pm, Sat 11am–3pm; ⓦwww.marstal -maritime-museum.dk; 35kr), a collection of maritime paintings and ship models from Marstal's nineteenth-century golden age, when it was one of the busiest harbours in Denmark.

Most people staying here sleep on yachts or in holiday-home rentals, but there are a few budget options including the **youth hostel** at Færgestræde 29 (☎63 52 63 58, ⓦwww.danhostel.dk/marstal; May–Aug), which has doubles (❶) and is conveniently close to the town centre and the harbour, and a **campsite**, *Marstal Camping* (☎63 52 63 69, ⓦwww.marstalcamping.dk; May–Oct), almost on the beach and with cabins, too. The nicest reasonably priced choice (rooms have shared bathrooms) is the small *Hotel Marstal* (☎62 53 13 52; ❸) at Dronningestræde 1A near the harbour. For local information, contact the **tourist office** (mid-June to Aug Mon–Fri 9am–5pm, Sat 9am–2pm, Sun 9.30am–12.30pm; rest of year Mon–Fri 9am–4pm, Sat 9am–12.30pm; ☎62 52 21 00. ⓦwww.langeland.com) on Havnegade 5, near the youth hostel. **Bikes** can be rented at Nørremark Cykelforretning, Møllevejen 77 (☎62 53 14 77) for 50kr per day.

The **rest of the island** is speckled with fine inns (*kros*) and working farms such as *Graasten Farmhouse*, half way between Ærøskøbing and Marstal (☎62 52 24 25; ❷), and the handsome *Vindeballe Kro* (☎62 52 16 13, 2) at the centre of the island in Vindeballe, simple but with a good restaurant and bar downstairs.

Travel details

Trains

Odense to: Århus (35 daily; 1hr 35min); Copenhagen (55 daily; 1hr 30min); Esbjerg (10 daily; 1hr 20min); Nyborg (40 daily; 15min); Svendborg (20 daily; 54min).

Buses

Kerteminde to: Nyborg (25 daily; 34min).
Odense to: Fåborg (40 daily; 58min–1hr 13min); Kerteminde (44 daily; 40min); Nyborg (39 daily; 52min); Svendborg (14 daily; 51min).
Rudkøbing to: Lohals (25 daily; 41min); Spodsbjerg (14 daily; 9min); Svendborg (53 daily; 25min).
Svendborg to: Fåborg (42 daily; 42min); Rudkøbing (53 daily; 25min); Nyborg (43 daily; 44min).

South coast ferries

Ferry connections are plentiful around the south coast archipelago and it's best to check the fine details locally. Some sailings continue all year, others only operate during the summer. One-way fares are 45–75kr per person. Frequencies given below are for weekdays; sailings are often reduced on weekends and public holidays.

Bøjden to: Fynshav (6–7 daily; 50min).
Søby to: Mommark (2–5 daily; 1hr).
Fåborg to: Lyø (2–4 daily via Avernakø; 1hr); Søby (3–6 daily; 1hr).
Marstal to: Rudkøbing (3–6 daily; 1hr).
Spodsbjerg to: Tårs (10–22 daily; 45min).
Svendborg to: Ærøskøbing (3–6 daily; 1hr 15min); Drejø (4–5 daily via Skarø; 1hr 15min).

International trains

Odense to: Hamburg (1 daily; 4hr 10min).

1.3

Jutland

Long ago, the people of **Jutland** (*Jylland*), the Jutes – pronounced "yutes" – were a quite separate tribe from the more warlike Danes who occupied the eastern islands. In pagan times, the peninsula had its own rulers and wielded considerable power, and it was here that the legendary ninth-century monarch Harald Bluetooth began the process that turned the two tribes into a unified Christian nation. By the dawn of the Viking era, however, the Danes had spread west, absorbing the Jutes, and real power in Denmark gradually shifted towards Zealand.

This is where it has largely stayed, making unhurried lifestyles and rural calm (except for a couple of very likeable cities) the overriding impression of Jutland. This is a friendly land, populated by locals who seem to relish their position outside the national spotlight. Yet there's much to enjoy in the unspoilt towns and villages, and Jutland's comparatively large size and distance from Copenhagen make it perhaps the most distinctive and interesting area in the country.

There are also more regional variations in Jutland than you'll find elsewhere in Denmark. **South Jutland** is a territory long battled over by Denmark and Germany, though beyond the immaculately restored town of **Ribe** it holds little of abiding interest. Further north, **Esbjerg** gives easy access to the windswept beaches on the western coast as well as the hills, meadows and woodlands of eastern Jutland, and to some of the peninsula's better-known sights – from the old military stronghold of **Fredericia** and the ancient runic stones at **Jelling** to the modern bricks of **Legoland**.

Århus, halfway up the eastern coast, is Jutland's main urban centre and Denmark's second city, and here, besides a wealth of history and cultural pursuits, you'll encounter the region's best nightlife. Just to the east, **Djursland** – the peninsula known as Denmark's nose – attracts thousands of visitors every year to its rolling hills and sandy beaches, the result of moraine formations after the last Ice Age. Århus is handy, too, for the optimistically titled **Lake District**, a small but appealing area between Skanderborg and **Silkeborg**. Further inland, the retreat of the ice sheets during the Ice Age left another terrain of sharp contrasts: stark heather-clad moors break suddenly into dense forests with swooping gorges and wide rivers – contrasts epitomized by the wild moorland at **Kongenshus** and the grassy vistas of **Hald Ege**. Ancient **Viborg** is a better base for seeing all this than dour **Randers**, and from here you can head north, either to the blustery beaches of **Limfjordslandet** or to old and vibrant **Aalborg**, which sits on the southern bank of the Limfjorden, a massive fjord that cuts through northern Jutland from Hals on the east coast to Thyborøn on the west coast, leaving the area north of the fjord separated from mainland Jutland

North of the Limfjorden, you'll get a taste of Jutland at its most dramatic: a sandy semi-wilderness stretching north to **Skagen**, at the very tip of the peninsula. **Frederikshavn**, on the way, is the port for boats to Norway and Sweden, and is usually full of those countries' nationals stocking up with (what is for them) cheap liquor.

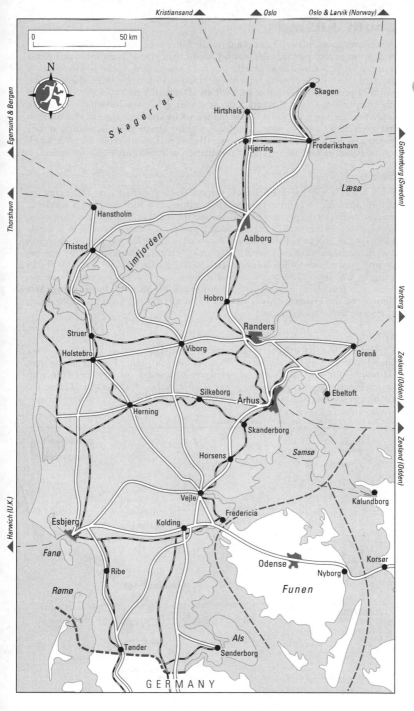

South Jutland

Best known as an entry and exit point (to the UK by sea and air, to Germany overland), more people pass through **south Jutland** than probably any other part of the country. Though many head straight out for Copenhagen or the holiday areas of the west coast, it's becoming increasingly popular to linger a little. The engaging and well-preserved medieval town of **Ribe**, Denmark's most visited conurbation after Copenhagen, is well worth a day's wander, while the beautiful coastline of sandy beaches and windswept dunes, backed up by some great seafood restaurants and a wonderful array of summer cottages, rightly attracts German tourists in their thousands. With the advent of **budget flights** to Esbjerg from London, south Jutland is also gaining something of a reputation as a weekend-break destination.

Esbjerg

South Jutland's only city is **ESBJERG** – and if this is your first view of the country, bear in mind it's an entirely untypical one. Esbjerg is a baby by Danish standards: purpose-built as a deep-water harbour during the nineteenth century, it went on to become one of the world's biggest fishing ports. Nowadays, it's used as a supply point for the North Sea oil industry and holds a large fish-oil factory, though it does maintain an air of its original Victorian-era charm, and handsome townhouses abound. Since both DFDS Seaways ferries and regular Ryanair and BMI flights from the UK arrive here, you may find yourself staying for a few days. If you do, there are a few places worth a nose, most notably the **Esbjerg Performing Arts Centre** and the **Fisheries Museum**. The town also makes a great base from which to explore the surrounding area.

Arrival, information and accommodation

The Esbjerg **tourist office**, at Skolegade 33 (mid-June to Aug Mon 10am–5pm, Tues–Fri 9am–6pm, Sat 9.30am–6.30pm; Sept to mid-June Mon–Fri 10am–5pm, Sat 10am–1pm; ☎75 12 55 99, ⊛www.esbjerg-tourist.dk), on a corner of the main square, Torvet, can give you all the practical information you might need, as well as a leaflet describing a short, self-guided walking tour of the city's early twentieth-

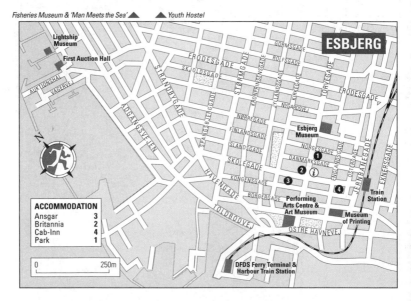

century buildings. The **passenger harbour** is a well-signposted ten-minute walk from the city centre, and trains to and from Copenhagen connect directly with the ferries at the **harbour train station**. Otherwise, there are frequent departures to all Danish cities from the **main train station** on Skolegade. Esbjerg **airport** is 9km south of the town centre. Buses (no number, marked "airport") leave every twenty minutes to and from the train station and cost 20kr one-way.

If you're staying, the tourist office can help in finding bed and breakfast-type **accommodation**; otherwise you'll find the cheapest good hotel is the twin-towered *Cab-Inn*, Skolegade 14 (☎75 18 16 00, ⓦwww.cabinn.dk; ❹), renovated into a mixture of simple, inexpensive cabin-style rooms and more traditional hotel accommodation. Another low-price option is the basic *Park Hotel* at Torvegade 31 (☎75 12 08 68, ☎75 13 56 99; ❹), while the central *Ansgar*, Skolegade 36 (☎75 12 82 44, ⓦwww.hotelansgar.dk; ❺), is a little more upmarket. The excellent *Britannia* on Torvet (☎75 13 01 11, ☎75 45 20 85, ⓦwww.britannia.dk; ❻) has furniture created by Danish design legend Arne Jacobsen in each room – stylish Swan chairs and sofas – as well as reductions of up to fifty percent on weekend packages. The **youth hostel**, which has some doubles (❸), is at Gammel Vardevej 80 (☎75 12 42 58, ⓦwww.danhostel.dk/esbjerg; closed Dec & Jan), 25 minutes' walk north of the city centre, or take a bus (#1, #4, #12, #40 or #41) from Skolegade. There's a well-equipped **campsite** with cabins, *Ådalens Camping*, at Gudenåvej 20 (☎75 15 88 22, ⓦwww.adal.dk), 6km north of the city towards Hjerting and reached by bus #1 from Skolegade.

The Town

The best way to get a sense of the city's newness is by dropping into the **Esbjerg Museum** (June–Aug daily 10am–4pm; Sept–May Tues–Sun 10am–4pm; ⓦwww.esbjergmuseum.dk; 30kr) at Torvegade 45, where the meatiest of the few displays recalls the so-called "American period" of the 1890s, when Esbjerg's rapid growth matched that of the US goldrush towns – albeit that the masses came here in search of herring, rather than gold. Also within easy reach of the centre is the **Esbjerg Performing Arts Centre**, Havnegade 20 (☎76 10 90 10, ⓦwww.mhe.dk), which houses various concert halls and exhibition areas, including the **Museum of Art** (daily 10am–4pm; 30kr), a modest collection of contemporary pieces of which the highlight is huge steel plates splattered in the blood of their creator, Danish *enfant terrible* Christian Lemmerz. The centre as a whole is one of Denmark's more groundbreaking cultural institutes and in recent times has exhibited – to much hand-wringing – Lemmerz's gory collection of dead pigs, and a forum on sex and pornography. The building itself is also something of an attraction, designed under the direction of Jorn Utzon, the architect responsible for the Sydney Opera House. A fascinating piece of modern architecture, it resembles a giant concrete tomb surrounded by massive white flowers. Less diverting is the nearby **Museum of Printing** (*Bogtrykmuseet*; June to mid-Sept daily noon–4pm; mid-Sept to May Tues–Fri noon–4pm; 15kr), at Borgergade 6, just off the pedestrianized strip of Kongensgade, which has an entertaining assortment of hand-, foot- and steam-operated presses, as well as more recent – and still functioning – printing machines.

If the Arts Centre has left you in the mood for more aesthetic appreciation, take a bus (#1, #6 or #8 from Skolegade) out along the coastal road until you arrive at the four 9m-high ghostly figures known as the **Man Meets the Sea**. Put in place in 1995 by artist Sven Wiig Hansen, this bizarre piece of public art reflects on Esbjerg's relationship to the sea and provides an excellent photo opportunity. Just around the corner is the wonderful **Fisheries and Maritime Museum and Sealarium** on Tarphagevej (daily: July–Aug 10am–6pm; Sept–May 10am–5pm; ⓦwww.fimus.dk; 70kr), where you can cast an eye over the old boats and other vestiges of the early Esbjerg fishing fleet. This is an excellent place to take the kids, not least because of the adjoining Sealarium, part of a seal research centre (feeding times

11am and 2.30pm). Some dark and spooky German wartime bunkers and an old working port – rebuilt brick by brick – make up the rest of this engaging museum.

With an hour to kill before your boat leaves, nip around the harbour to the **Lightship Museum** (May–Sept daily 10am–4pm; 20kr), which gives a vivid impression of the North Sea lightshipman's lot.

Eating, drinking and nightlife

Esbjerg's **eating** options are fairly limited if you're on a tight budget, though the usual run of hot-dog grills and bakeries is scattered throughout the town. You can get a decent two-course lunch for around 65kr at the *Park Hotel*, Torvegade 31. For traditional Danish food – and service – try *Sands*, Skolegade 60 (closed Sun). More expensively, for around 180kr you can sample Esbjerg-style *nouvelle cuisine* (basically well-prepared fresh fish with everything) at *Pakhuset*, Dokvej 3, in the dock area. A good place for lunch or an early-evening beer or coffee is the popular *Café Christian IX*, overlooking Torvet and named after the monarch commemorated by the square's equestrian statue – they sometimes have live music at weekends. Also decent value at lunchtime are the dependable chain restaurants *Jensens Bøfhus*, on Kongensgade, for steak; and *Den Grimme Ælling* ("The Ugly Duckling"), Kirkegade 21, which usually has lunch specials.

Nightlife in Esbjerg is geared to the thousands of sailors who pass through this busy port town. There are a run of strip bars on Skolegade, but these can get quite rowdy and aren't recommended for the fainthearted. If you've just arrived from Britain and want to make a more gentle transition to Danish culture (and prices), sip a beer or two at one of the town's pubs, such as the English-style *You'll Never Walk Alone*, Kongensgade 10, or the equally sedate *Kasket-Karl*, Skolegade 17 – the latter shares premises with the livelier *John Wayne Saloon* dance club, which attracts a younger crowd.

Around Esbjerg: Fanø

From Esbjerg it's a straightforward fifteen-minute ferry trip to **Fanø**, a long, flat island with superb beaches that draw German holidaymakers in droves during the summer. Scandlines ferries (℡33 15 15 15, ✆www.scandlines.dk; 12min; 30kr return) run frequently between Esbjerg and the island's main village, **Nordby**, where the **tourist office** at the harbour (June–Aug Mon–Fri 8.30am–6pm, Sat 8am–7pm, Sun 10am–5pm; Sept–May Mon–Fri 8.30am–5.30pm, Sat 9am–1pm; ℡75 16 26 00, ✆www.fanoeturistbureau.dk) can provide information on accommodation and the few sights (a couple of fairly ordinary local museums and a windmill). There are eight **campsites**, of which the best is *Feldberg Familie Camping* (℡75 16 36 80), almost on the beach.

Ribe

Just over half an hour by train south from Esbjerg lies the exquisitely preserved town of **RIBE**. In 856 Ansgar built one of the first Danish churches here as a base for his missionaries arriving from Germany; a hundred years later the town was a major staging post for pilgrims making their way south to Rome. Ribe's proximity to the sea allowed it to evolve into a significant trading port, but continued expansion was thwarted by the dual blows of the Reformation and the sanding-up of the harbour. Since then, not much appears to have changed. The surrounding marshlands, which have prevented the development of any large-scale industry, and a long-standing conservation programme have enabled Ribe to keep the appearance and size of medieval times, and its old town is a delight to wander in.

The Town

From Ribe's train station, Dagmarsgade cuts a straight path to Torvet and the **Domkirke** (June–Aug Mon–Sat 10am–6pm, Sun noon–5pm; May & Sept Mon–Sat 10am–5pm, Sun noon–5pm; Oct–April Mon–Sat 11am–4pm, Sun noon–4pm; 12kr), which towers above the town and dominates the wetlands for miles around. A sequel to Ansgar's original church, the cathedral was begun around 1150 using tufa – a suitably light material for the marshy base – brought, along with some of the Rhineland's architectural styles, by river from southern Germany.

Originally raised on a slight hill, the cathedral is now a couple of metres below the surrounding streets, their level having risen due to the many centuries' worth of debris accumulated beneath them. The **interior** is not as spectacular as the cathedral's size and long history might suggest, having been stripped of much of its decoration by Hans Tausen, Bishop of Ribe, during the mid-sixteenth century. The thirteenth-century "Cat's Head Door" on the south side, a good example of the imported Romanesque design, is one of the few early decorative remains. More recent additions that catch the eye are the butcher's-slab altar and the frescoes and mosaics by Carl-Henning Pedersen, added in the mid-1980s. After looking around, climb the 248 steps to peer out from the top of the red-brick **Citizens' Tower**, so named since it doesn't belong to the church but to the people whose taxes pay for its upkeep. The tower's predecessor toppled into the nave on Christmas morning, 1283.

Heading away from the cathedral along Overdammen, you cross three streams, channelled at around 1250 to provide water for a mill. The houses on the right are the best of Ribe's many half-timbered structures; one of them, **Quedens Gaard**, at the corner of Sortebrødregade, is now a museum (June–Aug daily 10am–5pm; March–May, Sept & Oct Tues–Sun 11am–3pm; Nov–Feb Tues–Sun 11am–1pm; 10kr), with sixteenth-century interiors and displays on medieval Ribe. Turn left off Overdammen and walk along the riverside Skibbroen and you'll spot the **Flood Column** (*Stormflodssøjlen*), a stout wooden pole showing the levels of the numerous floods that plagued the town before protective dykes were built a century ago.

Continuing along Overdammen, Skt Nicolaj Gade cuts right to **Ribe Art Gallery** (mid-June to Aug daily 11am–5pm; Sept to mid-June Tues–Sat 1–4pm, Sun 11am–4pm; 30kr), housing a reasonable display of works by Danish artists in a chronological progression that takes you from noble portraiture through pre-Raphaelite aestheticism to modern verism. On the first floor the highlight is *The Christening*, by Skagen painter Michael Ancher (see p.181). A handful of accomplished bronze sculptures is supplemented by larger pieces on the back lawn, from where paths and footbridges lead back across the river to the town centre.

Ribe has recently gained a couple of museums celebrating the town's Viking era. The **Ribes Vikinger** (July & Aug daily 10am–6pm, Wed until 9pm; April–June, Sept & Oct daily 10am–4pm; Nov–March Tues–Sun 10am–4pm; ⓦwww .ribesvikinger.dk; 50kr), opposite the train station, displays locally excavated

The Nightwatchman of Ribe

At 10pm every evening between May and mid-September – and also at 8pm from June to August – the **Nightwatchman of Ribe** emerges from the bar of the *Weis' Stue* inn, Torvet 2, and makes his rounds. Before the advent of gas lighting, a nightwatchman would patrol every town in Denmark to help keep the sleeping populace safe from fire and flood. The last real nightwatchman of Ribe made his final tour in 1902, but thanks to the early development of tourism in the town, the custom had been reintroduced by 1932.

Dressed in a replica of the original uniform and carrying an original morning-star pike and lantern (the sharp tip doubling as a weapon), the watchman – a role filled for the last 26 years by octogenarian Aage Gran – walks the narrow alleys of Ribe singing songs written by Thomas Kingo (a local priest who lived in Ribe in the mid-eighteenth century), and talking about the town's history while stopping at points of interest. One song tells people to go to bed and to be careful with lighting fires – sensible advice when most of the town's dwellings are built from wood. It's obviously laid on for the tourists, but the tour is free and good fun.

remains, along with a full-size reconstructed Viking ship. If you've not had your fill, head for the **Ribe Vikinge Centre** (July & Aug daily 11am–4.30pm; May, June & Sept Mon–Fri 11am–4pm; ☻www.ribevikingecenter.dk; 50kr), 3km south of the centre on Lystrupvej, which attempts to re-create the Viking lifestyle, with costumed attendants demonstrating traditional Viking crafts.

That's more or less all there is to Ribe, save for the paltry remains of **Ribehus Slotsbanke**, a twenty-minute walk away on the northern side of the town. The twelfth-century castle that stood here was a popular haunt with Danish royalty for a couple of centuries but was already fairly dilapidated when it was demolished by Swedish bombardment in the mid-seventeenth century. The **statue** of Queen Dagmar, a recent addition to the site and standing in bewitching isolation, is the only visible reward for the trek out here.

Practicalities

Besides the usual services, the **tourist office** (July & Aug Mon–Fri 9.30am–5.30pm, Sat 10am–5pm, Sun 10am–2pm; April–June, Sept & Oct Mon–Fri 9am–5pm, Sat 10am–2pm; Nov–March Mon–Fri 9.30am–4.30pm, Sat 10am–1pm; ☎75 42 15 00, ☻www.ribetourist.dk), across the road to the rear of the cathedral, offers the free *Denmark's Oldest Town* leaflet, a useful aid to self-guided exploration.

If you intend to stick around for the nightwatchman's tour, you'll need to **stay overnight**. There's a good range of interesting and affordable accommodation, though in summer be sure to book ahead as everything gets packed. First choice might be the *Weis Stue* (☎75 41 04 88; ❹), from where the nightwatchman begins his daily rounds, which also doubles as a teahouse-cum-restaurant filled with antique crockery and furniture. It's wonderfully atmospheric, with creaking floorboards and wood-panelled walls, but as there are only five rooms, advance booking is essential year-round. Another intriguing option is *Den Gamle Arrest*, Torvet 11 (☎75 42 37 00, ☻www.dengamlearrest.dk; ❹). Built originally as a girls' boarding school, it later served as the town's jail – its double rooms are in the former cells, which these days lock from the inside. Alternatively, if you can afford it, try the beautifully restored *Dagmar*, opposite the Domkirke (☎75 42 00 33, ☻www.hoteldagmar.dk; ❻), which dates from 1581 and claims to be the oldest hotel in Denmark; its gorgeous doubles come with period furniture and loads of character. There are several cheaper pensions as well, including the bright yellow pub *Frue Mathies* at Saltgade 15 (☎75 42 34 20, ☎75 41 02 44; ❹), right in the centre, with en-suite rooms, and the simpler *Restaurant Backhaus*, Grydergade 12 (☎75 42 11 01, ☻www.backhaus-ribe.dk; ❹), which has a few rooms above a restaurant. The **youth hostel** at Skt Pedersgade 16 (☎75 42 06 20, ☻www.danhostel.dk/ribe; May to mid-Sept) is a simple walk over the river from the town centre, and has some doubles (❷). The nearest **campsite** (☎75 41 07 77, ☻www.dk-camp.dk/ribe; April–Nov), 2km distant along Farupvej (take bus #771), is equipped with cabins. The tourist office also publishes a list of private rooms for about 220kr per person.

One reputable spot **to eat** close to the cathedral is *Vægterkælderen*, in the basement beneath the *Dagmar* hotel, serving two- (75kr) and three-course (95kr) lunches, and two-course dinners (150kr). *Café Nicolaj*, beside the art gallery, is open late for coffee and drinks and serves 60kr meals from noon to 2pm and from 6pm to 8pm. At night, *Vægterkælderen* (see above) has a lively bar, though the beer is cheaper at *Pepper's* and *Stenbohus*, which face each other just up the street. If you're looking for atmosphere, hit the tiny but distinctive *Strygejernet* pub at Dagmarsgade 1 (☎75 41 13 51), which serves light meals and snacks during the day and popular draught ales at night.

Rømø and Tønder

From Skærbæk, a few kilometres south of Ribe by train, bus #29 heads across 12km of tidal flats to the island of **Rømø**. The actions of sea and wind have given the island a wild and unkempt appearance, as well as creating a wide beach along the eastern side and allowing wildlife to flourish all over. There's a good chance of seeing seals basking during the spring, while at the end of the summer many migratory wading birds can be found, dodging the island's plentiful sheep.

Rømø's **tourist office** on Havnebyvej 30 (July to mid-Aug daily 9am–6pm; rest of the year 9am–5pm; ☎74 75 51 30, ⓦwww.romo.dk), just south of the causeway in the main village of **HAVNEBY**, can provide details on the island's bus service. There are several spots on Rømø **to stay**: ask at the tourist office for details of private rooms or summer cottages, for which you'll pay around 250kr per person per night. The best hotel on the island is the *Kommandørgården* (☎74 75 51 22, ⓦwww.kommandoergaarden.dk; ❻) in Østerby, a kilometre or so north of Havneby, which also has a **campsite** with four-person cabins for 575kr. Of the two other camping options, best is *Lakolk Camping* (☎74 75 52 28, ⓦwww.lakolkcamping .dk; April to mid-Oct), on the island's windswept west coast at Kongsmark and reachable via bus #29. There's a **youth hostel** in Havneby itself at Lyngvejen 7 (☎74 75 51 88, ⓦwww.romo-vandrerhjem.dk; mid-March to mid-Nov), which has some doubles (❸).

Besides enjoying the sands, and the fact that Rømø is a noted **nude bathing** spot, it's possible to **cross the border to Germany** without returning to the Danish mainland by using the ferry that sails from Havneby to List, on the German island of Sylt (information on ☎74 75 53 02, ⓦwww.romo-sylt.dk).

Tønder

Back on the mainland and heading south from Skærbæk brings you to **TØNDER**, the chief town on the Danish side of the border with Germany. Founded in the thirteenth century, the town's cobbled streets still contain many ancient gabled buildings, and Tønder makes an attractive and low-key base for a day or two, especially if you're around the end of August, when there's a terrific annual **jazz and folk festival**. In 2002, performers included Arlo Guthrie, The Dubliners, Runrig and a host of other international performers, and there are always many free outdoor events, too. Contact the Tønder Festival office (☎74 72 46 10, ⓦwww.tf.dk) for more details. Otherwise, the main sights in town are the **Tønder Museum** (June–Aug daily 10am–5pm; Sept–May Tues–Sun 10am–5pm; ⓦwww.tonder-net.dk/museerne; 30kr, includes entry to the Art Museum), in the gatehouse of the sixteenth-century castle, and the adjoining **South Jutland Art Museum** (same hours, 30kr including entrance to the Tønder Museum), with its changing exhibitions of twentieth-century Danish works. Danish Prince Joachim and Princess Alexandra live 4km to the west of Tønder in **Schackenborg Castle**, in the village of Møgeltønder (bus #66) – there's no entry to the public, but the castle park is good for an hour's strolling and there's the possibility, if you're lucky, of a royal sighting.

First call for local information should be the **tourist office** on Torvet (mid-June to Aug Mon–Fri 9.30am–5.30pm, Sat 9.30am–3pm; Sept to mid-June Mon–Fri 9am–4pm, Sat 9am–noon; ☎74 72 12 20, ⓦwww.visittonder.dk). There's a **youth hostel** at Sønderport 4 (☎74 72 35 00, ⓦwww.tonder-net.dk/danhostel; closed Christmas & Jan) with doubles (❷), 1km from the train station; a **campsite** at Holmevej 2a (☎74 72 18 49, ⓦwww.sydvest.dk; April–Sept); the functional *Hotel Tønderhus* at Jomfrustien 1, opposite the Tønder Museum (☎74 72 22 22, ⓦwww .hoteltoenderhus.dk; ❺), and the three-star, but somehow cheaper, *Hostrup Hotel*, Søndergade 30 (☎74 72 21 29, ⓦwww.hostrupshotel.dk; ❸).

Kolding

Even though it's handily placed on the main road and rail axes north of Tønder, **KOLDING** doesn't attract a lot of attention. If you do find yourself here with time to spare, head a short way north from the centre to the Slotsø lake and the imaginatively renovated **Koldinghus Museum** (daily 10am–5pm; ⓦwww.koldinghus.dk; 50kr), a harmonious mix of ruined and modern structures housing sparsely furnished period rooms as well as changing design exhibitions and a good café. Another worthwhile call in this direction, 3km beyond the lake (bus #4 from the train station), is the **Trapholt Art Museum** (daily 10am–5pm; ⓦwww.trapholt.dk; 50kr), its angular glass walls and shrill white interiors flooding the (mostly) modern art and design – including a fascinating chair exhibition – with natural light.

The **tourist office** is at Akseltorv 8 (July & Aug Mon–Fri 9.30am–7pm, Sat 9.30am–4.30pm; Sept–June Mon–Fri 9.30am–5.30pm, Sat 9.30am–2pm; ⓣ76 33 21 00, ⓦwww.visitkolding.dk). Predictably, the cheapest **accommodation** option is the youth hostel, Ørnsborgvej 10 (ⓣ75 50 91 40, ⓦwww.danhostel.dk/kolding; closed Dec & Jan), which has a few doubles (❶). Other relatively economical choices include the simple *Bramdrupdam Kro*, about 4km north of the town at Vejlevej 332 in Bramdrupdam (ⓣ75 56 82 88; ❸). Two more expensive options are the fairly central *Hotel Tre Roser*, at Grønningen 2 (ⓣ75 53 21 22, ⓦwww.treroser.dk; ❺), and *The Saxildhus* at Banegårdspladsen, opposite the train station (ⓣ75 52 12 00, ⓦwww.saxildhus.dk; ❺). The closest **campsite** is at Vonsildvej 19 (ⓣ75 52 13 88, ⓦwww.vonsild-camping.dk), 3km from the town centre via bus #3. There are several beachfront campsites farther afield – contact the tourist office for details.

For an inexpensive place **to eat**, try the outstanding spare ribs at *Joe's Diner*, Låsbygade 27. For Italian, head for *Bella Italia*, Jernbanegade 40 or *Italiano*, Søndergade 11. If you fancy a drink or a light meal, go to *Den Blå Café* on Lilletorv at Slotsgade 4, which has outdoor seating; for more excitement, head for *Jernbanegade*, a rock bar by the train station, or, also on Jernbanegade, *Crazy Daisy* at no. 13, or the *Pit Stop* disco at no. 54.

Sønderborg

Despite lush green landscapes subsiding gently into a peaceful coastline, the eastern section of southern Jutland holds comparatively few spots of interest and is best seen as part of a southerly route to Funen or Ærø (covered in the previous chapter). A lively provincial town in an area laden with campsites, **SØNDERBORG** straddles the once strategically important **Alssund**, a narrow but deep channel dividing the island of Als from the Jutland mainland. The campsites are evidence of the appeal of the region's sandy coastline, while the line of preserved earthworks on the mainland side of town is testament to Sønderborg's crucial place in Danish history. Beside them, the **Battlefield Centre** (*Historiecenter Dybbøl Banke*; mid-April to Sept daily 10am–5pm; ⓦwww.1864.dk; 40kr) has multimedia displays that trace the details of the battle that took place here on April 18, 1864, when the Danes were defeated by the Prussians and medieval Sønderborg was all but destroyed. From then until 1918, when a plebiscite returned it to Denmark, northern Schleswig (in which Sønderborg stands) became part of Germany.

The bulk of the town lies across the Alssund, where your attention should focus on **Sønderborg Slot**, which may not be the grandest but is certainly one of Denmark's oldest castles, thought to have been started by Valdemar I in 1170 as a defence against the Wends. Inside, the **Museum of South Jutland** (daily: May–Sept 10am–5pm; April & Oct 10am–4pm; Nov–March 1–4pm; 25kr) comprises room after room of military mementoes. One of the more interesting sections tells of the four-day Als Republic of 1918, born as the German Reich's dissenting northern ports – Sønderborg, Bremen, Hamburg and Kiel – rebelled against the Kaiser and, in emulation of the then-recent Russian Revolution, raised a red banner over the town's barracks.

Practicalities

Trains go no further than the mainland section of the town, though long-distance **buses** continue across the Alssund, via a graceful modern road bridge, to Als and the bus station on Jernbanegade. Just downhill from the bus station, you'll find the

tourist office, on Rådhustorvet 7 (mid-June to Aug Mon–Fri 9.30am–6pm, Sat 9.30am–2pm; Sept to mid-June Mon–Fri 9.30am–5pm, Sat 9.30am–1pm; ☎74 42 35 55, ⊛www.visitals.com). Of the central **hotels**, the *Arnkilhus*, Arnkilgade 13 (☎74 42 23 36, ⊛www.arnkilhus.dk; ❹), is best for price, though the grandest place in town is undoubtedly the *Comwell*, Rosengade 2 (☎74 42 19 00, ⊛www.comwell.com; ❺) – look for big discounts on weekends. The shiny modern **youth hostel** (☎74 42 31 12, ⊛www.danhostel.dk/sonderborg; Feb–Nov), which has some doubles (❷), is a twenty-minute walk along Perlegade and Kærvej, and is a little less centrally placed than the waterfront **campsite** on Ringgade 7 (☎74 42 41 89, ⊛www.sonderborgcamping.dk).

The town's main shopping street, **Perlegade**, is close to the tourist office; past here, its name changes twice, first to Store Rådhusgade, then to Christian den Andens Gade. All along its length, though, the street takes on a Mediterranean air on warm evenings as smartly dressed Danes mill from bar to bar; locals often begin a weekend by shopping at the Perlegade end, then **eating** their way down to the other end of the street. There's a branch of the ubiquitous steakhouse chain, *Jensens Bøfhus*, at Perlegade 36; *Café Druen*, at Store Rådhusgade 1, has filling, low-cost snacks, and next door there are good evening meals at English-style pub *Penny Lane* – both sometimes host live jazz and other music. Nearby on Bagergade 2, *Tortilla Flats* offers Mexican main courses for 80kr, and the *Bella Italia*, on Lille Rådhusstræde 31, has filling Italian meals. By the harbour, on Søndre Havnegade 22, *Café au Lait* by the harbour is also good for drinks. **Nightlife** is limited: along Store Rådhusgade, *Penny Lane* at no. 12 (with beers from all over the world), or *Café Druen* at no.1, are your best options. *Maybe Not Bob*, Rådhustorvet 5, is a slightly noisier place, popular with young locals.

Fredericia, Vejle and around

There's little that's unique about **east Jutland**, though its thick forests are a welcome change if you're coming directly from the windswept western side of the peninsula. As the main route between Funen and the big Jutland cities, it's a busy region with good transport links, but the area has only two sizeable towns: **Fredericia** is the more unusual, **Vejle** is more appealing – though neither justifies a lengthy stay.

Fredericia

FREDERICIA – junction of all the rail routes in east Jutland, and those connecting the peninsula with Funen – has one of the oddest histories (and layouts) in Denmark. It was founded in 1650 by Frederik III, who envisaged the town as a strategically placed reserve capital and a base from which to defend Jutland. Three nearby villages were demolished and their inhabitants forced to assist in the building of the new town – and afterwards they had no choice but to live in it. Military considerations required that Fredericia be built on a strict grid plan, with low buildings enclosed by high earthen ramparts, making it invisible to approaching armies. Even the town's later role as a railway hub hasn't destroyed its soldierly air, with memorials to victorious heroes and the only military tattoo in Denmark – an event that failed elsewhere in the country due to lack of interest.

The half-hour walk (or ten-minute ride on bus #3) from the **train station** along Vesterbrogade into the town centre takes you through the Danmarks Port, gateway to the most impressive section of the old ramparts. These stretch for 4km and rise 15m above the streets, and walking along the top gives a good view of the layout of the town. But it's the **Landsoldaten statue**, opposite Princes Port, that best exemplifies the local spirit. The bronze figure holds a rifle in its left hand, a sprig of leaves in the right, and its left foot rests on a captured cannon. The inscription on the statue reads "6 Juli 1849", the day the town's battalion made a momentous sortie against German troops in the first Schleswig war – an anniversary still celebrated as

FREDERICIA

Ramparts

Youth Hostel

Train Station

Landsoldaten Statue

DANMARKSGADE

Fredericia Museum

Trinitatis Kirke

Ramparts

N

HOLSTENSVEJ

OLDENBORGGADE

0   500m

ACCOMMODATION
Hotel Postgården   2
Sømandshjemmet   1

CAFÉS & RESTAURANTS
Bøf & Vino   B
Den Lille Hornblæser   C
Jensens Bøfhus   A

Fredericia Day. The downside of the battle was the five hundred Danes killed; they lie in a mass grave in the grounds of **Trinitatis Kirke** in Kongensgade.

Predictably, three hundred years of armed conflict form the core of the displays in the **Fredericia Museum** at Jernbanegade 10 (mid-June to Aug daily 11am–4pm; Sept to mid-June Tues–Sun noon–4pm; 20kr). There are also reconstructions of typical local house interiors from the seventeenth and eighteenth centuries, and a dreary selection of archeological finds only enlivened by a glittering cache of silverware in the crafts section.

Practicalities

Unless you want to laze around on Fredericia's fine **beaches**, which begin at the eastern end of the ramparts, there's little reason to hang around for very long. The cheapest **hotel** is the central *Hotel Postgården* on Oldenborggade 4 (☎75 92 18 55, ⊛www.postgaarden.dk; ❸), and there's also the family-oriented *Sømandshjemmet* (☎75 92 01 99, ⊛www.fsh.dk; ❺), near the harbour on Gothersgade 40, which can lay on meals. There's a modern **youth hostel** west of the town at Vestre Ringvej 98 (☎75 92 12 87, ⊛www.fredericia-danhostel.dk), with dorms and plenty of doubles (❷), and the *Trelde Næs* **campsite** (☎75 95 71 83, ⊛www.trelde.dk; April–Oct) on the Vejle fjord, though it's 15km north of town and adjacent to a public beach, so can get very crowded during fine weather and at holiday times. You can arrange private rooms with the centrally placed **tourist office**, Danmarksgade 2A (June–Aug Mon–Fri 9am–6pm, Sat 9am–2pm; Sept–May Mon–Fri 10am–5pm, Sat 10am–1pm; ☎75 92 13 77, ⊛www.visitfredericia.dk).

For **food**, there's the predictable *Jensens Bøfhus* steakhouse, Danmarksgade 8; *Den Lille Hornblæser*, Jyllandsgade 53, with a range of Danish offerings; and the Italian restaurant *Bøf & Vino*, Danmarksgade 36. For **nightlife**, try the popular *Laki Design* disco at Bjergegade 54 (☎75 91 54 88).

Vejle

A twenty-minute train ride north of Fredericia, **VEJLE**, a compact harbour town on the mouth of the Vejle fjord, is home to the Tulip factory, from where 400 million sausages a year begin their journey to British breakfast tables. It's also the best base for exploring the contrasting pleasures of the Viking burial mounds at Jelling and – rather more famously – the Legoland complex at Billund, both within easy reach by bus or train.

The chief attraction in Vejle itself is **Skt Nicolai Kirke** (Mon–Fri 9am–5pm, Sat & Sun 9am–noon) in Kirke Torvet, in which a glass-topped coffin holds the peat-preserved body of a woman found in the Haraldskur bog in 1835. Originally the body was thought to be the corpse of a Viking queen, Gunhilde of Norway, but the claim was disputed and tests carried out in 1977 dated the body to around 490 BC – too old to be a Viking, but nonetheless still the best preserved "bog body" in the country. Unfortunately, it's hidden away behind bars in the north transept; what you can see is mainly the feet. Another macabre feature of the church, though again you can't see it, are the 23 skulls hidden in sealed holes in the northern transept. Legend has it that they are the heads of thieves executed in 1630.

The **Museum of Art** and **Vejle Museum** are conveniently placed next to each other at Flegborg 16 and 18. The art museum (Tues–Sun 11am–4pm; @www .vejlekunstmuseum.dk; 20kr) specializes in graphics and drawings, has a collection of twentieth-century painting and sculpture, and often hosts innovative temporary exhibitions from around the world; the Vejle Museum (Tues–Fri 10am–3pm; ☎75 82 43 22; free) has a small collection of local historical and archeological finds. Also run by the museum, and perhaps a better destination on a sunny day, is **Vejle Vindmølle**, a disused windmill which maintains its full complement of ropes, shafts and pinions, and displays a through-the-ages account of milling, from Neolithic blocks to modern roller mills. From the windmill, reached by climbing Kiddesvej (which leads off Søndergade), there are stupendous views across Vejle and its fjord.

Practicalities

Tucked into a small courtyard on Banegårdspladsen 6, the **tourist office** (mid-June to Aug Mon–Fri 10am–5.30pm, Sat 10am–3pm; Sept to mid-June Mon–Thurs 9.30am–5pm, Fri 9.30am–4.30pm, Sat 9.30am–12.30pm; ☎75 82 19 55, @www .visitvejle.com) has a list of **accommodation** in private rooms for 175kr per person per night, but charges a steep 40kr booking fee. Otherwise, try for a room at the *Park* (☎75 82 24 66, @www.park-hotel.dk; ❺) at Orla Lehmannsgade 5, or the pricier four-star *Munkebjerg*, Munkebjergvej 125 (☎76 42 85 00, @www.munkebjerg .dk; ❼), which has a casino amongst its attractions. Much less convenient, but with some doubles (❷), is the **youth hostel** on Gammel Landevej (☎75 82 51 88, @www.vejle-danhostel.dk), a 5km journey on bus #2 from either the bus station on Nørretorv or the Vejle Trafikcentre outside the train station, opposite the tourist office. There's also a **campsite** at Helligkildevej 5 (☎75 82 33 35, @www.dk-camp.dk/vejlecamp), a few kilometres east and reachable on bus #4.

Central Vejle has plenty of inexpensive places **to eat**. In the same Smitskegård courtyard as a section of Vejle Museum, on Søndergade 14, *Conrad Café* serves substantial salads and *smørrebrød* through the afternoon, and drinks until midnight (sometimes with live music). Around the corner on Søndergade, the glass-walled *Madværkstedet* has simple food for around 50kr. For a fuller evening meal, make for *Café Biografen*, Klostergade 1, which is also a good place for a drink. There are a number of English-style **pubs** in town: try the *Irish Cat*, Nørregade 61, or – perhaps the most popular – the *Tartan Pub*, next door at Dæmningen 40.

Around Vejle: Jelling and Legoland

Twenty minutes by train northwest of Vejle, the village of **JELLING** is known to have been the site of pagan festivals and celebrations, and has two **burial mounds** thought to have contained King Gorm, Jutland's tenth-century ruler, and his queen, Thyra. The graves were found in the early twentieth century and, although only one coffin was actually recovered, there is evidence to suggest that the body of Gorm was removed by his son, Harald Bluetooth, and placed in the adjacent church – which Bluetooth himself built around 960 after his conversion to Christianity. In the grounds of the present church are two big **runic stones**, one erected by Gorm to the memory of Thyra, the other raised by Harald Bluetooth in honour of Gorm. The texts hewn into the granite record the era when Denmark began the transition to Christianity. Across the road from the stones on Gormsgade 23, the elegant new **Kongernes Jelling Exhibition Centre** (June–Aug daily 10am–5pm; April, May & Sept Tues–Sun 10am–5pm; Oct–March Tues–Sun 1–4pm; ⓦwww.kongernesjelling.dk; 30kr) provides a full breakdown of their history.

Train services from Vejle to Struer or Herning stop at Jelling: both run about once an hour on weekdays and less frequently at weekends. There's also a **vintage train** between Vejle and Jelling, running every Sunday in July and on the first three Sundays in August (for information call ⓣ75 58 60 60). By **bike**, it's a scenic ride through the hamlet of Uhre and along the shores of Fårup Sø lake – you can rent a bike in Vejle from Buhl Jensen, Gormsgade 14–16 (ⓣ75 82 15 09; 75kr per day). If you want **to stay**, the *Jelling Kro*, Gormsgade 16 (ⓣ75 87 10 06, ⓦwww.jellingkro.dk; ❸), is pleasant and serves filling meals, or head for Jelling's **campsite** (ⓣ75 87 16 53, ⓦwww.jellingcamping.dk; April to mid-Sept), about 1km west of the church on Mølvangsvej.

Legoland Park

Twenty kilometres west of Vejle – to which it's linked by bus #244 – the village of **Billund** has been transformed into a major tourist centre, complete with international airport and rows of pricey hotels. It's all thanks to **Legoland Park** (July to mid-Aug daily 10am–9pm; June & mid-Aug to Sept daily 10am–8pm; April, May & Oct Mon–Fri 10am–6pm, Sat & Sun 10am–8pm; ⓦwww.legoland.dk; 160kr), a theme park celebrating the tiny plastic bricks that have filled many a Christmas stocking since a Danish carpenter, Ole Kirk Christiansen, started making wooden toys collectively named "Lego", from the Danish phrase "*Leg Godt*", or "play well" (which also, by a happy coincidence, means "I study" and "I assemble" in Latin). In 1947, the Lego company began to manufacture its bricks in plastic, becoming the first company in Denmark to use the new plastic moulding-injection techniques – the Lego pieces (or "Automatic Binding Bricks", to be perfectly precise) we know today were first created in 1958. The park itself, featuring a cornucopia of elaborate model buildings, animals, planes and many other weird and wonderful things (such as Titania's Palace – home for the queen of the fairies), is aimed chiefly at kids, but anybody whose efforts at Lego construction have resulted in tears of frustration over missing corner bricks might like to discover what can be achieved when someone has 45 million pieces to play with.

If you want to stay, try the fine modern **youth hostel**, outside town at Ellehammers Allé (ⓣ75 33 27 77, ⓦwww.sima.dk/billund), which has a good supply of double rooms (❷) and other family accommodation. Without a car, it's best to take a bus from the city centre to Legoland and walk the remaining 300m to the hostel. The other options in town are rather more expensive, and can be laid out for you at Billund's **tourist office** (ⓣ76 50 00 55, ⓕ76 35 31 79), located by Legoland.

North of Vejle: Horsens

Travelling north from Vejle, there's every chance you'll pass through **HORSENS**, a likeable though hardly exciting town whose Søndergade is claimed to be the widest main street in Denmark. Horsens was also the birthplace, in 1681, of **Vitus Bering**, who discovered what became known as the Bering Strait whilst on a mission on behalf of Peter the Great to find an Asian–American land bridge. A memorial to him stands in the park which also bears his name.

In another park, Caroline Amalielunden, just north on Sundvej, is **Horsens Museum** (July & Aug daily 10am–4pm; Sept–June Tues–Sun 11am–4pm; ⓦwww.horsensmuseum.dk; 20kr), which contains a run-of-the-mill collection of local knick-knacks. Around the corner on Carolinelundsvej 2 is the more enticing **Art Museum** (July & Aug Mon–Fri 10am–4pm, Sat & Sun 10am–5pm; Sept–June Tues–Fri 11am–4pm, Sat & Sun 11am–5pm; ⓦwww.horsenskunstmuseum.dk; 20kr), displaying some Danish Golden Age masters and an honourable collection of works by local artists. In the town's former electricity and gas works, the new **Industrimuseet** on Gasvej 17–19 (July & Aug daily 10am–4pm; Sept–June Tues–Sun 11am–4pm; ⓦwww.industrimuseet.dk; 30kr) is also worth a visit, offering a captivating insight into how industrialization took place in Denmark from 1860 up until today.

There are plenty of **accommodation** options in Horsens, most expensively at the fancy pink *Jørgensens Hotel* (☏75 62 16 00, ⓦwww.jorgensens-hotel.dk; ⓞ), housed in an eighteenth-century palace at Søndergade 17. Fifteen minutes' walk from the centre overlooking Horsens Fjord are the more affordable dorms and doubles (❷) at the **youth hostel**, Flintebakken 150 (☏75 61 67 77, ⓦwww.danhostelhorsens.dk). Ask at the **tourist office**, Søndergade 26 (mid-June to Aug Mon–Fri 9.30am–5.30pm, Sat 9.30am–2.30pm; Sept to mid-June Mon–Fri 9.30am–4.30pm, Sat 9.30am–12.30pm; ⓦwww.visithorsens.dk), about walks in the area. Inexpensive **restaurants** include the Greek eatery *Kikos*, Kippervig 1, near the town's central pedestrian area, the Mexican *Tequila Sunrise*, Smedegade 10, and the lunch place *Teater Cafeen*, on Teatertorvet. There's also the usual *Jensens Bøfhus* at Åboulevarden 129 for steaks, with cheap afternoon specials on weekdays. During summer, local bars and cafés in the centre set chairs and tables outside for alfresco eating and drinking. The best include the *Corfitz* at Søndergade 23, an elegant place in the heart of town; quiet *Koks*, Nørregade 10; *Paddy's Irish Pub*, right in the centre at Torvet 2A; and another pub, *Camp David*, at Graven 12.

Århus

Geographically at the heart of the country, and often regarded as Denmark's cultural capital, **ÅRHUS** typifies all that's good about Danish cities. It's small enough to get to know in a few hours, yet big and lively enough to have plenty to fill both days and nights, and the combination of laid-back atmosphere with a surprising number of sights might keep you around longer than planned. Århus is also something of an architectural showcase, with several notable structures spanning a century of Danish and international design. A number of these buildings form the campus of the city's university, whose students contribute to a nightlife that's on a par with that of Copenhagen.

Despite Viking-era origins, the city's present prosperity is due to its long, sheltered bay, on which a harbour was first constructed during the fifteenth century, and the more recent advent of railways, which made Århus a nationally important trade and transport centre. It's easily reached by train from all the country's bigger towns, sits at one end of the only direct sea link between Jutland and Zealand (a fast catamaran service linking Århus with Odden, and a slower ferry linking it with Kalundborg), and also has an international airport.

Arrival, information and city transport

Whichever form of public transport brings you to Århus, you'll be deposited within easy reach of the hotels and main points of interest. **Trains** and **buses** stop at their respective stations (Banegårdspladsen and Nybanegårdsgade) on the southern edge of the city centre, from where it's a short walk to the **tourist office** on the first floor of the Rådhus (May to mid-June Mon–Fri 9.30am–5pm, Sat 10am–1pm; mid-June to Sept Mon–Fri 9.30am–6pm, Sat 9.30am–5pm, Sun 9.30am–1pm; Oct–April Mon–Fri 9.30am–4.30pm, Sat 10am–1pm; ☏89 40 67 00, ⓦwww.visitaarhus.com);

ferries from Zealand dock just west of the centre at the end of Nørreport, a short distance from the heart of Old Århus. Buses from **Tirstrup Airport**, some 45km northeast of the city, arrive at (and leave from) the train station; the one-way fare for the 45-minute journey is 55kr.

Getting around is best done on foot: the city centre is compact and you'll seldom need to use **buses** at all unless you're venturing out to the beaches or woods on the city's outskirts. If you do, note that the transport system divides into four zones: one and two cover the whole central area; three and four reach into the countryside. The basic ticket is the so-called "**cash ticket**", which costs 14kr from the machine at the rear of the bus and is valid for any number of journeys for up two hours from the time stamped on it. If you're around for several days and doing a lot of bus hopping (or using local trains, on which these tickets are also valid),

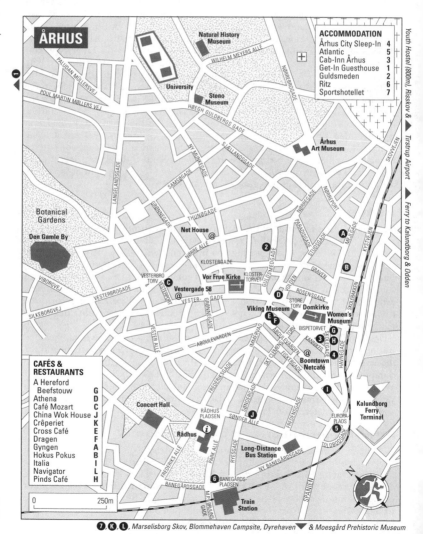

ÅRHUS

Natural History Museum

WILHELM MEYERS ALLÉ

PALUDAN MÜLLERSVEJ

POUL MARTIN MØLLERS VEJ

University

Steno Museum

HØEGH GULDBERGS GADE

NØRREBROGADE

SKOVVEJEN

KYSTVEJEN

Århus Art Museum

ACCOMMODATION

Århus City Sleep-In	4
Atlantic	5
Cab-Inn Århus	3
Get-In Guesthouse	1
Guldsmeden	2
Ritz	6
Sportshotellet	7

Youth Hostel (800m), Risskov & ▶ Tirstrup Airport ▶ Ferry to Kalundborg & Odden

LANGELANDSGADE

SAMSØGADE

SJÆLLANDSGADE

NY MUNKEGADE

GRØNNEGADE

THUNØGADE

NØRREBROGADE

PARADISGADE

MEJLGADE

Botanical Gardens

Den Gamle By

VIBORGVEJ

VESTERBROGADE

VESTER ALLÉ

SILKEBORGVEJ

Net House @

NØRRE ALLÉ

KLOSTERGADE

VESTERBRO TORV

C Vestergade 58 @

VESTER-GADE

GRØNNEGADE

Vor Frue Kirke

KLOSTER-TORVET

GULDSMEDGADE

STUDSGADE

GRAVEN

ROSENSGADE

VOLDEN

SKOLEGADE

SKOLEBAKKEN

A

B

2

D

STORE TORV

Domkirke

Viking Museum

E **F**

Women's Museum

BISPETORVET

3

KANNIKEG.

HAVNEGADE

G **H**

ABOULEVARDEN

IMMERVAD

ABOULEVARDEN

SCT. CLEMENS TORV

FISKERGADE

Boomtown Netcafé @

I

CAFÉS & RESTAURANTS

A Hereford Beefstouw	**G**
Athena	**D**
Café Mozart	**C**
China Wok House	**J**
Crêperiet	**K**
Cross Café	**E**
Dragen	**F**
Gyngen	**A**
Hokus Pokus	**B**
Italia	**I**
Navigator	**L**
Pinds Café	**H**

Concert Hall

RÅDHUS PLADSEN

J

SØNDER ALLÉ

FREDERIKSGADE

SØNDERGADE

RYESGADE

FREDENSGADE

Rådhus

i

Kalundborg Ferry Terminal

EUROPA-PLADS

5

TOLDBODGADE

FREDRIKS ALLÉ

PARK ALLÉ

Long-Distance Bus Station

NY BANEGÅRDSGADE

6 BANEGÅRDS-PLADSEN

BANEGÅRDSGADE

M.P. BRUUNS GADE

Train Station

SPANIEN

N

0   250m

7, **K**, **L**, Marselisborg Skov, Blommehaven Campsite, Dyrehaven ▼ & Moesgård Prehistoric Museum you have three good options. Either get an **Århus Pass**, which costs 88kr for 24 hours, 110kr for 48 hours, and 155kr for an entire week, and covers unlimited travel and entrance to most museums, including Den Gamle By, as well as sightseeing tours (though you must book these at the tourist office first); or a **multi-ride ticket** (78kr), valid for nine trips within the immediate city area and can be used by more than one person at once; or a **24-hour ticket** (50kr), which covers public transport in all four zones and nothing else. These tickets can be bought at newsstands, campsites and shops displaying the "Århus Sporveje" sign. The driver won't check your ticket but a roving inspector might, and there's an instant fine of 250kr if you're caught travelling without one. The **bus information office** is at Banegårdspladsen 20 (Mon–Fri 8am–6pm, Sat 9am–noon; ☎89 40 10 10).

Cycling is another viable way to get around, particularly if you're heading out along the coast to Moesgård. The most central place to rent a bicycle is Cykelværkstedet Morten Mengel, Mejlgade 41 (☎86 19 29 27) which charges 75kr for the first day, 45kr up to six following days, and 250kr for a full week.

Accommodation

Budget travelling has improved remarkably in Århus over the past few years – there are now some fairly reasonably priced hotel and hostel options, and the tourist office can help you find affordable **private rooms** (from 300kr a night plus a 25kr booking fee). The Århus Bed & Breakfast network (☎86 27 51 30, ⊛www.aarhus-bed-and-breakfast.dk) can also help with rooms for 300kr a night, and self-contained apartments for 550kr a night.

Another option is to stay at a farmhouse some 15km west of the city, but you'll need your own transport to get there. The *Tarskov Mølle*, at Tarskovvej 1 in Harlev (☎86 94 25 44, ⊛www.tarskovmolle.dk; ❸), has its own water mill, forest and lake frontage. Or try one of the inns surrounding Århus such as *Malling Kro*, Stationspladsen 2 in Malling, 12km south of Århus and half an hour by train towards Odder (☎86 93 10 25, ⊛www.mallingkro.dk; ❷). The tourist office has a full list of inns in the Århus area.

Hotels and guesthouses

Atlantic Europa Plads 10–14 ☎86 13 11 11, ⊛www.choicehotels.dk. Right next to the harbour and a one-minute walk from the bus station, *Atlantic* is hard to miss, set in one of Arhus' few multistorey buildings. Part of the Comfort Hotel chain, so rooms are, as you'd expect, standardized and adequate. ❺

Cab-Inn Århus Kannikegade 14 ☎86 75 70 00, ⊛www.cab-inn.dk. A stone's throw from the Århus Å River, the functional cabin-like rooms (everything folds up and packs away) are very good value. Breakfast is 50kr. ❹

Get-In Guesthouse Jens Baggesensvej 43 ☎86 10 86 14, ⊛www.get-in.dk. On the edge of town, this is a relaxed and friendly place with slightly scruffy rooms, some with shared bathrooms. Breakfast isn't included. Bus #7 or #26 from the station. ❷

Guldsmeden Guldsmedegade 40 ☎86 13 45 56, ⊛www.hotelguldsmeden.dk. One of the best-value hotels in the centre, ten minutes' walk from the station. Rooms are delicately decorated in French colonial style, and no two are the same; some have shared bath. Bus #1, #2, #6, #9 or #11. ❺

Ritz Banegårdspladsen 12 ☎86 13 44 44, ⊛www.hotelritz.dk. As the name implies, this place, just next to the train station, is both pricey and posh. Very elegant rooms with ornately carved furniture and plush bathrooms. ❻

Sportshotellet Stadion Allé 70 ☎86 14 30 00, ⊛www.aarhusidraetspark.dk. A functional hotel, part of the fancy new sports stadium complex in the Marlisborg forest. The rooms are basic but all are self-contained. Take bus #19 from the station. ❸

Sleep-ins and youth hostels

Århus City Sleep-In Havnegade 20 ☎86 19 20 55, ⊛www.citysleep-in.dk. Near both the city centre and harbour, offering dorm beds and doubles (❶). Guests without their own sleeping bags have to rent sheets and blankets (35kr); other facilities include a games room, café and bike rental (50kr per day). Bus #3 from the station, but you might as well walk.

Århus Youth Hostel Marienlundsvej 10 ☎86 16 72 98, ⊛www.hostel-aarhus.dk. Much more peaceful than the central Sleep-in, this is 4km northeast of town in the middle of Risskov wood, close to the popular Den Permanente beach. It has a hotel-style wing with double rooms (❷), too. Bus #1, #6 #8, #9, #56 or #58.

Campsites

Blommehaven Ørneredevej 35, Højbjerg ☏86 27 02 07, ⊛www.blommehaven.dk. Overlooking the bay, with access to a beautiful beach, and about 4km south of the city centre. Bus #6 or #19. Open April–Aug.

Århus Nord Randersvej 400, Lisbjerg ☏86 23 11 33, ⊛www.dk-camp.dk/aarhusnord. Some 8km north of the city centre and convenient for the E45 motorway, this campsite is only slightly cheaper than *Blommehaven* above, and not nearly as well situated. Bus #117 or #118.

The City

For reasons of simple chronology, Århus divides into two clearly defined parts: even combined, these fill a small and easily walkable area. The **old section**, close to the cathedral, is a tight cluster of medieval streets with several interesting churches and a couple of museums, as well as the bulk of the city's nightlife. The (relatively) **new sections** of Århus form a collar around the old centre, inevitably with less character, but nonetheless holding plenty that's worth seeing, not least the city's major architectural works.

Old Århus

Søndergade is Århus's main street, a pedestrianized strip lined with shops and overpriced snack bars that leads from the train station (where it's initially called Ryesgade), through Skt Clemens Torv and down into the main town square, Bispetorvet, and the old centre, whose streets form a web around the **Domkirke** (May–Sept Mon–Sat 9.30am–4pm; Oct–April Mon–Sat 10am–3pm). Take the trouble to push open the cathedral's sturdy doors, not just to appreciate the soccer-pitch length – this is easily the longest church in Denmark – but for a view of a couple of features that spruce up the plain Gothic interior, which is mostly a fifteenth-century rebuilding after the original twelfth-century structure was destroyed by fire. At the eastern end is one of few pre-Reformation survivors, a grand tripartite altarpiece by the noted Bernt Notke. Look also at the painted – as opposed to stained – glass window behind the altar, the work of Norwegian Emmanuel Vigeland (brother of Gustav); it's most effective when the sunlight falls directly on it.

From the time of the first settlement here, in the tenth century, the area around the cathedral has been at the core of Århus life. A number of Viking remains have been excavated on Skt Clemens Torv, across the road from the cathedral, and some of them are now displayed in the basement of the Nordea bank at Skt Clemens Torv 6 (entrance inside the bank on the left) as part of the **Viking Museum** (Mon–Fri 10am–4pm, Thurs until 6pm; free), which displays sections of the original ramparts and Viking tools alongside informative accounts of early Århus. Also close to the cathedral, in a former police station on Bispetorvet, the **Women's Museum** (*Kvindemuseet*; daily: June–Aug 10am–5pm; Sept–May Tues–Sun 10am–4pm; ⊛www.kvindemuseet.dk; 25kr) is one of Denmark's most innovative, staging temporary exhibitions on aspects of women's lives past and present. After visiting the museums, venture into the narrow and enjoyable surrounding streets, lined by innumerable old and well-preserved buildings, many of which now house browsable antique shops or chic boutiques. The area is also home to some of the city's most enjoyable drinking spots (see p.166).

West along Vestergade from the Domkirke, the thirteenth-century **Vor Frue Kirke** (Mon–Fri 10am–2pm, Sat 10am–noon) is actually the site of three churches, the most notable of which is the eleventh-century **crypt church** (go in through the main church entrance and walk straight ahead), which was discovered, buried beneath several centuries' worth of rubbish, during restoration work on the main church in the 1950s. There's not exactly a lot to see, but the tiny, rough-stone building – resembling a hollowed-out cave – is strong on atmosphere, especially during the candle-lit Sunday services. Except for Claus Berg's fine altarpiece, there's not much to warrant a look in the main church. However, you should make your way (to the left of the entrance) through the cloister that remains from the pre-Reformation monastery – now an old folk's home – to see the medieval frescoes inside the third church, which depict local working people rather than the more commonly found biblical scenes.

Modern Århus

If you've visited the tourist office, you've already been inside the least interesting section of one of the modern city's major sights: the functional **Rådhus**, completed in 1941 and as capable of inciting high passions – for and against – today as it was when it opened. From the outside, it's easy to see why opinions should be so polarized: the coating of Norwegian marble lends a sickly pallor to the building. But on the inside (enter from Rådhuspladsen), the finer points of architects Arne Jacobsen and Erik Møller's vision make themselves apparent, amid the harmonious open-plan corridors and the extravagant quantities of glass. You're free to walk in and look for yourself, but it's worth taking one of the fascinating **guided tours** (in English, mid-June to early Sept Mon–Fri at 11am; 10kr). You can also tour the bell tower at noon and 2pm daily (same months; 5kr).

Above the entrance hangs Hagedorn Olsen's huge mural, *A Human Society*, symbolically depicting the city emerging from the last war to face the future with optimism. In the council chamber, the lamps appear to hang suspended in mid-air (in fact they're held by almost invisible threads), and the shape of the council leader's chair is a distinctive curved form mirrored in numerous smaller features throughout the building, notably the ashtrays in the lifts – though many of these have been pilfered by visitors. Perhaps most interesting of all, however, if only for the background story, are the walls of the small Civic Room, covered by intricate floral designs in which artist Albert Naur, working during the Nazi occupation, concealed various Allied insignia.

A more recent example of Århus's municipal architecture is the glass-fronted **Concert Hall** (Musikhuset: daily 11am–9pm; ⊛www.musikhusetaarhus.dk), a short walk from the Rådhus, which has been the city's main venue for opera and classical music since it opened in 1982. It's worth dropping into, if only for the small café where you might be entertained for free by a string quartet or a lone fiddler. A monthly list of forthcoming concerts and events is available from the box office or the tourist office.

It's just a few minutes' walk from the Concert Hall to Viborgvej and the city's best-known attraction, **Den Gamle By** ("The Old Town"; Jan 11am–3pm; June–Aug 9am–6pm; April–May & Sept–Oct 10am–5pm; Feb, March, Nov & Dec 10am–4pm; ⊛www.dengamleby.dk; 70kr). An open-air museum of traditional Danish life, it consists of around seventy-five half-timbered townhouses (including a popular Mayor's House of 1597) from all over the country which have been moved here since the museum's inception in 1914. With many of the buildings used for their original purpose, the overall aim of the place is to give an impression of an old Danish market town, complete with bakers, craftsmen and the like. This is done very effectively, although sunny summer days bring big crowds, and the period flavour is strongest outside high season, when visitors are fewer.

If you're at all interested in Danish art, the **Århus Art Museum** (Tues & Thurs–Sun 10am–5pm, Wed 10am–8pm; ⊛www.aarhuskunstmuseum.dk; 40kr) on Høegh-Guldbergs Gade, at the northeastern edge of the city centre, gives a good overview of the main national trends, from late eighteenth-century formal portraits and landscapes by Jens Juel, and finely etched scenes of domestic tension by Jørgen Sonne, through to the works of more internationally renowned names, particularly Vilhelm Hammershoi, represented here by some of his moody interiors. There are lots of worthwhile modern pieces, too. Besides the radiant canvases of Asger Jorn and Richard Mortensen, don't miss Bjørn Nørgård's sculpted version of Christian IV's tomb: the original, in Roskilde Cathedral, is stacked with riches; this one features a coffee cup, an egg and a ballpoint pen.

Though it's so plain you'd barely notice it, the Art Museum building is often on the itinerary of architects visiting the city. It's reckoned to be a prime example of the modern Danish style: red bricks and white-framed rectangular windows, with no decoration at all. There's much more of this style on the **university campus**, which sprawls across a hillside overlooking the city a short way up Høegh-Guldbergs Gade – it's walkable from Den Gamle By, but from the centre take bus #2, #3, #11, #14, #54, #56 or #58. Most of the university buildings were designed by C.F. Møller and completed just after World War II. While on campus, there are two museums that might appeal: the **Natural History Museum** (July–Aug 10am–5pm; Sept–June 10am–4pm; ⓦwww.naturhistoriskmuseum.dk; 40kr) has a large collection of stuffed birds and animals alongside some exhibits on Danish ecology, while the **Steno Museum** (Tues–Sun 10am–4pm; ⓦwww.stenomuseet.dk; 40kr) focuses on medical matters and also includes a small planetarium.

Out from the centre

On Sundays Århus resembles a ghost town, with most locals spending the day in the parks, woodlands or beaches on the city's outskirts. If you're around on a Sunday – or, for that matter, any sunny day in the week – you could do much worse than join them. The closest beaches and woods are just **north of the city** at Risskov, near the youth hostel, easily reached on buses #6 or #16, or on any local trains headed for Grenå or Hornslets, some of which halt at the tiny Den Permanente train platform by the beach (but check before boarding, as not all trains stop here). Risskov's beach is narrow but scenic, and clean enough for swimming, while the thick forest behind is criss-crossed with walking and cycling trails.

For a more varied day, head **south** through the thick Marselisborg Skov forest and on to the prehistoric museum at Moesgård. This is also ideal territory for cycling or hiking – see p.161 for details of bicycle rental. Contact the tourist office for suggestions about routes and maps.

Marselisborg Skov and Dyrehaven

The **Marselisborg Skov**, 4km south of the city centre, is a large park that contains the city's sports and horse-trotting stadiums and sees a regular procession of people exercising their dogs. It also holds the diminutive **Marselisborg Slot**, summer home of the Danish royals, whose landscaped grounds can be visited during daylight hours (free) when they're not in residence (usually at all times outside Easter, Christmas and late June to early Aug). Further south, across Carl Nielsen Vej, the park turns into a dense forest, criss-crossed with footpaths but still easy to get lost in.

A simpler route to navigate, and one with better views, is along Strandvejen, which runs between the eastern side of the forest and the shore. Unbroken footpaths run along this part of the coast and there are many opportunities to scamper down to rarely crowded (though often pebbly) beaches. Also on this route, near the junction of Ørneredevej and Thorsmøllevej, is the **Dyrehaven**, or Deer Park – a protected section of the wood that's home to many deer. The animals can be seen (if you're lucky – they're not the most gregarious of creatures) from the marked paths running through the park from the gate on the main road.

Moesgård Prehistoric Museum

Occupying the buildings and grounds of an old manor house 10km south of Århus city centre, **Moesgård Prehistoric Museum** (April–Sept daily 10am–5pm; Oct–March Tues–Sun 10am–4pm; ⓦwww.moesmus.dk; 35kr) traces the story of Danish civilizations from the Stone Age onwards with copious finds and easy-to-follow illustrations. It's the Iron Age which is most comprehensively covered and produces the most dramatic single exhibit: the **Grauballe Man**, the remains of a body, dated to 80 BC, which was discovered in a peat bog west of Århus in a state of such excellent preservation that it was even possible to discover what the deceased had eaten for breakfast (burnt porridge made from rye and barley) on the day of his death. Only a roomful of imposing runic stones further on captures the imagination as powerfully, and you'll exhaust the museum in an hour. Bus #6 runs here direct from the city, while bus #19 takes a more scenic route along the edge of Århus Bay, leaving you with at least a two-kilometre walk through woods to the museum.

Outside the museum, the **prehistoric trail** runs from the far corner of the courtyard to the sea and back again (follow the red dots), a distance of about 3km each way, heading past a scattering of reassembled prehistoric dwellings, monuments and burial places – a trail guide is available in English (10kr) and there's a map on the back of your entry ticket. On a fine day, the walk itself is as enjoyable as the actual sights, and you could easily linger for a picnic when you reach the coast, or stop for a coffee and a snack at the small but popular *Skovmøllen* restaurant en route. Bus #19 goes back to the city from a stop about a hundred metres back to the north of the trail's end at the beach.

Eating

Central Århus is loaded with **eating** possibilities and, while nothing is particularly cheap, a good and affordable bite can still be found in the right places. In general, it's wise to follow locals and students away from the heavily touristed Domkirke and Store Torv to streets such as Mejlgade, Nørre Allé, Vestergade or Skolegade – the latter has a number of unpretentious eateries – so unpretentious, in fact, that they often look closed when they're open. You'll find the best **lunch** bargains, for around 55kr, simply by cruising the cafés and restaurants of the old city and reading the notices chalked up outside them. If you're prepared to pay a bit more, Åboule-varden – the northern bank of a newly uncovered section of the Århus River – offers a string of trendy eating and drinking venues, and is a good place to head for **dinner**.

If money is tight, or you just want to stock up for a **picnic**, try the *Special Smørrebrød* outlet at Nybanegårdsgade 53. For more general food shopping, there's a branch of Brugsen on Søndergade, and a **late-opening DSB supermarket** (8am–midnight) at the train station. There are several other downtown supermarkets of varying quality – try the decent Super Brugsen at Nørre Allé, or the slightly less good Aldi across the way; at the former, local merchants peddle berries and beans fresh from the fields when in season.

A Hereford Beefstouw Skolegade 5 ☎ 86 13 53 25. An expensive but venerable steak house offering grilled Australian beef and a French wine list. A short walk from Bispetorvet and the city centre.

Athena Store Torv 18. Good-value Greek restaurant on the first floor overlooking the city centre hustle and bustle of Store and Little Torv below.

Café Mozart Vesterport 10. On the corner of Nørregade, this is a good sandwich and juice place; take-away also available.

China Wok House Sønder Allé 9. As well as standard Chinese fare, this place is known for its 25kr takeaway China boxes, sold from the front window.

Crêperiet Marselisborg Havnevej 24. Upmarket-ish place by the harbour; try out the crêpes, fish soups or onion consommé (all 60–90kr). Take bus #6 from the station.

Cross Café Åboulevarden 66. On the trendy bit of Åboulevarden, overlooking the newly uncovered

Århus Å river, and serving up generous brunch platters at 75kr as well as oversized salmon sandwiches.

Dragen Åboulevarden 64. For 99kr, you choose your ingredients from the wok buffet and have them stir-fried in front of you.

Gyngen, Mejlgade 53. Good-value, highly rated vegetarian meals served up within the Fronthuset culture centre; local bands sometimes play after dinner.

Hokus Pokus Mejlgade 28. New vegetarian restaurant that does a filling and healthy lunchtime menu for only 25kr and a two-course evening meal for 59kr. Bring your own wine.

Italia Åboulevarden 9. At the harbour end of Åboulevarden, this is the best-value Italian restaurant in Århus.

Navigator Marselisborg Havnevej 46D. If you're prepared to splash out, this is a great fish restaurant with a fantastic view of the Århus bay area.

Pinds Café Skolegade 11. Although it often looks deceptively shut, *Pinds* nonetheless opens long hours and does excellent *smørrebrød*, as well as set lunches for 65kr.

Raadhus Kaféen Sønder Allé 3. Near the train station and across from the tourist office, offering all-day Danish specials for 75kr.

Nightlife

Århus is the only place in Denmark with a **nightlife** to match that of Copenhagen, offering a diverse assortment of ways to be entertained, enlightened, or just inebriated, almost every night of the week. And while things sparkle socially all year round, if you visit during the **Århus Festival** (*Århus Festuge*), an orgy of arts events held annually over the first week in September (check what's on with the tourist office or visit ⓦ www.aarhusfestuge.dk), you'll find even more to occupy your time.

The city has a wonderful endowment of **cafés**, with many situated in the recently restored medieval streets close to the cathedral. There's little to choose between the cafés themselves: each pulls a lively cosmopolitan crowd and the best plan is simply to wander around and try a few, but we've listed the most enduring options below. Between Thursday and Saturday, most cafés stay open until midnight (and some as late as 2am); we've specified these within the listings below.

Home to a music school that's produced some of the county's most successful performers, Århus boasts a music scene that's well known throughout Denmark – so if you're looking for **live music**, you won't have to look far. Basic details of all events are available from the tourist office, but a better source for rock music news is the Århus Billet Bureau, at Klostergade 20 (☏86 13 05 44), where you can pick up a variety of free local magazines and flyers advertising forthcoming gigs. Århus's clubbing scene is equally lively, with both *Voxhall* and *Train* (see opposite) staging club nights when they aren't hosting live bands, and plenty of more mainstream venues providing a less achingly cool place to dance. Early in the week, admission to any club is likely to be free; on Thursday, Friday or Saturday, you'll pay 40–60kr. Århus doesn't have the wide network of **gay clubs** you'll find in Copenhagen, though the long-established gay social centre *Pan Klubben*, south of the train station at Jægergårdsgade 42 (☏86 13 43 80), has a café (open Tues & Thurs–Sat) and disco (Thurs–Sat). Second Friday every month is lesbian-only night; otherwise there's a mixed crowd.

Cafés and bars

Bryggeriet Sct Clemens Kannikegade 10–12. An upmarket bar-cum-restaurant with a built-in brewery; serves some good steaks, too. Just off Bispetorvet next to Århus theatre. Closed Sunday.

Café Jorden Badstuegade 3. Popular café in the medieval cathedral area, which serves quality brunch until mid-afternoon, and gets very lively at night when the drinkers arrive. Open daily until 2am.

Café Paradis Paradisgade 9. Clubby café that's popular amongst local revellers with stamina. Open until at least midnight, usually 4am Thurs & Fri.

Café Svej. Åboulevarden 22. Tucked in among the thick row of cafés and bars lining Århus Å River, with chairs spilling out onto the pavement, this is *the* place to be seen on sunny summer evenings.

Carlton Rosengade 23. In the centre of this quaint, café-heavy medieval quarter, and always buzzing at night. The food is slightly pricey, so most people only come to drink.

Casablanca Rosengade 12. A good place to start the evening, this is Århus's oldest café, with movie-themed decorations and live jazz on Wednesday evenings. Open Mon–Sat until 2am.

Den Smagløse Klostertorv 7. An old-timer of the café scene. Busy with lunchers during the day, and crowded with some of Århus's sizeable student population at night.

Englen Studsgade 3. Near the old quarter's better shopping streets and a great place to rest your feet or sample some of the good food during the day. Local revellers liven things up in the evenings.

Ris Ras Mejlgade 24. Another student hangout, *Ris Ras* excels in good beer and cigars. There's also an art gallery in the basement that's well worth checking out.

Under Masken Bispegade 3. Just off Bispetorvet and next to the casino, this is a cosy yet quirky bar with masks from around the globe decorating the walls. Open daily until 2am.

Live music venues

Bent J Nørre Allé 66 ☏86 12 04 92, ⓦ www.bentj.dk. By far the best jazz venue in town, this smoky, atmospheric pub has free jam sessions several nights a week, and regular performances by bands (expect to pay 50–90kr). Closed Sunday.

Fatter Eskild Skolegade 25 ☏ 86 19 44 11, ⓦ www.fattereskild.dk. Piano bar hosting Danish bar-bands and R&B acts. Open until 5am Fri & Sat, closed Mon.

Musikcafeen Mejlgade 53 ☏ 86 76 03 44, ⓦ www.musikcafeen.dk. On the first floor of the Fronthuset cultural centre, this is Århus's main venue for up-and-coming Danish and international bands, as well as live jazz, rock and the odd techno act. Entrance fee varies between 20kr and 150kr depending on who's playing. Closed Sun.

Musikhuset Thomas Jensens Allé ☏ 86 40 90 50, ⓦ www.musikhusetaarhus.dk. City-centre concert hall which plays host to classical music, opera and, occasionally, mainstream pop bands.

Train Toldbogade 6 ☏ 86 13 47 22, ⓦ www.train.dk. Attracting an older crowd and slightly more well-established bands than its rival *Voxhall* (see below). Gigs take place three or four nights a week; admission runs from 100kr to 250kr, with doors opening at 9pm and the main band starting a few hours later.

Voxhall Vester Allé 15 ☏ 87 30 97 97, ⓦ www.voxhall.dk. Århus's premier venue, hosting the cream of Danish and international independent

acts from hip hop to world music. Tickets cost 50–200kr.

Clubs

Buddy Holly Frederiksgade 29 ☏ 86 18 08 55. Three storeys of different music styles: most of it's pretty mainstream, so no real surprises. A short walk from the town hall and tourist office. Closed Sun.

Café Stage Mejlgade 14 ☏ 86 13 02 54. Another popular disco playing mainstream tunes, this is right in the middle of the café quarter and an easy option if you don't fancy walking too far.

Hotel Royal Store Torv 4 ☏ 86 12 00 11. Glitzy hotel basement housing a combined casino/nightclub that's liveliest early in the week. Smart dress code applies. Open daily until 4am.

Loft M.P. Bruuns Gade 15 ⓦ www.l-o-f-t.dk. A great place to go if you fancy a night of 1950s and 60s nostalgia. Just behind the train station.

Showboat Nordhavnsgade 20 ☏ 86 13 14 29. Know locally as *Broen*, this club on a boat moored in the harbour is divided into five separate sections with different decor and styles of music. Fri & Sat only.

Social Club Klostergade 34 ☏ 86 19 42 50. The city's coolest club, playing the newest, hottest dance tunes. Massive discounts for students. Thurs, Fri & Sat only.

Listings

Airlines SAS (domestic ☏ 70 10 30 00, international ☏ 70 10 20 00, ⓦ www.scandinavian.net); Maersk Air (reservations ☏ 70 10 74 74, flight information ☏ 76 50 50 50, ⓦ www.maersk-air.com).

Airport Tirstrup Airport (☏ 87 75 70 00; ⓦ www.aar.dk) is 45km east of the city. Buses for the airport leave from outside the train station; the fare is 55kr and the journey takes 45 min.

Bookshops English Books and Records, Frederiks Allé 53 (☏ 86 19 54 55, Mon–Fri 11.30am–5.30pm, Sat 11am–2pm), fully lives up to its name.

Bus enquiries Local buses ☏ 89 40 10 10; Abildskou's Århus–Copenhagen coach reservations ☏ 70 21 08 88, ⓦ www.abildskou.dk.

Car rental Avis, Spanien 63 ☏ 86 19 23 99, ⓦ www.avis.dk; Europcar, Sønder Allé 35 ☏ 89 33 11 11, ⓦ www.europcar.dk.

Doctor Between 4pm and 8pm, call ☏ 86 20 10 22. Outside these hours, contact the Kommunehospital (see Hospitals, below).

Ferries and catamarans Mols Linien to either Odden or Kalundborg on Zealand ☏ 70 10 14 18, ⓦ www.mols-linien.dk.

Hospitals There are 24hr emergency departments

at Århus Kommunehospital, Nørrebrogade 44 (☏ 89 49 33 33), and Århus Amtssygehus, Tage-Hansens Gade 2 (☏ 89 49 75 75).

Internet cafés Boomtown, Åboulevarden 21 ☏ 89 41 39 30, ⓦ www.boomtown.net; Mon–Thurs 10am–2am, Fri & Sat 10am–8am, gates shut at midnight, Sun 11am–midnight; 25kr per hr; Gate 58, Vestergade 58 ☏ 87 30 02 80, ⓦ www.gate58.dk; Sun–Thurs 11am–midnight, Fri & Sat 11am–8am; 25kr per hr; Net House, Nørre Allé 66A ☏ 87 30 00 96, ⓦ www.net-house.dk; daily noon–midnight; 20kr per hr.

Market There's a fruit, veg and flower market every Wed and Sat on Bispetorv, beside the cathedral (early morning till noon), though the one on Sat mornings (until 2pm) along Ingerslevs Boulevard, south of the centre, is livelier.

Pharmacy Løve Apoteket, Store Torv 5 ☏ 86 12 00 22, is open 24 hours.

Police Århus Politisation, Ridderstræde 1 ☏ 87 31 14 48.

Post office Banegårdspladsen, by the train station (Mon–Fri 9.30am–6pm, Sat 10am–1pm).

Train enquiries ⓦ www.dsb.dk has details of all

services; you can also call ☎89 40 10 10 for info on regional services; ☎70 13 14 15 for inter-city services; and ☎70 13 14 16 for international trains.

Travel agents Kilroy Travels, Fredensgade 40 ☎70 15 40 15, ⓦwww.kilroytravels.com.

Randers and Djursland

From rolling hills and lush valleys to sandy beaches, **Djursland**, the nose-shaped peninsula east of Århus, boasts some of the prettiest landscapes in Denmark – suffi-cient ingredients for a couple of days' pleasurable exploration. The southern coastal stretch, known as **Mols**, is especially delightful, its hills affording some superb views. Base yourself in the countryside close to Randers, and see the area by bike (see opposite for details of rental outlets) or local buses.

Randers

A trading and manufacturing base since the thirteenth century, **RANDERS** is not a promising introduction to east Jutland. Its growth has continued apace over the years, leaving a tiny medieval centre miserably corralled by a bleak new industrial zone. The town's main historical sight is the house at **Storegade 13**, said to be the place where Danish nobleman Niels Ebbesen killed the German count, Gerd of Holstein, in 1340; a shutter on the upper storey is always left open to allow the count's ghost to escape lest the malevolent spirit should cause the house to burn down. However, Randers' biggest tourist attraction these days – one of the most popular in Jutland – is the **Randers Regnskov** ("Randers Rainforest"; mid-June to Aug daily 10am–6pm; Sept to mid-June Mon–Fri 10am–4pm, Sat & Sun 10am–5pm; ⓦwww.regnskoven.dk; 65kr), a re-creation of a tropical rainforest alongside the River Gudenå. Visitors wander through the dense, damp foliage, enclosed within two giant domes, watching out for the birds, animals and amphib-ians, which include a number of rare turtles and a flying fox, not to mention a for-midable assortment of vipers, boas, pythons, poison frogs and the like. The best part is undoubtedly the dark and spooky "night zoo", located in a dripping stone cave.

Otherwise, there are a couple of museums that are worth a visit, both in the Culture Centre near the bus station on Stenmannsgade 2. The grandly named **Museum of Danish Art** (Tues–Sun 11am–5pm; ⓦwww.randerskunstmuseum.dk; 40kr) on the second floor has a permanent collection of over 4000 pieces from the late eighteenth century up until today, mostly by Danish artists. You could easily kill a couple of hours here, if only for the wacky glass and mirror installation *Cosmic Space*, by the Faroese artist Trondur Patursson. The first floor holds the less captivat-ing **Museum of Cultural History** (same hours; ⓦwww.khm.dk; 25kr) which provides a solid, if uninspiring, historical introduction to the region.

Practicalities

The **bus station** is right in the centre at Dytmærsken 12, while the **train station** is ten minutes' walk out of town at Jernbanegade 29. First stop should be the **tourist office**, near Randers Regnskov at Tørvebryggen 12 (mid-June to Aug Mon–Fri 9am–5.30pm, Sat 9am–noon; Sept to mid-June Mon–Fri 9.30am–4.30pm, Sat 9am–noon; ☎86 42 44 77, ⓦwww.visitranders.com), from where you can get a list of private rooms which rent from 150kr per person – but be aware that some of them are a long way outside town. One of the best-value **hotels** is the *Hotel Gudenå* on Østervold 42 (☎86 40 44 11, ☎86 40 44 82; ❺), in the former seaman's home overlooking the harbour. More upmarket are *Hotel Randers*, Torvegade 11 (☎86 42 34 22, ⓦwww.hotel-randers.dk; ❺/❻), and the *Scandic Hotel Kongens Ege* (☎86 43 03 00, ⓦwww.scandic-hotels.com; ❺/❻), on Gammel Hadsundvej atop a wooded hill above the town, whose rooms give superb views over the city. Randers' status as "Conference City" means you'll pay a lot more for hotels during the week; the reviews above give the weekend rate followed by the weekday one. Randers' **youth hostel**, with dorms and private rooms (❷), is

1.3 | DENMARK | Jutland

only five minutes from the centre at Gethersvej 1 (☎86 42 50 44, ☻www.danhostel
.dk/randers; mid-Feb to Nov). The nearest **campsite**, with cabins and a swimming
pool, is at Fladbro, 6km west of the town (☎86 42 93 61, ☻www.fladbrocamping
.dk): take bus #10 to the golf course, from where it's a ten-minute walk. Note that
some #10 buses do go all the way to the campsite stop, so ask the driver.

Randers has plenty of relatively cheap **restaurants**: try the Greek dishes at *Hellas*,
Vester Kirkestræde 3, Mexican food at *Tortilla Flats*, Adelgade 2, or the filling
lunchtime deals at *Maren Knudsen Øl & Vinkælder* on Storegade. As for **nightlife**,
Storegade holds a good selection of bars where you can sample the local Thor beer,
such as the popular *Tante Olga*, Søndergade 6 (☻www.tanteolga.dk), which has live
rock at weekends, or the more peaceful *Café von Hatten*, at Von Hattenstræde 7. In
early August the town celebrates **Randers Ugen**, a week packed with all sorts of
cultural events; the rest of the year, major rock concerts and theatre performances
are put on regularly at Værket Musik & Teaterhus, a converted power station on
Mariagervej (ticket office ☎86 43 29 00, ☻www.vaerket.dk) – ask at the tourist
office for details of what's on, or visit the website.

The best way to see the countryside around Randers is by **bike**. Schmidt Cykler,
Vestergade 35 (☎86 41 29 03), rents them for 50kr per day.

Djursland

East of Randers stretches the **Djursland peninsula** – popularly known as
Denmark's nose. With its hilly, wooded landscape, edged by some fine beaches, the
southern area of **Mols** attracts huge numbers of tourists every year. **EBELTOFT** is
the most popular destination, easily reached by regular bus from Århus, or by frequent ferry services from Odden in Zealand. A thriving market centre in medieval
times, it was sacked by the invading Swedes in 1659 and has only recently emerged
from economic decline, thanks to tourism: try to arrive in early summer, before the
cobbled streets are overrun by (mostly German) tourists shopping for souvenirs.
The main sight in town is the **Fregatten Jylland** (daily: mid-June to Aug
10am–7pm; Sept–Oct & April to mid-June 10am–5pm; Nov–March 10am–4pm;
☻www.fregatten-jylland.dk; 60kr), moored just behind the bus station; a beautifully
restored nineteenth-century wooden frigate with lots of miniature famous sea battle scenarios on display downstairs in the galley. Nearby at Strandvejen 8, the **Glass
Museum** (July Mon–Wed & Fri–Sun 10am–7pm, Thurs 10am–9pm, Aug–June
daily 10am–5pm; ☻www.glasmuseet.dk; 40kr) provides the chance to see local artisans demonstrating the fabulous art of glass blowing. Should you fancy staying in
town, the best-value **hotel** is the small one-star *Ebeltoft* on Adelgade (☎86 34 10
90; ❹); there's also a **youth hostel** at Søndergade 43 (☎86 34 20 53, ☻www.dan-
hostel.dk/ebeltoft) with bunks and doubles (❶). There are several **campsites** along
the bay, the best being *Vibæk Camping* (☎86 34 12 14, ☻www.publiccamp.dk
/vibaek), right on the beach a little way north of town.

At Jutland's easternmost point, **GRENÅ** grew up around its harbour in the nineteenth century, and it's still an important port, with frequent ferry services to
Varberg in Sweden. Though the town centre is pleasant enough, the main draw is
the lush, wide and sandy beaches south of town. If you need **to stay** overnight, try
for a room at the yellow *Hotel Grenaa Strand*, close to the harbour (☎86 32 68 14,
☻www.grenaastrand.dk; ❹); alternatively, there's a **youth hostel** with bunks and
doubles (❷) at Ydesvej 4 (☎86 32 66 22, ☻www.danhostel.dk/grenaa; closed mid-
Dec to mid-Jan), while the best of the local **campsites** is *Grenå Strand Camping*,
south of the harbour at Fulgsangvej 58 (☎86 32 17 18, ☻www.grenaastrandcamp-
ing.dk; April–Sept). Grenå is reachable by train from Århus (1hr 25min), while bus
#214 runs hourly through the day from Randers bus station, the journey taking
about ninety minutes.

If it's really the beaches you're after, it's better to head 10km north of Grenå by
local bus to **GJERRILD**, a small and quiet village with an inn, bakery, grocery and
a small castle (Sostrup Slot). The beach here, **Nordstranden**, is one of the best in

the country, far preferable to the pebbly offerings in the opposite direction. Budget accommodation alternatives are pretty much limited to Gjerrild's **youth hostel** (☎86 38 41 99, ✆www.danhostel.dk/gjerrild), with bunks and doubles (**❷**), and an excellent **campsite** (☎86 38 42 00, ✆www.dk-camp.dk/gjerrild; April–Sept), 500m from the sands at Nordstranden.

The Lake District: Silkeborg, Viborg and around

Boundaried by a loose triangle formed by Vejle, Århus and Viborg, the grandly titled **Lake District** comprises several small lakes amid green, rolling woodlands which hold Denmark's highest point (147m Himmelbjerget). If you've only seen Denmark's larger towns, this is a region well worth a couple of days' rural exploration, and there are innumerable campsites if you want to linger. The north–south rail route passes first through missable Skanderborg, but it's the Lake District's other main town, **Silkeborg**, spreading handsomely across several inlets, which serves as the area's lively centre. The region is easily accessed by train, although if coming from Århus you'll need to change at Langå to get straight into the lush patch around historic **Viborg**.

Silkeborg

SILKEBORG has little history of its own – it was still a small village in 1845 when the local river was harnessed to power a paper mill that brought a measure of growth and prosperity – but the well-preserved body of an Iron Age woman, discovered 15km west of Silkeborg in 1928, adds greatly to the appeal of the town's **Silkeborg Museum**, at Hovedgården (May–Oct daily 10am–5pm; Nov–April Wed, Sat & Sun noon–4pm; ✆www.silkeborgmuseum.dk; 30kr). As preserved bodies go, however, the so-called **Elling Girl** has been overshadowed since 1952 by the discovery of the Tollund Man, a corpse of similar vintage also on display at the museum. Gruesome as it may sound, the man's head is in particularly good condition, with stubble still visible on the chin.

An equally worthwhile call is to see the excellent collection of abstract works by Asger Jorn and others in the **Museum of Art**, Gudenå 7 (April–Oct Tues–Sun 10am–5pm; Nov–March Tues–Fri noon–4pm, Sat & Sun 10am–5pm; ✆www .silkeborgkunstmuseum.dk; 40kr). It was to Silkeborg that Jorn, Denmark's leading modern painter and founder member of the influential CoBrA (Copenhagen-Brussels-Amsterdam) group, came to recuperate from tuberculosis. From the 1950s until his death in 1973, Jorn donated an enormous amount of his own and other artists' work to the town, which displays them proudly in this purpose-built museum.

For something less cultural, the **Aqua** fresh-water aquarium (June–Aug daily 10am–6pm; Sept–May Mon–Fri 10am–4pm, Sat & Sun 10am–5pm; ✆www .ferskvandscentret.dk/aqua; 70kr), set in the beautiful old tuberculosis sanatorium at Vejlsøvej 55 on the southern edge of town, has a variety of freshwater fish alongside numerous water birds and mammals, including some cute otters. You can get here by taking the *Helje* steamer (4–6 trips daily; 84kr return), the world's oldest coal burning paddle steamer, from the Silkeborg Museum. After the aquarium, the steamer carries on along the Gudenåen river to the foot of **Himmelbjerget** ("Sky Mountain"), Denmark's tallest hill; from here the trek to the top takes about thirty minutes, and your reward is magnificent views of the surrounding area.

Practicalities

The helpful **tourist office**, by the harbour at Åhavevej 2A (mid-June to Aug Mon–Fri 9am–5pm, Sat 9am–3pm, Sun 9.30am–12.30pm; Sept to mid-June Mon–Fri 9am–4pm, Sat 9am–noon; ☎86 82 19 11, ✆www.silkeborg.com), has a lengthy list of affordable **accommodation** in what's a surprisingly expensive town.

Reasonable options include the old and atmospheric *Dania*, on Torvet (☎86 82 01 11, ⓦwww.hoteldania.dk; ⓺), a central and typically priced four-star hotel offering reduced rates at weekends. There are many cheaper *kros* in the outlying countryside, such as *Signesminde Kro* at Viborgvej 145 (☎86 85 54 43; ⓸), reached by bus #60 and town buses #31 and #32 from the railway station; and *Linå Kro* (☎86 84 14 43; ⓷), 8km distant on the road to Århus (bus #113 and town bus #34). Budget accommodation is limited to the **youth hostel**, Åhavevej 55 (☎86 82 36 42, ⓦwww .danhostel.dk/silkeborg), which has dorms and affordable triples and quads, though no doubles, and several **campsites**: *Indelukkets* (☎86 82 22 01, ⓦwww.indelukket.dk), to the south on Vejlsøvej, and *Silkeborg Sø* (☎86 82 28 24, ⓦwww.seacamp.dk), on the Århus road, are closest to town. To get to the former, walk about 2km from the main square down Christian VIII Vej and turn left onto Marienlundsvej; for the latter, begin at the square and head down Østergade, through two traffic lights to Århusbakken (also know as Århusvej). The tourist office can also help to organize **canoe trips**, and book you in at campsites along the way. If you want to go it alone, many of the campsites rent out canoes, or try Slusekioskens Kanoudlejning (☎86 80 08 93; 300kr per day, 1600kr per week) at the harbour.

Viborg

For many years **VIBORG** was one of the most important communities in the country, at the junction of all the major roads across Jutland. From Knud in 1027 to Christian V in 1655, every Danish king was crowned here; Hans Tausen's Lutheran preaching began in Viborg in 1528, eight years before Denmark's official conversion from Catholicism; and until the early nineteenth century the town was the seat of a provincial assembly. As the national administrative axis shifted towards Zealand, however, Viborg's importance waned, and although it's still home to the high court of West Denmark, it's now primarily a market town for local farmers.

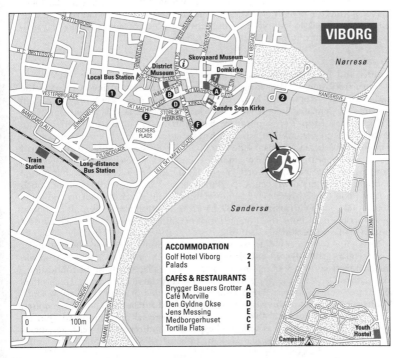

Viborg is cut in half by the Viborg Sø lake, which is spanned by the Randersvej bridge. The centre is concentrated in a small area, though, and most parts of the old town are within a few minutes' walk of each other. The twin towers of the **Domkirke** (June–Aug Mon–Sat 10am–5pm, Sun noon–5pm; April, May & Sept Mon–Sat 11am–4pm, Sun noon–4pm; Oct–March Mon–Sat 11am–3pm, Sun noon–3pm) are the town's most visible feature and the most compelling reminder of its former glories. Begun by Bishop Eskil in 1130, the original cathedral was destroyed by fire in 1726 and rebuilt in the Baroque style by one Claus Stallknecht, though so badly that it had to be closed for two years and the work begun again. The interior is now dominated by the brilliant frescoes of Joakim Skovgaard, an artist commemorated by the **Skovgaard Museum** (daily: May–Sept 10am–12.30pm & 1.30–5pm; Oct–April 1.30–5pm; 10kr May–Sept; free rest of the year) inside the former Rådhus across Gammel Torv from the cathedral – a neat building with which Claus Stallknecht made amends for his botched job of the cathedral. There's a good selection of Skovgaard's paintings in the museum – although they're a little anticlimactic after his splendid work in the cathedral – plus some works by other members of his family.

Two minutes' walk away on Kirke Stræde, the late-Romanesque **Søndre Sogn Kirke** is all that remains of the cloisters of the Dominican Black Friars, one of four monastic orders in Viborg abolished during the Reformation; it was undergoing renovation at the time of writing, but when works are finished (some time in 2004), visitors should be able to go inside, though you'll need to get the key from the building just to the right. Inside the church, the sixteenth-century Belgian altarpiece is the star turn, with 89 gilded oak figures in high relief around the central Crucifixion scene.

For a broader perspective of Viborg's past, keep an hour spare for exploring the **District Museum** (*Stiftsmuseum*; mid-June to Aug daily 11am–5pm; Sept to mid-June Tues–Fri 2–5pm, Sat & Sun 11am–5pm; ⓦwww.viborgstiftsmuseum.dk; 20kr), on the northern side of Hjultorvet between Vestergade and Skt Mathias Gade. The three well-stocked floors hold everything from prehistoric and archeological artefacts to clothes, furniture and household appliances.

Practicalities

Trains and long-distance buses arrive at their respective stations on Viborg's western side, roughly 1km from the centre. The **tourist office** is close to the cathedral on Nytorv (mid-May to mid-June Mon–Fri 9am–5pm, Sat & Sun 9.30am–12.30pm; mid-June to Aug Mon–Fri 9am–5pm, Sat & Sun 9am–3pm; Sept to mid-May Mon–Fri 9am–4pm, Sat 9.30am–12.30pm; ☎86 61 16 66, ⓦwww.viborg-egnen.dk). All Viborg's **hotels** are fairly pricey – best bets are the handsome *Palads*, Skt Mathias Gade 5 (☎86 62 37 00, ⓦwww.hotelpalads.dk; ❻); if a lake view appeals, try the even more expensive *Golf Hotel Viborg*, Randersvej 2 (☎86 61 02 22, ⓦwww.golf-hotel-viborg.dk; ❻). Also close to the lake, but on the opposite side to the town centre (a 2km walk or local bus #707), are the **youth hostel** (☎86 67 17 81, ⓦwww.danhostel.dk/viborg), which has dorms and some doubles (❷), and a **campsite** (☎86 67 13 11, ⓦwww.camping-viborg.dk). Contact the tourist office about the possibility of arranging private rooms, which cost around 130kr per person.

During the day, you could do worse than pick up some *smørrebrød* (the best outlet is at Jernbanegade 14) and **eat** alfresco in one of the numerous parks or on the banks of the lake. Plenty of reasonably priced eating places can also be found along Skt Mathias Gade; try the popular *Jens Messing* at no. 48 (closed Sun), which offers 89kr three-course dinners. For a lighter snack, coffee or salad try *Café Morville*, Hjultorvet 2, next to the Stiftsmuseum. A little further out, *Medborgerhuset*, Vesterbrogade 13, serves a 48kr *dagens ret* (daily special) from noon to 8pm on weekdays (Fri until 5pm), as well as cheap coffee and cakes. The cellar restaurant *Brygger Bauers Grotter*, Skt Mathias Gade 61 (☎86 61 44 88, closed Sun), is by far the

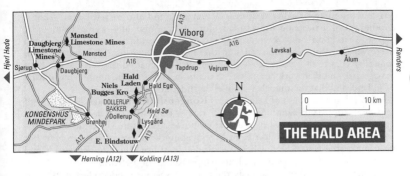

THE HALD AREA

▼ *Herning (A12)* ▼ *Kolding (A13)*

top spot in town for a candlelit dinner, although you'll find lower prices and a live-lier atmosphere at the Mexican restaurant *Tortilla Flats* on Sct Mikkelsgade 2 (closed Mon). For quality steak, try the small and expensive *Den Gyldne Okse* (☎86 62 27 44) on Store Sct Peder Stræde 11, with meals from around 100kr.

Around Viborg

The area **around Viborg** is excellent for cycling, with plenty of pleasant spots with-in easy reach; there's also a decent local bus service. Leaving Viborg, heading south on Koldingvej and turning west towards Herning brings you to **Hald**, a beautiful area of soft hills and meadows on the shores of **Hald Sø**. For all its peace, though, the district's history is a violent one. This is where Niels Bugge led a rebellion of Jutland squires against the king in 1351, and where the Catholic bishop, Jørgen Friis, was besieged by Viborgers at the time of the Reformation. Much of the action took place around the manor houses that stood here, the sites and ruins of which can be reached by following the **footpath** that runs along the western lake shore. The path starts close to **Hald Lade**, a restored barn by the side of the road, where an exhibi-tion (June–Aug daily noon–6pm; Sept–May Sat & Sun noon–6pm; free) details the history and geology of the area, and the battle against the pollution that is killing Hald Sø. All the text is in Danish, but the many photos are worth a peek. This is also where the hilly lakeside area of **Dollerup Bakker** starts. From June to August row-ing boats are available for rent from *Niels Bugges Kro*, which also does good, albeit expensive, meals. Just to the south of here, a road leads from the village of Dollerup to **LYSGÅRD**, home to **E. Bindstouw** (May to mid-Sept Tues–Sun 10am–5pm; 20kr), the old school house where **Steen Steensen Blicher** recorded his famous stories. Blicher would sit here in the evenings while poor locals wove socks beside the stove and told folk tales, which Blicher noted down for posterity. The small building still contains the fixtures and fittings of Blicher's time, including his writing board, stove, and even a few socks. To get here from Viborg, take the #54 bus.

West of Viborg

About 9km west of Viborg, beside the A16 between Mønsted and Raunstrup, the **Jutland Stone** marks the precise geographical centre of Jutland. There's not much to see, just a big inscribed rock and lots of cigarette ends. A few kilometres further, and markedly more interesting, are the **Mønsted Limestone Mines** (mid-May to Oct daily 10am–5pm; ⑩www.monsted-kalkgruber.dk; 40kr), which wind underground for 60km. The mines stay at a constant temperature, regardless of external weather, and wandering around their cool, damp innards can be magically atmospheric, although a century ago conditions for the workers here were so horrific that when Frederik IV visited the place he was sufficiently appalled to bring about reforms – the mines were subsequently known as "Frederik's Quarries" or, more venomously, "The King's Graves". The site closes in winter, when the mines are taken over by an enormous colony of hibernating bats. Bus #28 from Viborg runs here.

A few kilometres further west near Daugbjerg (and also served by bus #28) is another set of **limestone mines** (daily: June 10am–4pm; July & Aug 10am–6pm; Sept & Oct 11am–3pm; ⊕www.daugbjerg-kalkgruber.dk; 40kr), unlit and much narrower than those at Mønsted, and therefore quite spooky. The entrance was found by chance fifty years ago and no one has yet charted the full extent of the passages; it's said that work began here at the time of Gorm, the tenth-century King of Jutland, and that the tunnels were used as hideouts by bandits.

A few kilometres south of Daugbjerg is **Kongenshus Mindepark** (early May to mid-Sept daily 10am–6pm; 10kr, 25kr for cars) – three thousand acres of protected moorland on which there have been attempts at agriculture since the mid-eighteenth century, when an officer from Mecklenburg began keeping sheep here. For his troubles, the would-be shepherd received a grant from the king, Frederik V, and built the house that gives the park its name: Kongenshus (King's House). A few years later, a thousand or so German migrants (the so-called "potato Germans") also tried to cultivate the area, but to little avail. In the centre of the park is a memorial to the early pioneers; standing here, as the wind howls in your ears and you look around the stark and inhospitable heath, you can only marvel at their determination. Kongenshus has now opened up as a *kro* (⊕97 54 81 25; ⊕www.kongenshus.dk; ❸) and the delightful restaurant does fine Danish food. There are also several **campsites** nearby: *Hessellund-Sø* (⊕97 10 16 04, ⊕www.hessellund-camping.dk; April to mid-Oct) to the south near Karup, and *Haderup* (⊕97 45 21 88; mid-May to mid-Sept), off Jens Jensenvej to the west, are the closest and best.

Further west beyond Daugbjerg, and about 30km from Viborg, is one of the most successful of Denmark's heritage tourism projects, the **Hjerl Hedes Frilandsmuseum** (April–Oct daily 9am–5pm; 45kr, 75kr in July and Aug; ⊕www.hjerlhede.dk). This open-air museum attempts to re-create the development of a local village from the years 1500 to 1900, with examples of a forge, an inn, a school, mills, a vicarage, a dairy, a grocer's shop and farms, all relocated from their original sites around Jutland. By far the best time to come is during summer (mid-June to mid-Aug), when the place is brought to life by a hundred or so men, women and children dressed in traditional costumes, who provide demonstrations of the old crafts and farming methods. To get here from Viborg, take the train to Vinderup (5–10 daily; 30min), from where it's an eight-kilometre walk or taxi ride.

Northwest Jutland: Limfjordslandet and around

Limfjordslandet is the name given to the area around the western portion of the **Limfjorden**, the body of water that separates northern Jutland from the rest of the peninsula. In the northwestern half, both the North Sea coast and the shore of the Limfjorden itself – which here resembles a large inland lake – attract legions of holidaying northern Europeans during the summer months, at which time it's best to arrange accommodation in advance. At other times this is a rarely visited quarter of the country. There are fine beaches and plenty of opportunities to mess about in boats – and to catch them to Norway and beyond – and a number of small, neat old towns with a smattering of mildly diverting museums. But the weather here is unpredictable, with sharp winds blustering in off the North Sea, and getting around is difficult: trains only reach to the fringes, so you'll need to rely on buses if you're without your own transport.

For a quick taste of the area, take the train from Viborg and change at Struer for the short journey south to **HOLSTEBRO**, the largest town in the region, and one with an easy-going atmosphere and a small, walkable centre. There's a commendable **Art Museum** (July–Aug Tues–Sun 11am–5pm; Sept–June Tues–Fri noon–4pm, Sat & Sun 11am–5pm; ⊕www.holstebrokunstmuseum.dk; 30kr, includes entry to Holstebro Museum) in the town park, with a strong contemporary Danish collection and some quality international pieces, including works by Matisse and Picasso. In

the same building, the **Holstebro Museum** (same hours; ⓦwww.holstebro-museum
.dk; 30kr, includes entry to the Art Museum) has a fair local history collection. The
tourist office at Den Røde Plads 14 (Mon–Fri 9.30am–4.30pm, Sat 10am–1pm;
ⓣ97 42 57 00; ⓦwww.holstebro.dk) can supply information on travelling deeper
into Limfjordslandet. For **staying** overnight, there's a campsite equipped with cabins at Birkevej 25 (ⓣ97 42 20 68, ⓦwww.camping-mejdal.dk; April to Sept). The
cheapest hotel by far is the *Borbjerg Mølle Kro*, Borgbjerg Møllevej 3 (ⓣ97 46 10
10, ⓦwww.borbjergmill.dk; ❹), 12km northeast of town.

Also reachable from Struer, **Thisted**, at the end of the local rail line, has access to
good beaches and a youth hostel (ⓣ97 92 50 42, ⓦwww.danhostelnord.dk/thisted)
with dorms and doubles (❷), as well as a campsite at Iversensvej 3 (ⓣ97 92 16 35,
ⓦwww.thisted-camping.dk), but little else of interest beyond its link (by bus #40)
to **Hanstholm**, from where ferries leave for Egersund and Bergen in Norway.

Northeast Jutland

Much easier to get to and travel around than Limfjordslandet, **northeastern
Jutland** is nonetheless another portion of Denmark often ignored by foreigners.
It's a shame, as the region has a highly convivial major city in **Aalborg**, as well as
ferries to Sweden and Norway departing from **Frederikshavn**. What's more, once
you cross the Limfjorden, the northeast boasts a landscape wilder than anywhere
else on the peninsula: lush green pastures giving way to strangely compelling views
of bleak moorland and windswept dunes. The highlight here is **Skagen**, a uniquely
atmospheric place whose unusual natural light has long attracted artists.

Aalborg

Hugging the south bank of the Limfjorden, **AALBORG** is the obvious place to
spend a night or two before venturing into the wilder countryside further on. It's
the main transport terminus for northern Jutland, and boasts a notable modern art
museum, a well-preserved old section, and the brightest (indeed only) nightlife for
miles around.

The profits from the seventeenth-century herring boom briefly made Aalborg the
biggest and wealthiest Danish town outside Copenhagen, and much of what
remains of **old Aalborg** – chiefly the area within Østerågade (commonly
abbreviated to Østerå), Bispensgade, Gravensgade and Algade – dates from that era,
standing in stark contrast to the new roads that slice through it to accommodate
the traffic using the Limfjorden bridge.

> Some years ago, it was officially decreed that the Danish double "Aa" would be written
> as "Å". The mayor of Aalborg, and many locals, resisted this change and eventually
> forced a return to the previous spelling of their city's name – though you may still see
> some maps and a few road signs using the "Å" form.

Information and accommodation

The **tourist office** is centrally placed at Østerågade 8 (July Mon–Fri 9am–5.30pm,
Sat 10am–4pm; mid- to end-June & Aug Mon–Fri 9am–5.30pm, Sat 10am–1pm;
Sept to mid-June Mon–Fri 9am–4.30pm, Sat 10am–1pm; ⓣ98 12 60 22,
ⓦwww.visitaalborg.dk).

If you want **to stay** in Aalborg, be aware that bargain-priced hotels are hard to
find. The three cheapest are the plain-looking *Aalborg Sømandshjem*, Østerbro 27
(ⓣ98 12 19 00, ⓦwww.hotel-aalborg.com; ❺), just 600m east of the city centre
(bus #1, #3, #5, #7 or #9); *Prinsens*, Prinsensgade 14–16 (ⓣ98 13 37 33, ⓦwww
.prinsen-hotel.dk; ❹); and, some 2km west of the city centre, the slightly cosier
Krogen, Skibstedvej 4 (ⓣ98 12 17 05, ⓦwww.krogen.dk; ❹), where rooms have
shared bathrooms. If these are too costly, make for the large **youth hostel** (ⓣ98 11
60 44, ⓦwww.danhostelnord.dk/aalborg; closed mid-Dec to mid-Jan) to the west

of the town on the Limfjorden bank beside the marina, which also has doubles (❷) and rustic cabins sleeping up to five (325–460kr) – take bus #8 from the centre to the end of its route. The same bus takes you to the **campsite**, *Strandparken* (☎98 12 76 29, ⓦwww.strandparken.dk; mid-April to mid-Sept), about 300m from the youth hostel. For a little more adventure, catch the half-hourly **ferry** (☎98 11 78 23; 6.30am–11.15pm; 12kr) from near the campsite to Egholm, an island in Limfjord where there's free camping under open-sided shelters.

The Old Town

The tourist office on Østerågade is as good a place as any to start exploring, with one of the town's major seventeenth-century structures standing directly opposite. The **Jens Bangs Stenhus** is a grandiose five storeys in Dutch Renaissance style

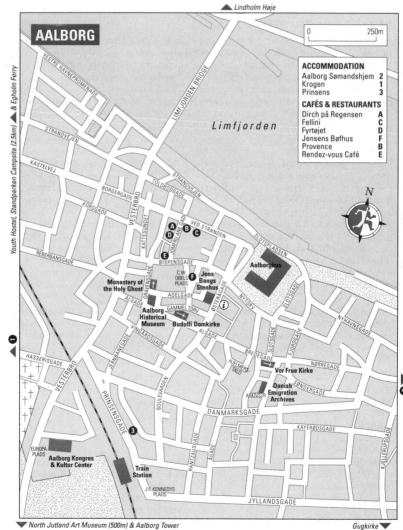

▲ Lindholm Høje

AALBORG

0   250m

ACCOMMODATION
Aalborg Sømandshjem   2
Krogen   1
Prinsens   3

CAFÉS & RESTAURANTS
Dirch på Regensen   A
Fellini   C
Fyrtøjet   D
Jensens Bøfhus   F
Provence   B
Rendez-vous Café   E

Limfjorden

Youth Hostel, Standparken Campsite (2.5km) ▲ & Egholm Ferry

VESTRE HAVNEPROMENADE
STRANDVEJEN
KASTELVEJ
BORGERGADE
KORSGADE
REBERBANSGADE
HASSERISGADE
LIMFJORDEN BRIDGE
STRANDVEJEN
TOLDBODGADE
VESTERBRO
KATTESUNDET
GRAVENSGADE
JERNBANEGADE
VESTERBRO
VINGÅRDSGADE
PRINSENSGADE
BOULEVARDEN
RANTZAUSGADE
AGADE
TOLDBODGADE
DANNEBROGSGADE
VED STRANDEN
BISPENSGADE
ADELGADE
ALGADE
GAMMEL TORV
ØSTERÅGADE
ALGADE
HJELMERS-TORV
BREDEGADE
DANMARKSGADE
SLOTSGADE
NYTORV
SLOTSGADE
SLOTSPLADSEN
NYHAVNSGADE
SLOTSGADE
FJORDGADE
NØRREGADE
SØNDERGADE
KAYERØDSGADE
JYLLANDSGADE
KJELLERUPSGADE
EUROPA PLADS
J.F. KENNEDYS PLADS

N

Aalborghus

Monastery of the Holy Ghost
C.W. OBELS PLADS
Jens Bangs Stenhus
Aalborg Historical Museum
Budolfi Domkirke
ⓘ
Vor Frue Kirke
Danish Emigration Archives
ARKIV STR.

❸

Aalborg Kongres & Kultur Center
Train Station

▼ *North Jutland Art Museum (500m) & Aalborg Tower*   *Gugkirke* ▼

and, incredibly, has functioned as a pharmacy ever since it was built. Jens Bang himself was Aalborg's wealthiest merchant but was not popular with the governing elite, who conspired to keep him off the local council. The host of goblin-like figures carved on the walls allegedly represent the councillors of the time, while another figure, said to be Bang himself, pokes out his tongue towards the former Rådhus, next door.

The commercial roots of the city are further evidenced by portraits of the town's merchants (rather than the more customary portraits of nobles) inside **Budolfi Domkirke** (May–Sept Mon–Fri 9am–4pm, Sat 9am–2pm; Oct–April Mon–Fri 9am–3pm, Sat 9am–noon), just a few steps behind the Jens Bangs Stenhus and easily located by its bulbous spire. A small but elegant specimen of sixteenth-century Gothic, the cathedral is built on the site of an eleventh-century wooden church; only a few tombs from the original remain, embedded in the walls close to the altar. Apart from these, there's little to see inside, but plenty to hear when the electronically driven bells ring out each hour – sending a cacophonous racket across the old square of **Gammel Torv**, on which the cathedral stands.

After viewing the cathedral, drop into the **Aalborg Historical Museum**, across the square at Algade 42 (Tues–Sun 10am–5pm; ⓦwww.aahm.dk; 20kr). The first exhibit here is a dramatic one: the peat-preserved skeleton of a forty-year-old woman who died around 400 AD. In comparison, the rest of the prehistoric section is fairly routine; make instead for the local collections, which provide a good record of Aalborg's early prosperity. The museum also has an impressive glassworks collection illustrating different designs from various Danish glass-working centres – look out for the armadillo-shaped bottle.

Just off Gammel Torv is the fifteenth-century **Monastery of the Holy Ghost** (*Helligåndsklostret*). Much of the building now serves as a senior citizens' home, and the remainder of the monastery can be seen only on one of the free guided tours which run during the summer (check details at the tourist office, as timings change frequently). These take in the monks' refectory, largely unchanged since the monks were thrown out in 1536, and the small Friar's Room, the only part of the monastery into which nuns (from the adjoining nunnery) were permitted entry. Indeed, this was one of the few monasteries where monks and nuns were allowed any contact at all, a fact which accounts for the reported hauntings of the Friar's Room – reputedly by the ghost of a nun who got too friendly with a monk, and as punishment was buried alive in a basement column (the monk was beheaded). Most interesting, however, are the **frescoes** of various biblical characters – dramatically posed images of Jesus, Samson, Mary and St John the Baptist amongst others – that cover the entire ceiling of the chapel. In more recent times, the corridor outside the chapel was used for shooting practice by the so-called "Churchill Gang", a group of local schoolboys who organized resistance to the Nazis.

The rest of old Aalborg lies to the east across Østerågade, and is a mainly residential area – with just a few exceptions. The sixteenth-century **Aalborghus** (grounds daily 8am–9pm; free) is technically a castle but looks much more like a country manor house, and has always had an administrative rather than a military function. Aside from the free theatrical productions staged here in summer, the castle is only worth visiting for the severely gloomy **dungeon** (May–Oct Mon–Fri 8am–3pm; free), to the right from the gateway, and the **underground passageways** (daily 8am–9pm; free) that run off it. From the castle, Slotsgade leads to the maze of narrow streets around **Vor Frue Kirke** (Mon–Fri 9am–2pm, Sat 9am–noon; ⓦwww.vorfrue.dk) a dull church that's surrounded by some meticulously preserved houses, many of which have been turned into upmarket craft shops. The best are along the oddly L-shaped Hjelmerstald: notice no. 2, whose ungainly bulge around its midriff has earned it the nickname "the pregnant house".

If you're of Danish descent, or particularly interested in Danish social history, visit the **Danish Emigration Archives**, nearby at Arkivstræde 1 (Mon–Thurs 9am–4pm, Fri 9am–2pm, plus until 8pm Mon May–Sept; ⓦwww.emiarch.dk). The story of Danish migration overseas is recorded through immense stacks of files and books; given enough background facts, details of individual migrants can be traced.

Outside the old centre

The old centre sets the pleasant tone of the city, but just outside it are a couple of other notable targets. One is the **North Jutland Art Museum** (Tues–Sun 10am–5pm; ⊛www.nordjyllandskunstmuseum.dk; 30kr), south from the centre on Kong Christians Allé, close to the junction with Vesterbro (bus #5, #8, #10 or #11, or a 15min walk from the centre). Housed in a building designed by the Finnish architect Alvar Aalto, this is one of the country's better modern art collections, strikingly contemporary in both form and content. Alongside numerous Danish contributions, it features works by Max Ernst, Andy Warhol, Le Corbusier and, imposingly stationed next to the entrance, Claes Oldenburg's wonderful *Fag-ends in a Colossal Ashtray*. After leaving the museum, you can get a cup of coffee and a grand view over the city and the Limfjorden by ascending the **Aalborg Tower** (July daily 10am–7pm; April–June, Aug & mid- to late Oct daily 11am–5pm; 20kr), on the hill just behind.

From the tower, you may, on a very clear day, be able to spot what looks like a set of large concrete bunkers on a hill to the southeast of the city. This is the **Gug Kirke** (Mon–Fri 9am–4pm; ⊛www.gugkirke.dk), designed by Inger and Johannes Exner and opened in the early 1970s. It's one of the most unusual churches in the country: except for the iron crucifix and the wooden bell tower, the whole thing, including the font, pulpit and altar – decorated by a collage of newspapers – is made of concrete. The idea was to blend the church into the mostly high-rise parish it serves, and for it to function also as a community centre: the perfectly square interior can be turned into a theatre, while the crypt doubles as a café and youth club. It's unique enough to merit a closer look; take bus #6 from the city centre.

Eating, drinking and nightlife

In pursuit of **food**, **drink** and **nightlife**, almost everybody heads for Jomfru Ane Gade, a small street close to the harbour between Bispensgade and Borgergade. Jomfru Ane (literally "young maiden Anne") was a noblewoman and reputed witch who, because of her social standing, was beheaded rather than burnt at the stake – though the street nowadays, at least by night, is more synonymous with getting legless than headless. Around midday, the restaurants crammed together here advertise their daily specials with signs: the most reliable are *Fyrtøjet*, at no. 17, and *Dirch på Regensen*, no. 16, both of which generally have lunches for 50–60kr, or try *Fellini* at no. 23, serving good-value pizzas and pastas. On the weekend, make a beeline for the *Rendez-vou Café* at no. 5, a bar with sandwiches, coffee and, on Saturdays, live music. Several other **bars** along this stretch also host live acts; just walk along, listen, and decide which appeals. For more downtown dining choices, try *Provence*, Ved Stranden 11 (☎98 13 51 33), a cosy French place near the Limfjorden with small, tightly packed tables (book ahead), or, in a 1585-built half-timbered merchants' house C.W. Obels Plads 9, *Jensens Bøfhus*, which has the usual steaks.

The better-known Danish and international **rock music** acts appear at *Skråen*, Strandvejen 19 (☎98 12 21 89, ⊛www.skraaen.dk), which also holds a café. For less mainstream rock music, make for *Café 1000 Fryd* at Kattesundet 10 (☎98 13 22 21; ⊛www.1000fryd.dk). The *Duus* wine bar, in the cellar of the Jens Bangs Stenhus (closed Sun), is the place for a quiet evening **drink**, while, at the opposite end of the scale, *Aalborg Kongres & Kultur Center* at Europa Pads 4 (☎99 35 55 65, ⊛www.akkc.dk) is the city's new theatre and concert venue.

Around Aalborg: Lindholm Høje and Rebild Bakker

A few kilometres north from Aalborg across the Limfjorden, **Lindholm Høje** (April–Oct daily 10am–5pm; Nov–March Tues–Sun 11am–4pm; 30kr) was a major Viking and Iron Age burial ground, and is a captivating place, especially at dawn or dusk. There are a number of very rare Viking "ship monuments" here – burial places with stones arranged in the outline of a ship – as well as more than six hundred Iron Age cremation graves. From Aalborg you can get to the site by bus #6 or #25 (every 30min for most of the day), or walk there in under an hour: go over the Limfjorden bridge, along Vesterbrogade into Thistedvej, right into Viaduktvej, and straight on until Vikingvej appears to the left.

About 30km south of Aalborg is **Rebild Bakker**, a heather-covered hill close to some scattered beech woods and the dense conifers that make up Rold Skov. The area is prime hiking territory, and has been a **national park** since a group of expatriate Danes in America purchased the land and presented it to the Danish government. It's also the site of the largest American Independence Day celebration outside the US every July 4, and is home to the somewhat tacky **Lincoln's Log Cabin** (June–Aug daily 11am–4.30pm; Sept–May Sat & Sun 11am–4.30pm; www.rebild.org; 15kr), a re-creation of Abraham Lincoln's log cabin filled with mundane articles from 49 American states and facts about Danish migration to the US. The Americana doesn't intrude on the natural beauty of the area, however, and the park can provide a couple of relaxing days. To get there from Aalborg, take a train to Skørping or bus #104 to Rebild, where there's a **youth hostel** at Rebildvej 23 (98 39 13 40, www.vandrerhjem.net; Feb–Nov) with dorm beds and doubles (❷); the adjacent **campsite** (98 39 11 10, www.dk-camp.dk/safari) is open year-round.

Continue 20km south of Rebild Bakker, via either the train or bus #53 from Aalborg, and you'll reach the town of **HOBRO**, worth visiting for the 1000-year-old **Fyrkat** (daily: June–Aug 10am–5pm; April–May & Sept–Oct 10am–4pm; www.fyrkat.dk; 50kr), a fortress said to have been built by the Viking king Harald Bluetooth. Fyrkat is a good place to get an impression of life during Bluetooth's era: houses and farms have been reconstructed, and in summer there are demonstrations of traditional Viking activities like bronze casting. Fyrkat is two kilometres' walk from the centre of Hobro, which has a **hostel** at Amerikavej 24 (98 52 18 47, www.danhostelnord.dk/hobro; closed mid-Dec to mid-Jan) with dorm beds and doubles (❷).

Frederikshavn

FREDERIKSHAVN, on north Jutland's east coast, is neither pretty nor particularly interesting, and as a major ferry port it's usually full of Swedes and Norwegians taking advantage of Denmark's liberal drinking laws. There's really not much here of interest except the ferry docks and a small train station with regular services to Skagen, but the town is virtually unavoidable if you're heading north, being at the end of the rail route from Aalborg (if you've an international sailing to meet at Hirtshals, change for the private train at Hjørring). If you're not catching a boat, speed straight on to Skagen (see p.181).

There are, however, a couple of things worth seeing. If you have half an hour, visit the **Krudttårnet** (June to mid-Sept daily 10.30am–5pm; 15kr), the squat, white tower near the train station, which has maps detailing the harbour's seventeenth-century fortifications (of which the tower was a part) and a collection of weaponry, uniforms and military paraphernalia from the seventeenth to the nineteenth centuries. With more time on your hands, take the twenty-minute ride on bus #3 to Møllehuset and walk on through Bangsboparken to the **Bangsbo-Museet** (June–Aug daily 10am–5pm; Sept & Oct daily 10.30am–5pm; Nov–May Tues–Sun 10.30am–5pm; www.bangsbo-museum.dk; 35kr). Here, comprehensive displays chart the development of Frederikshavn from the 1600s, alongside a slightly grotesque, but very engrossing, collection of pictures, bracelets, rings and necklaces – all made of human hair. The outbuildings store an assortment of maritime articles, distinguished only by the twelfth-century *Ellingåskibet*, a ship found north of Frederikshavn, plus a worthwhile exhibition covering the German occupation during World War II and the rise of the Danish resistance movement.

△ Viking Ship Museum, Roskilde

Practicalities

Buses and **trains** both terminate at the train station; crossing Skippergade and walking along Denmarksgade brings you to the town centre in a few minutes. Arriving **ferries** dock near Havnepladsen, also near the centre, and close to the **tourist office** at Skandiatorv 1, on the corner of Rådhus Allé and Havnepladsen (July to mid-Aug Mon–Sat 8.30am–7pm, Sun 8.30am–5pm; mid- to end-June & mid- to end-Aug daily 8.30am–5pm; Sept to mid-June Mon–Fri 9am–4pm, Sat 11am–2pm; ☎98 42 32 66, ⊛www.frederikshavn-tourist.dk). If you're forced to stay, the best-value **hotels** are the *Sømandshjemmet* at Tordenskjoldsgade 15B (☎98 42 09 77, ⊛www.fshotel.dk; ❹), and the central *Hotel Herman Bang*, Tordenskjoldsgade 3 (☎98 42 21 66, ⊛www.hermanbang.dk; ❹). There's also a **youth hostel** with dorms and doubles (❶) at Buhlsvej 6 (☎98 42 14 75, ⊛www.danhostel.dk /frederikshavn), 1500m from the train station (turn right), and a **campsite**, *Nordstrand*, at Apholmenvej 40 (☎98 42 93 50, ⊛www.nordstrand-camping.dk; April to mid-Oct); the site is 3km north of the town centre, just off Skagensvej.

Skagen

Forty kilometres north of Frederikshavn, **SKAGEN** perches at the very top of Jutland amid a desolate landscape of heather-topped sand dunes, its houses painted a distinctive bright yellow. It can be reached by bus or privately operated train (Scanrail, Eurail and InterRail not valid), both of which leave from Frederikshavn train station roughly once an hour – the bus is the best choice if you're planning to stay at the Skagen youth hostel.

The Town

Sunlight seems to gain extra brightness as it bounces off the two seas that collide off Skagen's coast, something that attracted the **Skagen artists** in the late nineteenth century. Painters Michael Ancher and Peder Severin (P.S.) Krøyer and writer Holger Drachmann arrived in the small fishing community during 1873 and 1874, and were later joined by Lauritz Tuxen, Carl Locher, Viggo Johansen, Christian Krogh and Oscar Björck. The painters often met in the bar of *Brøndum's Hotel*, off Brøndumsvej, and the owner's stepsister, Anna, herself a skilful painter, married Michael Ancher. The grounds of the hotel now house the impressive **Skagens Museum** (June–Aug daily 10am–6pm; May & Sept daily 10am–5pm; April & Oct Tues–Sun 11am–4pm; Nov–March Wed–Fri 1–4pm, Sat 11am–4pm, Sun 11am–3pm; ⊛www.skagensmuseum.dk; 50kr), the most comprehensive collection of these artists' work anywhere. The majority of the canvases depict local scenes, capturing subtleties of colour using the area's strong natural light. Many of the works, particularly those of Michael Ancher and Krøyer, are outstanding; but it's the work of Anna Ancher, though perhaps the least technically accomplished, which often comes closest to achieving the naturalism these artists sought.

A few strides away at Markvej 2, the **Michael & Anna Anchers Hus** (mid-June to mid-Aug daily 10am–6pm; May to mid-June & mid-Aug to Sept daily 10am–5pm; April & Oct daily 11am–3pm; Nov–March Sat & Sun 11am–3pm; ⊛www.anchershus.dk; 40kr) has been restored with the intention of evoking the atmosphere of their time through an assortment of squeezed tubes of paint, sketches, paintings, books, ornaments and piles of canvases. Less essential is **Drachmanns Hus** (July daily 10am–5pm; June & Aug to mid-Sept daily 11am–3pm; May & mid-Sept to mid-Oct Sat & Sun 11am–3pm; 25kr) at Hans Baghs Vej 21, on the junction with Skt Laurentii Vej, where Holger Drachmann lived from 1902. Inside the house is a large collection of Drachmann's paintings and sketchbooks, although it was for his lyrical poems – at the forefront of the early twentieth-century Danish Neo-Romantic movement – that he was best known. Such was Drachmann's cultural importance that, on his death, the major Danish newspaper *Politiken* devoted most of its front page to him; facsimiles are on display.

The arrival and subsequent success of these artists inadvertently made Skagen fashionable, and the town continues to be a popular holiday destination. But it still bears many marks of its past as a fishing community, a history that is well documented in the **Skagens By og Egnsmuseum** on P.K. Nielsensvej 8–10 (July daily 10am–6pm; Aug Mon–Fri 10am–5pm, Sat & Sun 11am–4pm; May–June Mon–Fri 10am–4pm, Sat & Sun 11am–4pm; March–April & Oct Mon–Fri 10am–4pm; Nov–Feb Mon–Fri 11am–3pm; ⓦwww.skagen-bymus.dk; 30kr), a fifteen-minute walk south along Skt Laurentii Vej (or the much nicer Vesterbyvej) from the town centre. Built on the tall dune where townswomen would watch for their husbands returning from sea during storms, the museum examines local fishing techniques in its main displays, reinforced by photos showing millions of fish strewn along the quay before being auctioned. Among the auxiliary buildings are reconstructions of rich and poor fishermen's houses: the rich house includes a macabre guest room kept cool to facilitate the storage of bodies washed ashore from wrecks, while the poor man's dwelling makes plain the contrast in lifestyles: it possesses just two rooms to accommodate the fisherman, his wife, and fourteen children.

Around Skagen: the Buried Church and Grenen

Amid the dunes to the south of town, about twenty minutes' walk along Skt Laurentii Vej, Damstedvej and Gammel Kirkestræde and onto a signposted footpath, is **Den Tilsandede Kirke**, or "the Buried Church" (June–Aug daily 11am–5pm; 10kr). The name is misleading since all that's here is the tower of a fourteenth-century church, built in what was then a minor agricultural area. From the beginning of the sixteenth century the church was assaulted by vicious sandstorms; by 1775 the congregation could only reach the church for services with the aid of shovels. In 1810 the nave and most of the fittings were sold, leaving just the tower as a marker to shipping – while not especially tall, its white walls and red roof are easily visible from the sea. Still under the sands are the original church floor and cemetery. Although part of the tower is open to the public, the great fascination is simply looking at the thing from outside, and appreciating the incredible severity of the storms which covered it.

Returning to Skagen, and carrying on straight through to the other side of the town, you'll reach Batterivej and the impressive new **Skagen Odde Naturcenter** (daily: June–Aug 10am–10pm; Sept–May 10am–4pm; ⓦwww.skagen-natur.dk; 65kr). Designed by Danish architect Jørn Utzon – best-known for the Sydney Opera House – this exploration of natural forces is beautifully centred around the themes of sand, water, wind and light, and you could easily spend a couple of hours here, exploring how these different forces interact with each other – something very evident just outside.

The forces of nature can be further appreciated at **Grenen**, at the northernmost tip of Denmark some 4km north of Skagen (reachable via hourly bus #79 during summer). From the bus stop and car park at the end of Fyrvej, the Sandormen tractor-drawn bus (April–Oct; 15kr return) runs along the beach to the tip, though it's nicer to walk the half-kilometre instead. This is the actual meeting point of two seas – the **Kattegat** and **Skagerrak** – and the spectacle of their clashing waves (the seas flow in opposing directions) is a powerful draw, although only truly dramatic when the winds are strong. On the way back, spare a thought for Holger Drachmann (see p.181), a man so enchanted by the thrashing seas that he chose to be buried in a dune close to them. His tomb is signposted from the car park.

Practicalities

Skagen's combined **bus and train station** is on Skt Laurentii Vej, a short walk from the **tourist office** at Skt Laurentii Vej 18 (July Mon–Sat 9am–7pm, Sun 10am–4pm; June & Aug Mon–Sat 9am–5pm, Sun 10am–2pm; May & Sept Mon–Fri 9am–4pm, Sat & Sun 10am–2pm; Oct–April Mon 9am–5pm,

Tues–Thurs 9am–4pm, Fri 9am–3pm, Sat & Sun 10am–1pm; ⓦwww.skagen
-tourist.dk; ⓣ98 44 13 77). **Staying overnight** in Skagen is infinitely preferable
to going back to Frederikshavn, and there are a number of options. For its artistic
associations, *Brøndum's Hotel*, Anchervej 3 (ⓣ98 44 15 55, ⓦwww.broendums
-hotel.dk; ❺), is by far the most atmospheric spot; the fact that few of the rooms
have their own bathrooms and all are far from luxurious keeps the price of doubles
down – but book well ahead in summer. A little cheaper and, also with shared bathrooms, is *Skagen Sømandshjem*, Østre Strandvej 2 (ⓣ98 44 25 88, ⓦwww.skaw.dk/
soemandshjem; ❺), which also serves up bargain meals. Alternatively, there's the small
Foldens Hotel, Skt Laurentii Vej 41 (ⓣ98 44 11 66, ⓦwww.skaw.dk/foldens-hotel;
❹); the equally pleasant *Den Gamle Skibsmedie*, Vestre Strandvej 28 (ⓣ98 44 67 16; ❹);
and, also with shared bathrooms, *Badepension Marienlund*, a simpler place right by
the beach in Old Skagen at Fabriciusvej 8 (ⓣ98 44 13 20, ⓦwww.marienlund.dk;
❹). There are two **youth hostels**: *Danhostel Skagen Ny Vandrehjem*, at Rolighedsvej
2 (ⓣ98 44 22 00; ⓦwww.danhostel.dk/skagen; closed Dec to mid-Feb), has dorms
and doubles (❸) and is only a couple of minutes west of the town centre. *Gammel
Skagen Vandrerhjem* (ⓣ98 44 13 56, ⓦwww.skawhostel.dk; Easter to mid-Oct), 3km
west of town (bus #79 towards Frederikshavn) at Højenvej 32 in Gammel Skagen,
has only double (❷) and quad rooms. Of the many **campsites**, most accessible are
Grenen, to the north along Fyrvej (ⓣ98 44 25 46, ⓦwww.grenencamping.dk; May
to early Sept), and *Poul Eeg's* (ⓣ98 44 14 70; mid-May to Aug), on Batterivej, left
off Oddenvej just before the town centre.

There are plenty of **eating** options in Skagen, though most of them are expensive.
For Italian food, try *Firenze* or *Alfredo*, both in Havnegade and serving reasonably
priced pizza and pasta dishes.

Travel details

Trains

Aalborg to: Århus (30 daily; 1hr 25min);
Frederikshavn (21 daily; 1hr 6min).

Århus to: Aalborg (30 daily; 1hr 25min);
Copenhagen (34 daily; 3hr 16min); Frederikshavn
(11 daily; 2hr 40min); Grenå (13 daily; 1hr 25min);
Randers (30 daily; 35min); Silkeborg (25 daily;
46min); Struer (29 daily; 2hr); Vejle (40 daily;
45min); Viborg (19 daily; 1hr 14min).

Esbjerg to: Århus (6 daily; 2hr 12min);
Copenhagen (10 daily; 3hr); Fredericia (23 daily;
1hr 5min); Ribe (25 daily; 35min).

Fredericia to: Århus (33 daily; 1hr 5min); Vejle (58
daily; 20min).

Frederikshavn to: Skagen (12 daily; 43min).

Ribe to: Tønder (15 daily; 50min).

Silkeborg to: Århus (25 daily; 46min).

Skagen to: Frederikshavn (12 daily; 43min).

Skanderborg to: Århus (64 daily; 15min);
Silkeborg (25 daily; 30min).

Struer to: Holstebro (37 daily; 15min); Thisted (8
daily; 1hr 20min); Vejle (15 daily; 1hr 50min);
Viborg (20 daily; 55min).

Tønder to: Ribe (15 daily; 50min).

Vejle to: Århus (40 daily; 45min); Fredericia (58
daily; 20min).

Viborg to: Struer (20 daily; 55min).

Buses

Aalborg to: Copenhagen (2–4 daily; 4hr 45min to
5hr).

Århus to: Copenhagen (via Ebeltoft: 1 daily; 3hr
50min; direct: 2hr 50min); Ebeltoft (13–17 daily;
1hr 17min).

Ebeltoft to: Copenhagen (2 daily; 2hr 50min);
Århus (13–17 daily; 1hr 17min).

Fjerritslev to: Copenhagen via Hobro, Randers
and Grenå (2–5 daily; 6hr 15min).

Frederikshavn to: Skagen (9 daily; 1hr).

Randers to: Ebeltoft (12 daily; 1hr 28min); Grenå
(19 daily; 1hr 35min); Viborg (19 daily; 45min to 1hr).

Silkeborg to: Århus (38 daily; 1hr 10min); Viborg
(20 daily; 1hr).

Skagen to: Frederikshavn (9 daily; 1hr).

Sønderborg to: Fynshav (17 daily; 25–40min).

Thisted to: Aalborg (16 daily; 1hr 40min to 2hr
10min); Hanstholm (19 daily; 40min).

Viborg to: Silkeborg (20 daily; 1hr).

Ferries

Århus to: Kalundborg (3–6 daily; 2hr 40min); Odden (5 daily; 1hr 5min).
Ebeltoft to: Odden (10–15 daily, 45min).
Frederikshavn to: Vesterø Havn (2–5 daily; 1hr 30min).
Fynshav to: Bøjden (8 daily; 50min).
Hov to: Sælvig (5–10 daily; 1hr 15min).
Grenå to: Anholt (1–2 daily; 2hr 45min).
Mommark to: Søby (2–5 daily in summer; 1hr).

International trains

Fredericia to: Flensburg (6 daily; 1hr 50min).

International ferries

Esbjerg to: Harwich (3–4 weekly in summer; 18hr).
Frederikshavn to: Gothenburg (up to 11 daily in summer; 3hr 15min); Oslo (1 daily; 8hr 30min); Larvik (1–2 daily; 6hr 15min).
Grenå to: Varberg (2 daily; 4hrs).
Hanstholm to: Egersund (4–7 weekly; 7hrs); Bergen (3 weekly; 16hr 30min).
Havneby to: List (July–Aug 11 daily; rest of the year 6 daily; 50min).
Hirtshals to: Oslo (1 daily; 8hr 30min); Kristiansand (2–5 daily; 4hr 30min).

Norway

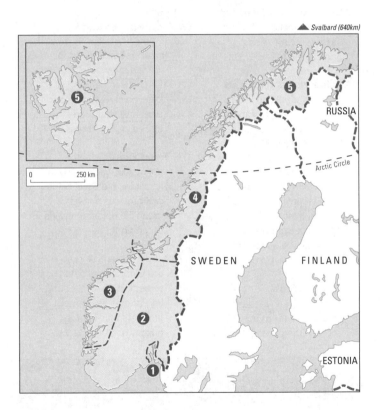

▲ Svalbard (640km)

RUSSIA

Arctic Circle

SWEDEN

FINLAND

ESTONIA

Norway highlights

✶ Oslo's Viking Ships Museum See Viking longships at close hand in this excellent museum. See p.244

✶ Oslo's Munch Museum A huge collection of works from Norway's finest artist. See p.246

✶ Oslo's Vigelandsparken Whatever you do, don't miss this phantasmagorical open-air sculpture park. See p.248

✶ Jotunheimen National Park Craggy and severe, this mountain range is the most sumptuously beautiful example of Norway's wild mountain scenery. See p.268

✶ Edvard Grieg's Troldhaugen Norway's most celebrated composer, Grieg lived just outside Bergen and his old house makes for a delightful visit. See p.304

✶ Urnes stave church Viking carvings are best seen at this country church. See p.322

✶ Norangsfjord The most immediately beautiful fjord, a serene band of blue-black water below dark and sharp ice-tipped peaks. See p.330

✶ Trondheim This easy-going, laid-back city with its stirring medieval cathedral provides a taste of urban life before the wilds of the north. See p.338

✶ Å Tiny village at the tip of the Lofoten that's hard to beat, both for its setting and its assortment of nineteenth-century buildings. See p.373

Introduction and basics

In many ways Norway is still a land of unknowns. Quiet for a thousand years since the Vikings stamped their distinctive mark on Europe, the country often seems more than just geographically distant nowadays. Beyond Oslo and the famous fjords, the rest of Norway might as well be blank for all many visitors know – and, in a manner of speaking, large parts of it are. Vast stretches in the north and east are sparsely populated and starkly vegetated, and it is, at times, possible to travel for hours without seeing a soul.

Despite this isolation, Norway has had a pervasive influence on the world outside. Traditionally its inhabitants were explorers, from the Vikings – the first Europeans to reach Greenland and North America – to more recent figures like Amundsen, Nansen and Heyerdahl. And Norse traditions are common to many other isolated fishing communities, not least northwest Scotland and the Shetlands. At home, too, the Norwegian people have striven to escape the charge of national provincialism, touting the disproportionate number of acclaimed artists, writers and musicians (most notably Munch, Ibsen and Grieg) who have made their mark on the wider European scene. It's also a pleasing discovery that the great outdoors – great though it is – harbours some lively historical towns.

Where to go

Beyond **Oslo**, one of the world's most prettily positioned capitals, the major cities of interest, in roughly descending order, are medieval **Trondheim**; **Bergen** in the heart of the fjords; hilly, southern **Stavanger**; and northern **Tromsø**. All are likeable cities, worth spending time in both for themselves and for the startlingly handsome countryside

---

Norway on the Net

ⓦ**www.visitnorway.com** The official site of the Norwegian Tourist Board, with links to all things Norwegian and good sections on outdoor activities and events.

ⓦ**odin.dep.no** Government site of ODIN (Official Documentation and Information from Norway) – despite the plain presentation this has everything you ever wanted to know about Norway and maybe more. Especially good on politics.

ⓦ**www.vandrerhjem.no** The official site of Norwegian Hostelling, providing clear and detailed information. You can make a reservation, order brochures and other publications, and there's a useful news section, too.

ⓦ**www.bike-norway.com** The best of the English-language cycling sites, with around a dozen suggested routes and lots of practical information about road conditions, traffic, cycle repair facilities and so forth.

ⓦ**museumsnett.kulturnett.no** Comprehensive information on the country's museums and current exhibitions. Click on "Museum Net Norway" for the English-language text.

ⓦ**www.turistforeningen.no** DNT – the Norwegian Mountain Touring Association – operates this excellent site detailing the country's most popular hiking routes, region by region. Also has comprehensive information on local affiliated hiking associations and DNT huts.

ⓦ**www.oslopro.no** Dedicated Oslo site with city listings and links.

ⓦ**www.unginfo.oslo.no** An English guide to Oslo specifically designed for young people. Strong on practical information geared to the budget traveller.

in which they're set. The perennial draw, though, is the **western fjords** – a must, and every bit as scenically stunning as they're cracked up to be. Dip into the region from Bergen or Åndalsnes, both accessible direct by train from Oslo, or take more time and appreciate the subtleties of the innumerable waterside towns and villages. The **south** of Norway, and in particular the long southern coast with its beaches and whitewashed wooden towns, is popular with holidaying Norwegians; the central, more remote regions are ideal for hiking and camping.

To the north, Norway grows increasingly barren. The vast lands of **Troms** and **Finnmark** boast wild and untamed tracts of breathtaking proportions. Here you'll find the Sámi people and their herds of reindeer, which you'll see on the thin, exposed road up to the North Cape, or **Nordkapp** – the northernmost point of mainland Europe. The Cape is the natural end to the long trek north, although there are still several hundred kilometres to be explored further east, right the way to Kirkenes and the Russian border.

When to go

Norway is still regarded as a remote, cold country – spectacular enough but climatically inhospitable. **When to go**, however, is not as clear-cut a choice as you'd imagine. There are advantages to travelling during the long, dark **winters** with their reduced everything: daylight, opening times and transport services. If you are equipped and hardy enough to reach the far north, seeing the phenomenal **Northern Lights** (aurora borealis) is a distinct possibility; later, once the days begin to get lighter, **skiing** is excellent; while **Easter** is the time of the colourful Sámi festivals. But – especially in the north – it is cold, often bitterly so, and this guide has been deliberately weighted towards the **summer** season, when most people travel and when it is possible to camp and hitch to keep costs down. This is the time of the **Midnight Sun**: the further north you go, the longer the day becomes, until at Nordkapp the sun is continually visible from mid-May to the end of July. (The box above lists the dates between which the Midnight Sun is

---

The midnight sun

Alta: May 16–July 26
Bodø: May 30–July 12
Hammerfest: May 13–July 29
Nordkapp: May 11–July 31
Tromsø: May 18–July 26

---

visible in different parts of the north.) Something worth noting is that the **summer season** in Norway is relatively short, stretching roughly from the beginning of June to mid-August. Come much later than 16–20 August and you'll find that tourist offices, museums and other sights cut back their hours, while buses, ferries and trains often switch to reduced schedules.

As regards **temperatures**, roughly speaking January and February are the coldest months, July and August the warmest; the Gulf Stream makes the coastal north surprisingly temperate during summer.

Getting there from the rest of Scandinavia

There's no problem in reaching Norway from the rest of **Scandinavia**. There are very regular train services from Sweden, year-round ferry connections from Denmark and frequent flights from Denmark, Sweden and Finland.

By train

By train you can reach **Oslo** from both Stockholm (3 daily; 7hr) and Copenhagen (2 daily; 8hr). There are also regular services from Stockholm to **Trondheim** (2 daily; 11hr) and **Narvik** (2 daily; 19hr). InterRail, ScanRail and Eurail passes are valid – for train pass details see "Basics", p.21.

Note that there are no direct train services from Finland.

By bus

Two **bus** companies provide regular daily services to Norway from **Copenhagen**, **Gothenburg** and **Stockholm**. They are NOR-WAY Bussekspress (⊛ www.nor-way.no)

and Safflebussen (⊛www.safflebussen.se). The main difference between the two services is price: Safflebussen are almost always less expensive, and both are cheaper than the train. As for **Finland**, there are no direct express buses, not even in the far north where Finland and Norway share a common border.

By ferry

Of the several **car ferry** services shuttling across the Skagerrak **from Denmark** to Norway, one of the most useful is DFDS Seaways' ferry (⊛www.dfdsseaways.com) from Copenhagen to Oslo (1 daily; 16hr). Alternatively, Stena Line (⊛www.stenaline .com) links Frederikshavn with Oslo (1–2 daily; 8hr 30min) and Color Line (⊛www .colorline.no) ferries depart Hirtshals for Oslo

(6–7 weekly; 8hr) and Kristiansand (1–3 daily; 4hr 30min). There's also a Color Line ferry service to Norway **from Sweden**, linking Strömstad, north of Gothenburg, with Sandefjord (2–6 daily; 2hr 30min).

Details of sailings and costs can be had via the company websites or from any travel agent or local tourist office. Prices tend to rise sharply in summer, though this is partly offset by all sorts of special deals; rail-pass holders get discounts on some routes, too.

By plane

Norway has international **airports** at Oslo (Gardermoen), Torp (Sandefjord), Bergen, Stavanger, Kristiansand, Trondheim and Tromsø; most flights from elsewhere in Scandinavia are with SAS (⊛www.sas.no) or

one of its subsidiaries, primarily Braathens (www.braathens.no). Standard unrestricted tickets are very expensive, but discounts are legion, mostly with caveats about the length of stay and so forth. That said, SAS has come under economic pressure from budget airlines in the rest of Europe, and domestic airfares look set to reduce in price in the near future. For details of pan-Scandinavian air discounts and deals, see "Getting around" (p.195).

Costs, money and banks

Norway has a reputation as one of the most **expensive** of European holiday destinations, and in some ways (but only some) this is entirely justified. Most of what you're likely to need – from a cup of coffee to a roll of film – is costly, though on the other hand certain major items are reasonably priced, most notably **accommodation**, which compared with other north European countries can be remarkably inexpensive. Norway's (usually) first-rate youth hostels, almost all of which have family, double and dormitory rooms, are particularly good value. **Getting around** is good news, too. Most travellers use some kind of rail pass, there is a fistful of discounts and internal deals, and the state subsidizes the more remote and longer bus hauls. Furthermore, **concessions** are almost universally available at attractions and on public transport, with infants (under 4) going everywhere free, children and seniors (over 67, sometimes 60) paying half the standard rate. **Food** is, however, a different matter. With few exceptions – such as tinned fish – it's expensive, while the cost of **alcohol** is enough to make even a heavy drinker contemplate abstinence.

On average, if you're prepared to buy your own picnic lunch, stay in youth hostels and stick to the less expensive cafés and restaurants, you could get by on around £25/$40 a day excluding the cost of public transport. Staying in three-star hotels, eating out in medium-range restaurants most nights (but avoiding drinking in a bar), you'll get through at least £50/$80 a day – with the main variable being the cost of your room. As always, if you're travelling alone you'll spend much more on accommodation than you would in a group of two or more: most hotels do have single rooms, but they're usually around sixty to eighty percent of the price of a double.

Currency and exchange rates

Norwegian currency consists of **kroner**, one of which, a krone (literally "crown"; abbreviated **kr** or **NOK**), is divided into 100 **øre**. Coins in circulation are 50 øre, 1kr, 5kr and 10kr; notes are for 50kr, 100kr, 200kr, 500kr and 1000kr. You can bring in up to 25,000kr in notes and coins (there's no limit on traveller's cheques).

At the time of writing the **exchange rate** was 11.54kr to one pound sterling; 7.38kr to one US dollar; 4.7kr to one Canadian dollar; 4.12kr to one Australian dollar; 3.62kr to one New Zealand dollar and 7.35kr to one euro.

Changing money

All but the tiniest of settlements in Norway have a **bank** or **savings bank**, and the vast majority will change foreign currency and traveller's cheques. **Banking hours** in Norway are usually Monday to Friday 8.15am–3pm, though they close thirty minutes earlier during the summer (June–Aug) and are open till 5pm on Thursday all year. All major **post offices** change foreign currency and traveller's cheques at rates that are competitive with those of the banks, and they have longer opening hours too, generally Monday to Friday 8am–5pm and Saturday 9am–1pm. Almost every bank and major post office charges a small commission for changing currency; if commission is waived, it probably means you're getting a poor exchange rate instead.

Outside banking and post office hours, most major hotels, many travel agents and some hostels and campsites will change money at less generous rates and with variable commissions, as will the **exchange kiosks** to be found in Oslo. In addition, **ATMs**, from which you can withdraw local currency using a credit or debit card, are commonplace right across Norway.

Tax-free shopping

Taking advantage of their decision not to join the EU, the Norwegians run a **tax-free shopping scheme** for tourists. If you spend more than 308kr at one of three thousand outlets in the tax-free shopping scheme you'll get a voucher for the amount of VAT you paid. On departure at an airport, ferry terminal or frontier crossing, present the goods, the voucher and your passport, and – provided you haven't used the item – you'll get an 11–18kr refund, depending on the price of the item. There isn't a reclaim point at every exit from the country, however – pick up a leaflet at any participating shop to find out where they are – and note that many of the smaller reclaim points keep normal shop hours, closing for the weekend at 2pm on Saturday.

Mail and telecommunications

Postal and telephone systems are both very efficient in Norway, and things are made even easier by the fact that any staff you'll need to deal with nearly always speak good English.

Post offices are plentiful; usual opening hours are Monday to Friday 8am/8.30am–4/5pm and Saturday 8am/9am–1pm. Some urban post offices open longer hours. **Postage** costs 5.5kr for either a postcard or a letter under 20g sent within Norway (7kr within Scandinavia, 9kr to the EU), and 10kr to countries outside. Mail to the USA takes a week to ten days, two to three days within Europe.

Norway has a reliable **telephone** system, run by Telenor. You can make domestic and international telephone calls with ease from public phones, which are plentiful and almost invariably work – if you can't find one, some bars have payphones. Most hotel rooms have phones too, but note that they always attract an exorbitant surcharge.

Public telephones are of the usual Western European kind, where you deposit the money before you make your call. They take 1kr, 5kr, 10kr and 20kr coins, though coin-operated public phones are gradually

being phased out in favour of those that only take **phonecards** (*TeleKort*). These can be purchased at newsstands, post offices, major train stations and some supermarkets, and come in 40kr, 90kr and 140kr denominations. An increasing number of public phones also accept major credit cards. Phone booths have English instructions displayed inside.

Local telephone calls **cost** a minimum of 2kr, while 10kr is enough to start an international telephone call, but not much more. Discount rates on international calls (of around fifteen percent) apply from 10pm to 8am. All Norwegian telephone numbers have eight digits and there's no area code.

You can access the **Internet** either at one of the country's growing number of Internet cafés (all major cities have at least a couple) or at public libraries. Library access is free, but Internet café charges vary wildly – 30kr per thirty minutes is a reasonable average.

Media

Most British and some American daily **newspapers**, plus the occasional periodical, are sold in most towns from Narvesen kiosks, large train stations and at airports. As for the **Norwegian media**, state advertising, loans and subsidized production costs sustain a wealth of smaller papers that would bite the dust elsewhere. Most are closely linked with political parties, although the

Useful numbers

International dialling code for Norway
☎0047
Directory enquiries (Scandinavia)
☎180
Directory enquiries (international)
☎181
Emergencies (fire) ☎110
Emergencies (police) ☎112
Emergencies (ambulance) ☎113
International operator assistance (including collect and reverse-charge calls) ☎115
Domestic operator assistance (including collect and reverse-charge calls) ☎117

bigger city-based papers tend to be independent. Highest circulations are claimed in Oslo by the independent *Verdens Gang* and the independent-conservative *Aftenposten*, and in Bergen by the liberal *Bergens Tidende*. There are no English-language titles.

The **television** network has expanded over the last few years, in line with the rest of Europe. Alongside the state channels, NRK and TV2, there are satellite channels like TV Norge, while TV3 is a channel common to Norway, Denmark and Sweden; you can also pick up Swedish TV broadcasts – though pornographic programmes are jammed. Many of the programmes are English-language imports with Norwegian subtitles, so there's invariably something on that you'll understand, though much of it is pretty unadventurous stuff. The big global cable and satellite channels like MTV and CNN are commonly accessible in hotel rooms.

Local tourist **radio**, giving details of events and festivals, is broadcast during the summer months; watch for signposts by the roadside and tune in. Otherwise, English radio broadcasts, featuring news from Norway, are repeated several times daily on FM (93 MHz). The BBC World Service is broadcast to all mainland Scandinavia. Frequencies vary according to area and often change every few months; visit ⊛www.bbc.co.uk/worldservice for updates.

Getting around

Norway's **public transport system** – a huge mesh of trains, buses, car ferries and passenger express ferries – is comprehensive and reliable. In the winter (especially in the north) services can be cut back severely, but no part of the country is unreachable for long. Bear in mind, however, that Norwegian villages and towns usually spread over a large distance, so don't be surprised if you end up walking a kilometre or two to get where you want to go. It's this sprawling nature of the country's towns and, more especially, the remoteness of many of the sights, that encourages visitors to rent a **car**. This is a very expensive business, but costs

are manageable if you hire locally for a day or two rather than for the whole trip.

Timetables for most of the principal air, train, bus and ferry services are detailed in the *NRI Guide to Transport and Accommodation*, a free and easy-to-use booklet available in your home country from the Norwegian Tourist Board. In Norway itself, almost every tourist office carries a comprehensive range of free local and regional public transport timetables. In addition, all major train stations carry the *NSB Togruter*, a brochure detailing Norway's principal train timetables, whilst long-distance bus routes operated by the national carrier, Nor-Way Bussekspress, are listed in the free *Rutehefte* (timetable), available at principal bus stations.

Trains

With the exception of the Narvik line into Sweden, operated by Tågkompaniet (☎0046 /690 69 10 17; ⊛www.tagkompaniet.se), all Norwegian **train** services are run by the state railway company, Norges Statsbaner (NSB; ☎81 50 08 88, then dial 4 for English, ⊛www.nsb.no). Apart from a sprinkling of branch lines, NSB services operate on three main domestic routes, linking Oslo to Stavanger in the southwest, to Bergen in the west and to Trondheim and on to Bodø in the north. In places, the rail system is extended by a *TogBuss* (literally train-bus) service, with connecting coaches continuing on from the train terminal. The nature of the country has made several of the routes engineering feats of some magnitude, worth the trip in their own right – the tiny **Flåm line** and the sweeping **Rauma line** from Dombås to Åndalsnes are exciting examples.

Prices are bearable, the popular Oslo–Bergen run, for example, costing around 600kr one way, Oslo–Trondheim 700kr. Both journeys take around six and a half hours. Costs can be reduced by purchasing a **rail pass** in advance (see pp.21 & 32); note that the Norway Rail Pass (see opposite) can be purchased either before or after arrival in Norway. Inside Norway, NSB offers a variety of special **discount fares**. The main ticket discount scheme is the **Minipris** (mini-price), under which you can cut up to fifty percent off the price of long-distance journeys. In general, the further you travel, the more economic they become. The drawback is that they must be purchased at least one day in advance, are not available at peak periods and on certain trains, and stopovers are not permitted (the trains you *can* take are indicated with a green dot on timetables). In addition, NSB offers a variety of special deals and discounts – inquire locally (and ahead of time) for details on any specific route.

In terms of **concessionary fares**, there are group and family reductions; children under 4 travel free provided they don't take up a seat, while under-16s pay half fare, as do senior citizens. It's worth noting that intercity trains and all overnight and international services require an advance **seat reservation** (30kr) whether you have a rail pass or not. In high season it's wise to make a seat reservation on main routes anyway as trains can be packed. **Sleepers** are reasonably priced if you consider you'll save a night's hotel accommodation: a bed in a three-berth cabin costs around 150kr, two-berth from 230kr.

NSB have two classes: **standard** and **economy** (the former is marketed abroad as "first class" on the reasonable assumption that the term "standard class" might be misunderstood). NSB **timetables** are available free at every train station. The general timetable, the *NSB Togruter*, is supplemented by individual timetables on each of the lines and, in the case of the more scenic routes, by leaflets describing the sights as you go.

For further advance advice about passes, discounts and tickets, either contact the specialist agents listed in "Getting there" (p.11).

Rail passes

Both the **InterRail** and **Eurail** passes (see p.21) are valid for the Norwegian railway system, as is the **ScanRail** pass (see p.32). The other alternative is the **Norway Rail Pass**, which allows unlimited travel on the railways of Norway on a specified number of days within a specific period. Three days in one month costs 1170kr, four days 1460kr,

five days 1620kr. The Norway Rail Pass can be bought from major train stations inside Norway and from agents abroad (see "Basics", p.22). Children under 4 travel free, under-16s get a fifty percent discount and seniors (60-plus) twenty percent.

All rail pass holders have to shell out a small additional surcharge on certain trains on certain routes and also have to pay the compulsory 30kr seat reservation fee on most intercity trains and all overnight and international services. On the plus side, rail passes are good for travel on connecting TogBuss services, while two of them (ScanRail and InterRail) give a fifty-percent discount on scores of intercity bus and boat routes.

Buses

Where the train network won't take you, **buses** will – and at no great cost, either: a substantial fjord journey, like the Sogndal–Florø trip, costs 259kr, while the ten-hour bus ride between Ålesund and Bergen is a reasonable 527kr. All tolls and ferry costs are included in the price of a ticket, which can represent a significant saving. You'll need to use buses principally in the western fjords and the far north, though there are also lots of long-distance express buses between major towns. Most long-distance buses are operated by the national carrier, **Nor-Way Bussekspress** (Norwegian-language info line ☎81 54 44 44, ⓦwww .nor-way.no), whose principal information office is at Oslo's main bus station. Their services are supplemented by a dense network of local buses, whose timetables are available at most tourist offices and bus stations. In general, most longer-distance routes tend to operate once or twice daily, with one bus leaving early in the morning, while shorter hauls, although more frequent, often tail off in the late afternoon. **Tickets** are usually bought on board, but travel agents sell advance tickets on the more popular long-distance routes; be sure to keep your ticket till the journey is completed.

In terms of **concessionary fares**, there are group and family reductions, children under 3 years travel free provided they don't take up a seat, youngsters under 16 pay half fare, and senior citizens over 67 get a 33 percent discount. Nor-Way Bussekspress offers InterRail and ScanRail pass holders a fifty percent reduction on certain bus services, and some local bus companies have comparable deals. Indeed, rail-pass and student-card holders should always ask about discounts when purchasing a ticket.

If you are going to travel much by bus, the Nor-Way Bussekspress **NOR-WAY BussPass** is excellent value – 21 days of unlimited travel for 2300kr. Valid on all Nor-Way Bussekspress services, the pass offers a guarantee of a seat without advance booking (except for groups of more than eight) – the idea is that if one bus gets full, they will lay on another. Again, all toll and ferry costs are covered, but not the majority of local bus services. Infants under 3 travel free; a pass for a child (4–15) is at 75 percent of the adult rate. The pass can be purchased at any of the larger bus stations in Norway and a complimentary timetable detailing all Nor-Way Bussekspress services is included.

Ferries

Using a **ferry** is one of the highlights of any visit to Norway – indeed among the western fjords and around the Lofotens they are all but impossible to avoid. The majority are roll-on, roll-off **car ferries**. These represent an economical means of transport, with prices fixed on a nationwide sliding scale: short journeys (10–15min) cost foot passengers 18–24kr, whereas car and driver will pay 45–65kr. Ferry procedures are straightforward: foot passengers walk on and pay the conductor, car drivers usually wait in line with their vehicles on the jetty till the conductor comes to the car window to collect the money (although some busier routes have a drive-by ticket office). One or two of the longer car ferries – in particular Bodø–Moskenes – take advance reservations, but the rest operate on a first-come, first-served basis. In the off-season, there's no real need to arrive more than twenty minutes before departure – with the possible exception of the Lofoten Island ferries – but in the summer allow two hours, two and a half to be really safe.

Passenger express boats

Norway's **Hurtigbåt passenger express boats** are catamarans that make up in speed what they lack in enjoyment: unlike the ordinary ferries, you're cooped up and view the passing landscape through a window, and in choppy seas the ride can be disconcertingly bumpy. Nonetheless, they're a convenient time-saving option: it takes just four hours on the Hurtigbåt service from Bergen to Balestrand, for instance, the same from Narvik to Svolvær, and a mere two and a half hours from Harstad to Tromsø. Hurtigbåt services are concentrated on the west coast around Bergen and the neighbouring fjords; the majority operate all year. There's no fixed tariff table, so rates vary considerably, though Hurtigbåt boats are significantly more expensive per kilometre than car ferries – Bergen–Stavanger, for instance, costs 590kr for the four-hour Hurtigbåt journey. There are **concessionary fares** on all routes, with infants up to the age of 3 travelling free, and children (4–15) and senior citizens (over 67) getting a fifty percent discount. In addition, rail-pass holders and students are often eligible for a fifty percent reduction on the full adult rate.

The Hurtigrute

Norway's most celebrated ferry journey is the long and beautiful haul up the coast from Bergen to Kirkenes on the **Hurtigrute** (literally "rapid route") **coastal boat** – or "coastal steamer" (in honour of its past rather than present means of locomotion). To many, the Hurtigrute remains the quintessential Norwegian experience, and it's certainly the best way to observe the drama of the country's extraordinary coastline. Eleven ships combine to provide one daily service in each direction and the boat stops off at over thirty ports on the way.

The whole trip lasts eleven days. **Tickets**, which include all meals, go for anything from 10,000kr to 25,000kr depending on whether you're sailing on one of the old or new vessels, where your cabin is on the boat and when you sail – departures between October and March are around forty percent cheaper than those in the summer. There are also **concessionary fares** offering fifty percent discounts for senior citizens (over 67), families, groups of ten or more, students and children (4–15). Infants up to 3 years old travel free providing they do not occupy a separate berth. Note that in the summertime these discounts are only valid for a limited number of cabins, which makes pre-booking pretty much essential. If you're over 16 and under 26 and travelling between September and April, another option is a **coastal pass**, which costs 1750kr for 21 days' unlimited travel on the Hurtigrute. Further details are available from, and bookings can be made with, most travel agencies back home. Making a Hurtigrute booking once you've got to Norway is easy too, though this does not apply to the coastal pass and other comparable deals. In Norway, contact either a travel agency or the general Hurtigrute number and website (☎81 03 00 00; @www .hurtigruten.com). Most city and coastal tourist offices have copies of the sailing schedule.

A **short or medium-sized hop** along the coast on a section of the Hurtigrute is also well worth considering. Fares are not particularly cheap, especially in comparison with the bus, but they are affordable. The standard, high-season, one-way passenger fare from Bergen to Trondheim (40hr), for example, costs about 1400kr; from Svolvær to Stokmarknes (3hr), 200kr. Last-minute bargains, however, can bring the rates right down to amazingly low levels. All the tourist offices in the Hurtigrute ports have the latest details and should be willing to telephone the captain of the nearest ship to make a reservation on your behalf. Note that prices for shorter trips don't include meals.

As for specifics, you don't need to have a cabin, as sleeping in the lounges or on deck is allowed. Bikes travel free. There's a 24-hour cafeteria supplying coffee and snacks and a first-rate restaurant on all Hurtigrute boats; the restaurant is very popular, so book as soon as you board.

Planes

Internal flights can prove a surprisingly inexpensive way of hopping about the country and are especially useful if you're short on time and want to reach, say, the far north: Tromsø to Kirkenes takes the best part of

two days by bus, but it's just an hour by plane. Domestic air routes are serviced by several companies, but the only big player is SAS (@www.sas.no) along with its many subsidiaries, primarily Braathens (@www .braathens.no). Regular standard fares are around 1600kr one-way from Oslo to Bergen, 3000kr from Oslo to Tromsø, and 2400kr from Bergen to Trondheim. SAS/Braathens operate a variety of **discount** schemes, such as Braathens' special fare for under-25s, which knocks 50–75 percent off the full price. The same airline also has special **excursion fares** bookable no less than seven days prior to departure and including a Saturday night away; these can discount the regular fare by fifty percent, sometimes more. Otherwise, check out Braathens' special offers, which often provide some great bargains. In terms of **concessionary fares**, SAS/Braathens permit infants under 2 to travel free on some flights, while on others ten percent of the regular fare is charged. In addition, people over 65, and children under 16 travelling in a family group including at least one full-fare-paying adult, receive a 33 percent discount on most flights. The details of these various discounts vary year to year, so it's always worth shopping around.

Both Braathens and SAS have excellent-value **air passes**. Braathens' "Northern Lights Pass" (not available to Scandinavian residents) is valid on all the company's routes and comprises discount coupons, with short one-way flights within southern or northern Norway costing around 500kr, long one-way flights between south and north costing about 1250kr (the dividing line between north and south is drawn through Trondheim, which is counted as belonging to both zones). The pass can be bought either before you get to Norway or when you're there. Further details are available direct from Braathens either in Britain (see p.14) or Norway (☎81 52 00 00). The SAS "**Visit Scandinavia AirPass**" can also be purchased either before or after you arrive in Scandinavia, but only if you fly to Scandinavia on an SAS flight; note that it is not available to Scandinavian residents. It entitles holders to purchase up to eight AirPass vouchers for internal flights within

Scandinavia for each return flight to Scandinavia (with SAS) you buy. The vouchers are good for all SAS flights within the region and cost about €70–90 each depending on the flight; airport taxes are extra.

Driving

Norway's main roads are excellent, especially when you consider the vagaries of the climate, and now that most of the more hazardous sections have been ironed out or tunnelled through, driving is comparatively straightforward. That said, you still have to be careful on some of the higher sections and in the longer, fume-filled tunnels. But once you leave the main roads for the narrow byroads that wind across the mountains, you'll be in for some nail-biting experiences – and that's in the summertime. In winter the Norwegians close many roads and concentrate their efforts on keeping the main highways open, but obviously blizzards and ice can make driving difficult to dangerous anywhere, even with winter tyres, studs and chains. At any time of the year, the more adventurous the drive, the better equipped you need to be: on remote drives you should pack provisions, have proper hiking gear, check the car thoroughly before departure, carry a spare can of petrol and take a mobile phone.

Norway's main highways have an E prefix – E6, E18 etc; all the country's other significant roads (*riksvei*, or *rv*) are assigned a number and, as a general rule, the lower the number, the busier the road. In our guide, we've used the E prefix, but designated other roads as Highways, or "Hwy" (followed by the number). Don't be too amazed if the road number we've given is wrong – the Norwegians are forever changing the numbers. **Tolls** are imposed on certain roads to pay for construction projects such as bridges and tunnels. Normally, once the costs are covered the toll is removed. The older projects levy a fee of around 20–30kr, but the toll for some of the newer works (like the tunnel near Fjaerland) runs to well over 100kr per vehicle. There's also a modest toll on entering the country's larger cities (15–20kr), but whether this is an environmental measure or a means of boosting city

coffers is a moot point. To avoid getting flustered at a toll booth, Norwegians carry a supply of coins ready to hand.

Fuel is readily available, even in the north, though here the settlements are so widely separated that you'll need to keep your tank pretty full; if you're using the byroads extensively, remember to carry an extra can. Current fuel prices are 8–10kr a litre and there are four main grades: unleaded (*blyfri*) 95 octane; unleaded 98 octane; super 98 octane; and diesel. It's worth remembering that many petrol stations don't accept credit cards, so make sure you have enough cash before filling up.

Major mountain passes opening dates

Obviously enough, there's no preordained date for opening **mountain roads** in the springtime – it depends on the weather, and the threat of avalanches is often much more of a limitation than actual snow falls. The dates below should therefore be treated with caution; if in doubt, seek advice from a local tourist office. If you do head along a mountain road that's closed, you'll sooner or later come to a barrier and have to turn round.

E6: Dovrefjell (Oslo–Trondheim). Usually open all year.

E69: Skarsvåg–Nordkapp. Closed late Oct to early April.

E134: Haukelifjell (Oslo–Bergen/Stavanger). Usually open all year.

Hwy 7: Hardangervidda (Oslo–Bergen). Usually open all year.

Hwy 51: Valdresflya. Closed Nov to early May.

Hwy 55: Sognefjellet. Closed Nov to early May.

Hwy 63: Grotli–Geiranger–Åndalsnes (Trollstigen). Closed late Sept to late May.

Documentation and rules of the road

EU **driving licences** are honoured in Norway, but other nationals will need an **International Driver's Licence** (available at minimum cost from your home motoring organization). No form of provisional licence is accepted. If you're bringing your own car, you must have vehicle registration papers, adequate insurance, a first-aid kit, a warning triangle and a green card (available from your insurers or motoring organization). Extra insurance coverage for unforeseen legal costs is also well worth having, as is an appropriate **break-down policy** from a motoring organization. In Britain, for example, the RAC and AA charge members and non-members about £110 for a month's Europe-wide breakdown cover, with all the appropriate documentation, including green card, provided.

Rules of the road are strict: you drive on the right, with dipped headlights required at all times; seat belts are compulsory for drivers and front-seat passengers (and for back-seat passengers too, if fitted). There's a speed limit of 30kph in residential areas, 50kph in built-up areas, 80kph on open roads and 90kph on motorways and some other main roads. Recently installed cameras monitor hundreds of kilometres of road – watch out for the *Automatisk Trafikk Kontroll* warning signs – they're far from popular and there are folkloric (and largely apocryphal) tales of men in masks returning at night with chain saws to chop them down. **Speeding fines** are so heavy that local drivers stick religiously within the speed limit. If you're filmed breaking the limit in a hire car, expect your credit card to be stung by the car hire company to the tune of at least 700kr. If you're stopped for speeding, large spot fines (700–3000kr) are payable; rarely is any leniency shown to unwitting foreigners. **Drunken driving** is also severely frowned upon. You can be asked to take a breath test on a routine traffic-check; if over the limit, you will have your licence confiscated and may face 28 days in prison.

If you **break down** in a hire car, you'll get roadside assistance from the particular repair company the car hire firm has contracted. The same principle works with your own vehicle's breakdown policy (see above). Two major **breakdown companies** in Norway are Norges Automobil-Forbund (NAF; 24hr assistance on ☎81 00 05 05) and Viking Redningstjeneste (24hr assistance on ☎80 03 29 00). There are emergency telephones along some motorways, and the NAF patrols all mountain passes between mid-June and mid-August.

Car rental

All the major international **car rental** companies are represented in Norway – contact details are given in the "Listings" sections of larger cities. To rent a car, you'll need to be 21 or over (and have been driving for at least a year), and you'll need a credit card. Rental **charges** are fairly high, beginning at around 3600kr per week for unlimited mileage in the smallest vehicle, but include collision damage waiver and vehicle (but not personal) insurance. To cut costs, watch for the special deals offered by the bigger companies – a Friday to Monday weekend rental might, for example, cost you as little as 800kr. If you go to a smaller, local company (of which there are many, listed in the telephone directory under *Bilutleie*), you should proceed with care. In particular, check the policy for the excess applied to claims and ensure that it includes collision damage waiver (applicable if an accident is your fault). Bear in mind, too, that it's almost always cheaper to rent a car before you leave home – see p.33.

Cycling

Cycling is a great way to take in Norway's scenery – just be sure to wrap up warm and dry, and don't be over-ambitious in the distances you expect to cover. Cycle tracks as such are few and far between, and are mainly confined to the larger towns, but there's precious little traffic on most of the minor roads and cycling along them is a popular pastime. Furthermore, whenever a road is improved or rerouted, the old highway is usually redesigned as a cycle route. At almost every place you're likely to stay in, you can anticipate that someone will **rent bikes** – either the tourist office, a sports shop, youth hostel or campsite. Costs are pretty uniform and you can reckon on paying between 120kr and 200kr a day for a seven-speed bike, plus a refundable deposit of up to 1000kr; mountain bikes are about thirty percent more.

A few tourist offices have maps of recommended cycling routes, but this is a rarity. It is, however, important to check your itinerary thoroughly, especially in the more mountainous areas. Cyclists aren't allowed through the longer **tunnels** for their own protection (the fumes can be life-threatening), so discuss your plans with whoever you hire the bike from. Bikes mostly go free on car ferries and attract a nominal charge on passenger express boats, but buses vary. The national carrier, Nor-Way Bussekspress, accepts bikes only when there is space and charges the appropriate child fare, whilst local, rural buses sometimes take them free, sometimes charge and sometimes do not take them at all. There's a fee of 50–180kr to take bikes on NSB trains.

If you're planning a **cycling holiday**, your first port of call should be the Norwegian Tourist Board (see p.230), where you can get general cycling advice, a map showing roads and tunnels inaccessible to cyclists and a list of companies offering all-inclusive **cycling tours**. Obviously enough, tour costs vary enormously, but as a baseline reckon on about 5000kr per week all-inclusive. The Syklistenes Landsforening, Storgata 23C, Oslo (☎22 47 30 30; ⊛www.slf.no), the Norwegian Cyclist Association, have an excellent range of specific cycling books and maps. Finally, Sykkelturisme i Norge (⊛www.bike-norway.com) has ideas for a dozen routes around the country from 100km to 400km, plus useful practical information about road conditions, repair facilities and places of interest en route.

Accommodation

Inevitably, hotel **accommodation** is one of the major expenses of a trip to Norway – and if you're after a degree of comfort, it's going to be the costliest item by far. There are, however, budget alternatives, including private rooms, campsites and cabins, and an abundance of HI hostels.

Hotels

Almost universally, Norwegian **hotels** are of a high standard: neat, clean and efficient. Summer prices and impromptu weekend deals also make many of them, by European standards at least, comparatively economical. Another plus is that the price of a hotel room always includes a buffet breakfast – in mid- to top-range hotels especially, these can be sumptuous banquets. The only negatives are the sizes of rooms, which tend to be small – singles especially – and their sameness: Norway abounds in mundanely modern concrete and glass skyrise hotels. In addition to the places we've detailed in the guide, most Norwegian hotels, along with their room rates, summer discounts and facilities, are listed in the free booklet *Transport og Overnatting*, available from the Norwegian tourist office.

Summer is the best time to use one of the several **hotel discount and pass schemes** which operate throughout Norway. There are five main ones to choose from; each serves to cut costs, though often at the expense of a flexible itinerary – advance booking is the norm. Most Norwegian hotels are members of one discount/pass scheme or another and you can usually join the scheme at one of the hotels, or at a tourist office; it's also worth checking what's available with your travel agent before leaving home.

Pensions, guesthouses and inns

For something a little more informal and less anonymous than the average hotel, **pensions** (*pensjonater*) are your best bet – small, sometimes intimate boarding houses which can usually be found in the larger cities and more touristy towns. Rooms go for 350–450kr single, 450–550kr double; breakfast is generally extra. A *gjestgiveri* or

---

Accommodation price codes

The hotels and guesthouses detailed in the Norway chapters of this guide have been graded according to the following price categories, based on the cost of the **least expensive double room during the high season** (usually June to mid-August). However, almost every hotel offers seasonal and/or weekend discounts, which can reduce the rate by one or even two grades. Wherever this is the case we've given two grades, covering both the regular and the discounted rate.

❶ under 350kr
❷ 350–600kr
❸ 600–800kr
❹ 800–1000kr

❺ 1000–1200kr
❻ 1200–1400kr
❼ over 1400kr

gjestehus is a **guesthouse** or **inn**, charging similar prices. Facilities in all are usually adequate without being overwhelmingly comfortable; at the cheaper establishments you'll share a bathroom with others. Some pensions and guesthouses also have kitchens available for the use of guests.

Hostels and private rooms

For many budget travellers, as well as hikers, climbers and skiers, the country's **hostels** (*vandrerhjem*) provide mainstay accommodation. There are almost a hundred in total, with handy concentrations in the western fjords, the central hiking and skiing regions and in Oslo. The Norwegian hostelling association, **Norske Vandrerhjem**, Torggata 1, Oslo (☎23 13 93 00, ⊛www.vandrerhjem .no), issues a free booklet, *Norske Vandrerhjem*, which details locations, opening dates, prices and telephone numbers; bear in mind that it's possible to make bookings via their website. The hostels themselves are invariably excellent – the only quibble, at the risk of being churlish, is that those occupying schools tend to be rather drab and institutional.

Prices per night vary from 100kr to 200kr, although the more expensive hostels nearly always include a grand breakfast. On average, reckon on paying 125kr a night for a bed, 50kr for breakfast and 80–100kr for a hot meal. Bear in mind also that almost all hostels have a few regular double and family rooms on offer: at 250–450kr a double, these are among the cheapest rooms you'll find in Norway. If you're not a member of Hostelling International (HI) you can still use the hostels, though it will cost you an extra 25kr or so a night – better to join up before you leave home. If you don't have your own sheet sleeping bag, you'll have to rent one for around 40–50kr a time.

It cannot be stressed too strongly that **pre-booking** a hostel bed will save you lots of unnecessary legwork. Many hostels are only open from mid-June to mid-August and most close between 11am and 4pm. There's sometimes an 11pm or midnight curfew, though this is less of a drawback in a country where carousing is so expensive. Where

breakfast is included – as it usually is – ask for a breakfast packet if you have to leave early to catch transport; otherwise note that hostel **meals** are nearly always tasty and excellent value. Most, though not all, hostels have small **kitchens**, but often no pots, pans, cutlery or crockery, so self-caterers should take their own.

Tourist offices in the larger towns and amongst the more touristy settlements can often fix you up with a **private room** in someone's house, which may include kitchen facilities. Prices are competitive – from 200–250kr single, 300–350kr double – though there's usually a booking fee (20–30kr) on top, and the rooms themselves are frequently some way out of the centre. Nonetheless, they're often the best bargain available and, in certain instances, an improvement on the local hostel. Where this is the case, we've said so. If you don't have a sleeping bag, check the room comes with bedding – not all of them do; and if you're cooking for yourself, a few basic utensils wouldn't go amiss either.

Campsites, cabins and mountain huts

Camping is a popular pastime in Norway and there are literally hundreds of sites to choose from, anything from a field with a few tent pitches through to extensive complexes with all mod cons. The Norwegian tourist authorities detail around 400 campsites in their free *Camping* brochure, classifying them on a one- to five-star grading depending on the facilities offered. Most sites are situated with the motorist (rather than the cyclist or walker) in mind, and a good few occupy key locations beside the main roads, though in summer these prime sites are occasionally inundated by seasonal workers. The majority of campsites are two- and three-star establishments, where prices are usually per tent, plus a small charge per person; on average expect to pay around 150kr for two people using a tent, with four- and five-star sites around twenty percent more. During peak season it can be a good idea to **reserve ahead** if you have a car and a large tent or trailer; contact details are listed in the free camping booklet and throughout the Guide.

Camping rough in Norway, as in Sweden, is a tradition enshrined in law. You can camp anywhere in open areas as long as you are at least 150m away from any houses or cabins. As a courtesy, ask farmers for permission to use their land – it is rarely refused. Fires are not permitted in woodland areas or in fields between April 15 and September 15, and camper vans are not allowed (ever) to overnight on lay-bys. A good sleeping bag is essential, since even in summer it can get very cold, and, in the north at least, mosquito repellent is vital.

The Norwegian countryside is dotted with thousands of timber **cabins/chalets** (called *hytter*), ranging from simple wooden huts through to comfortable lodges. They are usually two- or four-bedded affairs, with full kitchen facilities and sometimes a bathroom or even TV. Some hostels have them on their grounds, there are nearly always at least a handful at every campsite, and in the Lofoten islands they are the most popular form of accommodation, many occupying refurbished fishermen's huts called *rorbuer*. Costs vary enormously, depending on location, size and amenities, and there are significant seasonal variations, too. However, a four-bed *hytter* will rarely cost more than 600kr per night – a more usual average would be about 400kr. If you're travelling in a group, they are easily the cheapest way to see the countryside – and in some comfort. Hundreds of *hytter* are also rented out as holiday cottages by the week.

One further option for hikers is the chain of **mountain huts** (again called *hytter*) on hiking routes countrywide. Some are privately run, but the majority are operated by **Den Norske Turistforening** (DNT), Storgata 3, Oslo (℡22 82 28 00, ⊛www.turistforeningen.no), the Norwegian Mountain Hiking Association, and affiliated regional hiking organizations. Membership of DNT costs 400kr a year, and although you don't have to be a member of DNT to use their huts, you'll soon recoup your outlay through reduced hut charges for members. For members staying in staffed huts, a bunk in a dormitory costs 90kr, a family or double room 140–175kr, with meals starting at 70kr for breakfast, 165kr for dinner. At unstaffed huts, where you leave the money for your stay in a box provided, an overnight stay costs 135kr.

Food and drink

At its best, **Norwegian food** can be excellent: fish is plentiful, and carnivores can have a field day trying meats like reindeer and elk or even, conscience permitting, seal and whale. Admittedly it's not inexpensive, and those on a tight budget may have problems varying their diet, but by exercising a little prudence in the face of the average menu (which is almost always in Norwegian and English), you can keep costs down to reasonable levels. Vegetarians, however, will have slim pickings, except in Oslo, and drinkers will have to dig very deep into their pockets to maintain much of an intake. Indeed, most drinkers end up visiting the supermarkets and state off-licences (*Vinmonopolet*) so that they can sup away at home (in true Norwegian style) before setting out for the evening.

Food

Many travellers exist almost entirely on a mixture of picnic food and by cooking their own meals, with the odd café meal thrown in to boost morale. Frankly, this isn't really necessary (except on the tightest of budgets) as there are a number of ways to eat out inexpensively. To begin with, a good self-service buffet breakfast, served in almost every hostel and hotel, goes some way to solving the problem, whilst special lunch deals will get you a tasty, hot meal for 70–90kr. Finally, alongside the regular restaurants – which are expensive – there's the usual array of budget pizzerias and cafeterias in most towns.

Breakfast, picnics and snacks

At its best, **breakfast** (*frokost*) in Norway is a substantial self-service affair of bread, crackers, cheese, eggs, preserves, cold meat and fish, washed down with tea and ground coffee. It's usually first-rate at youth hostels, and often memorable in hotels, filling you up for the day for 60–80kr, on the rare occasions when it's not thrown in with the price of your room.

If you're buying your own **picnic food**, bread, cheese, yoghurt and local fruit are all relatively good value, but other staple foodstuffs – rice, pasta, meat, cereals and vegetables – can cost up to twice the price of British equivalents. Anything tinned is particularly dear, with the exception of tinned fish, but coffee and tea are quite reasonably priced. **Supermarkets** are ten-a-penny.

Fast food offers the best chance of a hot takeaway snack. The indigenous Norwegian stuff, served up from **gatekjøkken** – street kiosks or stalls – in every town, consists mainly of rubbery hot dogs (*varm pølse*), while pizza slices and chicken pieces and chips are much in evidence, too. American burger bars are also creeping in – both at motorway service stations and in the towns and cities. A better choice, and usually not much more expensive, is simply to get a sandwich, normally a huge open affair called a **smørbrød** (pronounced "smurrbrur"), heaped with a variety of garnishes. You'll see them groaning with meat or shrimps, salad and mayonnaise in the windows of bakeries and cafés, or in the newer, trendier sandwich bars in the cities. **Cakes and biscuits** are OK too: watch for doughnuts, Danish pastries (*wienerbrød*), butter biscuits (*kjeks*) and waffles (*vafler*).

Good **coffee** is available everywhere, rich and strong, and served black or with cream. **Tea**, too, is ubiquitous, but the local preference is for lemon tea or a variety of flavoured infusions; if you want milk, ask for it. All the familiar **soft drinks** are also available.

Lunch and dinner

For the best deals, you're going to have to eat your main meal of the day at lunch or possibly tea time, when **kafeterias** (often self-service restaurants) lay on daily specials, the *dagens rett*. This is a fish or meat dish served with potatoes and a vegetable or salad, often including a drink, sometimes bread, and occasionally coffee, too; it should go for 70–90kr. Dipping into the menu is more expensive, but not cripplingly so if you stick to omelettes and suchlike. Many department stores have *kafeterias*, as does every large railway station. You'll also find them hidden above shops and offices and adjoining hotels in larger towns, where they might be called *kaffistovas*. Most close at around 6pm, and many don't open at all on Sunday. As a general rule, the food these places serve is plain-verging-on-the-ordinary (though there are many excellent excep-

tions), but the same cannot be said of the continental-style **café-bars** which abound in Oslo and, increasingly, in all of Norway's larger towns and cities. These eminently affordable establishments offer much tastier and much more adventurous meals like pasta dishes, salads and vegetarian options.

In all of the cities, but especially in Oslo, there are first-class **restaurants**, serving dinner (*middag*) in quite formal surroundings. Apart from exotica such as reindeer and elk, the one real speciality is the seafood, simply prepared and wonderfully fresh – whatever you do, don't go home without treating yourself at least once. In the smaller towns and villages, gourmets will be harder pressed – many of the restaurants are pretty mundane, though the general standard is improving rapidly. Main courses begin at around 150kr, starters and desserts at around 60kr. If in doubt, smoked salmon comes highly recommended, as does the catfish and monkfish. Again, the best deals are at lunchtime.

In the towns, and especially in Oslo, there is also a sprinkling of **ethnic restaurants**, mostly Italian with a good helping of Chinese and Indian places. Other cuisines pop up here and there, too – Japanese, Moroccan and Persian to name but three. The most affordable are the Chinese restaurants and the pizza joints.

Vegetarians

Vegetarians are in for a hard time. Apart from a handful of specialist restaurants in the big cities, there's little option other than to make do with salads, look out for egg dishes in *kafeterias* and supplement your diet from supermarkets. If you are a **vegan** the problem is greater: when the Norwegians are not eating meat and fish, they are attacking a fantastic selection of milks, cheeses and yoghurts. At least you'll know what's in every dish you eat, since everyone speaks English. If you're self-catering, look for **health food shops** (*helsekost*), found in some of the larger towns and cities.

Drink

One of the less savoury sights in Norway – and especially common in the north – is the fall-over drunk: you can spot them at any time of the day or night zigzagging along the

Glossary of Norwegian food and drink terms

Basics and snacks

Appelsin-marmelade	marmalade
brød	bread
eddik	vinegar
egg	egg
eggerøre	scrambled eggs
flatbrød	crispbread
fløte	cream
grøt	porridge
iskrem	ice cream
kaffefløte	single cream (for coffee)
kake	cake
kaviar	caviar
kjeks	biscuits
krem	whipped cream
melk	milk
mineralvann	mineral water
nøtter	nuts
olje	oil
omelett	omelette
ost	cheese
pannekake	pancakes
pepper	pepper
pommes-frites	chips
potetchips	crisps
ris	rice
rundstykker	roll
salat	salad
salt	salt
sennep	mustard
smør	butter
smørbrødo	open sandwich
sukker	sugar
suppe	soup
syltetøy	jam
varm pølse	hot dog
yoghurt	yogurt

Meat (kjøtt) and game (vilt)

dyrestek	venison
elg	elk
kalkun	turkey
kjøttboller	meatballs
kjøttkaker	meatcakes
kylling	chicken
lammekjøtt	lamb
lever	liver
oksekjøtt	beef
pølser	sausages
postei	pâté
reinsdyr	reindeer
ribbe	pork rib

skinke	ham
spekemat	dried meat
stek	steak
svinekjøtt	pork
varm pølse	frankfurter/hot dog

Fish (fisk) and shellfish (skalldyr)

ål	eel
ansjos	anchovies (brisling)
blåskjell	mussels
brisling	sprats
hummer	lobster
hvitting	whiting
kaviar	caviar
krabbe	crab
kreps	crayfish
laks	salmon
makrell	mackerel
ørret	trout
piggvar	turbot
reker	shrimps
rødspette	plaice
røkelaks	smoked salmon
sardiner	sardines (brisling)
sei	coalfish
sild	herring
sjøtunge	sole
småfisk	whitebait
steinbit	catfish
torsk	cod
tunfisk	tuna

Vegetables (grønsaker)

agurk	cucumber/ gherkin/pickle
blomkål	cauliflower
bønner	beans
erter	peas
gulrøtter	carrots
hodesalat	lettuce
hvitløk	garlic
kål	cabbage
linser	lentils
løk	onion
mais	sweetcorn
nepe	turnip
paprika	peppers
poteter	potatoes
rosenkål	Brussels sprouts
selleri	celery
sopp	mushrooms

spinat	spinach	sitron	lemon
tomater	tomatoes	solbær	blackcurrants
		tyttbær	cranberries

Fruit (frukt)

ananas	pineapple	**Terms**	
appelsin	orange	blodig	rare, underdone
aprikos	apricot	godt stekt	well done
banan	banana	grillet	grilled
blåbær	blueberries	grytestekt	braised
druer	grapes	kokt	boiled
eple	apple	marinert	marinated
fersken	peach	ovnstekt	baked/roasted
fruktsalat	fruit salad	røkt	smoked
grapefrukt	grapefruit	stekt	fried
jordbær	strawberries	stuet	stewed
multer	cloudberries	sur	sour, pickled
pærer	pears	syltet	pickled
plommer	plums	saltet	cured

Norwegian specialities

brun saus	gravy served with most meats, meatcakes, fishcakes and sausages
fenalår	marinated mutton, smoked, sliced, salted, dried and served with crispbread, scrambled egg and beer
fiskekabaret	shrimps, fish and vegetables in aspic
fiskeboller	fish balls, served under a white sauce or on open sandwiches
fiskesuppe	fish soup
flatbrød	a flat unleavened cracker, half barley, half wheat
gammelost	a hard, strong smelling, yellow-brown cheese with veins
geitost/gjetost	goats' cheese, slightly sweet and fudge-coloured. Similar cheeses have different ratios of goats' milk to cows' milk
gravetlaks	salmon marinated in salt, sugar, dill and brandy
juleskinke	marinated boiled ham, served at Christmas
kjøttkaker med surkål	home made burgers with cabbage and a sweet-and-sour sauce
koldtbord	a midday buffet with cold meats, herrings, salads, bread and perhaps soup, eggs or hot meats
lapskaus	pork, venison (or other meats) and vegetable stew, common in the south and east, using salted or fresh meat, or leftovers, in a thick brown gravy
lutefisk	fish (usually cod) preserved in an alkali solution and flavoured; an acquired taste
multer	cloudberries – wild berries, mostly found north of the Arctic Circle and served with cream (med krem)
mysost	brown whey cheese made from cows' milk
nedlagtsild	marinated herring
pinnekjøtt	western Norwegian Christmas dish of smoked mutton steamed over shredded birch bark, served with cabbage; or accompanied by boiled potatoes and mashed swedes (kålrabistappe)
reinsdyrstek	reindeer steak, usually served with boiled potatoes and cranberry sauce
rekesalat	shrimp salad in mayonnaise

continued overleaf ↘

ribbe julepølse medisterkake	eastern Norwegian Christmas dish of pork ribs, sausage and dumplings
spekemat	various types of smoked, dried meat
Trondhjemsuppea	kind of milk soup with raisins, rice, cinnamon and sugar

Bread, cake and desserts

bløtkake	cream cake with fruit
fløtelapper	pancakes made from cream, served with sugar and jam
havrekjeks	oatmeal biscuits, eaten with goats' cheese
knekkebrød	crispbread
kransekake	cake made from almonds, sugar and eggs, served at celebrations
lomper	potato scones-cum-tortillas
riskrem	rice pudding with whipped cream and sugar, usually served with *frukt saus*, a slighly thickened fruit sauce
tilslørtbondepiker	stewed apples and breadcrumbs, served with cream
trollkrem	beaten egg whites (or whipped cream) and sugar mixed with cloudberries (or cranberries)
vafle	waffles

Drinks

akevitt	aquavit	sitronbrus	lemonade
appelsin saft/juice	orange squash/ juice	te med melk/sitron	tea with milk/lemon
brus	fizzy soft drink	vann	water
eplesider	cider	varm sjokolade	hot chocolate
fruksaft	sweetened fruit juice	vin	wine
kaffe	coffee	søt	sweet
melk	milk	tørr	dry
mineralvann	mineral water	rød	red
øl	beer	hvit	white
		rosé	rosé
		skål!	cheers!

street, a strangely disconcerting counter to the usual stereotype of the Norwegian as a healthy, hearty figure in a wholesome woolly jumper. For reasons that remain obscure – or at least culturally complex – many Norwegians can't just have a drink or two, but have to get absolutely wasted. The majority of their compatriots deplore such behaviour and have consequently imposed what amounts to alcoholic rationing: thus, although booze is readily available in the bars and restaurants, it's taxed up to the eyeballs (half a litre of beer costs 35kr or over) and the distribution of wines and spirits is strictly controlled by a state-run monopoly, **Vinmonopolet**. Whether this paternalistic type of control makes matters better or worse is a moot point, but the majority of Norwegians support it.

What to drink

If you decide to splash out on a few drinks, you'll find Norwegian **beer** is lager-like and comes in three strengths (class I, II or III), of which the strongest and most expensive is class III. Brands to look for include Hansa and Ringsnes. There's no domestically produced **wine** to speak of and most **spirits** are imported too, but one local brew worth experimenting with at least once is **aquavit** (*akevitt*), a bitter concoction served ice-cold in little glasses and, at forty percent proof, real headache material – though it's more palatable with beer chasers: Linie aquavit is one of the more popular brands.

Where to buy drink

Beer is sold in supermarkets and shops all over Norway, though some local communi-

NORWAY | Basics

ties, particularly in the west, have their own rules and restrictions; it's about half the price you'd pay in a bar. The strongest beer, along with wines and spirits, can only be purchased from the **Vinmonopolet** shops. There's generally one in each medium-size town, though there are more branches in the cities (twenty or so in Oslo). Opening hours are usually Monday to Wednesday 10am–4/5pm, Thursday 10am–5/6pm, Friday 9am–4/6pm, Saturday 9am–1pm, though these times can vary depending on the area, and they'll be closed the day before a public holiday. At these stores, wine is quite a bargain, from around 75kr a bottle, and there's generally a fairly bizarre choice of vintages from various South American countries on offer.

Where to drink

Wherever you **go for a drink**, a half-litre of beer should cost between 35kr and 45kr, and a glass of wine from 30kr. You can get a drink at most outdoor cafés, in restaurants and at bars, pubs and cocktail bars. That said, only in the towns and cities is there any kind of "European" bar life and in many places you'll be limited to a drink in the local hotel bar or restaurant. However, in Oslo, Bergen, Stavanger, Trondheim and Tromsø you will be able to keep drinking in bars until at least 1am, until 4am in some places.

Directory

Borders There is little formality at the Norway–Sweden border, slightly more between Norway and Finland. However, the northern border with Russia is a different story. Despite the break-up of the Soviet Union, border patrols (on either side) won't be overjoyed at the prospect of you nosing around. If you have a genuine wish to visit Russia, it's best to sign up for an organized tour from Kirkenes.

Kids There are no real problems with taking children to Norway. They go for half-price (infants under 3 or 4 go free) on all forms of public transport, and get the same discount on an extra bed in their parents' hotel room. Family rooms are widely available in youth hostels, while many of the summer activities detailed in this book are geared up to cater for kids as well. There are also baby compartments (with their own toilet and changing room) for kids under 2 and their escorts on most trains, and baby-changing rooms at most larger train stations. Many restaurants have children's menus; where they don't, it's always worth asking if there are cheaper, smaller portions.

Left luggage There are coin-operated lockers in most railway and bus stations and at all major ferry terminals.

Public holidays National public holidays are a noticeable feature of the Norwegian calendar and act as a unifying force in what remains an extremely homogeneous society. There are ten national public holidays per year, most of which are keenly observed, though the tourist industry carries on pretty much regardless. Some state-run museums adopt Sunday hours on the public holidays listed below, except on Christmas Day and New Year's Day (and often December 26) when they close. Otherwise most businesses and shops close, and the public transport system operates a skeleton or Sunday service. Most Norwegians take their holidays in the summer season, between mid-June and mid-August. Public holidays are: New Year's Day; Maundy Thursday; Good Friday; Easter Monday; Labour Day (May 1); Ascension Day (mid-May); National Day (May 17); Whit Monday; Christmas Day; Boxing Day.

Shopping hours Normal shopping hours are Monday to Friday 9am–4/5pm, with late opening on Thursdays till 6pm or 8pm, plus Saturdays 9am–1/3pm. Some supermarkets stay open much longer – until 8pm in the week and 6pm on Saturdays – and, in addition, the majority of kiosks-cum-newsstands stay open till 9pm or 10pm every night of the week (including Sundays), especially in cities and larger towns. Many petrol stations sell a basic range of groceries and stay open till 11pm daily.

Smoking Smoking is prohibited in all public buildings, including train stations, and it's forbidden on all domestic flights and bus services. Restaurants have to have non-smoking areas by law, and there are supposed to be dividing walls between smoking and non-smoking sections. Hoteliers have by law to designate fifty percent of their rooms as non-smoking.

Tipping A service charge is automatically included in hotel and restaurant bills, so any additional tip is not expected – but always welcome.

History

Despite its low contemporary profile, Norway has a fascinating past. As early as the tenth century its people had explored – and conquered – much of northern Europe, and roamed the Atlantic as far as the North American mainland. Though at first an independent state, from the fourteenth century Norway came under the sway of first Denmark and then Sweden.
Independent again from 1905, Norway was propelled into World War II by the German invasion of 1940, an act of aggression that transformed the Norwegians' attitude to the outside world. Gone was the old insular neutrality, replaced by a liberal internationalism typified by Norway's leading role in the environmental movement.

Early civilizations

The earliest signs of human habitation in Norway date from the end of the last Ice Age, around 10,000 BC. In the Finnmark region of north Norway, the **Komsa** culture was reliant upon seal-fishing, whereas the peoples of the **Fosna** culture, further south near present-day Kristiansund, hunted seals and reindeer. Both these societies were essentially static, dependent upon flint and bone implements. At Alta, the Komsa people left behind hundreds of **rock carvings** and drawings, naturalistic representations of their way of life dating from the seventh to the third millennia BC.

As the edges of the ice cap retreated from the western coastline, so new migrants slowly filtered north. These new peoples, of the **Nøstvet-økser** culture, were also hunters and fishers, but they were able to manufacture stone axes, examples of which were first unearthed at Nøstvet, near Oslo. Beginning around 2700 BC, immigrants from the east, principally the semi-nomadic **Boat Axe** and **Battle-**

Axe peoples – so-called because of the distinctive shape of their stone weapons/tools – introduced animal husbandry and agriculture. The new arrivals did not, however, overwhelm their predecessors; the two groups coexisted, each learning from the other how to survive in a land of harsh infertility. These late Stone Age cultures flourished at a time when other, more southerly countries were already using metal. Norway was poor and had little to trade, but the Danes and Swedes exchanged amber for copper and tin from the bronze-making countries. A fraction of the imported bronze subsequently passed into Norway, mostly to the Battle-Axe people, who appear to have had a comparatively prosperous aristocracy. This was the beginning of the Norwegian **Bronze Age** (1500–500 BC).

Around 500 BC Norway was affected by two adverse changes: the climate deteriorated, and trade relations with the Mediterranean were disrupted by the westward movement of the Celts across central Europe. The former encouraged the development of settled, communal farming in an attempt to improve winter shelter and storage; the latter cut the supply of tin and copper and subsequently isolated the country from the early **Iron Age**. Norway's isolation continued through much of the **classical period**, though the expansion of the Roman Empire in the first and second centuries AD did revive Norway's trading links with the Mediterranean. Evidence of these renewed contacts is provided across Scandinavia by **runes**, carved inscriptions dating from around 200 AD whose 24-letter alphabet – the *futhark* – was clearly influenced by Greek and Latin capitals. Initially, runes were seen as having magical powers, but gradually their usage became more prosaic. Of the 800 or so runic inscriptions extant across southern Norway, most commemorate events and individuals: mothers and fathers, sons and slain comrades.

The renewal of trade with the Mediterranean also spread the use of **iron**. Norway's agriculture was transformed by the use of iron tools, and the pace of change accelerated in the fifth century AD, when the Norwegians learnt how to smelt the brown iron ore, limonite, that lay in their bogs and lakes – hence its common name, **bog-iron**. Clearing the forests with iron axes was relatively easy and, with more land available, the pattern of settlement became less concentrated. Family homesteads leapfrogged up the valleys, and a class of wealthy farmers emerged, their prosperity based on fields and flocks. Above them in the pecking order were local **chieftains**, the nature of whose authority varied considerably. Inland, the chieftains' power was based upon landed wealth and constrained by feudal responsibilities, whereas the coastal lords, who had often accumulated influence from trade, piracy and military prowess, were less encumbered. Like the farmers, these seafarers had also benefited from the iron axe, which made boat-building much easier.

By the middle of the eighth century, Norway had become a country of small, **independent kingships**, its geography impeding the development of any central authority.

The Vikings

Overpopulation, clan discord and the lure of commerce all contributed to the sudden explosion that launched the **Vikings** (from the Norse word *vik*, meaning "creek", and -*ing*, "frequenter of") upon an unsuspecting Europe in the ninth century. The patterns of attack and eventual settlement were dictated by the geographical position of the various Scandinavian countries: the Swedish Vikings turned eastwards, the Danes headed south and southwest, while the Norwegians sailed west. Norwegian longships fell upon the Hebrides, Shetland, Orkney, the Scottish mainland and western Ireland. The Pictish population was able to muster little resistance and the islands were quickly overrun, forming the nucleus of a new Norse kingdom, which itself provided a base for further attacks upon Scotland and Ireland.

The Norwegians founded Dublin in 836, and from Ireland turned their attention eastward to northern Britain. Elsewhere, Norwegian Vikings settled the Faroe Islands and Iceland, and even raided as far south as Moorish Spain, attacking Seville in 844. The raiders soon became settlers, sometimes – as in Iceland and the Faroes – colonizing the entire country, but mostly intermingling with the local population. The speed of their assimilation is, in fact, one of the Vikings' most striking features: William the Conqueror (1027–87) was the epitome of the Norman baron, yet he was also the descendant of Rollo, the Viking warrior whose army had overrun Normandy just a century before.

The whole of Norway felt the stimulating effects of the Viking expeditions. The standard of living rose and the economy was boosted by the spoils of war. Farmland was no longer in such short supply; slaves assisted labour-intensive land clearance schemes; cereal and dairy farming extended into new areas in eastern Norway; new vegetables, such as cabbages and turnips, were introduced from Britain; and farming methods were improved by overseas contact – the Celts, for instance, taught the Norwegians how to thresh grain with flails.

The Vikings' brand of **paganism**, with its wayward, unscrupulous deities, underpinned their inclination to vendetta and clan warfare. Nevertheless, institutions slowly developed which helped regulate the bloodletting. Western Norway adopted the Germanic *wergeld* system of cash-for-injury compensation; every free man was entitled to attend the local *Thing* or parliament, while a regional *Lagthing* made laws and settled disputes. Justice was class-based, however, with society divided into three main categories: the lord, the freeman and the thrall or slave, who was worth about eight cows. Viking **decorative art** was pan-Scandinavian, with the most distinguished work being the elaborate and often grotesque animal motifs that adorned their ships, sledges, buildings and furniture. This craftsmanship is seen at its best in the **ship burials** of Oseberg and Gokstad, both on display in Oslo's Viking Ships Museum.

Norway's first widely recognized chieftain was **Harald Hårfagri** (Fair-Hair), who gained control of the coastal region as far north as Trøndelag around 900. This sparked an exodus of minor rulers, most of whom left to settle in Iceland. Harald's long rule was based on personal pledges of fealty; with the notable exception of the regional *Lagthings*, there were no institutions to sustain it, and when he died his kingdom broke up into its component parts. Harald did, however, leave a less tangible but extremely important legacy: from now on every ambitious chieftain was not content to be a local lord, but strove to be ruler of Harald's whole kingdom.

Harald's sons and grandsons warred over their inheritance for the rest of the tenth century, undermining Norway's independence by seeking military support in Denmark and Sweden. Meanwhile, Norwegian settlers were laying the foundations of independent Norse communities in the **Faroes** and **Iceland**, where they established a parliament, the *Althing*, in 930. Subsequently, Erik the Red, exiled from Norway and then banished from Iceland for three years for murder, set out in 985 with 25 ships, fourteen of which arrived in **Greenland**. The new colony prospered, and by the start of the eleventh century there were about three thousand settlers. This created a shortage of good farmland, making another push west inevitable. The two **Vinland sagas** provide the only surviving account of these further explorations, recounting the exploits of Leif Eriksson the Lucky, who founded a colony he called Vinland on the shore of **North America** (probably Newfoundland) around 1000 AD.

The arrival of Christianity

In 1015, a prominent Viking chieftain, **Olav Haraldsson**, sailed for Norway from England, intent upon conquering his homeland. Significantly, he arrived by merchant ship with just 100 men, rather than with a fleet of longships and an army, a clear sign of the passing of the Viking heyday. Pledged to him was the support of the yeoman farmers of the interior – a new force in Norway that was rapidly supplanting the old warrior aristocracy – and Haraldsson was soon recognized as king of much of the country.

For twelve years, Olav ruled in peace, founding Norway's first national government. His authority was based upon the regional *Things* – broadly democratic bodies which administered local law – and on his willingness to deliver justice without fear or favour. The king's most enduring achievement, however, was to make Norway **Christian**. Olav had been converted during his days in England and vigorously imposed his new faith on his countrymen.

It was foreign policy rather than pagan enmity, however, that brought about Olav's downfall. By scheming with the Swedish ruler against **King Knut** (Canute) of Denmark and England, Olav provoked a Danish invasion. The Norwegian chieftains who had suffered at the hands of Olav could be expected to help Knut, but even the yeomen failed to rally to the cause. In 1028, Olav was forced to flee, first to Sweden and then to Russia, while Knut's son Svein and his mother, the English Queen Aelfgifu, took the Norwegian crown. Two years later, Olav made a sensational return at the head of a scratch army, only to be defeated and killed by an alliance of wealthy landowners and chieftains at **Stiklestad**, the first major Norwegian land battle.

The petty chieftains and yeoman farmers who had opposed Olav soon fell out with their new king: Svein had no intention of relaxing the royal grip, and his chieftains' subsequent rebellion seems also to have had nationalistic undertones – many Norwegians had no wish to be ruled by a Dane. Svein had to flee the country, and Olav's old enemies popped over to Sweden to bring back Olav's young son, **Magnus**, who became king in 1035.

The chastening experience of Svein's short rule transformed the popular memory of Olav. With surprising speed, he came to be regarded as an heroic champion of Norway, and there was talk of miracles brought about by the dead king's body. The Norwegian church, looking for a local saint to enhance its position, fostered the legends and had Olav canonized. The remains of **St Olav** were then reinterred ceremoniously at Nidaros, today's Trondheim, where the miracles increased in scope, hastening the conversion of what remained of heathen Norway.

On Magnus's death in 1047, **Harald Hardråda** (Olav's half-brother) became king. The last of the Viking heroes, Hardråda dominated his kingdom by force of arms for over twenty years. Neither was Hardråda satisfied with being king of just Norway. In 1066, the death of Edward the Confessor presented Harald with an opportunity to press his claim to the English throne. The Norwegian promptly sailed on England, landing near York with a massive fleet, but just outside the city, at Stamford Bridge, his army was surprised and trounced by Harold Godwinson, the new Saxon king of England. Hardråda was killed in the battle and the threat of a Norwegian conquest of England had – though no one realized it at the time – gone forever. Not that the victory did much for Godwinson, whose weakened army trudged back south to be defeated by William of Normandy at the Battle of Hastings.

Medieval success

Harald's son, **Olav Kyrre** (the Peaceful) – whose life had been spared after Stamford Bridge on the promise that he never attack England again – went on to reign as king of Norway for the next 25 years. Peace engendered economic prosperity, and treaties with Denmark ensured Norwegian independence. Three native bishoprics were established, and cathedrals built at Nidaros, Bergen and Oslo. It's from this period, too, that Norway's surviving **stave churches** date: wooden structures resembling an upturned keel, they were lavishly decorated with dragon heads and scenes from Norse mythology, proof that the traditions of the pagan world were slow to disappear.

The first decades of the twelfth century witnessed the further consolidation of Norway's position as an independent power, despite internal disorder as the descendants of Olav Kyrre struggled to maintain their influence. Civil war ceased only when **Håkon IV** took the throne in 1240, ushering in what is often called "The Period of Greatness". Secure at home, Håkon strengthened the Norwegian hold on the Faroe and Shetland islands, and in 1262 both

Iceland and Greenland accepted Norwegian sovereignty. When his claim to the Hebrides was disputed by Alexander III of Scotland, Håkon assembled an intimidatory fleet, but died in 1263 in the Orkneys. Three years later the Hebrides and the Isle of Man (always the weakest links in the Norwegian empire) were sold to the Scottish crown by Håkon's successor, **Magnus the Lawmender** (1238–80).

Under Magnus, Norway prospered. Law and order were maintained, trade flourished and the king's courtiers even followed a code of etiquette compiled in the *King's Mirror* (*Konungs skuggsja*), in contrast to former rough-and-ready Viking ways. Neither was the power of the monarchy threatened by feudal barons as elsewhere in thirteenth-century Europe. Norway's scattered farms were not susceptible to feudal tutelage and, as a consequence, the nobility lacked local autonomy – castles remained few and far between – and were drawn into the centralized administration of the state. Norwegian **Gothic art** reached its full maturity in this period, as construction began on the nave at Nidaros Cathedral and on Håkon's Hall in Bergen.

Magnus was succeeded by his sons, first the undistinguished Erik and then by **Håkon V** (1270–1319), the last of medieval Norway's talented kings. Håkon continued the policy of his predecessors, making further improvements to central government and asserting royal control of Finnmark by the construction of a fortress at Vardø. His achievements, however, were soon to be swept away along with the independence of Norway itself.

Medieval failure

Norway's independence was threatened from two quarters. With strongholds in Bergen and Oslo, the **Hanseatic League** and its merchants had steadily increased their influence, holding a monopoly on imports and controlling inland trade. The power of their interna-

tional trading links was reinforced in Norway as the royal household grew increasingly dependent on the taxes paid to them by the League. The second threat was **dynastic**. When Håkon died in 1319 he left no male heir and was succeeded by his grandson, the three-year-old son of a Swedish duke. The boy, Magnus Eriksson, was elected Swedish king two months later, marking the virtual end of Norway as an independent country until 1905.

Magnus assumed full power over both countries in 1332, but his reign was a difficult one. When the Norwegian nobility rebelled he agreed that the monarchy should again be split: his three-year-old son, Håkon, would become Norwegian king when he came of age, while the Swedes agreed to elect his eldest son Erik to the Swedish throne. It was then, in 1349, that the **Black Death** struck, spreading quickly along the coast and up the valleys, and killing almost two-thirds of the Norwegian population. It was a catastrophe of almost unimaginable proportions, its effects compounded by the way the country's agriculture was structured. Animal husbandry was easily the most important part of Norwegian farming, and the harvesting and drying of sufficient winter fodder was labour-intensive. Without the labourers, the animals died in their hundreds and famine conditions prevailed for several generations.

Many farms were abandoned and, deprived of their rents, the petty chieftains who had once dominated rural Norway were, as a class, almost entirely swept away. The vacuum was filled by royal officials, the *syslemenn*, each of whom exercised control over a large chunk of territory on behalf of a Royal Council. The collapse of local governance was compounded by the dynastic toing and froing at the top of the social ladder. In 1380, Håkon died and Norway passed under Danish control with Olav, the son of Håkon and the Danish princess **Margaret**, becoming the ruler of the two kingdoms. It was a union that was to last 400 years.

The Kalmar union

Despite Olav's early death in 1387, the resourceful Margaret persevered with the union. Proclaimed regent by both the Danish and (what remained of the) Norwegian nobility, she engineered a treaty with the Swedish nobles that not only recognized her as regent of Sweden but also agreed to accept any king she should nominate. Her chosen heir, **Erik of Pomerania**, was foisted on the Norwegians in 1389. When he reached the age of majority in 1397, Margaret organized a grand coronation with Erik crowned king of all three countries at Kalmar in Sweden – hence the **Kalmar Union**.

After Margaret's death in 1412, all power was concentrated in Denmark. In Norway, foreigners were preferred in both state and church, and the country became impoverished by paying for Erik's wars. Incompetent and brutal in equal measure, Erik managed to get himself deposed in all three countries at the same time. In the meantime, Sweden had left the union, and eventually a Danish count, Christian of Oldenburg, was crowned king of Norway and Denmark in 1450. Thereafter, Norway ceased to take any meaningful part in Scandinavian affairs. Literature languished as the Old Norse **language** was displaced as the official language by Danish – and indeed it soon came to be regarded as the language of the ignorant and inconsequential. Only the Norwegian church retained any power, but this itself was overwhelmed by the Reformation.

Union with Denmark

In 1536 Christian III declared his kingdom Protestant and, although it was slow to take root among the Norwegian peasantry, **Lutheranism** soon came to be a powerful instrument in establishing Danish influence. The Bible, catechism and hymnal were all in Danish, the bishops were all Danes and,

after 1537, so were all the most important provincial Norwegian governors.

In many respects, Norway became simply a source of raw materials – fish, timber and iron ore – whose proceeds lined the royal purse. Naturally enough, the Swedes coveted these materials too, the upshot being a long and inconclusive war (1563–70) which saw much of Norway ravaged by competing bands of mercenaries. Among the Danish kings of the period, **Christian IV** (1588–1648) proved the most sympathetic to Norway. He visited the country often, improving the quality of its administration and founding new towns including Kongsberg, Kristiansand and Christiania (later Oslo).

At last, in the middle of the seventeenth century, the Norwegian economy began to pick up. The population grew, trade increased and, benefiting from the decline of the Hanseatic League, a native bourgeoisie began to take control of certain parts of the economy, most notably the herring industry. But Norwegian cultural self-esteem remained at a low ebb: the country's merchants spoke Danish, mimicked Danish manners and read Danish pot-boilers. What's more, Norway was a constant bone of contention between Sweden and Denmark, the result being a long series of wars in which its more easterly provinces were regularly battered by the competing armies.

The year 1660 marked a turning point in the constitutional arrangements governing Norway. For centuries, the Danish Council of State had had the power to elect the monarch and impose limitations on his or her rule. Now, a powerful alliance of merchants and clergy swept these powers away to make **Frederik III** an absolute ruler. This was not a reactionary coup, but an attempt to limit the power of the conservative-minded nobility. In addition, the development of a centralized state machine would, many calculated, provide all sorts of job opportunities to the low-born but adept. Norway was incorporated into the administrative structure of Denmark, with royal authority delegated to the *Stattholder*, who governed through what soon became a veritable army of professional bureaucrats. There were positive advantages for Norway: the country acquired better defences, simpler taxes, a separate High Court and doses of Norwegian law, but once again power was exercised almost exclusively by Danes.

The eighteenth and early nineteenth centuries

The **absolute monarchy** established by Frederik III soon came to concern itself with every aspect of Norwegian life. The ranks and duties of minor officials were carefully delineated, religious observances tightly regulated and restrictions were imposed on everything from begging and dress through to the food and drink that could be consumed at weddings and funerals. This extraordinary superstructure placed a leaden hand on imagination and invention. Neither was it impartial: there were some benefits for the country's farmers and fishermen, but by and large the system worked in favour of the middle class. The merchants of every small town were allocated the exclusive rights to trade in a particular area and competition between the towns was forbidden. These local monopolies placed the peasantry at a dreadful disadvantage, nowhere more iniquitously than in the Lofotens, where the fishermen not only had to buy supplies and equipment at the price set by the merchant, but also had to sell their fish at the price set by him too.

In the meantime, there were more wars between Denmark and Sweden. In 1700, **Frederik IV** (1699–1730) made the rash decision to attack the Swedes at the time when their king, Karl XII, was generally reckoned to be one of Europe's most brilliant military strategists. Predictably, the Danes were

defeated and only the intervention of the British saved Copenhagen from falling into Swedish hands. Undeterred, Frederik tried again, and this time Karl retaliated by launching a full-scale invasion of Norway. The Swedes rapidly occupied southern Norway, but after Karl was shot dead by a sniper, the two countries agreed the **Peace of Frederiksborg** (1720), which ended hostilities for the rest of the eighteenth century.

Peace favoured the growth of trade, but although Norway's economy prospered it was hampered by the trade monopolies exercised by the merchants of Copenhagen. In the 1760s, however, the Danes did a dramatic U-turn, abolishing monopolies, removing trade barriers and even permitting a free press – and the Norwegian economy boomed. Nonetheless, the bulk of the population remained impoverished and prey to famine whenever the harvest was poor. The number of landless agricultural labourers rose dramatically, partly because the more prosperous farmers were buying up large slices of land, and for the first time Norway had something akin to a lumpen proletariat.

Despite this, Norway was one of the few European countries little affected by the French Revolution. Instead of political action, there was a **religious revival**, with Hans Nielson Hauge emerging as an evangelical leader. The movement's characteristic hostility to officialdom caused concern, and Hauge was imprisoned, but in reality it posed little threat to the status quo. The end result was rather the foundation of a fundamentalist movement that is still a force to be reckoned with in parts of fjordland Norway.

The period leading up to the **Napoleonic Wars** was a good time for Norway: overseas trade, especially with England, flourished, with the demand for Norwegian timber and iron heralding a period of unparalleled prosperity. Denmark and Norway had remained neutral throughout the Seven Years' War (1756–63) between England and

France, and renewed that neutrality in 1792. However, when Napoleon implemented a trade blockade – the Continental System – against Britain, he roped in the Danes. As a result, the British fleet bombarded Copenhagen in 1807 and forced the surrender of the entire Dano-Norwegian fleet. Denmark, in retaliation, declared war on England and Sweden. The move was disastrous for the Norwegian economy, which had suffered bad harvests in 1807 and 1808, and the English blockade of its seaports ruined trade.

By 1811 it was obvious that the Danes had backed the wrong side in the war, and the idea of an equal union with Sweden, which had supported Britain, became increasingly attractive to many Norwegians. By latching on to the coat-tails of the victors, they hoped to restore the commercially vital trade with England. They also thought that the new Swedish king would be able to deal with the Danes if it came to a fight – just as the Swedes had themselves calculated when they appointed him in 1810. The man concerned, **Karl XIV Johan**, was, curiously enough, none other than Jean-Baptiste Bernadotte, formerly one of Napoleon's marshals. With perfect timing, he had helped the British defeat Napoleon at Leipzig in 1813. His reward came in the **Treaty of Kiel** the following year when the great powers instructed the Danes to cede all rights in Norway to Sweden (although they did keep the dependencies of Iceland, Greenland and the Faroes). Four hundred years of union had ended.

Union with Sweden 1814–1905

The high-handed transfer of Norway from Denmark to Sweden did nothing to assuage the growing demands for greater independence. Furthermore, the Danish Crown Prince Christian Frederik roamed Norway stirring up fears of Swedish intentions. The prince and his supporters convened a Constituent Assembly, which met at Eidsvoll in April 1814 and produced a **constitution**. Issued on May 17, 1814 (still a national holiday), this declared Norway to be a "free, independent and indivisible realm" with Christian Frederik as its king. Not surprisingly, Karl XIV Johan would have none of this and, with the support of the great powers, he invaded Norway. Completely outgunned, Christian Frederik mounted barely any resistance. In exchange for Swedish promises to recognize the Norwegian constitution and the Storting (parliament), he abdicated as soon as he had signed a peace treaty – the so-called **Convention of Moss** – in August 1814.

The ensuing period was marred by struggles between the Storting and Karl XIV Johan over the nature of the union. Although the constitution emphasized Norway's independence, Johan had a veto over the Storting's actions; the post of *Stattholder* in Norway could only be held by a Swede; and foreign and diplomatic matters concerning Norway remained entirely in Swedish hands. Despite this, Karl XIV Johan proved popular in Norway, and during his reign the country enjoyed a fair amount of independence. From 1836 all the highest offices in Norway were filled exclusively by Norwegians, and democratic local councils were established, in part due to the rise of peasant farmers as a political force.

The gradual increase in prosperity had important **cultural implications**. The layout and buildings of modern Oslo – the Royal Palace, Karl Johans gate and the university – date from this period, whilst Johan Christian Dahl, the most distinguished Scandinavian landscape painter of his day, was instrumental in the moves to establish the National Gallery in Oslo in 1836. Other prominent members of the bourgeoisie championed all things Norwegian. However, under both Oscar I (1844–59) and Karl XV (1859–72) it was **pan–Scandinavianism** that ruled the intellectual roost. This belief in the natural solidarity of Denmark, Norway and Sweden was espoused by the leading artists of the period, including Ibsen and Bjørnstjerne Bjørnson, but died a death in 1864, when the people of Norway and Sweden refused to help Denmark when it was attacked by Austria and Prussia (some of the loudest cries of treachery came from a young Henrik Ibsen, in his poetic drama *Brand*).

Domestic politics changed, too, with the rise to power in the 1850s of **Johan Sverdrup**, who started a long and ultimately successful campaign to wrest executive power from the king and transfer it to the Storting. By the mid-1880s, Sverdrup and his political allies had pretty much won the day, but a further bout of sabre-rattling between the supporters of Norwegian independence and the Swedish king, **Oscar II** (1872–1907), was necessary before both sides would accept a plebiscite. This took place in August 1905, when there was an overwhelming vote in favour of the **dissolution of the union**, which was duly confirmed by the Treaty of Karlstad. A second plebiscite determined that independent Norway should be a monarchy rather than a republic and, in November 1905, Prince Karl of Denmark (Edward VII's son-in-law) was elected to the throne as **Håkon VII**.

Dissolution came at a time of further economic advance, engendered by the introduction of hydroelectric power. Social reforms also saw funds being made available for unemployment relief, accident insurance schemes and a Factory Act (1909). An extension to the franchise gave the vote to all men over 25 and, in 1913, to women too. The education system was reorganized, and substantial sums were spent on new arms and defence matters. This prewar period also saw the emergence of a strong trade union movement and of a Labour Party committed to revolutionary change.

Culturally, the second half of the nineteenth century was fruitful for Norway, with the rediscovery of the Norwegian language and its folklore by a number of academics who formed the nucleus of the National Romantic movement, which did much to restore the country's cultural self-respect. Following on were well-known authors like **Alexander Kielland**, who wrote most of his works between 1880 and 1891, and **Knut Hamsun**, who published his most characteristic novel, *Hunger*, in 1890. In music, **Edvard Grieg** (1843–1907) made his debut in the first concert to consist entirely of works by Norwegian composers and was inspired by old Norwegian folk melodies, composing some of his most famous music for Ibsen's *Peer Gynt*. The artist **Edvard Munch** was also active during this period, completing many of his major works in the 1880s and 1890s, while the internationally acclaimed dramatist **Henrik Ibsen** returned to Oslo after a prolonged, self-imposed exile in 1891.

The early years of independence up to 1939

Since 1814 Norway had had little to do with European affairs, and at the outbreak of **World War I** declared herself strictly neutral. Sympathy, though, lay largely with the Western Allies, and the Norwegian economy boomed since its ships and timber were in great demand. By 1916, however, Norway had begun to feel the pinch, as German submarine action hit both enemy and neutral shipping, and by the end of the war Norway had lost half its chartered tonnage and 2000 crew. The Norwegian economy also suffered after the USA entered the war because the Americans imposed strict trade agreements in their attempt to prevent supplies getting to Germany, and rationing had to be introduced across Norway. Indeed, the price of neutrality was high: there was a rise in state expenditure, a soaring cost of living and, at the end of the war, no seat at the conference table. In spite of its losses, Norway got no share of the confiscated German shipping, although it was partly compensated by gaining sovereignty of **Spitsbergen** and its coal deposits – the first extension of the Norwegian frontiers for 500 years. In 1920 Norway also entered the new League of Nations.

Later in the 1920s, the decline in world trade led to a decreased demand for Norway's shipping. Bank failure and currency fluctuation were rife, and, as unemployment and industrial strife increased, a burgeoning Norwegian **Labour Party** took advantage. With the franchise extended to all those over 23 and the introduction of larger constituencies, it had a chance, for the first time, to win seats outside the large towns. At the 1927 election the Labour Party, together with the Social Democrats from whom they'd split, were the biggest grouping in the Storting. Nonetheless, because they had no overall majority and because many feared their revolutionary rhetoric, they were manoeuvred out of office after only fourteen days. **Trade disputes** and lockouts continued and troops had to be used to protect workers crossing picket lines.

During the war, **Prohibition** had been introduced as a temporary measure, and a referendum of 1919 showed a clear majority in favour of its continuation. But the ban did little to quell – and even exacerbated – drunkenness, and it was abandoned in 1932, to be replaced by the government sales monopoly of wines and spirits that remains in force today. The 1933 election gave the Labour Party more seats than ever. Having shed its revolutionary image, a campaigning reformist Labour Party benefited from the increasing conviction that state control and a centrally planned economy were the only answer to Norway's economic problems. In 1935 the Labour Party, in alliance with the Agrarian Party, took power – an unlikely combination since the Agrarians were profoundly nationalist in outlook, so much so that their

defence spokesman had been the rabid anti-Semite **Vidkun Quisling**. Frustrated by the democratic process, Quisling had left the Agrarians in 1933 to found the Nasjonal Samling (National Unification), a fascist movement which proposed, among other things, that both Hitler and Mussolini should be nominated for the Nobel Peace Prize. Quisling had good contacts with Nazi Germany but little support in Norway – local elections in 1937 reduced his local representation to a mere seven, and party membership fell to 1500.

The Labour government under **Johan Nygaardsvold** presided over an improving economy. By 1938 industrial production was 75 percent higher than it had been in 1914; unemployment had dropped as expenditure on roads, railways and public works increased. Social welfare reforms were implemented and trade union membership increased. When war broke out in 1939, Norway was lacking only one thing – adequate defence. A vigorous member of the League of Nations, the country had pursued disarmament and peace policies since the end of World War I and was determined to remain neutral.

World War II

In early 1940, despite the threatening rumblings of Hitler, the Norwegians were preoccupied with Allied mine-laying off the Norwegian coast – part of their attempt to prevent Swedish iron ore being shipped from Narvik to Germany. Indeed, such was Norwegian naivety that they made a formal protest to Britain on the day of the **German invasion**. Caught napping, the Norwegian army offered little initial resistance and the south and central regions of the country were quickly overrun. King Håkon and the Storting were forced into a hasty evacuation of Oslo and headed north, eventually taking refuge in Britain where they formed the Norwegian government-in-exile. Norway was rapidly brought under Nazi control, Hitler sending **Josef Terboven** to take full charge of affairs. The fascist Nasjonal Samling was declared the only legal party and the media, civil servants and teachers were brought under their control. As **civil resistance** grew, a state of emergency was declared: two trade union leaders were shot, arrests increased and a concentration camp was set up outside Oslo. In February 1942 Quisling was installed as "Minister President" of Norway, but it was soon clear that his government didn't have the support of the Norwegian people. The church refused to cooperate, schoolteachers protested and trade union members and officials resigned en masse. In response, deportations increased, death sentences were announced and a compulsory labour scheme was introduced.

Military resistance escalated. A military organisation (MILORG) was established as a branch of the armed forces under the control of the High Command in London. By May 1941 it had enlisted 20,000 men (32,000 by 1944) in clandestine groups all over the country. Arms and instructors came from Britain, radio stations were set up and a continuous flow of intelligence about Nazi movements sent back. Sabotage operations were legion, the most notable being the destruction of the heavy-water plant at **Rjukan**, foiling a German attempt to produce an atomic bomb.

The **government in exile** in London continued to represent free Norway to the world, mobilizing support on behalf of the Allies. Most of the Norwegian merchant fleet was abroad when the Nazis invaded, and by 1943 the Norwegian navy had seventy ships helping the Allied convoys. In Sweden, Norwegian exiles assembled in "health camps" at the end of 1943 to train as police troops in readiness for liberation.

When the Allies landed in Normandy in June 1944, overt action against the Nazis in Norway by the resistance was temporarily discouraged, since the Allies couldn't safeguard against reprisals. By late October, the Russians had crossed the border in the far north. The Germans, forced to retreat, burned everything in their path and drove the local population into hiding. To prevent the Germans reinforcing their beleaguered Finnmark battalions, the resistance – with renewed Allied support – planned a campaign of mass railway sabotage, stopping three-quarters of the troop movements overnight. As their control of Norway crumbled, the Germans finally **surrendered** on May 7, 1945. King Håkon returned to Norway on June 7, five years to the day since he'd left for exile.

Terboven committed suicide and the Nasjonal Samling collaborators were rounded up. A caretaker government took office, staffed by resistance leaders, and was replaced in October 1945 by a majority **Labour government**. The Communists won eleven seats, reflecting the efforts of Communist saboteurs in the war and the prestige that the Soviet Union enjoyed in Norway after liberation. Quisling was shot, along with 24 other high-ranking traitors, and thousands of collaborators were punished.

Postwar reconstruction

At the end of the war, Norway was on its knees: the far north – Finnmark – had been laid waste, half the mercantile fleet lost, and production was at a standstill. Recovery, though, fostered by a sense of national unity, was quick; it took only three years for GNP to return to its prewar level. Norway's part in the war had increased her prestige in the world. The country became one of the founding members of the **United Nations** in 1945, and the first UN Secretary-General, Tryggve Lie, was Norwegian Foreign Minister. With the failure of discussions to promote a Scandinavian defence union, the Storting also voted to enter **NATO** in 1949.

Domestically, there was general agreement about the form that social reconstruction should take. In 1948, the

Storting passed the laws that introduced the Welfare State virtually unanimously. The 1949 election saw the government returned with a larger majority and Labour administrations remained in power throughout the following decade, when the dominant political figure was **Einar Gerhardsen**. As national prosperity increased, society became ever more egalitarian, levelling up rather than down. Subsidies were paid to the agricultural and fishing industries, wages increased and a comprehensive social security system helped to eradicate poverty. The state ran the important mining industry, was the largest shareholder in the hydroelectric company and built an enormous steelworks at Mo-i-Rana to help develop the economy of the devastated northern counties. Rationing ended in 1952 and, as the demand for higher-level education grew, new universities were approved at Bergen, Trondheim and Tromsø.

Beyond consensus: modern Norway

The political consensus began to fragment in the early 1960s. Following changes in the constitution concerning the rural constituencies, the centre had realigned itself in the 1950s, the outmoded Agrarian Party becoming the **Centre Party**. Defence squabbles within the Labour Party led to the formation of the **Socialist People's Party** (the SF), which wanted Norway out of NATO and sought a renunciation of nuclear weapons. The Labour Party's 1961 declaration that no nuclear weapons would be stationed in Norway except under an immediate threat of war did not placate the SF who, unexpectedly, took two seats at the election that year. Holding the balance of power, the SF voted with the Labour Party until 1963, when it helped bring down the government over the mismanagement of state industries. A replacement coalition collapsed after only one month, but the writing was on the wall.

Rising prices, dissatisfaction with high taxation and a continuing housing shortage meant that the 1965 election put a **non-socialist coalition** in power for the first time in twenty years.

The new coalition's programme, under the leadership of **Per Borten** of the Centre Party, was unambitious. However, living standards continued to rise, and although the 1969 election saw a marked increase in Labour Party support, the coalition hung on to power. Also in 1969, **oil and gas** were discovered beneath the North Sea and, as the vast extent of the reserves became obvious, so it became clear that the Norwegians were to enjoy a magnificent bonanza – one which was destined to pay about 25 percent of the government's annual bills. Meanwhile, Norway's politicians, who had applied twice previously for membership of the **European Economic Community** (EEC) – in 1962 and 1967 – believed that de Gaulle's fall in France presented a good opportunity for a third application, which was made in 1970. There was great concern, though, about the effect of membership on Norwegian agriculture and fisheries, and in 1971 Per Borten was forced to resign following his indiscreet handling of the negotiations. The Labour Party, the majority of its representatives in favour of EEC membership, formed a minority administration, but when the 1972 referendum narrowly voted "No" to joining the EEC, the government resigned.

With the 1973 election producing another minority Labour government, the uncertain pattern of the previous ten years continued. Even the postwar consensus on **Norwegian security policy** broke down on various issues – such as the question of a northern European nuclear-free zone and the stocking of Allied material in Norway – although there remained strong agreement for continued NATO membership.

In 1983, the Christian Democrats and the Centre Party joined together in a non-socialist coalition, which lasted only two years. It was replaced in 1986 by a minority Labour administration, led by **Dr Gro Harlem Brundtland**, Norway's first woman prime minister. She made sweeping changes to the way the country was run, introducing seven women into her eighteen-member cabinet, but her government was beset by problems for the three years of its life: tumbling oil prices led to a recession, unemployment rose (though only to four percent) and there was widespread dissatisfaction with Labour's high taxation.

At the **general election** in September 1989, Labour lost eight seats and was forced out of office – the worst result that the party had suffered since 1930. More surprising was the success of the extremist parties on both political wings – the anti-NATO Left Socialist Party and the right-wing, anti-immigrant Progress Party both scored spectacular results, winning almost a quarter of the votes cast, and increasing their representation in the Storting many times over. This deprived the Conservative Party (one of whose leaders, bizarrely, was Gro Harlem Brundtland's husband) of the majority it might have expected, the result being yet another shaky minority administration – this time a **centre-right coalition** between the Conservatives, the Centre Party and the Christian Democrats, led by Jan Syse.

The new government immediately faced problems familiar to the last Labour administration. In particular, there was continuing conflict over joining the **European Community**, a policy still supported by many in the Norwegian establishment but flatly rejected by the Centre Party. It was this, in part, that signalled the end of the coalition, for after just over a year in office, the Centre Party withdrew its support and forced the downfall of Syse. In October 1990, Gro Harlem Brundtland was put back in power at the head of a **minority Labour administration**, remaining in office till her re-election for a fourth minority term in 1993. The 1993 elections saw a revival in Labour Party fortunes and, to the relief of the majority, the collapse of the Progress Party vote. However, it was also an untidy, confusing affair where the main issue, membership of the EU, cut across the traditional left versus right axis of the political parties.

Present-day Norway

Following the 1993 election, the country tumbled into a long and fiercely conducted campaign over membership of the EU. Brundtland and her main political opponents wanted in, but despite the near unanimity amongst politicians, the Norwegians narrowly rejected the EU in a **referendum** on November 28, 1994. It was a close call (52.5 percent versus 47.5 percent), but in the end farmers and fishermen afraid of the economic results of joining, as well as women's groups and environmentalists who felt that Norway's high standards of social care and "green" controls would suffer, came together to swing opinion against the EU. Afterwards, and unlike the Labour government of 1972, the Brundtland administration soldiered on, wisely soothing ruffled feathers by promising to shelve the whole EU membership issue until at least 2000. Nevertheless, the **1997 election** saw a move to the right, the main beneficiaries being the Christian Democratic Party and the ultra-conservative Progress Party. In itself, this was not enough to remove the Labour-led coalition from office – indeed Labour remained comfortably the largest party – but the right was dealt a trump card by the new Labour leader, **Thorbjørn Jagland**. During the campaign, Jagland had promised that the Labour Party would step down from office if it failed to elicit more than the 36.9 percent of the vote it had secured in 1993. Much to the chagrin of his colleagues, Jagland's political chickens came home to roost when Labour only received 35 percent of the vote – and they had to go, leaving the government in the hands of an unwieldy right-of-centre, minority coalition. Bargaining with its rivals from a position of parliamentary weakness, the new government found it difficult to cut a clear path – or at least one very different from its predecessor – apart from in managing to antagonize the women's movement by some of its reactionary social legislation during 1998 and 1999. In the Spring of 2000, the government resigned and Labour resumed command – but not for long: in the elections of the next year, they took a drubbing and the right prospered, paving the way for another ungainly centre-right administrative coalition.

In the long term, quite what Norway will make of its splendid **isolation from the EU** is unclear, though the situation is mitigated by Norway's membership of the European Eco-nomic Agreement (EEA), a free-trade deal of January 1994 which covers both Norway and the EU. Whatever happens, and whether or not there is another EU referendum, it's hard to imagine that the Norwegians will suffer any permanent economic harm. They have, after all, a superabundance of natural resources and arguably the most educated workforce in the world. Which isn't to say the country doesn't collectively **fret** – a modest increase in the amount of drug addiction and street crime has produced much heart-searching, the theory being that an advanced and progressive social policy should be able to eliminate such barbarisms. This thoughtful approach, so typical of Norway, is very much to the country's credit as is the refusal to accept a residual level of unemployment (of about 6–7 percent) that is the envy of many other Western governments.

Books

Books in English on Norway are surprisingly scant: few travellers have written well (or indeed at all) about the region over the years, and historical works tend to concentrate almost exclusively on the Vikings. That said, Norwegian literature is increasingly appearing in translation – notably the Icelandic sagas and selected modern novelists – and it's always worth looking out for a turn-of-the-century *Baedeker's Norway and Sweden*, if only for the phrasebook, from which you can learn the Norwegian for "Do you want to cheat me?", "When does the washerwoman come?" and "We must tie ourselves together with rope to cross this glacier."

In the UK, **Norvik Press** is an excellent source of old and new Scandinavian writing: for their catalogue write to the University of East Anglia, Norwich NR4 7TJ (☎01603/593356, ⊛www .uea.ac.uk/llt/norvik_press).

Most of the books listed below are paperbacks and in print – those that are out of print should be easy to track down in secondhand bookshops. Recommended titles are asterisked.

Travel and general

Thor Heyerdahl *The Kon-Tiki Expedition*. You may want to read this after visiting Oslo's Kon-Tiki Museum (p.245). The intrepid Heyerdahl's accounts of his expeditions aroused huge interest when they were first published, and remain ripping yarns though surprisingly few people care to read them today.

★ **Mark Kurlansky** *Cod: A Biography of the Fish that Changed the World*. This wonderful book tracks the life and times of the cod and the generations of fishermen who have lived off it. There are sections on over-fishing and the fish's breeding habits, and recipes are provided. Norwegians figure frequently – cod was their staple diet for centuries.

Constance Roos *Walking in Norway*. This well-researched and informative guide outlines hiking routes in almost every part of Norway, with useful sections on conditions in the mountains and equipment. It's easily the best of its type on the market, though the descriptions of some of the hiking routes lack detail.

Mary Wollstonecraft *Letters written during a Short Residence in Sweden, Norway and Denmark*. For reasons that have never been entirely clear, Wollstonecraft, the author of *A Vindication of the Rights of Women* and mother of Mary Shelley, travelled Scandinavia for several months in 1795. Her letters home represent a real historical curiosity, though her trenchant comments on Norway often get sidelined by her intense melancholia.

History and mythology

★ **Peter Christen Asbjørnsen and Jørgen Moe** *Norwegian Folk Tales*. Of all the many books on Norwegian folk tales, this is the edition you want – the illustrations by Erik Werenskiold and Theodor Kittelsen are superb.

Fredrik Dahl *Quisling: A Study in Treachery*. A comprehensive biography of the world's most famous traitor, Vidkun Quisling – the man is pre-sented in all his unpleasant fullness.

Rolf Danielsen (et al) *Norway: A History from the Vikings to Our Own Times*. Thoughtful and well-presented

account investigating the social and economic development of Norway – a modern and well-judged book that avoids the "kings and queens" approach to its subject.

★ **H.R. Ellis Davidson** *The Gods and Myths of Northern Europe*. A handy, first-rate companion to the sagas, this "who's who" of Norse mythology includes some useful reviews of the more obscure gods.

Gwyn Jones *A History of the Vikings*. Superbly crafted, erudite account of the Vikings with excellent sections on every aspect of their history and culture. The same author wrote *Scandinavian Legends and Folk Tales* (o/p), an excellent and enjoyable analysis of its subject.

Snorri Sturluson *Egil's Saga, Laxdaela Saga, Njal's Saga*, and *King Harald's Saga*. Icelandic sagas, written in the early years of the thirteenth century, and which tell of ninth- and tenth-century derring-do. There's clan warfare in the Laxdaela and Njal sagas, more bloodthirstiness in Egil's, and a bit more biography in King Harald's, penned to celebrate one of the last and most ferocious Viking chieftains – Harald Hardråda (see p.209).

Architecture and the visual arts

J.P. Hodin *Edvard Munch*. The best available general introduction to Munch's life and work, with much interesting historical detail.

Robert Layton *Grieg*. Clear, concise and attractively illustrated book on Norway's greatest composer. Essential reading if you want to get to grips with the man and his times.

Marion Nelson (et al) *Norwegian Folk Art: The Migration of a Tradition*.

Lavishly illustrated book discussing the whole range of folk art, from wood carvings through to bedspreads and traditional dress. It's particularly strong on the influence of Norwegian folk art in the USA, but the text sometimes lacks focus.

Literary fiction and biography

Kjell Askildsen *A Sudden Liberating Thought*. Short stories, in the Kafkaesque tradition, from one of Norway's most uncompromisingly modernist writers.

Jens Bjørneboe *The Sharks*. Set at the end of the last century, this is a thrilling tale of shipwreck and mutiny by a well-known Norwegian writer, who had an enviable reputation for challenging authoritarianism of any description. Also recommended is his darker trilogy – *Moment of Freedom*, *The Powderhouse* and *The Silence* – exploring the nature of cruelty and injustice.

Jostein Gaarder *Sophie's World*. Hugely popular novel that deserves all the praise heaped upon it – it's beautifully and gently written, with puffs of whimsy all the way through. It bears comparison with Hawking's *A Brief History of Time*, though the subject matter here is philosophy, and there's an engaging mystery story tucked in here too. Also try *Through A Glass Darkly*.

Knut Hamsun *Hunger*. Norway's leading literary light in the 1920s and early 1930s, Knut Hamsun was a writer of international acclaim until he disgraced himself by supporting Hitler. Of Hamsun's many novels, *Hunger* (1890) made his name, a trip into the psyche of an alienated and angst-ridden young writer, which shocked contemporary readers.

Henrik Ibsen *The Complete Major Prose Plays*. The key international figure of Norwegian literature, Ibsen was a social dramatist, keen to portray contemporary society, in all its forms and with all its hypocrisies, through his characters. Comparatively few of his plays are ever performed in Britain or the USA, apart perhaps from *A Doll's House* and *Hedda Gabler*. All his major plays are contained in this inexpensive volume.

Amalie Skram *Under Observation*. Confined to a mental hospital against her will, Skram (1846–1905) had a terrible time at the hands of her tyrannical male doctor, and based this chunky novel on her experiences. Similar themes are developed in her excellently written *Lucie*.

Herbjørg Wassmo *Dina's Book: A Novel*. Set in rural northern Norway in the middle of the nineteenth century, this strange but engaging tale has a plot centred on a powerful but tormented heroine.

A brief guide to Norwegian

There are two official Norwegian languages: *Riksmål* or *Bokmål* (book language), a modification of the old Dano-Norwegian tongue left over from the days of Danish dominance; and *Landsmål* or *Nynorsk*, which was codified during the nineteenth-century upsurge of Norwegian nationalism and is based on rural dialects of Old Norse provenance. Roughly eighty percent of schoolchildren have *Bokmål* as their primary language, and the remaining twenty percent, concentrated in the fjord country of the west coast and the mountain districts of central Norway, are *Nynorsk* users. Despite the best efforts of the government, *Nynorsk* is in decline – in 1944 fully one-third of the population used it. As the more common of the two languages, it is *Bokmål* we use here.

As elsewhere in Scandinavia, you don't really need to know any Norwegian to get by. Almost everyone speaks at least some English, and in the tourist industry many Norwegians are fluent. **Phrasebooks** are thin on the ground, but Berlitz's Norwegian–English mini-dictionary has a useful grammar section and a menu reader, while Routledge's more comprehensive (and much heavier) Norwegian dictionary has much the same.

Pronunciation

Pronunciation can be tricky. A **vowel** is usually long when it's the final syllable or followed by only one consonant; followed by two it's generally short. Unfamiliar ones are:

ae before an r, as in bad; otherwise as in say
ø as in fur but without pronouncing the r
å usually as in saw
øy between the ø sound and boy
ei as in say
consonants are pronounced as in English except:
c, q, w, z found only in foreign words and pronounced as in the original
g before i, y or ei, as in yet; otherwise hard
hv as in view
j, gj, hj, lj as in yet
rs usually as in shut
k before i, y or j, like the Scottish loch; otherwise hard
sj, sk before i, y, ø or øy, as in shut

Basic phrases

do you speak English? - **snakker du engelsk?**
yes - **ja**
no - **nei**
do you understand? - **forstår du?**
I don't understand - **jeg forstår ikke**
I understand - **jeg forstår**
please - **vær så god**
thank you (very much) - **takk (tusen takk)**
you're welcome - **vær så god**
excuse me - **unnskyld**
good morning - **god morgen**
good afternoon - **god dag**
good night - **god natt**
goodbye - **adjø**
today - **i dag**
tomorrow - **i morgen**
day after tomorrow - **i overmorgen**
in the morning - **om morgenen**
in the afternoon - **om ettermiddagen**
in the evening - **om kvelden**

Some signs

entrance - **inngang**
exit - **utgang**
gentlemen - **herrer** or **menn**
ladies - **damer** or **kvinner**
open - **åpen**
closed - **stengt**
arrival - **ankomst**
police - **politi**
hospital - **sykehus**
cycle path - **sykkelsti**
no smoking - **røyking forbudt**

no camping - **camping forbudt**
no trespassing - **uvedkommende forbudt**
no entry - **ingen adgang**
pull/push - **trekk/trykk**
departure - **avgang**
parking fees - **avgift**

Questions and directions

where? (where is/are?) - **hvor? (hvor er?)**
when? - **når?**
what? - **hva?**
how much/many? - **hvor mye/hvor mange?**
why? - **hvorfor?**
which? - **hvilket?**
what's that called - **hva kaller man det på**
in Norwegian? **norsk?**
can you direct me to ...? - **kan de vise meg**
veien til ...?
it is/there is (is it/is there) - **det er (er det)?**
what time is it? - **hvor mange er klokken?**
big/small - **stor/liten**
cheap/expensive - **billig/dyrt**
early/late - **tidlig/sent**
hot/cold - **varm/kald**
near/far - **i nærheten/langt borte**
good/bad - **god/dårlig**
vacant/occupied - **ledig/opptatt**
a little/a lot - **litt/mye**
more/less - **mer/mindre**
can we camp here? - **kan vi campe her?**
is there a youth hostel near here? - **er det et**
vandrerhjem i nærheten?
how do I get to ...? - **hvordan kommer jeg**
til ...?
how far is it to ...? - **hvor langt er det**
til ...?
ticket - **billett**
single/return - **en vei/tur-retur**
can you give me a lift to ...? - **kan jeg få**
sitte på til ...?
left/right - **venstre/høyre**
go straight ahead - **kjør rett frem**

Numbers

0 - **null**	17 - **sytten**
1 - **en**	18 - **atten**
2 - **to**	19 - **nitten**
3 - **tre**	20 - **tjue**
4 - **fire**	21 - **tjueen**
5 - **fem**	22 - **tjueto**
6 - **seks**	30 - **tretti**
7 - **sju**	40 - **førti**
8 - **åtte**	50 - **femti**
9 - **ni**	60 - **seksti**
10 - **ti**	70 - **sytti**
11 - **elleve**	80 - **åtti**
12 - **tolv**	90 - **nitti**
13 - **tretten**	100 - **hundre**
14 - **fjorten**	101 - **hundreogen**
15 - **femten**	200 - **to hundre**
16 - **seksten**	1000 - **tusen**

Days and months

Sunday - **søndag**
Monday - **mandag**
Tuesday - **tirsdag**
Wednesday - **onsdag**
Thursday - **torsdag**
Friday - **fredag**
Saturday - **lørdag**
January - **januar**
February - **februar**
March - **mars**
April - **april**
May - **mai**
June - **juni**
July - **juli**
August - **august**
September - **september**
October - **oktober**
November - **november**
December - **desember**

(Note: days and months are never capitalized)

Glossary of Norwegian terms and words

å - stream or creek
apotek - chemist
bakke - hill
bokhandel - bookshop
bro/bru - bridge
dal - valley/dale

domkirke - cathedral
drosje - taxi
e.Kr - AD
elv/bekk - river/stream
ferje/ferge - ferry
fjell/berg - mountain

f.Kr – BC
foss – waterfall
gate (gt.) – street
hav – ocean
havn – harbour
hytte – cottage, cabin
innsjø – lake
jernbanestasjon – railway station
KFUM/KFUK – Norwegian YMCA/YWCA
kirke/kjerke – church
klokken/kl. – o'clock
moderasjon – discount or price reduction
MOMS or MVA – Value Added Tax
museet – museum

NAF – Norwegian Automobile Association
rabatt – discount or price reduction
rådhus – town hall
sentrum – city or town centre
sjø – sea
skog – forest
slott – castle, palace
Storting – parliament
tilbud – special offer
torget – main town square, often home to an outdoor market
vann/vatn – water or lake
vei/veg/vn – road

2.1

Oslo and the Oslofjord

Oslo is an enterprising city. Something of a poor relation to Stockholm until Norway's break with Sweden at the beginning of the twentieth century, it remained dourly provincial until the 1950s, since when it has developed into a go-ahead and cosmopolitan commercial hub of half a million people. The new self-confidence is plain to see in the vibrant and urbane city centre, whose easy-going atmosphere compares favourably with any other capital in Europe. Inevitably, Norway's big companies are mostly based here, as a rash of concrete-and-glass towers testify, though these monoliths rarely interrupt the stately Neoclassical lines of the late nineteenth-century **town centre**. It's here you should head first, as Oslo's handsome older quarters notch up some excellent museums and field a cosmopolitan street-life and bar scene that surprises many first-time visitors; furthermore, they're also within easy reach of the **Bygdøy peninsula**, home to the world-famous Viking Ships Museum.

Oslo is also the only major metropolis in the country (its nearest rival, Bergen, is less than half its size), a distinction which gives the city an unusually powerful – some say overweening – voice in the nation's affairs, whether political, cultural or economic. The centre itself is compact, but the city's vast boundaries (453 square kilometres) encompass huge areas of forest and coastline, reflecting the deep and abiding affinity which the inhabitants have for the wide open spaces that surround their city. The waters of the **Oslofjord** to the south and the forested hills of the **Nordmarka** inland to the north are immensely popular for everything from boating and hiking to skiing, and on all but the shortest of stays there's ample opportunity to join in. The **island beaches** just offshore in the Oslofjord and the open forest and ski jumps at **Holmenkollen** are obvious targets, both within easy reach by ferry or underground train.

Oslo curves round the northernmost point of the Oslofjord, which extends for some 100km from the Skagerrak, the choppy channel separating Norway and Sweden from Denmark. As Norwegian fjords go, Oslofjord is not particularly beautiful, but amongst a string of workaday industrial settlements is Norway's only surviving fortified town, **Fredrikstad**, with its angular bastions and grid-iron of late sixteenth-century streets; it's best visited as a day-trip by train from the capital.

Oslo

The oldest of the Scandinavian capital cities, **OSLO** (the name is made up from *Às*, a Norse word for God, and *Lo*, meaning field) was founded, according to the medieval Norse chronicler Snorre Sturlason, around 1048 by Harald Hardråde. Harald's son, Olav Kyrre, established a bishopric and built a cathedral here, though the kings of Norway continued to live in Bergen – an oddly inefficient division of church and state, considering the difficulty of communications between the two settlements. At the start of the fourteenth century, Håkon V rectified matters by moving to Oslo, where he built himself the Akershus fortress. The town boomed until 1349 when the bubonic plague wiped out almost half the population, initiating a period of slow decline whose pace accelerated after Norway came under

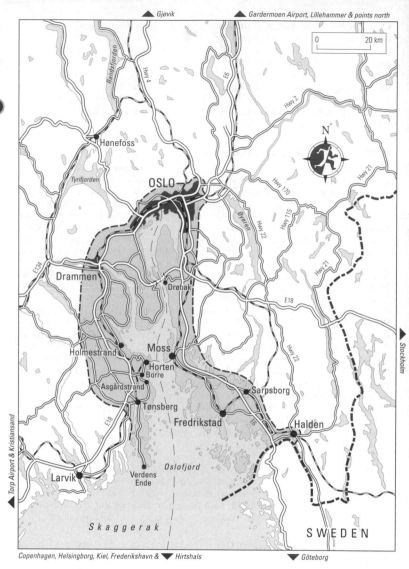

Danish control in 1397. No more than a neglected backwater, Oslo's fortunes were ultimately revived by the Danish king **Christian IV**, who in 1624 moved Oslo lock, stock and barrel, shifting it west to its present site and re-christening it "Christiania". The new city prospered and by the nineteenth century, Christiania (indeed Norway as a whole) was clamouring for independence, which it finally achieved in 1905 – though the city didn't revert to its original name for another twenty years.

Today's **city centre** embodies the urban elegance of the late nineteenth and early twentieth centuries: wide streets, dignified parks and gardens, solid buildings and long, consciously classical vistas combine to lend it a self-satisfied, respectable air.

Oslo's biggest single draw is its **museums**, which cover a hugely varied and stimulating range of topics: the fabulous Viking Ships Museum, the Munch Museum, the park devoted to the bronze and granite sculptures of Gustav Vigeland, and the moving historical documents of the Resistance Museum are enough to keep even the most battle-weary museum-goer busy for a few days. There's also a decent **outdoor life** – Oslo is enlivened by a good range of parks, pavement cafés, street entertainers and festivals. In summer, when virtually the whole population lives outdoors, the city is a real delight. It's also worth visiting in winter, when its prime location amid hills and forests makes it a thriving and affordable ski centre.

Arrival and information

Downtown Oslo is at the heart of a superb **public transport system**, which makes arriving and departing straightforward. The principal arrival hub is the area around Oslo S train station at the eastern end of the main thoroughfare, Karl Johans gate. The other hub is Nationaltheatret at the west end of Karl Johans gate. There's a tourist information office in Oslo S and another by the harbour close to Nationaltheatret.

Trains and buses

International and domestic **trains** use Oslo Sentralstasjon, known as **Oslo S** (train information and reservations on ☎177 or ⊛www.nsb.no), sited on the Jernbanetorget square at the eastern end of the city centre. There are money-exchange facilities here, as well as a post office, a tourist office, and **two train information offices**, one dealing with enquiries, the other selling tickets and making seat reservations (the latter are compulsory on many long-distance trains). Many domestic trains en route to and from Oslo S also pass through the **Nationaltheatret** station, at the west end of Karl Johans gate, which is handier for most of the city-centre sights and Oslo's main harbour. Trains to and from the airport (see below) stop at both Nationaltheatret and Oslo S.

The central **Bussterminalen** (bus terminal) is handily placed a short walk northeast of Oslo S, under the Galleriet Oslo shopping centre. It handles most of the bus services within the city as well as those to and from the airport. Long-distance buses also arrive and depart from here, but bus travellers should note that incoming services sometimes terminate on the south side of Oslo S, at the bus stands beside Havnegata. For all bus enquiries, consult the Nor-Way **Bussekspress Bussterminalen information desk** (Mon–Fri 7am–10pm, Sat 8am–5.30pm, Sun 8am–10pm; ☎23 00 24 00, ⊛www.nor-way.no); the desk also has information on Säfflebussen (☎22 19 49 00, ⊛www.safflebussen.se) international bus services to Copenhagen and Stockholm.

Airport

Oslo's gleamingly modern airport, **Gardermoen**, is a lavish affair very much in the Scandinavian style, with acres of cool wooden floor, soft angles and slender concrete pillars. Departures are processed on the upper and arrivals on the lower level, where there are also currency-exchange facilities, car-rental offices – see p.257 for details – and a tourist information office. Gardermoen is located 45km north of the city off the E6 motorway. If you're **driving** into Oslo, note that there's a 15kr toll on all approach roads into the city. From the airport, **express trains** run south to Oslo, stopping at Oslo S and Nationaltheatret stations (every 15–20min 5.30am–12.30am; 25min; 140kr). There are also ordinary inter-city trains into Oslo (every 1–2hr; 40min; 70kr) and trains north to Lillehammer, Røros and Trondheim. **Flybussen** buses (every 10–15min Mon–Sat 5.30am–1am, Sun noon–midnight; 45min; 95kr) also link the airport with Oslo, departing from outside the arrivals concourse and travelling via the main downtown bus station to Jernbanetorget,

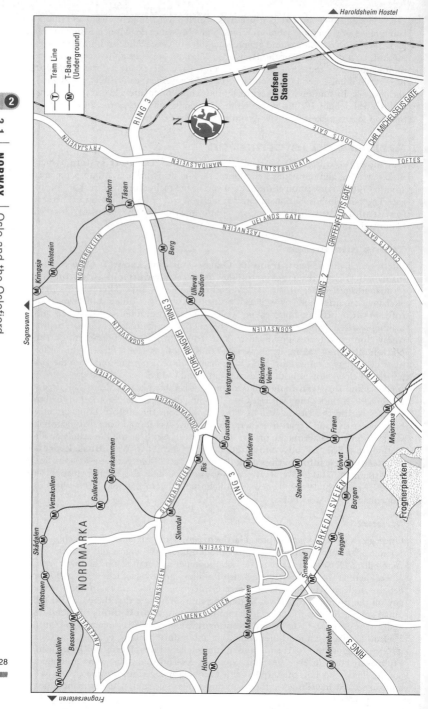

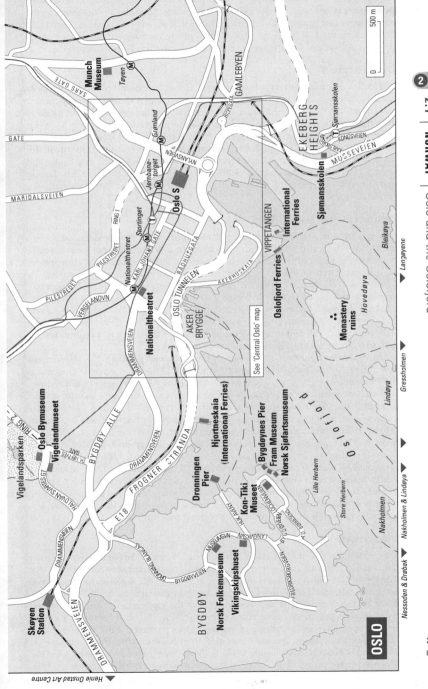

OSLO

229

Munch Museum

Tøyen

SARS GATE

GATE

MARIDALSVEIEN

Grønland

Gamlebyen

EKEBERG HEIGHTS

Sjømannskolen

KONGSVEIEN

MOSSEVEIEN

Sjømannsskolen

Jernbane-torget

Oslo S

NYLANDSVEIEN

RING 1

Stortinget

Nationaltheatret

PILESTREDET

RÅDHUSGATA

KARL JOHANS GATE

PILESTREDET

VERGELANDVN

DRAMMENSVEIEN

OSLO TUNNELEN

Nationaltheatret

AKER BRYGGE

AKERHUSKAIA

VIPPETANGEN

International Ferries

Oslofjord Ferries

Monastery ruins

Hovedøya

Bleikøya

Langøyene

Gressholmen

Lindøya

See 'Central Oslo' map

Oslofjord

Vigelandsparken

Oslo Bymuseum

Vigelandmuseet

RING 2

HALVDAN SVARTES GATE

TH. HEYERDS GATE

BYGDØY ALLE

DRAMMENSVEIEN

FROGNER STRANDA

Hjortneskaia (International Ferries)

Dronningen Pier

Kon-Tiki Museet

Bygdøynes Pier
Fram Museum
Norsk Sjøfartsmuseum

Lille Herbern

Store Herbern

Nakholmen

Nessoden & Drøbak

Nakholmen & Lindøya

Norsk Folkemuseum

Vikingskipshuset

BYGDØY

MUSEUMSVN

LANGVIKSVN

HUK AVENY

O. DECHENSVN

BYGDØYVEIEN

FREDRIKSBORGVEIEN

DRONNING BLANCAS

Skøyen Station

DRAMMENSVEIEN

E18

BYGDØY ALLE

DRAMMENSVEIEN

Henie Onstad Art Centre

500 m

0

Grensen and the *Radisson SAS Scandinavia* hotel. In addition, **Nor-Way Bussekspress** operate a variety of other bus services from the airport direct to the small towns surrounding Oslo. Finally, note that Ryanair fly from Stansted and Prestwick in the UK to **Torp** airport, just outside the town of Sandefjord, about 100km southwest of Oslo; there are bus connections from Torp to the capital.

Car ferries

DFDS Scandinavian Seaways **ferries** from Copenhagen and Stena ferries from Fredrikshavn, also in Denmark, arrive at the **Vippetangen quays**, a twenty-minute walk south of Oslo S: take Akershusstranda and Skippergata to Karl Johans gate and turn right, or catch bus #60 marked "Jernbanetorget" (every 20–30min Mon–Fri 6am–midnight, Sat from 7am, Sun from 8am; 10min; 22kr). On Color Line from Kiel in Germany and Hirsthals in Denmark you'll arrive at the **Hjortneskaia**, some 3km west of the city centre. From here, bus #56 goes to the city centre and Oslo S (every 30min Mon–Fri 6–9.20am & 2.30–5.30pm; 10min; 22kr). Failing that, a taxi to Oslo S will cost about 100kr (for ferry ticket office details see "Listings", p.257).

Driving into the city

Arriving **by car**, you'll have to drive through one of eighteen video-controlled toll-points which ring the city: it's 15kr to enter and there are spot-fines if you're caught trying to avoid the tolls. Passholder lanes (blue signs inscribed *Abonnement*) are always located on the left and are for drivers in possession of toll passes; the *Mynt/Coin* (yellow signs) lanes are for exact cash payments only, and frequently have a bucket-shaped receptacle where you throw your money; the *Manuell* (grey) lanes are also used for cash payments, but provide change. Oslo's ring roads circle and tunnel under the city; if you follow the signs for "Ring 1" you'll be delivered right into the centre and emerge (eventually) at the Ibsen P-hus, a multistorey car park two blocks north of Karl Johans gate.

You won't need your car to sightsee in Oslo. For **car parking**, the above-mentioned Ibsen P-hus, on C.J. Hambros Plass 1 (☎22 33 04 80), is open 24 hours, as is the Europark Aker Brygge P-hus, to the rear of the Aker Brygge complex, down near the main harbour at Sjøgata 4. There are half a dozen other multistorey car parks in the centre, though several of them operate restricted hours only. **Costs** are predictably expensive except during the evening and overnight: during peak hours (Mon–Fri 7am–5pm) it's 20kr for thirty minutes or 23kr for an hour up to a maximum of 190kr per day. Alternatively, you can park in **pay-and-display** car parks and metered spaces around the city (up to 15kr per hour, 32kr for two hours). Identified by blue "P" signs, on-street metered spaces are free from Monday to Friday between 5pm and 8am and over the weekend after 2pm Saturday. They're also free for Oslo Card holders at all times (see box, opposite) – but make sure to write your registration number, date and time on the card in the space provided, and note that you'll still have to observe parking time-limits.

Information

The main tourist information office, the **Norges Informasjonssenter** (Norwegian Information Centre; June–Aug daily 9am–7pm; May & Sept Mon–Sat 9am–5pm; Oct–April Mon–Fri 9am–4pm; ☎23 11 78 80, ⊛www.visitoslo.com) is housed in what used to be the Oslo Vestbane train station at Brynjulf Bull's plass 1, down by the waterfront at the western end of the city centre. It has some glossy visual displays and an extensive range of brochures relating to Norway as a whole, but also specializes in everything to do with Oslo, providing a full range of information, free city maps, guided tours and an accommodation-booking service. There's also a tourist office inside **Oslo S** (May–Sept daily 8am–11pm; Oct–April Mon–Sat 8am–5pm; ☎23 11 78 80) with similar services. Both offices sell the Oslo

The Oslo Card

The useful Oslo Card gives free admission to almost every museum in the city and unlimited free travel on the entire municipal transport system, including local trains, plus free on-street parking at metered parking places. It also provides some useful discounts in shops, hotels and restaurants. Valid for either 24, 48 or 72 hours, it costs 180kr, 270kr or 360kr respectively (children aged 4–15: 60kr, 80kr and 110kr); a 24hr family card for two adults and two children costs 395kr. Cards are sold at the city's tourist offices, most hotels, the Trafikanten office (see below) and downtown Narvesen newsagents. They are valid from the moment they're first used, at which time they should either be presented and stamped or (for example, if your first journey is by tram) you should ink in the date and time yourself. Bear in mind that in the winter, when opening hours for many sights and museums are reduced, you may well have to work hard to make the card pay for itself.

Card and have free copies of various booklets and leaflets, including the excellent and very thorough *Oslo Official Guide* and *What's On in Oslo*, an invaluable listings guide to events and services in the city. The **Norwegian Youth Hostel Association** (*Norske Vandrerhjem*) has its main office in the centre of town, not far from Oslo S at Torggata 1 (☎23 13 93 00, ✆www.vandrerhjem.no). They issue a free booklet detailing all the country's hostels.

City transport

Compared to other European capitals, Oslo is extremely **safe**, and you're unlikely to be hassled. However, the usual cautions apply to walking around on your own late at night, when you should be particularly careful in the vicinity of Oslo S (where the junkies gather) and on the tougher east side of town along and around Storgata. This sense of safety applies in equal measure to the **city transport** system, which is operated by AS Oslo Sporveier, whose information office, **Trafikanten**, is on Jernbanetorget, beneath the see-through high-tech clock tower outside Oslo S (Mon–Fri 7am–8pm, Sat 8am–6pm; ☎81 50 01 76, ✆www.trafikanten.no). Apart from selling Oslo Cards and public transport tickets (see box above), they give away a useful **transit route map**, the *Sporveiens hovedkart*, as well as a **timetable** booklet called *Rutebok for Oslo*, which details every timetable for every route in the Oslo system.

Oslo's public transport system consists of buses, trams, a modest underground rail system (the Tunnelbanen) and local ferries. Flat-fare **tickets** (bought on board buses, trams or ferries, or at Tunnelbanen stations) cost 22kr and are valid for unlimited travel within the city boundaries for one hour (children 4–16 travel half price; under-4s go free). There are several ways to cut costs, the best being the **Oslo Card** (see box above), which is valid on the whole network and on certain routes beyond – but not on trains or buses to the airport. If you're not into museums, however, a straight **travel pass** might be a better buy. A Dagskort, valid for unlimited travel within the city limits for 24 hours, costs 50kr, or there's the Flexikort (8 rides; 135kr), as well as passes for longer stays, available from the Trafikanten office in Jernbanetorget and downtown Narvesen kiosks. On buses, the driver will check your ticket; on trams you're trusted to have one. Flexikort tickets should be cancelled in the machine on every journey. Though **fare-dodging** might seem widespread, bear in mind that it is punished by some hefty spot fines.

Buses

Almost all city **bus** services originate at the Bussterminalen beside Oslo S. There are around fifty routes operating within the city limits, and other services out of Oslo, too. The vast majority of them pass through Jernbanetorget and many also stop at the Nationaltheatret (National Theatre), towards the west end of the city centre. Most buses stop running at around midnight, though at weekends **night buses** (*nattbussen*) take over on certain routes (flat-rate fare 50kr; Oslo Card and other passes not valid); for full details see the timetable, *Rutebok for Oslo*.

Trams

The city's **trams** run on eight routes through the city, criss-crossing the centre from east to west, and sometimes duplicating the bus routes. They are a bit slower than the buses, but are a handy and rather more interesting way of getting about. Major stops include Jernbanetorget, Nationaltheatret and Aker Brygge. Most operate regularly throughout the day from 6am to midnight.

Tunnelbanen and local trains

The Tunnelbanen – or **T-bane** – has eight lines, all of which converge to share a common slice of track which crosses the city centre from Majorstuen in the west to Tøyen in the east, with Jernbanetorget, Stortinget and Nationaltheatret stations in between. From this central section, four lines run westbound (*Vest*) and four eastbound (*Øst*). The system mainly serves commuters from the suburbs, but you'll find it useful for trips out to Holmenkollen and Sognsvann – where the trains travel above ground. The system runs from around 6am until 12.30am. A series of **local commuter trains**, run by NSB, link Oslo with Moss, Eidsvoll, Drammen and other outlying towns; departures are from Oslo S, with many also making a stop at Nationaltheatret.

Ferries

Numerous **ferries** shuttle across the northern reaches of the Oslofjord, connecting the city centre with outlying districts and the archipelago. Services to the Bygdøy peninsula (late April to Sept only) leave from the piers behind the Rådhus, while the all-year services to Hovedøya, Lindøya and the other offshore islets (except Langøyene, June–Aug only) leave from the Vippetangen quay, behind Akershus Castle. To get to the Vippetangen quay from Jernbanetorget, either take bus #60 or walk – it takes about twenty minutes. If you're venturing beyond the city limits, there are also boats to Nesodden (all year), and Drøbak (summer weekends only); these leave from the Aker Brygge piers.

Taxis

The speed and efficiency of Oslo's public transport system means that you should rarely have to resort to a **taxi**, which is probably just as well given how expensive they are. Fares are regulated, with the tariff varying according to the time of day: expect to pay around 100kr for a ten-minute, five-kilometre ride at night; about 25 percent less during the day. Taxi ranks can be found round the city centre and outside all the big hotels. For easy reference, there's one at the corner of Karl Johans gate and Lille Grensen. To call a cab ring Oslo Taxi on ☎02323.

Bicycles

Renting a **bicycle** is a pleasant option if you want to get about under your own steam: the city has a reasonable range of cycle tracks, while an increasing number of roads have cycle lanes. However at the time of writing, plans for a **municipal bike** rental scheme had collapsed, and there were no bike rental outlets in the city. This is sure to change quickly – ask at the tourist office for an update.

Accommodation

Oslo has the range of **hotels** you would expect of a capital city, as well as **B&B-cum-private rooms**, a smattering of **guesthouses** (*pensjonater*) and a quartet of **youth hostels**, unofficial and official. To appreciate the full flavour of the city, you're best off staying on or near the western reaches of Karl Johans gate – between the Stortinget and the Nationaltheatret – though the well-heeled area to the north and west of Det Kongelige Slott (the Royal Palace) is enjoyable, too. Many of the least expensive lodgings are, however, to be found in the vicinity of Oslo S, and this district – along with the grimy suburbs to the north and east of the station – is preferably avoided. That said, if money is tight and you're here in July and August, your choice of location may well be very limited as the scramble for **budget beds** becomes acute – or at least tight enough to make it well worth either ringing ahead or booking via an establishment's website. For peace of mind, it's advisable to make an **advance reservation**, particularly for your first night.

One way of cutting out the hassle is to use the **accommodation service** provided by the city's two tourist offices (see p.230). Both can give you accommodation lists, or make a booking on your behalf for 30kr per person, a real bargain when you consider that they often get discounted rates – the Oslo S office is especially good for B&Bs.

Hotels

The standard charge at the less expensive end of the **hotel** market is around 700–900kr; for this you'll get a fairly small and simple en-suite double room. You hit the comfort zone at about 900kr, and luxury from around 1000kr. However, **special offers and seasonal deals** often make the smarter hotels more affordable than this. Most of them offer discounts of up to thirty percent at weekends, while in July and August – when Norwegians leave town for their holidays – prices everywhere tend to drop radically. Where the discount is fixed, we've given codes for the reduced as well as the regular rate.

Expensive

Best Western Ambassadeur Camilla Colletts vei 15 ☎23 27 23 00, ⊛www.bestwestern.com/no /ambassadeur. One of a long row of attractive nineteenth-century town houses graced by wrought-iron balconies, though the slightly grimy facade doesn't do justice to the elegantly furnished interior. Each of the bedrooms has a different theme, such as "Shanghai" or "Amsterdam", and it's in a great location too, just three blocks west of the Slottsparken. ❻/❹

Bristol Kristian IV's gate 7 ☎22 82 60 00, ⊛www.bristol.no. Plush establishment distinguished by its sumptuous public rooms, with ornate nineteenth-century chandeliers, columns and fancifully carved arches. ❻/❹

Continental Stortingsgata 24 ☎22 82 40 00, ⊛www.hotel-continental.no. One of Oslo's most prestigious hotels, ideally located just steps from Karl Johans gate, with chic and glitzy public rooms and amazingly comfortable bedrooms furnished in immaculate modern style. ❼/❻

First Hotel Nobel House Kongens gate 5 ☎23 10 72 00, ⊛wwwfirsthotels.com. Deluxe place oozing style, from the smart wooden floors to the cool, modernist decor. Great downtown location too, footsteps from the restaurants and art museums of Bankplassen. ❼/❺

Frogner House Skovveien 8 ☎22 56 00 56,

⊛www.frognerhouse.com. Elegant hotel occupying a handsome Victorian town house in one of Oslo's ritziest neighbourhoods. Each of the comfortable bedrooms is individually decorated in tasteful modern style, with stripped wood and thick carpets throughout. It's 1km west of the centre off Frognerveien – trams #12 or #15. ❼/❺

Gabelshus Gabels gate 16 ☎23 27 65 00, ⓔgableshus.hotel@os.telia.no. Delightful and intimate hotel in a smart residential area a couple of kilometres west of the city centre. The beautifully maintained interior boasts ornate fireplaces and antique furnishings. It's off Drammensveien – take tram #10 or #13 from the centre. Highly recommended. ❻/❹

Grand Karl Johans gate 31 ☎23 21 20 00, ⊛www.grand.no. Over 100 years of tradition, comfort and style in a prime position on Oslo's main street translates into stratospheric room rates, though hefty weekend and summertime discounts can make it much more affordable. Breakfasts are sumptuous, the lobby opulent, and the rooms eminently comfortable. ❼/❹

Quality Savoy Universitetsgata 11 ☎23 35 42 00, ⊛www.choicehotels.no. Attractive and very comfortable choice with pleasant rooms and wood-panelled public areas. In an interesting area too, with bookshops and bars catering primarily for the city's students. ❻/❸

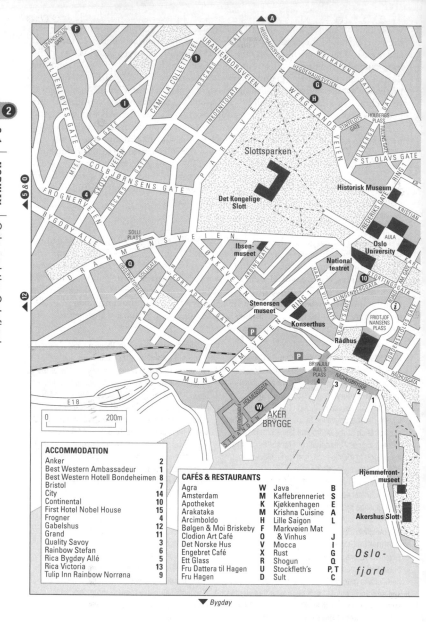

Slottsparken

Det Kongelige Slott

Historisk Museum

Ibsen-museet

Oslo University

National teatret

AULA

Stenersen museet

Konserthus

Rådhus

FRIDTJOF NANSENS PLASS

BRYNJULF BULL'S PLASS

AKER BRYGGE

Hjemmefront-museet

Akershus Slott

Oslo-fjord

E18

0   200m

ACCOMMODATION

Anker	2
Best Western Ambassadeur	1
Best Western Hotell Bondeheimen	8
Bristol	7
City	14
Continental	10
First Hotel Nobel House	15
Frogner	4
Gabelshus	12
Grand	11
Quality Savoy	3
Rainbow Stefan	6
Rica Bygdøy Allé	5
Rica Victoria	13
Tulip Inn Rainbow Norrøna	9

CAFÉS & RESTAURANTS

Agra	W	Java	B	
Amsterdam	M	Kaffebrenneriet	S	
Apotheket	K	Kjøkkenhagen	E	
Arakataka	M	Krishna Cuisine	A	
Arcimboldo	H	Lille Saigon	L	
Bølgen & Moi Briskeby	F	Markveien Mat		
Clodion Art Café	O	& Vinhus	J	
Det Norske Hus	V	Mocca	I	
Engebret Café	X	Rust	G	
Ett Glass	R	Shogun	Q	
Fru Dattera til Hagen	U	Stockfleth's	P, T	
Fru Hagen	D	Sult	C	

▼ Bygdøy

Rica Victoria Rosenkrantz gate 13 ☎ 24 14 70 00, ⓦ www.rica.no. Large, smart modern hotel just south of Karl Johans gate, popular with visiting business folk. Verging on the luxurious, its commodious rooms come with every convenience. ❼

Moderate and inexpensive hotels

Anker Storgata 55 ☎ 22 99 75 00, ⓦ www.anker.oslo.no. Large budget hotel in a glum high-rise block beside the murky river at the east end of Storgata, which caters predominantly

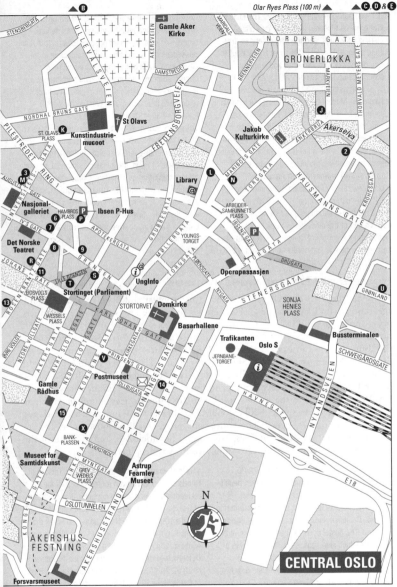

CENTRAL OSLO

Ferry to Hovedøya & ▼ *Langøyene* ▼ *Stena Ferry & DFDS Ferry to Denmark*   *Sjømannsskolen* ▼

for visiting Norwegians. The hotel's facilities are perfectly adequate, if somewhat frugal, but the surrounding area is cheerless. Twenty minutes' walk from Oslo S or five minutes by tram #10, #11, #12, #15 or #17. Part of the high-rise which also holds the *Albertine Hostel* – see below. ④

Best Western Hotell Bondeheimen Rosenkrantz gate 8 ☎ 23 21 41 00, ⊛ www.bondeheimen.com. One of Oslo's most delightful hotels, handily located just north of Karl Johans gate. Both the public areas and the comfortable bedrooms are tastefully decorated in a modern, Scandinavian style, with polished pine everywhere. The inclusive buffet breakfast, served in the *Kaffistova* (see p.251), is very good, and there's sometimes free coffee, soup and bread in the foyer throughout the evening. Look out for weekend and summer discounts of up to forty percent. ⑤/④

City Skippergata 19 ☎22 41 36 10, ⊛www .cityhotel.no. Modest but pleasant, this is a long-time favourite with budget travellers, located above shops and offices in a traditional Oslo apartment block near the train station. The surroundings are a little seedy, but the hotel is cheerful enough, and the rooms small but perfectly adequate. ④/③

Rainbow Stefan Rosenkrantz gate 1 ☎23 31 55 00, ⊛www.rainbow-hotels.no. Unremarkable but spick-and-span modern hotel with 210 rooms above the first-floor shops of a five-storey high-rise. It's one of the city's better deals, and its location, just a couple of minutes' walk north of Karl Johans gate, could hardly be bettered. ④/③

Rica Bygdøy Allé Bygdøy allé 53 ☎23 08 58 00, ⊛rica.hotel.bygdoey.alle@rica.no. With its late nineteenth-century forest of spiky towers, this *Rica* possesses the most imposing hotel facade in the city. Inside, each of the rooms is individually decorated in tasteful modern style and the public rooms are imaginative and engaging. In a busy residential area about 2km west of the centre – take bus #30, #31, #32 or #33. ⑤

Tulip Inn Rainbow Norrøna Grensen 19 ☎23 31 80 00, ⊛www.rainbow-hotels.no. Occupying part of a nineteenth-century apartment block right in the middle of town, this pleasantly renovated hotel offers straightforward modern rooms – nothing exciting but perfectly OK. The buffet breakfast is excellent and the breakfast room offers an attractive city view. At 850kr per double, it's a bargain that's made even more attractive by summer and weekend discounts of 15 percent. ④/③

Hostels, B&Bs and guesthouses

There are three HI **hostels** in Oslo, each very popular and open to people of any age, though you'll need to be an HI member to get the lowest rate (non-members pay a surcharge of 30kr); the fourth hostel is attached to one of the city's budget hotels. All of them have single and double rooms as well as dorm beds. Alternatively, the tourist office can book you into a **B&B/private room** – the supply rarely dries up. These cost around 225kr per single, and 350kr per double per night – something of a bargain, especially as many have cooking facilities. However, they do tend to be out of the city centre, and there's sometimes a minimum two-night stay. Broadly similar to the hostels and B&Bs are **guesthouses** – *pensjonater*. These start at around 450kr single, 600kr double, but they are few in number and there's only one near the city centre. They offer bare but generally adequate rooms, either with or without en-suite facilities; breakfast is not included, and at some of the more basic places you may need to supply your own sleeping bag.

Albertine Hostel Storgata 55 ☎22 99 72 00, ⊛www.albertine.no. Plain and simple dorm beds in 4-bedded and 6-bedded rooms; also doubles (②). Serves an adequate breakfast and has self-catering facilities. Bed linen and towels are for hire, or bring your own. The hostel occupies part of a glum high-rise block which also houses the *Anker* hotel in a cheerless neighbourhood at the east end of Storgata, twenty minutes' walk from Oslo S or five minutes by tram #11, #12, #15 or #17.

Cochs Pensjonat Parkveien 25 ☎23 33 24 00, ℱ23 33 24 10. On the third floor of a drab old block, this no-frills guesthouse is handily located behind Slottsparken, at the foot of Hegdehaugsveien. Singles, doubles (②), triples and quads are all available; some rooms have en-suite and cooking facilities.

Oslo Ekeberg Kongsveien 82 ☎22 74 18 90,

⊛oslo.ekeberg.hostel@vandrerhjem.no. This small HI hostel, with just eleven rooms, occupies the residential part of a school complex 4km southeast of Oslo S. Take tram #18 or #19 from outside Oslo S and it's 100m from the Holtet tram stop – ask the driver to put you off. Dorm beds 175kr, singles and doubles (②); all have shared facilities.

Oslo Haraldsheim Haraldsheimveien 4, Grefsen ☎22 22 29 65, ⊛www.haraldsheim.oslo.no. Best of Oslo's three HI youth hostels, 4km northeast of the centre, and open all year except Christmas week. There are 270 beds in 71 rooms, most of which are four-bedded. The public areas are comfortable and attractively furnished and the bedrooms clean and frugal, with about 40 having their own showers and WC. There are self-catering facilities, a restaurant and washing machines. The basic 170kr/190kr dorm bed price includes breakfast; single and double rooms (**2**) are also available. The only downside can be the presence of parties of noisy schoolkids. It's a very popular spot, so advance booking is essential throughout the summer. To get there, take tram #15 or #17 from the bottom of Storgata, near the Domkirke, to the Sinsenkrysset stop, from where it's a ten-minute signposted walk. By road, the hostel is situated close to – and signed from – Ring 3.

Oslo Holtekilen Michelets vei 55, Stabekk ☎67 51 80 40, ℮oslo.holtekilen.hostel@vandrerhjem .no. Another HI hostel, but much smaller than Haraldsheim, with kitchen facilities, a restaurant and a laundry. It's located 10km west of the city centre. From Oslo bus station, take bus #151 and the hostel is 100m from the Kveldsroveien bus stop. Dorm beds 180kr, including breakfast. Single and double rooms (**2**) are also available.

The City

At the time of their construction, the grand late nineteenth- and early twentieth-century buildings that populate **central Oslo** provided the country's emerging bourgeoisie with a sense of security and prosperity, an aura that survives today. Largely as a result, most of downtown Oslo remains easy and pleasant to walk around, its airy streets and squares accommodating the appealing remnants of the city's early days, as well as a clutch of good museums and dozens of bars, cafés and restaurants.

Despite the mammoth proportions of the Oslo conurbation, the city centre has stayed surprisingly compact and is easy to navigate by remembering a few landmarks. From the train station **Oslo S**, at the eastern end of the centre, **Karl Johans gate**, the main drag, heads directly up the hill, passing the **Domkirke** en route to the **Stortinget** (parliament building). From here it sweeps down past the **University** to the **Royal Palace**, which sits in parkland (the **Slottsparken**) at the western end of the centre. South of the palace, on the waterfront, is the brash harbourside development of **Aker Brygge** and the distinctive twin-towered **Rådhus** (City Hall). South of the Rådhus, on the lumpy peninsula overlooking the harbour, is the severe **Akershus Slott**, the city's castle. Between the castle, the Stortinget and Oslo S is a tight, slightly gloomy grid of streets and high buildings that was originally laid out by Christian IV in the seventeenth century. For many years this was the city's commercial hub and although Oslo's burgeoning suburbs undermined its position in the 1960s, the district is currently making a comeback, reinventing itself with specialist shops and smart restaurants.

Along Karl Johans gate

Heading west and uphill from Oslo S train station, **Karl Johans gate** begins unpromisingly with a clutter of tacky shops and groups of junkies. Things soon pick up, however, at the corner of Dronningens gate, where the **Basarhallene** is a curious two-tiered, nineteenth-century building built to house the city's food market. Its brick cloisters have recently been revived as a tiny shopping complex complete with art shops and cafés. The adjacent **Domkirke** (Cathedral; daily 10am–4pm; free) dates from the late seventeenth century, though its heavyweight tower was remodelled in 1850. Plain and dour from the outside, the cathedral's elegantly restored interior is in delightful contrast, with its homely, low-ceilinged nave and transepts awash with maroon, green and gold paintwork and, to either side of the high altar, the stained-glass windows created by Emanuel Vigeland in 1910 (for more on the Vigelands, see p.248). Outside the cathedral, **Stortorvet** was once the main city square, but it's no longer of much account, its statue of a portly Christian IV now serving merely as the forlorn guardian of a second-rate **flower market**.

Returning to Karl Johans gate, it's a brief stroll up to the **Stortinget**, the parliament building, an imposing chunk of neo-Romanesque architecture completed in 1866. It's open to the public for free guided tours (July to mid-Aug Mon–Sat English tours at 10am & 1pm; mid-Aug to mid-June Sat 10am & 1pm), though you see little more than can be gleaned from the outside. In front of the parliament, a narrow **park-piazza** runs west to the Nationaltheatret, filling in the gap between Karl Johans gate and Stortingsgata. In summer, the park brims with promenading city folk, who dodge between the jewellery hawkers, ice-cream kiosks and street performers; in winter the magnet is the park's dinky little open-air and floodlit ice-skating rinks (with cheap skate rental). Lurking at the western end of the park is the Neoclassical **Nationaltheatret** (National Theatre), built in 1899 and flanked by two stodgy statues of playwrights Henrik Ibsen and Bjørnstjerne Bjørnson.

Beyond the theatre, standing on the hill at the end of Karl Johans gate, **Det Kongelige Slott**, the Royal Palace, is a monument to Norwegian openness. Built between 1825 and 1848, at a time when other monarchs were nervously counting their friends, it still stands without railings and walls, the **Slottsparken** grounds which surround it open freely to the public. You can't actually go into the palace, but every day at 1.30pm there's a snappy changing of the guard. Bang in front of the palace is an equestrian statue of **Karl XIV Johan**. Formerly the French General Bernadotte, he abandoned Napoleon and, having been elected king of Sweden, assumed the Norwegian throne when Norway passed from Denmark to Sweden after the Treaty of Kiel in 1814. He had this whopping palace built for himself, seemingly not content with the terms of his motto (inscribed on the statue): "The people's love is my reward".

The Ibsen Museum

The grand old mansions bordering the southern perimeter of the Slottsparken were once home to Oslo's social elite. Here, in a fourth-floor apartment at Arbins gate 1, Ibsen spent the last ten years of his life. His old quarters are now maintained as the **Ibsen Museum** (*Ibsen-museet*; Tues–Sun guided tours at noon, 1pm & 2pm; 40kr). Both Ibsen and his wife died here: Ibsen paralyzed in bed; his wife, unwilling to expire in an undignified pose, dressed and sitting upright in a chair. Only the study looks much like it did in Ibsen's day, but the reverential one-hour tour provides a fascinating background to his work, and helps to explain the importance of the playwright to his emergent nation. For more on Ibsen, see p.214.

The University and its museums

Retracing your steps to Karl Johans gate brings you to the nineteenth-century buildings of the **University**, whose classical columns and imperial pediments fit perfectly with this monumental part of the centre. Within the university complex at Frederiks gate 2, the Historical Museum (*Historisk Museum*; mid-May to mid-Sept Tues–Sun 10am–4pm; mid-Sept to mid-May Tues–Sun 11am–4pm; free) contains the university's hotchpotch historical and ethnographical collections. The highlight is the **Viking and early medieval section**. In the rooms to the left of the entrance are several magnificent twelfth- and thirteenth-century stave-church porches and gateposts, alive with dragons and beasts emerging from swirling, intricately carved backgrounds. There are weapons, coins, drinking horns, runic stones, religious bric-a-brac and bits of clothing here too, as well as a superb vaulted room, dating from the late thirteenth century and originating in Ål, near Geilo. The rest of the ground floor is taken up by a pretty dire sequence of exhibitions on the Stone, Bronze, Iron and Viking ages. Geared up for school parties, the tiny dioramas are downright silly and detract from the actual exhibits, which (accompanied by long explicatory leaflets) illustrate various aspects of early Norwegian society – from religious beliefs and social structures through to military hardware and trade and craft.

On the second floor, the first part of the **Etnografisk Museum** (Ethnographical Museum) is devoted to the arctic peoples and features an illuminating section on the Sámi, who inhabit the northern reaches of Scandinavia. Incongruously, there's a coin collection here as well, while it's upstairs again for African and Asiatic art and culture – pretty standard stuff, though temporary exhibitions from around the world sometimes prove worth investigating.

The National Gallery

Norway's largest and best collection of fine art is only a step away from the university in the **National Gallery** (*Nasjonalgalleriet*; Mon, Wed & Fri 10am–6pm, Thurs 10am–8pm, Sat 10am–4pm, Sun 11am–4pm; free). An approachable collection shoehorned into a stolid nineteenth-century building, it's short on internationally famous painters – apart from a fine sample of work by Edvard Munch – but there's compensation in oodles of Norwegian art, including examples of the work of all the leading figures up until the end of World War II.

Something of a mishmash, the **ground floor** is home to a quirky series of collections, with the large room to the right of the entrance crammed with plaster casts of Greek, Roman and Italian Renaissance sculptures – including a massive and militaristic equestrian statue by Donatello. To the left of the main entrance, one room is devoted to Danish and Norwegian nineteenth-century sculpture, another holds a workaday selection of Norwegian paintings from 1870 to 1900, while others are set aside for temporary exhibitions.

Moving on, the wide and gracious stairway – look out for a tortured bronze relief, *Helvete* (Hell), by Gustav Vigeland – leads to the next level up and the kernel of the gallery's collection, which broadly divides between Norwegian painting on the right-hand side and European art to the left. The latter section contains an enjoyable sample of work by the **Impressionists**, assorted bursts of colour from Manet, Monet, Degas and Cézanne, as well as a distant, piercing Van Gogh self-portrait, and later works by the likes of Picasso and Braque. There's also a set of Novgorod medieval religious paintings and a rather timid selection of Old Masters, amongst which Lucas Cranach's *The Golden Age* and two warm and melodramatic canvases by El Greco stand out.

To the right of the staircase, the first room of **Norwegian paintings** displays the work of the country's most important nineteenth-century landscape painters, **Johan Christian Dahl** (1788–1857) and his pupil **Thomas Fearnley** (1802–42). Dahl's giant-sized canvas *Stalheim* is typical of his work, the soft and dappled hues of the mountain landscape framing a sleepy village dotted with tiny figures. His *Hjelle in Valdres* of 1851 adopts the same approach, though here the artifice suffusing the apparent naturalism is easier to detect: the year before, Dahl had completed another painting of Hjelle, but he returned to the subject to widen the valley and heighten the mountains, sprinkling them with snow. Fearnley often lived and worked abroad, but he always returned to Norwegian themes, painting no fewer than five versions of the *Labrofossen ved Kongsberg* ("The Labro Waterfall at Kongsberg"), a fine, moody canvas of dark, louring clouds and frothing water.

On the same floor, Room 23 is distinguished by **Gerhard Munthe** (1849–1929), whose cosy, folksy scenes are echoed – in the same room – by the paintings of **Erik Werenskiold** (1855–1938), who is well represented by *Peasant Burial* (1885). During this period, **Theodor Kittelsen** (1857–1914) defined the appearance of the country's trolls, sprites and sirens in his illustrations of Asbjørnsen and Moe's *Norwegian Folk Tales*, published in 1883. Two modest examples of his other work – a self-portrait and a fairytale landscape – are in Room 18. **Harald Sohlberg** (1869–1935) is represented by a series of sharply observed Røros streetscapes, and by more elemental themes such as the stunning *En blomstereng nordpå* ("A Northern Flower Meadow") and *Vinternatt i Rondane* ("Winter Night in the Rondane"). These are exhibited in Room 31, alongside the comparable *Opptrekkende uvaer* ("Approaching Storm") by **Halfdan Egedius** (1877–99).

Also on this floor is the museum's star turn – its **Munch** collection, which gathers together representative works from the 1880s through to 1916 in one central room, with several lesser pieces displayed elsewhere. His early work is very much in the naturalist tradition of his mentor Christian Krohg, though by 1885 Munch is already pushing the boundaries in *The Sick Child*, a heart-wrenching evocation of his sister Sophie's death from tuberculosis. Other works with this same sense of pain include *Mother and Daughter, Moonlight* and one of several versions of *The Scream*, a seminal canvas of 1893 whose swirling lines and rhythmic colours were to inspire the Expressionists. This sample of Munch's work serves as a good introduction to the artist, but for a more detailed appraisal – and a more comprehensive selection of his work – check out the Munch Museum (p.247).

Munch aside, the general flow of Norwegian art was reinvigorated in the 1910s by a new band of artists who had trained in Paris under Henri Matisse, whose emancipation of colour from naturalist constraints inspired his Norwegian students. **Henrik Sørensen** (1882–1962), the outstanding figure here, summed up the Frenchman's influence thirty years later: "From Matisse, I learned more in fifteen minutes than from all the other teachers I have listened to" – lessons that inspired Sørensen's surging, earthy portrayals of the landscapes of eastern Norway. **Axel Revold** (1887–1962) was trained by Matisse too, but also assimilated Cubist influences – in, for example, his *Sommernatt i Nordland* ("Summer Night in Nordland") of 1930 – whilst **Erling Enger** (1899–1990) maintained a gently lyrical approach to the landscape and its seasons. Examples of the work of these and other later artists are concentrated on the third floor, where there's also a large collection of paintings from the rest of Scandinavia, mostly dating from the first half of the twentieth century.

The Museum of Applied Art

The Museum of Applied Art (*Kunstindustrimuseet*; Tues–Sun 11am–4pm, Thurs till 7pm; ⑨www.kunstindustrimuseet.no; 25k) occupies an imposing nineteenth-century building some ten minutes' walk north from the National Gallery, at St Olavs gate 1: continue to the far end of Universitetsgata, veer to the right and it's at the end of the street. Founded in 1876, this was one of the first museums of its kind in Europe, its multifaceted collection (particularly strong on period furniture) spreading over four floors. The **first floor** accommodates temporary exhibitions (which sometimes raise the cost of admission), while on the **second floor** (in the first room to the left of the stairs) is an engaging hotchpotch of Viking tackle from drinking horns, brooches and belts through to religious statuettes and church vestments. The museum's top exhibit is here too, the brightly coloured **Baldishol Tapestry**, one of the finest early examples of woven tapestry in Europe. Next door, the "Norwegian Gallery" boasts an enjoyable sample of carved wooden furniture, amongst which the cheerily painted chests from Gudbrandsdal are especially fetching. Alongside is a charming selection of bedspreads sporting either religious or folkloric motifs. Upstairs, on the **third floor**, a sequence of period interiors illustrates foreign fashions from Renaissance and Baroque through to Chippendale, Louis XVI and Art Nouveau. The **fourth-floor** displays concentrate on ceramics and glassware from the early nineteenth century onwards, with other exhibits on textiles and fashions. The highlight here is the collection of extravagant costumes worn by Norway's royal family at the beginning of the twentieth century.

To the water: the Rådhus and Aker Brygge

Back in the city centre, rearing high above the waterfront south of the Nationaltheatret, is Oslo's City Hall, the **Rådhus** (daily: May–Aug 9am–5pm; Sept–April 9am–4pm; free, but guided tours, at 30kr, Jan–June & Sept–Dec Mon–Fri 10am, noon & 2pm; July & Aug daily 10am, noon & 2pm), a modernist, twin-towered construction of dark-brown brick designed by Arnstein Arneberg and Manus Poulsson. Opened in 1950 to celebrate the city's 900th anniversary, this grandiose statement of civic pride was nearly twenty years in the making. At first, few people had a good word for what they saw as an ugly and strikingly un-Norwegian addition to the city. But with the passing of time, the obloquy has fallen on more recent additions to the skyline – such as Oslo S – and the Rådhus has become one of the city's more popular buildings.

Initially, the interior was equally contentious. Many leading Norwegian painters and sculptors contributed to the decorations, which were intended to celebrate all things Norwegian. The **Rådhushallen** (main hall) is decorated with vast stylized – and for some, completely over-the-top – murals. On the north wall, Per Krohg's *From the Fishing Nets in the West to the Forests of the East* invokes the figures of polar explorer Fridtjof Nansen (on the left) and dramatist Bjørnstjerne Bjørnson (on the right) to symbolize, respectively, the nation's spirit of adventure and its intellectual development. On the south wall is the equally vivid *Work, Administration and Celebration*, which took Henrik Sørensen a decade to complete. The self-congratulatory nationalism of these murals is hardly attractive, although the effect is partly offset by the forceful fresco along the east wall honouring the Norwegian Resistance of World War II.

At the back of the Rådhus a line of six muscular bronze figures represent the trades – builders, bricklayers and so on – who worked on the building, while behind them, over the tram lines, stand four massive granite female sculptures surrounding a central fountain. Beyond that, and shadowed by the Akershus peninsula, is the central **harbour**, always busy with ferries and boats, with Bygdøy and the islands of the Oslofjord filling out the backdrop. This is one of downtown Oslo's prettiest spots, and handy for the **Norges Informasjonssenter** (see p.230), located steps from the Rådhus in the old, yellow Oslo V railway station. Metres away, the old Aker shipyard has been turned into the **Aker Brygge** shopping-cum-office complex, a gleaming concoction of circular staircases and glass lifts, trimmed with neon and plastic; the bars and restaurants here are some of the most popular in town.

Rådhusgata: the Museum of Contemporary Art and the Astrup Fearnley Museum of Modern Art

To the east of the Rådhus, the gridded streets to either side of **Rådhusgata** are a legacy of seventeenth-century Oslo, but it's only the layout that has survived as the old timber buildings were almost entirely demolished and replaced by larger stone structures in the nineteenth century. One block south of Rådhusgata along Kirkegata is **Bankplassen**, arguably the city's most attractive square, framed by Gothic Revival and Second Empire buildings, a perfect illustration of the grand tastes of the Dano-Norwegian elite who ran the country at the beginning of the twentieth century.

The square's proudest building, the 1907 Art Nouveau Norges Bank, at no. 4, has been superbly restored to house the enterprising **Museum of Contemporary Art** (*Museet for Samtidskunst*; Tues, Wed & Fri 10am–5pm, Thurs 10am–8pm, Sat 11am–4pm, Sun 11am–5pm; 40kr). The museum owns work by virtually every major postwar Norwegian artist and by many leading foreign figures, too. Each item is allowed a generous amount of space and so – given that some of the pieces are massive, and that the museum also hosts prestigious international exhibitions – only a fraction of the permanent collection can be shown at any one time. Norwegian names to look out for include Bjørn Carlsen, Frans Widerberg, Knut Rose and Bjørn Ransve. There are also three permanent installations, including the weird *Inner Room V*, the fifth in a series of angst-rattling rooms made from recycled industrial junk by the Norwegian Per Inge Bjørlo. Tucked away in a room of its own on the top floor, there's also the peculiar – and peculiarly engaging – *The Man Who Never Threw Anything Away*. This is the work of the Russian Ilya Kabakov, who spent over a decade collecting hundreds of discarded items from the recesses of his house – bits of toe nail, string, hairs, elastic bands, crumbs etc – and gathered them together here, each precisely labelled and neatly displayed. Kabakov continues turning up to add bits and pieces to his display, which occupies a sort of parallel reality – originally a retreat from the bureaucratic illogicalities of the Soviet system, but now a tribute to the anally retentive.

About 200m to the east of the Samtidskunst, at Dronningens gate 4, the **Astrup Fearnley Museum of Modern Art** (*Astrup Fearnley Museet for Moderne Kunst*; Tues, Wed & Fri 11am–5pm, Thurs 11am–7pm, Sat & Sun noon–5pm; 50kr) occupies a sharp modern building of brick and glass with six-metre-high steel entrance doors. It's meant to impress – a suitably posh setting for the display of several private collections and for eminent temporary exhibitions. The temporary exhibitions often leave little space for the permanent collection, which includes examples of the work of most major postwar Norwegian artists. There's also a smattering of notable foreign works by the likes of Francis Bacon, Damien Hirst and Anselm Kiefer.

Akershus castle and the Resistance Museum

Though very much part of central Oslo by location, the jutting thumb of land that holds the castle, the **Akershus Slott**, is quite separate from the city centre in feel, comprising the most significant reminders of the medieval city. Built on a rocky knoll overlooking the harbour in around 1300, the original castle was already the battered veteran of several unsuccessful sieges when Christian IV (1596–1648) took matters in hand. The king had a passion for building cities and a keen interest in Norway – during his reign he visited the country about thirty times, more than all the other kings of the Dano-Norwegian union together. So, when Oslo was badly damaged by fire in 1624, he took his opportunity and simply ordered the town to be moved round the bay from its location at the mouth of the river Alna beneath the Ekeberg heights. He had the town rebuilt in its present position, renamed it "Christiania" – which stuck until 1925 – and transformed the medieval castle into a Renaissance residence. Around the castle he also constructed a new fortress – the **Akershus Festning** – whose thick earth-and-stone walls and protruding bastions were designed to combat the threat of artillery bombardment. Refashioned and enlarged on several later occasions – and now bisected by Kongens gate – parts of the fortress have remained in military use to the present day.

There are several entrances to the Akershus complex, but the most interesting is from the **west end of Myntgata**, where there's a choice of two marked footpaths. Take the path leading up to a side gate in the perimeter wall and inside, just beyond the gate, is a cute little pond and a crashingly boring museum-cum-information centre that makes a strange attempt to tie in the history of the castle with modern environmental concerns. There's another choice of signed routes here, with one path offering heady views over the harbour as it worms its way up to the castle. The other path from Myntgata cuts along to the **Norwegian Resistance Museum** (*Norges Hjemmefrontmuseum*; mid-April to mid-June & Sept Mon–Sat 10am–4pm, Sun 11am–4pm; mid-June to mid-Aug Mon, Wed & Fri–Sat 10am–5pm, Tues & Thurs 10am–6pm; Oct to mid-April Mon–Fri 10am–3pm, Sat & Sun 11am–4pm; 25kr), which occupies a separate building just outside the castle entrance, an apt location as captured Resistance fighters were tortured and/or executed in the castle by the Gestapo. Labelled in English and Norwegian, the museum's mostly pictorial displays detail the history of the war in Norway from defeat and occupation through resistance to final victory. There are tales of extraordinary heroism here – the determined resistance of hundreds of the country's teachers to Nazi instructions, and the story of a certain Petter Moen, who was arrested by the Germans and imprisoned in the Akershus, where he kept a diary by picking out letters on toilet paper with a nail: the diary survived, but he didn't. Another section deals with Norway's Jews, of whom there were 1800 in 1939 – the Germans captured 760; 24 survived. There's also an impressively honest account of Norwegian collaboration – fascism struck a chord with the country's petit bourgeois, and hundreds of volunteers joined the Wehrmacht. The most notorious collaborator was **Vidkun Quisling**: pressing a button brings his radio announcement declaring his assumption of power at the start of the German invasion in April 1940.

Next door, the severe stone walls and twin spires of the **Slott** (Castle; May to mid-Sept Mon–Sat 10am–4pm, Sun 12.30–4pm; 25kr; guided tours in English at

11am, 1pm & 3pm, Sun at 1pm & 3pm) perch on a rocky ridge high above the zigzag fortifications that Christian IV added. The castle is approached through a narrow tunnel-gateway, beyond which the stone-flagged courtyard is overlooked by the main gate. The interior is, however, a real disappointment, with a series of bare and boring rooms only enlivened by the tapestries and bedspreads of the Romerike Hall. The guided tour takes in the royal chapel too, as well as the royal mausoleum, the last resting-place of Norway's current dynasty.

Back outside, a **path** leads off the courtyard, running down the side of the castle with the walls pressing in on one side and views out over the harbour on the other. At the foot of the castle, the path swings across a narrow promontory and soon reaches the footbridge over Kongens gate – keep straight for the string of ochre-painted barrack blocks that lead back to the pond and Myntgata.

Out from the centre

From the jetty behind the Rådhus, ferries shuttle southwest from central Oslo to the **Bygdøy peninsula**, home to the city's showpiece museums, whilst others head south from the Vippetangen quay behind Akershus Slott to the string of rusticated **islands** that necklace the inner waters of the Oslofjord. Back on the mainland, **east Oslo** is perhaps the least prepossessing part of town, a gritty sprawl whose main attraction is the superb Munch Museum. **Northwest Oslo** is far more prosperous, with big old houses lining the avenues immediately to the west of the Slottsparken. Beyond is the **Frognerparken**, a chunk of parkland with the stunning open-air sculptures of Gustav Vigeland displayed in the **Vigelandsparken**.

North of the centre is the **Nordmarka**, a massive forested wilderness that stretches inland, patterned by hiking trails and cross-country ski routes. Two T-bane lines provide ready access, clanking their way up into the rocky hills that herald the region. The more westerly grinds on past **Holmenkollen**, a resort whose ski jump forms a crooked finger on Oslo's skyline, before continuing to the **Frognerseteren** terminus, which is still within the municipal boundaries, though the forested hills and lochs around the station feel anything but urban. This atmosphere of remoteness is duplicated in neighbouring **Sognsvann**, at the end of the other T-bane line.

Southwest of the centre: the Bygdøy peninsula

Other than the centre, the place you're likely to spend most time in Oslo is the **Bygdøy peninsula**, across the bay to the southwest of the city, where five separate museums make up an absorbing cultural and historical display – allow at least a day or, less wearyingly, two half-days. The most enjoyable way to reach Bygdøy is by **ferry**. These leave from pier 3 behind the Rådhus (daily: late April & Sept every 40min 9.05am–6.25pm; May–Aug every 40min 9.05am–9.05pm; 22kr), and call at two places on the peninsula, stopping first at the Dronningen pier, then at the Bygdøynes pier. The two most popular attractions – the Viking Ships and Norwegian Folk museums – are within easy walking distance of the Dronningen pier; the other three are a stone's throw from Bygdøynes. If you decide to walk between the two groups, allow about fifteen minutes: the route is well signposted but dull. The alternative to the ferry is **bus** #30 (every 15min), which runs all year from Jernbanetorget and the Nationaltheatret to the Folk and Viking Ships museums, and, when the ferry isn't running, to the other three museums as well.

Norwegian Folk Museum

About 700m uphill from the Dronningen pier, the **Norwegian Folk Museum** at Museumsveien 10 (*Norsk Folkemuseum*; mid-May to mid-Sept daily 10am–6pm, 70kr; mid-Sept to mid-May Mon–Sat 11am–3pm, Sun 11am–4pm; ⓦwww .norskfolke.museum.no; 50kr) combines indoor collections focusing on folk art, furniture, dress and customs with an extensive open-air display of reassembled buildings, mostly wooden barns, stables, storehouses and dwellings from the seventeenth to the nineteenth centuries.

At the entrance, pick up a free map and English-language guide and begin by going upstairs to the Norwegian parliament chamber, a cosy nineteenth-century affair that has been reassembled here, complete with inkwells and quills at the members' seats. The adjoining complex of buildings holds a rather confusing sequence of exhibitions: some are eminently missable, but the **folk art** section has a delightful sample of quilted bedspreads and painted furniture, as well as an intriguing subsection devoted to **love gifts**, with fancily carved love spoons and mangle boards given by the boys, mittens and gloves by the girls. In rural Norway, it was considered improper for courting couples to be seen together during the day, but acceptable (or at least tolerated) at night – parents usually moved girls of marrying age into one of the farm's outhouses to assist the process. The **folk dress** section is excellent, too. Rural customs specified the correct dress for every social gathering from cradle to grave, but it's the extravagant and brightly-coloured bridal headdresses that grab the eye. Look out also for the temporary exhibitions – the museum has a well-deserved reputation for imaginative displays.

The **open-air collection** consists of more than 150 reconstructed buildings. Arranged geographically, they provide a marvellous sample of Norwegian rural architecture, somewhat marred by inadequate explanations. It's worth tracking down the **stave church**, particularly if you don't plan to travel elsewhere in Norway. Dating from the early thirteenth century but extensively restored in the 1880s, when it was moved here from Gol, the church is a good example of its type, with steep, shingle-covered roofs, dragon finials and a cramped, gloomy nave – which can only be viewed from the gallery outside. The interior is decorated with robust woodcarvings and there's a striking *Last Supper* behind the altar. Elsewhere, the cluster of buildings from **Setesdal** in southern Norway holds some especially well-preserved dwellings and storehouses from the seventeenth century, while the **Numedal** section contains one of the museum's oldest buildings, a late thirteenth-century house from Rauland, whose door posts are embellished with Romanesque vine decoration. In summer, many of the buildings are open for viewing and costumed guides roam the site to explain the vagaries of Norwegian rural life.

Viking Ships Museum

A five-minute walk south along the main road is the **Viking Ships Museum** (*Vikingskipshuset*; daily: May–Sept 9am–6pm; Oct-April 11am–4pm; Ⓦwww.ukm.uio.no/vikingskipshuset; 40kr), a large hall specially constructed to house a trio of ninth-century Viking ships, with viewing platforms to enable you to see inside the hulls. The three oak vessels were retrieved from ritual burial mounds in southern Norway; all were embalmed in a subsoil of clay, which accounts for their excellent state of preservation. The size of the Viking burial mound denoted the dead person's rank and wealth, while the possessions buried with the body were designed to make the afterlife as comfortable as possible. Implicit was the assumption that a chieftain in this world would be a chieftain in the next – slaves were frequently killed and buried with their master or mistress – a fact that would subsequently give Christianity an immediate appeal to those at the bottom of the Viking pile. That much is clear, but quite how the Vikings saw the transfer to the afterlife taking place is less certain. The evidence is contradictory: sometimes the Vikings stuck the anchor on board the burial ship in preparation for the spiritual journey; at other times the vessels were moored to large stones before they were buried. Nor was ship burial the only type of Viking funeral – far from it: the Vikings buried their dead in mounds and on level ground, with and without grave goods, in large and small coffins, both with and without boats – and they practised cremation, too.

The star exhibits are the Oseberg and Gokstad ships, named after the places on the west side of the Oslofjord where they were discovered in 1904 and 1880 respectively. The **Oseberg ship**'s ornately carved prow and stern rise high above the hull, where thirty oar-holes indicate the size of the crew. It is thought to be the burial ship of a Viking chieftain's wife; much of the treasure buried with it was retrieved, and can be seen on display at the back of the museum. The grave goods reveal an attention to detail and a level of domestic sophistication not usually associated with the Vikings: there are marvellous decorative items like the fierce-looking animal-head posts and exuberantly carved ceremonial sleighs, plus a host of smaller, more mundane household items such as agricultural tools and a cooking pot. Here also are finds from another burial mound at Borre in Vestfold, most notably a rare dark-blue glass beaker and a fancifully decorated bridle.

The Oseberg ship is 22m long and 5m wide, and probably represents the type of vessel the Vikings would have used to navigate fjords and coastal waters. The **Gokstad ship** is slightly longer and wider, and quite a bit sturdier and stronger – its seaworthiness was demonstrated in 1893 when a copy was sailed across the Atlantic to the USA. Like the Oseberg mound, the Gokstad burial chamber was raided by grave robbers long ago – and to greater effect – but a handful of items were unearthed and these are exhibited behind the third vessel, the **Tune ship**. Only fragments of this, the smallest of the three vessels, survive; these are displayed unrestored, much as they were discovered in 1867 on the eastern side of the Oslofjord.

The Kon-Tiki, Fram and Maritime museums

A few metres from the Bygdøynes pier, the **Kon-Tiki Museum** (daily: June–Aug 9.30am–5.45pm; April, May & Sept 10.30am–5pm; Oct–March 10.30am–4pm; ⓦwww.kon-tiki.no; 35kr) is most unusual. On display inside is the balsawood raft on which, in 1947, Thor Heyerdahl made his now legendary journey across the Pacific from Peru to Polynesia. Heyerdahl wanted to prove the trip could be done: he was convinced that the first Polynesian settlers had sailed from pre-Incan Peru, and rejected prevailing opinions that South American balsa rafts were unseaworthy. Looking at the flimsy raft *Kon-Tiki*, you could be forgiven for agreeing with Heyerdahl's doubters – and for wondering how the crew didn't murder each other after a week in such a confined space. Heyerdahl's later investigations of Easter Island statues and cave graves lent further weight to his ethnological theory, which has now received a degree of acceptance. The whole saga is outlined here in the museum, and if you're especially interested, the story is also told in his book *The Kon-Tiki Expedition* (see p.219). Preoccupied with trans-oceanic contact between prehistoric peoples, Heyerdahl went on to attempt several other voyages, sailing successfully across the Atlantic in a papyrus boat, *Ra II*, in 1970 to prove that there could have been contact between Egypt and South America. *Ra II* is displayed here and again Heyerdahl recorded the exploit in a book – *The Ra Expeditions*.

Just over the road, in front of the mammoth triangular display hall of the Fram Museum, stands the *Gjøa*, the one-time sealing ship in which **Roald Amundsen** made the first complete sailing of the Northwest Passage in 1906. By any measure, this was a remarkable achievement and the fulfilment of a nautical mission that had preoccupied sailors for several centuries. It took three years, with Amundsen and his crew surviving two ice-bound winters deep in the Arctic, but even this epic journey was eclipsed when, in 1912, the Norwegian dashed to the South Pole, famously beating the ill-starred Captain Scott. The ship that carried Amundsen to within striking distance of the South Pole, the *Fram*, is displayed inside the **Fram Museum** (*Frammuseet*; Nov–Feb Mon–Fri 11am–2.45pm, Sat & Sun 11am–3.45pm; March & April daily 11am–3.45pm; early May & Sept daily 10am–4.45pm; mid-May to mid-June daily 9am–5.45pm; mid-June to Aug daily 9am–6.45pm; Oct daily 10am-3.45pm; 30kr). Designed by Colin Archer, a Norwegian shipbuilder of Scots ancestry, and launched in 1892, the *Fram*'s design was unique, its sides made smooth to prevent the ice from getting a firm grip on the hull, while inside a veritable maze of beams, braces and stanchions held it all together. Living quarters inside the ship were necessarily cramped, but – in true

Edwardian style – the Norwegians still found space for a piano. Look out too for the assorted knick-knacks the explorers took with them, including playing cards, maps, notebooks, snowshoes and surgical instruments – although this was as nothing to the clobber carted there by Scott, one of the reasons for his failure. Scott's main mistake, however, was to rely on Siberian ponies to transport his tackle. The animals were useless in Antarctic conditions and Scott and his men ended up pulling the sledges themselves, whereas Amundsen wisely brought a team of huskies.

The adjacent **Norwegian Maritime Museum** (*Norsk Sjøfartsmuseum*; mid-May to Sept daily 10am–6pm; Oct to mid-May Mon–Wed & Fri–Sun 10.30am–4pm, Thurs 10.30am–6pm; 30kr) occupies two buildings, the larger of which is a well-designed brick structure with a fairly pedestrian collection of maritime artefacts. Its most popular attraction is the "Supervideograph", a widescreen movie that trucks over Norway's coastline in dramatic style. Otherwise, one of the more interesting exhibits allows visitors to track (but not change!) local shipping movements by means of an electronic link with the Oslofjord traffic control system. There's also the so-called Gibraltar boat, a perilously fragile canvas-and-board home-made craft on which a bunch of Norwegian sailors fled Morocco for British Gibraltar after their ship had been impounded by the Vichy French authorities. Moving on, the museum's second building, the **Båthallen** (boat hall), has an extensive collection of small and medium-sized wooden boats from all over Norway, mostly inshore sailing and fishing craft from the nineteenth century. Enthusiasts swear by the place, but non-sailors may find it rather heavy going – and head straight for the museum's fjordside café instead.

South of the centre: the inner Oslofjord

The compact archipelago of low-lying, lightly forested **islands** in the inner Oslofjord is the city's summer playground, and makes going to the beach a viable, if unusual, option for a European capital. Jumping on a ferry is a pleasant way of passing the time, whether in the heat of the day or in the evenings, when the more lightly populated islands become favourite party venues for the city's preening youth. **Ferries** to the islands (22kr each way, Oslo Card & all other transport passes valid) leave from the Vippetangen quay, beside the grain silo at the foot of Akershusstranda – a twenty-minute walk or a five-minute ride on bus #60 south from Jernbanetorget.

Conveniently, **Hovedøya** (ferry #92; mid-March to Sept every hour or ninety minutes 7.30am–7pm; Oct to mid-March 3 daily; 10min), the nearest island, is also the most interesting. Its rolling hills contain farmland and deciduous woods, as well as the overgrown ruins of a **Cistercian monastery**, built by English monks in the twelfth century, and other remains from the days when the island was garrisoned and armed to protect Oslo's harbour. A map of the island at the jetty helps with orientation, but on an islet of this size – it's just ten minutes' walk from one end to the other – getting lost is pretty much impossible. There are plenty of footpaths to wander, you can swim from the shingle beaches on the south shore, and there's a seasonal café opposite the monastery ruins. Camping is not permitted, however, as Hovedøya is a protected area – that's why there are no summer homes.

The pick of the other islands is H-shaped, wooded **Langøyene** (ferry #94; June–Aug hourly 9am–7pm; 30min), the most southerly of the archipelago and the one with the best beaches. There's a spartan **campsite**, *Langøyene Camping* (☎22 11 53 21; June-Aug), and at night the ferries are full of people with sleeping bags and bottles, on their way to join swimming parties.

East of the centre: the Munch Museum

Nearly everyone who visits Oslo makes time for the **Munch-museet** (Munch Museum) – and with good reason. In his will, Munch donated all the works in his possession to Oslo city council – a mighty bequest of several thousand paintings, prints, drawings, engravings and photographs, which took nearly twenty years to catalogue and organize for display in this purpose-built gallery. The museum is located to the east of the city centre at Tøyengata 53 (June to mid-Sept daily 10am–6pm; mid-Sept to May Tues–Fri 10am–4pm, Sat & Sun 11am–5pm; ⓦwww.munch.museum.no; 60kr) and is reachable by T-bane – get off at Tøyen and it's a signposted five-minute walk.

The museum

The collection is huge, and only a small part of it can be shown at any one time – an advantage, since you don't feel overwhelmed by what's on display. The space required by visiting exhibitions also often confines the Munch collection to one large gallery, which can appear cluttered, but at least you can reckon on seeing many of the more highly praised works. There's a basement display on Munch's life and times as well, with oodles of background information.

In the main gallery, the landscapes and domestic scenes of Munch's **early paintings** – such as *Tête à Tête* (1885) and *At the Coffee Table* (1883) – reveal the perceptive, if deeply pessimistic, realism from which Munch's later work sprang. Even more riveting are the great works of the **1890s**, which form the core of the collection and are considered Munch's finest achievements. Among many, there's *Dagny Juel*, a portrait of the Berlin socialite Ducha Przybyszewska, with whom both Munch and his friend Strindberg were infatuated; the searing representations of *Despair* and *Anxiety*; the chilling *Red Virginia Creeper*, a house being consumed by the plant; and, of course, *The Scream* – of which the museum holds several of a total of fifty versions. Consider Munch's words as you view it:

I was walking along a road with two friends. The sun set. I felt a tinge of melancholy. Suddenly the sky became blood red. I stopped and leaned against a railing feeling exhausted, and I looked at the flaming clouds that hung like blood and a sword over the blue-black fjord and the city. My friends walked on. I stood there trembling with fright. And I felt a loud unending scream piercing nature.

Munch's style was never static, however. **Later paintings** such as *Workers On Their Way Home* (1913), produced after he had recovered from his breakdown and had withdrawn to the tranquillity of the Oslofjord, reflect his renewed interest in nature

---

Edvard Munch

Born in 1863, **Edvard Munch** had a melancholy childhood in what was then Christiania, overshadowed by the early deaths of both his mother and a sister from tuberculosis. After some early works, including several self-portraits, he went on to study in Paris, a city he returned to again and again, and where he fell (fleetingly) under the sway of the Impressionists. In 1892 he moved to Berlin, where his style developed and he produced some of his best and most famous work, though his first exhibition there was considered so outrageous it was closed after only a week – his painting was, a critic opined, "an insult to art". Despite the initial criticism, Munch's work was subsequently exhibited in many of the leading galleries of the day. Generally considered the initiator of the Expressionist movement, Munch wandered Europe, painting and exhibiting prolifically. Meanwhile overwork, drink and problematic love affairs were fuelling an instability that culminated, in 1908, in a nervous breakdown. Munch spent six months in a Copenhagen clinic, after which his health improved greatly – and his paintings lost the hysterical edge characteristic of his most celebrated work. It wasn't until well into his career, however, that he was fully accepted in his own country, where he was based from 1909 until his death in 1944.

and physical work. His technique also changed: in works like the *Death of Marat II* (1907) he began to use streaks of colour to represent points of light. Still later paintings, such as *Winter in Kragerø* and *Model by the Wicker Chair*, reveal at last a happier – if rather idealized – attitude to his surroundings, also evident in works like *Spring Ploughing*, painted in 1919.

The exhibition is punctuated by **self-portraits**, a graphic illustration of Munch's state of mind at various points in his career. There's a palpable sadness in his *Self-portrait with Wine Bottle* (1906), along with obvious allusions to his heavy drinking, while the telling perturbation of *In Distress* (1919) and *The Night Wanderer* (1923) indicate that he remained a tormented, troubled man even in his later years. One of his last works, *Self-portrait by the Window* (1940), shows a glum figure on the borderline of life and death, the strong red of his face and green of his clothing contrasted with the ice-white scene visible through the window.

Munch's **lithographs and woodcuts** are shown in a separate section of the gallery: a dark catalogue of swirls and fogs, technically brilliant pieces of work and much more than simple copies of his paintings – indeed, they're often developments of them. In these he pioneered a new medium of expression, experimenting with colour schemes and a huge variety of materials, which enhance the works' rawness: wood blocks show a heavy, distinct grain, while there are colours like rust and blue drawn from the Norwegian landscape. As well as the stark woodcuts on display, there are also sensuous, hand-coloured lithographs, many focusing on the theme of love (in the form of a woman) bringing death.

West of the centre: Frogner Park and Vigeland Sculpture Park

The green expanse of **Frognerparken** (Frogner Park) lies to the west of the city centre – take tram #15 from Nationaltheatret and get off at Vigelandsparken, the stop after Frogner plass. The park incorporates one of Oslo's most celebrated and popular cultural attractions, the open-air sculpture park, which, along with the nearby museum, commemorates a modern Norwegian sculptor of world renown, **Gustav Vigeland** (1869–1943). Between them, they display a huge portion of his work, presented to the city in return for favours received in the shape of a studio and apartment during the years 1921–30.

A country boy, Vigeland began his career as a woodcarver but later, influenced by Rodin, turned to stone and bronze. He started work on the **Vigelandsparken** (open 24hr; free) in 1924, and was still working on it when he died in 1943. It's a literally fantastic work, medieval in spirit and complexity. Here he had the chance to let his imagination run riot and, when unveiled, many city folk were simply overwhelmed – and no wonder. From the monumental wrought-iron gates, the central path takes you into a world of frowning, fighting and posing bronze figures, which flank the footbridge over the river. Beyond, the **central fountain**, part of a separate commission begun in 1907, is an enormous bowl representing the burden of life, supported by straining, sinewy bronze Goliaths while, underneath, water tumbles out around clusters of playing, talking, resting and standing figures.

But it's the twenty-metre-high **obelisk** up on the stepped embankment, and the granite sculptures grouped around it, which really take the breath away. It's a humanistic work, a writhing mass of sculpture which depicts the cycle of life as Vigeland saw it: a vision of humanity teaching, playing, fighting, loving, eating and sleeping – and clambering on and over each other to reach the top. The granite children scattered around the steps are perfect: little pot-bellied figures who tumble over muscled adults, and provide an ideal counterpoint to the real Oslo toddlers who splash around in the fountain, oblivious and undeterred.

A five-minute walk from the obelisk, on the other side of the river at the southern edge of the park, the **Vigeland Museum** (*Vigeland-museet*; May–Sept Tues–Sat 10am–6pm, Sun noon–6pm; Oct–April Tues–Sun noon–4pm; 40kr), at the corner of Halvdan Svartes gate and Nobels gate, was the artist's studio and home during the 1920s. It's still stuffed with all sorts of items related to the sculpture park, including discarded or unused sculptures, woodcuts, preparatory drawings and scores of plaster casts. Here and there are scraps of biographical information, but Vigeland's last decades were defined by his creation: you get the feeling that given half a chance he would have had himself cast and exhibited – as it is, his ashes were placed in the museum's tower.

North of the centre: the Nordmarka

Criss-crossed by hiking trails and cross-country ski routes, the forested hills and lochs of the **Nordmarka** area occupy a tract of land that extends deep inland from downtown Oslo, but is still within the city limits for some 30km. A network of byroads provides dozens of access points to this wilderness, which is extremely popular with the capital's outdoor-minded citizens. **Den Norske Turistforening** (DNT), the Norwegian hiking organization, maintains a handful of staffed and unstaffed huts here. Their Oslo branch, in the city centre near Oslo S at Storgata 3 (Mon–Fri 10am–4pm, Thurs until 6pm, Sat 10am–2pm; ☎22 82 28 00, ⊛www .turistforeningen.no), has detailed **maps** and will arrange a year's DNT membership for 400kr. Members are offered substantial discounts at staffed huts and membership is a prerequisite if you want to get the key to one of their unstaffed, self-service huts (see p.40 for more on hiking).

For a day-trip, one of the easiest and most obvious departure points is **Sognsvann station**, the terminus of T-bane line #5, just twenty minutes from the city centre. Maps of the surrounding wilderness are posted at the station and show a network of hiking trails labelled according to the season – red for winter skiing, blue for summer. From the station, it's a signposted five-minute walk to **Sognsvannet**, an attractive lake flanked by forested hills and encircled by an easy four-kilometre hiking trail. The lake is iced-over until the end of March, but thereafter the hardy can go for a dip – treat Norwegian assurances about the warmth of the water with caution. With the proper hiking equipment (see p.40), it's possible to hike west over the hills to Frognerseteren station (see below), a tough and not especially rewarding trek of about 5km. Locals mostly shun this route in summer, but – approached from the other direction – it's really popular in winter with parents teaching their children to cross-country ski.

T-bane line #1 also delves into the Nordmarka, wriggling up into the hills to the **Frognerseteren** terminus, a thirty-minute ride north of the city centre. From the station, there's a choice of signposted trails across the surrounding countryside. The most popular is the easy but squelchy 2km stroll to the **Tryvannstårnet TV Tower** (daily: June 10am–6pm; July & Aug 10am–8pm; May & Sept 10am–5pm; Oct–April 10am–4pm; 40kr), where a lift whisks you up to an observation platform for panoramic views. Labels inside the platform point everything out for you, but note that this is a pointless excursion unless the weather is clear as even a light mist obscures the view. As an alternative to the TV tower, it's just a couple of hundred metres down from the T-bane station to the *Frognerseteren Restaurant* (opens 11am; ☎22 92 40 40), a delightful wooden lodge whose terrace offers splendid views out over the Nordmarka – and smashing food: coffee and cakes from 8kr, main dishes 120kr.

Forest footpaths link Frognerseteren with Sognsvannet, or it's a twenty-minute tramp downhill – either along the road or the adjacent footpath – to the flashy chalets and hotels of the **Holmenkollen ski resort**. The latter also has its own T-bane station, located at the very southern end of the resort. Holmenkollen's main claim to fame is its international **ski-jump**, a gargantuan affair that dwarfs its surroundings. At its base, the diligent **Skimuseet** (Ski Museum; daily: June–Aug 9am–8pm; May & Sept 10am–5pm; Oct–April 10am–4pm; 80kr) has a more entertaining display than its name suggests. As well as skis through the ages, the museum has clothes and equipment, from the latest in competition ski-wear to the seemingly makeshift garb of early polar explorers like Nansen and Amundsen. The Skimuseet also gives access to the mountain of metal steps which leads up the ski-jump for a peek straight down at what is, for most mortals, a horrifyingly steep, almost vertical, descent: it seems impossible that the tiny bowl at the bottom could pull the skier up in time – or that anyone could possibly want to jump off in the first place. The bowl is also the finishing point for the 8000-strong cross-country skiing race that forms part of the Holmenkollrennene (ski festival) every March.

Eating and drinking

There was a time when eating out in Oslo hardly set the pulse racing, but things are very different today. At the top end of the market, the city possesses dozens of fine **restaurants**, the pick of which feature Norwegian ingredients, especially fresh North Atlantic fish, but also more exotic dishes of elk, caribou and salted dried cod – for centuries Norway's staple food. Many of these restaurants have also assimilated the tastes and styles of other cuisines – especially those of the Mediterranean – and there is a smattering of foreign restaurants too, everything from Italian to Mongolian.

Many of the city's restaurants are fairly formal affairs with prices to burn your fingers, though the ethnic restaurants are usually much less expensive; Vietnamese places are currently very much in vogue. Equally affordable are the **cafés** and **café-bars**, which run the gamut from homely family places, offering traditional Norwegian stand-bys, to student haunts and ultra-fashionable hangouts. Nearly all serve inexpensive lunches, and many offer excellent, competitively priced evening meals as well, though the self-service cafés amongst them mostly close at 5 or 6pm. In addition, downtown Oslo boasts a vibrant **bar** scene, a boisterous but generally good-tempered affair, which is at its most frenetic at weekends in summer, when the city is crowded with visitors from all over Norway.

Finally, those carefully counting the kroner will find it easy to buy bread, fruit, snacks and sandwiches from stalls, supermarkets and kiosks across the city centre, while fast-food joints offering hamburgers and *pølser* (hot dogs) are legion, just not very exciting.

Cafés, coffeehouses and café-bars

Fast-food joints apart, **cafés** represent the best value in town. Traditional *kafeterias* (often self-service) offer substantial portions of Norwegian food in pleasant, crisply modern surroundings, though some are decidedly Scandinavian in appearance with oodles of pine panelling. In addition, Oslo has a slew of **café-bars** dishing up salads, pasta and the like in attractive, often modish premises. The most favourable buys are generally at **lunchtime**, when there's usually a dish of the day. As for **opening hours**, most of the cafés listed below are open until about 8 or 9pm, but predictably enough the café-bars stay open much later. The Norwegians have also developed a penchant for coffee and, like many other north European cities, Oslo now contains dozens of specialist **coffeehouses**. A couple of national chains are very well represented – *Kaffe & Krem* and the rather more appealing *Kaffebrenneriet* – and there's a smattering of more individualistic places too. Most coffeehouses are open from Monday through Friday 7 or 8am to 5 or 7pm, Saturdays 9 or 10am to 4 or 5pm and Sunday noon to 5pm.

Central

Amsterdam Universitetsgata 11, entrance on Kristian Augusts gate. Decorated in the style of a traditional Dutch bar, this busy and agreeable café-bar has a moderately priced menu with an international flavour. Offerings include lasagne, satay, and ciabatta with shellfish, and prices are in the 70–90kr range. Kitchen closes around 9pm.
Apotheket St Olavs Plass. Centrally located in a grand old building that used to be – yes – a

pharmacy, this café-bar comes complete with high ceilings, old wooden panels and antique furniture, and serves excellent Greek meze and other Mediterranean treats at very affordable prices, all washed down by a good range of beers.
Ett Glass Karl Johans gate 33, entrance round the corner on Rosenkrantz gate. Trendy, candle-lit café-bar with an imaginative menu focusing on Mediterranean-influenced light meals and lunches. Moderate prices.

Java Ullevålsveien 45B. Coffee connoisseur's paradise patronized by Norwegian royals – but without any of the pomp of other, more formal dynasties. Delicious sandwiches are on sale, too – as they are at the sister coffeehouse of *Mocca* (see below). North of the centre in the St Hanshaugen district. Closed Sun.

Kaffebrenneriet Grensen 45. Popular Norwegian coffeehouse chain with other branches scattered over central Oslo. Particularly good espressos, tasty snacks and great cakes, too. Bright, modern decor.

Kaffistova Rosenkrantz gate 8. Part of the *Hotell Bondeheimen* (see p.235), this spick-and-span self-service café serves reasonably tasty, traditional Norwegian cooking at very fair prices. There's usually a vegetarian option, too.

Stockfleth's Lille Grensen and C.J. Hambros plass. Many locals swear by the coffee served by this small chain. Regularly wins coffee-making and coffee-makers' competitions; their latte, either regular strength or strong, is the best in town.

Westside

Arcimboldo Wergelandsveien 17. Fashionable but unpretentious self-service café-bar inside the Kunstnernes Hus, the old art gallery facing onto the Slottsparken near the foot of Linstows gate. An imaginative menu featuring both Mediterranean-style and Norwegian dishes, with main courses in the region of 150kr.

Clodion Art Café Bygdøy allé 63, entrance round the corner on Thomas Heftyes gate. Well to the west of the city centre, not far from Frognerparken, this café-bar, with its brightly-

painted secondhand furniture, hosts regular art displays and has good food: soups at around 45kr, bowls of pasta for 70kr.

Mocca, Niels Juels gate 70. The only Oslo coffeehouse to roast its own beans – the results speak for themselves. Great sandwiches; sister coffeehouse is *Java* (see above). Closed Sun.

Rust Hegdehaugsveien 22. Smart, loungy kind of place that's good for lunches and light meals during the day and early evening. Turns into a chic bar at night – Calvados is the house speciality.

Eastside: Grünerløkka and Grønland

Fru Dattera til Hagen Grønland 10. Not too far from Oslo S, this is a spin-off venture of *Fru Hagen* (see below), serving tapas, beer and coffee in the daytime and turning into a happening bar at night with good – or usually good – DJ sounds on the first floor. There's an outdoor area at the back that's great on a hot summer's night. Don't fret – the toilets are indeed unisex.

Fru Hagen Thorvald Meyers gate 42. Trendy for years now, and still hanging on in there, this colourful place offers tasty snacks and meals from an inventive menu with a Mediterranean slant (main courses at 80–130kr). The kitchen opens till 9.30pm, after which the drinking gets going in earnest. Very popular spot – so go early to be sure of a seat.

Kjøkkenhagen Thorvald Meyers gate 40. Next door to Fru Hagen. Simple, straightforward snacks and light meals – tasty salads, quiche and so forth – at moderate prices.

Restaurants

Dining out at one of Oslo's **restaurants** can make a sizeable dent in the wallet unless you exercise some restraint. In most places, a main course will set you back between 150kr and 220kr – not too steep until you add on a couple of beers (at about 50kr a throw) or a bottle of wine (at least 240kr). On a more positive note, Oslo's better restaurants have creative menus marrying Norwegian culinary traditions with those of the Mediterranean – and a lousy meal is a rarity. Restaurant decor is often a real feature too, ranging from the predictable fishing photos and nets to sharp modernist styles, all pastel-painted walls and angular furnishings and fittings.

As regards **opening hours**, most restaurants open from 3 or 4pm to 10 or 11pm; where the hours are radically different, we've indicated below. Many places are closed on one day a week, often Sundays; again days of closure are detailed below. Finally, note that we've given phone numbers only for places where you need to **book in advance**.

Central

Agra Stranden 3, Aker Brygge. For Indian food and an authentic atmosphere, try this appealing, reasonably priced restaurant, hidden away in the Aker Brygge complex. Super tasty and (usually) good service, too.

Det Norske Hus, Prinsen gate 18 ☎22 41 12 10. First-rate restaurant serving traditional Norwegian cuisine, from reindeer through to salted cod. Main courses hover around 220kr. Smart decor in the restaurant and in the lunch bar, where meals are reasonably priced at around 100kr. Closed Sun.

Engebret Café Bankplassen 1 ☎22 82 25 25. Smart and intimate restaurant in an attractive old building across from the Museum of Contemporary Art, with seating outside on the pretty cobbled square In summer. Specializes in Norwegian delicacies such as elk and cod, with mouthwatering main courses in the region of 230kr. Closed Sun.

Grand Café Karl Johans gate 31. This is the café-restaurant where Ibsen once held court – and the murals prove the point. Now popular with pensioner-package tourists, the old-fashioned formality of the place, with its chandeliers, bow-tie waiters and glistening cutlery, is its main appeal, plus the reasonably priced set lunches. Also has a rooftop café with great views over Karl Johans gate, but occasionally slow service.

Westside

Bølgen & Moi Briskeby Løvenskioldsgate 26. Traditional Norwegian cuisine with a hint of Mediterranean/nouvelle crossover served both in the (expensive) gourmet section and at the (less expensive) bistro. Also offers fantastic breakfast buffets with everything you could wish for – and then some. Highly recommended. Løvenskioldsgate is on the west side of the city – take tram #12 or #15 from the centre.

Krishna Cuisine Kirkeveien 59B. Three-course vegetarian meals for around 100kr – and refills, too. Always tasty and filling, and by far the best vegetarian option in the city. West of the centre, near the Majorstuen T-bane station. Closed Sat & Sun.

Shogun Observatoriegaten 2B ☎22 44 07 45. Superfresh sushi at superlow prices, this offers a different and distinctive way to taste Norwegian fish. Good deals with soup and eight, ten or twelve pieces of maki and nigirisushi. West of the centre off Drammensveien – trams #10 or #12.

Eastside: Grünerløkka and Grønland

Arakataka Mariboes gate 7 ☎23 32 83 00. This smart, modern restaurant serves outstanding food, mostly fish, at unbeatable prices, both à la carte and with a set three-course menu for just 250kr. Highly recommended, though the service is patchy. A fifteen-minute walk north from the Domkirke or bus #34 or #38 from Jernbanetorget.

Lille Saigon Møllergata 32C. The best Vietnamese restaurant in the city. Simple surroundings, and delicious, inexpensive food – be sure to try the spring rolls. Møllergata runs north from near the Domkirke.

Markveien Mat & Vinhus Torvbakkgaten 26, entrance in Markveien ☎22 37 22 97. Mediterranean-influenced food and one of the best wine cellars in the city. High-quality and excellent service. On the southern edge of the Grünerløkka district. Closed Sun.

Sult Thorvald Meyers gate 26 ☎22 87 04 67. One of the city's most popular restaurants, named "Hunger" after the novel by Knut Hamsun. Features an inventive and moderately priced Norwegian-based menu, using only the freshest of ingredients. Thorvald Meyers gate is in the Grünerløkka district. Closed Mon.

Bars

Bar-hopping in Oslo is good fun. The more mainstream places are bang in the centre along and around Karl Johans gate, but the sharper, more fashionable spots are concentrated to the east in the Grünerløkka and Grønland districts; the westside of the city also chimes in with the smart and chic bars of Hegdehaugsveien and Bogstadveien. As for **opening hours**, many of Oslo's bars stay open until well after midnight on the weekend – in some cases 3–4am; on weekdays, they usually close around 1am. Drinks are uniformly expensive, so if you're after a big night out, it's a good idea to follow Norwegian custom and have a few warm-up drinks before you hit the tiles.

Central

Cruise Kafé Stranden 3, Aker Brygge. Standard-issue modern bar done out in pastel shades, with photographs of actors on the walls. It's all rather contrived, but the music – rock, and some rock and roll – is eclectic, and there are occasional live acts, too.

Last Train Karl Johans gate 45. The best rock-pub in town, with the music played at volume to a leather and jeans clientele.

Savoy Universitetsgata 11. With its stained-glass windows and wood-panelled walls, this small, intimate bar is an agreeably low-key spot to nurse a beer. Part of the *Quality Savoy Hotel*, on the corner of Kristian Augusts gate.

Studenten Karl Johans gate 45, corner of Universitetsgata. Micro-brewery pub with the copper vats to prove it. There are views across to the Nationaltheatret from the window seats, and a youthful crowd.

Westside

Barbeint Drammensveien 20. If you're familiar with Scandinavian bands and films, you may recognize a few faces in this jam-packed, fashionable bar. Loud sounds – everything from rap to rock. Close to Parkveien, about ten minutes' walk west of the Nationaltheatret.

Lorry Parkveien 12, corner of Hegdehaugsveien. Attracting a mixed crowd, this is a popular and enjoyable pub with old-fashioned fittings, a wide choice of beers and outdoor seating in the summer. A ten-minute walk west of the Nationaltheatret.

Palace Grill Solligata 2. Popular with everyone from yuppies to students, this is a small, American -style bar with Irish beers on draught. Roots, rock and jazz music, plus occasional live acts. Follow Drammensveien towards Solli Plass, turn left down Cort Adelers gate and it's first on the right.

Skaugum Solligata 2. This backyard behind the *Palace Grill* (which it shares an entrance with; see above) and *Bollywood Dancing* (see p.254) has been turned into a sort of Aladdin's cave with rack upon rack of multicoloured fairy lights illuminating the thirty-odd sinks – yes, sinks – that have been attached to the walls. It's all very modish and very successful, and it attracts an appreciative clientele. Open every day in summer when the weather is fine.

Eastside: Grünerløkka and Grønland

Bar Boca Thorvald Meyers gate 30, Grünerløkka. Tiny 1950s-style bar with perhaps the best cocktails in town – the bartenders take their work very seriously. Get there early and be prepared for the crush.

Café con Bar Brugata 11, Grønland. Hip-as-you-like with retro interior and a long bar, though this doesn't mean quick service – rather the reverse. Good atmosphere and loungy decor.

Elvis Pub Christian Kroghs gate 43. Not too easy to find (though hardcore Elvis fans will undoubtedly succeed), this tiny place is jam-packed with Elvis images and paraphernalia – no guesses as to what's on the jukebox. Down by the River Akerselva near the north end of Storgata.

Tea Lounge Thorvald Meyers gate 33B, Grønland. Lounge-type bar with velvety red couches and huge windows. Fine place to have a quiet (some would say romantic) night out.

Entertainment and nightlife

Oslo has a vibrant **nightclub** scene, which is hardly surprising given the number of Norwegians who flock to Ibiza every year. Tracking down live music is also straightforward. Though the domestic **rock** scene is far from inspiring, **jazz** fans are well served, with several first-rate venues dotted round the city centre, while **classical music** enthusiasts benefit from an ambitious concert programme. Throughout the summer, free outdoor and indoor musical events of every description are legion, and although things are much quieter (and always indoors) in the winter, there's usually something happening somewhere on every weekend. Most **theatre**

Rock and pop music festivals

The most prestigious annual event in the Oslo festival calendar is **Norwegian Wood** (℡81 53 31 33, ⊕www.norwegianwood.no), a three-day open-air rock festival held in June in the outdoor amphitheatre at Frogner Park, a ten-minute ride from the city centre on tram #12 or #15. Previous years have attracted the likes of Lou Reed, Van Morrison and Faithless, and the festival continues to pull in some of the best, supported by a variety of Norwegian acts. The arena holds around six thousand people, but tickets, costing around 350kr per day and available via the festival website, sell out long in advance. Oslo also hosts the more contemporary **Øyafestivalen** (⊕www.oyafestivalen.com), a three-day event that usually takes place in the middle of August. This showcases a wide range of artists, mostly Norwegian but with some imports, too – the 2002 lineup included Tortoise, Chicks On Speed and Saint Etienne – and a club night kicks the whole thing off in style. It's held outside in the Middelalderparken, not far from Oslo S train station – take tram #18 from Jernbanetorget. Tickets are available online or from Ticket Master (see above).

productions are in Norwegian, but English-language theatre companies visit often, and at the **cinema** films are shown in the original language with Norwegian subtitles.

For **entertainment listings** it's always worth checking out the weekly Norwegian-language listings leaflet *Plakaten*, available free from downtown cafés, bars, shops and the tourist office. More detailed information and reviews are provided by *Natt & Dag* (🖰www.nattogdag.no), a free Norwegian-language monthly broadsheet, which is also widely distributed downtown. The main alternative is *What's On in Oslo*, a monthly, somewhat anodyne English-language freebie produced by the tourist office.

For **tickets**, try Ticket Master ☎81 53 31 33, for whom larger Norwegian post offices act as agents; otherwise, contact the venue direct.

Nightclubs and live music venues

Oslo's hippest **nightclubs** are located on the east side of the city in the Grünerløkka and Grønland districts, but there's also a selection of more mainstream places right in the centre of town around Karl Johans gate and on Rosenkrantz gate. Entry will set you back in the region of 100kr, but quite a few places do not have a cover charge at all, and, surprisingly enough, drink prices are the same as anywhere else. Nothing gets going much before 11pm; closing times are generally around 3am. As for **live music**, big-name **rock bands** often include Oslo in their tours, leavening what would otherwise be a pretty dull scene.

Bollywood Dancing Solli gate 2 ☎22 55 11 66. Super-kitschy restaurant-bar-cum-disco that's one of the best – and trendiest – nightspots in town. Asian retro decor – fake red leather sofas and so forth – plus ingenious cocktails. Check out the excellent "Bollyburgers" and groove away on the dance floor until the early hours. West of the centre.

Blå Brenneriveien 9C ☎22 20 91 81, 🖰www.blx.no. Creative, cultured nightspot featuring everything from live jazz and cabaret through to public debates and poetry readings. Also features what many locals reckon to be the best DJs in town, keeping the crowd bopping until 3.30am on the weekend. In the summer, there's a pleasant riverside terrace. In Grünerløkka, a fifteen-minute walk north from the city along – and at the far end of – Møllergata.

Gloria Flames Grønland 18 ☎22 17 16 00. Not the easiest place to find – there's just a small sign on the door – but this hardcore rock and rockabilly club does its thing very well indeed. A short walk north of Oslo S.

Oslo Spektrum Sonja Henies plass 2 ☎22 05 29 00, 🖰www.oslospektrum.no. Major venue showcasing big international acts, as well as small-fry local bands. See listings magazines and/or press for programme. Central location, close to Oslo S.

Rockerfeller Music Hall Torggata 16 ☎22 20 32 32, 🖰www.rockefeller.no. With a capacity of 1500, this is one of Oslo's grandest club-cum-concert venues, occupying an imaginatively recycled former bathhouse. Hosts well-known and up-and-coming rock groups, with a good sideline in reggae and salsa. Torggata runs north from Stortorvet near the east end of Karl Johans gate; the entrance is round the back.

So What! Grensen 8 ☎22 33 64 66, 🖰www.sowhat.no. Something of a national institution and long a mecca for indie bands, *So What!* offers an ambitious programme of live music in its darker-than-dark basement. When there isn't a gig, the basement is used for some high-octane dancing, whilst the ground-floor bar features live rock and indie. Central location.

Jazz venues

Oslo has a strong **jazz** tradition, and in early or mid-August its week-long **Jazz Festival** (☎22 42 91 20, 🖰www.oslojazz.no) attracts internationally renowned artists and also showcases local talent. The Festival Office, at Tollbugata 28, and the website have full programme details both of the gigs, to which there's an admission charge, and the many free outdoor performances. At other times of the year, try one of the following for regular live jazz.

Herr Nilsen C.J. Hambros plass 5 ☎22 33 54 05 ⓦwww.herrnilsen.no. Small, intimate centrally located bar whose brick walls are awash with appropriate memorabilia. Live jazz – often traditional and bebop – most nights. Air-conditioned.

Original Nilsen Rosenkrantz gate 11 ☎22 72 12 21 ⓦwww.originalnilsen.no. Popular bar featuring regular live jazz, from traditional through to avant-garde. A favourite with visiting American artists – and has been so for years.

Classical music and opera

Oslo's major orchestra, the **Oslo Filharmonien** (ⓦwww.oslophil.com), gives regular concerts in the city's Konserthus, Munkedamsveien 14, and has an information office at Haakon VII's gate 2 (☎23 11 60 60). As you would expect, programmes often include works by Norwegian and other Scandinavian composers. Tickets for most performances cost around 300kr. In August and September, the orchestra traditionally gives a couple of free evening concerts in the Vigeland sculpture park – part of the city's summer entertainment programme, which also sees classical concerts at a variety of other venues, including the Domkirke, the Munch Museum and the University Aula. In October, there's also the ten-day **Ultima Contemporary Music Festival** (☎22 42 99 99, ⓦwww.ultima.no), which gathers together more Scandinavian and international talent in an extraordinarily ambitious programme of concerts featuring everything from modernist contemporary music to opera, ballet, classical and folk.

Den Norske Opera, the country's prolific opera company, offers the popular repertoire – Mozart, R. Strauss and the Italians – but also undertakes a number of contemporary works each year. Performances are usually held at the Opera House, Storgata 23 (information ☎23 31 50 00, booking office ☎81 54 44 88, ⓦwww.operaen.no).

Cinema

The ease with which most Norwegians seem to tackle other languages is best demonstrated at the **cinema**, where films are shown in their original language with Norwegian subtitles. Given that American (and British) films are the most popular, this has obvious advantages for visiting English speakers.

Oslo has its share of mainstream multiscreens, as well as a good art-house cinema. Prices are surprisingly reasonable, with tickets costing 65–75kr. Cinema **listings** – including details of late-night screenings – appear daily in the local press and the tourist office has programme times, too. The following is a selection of central screens.

Eldorado Torggata 9 ☎82 03 00 00. Mainstream multiplex.

Filmens Hus Dronningens gate 16 ☎22 47 45 00. Art-house.

Filmteateret Stortingsgata ☎82 03 00 00. Former theatre, with wonderful decor, and both mainstream and classic films.

Gimle Bygdøy allé ☎82 03 00 00. Sympathetically revamped old cinema with Oslo's most comfortable seats and a wine bar in the entrance area. Varied programme, mostly mainstream.

Saga Stortingsgata 28 at Olav V's gate ☎82 03 00 00. Mainstream; six screens.

Theatre

Nearly all of Oslo's **theatre** productions are in Norwegian, making them of limited interest to (most) tourists, though there are occasional English-language performances by touring theatre companies. The principal venue is the **Nationaltheatret**, Stortingsgata 15 (☎22 31 90 50, ⓦwww.nationaltheatret.no), which stages the prestigious annual **Ibsen Festival**. Touring companies may also appear at the more adventurous **Det Norske Teatret**, Kristian IV's gate 8 (☎22 42 43 44, ⓦwww.detnorsketeatret.no).

Sports

Surrounded by forest and fjord, Oslo is very much an outdoor city, offering a wide range of **sports** and related activities. In summer, locals take to the hills to **hike** the network of trails that lattice the forests and lakes of the Nordmarka (see p.249), where many also fish. Others use the city's open-air **swimming pool** and **tennis courts**, or head out to the offshore islets of the Oslofjord (see p.246) to sunbathe and swim. In winter, the cross-country ski routes of the Nordmarka are especially popular, as is downhill **skiing** at Holmenkollen. Indeed skiing is such an integral part of winter life here that the T-bane carriages all have ski racks. **Sleigh-riding** is possible too, and so is **ice skating**, with the handiest rinks right in the middle of town in front of the Stortinget (see p.237). An indoor option at any time of year is **ten-pin bowling** at – amongst several places – Oslo Bowlingsenter, Torggata 16 (☎22 20 44 42).

Summer sports

Oslo's main open-air **swimming pool**, Tøyenbadet (☎22 68 24 23; 50kr, children 30kr; free with the Oslo Card), is located to the northeast of the city centre, close to the Munch Museum at Helgesens gate 90. To get there, take the T-bane to Tøyen station, from where it's a five-minute walk. Tøyenbadet comprises four unheated, seasonal swimming pools, a sauna, solarium, diving boards, water chute and keep-fit facilities. It also has an all-year indoor swimming pool. Similar outdoor swimming facilities are provided from May to August at the newly redecorated Frognerbadet baths (☎22 44 74 29; 60kr; children 30kr; free with the Oslo Card), in Frognerparken, west of the centre and reached on tram #12 and #15. Also in Frognerparken is Oslo's one set of municipal **tennis courts** – an inexpensive supplement to the city's many private tennis clubs. The public courts only cost 50kr per person per hour (30kr for children) and as a result they're very popular, especially at weekends. Hiring a court is done locally at the kiosk.

As regards **fishing**, the freshwater lakes of the Nordmarka are reasonably well-stocked – trout, char, pike and perch are the most common species. The Oslomarkas Fiskeadministrasjon, Kongeveien 5 (☎22 49 07 99), near the Holmenkollen ski-jump, provides information on fishing in the Oslo area. In particular, they can advise about fishing areas and have lists of where local licences can be bought – as can the tourist office.

Winter sports

Skiing is extremely popular and skis and equipment can be rented for 200–300kr a day from Skiservice Tomm Murstad, Tryvannsveien 2 (☎22 13 95 00, ⊛www .skiservice.no), at the Voksenkollen T-bane station (the penultimate stop on line #1). Both cross-country and downhill enthusiasts should call by the **Skiforeningen** (Ski Association) office, at Kongeveien 5 (☎22 92 32 00, ⊛www.skiforeningen.no), near the Holmenkollen ski-jump, on T-bane #1. They have lots of information on Oslo's floodlit trails, cross-country routes, downhill and slalom slopes, ski schools (including one for children) and organized excursions to the nearest mountain resorts. Guided ski tours are organized by Uten Grenser (☎22 22 77 40). For spectators, March sees the annual Holmenkollen Ski Festival – tickets and information from the Skiforeningen.

Three other winter sports are worth noting. **Horsedrawn sleigh rides** in the Nordmarka can be arranged through either Vangen Skistue, PO Box 29, Klemetsrud, N-1212 Oslo (☎64 86 54 81); or Helge Torp, Sørbråten Gård, Maridalen, Oslo (☎22 23 22 21). **Ice fishing** is another Nordmarka option, but follow what the locals do as it can be dangerous (see above for information on fishing licences). Finally, there's a floodlit **skating rink**, Narvisen (Nov–March), in front of the Stortinget beside Karl Johans gate. Admission is free and you can hire skates on the spot at reasonable rates, with a modest discount if you have an Oslo Card.

Listings

Airlines British Airways, Gardermoen airport ☎80 03 31 42; Finnair, Jernbanetorget 4A ☎81 00 11 00; KLM, booking and information only by phone ☎82 00 20 02; SAS, Gardermoen airport and the airport train terminal at Oslo S ☎81 52 04 00; Widerøe's ☎81 00 12 00.

Banks and exchange Among many, Den Norske Bank has downtown branches at Stranden 1, Aker Brygge, and Karl Johans gate 2; Sparebanken is at Oslo S, Storgata 1 and Kirkegata 18. Normal banking hours are mid-May to mid-Sept Mon–Fri 8.15am–3pm, Thurs till 5pm; mid-Sept to mid-May Mon–Fri 8.15am–3.30pm, Thurs till 5pm. ATMs are liberally distributed across the city centre and at Gardermoen airport. There are also late-opening bureaux de change at the airport in Arrivals (Mon–Fri 8am–10.30pm, Sat 8.30am–7pm & Sun 10am–10.30pm) and Departures (Mon–Fri 5.30am–8pm, Sat 5.30am–6pm & Sun 6.30am–8pm); plus another at the airport train terminal at Oslo S (Mon–Fri 7am–7pm, Sat & Sun 8am–5pm). You can also change money and traveller's cheques at larger post offices, where the rates are especially competitive. There are 24hr credit-card cash machines at Oslo S and the airport.

Bookshops Tanum, Karl Johans gate 37, has the city's widest selection of English fiction. Nomaden, Uranienborgveien 4 (just behind the Slottsparken), has a first-rate selection of travel guides and maps, the best in Oslo. The shop of the Norwegian hiking organization, Den Norske Turistforening (DNT), Storgata 3, has a comprehensive collection of Norwegian hiking maps.

Buses For information on long-distance bus services, contact Nor-Way Bussekspress (@www.nor-way.no), at the Bussterminalen information desk (Mon–Fri 7am–10pm, Sat 8am–5.30pm, Sun 8am–10pm), or call ☎23 00 24 00 for details of their services to and from Oslo, ☎82 02 13 00 (premium-rate line) for their other services. For city buses, see p.231.

Car rental Avis, Munkedamsveien 27 ☎23 23 92 00, and at Gardermoen airport ☎64 81 06 60; Bislet Bilutleie, Pilestredet 70 ☎22 60 00 00; Europcar, Gardermoen airport ☎22 60 70 22. There are many others – see under *Bilutleie* in the Yellow Pages.

Email and Internet Free access is available at the main city library, Henrik Ibsen gate 1 (Mon–Fri 10am–8pm, Sat 9am–3pm).

Embassies and consulates Australia, Jernbanetorget 2 ☎22 47 91 70; Canada, Wergelandveien 7 ☎22 99 53 00; Ireland, c/o *Radisson SAS Scandinavia Hotel*, Holbergs gate 30 ☎22 20 43 70; Netherlands, Oscars gate 29 ☎23 33 36 00; Poland, Olav Kyrres plass 1 ☎22 55 55 36; UK, Thomas Heftyes gate 8 ☎23 13 27 00; USA, Drammensveien 18 ☎22 44 85 50. For others, look under *Ambassadeur og Legasjoner* in the Yellow Pages.

Emergencies Ambulance and medical assistance ☎113; police ☎112; fire brigade ☎110.

Ferries DFDS Seaways (to Helsingborg & Copenhagen), Vippetangen Utstikker (pier) #2, beside Akershusstranda (☎22 41 90 90, @www.dfds.no); Stena Line (to Frederikshavn in Denmark), Jernbanetorget 2 (☎02010, @www.stenaline.no); Color Line (to Kiel and Hirtshals, Denmark), Hjortneskaia (☎81 00 08 11, @www.colorline.com). Tickets from the companies direct or travel agents.

Gay Oslo Primarily because Oslo's gays and lesbians are mostly content to share pubs and clubs with heteros, there's no real scene in the city. Activities and events are organized – and advice given – by LLH (*Landsforeningen for lesbisk og homofil frigjøring*), 3rd Floor, Nordahl Brunsgate 22 (☎23 32 73 73). Their website, @www.llh.oslo.no, is Norwegian-only; for English information email on @post@llh.no. The main Oslo event is the annual Skeive Dager festival ("Queer Days"; @www.skeivedager.no), usually in late June, which includes parties, political meetings and a film festival. There's also a gay parade towards the end of July. The pick of the pubs and clubs are *London Pub*, C.J. Hambros plass 5 (☎22 70 87 00), with a bar on the first floor and a downstairs disco/club that gets packed at the weekend. *Soho*, Kirkegata 34 (☎22 42 91 00), is a pub-cum-club with a mixed gay crowd; while the prime lesbian spot in town, *Potpurriet*, Øvre Vollgate 13 (☎22 41 14 40), has club nights at weekends.

Hiking Den Norske Turistforening (DNT), Storgata 3 (Mon–Fri 10am–4pm, Thurs until 6pm, Sat 10am–2pm; ☎22 82 28 00, @www.turistforeningen.no), sells hiking maps and gives general advice and information on route planning – a useful first port-of-call before a walking trip in Norway.

Laundry Majorstua Myntvaskeri, Vibes gate 15 (Mon–Fri 8am–8pm, Sat 8am–5pm); Mr Clean, Parkveien 6, entrance on Welhavens gate (daily 7am–11pm); A-vask Selvbetjening, Thorvald Meyers gate 18, Grünerløkka (daily 10am–8pm).

Left luggage Coin-operated lockers (24hr) and luggage office at Oslo S.

Lost property (*hittegods*) Trams, buses and T-bane ☎22 08 53 61; NSB railways ☎23 15 00 00; police ☎22 66 98 65.

Markets and supermarkets Oslo's principal open-air market is on Youngstorget (Mon–Sat 7am–2pm), a brief stroll north of the Domkirke along Torggata. There's everything here from secondhand clothes to fresh fruit and veg. More convenient for the centre are the several fresh produce stalls in the Basarhallene, beside Karl Johans gate (see p.237). Supermarkets are thick on the ground in the suburbs, but rarer in the city centre. The biggest name is Rimi, which has a downtown outlet at Akersgata 45, near the corner with Grensen (Mon–Sat 8am–8pm, Sun 9am–5pm).

Newspapers Many English and American newspapers and magazines are widely available in downtown Oslo's convenience stores and Narvesen kiosks. There's an especially wide selection at Oslo S.

Pharmacy Jernbanetorgets Apotek, near Oslo S at Jernbanetorget 4b (☎22 41 24 82), is open 24-hours. All city pharmacies display a rota of late-opening places.

Post office The main post office, with poste restante, is at Dronningens gate 15 (Mon–Fri 8am–6pm, Sat 10am–3pm). There are lots of other post offices dotted across Oslo and usual opening hours are Mon–Fri 8am–5pm, Sat 9am–1pm. Downtown locations include Karl Johans gate 22, opposite the Parliament building; Universitetsgata 2; and inside Oslo S. All post offices exchange currency and cash cheques at very reasonable rates.

Taxis There are taxi ranks dotted all over the city centre. You can also telephone Oslo Taxi on ☎02 323 or Taxi 2 on ☎02 202.

Trains Enquiries and bookings on ☎81 50 08 88, ⊛www.nsb.no.

Vinmonopolet Klingenberggaten 4; Møllergaten 10–12; and at the Oslo City shopping complex, Stenersgaten 1.

Around Oslo

The forested uplands that surround Oslo have little of the splendour of other parts of the country, but you can get a hint of what the great Norwegian outdoors is about by exploring the narrow straits and chubby basins of the **Oslofjord**, which links the capital with the open sea. This waterway – around 100km from top to bottom – has long been Norway's busiest, an islet-studded channel whose sheltered waters were once crowded with steamers shuttling passengers along the Norwegian coast. The humdrum settlements that flank the fjord are, however, without much interest, except for the old garrison town of **Fredrikstad**, down the eastern side of the fjord on the train route to Sweden, whose antique grid-iron streets and earthen bastions have survived in remarkably good condition.

Fredrikstad

Roughly every two hours, trains leave Oslo to thump down the east side of the Oslofjord on their way to **FREDRIKSTAD**, named after the Danish king, Frederik II, who had the original fortified town built here at the mouth of the River Glomma in 1567. Norway was ruled by Danish kings from 1387 to 1814 and, with rare exceptions, the country's interests were systematically neglected in favour of Copenhagen's. A major consequence was Norway's involvement in the bitter rivalry between the Swedish and Danish monarchies, which prompted a seemingly endless and particularly pointless sequence of wars lasting from the early sixteenth century until 1720. The eastern approaches to Christiania (Oslo), along the Oslofjord, were especially vulnerable to attack from Sweden and the area was ravaged by raiding parties on many occasions. Indeed, Frederik II's fortress only lasted three years before it was burnt to the ground, though it didn't take long for a replacement to be constructed – and for the whole process to be repeated again. Finally, in the middle of the seventeenth century, Fredrikstad's fortifications were considerably strengthened. The central gridiron of cobbled streets was encircled on three sides by zigzag bastions, which allowed the defenders to fire across the flanks and into the front of any attacking force. In turn, these bastions were protected by a moat, concentric earthen banks and outlying redoubts. Armed with 130 cannon,

▲ Oslo   ▲ Oslo

Domkirke

Train & Bus Station

Victoria Hotel

FERJESTEDSVEIEN

Ferry

Balaklava Gjestgiveri

ISEGRAN

GAMLEBYEN

Museum

Fredrikstad Motel & Camping

Kongsten Fort

FREDRIKSTAD

0   200m

▶ Halden

Fredrikstad was, by 1685, the strongest fortress in all of Norway – and it has remained in military use ever since, which partly accounts for its excellent state of preservation. The fort was also left unaffected by the development of modern Fredrikstad, an offspring of the timber industry. This new town was built on the west bank of the Glomma while the old fort – now known as the **Gamlebyen** (Old Town) – was left untouched on the east.

From Fredrikstad **train** and **bus** station, located in the new part of town, it's a couple of minutes' walk to the Glomma river – head straight down Jernbanegata and take the first left along Ferjestedsveien. From the jetty, the **ferry** (Mon–Fri 5.30am–11pm, Sat 7am–11pm, Sun 9.30am–11pm; 5min; 8kr) shuttles over to the gated back wall of the Gamlebyen. Inside, the pastel-painted timber and stone houses of the old town, just three blocks deep and six blocks wide, make for a delightful stroll especially as very few tourists venture this way except in the height of the season. Indeed, on a drizzly day the streets echo with nothing but the sound of your own footsteps – plus the occasional army boot hitting the cobbles as the garrison moves about its duties. A **museum** (mid-June to Aug Mon–Sat 11am–5pm, Sun noon–5pm; 30kr), housed in the Gamle Slaveri (Old Slave House), where prisoners once did hard labour, dutifully outlines the history of the Old Town and displays a model of the fortress in its prime. Elsewhere, the main square holds an unfortunate **statue** of Frederik II, who appears to have a serious problem with his pantaloons, but it's the general appearance of the place that appeals rather than any specific sight. Make sure also to take in the most impressive of the town's outlying defences, the **Kongsten Fort**, about ten minutes' walk from the main fortress: go straight ahead from the main fortress gate, take the first right along Heibergsgate and it's clearly visible on the left. Here, thick stone and earthen walls are moulded round a rocky knoll which offers wide views over the surrounding countryside – an amiably quiet vantage point.

Back on the western side of the Glomma, follow Ferjestedsveien in the opposite direction to that taken before for the brief walk round to the small park beside the **Domkirke** (late June to mid-Aug Tues–Sat noon–3pm), a big, brown, brick building with stained glass by Emanuel Vigeland. Beyond the church is the centre of modern Fredrikstad, an uninteresting place plonked on a bend in the river.

Although it's preferable to treat a visit as a day-trip, there is a handful of **hotels** in Fredrikstad, including the *Victoria*, Turngaten 3 (☎69 31 11 65, ⓦwww .victoria-fredrikstad.com; ❻/❹), a comfortable place in a straightforward Art Nouveau building overlooking the park next to the Domkirke. Alternatively, the bargain-basement *Fredrikstad Motel & Camping*, Torsnesveien 16 (☎69 32 05 32, ⓕ69 32 36 66; ❷), is about 300m straight ahead from the main gate of the Gamlebyen; it provides tent space as well as inexpensive rooms.

Travel details

Trains

Oslo to: Åndalsnes (2–3 daily; 6hr 30min); Bergen (4–5 daily; 6hr 30min); Dombås (3–4 daily; 4hr 20min); Drammen (4–5 daily; 40min); Fredrikstad (8 daily; 1hr 15min); Geilo (4–5 daily; 3hr 20min); Halden (8 daily; 1hr 45min); Hamar (7 daily; 1hr 40min); Hjerkinn (3 daily; 4hr 45min); Kongsberg (4–5 daily; 1hr 20min); Kristiansand (4–5 daily; 5hr); Larvik (2–7 daily; 2hr 15min); Lillehammer (7 daily; 2hr 30min); Moss (8 daily; 50min); Myrdal (4–5 daily; 4hr 30min); Otta (4–5 daily; 4hr 10min); Røros (2–3 daily; 6hr); Stavanger (3 daily; 9hr); Trondheim (3–4 daily; 8hr 15min); Voss (4–5 daily; 5hr 40min).

Buses

Oslo to: Alta via Sweden (3 weekly; 27hr); Arendal (1 daily; 4hr 15min); Balestrand (3 daily; 8hr 15min); Bergen (1 daily; 11hr 40min); Drøbak (hourly; 40min); Fagernes (3 daily; 3hr 20min); Fjaerland (3 daily; 7hr 50min); Grimstad (1 daily; 4hr 40min); Hamar (1 daily; 2hr); Hammerfest via Sweden (3 weekly; 30hr); Haugesund (1 daily; 10hr); Kongsberg (1 daily; 2hr); Kristiansand (1 daily; 5hr 40min); Lillehammer (1 daily; 3hr); Lillesand (1 daily; 5hr); Odda (1 daily; 8hr); Otta (2 daily; 5hr); Risør (1 daily; 3hr 30min); Sogndal (3 daily; 7hr); Stavanger (1 daily; 10hr); Stryn (1 daily; 8hr); Voss (1 daily; 10hr 30min).

Ferries

Horten to: Moss (hourly 6am–1am; 30min).
Oslo to: Dronningen/Bygdøynes (May–Aug every 40min 9.05am–9.05pm; late April & Sept every 40min 9.05am–6.25pm; 10–15min); Hovedøya (mid-March to Sept every 60–90min; Oct to mid-March 3 daily; 10min); Langøyene (June–Aug hourly 10am–6pm; 30min).

International trains

Oslo to: Hamburg (1 daily; 14hrs); Copenhagen via Gothenburg (2 daily; 8hr 20min); Stockholm (3–5 daily; 6hr).

International buses

Oslo to: Amsterdam (2–3 weekly; 22hrs); Copenhagen (2–3 daily; 9hr 15min); Gothenburg (2–3 daily; 4hr 45min); London (3–5 weekly; 35hrs); Stockholm (3–4 daily; 10hr). Also services to Germany, Italy, Greece, Austria and Belgium.

International ferries

Oslo to: Copenhagen (1 daily; 16hr); Frederikshavn (1–2 daily; 8hr 30min); Hirtshals (6 weekly; 8hr); Kiel (1 daily; 19hr).

2.2

South and Central Norway

Preoccupied by the fjords and the long road to the Nordkapp, few tourists are tempted to explore **South and Central Norway**. The Norwegians know better. Trapped between Sweden and the fjords, this great chunk of land boasts some of the country's finest scenery, with forested dales trailing north and west from Oslo towards the rearing peaks inland. It's here, within shouting distance of the country's principal train line and the E6 – the main line of communication between Oslo, Trondheim and the north – that you'll find three of Norway's prime **hiking areas**. These are made up of a trio of mountain ranges, each partly contained within a **national park** – from south to north, Jotunheimen, Rondane and the Dovrefjell. Each park is equipped with well-maintained walking trails and DNT huts. **Otta** and **Kongsvoll**, on both the E6 and the train line, are particularly good starting points for hiking expeditions.

Entirely different, but just as popular with the Norwegians, is the **south coast**, an appealing region whose myriad islets and skerries, beaches and coves punctuate the shoreline that extends west from the Oslofjord. This coast is at its prettiest in the east where a handful of old timber ports – **Arendal**, **Lillesand** and **Mandal** – sport bright-white, antique clapboard houses along their harbourfronts. **Kristiansand**, easily the largest town on the coast, is different again, a brisk, modern place that successfully combines its roles as a resort and as a major ferry port with connections to Denmark. Beyond Kristiansand lies **Mandal**, an especially fetching holiday spot with a great beach, but thereafter the coast becomes harsher and less absorbing, heralding a sparsely inhabited region with precious little to detain you before **Stavanger**, a lively oil town and port within easy striking distance of some fine fjord and mountain scenery.

The south coast is traversed by the E18 (and its continuation the E39), linking Oslo with Stavanger. In between the E18/39 and the E6, three major roads – the E134, Hwy 7 and, fastest of the lot, the E16 – cut across the interior from the capital to the central fjords and Bergen. These highways can make the whole region seem rather like a transport corridor, but, whichever way you're heading, it would be a great pity not to allow at least a couple of days for the south coast or the national parks in the north.

As you might expect, **bus** services along these main highways are excellent and **trains** are fast and frequent, too. Away from the highways, however, the bus system thins out and travelling becomes a pain without your own vehicle – it can be worth renting a car locally for a few days. In terms of **accommodation**, roadside campsites are commonplace, there's a reasonable supply of youth hostels and every major town has at least one hotel or guesthouse.

North to Kongsvoll and Røros

Hurrying from Oslo to Trondheim and points north, the **E6** remains the most important highway in Norway, and is consequently kept in excellent condition – often with the roadworks to prove it. Inevitably, the road is used by many of the region's long-distance **buses**, and for much of its length it's also shadowed by

Norway's principal **train** line. Heading out of Oslo, both the E6 and the railway thump northwards across the lowlands to clip along the north bank of Lake Mjøsa en route to **Lillehammer**, site of the 1994 Winter Olympic Games and the country's best open-air folk museum. Thereafter, road and rail wriggle on between the **Jotunheimen** and **Rondane national parks**, whose magnificent mountains are both within easy reach of the amiable town of **Otta**. Further north still is the

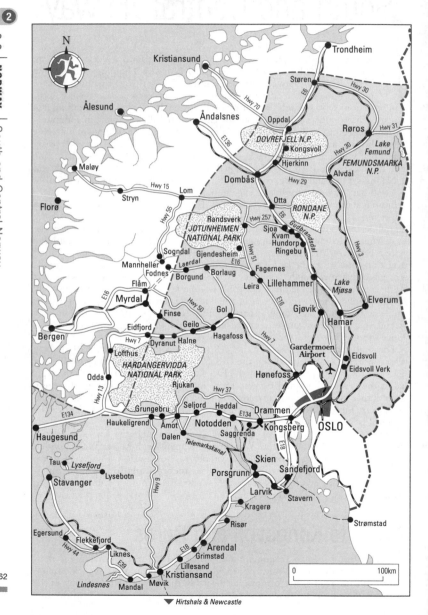

▼ *Hirtshals & Newcastle*

beautiful **Dovrefjell** range, which forms a third and equally stunning national park, and one that's best approached from tiny **Kongsvoll**. All three parks are famous for their hiking, and are criss-crossed by an extensive and well-planned network of **trails**. From Kongsvoll, the obvious route north is along the E6 to Trondheim (see p.338), though you might consider detouring east to the quaint old mining town of **Røros**.

Hamar

Beyond the flat farmlands north of Oslo, the E6 curves round the northern shore of Norway's largest lake, **Lake Mjøsa**, a favourite retreat for Norwegian families, with the surrounding farmland, woods and pastures harbouring numerous second homes. Before the railroad arrived in the 1880s, the lake was an important transport route, crossed by boats during the summer and by horse and sleigh in winter. It's also halfway country: the quiet settlements around the lake give a taste of small-town southern Norway before the E6 plunges on into wilder regions further north. Midway round the lake, some 130km from Oslo, lies **HAMAR**, an easy-going little place of 25,000 souls where marinas and waterside cafés make a gallant attempt to sustain a nautical flavour. The town was once the seat of an important medieval bishopric, and the substantial Gothic remains of the **Domkirke** (cathedral) are stuck out on the **Domkirkeodden** (Cathedral Point), a low, grassy headland towards the west end of town. The cathedral is thought to have been built by the "English pope" Nicholas Breakspear, who spent a couple of years in Norway as the papal legate before becoming Adrian IV in 1154, but the building, along with the surrounding episcopal complex, was ransacked during the Reformation, and local road-builders subsequently helped themselves to the stone. The ruins have now been incorporated into the **Hedmarksmuseet** (daily: mid-May to mid-June 10am–4pm; mid-June to mid-Aug 10am–6pm; mid-Aug to mid-Sept 10am–4pm; 60kr), which contains an archeological museum and an open-air folk museum. The latter holds fifty buildings collected from across the region and, although it's not as comprehensive as the one in Lillehammer (see p.264), it does contain one or two particularly fine buildings, including the parsonage of Bolstad with its beautifully decorated log walls. The most scenic approach to the headland is along the pleasant lakeshore footpath, which stretches 2km north from the train station.

Hamar is also as good a place as any to pick up the 130-year-old **paddle steamer**, the *Skibladner* (☎61 14 40 80, ⊛www.skibladner.no), which shuttles up and down Lake Mjøsa between late June and late August: on Tuesdays, Thursdays and Saturdays the boat makes the return trip across the lake from Hamar to Gjøvik and on up to Lillehammer, while on Mondays, Wednesdays and Fridays it chugs down to Eidsvoll and back; there's no Sunday service. Departure details are available direct or at any local tourist office. Tickets are bought on board: return trips from Hamar to Eidsvoll cost around 200kr and last two and a half hours, those to Lillehammer cost 250kr and last eight hours. One-way fares cost a little over half these rates. Travellers heading north may find the trip to Lillehammer tempting at first sight, but the lake is not particularly scenic, and after four hours on the boat you'll feel like jumping overboard with tedium. The best bet is to take the short bus or train ride instead.

Practicalities

Hamar's **train station** is in the town centre beside the lake; **buses** stop outside. Some trains from Oslo pause here before heading up the secondary branch line to Røros (see p.270), a fine three-and-a-half-hour ride over the hills and through huge forests. Some 600m from the train station – turn left out of the terminal building and head along Stangevegen – is the jetty for the *Skibladner* ferry.

There's a fair choice of central **hotels**, one pleasant and reasonably priced option being the lakeshore *First Hotel Victoria*, Strandgata 21 (☎62 02 55 00, ⊛www.firsthotels.com; ❹), which also has a competent restaurant serving

Norwegian favourites. Part of the same complex is employed as a **motel**, with slightly cheaper rooms (**❸**). There's also an all-year HI **hostel**, Åkersvikaveg 24 (☎62 52 60 60, ✉hamar.hostel@vandrerhjem.no), which occupies smart modern buildings about 2km south along the lakeshore from the train station. It's in the middle of nowhere, just across from the massive skating arena built for the 1994 Winter Olympics in the shape of an upturned Viking ship.

LILLEHAMMER (literally "Little Hammer"), 50km north of Hamar and 180km from Oslo, is Lake Mjøsa's most worthwhile destination. In **winter**, it's *the* Norwegian ski centre, a young and vibrant place whose rural, lakeshore setting and extensive cross-country ski trails contributed to its selection as venue for the 1994 Winter Olympic Games. In preparation for the games, the Norwegian government spent a massive two billion kroner on the town's **sporting facilities**, which are now the best in the country. Spread along the hillsides above and near the town, they include a ski-jumping tower and chair lift; a ski-jumping arena with two jumping hills and chairlift; an ice hockey arena; a bobsleigh track and a cross-country skiing stadium which gives access to about 30km of cross-country ski trails. Several local companies, including Saga Arrangement, Gudbrandsdalsvegen 203 (☎61 26 92 44, ✇www.sagaarrangement.no), operate all-inclusive winter sports and activity holidays, though if this is what you have in mind, you may as well book your holiday with an agent back home. As you would expect, most Norwegians arriving here in winter come fully equipped, but it's possible to rent (or purchase) equipment when you get here – the tourist office (see opposite) will advise.

Lillehammer remains a popular holiday spot in **summer** too. Hundreds of Norwegians hunker down in their second homes in the hills, dropping into the town centre for a drink or a meal. Cycling, walking, fishing and canoeing are popular pastimes at this time of year, with all sorts of possibilities for guided tours and equipment hire. But, however appealing the area may be to Norwegians, the countryside round here has little of the wonderful wildness of other parts of Norway, and unless you're someone's guest or bring your own family, you'll probably feel rather out on a limb. That said, Lillehammer is not a bad place to break your journey, and there are a couple of attractions to keep you busy for a day – but not two.

The Kunstmuseum and Maihaugen

Lillehammer's briskly efficient centre, just a few minutes' walk from one end to the other, is tucked into the hillside above the lake, the E6 and the railway. It has just one really notable attraction, the municipal art gallery, the **Kunstmuseum**, at Stortorget 2 (late June to late Aug daily 11am–5pm; late Aug to late June Tues–Sun 11am–4pm; 50kr). Housed in a flashy modern edifice, the gallery's speciality is its temporary exhibitions of contemporary art (which attract an extra admission charge), but the permanent collection is also very worthwhile, with a small but representative sample of the works of most major Norwegian painters from Johan Dahl and Christian Krohg to Munch and Erik Werenskiold.

The much-vaunted **Maihaugen** open-air folk museum – the largest of its type in northern Europe – is located a twenty-minute walk or a quick bus ride southeast from the Skysstasjon along Anders Sandvigsgate (late May & late Aug to Sept daily 10am–5pm; June to mid-Aug daily 9am–6pm; June to mid-Aug 90kr, rest of the year 75kr). Incredibly, the whole collection represents the lifetime's work of one man, a magpie-ish dentist by the name of Anders Sandvig. The Maihaugen holds around 140 reconstructed buildings, brought here from all over the region, including a charming seventeenth-century presbytery (*prestegårdshagen*), a thirteenth-century stave church from Garmo, log stores and smokehouses, summer grazing huts and various workshops. The key exhibits, however, are the two **farms** dating from the late seventeenth century, complete with their various outhouses and living areas.

The outside area is stocked with farmyard animals, while guides dressed in traditional costume give the lowdown on traditional rural life, and in the summertime there's often the chance to have a go at homely activities such as spinning, baking, weaving and pottery – good, wholesome fun. The main museum building features temporary exhibitions on folkloric themes. Allow a good half-day for a visit and take advantage of the free guided tour (in English every other hour, on the hour).

Practicalities

The E6 runs along the lakeshore about 500m below the centre of Lillehammer, where the ultramodern **Skysstasjon**, on Jernbanetorget at the bottom of Jernbanegata, incorporates the **train station** and the **bus terminal**. The **information kiosk** here has public transport timetables and some tourist information. The main **tourist office** is a five-minute walk away up the hill and off the main street, Storgata, at Elvegata 19 (mid June to late Aug Mon–Sat 10am–8pm, Sun 11am–6pm; late Aug to mid-June Mon–Fri 10am–4pm, Sat 10am–2pm; ☎61 25 02 99, ⊛www.lillehammerturist.no). Staff have bucketloads of free brochures, information on local events and activities, and will help with finding accommodation. **Orientation** couldn't be easier, with all activity focused on the pedestrianized part of Storgata which runs north from Bankgata, across Jernbanegata to the tumbling River Mesnaelva; Anders Sandvigsgate and Kirkegata run parallel on either side to east and west respectively.

For a place to stay, the popular HI **hostel** (☎61 24 87 00, ⊕lillehammer.hostel @vandrerhjem.no) is perfect for an overnight visit. It occupies part of the Skysstasjon, and the thirty or so four-bunk rooms are kitted out with smoked-glass windows and smart modern furnishings; there are also private doubles (❷). If you're around for longer, you may want something rather more cosy: *Gjestehuset Ersgaard*, Nordseterveien 201 (☎61 25 06 84, ☏61 25 31 09, ⊛www.ersgaard.no; ❸), a couple of kilometres above town (in the Nordseter direction), is a pleasant **guesthouse** which serves excellent breakfasts in its dining room overlooking the town and lake. In the centre, the *First Hotell Breiseth*, across from the Skysstasjon at Jernbanegata 3 (☎61 24 77 77, ⊛www.breiseth.com; ❺), is a large chain **hotel** with comfortable rooms.

Downtown Lillehammer has a good supply of **restaurants** and **cafés**. The busy *Bøndernes Hus Kafeteria*, Kirkegata 68, is a big, old-fashioned sort of place with cheap and filling self-service meals. Moving up a rung, the *Vertshuset Solveig*, down an alley off the pedestrianized part of Storgata, is cafeteria-style too, but the meals are first-rate, with main courses averaging around 120kr. If it's sunny, head for the *Terrassen*, a large and moderately priced outdoor restaurant by the river at Storgata 84 serving all the Norwegian favourites. The town has an animated nightlife, with **bars** clustered around the western end of Storgata – try *Nikkers*, a stone's throw from the main tourist office.

The Gudbrandsdal: Hundorp and Sjoa

Heading north from Lillehammer, the E6 and the railway leave the shores of Lake Mjøsa for the **Gudbrandsdal**, the 160-kilometre-long river valley which was for centuries the main route between Oslo and Trondheim. Enclosed by mountain ranges, the valley has a comparatively dry and mild climate, and its fertile soils have nourished a string of farming villages since Viking times – though there was some industrialization at the beginning of the twentieth century.

The first part of the Gudbrandsdal is fairly uninspiring, but after 70km the road swings past **HUNDORP**, where a neat little quadrangle of old farm buildings has been tastefully turned into a roadside tourist stop, with a café, art gallery and shop. There has been a farm here since prehistoric times, its most famous owner a Viking warrior by the name of Dalegudbrand, who became a bitter enemy of St Olav after his enforced baptism in 1021. With a little time to spare, you could ramble down towards the river from the compound and nose around a couple of Viking burial mounds. Three kilometres further north, amongst the orchards overlooking the E6, is **Sygard Grytting** (T & F 61 29 85 88; mid–June to mid–Aug), an ancient farmstead whose eighteenth-century buildings are in an almost perfect state of preservation – a beautiful ensemble with assorted barns and outhouses facing onto a tiny courtyard. One barn dates from the fourteenth century, when its upper storey was used to shelter pilgrims on the long haul north to Trondheim – it now offers inexpensive dormitory accommodation (300kr per person), whilst the rooms in the main farmhouse (❹) provide some of the most attractive lodgings in the region. The nearest train station is Hundorp, which is where long-distance buses will drop you, too.

Pressing on, the E6 weaves north along the course of the river to reach, after 35km, **SJOA** train station, which sits beside the E6 at its junction with Hwy 257. The latter cuts west along the Heidal valley, which boasts some of the country's most exciting **whitewater rafting** on the River Sjoa. If you want to come to grips with the Sjoa's gorges and rapids, contact the local specialists Heidal Rafting (T 61 23 60 37, W www.heidalrafting.no). An all-inclusive one-day rafting excursion costs around 800kr; a more strenuous two-day expedition inclusive of meals and lodgings will set you back almost three times that amount. The season lasts from May to September and reservations are recommended, though there's a reasonably good chance of being able to sign up at the last minute. Heidal Rafting are based at the Sjoa HI **hostel** (T 61 23 62 00, F 61 23 60 14; mid–May to Sept), itself worth a second look. Perched on a wooded hillside high above the river, the main building is a charming old log farmhouse dating from 1747 and, although visitors sleep elsewhere, you do eat here. Breakfasts are banquet-like and dinners (by prior arrangement only) are reasonably priced if rather less spectacular. The hostel offers no-frills dormitory accommodation and a handful of spacious and comfortable double rooms and chalets (both ❷). Advance reservations are recommended for the chalets at weekends. The hostel is situated just 1300m west of Sjoa train station near Hwy 257 – note that some trains only stop at Sjoa on request: check with the conductor.

Otta and the Rondane and Jotunheimen national parks

Just 10km beyond Sjoa lies **OTTA**, an unassuming and unexciting little town at the confluence of the rivers Otta and Lågen. It may be dull, but Otta makes a handy base for hiking in the nearby Rondane and Jotunheimen national parks, especially if you're reliant on public transport – though staying in one of the parks' mountain lodges is to be preferred. In Otta, everything you need is within easy reach: the E6 passes within 200m of the centre, sweeping along the east bank of the Lågen, while the **train station**, **bus terminal** and **tourist office** (July & Aug Mon–Fri 8.30am–7pm, Sat & Sun 11am–6pm; Sept–June Mon–Fri 8.30am–4pm; T 61 23 66 50) are all clumped together on the west bank in the Skysstasjon, just 100m from the small grid of streets that pass for the town centre. There are no sights as such, but the stiff hike along the footpath up the forested slopes to the summit of nearby **Pillarguritoppen** (853m), across the Otta River south of the centre, is a popular outing.

Otta tourist office is exceptionally helpful, providing local bus timetables, booking accommodation, reserving boat tickets, selling DNT membership and fishing licences, offering hiking tips and selling a range of hiking maps. As for **accommodation**, the *Grand Gjestegård* (T 61 23 12 00, F 61 23 04 62; ❸), across from the train station at the corner of Ola Dahls gate, is a large pension-cum-hotel with simple but perfectly adequate rooms furnished in brisk modern style. If they're full, try the *Norlandia Otta Hotell* (T 61 23 00 33, F 61 23 15 24; ❹), which occupies a recently spruced up concrete block a few metres to the west along Ola Dahls gate. The nearest **campsite**, the all-year *Otta Camping* (T 61 23 03 09), occupies a

Moving on from Otta and the western fjords

Running west from Otta, **Hwy 15** sweeps along the wide and fertile Hjelledal river valley over to Lom (see p.323), where there's a choice of wonderful routes on into the western fjords. From Lom, **Hwy 55** climbs steeply to the south, travelling along the western flank of the Jotunheimen National Park and offering breathtaking views of its jagged peaks before careering down to Sogndal (see p.321). Alternatively, Hwy 15 forges ahead from Lom to Stryn (see p.325), passing the nerve-jangling **Ørnevegen** (Eagle's Highway) – Hwy 63 – turning to **Geiranger** (see p.330). In terms of public transport, the Oslo–Måløy Nor-Way Bussekspress **bus** (2–3 daily) passes through Otta and Lom en route to Stryn; from mid-June to August, one of these three buses connects at Grotli with the bus down to Geiranger. The journey time from Otta to Lom is one hour, three hours to Stryn. There are no bus services along Hwy 55.

small riverside site with pitches and cabins (❷) in a scenic spot on the wooded banks of the River Otta about 1500km from the town centre. To get there, cross the bridge on the south side of the centre, turn right and keep going. Otta doesn't have much in the way of **restaurants**, but the *Pillarguri Café* on Storgata musters a more-than-competent range of Norwegian standbys.

Rondane National Park

Spreading north and east from Otta towards the Swedish border, the **Rondane National Park** (*Rondane Nasjonalpark*), established in 1962 as Norway's first national park, is now one of the country's most popular hiking areas. Its 580 square kilometres, one-third of which are in the high alpine zone, appeal to walkers of all ages and abilities. The soil is poor, so vegetation is sparse and lichens, especially reindeer moss, predominate, but the views across this bare landscape are serenely beautiful, and a handful of lakes and rivers along with patches of dwarf birch forest provide some variety.

Wild mountain peaks divide the Rondane into three distinct areas. To the west of the centrally located lake, **Rondvatn**, are the wild cirques and jagged peaks of Storsmeden (2017m), Sagtinden (2018m) and Veslesmeden (2015m), while to the east of the lake tower Rondslottet (2178m), Vinjeronden (2044m) and Storronden (2138m). Further east still, the park is dominated by Høgronden (2115m). Most of the mountains, ten of which exceed the 2000-metre mark, are accessible to any reasonably fit walker via a dense network of trails and hiking huts.

Buses to the park from Otta depart daily in summer (late June to mid-Aug 2 daily; 50min), travelling the 25km to the Spranghaugen car park, the starting point for hikes into the Rondane. One bus leaves in the morning, the other in the afternoon. If you opt for the latter, you'll need to overnight at Rondvassbu hut (see below). The return bus leaves Spranghaugen for Otta in the late afternoon. Taking a **taxi** is also a possibility, especially if you're in a group – enquire at the tourist office, where you can also get details of local **car rental** companies. If you want to do things yourself, taxis are available from Otta Skysstasjon (☎61 23 05 01) and rental cars from Otta Auto (☎61 23 64 50).

Accommodation in the Rondane is limited to the **Rondvassbu hut** (☎ & ☎61 23 18 66; late June to mid-Sept) at the southern end of Rondvatn. This is a typical DNT staffed lodge, with over one hundred dorm beds, filling meals and pleasant service. If visibility is poor or you don't fancy a climb, there is a charming summer **boat service** (July to late Aug 2–3 daily; 1hr return; 35kr one-way, 50kr return) to the far end of Rondvatn, from where it takes about two and a half hours to walk back to Rondvassbu along the lake's steep western shore.

Norway's most celebrated walking area, the national park of **Jotunheimen** ("Home of the Giants") lives up to its name: pointed summits and undulating glaciers dominate the skyline, soaring high above river valleys and lake-studded plateaux. The park offers an amazing concentration of high peaks, more than two hundred of them rising above 1900 metres, including Norway's and northern Europe's two highest mountains, Galdhøpiggen (2469m) and Glittertind (2464m), while Norway's highest waterfall, the 275-metre-high Vettisfossen, is here too, a short walk from the Vetti lodge on the west side of the park. A network of footpaths and mountain lodges lattices the park, but be warned that the weather is very unpredictable and the winds can be bitingly cold – be cautious if you're new to mountain hiking and always come well-equipped (see "Basics", p.40).

There are no public roads into the park; visitors usually walk or ski into the interior from Hwy 55 in the west or make the slightly easier approach via **GJENDESHEIM**, off Hwy 51 in the east of the park about 90km from Otta. In summer, there's an early-morning **bus** from Otta to Gjendesheim (late June to mid-Aug Mon–Sat 1 daily; 2hr) and another leaving around noon (late June to Aug 1 daily; 2hr). Gjendesheim is no more than a couple of buildings, one of which is the excellent DNT **Gjendesheim lodge** (℡61 23 89 10, ℻61 23 89 65; mid-June to mid-Sept), which sits at the eastern tip of long and slender Lake Gjende. **Boats** (late June to early Sept 1–3 daily; ℡61 23 85 09) travel the length of the lake, reaching deep into the park to connect with mountain trails and dropping passengers off at two more lodges, the privately owned **Memurubu** (late June to early Sept; ℡61 23 89 99; ⓦwww.memurubu.no), halfway along the lake with double rooms (❷) as well as dorms, and the DNT's **Gjendebu** (℡61 23 89 44; mid-June to mid-Sept), right at the other end. It takes the boat twenty minutes to reach Memurubu, forty-five minutes to Gjendebu. Naturally, you can see a slice of the Jotunheimen and avoid a hike by riding the boat and sleeping at the lodges – a useful option in bad weather.

North along the E6

If you avoid the temptation of heading west from Otta along Hwy 15 to the fjords, you might want to follow the E6 and the railway 45km north to **DOMBÅS**, a mundane crossroads settlement that has a couple of good places to stay, if not much else. Close to the train and bus station as well as the E6/E136 junction is the *Dombås Hotell* (℡61 24 10 01, ⓦwww.dombas-hotel.no; ❺/❹), whose distinctive high gables look back down the Gudbrandsdal. A hotel of two halves, most of the bedrooms are tucked away in the modern annexe round the back, but the old main building holds a handsome series of long public rooms dating from the beginning of the twentieth century. The bedrooms in this part of the hotel tend to be a little the worse for wear, but the views down the valley more than compensate. Also offering valley views is Dombås's HI **hostel** (℡61 24 09 60, ℮dombaas.hostel @vandrerhjem.no), a comfortable complex of mountain huts, which hold some double rooms (❷), way up on the hillside above the E6. To get there, head north out of town along the E6 for around 1km and follow the signs up the hill; on foot, it's a hard slog from the train and bus station, down in the valley below. Both routes out of Dombås offer tantalizing prospects: E136 leads the 110km west to Åndalsnes and the Romsdalsfjord (see p.329), whilst the E6 plunges north through the mountains towards Trondheim (see p.338); you can complete either journey by rail as well, though the Åndalsnes train only runs a couple of times a day.

Staying on the E6 north from Dombås, it's just 30km to the outpost of **HJERKINN**, stuck out on bare and desolate moorland, its pocket-sized military base battened down against the wind-blasted ice and snow of winter. The base overlooks the E6/Hwy 29 junction, as does the adjacent train station, a perky wooden affair with brightly painted window frames. There's been a mountain inn

△ Stave church

here since medieval times, a staging post on the long trail to Trondheim, now just 170km away. The present inn, the *Hjerkinn Fjellstue* (☎61 24 29 27, ⓦwww.hjerkinn.no; ❹), continues this tradition in a becoming manner, with two expansive wooden buildings with big open fires and breezy pine furniture. The restaurant is good, too – try the reindeer culled from local herds – and there's horse-riding from the stables next door. The inn is set on a hill overlooking the moors just over 2km from the train station beside Hwy 29.

Kongsvoll

Beyond Hjerkinn, the E6 slices across the barren uplands before descending into a narrow ravine, the **Drivdal**. Hidden here, just 12km from Hjerkinn, is **KONGSVOLL**, home of a tiny train station and the delightful *Kongsvold Fjeldstue* (☎72 40 43 40, ⓦwww.kongsvold.no; ❹), which provides some of the most charming accommodation in the whole of Norway. There's been an inn here since medieval times and the present complex, a huddle of tastefully restored old timber buildings with sun-bleached reindeer antlers tacked onto the outside walls, dates back to the eighteenth century. Dinner is served in the excellent, reasonably priced **restaurant**, and the complex also includes a **café** and a small **park information centre**. The inn is a lovely spot to break your journey and an ideal base for hiking into the Dovrefjell National Park which extends to east and west. If you're arriving by **train**, note that only some of the Oslo–Trondheim trains stop at Kongsvoll station, 500m down the valley from the inn – and then only by prior arrangement with the conductor.

Beyond Drivdal, 35km north of Kongsvoll, **OPPDAL** is a crossroads town where Hwy 70 forks west for the coast, while the E6 presses on north the 120km to Trondheim (see p.338).

Dovrefjell National Park

Bisected by the railroad and the E6, **Dovrefjell National Park** (Dovrefjell Nasjonalpark) is one of the more accessible of Norway's national parks. Just 265 square kilometres in area, it comprises two distinct zones: the marshes, open moors and rounded peaks that characterize much of eastern Norway spread east from the E6, while to the west the mountains become increasingly steep and serrated as they approach the jagged spires of the Romsdal. Beyond the park's western limits, backing on to the Romsdalsfjord, is the greatest concentration of high peaks outside the Jotunheimen; this is a favourite destination for European mountaineers, who clamber perpendicular rock faces reckoned to be some of the world's most difficult.

Hiking trails and **huts** are spread throughout the western part of the Dovrefjell. Kongsvoll makes an ideal starting point: it's possible to hike all the way from here to the coast at Åndalsnes, but this takes all of nine or ten days; a more feasible expedition for most visitors is the two-day hike there and back to one of the four snow-tipped peaks of mighty **Snøhetta**, at around 2200m. There's accommodation five hours' walk west from Kongsvoll at the unstaffed **Reinheim** hut (mid-Feb to mid-Oct). Further hiking details and maps are available at the park information centre in the *Kongsvold Fjeldstue*.

Røros and around

Located on a treeless mountain plateau 160km east of Kongsvoll, **RØROS** is a blustery place even on a summer's afternoon, when it's full of day-tripping tourists surveying the old part of town, little changed since its days as a copper-mining centre. Røros is a unique and remarkable survivor – until the mining company went bust a decade or two ago, mining had been the basis of life here since the seventeenth century. This dirty and dangerous work was supplemented by a little farming and hunting, and life for the average villager can't have been anything but hard. Furthermore, Røros' wooden houses, some of them 300 years old, have escaped the

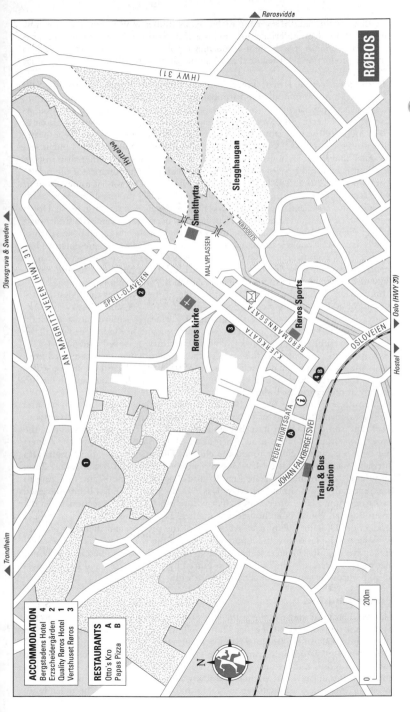

RØROS

▲ Rørosvidda

Olavsgruva & Sweden ▲

AN-MAGRITT-VEIEN (HWY 31)

(HWY 31)

Hyttelva

▲ Trondheim

Slegghaugan

Smelthytta

MALMPLASSEN

SLEGGVEIEN

SPELL-OLAVEIEN

Røros kirke

Oslo (HWY 30) ▶

Røros Sports

Hostel ▶

OSLOVEIEN

KJERKGATA

BERGMANNSGATA

PEDER HIORTSGATA

JOHAN FALKBERGETSVEI

Train & Bus
Station

ACCOMMODATION
Bergstadens Hotel 4
Erzscheidergården 2
Quality Røros Hotel 1
Vertshuset Røros 3

RESTAURANTS
Otto's Kro A
Papas Pizza B

N

0   200m

fires that have devastated so many of Norway's timber-built towns. Røros is now on UNESCO's World Heritage List, and there are firm regulations limiting changes to its grass-roofed cottages. Film companies regularly use the town as a backdrop for their productions – it featured as a labour camp in the film of *One Day in the Life of Ivan Denisovich*.

In the town centre, **Røros kirke** (early to mid-June & mid-Aug to mid-Sept Mon–Sat 11am–3pm; mid-June to mid-Aug Mon–Sat 10am–5pm, Sun 2–4pm; mid-Sept to May Sat 11am–1pm; 25kr) is the most obvious target for a stroll, its heavy tower reflecting the wealth of the eighteenth-century mine owners. Built in 1784, and once the only stone building in Røros, the church is more like a theatre than a religious edifice. A huge structure capable of seating 1600 people, it was designed, like the church at Kongsberg (see p.275), to overawe rather than inspire. Its pulpit is built directly over the altar to emphasize the importance of the priest's word, and a two-tiered gallery runs around the nave. Occasional mine labourers were accommodated in the gallery's lower level, while "undesirables" were compelled to sit above, and even had to enter via a separate, external staircase. Down below, the nave exhibited even finer distinctions: every pew nearer the front was a step up the social ladder, while mine managers vied for the curtained boxes, each of which had a well-publicized annual rent; the monarch (or royal representative) had a private box commanding views from the back. These byzantine social arrangements are explained in depth during the **guided tour** (late June to mid-Aug 1 daily in English), the cost of which is included in the admission fee.

Immediately below the church, on either side of the river, lies the oldest part of Røros. A huddle of sturdy cross-timbered smelters' cottages, storehouses and workshops squat in the shadow of the **slegghaugan** (slagheaps) – more tourist attraction than eyesore, and providing fine views over the town and beyond. Here, next to the river, the rambling main works have been tidily restored and face on to **Malmplassen** ("ore-place"), the wide earthen square where drivers arrived from across the mountains to have their cartloads of ore weighed on the outdoor scales. Also in the square, hung in a rickety little tower, is the smelters' bell, which used to be rung at the start of each shift.

Malmplassen is at the top of Bergmannsgata which, together with parallel Kjerkgata, forms the heart of today's Røros. Conspicuously, the smaller artisans' dwellings, some of which have become **art and craft shops**, are set near the works, away from the rather more spacious dwellings once occupied by the owners and overseers, which cluster round the church. The main works, the **Smelthytta** (literally "melting hut"; Jan–May Mon–Fri noon–2.30pm, Sat & Sun 11am–2pm; early June daily 10am–4pm; late June to mid-Aug daily 10am–7pm; mid-Aug to late Sept daily 10am–4pm; Oct–May daily 11am–2pm; 60kr), has been converted into a museum, a large three-storey affair whose most interesting section, set in the cavernous hall which once housed the smelter, explains the intricacies of copper production. Dioramas illuminate every part of the process, and there are production charts, samples of ore and a potted history of the company; pick up the comprehensive English-language leaflet available free at reception. There's actually not that much to look at – the building was gutted by fire in 1975 – and so the museum is perhaps for genuine copper enthusiasts only.

Practicalities

The **train** and **bus stations** are at the foot of the town centre, a couple of minutes' walk from the **tourist office** (late June to mid-Aug Mon–Sat 9am–6pm, Sun 10am–4pm; mid-Aug to late June Mon–Fri 9am–4pm, Sat 10.30am–12.30pm; ☎72 41 00 50, ⊛www.rorosinfo.com), where you can pick up a comprehensive free booklet on Røros and the surrounding region. They also have details of local **hikes** out across the uplands that encircle the town, one of the more popular being the five-hour trek east to the self-service DNT hut at Marenvollen. The uplands are also popular with **cross-country skiers** in the winter, and the tourist office has a leaflet mapping out several possible routes. To get around town, pick up one of the free municipal **bicycles** available at the train station and tourist office; for those venturing further afield, **mountain bikes** can be rented from Røros Sports, Bergmannsgata 13 (☎72 41 12 18), for around 150kr a day (plus 100kr deposit).

Because of the long drive here and the infrequency of trains to Trondheim and Oslo, you may well want to stay the night. Fortunately, there's a reasonable range of centrally located **accommodation**. Easily the best deal in town is the *Erzscheidergården* guesthouse, Spell-Olaveien 6 (☎72 41 11 94, ☎72 41 19 60; ❸), with some charming, unassuming rooms in its wooden main building. Some rooms also have fine views over town, and there's an attractive subterranean breakfast area and a cosy lounge. Also worth considering are the *Quality Røros Hotel*, An-Magritt veien (☎72 40 80 00, ☎www.roroshotel.no; ❻/❹), a big modern place on the northern edge of the centre, and *Vertshuset Røros*, Kjerkgata 34 (☎72 41 24 11, ☎www.roroshotel.no; ❹), a guesthouse with cramped doubles that's bang in the centre of town. Less appealing is *Bergstadens Hotel*, Osloveien 2 (☎72 40 60 80, ☎www.bergstaden.no; ❺/❹), conveniently located at the foot of Bergmannsgata, but otherwise a routine, modern hotel with workaday double rooms. There's also the unappealing *Røros Vandrerhjem*, Øraveien 25 (☎72 41 10 89, ☎roros.hostel @vandrerhjem.no), an all-year HI **hostel** with dorm beds and doubles (❷) in a concrete block about 800m south of the train station next to the sports ground.

When it comes to **food**, Røros is no gourmet's paradise, but there's just enough choice to get by. The *Quality Røros Hotel* has a good, if slightly formal, restaurant that's generally reckoned to serve the best meals in town; it's expensive though and closes at 10pm. In contrast, the busy and competent *Papas Pizza*, at the foot of Bergmannsgata in the back of the *Bergstadens Hotel*, is open late. For substantial meals at fairly reasonable prices there's also *Otto's Kro Restaurant*, Peder Hiortsgata 4, just west of the tourist office – try the *entrecôte*.

Olavsgruva copper mine

Thirteen kilometres east of Røros off Highway 31, the **Olavsgruva**, one of the old copper mines, has been kept open as a museum, and there are daily guided tours of the workings throughout the summer (early June & late Aug to early Sept Mon–Sat 2 daily, Sun 1 daily; late June to late Aug 6 daily; early Sept to Dec Sat 1 daily; 60kr). Special **buses** timed to coincide with the guided tours make the journey once daily from Røros' train station and Smelthytta to the mine in July and early August, returning to town afterwards. The temperature down the mine is a constant 5°C, so take something warm to wear – you'll need sturdy shoes, too.

West towards the fjords

The forested dales and uplands which fill the interior of southern Norway between Oslo and the western fjords (see pp.292–336) rarely inspire: in almost any other European country, these elongated valleys would be attractions in their own right, but here in Norway they simply can't compare with the mountains and fjords of the north and west. Almost everywhere, the architecture is routinely modern and most of the old timber buildings that once lined the valleys are long gone – except in the ten-a-penny open-air museums that are a feature of nearly every town.

Of the three major trunk roads crossing the region, the **E16** is the fastest, a quick 350-kilometre haul up from Oslo to the fjord ferry point near Sogndal and the colossal 24km-long tunnel that leads to Flåm and ultimately Bergen. Otherwise, the E16's nearest rival, the slower **Hwy 7**, branches off the E16 at Hønefoss and, after a scenic wriggle along the edge of the Hardangervidda plateau, finally reaches the coast at Eidfjord near Hardangerfjord, a distance of 334km. Hwy 7 also intersects with Hwy 50, offering another possible route to Flåm. For most of its length, Hwy 7 is shadowed by the **Oslo–Bergen railway**, though they part company when the train swings north for its spectacular traverse of the mountains. The third road, the **E134**, stretches the 418km from Drammen near Oslo to Haugesund, passing near Odda on the Sørfjord (323km); it's another slower route, and has the advantage of passing through **Kongsberg**, an attractive town that makes for a pleasant overnight stay. There are regular long-distance **buses** along all three major roads.

West along the E16 to Leira and Borgund

Clipping along the **E16** from Oslo, it's 180km up through a sequence of river valleys to ribbon-like **LEIRA**, where you can break your journey economically – if not exactly thrillingly – at the HI **hostel** (☎61 35 95 00, ✉leira.hostel@vandrerhjem .no; late May to early Aug), which occupies part of the high-school complex beside the road and has double rooms (❷) as well as dorm beds. Hwy 51 branches north at the next village of **Fagernes**, running along the eastern edge of the Jotunheimen National Park, passing near Gjendesheim and its lodge (see p.268) before finally joining Hwy 15 west of Otta (see p.266).

About 30km west of Fagernes along the E16, the scenery improves as you approach the coast. The road dips and weaves from dale to dale, slipping between the hills until it reaches the **Laerdal** valley, whose forested sides frame the stepped roofs and angular gables of the **Borgund stave church** (daily: June–Aug 8am–8pm; May & Sept 10am–5pm; 50kr). One of the best preserved stave churches in Norway, Borgund was built beside what was – until bubonic plague wiped out most of the local population in the fourteenth century – one of the major pack roads between east and west. The church has preserved much of its medieval appearance, its tiered exterior protected by shingles and decorated with finials in

Stave churches

Of the 29 surviving **stave churches** in Norway, all but a handful are in the southern and central areas. Together, they represent the country's most distinctive architectural feature. Their key characteristic is that their timbers are placed vertically into the ground – in contrast to the log-bonding technique used by the Norwegians for everything else. Thus, a stave wall consists of vertical planks slotted into sills above and below, with the sills connected to upright posts – or **staves** (hence the name) – at each corner. The general design seems to have been worked out in the twelfth century and regular features include external wooden galleries, shingles and finials. However, the most fetching churches are those where the central section of the nave has been raised above the aisles to create – from the outside – a distinctive, almost pagoda-like effect. In virtually all stave churches, the **door frames** (where they survive) are decorated from top to bottom with surging, intricate carvings – fantastic long-limbed dragons, entwined with tendrils of vine – that clearly relate back to Viking design.

The **origins** of stave churches have attracted an inordinate amount of academic debate. Some scholars argue that they were originally pagan temples, converted to Christian use by the addition of a chancel, whilst others are convinced that they were inspired by Russian churches. In the nineteenth century, they also developed a symbolic importance as reminders of the time when Norway was independent. Many had fallen into a dreadful state of repair and were clumsily renovated – or even remodelled – by enthusiastic medievalists with a nationalistic agenda. Undoing this repair work has been a major operation that continues today. For most visitors, seeing one or two will suffice – two of the finest are those at Heddal (see p.276) and Borgund (see above).

the shape of dragons and Christian crosses, culminating in a slender ridge turret. A rickety wooden gallery runs round the outside of the church, and the doors sport a swirling abundance of carved animals and foliage. Inside, the dark, pine-scented nave is framed by the upright wooden posts that define this style of church architecture.

Beyond the church, the valley grows wilder as the E16 travels the 45km down to Fodnes, where a 24hr car ferry zips over to Manheller, some 18km from Sogndal (see p.321). On the way, you'll pass the entrance to the 24.3km-long tunnel that extends the E16 to Flåm (see p.315) and Bergen (see p.293).

West along Highway 7 to Geilo

Highway 7 branches off the E16 about 60km from Oslo at **Hønefoss**, and then cuts an unexciting course along the **Hallingdal** valley, as does the main Oslo–Bergen railway. Some 180km from Hønefoss, the road forks at **Hagafoss**, with Hwy 50 descending the dales to reach, after 100km, the Aurlandsfjord just round the coast from Flåm. Meanwhile, Hwy 7 presses on west to the winter ski resort of **GEILO**, 250km from Oslo – it's a boring town out of the skiing season, but it does have several inexpensive places to stay, including an HI **hostel** (☎32 08 70 60, ☏32 08 70 66; mid-June to Aug & Dec–April), housed in large barrack-like buildings in the town centre just off the main drag, and with dorms as well as doubles (❷). Details of other accommodation are available from the **tourist office** nearby (July to mid-Aug daily 8.30am–8pm; June & late Aug Mon–Fri 8.30am–6pm, Sat 9am–3pm; Sept–May Mon–Fri 8.30am–4pm; ☎32 09 59 00).

Beyond Geilo, the rail line ceases to follow the road, breaking off to tunnel its way through the mountains to Finse, Myrdal (where you change for the scenic branch line down to Flåm; see p.315), and points to Bergen. Hwy 7 continues west for a further 100km, slicing across the peripheries of the Hardangervidda national park (see p.312). It's a lonely, handsome road and on the way you'll pass several places – such as Halne and Dyranut – where you can pick up the Hardangervidda's network of hiking trails (for more on hiking in the Hardangervidda, see p.312). On the far side of the plateau, Hwy 7 rushes down a steep valley to reach the fjords at Eidfjord (see p.312).

West along the E134: Kongsberg and around

After about 80km, the **E134**, a third main route west from Oslo to the fjords, has the advantage of passing through **KONGSBERG**, one of the most interesting towns in the region. A local story claims that the silver responsible for its existence was discovered by two goatherds, who stumbled across a vein of the metal laid bare by the scratchings of an ox. True or not, Christian IV, his eye on the main chance, was quick to exploit the find, sponsoring the development of mining here – the name means "King's Mountain" – at the start of what became a seventeenth-century silver rush. In the event, it turned out that Kongsberg was the only place in the world where silver was to be found in its pure form, and there was enough of it to sustain the town for a couple of centuries. Indeed, by the 1750s the town was the largest in Norway, with half of its 8000 inhabitants employed in and around the 300-odd mine shafts that littered the area. The silver works closed in 1805, but by this time Kongsberg was also the site of a royal mint and then an armaments factory, which still employs people to this day.

To appreciate the full economic and political clout of the mine owners, visit the church they funded, **Kongsberg kirke** (mid-May to mid-Aug Mon–Fri 10am–4pm, Sat 10am–1pm & Sun 2–4pm; late Aug Mon–Fri 10am–noon; Sept to mid-May Tues–Thurs 10am–noon; 30kr), the largest and arguably the most beautiful Baroque church in Norway. It dates from 1761, when the mines were at the peak of their prosperity, and sits impressively in a square surrounded on three sides by period wooden buildings. Inside, too, it's a grand affair, with an enormous and showily mock-marbled western wall incorporating altar, pulpit and organ. This arrangement was dictated by political considerations: the pulpit is actually *above* the altar, to ram home the point that the priest's stern injunctions to work harder on behalf of the mine owners were an expression of God's will.

Kongsberg itself is an agreeable if quiet place in summer, with plenty of green spaces. The **River Lågen** tumbles through the centre, and statues on the town bridge at the foot of Storgata commemorate various local activities, including foolhardy attempts to locate new finds of silver – one of them involving the use of divining rods. Enthusiasts will enjoy the **Norwegian Mining Museum**, Hyttegata 3 (Norsk Bergverksmuseet; mid-May to Aug daily 10am–4pm; Sept daily noon–4pm; Oct to mid-May Sun only noon–3pm; 50kr), housed in the old smelting works at the river's edge along with a pocket-sized ski museum and coin collection, but merely pottering around is as enjoyable a way as any of spending time in Kongsberg.

The **silver mines** themselves, the Sølvgruvene, are open for tours and make a fine excursion, especially if you have children to amuse. They're hidden in green surroundings 8km west of town in the hamlet of **SAGGRENDA** – drive along the E134 in the Notodden direction and look for the sign leading off to the right. The informative 80-minute **tour** (mid-May to Aug; 50kr) includes a ride on a miniature train through black tunnels to the shafts. There are three or four departures a day (call ☏32 29 90 50 for timings); take a sweater as it's cold underground. Back outside, just 350m down the hill, the old ochre-painted, timber workers' compound – the **Sakkerhusene** – has been restored and holds some rather half-hearted displays on the history of the mines, as well as a café.

Practicalities

Kongsberg **tourist office**, at Karsches gata 3 (May to late June & mid-Aug to mid-Sept Mon–Fri 9am–4pm, Sat 10am–2pm; late June to mid-Aug Mon–Fri 9am–7pm, Sat & Sun 10am–4pm; mid-Sept to April Mon–Fri 9am–4pm; ☏32 29 90 50, ☻www.kongsberg-turistservice.no), is a brief walk from the **train and bus station**, and can help with accommodation – not that there's much of a decision to be made. The HI **hostel** at Vinjesgata 1 (☏32 73 20 24, ☻kongsberg.hostel @vandrerhjem.no) is *the* place to stay, with both dorm beds and comfortable en-suite double rooms (**②**) in an attractive timber lodge close to the town centre. Drivers need to follow the signs on the E134; train and bus users need to walk south from the station along Storgata, cross the bridge and walk round the back of the church on the right-hand side. At the back of the church, head down the slope and over the footbridge – about a ten-minute walk in all. As for central **hotels**, there is just one appealing option, the *Quality Hotel Grand*, down near the river at Christian Augusts gate 2 (☏32 77 28 00, ☻www.quality-grand.no; **③/④**), which also has a first-class **restaurant**. If the weather's good, the *Gamle Kongsberg Kro* café-restaurant has a pleasant riverside terrace below the church.

West of Kongsberg: Heddal, Seljord and Åmot

A few kilometres west of Kongsberg, the E134 passes into **Telemark**, a county that covers a great forested chunk of southern Norway. Just inside its borders is industrial **Notodden** and, 6km beyond that, beside the main road, is the **stave church of Heddal** (late May to late June & late Aug to mid-Sept Mon–Sat 10am–5pm; late June to late Aug Mon–Sat 9am–7pm; plus Sun all year 1–5/7pm; 30kr). Surrounded by a neat cemetery and rolling pastureland, Heddal is actually the largest surviving stave church in Norway. Its pretty tumble of shingle-clad roofs was restored to something like its medieval appearance in 1955, rectifying a heavy-handed nineteenth-century remodelling. The crosses atop the church's gables alternate with dragon-head gargoyles, a mix of Christian and pagan symbolism that is typical of many stave churches. Inside, the twenty masts of the nave are decorated at the top by masks, and there's some attractive seventeenth-century wall decoration in light blues, browns and whites. Pride of place, however, goes to the ancient bishop's chair in the chancel. Dating from around 1250, the chair carries a relief retelling the saga of Sigurd the Dragonslayer, a pagan story that Christians turned to their advantage by recasting the Viking as Jesus and the dragon as the Devil. Across from the church, there's a café and a modest museum illustrating further aspects of Heddal's history.

There's another fine church around 55km further west just off the E134 in **SELJORD**, a small industrial town of ancient provenance that spreads between the forested hills and lake Seljordsvatnet. Dating from the twelfth century, the church is built of stone (open for free guided tours, call ☎35 06 59 88), and as such is something of a medieval rarity. The town also seems to have attracted more than its fair share of "Believe It or Not" stories: a monster is supposed to lurk in the depths of the lake; elves are alleged to gather here for some of their soirées; and the 570kg stone outside the church was, so the story goes, only lifted once, by an eighteenth-century strongman by name of Nils Langedal. Elves and sea serpents apart, there's nothing much to delay you.

Beyond Seljord, it's a further 80km west along E134 to the handsome **Grungedal valley**, home to several antique farmsteads. Pushing on, the scenery bordering E134 becomes wilder and more dramatic as the road slips across the southern peripheries of the Hardangervidda plateau before tunnelling through the mountains to meet the coastal Hwy 13. Branching off to the north, Hwy 13 passes, in 5km, the waterfalls at **Latefossen**, two huge torrents that empty into the river with a deafening roar. From here, it's a further 14km to Odda, an ugly industrial centre that is a particularly unfortunate introduction to the fjords: try to allow enough time to avoid the place altogether and keep going north to the much more appealing hamlet of Lofthus (see p.311). Alternatively, if you ignore Hwy 13 and keep on along the E134, it's 115km from the crossroads to the coast at Haugesund.

The south coast

Stretching from the Oslofjord to Stavanger, Norway's **south coast** may have little of the imposing grandeur of other, wilder parts of the country, but its island-shredded eastern half, running down to Kristiansand, is undeniably lovely. Backed by forests and lakes, this part of the coast attracts Norwegians in droves, equipped not so much with a bucket and spade, but more with a **boat** and navigational aids – these waters, with their narrow inlets, islands and skerries, make for particularly enjoyable sailing. **Camping** on the offshore islands is easy too, the only restrictions being that you shouldn't stay in one spot for more than 48 hours, shouldn't get close to anyone's home or light a fire on bare rock or among vegetation. Leaflets detailing coastal rules and regulations are available at any local tourist office.

If boats and tents aren't your thing, the white-painted clapboard houses of tiny towns like **Lillesand**, **Arendal** and, to a lesser degree, **Grimstad** have an appropriately nautical, almost jaunty air. This portion of the coast is also important for Norway's international trade: it's just a short hop to Denmark from here, and larger towns such as Sandefjord, Larvik and Porsgrunn have kicked over their seventeenth-century traces as rustic timber ports to become industrial centres in their own right. Most of these manufacturing towns are run-of-the-mill, except for the biggest of them, **Kristiansand**, a lively port and resort with enough sights, restaurants, bars and beaches to while away a night, possibly two. Beyond Kristiansand lies **Mandal**, an especially fetching holiday spot with a great beach, but thereafter the coast becomes harsher and less absorbing, heralding a sparsely inhabited region with little to detain you. A possible exception is the old port of **Flekkefjord**, which does warrant a pit-stop, though most visitors push on to the bustling, oil-rich city of **Stavanger**, 250km from Kristiansand.

There are regular **trains** from Oslo to Kristiansand and Stavanger, but the rail line runs inland for most of its journey, only dipping down to the coast at the major resorts – a disappointing ride, the sea views shielded much of the time behind bony, forested hills. The same applies to the main **road** and **bus** route – the **E18/E39** – which also sticks stubbornly inland for most of the 300km from Oslo to Kristiansand (E18) and again for the 250km on to Stavanger (E39). It does, however, make for easy and fast travel to the main destinations, even if exploring the smaller coastal settlements is awkward without your own vehicle.

All the places in this section are easily accessed from the E18/E39, and all provide boat trips along the neighbouring coastline and offer accommodation in some form or another. Note, though, that the season is short – from late June to the end of August. At other times of the year, many museums are closed and boat trips curtailed.

Arendal

The first place that really merits a stop on the E18 is **ARENDAL**, 260km from Oslo and one of the most appealing spots on the coast, its sheltered harbour curling right into the town centre, which is itself pushed up tight against the forested hills behind. The town's heyday was in the eighteenth century when its shipyards churned out dozens of the sleek wooden sailing ships that then dominated international trade. There's an attractive reminder of the boom times in the grand **Rådhus** (Mon–Fri 9am–3pm; free), a four-storey, white timber building from 1812 that faces out over what was once the main city dock. The Rådhus was actually built as a private mansion for a wealthy family of merchants – as the formal rooms inside demonstrate – and there are more elegant old buildings immediately behind it in the oldest part of town, known as **Tyholmen**. You can wander these few blocks and then stroll along the boardwalk flanking **Pollen**, a short rectangular inner harbour bordered by outdoor cafés. For the architectural low-down on Tyholmen, call in at the tourist office (see below) and sign up for one of their city walking tours (late June to early Aug 3 weekly; 1hr 30min; 50kr).

Also available at the tourist office are details of all sorts of **boat trips**, which leave the Pollen to explore the surrounding coastline. The most enjoyable excursion is to **Merdø**, a low-lying, lightly wooded islet stuck out in the Skagerrak. Footpaths network the island, and there's a beach, a café and the **Merdøgaard Museum** (late June to mid-Aug daily noon–4pm; 30kr), which occupies a sprightly eighteenth-century sea captain's house, its period rooms liberally sprinkled with appropriate bygones. **Ferries** leave Pollen for Merdø every hour or so; the return fare is 30kr.

Practicalities

From Arendal **train station**, it's a five- to ten-minute walk west to the main square, Torvet – either through the smoky tunnel or up and over the steep hill along Iuellsklev and then Bendiksklev, the latter being a distinctly healthier route. Torvet is about 150m north of the Pollen inner harbour. **Buses** stop in the larger square, west of Torvet and across from the huge red-brick church with the copper-green steeple. Arendal **tourist office** is on the east side of Pollen on Langbryggen (mid-June to mid-Aug Mon–Sat 9am–7pm, Sun noon–7pm; mid-Aug to mid-June Mon–Fri 9am–4pm; ☎37 00 55 44, ⍟www.arendal.com).

Easily the nicest place **to stay** is the luxurious *Clarion Hotel Tyholmen*, Teaterplassen 2 (☎37 02 68 00, ⍟www.tyholmenhotel.no; **❼**/**❹**), which occupies a handsome wooden building in the style of an old warehouse on the Tyholmen quayside. The more modest *Scandic Hotel Arendal*, Friergangen 1 (☎37 02 51 60, ⍟www.scandic-hotels.com; **❻**/**❹**), is a straightforward modern place just off the west side of Pollen, with well-appointed rooms. For **food**, there are a couple of inexpensive cafés on Torvet and a string of more tempting places along and around Pollen, including *Madam Reiersen*, which offers delicious seafood and fresh pasta dishes from its harbourside premises at Nedre Tyholmsvei 3; mains average at 130kr. Later on, the café-bars lining Pollen become lively **drinking** haunts till the early hours, especially on a warm summer's night.

Grimstad

From Arendal, it's a short 20km hop south on the E18 by bus or car to **GRIM-STAD**, a brisk huddle of white houses with orange-tiled roofs stacked up behind the harbour. At the beginning of the nineteenth century the town had no less than forty shipyards and carried on a lucrative trade with France. It wasn't particularly surprising, therefore, that when Henrik Ibsen left his home in nearby Skien in 1844 at the age of sixteen he should come to Grimstad, where he worked as an apprentice pharmacist for the next six years. The careless financial dealings of Ibsen's father had impoverished the family, and Henrik's already jaundiced view of Norway's provincial bourgeoisie was confirmed here in the port, whose worthies Ibsen mocked in poems like *Resignation* and *The Corpse's Ball*. It was here too that Ibsen picked up first-hand news of the Paris Revolution of 1848, an event that radicalized him and inspired his paean to the insurrectionists of Budapest, *To Hungary*, written in 1849. Nonetheless, Ibsen's stay on the south coast is more usually recalled as providing the setting for some of his better known plays, particularly *Pillars of Society*. The pharmacy where Ibsen lived and worked, just up from the harbour in the centre of town on Henrik Ibsens gate, has been turned into the pocket-sized **Ibsen House and Grimstad Town Museum** (*Ibsenhuset og Grimstad Bymuseet*; Jan–May & Aug–Dec Mon–Fri 10am–3pm; June & July Mon–Sat 11am–5pm, Sun 1–5pm; 40kr). With creaking wooden floors and narrow beamed ceilings, the premises have maintained their nineteenth-century appearance and come complete with various Ibsen memorabilia – look out for the glass case displaying the playwright's hat, coat, umbrella and boots as worn on his daily stroll down to Oslo's *Grand Hotel*.

Practicalities

Grimstad **bus station** is at the south end of the harbour, a couple of hundred metres along from the **tourist office** (Jan–May & Aug–Dec Mon–Fri 8.30am–4pm; June & July Mon–Fri 9am–6pm, Sat & Sun 10am–4pm; ☎37 04 40 41, ⓦwww.grimstad.net), from where you can pick up all the usual bumph as well as detailed maps of the islands that clutter the seaward approaches to Grimstad harbour. Many of the islands – or parts of them – are publicly owned and protected within the **Skjærgårdspark**. Within the park, public access moorings are commonplace and so are picnic and bathing facilities, though, of course, you do need a boat to get there. Boat hire is available from several local companies via the tourist office. In addition, there is a handful of **boat cruises** to choose from, though these don't stop at any of the islands. The most popular is the two-hour coastal cruise around the offshore islands and skerries with the *M/S Bibben* (July Sun–Fri 1 daily; 150kr); call ☎37 04 31 85 to sign up.

Grimstad has an attractive and central **hotel**, the *Grimstad*, Kirkegaten 3 (☎37 25 25 25, ⓦwww.grimstadhotell.no; ⑥), in an old and cleverly converted clapboard complex amongst the narrow lanes near the Ibsen house; the hotel has the best **restaurant** in town, too. Wine buffs can seek out the fruit wines produced by Fuhr, a local firm – with Fuhr Rhubarb and Fuhr Vermouth representing two daunting challenges for the palate.

Lillesand

Bright, cheerful **LILLESAND**, just 20km south of Grimstad, is one of the most popular holiday spots on the coast, the white clapboard houses of its tiny centre draped prettily round the harbourfront. One or two of the buildings, notably the sturdy **Rådhus** of 1734, are especially good-looking, but it's the general appearance of the place which appeals, best appreciated from the terrace of one of the town's waterfront café-restaurants: the *Sjøbua*, midway round the harbour, does very nicely.

To investigate Lillesand's architectural nooks and crannies, sign up at the tourist office (see below) for one of their hour-long **guided walks** (1 daily mid-June to Aug; 30kr). The tourist office also has information on – and sailing schedules for – a wide variety of local **boat trips**. These include cruises along the coast, fishing trips and the *badeboot* (bathing boat; July 4 daily; 15min; 40kr return), which shuttles across to **Hestholm bay**, on the island of **Skaurøya**, where swimmers don't seem to notice just how cold the Skagerrak actually is. Even better, take a three-hour cruise with **M/S Øya** (late June to early Aug Mon–Sat at 10am; 170kr each way; ☎94 58 33 97), a dinky little passenger ferry which wiggles its way south to Kristiansand (see p.280) along the narrow channel separating the mainland from the offshore islets. Sheltered from the full force of the ocean, this channel – the **Blindleia** – was once a major trade route, but today it's trafficked by every sort of pleasure craft imaginable, from replica three-mast sail ships to the sleekest of yachts. Other, faster boats make the trip too, but the *M/S Øya* is the most charming.

Practicalities

Lillesand cannot be reached by train, but it is on the main Oslo–Arendal –Kristiansand bus route. **Buses** pull in near the south end of the harbour, a brief stroll from the **tourist office**, located in the old waterfront customs house (mid-June to mid-Aug Mon–Fri 9am–6pm, Sat 10am–4pm, Sun noon–4pm; mid-Aug to mid-June Mon–Fri 9am–4pm; ☎37 26 16 80; ⊛www.lillesand.com). Lillesand has one central **hotel**, the first-rate *Norge*, Strandgaten 3 (☎37 27 01 44, ⊛www .hotelnorge.no; ❹/❼), which occupies a grand old wooden building near the bus stop. Refurbished in attractive period style, the interior holds some charming stained-glass windows and the rooms are named after some of the famous people who have stayed here – the novelist Knut Hamsun and the Spanish king Alfonso XIII for starters. Otherwise, *Tingsaker Familiecamping*, on Øvre Tingsaker (☎37 27 04 21, ⊛www.tingsakercamping.no; May–Aug), is a well-equipped waterfront campsite with tent and caravan pitches as well as cabins (❸). Amongst its facilities, there's a communal kitchen area, canoe hire, a pool and a playground; it's situated about 1km north of the centre – take Storgata and keep going. For **food**, the *Hotel Norge* has an excellent restaurant, but it's more expensive and formal than the harbourfront *Sjøbua*, which serves up excellent fish dishes for around 160kr in breezily naff surroundings – the interior is kitted out like an old sailing ship.

Kristiansand

With 75,000 inhabitants, **KRISTIANSAND**, some 30km on from Lillesand, is Norway's fifth largest town and a part-time holiday resort, a genial, energetic place which thrives on its ferry connections with Denmark, its busy marinas and passable sandy beaches. In summer, the seafront and adjoining streets are a frenetic bustle of cocktail bars, fast-food joints and flirting holidaymakers, and even in winter Norwegians come here to live it up. Like so many other Scandinavian towns, Kristiansand was founded by and named after **Christian IV**, who saw an opportunity to strengthen his coastal defences here. Building started in 1641, and the town has retained the spacious quadrant plan that characterized all Christian's projects. There are few specific sights, but it's worth a quick look around, especially when everyone else has gone to the beach and left the central pedestrianized streets relatively uncluttered. Kristiansand is also just a few kilometres from the **Kristiansand Kanonmuseum**, the forbidding remains of a large coastal gun battery built during the German occupation of World War II.

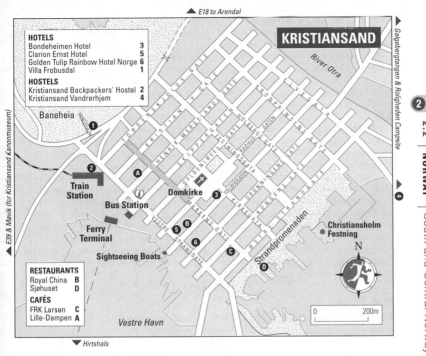

HOTELS
Bondeheimen Hotel   3
Clarion Ernst Hotel   5
Golden Tulip Rainbow Hotel Norge   6
Villa Frobusdal   1
HOSTELS
Kristiansand Backpackers' Hostel   2
Kristiansand Vandrerhjem   4

Baneheia

River Otra

◄ E39 & Møvik (for Kristiansand Kanonmuseum)

Train Station
Bus Station
Ferry Terminal
Domkirke
Sightseeing Boats
Christiansholm Festning
Strandpromenaden

RESTAURANTS
Royal China   B
Sjøhuset   D
CAFÉS
FRK Larsen   C
Lille-Dampen   A

N

0   200m

Vestre Havn

▼ Hirtshals

Arrival and information

Trains, **buses** and **ferries** all arrive close to each other, by Vestre Strandgate on the edge of the town grid. The main regional **tourist office** is here also, at Vestre Strandgate 32 (mid-June to mid-Aug Mon–Fri 8am–6pm, Sat 10am–6pm & Sun noon–6pm; mid-Aug to mid-June Mon–Fri 8.30am–3.30pm; ☎38 12 13 14, ⓦwww.sorlandet.com). Staff issue free town maps and a useful guide to the whole of the Sørlandet area, carry public transport timetables and have information on boat sailing times, island bathing and beaches. **Parking** is easy throughout town, with car parks concentrated along Vestre Strandgate. The best way to explore the centre is on **foot** – it only takes about ten minutes to walk from one side to the other – but **bike rental** is available on the edge of town at Kristiansand Sykkelsenter, Grim Torv (☎38 03 68 35); 21-gear bikes cost 150kr per day, 490kr for a week.

Accommodation

Kristiansand has a reasonably good choice of **accommodation** with a fair sprinkling of hotels, a guesthouse or two and a youth hostel, all either in or fairly near the centre. There's also a large and quite formal **campsite**, *Roligheden Camping*, Framnesveien (☎38 09 67 22 ☎38 09 11 17 ⓦwww.roligheden.no; late June to mid-Sept), 3km east of the centre behind a yacht jetty. To get there, drive over the bridge at the end of Dronningens gate, turn right along Marviksveien, then right again near the end, following the signs.

Hotels

Centrum Park Hotel Bondeheimen Kirkegata 15 ☎38 02 44 40, ⓦwww.centrumpark.no. Located right in the middle of town, near the Domkirke, this hotel offers modern and comfortable if uninspiring

rooms in a converted nineteenth-century town house. ❺/❹

Clarion Ernst Hotel Rådhusgaten 2 ☎38 12 86 00, ⓦwww.ernst.no. Housed in a flashily modernized building, this hotel has large doubles with standard-issue modern furnishings and fittings. The air conditioning can be stuffy, so try to get a room where you can open a window and one which doesn't face the interior courtyard. ⑥/⑤

Golden Tulip Rainbow Hotel Norge Dronningens gate 5 ☎38 17 40 00, ⓦwww.hotel-norge.no. Pleasant modern hotel with attractively furnished rooms in lively colours. A good downtown choice. ⑤/④

Villa Frobusdal Frobusdalen 2 ☎38 07 05 15, ⓦwww.bednbreakfast.no. Occupying a shipowner's mansion of 1917 near the west end of Kirkegata, this delightful family-run hotel is undoubtedly the best in town, with a sensitively restored interior that's crammed with period antiques. The only problem is location: it's only five minutes' walk from the train station, but tucked away down a hard-to-find side street off the ring road on the edge of the town centre. Drivers should head north along three-lane Festningsgata and, at the traffic lights at the end, follow the sign to Evje. ④

Hostels
Kristiansand Backpackers' Hostel Jernbanetomta, Vestre Strandgate 49 ☎38 02 79 69, 96 ⓦwww.backpackers.no. Metres from the train station, this hostel provides frugal lodgings at budget-basement prices, though all the rooms – from singles to doubles (❸/❷) or six-bunk rooms – are en suite. There are self-catering facilities and a laundry on site.

Kristiansand Vandrerhjem Skansen 8 ☎38 02 83 10, ⓔKristiansand.hostel@vandrerhjem.no. Pricey for what you get – cramped rooms in ugly, prefabricated 1960s boxes in the middle of an industrial estate. The facilities are quite good, however, with dorm beds as well as doubles (❷), a communal kitchen, a laundry and a café. The hostel is about fifteen minutes' walk east of the ferry terminal on the tiny peninsula – Tangen – edging the marina. Take any street up to Elvegata, turn right and keep going: Skansen is a turn on the left. Open all year. Dorm beds 190kr, doubles 420kr.

The Town

Neat and trim, the gridiron streets of Kristiansand's compact centre hold one architectural high point, the **Domkirke** (June–Aug Mon–Fri 10am–2pm; free) on Kirkegata at Rådhusgaten, an imposing neo-Gothic edifice dating from the 1880s and seating nearly 2000. Its only rival is the **Christiansholm Festning** on Strandpromenaden (mid-May to mid-Sept daily 9am–9pm; free), a squat fortress whose sturdy circular tower and zigzagging earth-and-stone ramparts overlook the marina in the east harbour. Built in 1672, the tower's walls are five metres thick, a precaution that proved unnecessary since it never saw action. These days it plays host to arts and crafts displays.

If you fancy a **swim**, head off to **Galgebergtangen** (Gallows' Point), an attractive rocky cove with a small sandy beach on the edge of a residential area, 2km east of the town centre. To get there, go over the bridge at the end of Dronningens gate, take the first major right (at the lights) and follow the signs.

The Kristiansand Kanonmuseum

Despite the inveigling of the German admiralty, who feared the British would occupy Norway and thus trap their fleet in the Baltic, **Hitler** was lukewarm about invading Norway until he met Vidkun Quisling in Berlin in late 1939. Hitler took Quisling's assurances about his ability to stage a coup d'état at face value, no doubt encouraged by the Norwegian's virulent anti-Semitism, and was thereafter keen to proceed. In the event, the invasion went smoothly enough – even if Quisling was soon discarded – but for the rest of the war Hitler overestimated both Norway's strategic importance and the likelihood of an Allied counter-invasion in the north. He garrisoned the country with nigh on half a million men and built several hundred artillery batteries round the coast – a huge waste of resources that were desperately needed elsewhere.

Work began on the coastal battery that is now conserved as the **Kristiansand Kanonmuseum** (May to mid-June Mon–Wed 11am–3pm; mid-June to mid-Aug daily 11am–6pm; mid-Aug to Sept Wed–Sun 11am–6pm; 50kr) in 1941, using – like all equivalent emplacements in Norway – the forced labour of POWs. Around 1400 men worked on the project, which involved the construction of protective

Moving on from Kristiansand

When it comes to **moving on from Kristiansand**, the obvious choice – the 240km trip west to Stavanger – is also the best. It's a journey that can be made by train as well as by bus or car along the E39, though both the railway line and the highway only afford glimpses of the coast, travelling for the most part a few miles inland. It may not be a gripping journey, but it's certainly a lot more pleasant than the dreary 240km haul north up **Setesdal** on Highway 9 to the E134. If, on the other hand, you're travelling north to Oslo between late June and early August, it might be worth considering the three-hour cruise up to Lillesand on the *M/S Øya* (see p.280).

housings for four big guns at the narrowest part of the Skagerrak. Guns on the Danish shore complemented those here, so that any enemy warship trying to slip through the straits could be shelled. Only a small zone in the middle was out of range, and this the Germans mined. The complex once covered 220 acres, but today the principal remains hog a narrow ridge, with a massive, empty artillery casement at one end, and a whopping 38cm-calibre **gun** in a concrete well at the other. The gun, which could fire a 500kg shell almost 55km, is in pristine condition, and visitors can explore the loading area, complete with the original ramrods, wedges, trolleys and pulleys. Below is the underground command post and soldiers' living quarters, again almost exactly as they were in the 1940s – including the odd bit of German graffiti.

The Kanonmuseum is situated an easy 10km drive south along the coast at **Møvik**: take Highway 456 out of Kristiansand, turning down Highway 457 for the last 3km of the journey.

Eating and drinking

There are lots of **restaurants** and **cafés** in the centre, but the standard is very variable – we've listed a few of the choicer places below. There's also a fairly active nightlife based around a handful of **bars** which stay open until 2am.

FRK Larsen Markens gate 5. Near the corner of Kongens gate, this laid-back café-bar is an appealing, fashionable place. Also serves meals – salted cod (*bacalao*), for instance, at a very reasonable 175kr.
Lille-Dampen Henrik Wergelandsgate 15. First-rate and inexpensive bakery, where the takeaway baguettes are delicious.
Royal China Tollbodgaten 7 ☎ 38 07 02 77.

Surprisingly plush Chinese restaurant offering tasty main courses from as little as 90kr.
Sjøhuset Østre Strandgate 12A ☎ 38 02 62 60. In an old converted warehouse by the harbour at the east end of Markens gate, this excellent restaurant serves superb fish courses for 190–210kr. Nautical fittings and wooden beams set the scene. Open daily in summer; closed Sun rest of the year.

West to Flekkefjord

West of Kristiansand lies a sparsely inhabited region, where the rough uplands and long valleys of the interior bounce down to a shoreline that is pierced by a string of inlets and fjords. The highlight is undoubtedly **Mandal**, a fetching seaside resort with probably the best sandy beach in the whole of Norway, but thereafter it's a struggle to find much inspiration. The best you'll do is the old harbour town of **Flekkefjord**, though frankly there's not really much reason to pause anywhere between Mandal and Stavanger.

The **E39** weaves its way across the region, staying deep inland for the most part and offering views of not very much at all; the same applies to the Kristiansand–Stavanger **train line**, which doesn't include Flekkefjord on its itinerary.

Mandal

MANDAL, just 40km from Kristiansand along the E39, is Norway's southernmost town. This old timber port reached its heyday in the eighteenth century, when pines and oaks from the surrounding countryside were much sought-after by the Dutch to support their canal houses and build their trading fleet. Although it's now bordered by a modern mess, Mandal has preserved its quaint **old centre**, a narrow strip of white clapboard buildings spread along the north bank of the Mandalselva River just before it rolls into the sea. It's an attractive spot that's well worth a few minutes' ramble, and you can also drop by the municipal **museum** (late June to mid-Aug Mon–Fri 11am–5pm, Sat 11am–2pm & Sun 2–5pm; March to late June & mid-Aug to Oct Sun 2–5pm; 20kr), whose rambling collection – from agricultural implements to seafaring tackle – occupies an old riverside merchant's house. It's not its antiquities that make Mandal a popular tourist spot, however, but its fine beach, **Sjøsanden**. An 800-metre stretch of golden sand backed by pine trees and framed by rocky headlands, it's touted as Norway's best – and although this isn't saying a lot, it's a perfectly enjoyable place to unwind for a few hours. The beach is about 1.5km from the town centre: walk along the harbour, past the tourist office to the end of the road and turn left; keep going and you'll reach the car park at the beach's eastern end.

Practicalities

Mandal hasn't got a train station, but there is a fast and fairly frequent **bus** service from Kristiansand (Mon–Sat hourly, 6 on Sun; 50min). The town's ugly modern **bus station** is by the bridge on the north bank of the Mandalselva River; from here it's a brief walk west to the old town centre, just beyond which is the **tourist office**, facing the river at Bryggegata 10 (mid-June to Aug Mon–Fri 9am–7pm; Sept to mid-June Mon–Fri 9am–4pm; ☎38 27 83 00; ✆www.visitregionmandal .com). There are a couple of good places to **stay**, beginning with the handy and economical *Kjøbmandsgaarden Hotel* (☎38 26 12 76, ✆www.kysthotel.no; ④), which occupies an old and intelligently renovated timber house across from the bus station at Store Elvegaten 57. All the dozen or so rooms are spick and span and the decor is bright and cheerful. Moving upmarket, the appealing *First Hotel Solborg*, Neseveien 1 (☎38 26 66 66, ℻38 26 48 22; ⑦/⑤), is an odd-looking but somehow rather fetching modern structure with every mod con; it's on the west side of the town centre, a good ten-minute walk from the bus station, tight against a wooded escarpment. Alternatively, you can camp or rent a cabin (②) very close to the western end of the beach at the *Sjøsanden Feriesenter*, Sjøsandvei 1 (☎38 26 14 19), a signposted 2km from the town centre.

The *First Hotel Solborg* has the best **restaurant** in town, but for something less pricey and more informal, head into the centre where you'll find several places, including the lively pizzeria-restaurant, *Jonas B Gundersen*. The café-restaurant of the *Kjøbmandsgaarden* comes highly recommended too, offering a tasty range of Norwegian dishes at inexpensive prices.

From Mandal, there are daily **express buses** along the E39 to Flekkefjord and Stavanger, respectively 90km and 210km away to the west. **Train** travellers have to return to Kristiansand to rejoin the rail network.

Flekkefjord

Moving on from Mandal, the **E39** hurries west, proceeding over the hills to workaday **Lyngdal** and then **Liknes**, the latter an inconsequential village at the foot of Kvinesdal and the head of the slender Fedafjord. Thereafter, the highway offers a rare glimpse of the ocean as it travels the western shore of the Fedafjord before turning inland again to snake over the hills to **FLEKKEFJORD**, 80km from Mandal. With a population approaching 6000, Flekkefjord is the big deal hereabouts, the old and picturesque timber houses of its tiny centre strung along the banks of a short (500m) channel that connects the Lafjord and the Grisefjord. Flekkefjord boomed in the sixteenth century on the back of its trade with the Dutch, who purchased the town's timber for their houses and granite for their dykes and harbours. The herring came later, in the 1750s, along with shipbuilding and tanning, but the Flekkefjord economy pretty much collapsed at the end of the nineteenth century when sailing ships gave way to steam. Recalling the Dutch connection by its nickname, "Hollenderbyen", the oldest and prettiest part of Flekkefjord lies on the west side of the channel. It only takes a few minutes to explore the area, though you can extend this pleasantly enough by examining the nineteenth-century period rooms of the **Flekkefjord Museum** (June–Aug Mon–Fri 11am–5pm, Sat & Sun noon–5pm; 15kr).

Buses pull in on Løvikgata, about 200m east of the central channel. The **tourist office** is on the west side of this same waterway at Elvegaten 15 (mid-June to mid-Aug Mon–Fri 9am–6pm, Sat & Sun 10am–2pm; mid-Aug to mid-June Mon–Fri 9am–4pm; ☎38 32 21 31). There's no pressing reason to overnight here, but there is one recommendable **hotel**, the unassuming *First Hotel Maritim* (☎38 32 33 33, ⓦwww.firsthotels.com; ❻/❸) at Sundgaten 15.

Stavanger and around

STAVANGER, 120km from Flekkefjord, is something of a survivor. While other Norwegian coastal towns have fallen foul of the precarious fortunes of fishing, Stavanger has grown and flourished, and is now the proud possessor of a dynamic economy which has swelled the population to over 100,000. It was the herring fishery that first put money into the town, crowding its nineteenth-century wharves with coopers and smiths, net makers and menders. When this industry failed the town moved into shipbuilding and ultimately oil: the port builds the rigs for the offshore oilfields and afterwards refines the oil before dispatch.

None of which sounds terribly enticing, and certainly no one could describe Stavanger as picturesque. That said, if you find yourself at the end of the south coast's railway line or, indeed, have arrived here from abroad by ferry or plane, Stavanger is an easy city to adjust to, has a couple of enjoyable museums, and holds a raft of excellent restaurants and lively bars. If you stay longer, you can sally out into the surrounding fjords, where the hike to the **Preikestolen** rock is one of the most popular jaunts in the whole of southern Norway. Finally, you'll hear lots of English spoken – well-paid foreign oil-workers gather here for their R&R.

Arrival, information and city transport

Stavanger's international **airport** is 14km southwest of the city centre at **Sola**. There's a Flybussen into Stavanger (Mon–Fri 6am–9pm, Sat 6am–8pm, Sun 7am–9pm every 20–30min; 45kr) and this stops at major downtown hotels, the ferry terminals and the bus and train stations. The **bus terminal** is on the southern side of the Breiavatnet, a tiny lake that's the most obvious downtown landmark; the **train station** (☎51 56 96 10) is adjacent. Also at the bus station is Rogaland Kollektivtrafikk, an agency run collectively by several transport companies (Mon–Fri 7am–9pm, Sat 8am–3.30pm, Sun noon–7pm; ☎51 53 96 00, ⓦwww.rkt.no), which provides comprehensive details of buses, boats and trains in the city and surrounding area.

Fjord Line **ferries** (☎815 33 500, ⓦwww.fjordline.com) from Newcastle, Haugesund and Bergen berth on the west side of the harbour, beside Strandkaien, a five-minute walk from the main square, Torget. The latter is immediately to the north of the central lake. All **Hurtigbåt passenger express boats** and **car ferries** bound for the islands and fjords around Stavanger use the Fiskepiren terminal, about 800m northeast of the train and bus stations. Finally, most pleasure cruises depart from Skagenkaien, on the east side of the main harbour.

Information

The **tourist office** overlooks the Torget from its bright and breezy premises at Rosenkildetorget 1 (Jan–May & Sept–March Mon–Fri 9am–4pm, Sat 9am–2pm; June–Aug daily 9am–8pm; ☎51 85 92 00, ⓦwww.visitstavanger.com). They publish the useful, thorough and free *Stavanger Guide* and supply free copies of *På Gang*, a monthly brochure detailing up-and-coming cultural events. They also carry a large

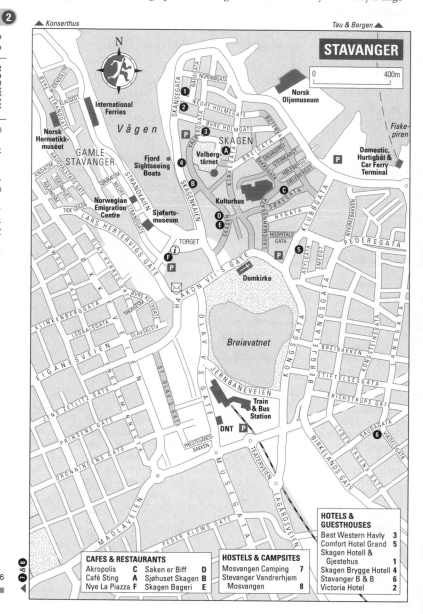

▲ *Konserthus*　　　　　　　　　　　　　　　　　　　　　　　　Tau & Bergen ▲

STAVANGER

0　　　　　　400m

Norsk
Oljemuseum

*Fiske-
piren*

International
Ferries

Vågen

Norsk
Hermetikk-
muséet

GAMLE
STAVANGER

SKAGEN

Domestic,
Hurtigbåt &
Car Ferry
Terminal

Fjord
Sightseeing
Boats

Valberg-
tårnet

Norwegian
Emigration
Centre

Sjøfarts-
museum

Kulturhus

TORGET

Domkirke

Breiavatnet

Train
& Bus
Station

DNT

CAFES & RESTAURANTS

Akropolis	**C**	Saken er Biff	**D**
Café Sting	**A**	Sjøhuset Skagen	**B**
Nye La Piazza	**F**	Skagen Bageri	**E**

HOSTELS & CAMPSITES

Mosvangen Camping	**7**
Stevanger Vandrerhjem	
Mosvangen	**8**

**HOTELS &
GUESTHOUSES**

Best Western Havly	**3**
Comfort Hotel Grand	**5**
Skagen Hotell &
Gjestehus	**1**
Skagen Brygge Hotell	**4**
Stavanger B & B	**6**
Victoria Hotel	**2**

range of leaflets from elsewhere in Norway, provide local bus and ferry timetables, have free cycling maps of both the city and its surroundings, along with route suggestions, and can book visitors on guided tours.

City transport and tours

All of Stavanger's key attractions are clustered in or near the centre within easy **walking** distance of each other, while the town's watery surroundings can be reached by a variety of local boats and buses departing from the terminals detailed above. A number of operators also provide regular summertime **fjord sightseeing tours** of one description or another, though the prime objective is almost invariably the **Lysefjord** (see p.290). Most of these tours depart from Skagenkaien and prices start at around 250kr for the more straightforward (3–4 hour) excursions; tickets are available at the quayside.

Accommodation

There's plenty of choice of **accommodation** in Stavanger. Half a dozen hotels are dotted around the centre, and each offers substantial weekend and/or summer discounts. Alternatively, there are a couple of convenient, no-frills guesthouses and, further afield, an HI hostel and campsite. All the classier hotels offer whopping summer and weekend discounts.

Hotels and guesthouses

Best Western Havly Valberggata 1 ☎51 89 67 00, ⊛www.havly-hotell.no. Unassuming, recently refurbished modern hotel in the narrow side streets off Skagenkaien. Comfortable, quiet rooms. ❸

Comfort Hotel Grand Klubbgata 3 ☎51 20 14 00, ⊛www.choicehotels.no. A good central choice, close to all the bars and restaurants. The rooms are smart, modern and spacious and the price includes a very good buffet breakfast. ❹/❸

Skagen Brygge Skagenkaien 30 ☎51 85 00 00, ⊛www.skagenbryggehotell.no. A delightful quayside hotel, built in the general style of an old warehouse but with lots of glass, and offering enjoyable views over the harbour. The rooms are modern and tastefully decorated, the buffet breakfast outstanding and delicious mid-afternoon nibbles are on offer, free – cheese, pickled herring etc. The only quibble is noise from outside on summer weekends, when it's advisable to get a room at the back or on the top floor. ❼/❹

Skagen Hotell & Gjestehus Skansegata 7 ☎51 93 85 00, ⊛www.shg.no. This hotel-cum-guesthouse in an old wooden building on the east side of the harbour has recently been revamped. Of its 28 en-suite rooms, the best are kitted in brisk and pleasant modern style. ❸

Stavanger B&B Vikedalsgaten 1A ☎51 56 25 00, ⊛www.stavangerbedandbreakfast.no. Straightforward, contemporary place in an unexciting residential area five minutes' walk southeast of the central lake. An inexpensive option. ❸

Victoria Hotel Skansegata 1 ☎51 86 70 00, ⊛www.victoria-hotel.no. Part of the *Rica* chain, this large hotel occupies a big old building with a fancy portico, overlooking the east side of the harbour. The foyer has kept much of its Victorian appearance, complete with wood panelling, leather sofas and ships' models – and the comfortable rooms beyond are in a broadly period style. ❼/❸

Hostel and campsite

Mosvangen Camping Tjensvollveien 1 ☎51 53 29 71. This large lakeside campsite next to the youth hostel has cabins (❷) as well as spaces for tents and caravans. Open mid-May to mid-September.

Stavanger Vandrerhjem Mosvangen Henrik Ibsens gate 21 ☎51 87 29 00, @stavanger.mosvangen.hostel@vandrerhjem.no.

Plain HI youth hostel at the waterside, a 3km walk from the centre: take Madlaveien west from near the station and turn left just beyond the lake, Mosvatnet, on to Tjensvollveien – Henrik Ibsens gate is its continuation. The hostel has some double rooms (❷), as well as self-catering and laundry facilities; advance reservations are advised. Open June–Aug.

The City

Built with oil money, much of central Stavanger is modern, a flashy but surprisingly likeable ensemble of mini tower-blocks. The only relic of the medieval city is the twelfth-century **Domkirke** (mid-May to mid-Sept Mon & Tues 11am–6pm, Wed–Sat 10am–6pm, Sun 1–6pm; mid-Sept to mid-May Wed–Sat 10am–3pm; free), up above the Torget, whose pointed-hat towers signal a Romanesque church that has suffered from several poorly conceived renovations. The simple interior, originally the work of English craftsmen, has fared badly, too, spoilt by ornate seventeenth-century additions including an intricate pulpit and five huge memorial tablets adorning the walls of the aisles – a jumble of richly carved angels, crucifixes, death's-heads, animals and apostles. Organ recitals are held here every Thursday at 11.15am.

A brief stroll away, beyond the fresh fish and flower stalls of **Torget**, is the **Skagen** area, built on the bumpy promontory that forms the eastern side of the harbour. It's an oddly discordant district, a clumsy mixture of the old and new incorporating the town's main shopping zone, whose mazy street plan is the only legacy of the original Viking settlement. The spiky **Valbergtårnet** (Valberg tower), atop the highest point and guarded by three rusty cannons, is the one specific sight, a nineteenth-century firewatch offering sweeping views of the city and its industry.

Beside the waterfront on the far side of Skagen, the oil industry celebrates its achievements by way of the gleaming **Norwegian Petroleum Museum** (*Norsk Oljemuseum*; June–Aug daily 10am–7pm, Sept–May Mon–Sat 10am–4pm & Sun 10am–6pm; 75kr; ⊕ www.norskolje.museum.no). Housed in a hangar-like building, the museum has displays on North Sea geology, oil extraction and the like, complete with drill bits and other oil-rig paraphernalia. There are several hands-on exhibits, too – including a diving bell – plus an honest account of the accidents and occasional disasters that have befallen the industry.

Gamle Stavanger

The city's star turn is **Gamle Stavanger** (Old Stavanger) area, on the western side of the harbour. Though very different in appearance from the modern structures back in the centre, the buildings here were also the product of a late nineteenth-century boom when herring turned up just offshore in their millions. Benefiting from this slice of luck, Stavanger flourished and expanded, and the number of merchants and ship owners in the town increased dramatically. Huge profits were made from the exported fish, which were salted and later, as the technology improved, canned. Today, some of the wooden stores and warehouses flanking the western quayside hint at their nineteenth-century pedigree, but it's the succession of narrow, cobbled lanes behind them that shows Gamle Stavanger to best advantage. Formerly home to local seafarers, craftsmen and cannery workers, the area has been maintained as a residential quarter, mercifully free of tourist tat; the long rows of white-painted, clapboard houses are immaculately maintained, complete with gas lamps, picket fences and tiny terraced gardens.

The **Canning Museum** (*Norsk Hermetikkmuséet*; early June & late Aug Mon–Thurs 11am–3pm; mid-June to mid-Aug daily 11am–4pm; Sept–May Sun 11am–4pm; 40kr), right in the heart of Gamle Stavanger at Øvre Strandgate 88, occupies an old **sardine-canning factory** and gives a glimpse of the industry that saved Stavanger from collapse at the end of the nineteenth century. The herring largely disappeared from local waters in the 1870s, but the canning factories switched to imported fish, thereby keeping the local economy afloat. They remained Stavanger's main source of employment until as late as 1960: in the 1920s there were seventy canneries in the town, and the last one only closed down in 1983. A visit to an old canning factory may not seem too enticing, but actually the museum is very good, not least because of its collection of **sardine tin labels**. The variety of design is extraordinary – anything and everything from representations of the Norwegian royal family to surrealistic fish with human qualities. You can watch the museum **smoking its own sardines** on the first Sunday of every month and every Tuesday and Thursday from mid-June to mid-August – and very tasty they are, too.

Eating

Although prices are marginally inflated by oil-industry expense accounts, Stavanger is a great place to **eat**, with several fine seafood restaurants clustered on the east side of the harbour along Skagenkaien. For something less expensive, the best option is to stick to the more mundane cafés and restaurants near the Kulturhus in the heart of the Skagen shopping area.

Cafés and restaurants

Akropolis Sølvberggata 14. Near the Kulturhus, this is a medium-priced Greek restaurant housed in a white wooden building on a cobbled street. Closed Mon.

Café Sting Valbergjet 3 ☎51 89 38 78. Right next to the Valbergtårnet, this laid-back café-bar is probably the coolest place in town. Tasty, inexpensive food with Mediterranean and Norwegian dishes. Also doubles as an art gallery and live music (indie through rock) venue.

Nye La Piazza Rosenkildetorget 1. Above the tourist office, this smart Italian restaurant serves delicious pizzas, pasta and more; main courses from 90kr.

Saken er Biff Skagen 28 ☎51 89 60 80. No self-

respecting oil town could do without a steakhouse – and this is it. A couple of stuffed cattle heads remind you what you're eating, and fish dishes, reindeer and ostrich are available too. Around 200kr for a main course.

Sjøhuset Skagen Skagenkaien 16 ☎51 89 51 80. Fine fish and seafood restaurant on the harbour, with monkfish a speciality. Main dishes are around 200kr.

Skagen Bageri Skagen 18. This pleasant coffee house, with its finely carved antique door and lintel, occupies the prettiest of the old wooden buildings on Skagen, one block up from the quayside. Great pastries, cakes and snacks at reasonable prices.

Drinking and nightlife

Stavanger is lively at night, particularly at weekends when a rum assortment of oil workers, sailors, fishermen, executives, tourists and office workers gather in the **bars and clubs** on and around Skagenkaien to live (or rather drink) it up. Most places stay open until 2am or later, with rowdier – but usually amiable – revellers lurching from one bar to the next.

For more subdued evenings, check out the programme at the concert hall, **Stavanger Konserthus** (☎51 53 70 00, ✆www.stavanger-konserthus.no), in Bjergsted park, north of the centre beyond Gamle Stavanger, where there are regular concerts by the Stavanger Symphony Orchestra and visiting artists. There's an eight-screen **cinema**, Stavanger Kinematografer, inside the Kulturhus (☎51 51 07 00).

Bars and clubs

Hansen Hjørnet Skagenkaien 18. Whenever the sun pops out, the outside terrace of this harbour bar fills up fast; one of Stavanger's most popular spots.

Newsman Skagen 14. One block up from the east side of the harbour, this attractive, busy bar has a newspaper theme, which means papers to read and a well-heeled clientele.

Taket Nedre Strandgate 15 ☎51 84 37 20. The best club in town, across the harbour from most of the bars and metres from the tourist office. Don't be surprised if you have to queue. Closed Sun.

Timbuktu Nedre Strandgate 15. Flashy café-bar beneath *Taket*. Noted for its imaginative modern decor and groovy atmosphere.

Listings

Airlines Braathens ☎815 20 000; SAS ☎81 00 33 00; Widerøes ☎81 00 12 00.

Car rental Avis, Skansegaten 15 ☎51 93 93 60; Hertz, Olav V's gate 13 ☎51 52 00 00, and at the airport ☎51 65 10 96.

Emergencies Fire ☎110, Police ☎112, Ambulance ☎113.

Exchange Competitive rates at the main post office (see below).

Ferries: International: Fjord Line, Strandkaien ☎81 53 35 00. **Domestic**: Rogaland Kollektivtrafikk enquiries ☎51 53 96 00; locally also ☎177; Hurtigbåt passenger express boat ☎51 86 87 80.

Hiking The DNT-affiliated Stavanger Turistforening, Olav V's gate 18 (Mon–Wed & Fri 10am–4pm, Thurs 10am–6pm; ☎51 84 02 00, @www.stavanger-turistforening.no), will advise on local hiking routes and sells a comprehensive range of hiking maps. They maintain around 900km of hiking trails and run over thirty cabins in the mountains east of Stavanger – as well as organizing ski schools on winter weekends. They also offer general advice about local conditions, weather etc, and you can obtain DNT membership here.

Laundry Renseriet, Kongsgata 40, by Breiavatnet.

Left luggage Fiskepiren Hurtigbåt express boat terminal (Mon–Fri 6.30am–11.30pm, Sat 6.30am–8pm, Sun 8am–10pm); and at the bus/train station (Mon–Fri 8am–5pm, Sat 8am–2.30pm).

Pharmacist Løveapoteket, Olav V's gate 11 (daily 9am–11pm; ☎51 52 06 07).

Post office The main post office is at Haakon VII's gate 9 (Mon–Fri 8am–5pm & Sat 9am–1pm).

Taxis Norgestaxi ☎08000.

Vinmonopolet Olav V gate 13, across the street from Stavanger Turistforening.

Around Stavanger: Lysefjord

Stavanger sits on a long promontory that pokes a knobbly head north towards the Boknafjord, whose wide waters form a deep indentation in the coast speckled with islets and islands. To the east of the town, longer, narrower fjords drill far inland. The most diverting of them is the blue-black **Lysefjord**, famous for its precipitous cliffs and an especially striking rock formation, the **Preikestolen**, a distinctive 25-metre-square table of rock with a sheer 600m drop down to the fjord on three of its sides.

Along the Lysefjord to Lysebotn

There are several ways to visit Lysefjord **by boat** from Stavanger. One option is with **Rødne Clipper Fjord Sightseeing** (☎51 89 52 70, @www.rodne.no), which runs a circular trip up about half its length, departing from the Skagenkaien (Jan–April & Oct–Dec 4–7 monthly, May & Sept 3 weekly; June–Aug 1–2 daily; 3hr 30min; 280kr). Despite the gushing multilingual commentary, however, the fjord seems disappointingly gloomy when seen from the bottom of its cliffs, and from this angle the Preikestolen hardly makes any impression at all. Rather more worthwhile is the same company's excursion to **Lysebotn**, at the east end of the fjord (June–Aug 1–2 weekly; 7hr; 450kr). At Lysebotn, a connecting bus heads up the mountainside, tackling no less than 27 switchbacks on its way to the minor road that leads back to Stavanger. Predictably, it's much less expensive to do the Lysebotn trip **independently**. Ruteservice Rogaland operates ferries to Lysebotn from Stavanger's Fiskepiren once daily from June to September. The journey takes four hours and costs 135kr per person, 305kr for car and driver; advance booking is required for vehicles. If you're returning to Stavanger by bus from Lysebotn, the tourist office will advise which ferries match the bus times.

The road from Lysebotn offers grand views as it wriggles its way up the mountainside, but adventurous souls prefer the very demanding **hiking trail** which leads west from the car park of the **Øygardstøl** café and information centre, just above the last hairpin, to a much-photographed boulder, the **Kjeragbolten**. The latter is wedged between two rock faces high above the ground. Allow between five and six hours for the round trip – and steel your nerves.

From Stavanger to Bergen

With great ingenuity, Norway's road builders have cobbled together the E39 coastal road, the **Kystvegen**, which traverses the west coast from Stavanger to Haugesund and Bergen, a distance of about 190km with two ferry trips breaking up the journey. The highway slips across a string of islands, which provide a pleasant introduction to the scenic charms of western Norway, and hint at the sterner beauty of the fjords beyond.

By **car**, it takes between five and six hours to get from Stavanger to Bergen. A fast and frequent **bus** service – the Kystbussen – plies the E39 too, taking a little under six hours to get to Bergen (8–11 daily; 390kr); you'll get to see far more of the coast this way than by using the **Hurtigbåt passenger express boat** on the same route (2–4 daily; 4hr; 590kr).

Preikestolen

Lysefjord's most celebrated vantage point, **Preikestolen** ("Pulpit Rock"), offers breathtaking views, though on sunny summer weekends you'll find yourself sharing them with a fair old crowd. To get to the rock, take the **ferry** east from Stavanger to **Tau** (every 30min to 1hr; 40min; passengers 30kr, car & driver 90kr) and then drive south along Highway 13 until, after about 14km, you reach the signed side road leading to Preikestolen. A local **bus** covers the Tau–Preikestolen road, too (4 daily; 25min), but you'll need to check with the tourist office as to which of the ferries connects with the bus. From the car park at the end of the road, it's a four-hour hike there and back to Preikestolen along a clearly marked trail. The first half is steep in parts and paved with uneven stones, the second half – over bedrock – is a good bit easier. The change in elevation is 350m; take food and water.

If you want to hang around, a first-rate HI hostel, **Preikestolen Vandrerhjem** (June–Aug; ☏97 16 55 51, ☜www.preikestolhytta.no), is located by the car park. Perched high up on a hillside, with great views over the surrounding mountains, the hostel was built on the site of an old mountain farm, the scant remains of which are visible all around. It comprises a small complex of turf-roofed lodges, each of which has a spick-and-span pine interior. There are some doubles (❷), self-catering facilities and boat rental, but no laundry; reservations are advised as the place is popular with school groups.

Travel details

Trains

Kristiansand to: Oslo (3–5 daily; 4hr 40min); Stavanger (3–5 daily; 3hr).
Oslo to: Arendal, change at Nelaug (3–5 daily; 4hr 40min); Egersund (3–5 daily; 6hr 40min); Kristiansand (3–5 daily; 4hr 40min); Stavanger (3–5 daily; 7hr 30min).
Stavanger to: Kristiansand (3–5 daily; 3hr); Oslo (3–5 daily; 7hr 30min).

Long-distance buses

Arendal to: Lillesand (4–5 daily; 45min); Oslo (4–5 daily; 4hr).
Grimstad to: Lillesand (4–5 daily; 15min); Oslo

(4–5 daily; 4hr 30min).
Kristiansand to: Flekkefjord (1–3 daily; 2hr); Mandal (Mon–Sat hourly, Sun 6 daily; 50min); Oslo (4–5 daily; 5hr 30min); Stavanger (1–3 daily; 4hr).
Oslo to: Arendal (4–5 daily; 4hr); Grimstad (4–5 daily; 4hr 30min); Kristiansand (4–5 daily; 5hr 30min); Lillesand (4–5 daily; 4hr 45min).
Lillesand to: Arendal (4–5 daily; 145min); Kristiansand (4–5 daily; 45min); Grimstad (4–5 daily, 15min); Oslo (4–5 daily; 4hr 45min).
Mandal to: Kristiansand (Mon–Sat hourly, Sun 6 daily; 50min); Stavanger (1–3 daily; 3hr 30min).
Stavanger to: Bergen (8–11 daily; 5hr 40min); Kristiansand (1–3 daily; 4hr); Mandal (1–3 daily; 3hr 30min).

Car ferries	Hurtigbåt passenger express boats
Egersund to: Bergen (2–4 weekly; 8hr). With Fjord line; originates in Hantsholm, Denmark. **Stavanger** to: Bergen (2–6 weekly; 7hr). With Fjord Line; originates in Newcastle, UK.	**Stavanger** to: Bergen (2–4 daily; 4hr).

2.3

Bergen and the western fjords

I f there's one familiar and enticing image of Norway it's the **fjords**: huge clefts in the landscape running from the coast deep into the interior. Wild, rugged and serene, these water-filled wedges are visually stunning; indeed, the entire fjord region elicits inordinate amounts of purple prose from tourist office handouts, and for once it's rarely overstated. The fjords are undeniably beautiful, especially around early May after the brief Norwegian spring has brought colour to the landscape.

The fjords run all the way up the coast to the Russian border, but are most easily – and impressively – seen on the west coast near **Bergen**, the self-proclaimed "Capital of the Fjords". Norway's second largest city, Bergen is a welcoming place with an atmospheric old warehouse quarter, a relic of the days when it was the northernmost port of the Hanseatic trade alliance. It's also a handy springboard for the nearby fjords, including the Flåmsdal valley to the east, where the inspiring **Flåmsbana** mountain railway trundles down to the **Aurlandsfjord**, a small arm of the mighty **Sognefjord**. Lined with pretty village resorts, the Sognefjord is the longest, deepest and most celebrated of the country's waterways, and is certainly one of the most beguiling. North of here lies the **Jostedalsbreen** glacier, mainland Europe's largest ice sheet, the relatively uninspiring **Nordfjord**, and the narrow, S-shaped **Geirangerfjord**, perhaps the most scenically impressive of all the fjords, though the tourist hordes can be off-putting. Further north, towards the **Romsdalsfjord**, the landscape becomes more extreme still, reaching pinnacles of isolation in the splendid **Trollstigen** mountain highway, a stunning prelude to the amenable little town of **Åndalsnes**.

Bergen

As it has been raining ever since she arrived in the city, a tourist stops a young boy and asks him if it always rains here. "I don't know," he replies, "I'm only thirteen." The joke isn't brilliant, but it does tell at least part of the truth. Of all the things to contend with in the western city of **BERGEN**, the weather is the most predictable: it rains relentlessly even in summer, and the surroundings are often shrouded with mist. But despite its dampness, Bergen is one of Norway's most enjoyable cities. Its setting – between seven hills, sheltered to the north, south and west by a series of straggling islands and fjords – is spectacular. There's plenty to see in town too, from sturdy **medieval buildings** to a whole series of good **museums**, and just outside the city limits is **Troldhaugen**, Edvard Grieg's charming old home.

More than anything else, though, it's the general flavour of the place that appeals. Although Bergen has become a major port and minor industrial centre in recent years, it remains a laid-back, easy-going town with a nautical air. Fishing continues to underpin the local economy, and the bustling main harbour, **Vågen**, is still very much the focus of attention. If you stay more than a day or two – perhaps using Bergen as a base for visiting the local fjords – you'll soon discover that the city also has the region's best choice of **restaurants**, some impressive art galleries, and a decent nightlife.

Arrival

Bergen's sturdy stone **train station** (local ☎55 96 69 00, national ☎81 50 08 88) is located on Strømgaten, just along the street from the entrance to the Bergen Storsenter shopping mall, within which is the **bus station** (☎177). From Strømgaten, it's a five- to ten-minute walk west to the most interesting part of the city, the waterfront at Bergen's main harbour, **Vågen**, via the pedestrianized shopping street Marken; a taxi to the harbour will set you back about 60kr. The **airport** is 20km south of the city at Flesland, and is connected to the centre by the **Flybussen** (Mon–Fri & Sun 5am–9pm, Sat 5am–4pm; every 15–20min; 45min; 60kr). This pulls in beside the *SAS Hotel Norge* on Ole Bulls plass and then at the bus station, before proceeding to the harbourfront *SAS Royal Hotel*. Taxis from the rank outside the airport arrivals hall charge around 300kr for the same trip.

By boat

As well as being a hub for ferry and catamaran links with the fjords, Bergen is a busy international port. **Ferries** from Denmark, Iceland, Shetland and the Faroe Islands all arrive at Skoltegrunnskaien, the quay just beyond Bergenhus fortress, as do those from Newcastle, which call at Stavanger and Haugesund on the way here. **Hurtigbåt passenger express boats** from Haugesund, Stavanger and the Hardangerfjord, as well as those from Sognefjord and Nordfjord, line up on the opposite side of the harbour at the Strandkaiterminalen; local **ferries** from islands and fjords immediately north of Bergen mostly arrive here too, though short excursions round the Byforden, adjoining Bergen harbour, leave from beside the Torget.

Bergen is also a port of call for the **Hurtigrute coastal boat**, which arrives at the Frieleneskaien harbour on the southern edge of the city centre, beyond the university and close to the Puddefjordsbroen bridge (Highway 555). City bus #5 links the Frieleneskaien with the central Torget (Mon–Sat 6am–11pm every 30min to 1hr, Sun 8am–10pm hourly; 20kr); by taxi the journey costs about 70kr. Alternatively, it's a steep 25-minute walk to the centre up through the university and down the other side.

For ferry and boat **ticket and timetable information**, see "Ferries" under "Listings" (p.307).

▲ *Trondheim*

▲ *Trondheim*

Oppdal

Dombås

E6

Otta

Lom

Hwy 70

Hwy 15

Hwy 55

Kristiansund

Hwy 70

E39

Hwy 64

Andalsnes

E136

Trollstigveg

Molde

Grotli

Tafjord

Sylte

Geiranger

Hwy 15

Hwy 258

Liabygda

Eidsdal

Linge

Hwy 63

Geiranger's
fjord

Stranda

Hellesylt

Hwy 60

Stryn

Loen

Olden

Jostedalsbreen

Kronndalsbreen

Nigardsbreen

Ålesund

E39

Nordfjordeid

Hwy 15

Nordfjord

Byrkjelo

Hwy 60

Skei

Hwy 5

Runde

E39

N O R W E G I A N   S E A

Måløy

Hwy 15

Flora

Hwy 5

E39

N

50 km

0

- - - - - Hurtigrute

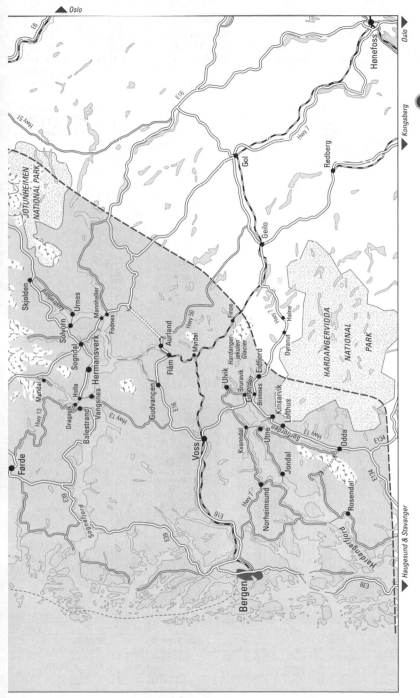

By car

If you're driving into Bergen, note that a **toll** (10kr) is charged on all vehicles over 50cc entering the city centre from Monday to Friday between 6am and 10pm; pay at the tollbooths. There's no charge for driving out of the city. In an attempt to keep the city centre relatively free of traffic, there's a confusing and none-too-successful one-way system in operation, supplemented by rigorously

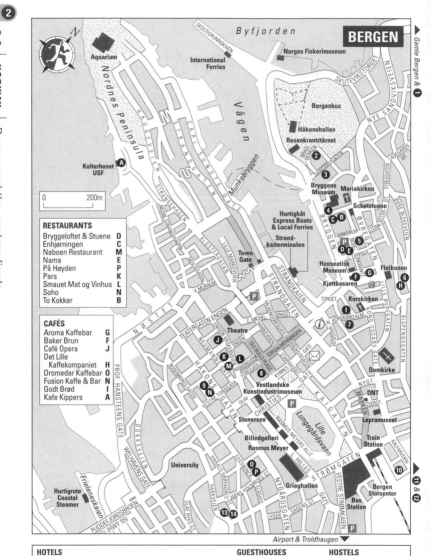

RESTAURANTS

Bryggeloftet & Stuene	D
Enhjørningen	C
Naboen Restaurant	M
Nama	E
På Høyden	P
Pars	K
Smauet Mat og Vinhus	L
Soho	N
To Kokker	B

CAFÉS

Aroma Kaffebar	G
Baker Brun	F
Café Opera	J
Det Lille Kaffekompaniet	H
Dromedar Kaffebar	O
Fusion Kaffe & Bar	N
Godt Brød	I
Kafe Kippers	A

Airport & Troldhaugen ▼

HOTELS				GUESTHOUSES		HOSTELS	
Dreggen	3	Radisson SAS Hotel Norge	8	Crowded House Travel		Bergen Vandrerhjem	
Golden Tulip Rainbow		Radisson SAS Royal Hotel	4	Lodge Sandviken	1	Montana	12
Rosenkrantz	5	Steens	13	Crowded House Travel		Bergen Vandrerhjem	
Grand Hotel Terminus	10	Tulip Inn Rainbow Bryggen		Lodge Sentrum	9	YMCA	7
Hotel Park Pension	14	Orion	2	Skansen Pensjonat	6	Intermision	11

enforced on-street parking restrictions. During peak periods (Mon–Fri 8am–5pm, Sat 8am–6pm), on-street parking for a maximum of two hours costs 18kr per hour (pay at the meters) and the best advice is to make straight for one of the four central **car parks**. The largest is the 24hr ByGarasjen on Vestre Strømkaien, a short walk from the centre behind the Storsenter shopping mall and bus station. The Parkeringshuset, on Rosenkrantzgaten (Mon–Fri 7am–11pm, Sat 8am–6pm, Sun 9am–6pm), has shorter opening hours but is handier for the harbourfront. To get there, follow the international ferry signs until you pick up the car park signs. **Tariffs** vary, but reckon on 13kr per hour up to a maximum of 130kr for 24hrs. Outside of peak periods, on-street parking is relatively easy and free.

Information

The **tourist office** is in a large, mural-decorated hall at Vågsallmenningen 1 (May & Sept daily 9am–8pm; June–Aug daily 8.30am–10pm; Oct–April Mon–Sat 9am–4pm; ☎55 55 20 00, ⓦwww.visitbergen.com), across the road from Torget, at the east end of Vågen, the main harbour. Staff give away copies of the *Bergen Guide*, an exhaustive listings booklet, and numerous other free brochures. Here you can also book hotels and rooms in private houses, reserve places on guided tours, buy tickets for fjord sightseeing boats, and change foreign currency – in high season, expect long queues. Bergen has one very good, and free, bi-monthly **newssheet** containing local news, entertainment listings and reviews – the Bergen edition of the Oslo-based *Natt & Dag*. Naturally enough, it's in Norwegian, but the listings section is still easy to use. It's widely available across the city centre.

City transport

Most of Bergen's key attractions are located in the compact city centre, which is best explored **on foot**. For outlying sights and accommodation, however, you'll need to take a city **bus**. Bergen and its surroundings are served by a dense network of local buses, whose hub is the bus station in the Storsenter shopping mall on Strømgaten (☎177). Flat-fare tickets, available from the driver, cost 20kr and are valid for an hour; if your journey involves more than one bus, ask the driver for a free transfer. Another useful link is the **Attractions bus**, which links the city centre with most of the outlying points of interest, including Grieg's Troldhaugen and Gamle Bergen; it runs hourly between 10am and 5pm daily from June to August and stops, amongst several places, outside the tourist office and on the Bryggen near the *SAS Royal Hotel*. A hop-on, hop-off day ticket costs 40kr, but note that the Attractions bus was only launched in 2002 and its future is not secure – it depends how many people use it. Finally, a tiny **orange ferry** (Mon–Fri 7am–4.15pm; 12kr) bobs across Vågen to provide a shortcut between Munkebryggen, along Carl Sundts gate, and a point near the *SAS Royal Hotel* on the Bryggen.

The Bergen Card

The **Bergen Card** is a 24-hour (165kr) or 48-hour (245kr) pass which provides free use of all the city's buses and free or substantially discounted admission to most of the city's sights, and reductions on many sightseeing trips. It also gives free on-street parking – if you can find a space and within the two-hour maximum parking time. The pass comes with a booklet listing all the various concessions. Obviously, the more diligent a sightseer you are, the better value the card becomes, doubly so if you're staying a bus ride from the centre. The card is sold at a wide range of outlets, including the tourist office, major hotels and the train station.

Accommodation

Budget **accommodation** is no great problem in Bergen. There are three hostels, a choice of private rooms in local houses and guesthouses, and some of the central hotels are surprisingly good value. Among the better deals are the **private rooms**, bookable through the tourist office. The vast majority provide self-catering facilities and some are fairly central, though most are stuck out in the suburbs. Prices are at a fixed nightly rate, currently 340kr for a double room without en-suite facilities (230kr single), 400kr en suite (260kr single). There are some apartments, too (500kr). They are very popular, so in summer you'll need to arrive at the tourist office early to secure one for the night.

Camping is also an option, and there are several campsites on the outskirts of the city, but you'll be far from the action at any of them. Most campsites have four-bunk timber **cabins**.

Hotels

Dreggen Sandbrugaten 3 ☎55 31 61 55, ⊛www.hotel-dreggen.no. Modest, three-star hotel in a plain modern block, but with a great location just off the Bryggen. Thirty plain and fairly small rooms kitted out in routine modern style, both with shared facilities and, costing a bit more, en suite. Rates include breakfast. ❸

Golden Tulip Rainbow Rosenkrantz Rosenkrantzgaten 7 ☎55 30 14 00, ⊛www.rainbow-hotels.no. Efficient and extremely competent mid-range hotel in an old building just behind the Bryggen. Rooms are tidy and trim, and the best ones on the upper floors have pleasing views over the harbour. Shame about the aluminium windows stuck in the attractive facade. ❼/❹

Grand Hotel Terminus Zander Kaaes gate 6 ☎55 21 25 00, ⊛www.grand-hotel-terminus.no. There was a time when the tweed-jacketed visitors of prewar England headed straight for the *Grand* as soon as they arrived in Bergen – and not just because the hotel is next door to the train station. Those ritzy days are long gone, but the hotel has reinvented itself, making the most of its quasi-baronial flourishes, notably its extensive wood panelling, chandeliers and stained glass. Breakfasts are superb and the bedrooms attractive and quiet, though some are rather pokey – if you can, have a look before you commit. ❺/❹

Hotel Park Pension Harald Hårfagres gate 35 ☎55 54 44 00, ⊛www.parkhotel.no. This excellent, family-run hotel occupies two handsome late nineteenth-century town houses on the edge of the town centre near the university. The charming interior is painted in soft pastel colours and the public areas are dotted with antiques. The bedrooms are smart, neat and appealing. It's a very popular place, so advance reservations are advised. ❹

Radisson SAS Hotel Norge Ole Bulls plass 4 ☎55 57 30 30, ⊛www.radissonsas.com. Swish and swanky top-class hotel, right in the thick of things and with a full range of facilities from bar to heated swimming pool. ❼

Radisson SAS Royal Hotel Bryggen ☎55 54 30 00, ⊛www.radissonsas.com. Full marks here to the architects, who have built an extremely smart, first-rate hotel behind a brick facade that mirrors the style of the old timber buildings that surround it. All facilities – pool, health club and so forth, plus attractively appointed rooms. Popular with visiting business folk. ❼

Steens Parkveien 22 ☎55 31 40 50, ☏55 32 61 22. One of an attractive terrace of high-gabled town houses, overlooking a mini-lake on the edge of the town centre near the university, this well-established hotel offers inexpensive lodgings. The interior has lots of late Victorian flourishes, but the overall effect is a tad gloomy. ❹/❸

Tulip Inn Rainbow Bryggen Orion Bradbenken 3 ☎55 30 87 00, ⊛www.rainbow-hotels.no. Deservedly popular mid-range hotel with unassuming but perfectly comfortable modern rooms. Has a handy location, a stone's throw from the Bergenhus fort, and breakfasts are magnificent banquets – with every type of pickled herring you can think of – and then some. Hard to beat. ❺/❹

Guesthouses

Crowded House Travel Lodge Håkons gaten 2794 ☎55 90 72 00, ⊛www.crowded-house.com. Traditionally, Bergen's guesthouses have been a little dowdy, but this lively, appealing place is the opposite – from the pastel-painted foyer to the bright and airy, if admittedly spartan, bedrooms. There are thirty-three rooms in total – singles, doubles and triples, all with shared bathrooms. There are self-catering facilities and a laundry, too. Located halfway along traffic-clogged Håkons gaten, about five minutes' walk from the city centre. ❷

Crowded House Travel Lodge Sandviken Sandviksveien; same details as *Crowded House* above. Similar in style and substance to its sister, but with parking. Located about 2km north from the city centre. ❷

Skansen Pensjonat Vetrlidsallmenningen 29 ☎ 55 31 90 80, ✉ mail@skansen-pensjonat.no. This simple little guesthouse occupies a nineteenth-century stone house of elegant proportions just above – and up the steps from – the terminus of the Fløibanen funicular railway, near Torget. It's a great location, in one of the most beguiling parts of town. The guesthouse has eight perfectly adequate if simple rooms, one of which is en suite. A real snip. ❷

Hostels

Bergen Vandrerhjem Montana Johan Blyttsveien 30, Landås ☎ 55 20 80 70, ⓦ www.montana.no. This large and comfortable HI hostel which occupies lodge-like premises in the hills overlooking the city is popular with school

parties, who are (usually) housed in a separate wing. Great views and great breakfasts, plus self-catering facilities, a laundry and Internet/email access. Dorm accommodation, family rooms, and doubles (❷), the pick of which are en suite and in a newly added wing. The hostel is 6km east of the centre – 15min on bus #31 (stop Montana) from Nygaten.

Bergen Vandrerhjem YMCA Nedre Korskirkealmenning 4 ☎ 55 60 60 55, ✉ bergen.ymca.hostel@vandrerhjem.no. No-frills HI hostel in the centre, a short walk from Torget, whose 175 beds (including private singles and doubles at ❷) fill up fast in summer. Facilities include a café, communal kitchen and a laundry; breakfast costs 40kr. Open May to mid-Sept.

Intermission Kalfarveien 8 ☎ 55 30 04 00. Christian-run private hostel in a two-storey, oldish wooden building five minutes' walk from the train station, just beyond one of the old city gates. Open mid-June to mid-Aug. Breakfast is 30kr.

The City

Founded in 1070 by King Olav Kyrre ("the Peaceful"), **Bergen** was the largest and most important town in medieval Norway, a regular residence of the country's kings and queens and, from the fourteenth century, a Hanseatic League port, connected to other European and Baltic cities by vigorous trading links. The League was controlled by German merchants, however, and although Hansa and local interests initially coincided, the picture slowly changed. Eventually, Germans came to dominate the region's economy, reducing the locals to a state of dependency by fixing the price of fish, the region's main commodity. Their trading station, which flourished on Bergen's main wharf, the Bryggen, became wealthy and hated in equal measure. In the 1550s, with Hansa power evaporating, a local lord, one Kristoffer Valkendorf, finally reasserted Norwegian control. Unfortunately, Valkendorf and his cronies simply took over the monopolies that had enriched their German predecessors, operating a system which continued to pauperize the region's fishermen right down to the nineteenth century.

Very little of medieval Bergen has survived, although parts of the fortress – the **Bergenhus** – which commands the entrance to the harbour, date from the thirteenth century. The rest of the city centre divides into several distinct parts, the most interesting being the wharf area, the **Bryggen**, which houses an attractive ensemble of eighteenth- and nineteenth-century merchants' trading houses. The Bryggen ends at the bottom of the central harbour, **Vågen**, where the **Torget** is home to an open-air fish market. East of here, stretching up towards the train station, is one of the older districts, a mainly nineteenth-century quarter at its prettiest along **Lille Øvregaten** and amongst the narrow lanes that clamber up the adjacent hillside. The main thoroughfare of this quarter, **Kong Oscars gate**, leads to the city's most endearing museum, the Leprosy Museum, itself little more than a stone's throw from the modern concrete blocks surrounding the city's central lake, **Lille Lungegårdsvann**. The high-rises here form the cultural focus of the city, holding Bergen's main concert hall and art galleries, whilst the main commercial area is just to the west along pedestrianized **Torgalmenningen**. The steep hill to the south of Lille Lungegårdsvann is crowned by the **university**.

Most of the main sights and museums are concentrated in these areas, but no tour of the city is complete without a stroll out along the **Nordnes peninsula**, where fine timber houses dot the bumpy terrain, and whose old USF sardine factory now contains a first-rate arts complex and café.

Torget

The nineteenth-century traveller Lilian Leland, writing about Bergen in 1890, complained that "Everything is fishy. You eat fish and drink fish and smell fish and breathe fish." Those days are long gone, but even now that Bergen is every inch the go-ahead, modern city, tourists still flock here to seek out all things piscine. The nearest you'll get to those fishy days now is the open-air **fish market** on the **Torget** (June–Aug daily 7am–5pm; Sept–May Mon–Sat 7am–4pm). It's not a patch on the days when scores of fishing smacks moored up against the quayside to empty their bulging holds, but the stalls still display huge mounds of prawns and crab-claws, buckets of herring and a hundred other varieties of marine life on slabs, in tanks and under the knife. Load up or eat up and hang around for a while to assess the comings and goings of the local boats and ferries.

Bryggen and around

From Torget, central Bergen spears right and left around the Vågen, with **Bryggen**, on the northerly side of the harbour, the obvious historical and cultural target. The site of the original settlement at Bergen, this is the city's best-preserved quarter, containing, among other things, the distinctive wooden gabled trading posts that front the wharf. The area was once known as Tyskebryggen, or "German Quay", after the Hansa merchants who operated their trading station here, but the name was unceremoniously dumped at the end of World War II.

The medieval buildings of Bryggen were destroyed by fire in 1702, to be replaced by another set of wooden warehouses. In turn, many of these were later replaced by high-gabled stone warehouses in a style modelled on that of the Hansa period, but a small section of the eighteenth-century **timber buildings** has survived and now houses shops, restaurants and bars. It's well worth nosing around here, wandering down the passageways in between wherever you can. Interestingly, these eighteenth-century buildings carefully follow the original building line: the governing body of the Hansa trading station stipulated the exact depth and width of each merchant's building, and the width of the passage separating them – a regularity that's actually best observed from Øvregaten (see opposite). The planning regulations didn't end there. Trade had to be carried out in the front section of the building, with storage rooms at the back; above could be found the merchant's office, bedroom and dining room, and above that, on the top floor, the living quarters of the employees, arranged by rank: merchants, journeymen/clerks and foremen, wharf hands and, last and least, house boys. At the near end of the Bryggen, just off Torget, the **Hanseatisk Museum** (daily: June–Aug 9am–5pm; Sept–May 11am–2pm; 40kr) is the best-preserved of the early eighteenth-century merchants' dwellings, and, kitted out in late Hansa style, gives an idea of how things worked. Among the assorted bric-a-brac are the possessions and documents of contemporary families, including several fine pieces of furniture, but more than anything else it's the gloomy, warren-like layout of the place that impresses, as well as the all-pervading smell of fish.

Guided tours of the Bryggen

Informative and amusingly anecdotal English-language **guided tours** of the Bryggen start from the Bryggens Museum (see opposite) daily between June and August at 11am and 1pm, and take roughly an hour and a half. Tickets (70kr) are on sale at the museum, and after the tour you can reuse them to get back into the Bryggens and Hanseatic museums as well as the Schøtstuene – but only on the same day.

Just round the corner, the basement of the **Bryggens Museum** (May–Aug daily 10am–5pm; Sept–April Mon–Fri 11am–3pm, Sat noon–3pm, Sun noon–4pm; 30kr) features all manner of things dug up in archeological excavations that started on the Bryggen in 1955. A wide range of artefacts – domestic implements, handicrafts, maritime objects and trade goods – illustrates the city's early history and the whole Hansa caboodle is put into context by a set of twelfth-century foundations, left *in situ* where they were unearthed. The floors above are given over to temporary exhibitions, which explore other aspects of Bergen's past with panache.

Mariakirken and the Schøtstuene

Beside the Bryggens Museum, the perky twin towers of the **Mariakirken** (late May to Aug Mon–Fri 11am–4pm; Sept to late May Tues–Fri noon–1.30pm; late May to Aug 10kr, rest of the year free) are the most distinctive features of what is Bergen's oldest extant building, a Romanesque-Gothic church dating from the twelfth century. Still used as a place of worship, Mariakirken is now firmly Norwegian, but from 1408 to 1706 it was the church of the Hanseatic League merchants. Inside, several of the ecclesiastical bits and pieces exhibited in the nave and choir date from medieval times, most notably the choir's fifteenth-century altar reredos, a gaudy north German triptych with crude depictions of saints and apostles but exquisite framing.

Directly opposite at Øvregaten 50, the **Schøtstuene** (May & Sept daily 11am–2pm; June–Aug daily 10am–5pm; Oct–April Sun 11am–2pm; 40kr, includes Hanseatisk Museum) comprises the old Hanseatic assembly rooms where the merchants would meet to lay down the law or just relax – it was the only building in the trading post whose occupants were allowed to have heating. As you explore the comfortable rooms, it's hard not to conclude that the merchants cared not a jot for their employees shivering away nearby – though, to be fair, the wooden warehouses were a very real fire hazard.

Øvregaten and the Fløibanen funicular railway

Saving the mildly interesting Bergenhus fortress for later (see below), stroll east from the Schøtstuene along **Øvregaten**, an attractive cobbled street which has marked the boundary of the Bryggen for the last 800 years. The Hanseatic warehouses once stretched back from the quayside to this street but no further and in medieval times – despite the fulminations of the Hansa merchants – this was the haunt of the city's prostitutes. From Øvregaten, the old layout of the trading station is still easy to discern, a warren of tiny passages separating warped and crooked buildings. On the upper levels, the eighteenth-century loading bays, staircases and higgledy-piggledy living quarters are still much in evidence, while the overhanging eaves of the passageways were designed to shelter trade goods.

At the far end of Øvregaten, back near the Torget, stands the terminus of the infinitely quaint **Fløibanen** funicular railway (every 30 minutes May–Aug Mon–Fri 7.30am–midnight, Sat 8am–midnight, Sun 9am–midnight; Sept–April Mon–Fri 7.30am–11pm, Sat 8am–11pm, Sun 9am–11pm; 50kr return), which shuttles up to the top of **Mount Fløyen** – "The Vane" – at 320m above sea level. When the weather is fine you get a bird's-eye view of Bergen and its surroundings from the top, where there's also a popular if rather staid café-restaurant. Several well-marked, colour-coded footpaths head off through the woods or you can hoof it back down to the city in about 45 minutes. Walking maps are displayed here and there, or you can pick up a free (and very simple) walking map from the tourist office.

From the funicular, you can either push on along Lille Øvregaten (see p.302) or double back to the Bergenhus.

The Bergenhus

Just to the west of the Bryggens Museum lies the **Bergenhus**, a large and roughly star-shaped fortification now used mostly as a park (daily 7am–11pm). Its thick stone-and-earth walls date from the nineteenth century, but they enclose the remnants of earlier strongholds – or rather their copies: the Bergenhus was wrecked when a German ammunition ship exploded just below the walls in 1944. Of the two main medieval replicas, the more diverting is the **Rosenkrantztårnet** (mid-May to Aug daily 10am–4pm; Sept to mid-May Sun noon–3pm; 20kr), a sturdy stone tower whose thirteenth-century spiral staircases, medieval rooms and low rough corridors make an enjoyable gambol. A doughty exhibition on medieval life occupies the top floor and it's also possible to walk out onto the rooftop battlements, from where there's an attractive view out over the harbour.

Across the cobbled courtyard, flanked by nineteenth-century officers' quarters, is the **Håkonshallen** (mid-May to Aug daily 10am–4pm; Sept to mid-May Mon–Wed & Fri–Sun noon–3pm, Thurs 3–6pm; 20kr), a careful reconstruction of the Gothic ceremonial hall built for King Håkon Håkonsson in the middle of the thirteenth century. Surplus to requirements once Norway lost its independence, no-one knew quite what to do with the capacious hall for several centuries, but it was revamped in 1910 and rebuilt after the 1944 explosion – it's now in use once again for public ceremonies.

From the Bergenhus, it's a five-minute walk back to Torget and the Fløibanen terminal.

Along Lille Øvregaten and Kong Oscars gate to the Leprosy Museum

Lille Øvregaten runs east from the Fløibanen terminal, lined by an appealing mix of expansive nineteenth-century villas and dinky timber houses, all bright-white clapboard planking and tiny windows. Soon it curves round to the **Domkirke** (mid-May to Aug Mon–Sat 11am–5pm, Sun 10am–1pm; Sept to mid-May Tues–Fri 11am–2pm, Sat 11am–3pm, Sun 10am–1pm; free), a solemn edifice whose stern exterior has been restored and rebuilt several times since its original construction in the thirteenth century. Neither does the interior set the pulse racing, but there's a noticeable penchant for fancy wooden staircases – two leading to the organ and one to the pulpit – which seems a little flippant given the dour surroundings.

Just up from the Domkirke at Kong Oscars gate 59, the fascinating **Leprosy Museum** (*Lepramuseet*; late May to Aug daily 11am–3pm; 30kr) is far more promising. This endearingly antiquated collection is housed in the eighteenth-century buildings of **St Jørgens Hospital**, ranged around a charming cobbled courtyard, and tells the tale of the Norwegian fight against leprosy. The disease first appeared in Scandinavia in Viking times and became especially prevalent in the coastal districts of western Norway, with around three percent of the population classified as lepers in the early nineteenth century. St Jørgens specialized in the care of lepers, assuming a more proactive role from 1830, when a series of Norwegian medics tried to find a cure for the disease. The most successful of them was Armauer Hansen, who in 1873 was the first person to identify the leprosy bacillus. The last lepers left St Jørgens in 1946 and the hospital has been left untouched, the small rooms off the central gallery revealing the patients' cramped living quarters. Also on display are medical implements (including cupping glasses for drawing blood) and a few gruesome sketches and paintings of sufferers. Dating from 1702, the adjoining hospital **chapel** is delightful, its rickety, creaking timbers holding a lovely folksy pulpit and altarpiece decorated with cherubs and dainty scrollwork. The two altar paintings are crude but appropriate – *The Ten Lepers* and *Canaanite's Daughter Healed*.

Lungegårdsvann: Bergen's art galleries

Bergen's central lake, **Lille Lungegårdsvann**, is a focus for summertime festivals and events, and its southern side is flanked by the city's four principal art galleries. The first – and the most diverting – of the quartet, working east to west, is the **Bergen Art Museum – the Rasmus Meyer Collection**, Rasmus Meyers Allé 7 (mid-May to mid-Sept daily 11am–5pm; mid-Sept to mid-May Tues–Sun 11am–5pm; 50kr combined ticket with the Art Gallery and the Stenersen Collection), housed in a large building with a pagoda-like roof. Gifted to the city by one of its old merchant families, the collection contains an extensive range of Norwegian painting from early landscape painters like Dahl and Fearnley (see p.239) through Christian Krohg to later figures such as Alex Revold and Henrik Sørensen. It is, however, for its large sample of the work of **Edvard Munch** that the museum is usually visited – if you missed out in Oslo (see p.247), this is the place to make amends. There are examples from all of Munch's major periods, with the disturbing – and disturbed – works of the 1890s stealing the spotlight from the calmer paintings that followed his recovery from the nervous breakdown of 1908. Apart from the paintings, there's also a substantial collection of his woodcuts and lithographs.

Just along the street, the **Bergen Art Gallery** (*Bergen Billedgalleri*; ⊛ www .galleribryggen.no; same times & ticket as Rasmus Meyer) is noted for its temporary exhibitions of contemporary art, whilst the adjacent **Bergen Art Museum – the Stenersen Collection** (⊛ www.bergenartmuseum.no; same times and ticket as Rasmus Meyer) features both changing exhibitions and the modern art collection of Rolf Stenersen. Something of a Renaissance man, Stenersen (1899–1978) – one-time athlete, financier and chum of Munch – seems to have had a successful stab at almost everything; he even wrote some highly acclaimed short stories in the 1930s. In 1936 he donated his first art collection to his home-town of Oslo (see p.247), and 35 years later he was in a similar giving mood, the beneficiary being his adopted town of Bergen. The collection is especially strong on one of Stenersen's favourites, the Bauhaus painter Paul Klee, and there's a smattering of work by more familiar artists too, featuring the likes of Toulouse-Lautrec, Picasso, Miró, Ernst and Léger.

Behind the museums lurks the **Grieghallen** concert hall, an ugly concrete structure that serves as the main venue for the annual Bergen Festival (see p.307).

The westernmost gallery of the four, the **West Norway Applied Art Museum** (*Vestlandske Kunstindustrimuseum*; mid-May to mid-Sept Tues–Sun 11am–4pm; mid-Sept to mid-May Tues-Sun noon–4pm; ⊛ www.vk.museum.no; 40kr), occupies the Permanenten building, a whopping neo-Gothic structure at the corner of Christies gate and Nordahl Bruns gate. A lively exhibition programme with the focus on contemporary craft and design brings in the crowds, and some of the displays are very good indeed – which is more than can be said for the permanent collection and its Chinese marble statues. Fans of Ole Bull (see below) will, however, be keen to gawp at one of the great man's violins, made in 1562 by the Italian Salò.

Torgalmenningen and the Nordnes peninsula

The broad sweep of pedestrianized **Torgalmenningen** is a suitable setting for the commercial heart of modern Bergen, lined with shops and department stores and decorated at its harbour end by a vigorous large-scale sculpture celebrating figures from the city's history. Around the corner, **Ole Bulls plass**, also pedestrianized, sports a rock pool and fountain, above which stands a rather jaunty statue of local boy Ole Bull, the nineteenth-century virtuoso violinist and heart-throb – his island villa just outside Bergen is the target of a popular day-trip. Ole Bulls plass stretches up to the municipal **theatre**, Den Nationale Scene, at the top of the hill, worth the short walk for a look at the fearsome, saucer-eyed statue of Henrik Ibsen that stands in front. Near here too, just down the hill, at the east end of Strandgaten, is the imposing bulk of an old **town gate**, built in 1628 to control access to the city but soon used by the authorities to increase their revenues by the imposition of a toll.

Beyond the theatre, the hilly **Nordnes peninsula** juts out into the fjord, its western tip accommodating the large **Aquarium** (*Akvariet*; May–Sept daily 9am–8pm; Oct–April daily 10am–6pm; ⊛ www.akvariet.com; 80kr; bus #11) and a pleasant park. It takes about fifteen minutes to walk there from Ole Bulls plass – via

Klostergaten/Haugeveien – but the effort is much better spent in choosing a differ-ent, more southerly route along the peninsula. This takes you past the charming timber villas of Skottegaten and Nedre Strangehagen before it cuts through the bluff leading to the old, waterside United Sardines Factory, imaginatively converted into an arts complex, the **Kulturhuset USF** (see p.307), often called Verftet; this incorporates a groovy café-bar, *Kafe Kippers* (see p.306).

❷ Out from the centre - Troldhaugen

The lochs, fjords and rocky wooded hills surrounding central Bergen have chan-nelled the city's **suburbs** into long ribbons that trail off in every direction. These urban outskirts are not in themselves appealing, but tucked away among them is **Troldhaugen** (Hill of the Trolls; May–Sept daily 9am–6pm; Oct & Nov Mon–Fri 10am–2pm, Sat & Sun noon–4pm; mid-Jan to April Mon–Fri 10am–2pm; ⓦwww.troldhaugen.com; 50kr), Edvard Grieg's lakeside home and one of the region's most popular attractions. Located about 7km south of downtown off the E39, it's accessible by public transport (see below), though this is a bit of a pain out-side June to August, and there are organized excursions from Bergen too, from about 250kr. Norway's only composer of world renown, Grieg has a good share of commemorative monuments in Bergen – a statue in the city park, the Grieghallen concert hall – but it's here that you get a sense of the man, an immensely likeable and much-loved figure of leftish opinions and disarming modesty: "I make no pre-tensions of being in the class with Bach, Mozart and Beethoven. Their works are eternal, while I wrote for my day and generation."

A visit begins at the **museum**, where Grieg's life and times are exhaustively chronicled and a short film provides yet further insights. From here, it's a brief walk to the **house**, a pleasant and unassuming villa built in 1885, and still pretty much as Grieg left it, with a jumble of photos, manuscripts and period furniture. Grieg didn't, in fact, compose much at home, but preferred to walk round to a tiny **hut** he had built just along the shore. The hut has survived, but today it stands beside a modern concert hall, the **Troldsalen**, where there are **recitals** of Grieg's works from mid-June through to November. Recital tickets (200kr), covering admission and transport, can be bought from Bergen tourist office.

In summer the **Attractions bus** (see p.297) makes visiting Troldhaugen quick and straightforward, departing from outside the tourist office, amongst several cen-tral locations; tickets and bus route maps from either the driver or the tourist office. Otherwise, go to the city bus station and take any bus leaving from platforms 19, 20 or 21. Get off at the Hopsbroen stop, walk back along the road for about 200m and then turn left up Troldhaugsveien for a stiff and uninteresting twenty-minute walk.

Eating, drinking and nightlife

Bergen has a good supply of **restaurants**, the pick of which focus mostly on seafood – the city's main gastronomic asset. The pricier tourist haunts are concen-trated on the Bryggen, but these should not be dismissed out of hand – several are first-rate. Other, marginally less expensive restaurants dot the side streets behind the Bryggen and the narrow lanes east of Torget, though many locals prefer to eat more economically and informally at the city's **café-bars**. Some of the best of these are in the vicinity of Ole Bulls plass, where you'll also find groovy **cafés** and **bars** – though the distinction between these categories is often very blurred, with both catering for both eaters and drinkers. As regards **opening hours**, the city's restau-rants mostly open daily from 4pm to 10pm or 11pm, though quite a few close one day a week – mostly Sunday – and a minority start at 11am; cafés and bars open much longer, usually daily from 11am to the early hours of the morning.

Entertainment listings (in Norwegian), including club, restaurant and café reviews, are provided by *Natt & Dag* (ⓦwww.nattogdag.no), a free monthly newssheet widely available across the city centre.

305

△ Stavanger

Cafés, coffee houses, bars and café-bars

Aroma Kaffebar Rosenkrantzgaten 1. Specialist coffee house with a good line in lattes and cappuccinos; snacks are available, too. Convivial atmosphere, frugal decor.

Baker Brun Kjøttbasaren. There are several Baker Brun café-bakery franchises in Bergen, but this is probably the best, inside the covered market – the Kjøttbasaren – at the Torget end of the Bryggen. Closed Sun.

Café Opera Engen Vaskerveien 24. Fashionable café-cum-bar in a rickety old wooden building near Ole Bulls plass, serving tasty, filling snacks from as little as 50kr. DJ sounds – mostly house – at weekends.

Det Lille Kaffekompaniet Nedre Fjellsmug 2. Many locals swear by the coffee here, reckoning it to be the best in town. Great selection of teas too, and charming premises – just one medium-sized room in an old wooden building one flight of steps above the funicular terminal.

Dromedar Kaffebar Fosswinkels gate 16. Good coffee, and excellent cheesecake and carrot cake. A student favourite.

Fusion Kaffe & Bar Håkons gaten 27. Snacks, salads, juices and coffees during the day, a busy bar at night. Attached to – and in the same stylistic vein as – the *Soho Restaurant* (see below).

Godt Brød Vestre Torggate 2. Eco-bakery and café (in that order), with great bread and good pastries, plus coffee and made-to-order sandwiches. Also at Nedre Korskirkealmenning 12. Closed Sun.

Kafe Kippers Kulturhuset USF Georgernes Verft ☎55 31 55 70. Part of the city's adventurous contemporary arts complex on the Nordnes peninsula, this laid-back café-bar serves tasty, inexpensive food (the reindeer is especially delicious), lays on occasional barbecues and, with its sea views and terrace, is *the* place to come on a sunny evening, when it's jam-packed. Puts on live music too, notably during its own jazz festival in late May.

Restaurants

Bryggeloftet & Stuene Bryggen ☎55 31 06 30. This restaurant may be a little old-fashioned, but it serves the widest range of seafood in town – delicious, plainly served meals featuring every North Atlantic fish you've ever heard of, and some you might not have heard of at all. Main courses around 190kr.

Enhjørningen Bryggen ☎55 32 79 19. On the second floor of a superbly restored eighteenth-century merchants' house – all low beams and creaking floors – this smart restaurant serves a mouthwatering range of fish and shellfish, with main courses from 220kr. Worth every krone for an indulgent evening out. The buffet lunch (June–Aug only) is a slightly more affordable alternative, with heaps of salmon, prawns and herring, along with salads, hot dishes, bread, cheese and desserts. Closed Sun.

Naboen Restaurant Neumanns gate 20. Easy-going restaurant featuring a lively, inventive menu that includes Swedish specialities and a wide range of fish dishes, including such extravagances as sea bass with blood-orange sauce; the pollack is especially good. Reckon on 170–200kr for a main course. Closed Sun.

Nama Lodin Lepps gate 2B. Behind the Bryggen, this popular sushi and noodle restaurant is a modern affair, crisply decorated with pastel-painted walls and angular furniture. It may be popular, but it's not cheap – each piece of sushi will cost you some 25kr.

På Høyden Fosswinckelsgate 18. Café-restaurant near the Grieghallen with modern decor and a student clientele. Straightforward food – burgers, chicken and so forth – at inexpensive prices. The Greek salad (75kr) is particularly good. Closed Sun.

Pars Sigurdsgate 5. First-rate Persian food in pleasantly kitsch surroundings. A good range of vegetarian dishes – aubergine casserole with rice, for instance, at 90kr; meat dishes are in the region of 130kr. Closed Mon.

Smauet Mat og Vinhus Vaskerelvsmuget, off Ole Bulls plass ☎55 21 07 10. Excellent, smart and fairly formal restaurant offering traditional Norwegian cuisine – including oodles of seafood – plus more exotic dishes like ostrich and antelope. Reckon on 220kr for a main course.

Soho Håkons gaten 27. Chic and ultra-modern restaurant with a creative and flexible menu – from full set meals to a one-course pit stop. Has a great line in traditional Norwegian dishes: try the *klippfisk* (dried and salted fish). Main courses average at 190kr.

To Kokker Bryggen ☎55 32 28 16. Similar to – and metres from – the *Enhjørningen*, but without the buffet. First-class seafood, plus regional dishes – the oven-baked reindeer is a house speciality. Main courses around 230kr. Closed Sun.

Festivals and the performing arts

Bergen takes justifiable pride in its **performing arts**, especially during the **Bergen International Festival** (*Festspillene i Bergen*; ☎55 21 06 30, ⊛www.festspillene.no), held for twelve days at the end of May and presenting an extensive programme of music, ballet, folklore and drama. The principal venue for the festival is the **Grieghallen**, on Lars Hille gate (☎55 21 61 50), where you can pick up programmes, tickets and information, as you can at the tourist office. The city's contemporary arts centre, the **Kulturhuset USF**, down on Georgernes Verft on the Nordnes peninsula (☎55 31 55 70, ⊛www.kulturhuset-usf.no), contributes to the festival by hosting **Nattjazz** (☎55 30 72 50, ⊛www.nattjazz.no), a prestigious and long-established international jazz festival held over the same period. The International Festival is the main player in the wide-ranging programme of cultural events that are tabulated and promoted by the tourist office in their **Sommer Bergen** leaflet and website (⊛www.sommerbergen.no). Part of this summer programme is devoted to **folk music** and **folk events** – singing, dancing and costumed goings-on of all kinds. Catch folk dancing at either the Bryggens Museum (mid-June to late Aug, once weekly at 9pm; 95kr) or at **Fana Folklore**'s "country festivals" (☎55 91 52 40), a mix of Norwegian music, food and dancing held on a private estate outside the city. These take place at 7pm several times a week from June to August and cost 260kr per person, including meal and transport; tickets from hotels and Fløio, Torgalmenning 9. There are also **chamber music and organ recitals** at the Mariakirken in June, July and August, and **Grieg recitals** at Grieg's home, Troldhaugen, from mid-June to October.

Out of summer, the Kulturhuset (see above) puts on an ambitious programme of concerts, art-house films and contemporary plays; the **Bergen Philharmonic** performs regularly in the Grieghallen from September to May (☎55 21 61 00, ⊛www.harmonien.no); and Bergen's main **theatre**, Den Nationale Scene, Engen (☎55 54 97 10; Sept–June only), offers performances on three stages. Most productions are, of course, in Norwegian, but there are occasional appearances by English-speaking troupes. Finally, Bergen has one large city-centre **cinema**, Bergen Kino, Konsertpaleet, Neumannsgate 3 (☎82 05 00 05), a five-minute walk south of Ole Bulls plass. Predictably, American films rule the roost, so English speakers are at an advantage. **Entertainment listings** (in Norwegian) are provided in *Natt & Dag* (⊛www.nattogdag.no), a free monthly newssheet widely available across the city centre.

Listings

Airlines Braathens, Bergen airport ☎81 52 00 00; SAS, Bergen airport ☎81 00 33 00.

Bookshop Norli, Torgalmenningen 7, right in the city centre (Mon–Fri 9am–8pm, Sat 9am–4pm), is easily the best bookshop in town, with a wide range of English books and French, German and Spanish titles, too. The travel section is especially good and the staff extremely helpful. Very competitive prices also.

Bus enquiries Timetable information on ☎177.

Car rental Hertz, Nygårdsgaten 89 ☎55 96 40 70; Avis, Lars Hilles gate 20B ☎55 55 39 55. At the airport, there's Statoil Bilutleie ☎55 99 14 90; and Budget ☎55 14 39 00.

Emergencies Ambulance ☎113, Fire ☎110, Police ☎112.

Exchange The main post office (see p.308) offers competitive exchange rates for foreign currency and traveller's cheques, with longer opening hours (Mon–Fri 8am–6pm, Sat 9am–3pm) than those of banks. The tourist office will also change foreign currency and traveller's cheques but their rates are poor, as are rates at the city's big hotels. There are ATMs dotted all over the city centre.

Ferries: Domestic: Hurtigbåt passenger express boats depart from the Strandkaiterminalen. The principal operators are HSD (south to Haugesund & Stavanger; north to Hardangerfjord; ☎55 23 87 80) and FSF (Sognefjord & Nordfjord; ☎55 90 70 70). The Hurtigrute coastal boat (☎81 03 00 00, ⊛www.hurtigruten.com) sails daily at 8pm from the Frieleneskaien on the southern edge of the city centre, about 1500m from the train station. Tickets from local travel agents or the operator.

Ferries: International: Fjord Line, Skoltegrunnskaien (℡81 53 35 00, ⓦwww.fjordline.no), operates a car ferry service to Haugesund, Stavanger and Newcastle, and another to Egersund and Hantsholm in Denmark; Smyril Line, Slottsgaten 1 (℡55 32 09 70, ⓦwww.smyril-line.fo), has car-ferry sailings from the Skoltegrunnskaien to Shetland, the Faroes and Iceland.

Hiking The DNT-affiliated Bergen Turlag, Tverrgaten 4–6 (Mon–Wed & Fri 10am–4pm, Thurs 10am–6pm; ℡55 32 22 30), will advise on hiking trails in the region, sells hiking maps and arranges guided weekend walks.

Internet The Cyberhouse Internet Café (℡55 36 66 16, ⓦwww.cyberhouse.no), just 30m below the funicular at Vetrlidsalmenning 30, has lots of terminals and is open every day and till late at night.

Laundry Coin operated and service wash at Jarlens Vaskoteque, Lille Øvregate 17, near the funicular (℡55 32 55 04).

Pharmacy Apotekel Nordstjernen, at the bus station (Mon–Sat 8am–midnight, Sun 9.30am–midnight; ℡55 21 83 84).

Post office Main post office on Olav Kyrres gate at the corner of Rådhusgaten (Mon–Fri 8am–6pm, Sat 9am–3pm).

Taxi Bergen Taxi ℡07000.

Trains National timetable information on ℡81 50 08 88.

Vinmonopolet Bergen Storsenter, Strømgarten.

The western fjords

Heading out from Bergen, the western fjords beckon. The most popular initial target is the **Hardangerfjord**, a delightful and comparatively gentle introduction to the wilder fjords that lie beyond. Also popular is **Voss**, inland perhaps, but still a sports centre of some renown, and a useful halfway house en route to **Flåm**, draped beside the **Aurlandsfjord** and at the end of a spectacularly exciting train ride down the valley from Myrdal. Nonetheless, scenic as all this is, it's the **Sognefjord**, further to the north, that captivates most visitors, its stirring beauty amplified by its sheer size, stretching inland from the coast for some 200km. Beyond, and running parallel, lies the **Nordfjord**, smaller at 120km long and less intrinsically enticing, though its surroundings are more varied with patches of the **Jostedalsbreen glacier** visible and visitable nearby. From here, it's another short journey to the splendid **Geirangerfjord** – narrow, sheer and rugged – whilst, hopping over a mountain range or two, the town of **Åndalsnes** boasts an exquisite setting with rearing peaks behind and the tentacular Romsdalsfjord in front. At the west end of the Romsdalsfjord is the region's prettiest town, **Ålesund**, whose centre is liberally sprinkled with charming Art Nouveau buildings – courtesy of Kaiser Bill.

This is not a landscape to be hurried – there's little point in dashing from fjord to fjord. Stay put at least for a while, go for at least one hike or cycle ride, and you'll really appreciate the western fjords in all their grandeur. The sheer size is breathtaking – but then the geological movements that shaped them were on a grand scale. During the Ice Age, around three million years ago, the whole of Scandinavia was covered in ice, the weight of which pushed the bottom of what would become the fjords down to depths well below that of the ocean floor – the Sognefjord, for example, descends to 1250m, ten times deeper than most of the Norwegian Sea. Later, as the ice retreated, it left huge coastal basins that filled with seawater to become the fjords, which the warm Gulf Stream keeps free of ice.

Where to stay in the fjords
Bergen advertises itself as "Capital of the Fjords", and the tourist office does organize a barrage of excursions from the city. These are an expensive option, however, since most can be done independently and far more cheaply. Also, as Bergen is in fact on the western edge of the fjords, the bulk of the day-trips from here involve too much travelling for comfort. This is doubly true as the main road east from Bergen – the E16 – is prone to congestion and possesses over twenty tunnels, many of which are horribly noxious. Avoid the E16 east of Bergen if you can, and cer-

tainly aim to branch off onto the relatively tunnel-free and much more scenic **Hwy 7** the first chance you get – about 30km east of the city. For all these reasons, one of the small towns that dot the fjords are far better as a base than Bergen, especially as distances once you're actually amidst the fjords are – at least by Norwegian standards – quite modest. In the Hardangerfjord, **Ulvik** and **Lofthus** are the most appealing bases, Sognefjord has **Mundal** and **Balestrand**, while further north **Loen**, **Åndalsnes** and **Ålesund** all have their advantages.

Getting around the fjords

The convoluted topography of the western fjords has produced a dense and complex **public transport** system that is designed to reach all the larger villages and towns at least once every weekday, whether by train, bus, ferry, Hurtigrute coastal boat or Hurtigbåt express passenger boat. By **train**, you can reach Bergen and Flåm in the south and Åndalsnes in the north. For everything in between – the Nordfjord, Jostedalsbreen glacier and Sognefjord – you're confined to buses and ferries, and although virtually all services connect up with each other, it means that there is no set way of reaching or exploring the fjord region. General travel details for this chapter are given on p.398, and in the text itself we've included local connections where they are especially useful; this information should be used in conjunction with the timetables that are widely available across the region. Bear in mind also that although there may be a transport connection to the town or village you want to go to, many Norwegian settlements are scattered and you may be in for a long walk after you've arrived – a particularly dispiriting experience if it's raining.

We've covered the region **south to north** – from the Hardangerfjord to Sognefjord, Nordfjord, Geirangerfjord, Åndalsnes and Ålesund. There are certain obvious connections – from Bergen to Flåm, and from Geiranger over the Trollstigen to Åndalsnes, for example – but routes are really a matter of personal choice; the text lists the options. It's a good idea to pick up full **bus and ferry timetables** from the local tourist offices whenever you can. The shorter bus routes are often part of a longer chain of linked buses and ferries, so you shouldn't get stranded anywhere.

The Hardangerfjord

To the east of Bergen, the obvious initial target is the 100-kilometre **Hardangerfjord**, whose wide waters are overlooked by a rough, craggy shoreline and a scattering of tiny settlements. At its eastern end the Hardanger divides into several lesser fjords, and it's here you'll find the district's most appealing villages,

---

Fjord ferries

Throughout the text there are numerous mentions of fjord **car ferries** and **Hurtigbåt passenger express boats**. The details given in parentheses concern the frequency of operation and the duration of the crossing: for example (hourly; 45min). Hurtigbåt services are usually fairly infrequent – three a day at most – whereas many car ferries shuttle back and forth every hour or two from around 7am in the morning until 10pm at night every day of the week; we've given times of operation where they are either different from the norm or particularly useful. **Hurtigbåt fares** are fixed individually with prices starting at around 100kr for every hour travelled: the four-hour trip from Bergen to Balestrand, for example, will cost you around 400kr. ScanRail and InterRail pass holders (see pp.21 & 32) are often entitled to discounts of up to fifty percent, and on some routes there are special excursion deals – always ask. **Car ferry fares**, on the other hand, are priced according to a nationally agreed sliding scale, with ten-minute crossings running at around 17kr per person and 41kr per car and driver, 19kr and 49kr respectively for a twenty-five minute trip.

Utne, **Lofthus** and **Ulvik**, each of which has an attractive fjordside setting and at least one especially good place to stay. To the east of these tributary fjords rises the **Hardangervidda**, a mountain plateau of remarkable, lunar-like beauty and a favourite with Norwegian hikers. The plateau can be reached from almost any direction, but one favourite starting point is **Kinsarvik**.

Of the two principal **car ferries** negotiating the Hardangerfjord, one shuttles in triangular fashion between Kvanndal, Utne and Kinsarvik, the other links Brimnes with Bruravik. There are no trains in the Hardangerfjord area but **buses** are fairly frequent, allowing you to savour the scenery and get to the three recommended villages without too much difficulty, except possibly on Sundays when services are reduced. Finally, if you're planning to travel south down Highway 13 from Kinsarvik bound for either Stavanger or Oslo, be sure your itinerary does not involve an overnight stay at the eminently missable zinc-producing and iron-smelting town of **Odda**, at the head of the Sørfjord.

East from Bergen to Norheimsund and the Kvanndal ferry

Heading east from Bergen by bus or car along the **E16** bound for the Hardangerfjord, the road first has to clear a string of polluted tunnels, an unpleasant 30km journey before you can fork off along **Highway 7**. By contrast, Hwy 7 is a rattling trip, with the road twisting up over the mountains and down the valleys, gliding past thundering waterfalls and around tight bends before racing down to **NORHEIMSUND** on the Hardangerfjord. A small-time port and furniture-making town, Norheimsund makes a gallant effort to bill itself as the gateway to the fjords, but in truth it's a very modest little place and there's precious reason to hang around: like many fjord settlements, it's the travel in between that is the real attraction. Norheimsund does, however, have its uses as a minor transport hub, principally for its Hurtigbåt passenger express boat service to Utne, Kinsarvik, Lofthus, Ulvik and Eidfjord.

Leaving Norheimsund by road, Highway 7 sticks to the rugged shoreline as it travels east to the ferry dock at **Kvanndal**, another pleasant journey with every turning bringing fresh mountain and fjord views as the Hardangerfjord begins to split into its various subsidiaries. There's a choice of routes from Kvanndal: you can either press on down the northern shore of the Hardangerfjord towards Ulvik and ultimately Voss (see pp.313 and 314), or take the Kvanndal **ferry** over to Utne and/or Kinsarvik (1 or 2 hourly; 20min/50min).

Utne

The tiny hamlet of **UTNE**, the Kvanndal ferry's midway point, occupies a splendid location, its huddle of houses overlooking the fjord from the tip of the rearing peninsula that divides the Hardangerfjord from the slender Sørfjord. Utne was long reliant on the orchards that still trail along the Sørfjord's sheltered slopes, its inhabitants making enough of a living to support themselves in some comfort, especially when supplemented by fishing and furniture-making: the brightly painted furniture that once haled from the district made a popular export. Classic examples of this furniture are on display in the delightful *Utne Hotel* (☎53 66 10 88, ⓔkildehot @online.no; ❹), whose twenty-four rooms, mostly en suite, occupy an immaculately maintained old clapboard complex metres from the ferry dock. It's a lovely place – family-owned and very relaxing – and the food, traditional Norwegian cuisine at its best, is top-notch too, served amidst the ancient panelling of the dining room.

Utne's heritage is celebrated at the **Hardanger Folkemuseum** (May, June & Aug Mon–Fri 10am–3pm, Sun noon–4pm; July Mon–Sat 10am–6pm, Sun noon–4pm; Sept–April Mon–Fri 10am–3pm; 40kr; ⓦwww.hardanger.museum.no), a five-minute walk along the fjord from the hotel. One of the largest and best-appointed folk museums in the region, it begins inside with an assortment of displays on various aspects of traditional Hardanger life, from fishing and farming through to fruit growing and trade. There's also a large display on local **folk costume** – the women's headdresses hereabouts were amongst the most elaborate in Norway and a popular subject for the romantic painters of the nineteenth century, notably Adolph Tidemand and Hans Frederik Gude. Outside, an assortment of old wooden buildings – farmhouses, cottages, store houses and so forth – rambles over the hillside in an **open-air section** whose logic is hard to fathom, though in summertime things make much more sense when there are demonstrations of farming and craft skills in and around them.

Kinsarvik and Lofthus

From Utne, the car ferry (every 1–2hr; 30min) bobs over the mouth of the Sørfjord to **KINSARVIK**, a humdrum little town which was once an important Viking marketplace. The Vikings stored their boats in the loft of the town's sturdy stone church (May–Aug daily 10am–7pm; free), though the building was clumsily restored in the 1880s, leaving only hints of its previous appearance, most notably a series of faint chalk wall paintings dating from the thirteenth century. Kinsarvik also lies at the mouth of the forested **Husedalen valley**, with its four crashing waterfalls. The valley makes an enjoyable hike in itself, though it's mostly used as an access route up to the Hardangervidda plateau. From Kinsarvik, it takes seven hours to reach the nearest DNT hut, the self-service **Stavali**, but be warned that the going is very steep and, in rainy conditions, intermittently very slippery. Hiking maps can be purchased at Kinsarvik **tourist office**, near the ferry jetty (early & mid-May Mon–Fri 9am–3pm; late May to late June & late Aug to late Sept Mon–Fri 9am–5pm; late June to late August daily 9am–7pm; ☎53 66 31 12). Nearby Lofthus is a lot more enticing, but Kinsarvik does have a couple of places with the obvious choice being the *Best Western Kinsarvik Fjord Hotel* (☎53 66 31 00, ⓦwww.kinsarvikfjordhotel.no; ❺/❻), which occupies a large and reasonably attractive ivy-clad modern block by the ferry dock.

Lofthus

Draped beside the Sørfjord 11km to the south of Kinsarvik, with the Folgefonna glacier glinting in the distance, **LOFTHUS** is an idyllic hamlet of narrow lanes and mellow stone walls, where a scattering of old grass-roofed houses sits among the orchards, pinky-white with blossom in the springtime. It's the overall impression which counts, though the church (May to Aug daily 10am–7pm; free), dating from 1250, is a good-looking stone structure with immensely thick walls and several bright but crude wall and wood paintings on the walls and the supporting timbers. A stream gushes through the village, tumbling down the steep escarpment behind it to bubble past the delightful *Ullensvang Gjesteheim* (☎53 66 12 36, ⓔullensvang .gjesteheim@c2i.net; ❸), a huddle of antique timber buildings with thirteen cosy and unassuming rooms – and great food. Another option is the modern, plush but much less distinctive *Hotel Ullensvang* (☎53 67 00 00, ⓦwww.hotel-ullensvang.no; ❼/❺), a massive, solitary affair plonked on the water's edge 1km to the north of Lofthus. As at Kinsarvik, a steep **hiking trail** leads up from Lofthus to the Hardangervidda plateau. It takes about four hours to reach the plateau at Nosi (950 metres above sea level) and part of the trail – at 650–700 metres – includes the **Munketreppene**, stone steps laid by the monks who farmed this remote area in medieval times. You can also hike up to the Stavali self-service DNT hut, a trek which takes about seven or eight hours.

North to Eidfjord

Heading north from Kinsarvik, **Highway 13** fidgets along the coastline to reach, after 19km, Brimnes, where a **car ferry** (1–2 hourly; 10min) shuttles over the fjord to Bruravik, for Ulvik (see p.313) and Voss (see p.314). Beyond Brimnes, Highway 13 becomes **Highway 7**, whose first significant port of call, after another 11km, is the village of **EIDFJORD**, which straggles over a narrow and hilly neck of land in between the fjord and a large and deep lake, the Eidfjordvatnet. There's been a settlement here since prehistoric times and for centuries the village prospered as a trading centre at the end of one of the main routes over the Hardangervidda – though this was a two-edged sword: from the seventeenth until the mid-nineteenth century, the villagers were obliged to build and repair foot and cart tracks up to the plateau, forced labour for which they weren't paid. Nowadays, Eidfjord and its environs rustle up a couple of good attractions, beginning with the **Hardangervidda Natursenter** in the village itself (daily: April–May & Sept–Oct 10am–6pm, June–Aug 9am–8pm; 70kr), whose displays focus on the plateau's natural history and geology. Secondly, a byroad leads northeast from Eidfjord up the **Simdal valley** to reach, after about 6km, the tortuous turning that wriggles up to the **Kjeåsen mountain farm**, a lonely complex of old farm buildings from where there are wondrous views over the Simadalsfjord rippling way down below. The road is much too narrow to take two-way traffic, but drivers can relax (a little) – you can only drive up to the farm on the hour and descend on the half hour.

The best hotel hereabouts is the *Eidfjord Hotell* (☎53 66 52 64, ☻www.eidfjordhotel .no; ❹), a crisply designed, medium-sized modern place with tastefully furnished rooms that perches on a knoll high above the Eidfjord. The **restaurant** is very good here, too. In addition, the village **tourist office** (late June & late Aug Mon–Sat 9am–6pm; July to mid-Aug Mon–Fri 9am–8pm, Sat 9am–6pm & Sun 11am–8pm; Sept to mid-June Mon–Fri 8.30am–4pm; ☎53 67 34 00, ☻www.eidfjordinfo.com/ index_n.asp) has the details of a handful of **private rooms** as well as a veritable raft of information on the area as a whole.

Heading east from Eidfjord, Highway 7 weaves and tunnels its way up to the Hardangervidda, the first part of its journey to Geilo. En route, it passes the Hardangervidda hiking bases of Dyranut and Halne.

The Hardangervidda plateau

The **Hardangervidda** is Europe's largest mountain plateau, occupying a one-hundred-dred-square-kilometre slab of land east of the Hardangerfjord and south of the Oslo–Bergen railway. The plateau is characterized by rolling fells and wide stretches of level ground, its rocky surfaces strewn with pools, ponds, lakelets and rivers. The whole plateau is above the treeline, and at times has an almost lunar-like appearance, although even within this elemental landscape there are variations. To the north, in the vicinity of Finse, there are mountains and a glacier, the **Hardangerjøkulen**, while the west is wetter – and the flora somewhat richer – than the barer moorland to the east. The lichen that covers the rocks is savoured by herds of reindeer, who leave their winter grazing lands on the east side of the plateau in the spring, chewing their way west to their breeding grounds before returning east again after the autumn rutting season.

Stone Age hunters once followed the reindeer on their migrations and traces of their presence – arrowheads, pit-traps, etc – have been discovered over much of the plateau. Later, the Hardangervidda became one of the main crossing points between east and west Norway, with horse traders, cattle drivers and Danish dignitaries all cutting across along cairned paths. These are often still in use as part of a dense network of trails and tourist huts that has been developed by several DNT affiliates in recent decades. Roughly one third of the plateau has been incorporated within the **Hardangervidda National Park**, but much of the rest is protected too, so hikers won't notice a deal of difference between the park and its immediate surroundings. The entire plateau is also popular for winter cross-country hut-to-hut ski touring. Many hikers and skiers are content with a day on the Hardangervidda, but some find the wide-skied, lichen-dappled scenery particularly enchanting and travel from one end of the plateau to the other, a seven- or eight-day expedition.

In terms of **access**, the Oslo–Bergen **train** line cuts across the northern edge of the plateau, calling at Finse train station, from where hikers and skiers head off across the plateau in all directions. Finse is not, however, accessible by road, so motorists (and bus travellers) use **Highway 7**, which runs across the plateau between **Eidfjord** (see p.312) and **Geilo**. There's precious little in the way of human habitation on this lonely 100km-long stretch of road, but you can pick up the plateau's hiking trails easily enough at several points. **Dyranut** and **Halne** are two such places, respectively 39km and 47km from Eidfjord. Some hikers prefer to walk eastwards onto the Hardangervidda from Kinsarvik and Lofthus (see p.311), but this does involve an arduous day-long trek up to the plateau from the fjord.

Ulvik

Tucked away in a snug corner of the Hardangerfjord, the pocket-sized village of **ULVIK** strings prettily along the shoreline, with orchards dusting the green hills behind. There's nothing specific to see – the town's main claim to fame as the place where potatoes were first grown in Norway in 1765 just about sums things up – but it's an excellent place to unwind, a popular little resort with a cluster of good hotels. **Hiking trails** lattice the rough uplands to the north of Ulvik and explore the surrounding shoreline. Indeed the local council have gone to some trouble here in their "kulturlandskapsplan" (culture landscape plan), in which four designated areas incorporate both footpaths and historic sights, most enjoyably the **Ljonakleiv crofter's farm** in the hills above the village; hiking maps are available at the tourist office (see below).

Practicalities

Ulvik is off the main **bus** routes, but there are regular local buses here from Voss (Mon–Sat 2–5 daily, Sun 1 daily; 1hr). These are routed via Bruravik to pick up passengers on the Brimnes–Bruravik ferry, coming from the likes of Odda, Lofthus, Kinsarvik and Eidfjord (1–4 daily). There are also **Hurtigbåt passenger express boat** services to Ulvik from Norheimsund via Kinsarvik, Lofthus (1 daily; 2hr 10min). Buses pull into the centre of the village, metres from the jetty, from where it's a couple of minutes' walk along the waterfront to the **tourist office** (late May to late Sept Mon–Sat 8.30am–5pm, Sun 1–5pm; late Sept to late May Mon–Fri 8.30am–1.30pm; ☎56 52 63 60, ⊕www.ulvik.org/ulvikinfo). Staff issue all the usual information, including bus and ferry timetables, sell detailed hiking maps and rent out bikes (150kr per day).

Among the **hotels**, the big deal hereabouts is the *Rica Brakenes* (☎56 52 61 05, ⊕www.brakanes-hotel.no; ❻/❹), a large and luxurious modern hotel occupying a lovely fjordside location in the centre of the village. If the *Brakenes* is a bit too big and domineering for your liking, the *Rica Ulvik* (☎56 52 62 00, ⊕www.rica.no; ❺/❹), five minutes' walk east along the waterfront, is a good deal less overpowering. Again, it's the setting rather than the architecture that appeals, with the fjord stretching out in front of the hotel, overlooked by the balconies of the fifty-odd modern bedrooms. Different again is the *Ulvik Fjord Pensjonat* (☎56 52 61 70, ☎56 52 61 60; ❹; May to late Sept), a well-maintained and appealing **guesthouse** situated a ten-minute walk west from the centre along the waterfront. The rooms in the main building are plain but comfortable, and there's a modern annexe, too. Breakfasts are first-rate and evening meals are available by prior arrangement. Otherwise, **eat** at either of the *Rica* hotels – the *Ulvik* edges the other in terms of price and informality.

Voss

Travelling east from Bergen on either the E16 or the train, it's an enjoyable 100km jaunt over the hills and round the mountains to **VOSS**, which boasts an attractive lakeside setting and a splendid thirteenth-century church. Voss is, however, best known as an adventure sports and winter skiing centre, with everything from skiing and snowboarding through to summertime rafting, kayaking and horse riding. Consequently, unless you're here for a sweat, your best bet is to have a quick look round and then move on, though there is a caveat: Voss is the ideal base for a **day trip by train** east up the Raun Valley, an especially scenic part of the Bergen–Oslo rail line. The most popular target on this stretch of the line is the Myrdal junction, where you change for the dramatic train ride down to Flåm (see box on p.316).

The town

With the lake on one side and the River Vosso on the other, **Voss** has long been a trading centre on one of the main routes between west and east Norway – though you'd barely guess this from the modern appearance of the town centre. In 1023, King Olav visited to check that the population had all converted to Christianity, and stuck a big stone cross here to make his point. Two centuries later another king, Magnus Lagabøte, built a church in Voss to act as the religious focal point for the whole region. The church, the **Vangskyrkja** (mid-May to mid-Sept Mon–Sat 10am–4pm, Sun 2–5pm; 15kr), still stands, its eccentric octagonal spire rising above stone walls which are up to two metres thick. The interior is splendid, a surprisingly flamboyant and colourful affair with a Baroque reredos and a folksy rood screen showing a crucified Jesus attended by two cherubs. The ceiling is even more unusual, its timbers painted in 1696 with a cotton-wool cloudy sky inhabited by flying angels – and the nearer you approach the high altar, the more of them there are. That's pretty much it as far as specific sights go, though you could take a stroll along the leafy Prestegardsalléen footpath, which heads south along the shore of **Vangsvatnet** lake from opposite the church; or wander the central shops and cafés – if you've come from the hamlets and villages further north, the shopping might seem something of a treat.

Practicalities

Buses stop outside the **train station** at the western end of the town centre. From the train station, it's a five-minute walk to the **tourist office** (June–Aug Mon–Sat 9am–7pm, Sun 2–7pm; Sept–May Mon–Fri 9am–4pm; ☎56 52 08 00, ⊛www .visitvoss.no) on the main street, Uttrågata – veer right round the Vangskyrkja church and it's on the right. There's oodles of information on hiking, rafting, skiing and local touring, the bones of which are detailed in the free *Voss Guide*.

To cater for all the visiting sportsfolk, Voss has lots of inexpensive **accommodation**, from guesthouses through to camping. The best budget bet is the excellent HI **hostel**, *Voss Vandrerhjem* (☎56 51 20 17, ⒺVoss.hostel@vandrerhjem.no; Feb to mid-Nov), which has both double rooms (❷) and dorms, and is sited in a modern chalet/lodge complex overlooking the water about 700m from the train station. To get there, turn right outside the station building and head along the lake away from the town centre – a ten-minute walk. The hostel serves large, inexpensive evening meals and good breakfasts, has its own sauna, laundry, Internet access and a kitchen for guests to use; it also rents out bikes and canoes. Advance booking is strongly recommended. The pick of the town's **guesthouses** is the *Kringsjå Pensjonat* (☎56 51 16 27, ⊛www.kringsjaa.no; ❷), just to the north of – and up above – the town centre and the railway line on Strengjarhaugen. The seventeen rooms here are themselves plain and straightforward, but the public areas are bright, cheerful and modern; the dining room offers tasty Norwegian food and pleasing views over Voss – again, advance booking is recommended. A third budget option is the rudimentary

Voss sports

Every summer, hundreds of Norwegians make a beeline for Voss on account of its **watersports**. The rivers near the town offer a wide range of conditions, suitable for everything from a quiet paddle to a finger-chewing whitewater ride. There are several operators, but **Voss Rafting Senter** (☎56 51 05 25, ⊛www.vossrafting.no) set the benchmark. Their four-hour whitewater rafting trips venture out onto three rivers – the relatively placid Vosso and the much rougher Stranda and Raundalen; the price, including swimming test and a snack, is 650kr, 690kr on Saturdays. Other options with the same operator and at about the same price include river-boarding (5hr), sports rafting, which is akin to canoeing (4hr), and whitewater rappelling (4hr). In addition, Nordic Ventures (☎56 51 00 17, ⊛www.nordicventures.com) offers all sorts of **kayaking** excursions as well as **tandem paragliding**; Voss Fallskjermklubb (☎56 51 10 00, ⊛www.skydivevoss.no) does **parachuting**; and Stølsheimen Fjellridning (☎56 51 91 66, ⊛www.engjaland.no) specializes in mountain **horseback riding**.

Skiing in Voss starts in late November and continues until mid-April – nothing fancy, but good for an enjoyable few days. From behind and above the train station, a **cable car** – the Hangursbanen – climbs 700m to give access to several short runs as well as the first of three chair lifts which take you up another 300m. A one-day lift pass costs 240kr (200kr per half-day), and in January and February some trails are floodlit. There's a choice of red, green and blue downhill ski routes, and amongst the latter is a long and fairly gentle route through the hills above town. Full **equipment** for both downhill and cross-country skiing can be rented for 200–300kr per day from Voss Skiskule & Skiutlege, at the upper Hangursbanen station (☎56 51 00 32). They also offer lessons in skiing and snowboarding techniques.

Voss Camping (☎56 51 15 97), located a short walk south of the Vangskyrkja church – turn left from the train station, take the right fork at the church and then turn right again, along the Prestegardsalléen footpath. It's open all year round and has a few cabins (❷), bicycle and boat rental, and washing machines. As for the town's **hotels**, one or two barely pass muster: easily the best bet is *Fleischer's* (☎56 52 05 00, ⊛www.fleischers.no; ❻), next door to the train station. Dating from the 1880s, the hotel's high-gabled and towered facade overlooks the lake and consists of the original building and a modern wing built in the same style. Parts of the hotel – and many of the bedrooms – have the whiff of real luxury, but others can seem a little downmarket and jaded – further renovations are planned. The hotel **restaurant** serves the best food in town and there's a terrace bar as well. Their all-inclusive food-and-lodging deals offer substantial savings on the normal rate.

North to Flåm

Heading north along the E16 from Voss, it's a short, scenic hop to **Flåm**, one of the region's most visited villages and justifiably famous for its railway. Flåm is an excellent base for further explorations, whether it be the train ride up to – or down from – Myrdal, the ferry trip up along the **Nærøyfjord** or a day-long hike in the surrounding mountains. Nearing Flåm you'll pass through two spirited pieces of tunnelling, with stretches of 11km and 5km bored through the mountainside at colossal expense. However, these are but pip-squeaks when compared with the newly completed 24-kilometre-long **tunnel** that links Aurlandsdal – from a point just east of Flåm – with Lærdal and, more importantly, completes the fast road, the E16, from Bergen to Oslo. Even better, it's free.

As for public transport, **express buses** (2–6 daily) scuttle north from Voss bound for Flåm and ultimately Sogndal. Eastbound **trains** from Voss stop at Myrdal, where you change for the branch line down to Flåm.

Flåm and the Nærøyfjord

Fringed by meadows and orchards, **FLÅM** village sits beside the Aurlandsfjord, a slender branch of the Sognefjord (see opposite), with the mountains glowering behind. It's a splendid setting, but initially you could still be excused for wondering why you bothered coming here. The fjordside complex adjoining the train station is crass and commercial – souvenir trolls and the like   and on summer days the tiny village heaves with tourists, who pour off the train, have lunch, and then promptly head out by bus and ferry. But a brief stroll is enough to leave the crowds behind at the harbourside, while out of season or in the evenings when the day-trippers have all moved on, Flåm is a pleasant spot – and an eminently agreeable place to spend the night. If you're prepared to risk the weather, mid-September is perhaps the best time to visit; the peaks already have a covering of snow and the vegetation is just turning its autumnal golden brown.

Flåm is the starting point for one of the most stupendous **ferry trips** in the fjords, the two-hour cruise up the Aurlandsfjord and down its narrow offshoot, the **Nærøyfjord** (1–4 daily; 170kr single, 210kr return). With high rock faces keeping out the sun throughout the winter, Nærøyfjord is the narrowest fjord in Europe, and its stern beauty makes for a magnificent excursion.

Practicalities

Flåm's harbourside complex may be ugly, but it is convenient, holding a supermarket, a train ticket office and the **tourist office** (daily: May, June & Sept 8.30am–3.30pm & 4–8pm; July–Aug 8.30am–8pm; ☎57 63 21 06, ⊛www.visitflam .com), where you can pick up a very useful free booklet on Aurland, Flåm and Lærdal, which includes public transport timetables as well as all sorts of local information. Staff also provide hiking hints, sell hiking maps and will purchase fjord ferry tickets on your behalf. If you do decide to stay, neat and trim *Flåm Camping*, a couple of minutes' signposted walk from the train station, has tent spaces and cabins (**❶**). It also incorporates a small and well-kept HI **hostel** (May–Sept; ☎57 63 21 21, ✉flaam.hostel@vandrerhjem.no), which has inexpensive double rooms (**❷**) as well as dorms. Alternatively, the *Heimly Pensjonat* (☎57 63 23 00, ☎57 63 23 40; **❸/❹**) provides simple but adequate lodgings in a mundane, modern block that overlooks the fjord, about 450m east of the train station along the shore. Set back

---

The Flåm railway – the Flåmsbana

Lonely **Myrdal**, just forty minutes by train from Voss, is the start of one of Europe's most celebrated branch rail lines, the **Flåmsbana** (⊛www.flaamsbana.no), a twenty-kilometre, 900-metre plummet down the Flåmsdal valley to **Flåm** – a fifty-minute train ride not to be missed under any circumstances. The track, which took four years to lay in the 1920s, spirals down the mountainside, passing through hand-dug tunnels and, at one point, actually travelling through a hairpin tunnel to drop nearly 300m. The gradient of the line is one of the steepest anywhere in the world and as the tiny train squeals its way down the mountain, past cascading waterfalls, it's reassuring to know that it has five separate sets of brakes, each capable of bringing it to a stop. The service runs all year round, a local lifeline during the deep winter months. There are ten departures daily from mid-June to mid-September, four the rest of the year; fares are 125kr single, 205kr return.

In the past, the athletic have risen to the challenge and undertaken the five-hour **walk** from the railway junction at Myrdal down the old road into the valley, instead of taking the train, but much the better option is to disembark about halfway down and walk in from there. **Berekvam** station, at an altitude of 343m, will do very nicely, leaving an enthralling two- to three-hour hike through changing mountain scenery down to Flåm. **Cycling** down the valley road is also perfectly feasible, though it's too steep to be relaxing.

From Flåm, there are daily **Hurtigbåt passenger express boat** services up the Aurlandsfjord and along the Sognefjord to Balestrand and Bergen. The one-way trip to Bergen takes five-and-a-half hours and costs 490kr; Balestrand is an hour and a half away and costs 140kr. By **train**, Myrdal, at the top of the Flåmsbana, is on the main Oslo–Bergen line, while Sognebussen **express buses** pass through Flåm bound for a variety of destinations, including Bergen, Voss and Sogndal (2–6 daily). Heading east by car, it's tempting to use the brand new free tunnel to Lærdal, but the 45km-long **mountain road** that the tunnel replaced has survived to provide splendid views and some hair-raising moments.

from the water a couple of hundred metres from the station, Flåm's only **hotel** is the *Fretheim* (☎57 63 63 00, ⍟www.fretheim-hotel.no; ❺), a rambling structure whose attractive older part, with high-pitched roofs and white-painted clapboard, is now flanked by a matching extension with well-appointed rooms furnished in brisk modern style. The hotel is the only good place to **eat** in town, with a banquet-like buffet every night; go early to get the pick of the buffet crop.

The Sognefjord

Profoundly beautiful, the **Sognefjord** drills in from the coast for some 200km, its inner recesses splintering into half a dozen subsidiary fjords. Perhaps inevitably, none of the villages and small towns that dot the fjord quite lives up to the splendid setting, but **Balestrand** and **Mundal**, on the Fjærlandsfjord, come mighty close and are easily the best bases. Both are on the north side of the fjord which, given the lack of roads on the south side, is where you want (or pretty much have) to be – Flåm (see p.315) apart. Mundal is also near two southerly tentacles of the Jostedalsbreen glacier: **Flatbreen** and easy-to-reach **Bøyabreen**.

The Sognefjord's north bank is hugged by Hwy 55 for almost the whole of its length and at **Sogndal** this same highway slices northeast to clip past the **Lustrafjord**. Side roads lead off this part of the highway to a pair of top-notch attractions, **Urnes stave church** – via a quick ferry ride from **Solvorn** – and, further north, to the east side of the Jostedalsbreen glacier at **Nigardsbreen**. Thereafter Hwy 55 – as the **Sognefjellsveg** – climbs steeply to run along the western side of the **Jotunheimen mountains**, an extraordinarily beautiful journey even by Norwegian standards and one which culminates with the road thumping down to **Lom** on the flatlands beside Hwy 15.

Public transport to and around the Sognefjord is generally excellent. Operating about halfway along the fjord, perhaps the most useful of the **car ferries** links Vangsnes, Hella and Dragsvik (for Balestrand), but in the east of the fjord the 24-hour shuttle between Fodnes and Mannheller is convenient too, especially if you're arriving from Oslo on the E16. **Hurtigbåt passenger express boat** services connect Bergen, Balestrand and Flåm, and long-distance **buses** come up from Bergen via Voss and the Fodnes–Mannheller ferry bound for Sogndal. At Sogndal, passengers change for onward services west along the north shore of the Sognefjord to Hella and Balestrand or run east to Oslo; other buses run up Hwy 5 to the peripheries of Mundal and the Nordfjord (see p.324). There is, however, no bus service across the Sognefjellsveg (Hwy 55).

Balestrand and around

An appealing first stop along the Sognefjord, **BALESTRAND** has been a tourist destination since the middle of the nineteenth century, when it was discovered by European travellers in search of cool, clear air and picturesque mountain scenery. Kaiser Wilhelm II got in on the act too, becoming a frequent visitor and sharing his

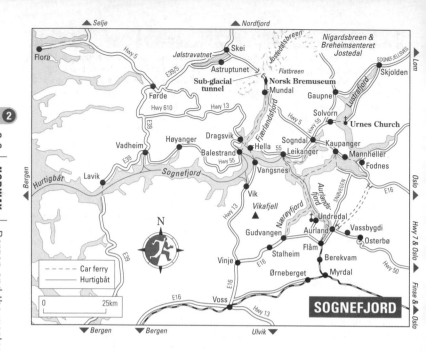

Selje ▲　　　Nordfjord ▲

Florø
Hwy 5
Jølstravatnet
Skei
Jostedalsbreen
Nigardsbreen &
Breheimsenteret
Jostedal
SOGNEFJELLSVEG
Lom ▶

Astruptunet
E39/5
Flatbreen
Skjolden

Norsk Bremuseum
Sub-glacial
tunnel
Førde
Mundal
Gaupne
Solvorn

Hwy 610
Hwy 13
Hwy 5
Hwy 55
Urnes Church

Høyanger
Dragsvik
Sogndal
Kaupanger

Vadheim
Hella
55
Leikanger
Mannheller

Balestrand
Fodnes

Lavik
Hwy 55
Vangsnes
E16

Sognefjord
Aurlands-
fjord
SNØVEGEN
Oslo ▶

Hurtigbåt
Vik
Nærøyfjord
Hwy 7 & Oslo ▶

Bergen
Vikafjell ▲
Undredal
Vassbygdi

N
Gudvangen
Aurland
Østerbø
Finse & Oslo ▶

Flåm
Vinje
Stalheim
Berekvam
Hwy 50

E16
Ørneberget
Myrdal

Car ferry
Hurtigbåt
Voss

0　　25km
E16
Hwy 13
SOGNEFJORD

Bergen ▼　　Bergen ▼　　Ulvik ▼

holiday spot with the tweeds and hobnail boots of the British bourgeoisie. These days, the village is used as a touring base for the immediate area, as the battery of small hotels and restaurants above the quay testifies, but it's all very small-scale, and among the 1000-strong population farming still remains the principal livelihood.

An hour or so will suffice to take a peek at Balestrand's two attractions. The **English church of St Olav** is a spiky brown-and-beige wooden structure built in 1897 in the general style of a stave church at the behest of a British émigré, a certain Margaret Kvikne, who moved here after she married a local curate. In one of those curious hand-me-downs from Britain's imperial past, the church remains part of the Diocese of Gibraltar, which arranges English-language services during the summer. The Germans have left their mark, too. About 300m south of the church along the fjord are two humpy **Viking burial mounds**, supposedly the tombs of King Bele and his wife. On the larger of them is a statue of the king in heroic pose, plonked there by the Kaiser in 1913 to match the statue of Bele's son-in-law that stands tall across the fjord in Vangsnes.

Practicalities

The only **car ferry** to Balestrand is the summertime service south from Mundal, on the Fjærlandsfjord (see p.320); otherwise, the nearest you'll get is Dragsvik, 9km to the north of Balestrand, and reached by ferry from either Hella or Vangsnes on the fjord's south shore (every 40min to 1hr). Both the Mundal ferry and **Hurtigbåt** services dock at the village quayside, plumb in the centre. **Buses** stop beside the quayside too, but there no services direct from Bergen and Voss; coming from the south it's necessary to change at Sogndal. The bus stop is in front of the Spar supermarket and the village **tourist office** is at the back of the shop (late June to late Aug Mon–Fri 7.30am–1pm & 3.30–9pm, Sat 7.30am–1pm & 3.30–6.30pm, Sun 8am–12.30pm & 3.30–6.30pm; early June & late Aug to Sept Mon–Fri 7.30am–1pm & 3.30–6pm, Sat 7.30am–1pm & 3.30–6.30pm, Sun 8am–12.30pm & 3.30–5.30pm; Oct–May Mon–Fri 9am–3pm;

☏57 69 12 55, ⊛www.sognefjorden.no). Staff hand out a wide range of fjord leaflets, sell local hiking maps (70kr), issue bus and ferry timetables and rent bikes (30kr per hour, 75kr per half day, 150kr per day).

For **accommodation**, the *Midtnes Pensjonat* (☏57 69 11 33, ℗57 69 15 84; ❸), about 300m from the dock behind the English church, is a low-key, pleasantly sedate affair with a few slightly dowdy but spacious rooms in a modern wing adjoining the original clapboard house; make sure to get a room with a fjord view. Close by, the *Balestrand Pensjonat* (☏57 69 11 38, ⊛www.balestrand.net; May-Sept; ❸) is very similar. Another good choice, just 150m uphill from the dock and with private doubles (❷) as well as dorms, is the HI **hostel** (☏57 69 13 03, ℮balestrand.hostel @vandrerhjem.no; late June to mid-Aug), part of the neat and trim *Kringsjå Hotell* (same number; ⊛www.kringsja.no; ❷). This complex occupies a pleasant modern building and its long verandah overlooks the fjord; there's a communal kitchen, a more-than-competent café-restaurant and a laundry; rowing boat rental is available, too. The big deal hereabouts, though, is *Kvikne's Hotel* (☏57 69 42 00, ⊛www .kviknes.no; ❹; May–Sept), whose various buildings dominate much of the waterfront. It's worth popping into the bar to take a look at the fancy fittings – some of which are in a sort of Victorian Viking-baronial style – but don't take a room without having a gander first: the best and most expensive overlook the fjord, but some are at the back of the modern annexe. Finally, the town **campsite**, *Sjøtun Camping* (☏57 69 12 23, ℮sjotun_camping@hotmail.com; June to mid-Sept) occupies a treeless field just beyond the burial mounds, a kilometre or so south of the dock.

For **food**, both the *Kringsjå* and the *Midtnes* serve tasty, excellent-value dinners and there are competent snacks and light lunches at *Gekkens Café*, upstairs in the shopping centre on the quayside. The cream of the gastronomic crop, however, is the restaurant at *Kvikne's Hotel*, where they serve up a banquet-sized buffet (300kr) every night – go early to get the pick and be sure to try the earth-shattering mousse.

Moving on from Balestrand

When it comes to **moving on from Balestrand** you're spoiled for choice. In the summertime, one especially tempting proposition is the **car ferry** (late May to early September 2 daily; 1hr 25min; passengers 140kr one-way 210kr return; car & driver 245kr one-way, 490kr return) north up along the stunningly beautiful Fjærlandsfjord to the eminently appealing hamlet of Mundal (see p.320), from where there's the possibility of an onward bus trip to the Norsk Bremuseum and the Bøyabreen glacier arm (see p.320). There is also a **Hurtigbåt passenger express boat** service linking Balestrand with Bergen in one direction, Sogndal and Flåm in the other (2–3 daily). **Driving** north from Balestrand, **Hwy 13** cuts a scenic route over the mountains on its way to its junction with the E39 near Førde, which itself proceeds north to the Nordfjord (see p.324). But **Hwy 55** to Sogndal and the eastern reaches of the Sognefjord has much more to offer, not least the Sognefjellsveg mountain road (Hwy 55; see p.317). To get to Sogndal from Balestrand, it's necessary to cross the mouth of the Fjærlandsfjord by ferry from Dragsvik, 9km along the coast to the north. This **Dragsvik car ferry** operates a triangular service shuttling both east across the fjord to Hella (15min; 19kr passengers, 50kr car & driver) and south to Vangsnes (25min; 21kr passengers, 57kr car & driver); sailings to both destinations are every forty minutes or so from mid-June to mid-August, hourly the rest of the year. The other significant cost for drivers is the 150kr toll payable on Hwy 5 just south of the Mundal turning.

Finally, the Sogn og Fjordane **express bus** travels west from Balestrand to Førde (Mon–Fri 1 daily; 2hr), where passengers change for Stryn and the Nordfjord (see p.324). This same bus also heads east (3 daily) from Balestrand to Sogndal and ultimately Oslo. At Sogndal, passengers change for Mundal and Lom (see p.323). Note, however, that connecting services are few and far between – mostly you'll have to hang around for an hour or two (at least) between buses.

North to the Fjærlandsfjord and Mundal

To the north of Balestrand, the **Fjærlandsfjord** is a wild place, its flanks blanketed with a thick covering of trees extending down to the water's edge, while a succession of thundering waterfalls tumbles down vast clefts in the rock up above. The village of **MUNDAL** – sometimes inaccurately referred to as Fjærland – matches its surroundings perfectly, a gentle ribbon of old wooden houses edging the fjord, with the mountains as a backcloth. It's one of the region's most picturesque places, saved from the developers by its isolation: it was one of the last settlements on the Sognefjord to be connected to the road system, with Hwy 5 from Sogndal only being completed in 1986. Moreover, it has eschewed the crasser forms of commercialism to become the self-styled "Norwegian Book Town", with a dozen old buildings accommodating antiquarian and secondhand bookshops. Naturally enough, most of the books are in Norwegian, but there's a liberal sprinkling of English editions, too. The bookselling season runs from mid-May to early September and the bookshops are mostly open daily from 10am to 6pm.

Bookshops aside, the village has two good-looking buildings, the first of which is the **Hotel Mundal** (see below), whose nineteenth-century turrets, verandahs and high-pitched roofs overlook the fjord from amongst the handful of buildings that amount to the village centre. Next door, the **church** (June–Aug daily 10am–6pm; free) is a serious affair dating from 1861, lacking in ornamentation but immaculately maintained; its graveyard hints at the hard but healthy life of the district's farmers – most of them seem to have lived to a ripe old age. Many locals are still farmers, but in summer hardly any of them herd their cattle up to the mountain pastures as was the custom until the 1960s. The disused tracks to these summer farms (*støls*) now serve as **hiking trails** of varying length and difficulty – the tourist office (see below) will advise.

Around Mundal: the Flatbreen and Bøyabreen

About 2.5km north of the village, along the quiet byroad that links it with Hwy 5, is the **Norwegian Glacier Museum** (*Norsk Bremuseum*; daily: April, May, Sept & Oct 10am–4pm; June–Aug 9am–7pm; information and enquiries free but displays 75kr; ☎57 69 32 88, ✆www.bre.museum.no), which tells you more than you ever wanted to know about glaciers. It features several lavish hands-on displays – a simulated walk below a glacier, for example – and screens films about glaciers; package tourists turn up in droves.

The museum is one of the Jostedalsbreen National Park's three information centres (see p.325 for details of the others), and as such has the details of all the various **guided glacier walks** on offer across the park as outlined in their *Breturar* (glacier walks) leaflet. The usual target from Mundal is the **Supphellebreen**, the Jostedalsbreen's nearest hikeable arm, or, to be precise, that part of it called **Flatbreen**, but this is a challenging part of the glacier and neither is it easy to get to. Flatbreen excursions take between six and eight hours and only take place in July. Advance reservations, at least a day beforehand, are essential on ☎57 69 32 33; the cost is 400kr per person. At the other extreme, you can get close to the glacier without breaking sweat just 10km north of Mundal on Hwy 5. Here, just before you enter the tunnel, look out for the signposted side road on the right, leading the 200m to the *Brævasshytta* restaurant (May–Sept daily 9am–5/8pm). This smart, modern place, a tour-package favourite, overlooks the slender glacial lake fed by the **Bøyabreen** arm of the glacier up above. It takes a couple of minutes to stroll down from the restaurant to the lake, close to the sooty shank of the glacier.

Practicalities

Arriving **by car** from the south, there's a whopping 150kr toll to pay on Hwy 5, just before you reach the turning for Mundal. The nearest you'll get to Mundal by regular **bus** is the Norwegian Glacier Museum on Hwy 5, from where it's an easy 2.5km stroll south along the fjord to the village. **Car ferries** arriving from Balestrand dock in the centre of Mundal and connect with special excursion buses – bookable either here or in Balestrand – which take passengers on to the Bremuseum and then, after a stop-off of over an hour, to the Bøyabreen. Mundal **tourist office**, metres from the boat dock (late May to early Sept daily 9.30am–5.30pm; ☎57 69 32 33), advises on local hiking routes, sells hiking maps and has bus and ferry timetables. **Cycle rental** is available from them too, at 25kr per hour, 125kr per day.

There are two fjordside **hotels** in Mundal The obvious choice is the splendid *Hotel Mundal* (☎57 69 31 01, ⊛www.fjordinfo.no/mundal; May to late Sept; ⑤), a quirky sort of place whose public rooms display many original features, from the parquet floors and fancy wooden scrollwork through to the old-fashioned sliding doors of the cavernous dining room. The rooms are frugal and some show their age, but somehow it doesn't matter much. If you do stay, look out for the old photos on the walls of men in plus-fours and hobnail boots clambering round the glaciers – only softies bothered with gloves. Nearby, the *Fjærland Fjordstue Hotell* (☎57 69 32 00; ❸) is very different – a well-tended family hotel with smart modern furnishings and a conservatory overlooking the fjord. A third option is *Bøyum Camping* (☎57 69 32 52) near the Bremuseum, which has huts (❶) as well as spaces for tents. Both hotels offer good, wholesome **food**.

Leaving Mundal, long-distance **buses** travelling along Hwy 5 can be picked up from the bus stop close to the Glacier Museum. There are services south to Sogndal and Oslo along the E16 (3–4 daily) and north to Skei and Førde (3 daily). Change at Skei for onward services north to Stryn and the Nordfjord (see p.324).

East to Sogndal

From Balestrand it's 9km north along the fjord to **Dragsvik**, where ferries shuttle over to the jetty at **Hella**, which is itself 40km from **SOGNDAL** – bigger and livelier than Balestrand, but still hardly a major metropolis, with a population of just 6000. Neither is Sogndal as appealing: it has a pleasant fjord setting in a broad valley, surrounded by low, green hills dotted with apple and pear trees, but its centre is a rash of modern concrete and glass. Frankly, there are other much more agreeable spots within a few kilometres' radius and your best option is to keep going.

Buses drop passengers at the **station** – a major interchange – on the west side of the town centre at the end of Gravensteinsgata, the long main drag. From here, it's about 500m east along Gravensteinsgata to the **tourist office** (late June to late Aug Mon–Fri 9am–8pm, Sat 10am–5pm, Sun 3–8pm; late Aug to late June Mon–Fri 9am–4pm; ☎57 67 30 83, ⊛www.sognefjorden.no), housed in one of the street's flashy modern buildings. Staff issue bus and ferry timetables, and have a list of local **accommodation**, though pickings are fairly slim. The nicest place to stay – though it's no great shakes – is the *Hofslund Fjord Hotel*, a stone's throw from the tourist office at Fjøregata 37 (☎57 67 10 22, ⊛www.hofslund-hotel.no; ❸). It comprises an old wooden building and a modern annexe; ask for a room with a fjord view. Another palatable and certainly economical option, with double rooms (❷) as well as dorms, is the HI **hostel** (☎57 67 20 33, ⊛sogndal.hostel@vandrerhjem.no; mid-June to mid-Aug), which manages to feel quite homely despite being housed in a residential folk high school, *Folkehøgskule*. It's well signposted and situated near the bridge at the east end of town and about 400m beyond the roundabout that marks the east end of Gravensteinsgata. This same roundabout is about 50m from the tourist office and it also marks the start of Fjøravegen, the town's other main drag, which cuts through the commercial heart of Sogndal. For **food**, the choice is uninspiring, but the restaurant of the *Quality Hotel Sogndal*, Gravensteinsgata 5 (☎57 62 77 00), is reliable, offering tasty Norwegian dishes at affordable prices.

Moving on from Sogndal

From Sogndal, there is a **Hurtigbåt passenger express boat** service to Flåm in one direction, Balestrand and Bergen in the other. There are also **express buses** northwest to Mundal and Skei (for Stryn) and southeast to Oslo via the E16. **Local buses** offer limited services from Sogndal up along Hwy 55 to the beginning of the Sognefjellsveg (see p.317), the highest parts of which are closed by snow from late October to May. These include buses to Solvorn (Mon–Sat 1–2 daily; 25min) and Elvekrok, within easy walking distance of the Nigardsbreen glacier nodule (2–5 daily; 1hr 30min). There are, however, currently no through services to Lom.

Finally, drivers should remember that the road to Oslo is interrupted some 18km southeast of Sogndal by the round-the-clock Manheller–Fodnes **car ferry** (every 30min; 15min; passengers 27kr, car & driver 80kr).

Northeast to Solvorn and Urnes stave church

Some 15km northeast of Sogndal on Hwy 55, a steep 3km-long turning leaves the main road to snake its way down to **SOLVORN**, an attractive little hamlet clustered beneath the mountains on the sheltered foreshore of the **Lustrafjord**. Solvorn is the site of the *Walaker Hotell* (☎57 68 20 80, ⊛www.walaker.com; ❹), the most conspicuous part of which is an ugly motel-style block. Don't let this put you off from staying here, since the old house, a comely pastel-painted building with a lovely garden, has first-rate period bedrooms.

From Solvorn, a local **car ferry** (early June to Aug Mon–Fri 10am–4pm hourly, plus Sat & Sun 11am–4pm hourly; Sept to early June Mon–Fri 2–4 daily, Sun 1 daily; 20min; 22kr passenger, 60kr car & driver) shuttles across the Lustrafjord to **Ornes**, from where it's a stiff, ten-minute hike up the hill to **Urnes stave church**, which is open for guided tours only (early June–Aug daily 10.30am–5.30pm; 40kr). Magnificently sited with the fjord and the snow-dusted mountains as its backdrop, this is the oldest and most celebrated stave church in Norway. Parts of the building date back to the twelfth century and its most remarkable feature is its wonderful medieval **carvings**. On the outside, incorporated into the north wall, are two exquisite door panels, the remains of an earlier church dating from around 1070 and alive with a swirling filigree of strange beasts and delicate vegetation. These forceful, superbly crafted panels bear witness to the sophistication of Viking woodcarving – indeed the church has given its name to this distinctively Nordic art form, found in many countries where Viking influence was felt and now generally known as the "Urnes" style. Most of the interior is seventeenth-century, but there is Viking woodcarving here too, notably the strange-looking figures and beasts carved on the capitals of the staves and the sacred-heart bench-ends. The guided tour fills in all the details and a small display in the house-cum-ticket office has photographic enlargements of carvings that are hard to decipher inside the poorly-lit church.

If you're driving, there's a choice of routes on from the church. You can head north along the minor road that tracks along the east shore of the Lustrafjord to rejoin Hwy 55 at Skjolden. Or you can retrace your steps back to Hwy 55 via Solvorn. The latter is the route you'll need to take if you're heading to the Nigardsbreen arm of the Jostedalsbreen glacier.

Onto the Nigardsbreen

From the Solvorn turning, it's about 15km north along Hwy 55 to **Gaupne**, where Hwy 604 forks north for the delightful 34km trip up the wild, forested river valley leading to the **Breheimsenteret Jostedal information centre** (daily: May to late June & late Aug to Sept 10am–5pm; late June to late Aug 9am–7pm; ☎57 68 32 50, ⊛www.jostedal.com; displays 50kr). This bleak, ultra-modern structure fits in well with the bare peaks that surround it and, as you sip a coffee on the terrace, you can admire the glistening glacier dead ahead – the **Nigardsbreen**, an eastern arm of the Jostedalsbreen. From the centre, it's an easy 3km drive or walk along the toll road to the shores of an icy green lake, where a tiny **boat** (early June to Aug daily 10am–6pm; 20kr) shuttles across to the bare rock slope beside the glacier, a great rumpled and seamed wall of ice that sweeps between high peaks. It's a magnificent spectacle and most visitors are satisfied with the forty-minute hike up from the jetty to the glacier's shaggy flanks, but others plump for a **guided glacier walk**. There is a plethora to choose from, beginning with a quick and easy one- to two-hour jaunt suitable for children over 6 (daily July to mid-Aug; 140kr, children 60kr), and tougher four-hour trips (daily late May to mid-Sept; 285kr including boat). Prices include equipment, and all these walks start at the car park at the end of the toll road. Tickets for the family walks can be purchased direct from the guides at the starting point, right beside the glacier, but other day-trip tickets must be pre-purchased at the information centre at least one hour before departure. Advance reservations for the longer, overnight trips are essential and must be made at least four weeks beforehand. For more on the Jostedalsbreen glacier, see p.320; further information on glacier walks is given on p.326.

Along the Sognefjellsveg

Back at Gaupne, Hwy 55 continues 26km northeast to **SKJOLDEN**, a dull little town that is bang at the head of the Lustrafjord and at the start of the 85km-long **Sognefjellsveg** over the mountains to Lom. Despite the difficulty of the terrain, the Sognefjellsveg marks the course of one of the oldest trading routes in Norway, with locals transporting goods by mule or, amazingly enough, on their shoulders: salt and fish went east, hides, butter, tar and iron went west. That portion of the road that clambers over the highest part of the mountains – 1434 metres above sea level – was only completed in 1938 under a Depression "make-work" scheme, which kept a couple of hundred young men busy for two years. Tourist literature hereabouts refer to the lads' "motivation and drive", but considering the harshness of the conditions and the crudeness of their equipment – pickaxes, spades and wheelbarrows – their purported enthusiasm seems unlikely.

Beyond Skjolden, the Sognefjellsveg wriggles and worms its way up the valley to a mountain plateau which it traverses, providing absolutely stunning views of the jagged, ice-crusted Jotunheimen peaks to the east. En route are several roadside lodges, easily the best of which is the comfortable and very modern *Turtagrø Hotel* (☎57 68 08 00, ⊛www.turtagro.no; ⑥; Easter–Oct), just 15km out from Skjolden. The hotel is a favourite haunt for mountaineers, but it also provides ready access to the **hiking trails** that lattice the Jotunheimen National Park (see p.268). However, the terrain is unforgiving and the weather unpredictable, so novice hikers beware. In addition, the *Turtagrø* is the base for Turtagrø Føring (☎57 68 08 08), whose mountain guides offer an extensive programme of guided mountain and glacier walks as well as summer **cross-country skiing**; the season begins at Easter and extends until October.

Onto Lom

Pushing on along the Sognefjellsveg, it's another short hop to the Bøverdalen hostel (see below) and then the crossroads settlement of **LOM**, a trading and transport centre for centuries, benefiting – in a modest sort of way – from the farms which dot the surrounding valleys. Today, with a population of just 700, it's hardly a boom town, but it does make a comfortable living from the passing tourist trade. Lom's eighteenth-century heyday is recalled by its **stave church** (daily: late May to mid-June & mid-Aug to mid-Sept 10am–4pm; mid-June to mid-Aug 9am–9pm; 40kr), an enormous structure perched on a grassy knoll above the river. The original church was built here about 1200, but it was remodelled and enlarged after the Reformation, when the spire and transepts were added and the flashy altar and pulpit

Routes on from Lom

Heading west along Hwy 15, Lom is within comfortable striking distance of either the Geirangerfjord (see p.328) or the Nordfjord and the western flanks of the Jostedalsbreen glacier (see p.320). In the opposite direction, also along Hwy 15, it's another very manageable drive to Otta (see p.266) and the main E6 highway between Oslo and Trondheim. A tantalizing choice perhaps, but, if you're after more fjord scenery, the Geirangerfjord definitely has the edge.

By **bus** from Otta, there are daily express services west to Grotli and Stryn, and east to Otta, Lillehammer and Oslo. From mid-June to the end of August, you can change onto a local bus at Grotli for the Geirangerfjord – but check connections with Lom tourist office before you depart. There are no buses from Lom to Sogndal along the Sognefjellsveg.

installed. Its most attractive features are the dinky, shingle-clad roofs, adorned by dragon finials, and the Baroque acanthus vine decoration inside.

Nearby is the town's open-air museum, the **Lom Bygdamuseum Presthaugen** (July daily 1–4pm; 20kr), a surprisingly enjoyable collection of old log buildings in a forest setting. Norway teems with this type of museum – stay in the country long enough and the very sight of one will make you want to scream – but Lom's is better than most. It is distinguished by the Olavsstugu, a modest hut where St Olav is said to have spent a night, and also by what must be the biggest and ugliest Storstabburet (large storehouse) in the country. Museum enthusiasts will also want to visit the **Norwegian Mountain Museum** (*Norsk Fjellmuseum*; Jan–April & Oct–Dec Mon–Fri 9am–4pm; May & Sept Mon–Fri 9am–4pm, Sat & Sun 10am–5pm; early June & late Aug Mon–Fri 9am–6pm, Sat & Sun 10am–5pm; late June to mid-Aug Mon–Fri 9am–9pm, Sat & Sun 10am–8pm; Oct–April Mon–Fri 9am–4pm; 60kr), a modern place which focuses on the Jotunheimen mountains. It's all here in admirable detail, from the fauna and the flora to the landscapes, farmers and past mountaineers.

Buses to Lom pull in a few metres west of the main crossroads, and most of what you're likely to need is within easy walking distance of here. The church and the open-air museum are across the bridge on the other side of the river, as is the mountain museum, which shares its premises with the **tourist office** (Jan–April & Oct–Dec Mon–Fri 9am–4pm; May & Sept Mon–Fri 9am–4pm, Sat & Sun 10am–5pm; early June & late Aug Mon–Fri 9am–6pm, Sat & Sun 10am–5pm; mid-June to mid-Aug Mon–Fri 9am–9pm, Sat & Sun 10am–8pm; ⓣ61 21 29 90, ⓦwww.visitlom.com). The choicest **accommodation** is the *Fossheim Turisthotell* (ⓣ61 21 10 05, ⓦwww.fossheimhotel.no; ❹), about 300m east of the crossroads along Hwy 15. The main lodge here is neat and smart, with an abundance of pine, and behind, trailing up the wooded hillside, are some delightful little wooden cabins (also ❹), some of which are very old and all of which are en suite. The hotel **restaurant** is excellent and reasonably priced; it specializes in traditional Norwegian cuisine. A palatable second-choice hotel is the modern *Fossberg* (ⓣ61 21 22 50, ⓦwww.fossberg.no; ❹), a large, mostly wooden place by the crossroads. For bargain-basement lodgings, the nearest HI **hostel**, *Bøverdalen Vandrerhjem* (ⓣ61 21 20 64, ⓔboeverdalen.hostel@vandrerhjem.no; June-Sept) is about 20km back down the Sognefjellsveg and occupies a series of glum modern buildings right by the roadside; there are double rooms (❷) as well as dorm beds.

The Nordfjord and the Jostedalsbreen glacier

Emerge from Hwy 5's Fjærland tunnel heading north from Mundal (see p.320), and you've just journeyed under the Jostedalsbreen glacier, which somehow seems a bit of a cheek – and environmentally dubious. That said, the highway is the handiest way to get between the Sognefjord and the **Nordfjord**, the next great fjord system to the north. The inner recesses of the Nordfjord are readily explored along **Hwy 60**, which weaves a tortuous course through a string of unexciting little towns in between the fjord and the glacier. Amongst them, **Loen** is the best base for further explorations, including the glacier, though dreary **Stryn** is larger and more important. Stryn is also where Hwy 60 meets **Hwy 15**. The former presses on north to Hellesylt (see p.329), the latter runs west along the Nordfjord, with the road dipping and diving along the northern shore in between deep-green reflective waters and severe peaks. It's a handsome enough journey, but the Nordfjord does not have the allure of its more famous neighbours, at least in part because its roadside hamlets lack real appeal.

High up in the mountains, dominating the whole of the inner Nordfjord region, lurks the **Jostedalsbreen glacier**, a five-hundred-square-kilometre ice plateau that creaks, grumbles and moans out towards the Sognefjord and the Jotunheim mountains. The glacier stretches northeast in a lumpy mass between Hwy 5 and Hwy 15, its myriad arms – or "nodules" – nudging down into the nearby valleys, the clay particles of its meltwater giving the local rivers and lakes their distinctive light-green colouring. Catching sight of the ice nestling between peaks and ridges can be unnerving - the overwhelming feeling being that somehow it shouldn't really be there.

For centuries, the glacier presented an impenetrable east–west barrier, crossed only at certain points by determined farmers and adventurers. It's no less daunting today, but access is much freer, a corollary of the creation of the **Jostedalsbreen National Park** in 1991. Since then, roads have been driven deep into the glacier's flanks, the comings (but mostly goings) of the ice have been closely monitored and there has been a proliferation of officially licensed **guided glacier walks** (*breturar*) on its various arms (see box on p.326). If that sounds too energetic and all you're after is a **close look at the glacier**, then this is possible at several places. The easiest approach is the five-minute stroll to the Bøyabreen on the south side of the glacier near Mundal (see p.320), whereas the east side's Nigardsbreen (see p.323) requires much more commitment – getting to the ice involves a boat ride and a stiff forty-minute hike. Here on the west side, off Hwy 60, the **Briksdalsbreen** requires a forty-five minute walk from the end of the road, but is still the most visited approach by a long chalk, partly on account of its horse-and-carriage rides up towards the ice. Much less crowded and far prettier is the easy fifteen-minute walk to the **Kjenndalsbreen**, near Loen – a charming way to spend a morning or afternoon. Incidentally, these vantage points often double as the designated starting points for the guided glacier walks.

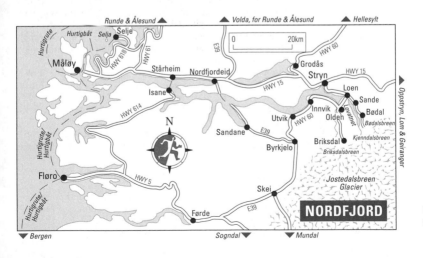

Guided glacier walks and national park information centres

Most **guided glacier walks** on the Jostedalsbreen are scheduled between early July and mid-August, though on some arms of the glacier the season extends from May until late September, even longer on the Briksdalsbreen. The walks range from two-hour excursions to five-day expeditions. Day-trip prices start at around 140kr per person for a two-hour gambol, rising to 400kr for six to eight hours. A comprehensive leaflet detailing all the various walks is widely available across the region and at the national park's three **information centres**. These are the **Norsk Bremuseum**, on the south side of the glacier near Mundal (see p.320); the **Breheimsenteret Jostedal** on the east side at the Nigardsbreen (see p.323); and the **Jostedalsbreen Nasjonalparksenter** (daily: early to mid-May 10am–4pm; mid-May to mid-Aug 10am–6pm; mid-Aug to Sept 10am–6pm; ☎57 87 72 00, ⊛www.museumsnett.no /jostedalsbreen; exhibitions 60kr) in Oppstryn, 20km east of Stryn on Hwy 15. Each of the centres has displays on all things glacial and sells books, souvenirs and hiking maps.

Booking arrangements for the shorter glacier walks vary considerably. On some of the trips – for example those at the Nigardsbreen – it's sufficient to turn up at the information centre an hour or two beforehand, but in general it's a good idea to make a reservation at least a day ahead. Sometimes this is best done through the information centre, sometimes direct with the tour operator. In the case of the overnight trips, however, advance booking is essential, often a minimum of four weeks beforehand. In all cases, basic **equipment** is provided, though you'll need to take good boots, waterproofs, warm clothes, gloves, hat, sunglasses – and your own **food** and **drink**.

Travelling around the area by **bus** presents few problems if you stick to the main highways, but services from Hwy 60 to the glacier are limited. There's a once daily bus to and from Briksdalsbreen, which gives you three hours there, but nothing at all to Kjenndalsbreen – the bus, again once daily, stops at Bødalseter, about 8km short of the end of the road.

North to Olden and the Briksdalsbreen

From Mundal on the Fjærlandsfjord (see p.320), it's 90km north along Hwy 5, the E39 and then Hwy 60 to the hamlet of **OLDEN** on the shores of the Nordfjord. The village doesn't have much going for it, but it is at the start of the 24km byroad south to **BRIKSDAL**, a scattering of mountain chalets that serves as the starting point for the easy 45-minute walk to the **Briksdalsbreen**. The path skirts waterfalls and weaves up the river until you finally reach the glacier, surprisingly blue except for streaks of dust and dirt. It's a simple matter to get close to the ice as the only precaution is a flimsy rope barrier with a small warning sign – be careful. Alternatively, you can hire a pony and trap at the café area at the start of the trail, something that will cost you 250kr – steep considering that you still have to hike the last bit of the path. Guided glacier walks begin at the café area, too. There are several operators to choose from; Briksdal Breføring (☎57 87 68 00, ⊛www .briksdalsbre.no) are as good as any.

Local **buses** link Stryn, Loen and Olden with Briksdal once daily throughout the year. Passengers get about three hours at Briksdal before the departure of the return service, again once daily.

Loen and the Kjenndalsbreen

LOEN spreads ribbon-like along the Nordfjord's low-lying, grassy foreshore with ice-capped mountains breathing down its neck. The village is also home to one of Norway's most famous hotels, the outstanding *Alexandra* (☎57 87 50 00, ⊛www.alexandra.no; ❼/❺), whose exterior barely does it justice. The hotel occupies a large and fairly undistinguished modern block overlooking the fjord, but inside the lodge-like public rooms are splendid – wide, open and extremely well-appointed. There's every convenience, including a sauna and solarium, while the bedrooms are spacious, infinitely comfortable and furnished in bright modern style. Breakfasts are banquet-like, but the evening **buffets** (from 7pm; 375kr) are even better, a wonderful selection that lays fair claim to being the best in the fjords. The *Alexandra* is, of course, fairly pricey, but across the road and right on the water's edge, the *Hotel Loenfjord* (☎57 87 57 00, ⓦwww.loenfjord.no; ❺/❹) is an excellent and less expensive second choice. A happy cross between a motel and a lodge, the *Loenfjord* comprises a long and low modern building in a vernacular version of traditional Norwegian style. The public rooms are expansive, and the evening buffet (250kr) very good.

Beginning beside the *Hotel Alexandra*, the 21km byroad leading south to the **Kjenndalsbreen** nodule of Jostedalsbreen starts by slipping up the river valley past lush meadows before pressing on along the northerly shore of **Lovatnet**, a long and slender lake of glacial blue. After 4.4km, the road reaches the ferry point for boat cruises along the lake (see box below) and then scuttles on to **Bødal**. There are no guided glacier walks on the Kjenndalsbreen itself, but they do take place near Bødal on the **Bødalsbreen** (June to mid-Sept; ☎57 87 68 00). The meeting point is **Bødalseter**, a DNT self-service hut about 5km from Bødal up a bumpy, signposted road and a ten-minute walk from the car park at the road end. From the hut to the glacier, it's another 2.5-kilometre walk.

Back on the Kjenndalsbreen road, it's a further 3km or so to a toll post (30kr) and a couple of hundred metres more to the **Kjendalsstova café** at the very end of the Lovatnet – and where the boat docks. Pushing on, it's 5km more to the car park, from where it's an easy and very pleasant fifteen-minute ramble through rocky terrain to the **ice**, whose fissured, blancmange-like blue and white folds tumble down the rock face, with a furious white-green river, fed by plummeting meltwater, flowing underneath. If the weather holds, it's a lovely spot for a picnic.

There are no local **buses** to the Kjenndalsbreen; the nearest you'll get is the once daily service – in each direction – from Stryn and Loen to Bødal and the Bødalseter car park.

Stryn

STRYN, just 12km around the fjord from Loen, is the biggest town hereabouts, though with a population of 1200 that's hardly a major boast. For the most part, it's a humdrum modern sprawl straggling beside its long main street, but there is a pleasant pocket of antique **timber houses** huddled round the old bridge, down by the river on the west side of the centre, just to the south of the main drag. Take a few moments to have a look.

Loen boat trips

From early June to August, a small **passenger boat** (1 daily) weaves a leisurely course from one end of lake **Lovatnet** to the other, a delightful cruise through beguiling scenery. The departure point is the pint-sized Sande jetty, 4.4km down the Kjenndalsbreen road from the *Hotel Alexandra* in Loen, and the boat docks beside the *Kjendalsstova* café, 5km from the Kjenndalsbreen ice-face. The excursion costs 120kr, including onward transportation by bus from the café to the car park at the end of the Kjenndalsbreen road and the return journey – again by bus and boat – back to Sande; in total the round-trip takes four hours. The *Hotel Alexandra* (see above) issues tickets and takes bookings and will, at a pinch, give you a lift down to Sande, though the Stryn–Loen–Bødal bus connects with boat departures.

The **bus station** is beside the river to the west of the town centre on Hwy 15/60. From here, it's a 600m walk to the **tourist office**, bang in the centre just off the main street, Tonningsgata, and behind *Johan's Kafeteria* (June & Aug daily 8.30am–6pm; July daily 8.30am–8pm; Sept–May Mon–Fri 8.30am–3.30pm; ☎57 87 40 40, ☺www.nordfjord.no). Staff issue free town maps, rent mountain bikes, have a wide range of local brochures and sell hiking maps. There's no strong reason to overnight here, but Stryn does have a better-than-average HI **hostel**, *Stryn Vandrerhjem* (☎57 87 13 36, ☺stryn.hostel@vandrerhjem.no; June–Aug), perched high above the centre at Geilevegen 14. The chalet-like hostel has private rooms (❷) and dorms, self-catering facilities, a laundry and Internet access plus splendid views over Stryn and its surroundings – compensation for the lung-wrenching one-kilometre-long trek up here. The hostel is signposted from the main drag – north up Bøavegen – on the east side of the centre. Four-star *Stryn Camping* (☎57 87 11 36, ☺57 87 20 25) is handier, just a couple of hundred metres up Bøavegen; it's well-equipped and has tent pitches as well as cabins (❷). As for **food**, Stryn is short of decent cafés and restaurants; the best you'll do is the routine Italian dishes of the *Restaurant Bacchus*, on the east side of the centre at Tonningsgata 33.

Heading west out of Stryn, highways 15 and 60 share the same stretch of road until, after 16km, Hwy 60 spears north to reach, after about 30km, Hellesylt, on the Geirangerfjord.

The Geirangerfjord and Norangsdalen

The **Geirangerfjord** is one of the region's smallest fjords, but also one of its most breathtaking. A convoluted branch of the Storfjord, the Geirangerfjord cuts well inland and is marked by impressive waterfalls, with a village at either end of its snake-like profile – **Hellesylt** in the west and **Geiranger** in the east. Of the two, Geiranger has the smarter hotels as well as the tourist crowds, Hellesylt is smaller and quieter with the added bonus of its proximity to the magnificent **Norangsdal** valley, where the hamlet of **Øye** boasts one of Norway's most enjoyable hotels.

You can reach Geiranger in dramatic style from both north and south along the rip-roaring, nerve-jangling Hwy 63 – the aptly named **Ørnevegen** ("Eagle's Highway"). The approach to Hellesylt along Hwy 60 is comparatively demure, though taken as a whole this highway is an especially appealing route between the Nordfjord and Ålesund. In addition, **car ferries** (May–Sept 4–8 daily; 1hr; passengers 90kr one-way, car & driver 180kr) run between Hellesylt and Geiranger. This is one of the most celebrated trips in the entire region, the S-shaped waters about 300m deep and fed by a series of plunging waterfalls up to 250m in height. The falls are all named, and the multilingual commentary aboard the ferry does its best to ensure that you become familiar with every stream and rivulet. More interesting are the scattered ruins of abandoned farms, built along the fjord's sixteen-kilometre length by fanatically optimistic settlers during the eighteenth and nineteenth centuries. The cliffs backing the fjord are almost uniformly sheer, making farming of any description a short-lived and back-breaking occupation – and not much fun for the children either: when they went out to play, they were roped to the nearest boulder to stop them dropping into the fjord.

Long-distance **buses** travelling west along Hwy 15 link Otta (see p.266) and Lom (see p.323) with Grotli and Langvatn, at one of which – depending on the service – you change for the **local bus** north to Geiranger, though note that this connecting service only operates from mid-June to August. The same local bus pushes on from Geiranger to Åndalsnes (see p.332). Hellesylt is on the main Bergen–Ålesund bus route, which passes along Hwy 60 through Loen and Stryn; there are at least a couple of services daily. Finally, there's a limited local bus service from Hellesylt down along the Norangsdal valley to Øye and Leknes (late June to mid-Aug Mon–Fri 1 daily); in the opposite direction, the bus runs all year, but it departs well before the other bus arrives, which is really rather hopeless.

Hellesylt

In Viking times, **HELLESYLT** was an important and well-protected port. Traders and warriors sallied forth from the village to England, France and Russia, and many old Viking names survive in the area. Nowadays it's primarily a stop-off on tourist itineraries, most visitors staying just long enough to catch the ferry down the fjord to Geiranger. For daytime entertainment, there is a tiny **beach** near the ferry quay and beyond the mini-marina, the prelude to some very cold swimming. Or you could splash about (as many do) in the waterfall in the village centre. By nightfall, when the day-trippers have departed, Hellesylt is quiet and peaceful.

The **tourist office** (June & late Aug to Sept Mon–Fri 9am–6pm, Sat & Sun noon–6pm; July to late Aug daily 9am–8pm; ☎70 26 38 80) is a five-minute walk from the jetty in a modern building that doubles as an **art gallery** (same times; 50kr). On display is a set of kitsch-meets-Baroque woodcarvings illustrating Ibsen's *Peer Gynt* by a certain Oddvin Parr. It's all rather strange, but good fun all the same. Hellesylt has one **hotel**, the *Grand* (☎70 26 51 00, ☎70 26 52 22; ❸), whose fancy wooden scrollwork and high-pitched gables have been a local landmark since 1871. However, the interior has been patchily restored and guests are put up in the modern annexe next door. The hotel's main competitor is the HI **hostel** (☎70 26 51 28, ☎ 70 26 36 57; June–Aug), pleasantly set on the hillside above the village beside Hwy 60 – a steep 350-metre walk up the signed footpath from the jetty. They have cabins (❶) which suit a family of four nicely, as well as both double rooms (❷) and dorms, and self-catering facilities. Rowing boats can be rented here and from the *Grand*; the latter also sells fishing licences and rents out fishing equipment. *Hellesylt Camping* (℡70 26 51 88) fills out the shadeless field beside the fjord, about 400m from the quay.

The Norangsdal valley and Øye

A century ago, pony and trap took cruise-ship tourists from Hellesylt down through the majestic **Norangsdal** valley to what was then the remote hamlet of ØYE, a distance of 24km. By car, it's a simple journey today, but the scene appears not to have changed at all: steep, snow-tipped peaks rise up on either side of a wide, boulder-strewn and scree-slashed valley, dented by a thousand rock falls. Near the top of the valley, the road, 8km of which is gravel, slips through mountain pastures, where local women once spent every summer with their cows. The women slept in spartan timber cabins and today roadside plaques at a couple of surviving cabins flesh out the details. Pushing on, the road soon dips down into Øye, whose pride and joy is the splendid *Hotel Union* (℡70 06 21 00, ⓦwww.unionoye.no; closed mid-Oct to April; ❺), a delightfully restored High Victorian establishment, built in 1891 to accommodate touring aristocrats. Its interior is crammed with period antiques and bygones seemingly hunted down from every corner of the globe by the present owner. Each of the bedrooms is individually decorated in elaborate style and most celebrate the famous people who stayed here, like King Haakon VII and Kaiser Wilhelm II, not to mention the Danish author Karen "*Out Of Africa*" Blixen: enthusiasts might be pleased to see a pair of her lover's boots. It's a great place to spend the night – though you do have to turn a blind eye to the occasional period excesses, like the four-posters – and the food is first-rate, too. Telephones are banned, which is inducement enough to sit on the terrace and watch the weather fronts sweeping in off the glassy green **Norangsfjord**, or have a day's fishing – the hotel sells licences and dispenses advice.

Geiranger

Any approach to **GEIRANGER** is spectacular. Arriving by ferry slowly reveals the little village tucked in a hollow at the eastern end of the fjord, while approaching from the north by road involves thundering along a fearsome set of switchbacks on the Ørnevegen (Hwy 63) for a first view of the village and the fjord glinting in the distance. Similarly, the road in from Hwy 15 to the south begins innocuously enough, but soon you're squirming round and down the zigzags to arrive in Geiranger from behind. It's a beautiful setting, one of the most magnificent in western Norway, the only fly in the ointment being the excessive number of tourists at the peak of the season. That said, the congestion is limited to the centre of the village and it's easy enough to slip away to appreciate the true character of the fjord, hemmed in by sheer rock walls interspersed with hairline waterfalls, with tiny-looking ferries and cruise ships bobbing about on its blue-green waters.

The only specific sight is the brand new **Norsk Fjordsenter** (daily: mid-June to mid-Aug 10am–10pm, May to mid-June & mid-Aug to Sept 10am–5pm ⓦwww.fjordsenter.info; 75kr), just across from the *Union Hotel*. The centre follows the usual pattern of purpose-built museums, with separate sections exploring different aspects of the region's history from communications and transportation through to fjord farms and the evolution of tourism. Perhaps the most interesting display examines the problem of fjordland avalanches – whenever there's a major rock fall into a fjord, the resulting tidal wave threatens disaster.

The fjord centre is, however, small beer when compared with the scenery. A network of **hiking trails** lattices the mountains that crimp and crowd Geiranger: some make their way to thundering waterfalls, while others visit abandoned mountain farmsteads or venture up to vantage points where the views over the fjord are exhilarating if not downright scary. One popular excursion, to the mountain farm of **Skageflå**, involves both a boat ride – on one of the sightseeing boats – and a stiff hour-long hike up from the fjord to the farm, followed by a three-hour trek back to Geiranger. There's also the short but precarious trail to the **Flydalsjuvet**, an overhanging rock high above the Geirangerfjord that features in a thousand leaflets. To get there, drive south up from the Geiranger jetty and watch for the sign after about 5km; the car park offers extravagant views, but the Flydalsjuvet is about 200m away, out at the end of a slippery and somewhat indistinct track.

Practicalities

Buses to Geiranger stop a stone's throw from the waterfront and a couple of hundred metres from the **ferry terminal**. The latter is used by both the ferry from Hellesylt and the **Hurtigrute**, which detours from – and returns to – Ålesund on its northbound route only; it leaves Geiranger at 1.30pm. The **tourist office** (May–Sept daily 9am–7pm, Oct–April Mon–Fri 9am–5pm; ☎70 26 30 99, ⓦwww.geiranger.no) is close by, also on the waterfront, beside the sightseeing boat dock. Staff issue bus and ferry timetables, sell hiking maps and supply free village maps, which usefully outline local hiking routes. They also promote expensive boat tours of the fjord, though the car ferry from Hellesylt is perfectly adequate.

There are several **hotels** to choose from, but advance reservations are strongly advised in July and August. Cream of the crop is the large and lavish *Union* (☎70 26 83 00, ⓦwww.union-hotel.no; ❼/❺; March to late Dec), high up the hillside but just 300m up the road from the jetty. There's been an hotel here since 1891 and although the present building, with its retro flourishes, is hardly startling, the public rooms are large and lodge-like, there's a sauna and both indoor and outdoor pools. In addition, the bedrooms are pleasantly furnished in modern style and the best have fjord-view balconies; those on floor four are the best. In addition, the *Union* does a first-rate help-yourself buffet dinner at 325kr – easily the best **food** around. Another good hotel option is the ultramodern timber-built *Grande Fjordhotell* (☎70 26 30 90, ☎70 26 31 77; ❹; May–Sept), which has a pleasant fjordside location about 2km north of the centre on the road to Eidsdal. They also have **cabins** (❸) and a **campsite**, which is adjacent to the very similar *Grande Turisthytter og Camping* (☎70 26 30 68, ☎70 26 31 17). The main campsite, *Geiranger Camping* (☎ & ☎70 26 31 20), sprawls along the fjordside fields a couple of hundred metres to the east of the tourist office. In summer it's jam-packed with caravans, cars and motorbikes – not much fun at all. Finally, there's an unofficial **hostel**, the family-run *Vinjebakken* (☎70 26 32 05; July to mid-Aug), near the old (octagonal) church up the road from the jetty and off to the left.

From mid-June to August, local **buses** run north into Geiranger from either Grotli or Langvatn on Hwy 15 – it depends on the service. There are two buses daily, one going straight into Geiranger (1hr), the other (2hr) making a dramatic detour up a rough mountain toll-road to the **Dalsnibba viewpoint**, overlooking the Geirangerfjord at 1476m. This same local bus pushes north out of Geiranger heading for Åndalsnes (see p.332) via the Trollstigen, a journey that takes just over three hours. Åndalsnes can also be reached by a number of other routes, including trains from Oslo.

North to Åndalsnes via the Trollstigen

Promoted as the "Golden Route", the 80km journey **from Geiranger to Åndalsnes** along Hwy 63 is famous for its mountain scenery – no wonder. Even by Norwegian standards, the route is of outstanding beauty, the road bobbing past a whole army of austere peaks whose cold severity is daunting. The journey also incorporates a ferry ride across the Norddalsfjord, a shaggy arm of the Storfjord, but the most memorable section is the **Trollstigen**, a mountain road that cuts an improbable course between the Valldal valley and Åndalsnes. At the end of the trip,

2.3 | NORWAY | Bergen and the western fjords

331

small-town **Åndalsnes** is an ideal base for further fjordland explorations and has a couple of smashing places to stay. It's also the northern terminus of the dramatic **Rauma train line** (see p.725) from Dombås to the east.

Twice-daily from mid-June to August, a special **bus** travels the length of the Golden Route, taking the sweat out of driving round its hairpins and hairy-scary corners. The higher parts of the road are generally closed from early October to mid-May – earlier/later if the snows have been particularly heavy.

Over the Trollstigen

Heading north from Geiranger, the first part of the Golden Route is the 22-kilometre, knuckle-whitening jaunt up the **Ørnevegen** (Hwy 63) to **Eidsdal** on the Norddalsfjord. From here, a **car ferry** (every 30–45min; 10min; passengers 18kr, car & driver 43kr) shuttles over to the **Linge** jetty, from where it's just 3km east to **SYLTE**, a shadowy, half-hearted village that straggles along the fjord. More importantly, Sylte marks the start of the road over the **Trollstigen** ("Troll's Ladder"), a dramatic trans-mountain route that is equally compelling in either direction. The road negotiates the mountains by means of eleven hairpins with a maximum gradient of 1:12, but it's still a pretty straightforward drive until, that is, you meet a tour bus coming the other way – followed by a bit of nervous backing up and re-positioning. Drivers (and cyclists) should also be particularly careful in wet weather.

From Sylte, the southern end of the Trollstigen starts gently enough with the road rambling up the **Valldal** valley, passing dozens of fresh strawberry stalls in June and July – many Norwegians reckon these are the best strawberries in the country, some say the world. Thereafter, the road swings north, building up a head of steam as it bowls up **Meiadal** valley bound for the barren mountains beyond. It's here that the road starts to climb in earnest, clambering up towards the bleak and icy plateau-pass marking its high point. At the top, there are the inevitable cafés and souvenir shops, but it's all pretty low-key and a fast-flowing river muffles every untoward sound as it rushes off the plateau to barrel down the mountain below. A five-minute walk leads over to the **Utsikten** (viewing point), from where there's a magnificent panorama over the surrounding mountains and valleys. From here, the sheer audacity of the road becomes apparent, zigzagging across the face of the mountain and somehow managing to wriggle round the tumultuous, 180-metre **Stigfossen Falls**. Clearly visible to the west are some of the region's most famous mountains peaks: Bispen and Kongen (the "Bishop" and the "King") are the nearest two, at 1462m and 1614m respectively. If you're feeling extremely energetic, the pass is one place you can pick up the **Kløvstien**, the original drovers' track over the mountains – abandoned when the road was completed in 1936. It is not, however, an easy route to follow and parts are very steep with chains to assist. Consequently, most hikers prefer to undertake more manageable outings west to nearby peaks and mountain lakes. By contrast, the mountains to the east are part of the **Trollveggen** mountain wall and remain the preserve of climbers. As usual, prospective hikers should come properly equipped and watch for sudden weather changes.

Beyond the hairpins on the north side of the Trollstigen, the road resumes its easy ramblings, scuttling along the Isterdal to meet the E136 just 6km from Åndalsnes.

Åndalsnes

Almost six hours by train from Oslo, **ÅNDALSNES** is, for many travellers, their first – and sometimes only – contact with the fjord country, a distinction it doesn't really warrant. Despite a wonderful setting between lofty peaks and chill waters, the town itself is unexciting: small (with a population of just 3500), modern and industrial, and sleepy at the best of times. That said, Åndalsnes is an excellent place to orientate yourself and everything you're likely to need is near at hand, not least some first-rate accommodation. Åndalsnes also makes an ideal base for further fjord explorations. Within easy reach by ferry, bus and/or car is some wonderful scenery, from the stern peaks that bump away inland through to the fretted fjords that stretch towards the open sea. There's also the matter of **Rødven stave church** (late June to late Aug daily 11am–4pm; 30kr), just half an hour's drive away - from Åndalsnes, head east round the Isfjord and after 22km take the signed turning which covers the final 10km. In an idyllic setting amid meadows, by a stream and overlooking a slender arm of the Romsdalsfjord, the church dates from around 1300, though its distinctive wooden supports may have been added in 1712 during the first of several subsequent remodellings. Every inch a country church, the place's creaky interior holds boxed pews, a painted pulpit and a large medieval crucifix, but it's the bucolic setting which most catches the eye.

Practicalities

Buses all stop outside the **train station**, where you'll also find the **tourist office** (late June to Aug Mon–Sat 10am–7pm, Sun 1–7pm; Sept to late June Mon–Fri 9am–5pm; ☏71 22 16 22, ✆www.andalsnes.net). Staff provide bus timetables, regional guides and a wide range of local information geared to make you use Åndalsnes as a base. Their free *Dagsturer* (day-trips) booklet gives details of all sorts of motoring excursions, and most recommendations include a short hike, too. There's also details of fishing trips to the fjord (3 daily; 4hr; 250kr), local day-long hikes and guided climbs (from 1500kr), and fixed-rate sightseeing expeditions with Åndalsnes Taxi (☏71 22 15 55), which charges, for example, 500kr for a brief scoot down the Trollstigen. This is, however, hardly a bargain when you consider the special deals offered by local car hire firms. Åndal Bil (☏71 22 22 55), for instance, charge around 650kr for a 24-hour car rental. The tourist office has all the latest information on local deals. Local **hiking maps** are sold at *Romsdal Libris*, a couple of minutes' walk from the tourist office in the centre of town.

The tourist office also has a small supply of en-suite **private rooms** which go for around 450kr per double, with self-catering facilities and bed linen provided – but note that most are a good walk from the town centre. Alternatively, Åndalsnes has a delightful HI **hostel** (mid-May to mid-Sept; ☏71 22 13 82, ✉aandalsnes.hostel @vandrerhjem.no), a two-kilometre hike west out of town on the E136. To get there, head up the hill out of the centre, keep straight onto the E136 at the traffic island at the top, go past the turning to Dombås, staying on the E136 in the direction of Ålesund; cross the river and it's signed on the left-hand side. The hostel has a pleasant rural setting and its simple rooms (including some doubles; ➋), in a group of modest wooden buildings, are extremely popular, making reservations pretty much essential. The buffet-style **breakfast**, with its fresh fish, is one of the best hostellers are likely to get in the whole country. Note that the hostel doesn't do evening meals (though there are cooking facilities) and reception is closed from 10am–4pm. Bikes can also be rented here. The other excellent choice, the *Grand Hotel Bellevue*, Åndalsgata 5 (☏71 22 75 00, ✆www.grandhotel.no; ➎), occupies a large whitewashed block, with attractive Art Deco touches, on a hillock just up from the train station; it's the second hotel here – its predecessor was bombed to bits in 1940. The rooms on the top floors – four and five – have great views, well worth the extra 100kr or so. Otherwise, the modern *Rauma Hotell*, Vollan 16, is right in the centre of town in the mini-pedestrianized area near the station (☏71 22 32 70, ✆71 22 32 71; ➍); it's a bit cheaper, but despite its recent refurbishment lacks character. Among several local **campsites**, *Åndalsnes Camping og Motell* (☏71 22 16 29, ✆www.andalsnescamp.no) has a fine riverside setting about 3km from the town centre – follow the route to the youth hostel but turn first left immediately after the river. It's a well-equipped site with cabins (➊) as well as bikes, boats, canoes and cars available for rent. For **food**, the *Buona Sera* pizzeria, a brief walk from the station up the hill out of town, serves filling Italian food at reasonable prices, but much better is the evening buffet served at the *Grand Hotel Bellevue* for 175kr from 6pm to 9.45pm; go early to catch the best of the spread.

From Åndalsnes, there are regular **express buses** to Ålesund (3–4 daily; 2hr 25min).

Ålesund

On the coast at the end of the E136, some 120km west of Åndalsnes, the fishing and ferry port of **ÅLESUND** is immediately – and distinctively – different from any other Norwegian town. Neither old clapboard houses nor functional concrete and glass is much in evidence, but instead the centre boasts a proud conglomeration of pastel-painted facades, lavishly decorated and topped off by a forest of towers and turrets. There are dragons and human faces, Neoclassical and mock-Gothic facades, decorative flowers and even a pharaoh or two, the whole ensemble set amid the town's several harbours. These architectural eccentricities sprang from disaster: in 1904, a dreadful fire left 10,000 people homeless and the town centre destroyed, but within three years a hectic reconstruction programme saw almost the entire area rebuilt in a bizarre Art Nouveau style, which borrowed heavily from the German *Jugendstil* movement. Many of the Norwegian architects who undertook the work had been trained in Germany, so the Jugendstil influence is hardly surprising, but this was no simple act of plagiarism: the Norwegians added all sorts of whimsical, often floric flourishes to the Ålesund stew. The result was – and remains – an especially engaging stylistic hybrid and Kaiser Wilhelm II, who footed the bill, was mightily pleased.

Arrival and information

From north to south, Ålesund's town centre is about 700m wide. The **bus station** is situated on the southern waterfront, across from the **tourist office** in the Rådhus (June–Aug Mon–Fri 8.30am–7pm, Sat 9am–5pm, Sun 11am–5pm; Sept–May Mon–Fri 8.30am–4pm; ☎70 15 76 00, ⊛www.visitalesund.com). Southbound local ferries depart from beside the bus station, northbound from the other side of the harbour, just metres from the quay for the **Hurtigrute coastal boat** (southbound 12.45am, northbound 9.30am for Geiranger, 6.45pm for Trondheim).

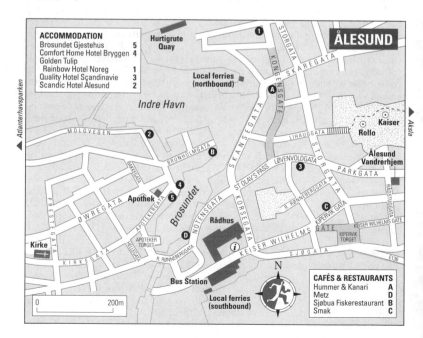

Accommodation

One of Ålesund's real pleasures is the quality of its downtown **hotels**, but the town is equipped with other, less expensive options too, most temptingly a waterfront **guesthouse** and an HI **hostel**, *Ålesund Vandrerhjem*, in the centre at Parkgata 14 (☎70 11 58 30, ✉aalesund.hostel@vandrerhjem.no; May–Sept). The hostel is small and clean verging on the cosy, and has double rooms (**②**) as well as dorm beds.

Brosundet Gjestehus Apotekergata 5 ☎70 12 10 00, ⓦwww.brosundet.no. Excellent guesthouse, occupying an attractively converted waterside warehouse, with a sauna, washing machines and self-catering facilities and offering an excellent breakfast (included in the rates). **④**

Comfort Home Hotel Bryggen Apotekergata 1 ☎70 12 64 00, ⓦwww.choicehotels.no. Smart hotel in a carefully modernized old waterside warehouse, with good facilities and well-appointed rooms. **②/④**

Golden Tulip Rainbow Hotel Noreg Kongens gate 27 ☎70 12 29 38, ⓦwww.rainbow-hotels.no. Suffers by comparison with its rivals, but the upper floors of this modern block do offer sea views and the rooms are perfectly adequate. **⑤/③**

Quality Hotel Scandinavie Løvenvoldgata 8 ☎70 15 78 00, ⓦwww.choicehotels.no. Efficient chain hotel inhabiting a grand old Art Nouveau edifice, unfortunately spoiled by an especially horrid set of automatic front doors. Brisk bedrooms. **④/③**

Scandic Hotel Ålesund Molovegen 6 ☎21 61 45 00, ⓦwww.scandic-hotels.com. It may be one of a chain and occupy a modern block, but there's something very appealing about this relaxed and friendly hotel. The rooms are bright and cheerful – but be sure to ask for one with a sea view. **②/④**

The town

Pedestrianized **Kongens gate**, the main drag, features several of the town's architectural highlights, as does **Apotekergata**, where the old "Apothek" (pharmacy) building, at the corner of Bakkegata, has, with its bay windows and sturdy circular tower, a decidedly neo-baronial appearance. Neighbouring **Kirkegata** is perhaps the most harmonious street of all, its long line of Art Nouveau houses decorated with playful turrets and towers reminiscent of a Ruritanian film set. Up along Kirkegata is Ålesund's finest building, its **kirke** (church; June–Aug Tues–Sun 10am–2pm; free). Completed in 1909, the church is decidedly Romanesque in style, from the hooped windows through to the roughly dressed stone blocks and the heavy-duty tower, but inside the high altar is flanked by the most wonderful of **frescoes**, a blaze of colour that fair takes the breath away; it was the work of one Enevold Thømt in the 1920s.

Further architectural intricacies are covered in the free but verbose *On Foot in Ålesund*, available at the tourist office (see below), though you'd be much better off signing up for one of their **guided walking tours** (mid-June to mid-Aug 1 daily; early May to early June & late Aug to late Sept Sat only; 1hr 30min; 60kr). The other obvious objective in the town centre is the **park** at the top of Lihauggata. It's a surprise to find monkey puzzle and copper beech trees here, as well as a large statue of **Rollo**, a Viking chieftain born and raised in Ålesund, who seized Normandy and became its first duke in 911; he was an ancestor of William the Conqueror. Nearby, there's also a much smaller bust of the town's benefactor, the kaiser, in which – if you're used to images of him as a grizzled older figure in a helmet – he looks disarmingly youthful. From the park, several hundred steps lead to the top of the **Aksla hill**, where the view out along the coast and its islands is fabulous. Otherwise, Ålesund's lively centre, which drapes around its oldest harbour, the **Brosundet**, makes for a pleasant stroll, and you can watch the ferries and Hurtigbåt coming and going to the islands just offshore.

Ålesund also possesses one of those prestige tourist attractions so beloved of development boards and councillors. It's the **Atlantic Sea-Park** (*Atlanterhavsparken*; mid-June to mid-Aug Mon–Fri & Sun 10am–7pm, Sat 10am–4pm; mid-Aug to mid-June Mon–Sat 11am–4pm, Sun noon–5pm; ⓦwww.atlanterhavsparken.no; 85kr), a large-scale recreation of the Atlantic marine environment including several enormous fish tanks; there's also an outside area with easy footpaths and bathing sites. The Sea-Park is located 3km west of Ålesund on a low-lying headland; there are no public transport links.

Eating and drinking

For **food**, the *Sjøbua Fiskerestaurant*, Brunholmgata 1 (℡70 12 71 00; closed Sun), round the corner from the *Comfort Home Hotel Bryggen*, serves wonderful seafood in chic surroundings and even has its own lobster tank. It's expensive but very popular, so reservations are advised. Similarly excellent is *Hummer & Kanari*, Kongens gate 19 (℡70 12 80 08), where a house speciality is *klippfisk* (salted and dried cod) cooked every which way. In sunny weather, everyone flocks to the **terrace bar** of the *Metz*, by the Brosundet harbour at Notenesgata 1. The interior is, however, rather tacky, so in poorer weather, take a drink instead at *Smak*, Kipervik gata 5.

Travel details

Trains

Åndalsnes to: Dombås (2 daily; 1hr 30min); Oslo (2 daily; 6hr 30min).
Bergen to: Geilo (4–5 daily; 3hr); Myrdal (4–5 daily; 1hr 50min); Oslo (4–5 daily; 6hr 30min); Voss (4–5 daily; 1hr 10min).
Dombås to: Trondheim (3–4 daily; 2hr 30min); Åndalsnes (2 daily; 1hr 30min).
Myrdal to: Flåm (June to late Sept 11–12 daily; Oct–May 2–4 daily; 50min).

Buses

Ålesund to: Bergen (1–2 daily; 10hr); Hellesylt (1–2 daily except Sat; 2hr 40min); Stryn (1–2 daily except Sat; 4hr); Trondheim (1–2 daily; 8hr 10min); Åndalsnes (3–4 daily; 2hr 20min).
Åndalsnes to: Geiranger (mid-June to late Aug 2 daily; 3–4hr); Kristiansand (2 daily; 3hr); Ålesund (3–4 daily; 2hr 20min).
Balestrand to: Oslo (3 daily; 8hr 15min); Sogndal (2 daily; 1hr 10min).
Bergen to: Dombås (1 daily; 12hr); Grotli (1 daily; 8hr); Hellesylt (1–2 daily; 8hr 15min); Kinsarvik (2 daily; 2hr 40min); Loen (3 daily; 6hr 30min); Lofthus (2 daily; 3hr); Norheimsund (3 daily; 2hr); Oslo (1 daily; 11hr); Skei (3 daily; 5hr); Sogndal (3 daily; 4hr 15min); Stavanger (1–5 daily; 5hr 40min); Stryn (3 daily; 6hr 45min); Trondheim (1 daily; 14hr); Utne (2 daily; 2hr 45min); Voss (4 daily; 1hr 45min); Ålesund (1–2 daily; 10hr).
Mundal to: Oslo (3 daily; 7hr 50min).
Geiranger to: Åndalsnes (mid-June to late Aug 2 daily; 3–4hr).
Sogndal to: Balestrand (2 daily; 1hr 10min); Bergen (3 daily; 4hr 15min); Mundal (3 daily; 35min); Oslo (3 daily; 7hr); Stryn (1–2 daily; 4hr 30min); Voss (3 daily; 3hr).
Stryn to: Bergen (2 daily; 7hr); Hellesylt (1–2 daily; 1hr); Oslo (1 daily; 8hr 30min); Trondheim (1 daily; 8hr).

Ulvik to: Voss (2–4 daily; 1hr).
Voss to: Bergen (4 daily; 1hr 45min); Norheimsund (3 daily; 2hr); Sogndal (2 daily; 3hr); Ulvik (2–4 daily; 1hr).

Boats

A plethora of boats shuttles between the settlements dotting the western fjords. There are two main types of service, **car ferries** and **Hurtigbåt express passenger boats**. They are supplemented by the **Hurtigrute coastal boat**.

Principal car ferries

Balestrand to: Mundal, Fjærland (late May to early Sept 2 daily; 1hr 25min).
Bruravik to: Brimnes (1–2 hourly; 10min).
Dragsvik to: Hella (every 30min; 15min); Vangsnes (hourly; 25min).
Fodnes to: Manheller (hourly; 15min).
Geiranger to: Hellesylt (May–Sept 4–8 daily; 1hr).
Hella to: Dragsvik (every 30min; 15min); Vangsnes (hourly; 15min).
Utne to: Kinsarvik (2 hourly; 25min).

Hurtigbåt

Bergen to: Balestrand (1–2 daily; 4hr); Flåm (1–2 daily; 5hr 30min); Sogndal (1–2 daily; 5hr).
Bergen to: Kinsarvik (1–3 daily; 2hr 20min); Lofthus (1–3 daily; 2hr 35min); Utne (1–3 daily; 1hr 50min).
Flåm to: Balestrand (1–2 daily; 1hr 30min); Bergen (1–2 daily; 5hr 15min); Sogndal (Mon–Sat 1–3 daily; 1hr 10min).

Hurtigrute

Northbound departures: daily from Bergen at 8pm; Ålesund at 9.30pm & 6.45pm; Trondheim at noon.
Southbound departures: daily from Trondheim at 10am; Ålesund at 12.45am; arrives Bergen, where the service terminates, at 2.30pm.

2.4

Trondheim to the Lofoten

Marking the transition from the rural south to the blustery north is the 900-kilometre-long stretch of Norway that extends from Trondheim to the island-studded coast near Narvik. Easily the biggest town hereabouts is **Trondheim**, a charming place of character and vitality which boasts an imposing cathedral – the finest medieval building in the country. Trondheim is also the capital of the **Trøndelag** province, whose sweeping valleys are – by Norwegian standards at least – very fertile, and it is, to boot, readily accessible from Oslo by train. But travel on one of the express trains that thunder further north, and you begin to feel far removed from the more intimate south. Distances between places grow ever greater, the travelling becomes more of a slog, and as Trøndelag gives way to the province of **Nordland** the scenery becomes ever wilder and more forbidding – "Arthurian", thought Evelyn Waugh.

The **E6** thrashes north from Trondheim over the hills and down the dales, but with the exception of the rugged landscape there's not much to detain you until you reach **Mo-i-Rana**, an industrial town that has partly – and successfully – rejigged and reinvented itself to attract the passing tourist. Just north of Mo-i-Rana on the E6, you cross the **Arctic Circle** – one of the principal targets for many travellers – at a point where the cruel and barren scenery seems strikingly appropriate. The circle marks the southernmost point at which the sun does not sink below the horizon in summer, or rise above it in winter – the Midnight Sun and the Polar Night. Here, they occur on one day each every year – at the summer and winter solstices – but the further north you go, the longer the phenomena last.

Beyond the Arctic Circle, the mountains of the interior lead down to a fretted, craggy coastline and even the towns, the largest of which is the port of **Bodø**, have a feral quality about them. The iron-ore port of **Narvik**, in the far north of Nordland, has perhaps the wildest setting of them all, and was the scene of some of the fiercest fighting between the Allied and Axis forces in World War II. To the west lies the offshore archipelago that makes up the **Vesterålen and Lofoten islands**. In the north of the Vesterålen, between **Harstad** and **Andenes**, the coastline of this island chain is mauled by massive fjords, whereas to the south, the Lofoten are backboned by a mighty and ravishingly beautiful mountain wall – a highlight of any itinerary. Among a handful of idyllic fishing villages the pick is the tersely named **Å**, though **Henningsvær** and **Stamsund** come a very close second.

Transport is good, which is just as well given the isolated nature of much of the region. The **Hurtigrute coastal boat** stops at all the major settlements on its route up the Norwegian coast from Bergen to Kirkenes, while the islands are accessed by a variety of **ferries** and **Hurtigbåt passenger express boats**. The E6 – sometimes known as the "Arctic Highway" – is the major road north from Trondheim; it's kept in excellent condition, though caravans can make the going very slow. The **train** network reaches as far north as Fauske and nearby Bodø, from either of which **buses** make the trip on to Narvik, itself the terminal of a separate rail line which runs the few kilometres to the border and then south through Sweden. The only real problem is likely to be **time**. It's a day or two's journey from Trondheim to Fauske, another to Narvik, and without time to spare you should think twice before venturing further: the travelling can be arduous, and in any case it's pointless if done at a hectic pace.

Trondheim

An atmospheric city with much of its antique centre still intact, **TRONDHEIM** was known until the sixteenth century as Nidaros ("mouth of the river Nid"), its importance as a military and economic power base underpinned by the excellence of its harbour and its position at the head of a wide and fertile valley. The early Norse parliament, or *Ting*, met here, and the cathedral was a major pilgrimage centre

at the end of a route stretching all the way back to Oslo. After a fire destroyed much of the city in 1681, Caspar de Cicignon, a military engineer from Luxembourg, rebuilt Trondheim on a gridiron plan, with broad avenues radiating from the centre to act as firebreaks. Cicignon's layout has survived intact, giving the city centre an airy, elegant air, though most of the buildings date from the commercial boom of the late nineteenth century. With timber warehouses lining the river and doughty stone structures dotting the main streets, the city centre is a suitably dignified and prosperous setting for the cathedral, one of Scandinavia's finest medieval structures.

Trondheim is now Norway's third city, but the pace is slow and easy and the main sights are best appreciated in leisurely fashion over a couple of days. Genial and eminently likeable, Trondheim is also a pleasant place to wave goodbye to city life if you're heading for the wilds of the north.

Arrival, information and city transport

Trondheim is on the E6 highway, seven or eight hours' drive (500km) from Oslo. It's a major stop for the **Hurtigrute coastal boat** (@www.hurtigruten.com), which docks at the harbour north of the centre, from where it's a dull fifteen-minute walk to **Sentralstasjon**, the gleaming bus and train terminal, where there's an **information kiosk** (☎177) dealing with all transport enquiries. You can save yourself the walk from the Hurtigrute quay by taking a taxi – it's about 60kr to the city centre. The all-year **Kystekspressen passenger express boat** from Kristiansund docks at the Hurtigbåt dock, which is also behind Sentralstasjon. From Sentralstasjon, you simply cross the bridge to reach the triangular island that holds all of central Trondheim.

If you're **driving**, a toll of 35kr is levied in either direction on the E6 near Trondheim, and there's another municipal toll of 15kr (Mon–Fri 6am–6pm) as you approach the city itself. **Parking** can be a pain. On-street parking during restricted periods (mostly Mon–Fri 8am–6pm, Sat 10am–1pm) is expensive and hard to find, so it's best to head for a car park: try the handy Torvet P-hus, in the centre at Erling Skakkes gate 16, or the marginally cheaper (and slightly less convenient) Bakke P-hus, east across the bridge from the centre at Nedre Bakklandet 60. Rates are around 10kr an hour. At other times, on-street parking is free and spaces are easy to find.

Trondheim **airport** is 35km northeast of the city at Værnes. From here, Flybussen buses (Mon–Fri 5am–9pm every 15min, Sat 5am–5.45pm every 30min, Sun 6.45am–9pm every 15–30min; 55kr) run to Sentralstasjon and points in the city centre, including the *Radisson SAS Royal Garden* hotel; journey time is about 45 minutes.

Information

The **tourist office**, Munkegata 19, sits right in the centre of town on the corner of the main square, Torvet (Sept to mid-May Mon–Fri 9am–4pm; mid-May to early June & late Aug Mon–Fri 8.30am–6pm, Sat & Sun 10am–4pm; mid- to late June & mid-Aug Mon–Fri 8.30am–8pm, Sat & Sun 10am–6pm; early Aug Mon–Fri 8.30am–10pm, Sat & Sun 10am–8pm; ☎73 80 76 60, @www.trondheim.com). Staff provide the free and very useful *Trondheim Guide* (also available from the information racks at Sentralstasjon) and a wide range of other free tourist literature including a cycle map of the city and its surroundings; they also have a limited supply of private rooms, though these are almost entirely out in the suburbs. You can also buy hiking maps and change money here.

City transport

The best way of exploring the city centre is **on foot** – it only takes about ten minutes to walk from one end to the other – but a convenient alternative is to take advantage of the city's **free bicycle rental**. Bright green municipal bikes are available from racks all over the city centre and are released upon payment of a small deposit (20kr); the money is returned automatically when you return the bike – just like a shopping trolley. The bikes are popular, so don't be surprised if you come across a rack that's empty. A map marking the locations of the racks is available from the tourist office. For longer excursions, **mountain bikes** can be rented from Ila Sykkelsenter, Steinberget 1 (☎73 51 09 40), at about 160kr a day. Otherwise, transport in town is by **buses** and **trams** with flat-fare tickets, from the

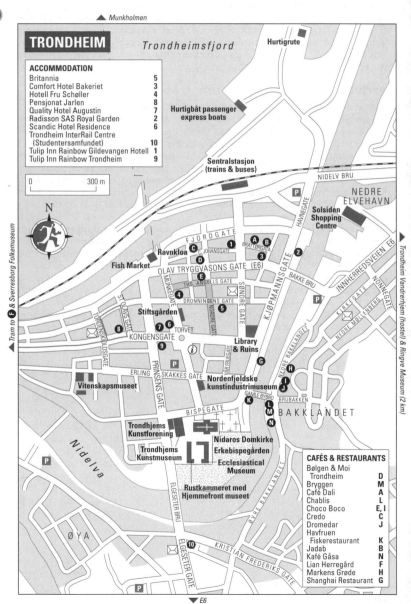

TRONDHEIM

Trondheimsfjord

Hurtigrute

ACCOMMODATION

Britannia	5
Comfort Hotel Bakeriet	3
Hotell Fru Schøller	4
Pensjonat Jarlen	8
Quality Hotel Augustin	7
Radisson SAS Royal Garden	2
Scandic Hotel Residence	6
Trondheim InterRail Centre (Studentersamfundet)	10
Tulip Inn Rainbow Gildevangen Hotell	1
Tulip Inn Rainbow Trondheim	9

0   300 m

N

▲ Munkholmen

Hurtigbåt passenger express boats

Sentralstasjon (trains & buses)

NIDELV BRU

NEDRE ELVEHAVN

Solsiden Shopping Centre

◄ Tram to F & Sverresborg Folkemuseum

FJORDGATE

Ravnkloa

Fish Market

OLAV TRYGGVASONS GATE (E6)

THS. ANGELLS GATE

DRONNINGENS GATE

Stiftsgården

KONGENSGATE

TORVET

Library & Ruins

Vitenskapsmuseet

ERLING SKAKKES GATE

Nordenfjeldske kunstindustrimuseum

GAMLE BYBRO

BRUBAKKEN

BAKKLANDET

BISPEGATE

Trondhjems Kunstforening

Trondhjems Kunstmuseum

Nidaros Domkirke

Erkebispegården

Ecclesiastical Museum

Rustkammeret med Hjemmefront museet

Nidelva

ØYA

KRISTIAN FREDERIKS GATE

ELGESETER GATE

▼ E6

▲ Trondheim Vandrerhjem (hostel) & Ringve Museum (2 km)

CAFÉS & RESTAURANTS

Bølgen & Moi Trondheim	D
Bryggen	M
Café Dali	A
Chablis	L
Choco Boco	E, I
Credo	C
Dromedar	J
Havfruen Fiskerestaurant	K
Jadab	B
Kafé Gåsa	N
Lian Herregård	F
Markens Grøde	H
Shanghai Restaurant	G

driver, costing 22kr. If you need to travel outside town, to one of the outlying museums or the campsite, it might be worth buying the unlimited 24-hour public transport ticket, the *dagskort*, which costs 55kr from the driver and is valid on all local buses and trams.

Accommodation

Accommodation is plentiful in Trondheim, with a choice of private rooms, two hostels and a selection of reasonably priced hotels and guesthouses (*pensjonater*). What's more, most of the more appealing places are dotted round the city centre, though the private rooms booked via the tourist office are usually out in the suburbs. These **private rooms** are good value, however, at a fixed rate of 400–440kr per double per night (250–320kr single), plus a 20kr booking fee and a 30kr deposit.

Hotels

Britannia Dronningens gate 5 ☎73 80 08 00, ⓦ www.britannia.no. Right in the middle of town, this long-established hotel has a magnificent Art Nouveau breakfast room, complete with a Moorish fountain, Egyptian-style murals and Corinthian columns. The comfortable rooms are heavily discounted in summer. ❼/❹

Comfort Hotel Bakeriet Brattørgata 2 ☎73 99 10 00, ⓦ www.choicehotels.com. Competent chain hotel in a pleasantly modernized former bakery. Central location. ❺/❸

Hotell Fru Schøller Dronningens gate 26 ☎73 87 08 00, ⓦ www.scholler.no. Spick and span hotel in a central location above a café, with just 25 rooms. Modern furnishings and fittings. ❺/❹

Quality Hotel Augustin Kongens gate 26 ☎73 54 70 00, ⓦ www.hotel-augustin.no. Routine chain hotel in a big, old brick building not far from the Torvet. Functional and perfectly adequate rooms. ❺/❹

Radisson SAS Royal Garden Kjøpmannsgata 73 ☎73 80 30 00, ⓦ www.radissonsas.com. Stylish modern hotel with sweeping architectural lines and wonderfully comfortable beds. Good summer deals make this more affordable than you might expect. Banquet-like breakfasts, too. Highly recommended. ❼/❹

Scandic Hotel Residonce Torvet ☎73 52 83 80, ⓦ www.scandic-hotels.com. Package-tour favourite, with standard double rooms. More expensive than most of its competitors until the summer, when there's a discount of thirty percent. ❼/❹

Tulip Inn Rainbow Gildevangen Hotell Søndre gate 22B ☎73 87 01 30, ⓦ www.rainbow-hotels .no. In a sturdy Romanesque Revival stone building, a couple of minutes' walk northeast of Torvet, this chain hotel offers eighty or so comfortable, modern rooms with a touch of style. ❻/❹

Tulip Inn Rainbow Trondheim Kongens gate 15 ☎73 50 50 50, ⓦ www.rainbow-hotels.no. Big and popular chain hotel in a plain and chunky modern block, right in the centre. The bar here is one of the few places where you can get home-made mead (*mjød*); as in medieval England, this was once Norway's most popular brew. ❺/❹

Hostels

Trondheim InterRail Centre Elgeseter gate 1 ☎73 89 95 38, ⓦ www.stud.ntnu.no/studorg/tirc. In the unusual, big, red and round building – the Studentersamfundet (university student centre) – just over the bridge at the south end of Prinsens gate, a five-minute walk from the cathedral. Offers basic bed-and-breakfast dormitory accommodation at 120kr per person per night; there's an inexpensive café, too.

Trondheim Vandrerhjem Rosenborg Weidemannsvei 41 ☎73 87 44 50, ⓦ www.trondheim-vandrerhjem.no. Mostly parcelled up into four-bed dorm rooms, this large and well-equipped HI hostel looks more like a hospital than somewhere you'd want to stay from the outside, but the interior is pleasant enough – especially the comfortable, newer rooms. There are self-catering facilities, a laundry and a canteen. A twenty-minute, 2km hike east from the centre: cross the Bakke bru onto busy Innherredsveien (the E6) and walk uphill; turn right onto Wessels gate and it's on the left at the fourth crossroads. To save your legs, take any bus up Innherredsveien and ask the driver to let you off as close as possible. Open all year.

The City

The historic centre of Trondheim sits on a small triangle of land bordered by the River Nid, with the curve of the long and slender Trondheimsfjord beyond. **Torvet** is the main city square, a spacious open area anchored by a statue of St Olav perched on a tall stone pillar like some medieval Nelson. The broad avenues that radiate out from here were once flanked by long rows of wooden buildings, which served all the needs of the small town and administrative centre. Most of these older structures are long gone, replaced for the most part by uninspiring modern constructions, though one notable survivor is the **Stiftsgården**, a fine timber mansion erected in the late eighteenth century. Nevertheless, this is small beer compared with the **Nidaros Domkirke** (cathedral), an imposing, largely medieval structure that is the city's architectural high point. The cathedral dominates the southern part of the centre and close by are the much-restored **Erkebispegården** (Archbishop's Palace) and the pick of Trondheim's several museums, the **Nordenfjeldske Kunstindustrimuseum** (Museum of Decorative Arts) and the **Trondheim Kunstmuseum** (City Art Gallery). Near here too, on the far side of the **Gamle Bybro** – the old town bridge – is a clutter of old warehouses and timber dwellings that comprises the prettiest and most fashionable part of town, **Bakklandet**, home to its best restaurants and bars.

Nidaros Domkirke

The goal of Trondheim's pilgrims in times past was the colossal cathedral, **Nidaros Domkirke**, Scandinavia's largest medieval building (May to mid-June & late Aug to mid-Sept Mon–Fri 9am–3pm, Sat 9am–2pm, Sun 1–4pm; late June to late Aug Mon–Fri 9am–6pm, Sat 9am–2pm, Sun 1–4pm; mid-Sept to April Mon–Fri noon–2.30pm, Sat 11.30am–2pm, Sun 1–3pm; 35kr, includes entry to Erkebispegården). Gloriously restored following several fires and the upheavals of the Reformation, it remains the focal point of any visit to the city and is best explored in the early morning, when it's reasonably free of tour groups. The building, still known by Trondheim's former name, is dedicated to King – later Saint – Olav. Born in 995, **Olav Haraldsson** followed the traditional life of the Viking chieftain from the tender age of 12, "rousing the steel-storm" (as the saga writers put it) from Finland to Ireland. He also served as a mercenary to both the duke of Normandy and King Ethelred of England, and it was during this time that he was converted to Christianity. In 1015 he invaded Norway, defeated his enemies and became king, though his zealous imposition of Christianity alienated many of his followers and the bribes of Olav's rival Knut (Canute), King of England and Denmark, did the rest: Olav's retainers deserted him and he was forced into exile in 1028. Two years later, he was back in the Trøndelag, but the army he had raised was far too weak to defeat his enemies, and Olav was killed in battle near Trondheim.

Olav may have lost his kingdom, but the nationwide church he founded had no intention of losing ground. Needing a local **saint** to consolidate its position, the church carefully nurtured the myth of Olav, a beatification assisted by the oppressive rule of the "foreigner" Knut. After the final battle, Olav's body had been spirited away and buried on the banks of the River Nid at what is today Trondheim. There were rumours of miracles in the vicinity of the grave and, when the bishop arrived to investigate these strange goings-on, he exhumed the body and found it uncorrupted. Olav was declared a saint, his body was placed in a silver casket and Olav Kyrre, who became King of Norway in 1066, started work on the grand church that was to house the remains in appropriate style. Over the years the church was altered and enlarged to accommodate the growing bands of medieval tourists. It achieved cathedral status in 1152 and subsequently became the traditional burial place of Norwegian royalty.

The cathedral itself is a magnificent blue- and green-grey soapstone edifice with a copper-green spire and roof and a fancy set of gargoyles on the choir. It's also a true amalgam of architectural styles. The original eleventh-century church was a simple basilica, but subsequent alterations enlarged it considerably. The Romanesque transepts, with their heavy hooped windows and dog-tooth decoration, were built by English stonemasons from Lincoln in the twelfth century, while the early Gothic choir, with its flying buttresses and intricate tracery, is clearly influenced by contemporaneous churches in England. The nave was built in the early thirteenth century, also in the early Gothic style, but was destroyed by fire in 1719; the present structure is a painstakingly accurate late nineteenth-century replica.

Inside the cathedral, the gloomy half-light hides much of the lofty decorative work, but it is possible to examine the striking **choir screen**, whose wooden figures are the work of Gustav Vigeland. The other item of particular interest is a famous fourteenth-century **altar frontal** (the front panel of an altar painting) displayed in a chapel off the ambulatory, directly behind the high altar. This is the earliest surviving representation of Olav's life and times, created during a period when few Norwegians could read or write and the saint's cult had to be promoted visually.

You can also take a peek at the assorted Norwegian **crown jewels** (April–May & late Aug to Oct Fri noon–2pm; June to late Aug Mon–Thurs & Sat 9am–12.30pm, Sun 1–4pm; free), kept at the west end of the church. What you won't see, however, is St Olav's silver casket-coffin: this was taken to Denmark and melted down for coinage in 1537. Two other features are the English-language **guided tours** of the cathedral (mid-June to mid-Aug at 11am, 2pm & 4pm; 30min), and the climb up the cathedral **tower** (every half-hour late June to late Aug Mon–Fri 10am–5pm, Sat 10am–12.30pm, Sun 1–3.30pm; 5kr). From the top, there's a fine view of the city and the forested hills that surround it, with the fjord trailing away in one direction, the river valley in the other.

Archbishop's Palace

Behind the Domkirke lies the heavily restored **Archbishop's Palace** (*Erkebispegården*). This courtyard complex was originally built in the twelfth century for the third archbishop, Øystein, but two stone-and-brick wings are all that survive of the original quadrangle – the others were added later. After the archbishops were kicked out during the Reformation, the palace became the residence of the Danish governors. It was subsequently used as the city armoury, and many of the old weapons are now displayed in the **Army and Resistance Museum** (*Rustkammeret med Hjemmefrontmuseet*; June–Aug Mon–Fri 9am–3pm, Sat & Sun 11am–4pm; Sept–Oct & March–May Sat & Sun 11am–4pm; free), which occupies the west wing. The first floor gives the broad details of Norway's involvement with the interminable Dano–Swedish wars that wracked Scandinavia from the fifteenth to the nineteenth century. Of more general interest, the second floor describes the German invasion and occupation of Norway during World War II, dealing respectfully with the sensitive issue of collaboration: you can turn on the radio to hear **Vidkun Quisling**'s radio speech announcing his coup d'état of April 9, 1940. There are also some intriguing displays on the daring antics of the Norwegian Resistance, notably in an extraordinary – perhaps hair-brained – attempt to sink the battleship *Tirpitz* as it lay moored in an inlet of the Trondheimsfjord in 1942. This escapade, like so many others, involved **Leif Larsen**, the Resistance hero who is commemorated by a statue on the Torget in Bergen. Larsen worked closely with the Royal Navy, who organized covert operations in occupied Norway from their base in the Shetlands. Supplies and personnel were transported across the North Sea by Norwegian fishing boats – a lifeline known, in that classically understated British (and Norwegian) way, as the "Shetland bus".

Moving on, the **south wing** now holds a smart ecclesiastical **museum** (early June & late Aug Mon–Fri 11am–3.30pm, Sat 11am–3pm, Sun noon–4.30pm; late June to late Aug Mon–Fri 10am–5pm, Sat 10am–3pm, Sun noon–5pm; May & early Sept Tues–Fri 11am–3.30pm, Sat 11am–3pm, Sun noon–4.30pm; mid-Sept to April Tues–Sat 11am–3pm Sun noon–4pm; 35kr or free with cathedral ticket), which is largely devoted to a few dozen medieval statues originally retrieved and put away for safekeeping during the nineteenth-century reconstruction of the nave and west facade. Many of the statues are too battered and bruised to be engaging, but they are well displayed and several are finely carved. In particular, look out for a life-size sculpture of poor old **St Denis**, his head in his hands (literally) in accordance with the legend that, after he was beheaded, he irritated his executioners no end by carrying his head to his grave. Downstairs, an assortment of finds unearthed during a lengthy 1990s archeological investigation of the palace demonstrates the economic power of the archbishops: they employed all manner of skilled artisans – from glaziers and shoemakers to rope-makers, armourers and silversmiths – and even minted their own coinage.

From the back of the Archbishop's Palace, you can stroll out onto the grassy lawns beside the **River Nid**. A trio of rusting bastions offers a reminder of the military defences that once protected this side of town, while footpaths snake round to the sturdy old tombs and wild flowers of the **graveyard**, just to the east of the cathedral's main entrance, but it's the setting that really appeals.

The Museum of Decorative Arts and City Art Museum

A couple of museums close to the Domkirke provide some varied entertainment, in particular the delightful **Museum of Decorative Arts**, a couple of minutes' walk away at Munkegata 5 (*Nordenfjeldske Kunstindustrimuseum*; June to late Aug Mon–Sat 10am–5pm, Sun noon–5pm; late Aug to May Tues–Wed & Fri–Sat 10am–3pm, Thurs 10am–5pm, Sun noon–4pm; ⊛www.nkim.museum.no; 40kr). The museum's collection is too extensive to be shown in its entirety at any one time, so displays are rotated regularly, and there's also an ambitious programme of temporary exhibitions focusing on contemporary arts, craft and design. Start in the basement, where bourgeois life in Trøndelag from the sixteenth century to 1900 is illustrated via an eclectic assemblage of furniture, faïence, glassware and silver, along with some twentieth-century pieces, notably a fine selection of **Art Nouveau** ceramics and furniture. The domestic theme is developed on the first floor, where there's a room kitted out by the Belgian designer and architect Henri van de Velde. An unusual display of folkloric tapestries produced in Trondheim in the early years of the twentieth century is also generally on display on this floor – they're modelled on original paintings by the Norwegian Gerhard Munthe, one of whose specialities was the portrayal of medieval folk tales. More modern works can be found on the second floor, but the highlight here is the room devoted to fourteen stunning tapestries by **Hannah Ryggen**, each done in a naive style with flair and vigour.

The **City Art Museum** (*Trondhjems Kunstmuseum*; June–Aug daily 10am–5pm; Sept–May Tues–Sun 11am–5pm; 30kr), near the cathedral at Bispegata 7B, is quite small, but features an enjoyable selection of works by Johan Dahl and Thomas Fearnley, the leading figures of nineteenth-century Norwegian landscape painting, as well as the romantic canvases of Hans Gude and his chum Adolph Tidemand. Also displayed is the first overtly political work by a Norwegian artist: *Streik* (*The Strike*) was painted in 1877 by the radical Theodor Kittelsen, better known for his illustrations of the folk tales collected by Jorgen Møe and Pieter Asbjørnsen. If you missed the work of Edvard Munch in Oslo, there's a diverting selection of his woodcuts, sketches and lithographs here, including several of those disturbing, erotically charged personifications of emotions – *Lust, Fear* and *Jealousy* – that were so characteristic of his oeuvre. Munch's works are not clearly labelled, but an inventory is available free at reception. The bad news is that most of the permanent collection is not on view during some of the larger temporary exhibitions – even Munch gets the heave-ho.

From the Stiftsgården to Bakklandet

One conspicuous remnant of old timber-town Trondheim survives in the city centre – the **Stiftsgården** (early to mid-June Mon–Sat 10am–3pm, Sun noon–5pm; late June to late Aug Mon–Sat 10am–5pm, Sun noon–5pm; guided tours every hour on the hour till 1hr before closing: 50kr), which stretches out along Munkegata just north of Torvet. Built in 1774–78, this good-looking yellow creation is claimed to be the largest wooden building in northern Europe. These days it serves as an official royal residence – a marked social improvement on its original function as home to the provincial governor. Inside, a long series of period rooms with fanciful Italianate wall-paintings and furniture comes in a range of late eighteenth- to early nineteenth-century styles, from Rococo to Biedermeier, that reflect the genteel tastes of the early occupants. The anecdotal guided tour brings a smile – but not perhaps 50kr wide.

From the Stiftsgården, it's a couple of minutes' walk east to the **medieval church ruins** discovered under the library at the far end of Kongens gate. A twelfth-century relic of the days when Trondheim had fifteen or more religious buildings, it is thought to have been a chapel dedicated to St Olav, although the evidence for this is a bit shaky. Excavations revealed nearly 500 bodies in the immediate area, which was once the church graveyard, and the skeletons on display are neatly preserved under glass. Entry is free and the site is accessible during library opening hours (July to mid-Aug Mon, Tues, Thurs & Fri 9am–4pm, Wed 9am–7pm, Sat 10am–3pm; mid-Aug to June Mon–Thurs 9am–7pm, Fri 9am–4pm, Sat 10am–3pm; plus Sept–April Sun noon–4pm).

Following the river south from the library, it's a short walk to the **Gamle Bybro** (Old Town Bridge), an elegant wooden reach with splendid views over the early eighteenth century gabled and timbered warehouses which flank Kjøpmannsgata. Most of these are now restaurants and offices, and there are more restaurants and several groovy bars at the far end of the bridge in the brightly painted old timber houses of the **Bakklandet** area, Trondheim's own "Left Bank".

Out from the centre: the Ringve museum

The **Ringve Museum** (late May to June & Aug to mid-Sept daily 11am–3pm; July daily 11am–5pm; mid-Sept to mid-May Sundays 11am–4pm; ⓦ www.ringve.com; 70kr) occupies a delightful eighteenth-century country house and courtyard complex on the hilly Lade peninsula, some 4km northeast of the city centre. Devoted to musical history and to musical instruments from all over the world, the museum is divided into two sections. In the main building, the collection focuses on **antique European instruments** in period settings, with several demonstrations included in a lengthy – and obligatory – guided tour. The second section, in the old barn, contains an **international selection of musical instruments** and offers a self-guided zip through some of the key moments and movements of **musical history**. There are themes like "the invention of the piano" and "pop and rock", not to mention the real humdinger, "the marching band movement in Norway". Immaculately maintained, the surrounding **botanical gardens** (daily; free) make the most of the scenic setting. To get there, take bus #3 or #4 to Lade from Munkegata.

Eating and drinking

As befits Norway's third city, Trondheim has a healthy selection of first-rate **restaurants**, but although they offer a variety of cuisines, the Norwegian places almost always have the gastronomic edge. In the particular, there's a cluster of excellent restaurants in the **Bakklandet** district, by the east end of the Gamle Bybro; the area also holds a string of laid-back and fashionable **café-bars**, where the food is usually very good and much less expensive than in the restaurants. There's another cluster of very recommendable café-bars and **bars** – Trondheim boasts a hectic weekend scene – in the **Brattørgata** district, in the centre near the west end of Bakke bru, and yet more of both in **Nedre Elvehavn**, an imaginatively revamped old industrial area on the water's edge near the east end of Bakke bru and the location of the whopping Solsiden shopping centre. As for **opening hours**, some restaurants open for a couple of hours at lunch times and then in the evening, but many just stick to the evenings and some are closed one day a week. Café-bars and bars almost invariably stay open from 11am or noon till the early hours of the morning – or at least until there's no-one left, while restaurants mostly open up at about 5pm or 6pm.

Finally – if needs must – the city's mobile **fast-food** stalls are concentrated around Sentralstasjon and along Kongens gate, on either side of Torvet.

Restaurants

Bryggen Øvre Bakklandet 66 ☎73 87 42 42. Superb, smart and classy seafood restaurant at the east end of the Gamle Bybro, where daily specials, mostly featuring the catch of the day, are a delight. Main courses average about 200kr. Closed Sun.

Bølgen & Moi Trondheim Carl Johans gate 5 ☎73 56 89 00. The new kid on Trondheim's (upmarket) restaurant block. Top-notch seasonal ingredients are used to create a stylish and innovative menu featuring both Norwegian and international dishes. As way of recommendation, this is where the Norwegian princess Mærtha Louise had her pre-wedding party when she married the writer Ari Behn in 2002.

Chablis Øvre Bakklandet 62 ☎73 87 42 50. Just metres from the Gamle Bybro, this polished brasserie-restaurant with its modish furnishings and fittings serves up excellent food: Norwegian but with a Mediterranean slant. Shares a kitchen with the neighbouring *Bryggen* (see above), but the prices are a good deal lower.

Credo Ørjaveita 4 ☎73 53 03 88. Smart and very popular Mediterranean/Spanish influenced place with delicious daily specials at very competitive prices. Ground-floor premises, with a stylishly modern bar upstairs.

Havfruen Fiskerestaurant Kjøpmannsgata 7 ☎73 87 40 70. An excellent fish restaurant near the cathedral – one of the best in town, with prices to match – main courses from 200kr. Try to book in advance. Closed Sun.

Jadab Brattørgata 3A. Indian food without the kitsch decor; all the standard dishes, friendly service and inexpensive prices.

Lian Herregård Lianveien 36 ☎72 55 90 77. Up in the forested hills about 8km west of the city centre, this traditional Norwegian restaurant has a terrace bar affording panoramic views over the Trondheimsfjord. Getting there is enjoyable, too: catch the Lian tram (the Gråkallbanen) from St Olavs gate and stay on till you reach the terminus, from where it's a couple of minutes' walk up the hill to the restaurant; note that at weekends the place is often too busy to be much fun. Open April–September Tues–Sun noon–6pm; rest of year, telephone for times.

Markens Grøde Nedre Bakklandet 58. The city's main vegetarian restaurant, featuring tasty food, a creative menu and a friendly atmosphere. Main courses at around 70kr.

Shanghai Restaurant Kjøpmannsgata 21 ☎73 51 47 77. Excellent Chinese restaurant, offering Szechuan dishes at affordable prices.

Cafés

Café Dali Brattørgata 7. Ground-floor café serving small portions of international food, from Tom Yam soup through to tapas. Good place for a coffee and/or a light meal and lunch. See also bars, below.

Choco Boco Nedre Bakklandet 5; Tryggvassons gate 29; TMV-Kaia 3; Nedre Elvehavn. Of the three locations, the pick is the Nedre Elvehavn branch with plenty of indoor and outdoor seating, plus entertainingly arty decor. Serves coffee, cakes and light meals – salads, sandwiches and so forth.

Patchy service, but still a good place to hang out.

Dromedar Nedre Bakklandet 3A. A modern café-bar with a laid-back atmosphere located a few metres north of the Gamle Bybro. The best coffee in the city plus snacks and light meals: filled bagels, sandwiches and the like.

Kafé Gåsa Øvre Bakklandet 58. With its traditional Norwegian decor and clutter of folksy bygones, this intimate café-bar is a charming place. Good local food and a great terrace in sunny weather.

Bars and nightclubs

BarMuda TMV-Kaia 11 Nedre Elvehavn. Relaxed cocktail bar with comfortable couches and an arty, punk-meets-New-Age clientele.

Brukbar Munkegata 26. Interesting, colourful bar catering for just about everyone – from business

folk dropping in for an after-work snifter through to hardcore student boozers. Note the peculiar bee-shaped wall-lamps.

Café Dali Brattørgata 7. First-floor bar above *Café Dali* (see above), offering a nice combination of industrial decor and cocktails.

Credo Bar Ørjaveita 4. Modish first-floor bar above the *Credo* restaurant (see opposite).

Frakken Dronningens gate 12 ☎73 52 24 42. High-octane bar and nightclub – all tight trousers and highlight hairdos. Popular generally, and raucous at the weekend. At the corner with Nordre gate.

Metro Kjøpmannsgata 12 ☎73 52 05 52. Trondheim's only gay and lesbian bar. DJ sounds on the weekend. Wed, Fri & Sat.

3B Brattørgata 3B ☎73 51 15 50. Rock'n'roll/indie club-cum-bar for drinking well into the wee hours.

Trondheim Mikrobryggeri Prinsens gate 39. Mainstream bar serving its own microbrewery ales. Filling pub food too, and a friendly atmosphere.

Listings

Car rental Avis, Kjøpmannsgata 34 ☎73 84 17 90; Budget, Elgeseter gate 21 ☎73 94 10 25; and at the *Radisson SAS Royal Garden Hotel*, Kjøpmannsgata 73 ☎73 52 69 20; Europcar, Trondheim airport ☎74 82 67 00.

Consulates UK, Beddingen 8 ☎73 60 02 00; Poland, TMV-Kaia 23 ☎73 87 69 00.

Emergencies Ambulance ☎113; Fire ☎110; Police ☎112.

Hiking Trondhjems Turistforening, just west of the centre at Sandgata 30 (☎73 92 42 00, ⊛www.tt.no), is the DNT's local branch, offering advice on the region's hiking trails and huts. Guided walks and cross-country skiing trips, with activities concentrated in the mountains to the south and east of the city, are also available, from one-day excursions to longer expeditions that suit different levels of skill and fitness.

Internet access Free Internet access at the

library, Peter Egges plass 1 (☎72 54 75 00; July to mid-Aug Mon, Tues, Thurs & Fri 9am–4pm, Wed 9am–7pm, Sat 10am–3pm; mid-Aug to June Mon–Thurs 9am–7pm, Fri 9am–4pm, Sat 10am–3pm; plus Sept–April Sun noon–4pm).

Pharmacy The main late- and weekend-opening pharmacy is St Olav Vaktapotek, Kjøpmannsgata 65 (☎73 88 37 37). Also Løveapoteket Ryhaven, Olav Tryggvasons gate 28 (☎73 83 32 83).

Police station Kongens gate 87 ☎73 89 90 90.

Post office Main office, with poste restante, at Dronningens gate 10 (Mon–Fri 8am–5pm, Sat 9am–2pm).

Taxis Eight ranks in and around the city centre including those at Torvet, Sentralstasjon, Søndre gate and the Radisson SAS Royal Garden Hotel; or call Trønder Taxi ☎73 90 90 73.

Vinmonopolet There's a city-centre branch at Kjøpmannsgata 32.

North from Trondheim to Fauske

North of Trondheim, it's a long haul up the coast to the next major places of interest: **Bodø**, the main ferry port for the Lofoten, and the gritty but likeable town of **Narvik**, respectively 720km and 910km distant. The easiest way to make the bulk of the trip is by **train**, a rattling good journey with the scenery becoming wilder and bleaker the further north you go – and you'll usually get a blast from the whistle as you cross the Arctic Circle. The train takes nine hours to reach **Fauske**, where the line reaches its northern limit and turns west for the last 65-kilometre dash to Bodø. At Fauske, there are **bus** connections north to Narvik, a further five-hour drive, but many travellers take an overnight break here – though in fact nearby Bodø is a far more pleasant place.

If you're **driving**, you'll find the E6 – which runs all the way from Trondheim to Narvik and points north – too slow to make more than three or four hundred kilometres comfortably in any one day – more, and the journey becomes a tiresome thrash. Fortunately, there are several pleasant places to stop, beginning with Trøndelag's **Snåsa**, a relaxing village beside the E6 with somewhere good to stay. Further on, in Nordland, the next region up, lies **Mo-i-Rana**, once a grimy steel town, but now attractively rehashed and the obvious starting point for a visit to the **Svartisen glacier,** which crowns the coastal peaks close by.

The only alternative to the E6 is the coastal Highway 17, the **Kystriksveien**, an ingenious and extremely scenic cobbling together of road, tunnel, bridge and ferry that negotiates the shredded coastline from **Steinkjer**, just north of Trondheim, all the way up to Bodø, a distance of nigh on 700km. Join the Kystriksveien just west of Mo-i-Rana for the best of the scenery.

Hell to Snåsa

Leaving Trondheim, the **E6** tunnels and twists its way round the Trondheimsfjord to **Hell**, a busy rail junction where one line forks north to slice through the dales and hills of Trøndelag en route to Fauske, while the other heads east for the seventy-kilometre haul to the Swedish frontier, with Östersund (see p.349) beckoning beyond. Just beyond Hell, the road forks too, with the E6 thumping north and the E14 zipping east. Hell itself has nothing to recommend it, except its name, though even this is a bit of a let-down when you realise that *hell* in Norwegian means good fortune: don't despair, the locals still sell postcards of the train station's freight depot tagged "Hell – gods ekspedisjon". Pressing on along the E6, it's about 160km to **SNÅSA**, a sleepy, scattered hamlet, whose farms roll over the gentle, lightly wooded countryside. It looks as if nothing much has happened here for decades, yet there is one sight of note, a pretty little hilltop **church** of softly-hued grey stone, dating from the Middle Ages and very much in the English style. On the west side of the village – 6km from the E6 – is the *Snåsa Hotell* (℡74 15 10 57, www.snasahotell .no; ❹/❸), a modern place with somewhat spartan decor, but comfortable bedrooms and a lovely setting overlooking the lake; it's a peaceful spot, ideal if you want to rest after a long drive. The hotel also operates a small **campsite** (same numbers; all year) with cabins (❷) as well as spaces for tents and caravans. There's a restaurant here too, serving mundane but filling Norwegian staples, but note that if you're likely to arrive hungry and late (after 7pm), you should telephone ahead to check it will still be open.

Mo-i-Rana and around

Beyond Snåsa, the E6 leaves the wooded valleys of the Trøndelag for the wider, harsher landscapes of **Nordland**. The road bobs across bleak plateaux, scuttles along rangy river valleys and eventually – after 300km – reaches **MO-I-RANA**, or "Mo", hugging the head of the Ranafjord. A minor port and market town until World War II, Mo was transformed by the construction of a large steel plant in the postwar period. The plant dominated proceedings until the 1980s, when there was some economic diversification and the town began to clean itself up. The fjord shore was cleared of its industrial clutter and the E6 was rerouted to create the pleasantly spacious and surprisingly leafy town centre of today. Most of Mo is resolutely modern, but look out for the pretty **Mo kirke**, a good-looking structure of 1832 with a pitched roof and onion dome, perched on a hill on the eastern edge of the town centre. Otherwise, Mo is first and foremost a handy base for visiting the east side of the Svartisen glacier (see p.349) and/or exploring the region's lakes, fjords and mountains, though it does possess a couple of minor surprises: it's home to the main archives of the **National Library** (*Nationalbiblioteket*), and its waterfront sports an Antony Gormley sculpture, **Havmannen**, who stands facing the sea "getting the waves up and down his legs".

Practicalities

Mo's **bus** and **train stations** are close together, down by the fjord on Ole Tobias Olsens gate. The compact town centre lies east of this street, with the foot of the main pedestrianized drag, Jernbanegata, opposite the bus station. The **tourist office** is about 300m to the south of the bus and train stations, also on Ole Tobias Olsens gate (mid-Aug to mid-June Mon–Fri 9am–4pm; mid-June to mid-Aug Mon–Fri 9am–8pm, Sat 9am–4pm, Sun 1–7pm; ℡75 13 92 00, www.arctic-circle.no). Staff have the usual local leaflets, provide free town maps and issue the free booklet that details the Kystriksveien (the Highway 17 Coastal Route; see box on p.350). Bus timetables are available, too, but local services are much too patchy to allow you to explore the town's environs without your own transport. In this regard, there's **car rental** – at around 700kr a day – from Avis, located at the Hydro Texaco Røssvoll gas station (℡75 14 81 57). If that looks too expensive, note that the tourist office is

The Grønligrotta cave

The limestone and marble mountains to the northwest of Mo are pocked by **caves**. The most accessible is the limestone **Grønligrotta** (mid-June to mid-Aug daily 10am–7pm; 70kr), where the easy forty-minute guided tour follows a subterranean river. Grønligrotta is lit by electric lights – it's the only illuminated cave in Scandinavia – and it's reached via (and signposted off) the road between the E6 and the Svartisen glacier (see below).

usually able to arrange a shared taxi ride to the most popular local attraction, the Svartisen glacier – there are no buses – and while you're here be sure to check that the boats that give access to the glacier are running.

The best of the town's several **hotels** is the excellently run and very comfortable *Meyergården*, at the north end of Ole Tobias Olsens gate (☏75 13 40 00, ⓦwww.meyergarden.no; ❺/❸). Most of the building is modern, but the original lodge has survived and is maintained in period style, with stuffed animal heads on the wall and elegant panelled doorways. Much less expensive – and much plainer – is the *Fjordgården Hotell Mo i Rana*, down by the waterfront at Søndregate 9 (☏75 15 28 00, ⓦwww.fjordgarden.no; open May to Aug; ❸). A happy medium – don't be deterred by the exterior – is the cosy rooms of the *Fammy Leilighetshotell*, Ole Tobias Olsens gate 4 (☏75 15 19 99, ⓦwww.fammy.no; ❸). A fourth and final option, located about 12km north of town along the E6, is *Anna's Camping & Rom* (☏75 14 80 74; mid-May to mid-Sept), a riverside site where there are cabins (❷) as well as tent pitches.

For **food**, first choice must be the *Meyergården Hotell*, where the restaurant serves an excellent range of Norwegian dishes featuring local ingredients; main courses average around 150kr. There's also the *China Kro*, in the centre of town at Nordahl Griegs gate 9 (☏ 75 15 15 93), where the Chinese food is renowned across Nordland and even pulls in punters from Sweden; main courses are around 100kr. Alternatively, the *Abelone mat & vinstue*, Ole Tobias Olsens gate 6, does competent pizzas and steaks, whilst *Babettes*, in the centre at Ranheimgata 2, is good for light meals and coffee.

The Svartisen glacier

Norway's second largest glacier, **Svartisen** – literally "Black Ice" – covers roughly 370 square kilometres of mountain and valley between the E6 and the coast. It's actually divided into two sections – east and west – by the Vesterdal valley, though this cleft is a recent phenomenon: when it was surveyed in 1905, the glacier was one giant block, about 25 percent bigger than it is today; the reasons for this change are still obscure. The highest parts of the glacier lie at around 1500m, but its tentacles reach down to about 170m – the lowest-lying glacial arms in mainland Europe. Mo is within easy reach of one of the glacier's eastern nodules: to get there, drive north from town on the E6 for about 12km and then take the signed turning to the glacier, a straightforward 23-kilometre trip ending beside the ice-green, glacial lake **Svartisvatnet**. Here, **boats** (late June to Aug, hourly or every 2hr 10am–4pm; 20min each way; 75kr return) shuttle across the lake, but note that services can't begin until the ice has melted – usually by late June, so check with Mo tourist office before you set out. Viewed from the boat, the great convoluted folds of the glacier look rather like bluish-white custard, but close up, after a stiff three-hour hike past the rocky detritus left by the retreating ice, the sheer size of the glacier becomes apparent: a mighty grinding and groaning wall of ice edged by a jumble of ice chunks, columns and boulders.

The west side of the Svartisen can be seen and visited via the coastal highway, the Kystriksveien (see box on p.350).

The Kystriksveien Coastal Route on Highway 17

Branching off the E6 just beyond Steinkjer, the tortuous **Kystriksveien** – the coastal route along Highway 17 – threads its way up the west coast, linking many villages that could formerly only be reached by sea. This is an obscure and remote corner of the country, but apart from the lovely scenery there's little of special appeal, and the seven ferry trips that interrupt the 688-kilometre drive north to Bodø (there are no buses) make it both expensive and time-consuming in equal measure. A free **booklet** describing the Coastal Route can be obtained at tourist offices throughout the region – including Mo – and it contains all of Highway 17's car-ferry timetables. You can also get information online at ⓦwww.rv17.no.

Conveniently, the stretch of Highway 17 between **Mo-i-Rana** and **Bodø** takes in (most of) the scenic highlights, can be negotiated in a day and saves a packet on ferry fares to boot. To sample this part of the route, drive 37km west from Mo along the E12 for the Highway 17 crossroads, from where it's some 60km north to the **Kilboghamn–Jektvik** ferry (3–6 daily; 1hr; driver and car 112kr) and a further 30km to the ferry linking **Ågskardet** with **Forgøy** (5–14 daily; 10min; driver and car 43kr). On the first ferry you cross the Arctic Circle with great views of the beautiful **Melfjorden**, and on the second, after arriving at Forgøy, you get a chance to see a westerly arm of the **Svartisen** glacier (see box on p.349), viewed across the slender Holandsfjorden. For an even closer look at the glacier, stop at the information centre in **HOLAND**, 12km beyond Forgøy, and catch the **passenger boat** (June to early Sept Mon–Fri 8am–9pm, Sat–Sun 10am or 11am to 5.30pm or 6.40pm; every 45min to 1hr 30min; 15min; 40kr return; ⓣ94 86 55 16), which zips across the fjord to meet a connecting bus; this travels the couple of kilometres up to the Svartisen Turistsenter (ⓣ75 75 00 11, ⓦsvartisen.no), merely 250m from the ice. The Turistsenter has a café, rents cabins (❷) and is the base for four-hour guided **glacier walks** (mid-June to mid-Aug only; prior booking is essential). For more on glacier walks see p.326. From Holand, it's 140km to the Saltstraumen (see p.355) and then 30km more to Bodø (see p.351).

The Arctic Circle

Given its appeal as a travellers' totem, and considering the amount of effort it takes to actually get here, crossing the **Arctic Circle**, about 80km north of Mo, is a bit of a disappointment. Uninhabited for the most part, the landscape is undeniably bleak, but the gleaming **Arctic Circle Centre** (*Polarsirkelsenteret*; daily: May to early June & Aug 9am–8pm; late June to July 8am–10pm; early Sept 10am–6pm; ⓦwww.polarsirkelsenteret.no) disfigures the scene: a giant lampshade of a building plonked by the roadside and stuffed with every sort of tourist bauble imaginable. You'll whizz by on the bus, the train toots its whistle as it passes by, and drivers can, of course, shoot past too – though the temptation to brave the crowds is strong and, even if you resist the Arctic exhibition (60kr), you'll probably get snared by either the "Polarsirkelen" certificate, or the specially stamped postcards. Outside the centre, a couple of simple stone memorials are poignant reminders of crueller times: they pay tribute to the Yugoslav and Soviet POWs who laboured under terrible conditions to build the Arctic railroad (Nordlandsbanen) to Narvik for the Germans in World War II.

Fauske

But for a brief stretch of line from Narvik into Sweden further north, **FAUSKE** marks the northernmost point of the Norwegian rail network and is, consequently, an important transport hub. Along with Bodø, the town is a departure point of the **Nord–Norgeekspressen**, the express bus service that carries passengers to Narvik and Tromsø, where you change – and stay overnight – before embarking on the next leg of the journey up to Alta (for Honningsvåg and Nordkapp). The bus leaves twice daily from beside Fauske train station, and tickets can be purchased from the driver or at any bus station. There are left-luggage lockers at the train station, and you can pick up information on the region's ferries there too from a leaflet-stuffed rack. Note that there is a fifty percent discount for InterRail and Scanrail pass holders on the route to Narvik (see p.355), a gorgeous five-hour run past fjords, peaks and snow. Most northbound **train travellers** spend the night in Fauske rather than making a quick change onto the connecting bus to Narvik or travelling on by train to Bodø, just forty minutes away to the west and a much more palatable place to stay.

From Fauske's **train station**, it's a five- to ten-minute walk down the hill and left at the T-junction to the local bus station, and a few metres more to the main drag, **Storgata**, which doubles as the E6. Storgata runs parallel to the fjord and holds the handful of shops that pass for the town centre. The **tourist office** (late Aug to mid-June Mon–Fri 8.30am–3.30pm; mid- to late June & mid-Aug–4pm; July to early Aug Mon–Fri 9am–7.30pm, Sat–Sun 10am–7pm; ☏75 64 33 03, ⓦwww.saltenreiseliv.no) is at the east end of Storgata at Sjøgata 86. Storgata holds the better of the town's two **hotels**, the *Fauske Hotell*, Storgata 82 (☏75 60 20 00, ⓔfirmapost@fauskehotell.no; ❻/❹), a chunky square block whose interior is made slightly sickly by a surfeit of salmon-coloured streaky marble. Quarried locally, the marble is exported all over the world, but is something of an acquired taste. Marble apart, the hotel rooms are comfortable enough, and the big, tasty breakfast is a real snip at 70kr. The most popular budget choice is the hostel-like *Seljestua*, just 500m from the train station at Seljeveien 2 (☏90 73 46 96; late June to mid-Aug; ❷), but much, much better is the *Lundhøgda* **campsite** (☏75 64 39 66, ⓔlundhogda@c2i.net; May–Sept). This occupies a splendid location about 3km west of the town centre, overlooking the mountains and the fjord: head out of town along the E80 (the Bodø road), turn off down a signposted country lane, ablaze with wild flowers in the summertime and flanked by old timber buildings. The campsite takes caravans, has spaces for tents and also offers cabins (❷).

Bodø and around

Readily reached by train or bus from Fauske, **BODØ**, 63km west of Fauske along the E80, is the terminus of the Trondheim train. Founded in 1816, the town struggled to survive in its early years, but was saved from insignificance by the herring boom of the 1860s. It later accrued several industrial plants and became an important regional centre, but was then heavily bombed during World War II, and nowadays there's precious little left of the proud nineteenth-century buildings that once flanked the waterfront. Nonetheless, Bodø manages a cheerful modernity, a bright and breezy place within comfortable striking distance of the old trading post of **Kjerringøy**, one of Nordland's most delightful spots. Bodø is also a regular stop on the Hurtigrute coastal boat route and, importantly, much the best place from which to hop over to the most interesting part of the Lofoten Islands.

Arrival and information

Bodø's **train station** is at the eastern end of the town centre, just off the long main street, Sjøgata. The southern **Lofoten ferry** (to and from Moskenes plus the islets of Værøy and Røst) and the **Hurtigrute coastal boat** use the docks (respectively) 500m and 700m northeast along the waterfront from the train station. The **bus station** is 700m west along Sjøgata from the train station, across from the gigantic *Radisson SAS Hotel Bodø*. Adjoining the bus station is the dock handling **Hurtigbåt passenger express boat** services for the Lofoten, most usefully to and from Svolvær.

The **tourist office** (June–Aug Mon–Fri 9am–8pm, Sat 10am–8pm, Sun noon–8pm; Sept–May Mon–Wed & Fri 9am–4pm, Thurs 9am–6pm, Sat 10am–3pm;

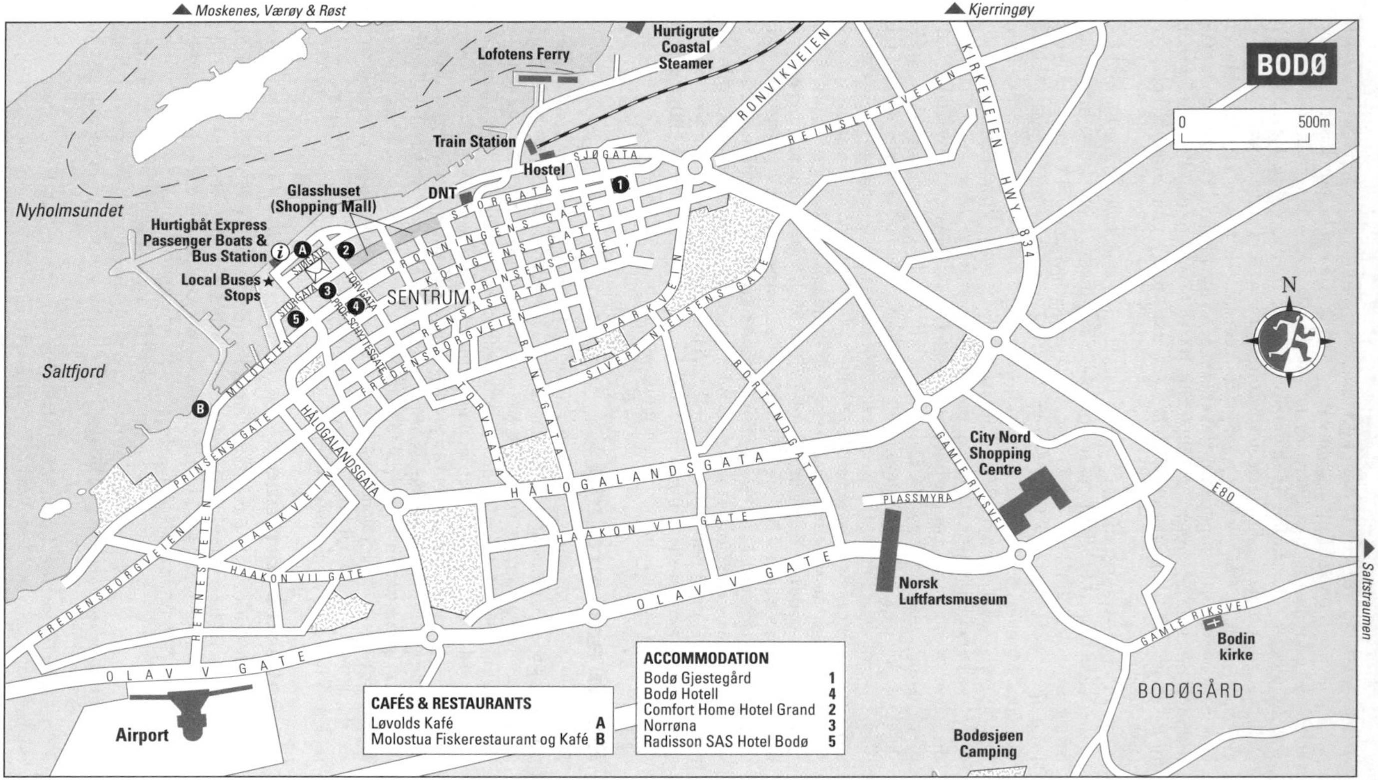
BODØ
0 500m
N
Moskenes, Værøy & Røst
Kjerringøy
Saltstraumen
Hurtigrute Coastal Steamer
Lofotens Ferry
Train Station
Hostel
DNT
Glasshuset (Shopping Mall)
Hurtigbåt Express Passenger Boats & Bus Station
Local Buses Stops
SENTRUM
Nyholmsundet
Saltfjord
City Nord Shopping Centre
Norsk Luftfartsmuseum
Bodin kirke
BODØGÅRD
Bodøsjøen Camping
Airport
KIRKEVEIEN HWY. 834
RONVIKVEIEN
REINSLETTVEIEN
SJØGATA
STORGATA
DRONNINGENS GATE
KONGENS GATE
PRINSENS GATE
RENSÅSGATA
RENSBORGVEIEN
FREDENSBORGVEIEN
TORVGATA
PROF. SCHYTTESGATE
MOLOVEIEN
PARKVEIEN
NIELSENS GATE
SIVERT
BANKGATA
BORTINDGATA
HÅLOGALANDSGATA
HAAKON VII GATE
OLAV V GATE
PLASSMYRA
GAMLE RIKSVEI
E80
PRINSENS GATE
HERNESVEIEN
ACCOMMODATION
Bodø Gjestegård 1
Bodø Hotell 4
Comfort Home Hotel Grand 2
Norrøna 3
Radisson SAS Hotel Bodø 5
CAFÉS & RESTAURANTS
Løvolds Kafé A
Molostua Fiskerestaurant og Kafé B

☎75 54 80 00, ⊛www.bodoe.com) shares the Hurtigbåt and bus station terminal building at Sjøgata 3; information on connections to the Lofoten Islands is available, as is an excellent town and district guide (free) and bike rental.

Accommodation

Bodø has a reasonable supply of **accommodation**, including half a dozen hotels and a couple of guesthouses. In addition, the tourist office has a small supply of **private rooms** in the town and its environs, with a fixed tariff of 300–350kr per double, plus a modest booking fee. There's also an HI **hostel**, *Bodø Vandrerhjem*, a spartan place next door to the train station at Sjøgata 55 (☎75 52 11 22, ⊕bodo.hostel@vandrerhjem.no; May–Sept). Finally, the town's **campsite**, *Bodøsjøen Camping*, Bodøsjøen (☎75 56 36 80, ⊕75 56 36 89), has a pleasant lakeside setting about 3.5km to the southeast of the centre, not far from the Bodin kirke. It has tent pitches, caravan hook-ups and cabins (**2**).

Bodø Gjestegård Storgata 90 ☎75 52 04 02, ⊕johansst@online.no. Bargain accommodation in this twenty-room guesthouse not far from the railway station. Breakfast included. **2**
Bodø Hotell Professor Schyttes gate 5 ☎75 54 77 00, ⊛www.bodohotell.no. Reasonably priced, mid-sized, mid-range hotel in a five-storey block right in the centre of town. Well-kept rooms with the usual mod cons plus oodles of pine in the Scandinavian style. **4**/**3**
Comfort Home Hotel Grand Storgata 3 ☎75 54 61 00, ⊛www.grand-bodo.no. Upmarket chain hotel in a smartly turned out building with appealing Art Deco flourishes. **6**/**4**
Norrøna Storgata 4B ☎75 52 55 50, ⊛www.norrona-hotell.bedre.no. Standard-issue chain hotel in a large modern block just metres from the bus station. At the lower end of the market, but still reliably comfortable. **3**/**2**
Radisson SAS Hotel Bodø Storgata 2 ☎75 52 41 00, ⊛www.radissonsas.com. The best hotel in town. Occupies an overly-large, modern concrete and glass tower block, but has commodious and well-appointed rooms – and those on the upper floors have great views out to sea. **7**/**4**

The Town

Bodø rambles over a low-lying, tapering peninsula that pokes out into the Saltfjorden, its long and narrow **centre** marked by two parallel main streets, Sjøgata and Storgata. The town is short of specific sights, but on the outskirts there is the imaginative **Norwegian Aviation Museum** (*Norsk Luftfartsmuseum*; mid-June to mid-Aug Sun–Fri 10am–7pm, Sat 10am–5pm; mid-Aug to mid-June Mon–Fri 10am–4pm, Sat & Sun 11am–5pm; ⊛www.aviation-museum.com; 70kr), which tracks through the general history of Norwegian aviation. It's housed in a building shaped like a two-bladed propeller: one blade houses air force and defence exhibits, the other concerns itself with civilian displays. The hub of the two blades straddles the outer ring road – Olav V's gate – and is topped by part of the old Bodø airport control tower. Among the planes to look out for are a Spitfire, a reminder that two RAF squadrons were manned by Norwegians during World War II, a rare Norwegian-made Hønningstad C-5 Polar seaplane and an American U2 spy plane – the US air force made regular use of Bodø throughout the Cold War. The museum is situated about 2km southeast of the centre, a dreary walk that you can avoid by catching one of several city buses – details from the bus station or the tourist office.

From the museum, it's a short drive east along the ring road to the Gamle Riksvei roundabout, where you turn right for the detour south to the onion-domed **Bodin kirke** (late June to mid-Aug Mon–Fri 10am–3pm; free), a pretty little stone church sitting snugly among clovery meadows. Dating from the thirteenth century, the church was modified after the Reformation by the addition of a tower and the widening of its windows; dark, gloomy churches were then associated with Catholic "superstition". It is, however, the colourful seventeenth-century fixtures that catch the eye, plus the lovingly carved Baroque altarboard and pulpit.

Eating and drinking

Bodø is hardly a gourmet's paradise, but there are one or two very competent **cafés** and **restaurants**, kicking off with the traditional and inexpensive Norwegian menu of *Løvolds Kafé* (closed Sun), down by the quay at Tollbugata 9; main courses here feature local ingredients and average around 100kr, daily specials 70kr. Moving upmarket, the first-rate, waterfront *Molostua Fiskerestaurant og Kafé*, Moloveien 9, is a café in the daytime and restaurant at night, when there's a tasty line in seafood and classic Norwegian dishes, often enlivened by French-style sauces; main courses are around 120kr. In addition, the *Radisson SAS Hotel* chimes in with both the *En Kopp* coffee bar, which makes the best coffee in town, and the **bar** with the best view, the swish *Top 13*.

Out from Bodø: Kjerringøy, Saltstraumen and the Svartisen glacier

There are three obvious excursions from Bodø: one northeast to the old trading station at **Kjerringøy**, another southeast to the tidal phenomenon known as the **Saltstraumen**, and a third south to the **Svartisen glacier**. The first two can be done by public transport, but are much easier with your own vehicle, while Bodø tourist office coordinate bus and ferry day-trips to Svartsen from June to August, every day except Saturdays. Excursions take twelve hours, departing Bodø bus station at 7.45am and arriving at the glacier at 11.30am; the cost is 390kr, but this doesn't include food. Be sure to have warm clothing. The glacier and the Saltstraumen can also be reached by car or bike on Highway 17 – the Kystriksveien – between Bodø and Mo-i-Rana (see p.348).

Kjerringøy

The **Kjerringøy trading post** (late May to mid-Aug daily 11am–5pm; 40kr), just 40km north along the coast from Bodø by road and ferry, boasts a superbly preserved collection of nineteenth-century timber buildings set beside a slender, islet-sheltered channel. This was once the domain of the Zahl family, merchant suppliers of everything from manufactured goods, clothes and farmyard foodstuffs to the fishermen of Lofoten. It was not, however, an equal relationship: the Zahls, who operated a local monopoly until the 1910s, could dictate the price they paid for the fish, and many of the islanders were permanently indebted to them. This social division is still very much in evidence at the trading post, where there's a marked distinction between the guestrooms of the main house and the fishermens' bunkbeds in the boat- and cookhouses. Indeed, the family house is remarkably fastidious, with its Italianate busts and embroidered curtains – even the medicine cabinet is well-stocked with formidable Victorian remedies like the bottle of "Sicilian Hair Renewer". There are enjoyable, hour-long **guided tours** around the main house throughout the summer (late May to mid-Aug daily, every hour on the hour; 25kr) and afterwards you can nose around the reconstructed general store, drop in at the café and stroll the fine sandy beach.

Getting here by car is easy enough – a straightforward coastal drive along Highway 834 with the added treat of a ferry ride (Festvåg to Misten, every half-hour or hour, less frequently on Sun; 10min; passengers 18kr, car and driver day return 43kr; ☎94 89 42 88). **By bus** (1–2 Mon–Fri & Sun; 73kr return including ferry), things are a tad more complicated, but a day-return trip beginning at Bodø bus station is possible Monday through Friday – pick up a combined bus-and-ferry schedule from Bodø tourist office. There's **accommodation** in Kjerringøy in the old parsonage, *Kjerringøy prestegård*, about 1km north of the trading post along the main road (☎75 51 07 80, ☎75 50 77 10; ✉ronvik.menighet@kirken.bodo.no). There are simple double rooms in the main building (❶) and slightly pleasanter ones in the renovated cowshed next door (❷).

Saltstraumen

Less interesting, but more widely publicized, is the maelstrom known as the **Saltstraumen**, 33km southeast of Bodø round the bay on Hwy 17. Billions of gallons of water are forced through this narrow, 150m-wide channel four times daily, making a headlong rush between inner and outer fjord. The creamy water is at its most turbulent at high tide, and its most violent when the moon is new or full – a timetable is available from Bodø tourist office. But although scores of tourists troop here for every high tide, you can't help but feel they wish they were somewhere else – the scenery is, in Norwegian terms at least, flat and dull, and the view from the bridge which spans the channel unexciting. There's a local **bus** service from Bodø to the Saltstraumen (Mon–Sat 5–7 daily, Sun 1 daily; 1hr), but the times rarely coincide with high tides, which means you'll end up hanging around. To pass the time you might drop by the **Saltstraumen Experience Centre** (*Saltstraumen Opplevelsessenter*; May–Aug daily 11am–6pm; Sept Sat & Sun 11am–6pm; 60kr), housed in two adjoining buildings near the east end of the bridge. The centre tells you all you'd ever wanted to know about tidal currents and also has several pools where you can take a close look at local fish, seals and tidepool life.

North to Narvik

The 240-kilometre journey north from Fauske to Narvik is spectacular, with the **E6** rounding the fjords, twisting and tunnelling through the mountains and rushing over high, pine-studded plateaux. This stretch of the highway presents two opportunities to catch a **car ferry** to the Lofoten – one at Skutvik, the other at Bognes. The more southerly of the two is **Skutvik**, 37km to the west of the E6, with ferries to Svolvær. At **Bognes**, where the E6 is interrupted by the Tysfjord, there's a choice of ferries. One sails to Lødingen and the E10 on the Lofoten, while a second hops over to **Skarberget** for the E6 and, after a further 80km, Narvik. Long-distance **buses** link Bodø, Fauske and Narvik twice daily.

Narvik

NARVIK, six hours from Fauske by bus along the E6, is a relatively modern town established less than a century ago to handle the iron ore brought by train from northern Sweden. It makes no bones about its main function: the **iron ore docks** are immediately conspicuous, slap bang in the centre of town and totally overwhelming the whole waterfront. Yet, for all the mess, the industrial complex is strangely impressive, its cat's cradle of walkways, conveyor belts, cranes and funnels oddly beguiling and giving the town a frontier, very Arctic feel. Not content with its iron, Narvik has also had a fair old stab at re-inventing itself as a **sports** centre with the emphasis on the extreme, becoming a popular destination for skiers, paragliders and scuba divers – and developing a good range of guesthouses to match.

Arrival and information

Fifteen minutes' walk from one end to the other, Narvik's sloping centre straggles along the main street, **Kongens gate**, which doubles as the E6. The **train station** is at the north end of the town, and from here it's a five- to ten-minute walk along Kongens gate to the **bus station**, in the basement of the Amfi shopping centre on the west side of the street. A few metres further along Kongens gate on the main square, the **tourist office** (early June Mon–Fri 9am–5pm, Sat & Sun 11am–5pm; mid-June to mid-Aug Mon–Fri 9am–5pm, Sat 10am–5pm, Sun 11am–5pm; late Aug Mon–Fri 9am–5pm, Sat 10am–3pm; Sept–May Mon–Fri 8.30am–3.30pm; ☎76 94 33 09, ⓦwww.narvikinfo.no) has a full range of bus and ferry timetables, and can provide lots of information on outdoor pursuits; staff will also assist with ferry and activity reservations. Amongst many outdoor options, there's **mountain climbing** and guided **glacier walking** with Nord-Norsk Klatreskole (☎76 95 13 53), who

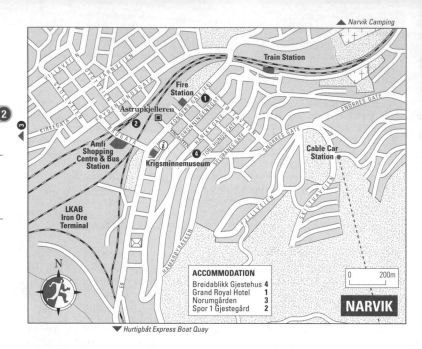

▲ *Narvik Camping*

Train Station

Fire Station ❶

Astrupkjelleren ❷

Amfi Shopping Centre & Bus Station

ⓘ

Krigsminnemuseum ❹

Cable Car Station

LKAB Iron Ore Terminal

N

0   200m

NARVIK

ACCOMMODATION
Breidablikk Gjestehus 4
Grand Royal Hotel 1
Norumgården 3
Spor 1 Gjestegård 2

▼ *Hurtigbåt Express Boat Quay*

also rent out the appropriate tackle, and **scuba diving** amidst the wreck-studded local waters with Narvik Dykk & Eventyr (☎99 51 22 05); they rent out equipment too, and provide diving tuition. From the tourist office, it's another five-minute walk down along Kongens gate to the south end of the town centre and the dock for the **Hurtigbåt passenger express boat** service to Svolvær on the Lofoten.

Accommodation

Narvik is a tad short of **hotels**, but it does have several very recommendable **guesthouses** and a reasonably convenient **campsite**, *Narvik Camping*, about 2km north of the centre on the E6 at Rombaksveien 75 (☎76 94 58 10, ⓦwww.opofoten.no), It's open all year and has tent and caravan pitches, hook-ups, and cabins at ❶.

Breidablikk Gjestehus Tore Hunds gate 41 ☎76 94 14 18, ⓦwww.narviknett.no/breida. Pleasant, unassuming guesthouse with homely, neat and trim en-suite rooms. Those on the upper floors have attractive views over town, and a good, hearty breakfast is included in the rates. It's located at the top of the steps at the end of Kinobakken, a side road leading east off Kongens gate, just up from the main town square. ❷

Grand Royal Kongens gate 64 ☎76 97 77 00, ⓦwww.grandroyalhotelnarvik.no. Some of Narvik's hotels have seen better days, but the *Grand*, just up from the tourist office, puts on a good show of wood-panelled elegance and has perfectly adequate rooms. ❻/❹

Norumgården B&B Framnesveien 127 ☎76 94 48 57, ⓦhttp://norumgaarden.narviknett.no. Lavish B&B in a fancy 1920s timber villa. The Germans used the place as an officers' mess during the war, and today, tastefully restored, it holds three large guest rooms, two of which have kitchenettes. Antiques are liberally distributed and breakfast is included in the (surprisingly low) room rate. ❸

Spor 1 Gjestegård Brugata 2A ☎76 94 60 20, ⓦwww.spor1.no. Set in a creatively recycled railway building just below the main town bridge, this trim guesthouse is the pick of the budget/backpacker options, with clean and comfortable double rooms in brisk, modern style; quads and a larger dorm room are also available. Kitchen facilities, a sauna and a bar on site. ❷

The town

Narvik's first modern settlers were the labourers who built the railway line to the mines in Kiruna, over the border in Sweden – a herculean task commemorated every March by a week of singing, dancing and drinking, when the locals dress up in nineteenth-century costume. The town grew steadily up to World War II, when it was demolished during fierce fighting for control of the harbour and iron ore supplies. Rebuilt, the town centre is, perhaps inevitably, rather lacking in appeal, with modern concrete buildings replacing the wooden houses that went before. Nevertheless, try to devote an hour or so to the **Red Cross War Memorial Museum** (*Nordland Røde Kors Krigsminnemuseum*; daily: early June to late Aug 10am–10pm; March to early June & late Aug to Sept 10am–4pm; 35kr), just along from the tourist office. Run by the Red Cross, the museum documents the wartime German saturation bombing of the town, and the bitter and bloody sea and air battles in which hundreds of foreign servicemen died alongside a swathe of the local population. In total, the fight for Narvik lasted two months, a complicated campaign beginning with the German invasion of April 1940, followed by an allied counterattack spearheaded by the Royal Navy. The Allies actually recaptured Narvik, driving the Germans into the mountains, but were hurriedly evacuated when Hitler launched the invasion of France. The story is movingly related by the museum, which then tracks through the German occupation of Norway until liberation in 1945.

There are also guided tours of the LKAB mining company's **ore-terminal complex** (mid-June to mid-Aug 1 daily; 30kr), interesting if only for the opportunity to spend ninety minutes amid such giant, ore-stained contraptions. After its arrival by train, the ore is carried on the various conveyor belts to the quayside, from where some thirty million tons of it are shipped out each year. Sign up for the tours at the tourist office.

Moving on from Narvik

There's a choice of several routes on from Narvik. By **bus**, the Nord-Norgeekspressen (North Norway Express bus; 1–2 daily) makes the four-hour hop north to Tromsø (see p.378), where you change (and stay overnight) before embarking on the next leg of the journey up to Alta (see p.383). There's also a bus direct from Narvik to Alta (Mon–Fri & Sun 1 daily; 10hr). Both trips give sight of some wonderfully wild and diverse scenery, from craggy mountains and blue-black fjords to gentle, forested valleys, though it's not perhaps quite as scenic a journey as the E6 from Fauske to Narvik. A third bus service, the Narvik-Lofoten Ekspressen (1–2 daily), runs west from Narvik to Sortland, Stokmarknes and Svolvær in the Lofoten Islands (see p.350). On all these buses, plus the bus trip south from Narvik to either Fauske (for connecting trains to Trondheim) or Bodø, rail-pass holders get a fifty percent discount. Narvik's **Hurtigbåt passenger express boat** service to Svolvær operates all year (Mon–Fri & Sun 1 daily; 3–4hr; 290kr one-way). Again, rail-pass holders get a fifty percent discount.

One of the real treats of a visit to Narvik is the **train ride** into the mountains that back the town and spread east across the Swedish border. Called the **Ofotbanen**, the line passes through some wonderful scenery, slipping between hostile peaks before reaching the barren, loch-studded plateau beyond. Operated by a private company, Tågkompaniet (☎0046/690 69 10 17; ⊚www.tagkompaniet.se), trains leave Narvik two or three times daily and take fifty minutes to reach the Swedish border settlement of **Riksgränsen**, a hiking and skiing centre on the plateau; the fare is 130kr return. You can either nose around here before returning by train to Narvik or travel east on to Kiruna and, ultimately, Stockholm; the ride to Stockholm takes around eighteen hours.

△ Viking carving, Urnes stave church

Fagernesfjellet

Located a stiff fifteen-minute walk up above the town behind the train station, Narvik's **cable car** (daily: mid-June to July noon–1am; Aug 1–9pm; 85kr return) whisks passengers up the first 650m of the mighty **Fagernesfjellet**. There's a restaurant and viewing point at the top of the cable-car run and from here, on a clear day, you can spy the Lofoten Islands on the horizon and, from the end of May to mid-July, experience the Midnight Sun. In addition, **hiking trails** that delve further into the mountains start here and, even more adventurously, **hang- and paragliders** have established a designated take-off point metres from the restaurant. Indeed, there's even a local club to advise on conditions: the Hang og Paragliderklubb (☎90 61 81 15). The cable car also provides a shuttle service for **skiers and snowboarders** during the season (late November to early June). The network of skiing slopes and trails includes five ski lifts, 7km of prepared courses and unlimited off-piste skiing, and some areas are floodlit; for further details contact Narvik ski centre (☎76 96 04 94, ✆skinarvik@narviknett.no). Finally, one word of caution: the cable car stops running in windy conditions.

Eating

Things are likely to change, but at present Narvik is very short of recommendable **cafés** and **restaurants**. The best bet is the *Astrupkjelleren*, Kinobakken 1, where the mostly meaty main courses start at 150kr.

The Vesterålen islands

A raggle-taggle archipelago in the Norwegian Sea, the **Vesterålen**, and their neighbours the Lofoten, are like western Norway in miniature: the terrain is hard and unyielding, the sea boisterous and fretful, and the main – often the only – industry is fishing. The weather is temperate but wet, and the islanders' historic isolation has bred a distinctive culture based, in equal measure, on Protestantism, the extended family and respect for the ocean.

The islands were first settled by semi-nomadic hunter-agriculturalists some 6000 years ago, and it was they and their Iron Age successors who chopped down the birch and pine forests that once covered the coasts. It was **boat-building**, however, which brought a brief golden age: by the seventh century, the islanders were able to build ocean-going vessels, a skill that enabled them to join in the bonanza of Viking exploration. In the early fourteenth century, the islanders **lost their independence** and were placed under the control of Bergen: by royal decree, all fish caught by the islanders had to be shipped to Bergen for export. This may have suited the economic interests of the Norwegian monarch and the Danish governors who succeeded them, but it put the islanders at a terrible disadvantage. With their monopoly guaranteed, Bergen's merchants controlled both the price they paid for the fish and the price of the goods they sold to the islanders – a system that was to survive, increasingly under the auspices of local merchants, until the early years of the twentieth century. Since World War II, improvements in fishing techniques and, more latterly, the growth in tourism and the extension of the road system have all combined to transform island life.

The Vesterålen are the less rugged of the two island groups: greener, gentler and less mountainous than the Lofoten to the south, with more of the land given over to agriculture, though this gives way to vast tracts of peaty moorland in the far north. The villages are less appealing too, often no more than formless ribbons straggling along the coast and across any available stretch of fertile land. Many travellers simply rush through on their way to the Lofoten, demoralized by the sheer mediocrity of the main settlements, a mistake primarily in so far as the fishing port of **Andenes**, tucked away at the far end of the island of Andøya, has a strange but enthralling back-of-beyond charm and is noted for its whale-watching expeditions. The other highlight is the magnificent but extremely narrow **Trollfjord**, where cruise ships and the Hurtigrute coastal boat perform some nifty manoeuvres.

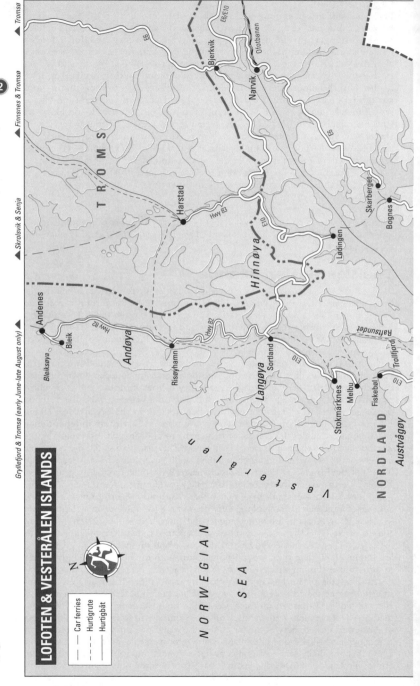

LOFOTEN & VESTERÅLEN ISLANDS

— — Car ferries
– – – Hurtigrute
——— Hurtigbåt

N

NORWEGIAN SEA

Vesterålen

Langøya

Andøya

Hinnøya

Austvågøy

T R O M S

N O R D L A N D

Andenes
Bleik
Bleiksøya
Risøyhamn
Sortland
Stokmarknes
Melbu
Fiskebøl
Trollfjord
Raftsundet
Harstad
Lødingen
Bognes
Skarberget
Narvik
Bjerkvik

E6
E6/E10
Ofotbanen
E10
E6
Hwy 83
Hwy 82

▲ Tromsø
▲ Finnsnes & Tromsø
▲ Skrolsvik & Senja
Gryllefjord & Tromsø (early June–late August only) ▲

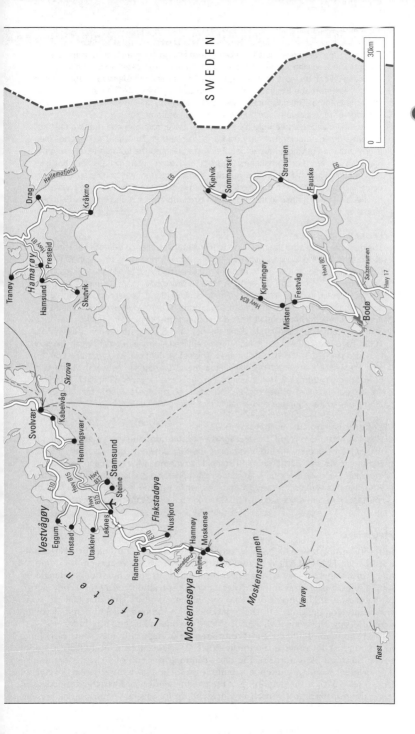

Getting to and around the Vesterålen Islands

Getting to the Vesterålen Islands from the mainland by **public transport** is easy enough – indeed, the number of permutations is almost bewildering – but getting around them can be more troublesome. The **E10** is the main island road, running the 370km west from the E6 just north of Narvik across the Vesterålen to the southern tip of the Lofoten. The only interruption is the **car ferry** linking Melbu, on the southern edge of the Vesterålen, with Fiskebøl in the Lofoten.

If you have your own **vehicle** it's possible to drive from one end of the archipelago to the other, catching the ferry from the mainland at Gryllefjord to Andenes (see p.366) and then driving south across the Vesterålen and the Lofoten to return to the mainland by ferry from Moskenes (see p.373). Drivers intent on a somewhat less epic trip could investigate the **car rental** outlets at Harstad, which offer special short deals from around 600kr a day. No single itinerary stands out, but Andenes has most to offer as a base thanks to its whale- and birdwatching trips and choice of accommodation.

By car ferry

The main **car ferry** from the mainland to the Vesterålen Islands departs from the jetty at **Bognes**, on the E6 between Fauske and Narvik, and sails to **Lødingen** (first-come, first-served; early June to mid-Aug 12 daily; mid-Aug to mid-June 5 daily; 1hr; passengers 39kr, car and driver 122kr; ☎177). From Lødingen, it's just 4km to the E10 at a point midway between Harstad and Sortland. A second, but this time seasonal, car ferry runs from remote **Gryllefjord**, 110km west of the E6 well to the north of Narvik, to **Andenes** at the northern tip of the Vesterålen (early to late June & mid- to late Aug 2 daily; late June to early Aug 3 daily; 1hr 40min; passengers 100kr, car 275kr). Reservations are strongly advised – phone or email Andøy Reiseliv in Andenes (☎76 14 18 10, ✉a-turist@online.no). A third car ferry links the Lofoten with the Vesterålen about halfway along the E10, running between Melbu and Fiskebøl (every 90min; 25min; passengers 24kr, driver and car 68kr; ☎177). Tickets are issued on a first-come, first-served basis, so get there twenty minutes or so before departure – an hour and a half in high season.

By boat: Hurtigrute and Hurtigbåt

Heading north from Bodø, the **Hurtigrute coastal boat** threads a scenic route up through the Lofoten to the Vesterålen Islands, where it calls at four places: **Stokmarknes** and **Sortland** in the south, **Risøyhamn** in the north and **Harstad** in the east. None of the four is an especially appealing destination, but workaday Risøyhamn is well on the way to Andenes, while Harstad is a regional centre and transport hub with a fine old church. Cruising southwards from Tromsø (see p.378),

Harstad

Just 130km northwest of Narvik, and easily reached by bus and the Hurtigrute coastal boat, **HARSTAD** is easily the largest town on the Vesterålen. It's home to much of northern Norway's engineering industry, its sprawling docks a tangle of supply ships, repair yards and cold-storage plants spread out along the gentle slopes of the Vågsfjord. This may not sound too enticing, and it's true that Harstad wins few beauty competitions, but the town does have the odd attraction and, if you're tired of sleepy Norwegian villages, it at least provides a bustling interlude.

The main item of interest, the **Trondenes kirke** (regular guided tours early June to late Aug; ask for times at the tourist office; 25kr), occupies a lovely, leafy location beside the fjord 3km north of the town centre at the end of a slender peninsula. The original wooden church was built at the behest of King Øystein (of *rorbuer* fame – see p.370) at the beginning of the twelfth century and had the distinction of being the northernmost church in Christendom for several centuries. The present the Hurtigrute follows the same itinerary, but in reverse. Scenically, the highlight is the **Raftsundet**, a narrow sound between Svolvær and Stokmarknes, off which branches the magnificent Trollfjord. Unfortunately, though, the Hurtigrute leaves Svolvær heading north at 10pm, so the Raftsundet is only visible during the period of the Midnight Sun (late May to mid-July); things are, however, easier in the opposite direction with boats leaving Stokmarknes at a much more convenient 3.15pm. This stretch of the journey takes three hours and costs 200kr for passengers, and 300kr for cars.

Sailing north, the Hurtigrute leaves Bodø for the Lofoten and the Vesterålen at 3pm and departs Tromsø heading south at 1.30am daily. Passenger tickets are reasonably priced, with the sixteen-hour journey from Bodø to Harstad costing around 700kr, Tromsø to Harstad (6.5hr) 470kr in summer, with significant off-season discounts. The fare for transporting a car from Bodø to Harstad is 380kr, from Tromsø to Harstad 320kr. Advance reservations are essential, but can be made just a few hours beforehand by telephoning the captain – ask down at Bodø harbour or at the port's tourist office for assistance. Special deals, which can reduce costs dramatically, are advertised at local tourist offices.

Hurtigbåt passenger express boat services provide a speedy and economic alternative to the car ferries and Hurtigrute. Principal Hurtigbåt services are **Tromsø to Harstad** (2 daily; 2hr 45min; 365kr); **Narvik to Svolvær** in the Lofoten (Mon–Fri & Sun 1 daily; 4hr; 286kr); and **Bodø to Svolvær** (Mon–Fri & Sun 1 daily; 3hr 30min; 250kr). In all cases, advance booking – most easily done via the local tourist office – is recommended.

By bus

A long-distance **bus** leaves **Narvik** once or twice daily to run along the E6 and then the E10 as far as Sortland. Here, passengers can usually – but not always – change, after an hour or two's wait, for the onward bus to **Stokmarknes**, the Melbu–Fiskebøl ferry and then **Svolvær**. Once daily, another long-distance bus runs up the E6 from **Bodø** and **Fauske** to meet the **Bognes–Lødingen** car ferry. At Lødingen, there's a choice of two onward connecting buses: one service continues north to **Harstad**, the other heads west for **Stokmarknes**, the Melbu–Fiskebøl ferry and **Svolvær**. As examples of journey times, Narvik to Sortland takes three hours, Bodø to Sortland seven, Bodø to Svolvær ten.

Generally speaking, **local buses** across the Vesterålen are no more than reasonable in the summer and very patchy out of season. Most are operated by Nordtrafikk (☎177 in Nordland, otherwise ☎75 77 24 10). One of their most useful services links Sortland with Andenes (1–3 daily; 2hr).

stone church was erected in the 1300s, its thick walls and the remains of its surrounding ramparts reflecting its dual function as both church and fortress – these were troubled and violent times. After the necessarily stern exterior, the warm and homely interior comes as a surprise. Here the dainty arches of the rood screen lead into the choir, where each of the three altars is surmounted by a late medieval wooden triptych in bas relief. Of the trio, the central triptych is the most charming: the main panel, depicting the Holy Family, is fairly predictable, but down below is a curiously cheerful sequence of biblical figures, each wearing a turban and sporting a big, bushy and exquisitely carved beard.

There's a reminder of World War II in the **Adolfkanonen** (Adolf Gun), a massive artillery piece stuck on a hilltop to the north of the church in the middle of the peninsula. It's inside a military zone, and the obligatory **guided tour** (early June to mid-Aug 4 daily; mid-Aug to late Aug 1 daily; 55kr; times vary – contact the tourist office), which begins at the gate of the compound 1km up the hill from the

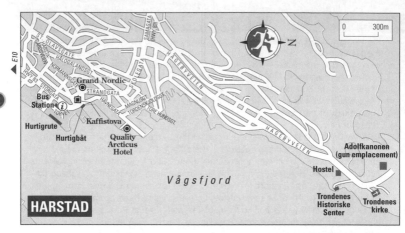

church, stipulates that you have to have your own vehicle to cross from the gate to the gun, a distance of 3km. A third attraction, near the church and just south along the fjord, is the **Trondenes Historical Centre** (*Trondenes Historiske Senter*; mid-June to early Aug daily 10am–5pm; early Aug to mid-June Mon–Fri 10am–noon, Sun 11am–5pm; 65kr), a plush modern complex with exhibitions on the history of the locality – dioramas, mood music, incidental Viking artefacts and the like.

Frankly, **downtown Harstad** doesn't have much going for it, though the comings and goings of the ferry boats are a diversion. In late June, the ten-day **North Norway Arts Festival** (*Festspillene i Nord-Norge*; ⑩www.festspillnn.no) provides a spark of interest with its concerts, drama and dance, but there again the town's hotels are full to overflowing throughout the proceedings.

Practicalities

Although Harstad is easy to reach by bus or boat from Sortland, Tromsø and Narvik, it's actually something of a cul-de-sac for car drivers, who have to leave the E10 for the final thirty-kilometre drive north into town along Highway 83, though in summertime the ferry to Skrolsvik does offer another route out (see box below). Once you've arrived, however, you'll find almost everything you need in the immediate vicinity of the **bus station**. Jetties for the **Hurtigbåt passenger express** and **Hurtigrute coastal boat** services are just metres away, and next to the bus station at Torvet 8, the **tourist office** (early June to mid-Aug Mon–Fri 7.30am–6pm, Sat & Sun 10am–3pm; mid-Aug to May Mon–Fri 8am–4pm; ☎77 01 89 89, ⑩www.destinationharstad.no) has a wide selection of tourist literature on the Vesterålen.

As regards **accommodation**, the centre is dotted with modern chain hotels. Among them, the *Quality Arcticus* has an attractive quayside location a short walk from Torvet at Havnegata 3 (☎77 04 08 00, ⑩www.choicehotels.no; ❼/❹). A good alternative is the neat and trim *Grand Nordic*, a couple of minutes' walk from Torvet at Strandgata 9 (☎77 00 30 00, ⑩www.nordic.no; ❻/❸). The HI **hostel** (June to late Aug; ☎77 07 28 00, ✉harstad.hostel@vandrerhjem.no; reception closed 4–6pm) has the advantage of a pleasant fjordside location, near the Trondenes church. It's easy to reach by the local "Trondenes" bus from the station (Mon–Sat 1 hourly; 10min), has self-catering facilities, washing machines, and large, comfortable and pleasantly furnished double rooms (❶); the only problem is that the building is a school for most of the year and so has a rather cold, institutional feel.

From Harstad, the **Hurtigrute** sails north for Tromsø at 8am and south for points in the Vesterålen and Lofoten Islands at 8.30am. Alternatively, there's a **Hurtigbåt** service to Tromsø (1–3 daily; 2hr 45min; 365kr) and frequent **buses** to Narvik, Sortland (for Andenes) and the Lofoten. In Harstad, several local **car rental** firms offer special short-term deals: try Europcar, Samagata 33 (☎77 01 86 10), or Hertz, Torvet 8 (☎77 06 13 46).

Harstad is no gastronomic nirvana, but the *Kaffistova* (Mon–Fri 8am–6pm, Sat 9.30am–2.30pm, Sun 11.30am–4.30pm), across from the Hurtigbåt terminal, serves traditional Norwegian standbys at inexpensive prices, and in the evening *Gallionen*, the restaurant of the *Quality Arcticus Hotel*, offers a reasonable line in seafood and pleasing fjord views.

Sortland, Stokmarknes, the Trollfjord and Melbu

Back on the E10 south of Harstad, it's 50km southwest along the fjord to the turning for the Lødingen ferry, and 50km more to **SORTLAND**, an unappetizing modern sprawl straggling along the shore near the bridge linking the islands of Langøya and Hinnøya. Sortland's location makes it something of a transport centre: bus travellers have to change here for the onward journey south to Stokmarknes and the Lofoten, or to catch the local bus north to Andenes, which originates here. If you've a little time to spare, visit the **tourist office** (mid-June to late Aug Mon–Fri 10am–6pm, Sat & Sun 11am–5pm; Sept to mid-June Mon–Fri 10am–5pm; ☎76 11 14 80, ⚲www.visitvesteralen.com), a five-minute walk from the bus station in the centre of town at Kjøpmannsgata 2, which has the full range of regional information.

Pushing south along the E10 from Sortland, the road hugs the shoreline for 30km before shooting over the two bridges that span the straits to reach **STOKMARKNES** on Hadseløya. The main reason for stopping in Stokmarknes is to catch the Hurtigrute south to Svolvær via the Trollfjord. The boat leaves at 3.15pm, sailing down the narrow sound – the Raftsundet – separating the harsh, rocky shanks of Hinnøya and Austvågøy. Towards the southern end of the sound, the ship usually makes the short detour to the **Trollfjord**, a majestic, two-kilometre-long tear in the landscape. Slowing to a mere chug, the vessels inch up the narrow gorge, smooth stone towering high above and blocking out the light. At its head, the boats effect a nautical three-point turn and then crawl back to rejoin the main waterway. It's very atmospheric, and the effect is perhaps even more extraordinary when the weather is up. One caution: the Hurtigrute does not enter the Trollfjord when there's the danger of a rock fall, but pauses at the fjord's mouth instead. Check locally before you embark, though this is most likely to happen in spring. The Hurtigrute cruise from Sortland to Svolvær takes three hours and costs 200kr per passenger.

If you stay the night in Stokmarknes awaiting the Hurtigrute, you'll find most things conveniently close, with **buses** pulling in near the harbourfront **tourist office** (mid-June to late Aug Mon–Fri 10am–5pm; ☎76 15 00 00). Staff have details of local **accommodation**, though there's not much on offer. The obvious choice is the *Hurtigrutens Hus* (☎76 15 29 99, ⚲www.hurtigrutenshus.com; ❺), a brassy, modern hotel-cum-conference centre plonked on the Børøya islet, about fifteen minutes' walk from the tourist office and at the end of the first of the two bridges back over to Langøya.

From Stokmarknes, it's 15km along the E10 to **MELBU**, from where there's a **car ferry** (every 90min; 25min; passengers 24kr, driver and car 68kr; ☎177) over to Fiskebøl on the Lofoten; Melbu is on the main bus routes to Svolvær from Fauske, Narvik and Tromsø.

North to Andenes

From Sortland, Hwy 82 begins its 100-kilometre trek north, snaking along the craggy peripheries of the ocean before crossing the bridge over to humdrum **RISØYHAMN**, the only Hurtigrute stop on **Andøya**, itself the most northerly of the Vesterålen Islands. Beyond Risøyhamn, the scenery is much less dramatic, as the mountains give way to hills in the west and a vast, peaty moor in the east. Hwy 82 crosses this moorland and, despite fine panoramic views of the mountains back on the mainland, it's an uneventful journey on to Andenes.

At the old fishing port of **ANDENES**, lines of low-slung buildings trail up to the clutter of wooden warehouses and small boat repair yards that edge the harbour and its prominent breakwaters. Andenes is famous for its **whale safaris**, four- to five-hour cruises off the coast with a marine biologist on board to point out sperm, killer and minke whales, as well as dolphins – there's reckoned to be a ninety per-cent chance of seeing the whales. Trips take place daily between late May and mid-September, with departures at 10.30am (subject to demand, there are additional departures at 8.30am, 3.30pm & 5.30pm); tickets are 650kr each and cover both lunch and a guided tour of the Whale Centre (see below) beforehand. **Booking** (☎76 11 56 00, ⊛www.whalesafari.no) at least a day in advance is strongly advised as the trips are popular, and indeed some are booked up weeks beforehand. The **Whale Centre** (*Hvalsenter*; daily: late May to mid-June & mid-Aug to mid-Sept 8am–4pm; mid-June to mid-Aug 8am–7.30pm; 60kr), metres from the harbour, is actually a somewhat disappointing way to start. Its incidental museum displays on the life and times of the animal hardly fire the imagination, and neither does the massive, and deliberately dark and gloomy, display of a whale munching its way though a herd of squid. Much more diverting is the **Hisnakul/Northern Lights Centre** (mid-June to mid-Aug daily noon–6pm; 40kr), in a refurbished timber warehouse near the Whale Centre, which explores various facets of Andøya life. It's short on historical artefacts, plumping instead for imaginative displays such as the two hundred facial casts of local people made in 1994 and an assortment of giant replica bird beaks. There's also a comprehensive explanation of the northern lights (see box on p.v) – Andenes is a particularly good spot to see them – illustrated by first-class photographs and a slide show.

The other recommended **boat trip** is a cruise round the **bird island of Bleiksøya** (June to late Aug 1 daily at 3.30pm, additional departures as required; 1hr 30min; 250kr; bookings through the tourist office or direct on ☎95 25 29 98), a pyramid-shaped hunk of rock populated by thousands of puffins, kittiwakes, razorbills and, sometimes, white-tailed eagles. Cruises leave from the jetty at **Bleik**, an old and picturesque fishing hamlet around 7km southwest of Andenes; a local bus often makes the trip from Andenes to coincide with sailings.

Practicalities

Bisecting the town, Andenes' long and straight main street, Storgata, ends abruptly at the seafront. The **bus station** is just a few metres to the east of Storgata, just back from the seafront, and the **tourist office** is right on Storgata, just before the seafront (June–Aug daily 8am–8pm; Sept–May Mon–Fri 8am–4pm; ☎76 14 18 10, ⊛www.andoy.net). Staff have a comprehensive range of local information and can make reservations for bird-island boat trips, whale safaris and the car ferry to Gryllefjord; there's a booking fee for the car ferry, but not the others.

Andenes has a fair sprinkling of inexpensive **accommodation** and several house-holds offer **private rooms** – look out for the signs – but, considering how isolated a spot this is, you'd be well advised to make an advance reservation either directly or via the tourist office. One of the nicest places to stay is the *Sjøgata Gjestehus*, Sjøgata 4 (☎76 14 16 37, ⊜tovekhan@online.no; May–Sept; ❷), which provides simple, inexpensive rooms in a pleasant old timber building just 200m east from the tourist office. Nearby, on the seafront, is the *Norlandia Lankanholmen Sjøhus* (☎76 14 28 50, ℗76 14 28 55), an unenticing modern complex which includes chalet- style

The coastal route north from Andenes to Tromsø

From early June to late August, two **car ferries** operated by Senjaferries (☎76 14 66 00, ⓦwww.senjafergene.no) make it possible to head up the coast from **Andenes to Tromsø** without having to double back inland. This scenic coastal route begins with the (often choppy) ferry ride from Andenes to the remote fishing village of **Gryllefjord** (early June to late Aug 2–3 daily; 1hr 40min; passengers 100kr, cars 275kr), on the island of **Senja**. From here, Highway 86 weaves a handsome route across the island's mountains to reach, after about 70km, the main town hereabouts, the boring Hurtigrute port of **FINNSNES**. Keep going – or rather turn north along Highway 861 just before Finnsnes – for the lovely 55 kilometre-long fjordside drive that leads up to **BOTNHAMN**, where a second **car ferry** crosses over to **BRENSHOLMEN** (June to late Aug 4–7 daily; 35min; passengers 50kr, cars 130kr). Brensholmen is within easy driving distance of Tromsø (see p.379). The whole journey is easily completed in a day – Gryllefjord to Tromsø is 230km.

huts (❸), apartments and doubles (❸), and a very small and very spartan HI **hostel** (same number; June–Aug); the hostel also has a few doubles (❶). There are two hotels, the better of which is the *Norlandia Andrikken*, about 900m from the harbour at Storgata 53 (☎76 14 12 22, ⓦwww.norlandia.no; ❺/❹), whose main building is a routine modern concrete block with rooms to match. More positively, the hotel **restaurant** is easily Andenes' best place to eat – the Arctic char is superb – and prices are reasonable. For daytime snacks, head for *Juhl Nilsens Bakeri*, close to the bus station at Kong Hansgata 1.

Leaving Andenes by **bus**, there are daily services south to Risøyhamn and Sortland, though the latter are few and far between on the weekend. In the summer, there's also the possibility of catching the **ferry** north to Gryllefjord (see box above).

The Lofoten Islands

A skeletal curve of mountainous rock stretched out across the Norwegian Sea and fretted by seastacks and skerries, the **Lofoten Islands** (ⓦwww.lofoten-tourist.no) are the focal point of northern Norway's winter fishing season. At the turn of every year, cod migrate from the Barents Sea to spawn here, where the coldness of the waters is tempered by the Gulf Stream. The season lasts from February to April, though it impinges on all aspects of the islands' life and is impossible to ignore at any time of year. At almost every harbour stand the massed ranks of wooden racks used for drying the catch; full and odiferous in winter, empty in summer like so many abandoned climbing frames.

Sharing the same history, but better known and more beautiful than their neighbours the Vesterålen, the Lofoten Islands have everything from seabird colonies in the south to beaches and fjords in the north, not to mention the 160-kilometre **Lofotenveggen** (Lofoten Wall), a chain of rearing mountains whose grandeur simply takes your breath away. The Lofoten have their own relaxed pace, and are perfect for a simple, uncluttered few days. For somewhere so far north, the weather is exceptionally mild: summer days can be spent sunbathing on the rocks or hiking around the superb coastline; and when it rains, as it does frequently, life focuses on the *rorbuer* (fishermen's huts), where freshly caught fish are cooked over wood-burning stoves, stories are told and time gently wasted. If that sounds rather contrived, in a sense it is – the way of life here is to some extent preserved like this for tourists. But it's rare to find anyone who isn't less than completely enthralled by it all.

The **E10** weaves a scenic route across the Lofoten, running the 170km from Fiskebøl in the north to Å in the south, hopping from island to island by bridge and causeway and occasionally tunnelling through the mountains and under the sea. The highway passes through or within a few kilometres of all the islands' main villages, amongst which **Henningsvaer** and **Å** are breathtakingly beautiful, with **Stamsund** coming in just behind – all three make great bases for further exploration. **Boat trips** along the coast (with or without birdwatching and fishing) are popular, as is **mountaineering** – Austvågøy island has the best climbing, and the best climbing school is at Henningsvaer. There's **walking**, too: the islands do not have a well-developed system of huts and hiking trails, but the byroads are quiet and delve into the heart of the scenery.

As regards **accommodation**, the Lofoten have a sprinkling of **hotels** as well as four HI **hostels** and numerous **campsites**, along with the local speciality, the *rorbuer* (see box below).

Svolvær

On the east coast of **Austvågøy**, the largest of the Lofoten, **SVOLVÆR** provides a disappointing introduction to the islands. The administrative and transport centre of the Lofoten, it has all the bustle but little of the charm of the other fishing towns, though it does have more accommodation than its neighbours and, despite the poor aspect of the town itself, Svolvær's surroundings are delightful. Two local **boat trips** provide an excellent taster. Every day several **cruises** leave Svolvær for the **Trollfjord** (for more on which, see p.365), an impossibly narrow, two-kilometre-

---

Getting to and around the Lofoten Islands

The Lofoten can be reached by car ferry, Hurtigbåt passenger express boat and the Hurtigrute coastal boat, but once you've got there you'll find **public transport** thin on the ground. What local **bus** services there are stick almost exclusively to the **E10**, the islands' only main road. Leave the main highway, however, and you'll mostly have to **walk** – hardly an onerous task in such beautiful surroundings. Alternatively, **bike rental** is available at the Svolvær tourist office (see p.368), as well as at many hotels, campsites and hostels, while the detailed *Cycling in Lofoten* booklet, which includes route maps, is sold at all tourist offices.

If you have your own **vehicle**, village-hopping is easy and quick, but do allow time for at least one walk or sea trip. Conversely, if you don't have a vehicle and want to reach the islands' remoter spots, it's worth considering renting a car, an inexpensive option if a few people share the cost. There are local **car rental** outlets at Svolvaer, Stamsund and Leknes airport, and special short-term deals can bring costs down to around 600kr a day.

For **timetable enquiries** for all public transport in the province of Nordland, which covers the Lofoten, call ☎177 or visit ⓦwww.177nordland.com.

By car ferry

From the mainland, the principal **car ferry** service to the Lofoten connects tiny Skutvik, 40km west of the E6 midway between Fauske and Narvik, with Svolvær (June to mid-Aug 8 daily; mid-Aug to May 2–3 daily; 2hr; passengers 60kr, car and driver 200kr; ☎177). Queues are commonplace and, as it's a first-come first-served ferry, it's best to arrive about two hours before departure to make sure of a place. A second car ferry service links **Bodø** with three destinations in the southern peripheries of the Lofoten: **Moskenes**, a tiny port just a few kilometres from the end of the E10, and the islets of Røst and Værøy. The route varies, but there's almost always one ferry a day (and sometimes more) to Moskenes throughout the year, with marginally less frequent services to Røst and Værøy. Moskenes is usually the first port of call. The trip from Bodø to Moskenes takes about four hours; allow a further two hours to Værøy and two more for Røst. Don't be surprised if it's a rough crossing. The fare from Bodø to Moskenes is 125kr for passengers, 440kr for a car and driver. These ferries are operated by OVDS (☎177; ⓦwww.ovds.no). **Advance reservations** long stretch of water up and down which countless excursion boats inch a careful way. The excursion takes three hours and costs 300kr.

Svolvær also boasts one of the archipelago's most famous **climbs**, the haul up to the top of the **Svolværgeita** (the "Svolvær goat"), a twin-pronged peak that rises high above the E10 just to the northeast of town. The lower slopes of the mountain are difficult enough, but the last 40m – up the horns of the "goat" – require considerable expertise. Daring-daft mountaineers then finish it off by jumping from one pinnacle to the other.

Practicalities

Ferries to Svolvær from Skutvik dock on the edge of town, about 1km from the town centre, whereas the Hurtigrute docks in the centre, the briefest of walks from both the **bus station** and the busy **tourist office**, which is beside the main town square by the harbour (late May to mid-June Mon–Fri 9am–4pm, Sat 10am–2pm; mid- to late June Mon–Fri 9am 4pm & 5–7.30pm, Sat 10am–2pm, Sun 4–7pm; late June to mid-Aug Mon–Fri 9am–4pm & 5–9.30pm, Sat 9am–4pm & 5–8pm, Sun 10am–9.30pm; mid-Aug to late Aug Mon–Fri 9am–7pm, Sat 10am–2pm; Sept to mid-May Mon–Fri 9am–4pm; ☎76 06 98 00, ⊛www.lofoten-tourist.no). Staff will reserve accommodation anywhere in the Lofoten (for a 50kr booking fee) and can reserve ferry tickets for a fee of 130kr. Svolvær is a good place to **rent a car**,

can be made online, or through Bodø tourist office for a fee of 100kr (ferry staff don't always speak English, and the website currently has no English-language option); otherwise drivers should arrive at least two hours before departure to make sure of a place. If you're driving to the Lofoten on the **E10**, which branches off the E6 north of Narvik, you'll use a third car ferry linking **Melbu** on the Vesterålen Islands with **Fiskebøl** on the Lofoten (first-come, first served; every 90min; 25min; passengers 24kr, driver and car 68kr; ☎177).

By Hurtigrute and Hurtigbåt

Heading north from Bodø at 3pm, the **Hurtigrute coastal boat** calls at two ports in the Lofoten – Stamsund and Svolvær – before nudging through the Raftsundet en route to Stokmarknes. Advance reservations for cars are essential, though these can be made up to a few hours before departure by telephoning the captain – ask down at the harbour or at the port's tourist office for assistance. Special deals, which can reduce costs dramatically, are commonplace.

Hurtigbåt passenger express boats operate from **Bodø to Svolvær** (Mon–Fri & Sun 1 daily; 3hr 30min; 250kr) and **Narvik to Svolvær** (Mon–Fri & Sun 1 daily; 4hr; 286kr). In both cases, advance booking (via the local tourist office) is recommended.

Buses

There are three long-distance **bus** services linking the mainland with the Lofoten. One is from **Fauske to Svolvær** (1 daily; 8hr 30min; one-way 433kr) via the Bognes-Lødingen and Melbu–Fiskebøl ferries; you can also start the journey in **Bodø**. The second service runs from **Narvik to Svolvær** (1–2 daily; 7–9hr; 370kr) via the Melbu–Fiskebøl ferry, while the third plies between **Tromsø** and **Svolvær** (Mon–Fri 1 daily; 15hr), though you have to change onto a local bus – and hang around for three and a half hours – just north of Narvik at the Bjerkvik crossroads.

On the Lofoten, there are at least a couple of **local buses** on weekdays between most of the larger villages, but often nothing at all on Sunday, and sometimes Saturday as well. One useful service travels south from Svolvær to Leknes and Å (Mon–Sat 1–2 daily). To avoid getting stuck, be sure to pick up a bus and ferry **timetable** from any island tourist office or bus station.

Staying in a rorbu

Right across the Lofoten, **rorbuer** (fishermen's shacks) are rented out to tourists for both overnight stays and longer periods. Traditionally, *rorbuer* were built on the shore, often on poles sticking out of the sea, and usually coloured with a red paint based on cod-liver oil. They consisted of two sections, a sleeping and eating room and a smaller storage area. At the peak of the fisheries in the 1930s, some 30,000 men were accommodated in *rorbuer*, but in the 1960s the fishing boats became more comfortable and since then many fishermen have preferred to sleep aboard. Most of the original *rorbuer* disappeared years ago and, although a few have survived, visitors today are much more likely to stay in a modern version, mostly prefabricated units churned out by the score. At their best, they are comfortable and cosy seashore cabins, sometimes a well-planned conversion of an original rorbu with bunk beds and wood-fired stoves; at their worst, they're little better than prefabricated hutches – or even garages – in the middle of nowhere. Most have space for between four and six guests and the charge for a hut is in the region of 600kr per night – though some cost as little as 400kr, while others rise to about 1000kr. Similar rates are charged for the islands' **sjøhus** (literally, sea-houses), bigger buildings that originated in the quayside halls where the catch was processed and the workers slept. A full list of *rorbuer* and *sjøhus* is given in the *Lofoten Info-Guide*, a free pamphlet that you can pick up at any local tourist office.

with both Avis (☏76 07 11 40) and Europcar (☏76 06 83 33), among others, offering some economic short-term deals from around 600kr per day.

Svolvær's flashiest **accommodation** is the gleaming and justifiably popular *Rica Hotel Svolvær* (☏76 07 22 22, ☻www.rica.no; ❹), whose various buildings, in the style of the traditional sjøhus, occupy a prime location on a tiny islet at the end of a causeway in the middle of the harbour. Not to be outdone, a longer causeway now leads out from the east end of the harbour to the slender islet of Svinøya, where *Svinøya Rorbuer* (☏76 06 99 30, ☻www.svinoya.no) has everything from plain and simple *rorbuer* (❸) through to the deluxe models (❼), all in a modern version of traditional style. Back in town, there are more modest rooms at the long-established – and much smaller – *Svolvær Sjøhus*, by the seashore at the foot of Parkgata (☏76 07 03 36, ☻www.svolver-sjohuscamp.no; ❷): to get there from the square, turn right up the hill along Vestfjordgata and it's to the right, past the library. Svolvær also has a handful of **hotels**, for the most part surly modern blocks that hardly set the architectural pulse racing, though the *Norlandia Royal Hotel* (☏76 07 12 00, ☻www.norlandia.no; ❹), a few metres up from the main square at the end of Torggat, has comfortable rooms and a convenient location.

There are several good **eating** options. Down on the quay, *Café Bacalao* is a spacious café-restaurant with snappy service and a menu that mixes Mediterranean and Norwegian cuisine with flair and imagination. Lunches and main courses in the evening hover around 80kr, while huge salads cost 125kr; there's excellent coffee, too, and the place turns into the town's liveliest **bar** at night, jam-packed on the weekend. In addition, the restaurants of the *Rica Hotel Svolvær* and the *Svinøya Rorbuer* are both highly competent, with seafood their forte, but the classiest and smartest restaurant is *Du Verden*, in the centre at J.E. Paulsens gate 12 (☏76 07 70 99), where a creative menu features the freshest of local ingredients. In the evening, prices are high, but not unreasonable – either à la carte or with the set menu – and at lunch time the place is a bit of a snip: try the mouthwatering, taste-bud-symphony-making fish soup.

Henningsvær

A beguiling headland village, **HENNINGSVÆR** lies 24km southwest of Svolvær, its cobweb of cramped and twisting lanes lined with brightly painted wooden houses. These frame a tiny inlet that literally cuts the place in half, forming a sheltered, postcard-pretty harbour. Almost inevitably, coach parties are wheeled in and out, despite the narrowness of its two high-arched bridges, but for all the tourist bustle the village is well worth an **overnight stay**.

The smartest **hotel** is the quayside *Heningsvær Bryggehotell* (☎76 07 47 50, ⓦwww.dvgl.no; ⑤), an attractive modern building in traditional style right on the waterfront, but the more economical – and frugal – choice is *Den siste Viking*, Misværveien 10 (☎76 07 49 11, ⓔpostmaster@nordnorskklatreskole.no; ①), which provides unadorned lodging right in the centre. The latter doubles as the home of the Lofoten's best **mountaineering school**, Nord Norsk Klatreskole (same number; ⓦwww.nordnorskklatreskole.no). The school operates a wide range of all-inclusive climbing holidays in the mountains near Henningsvær, catering to various degrees of fitness and experience. Prices vary greatly depending on the trip, but a three-day, one-climb-a-day holiday costs in the region of 4200kr per person, including equipment, food and accommodation.

Much less strenuous are **fishing trips**, a morning or afternoon's excursion for around 300kr, booked down at the harbour, or you could drop by the **Galleri Lofoten Hus** (daily: March noon–3pm, late May to early June & mid-Aug 10am–6pm, mid-June to early Aug 9am–9pm; late Aug 11am–4pm; 60kr), which exhibits and sells the work of the contemporary artist Karl Erik Harr alongside a scattering of earlier paintings.

For **food**, the *Klatrekafeen*, at Den siste Viking on the main street just back from the waterfront, serves up a good range of Norwegian standbys from 80kr, plus soup and salads and some ethnic options, all washed down with first-rate coffee. Much classier, however, is the waterside *Fiskekrogen Restaurant*, Dreyersgate 19, where the fish soup in particular and the seafood in general are simply superb; main courses from 160kr.

Vestvågøy: Stamsund

It's the next large island to the southwest of Austvågøya, **Vestvågøy**, that captivates many travellers to the Lofoten. This is due in no small part to the laid-back charm of **STAMSUND**, whose older buildings string along the rocky, fretted seashore in an amiable jumble of crusty port buildings, wooden houses and *rorbuer*. There have been some recent additions to the Stamsund stew, but it's all pretty low-key and the new art gallery, **Galleri 2**, about 100m from the Hurtigrute dock (mid-June to mid-Aug Tues–Sun noon–4pm & 7–9.30pm; 20kr), is well worth a quick rummage. Stamsund is also the first port at which the **Hurtigrute coastal boat** docks on its way north from Bodø, and is much the best place to stay on the island. Getting there **by bus from Austvågøya** is reasonably easy too, with several buses making the trip daily, though you do have to change at **LEKNES**, 15km away to the west and the site of the airport. Leknes itself is the dull and boring administrative centre of Vestvågøy – something you're likely to discover fairly immediately as you wait the hour or two it usually takes to change buses.

The village **tourist office** is situated just 200m from the ferry dock (mid-June to mid-Aug daily 6–9.30pm; ☎76 05 69 96), but it's hardly over-burdened with information and you may well get as much, if not more, advice at the friendly HI **hostel** (☎76 08 93 34, ⓕ76 08 97 39; late Dec to mid-Oct), about 1km down the road from the port and 200m from the nearest bus stop – ask to be let off. The warden, who is something of a one-off, knows everything there is to know about Vestvågøy and then some, from hiking through to fishing and beyond, while the hostel itself is made up of several *rorbuer* and a *sjøhus* perched over a bonny, pin-sized bay, and has some double rooms (①). The **fishing** hereabouts is first-class: the hostel rents out rowing boats and lines to take out on the (usually still) water, or you can head off on an organized half-day fishing trip for just 200kr. Afterwards you can cook your catch on the wood-burning stoves and eat alfresco on the veranda overlooking the bay. Unsurprisingly, many travellers return time and again – though no one could say the hostel was spick or span and the general sense of chaos is not to everyone's taste. The safer and smoother option is *Skjærbrygga* (☎76 05 46 00, ⓦwww .skjaerbrygga.no; ❺), a combined **hotel**, *sjøhus* and *rorbuer* facility right in the centre of Stamsund by the harbour. Most of the nineteen *rorbuer* (❺) are tastefully revamped old cabins dating back to the 1940s; others are more modern but all are comfortable. The Skjærbrygga itself is a pleasantly recycled former warehouse that now contains a café and a very good **restaurant**, with main courses, featuring local ingredients, costing around 150kr.

Pushing west along the coast, it's just 3km from the Stamsund ferry port to the hamlet of **STEINE**, where an offshore archipelago of islets confettis the coastline and where the cosy if rather spartan *Steine Rorbuer & Hytter* (☎ & ☎76 08 92 83; ❶) snuggle up to the seashore. Note that there are no buses connecting Stamsund with Steine.

The west coast and the Lofotr Vikingmuseum

Admirers of wild scenery should consider heading out to Vestvågøy's blustery **west coast**, where a few hardy fishing villages hung on until they finally abandoned the land to the birds, the wind and the sea in the 1950s. This coast is accessed by a series of turnings off the **E10** as it slices across Vestvågøy's drab central valley; from Stamsund, follow the E10 for a hilly 15km to **Leknes** (see above). Keep going north along the E10 for a few more kilometres and you'll come to the second sign-posted byroad which leads to **UNSTAD**, a huddle of houses in a diminutive river valley set right beneath the mountains and with wide views out to sea. A popular and comparatively straightforward nine-kilometre-long **hiking trail** runs along the seashore from Unstad with mountains and lakes on one side, the surging ocean on the other, until it slips into **EGGUM**. This tiny hamlet is an especially pretty spot, its handful of houses hanging onto a precarious headland dwarfed by the mountains behind and with a whopping pebble beach in front. Eggum can also be reached by road off the E10 – it's the next turning along from the Unstad turn – but note that without a car, all these places are difficult to reach: cyclists will face stiff gradients and often strong winds and, although the bus service along the E10 itself is fairly good, there are no buses off it to the west coast. More accessible, in that it's on the E10 between the Unstad and Eggum turnings, 14km from Leknes, is the flashy **Lofotr Vikingmuseum** (mid-May to Aug daily 10am–7pm; Sept to mid-May Fri 1–3pm; ⓦwww.lofotr.no; 80kr), where the accidental discovery of the site of a Viking chieftain's house by a local farmer in 1981 has inspired the creation of a full-blooded Viking museum. The 83-metre Viking house has been reconstruct-ed and all sorts of gimcrackery – flickering lights, wood tar smells and so forth – add to the atmosphere, though some visitors prefer the permanent exhibition of actual archeological finds. "Viking" animals graze the grounds and the boathouse contains a full-size replica of the Gokstad ship displayed in Oslo (see p.244).

South to Nusfjord

By any standard the next two islands of the archipelago, **Flakstadøya** and **Moskenesøya**, are extraordinarily beautiful. As the Lofoten taper towards their southerly conclusion, the rearing peaks of the Lofotenveggen crimp the sea-shredded coastline, providing a thunderously scenic backdrop to a necklace of tiny fishing villages. The E10 travels along almost all of this shoreline, leaving Leknes to tunnel west under the sound separating Vestvågøy from Flakstadøya (toll 80kr). About 20km from Leknes, an even more improbable byroad manages somehow to worm its way 6km up through the mountains to **NUSFJORD**, an extravagantly picturesque fishing village in a tight and forbidding cove. Unlike many fishermen's huts elsewhere in the Lofoten, the ones here are the genuine nineteenth-century article, and the general store, with its wooden floors and antique appearance, fits in nicely, too. Inevitably, it's tourism that keeps the local economy afloat, and the vil-lage is firmly on the day-trippers' itinerary, but it's still an incredibly beguiling place.

Accommodation is available in more than thirty comfortably refurbished – and chain-hotel owned – *rorbuer*. The one-bedroom versions hold two to four people (490kr), while the two-bedroom ones have space for five (from 800kr). There's also a **bar-restaurant**. Advance reservations are strongly advised via *Nusfjord Rorbuanlegg* (☎76 09 30 20, ⊛www.rica.no).

Hamnøy and Reine

Back on the E10, it's a further 5km to the **Flakstad kirke**, a distinctive onion-domed, red-timber church built of driftwood in 1780. The church marks the start of **RAMBERG**, the island's administrative centre – if that's what you can call the smattering of services (garage, supermarket and suchlike) straggling the sandy beach. Pressing on south, over the first of several narrow bridges, you're soon on **Moskenesøya**, where the road squeezes along the coast before squirming across the mouth of the Reinefjord, hopping from islet to islet to link **HAMNØY**, on the north side of the inlet, with **REINE** to the south. Both villages boast impossibly picturesque settings, and Hamnøy also lays claim to an excellent restaurant, *Hamnøy Mat & Vinbu* (early March to Sept), which offers traditional Norwegian cuisine at its best. The menu is short, but the food is first-rate and this is as good a place as any to try a traditional island delicacy, fried cods' tongues. Hamnøy also holds the very plain *Hamnøy Rorbuer* (☎76 09 23 20, ☎76 09 21 54, ❸), but these are not nearly as appealing as those on the tiny islet of **Sakrisøya**, midway between Hamnøy and Reine, where the pretty yellow cabins of *Sakrisøy Rorbuer* (☎76 09 21 43, ⊛www.rorbu.as; ❸) are well-kept and cosy.

Stuck on a promontory just off the E10 immediately to the south of Sakrisøya, **REINE** conspires to look a tad seedy despite the scenery. It is, however, very useful as the departure point for a variety of **boat trips**. These include Midnight Sun cruises (late May to mid-July 1 weekly; 5hr; 420kr), coastal voyages (June to mid-Aug 1 weekly; 4hr; 300kr), fishing expeditions and excursions to the Moskenstraumen (see overleaf). Further information about these trips, including sailing schedules, is easy to come by locally – phone or visit the Moskenes tourist office (see below), or ask at wherever you're staying.

Moskenes

From Reine, it's about 5km to **MOSKENES**, the main island port from Bodø – not that there's much here beyond a handful of houses dotted round a horseshoe-shaped bay. There is, however, a helpful **tourist office** by the jetty (early to late June Mon–Fri 10am–5pm; late June to early Aug daily 10am–7pm; early to mid-Aug Mon–Fri 10am–5pm; mid-Aug to early June Mon–Fri 10am–2pm; ☎76 09 15 99), and a basic **campsite** (☎76 09 13 44; June-Aug), a five-minute walk away some 400m up a gravel track. A local **bus** runs along the E10 linking Leknes, Moskenes and Å (see below) at least once or twice daily from late June to late August, less frequently the rest of the year. Times do not, however, usually coincide with ferry sailings.

Å

Five kilometres further south the road ends abruptly at the tersely named **Å**, one of the Lofoten's most delightful villages, its old buildings rambling along a foreshore that's wedged in tight between the grey-green mountains and the surging sea. Unusually, so much of the nineteenth-century village has survived that a goodly portion has been incorporated into the **Norwegian Fishing Village Museum** (*Norsk Fiskevaersmuseum*; late June to late Aug daily 11am–6pm; late Aug to late June Mon–Fri 11am–3pm; 40kr), an engaging attempt to recreate life here at the end of the nineteenth century. There are about fifteen buildings to examine – though some seem to be permanently closed – including a boathouse, forge, cod-liver oil processing plant, *rorbuer* and the houses of the two traders who dominated things hereabouts and the fishermen who did their bidding. The museum has a series of displays which detail every aspect of village life – and very well presented it is, too. Afterwards, you can extend your knowledge of all things fishy by visiting the **Stockfish Museum** (*Tørrfiskmuseum*; early to late June daily 11am–5pm; late June to late Aug daily 10am–5pm; 35kr), stockfish being the air-dried fish that was the staple diet of most Norwegians well into the twentieth century.

Å also weighs in with several **boat trips**. There are day-long fishing expeditions (June–Aug Mon–Sat 1 daily; 3hr; 280kr) and, weather and tides permitting, regular cruises (June to mid-Aug 1 weekly; 4hr; 400kr) to the **Moskenstraumen**, the maelstrom at the southern tip of Moskenesøya. There are other places to see similar phenomena in Norway – the Saltstraumen near Bodø (see p.351) springs to mind – but the swirling, hissing, spinning waters of the Moskenstraumen are the most dramatic.

Practicalities

Reachable by local **bus** at least once or twice daily from late June to late August, less frequently the rest of the year, Å is at the very end of the E10. Irritatingly, bus times do not usually coincide with the Moskenes ferry sailings to and from the mainland, so to get from Moskenes to Å you'll either have to walk – it's an easy 5km – or take a taxi.

All the **accommodation** in Å is run by one family, who own the all-year HI **hostel**, which has doubles (**①**) as well as dorms; the assortment of smart three- to ten-bedded *rorbuer* (550–1550kr per *rorbu*) surrounding the dock; and the adjacent *sjøhus*, which offers very comfortable and equally smart, hotel-standard rooms (from **②**). There's also the possibility of some informal **camping** within the Norsk Fiskevaersmuseum. The same family also run the cosy **bar** and the only **restaurant**, where the seafood is first-rate and main courses average around 120kr. Bookings for all these on ☎76 09 11 21, though off-season (September–May) you may have better luck on ☎22 50 97 84 or via ⓦwww.lofoten-rorbu.com. Finally, Å has a grocery store, an old-style bakery and bikes can be rented at 180kr per day.

Travel details

Trains

Narvik to: Riksgränsen (2–3 daily; 50min); Stockholm (1 daily; 18hr).
Trondheim to: Bodø (2–3 daily; 11hr); Dombås (3–4 daily; 2hr 30min); Fauske (2–3 daily; 10hr); Mo-i-Rana (2–3 daily; 7hr); Oslo (3–4 daily; 6hr); Otta (3 daily; 3hr); Røros (1–2 daily; 2hr 30min); Steinkjer (2–3 daily; 2hr); Stockholm (2 daily; 12hr).

Principal buses

Bodø to: Fauske (2–4 daily; 1hr 10min); Harstad (1 daily; 7hr 30min); Narvik (1–3 daily; 7hr 30min); Sortland (1–2 daily; 7hr); Svolvær (1 daily; 10hr 40min).
Fauske to: Bodø (2–5 daily; 1hr 10min); Harstad (1 daily; 6hr 30min); Narvik (1–3 daily; 5hr 30min); Sortland (1–2 daily; 6hr); Svolvær (1 daily; 9hr).
Harstad to: Fauske (1 daily; 6hr 30min).
Narvik to: Alta (Mon–Fri & Sun 1–3 daily; 9hr);

Bodø (1–3 daily; 7hr); Fauske (1–3 daily; 5hr 30min); Sortland (1–2 daily; 4hr); Svolvær (1–2 daily; 6hr 40min); Tromsø (1–2 daily; 4hr 10min).
Sortland to: Andenes (1–3 daily; 2hr 15min).
Svolvær to: Å (Mon–Fri 1–2 daily; 3hr 20min).
Trondheim to: Bergen (2 daily; 14hr); Kristiansund (1–3 daily; 5hr); Otta (2 daily; 4hr); Stryn (2 daily; 7hr 20min); Ålesund (1–3 daily; 8hr).

Nord-Norgeekspressen

The **Nord-Norgeekspressen** (North Norway Express Bus) complements the railway system. It runs north from Bodø and Fauske to Narvik and Tromsø, where you change – and stay overnight – before embarking on the next leg of the journey up to Alta. In Alta, passengers change again for the connecting **Nordkappekspressen** bus onto Honningsvåg and Nordkapp. For further details of the northern parts of this epic bus journey, see "Travel Details" at the end of the North Norway chapter.

Andenes to: Gryllefjord (early June to late Aug 2–3 daily; 1hr 40min).
Bodø to: Moskenes (June–Aug 2–4 daily; Sept–May Mon–Fri & Sun 1–2 daily; 4hr 15min or 8hr depending on routing); Røst (5 weekly; 8hr); Værøy (5 weekly; 7hr).
Botnhamn to: Brensholmen (June to late Aug 4–7 daily; 35min).
Bognes to: Lødingen (early June to mid-Aug 12 daily, mid-Aug to mid-June 5 daily; 1hr); Skarberget (15–21 daily, usually every 1hr or 1hr 30min; 25min).
Fiskebøl to: Melbu (every 90min; 25min).
Harstad to: Skrolsvik (early June to late Aug 2–4 daily; 1hr 50min).
Skutvik to: Svolvær (June to mid-Aug 8 daily; mid-Aug to May 2–3 daily; 2hr).
Svolvær to: Skutvik (June to mid-Aug 8 daily; mid-Aug to May 2–3 daily; 2hr).

Bodø to: Svolvær (Mon–Fri & Sun 1 daily; 5hr 30min).
Harstad to: Tromsø (1–2 daily; 2hr 45min).
Narvik to: Svolvær (Tues–Fri & Sun 1 daily; 3hr 30min).
Trondheim to: Kristiansund (1–3 daily; 3hr 30min).

Northbound departures: daily from Trondheim at noon; Bodø at 3pm; Stamsund at 7.30pm; Svolvær at 10pm; Stokmarknes at 1am; Sortland at 3am and Harstad at 8am.
Southbound departures: daily from Harstad at 8am; Sortland at 1pm; Stokmarknes at 3.15pm; Svolvær at 7.30pm; Stamsund at 9.30pm; Bodø at 4am and Trondheim at 10am.
Journey time Trondheim–Harstad 43hr, Trondheim–Tromsø 51hr.

2.5

North Norway

aedeker, writing 100 years ago about Norway's remote **northern provinces** of Troms and Finnmark, observed that they "possess attractions for the scientific traveller and the sportsman, but can hardly be recommended for the ordinary tourist" – a comment which isn't too wide of the mark even today. These are enticing lands, no question, the natural environment they offer stunning in its extremes, but the travelling can be hard, the specific sights well distanced and, when you reach them, subtle in their appeal.

Troms's intricate, fretted coastline has shaped its history since the days when powerful Viking lords operated a trading empire from its islands. Indeed, over half the population still lives offshore in dozens of tiny fishing villages, but the place to aim for is **Tromsø**, the so-called "Capital of the North" and a lively university town where King Håkon and his government proclaimed a "Free Norway" in 1940 before fleeing into exile. Beyond Tromsø, the long trek north begins in earnest as

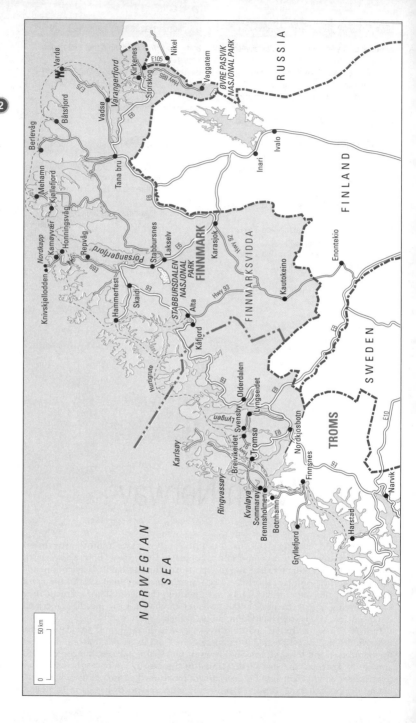

Finnmark: The midnight sun and polar night

On clear nights, the **Midnight Sun** is visible at Alta, Hammerfest and Nordkapp from mid-May until the end of July; the long **Polar Night** runs from the last week in November until the third week in January.

you enter **Finnmark**, a vast wilderness covering 48,000 square kilometres, but home to just two percent of the Norwegian population. Much of the land was laid waste during World War II, the combined effect of the Russian advance and the retreating German army's scorched-earth policy, and it's now possible to drive for hours without coming across a building more than sixty years old. The first obvious target in Finnmark is **Alta**, a sprawling settlement that's famous for its prehistoric rock carvings. Alta is also an important crossroads. From here, most visitors head straight for the steely cliffs of **Nordkapp** (the North Cape), mainland Europe's northernmost point, with or without a detour to the likeable port of **Hammerfest**, and leave it at that; but some doggedly press on to **Kirkenes**, the last town before the Russian border, which feels as if it's about to drop off the end of the world. From Alta, the other main alternative is to travel inland across the eerily endless scrubland of the **Finnmarksvidda**, where winter temperatures plummet to -35°C. This high plateau is the last stronghold of the **Sámi**, northern Norway's indigenous people, many of whom still live a semi-nomadic life tied to the movement of their reindeer herds. You'll spot Sámi in their brightly coloured traditional gear all across the region, but especially in the remote towns of **Kautokeino** and **Karasjok**, strange, disconsolate places in the middle of the plain.

Finally, and even more adventurously, there is the **Svalbard** archipelago, whose icy mountains rise out of the Arctic Ocean 640km north of mainland Norway. Once the exclusive haunt of trappers, fishermen and coal miners, Svalbard now makes a tidy income from adventure tourism – everything from guided glacier walks to snowmobile excursions and whale-watching. You can fly there independently from most of Norway's larger towns, including Tromsø, at prices that are bearable, though most people opt for a package tour.

Transport and accommodation

Public transport in Troms and Finnmark is by bus, Hurtigrute coastal boat and plane – there are no trains. For all but the most truncated of tours, the best idea is to pick and mix these different forms of transport – for example by flying from Tromsø to Kirkenes and then taking the Hurtigrute back, or vice versa. It's best to avoid endless doubling back on the E6, though this is often difficult, as this is the only road to run right across the region. To give an idea of the distances involved, it's 400km from Tromsø to Alta, 600km to Nordkapp and 950km to Kirkenes.

The principal long-distance bus is the **Nord-Norgeekspressen**, which links Tromsø with Alta, from where there are onward services to Honningsvåg and – from late June to mid-August – Nordkapp. Alta is also handy for local buses to Karasjok and Kirkenes. North of Alta, just about every bus uses the E6 to pass through Skaidi, where you change for Hammerfest and Olderfjord. The bus linking Hammerfest with Karasjok and Kirkenes also runs through Olderfjord. Bus **timetables** are available at most tourist offices and bus stations. On the longer rides, it's a good idea to buy **tickets** in advance.

The main **highways** are all well-maintained, but **drivers** will find the going a little slow as they have to negotiate some pretty tough terrain. You can cover 250–300km in a day without any problem, but much more and it all becomes rather wearisome. Be warned also that in July and August, the E6 north of Alta can get congested with caravans and motor homes on their way to Nordkapp. You can avoid the crush by starting early or, for that matter, by driving overnight – an eerie experience when it's bright sunlight in the wee hours of the morning. In **winter**, driving conditions can be appalling and, although the Norwegians make a spirited effort to keep the E6 open, they don't always succeed. If you're not used to driving in these sorts of conditions, don't start here – especially during the Polar Night. If you intend to use the region's **unpaved roads**, be prepared for the worst and certainly take food and drink, warm clothes and, if possible, a mobile phone. Keep an eye on the fuel indicator too, as petrol stations are confined to the larger settlements and these are often 100–200km apart. Car repairs can take time since workshops are scarce and parts often have to be ordered from the south.

Much more leisurely is the **Hurtigrute coastal boat**, which takes the best part of two days to cross the huge fjords between Tromsø and Kirkenes. En route, it calls at eleven ports, mostly remote fishing villages, but also Hammerfest and Honningsvåg, where it pauses for two or three hours so that special buses can cart passengers off to Nordkapp and back. With regard to **air travel**, the region has several **airports**, including those at Alta, Hammerfest, Honningsvåg, Kirkenes, Tromsø and Longyearbyen, on Svalbard. Via its subsidiary, Braathens/Widerøe, SAS flies in and out of a string of small northern airstrips with summer discounts and special deals and passes making flying an economic possibility.

As for **accommodation**, all the major settlements have at least a couple of hotels and the main roads are sprinkled with campsites. If you have a tent and a well-insulated sleeping bag you can, in theory, bed down more or less where you like, but the hostility of the climate and the ferocity of the mosquitoes, which breed in marshy areas of the Finnmarksvidda, make most people think (at least) twice. There are HI **hostels** at Tromsø, Alta, Lakselv and Karasjok.

Tromsø

TROMSØ has been called, rather preposterously, the "Paris of the North", and though even the tourist office doesn't make any pretence to such grandiose titles today, the city is without question the effective capital of northern Norway. Easily the region's most populous town, Tromsø received its municipal charter in 1794, when it was primarily a fishing port and trading station, and flourished in the middle of the nineteenth century when its seamen ventured north to Svalbard to reap rich rewards hunting arctic foxes, polar bears and, most profitable of all, seals. Subsequently, Tromsø became famous as the jumping-off point for a string of arctic expeditions, its celebrity status assured when the explorer Roald Amundsen flew from here to his death somewhere on the Arctic ice cap in 1928. Since those heady days, Tromsø has grown into an urbane and likeable small city with a population of 60,000 employed in a wide range of industries and at the university. Give or take the odd museum, Tromsø is short on specific sights, but its amiable atmosphere and fine mountain and fjord setting more than compensate. It also possesses a clutch of good restaurants, lively bars and several enjoyable hotels.

Arrival and information

At the northern end of the E8, 73km from the E6 and 250km north of Narvik, Tromsø's compact centre slopes up from the waterfront on the hilly island of Tromsøya. The island is connected to the mainland by bridge and tunnel. The **Hurtigrute** docks in the town centre at the foot of Kirkegata; **Hurtigbåt** boats arrive at the quay about 150m to the south. Long-distance **buses** arrive and leave from the car park a few metres away. The **airport** is 5km west of the centre on the other side of Tromsøya. From the airport, frequent Flybussen airport buses (Mon–Fri hourly 7.30am–8pm, Sat 6 daily, Sun hourly 9am–8pm; 40kr) run into the city, stopping at the *Radisson SAS Hotel Tromsø* on Sjøgata and at several other central hotels; the taxi fare is 90kr.

Tromsø's **tourist office**, Storgata 61 (mid- to late May & mid-Aug to mid-Sept Mon–Fri 8.30am–4pm, Sat & Sun 10.30am–2pm; June to mid-Aug Mon–Fri 8.30am–6pm, Sat 10am–5pm & Sun 10.30am–5pm; mid-Sept to mid-May

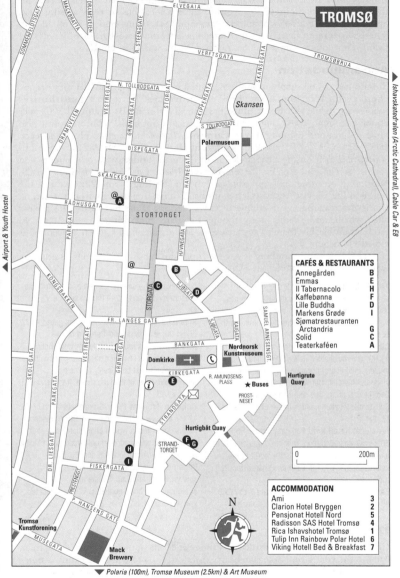

TROMSØ

CAFÉS & RESTAURANTS

Annegården	B
Emmas	E
Il Tabernacolo	H
Kaffebønna	F
Lille Buddha	D
Markens Grøde	I
Sjømatrestauranten	
Arctandria	G
Solid	C
Teaterkaféen	A

ACCOMMODATION

Ami	3
Clarion Hotel Bryggen	2
Pensjonat Hotell Nord	5
Radisson SAS Hotel Tromsø	4
Rica Ishavshotel Tromsø	1
Tulip Inn Rainbow Polar Hotel	6
Viking Hotell Bed & Breakfast	7

0   200m

Polaria (100m), Tromsø Museum (2.5km) & Art Museum

Mon–Fri 8.30am–4pm, Sat 10.30am–2pm, closed Sun; ☏77 61 00 00, ⓦwww
.destinasjontromso.no), is a couple of minutes' walk straight up Kirkegata from
where the long-distance buses stop. Staff can supply free town maps and oodles of
local information, and also sell a one-day **tourist ticket** (60kr, valid 24hr from
when it's first used) offering unlimited city bus travel, though most places of interest
can easily be reached on foot.

It only takes five minutes to walk from one side of the centre to the other, but for the outlying attractions you can either catch a local bus or **rent a bike** from Sportshuset, Storgata 87 (Mon–Fri 9am–5pm, Sat 10am–4pm; ☎77 66 11 00). There's **Internet** access at the *Amtmannens Datter* café-bar, Grønnegata 81 (Mon–Thurs noon–2am, Fri & Sat noon–3.30am, Sun 3pm–2am).

Accommodation

Tromsø has a good supply of modern, central **hotels**, though the majority occupy chunky concrete high-rises. Less expensive are the town's **guesthouses** (*pensjonater*), while the tourist office has a small list of **B&Bs** at around 300kr per double per night (200kr single), but most are stuck out in the suburbs. Tromsø also possesses a reasonably handy all-year **campsite**, *Tromsdalen Camping*, Elvestrandvegen (☎77 63 80 37, ☏77 63 85 24), about 2km east of the Arctic cathedral (*Ishavskatedralen*) on the mainland side of the main bridge, with tent pitches and cabins (❶); and a barracks-like HI **hostel**, *Tromsø Vandrerhjem* (☎77 65 76 28, ⓔtromso.hostel@vandrerhjem.no; late June to late Aug), some 2km west of the centre in Elverhøy at Åsgårdsveien 9. It's a stiff thirty-minute walk from the centre, and is also reachable via a couple of city buses; ask at the bus station. It's a basic affair which can be rather noisy, though there are some private doubles (❶). No food is available, but there's a store close by and a communal kitchen. Reception is closed 11am–5pm.

Note that advance booking is a very good idea for all the options listed here, especially in the summer.

Ami Skolegata 24 ☎77 68 22 08, ⓦwww.amihotel.no. This guesthouse/hotel has wide views over the city from the hillside behind the town centre. Seventeen simple rooms. Worth booking ahead in summer. ❷

Clarion Hotel Bryggen Sjøgata 19–21 ☎77 78 11 00, ⓦwww.choicehotels.no. Polished, super-modern chain hotel down on the waterfront with small but tastefully furnished rooms. The fifth-floor jacuzzi offers fine sea (and sky) views. Substantial weekend and summer discounts. ❻/❸

Pensjonat Hotell Nord Parkgata 4 ☎77 66 83 00, ⓦwww.hotellnord.no. This basic guesthouse is a good, stiff walk up the hill to the north of the centre, and has both en-suite and shared-facility rooms. ❷

Radisson SAS Hotel Tromsø Sjøgata 7 ☎77 60 00 00 ⓦwww.radissonsas.com. This plush,

downtown high-rise offers smart and comfortable modern rooms, and ultra-efficient service. ❻ s/r ❹

Rica Ishavshotel Tromsø Fr. Langes gate 2 ☎77 66 64 00, ⓦwww.rica.no. Perched on the harbourfront, this imaginatively designed hotel is partly built in the style of a ship, complete with a sort of crow's nest bar. Lovely rooms and unbeatable views of the waterfront. Best place in town. ❺/❸

Tulip Inn Rainbow Polar Grønnegata 45 ☎77 75 17 00, ⓦwww.rainbow-hotels.no. Small, modern rooms decorated in typical chain-hotel style, but summer and weekend discounts make this place a real bargain; central location, too. ❹/❷ .

Viking Grønnegata 18 ☎77 65 76 22, ⓦwww.viking-hotell.no. Simple and straightforward hotel-cum-B&B, centrally located and with very good prices. ❷

The City

Completed in 1861, the **Domkirke** (Tues–Sat 10am–4pm, Sun 10am–2pm; free), bang in the centre on Kirkegata, bears witness to the prosperity of Tromsø's nine-teenth-century merchants, who became rich on the back of the barter trade with Russia. They part-funded the cathedral's construction, resulting in the large and handsome structure of today, whose imposing spire pokes high into the sky. Behind the church, at Sjøgata 1, stands the **Art Museum of Northern Norway** (*Nordnorsk Kunstmuseum*; Tues, Wed & Fri 10am–5pm, Thurs 10am–7pm, Sat & Sun noon–5pm; ⓦwww.museumsnett.no/nordnorsk-kunstmuseum; 30kr), a well-pre-sented collection of fine art and northern handicrafts from the 1850s onwards. It's not a large ensemble, but it does contain the work of many Norwegian painters, from lesser-known figures like Axel Revold and Christian Krohg to a handful of works by Edvard Munch (for more on whom, see p.247). There are also several Romantic peasant scenes by Adolph Tidemand and a couple of ingenious landscapes by both the talented Thomas Fearnley and Johan Dahl. The permanent collection is enhanced by frequent loans from the National Gallery in Oslo and by a lively programme of temporary exhibitions.

Back at the front of the Domkirke, it's a gentle five-minute stroll north past the shops of Storgata to the main square, **Stortorget**, site of a daily open-air flower and knick-knack **market**. The square nudges down to the waterfront, where fresh fish and prawns are sold direct from inshore fishing boats throughout the summer. Follow the harbour round to the north and you're in the heart of old Tromsø: the raised ground close to the water's edge was the centre of the medieval settlement and it was here that the locals built the first fortifications. Nothing now remains of the medieval town, but you can discern the shape of a later, eighteenth-century **fort** in the modest knoll, Skansen, at the end of Skansegata.

Close by, in an old wooden waterfront warehouse, is the city's most enjoyable museum, the **Polar Museum** (daily: mid-May to mid-June & mid-Aug to mid-Sept 11am–5pm; mid-June to mid-Aug 10am–7pm; mid-Sept to mid-May 11am–3pm; ⓦwww.polarmuseum.no; 40kr). The collection begins with a rather unappetizing series of displays on trapping in the Arctic, but beyond is an outstanding section on Svalbard, including archeological finds recently retrieved from an eighteenth-century Russian trapping station – most come from graves in which they were preserved by permafrost. Two other sections on the first floor focus on seal hunting, an important part of the local economy until the 1950s. Upstairs, on the second floor, a further section is devoted to the polar explorer **Roald Amundsen** (1872–1928). Amundsen spent thirty years searching out the secrets of the polar regions, and on December 14, 1911, he and four of his crew became the first men to reach the South Pole, famously just ahead of his British rival Captain Scott. The museum exhibits all sorts of oddments used by Amundsen and his men – from long johns and pipes through to boots and ice picks – but it's the photos that steal the show, both for the fascinating insight they give into the expeditions and their hardships, and for their images of a heroically posed Amundsen, complete with the finest set of eyebrows north of Oslo.

To the south of the city centre, the eminently profitable **Mack brewery**, at the corner of Storgata and Musegata, proudly lays claim to being the northernmost brewery in the world – and dreams up all sorts of bottle labels with ice and polar bears to hammer home the point. Nearby, just up Musegata, the **Tromsø Art Institute** (*Kunstforening*; Tues–Sun noon–5pm; 30kr) occupies part of a large and attractive late nineteenth-century building that started out as the municipal museum. Today, the gallery showcases imaginative temporary exhibitions of Norwegian contemporary art with the emphasis on the work of Nordland artists.

Doubling back down Musegata, it's a couple of hundred metres south along Storgata to **Polaria** (daily: mid-May to mid-Aug 10am–7pm; mid-Aug to mid-May noon–5pm; ⓦwww.polaria.no; 75kr), a lavish waterfront complex which deals with all things Arctic. There's an aquarium filled with Arctic species, a 180-degree cinema showing a gripping film on Svalbard and several exhibitions on polar research.

Eating and drinking

With a clutch of first-rate **restaurants**, several enjoyable **cafés** and a good supply of late-night **bars**, Tromsø is certainly as well served as any comparable Norwegian city. The best of the cafés and restaurants are concentrated in the vicinity of the tourist office, on Storgata, and most of the livelier bars – many of which sell Mack, the local brew – are in the centre, too.

Cafés and restaurants

Aunegården Sjøgaten 29. Large(ish) café-restaurant situated in the listed Aunegården building. Serves all the Norwegian standard dishes at moderate prices, but these are as nothing when compared with the cakes, wonderful confections which are made at their own bakery. Weep with pleasure as you nibble at the cheesecake.

Emmas Drømmekjøkken Kirkegata 8 ☏77 63 77 30. Much praised in the national press as a gourmet treat, "Emma's dream kitchen" lives up to its name, with an imaginative and wide-ranging menu. Expensive, and smart, too. Closed Sun.

Il Tabernacolo Storgata 36. Claims to be the world's northernmost and Tromsø's only authentic Italian restaurant – few would dispute either tag. Serves first-class, reasonably priced pasta and pizza dishes plus all the other Italian classics in cosy, pastel-painted surroundings. Closed Tues.

Kaffebønna Strandtorget 1. Smart, specialist coffee house with definitively the best brew in town, plus tasty snacks from their own bakery.

Lille Buddha Sjøgata 25. Different kinds of Asian cuisine, everything from Chinese to Indian, at affordable prices – main courses from 100kr.

Markens Grøde Storgata 30 ☏77 68 25 50. Classy and expensive Norwegian cuisine featuring innovative preparations of local fish and game, and lots of seasonal specialities. Closed Mon.

Sjømatrestauranten Arctandria Strandtorget 1 ☏77 60 07 20. Some of the best food in town. The upstairs restaurant serves a superb range of fish, with the emphasis on Arctic species, and there's also reindeer and seal; main courses start at around 200kr. Prices are about twenty percent less at the café-bar *Skarven*, downstairs, where there's a slightly less varied menu. Closed Sun.

Solid Storgata 73. Brisk, modern café in the daytime, busy bar at night. Tasty snacks and light meals at lunch time.

Bars

Amtmannens Datter Grønnegata 81. Café-bar with arty student clientele, newspapers, Internet access and lots of different types of beer.

Blå Rock Café Strandgata 14. Definitely the place to go for loud rock music – with and without the roll. Occasional live acts too, not to mention the best burgers in town.

Mackkjelleren Sjøgata 12, but entrance on Storgata. Popular beer haunt in a basement whose whitewashed walls are covered with old Tromsø aphorisms and proverbs. The locals are (usually) keen to translate. Some karaoke, plus DJ nights, where the emphasis is mostly 1980s, and live acts.

Skipsbroen Fr. Langes gate 2. Inside the *Rica Ishavshotel* (see p.380), this smart little bar overlooks the waterfront from on high – it occupies the top of a slender tower with wide windows that afford sea views. Relaxed atmosphere; lots of tourists.

Teaterkaféen Grønnegata 87, corner of Stortorget. Inside the Kulturhus, this arts-centre café-bar is long on conversation and (student) style. Open until 1am daily.

Ølhallen Pub Storgata 4. Solid (some would say staid) pub adjoining the Mack brewery, whose various ales are its speciality. Closed Sun.

Into Finnmark: Alta

Northeast of Tromsø, the vast sweep of the northern landscape slowly unfolds, with silent fjords gashing deep into the coastline beneath ice-tipped peaks which themselves fade into the high plateau of the interior. This forbidding, elemental terrain is interrupted by the occasional valley where those few souls hardy enough to make a living in these parts struggle on – often by dairy farming. In summer, cut

---

Routes north from Tromsø

Northbound, the **Hurtigrute** leaves Tromsø daily at 6.30pm, taking eleven hours to reach Hammerfest. The **Nord-Norgeekspressen** (North Norway Express Bus) runs north from Tromsø to Alta, where passengers change again for the connecting **Nordkappekspressen** bus onto Honningsvåg and Nordkapp. The Nord-Norgeekspressen operates all year, the Nordkappekspressen from late June to mid-August. At other times of the year, FFR, the local transport company, operates a bus from Alta to Honningsvåg, but not Nordkapp.

grass dries everywhere, stretched over wooden poles that form long lines on the hillsides like so much washing drying.

Slipping along the valleys and traversing the mountains in between, the **E8** and then the **E6** follow the coast pretty much all the way to Alta, some 420km – about nine hours' drive – to the north. Drivers can save around 120km (although not necessarily time, and certainly not money) by turning off the E8 25km south of Tromsø onto **Highway 91** – a quieter, arguably even more scenic route, offering yet more extravagant fjord and mountain views. Highway 91 begins by cutting across the rocky peninsula that backs onto Tromsø to reach the **Breivikeidet–Svendsby car ferry** (every 1–2hr: Mon–Thurs 6am–8pm, Fri 6am–9pm, Sat 8am–8pm, Sun 10am–9pm; 25min; 60kr car and driver; ☎77 71 14 00) over to the glaciated Lyngen peninsula. From the Svensby ferry dock it's just a 22-kilometre drive across the Lyngen to the **Lyngseidet–Olderdalen car ferry** (every 1–2hr: Mon–Thurs 7am–7pm, Fri 7am–9pm, Sat 9am–7pm, Sun 11am–9pm; 40min; 80kr car and driver), by means of which you can rejoin the E6 at **Olderdalen**, some 220km south of Alta. This is the route used by most long-distance buses.

Beyond Olderdalen, the E6 enters **Finnmark** as it approaches the hamlet of **Langfjordbotn**, at the foot of the long and slender Langfjord. Thereafter, the road sticks tight against the coast to reach, after another 60km, the tiny village of **KÅFJORD**, whose recently restored nineteenth-century church was built by the English company who operated the area's copper mines until they were abandoned as uneconomic in the 1870s. From here, it's just 20km further to Alta.

Alta

Despite the long haul to get here, first impressions of **ALTA** are not encouraging. With a population of just 16,000, the town spreads unenticingly along the E6 for several kilometres, at its ugliest part in **Alta Sentrum**, now befuddled by a platoon of concrete blocks. Alta was at least interesting once, and for decades was not Norwegian at all, but Finnish and Sámi, and host to an ancient Sámi fair. World War II polished off the fair and destroyed all the old wooden buildings that once clustered together in Alta's **Bossekop**, where Dutch whalers settled in the seventeenth century.

For all that, Alta does have one remarkable feature, the most extensive area of **prehistoric rock carvings** in northern Europe, the Helleristningene i Hjemmeluft, which has been designated a UNESCO World Heritage site. The carvings are located beside the E6 as you approach Alta from the southwest, some 2.5km before the Bossekop district, and form part of **Alta Museum** (May daily 9am–6pm; early June and late Aug daily 8am–8pm; mid-June to mid-Aug daily 8am–11pm; Sept daily 9am–6pm; Oct–April Mon–Fri 9am–3pm, Sat & Sun 11am–4pm; 70kr May–Sept, otherwise 35kr). The **museum** itself provides a wealth of background information on the carvings in particular and prehistoric Finnmark in general, as well as a potted history of the Alta area, with exhibitions on the salmon-fishing industry, copper mining and so forth. Outside, the **rock carvings** extend down the hill from the museum building to the fjordside. A clear and easy-to-follow footpath and boardwalk circumnavigate the site, taking in all the carvings in about an hour. On the trail, there are **thirteen vantage points** offering close-up views of the carvings, recognizable though highly stylized representations of boats, animals and people picked out in red pigment (the colours have been retouched by researchers). They make up an extraordinarily complex tableau, whose minor variations – there are **four identifiable bands** – in subject matter and design indicate successive historical periods. The carvings were executed, it's estimated, between 6000 and 2500 years ago, and are indisputably impressive: clear, stylish and touching in their simplicity, offering an insight into a prehistoric culture that was essentially settled and largely reliant on the hunting of land animals.

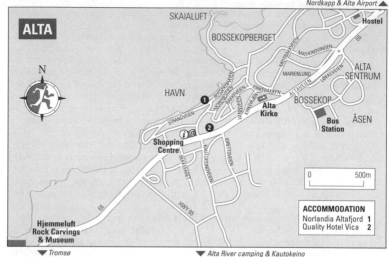

Tromsø ▼   ▼ *Alta River camping & Kautokeino*

Practicalities

Long-distance **buses** make two stops in Alta – one at Alta Sentrum, where they pause at the **bus station**, the other at Alta airport, further north along the E6 in the Elvebakken district. Get off at Alta Sentrum for the rock carvings, which are reachable via a 4.5-kilometre walk back along the E6. Alternatively, you can catch a **local bus** (every half-hour Mon–Fri 6am–8pm, Sat 10am–3pm) from the bus station (or the airport) to Bossekop, from where you walk the final 2.5km. If you want to call a taxi, ring Alta Taxi on ☎78 43 53 53.

Alta's **tourist office** is near the Rimi supermarket in the Bossekop shopping centre (early June Mon–Fri 8am–4pm; mid-June to early Aug Mon–Fri 8am–6pm, Sat 10am–4pm, Sun noon–4pm; early Aug to end Aug Mon–Fri 8am–4pm & Sat 10am–3pm; ☎78 45 77 77, ⊛ www.destinasjonalta.no). They offer the public Internet access (1kr per minute, minimum charge 30kr for 30min), will advise on hiking the Finnmarksvidda (see opposite) and help with finding **accommodation**.

There are two excellent **hotels** in town, both in Bossekop and within comfortable walking distance of the tourist office. The first, a couple of hundred metres away, is the *Quality Hotel Vica*, Fogdebakken 6I (☎78 43 47 11, ⊛ www .vica.no; ⑤/❹), a small, cosy place decorated in the style of a mountain lodge, with lots of pine panelling; Internet access is included in the rates. Alternatively, the *Norlandia Altafjord Hotell* (☎78 43 70 11, ⊛ www.norlandia.no; ❹), a five- to ten-minute walk away to the west, down by the fjord, offers three sorts of rooms: run-of-the-mill in the main building, cottage-style down by the fjord (the best choice) and in turf-roofed buildings, a spick-and-span version of the traditional-style house. Less costly by far is the HI **hostel**, in a plain chalet about 700m north of Alta Sentrum at Midtbakkveien 52 (☎78 43 44 09, ⊛alta.hostel @vandrerhjem.no; mid-June to mid-Aug), which has doubles (❶) as well as dorms. To get there from Alta Sentrum, drive or walk east up the E6 to the next roundabout, where you turn left and then first left again – a fifteen-minute stroll. Food isn't available, but there are self-catering facilities. There are also several **campsites** in the vicinity of Alta. The best is the well-equipped, four-star *Alta River Camping* (☎78 43 43 53, ⊛annjenss@online.no), by the river about 4km out of town along Highway 93, which cuts off the E6 in between Bossekop and the rock paintings.

Easily the best **restaurant** in town is at the *Hotel Vica*, which specializes in regional delicacies – cloudberries, reindeer and the like. Prices are very reasonable and traditional Sámi dishes are often on the menu, too.

The Finnmarksvidda

Venture far inland from Alta and you enter the **Finnmarksvidda**, a vast mountain plateau which spreads southeast up to and beyond the Finnish border. Rivers, lakes and marshes criss-cross the region, but there's barely a tree, let alone a mountain, to break the contours of a landscape whose wide skies and deep horizons are eerily beautiful. Distances are hard to gauge – a dot of a storm can soon be upon you, breaking with alarming ferocity – and the air is crystal-clear, giving a white-ish lustre

---

The Sámi

The northernmost reaches of Norway, Sweden and Finland, and the Kola peninsula of northwest Russia, are collectively known as **Lapland**. Traditionally, the indigenous people were called "Lapps", though in recent years this name has fallen out of favour and been replaced by the term **Sámi**, although the change is by no means universal. (The new name comes from the Sámi word *sámpi*, meaning both the land and its people.) There are around 70,000 Sámi spread across the whole of the region. Among the oldest peoples in Europe, the Sámi are probably descended from prehistoric clans who migrated here from the east by way of the Baltic. Their language is closely related to Finnish and Estonian, though it's somewhat misleading to speak of a "Sámi language" as there are, in fact, three distinct versions, and each of these breaks down into a number of markedly different regional dialects. All three share many common features, however, including a superabundance of words and phrases to express variations in snow and ice conditions.

Originally, the Sámi were a semi-nomadic people, living in small communities (*siidas*), each of which had a degree of control over the surrounding hunting grounds. They mixed hunting, fishing and trapping, but it was the wild reindeer that supplied most of their needs. This changed in the sixteenth century when the Sámi switched over to **reindeer herding**, with communities following the seasonal movements of the animals.

What little contact the early Sámi had with other Scandinavians was almost always to their disadvantage, but these early depredations were nothing compared with the **dislocation of Sámi culture** that followed the efforts of Sweden, Russia and Norway to control and colonize Sámi land from the seventeenth century onwards. Things got even worse for the Norwegian Sámi towards the end of the nineteenth century, when the government, influenced by the Social Darwinism of the day, embarked on an aggressive policy of **"Norwegianization"**. New laws banned the use of the Sámi languages in schools, and stopped Sámi from buying land unless they could speak Norwegian. This policy was only abandoned and slowly replaced by a more considerate and progressive approach in the 1950s.

Since the international anti-colonial struggles of the 1960s, the Norwegians have been obliged to re-evaluate their relationship with the Sámi. In 1988, the country's **constitution** was amended with an article that stated "It is the responsibility of the authorities of the state to create conditions enabling the Sámi people to preserve and develop its language, culture and way of life", and the following year the **Sameting** (Sámi Parliament) was opened in Karasjok. Certain deep-seated problems do remain and, in common with other aboriginal peoples marooned in industrialized countries, there have been heated debates about land and mineral rights and the future of the Sámi as a people, above and beyond one country's international borders. Neither is it clear quite how the Norwegian Sámi will adjust to having something akin to dual citizenship – but at least Oslo is asking the right questions.

to the sunshine. A couple of roads cross this expanse, but for the most part it remains the preserve of the few thousand semi-nomadic **Sámi** who make up the majority of the local population. Many still wear traditional dress, a brightly coloured affair of red bonnets and blue jerkins or dresses, all trimmed with red, white and yellow embroidery. You'll see permutations on this traditional costume all over Finnmark, but especially at roadside souvenir stalls and on Sundays outside Sámi churches.

Setting aside the slow encroachments of the tourist industry, lifestyles on the Finnmarksvidda have remained remarkably constant for centuries. The main occupation is reindeer-herding, supplemented by hunting and fishing, and the pattern of Sámi life is mostly still dictated by the movements of their animals. During the winter, the reindeer graze the flat plains and shallow valleys of the interior, migrating towards the coast in early May as the snow begins to melt. By October, both people and reindeer are journeying back from their temporary summer quarters. The long, dark winter is spent in preparation for the great **Easter festivals**, when weddings and baptisms are celebrated in the region's two main settlements, Karasjok and, more especially, Kautokeino. As neither settlement is particularly engaging in itself, Easter is without question the best time to be here – a celebration of the end of the Polar Night and the arrival of spring. There are folk-music concerts, church services and traditional sports, including the famed reindeer races – not, thank goodness, reindeers racing each other (they would never cooperate), but reindeer pulling passenger-laden sleighs. Details of these Easter festivals are available at any Finnmark tourist office, and there's a **Kautokeino festival website** (ⓦwww .saami-easterfestival.org). Summer visits, on the other hand, can be disappointing, since many families and their reindeer are at coastal pastures and there is precious little activity.

From Alta, the only direct route into the Finnmarksvidda is south along Hwy 93 to **Kautokeino**, a distance of 130km. Thereafter, there's a bit more choice, with Hwy 93 pressing on into Finland, whilst Hwy 92 travels the 130km east to **Karasjok**, where you can rejoin the E6 (but well beyond the road to Nordkapp). **Bus** services across the Finnmarksvidda are patchy: there are one or two buses from Alta to Kautokeino every day except Saturday, and a limited service along the E6 from Alta to Karasjok (late June to mid-Aug Mon–Fri & Sun 2 daily; late Aug to early June 1–2 daily 4 variable days a week). A further service links Karasjok with Hammerfest once or twice daily except on Saturdays, but there are no buses between Karasjok and Kautokeino. Local buses are operated by FFR (⑦78 43 36 77, ⓦwww.ffr.no).

The best time to **hike** in the Finnmarksvidda is in August and early September – after the peak mosquito season and before the weather turns cold. For the most part the plateau vegetation is scrub and open birch forest, which makes the going fairly easy, though the many marshes, rivers and lakes often impede progress. There are a handful of clearly demarcated **hiking trails** and a smattering of appropriately sited but unstaffed huts; for detailed information, ask at Alta tourist office.

Kautokeino

It's a two- and a half-hour drive or bus ride from Alta across the Finnmarksvidda to **KAUTOKEINO** (*Guovdageaidnu* in Sámi), the principal winter camp of the Norwegian Sámi and the site of a huge reindeer market in spring and autumn. The Sámi are not, however, easy town dwellers and although Kautokeino is very useful to them as a supply base, it's still a desultory, desolate-looking place that straggles along the banks of the Kautokeinoelva river. Nevertheless, the settlement has become something of a tourist draw on account of the **jewellers** who have moved here from the south. Every summer, their souvenir booths line long main street, attracting Finnish day-trippers like flies. The jewellery bigwigs hereabouts are **Frank and Regine Juhls**, who braved all sorts of difficulties to set up their workshop here in 1959. It was a bold move at a time when the Sámi were very much a neglected minority, but the Juhls had a keen interest in nomadic cultures and, although the

Sámi had no tradition of jewellery-making, they did adorn themselves with all sorts of unusual items traded in from the outside world. The Juhls were much influenced by the Sámi style of self-adornment, repeating and developing it in their own work, and their business prospered – perhaps beyond their wildest dreams. As testimony to the Juhls' commercal success, the plain and simple workshop they first built has been replaced by the **Juhl's Silver Gallery** (daily: early June to early Aug 9am–7pm; mid-Aug to May 9am–6pm, ring in winter to confirm hours on ☎78 48 61 89, ⓦwww.juhls.no), an extensive complex of low-lying showrooms and workshops, whose pagoda-like roofs are derived from the Sámi, where exquisitely beautiful, high-quality silver work is made and sold alongside a much broader range of classy craftwork. The complex's **interior** (regular, free guided tours; 20min) is intriguing in its own right, with some rooms decorated in crisp, modern pan-Scandinavian style, others done out in an elaborate version of Sámi design. The gallery is located on a ridge above the west bank of the Kautokeinoelva, 2.5km south from the handful of buildings that passes for the town centre – follow the signs.

Practicalities

Doubling as Highway 93, Kautokeino's main street is 1500m long, and most of the town's facilities are clustered on the north side of the river, about 350m south of the **bus stop** in the vicinity of the **tourist office** (daily: June & Aug 9am–4pm, July 9am–7pm; ☎78 48 65 00, ⓔe-mail@kautokeino.kommune.no), which marks what is effectively the town centre. The tourist office provides town maps and has details of local events and activities, from fishing and hiking through to "**Sami adventures**", which typically include a boat trip and a visit to a *lavvo* ("tent") where you can sample traditional Sámi food and listen to *joik* (rhythmic song poems), from around 300kr. The main local tour operator is Cavzo Safari (☎78 48 75 88, ⓦwww.samitour.com/norsk/cavzo).

The only **hotel** is the modest and modern *Norlandia Kautokeino* (☎78 48 62 05, ☎78 48 67 01; ❺/❹), on the north side of town just off Highway 93. There are also a couple of **campsites** near the river on the southern edge of town, primarily *Kautokeino Camping og Motell* (☎78 48 54 00, ☎78 48 75 05), with cabins (❶) and a few frugal motel rooms (❷). The *Norlandia Kautokeino* has a competent **restaurant** – it's the only one in town.

Karasjok

The only other settlement of any size on the Finnmarksvidda is **KARASJOK** (*Kárásjohka* in Sámi), Norway's Sámi capital, which straddles the E6 on the main route from Finland to Nordkapp and consequently sees plenty of tourists. Spread across a wooded river valley, it has none of the desolation of Kautokeino, yet it still conspires to be fairly mundane despite the presence of the Sámi parliament and the country's best Sámi museum. The busiest place in town is the **tourist office**, Karasjok Opplevelser (early June & late Aug daily 9am–4pm; mid-June to late Aug daily 9am–7pm; Sept–May Mon–Fri 9am–4pm; ☎78 46 88 10, ⓦwww.koas.no), located on the north side of the river beside the E6 and Highway 92 crossroads, which is, to all intents and purposes, the centre of town. Staff issue free town maps, book overnight accommodation and organize authentic(ish) Sámi expeditions. The office is also incorporated within a miniature Sámi theme park, **Sámpi** (same times; 90kr), which offers a fancy multimedia introduction to the Sámi in the Stálubákti ("Magic Theatre"), as well as examples of traditional dwellings, Sámi shops and a restaurant. It also features displays of various ancient Sámi skills with the obligatory reindeer brought along as decoration or to be roped and coralled.

You may also want to take a peek at the **Gamle kirke** (June–Aug daily 8am–9pm; free), just off Highway 92 on the south side of the river and not to be confused with the more modern church on the north side. Gamle kirke was the only building left standing here at the end of World War II. Of simple design, it dates from 1807, making it easily the oldest surviving church in Finnmark.

Practicalities

There is a limited **bus** service to Karasjok along the E6 from Alta and Kirkenes (late June to mid-Aug Mon–Fri & Sun 2 daily; late Aug to early June 1–2 daily 4 variable days a week), and another bus links Hammerfest with Karasjok once or twice daily except on Saturdays; there are no buses from Kautokeino, however. Schedules mean that it's often possible to spend a couple of hours in Karasjok before moving on, which is quite enough to see the sights, but not nearly long enough to get the real flavour of the place. Buses pull in at the **bus station** on Storgata. From here, it's a signposted five- to ten-minute walk west to the **tourist office** (see p.387).

The best **hotel** in town is the *Rica Hotel Karasjok* (☎78 46 74 00, ⊛www.rica.no; ❻/❹), a breezy modern establishment a short stroll north of the tourist office along the E6. More modest and less expensive accommodation is provided by the unassuming *Annes Overnatting og Motell* (☎78 46 64 32; ❷), east of the tourist office along the E6 towards Kirkenes. There's also the all-year *Karasjok Camping*, a ten-minute walk west from the tourist office on the Kautokeino road (☎78 46 61 35, ☎78 46 66 97); the latter has cabins (❷) as well as spaces for tents. Some 7km out of town on the Kautokeino road (Hwy 92) *Engholm Husky Vandrerhjem* (☎78 46 71 66, ⊛www.engholm.no) is an all-year HI **hostel**, which in addition to dorms has cosy home-made four- to six-bed **cabins** (300kr per night plus 100kr per person). The hostel is open all year and offers self-catering facilities, a sauna and Arctic dinners, sitting on reindeer skins around an open fire. The owner, the eponymous Sven, is an expert dog-sled racer and keeps about forty huskies; he uses them on a variety of winter guided tours – dog sledding and so forth – and in summer organizes everything from fishing trips and guided wilderness hikes to horseback riding; he will pick up guests from Karasjok by prior arrangement, too.

For **food**, the *Rica Hotel Karasjok* has the unusual *Gammen* restaurant, a set of turf-covered huts where Sámi-style meals are served. It's all good fun, unless, that is, you dislike reindeer meat, inevitably the staple ingredient.

From Karasjok, it's 130km west to Kautokeino; 270km north to Nordkapp; 220km northwest to Hammerfest and 330km east to Kirkenes.

Hammerfest

HAMMERFEST, some 150km north of Alta, is, as its tourist office takes great pains to point out, the world's northernmost town. It was also, they add, the first town in Europe to have electric street-lighting. Hardly fascinating facts perhaps, but both give a glimpse of the pride that the locals take in making the most of what is, indisputably, an inhospitable location. Indeed, it's a wonder the town has survived at all: a hurricane flattened the place in 1856; it was burnt to the ground in 1890; and the retreating Germans mauled it at the end of World War II. Yet, instead of being abandoned, Hammerfest was stubbornly rebuilt for a third time. Nor is it the grim industrial town you might expect from the proximity of the offshore oil wells, but a bright, cheerful port that drapes around a **horseshoe-shaped harbour** sheltered from the elements by a steep rocky hill. But don't get too carried away: Bill Bryson, in *Neither Here Nor There*, hit the nail on the head with his description of Hammerfest as "an agreeable enough town in a thank-you-God-for-not-making-me-live-here sort of way".

The Town

Running parallel to the waterfront, **Strandgata**, the town's principal street, is a busy, 500-metre-long run of supermarkets, clothes and souvenir shops, partly inspired by the town's role as a stop-off for cruise ships on the way to Nordkapp. However, most of the activity takes place on the **town quay**, off Sjøgata, with tourists emerging from the liners to beetle around the harbourfront, eating shellfish

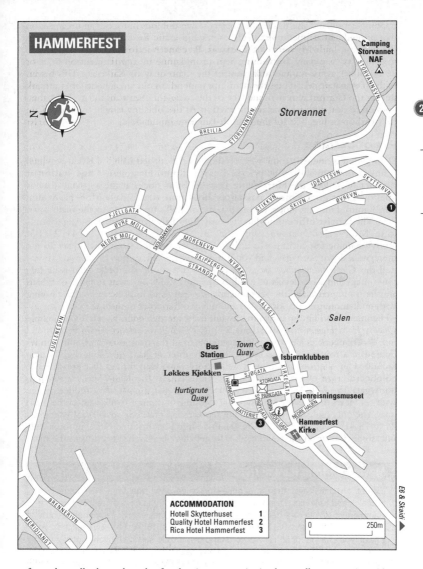

HAMMERFEST

Camping
Storvannet
NAF

Storvannet

BREILIA

STORVANNSVN

IDRETTSVN

SKYTTERVN

STIKKVN SKIVN ØVREVN

FJELLGATA

ØVRE MOLLA

NEDRE MOLLA

SKOLEBAKKEN

MORENEVN

SKIPPERGT

STRANDGT

NYBAKKEN

SALSGT

FUGLENESVN

Salen

Bus
Station

Town
Quay

Isbjørnklubben

Løkkes Kjøkken

SJØGATA

KIRKEGATA

STORGATA

Hurtigrute
Quay

HAMNEGATA

BATTERIET

PARKGATA

STRANDGATA

KIRKEGATA

KIRK.VEISTAG

NEDRE HAUEN

Gjenreisningsmuseet

Hammerfest
Kirke

BRENNERIVN

MERIDIANGT

ACCOMMODATION
Hotell Skytterhuset   1
Quality Hotel Hammerfest   2
Rica Hotel Hammerfest   3

0   250m

E6 & Skaidi ▶

from the stalls along the wharf or buying souvenirs in the small, summertime Sámi market. The Hurtigrute spends a couple of hours here too, arriving at an unsociable 5.15am on its way north, 11.45am heading south.

Beyond that, it's the general atmosphere of the place that appeals rather than any specific sight, though Hammerfest's tiny town centre does muster a couple of attractions, beginning with the **Royal and Ancient Polar Bear Society** (*Isbjørnklubben*; Jan to mid-May & Sept–Dec Mon–Fri 11.30am–1.30pm; mid-May to late June & late Aug Mon–Fri 10am–3pm, Sat & Sun 11am–2pm; late June to early Aug daily 6am–5.30pm; 20kr), up from the quay in the basement of the town hall on Sjøgata. The society's pint-sized museum tells the story of Hammerfest as a trapping centre and also relates the Society's own dubious history as an organization that hunted and trapped polar bears, eagles and arctic foxes. A good deal better is the purpose-built **Museum of Postwar Reconstruction** (*Gjenreisningsmuseet*; mid-June to Aug daily 10am–6pm, Sept to mid-June by appointment on ☏78 42 26 30; 40kr), a five-minute walk west of the main quay up Kirkegata. This begins with a fascinating section on the hardships endured by the inhabitants of Finnmark during the German retreat, in the face of the advancing Russians in late 1944, then goes on to deal with postwar reconstruction. As the labelling is only in Norwegian, it's worth investing 20kr for the English-language guidebook.

Practicalities

Hammerfest is situated on the western shore of the rugged island of Kvaløya, which is linked to the mainland by bridge. Buses pull into Hammerfest **bus station** at the foot of Sjøgata; the **Hurtigrute coastal boat** docks at the adjacent quay, as does the **Hurtigbåt express passenger boat** from Alta (1 daily Mon–Fri & Sun; 1hr 30min). From the dock, it's the briefest of walks up Sjøgata to the main town quay. The **tourist office** (mid-June to early Aug daily 9am–5pm; mid-Aug to mid-June Mon–Fri 8.30am–3.30pm, Sat & Sun 10am–3pm; ☏78 41 21 85, @www.hammerfest-turist.no) is a short walk west of the main town quay. To get there, walk down Sørøygata and you'll spot it on the left, or pop in after you've visited the *Gjenreisningsmuseet* (see above) – it's just round the back. Staff issue free town maps and have details of local excursions, easily the most popular of which are the fishing trips and the summertime sea cruises to local nesting cliffs, heaving with guillemots, gannets, kittiwakes and many other types of seabird.

Hammerfest is light on places to stay, but there are two good **hotels**: the enjoyable *Quality Hotel Hammerfest*, Strandgata 2–4 (☏78 42 96 00, @www.hammerfesthotel .no; ❻/❺), occupies a prime spot just metres from the main quay, and, although it's housed in a routine modern block, the cosy interior has a pleasant, slightly old-fashioned air, the rooms equipped with chunky wooden fittings that pre-date the chipboard craze of the 1960s. Equally appealing is the *Rica Hotel Hammerfest*, Sørøygata 15 (☏78 41 13 33, @www.rica.no; ❺/❸), an attractive modern place with sea views that sits on a grassy knoll a couple of minutes' walk west of the main quay. The only budget option is the unprepossessing *Hotell Skytterhuset*, Skytterveien 24 (☏78 41 15 11, ℻78 41 19 26; ❸), in a large prefabricated block up on a hillside, some 3km from the town centre. To get there by car, head east from the main

Moving on from Hammerfest

Except on Saturdays, there's a once- or twice-daily **bus** from Hammerfest to Karasjok and Kirkenes. This passes through Skaidi, on the E6, as does the bus from Hammerfest to Alta (1–2 daily Mon–Fri & Sun). Both these services are operated by Finnmark Fylkesrederi og Rutesselskap (FFR; ☏78 40 70 00, @www.ffr.no). At Skaidi, you change for either the Nordkappekspressen service to Honningsvåg and Nordkapp, or FFR's Skaidi–Honningsvåg bus (see below). Note that not all the buses make the connection, so be sure to check at Hammerfest bus station before you set out. The **Hurtigrute coastal boat** departs Hammerfest heading south at 1pm and takes 10.5 hours to reach its next major port of call, Tromsø (passengers 690kr one-way, car 340kr). Sailing north, the Hurtigrute departs at 6.45am and reaches Honningsvåg at 11.45am (passengers 360kr, car 318kr). At Honningsvåg, it stops for three and three-quarter hours, plenty time enough for special connecting buses to make the return trip to Nordkapp. Finally, Hammerfest has several **car rental** companies and these frequently offer attractive short-term deals from around 650kr a day; try Hertz, Rossmollgate 48 (☏78 41 71 66). If, however, Nordkapp is your goal, comparable rental deals are available at Honningsvåg (see opposite), 180km north from Hammerfest.

quay along Strandgata and, after about 400m, just over the stream, turn right along Skolebakken. This leads round a lake, Storvannet, which lies at the bottom of a steep-sided valley dotted with the houses of Hammerfest's one and only suburb. The road then climbs up the east side of Salen hill to run past the hotel. On the way to the hotel, you'll pass the tiny lakeshore *Storvannet Camping NAF* (☎78 41 10 10; June to mid-Sept), with tent spaces and a few cabins (❶). Unless you're particularly energetic, you'll not want to walk to either of these places from the centre – take a taxi.

For **food**, the *Rica Hotel Hammerfest* possesses the best **restaurant** in town, with sea views and delicious seafood; main courses start at around 190kr. More economical is *Løkkes Kjøkken*, across from the Hurtigrute quay at Storgata 2, a well-tended, family-run café providing tasty standard-issue Norwegian meals.

North to Magerøya and Nordkapp

At the northern tip of Norway, the treeless and windswept island of **Magerøya** is mainly of interest to travellers as the location of the **Nordkapp** (North Cape), generally regarded as mainland Europe's northernmost point – though in fact it isn't; that distinction belongs to the neighbouring headland of **Knivskjellodden**. Somehow, everyone seems to have conspired to ignore this simple fact of latitude and now, whilst Nordkapp has become one of the most popular tourist destinations in the country, there isn't even a road to Knivskjellodden. Neither has the development of the Nordkapp as a tourist spot been without its critics, who argue that the large and lavish visitor centre – **Nordkapphallen** – is crass and grossly overpriced; their opponents simply point to the huge number of people who visit. Whatever, it's hard to imagine making the long trip to Magerøya without at least dropping by Nordkapp, and the island has other charms too, notably a bleak, rugged beauty that's readily appreciated on the E69 as it threads across the mountainous interior from Honningsvåg, on the south coast, to Nordkapp, a distance of 34km.

The obvious base for a visit to Nordkapp is **Honningsvåg**, the island's main settlement and a middling fishing village with a clutch of chain hotels. More appealing, however, is the tiny hamlet of **Kamøyvær**, nestling beside a narrow fjord just off the E69 between Honningsvåg and Nordkapp, and with a couple of family-run guesthouses. Bear in mind also that Nordkapp is within easy striking distance of other places back on the mainland, including the picturesque fishing station-cum-hotel at **Repvåg** – and maybe even Alta and Hammerfest, respectively 210km and 240km distant.

Arriving by bus from Alta and Skaidi (for Hammerfest), the Nordkappekspressen stops at both Honningsvåg and Nordkapp twice daily between Monday and Friday and once on Saturday and Sunday, but only between late June and mid-August. The schedule is such that on weekdays you can take the first bus to Nordkapp, spend a couple of hours there and then catch the second bus back. If you catch the second bus, or the weekend bus, you'll have three hours at Nordkapp, from 9pm to 12.15am – which means, of course, that you can view the Midnight Sun. Supplementing this service is FFR's Alta–Skaidi–Honningsvåg bus route (late June to mid-Aug 1–5 daily, mid-Aug to late June 1–2 daily on 4 variable days a week), but obviously this leaves you well short of Nordkapp. If Honningsvåg is as far as you can get by bus, the best way of proceeding onto Nordkapp is to rent a car or take a taxi. Honningsvåg tourist office has the details of local **car hire** companies offering special deals – reckon on 650kr for a four-hour rental. The **taxi fare** to Nordkapp, including an hour's waiting time after you get there, is 700kr return, 900kr after 10pm, and 450kr one-way; contact Nordkapp Taxisentral (☎78 47 52 48). In **winter**, Nordkapp Opplevelser (☎78 47 52 48) organize snowmobile trips to Nordkapp from the hamlet of Skarsvåg, 24km north of Honningsvåg; they also arrange transport from Honningsvåg to Skarsvåg. To stand a chance of seeing the northern lights, try to go when the weather's clear.

Arriving by car, bear in mind that the last stretch of the Honningsvåg–Nordkapp road is closed by snow in winter, roughly from mid-October to mid-April, though the (fanatically) determined can still get there on a guided **snowmobile excursion** with Nordkapp Opplevelser (see p.391).

North from Skaidi to Repvåg and Nordkapp

At the **Skaidi** crossroads at the end of Highway 94 from Hammerfest, the **E6** veers east to clip across a bleak plateau that brings it, 23km later, to the turning for Nordkapp. This turning, the **E69**, scuttles north along the shore of the **Porsangerfjord**, a deep and wide inlet flanked by bare, low-lying hills whose stone has been fractured and made flaky by the biting cold of winter. After 48km, the E69 zips past the byroad to **REPVÅG**, an old timber fishing station on a promontory just 2km off the main highway. A rare and particularly picturesque survivor from prewar days, the station is painted red in the traditional manner and perches on stilts at the water's edge. The whole complex has been turned into the *Repvåg Fjordhotell og Rorbusenter* (☎78 47 54 40, ☎78 47 27 51; April–Oct), with simple, unassuming rooms (❸) in the main building, as well as a cluster of old fishermen's shacks – *rorbuer* (❷). It's a charming place to stay and an ideal base from which to reach the Nordkapp. Almost inevitably, the hotel **restaurant** specializes in seafood – and very good it is, too.

Back on the E69, it's about 25km to the ambitious – and amazingly expensive – series of tunnels and bridges (125kr toll) that spans the straits between the mainland and Honningsvåg, on the island of **Magerøya**; you'll see the island long before you arrive, a hunk of brown rock looking like an inverted blancmange.

Honningsvåg

HONNINGSVÅG, 180km from Hammerfest, is officially classified as a village, which robs it of the title of the world's northernmost town – hard luck considering it's barely any smaller or less hardy in the face of adversity than its neighbour. Largely made up of a jumble of well-worn modern buildings, the village straggles along the seashore, sheltered from the blizzards of winter by the surrounding crags – though, given the conditions, sheltered is a comparative term. Its prettiest area is at the **head of the harbour**, where an assortment of timber warehouses, dating back to the days when the village was entirely reliant on fish, makes an attractive ensemble.

Honningsvåg strings out along its main drag, Storgata, for about one kilometre. Buses from the mainland, including the long-distance Nord-Norgeekspressen, pull in to the **bus station** at the west end of Storgata. **Hurtigrute coastal boats** dock at the adjacent jetty and are met by special Nordkapp excursion buses. The **tourist office** is here, too (mid-June to mid-Aug Mon–Fri 8.30am–6pm, Sat & Sun noon–6pm; mid-Aug to mid-June Mon–Fri 8.30am–4pm; ☎78 47 25 99, ⓦwww.northcape.no).

All of Honningsvåg's **hotels** are along or near Storgata. Walking east from the bus station, it's a few metres to the first, the *Rica Hotel Honningsvåg* (☎78 47 23 33, ⊛www.rica.no; mid-May to Aug; ❺), a routine modern block with nearly two hundred modern rooms. Its sister hotel, the all-year *Rica Bryggen* (☎78 47 28 88, ⊛www.rica.no; ❺), occupies a similar but slightly smarter concrete high-rise about 500m to the east, down at the head of the harbour. Again, the rooms are bright, modern and comfortable, but hardly inspiring. More appealing is the adjacent *Honningsvåg Brygge Hotel* (☎78 47 64 64, ⊛www.hvg.brygge.no; ❺), a tasteful and intelligent conversion of a set of wooden warehouses perched on one of the old jetties. The rooms here are smart and cosy – and advance reservations are strongly advised. Alternatively, *NAF Nordkapp Camping* (☎78 47 33 77, ⊕nordkapp.camping @nordkapp.com; late May to mid-Sept), comprising a **campsite** and **cabins** (❷), is located about 8km from Honningsvåg on the road to Nordkapp. Right next door is the sprawling, chalet-style *Rica Hotel Nordkapp* (☎78 47 33 88, ⊛www.rica.no; June to mid-Aug; ❺).

For **food**, the *Honningsvåg Brygge Hotel's Sjøhuset* is the best **restaurant** by far: seafood is delicious and main courses hover around 170kr; reservations are advised.

North from Honningsvåg

The E69 winds out of Honningsvåg staying close to the shore and, just beyond the conspicuous *Rica Hotel Nordkapp* (see p.396), some 9km on, passes the turning for **KAMØYVÆR**, a pretty little village 2km from the main road, tucked in tight between the sea and the hills. Here, right on the jetty, the old timber fishing station has been converted into the charming *Havstua* (☎78 47 51 50, ⊛www.havstua.no; ❸; May to mid-Sept), with twenty simple but smart and extraordinarily cosy rooms. It's a delightful spot and the food is also first-rate – but note that it's advisable to book dinner in advance. A few metres away, just back from the jetty, is the *Árran Nordkapp Gjestehus* (☎78 47 51 29, ⊛www.arranhotels.com; ❷; May to mid-Sept), not quite as appealing perhaps, but still a pleasant, family-run guesthouse in a brightly painted and well-tended home.

Beyond the Kamøyvær turning, the E69 twists a solitary course up through the hills to cross the high-tundra plateau, the mountains stretching away on either side. It's a fine run, with snow and ice lingering well into the summer and impressive views over the treeless and elemental Arctic terrain. From June to October this is pastureland for herds of reindeer, who graze right up to the road, paying little heed to the occasional vehicle unless they get very close. The Sámi, who bring them here by boat, combine herding with souvenir selling, setting up camp at the roadside in full costume to peddle clothes, jewellery and antler sets, which some motorists are daft enough to attach to the front of their vehicles. About 29km from Honningsvåg, the E69 passes the start of the well-marked **hiking trail** that leads to the tip of Europe, the headland of **Knivskjellodden**, stretching about 1500m further north than its famous neighbour. The 16-kilometre-long hike – there and back – takes between two and three hours each way, but the terrain is too difficult and the climate too unpredictable for the inexperienced or poorly equipped hiker.

The Nordkapp

Many visitors, when they finally reach the **Nordkapp**, feel desperately disappointed – it is, after all, only a cliff and, at 307 metres, it isn't even all that high. But for others there's something about this greyish-black hunk of slate, stuck at the end of a bare, wind-battered promontory, that exhilarates the senses – and some such feeling must have inspired the prehistoric Sámi when they established a sacrificial site here.

The "North Cape" was actually named by the English explorer Richard Chancellor in 1553, as he drifted along the Norwegian coast in an attempt to find the Northeast Passage from the Atlantic to the Pacific. He failed, though the name stuck, and the visit of the Norwegian king Oscar II in 1873 opened the tourist floodgates.

Nowadays the lavish **North Cape Hall** (*Nordkapphallen*; daily: April to late May & Sept to early Oct noon–5pm; late May to mid-June noon–1am; mid-June to early Aug 9am–2am; early Aug to end Aug noon–midnight; 185kr for 48 hours, including parking), cut into the rock of the Cape, entertains hundreds of visitors every day, who all pay handsomely for the pleasure of standing at mainland Europe's supposed northernmost extremity. Fronted by a statue of King Oscar II, the main building contains a restaurant, cafés, souvenir shops, a post office where you can get your letters specially stamped, and a cinema showing – you guessed it – films about the cape. There's a viewing area too, but there's not much to see except the sea – and, weather permitting, the Midnight Sun (May 11 to July 31). A **tunnel** runs from the main building to the cliff face. It's flanked by a chapel, where you can get married, and a series of displays detailing past events and visitors, including the unlikely appearance of the King of Siam in 1907, who was so ill that he had to be carried up here on a stretcher. At the far end, the cavernous **Grotten Bar** offers caviar and champagne, long views out to sea through the massive glass wall and (of all things) a mock bird cliff. Alternatively, to escape the hurly-burly, you may decide to walk out onto the surrounding headland, though this is too bleak a spot to be much fun.

East to Kirkenes

East of Nordkapp the landscape is more of the same: a relentless expanse of barren plateaux and ocean. Occasionally the picture is relieved by a determined village commanding sweeping views over the fjords that slice into the mainland, but generally there's little for the eyes of a tourist. Nor is there much to do in what are predominantly fishing and industrial settlements, and few tangible attractions beyond the sheer impossibility of the chill wilderness.

The **E6** weaves a circuitous course across this vast territory, travelling close to the Finnish border for much of its length. The only obvious target is the Sámi centre of **Karasjok** (see p.387), 270km from Nordkapp and 220km from Hammerfest and easily the region's most interesting town. Frankly, there's not much reason to push on further east unless you're intent on picking up the **Hurtigrute coastal boat** as it bobs along the remote and spectacular shores of the Barents Sea. Amongst the Hurtigrute's several ports of call, perhaps the most diverting is **Kirkenes**, 320km to the east of Karasjok near the Russian frontier and a town that comes close to defining remoteness. Kirkenes is actually the northern terminus of the Hurtigrute, from where it begins its long journey back to Bergen. Taking the boat also means that you can avoid the long haul back the way you came – and by the time you reach Kirkenes you'll probably be heartily sick of the E6. The other shortcut is to **fly** – SAS's Braathens (ⓦwww.braathens.no; ☎78 97 35 20) operates regular flights between Kirkenes and various Norwegian cities including Alta, Oslo and Tromsø; as a sample fare, a single economy ticket from Kirkenes to Alta currently goes for around 2300kr.

Accommodation in this part of Norway is very thin on the ground, with campsites being the main option; they usually have cabins, but the sites are mostly stuck in the middle of nowhere. The main **long-distance bus** links Alta with Kirkenes via Skaidi, Karasjok and Tana Bru three times weekly and takes eleven hours to do it.

East from Nordkapp: by land

Beyond the junction of the E69 Nordkapp road, the **E6** bangs along the western shore of the **Porsangerfjord**, a wide inlet that slowly shelves up into the sticky marshes and mudflats at its head. After about 45km, the road reaches the hamlet of **STABBURSNES**, which is home to the small but enjoyable **Stabbursnes Natural History Museum** (*Stabbursnes Naturhus og Museum*; early June & mid- to late Aug daily 10am–5pm; mid-June to early Aug daily 9am–8pm; Sept–May Tues & Thurs noon–3pm, Wed noon–6pm; 30kr), which provides an overview of the region's flora and fauna.

From Stabbursnes, it's about 15km to **LAKSELV**, an inconsequential fishing village at the head of the Porsangerfjord, and another 80km to Karasjok (see p.387), the best place to spend the night. Pushing on, the E6 weaves its way northeast along the Finnish border to reach, in 180km, **TANA BRU**, a Sámi settlement clustered round the suspension bridge over the River Tana, one of Europe's best salmon rivers, which sweeps down to the Tanafjord and the Barents Sea. Beyond the village, the E6 follows the southern shore of the **Varangerfjord**, a bleak, weather-beaten run, all colour and vegetation confined to the opposite coastline with its scattered farms and painted fishing boats. As the road swings inland, it's something of a relief to arrive in Kirkenes.

East from Nordkapp: by sea

Beyond Nordkapp, the **Hurtigrute** steers a fine route round the top of the country, nudging its way between tiny islets and craggy bluffs and stopping at a series of remote fishing villages. Amongst these, the prettiest is **BERLEVÅG**, which sits amidst a landscape of eerie greenish-grey rock, splashes of colour in a land otherwise stripped by the elements. It's a tiny village, with a population of just 1200, but its cultural traditions and tight community spirit were deftly explored in Knut Jensen's fine documentary film *Heftig og Begeistret* ("Cool & Crazy"), released in 2001. The film received rave reviews both here in Norway and across Europe, a welcome fillip to Berlevåg in general and the subject of the film – the local men's choir, the **Berlevåg Mannsangforening** – in particular.

From Berlevåg, it's five hours more to **VARDØ**, Norway's most easterly town, built on an island a couple of kilometres from the mainland, to which it's connected by a tunnel. Like every other town in Finnmark, Vardø was savaged in World War II and subsequently rebuilt. Its present population is just 3000 and its main attraction, located about 500m to the west of the Hurtigrute quay, is the **Vardø fortress** (*Vardøhus Festning*; daily: mid-June to mid-Sept 8am–9pm, mid-Sept to mid-June 8am–6pm; 20kr), a well-preserved if tiny star-shaped fortress built in the 1730s at the behest of Christian VI.

Northbound, the **Hurtigrute** reaches Vardø at 5am and leaves just thirty minutes later; heading south, it docks here at 4.45pm and hangs around for an hour – quite enough time to make it to the fortress and back.

Kirkenes

During World War II the mining town and ice-free port of **KIRKENES** suffered more bomb attacks than any other place in Europe apart from Malta. What was left was torched by the German army retreating in the face of liberating Soviet soldiers, who found 3500 locals hiding in the nearby iron-ore mines. The mines were finally closed in 1996, threatening the future of the 6000-strong community, which is desperately trying to kindle trade with Russia to keep itself afloat.

Kirkenes is almost entirely modern, with long rows of uniform houses spreading out along the Bøkfjord. If that sounds dull, it's not to slight the town, which makes the most of its inhospitable surroundings with some pleasant public gardens, lakes and residential areas – it's just that it seems an awfully long way to come for not very much. That said, once you've finally got here it seems churlish to leave quickly and it's certainly worth searching out the **Savio Museum** (*Saviomuseet*; late June to late Aug daily 10am–6pm; late Aug to late June Mon–Fri 10am–3pm; 25kr), housed in the old library about 300m south of the tourist office at Kongensgate 10B. This small museum displays the work of the local Sámi artist, **John Savio** (1902–38). Savio's life was brief and tragic – orphaned at the age of three, he was ill from childhood onwards and died in poverty of tuberculosis aged 36 – a fact which lends poignancy to his woodcuts and paintings, with their lonely evocations of the Sámi way of life and the overbearing power of nature. The museum also hosts travelling contemporary art exhibitions.

Practicalities

Kirkenes is the northern terminus of the **Hurtigrute coastal boat**, which arrives here at 10.30am and departs for Bergen at 1.30pm. It uses the quay just over 1km east of the town centre; a local bus shuttles between the two. Kirkenes **airport** is 14km southwest of town; Flybussen (50kr) connect the airport with the centre, or you can take a taxi. Long-distance and local buses share the same **bus station** on the west side of the town centre, at the end of Kirkegata. From here, it's about 300m southeast to the **tourist office** (early June to mid-Aug Mon–Fri 8.30am–6pm, Sat & Sun 11am–6pm; mid-Aug to early June Mon–Fri 8.30am–4pm; ☎78 99 25 44, ☻www.sor-varanger.kommune.no), in the centre of town on Kjelland Torkildsens gate, next to the *Rica Arctic Hotel*. Staff issue free town maps, have lots of ideas as to how to while away the time here and provide general information about excursions to Russia.

The town's best **hotel** is the *Rica Arctic*, whose eighty well-appointed rooms occupy a smart modern block in the centre at Kongensgate 1 (☎78 99 29 29, ☻www .rica.no; ❻). More individual – and affordable – are *Barbara's Bed & Breakfast*, with just two cosy rooms at loft level in one of the town's older buildings, about 500m east of the tourist office at Henrik Lunds gate 13 (☎78 99 32 07; http://home.troll-net.no/barbara; ❷); or *Barents Frokost Hotell*, Presteveien 3 (☎78 99 32 99, ☻gcelsius@frisurf.no; ❷), with frugal rooms both en suite and with shared facilities; Presteveien is on the east side of the centre. As for **food**, the *Rica Arctic Hotel* has a very competent restaurant, though it's slightly bettered by *Vin og Vilt*, Kirkegata 5 (☎78 99 38 11), where they serve up an excellent range of Arctic specialities from reindeer to char and beyond. Main courses at both hover at around 110kr.

Svalbard

During the long Arctic winter, the **Svalbard archipelago** is one of the most hostile places on earth. Some 640km north of the Norwegian mainland (and just 1300km from the North Pole), two-thirds of its surface is covered by glaciers, the soil frozen to a depth of up to 500m. It was probably discovered in the twelfth century by Icelandic seamen, though it lay ignored until 1596 when the Dutch explorer Willem Barents named the main island, **Spitsbergen**, after its needle-like mountains. However, apart from a smattering of determined adventurers few people ever lived here until, in 1899, rich coal deposits were discovered, the geological residue of a prehistoric tropical forest. The first **coal mine** was opened by an American seven years later and passed into Norwegian hands in 1916. Meanwhile, other countries, particularly Russia and Sweden, were getting into the coal-mining act, and when, in 1920, Norway's sovereignty over the archipelago was ratified by international treaty, it was on condition that those other countries who were operating mines could continue to do so. It was also agreed that the islands would be a demilitarized zone.

Despite the hardships, there are convincing reasons to make a trip to this oddly fertile land, covering around 63,000 square kilometres. Between late April and late August there's continuous daylight, with temperatures regularly bobbing up into the late teens of degrees centigrade; the snow has virtually all melted by July, leaving the valleys covered in flowers; and there's an abundance of wildlife – over a hundred species of migratory birds, arctic foxes, polar bears and reindeer on land, and seals, walruses and whales offshore. In winter, it's a different story: the polar night, during which the sun never rises above the horizon, lasts from late October to mid-February; and the record low temperature is a staggering -46°C, not counting the wind-chill factor.

Getting there and getting around

The simplest way to reach Svalbard is to **fly** to the archipelago's airport at Longyearbyen on the main island, Spitsbergen. Braathens (☎79 02 45 00,

@www.braathens.no), an SAS subsidiary, operates services there from a variety of Norwegian cities, including Oslo, Bergen, Trondheim, Alta and Tromsø, on average four or five times weekly. SAS also flies to Longyearbyen, but only from Oslo via Tromsø. The Tromsø–Longyearbyen flight takes an hour and thirty minutes and a standard fare with no restrictions with Braathens is 5400kr return, though special deals are commonplace and reduce this to 1800–2000kr. However, before you book your flight, you'll need to reserve accommodation in Longyearbyen (see p.397) and – unless you're happy to be stuck in your lodgings – you'd be well-advised to pre-book one of the **guided excursions** that take your fancy, too. There's a wide range on offer, from hiking and climbing through to kayaking, snowmobiling, glacier walking, helicopter rides, Zodiac boat trips, wildlife "safaris" and ice caving. In the first instance, further **information**, including details of all the tour companies, is available from Info-Svalbard, Postboks 323, N-9171 Longyearbyen (☎79 02 55 50, @www.svalbard.net). A very good travel and tour agency is Spitsbergen Travel, Postboks 548, N-9171 Longyearbyen (☎79 02 61 00, @www.spitsbergentravel.no). You can, of course, take pot luck when you get there, but be warned that wilderness excursions are often fully booked weeks in advance.

Otherwise, there are **adventure cruises** around Svalbard, involving polar-bear spotting and the like. A five-day package with four days' cruising and one night in a Longyearbyen hotel costs anywhere between 6700kr and 15700kr, depending on the standard of the boat – seven nights works out at between 17900kr and 32500kr. (Prices don't include the flight to Longyearbyen.) In addition, adventure tour operators abroad offer all sorts of Svalbard **holidays**; one of the best is Britain's Arctic Experience (see p.15 for address and details), which runs an excellent range of all-in camping and hiking tours to the archipelago in July and August; prices vary with the itinerary and length of stay, but a ten-day trip costs around £2000.

Finally, if you are determined to strike out into the wilderness **independently**, you first have to seek permission from, and log your itinerary with, the governor's office, Sysselmannen på Svalbard, Postboks 633, N-9171 Longyearbyen (☎79 02 31 00, ☎79 02 11 66); they will certainly expect you to carry a gun on account of the polar bears. Note also that there are no road connections between any of Svalbard's settlements, though there's about 45km of road around Longyearbyen. The only public transport, apart from the airport bus, is a pricey, privately run air service from Longyearbyen to minuscule Ny Ålesund (1400kr each way); it's primarily used to shuttle scientists around, but paying passengers are sometimes accepted.

Spitsbergen

The main island of the Svalbard archipelago, **Spitsbergen**, is the only one that is permanently inhabited; its three Norwegian and one Russian settlements have a total population of around 3000. With just over 1500 inhabitants, the only Norwegian settlement of any size is **LONGYEARBYEN**, which huddles on the narrow coastal plain below the mountains and beside the Isfjorden, roughly in the middle of the island. It was founded in 1906, when John M. Longyear, an American mine owner, established the Arctic Coal Company here. Longyearbyen is now well equipped with services, including shops, cafés, a post office, bank, swimming pool, several tour companies, a campsite, a couple of guesthouses and three hotels – but note that advance reservations are essential for all accommodation.

There are **three other settlements** on Spitsbergen – two Norwegian and one Russian. The former consist of **Ny Ålesund** (40–100 inhabitants, depending on the season); a **polar research centre** to the northwest of Longyearbyen; and the **Sveagruva** mining community (200 day-workers) to the southeast. The only Russian settlement is coal-mining Barentsburg (900) to the west of Longyearbyen. If you do make it to Barentsburg, you'll find that Norwegian kroner are accepted.

Longyearbyen practicalities

Longyearbyen **airport** is 5km west of town and both Braathens (☎81 52 00 00) and SAS (☎79 02 16 50) have offices there. An **airport bus**, the Flybussen (March–Sept; 45kr), runs from the airport into town, or you can take a **taxi** (80–100kr). The settlement trails inland from the Isfjorden for a couple of kilometres. The few buildings that pass for the centre are located about 600m in from the fjord; one of them contains the all-year **tourist office** (no set hours; ☎79 02 55 50, ⊛www.svalbard.net). There's a full range of leaflets on the archipelago as well as information on a wide range of trips.

Longyearbyen has a healthy supply of **accommodation**. Cream of the crop is the plush *Radisson SAS Polar Hotel* (☎79 02 34 50, ⊛www.longyearbyen.radissonsas .com), just to the north of the tourist office. More distinctive, if frugal, lodgings are available in old miners' quarters to the west of the centre, across the river, at the *Mary-Ann Riggen* guesthouse (☎79 02 37 02, ⓔnggen@longyearbyen.net; ❸). Similarly economic, though not perhaps as agreeable, is the *Spitsbergen Nybyen Gjestehus*, on the southern edge of town (☎79 02 63 00, ⓔnybyen@spitra.no; ❹). Finally, *Longyearbyen Camping* (☎79 02 10 68, ⓔinfo@terrapolaris.com; late June to early Sept), out near the airport, charges just 70kr per person per night. Surprisingly, they don't have any cabins, but there is a kitchen, laundry and (thank goodness) heated toilets. Obviously enough, you must come fully equipped to survive what can be, at any time of the year, a cruel climate.

For **food**, the *Radisson SAS Polar Hotel's Restaurant Nansen* is the best place in town, serving all manner of Arctic specialities from char through to seal and (like it or not) whale. Other less expensive options include the straightforward *Kafé Busen*, near the tourist office, and, across the river at the southern edge of town, the *Huset* (☎79 02 25 00), which also specializes in Arctic dishes and is attached to a bar and the town cinema. For **drinking**, the liveliest hangout is the *Funken Bar*, part of the hotel from which it takes its name and situated just to the south of the centre. The *Radisson SAS Polar Hotel's Barents Pub* is both smarter and more sedate.

Travel details

Buses

Alta to: Hammerfest (1–3 daily except Sat; 2hr 30min); Honningsvåg (late June to mid-Aug 1–2 daily, mid-Aug to late June 1–2 daily except Thurs & Sat; 4hr); Karasjok (late June to mid-Aug 1–2 daily; mid-Aug to late June 1–2 daily except Thurs & Sat; 5hr); Kautokeino (1–2 daily except Sat; 2hr 30min); Kirkenes (late June to mid-Aug 1–2 daily; mid-Aug to late June 1–2 daily except Thurs & Sat; 10hr); Skaidi (late June to mid-Aug 1–3 daily, mid-Aug to late June 1–3 daily except Tues, Thurs & Sat; 1hr 40min); Tromsø (April to late Oct 1–2 daily; 7hr).

Hammerfest to: Alta (1–3 daily except Sat; 2hr 30min); Karasjok (late June to mid-Aug 1–2 daily, mid-Aug to late June 1–2 daily except Thurs & Sat; 4hr 30min); Kirkenes (late June to mid-Aug 1–2 daily, mid-Aug to late June 1–2 daily except Thurs & Sat; 10hr 30min); Skaidi (late June to mid-Aug 1–2 daily, mid-Aug to late June 1–2 daily except Thurs & Sat; 1hr 30min).

Honningsvåg to: Alta (late June to mid-Aug 1–2 daily, mid-Aug to late June 1–2 daily except Thurs & Sat; 4hr); Nordkapp (late June to mid-Aug 1–2 daily; 50min).

Karasjok to: Hammerfest (late June to mid-Aug 1–2 daily, mid-Aug to late June 1–2 daily except Thurs & Sat; 4hr 30min); Kirkenes (late June to mid-Aug 1–2 daily, mid-Aug to late June 1–2 daily except Thurs & Sat; 5hr 15min).

Kautokeino to: Alta (1–2 daily except Sat; 2hr 30min).

Kirkenes to: Alta (late June to mid-Aug 1–2 daily; mid-Aug to late June 1–2 daily except Thurs & Sat; 10hr); Hammerfest (late June to mid-Aug 1–2 daily, mid-Aug to late June 1–2 daily except Thurs & Sat; 10hr 30min); Karasjok (late June to mid-Aug 1–2 daily, mid-Aug to late June 1–2 daily except Thurs & Sat; 5hr 15min); Vadsø (1–2 daily except Sat; 3hr 30min).

Skaidi to: Alta (late June to mid-Aug 1–3 daily, mid-Aug to late June 1–3 daily except Tues, Thurs & Sat; 1hr 40min); Hammerfest (late June to mid-Aug 1–2 daily, mid-Aug to late June 1–2 daily except Thurs & Sat; 1hr 30min).

Tromsø to: Alta (April to late Oct 1–2 daily; 7hr); Narvik (2 daily; 7hr); Nordkapp (late June to mid-Aug 1–2 daily; 13hr); Skaidi (late June to mid-Aug 1–2 daily; 9hr).

Hurtigrute coastal boat

Northbound from: Tromsø at 6.30pm; Hammerfest at 6.45am; Honningsvåg at 3.30pm; terminates at Kirkenes at 10.30am.

Southbound from: Kirkenes at 1.30pm; Honningsvåg at 7am; Hammerfest at 1pm; Tromsø at 1.30am.
The Tromsø–Kirkenes journey time is 42hrs.

Hurtigbåt passenger express boats

Alta to: Hammerfest (1–2 daily; 1hr 30min).
Tromsø to: Harstad (1–3 daily; 2hr 45min).

Sweden

Sweden highlights

✴ **Gamla Stan, Stockholm** Stroll through some of the best-preserved medieval city streets in Europe. See p.444

✴ **Fürstenburg Galleries, Gothenburg Art Museum** Gloriously evocative, beautifully displayed paintings by Sweden's finest nineteenth-century artists. See p.488

✴ **Classic car show, Norrvikens Gardens** Antique Swedish sports models paraded against a magnificent garden backdrop. See p.519

✴ **Nimis, Kullen peninsula** This oceanside stairway-and-tower sculpture, made entirely of driftwood, makes an extraordinary sight. See p.520

✴ **Kalmar Castle** A sensational twelfth-century stronghold remodelled into a Renaissance Palace. See p.557

✴ **Visby, Gotland** Amble through the remarkable walled old town and soak up the vibrant summer atmosphere. See p.588

✴ **Gammelstad parish village** Dozens of superbly preserved wooden cottages around a beautiful church. See p.617

✴ **Inlandsbanan** This single-track railway traverses some dramatic landscapes before crossing the Arctic Circle. See p.627

Introduction and basics

In geographical terms, Sweden is easily the biggest of the Scandinavian countries – a massive 450,000 square kilometres, larger than California and twice as big as Britain – although its population numbers barely nine million. Essentially one vast coniferous forest punctuated by some 100,000 crystal-clear lakes, Sweden reposes contentedly within an endless natural beauty. Remote, austere, cold – all these generalizations may be partly true, but Sweden is also friendly and efficient and, as it boasts no single concentration of sights (other than in Stockholm), you're as likely to fetch up on a sunny Baltic beach as camp in the forest or hike through the national parks of Swedish Lapland.

One aspect of the country most likely to impinge on the cluttered eye of Europeans is the sense of space. Away from the relatively densely populated south, it's easy to travel for miles without seeing a soul, and taking in these vast, unpopulated stretches in a limited time can be exhausting and unrewarding. Better, on a short trip, to delve into one or two regions and experience the natural beauty that pervades and shapes the Swedes' attitude to life: once you've broken through the oft-quoted reserve of the people there's a definite emotive feel to the country. And initial contact is easy, as almost everyone speaks English.

Where to go

The **south and southwest** of the country are flat holiday lands. For so long territory disputed with Denmark (which the landscape closely resembles), the provinces now harbour a host of historic ports – including **Gothenburg**, **Helsingborg** and **Malmö** – and less frenetic beach towns, all old and mostly fortified. Off the **southeast** coast, the Baltic islands of **Öland** and **Gotland** are the country's most hyped resorts – and with good reason, supporting a lazy beach-life to match that of the best southern European spots, but without the hotel blocks, crowds and tat.

Central and northern Sweden is the stuff of tourist brochures: great swaths of forest, inexhaustible lakes ideal for nude bathing and some of the best wilderness hiking in Europe. Two train routes link north with south. The eastern run, close to the

Bothnian coast, passes old wood-built towns and is handy for the city of **Umeå**, with its ferry connections to Vaasa in Finland. In the centre of the country, the trains of the **Inlandsbanan** (inland railway) strike off through some remarkably changing landscapes of lakelands to mountains, clearing reindeer off the track as they go. Both routes meet in Sweden's **far north**, home of the Sami, the oldest indigenous Scandinavian people, and of the Midnight Sun, which in high summer never sets.

Of the cities, **Stockholm** is supreme. A bundle of islands housing regal and monumental architecture, fine museums and the country's most active culture and nightlife, it's a likely point of arrival and a vital stop-off. Two university towns, **Uppsala** and **Lund**, also demand a visit, while nearly all the other major cities – chiefly Östersund, Umeå, Gällivare and Kiruna – can make some sort of cultural claim on your attention. Time is rarely wasted in humbler towns either, as the beauty of the local surroundings adequately compensates for any lack of specific sights.

When to go

Summer in Sweden is short and hectic. Generally speaking, Swedes consider summer to run from mid-June to mid-August, and during this time accommodation is reduced in price (to fill rooms occupied by business people during the rest of the year) and most of the country's attractions are open for business. Conversely, though, summer also sees something of a shutdown: many bus timetables are at their most skeletal, and facilities such as swimming pools and cinemas in sparsely populated parts of the country close completely. Most Swedes take their holidays during the summer, with the result that popular destinations such as Dalarna can be tediously overcrowded. From rowdy Midsummer's Night (June 21) onwards, accommodation is scarce and trains packed as Swedes head out into the country and to the beaches. Outside the peak month of **July**, however, things are noticeably quieter; by mid-August, most Swedes have returned to work and the feeling of summer has gone – by late August, some parts of northern Sweden see their first frost. To avoid the rush, try visiting in September or late May – both are usually bright and warm. The **Midnight Sun** extends the days in June and July, and north of the Arctic Circle it virtually never gets dark. Elsewhere it stays light until very late, up to midnight and beyond. Thanks to the Gulf Stream, temperatures in Sweden are surprisingly high – see the temperature chart on p.ix – and on the south coast it can be as hot as any southern European resort.

Winter, on the other hand, can be a miserable experience. It lasts a long time (November to April solid) and gets very cold indeed: temperatures of -15°C and below are not unusual even in Stockholm. Further

north it is positively arctic. Days are short and dark (in the far north the sun barely rises at all) and biting winds cut through the most elaborate of padded coats. On the plus side, the snow stays crisp and white, the air is clean, the water everywhere frozen solid: a paradise for skaters and skiers. Stockholm, too, is particularly beautiful with its winter covering of snow and ice.

Getting there from the rest of Scandinavia

The cheapest **Scandinavian connection** with Sweden is from Denmark, by bus and ferry, and regular trains and ferries connect other mainland countries.

By train

There are four possible **train** routes into Sweden **from Norway**. Cheapest are the five-hour run from Oslo to Gothenburg and the slightly longer route from Oslo to Stockholm; the other options are the twelve-hour ride from Trondheim to Stockholm and the day-long (23hr) haul from Narvik. Through-trains **from Denmark** (Copenhagen and Kastrup airport) to Malmö, Gothenburg

or Stockholm use the new Öresunds Link between the Danish coast and Malmö. **Rail passes** (InterRail, Eurail and ScanRail) are valid on all these routes. Note that the ScanRail pass gives free or discounted travel on various ferry lines between Denmark or Finland and Sweden.

By bus

There are several **bus** routes into Sweden from other Scandinavian cities, though the frequent services **from Denmark** are the only ones that will get you there quickly. The easiest – and cheapest – connection is on one of the several daily buses **from Copenhagen** to Helsingborg, using the ferry from Helsingør – this bus then continues up the southwestern coast of Sweden to Halmstad, connecting there with trains to

Gothenburg. Frankly, though, you're better off using the train.

It's a longer haul **from Norway**, and much more expensive, too: there are several daily buses from Oslo to Gothenburg, the journey taking five or six hours, and one daily bus from Oslo to Stockholm, a nine-hour ride. **From Finland** most routes converge upon Helsinki or Turku and then use the ferry crossings to Stockholm.

By ferry

Ferry or **fast ferry** (**HSS**) services to Sweden are plentiful, but can be confusing – not least because several operators run rival services on the same route. To make any sense of the timetables and prices, which change from year to year, check the ferry company websites, or consult their brochures at any local tourist office. You'll find other details – frequencies and journey times – in the "Travel Details" at the end of each chapter.

In addition, rail passes give **discounts and free travel** on some of the ferry routes. The ScanRail pass currently gives free passage on ferries between Helsingør and Helsingborg, and a fifty percent discount on the Frederikshavn–Gothenburg, Turku–Stockholm, Helsinki–Stockholm and Rønne–Ystad routes.

From Denmark

The shortest and cheapest ferry crossing is **Helsingør–Helsingborg** (@www.scandlines.com; 20min; foot passengers 24Dkr, cars 400Dkr); just walk on board and go. There are also year-round HSS sailings and slower connections via regular ferry to Gothenburg **from Frederikshavn** (@www.stenaline.com; 2hr HSS, 3hr 15min regular ferry; both 288Dkr for foot passengers, 1260Dkr for cars). Stena Line also sail daily to Varberg **from Grenå** (4hr; foot passengers 288Dkr, cars 1176Dkr). Quicker are the Scandlines catamaran services to Malmö and Helsingborg **from Copenhagen** (45min; foot passengers 96Dkr, no cars carried), though these crossings are often disrupted by frozen sea between November and March.

The other approach from Denmark is to come via the Danish island of **Bornholm**. Ferries and catamarans from Copenhagen run to Rønne (@www.bornholmferries.dk; foot passengers 252Dkr, plus 50 percent discount with ScanRail pass; cars from 852Dkr), from where you can cross daily to Ystad, on the Swedish coast.

From Finland

Longer ferry journeys link Sweden with Finland, the major crossing being the **Helsinki–Stockholm** route, a sixteen-hour trip with either Silja (@www.silja.com; 16hr; foot passengers €96, cars €54) or Viking (@www.vikingline.fi; foot passengers €69, cars €62). There are also regular crossings **from Turku** and **from Mariehamn** in the Finnish Åland Islands to Stockholm (both Silja and Viking; 4hr; foot passengers €11, cars €15). If you're aiming for the north of

Sweden, you might be better off crossing **from Vaasa** (@www.rgline.com; foot passengers €72; cars €232): there are year-round services to Umeå, a journey of four hours.

From Norway

There are two year-round crossings from Norway to Sweden, **from Sandefjord** to Strömstad, north of Gothenburg (@www.scandline.no; 2hr; foot passengers 96Nkr, cars 492Nkr) and from Oslo to Helsingborg (@www.dfdsseaways.com; 14hr; foot passengers 984Nkr, cars 3576Nkr).

By plane

Although it's possible to **fly** to Sweden from each of the other Scandinavian countries, the cost of these short flights (generally no more than an hour) makes them prohibitively expensive when compared to travel by train or bus. If time is of the essence and you need to fly, however, make sure you include a Saturday night stay on your ticket and don't consider buying a single, which will always cost more than the cheapest return. When flying between Norway and Sweden, Finnair generally have slightly cheaper fares than SAS, and on the Copenhagen–Stockholm route you can save a few hundred kroner by taking the once daily TAP flight originating in Lisbon, which lands in Denmark before continuing to Sweden.

SAS (@www.scandinavian.net) operates regular daily flights **from Copenhagen** to Gothenburg, Kalmar, Karlstad, Linköping, Norrköping, Stockholm, Västerås, Växjö and Örebro. A return flight on all the above routes is around 2400Dkr, but Copenhagen–Stockholm is usually a little less, approximately 1800Dkr.

From Oslo SAS operates hourly direct flights to Stockholm and twice daily services to Gothenburg – the cheapest return costs around 1800Nkr on both routes. Finnair (@www.finnair.com) flies once-daily between Oslo and Stockholm, generally for a few hundred kroner less than SAS, as well as flying three times a week from Bergen to Stockholm. The Norwegian airline Widerøe (@www.wideroe.no) also runs services from Oslo to Gothenburg four times daily.

Of all the Scandinavian countries, **Finland** has the greatest number of regional flights to Sweden. Services are operated by either SAS or Finnair but are too numerous to list here. However, the following Finnish cities all have direct air links with Stockholm: Jyväskylä, Kokkola, Tampere, Turku, Mariehamn, Oulu and Vaasa.

Costs, money and banks

Sweden is no more expensive than, say, France or Germany, and certainly much cheaper than neighbouring Norway. If you don't already have a rail pass, flying on standby (at least for under-25s) is a fast and affordable option in cutting travel **costs**, while regional and city discount travel passes ease what could otherwise be a burden. Accommodation, too, can be good value: a bed in one of Sweden's well-appointed youth hostels costs an average of 130kr (£9/$15) per night for members (another 50kr or so for non-members), while camp-sites are plentiful and cheap. Virtually every hotel in Sweden halves its prices in summer, bringing even the most palatial places within reach of most travellers, and the cost of eating is made bearable by the three-course daily lunch offers found throughout the country on weekdays – around £6/$9 for a main dish with a side salad, bread, coffee and a soft drink.

Put all this together and you'll find you can exist – camping, self-catering, hitching, no drinking – on around £15/$22 a day. Stay in hostels, eat lunch, get out and see the sights and this will rise to at least £25/$40. Add on £3/$5 for a drink in a bar, around £2/$3 for coffee and cake and £40/$65 minimum a night in a hotel (for a double room) and you're looking at a figure of more like £60–75/$90–115 a day. Remember, though, that the countryside (and much of your camping) is free, museums usually have low (or no) admission charges, and that everything everywhere is clean, bright and works.

Swedish **currency** is the **krona** (plural kronor), made up of 100 öre. It comes in coins of 50 öre, 1kr, 5kr and 10kr; and notes of 20kr, 50kr, 100kr, 500kr, 1000kr and 10,000kr. You can **change money** in **banks** all over Sweden, which open Monday to Friday from 9.30am until 3pm (plus late opening on Thursdays until 5.30pm); branches in Stockholm and Gothenburg have longer summer hours – see the various city "Listings" sections). Outside normal banking hours you'll also be able to change money in **exchange offices** at airports and ferry terminals, and in post offices, as well as at Forex exchange offices, where rates are generally a little better than at banks. At both Forex offices and in banks, commission is roughly 30–40kr. Forex offices are detailed in the relevant "Listings" sections.

Mail and communications

Communications within Sweden are good, and as most people speak at least some English, you won't go far wrong in the post or telephone office.

Post offices are open Mon–Fri 9am–6pm, Sat 10am–1pm, with some branches closed on Saturday throughout July, Sweden's holiday month. You can buy **stamps** at post offices, most newspaper kiosks, supermarkets, tobacconists and hotels; a letter under 20g costs 7kr to Europe and 8kr to the rest of the world. **Poste restante** is available at all main post offices; take your passport along to claim mail.

For international **telephone calls** dial direct from public **cardphones** – payphones no longer exist in Sweden. This is very easy: buy a card from a Pressbyrå newsagent for 120 units (100kr) for the best value for money (the larger the card's denomination, the cheaper the cost per unit). English instructions on how to use a cardphone are generally displayed inside each booth. You can also pay for calls using your credit card – look out for phones marked "CCC". Note that numbers prefixed by ☎020 (often transport information numbers) are all toll-free.

International dialling codes for calling **from and to Sweden** are given on p.27. For reverse-charge international calls, ring the **overseas operator** on ☎118 119. For **directory enquiries**, dial ☎118 118 for domestic numbers, ☎118 119 for international enquiries.

Internet cafés are surprisingly thin on the ground, restricted primarily to the bigger cities. However, most local libraries have Net access, and it's a good idea to book a timeslot to save hanging around. Access at libraries is free, while you'll pay 40–60kr per hour in cafés.

The media

You'll easily be able to keep in touch with home by tuning into the TV – which relies heavily on English and American programmes – or listening to one of the English-language radio stations. Assuming that you don't read Swedish, you can also keep abreast of world events by buying **foreign newspapers** in the major towns and cities, sometimes on the day of issue, more usually the day after. Of **Swedish newspapers**, the *Dagens Nyheter* broadsheet is the best source of non-biased Swedish-language news. Recently transformed into tabloid format, its main competitor, *Svenska Dagbladet*, is still a serious source of news, albeit with a slight right-of-centre slant. The true tabloids *Aftonbladet* and *Expressen* contain less demanding Swedish.

Swedish **television** is fairly unchallenging. On top of the two state channels, SVT1 and 2, there are two commercial stations, TV4 and TV5, while the dire cable station TV3 is shared with Denmark and Norway.

On the **radio**, there's national (Swedish) news in English on **Radio Sweden**. Their English-language programming can be heard daily in Stockholm on 89.6FM at 3.30pm, 7.30pm, 9.30pm and 2.30am. The evening broadcasts should be audible on 1179kHz medium wave throughout southern Sweden, although reception can vary considerably. You can also hear BBC World Service on the same frequency (Mon–Fri 6–7.30am; Sat 6–6.30am & 7–7.30am; Sun 5–5.30am and 6–6.30am) and at all other times by tuning to either 6195, 9410, 12095 or 15070kHz short wave.

Getting around

Sweden's internal **transport** system is quick, efficient and runs through all weathers. Services are often reduced in the winter (especially on northern bus routes), but it's unlikely you'll ever get stranded. In summer, when everyone is on holiday, trains and, to a lesser extent, buses are packed, making seat reservations a good idea on long journeys.

All train, bus, ferry and plane schedules are contained within the giant **Rikstidtabellen** ("timetable"); every tourist office and travel agent has a copy. It costs 80kr and isn't worth buying and carrying around; just ask for photocopies of the relevant pages.

Keep an eye out for city and regional **discount cards**. One payment gets a card valid for anything from a day up to a week, and it usually covers **unlimited local travel** (bus, tram, ferry, sometimes train), museum entry and other discounts and freebies. Cards are often only available during the summer (valuable exceptions being the Stockholm, Gothenburg and Malmö cards), and where useful are detailed in the text. Otherwise it's worth asking at tourist offices, as schemes change frequently.

Trains

Apart from flying, **trains** are the quickest way to get around Sweden's vast expanses. The service is excellent, especially on the main routes, and prices not too expensive – a standard-class single from Stockholm to Gothenburg, for example, will cost you 518kr. **Swedish State Railways** (SJ – *Statens Järnvägar*; from abroad ☎00 46 771 75 75 75, in Sweden ☎0771/75 75 75, ⓦwww.sj.se) have an extensive network of routes, running right from the far south of the country up to Östersund and Sundsvall in central Sweden. If you're trying to work out a train-and-bus journey and want to ensure smooth connections, visit ⓦwww.tagplus.se. For trains to Swedish Lapland and across the border to Narvik in Norway, services are operated by the private company, **Tågkompaniet** (☎020/44 41 11, ⓦwww.tagkompaniet.se), although rail passes are valid on these services too. The luxurious, high-speed **X2000** train services can often shave a couple of hours off the normal journey time, particularly on the Stockholm–Gothenburg run, though prices are naturally higher: Stockholm–Gothenburg, for instance, costs a hefty 993kr one-way. Note that one-way train tickets cost half the price of returns, and that you need to make a **seat reservation** on inter-city services (included in the price).

Buying individual **train tickets** is rarely cost-effective, despite the comprehensive system of discounts, which seem to be in continual flux. If you're planning to travel a lot by train, you're generally better off buying a **train pass**, such as a multicountry InterRail, Eurail or ScanRail **pass**, which needs to be purchased before you leave home (for details see "Basics", p.32). If you're planning to travel only in Sweden, then it might be worth considering a Sweden-only rail pass; you need to pre-purchase before arriving in Sweden, and it currently costs 1810kr for six days' economy class travel in one calendar month, 1630kr for five days and 1430kr for four days – seat reservations are payable on X2000 services. The pass should be available from the train ticket agents detailed in "Basics", p.32 – contact the Swedish tourist board (see p.437) if you have difficulties. You can also buy online with a non-Swedish credit card by sending an email to © swedenbooking@gtsab.se.

If you don't have a pass, check for any special deals that may be available. Alternatively, it's worth being aware of the main discount system for SJ train tickets, the **förköpsbiljett** (advance purchase ticket), which is available every day (higher prices apply, however, on Fri and Sun) for most trains in second class. This ticket can be bought between ninety and seven days before departure and includes all seat reservations. **Under-26s** are entitled to a thirty percent discount on most fares, but must be able to prove their age. On long **overnight** train journeys it's worth paying for a couchette or a sleeping car. Prices are low: the cost of either a couchette in a six-berth cabin or a sleeping berth in a two- or three-person cabin depends on the length of the journey: from Stockholm to Malmö, for example, a ticket including a couchette

costs 750kr, while 950kr buys a berth in a three-berth cabin, and 1150kr in a two-berth. Note that night-train services between Stockholm and Copenhagen or Oslo have been discontinued. Fares on overnight Tågkompaniet trains are set regardless of distance: 350kr for a seat, 600kr for a couchette, and 750kr per berth for a sleeping car with up to three berths. Daytime tickets are as follows: Luleå–Gällivare 145kr; Luleå–Kiruna 215kr; Umeå–Luleå 250kr.

It's worth picking up the SJ **Tågtider timetable**, free from any train station. Published twice yearly, this is an accurate and comprehensive list of the most useful train services in the country. Otherwise, each train route has its own timetable leaflet, also available free from any station.

The Inlandsbanan

If you're in the country during the summer months, then travelling at least a section of the **Inlandsbanan** (inland railway) is a must: a single track route, it runs for over a thousand kilometres from central Sweden to arctic Gällivare. The line was saved from closure in 1992 when it was bought by the local authorities along its length, but it now operates from late June to early August only. InterRail holders under 26 travel free; ScanRail pass holders get a 25 percent discount on the **Inlandsbanankort** (Inland Railway Card; full price 950kr). Available on board the trains, this card gives unlimited travel on the line for fourteen days. Tickets cost 75kr per 100km, and seat reservations can be made for 50kr. **Timetables** vary from year to year: get the latest information by calling ℡020/53 53 53 (outside Sweden ℡00 46/63 19 44 09) or visiting ⊛ www .inlandsbanan.se.

The Pågatåg

In Skåne in southern Sweden, a local company, **Pågatåg** (⊛ www.sj.se), operate trains between Helsingborg, Lund and Malmö, and Ystad and Simrishamn. Trains are fully automated and you buy your tickets from a machine on the platform which accepts coins and notes. Prices on the short hops are low, and InterRail cards are valid.

Buses

The main **long-distance bus** companies are Swebus Express (☎020/218 218, ⓦwww.swebusexpress.se) and Svenska Buss (☎0771/67 67 67, ⓦwww.svenskabuss.se). There are two types of bus: *expressbussar* (express buses) run daily, complementing rather than competing with the train system, while the cheaper *veckoslutsbussar* (weekend buses) often only run at weekends (usually Fri & Sun). The main routes and one-way fares are: Stockholm–Gothenburg 350kr; Stockholm–Malmö 435kr; and Gothenburg–Malmö 260kr. In the north of Sweden, there are a number of smaller companies running only one or two routes, including **Y-Bussen** (☎08/440 85 70 in Stockholm, ☎060/17 19 60 in Sundsvall; ⓦwww.ybuss.se), the only company operating services from Stockholm to Sundsvall (200kr), the High Coast (270kr), Örnsköldsvik (280kr) and Umeå (320kr), as well as across to Östersund (255kr); and **Lapplandspilen** (☎0951/779 50, ⓦwww.lapplandspilen.se), which operates buses between Stockholm and Vilhelmina (510kr), Storuman (525kr), Tärnaby (545kr) and Hemavan (545kr). There are also many regional bus companies in the north, charging 150–200kr for a one- to two-hour journey. Major routes are listed in the "Travel Details" at the end of each chapter, and you can pick up a comprehensive **timetable** at any bus terminal.

Local buses, too, are frequent and regular. Count on using them, as many hostels and campsites are a fair distance from town centres. Flat **fares** cost 15–20kr, with tickets usually valid for an hour. Most large towns operate some sort of discount system where you can buy cheaper books of tickets – these are detailed in the text where useful, and more information is available from local tourist offices.

Ferries and cruises

Unlike Norway and Finland, there are few domestic **ferry** services in Sweden. The various archipelagos on the southeast coast are served by small ferries, the most comprehensive network being within the **Stockholm archipelago**, for which you can buy a boat pass (see p.468). The other major link is between the Baltic island of **Gotland** and the mainland at Nynäshamn and Oskarshamn, both very popular routes for which you should book ahead in summer: all routes are operated by Destination Gotland ☎0498/20 10 20; ⓦwww.destinationgotland.se), and there's a choice of faster catamarans (2hr 30min–2hr 50min; foot passengers 420kr, cars 574kr) and regular car ferries (4–5hr; foot passengers 252kr, cars 504kr). There are discounts for rail pass holders; see "Basics", p.32, for details on routes. With your own boat it's possible to cross Sweden between Stockholm and Gothenburg on the **Göta Canal** or, alternatively, you can take an expensive **cruise** along the same route; ticket and journey details are given on p.503. Cheaper **day cruises** are possible along stretches of the Göta Canal and the Trollhättan Canal (see p.503).

Planes

The **domestic flight** network is operated by SAS and several smaller companies, such as Skyways (☎020/95 95 00, ⓦwww.skyways.se), and various deals can make flying a real steal, especially those long slogs north – contact the airlines direct for the latest details. Regular return **fares** for daily off-peak departures from Stockholm are: Gothenburg 1980kr; Kiruna 2787kr; Sundsvall 2130kr; and Malmö 2148kr. **Under-26s** can fly on standby with SAS anywhere in Sweden – the flight from Stockholm to Luleå, for example, currently costs a ridiculously cheap 340kr one-way – while for 470kr you can book yourself onto a particular flight. If you buy eight single standby tickets you also get two single standby tickets within Sweden free. Buy sixteen single tickets and you're entitled to a free return ticket from Sweden to any SAS European destination north of the Alps. You can avoid lengthy waits at airports by checking seat availability; phone (in Swedish only) ☎020/72 78 88, or visit ⓦwww.sas.se/ungdom. **Children** under two travel free. It's also worth considering an **air pass**, which you'll need to buy in conjunction with your ticket to Scandinavia – SAS and Skyways offer a "Visit Scandinavia" pass that's valid on all their routes in Sweden, Denmark, Norway and Finland. See "Basics", p.11, for more information.

Driving and hitching

Driving presents few problems: roads are good and generally reliable, and the only real danger are the reindeer and elk that can wander onto the tarmac. Watch out in bad light particularly – if you hit one, you'll know about it. As for **documentation**, you need a full licence and the vehicle registration document; an international driving licence and insurance "green card" are not essential. **Speed limits** are 110kph on motorways, 90kph and 70kph on other roads, 50kph in built-up areas. It's compulsory to use **dipped headlights** during daylight hours (on rented cars they will probably come on automatically) and, if you are taking your own car from Britain, remember to get the beam of your headlights adjusted to suit **driving on the right**. If you're motoring into northern Sweden then it's recommended that you fit mud flaps to your wheels and stone guards on the front of caravans. Swedish **drink-driving laws** are among the toughest in Europe and random breath tests the norm. Even the smallest amount of alcohol can lead to lost licences (always), fines (often) and prison sentences (not infrequently).

If you **break down**, call either the police or the Larmtjänst (☎020/91 00 40), a 24-hour rescue organization run by Swedish insurance companies. You should only use the emergency telephone number (☎112) in the event of an accident.

Car rental and petrol

Car rental is uniformly expensive, though most companies have special weekend tourist rates – from around 600kr, Friday to Monday, for a small car. It's worth checking out local tourist offices in the summer, as they sometimes recommend or operate reasonable weekly deals; otherwise, expect to pay around 3500kr a week, unlimited mileage, for a VW Golf or similar-sized car. The major international companies are represented in all the large towns and cities – details are under the various city "Listings".

Fuel currently costs around 9.5kr per litre; lead-free fuel is widely available and slightly cheaper. Most filling stations are self-service (*tanka själv*) and lots of them have automatic pumps (*sedel automat*), where you can fill up at any time using 100kr, 50kr and 20kr notes.

Cycling

A much better way to get around independently is to **cycle**. Some parts of the country were made for it, the southern provinces (and Gotland in particular) being ideal for a leisurely pedal. Many towns are best explored by bike, too, and tourist offices, campsites and youth hostels often **rent** out machines from around 100kr a day, 400kr a week; you may have to pay a returnable deposit as well. If you're touring, be prepared for long-distance hauls in the north and for rain in summer. **Taking a bike on a train** will cost you 375kr; you need to check bikes in ahead of your journey – the Swedish word for this is "*pollettera*".

The Svenska Cykelsällskapet (Swedish Cycling Association), Box 6006, S-164 06 Kista, Stockholm (☎08/751 62 04, ☯www.svenska-cykelsallskapet.se), signpost cycle routes in central and southern Sweden and can provide maps of these routes as well as general information. The STF can also advise on cycling package holidays in Sweden, which usually include youth hostel accommodation, meals and bike rental.

Accommodation

Finding somewhere cheap to sleep is not difficult provided you're prepared to do some advance planning. There's an excellent network of **youth hostels**, **pensions** and **campsites**, while **private rooms** and **bed-and-breakfast** places are common in the cities. Year-round discounts even make **hotels** affordable, an option certainly worth considering in the large cities where a city discount card is thrown in as part of the package.

Hotels and pensions

Hotels and **pensions** (the latter usually family-run B&B-type places) come cheaper than you'd think in Sweden. Although there's little

The hotels and guesthouses listed in the Sweden chapters of this Guide have been graded according to the following price bands, based on the cost of the **least expensive double room during the summer season** (mid-June to mid-Aug) and on winter weekends. Where winter weekday rates are higher, we've given two grades, covering both the summer and winter rate (ie ❷/❸).

❶ Under 500kr
❷ 500–700kr
❸ 700–900kr

❹ 900–1200kr
❺ 1200–1500kr
❻ Over 1500kr

chance of a room under 450kr a night anywhere, you'll find that rates vary according to season and the day of the week. Outside the summer period (roughly mid-June to mid-Aug), rates are reduced at weekends (usually Fri and Sat), while a higher price is applied from Sunday to Thursday to take advantage of business travellers. During the summer, winter weekend rates generally apply throughout the week. Bear in mind, though, that this is a general rule that varies from place to place.

In summer and at weekends outside of summer, expect to pay from 450kr for a single, 600kr for a double room with a TV and private bathroom. From Sunday to Thursday outside of summer, prices average at around 700kr for a single and 1000kr for a double. Nearly all hotels include a self-service buffet breakfast in the price – which, given its size, can make for a useful saving.

The best local **package deals** are available through the tourist offices in Malmö, Stockholm and Gothenburg: 400–500kr (minimum) gets you a double room for one night, breakfast and the relevant city discount card thrown in. These schemes are generally valid from mid-June to mid-August and at weekends throughout the rest of the year; see the accommodation details under the city accounts within the Guide for more detailed information.

The other option to consider is buying into a **hotel pass** scheme, where you pay in advance for a series of vouchers or cheques which then allow discounts or "free" accommodation in various hotel chains throughout the country. Further details can be found in the free booklet *Hotels in Sweden*, available from the Swedish Tourist Board, which also lists every hotel in the country.

Youth hostels

The biggest choice (indeed, quite often the only choice) of accommodation lies with the country's huge chain of youth hostels (vandrarhem), operated by the Svenska Turistföreningen (STF), Box 25, S-101 20 Stockholm (☎08/463 22 70, ⓦwww.meravsverige.nu). There are over 300 hostels in the country, mainly in southern and central Sweden, but also at regular and handy intervals throughout the north. Forget any preconceptions about youth hostelling: in Sweden rooms are family oriented, modern, clean and hotel-like, existing in the unlikeliest places – old castles, schoolrooms, country manors, and even on boats. Virtually all have well-equipped self-catering kitchens and serve a buffet breakfast. Prices are low, at abut 120–200kr for a bed; depending on the hostel, the bed can be either in a room (generally shared with one to three others), or in a larger dorm. Some hostels have private double rooms, and we've given price codes for these where they exist. Note that non-members of Hostelling International (see p.34) pay an extra 50kr or so per night), and that some hostels apply the same seasonal reductions to rates as hotels (see above). It would be impossible to list every hostel in this guide, so consult the Hostelling International handbook, or the one published by the STF, available from hostels, tourist offices and large bookshops, or directly from STF. Apart from the STF hostels, there are a number of independently run hostels, usually charging similar prices; local tourist offices will have details, and we've included the best places in the Guide.

Bear in mind that hostels are used by Swedish families as cheap, hotel-standard accommodation and can fill quickly, so always **book ahead** in the summer; it's also worth noting that hostels are sometimes closed between 10am and 5pm and have curfews around 11pm/midnight.

Private rooms and B&Bs

A further option is the **private rooms** in people's houses. Affordable and usually pleasant, these have access to showers and/or baths, sometimes a kitchen too, and hosts are rarely intrusive. Where rooms are available they are mentioned in the text, or look for the words *rum* or *logi* by the roadside. in any reasonably sized town, though, the tourist office can book private rooms for you; rates are anything from 100kr to 2000kr per person per night, plus a 30–50kr booking fee.

Farms throughout Sweden offer **B&B** accommodation and self-catering facilities; lists are available from Bo på Lantgård, Box 8, S-668 21 Ed, Sweden (☎0534/120 75, ✆www.bopalantgard.org), or from local tourist offices. Farm accommodation costs roughly 250–300kr per night per person, with discounts for children. If you want to book before you leave, the Swedish Tourist Board should be able to point you in the right direction.

Campsites

Practically every town or village has at least one **campsite**. These are generally of a high standard and will usually have a shower block, though you may have to pay for hot water. The larger campsites may have outdoor pools, too. Pitching a tent costs 80–160kr a night and there's often a charge of 10–20kr per person, too. Most sites are open from June to September; some (in winter sports areas) throughout the year. The bulk of the sites are approved and classified by the Swedish Tourist Board, and a comprehensive listings book, *Camping Sverige*, is available at larger sites and most Swedish bookshops (or, in advance, try one of the map outlets listed in "Basics"). The Swedish Tourist Board also puts out a short free list.

Note that you'll need a **camping card** (60kr from your first stop) at most sites and that **camping gaz** can be tricky to get hold

of in Sweden – take your own if possible.

Thanks to a tradition known as *Allemansrätt* ("Everyman's Right"), it's perfectly possible to **camp rough** throughout the country. This gives you the right to camp anywhere for one night without asking permission, provided you stay a reasonable distance (100m) away from other dwellings. In practice (and especially if you're in the north) no-one will object to discreet camping for longer periods, although it's as well, and polite, to ask first. The wide open spaces within most town and city borders make free camping a distinct possibility in built-up areas, too.

Cabins and mountain huts

Many campsites also boast **cabins**, usually decked out with bunk beds, kitchen and equipment, but not sheets. These make an excellent alternative to camping for groups or couples; cabins go for around 350–450kr for a four-bed affair. Again, it's wise to ring ahead to secure one. Sweden also has a whole series of **chalet villages**, which – on the whole – offer high-standard accommodation at prices to match. If you're interested in a package along these lines, contact the Swedish Tourist Board for more details.

In the more out-of-the-way places, STF operate a system of **mountain huts**, strung along hiking trails and in national parks. Usually staffed by a warden, and with cooking facilities, the huts cost around 170–190kr per person per night for members. More information and membership details are available from STF.

Food and drink

There's no escaping the fact that **eating** and **drinking** is going to take up a large slice of your daily budget in Sweden. However, if you choose to eat your main meal of the day at lunchtime, as the Swedes do, you'll save a small fortune.

At its best, **Swedish food** is excellent. It's largely meat-, fish- and potato-based, but varied for all that, and generally tasty and filling. There are unusual northern delicacies to look out for as well – reindeer and elk meat, and wild berries – while herring comes in so many different guises that fish fiends will always be content. **Drinking** is more uniform, the lager-type beer and imported wine providing no surprises, although the local spirit, *akvavit*, is worth trying at least once – it comes in dozens of different flavours.

Food

Eating well and cheaply in Sweden are often mutually exclusive aims, at least as far as a sit-down restaurant meal is concerned. The best strategy is to fuel up on breakfast and lunch, both of which offer

Glossary of Swedish food and drink terms

Basics and snacks

Ägg	Egg
Bröd	Bread
Glass	Ice cream
Grädde	Cream
Gräddfil	Sour cream
Gröt	Porridge
Jus	Fruit juice
Kaffe	Coffee
Knäckebröd	Crispbread
Mineralvatten	Mineral water
Mjölk	Milk
Olja	Oil
Omelett	Omelette
Ost	Cheese
Pastej	Pâté
Peppar	Pepper
Ris	Rice
Salt	Salt
Senap	Mustard
Småkakor	Biscuits
Smör	Butter
Smörgås	Sandwich
Socker	Sugar
Soppa	Soup
Strips	Chips
Sylt	Jam
Te	Tea
Våfflor	Waffles
Vinäger	Vinegar

Meat (*Kött*)

Älg	Elk
Biff	Beef steak
Fläsk	Pork
Kalvkött	Veal
Korv	Sausage
Kotlett	Cutlet/chop
Köttbullar	Meatballs
Kyckling	Chicken
Lammkött	Lamb
Lever	Liver
Oxstek	Roast beef
Renstek	Roast reindeer
Skinka	Ham

Fish (*Fisk*)

Ål	Eel
Ansjovis	Anchovies
Blåmusslor	Mussels
Fiskbullar	Fishballs
Forell	Trout
Hummer	Lobster
Kaviar	Caviar
Krabba	Crab
Kräftor	Freshwater crayfish
Lax	Salmon
Makrill	Mackerel
Räkor	Shrimps/prawns
Rödspätta	Plaice
Sardiner	Sardines
Sik	Whitefish
Sill	Herring
Strömming	Baltic herring
Torsk	Cod

Vegetables (*Grönsaker*)

Ärtor	Peas
Blomkål	Cauliflower
Bönor	Beans
Brysselkål	Brussels sprouts
Gurka	Cucumber
Lök	Onion
Morötter	Carrots
Potatis	Potatoes
Rödkål	Red cabbage
Sallad	Salad
Spenat	Spinach
Svamp	Mushrooms
Tomater	Tomatoes
Vitkål	White cabbage
Vitlök	Garlic

Fruit (*Frukt*)

Ananas	Pineapple
Apelsin	Orange
Äpple	Apple
Aprikos	Apricot
Banan	Banana
Citron	Lemon

good-value options. There's also a large number of foreign restaurants – principally pizzerias and Chinese restaurants – which are more likely to serve decently priced evening meals.

Breakfast, snacks and self-catering

Breakfast (*frukost*) in most youth hostels and hotel restaurants is almost invariably a help-yourself buffet; it usually costs around 50kr in hostels, and is free in hotels. If you

Hallon	Raspberry	*Rökt*	Smoked
Hjortron	Cloudberry	*Stekt*	Fried
Jordgrubbar	Strawberries	*Ugnstekt*	Roasted/baked
Lingon	Cranberries	*Varm*	Hot
Päron	Pear		
Persika	Peach	**Drinks**	
Vindruvor	Grapes	*Apelsin juice*	Orange juice
		Choklad	Hot chocolate
General terms		*Citron*	Lemon
Ångkokt	Steamed	*Frukt juice*	Fruit juice
Blodig	Rare	*Kaffe*	Coffee
Filó	Fillet	*Mineralvatten*	Mineral water
Friterad	Deep fried	*Mjölk*	Milk
Genomstekt	Well-done	*Öl*	Beer
Gravad	Cured	*Saft*	Squash
Grillat/Halstrad	Grilled	*Te*	Tea
Kall	Cold	*Vatten*	Water
Kokt	Boiled	*Vin*	Wine
Lagom	Medium	*Skål!*	Cheers!
Pocherad	Poached		

Swedish specialities

Ål	Eel, smoked and served with creamed potatoes or scrambled eggs (*äggröra*).
Ärtsoppa	Yellow pea soup with pork; a winter dish traditionally served on Thursdays.
Björnstek	Roast bear meat; fairly rare, but occasionally served at Orsa.
Bruna bönor	Baked, vinegared brown beans, usually served with bacon.
Fisksoppa	Fish soup.
Getost	Goat's cheese.
Gravadlax	Salmon marinaded in dill, sugar and seasoning, and served with mustard sauce.
Hjortron	A wild, northern berry served with fresh cream and/or ice cream.
Köttbullar	Meatballs served with a brown sauce and cranberries.
Kryddos	Hard cheese with caraway seeds.
Lövbiff	Sliced, fried beef with onions.
Mesost	Brown, sweet cheese; a breakfast favourite.
Potatissallad	Potato salad.
Pytt i panna	Cubes of meat and fried potatoes with a fried egg.
Sillbricka	Various cured and marinaded herring dishes; often appears as a first course at lunchtime in restaurants.
Sjömansbiff	Beef, onions and potato stewed in beer.

can eat vast amounts between 7am and 9.30am, it's nearly always good value. Juice, milk, cereals, bread, jam, boiled eggs, salami, tea and coffee appear on even the most limited tables. Swankier venues will also add herring, porridge, yoghurt, pâté and fruit. Something to watch out for is the jug of *filmjölk* next to the ordinary milk – it's thicker, sour milk for pouring on cereals. **Coffee** in Sweden is always freshly brewed and very good; often it's free after the first cup, or at least greatly reduced in price – look for the word *påtår*. **Tea** is less exciting – weak Lipton's as a rule – but costs around the same: 15kr a cup.

For **snacks** and lighter meals the choice expands, although availability is inversely related to health value. A *gatukök* (street kitchen) or *korvstånd* (hot-dog stall) will serve a selection of hot-dogs, burgers, pizza slices, chicken bits, chips, ice cream, Coke, crisps and ketchup – something and chips will cost around 50kr. These stalls and stands are on every street in every town and village. A hefty burger and chips meal in a **burger bar** goes for around 55kr: the local *Clockburger* is cheaper than *McDonald's*, but both are generally the source of the cheapest coffee in town.

It's often nicer to hit the **konditori**, a coffee shop with succulent pastries and cakes. They're not particularly cheap (coffee and cake cost 35–50kr) but are generally as good as they look, and the coffee is often free after you've paid for the first cup. This is also where you'll come across *smörgåsar*, open **sandwiches** piled high with an elaborate variety of toppings. Favourites include shrimps, smoked salmon, eggs, cheese, pâté and mixed salad – around 50–60kr a time.

Restaurants: lunch and dinner

Eating in a **restaurant** (*restaurang*) needn't be out of your price range, but remember that **lunch** is always around a third cheaper than dinner. Most restaurants offer something called the **dagens rätt** ("daily dish") at 60–70kr, an excellent way to sample real Swedish *husmanskost* – "home cooking". Served Monday to Friday between 11am and 2pm, this is simply a choice of main meal (usually one meat and one fish dish)

which comes with bread/crispbread and salad, sometimes a soft drink or light beer, and usually coffee. Some Swedish dishes, like *pytt i panna* and *köttbullar* (see p.415), are standards. On the whole, though, more likely offerings in the big cities are pizzas, basic Chinese meals and meat or fish salads. If you're travelling **with kids**, look out for the word *barnmatsedel* (children's menu).

More expensive – but good for a blowout – are restaurants and hotels that put out the **smörgåsbord** at lunchtime. Following the breakfast theme, you help yourself to unlimited portions of herring, hot and cold meats, eggs, fried and boiled potatoes, salad, cheese, desserts and fruit for 150–250kr. To follow local custom you should start with *akvavit*, drink beer throughout and finish with coffee, although this will add to the bill unless it is a fancier all-inclusive spread (usually found on Sunday). A variation on the buffet theme is the **sillbricka**, a specialist buffet where the dishes are all based on cured and marinated herring – it might simply be called the "herring table" on the menu.

If you don't eat the set lunch, meals in restaurants, especially at **dinner** (*middag*), can be expensive. Expect to pay at least 400kr per head for a three-course affair, to which you can add 40–50kr for a beer, and 150kr for the cheapest bottle of house wine. The food in Swedish restaurants is generally *husmanskost*, although the latest trend is for "crossover" cuisine: Swedish cooking with an international edge that's usually delicious.

Swedes eat early and lunch in most restaurants is served from around 11am, dinner from around 6pm.

Ethnic restaurants

For years the only **ethnic** choice in Sweden was between the pizzeria or the odd Chinese restaurant, and these still offer the best-value dinners. In **pizzerias** you'll get a large, if not strictly authentic, pizza for around 50kr, usually with free coleslaw and bread, and the price generally remains the same whether it's lunch or dinner. Branches of *Pizza Hut* can sometimes be found, though they're much more expensive. **Chinese** restaurants nearly always offer a set lunch for around 50kr, and though pricier in the evenings (80–100kr a dish), a group of people can usually put together quite a good-value meal.

Vegetarians

It's not too tough being **vegetarian** in Sweden, given the preponderance of buffet-type meals, most of which are heavy with salads, cheeses, eggs and soups. The cities, too, have salad bars and sandwich shops where you'll have no trouble feeding yourself, and if all else fails the local pizzeria will always deliver the meat-free goods. At lunchtime you'll find that the *dagens rätt* in many places has a vegetarian option; don't be afraid to ask.

Drinking

Drinking in Sweden is no longer the notoriously pricey pursuit it once was – in fact, a beer in Stockholm now costs roughly the same as in London. Nonetheless, it's still cheaper to forgo bars every once in a while and buy your booze from the state-licensed *Systembolaget* liquor stores – though doing so is, of course, not nearly as enjoyable. Swedes still perceive drinking to be an expensive activity: consequently, you won't find yourself stuck buying rounds at the bar which demand a bank loan to pay off, and it's perfectly acceptable to nurse your drink as long as you like. It's worth noting, though, that some bars have happy hours, when half a litre of beer goes for around half-price.

What to drink

If you drink anything alcoholic in Sweden, a good choice is **beer**, which, while expensive, at least costs the same almost everywhere, be it a café, bar or restaurant. Around 40–45kr will get you a half-litre of good, lager-type brew – unless you specify, it will be *starköl*, the strongest Class III beer; cheaper will be *folköl*, Class II and weaker; whilst cheapest (around half the price of *folköl*) is *lättöl*, a Class I concoction notable only for its virtual absence of alcohol. Classes I and II are available in supermarkets, although the real stuff is only on sale in the *Systembolaget* state-licensed liquor stores – see opposite – where it's around a third of the price you'll pay in a bar. **Wine** is

good value when bought in the *Systembolaget* but can be expensive in restaurants and bars, where you'll pay around 45kr for a glass and upwards of 150kr for a bottle. **Spirits** are the most expensive alcoholic drinks; vodka, for example, costs around 50kr a shot. For experimental drinking, **akvavit** – clear, and tasteless – is a good bet. Served ice cold in tiny shots, it's washed down with beer; hold onto your hat. There are various different "flavours" too, in which spices and herbs are added to the finished brew to produce some unusual headaches. Or try **glögg**: served at Christmas, it's a mulled red wine with cloves, cinnamon, sugar and more than a dash of *akvavit*.

Where to drink

You'll find **bars** in all towns and cities and most villages. In Stockholm and the larger cities the move is towards brasserie-type places – smart and flash – and British-style pubs. Elsewhere, you still come across more down-to-earth drinking dens, often sponsored by the local union or welfare authority, but the drink's no cheaper and the clientele heavily male and drunk. Either way, the bar is not the centre of Swedish social activity – if you really want to meet people, you'd be better off heading for the campsite or the beach.

In the summer, **café-bars** spread out onto the pavement, better for kids and handy for just a coffee. In out-of-the-way places, when you want a drink and can't find a bar, head for a hotel. Things close down at 11pm or midnight except in Gothenburg and Stockholm where – as long as your wallet is bottomless – you can drink all night.

The Systembolaget

Venturing into a **Systembolaget** (a state-run off-licence) is a move into a twilight world. Buying alcohol is made as unattractive as possible, with everything behind glass and grilles, and service often dour and disapproving. There is still a real stigma attached to alcohol and its (public) consumption, and punters sneaking out with a plastic bag full of the hard stuff is not a rare sight. Buying from the *Systembolaget* is, however, the only option for many budget travellers, although apart from strong beer (15kr or so for a third of a litre), the only bargain is the wine – from around 50kr a bottle for some surprisingly good European and New World imports. *Systembolaget* shops are open Monday to Saturday only (10am–6pm or 7pm, Sat until 2pm); minimum age for being served is 20, and you may need to show ID, although in bars and pubs the age limit is 18.

Directory

Customs From another European Union country where tax has been paid, your customs allowance entering Sweden is two litres of spirits, 26 litres of wine and 32 litres of strong beer.

Emergencies Dial ☎112 for police (*polis*), fire brigade (*brandkår*) or ambulance (*ambulans*), free of charge from any phone box.

Public holidays Banks, offices and shops are closed on the following days and may shut early on the preceding day: January 1, January 6 (Epiphany), Good Friday, Easter Monday, May 1 (Labour Day), Ascension Day (fortieth day after Easter), Whit Monday (eighth Monday after Easter), Midsummer's Day, All Saint's Day, Christmas Day, Boxing Day.

Shops Opening hours are Mon–Fri 9am–6pm, Sat 9am–4pm. Some department stores stay open until 8–10pm in cities, and may open on Sunday afternoons as well.

Tipping Hotels and restaurants include their service charge (usually ten percent) in the bill. You should tip cloakroom attendants in bars and discos around 10kr a time.

History

Sweden has one of Europe's longest documented histories, but for all the upheavals of the Viking times and the warring of the Middle Ages, during modern times the country has seemed to delight in taking an historical back seat. For one brief period, when Prime Minister Olof Palme was shot dead in 1986, Sweden was thrust into the international limelight. Since then, however, it's regained its poise, even though the current situation is fraught. Political infighting and domestic disharmony are threatening the one thing that the Swedes have always been proud of and that other countries aspire to: the politics of consensus. The passing of this, arguably, is of far greater importance than even the assassination of their prime minister.

Early civilizations

It wasn't until around 6000 BC that the **first settlers** roamed north and east into Sweden, living as nomadic reindeer-hunters and herders. By 3000 BC people had settled in the south of the country and were established as farmers; whilst from around 2000 BC occurred a development in burial practices, with **dolmens** and **passage graves** being found throughout the southern Swedish provinces. Traces also remain of the **Boat Axe People**, named after their characteristic tool/weapon shaped like a boat. The earliest Scandinavian horse-riders, they quickly held sway over the whole of southern Sweden.

During the **Bronze Age** (1500–500 BC) the Boat Axe People traded furs and amber for southern European copper and tin. Large finds of ornaments and weapons attest to a comparatively rich culture, exemplified by elaborate burial rites, with the dead laid in single graves under mounds of earth and stone.

The deterioration of the Scandinavian climate in the last millennium before Christ coincided with the advance across Europe of the Celts, which halted the flourishing trade of the Swedish settlers. With the new millennium, Sweden made its first mark upon the classical world when Pliny the Elder (23–79 AD), in the *Historia Naturalis*, mentioned the "island of Scatinavia" far to the north. Tacitus was more specific: in 98 AD he referred to a powerful people, the Suiones, who were strong in men, weapons and ships: a reference to the **Svear**, who were to form the nucleus of an emergent Swedish kingdom by the sixth century.

Rulers of the whole country except the south, the Svear settled in the rich land around Lake Mälaren. The modern Swedish name for Sweden, *Sverige*, is a derivation "Svear rike", meaning the kingdom of the Svear. More importantly, the Svear gave their first dynastic leaders a taste for expansion, trading with Gotland and holding suzerainty over the Åland Islands.

The Viking period

The Vikings – raiders and warriors who dominated the political and economic life of Europe and beyond from the ninth to the eleventh centuries – came from all parts of southern Scandinavia. But there is evidence that the **Swedish Vikings** were among the first to leave home, impelled by a rapid population growth, domestic unrest and a desire for new lands. The raiders (and, later, traders) turned their attention largely eastwards, and by the ninth century trade had developed along well-established routes, with Swedes reaching the Black and Caspian seas and making valuable contact with the **Byzantine Empire**. Although more commercially inclined than their Danish and Norwegian counterparts, Swedish Vikings were quick to use force if profits were slow to materialize. From 860 onwards Greek and Muslim records relate a series of raids across the Black

Sea against Byzantium, and across the Caspian into northeast Iran.

But the Vikings were settlers as well as traders and exploiters, and their long-term influence was marked. Embattled Slavs to the east gave them the name **Rus**, and their creeping colonization gave the area in which the Vikings settled its modern name, Russia. Russian names today – Oleg, Igor, Vladimir – can be derived from the Swedish – Helgi, Ingvar, Valdemar.

Domestically, **paganism** was at its height. Freyr was "God of the World", a physically potent god of fertility from whom dynastic leaders would trace their descent. It was a bloody time. Nine **human sacrifices** were offered at the celebrations held every nine years at Uppsala. Adam of Bremen recorded that the great shrine there was adjoined by a sacred grove where "every tree is believed divine because of the death and putrefaction of the victims hanging there".

Viking **law** was based on the Thing, an assembly of free men to which the king's power was subject. Each largely autonomous province had its own assembly and its own leaders: where several provinces united, the approval of each Thing was needed for any choice of leader. For centuries in Sweden the new king had to make a formal tour to receive the homage of each province.

The arrival of Christianity

Christianity was slow to take root in Sweden. Whereas Denmark and Norway had accepted the faith by the beginning of the eleventh century, Swedish contact was still with the peoples to the east, who remained largely heathen. Missionaries met with limited success and no Swedish king was converted until 1008, when **Olof Skötonung** was baptized. He was the first known king of both Swedes and Goths (that is, ruler of the two major provinces of Västergötland and

Östergötland) and his successors were all Christians. Nevertheless, paganism retained a grip on Swedish affairs, and as late as the 1080s the Svear banished their Christian king, Inge, when he refused to take part in the pagan celebrations at Uppsala. By the end of the eleventh century, though, the temple at Uppsala had gone and a Christian church was built on its site. In the 1130s Uppsala replaced Sigtuna – original centre of the Swedish Christian faith – as the main episcopal seat and, in 1164, Stephen (an English monk) was made the first archbishop.

The warring dynasties

The whole of the early Middle Ages in Sweden was characterized by a succession of struggles for control of a growing central power. Principally two families, the Sverkers and the Eriks, waged battle throughout the twelfth century. **King Erik the Holy** was the first notable Sverker ruler to make his mark: in 1157 he led a crusade to heathen Finland, but was killed at Uppsala in 1160 by a Danish pretender to his throne. Within a hundred years he was to be recognized as patron saint of Sweden, and his remains interred in the new Uppsala Cathedral.

Erik was succeeded by his son **Knut**, whose stable reign lasted until 1196 and was marked by commercial treaties and strengthened defences. Following his death, virtual civil war weakened the royal power with the result that the king's chief ministers, or **Jarls**, assumed much of the executive responsibility for running the country; so much so that when Erik Eriksson (last of the Eriks) was deposed in 1229, his administrator **Birger Jarl** assumed power. With papal support for his crusading policies, Jarl confirmed the Swedish grip on the southwest of Finland. His son Valdemar succeeded him, but proved a weak ruler and didn't survive the family feuding after Birger Jarl's death. Valdemar's brother Magnus assumed power in 1275.

Magnus Ladulås represented a peak of Swedish royal power not to be repeated for three hundred years. His enemies dissipated, he forbade the nobility to meet without his consent and began to issue his own authoritative decrees. Preventing the nobility from claiming maintenance at the expense of the peasantry as they travelled from estate to estate earned him his nickname Ladulås or "Barn-lock". He also began to reap the benefits of conversion: the clergy became an educated class upon whom the monarch could rely for diplomatic and administrative duties. By the thirteenth century, there were ambitious Swedish clerics in Paris and Bologna, and the first stone churches were appearing in Sweden, among them the monumental early Gothic cathedral at Uppsala.

The nobility, meanwhile, had come to form a military class, exempted from taxation on the understanding that they would defend the crown. In the country the standard of living was still low, although a burgeoning population stimulated new cultivation. The forests of Norrland were pushed back, southern heathland was turned into pasture, and crop rotation introduced. Noticeable, too, was the increasing **German influence** within Sweden as the Hanseatic League traders spread. Their first merchants settled in Visby and, by the mid-thirteenth century, in Stockholm.

The fourteenth century – towards unity

When Magnus died in 1290, power shifted to a cabal of magnates led by **Torgil Knutsson**. As Marshal of Sweden, he pursued an energetic foreign policy, conquering western Karelia to gain control of the Gulf of Finland and building the fortress at Viborg, which was lost only with the collapse of the Swedish Empire in the eighteenth century.

Magnus's son Birger came of age in 1302 but soon quarrelled with his brothers Erik and Valdemar. They had

Torgil Knutsson executed, then rounded on Birger, who was forced to divide Sweden among the three of them. An unhappy arrangement, it lasted until 1317, when Birger had his brothers arrested and starved to death in prison – an act that prompted a shocked nobility to rise against Birger and force his exile to Denmark. The Swedish nobles restored the principle of elective monarchy by calling on the three-year-old **Magnus** (son of a Swedish duke and already declared Norwegian king) to take the Swedish crown. While Magnus was still a boy, a treaty was concluded with Novgorod (1323) to fix the frontiers in eastern and northern Finland. This left virtually the whole of the Scandinavian peninsula (except the Danish provinces in the south) under one ruler.

Yet Sweden was still anything but prosperous. The **Black Death** reached the country in 1350, wiping out whole parishes and killing around a third of the population. Subsequent labour shortages and troubled estates meant that the nobility found it difficult to maintain their positions. German merchants had driven the Swedes from their most lucrative trade routes and even the copper and iron-ore **mining** that began around this time in Bergslagen and Dalarna relied on German capital.

Magnus soon ran into trouble, threatened further by the accession of Valdemar Atterdag to the Danish throne in 1340. Squabbles over the sovereignty of the Danish provinces of Skåne and Blekinge led to Danish incursions into Sweden and, in 1361, Valdemar landed on Gotland and sacked **Visby**. The Gotlanders, refused refuge by the Hanseatic League, were massacred outside the city walls.

Magnus was forced to negotiate and his son **Håkon** – now King of Norway – was married to Valdemar's daughter Margrethe. With Magnus later deposed, power fell into the hands of a group of magnates, who shared out the country. Chief of the ruling nobles was the

Steward **Bo Jonsson Grip**, who controlled virtually all Finland and central and southeast Sweden. Yet on his death, the nobility turned to Håkon's wife **Margrethe**, already regent in Norway (for her son Olof) and in Denmark since the death of her father, Valdemar. In 1388 she was proclaimed "First Lady" of Sweden and, in return, confirmed all the privileges of the Swedish nobility. They were anxious for union, to safeguard those who owned frontier estates and strengthen the crown against any further German influence. Called upon to choose a male king, Margrethe nominated her nephew, **Erik of Pomerania**, who was duly elected king of Sweden in 1396. As he had already been elected to the Danish and Norwegian thrones, Scandinavian unity seemed assured.

The Kalmar Union

Erik was crowned King of Denmark, Norway and Sweden in 1397 at a ceremony in **Kalmar**. Nominally, the three kingdoms were now in union but, despite Erik, real power remained in the hands of Margrethe until her death in 1412.

Erik was at war throughout his reign with the Hanseatic League. Vilified in popular Swedish history as an evil and grasping ruler, the taxes he raised went on a war that was never fought on Swedish soil. He spent his time instead in Denmark, directing operations, leaving his queen Philippa (sister to Henry V of England) behind. Erik was deposed in 1439 and the nobility turned to **Christopher of Bavaria**, whose early death in 1448 led to the first major breach in the union.

No one candidate could fill the three kingships satisfactorily, and separate elections in Denmark and Sweden signalled a renewal of the infighting that had plagued the previous century. Within Sweden, unionists and nationalists skirmished, the powerful unionist **Oxenstierna** family opposing the claims of the nationalist **Sture** family until 1470, when **Sten Sture** (the Elder) became "Guardian of the Realm". His victory over the unionists at the **Battle of Brunkeberg** (1471) – in the middle of modern Stockholm – was complete, gaining symbolic artistic expression in the **statue of St George and the Dragon** that still adorns the Great Church in Stockholm.

Sten Sture's primacy fostered a new cultural flowering. The first **university** in Scandinavia was founded in Uppsala in 1477, and the first printing press appeared in Sweden six years later. Artistically, German and Dutch influences were great, traits seen in the decorative art of the great Swedish medieval churches. Only remote **Dalarna** kept alive a native folk art tradition.

Belief in the union still existed though, particularly outside Sweden, and successive kings had to fend off almost constant attacks and blockades emanating from Denmark. With the accession of **Christian II** to the Danish throne in 1513, the unionist movement found a leader capable of turning the tide. Under the guise of a crusade to free Sweden's imprisoned archbishop Gustav Trolle, Christian attacked Sweden and killed Sture. After Christian's coronation, Trolle urged the prosecution of his Swedish adversaries who, gathered together under an amnesty, were found guilty of heresy. Eighty-two nobles and burghers of Stockholm were executed and their bodies burned in what became known as the **Stockholm Bloodbath**. A vicious persecution of Sture's followers throughout Sweden ensued, a move that led to widespread reaction and, ultimately, the downfall of the union.

Gustav Vasa and his sons

Opposition to Christian II was vague and unorganized until the appearance of the young **Gustav Vasa**. Initially unable to stir the locals of the Dalecarlia region into open revolt, he left for exile in Norway, but was chased on skis and recalled after the people had had a change of heart. The chase is celebrated still in the **Vasalopet** race, run each year by thousands of Swedish skiers.

Gustav Vasa's army grew rapidly and in 1521 he was elected regent, and subsequently, with the capture of Stockholm in 1523, king. Christian had been deposed in Denmark and the new Danish king, Frederik I, recognized Sweden's de facto withdrawal from the union. Short of cash, Gustav found it prudent to support the movement towards religious reform propagated by Swedish Lutherans. More of a political than a religious **Reformation**, the result was a handover of church lands to the crown and the subordination of church to state. It's a relationship that is still largely in force today, the clergy being civil servants paid by the State. In 1541 the first edition of the Bible in the vernacular appeared. Suppressing revolt at home, Gustav Vasa strengthened his hand with a centralization of trade and government. On his death in 1560 Sweden was united, prosperous and independent.

Gustav Vasa's heir, his eldest son **Erik**, faced a difficult time, not least because the Vasa lands and wealth had been divided among him and his brothers Johan, Magnus and Karl (an atypically imprudent action of Gustav's before his death). The Danes, too, pressed hard, reasserting their claim to the Swedish throne in the inconclusive **Northern Seven Years' War**, which began in 1563. Erik was deposed in 1569 by his brother who became **Johan III**, his first act being to end the war at the **Peace of Stettin**. At home Johan ruled more or less with the goodwill of the nobility, but upset matters with his Catholic sympathies. He introduced the liturgy and Catholic-influenced Red Book, and his son and heir Sigismund was the Catholic king of Poland. On Johan's death in 1592, Sigismund agreed to rule Sweden in accordance with Lutheran practice but failed to do so. When Sigismund returned to Poland the way was clear for Duke Karl (Johan's brother) to assume the regency, a role he filled until declared King **Karl IX** in 1603.

Karl had ambitions eastwards but, routed by the Poles and staved off by the Russians, he suffered a stroke in 1610 and died the year after. The last of Vasa's sons, his heir was the seventeen-year-old Gustav II Adolf, better known as Gustavus Adolphus.

The rule of Vasa and his sons made Sweden a nation, culturally as well as politically. The courts were filled with men of learning and the arts flourished. The **Renaissance** style appeared for the first time in Sweden, with royal castles remodelled – Kalmar being a fine example. Economically, Sweden remained mostly self-sufficient, its few imports being luxuries like cloth, wine and spices. With around 8000 inhabitants, Stockholm was its most important city, although **Gothenburg** was founded in 1607 to promote trade to the west.

Gustav II Adolf: the rise of the Swedish empire

During the reign of **Gustav II Adolf**, Sweden became a European power. Though still a youth, he was considered able enough to rule, and proved so by concluding peace treaties with Denmark (1613) and Russia (1617), the latter isolating Russia from the Baltic and allowing the Swedes control of the eastern trade routes into Europe.

In 1618 the **Thirty Years' War** broke out in Germany. It was vital for Gustavus that Germany should not become Catholic, given the Polish king's continuing pretensions to the Swedish crown, and the possible threat it could pose to Sweden's growing influence in the Baltic. The Altmark treaty with a defeated Poland in 1629 gave Gustavus control of Livonia and four Prussian sea ports, and the income this generated financed his entry into the war in 1630 on the Protestant side. After several convincing victories

Gustavus pushed through Germany, delaying an assault upon undefended Vienna. It cost him his life. At the **Battle of Lützen** in 1632 Gustavus was killed, his body stripped and battered by the enemy's soldiers. The war dragged on until the **Peace of Westphalia** in 1648.

With Gustavus away at war for much of his reign, Sweden ran smoothly under the guidance of his friend and chancellor, **Axel Oxenstierna**. Together they founded a new Supreme Court in Stockholm (and the same, too, in Finland and the conquered Baltic provinces); reorganized the national assembly into four Estates of nobility, clergy, burghers and peasantry (1626); extended the university at Uppsala (and founded one at Åbo – modern Turku); and fostered the mining and other industries that provided much of the country's wealth. Gustavus had many other accomplishments, too: he spoke five languages and designed a new light cannon, which assisted in his routs of the enemy.

The Caroleans

The Swedish empire reached its territorial peak under the **Caroleans**. Yet the reign of the last of them was to see Sweden crumble.

Following Gustav II Adolf's death and the later abdication of his daughter Christina, **Karl X** succeeded to the throne. War against Poland (1655) led to some early successes and, with Denmark espousing the Polish cause, gave Karl the opportunity to march into Jutland (1657). From there his armies crossed the frozen sea to threaten Copenhagen; the subsequent **Treaty of Roskilde** (1658) broke Denmark and gave the Swedish empire its widest territorial extent.

However, the long regency of his son and heir, **Karl XI**, did little to enhance Sweden's vulnerable position, so extensive were its borders. On his assumption of power in 1672 Karl was almost immediately dragged into war: beaten by a smaller Prussian army at Brandenberg in 1675, Sweden was suddenly faced with war against both the Danes and Dutch. Karl rallied, though, to drive out the Danish invaders, the war ending in 1679 with the reconquest of Skåne and the restoration of most of Sweden's German provinces.

In 1682 Karl XI became **absolute monarch** and was given full control over legislation and *reduktion* – the resumption of estates previously alienated by the crown to the nobility. The armed forces were reorganized too, and by 1700 the Swedish army had 25,000 soldiers and twelve regiments of cavalry; the naval fleet was expanded to 38 ships and a new base built at **Karlskrona** (nearer than Stockholm to the likely trouble spots).

Culturally, Sweden began to benefit from the innovations of Gustav II Adolf. *Gymnasia* (grammar schools) continued to expand and a second university was established at **Lund** in 1668. A national literature emerged, helped by the efforts of **George Stiernhielm**, "father" of modern Swedish poetry, while the same period saw the work of **Olof Rudbeck** (1630–1702), a Nordic polymath whose scientific reputation lasted longer than his attempt to identify the ancient Goth settlement at Uppsala as Atlantis. Architecturally, this was the age of **Tessin**, both father and son. Tessin the Elder was responsible for the glorious palace at **Drottningholm**, work on which began in 1662, as well as the cathedral at **Kalmar**. His son, Tessin the Younger, succeeded him as royal architect and was to create the new royal palace at Stockholm.

In 1697 the 15-year-old **Karl XII** succeeded to the throne and under him the empire collapsed. Faced with a defensive alliance of Saxony, Denmark and Russia, there was little the king could have done to avoid eventual defeat. However, he remains a revered figure for his valiant (often suicidal) efforts to prove Europe wrong. Initial victories against Peter the Great and Saxony led him to march on Russia,

where he was defeated and the bulk of his army destroyed. Escaping to Turkey, where he remained as guest and then prisoner for four years, Karl watched the empire disintegrate. With Poland reconquered by Augustus of Saxony, and Finland by Peter the Great, he returned to Sweden, only to have England declare war on him.

Eventually, splits in the enemy's alliance led Swedish diplomats to attempt peace talks with Russia. Karl, though, was keen to exploit these differences in a more direct fashion. In order to strike at Denmark, but lacking a fleet, he besieged Fredrikshald in Norway in 1718 and was killed by a sniper's bullet. In the power vacuum thus created, Russia became the leading Baltic force, receiving Livonia, Estonia, Ingria and most of Karelia from Sweden.

The age of freedom

The eighteenth century saw absolutism discredited in Sweden. A new constitution vested power in the Estates, who reduced the new king **Fredrik I**'s role to that of nominal head of state. The chancellor wielded the real power and under **Arvid Horn** the country found a period of stability. His party, nicknamed the "Caps", was opposed by the hawkish "Hats", who forced war with Russia in 1741, a disaster in which Sweden lost all of Finland and had its whole east coast burned and bombed. Most of Finland was returned with the agreement to elect **Adolf Fredrik** (a relation of the crown prince of Russia) to the Swedish throne on Fredrik I's death, which duly occurred in 1751. During his reign Adolf repeatedly tried to reassert royal power, but found that the constitution was only strengthened against him. The resurrected "Hats" forced entry into the **Seven Years' War** in 1757 on the French side, another disastrous venture as the Prussians repelled every Swedish attack.

The aristocratic parties were in a state of constant flux. Although elections of sorts were held to provide delegates for the Riksdag (parliament), foreign sympathies, bribery and bickering were hardly conducive to a democratic administration. Cabals continued to rule Sweden, the economy was stagnant, and reform delayed. It was, however, an age of intellectual and scientific advance, surprising in a country that had lost much of its cultural impetus. **Carl von Linné** (better known by the Latinized version of his name, Linnaeus), the botanist whose classification of plants is still used, was professor at Uppsala from 1741 to 1778. **Anders Celsius** initiated the use of the centigrade temperature scale; **Carl Scheele** discovered chlorine. A royal decree of 1748 organized Europe's first full-scale census, and by 1775 the census had become a five-yearly event. Other fields flourished, too. **Emmanuel Swedenborg**, the philosopher, died in 1772, his mystical works encouraging new theological sects; and the period encapsulated the life of **Carl Michael Bellman** (1740–95), the celebrated Swedish poet, whose work did much to identify and foster a popular nationalism.

With the accession of **Gustav III** in 1771, the crown began to regain the ascendancy. A new constitution was forced upon a divided Riksdag and proved a balance between earlier absolutism and the later aristocratic squabbles. A popular king, Gustav founded hospitals, granted freedom of worship and removed many of the state controls over the economy. His determination to conduct a successful foreign policy led to further conflict with Russia (1788–90) in which, to everyone's surprise, he managed to more than hold his own. But with the French Revolution polarizing opposition throughout Europe, the Swedish nobility began to entertain thoughts of conspiracy against a king whose growing powers they now saw as those of a tyrant. In 1792, at a masked ball in the Stockholm Opera House, the king was shot by an assassin hired by the disaffected aristocracy. Gustav died two

weeks later and was succeeded by his son **Gustav IV**, the country led by a regency for the years of his minority.

The wars waged by revolutionary France were at first studiously avoided in Sweden but, pulled into the conflict by the British, Gustav IV entered the **Napoleonic Wars** in 1805. However, Napoleon's victory at Austerlitz two years later broke the coalition and Sweden found itself isolated. Attacked by Russia the following year, Gustav was later arrested and deposed, his uncle elected king.

A constitution of 1809 established a liberal monarchy in Sweden, responsible to the elected Riksdag. Under this constitution **Karl XIII** was a mere caretaker, his heir a Danish prince who would bring Norway back to Sweden – some compensation for finally losing Finland and the Åland Islands to Russia (1809) after five hundred years of Swedish rule. On the prince's sudden death, however, Marshal Bernadotte (one of Napoleon's generals) was invited to become heir. Taking the name of **Karl Johan**, he took his chance in 1812 and joined Britain and Russia to fight Napoleon. Following Napoleon's first defeat at the Battle of Leipzig in 1813, Sweden compelled Denmark (France's ally) to exchange Norway for Swedish Pomerania.

By 1814 Sweden and Norway had formed an uneasy union. Norway retained its own government and certain autonomous measures. Sweden decided foreign policy, appointed a viceroy and retained a suspensive (but not absolute) veto over the Norwegian parliament's legislation.

The nineteenth century

Union under Karl Johan, or **Karl XIV** as he became in 1818, could have been disastrous. He spoke no Swedish and just a few years previously had never visited either kingdom. However, under him and his successor **Oscar I**, prosperity ensued. The **Göta Canal** (1832) helped commercially, and liberal meas-

ures by both monarchs helped politically. In 1845 daughters were given an
equal right of inheritance, a poor law
was introduced in 1847, restrictive craft
guilds were reformed and an education
act passed.

The 1848 revolution throughout
Europe cooled Oscar's reforming
ardour, and his attention turned to
reviving **Scandinavianism**. There was
still a hope, in certain quarters, that
closer cooperation between Denmark
and Sweden–Norway could lead to
some sort of revived Kalmar Union.
Expectations were raised with the
Crimean War of 1854 that Russia –
Sweden's main enemy in the eighteenth
century – could be weakened for good.
But peace was declared too quickly (at
least for Sweden) and there was still no
real guarantee that Sweden would be
sufficiently protected from Russia in the
future. With Oscar's death, talk of political union faded.

His son **Karl XV** presided over a
reform of the Riksdag that put an end to
the Swedish system of personal monarchy. The Four Estates were replaced by a
representative two-house parliament
along European lines. This, together with
the end of political Scandinavianism (following the Prussian attack on Denmark
in 1864 in which Sweden refused to
offer assistance), marked Sweden's entry
into modern Europe.

Industrialization was slow to take
root in Sweden. No real industrial revolution occurred, and developments such
as mechanization and the introduction
of railways were piecemeal. One result
was widespread **emigration** amongst
the rural poor, who had been hard hit
by famine in 1867 and 1868. Between
1860 and 1910 over one million people
left for America (in 1860 the Swedish
population was only four million).
Given huge farms to settle, the emigrants headed for land similar to that
they had left behind – to the Midwest,
Kansas and Nebraska.

At home, Swedish **trade unionism**
emerged to campaign for better conditions. Dealt with severely, the unions
formed a confederation (1898) but
largely failed to make headway. Even
peaceful picketing carried a two-year
prison sentence. Hand in hand with the
fight for workers' rights went the
temperance movement. The level of
spirit consumption was alarming and
various abstinence programmes
attempted to educate the drinkers and,
where necessary, eradicate the stills.
Some towns made the selling of spirits a
municipal monopoly – not a big step
from the state monopoly that exists
today.

With the accession of **Oscar II** in
1872, Sweden continued on an even, if
uneventful, keel. Keeping out of further
European conflict (the Austro–Prussian
War, Franco–Prussian War and various
Balkan crises), the country's only worry
was a growing dissatisfaction in Norway
with the union. Demanding a separate
consular service, and objecting to the
Swedish king's veto on constitutional
matters, the Norwegians brought things
to a head, and in 1905 declared the
union invalid. The Karlstad Convention
confirmed the break and Norway
became independent for the first time
since 1380.

The late nineteenth century was a
happier time for Swedish culture.
August Strindberg enjoyed great
critical success and artists like **Anders
Zorn** and **Prince Eugene** made their
mark abroad. The historian **Artur
Hazelius** founded the Nordic and
Skansen museums in Stockholm; and
the chemist, industrialist and dynamite
inventor **Alfred Nobel** left his fortune
to finance the Nobel Prizes. An
instructive tale, Nobel hoped that the
knowledge of his invention would help
eradicate war – optimistically believing
that mankind would never dare unleash
the destructive forces of dynamite.

Two world wars

Sweden declared a strict neutrality on
the outbreak of **World War I**, tempered
by much sympathy within the country

for Germany, sponsored by long-standing language, trade and cultural links. It was a policy agreed with the other Scandinavian monarchs, but a difficult one to pursue. Faced with British demands to enforce a blockade of Germany and the blacklisting and eventual seizure of Swedish goods at sea, the economy suffered grievously; rationing and inflation mushroomed. The **Russian Revolution** in 1917 brought further problems to Sweden. The Finns immediately declared independence, waging civil war against the Bolsheviks, and Swedish volunteers enlisted in the White army. But a conflict of interest arose when the Swedish-speaking Åland Islands wanted a return to Swedish rule rather than stay with the victorious Finns. The League of Nations overturned this claim, granting the islands to Finland.

After the war, a Liberal–Socialist coalition remained in power until 1920, when **Branting** became the first socialist prime minister. By the time of his death in 1924, the franchise had been extended to all men and women over 23 and the state-controlled alcohol system (*Systembolaget*) set up. Following the Depression of the late 1920s and early 1930s, conditions began to improve after a Social Democratic government took office for the fourth time in 1932. A **Welfare State** was rapidly established, meaning unemployment benefit, higher old-age pensions, family allowances and paid holidays. The **Saltsjöbaden Agreement** of 1938 drew up a contract between trade unions and employers to help eliminate strikes and lockouts. With war again looming, all parties agreed that Sweden should remain neutral in any struggle and rearmament was negligible, despite Hitler's apparent intentions.

World War II was slow to affect Sweden. Unlike 1914, there was little sympathy for Germany, but neutrality was again declared. The Russian invasion of Finland in 1939 brought Sweden into the picture, providing weapons, volunteers and refuge for the Finns. Regular Swedish troops were refused though, fearing intervention from either the Germans (then Russia's ally) or the Allies. Economically, the country remained sound – less dependent on imports than in World War I and with no serious shortages. The position became stickier in 1940 when the Nazis marched into Denmark and Norway, isolating Sweden. Concessions were made – German troop transit allowed, iron ore exports continued – until 1943–44 when Allied threats became more convincing than the failing German war machine. Sweden became the recipient of countless refugees from the rest of Scandinavia and the Baltic. Instrumental, too, by rescuing Hungarian Jews from the SS, was **Raoul Wallenberg**, who persuaded the Swedish government to give him diplomatic status in 1944. Unknown thousands (anything up to 35,000) of Jews in Hungary were sheltered in "neutral houses" (flying the Swedish flag), fed and clothed by Wallenberg. But when Soviet troops liberated Budapest in 1945, Wallenberg was arrested as a suspected spy and disappeared – he was later reported to have died in prison in Moscow in 1947, although unconfirmed accounts had him alive in a Soviet prison as late as 1975.

The end of the war was to provide the country with a serious crisis of conscience. Physically unscathed, Sweden was now vulnerable to Cold War politics. Proximity to the Soviet Union meant that Sweden refused to follow the other Scandinavian countries into **NATO** in 1949. The country did, however, much to Conservative disquiet, return most of the Baltic and German refugees who had fought against Russia during the war into Stalin's hands – their fate is not difficult to guess.

Postwar politics

The wartime coalition quickly gave way to a purely **Social Democratic** government committed to welfare provision and increased defence expenditure – non-participation in military alliances didn't mean a throwing down of weapons.

Sweden regained much of its international moral respect (lost directly after World War II) through the election of **Dag Hammarskjöld** as Secretary-General of the United Nations in 1953. His strong leadership greatly enhanced the prestige (and effectiveness) of the organization, participating in the solution of the Suez crisis in 1956 and the Lebanon–Jordan affair in 1958. He was killed in an air crash in 1961, towards the end of his second five-year term.

Throughout the 1950s and 1960s, domestic reform continued unabated. It was in these years that the country laid the foundations of its much-vaunted social security system, although at the time it didn't always bear close scrutiny. A **National Health Service** gave free hospital treatment, but only allowed for a small refund of doctor's fees, medicines and dental treatment – hardly as far-reaching as the British system introduced immediately after the war.

The Social Democrats stayed in power until 1976, when a **non-Socialist coalition** (Centre–Liberal–Moderate) finally unseated them. In the 44 years since 1932, the Socialists had been an integral part of government in Sweden, tempered only by periods of war and coalition. It was a remarkable record, made more so by the fact that modern politics in Sweden has never been about ideology so much as detail. Socialists and non-Socialists alike share a broad consensus on foreign policy and defence matters, and even on the need for the social welfare system.

Olof Palme

The Social Democrats regained power in 1982, subsequently devaluing the krona, introducing a price freeze and cutting back on public expenditure, but lost their majority in 1985, having to rely on Communist support to get

their bills through. Presiding over the party since 1969, and prime minister for nearly as long, was **Olof Palme**. Assassinated in February 1986, his death threw Sweden into modern European politics like no other event. Proud of their open society (Palme was returning home unguarded from the cinema), the Swedes were shocked by the gunning down of a respected politician, diplomat and pacifist. Shock turned to anger and then ridicule as the months passed without his killer being caught. Police bungling was criticized and despite the theories – Kurdish extremists, right-wing terror groups – no one was charged with the murder.

Then, finally, the police came up with **Christer Pettersson**, who – despite having no apparent motive – was identified by Palme's wife as the man who had fired the shot that night. Despite pleading his innocence, claiming he was elsewhere at the time of the murder, Pettersson was convicted of Palme's murder and jailed. There was great disquiet about the verdict, however, both at home and abroad: the three legal representatives in the original jury had voted for acquittal at the time; and it was believed that Palme's wife couldn't possibly be sure that the man who fired the shot was Pettersson, since by her own admission she had only seen him once, on the dark night in question and then only very briefly. In 1989, on appeal, Pettersson was acquitted and released. The Swedish police appear to believe that they had the right man but not enough evidence to convict; more recent evidence has pointed to South African involvement, Palme having been a vocal opponent of apartheid.

Carlsson and Bildt

Ingvar Carlsson was elected prime minister after Palme's murder, a position confirmed by the **1988 general election** when the Social Democrats – for the first time in years – scored more seats than the three non-Socialist parties combined. However, Carlsson's was still a minority government, the Social Democrats requiring the support of the Communists to command an overall majority – support that was usually forthcoming but that, with the arrival of the **Green Party** into parliament in 1988, could no longer be taken for granted. The Greens and Communists jockeyed for position as protectors of the Swedish environment, and any Social Democrat measure seen to be anti-environment cost the party Communist support. Perhaps more worryingly for the government, a series of **scandals** swept the country, leading to open speculation about a marked decline in public morality. The Bofors arms company was discovered to be involved in illegal sales to the Middle East, and early in 1990 the Indian police charged the company with paying kickbacks to politicians to secure arms contracts in the subcontinent. In addition, there was insider dealing at the stock exchange and the country's ombudsman resigned over charges of personal corruption.

The real problem for the Social Democrats, though, was the **state of the economy**. With a background of rising inflation and slow economic growth, the government announced an austerity package in January 1990 which included a two-year ban on strike action, and a wage, price and rent freeze – measures whose severity astounded most Swedes. The Greens and Communists would have none of it and the Social Democrat government resigned a month later. Although the Social Democrats were soon back in charge of a minority government, having agreed to drop the most draconian measures of their programme, the problems didn't go away.

The **general election of 1991** merely confirmed that the consensus model of politics had finally broken down. A four-party centre-right coalition came to power, led by **Carl Bildt**,

which promised tax cuts and economic regeneration, but the recession sweeping western Europe didn't pass Sweden by. Unemployment hit a post-war record and in autumn 1992 – as the British pound and Italian lira collapsed on the international money markets – the krona came under severe pressure. Savage austerity measures did little to help: VAT on food was increased, statutory holiday allowances cut, welfare budgets slashed, and – after a period of intense currency speculation – short-term marginal interest rates raised to a staggering 500 percent. In a final attempt to steady nerves, Prime Minister Bildt and the leader of the Social Democratic opposition, Ingvar Carlsson, made the astonishing announcement that they would ignore party lines and work together for the good of Sweden – and then proceeded with drastic public expenditure cuts.

However, it was too little too late. Sweden was gripped by its worst **recession** since the 1930s and unemployment reached record levels of fourteen percent. Poor economic growth coupled with generous welfare benefits, runaway speculation by Swedish firms on foreign real estate, and the world recession, all contributed to Sweden's economic woes. With the budget deficit growing faster than that of any other western industrialized country, Sweden also decided it was time to tighten up its asylum laws and introduced controversial new visa regulations to prevent a flood of Bosnian refugees.

To the millennium

Nostalgia for the good old days of Social Democracy swept the country during the general election of September 1994 and Carl Bildt's minority Conservative government was pushed out, allowing a return to power by Sweden's largest party, headed by **Ingvar Carlsson**. Social Democracy was well and truly back, with Carlsson choosing a cabinet composed equally of men and women. New social reforms were implemented, most significantly the 1995 law allowing gay couples to marry, which gives them virtually equal rights with heterosexual couples.

During 1994, negotiations on Sweden's planned membership of the **European Union** were completed and put to a referendum that saw public opinion split right down the middle. While some thought that EU membership would allow Sweden a greater influence within Europe, others were concerned that the country's standards would be forced downwards, affecting the quality of life Swedes had come to expect. However, in November the vote for membership was won, albeit by the narrowest of margins – just five percent – and Sweden joined the Union as of January 1, 1995.

Meanwhile, the welfare state was trimmed back further and new taxes announced to try to rein in the spiralling debt: unemployment benefit was cut to 75 percent of previous earnings, sick-leave benefits reduced, and lower state pension payments came into force, though Finance Minister **Göran Persson** did at least reduce taxes on food from a staggering 21 percent to 12 percent to try to retain some public support. Just when everything appeared to be under control, Carlsson announced his resignation in order to spend more time with his family, to be replaced by the domineering Persson.

Following elections in September 1998, Göran Persson clung on to power but with a much reduced majority. The election was a disaster for Sweden's Social Democrats, who recorded their worst result since World War II after losing support to the far left. Many voters complained that the Social Democrats had slashed the welfare state too far in an effort to revive the flagging economy.

Sweden today

Sweden's export-led **economy** has rendered the country extremely susceptible to changes in world finances. As globalisation has gathered momentum since the turn of the millennium, the country has faced a number of difficult choices which would have been totally unthinkable during the heady days of Social Democracy. Over the past couple of years, privatizations, mergers and general cost-cutting measures – most visibly the virtual disappearance of the post office from Swedish high streets and the much-lamented fragmentation of the national rail network – have brought Sweden more into line with countries that went through equally painful economic change decades ago. Some economists argue that it's this enforced shaking up of the business environment from outside, rather than any direct government measures, that's responsible for Sweden's improved economic fortunes since 1998 – today, Swedish markets are once again flourishing. As the country prepares for a heated debate on whether or not to adopt the **euro**, this refound growth and prosperity will be at the centre of discussion. Polls have consistently shown divided public opinion on the issue, but things look set to come to a head during 2003 when a public referendum on the question is expected. At stake, naturally, is not only Sweden's blossoming economy but also the amount of influence the Swedes can bring to bear on events inside the European Union, should the country opt to stay outside the single currency. The Prime Minister, Göran Persson, is strongly pro-euro and following his resounding general election success in September 2002, he's likely to throw his weight behind the campaign for the single currency, making a "yes" vote the most likely outcome.

Books

There's a surprisingly small number of books available in English on all matters Swedish, but what follows is a summary of some of the more readily available publications. Titles that are out of print (listed as "o/p") may be available second-hand, or on websites such as ⊛www.amazon.com. For books on Scandinavia in general, see "Basics", p.43.

History and politics

★ **Sheri Berman** *The Social Democrat Movement*. A comparison of the Swedish and German social democratic system between the First and Second World Wars.

Eric Elstob *Sweden: A Traveller's History* (o/p). An introduction to Swedish history from the year dot, with useful chapters on art, architecture and cultural life.

★ **Lee Miles** *Sweden and European Integration*. A political history of Sweden focusing on the period 1950–66, and the accession to the European Union in 1995.

Alan Palmer *Bernadotte* (o/p). First English biography for over fifty years of Napoleon's marshal, later Sweden's King Karl Johan XIV. It's lively and comprehensive, though probably for enthusiasts only.

Michael Roberts *The Early Vasas: A History of Sweden 1523–1611* (o/p). This general account of the period is complemented by Roberts' more recent *Gustavus Adolphus and the Rise of Sweden* (Addison Wesley), which, more briefly and enthusiastically, covers the period from 1612 to the king's death in 1632.

Vilhem Moberg *The Emigrants*. A series of emotionally poignant historical novels, centred on a husband and wife, that tell the story of the one million Swedes who emigrated to the United States in the late nineteenth and early twentieth centuries. Moberg himself chose to stay in Sweden, and is recognised as a major social chronicler of his time.

Franklin Daniel Scott *Sweden: The Nation's History*. A good all-round account of Sweden's history from a poor, backward warrior nation to the prosperous modern one of today.

Literature

Sigrid Cambüchen *Byron* (o/p). A highly regarded Swedish literary critic, Cambüchen has taken as her starting point the exhumation of the poet Byron's body by devotees in the 1930s – developing this into a brilliantly realized biography.

Stig Dagerman *The Games of Night*. Intense short stories by a prolific young writer who had written four novels, four plays, short stories and travel sketches by the time he was 26. He committed suicide in 1954 at the age of 31. This is some of the best of his work.

★ **Kerstin Ekman** *Under the snow*. In a remote Lapland village, a police constable investigates the death of a teacher following a drunken brawl – the dark deeds of winter finally come to light under the relentless summer sun. An excellent means of getting to grips with the mentality of northern Swedes.

Robert Fulton (trans.) *Preparations for Flight*. Eight Swedish short stories from the last 25 years, including two rare prose outings from the poet Niklas Rådström.

P.C. Jersild *A Living Soul.* Social satire based around the "experiences" of an artificially produced, bodiless human brain floating in liquid. Entertaining, provocative reading from one of Sweden's best novelists.

Sara Lidman *Naboth's Stone.* A novel set in 1880s Västerbotten, in Sweden's far north, charting the lives of settlers and farmers as the industrial age – and the railway – approaches.

Agneta Pleijel *The Dog Star.* Powerful tale of a young girl's approach to puberty. One of Pleijel's finest novels, full of fantasy and emotion.

Clive Sinclair *Augustus Rex* (o/p). August Strindberg dies in 1912 – and is then brought back to life by the Devil in 1960s Stockholm. Bawdy, imaginative and very funny treatment of Strindberg's well-documented neuroses.

Bent Söderberg *The Mysterious Barricades.* Leading Swedish novelist writes of the Mediterranean during the wars – a part of the world he's lived in for over thirty years.

Hjalmar Söderberg *Short Stories.* Twenty-six short stories from the stylish pen of Söderberg (1869–1941). Brief, ironic and eminently ripe for dipping into.

August Strindberg *Strindberg Plays: Two*; *Strindberg Plays: Three*; *Three Plays*; *Inferno/From an Occult Diary; By the Open Sea.* Strindberg is now seen as a pioneer in both his subject matter and style. His early plays were realistic in a manner not then expected of drama, and confronted themes that weren't

considered suitable viewing at all, with psychological examinations of the roles of the sexes both in and out of marriage. A fantastically prolific writer, only a fraction of his sixty plays, twelve historical dramas, five novels, short stories, numerous autobiographical volumes and poetry has ever been translated into English.

Criticism and biography

Peter Cowie *Ingmar Bergman.* New edition of a well-written and sympathetic account of the director's life and career.

Michael Meyer *Strindberg on File* (o/p). A useful brief account of Strindberg's life and work, though for a more stirring biography the same author's *Strindberg* (o/p) is the best and most approachable source.

Art and architecture

Henrik O. Andersson and Frederic Bedoure *Svensk Arkitektur* (o/p). Seminal book on Swedish architectural history from 1640 to 1970, with text in English and Swedish. Colour plates illustrate the works of each architect. One to borrow from the library.

Barbro Klein and Mats Widbom (eds) *Swedish Folk Art – All Tradition Is Change* (o/p). Lavishly produced volume on the folk art movement, illustrating the influences of local culture on art and design up to and including IKEA.

Roger Tanner (trans.) *A History of Swedish Art* (o/p). Covers architecture, design, painting and sculpture, ranging from prehistoric rock carvings to postmodernism. Well illustrated.

A brief guide to Swedish

Nearly everyone, everywhere in Sweden speaks English, the tourist offices often staffed with what appear to be native Americans (most pick up the accent from films and TV). Still, knowing the essentials of Swedish is useful, and making an effort with the language certainly impresses. If you already speak either Danish or Norwegian you should have few problems being understood; if not, then a basic knowledge of German is a help too. Of the phrasebooks, most useful is *Swedish for Travellers* (Berlltz), or use the section in *Travellers' Scandinavia* (Pan).

Pronunciation

Pronunciation is even more difficult than Danish or Norwegian. A **vowel** sound is usually long when it's the final syllable or followed by only one consonant; followed by two it's generally short. Unfamiliar combinations are:

ej as in mate.
y as in ewe.
å when short as in hot; when long as in raw.
ä when before r as in man; otherwise as in get.
ö as in fur but without the r sound.

Consonants are pronounced as in English except:
g usually as in yet; occasionally as in shut.
j, dj, gj, lj as in yet.
k before i, e, y, ä, or ö, like the Scottish loch; otherwise hard.
qu as **kv**.
sch, skj, stj as in shut; otherwise hard.
tj like loch.
z as in so.

Basics

Hello – **Hej**
Good morning – **God morgon**
Good afternoon – **God middag**
Good night – **God natt**
Goodbye – **Hejdå**
Do you speak English ? – **Talar du engelska?**
Yes – **Ja**
No – **Nej**
I don't understand – **Jag förstår inte**
Please – **Var så god**
Thank you (very much) – **Tack (så mycket)**
You're welcome – **Var så god**
Today – **I dag**
Tomorrow – **I morgon**

Day after tomorrow – **I övermorgon**
In the morning – **På morgonen**
In the afternoon – **På eftermiddagen**
In the evening – **På kvällen**

Some signs

Entrance – **Ingång**
Exit – **Utgång**
Men – **Herrar**
Women – **Damer**
Open – **Öppen, öppet**
Closed – **Stängt**
Push – **Skjut**
Pull – **Drag**
Arrival – **Ankomst**
Departure – **Avgång**
No smoking – **Rökning förbjuden**
No camping – **Tältning förbjuden**
No trespassing – **Tillträde förbjudet**
No entry – **Ingen ingång**
Police – **Polis**

Questions and directions

Where is … ? – **Var är … ?**
When? – **När?**
What? – **Vad?**
Can you direct me to … – **Skulle du kunna visa mig vägen till …**
It is/There is (Is it/Is there?) – **Det är/det finns (Är det/Finns det?)**
What time is it? – **Hur mycket är klockan?**
Big/small – **Stor/liten**
Cheap/expensive – **Billig/dyr**
Early/late – **Tidig/sen**
Hot/cold – **Varm/kall**
Near/far – **Nära/avlägsen**
Good/bad – **Bra/dålig**
Left/right – **Vänster/höger**
Vacant/occupied – **Ledig/upptagen**

A little/a lot - **Lite/en mängd**
I'd like - **Jag skulle vilja ha ...**
... a single room - **... ett enkelrum**
... a double room - **... ett dubbelrum**
How much is it? - **Vad kostar det?**
Can we camp here? - **Får vi tälta här?**
Campsite - **Campingplats**
Tent - **Tält**
Is there a youth hostel near here? - **Finns det något vandrarhem i närheten?**

Numbers

0 - **noll**	14 - **fjorton**
1 - **ett**	15 - **femton**
2 - **två**	16 - **sexton**
3 - **tre**	17 - **sjutton**
4 - **fyra**	18 - **arton**
5 - **fem**	19 - **nitton**
6 - **sex**	20 - **tjugo**
7 - **sju**	21 - **tjugoett**
8 - **åtta**	22 - **tjugotvå**
9 - **nio**	30 - **trettio**
10 - **tio**	40 - **fyrtio**
11 - **elva**	50 - **femtio**
12 - **tolv**	60 - **sextio**
13 - **tretton**	70 - **sjuttio**

80 - **åttio**	200 - **tvåhundra**
90 - **nittio**	500 - **femhundra**
100 - **hundra**	1000 - **tusen**
101 - **hundraett**	

Days and months

Monday - **måndag**
Tuesday - **tisdag**
Wednesday - **onsdag**
Thursday - **torsdag**
Friday - **fredag**
Saturday - **lördag**
Sunday - **söndag**
January - **januari**
February - **februari**
March - **mars**
April - **april**
May - **maj**
June - **juni**
July - **juli**
August - **augusti**
September - **september**
October - **oktober**
November - **november**
December - **december**
(Days and months are never capitalized)

Glossary of Swedish terms and words

Bastu - Sauna
Berg - Mountain
Bokhandel - Bookshop
Bro - Bridge
Cykelstig - Cycle path
Dal - Valley
Domkyrka - Cathedral
Drottning - Queen (as in Drottninggatan, Queen Street)
Färja - Ferry
Gamla - Old (as in Gamla Stan, old town)
Gata (gt) - Street
Hamnen - Harbour
Järnvägsstation - Railway station
Klockan (kl) - o'clock
Kyrka - Church
Lilla - Little (as in Lilla Torget, small square)
Muséet - Museum

Pressbyrå - Newsagent
Rabatt - Rebate/discount
Rea - Sales (and Vrakpriser, bargain)
Riksdagshus - Parliament building
Sjö - Lake
Skog - Forest
Slott - Castle
Spår - Platform (at railway station)
Stadshus - Town hall
Stora - Great/big (as in Storatorget, main square)
Strand - Beach
Stugor - Chalet, cottage
Torg - Central town square, usually the scene of daily/weekly markets
Universitet - University
Väg (v) - Road

3.1

Stockholm and around

S tockholm is one of the most beautiful cities in Europe. Built on no fewer than fourteen islands, where the fresh water of Lake Mälaren meets the brackish Baltic Sea, it has clean air and open space in plentiful supply: one-third of the area inside the city limits is made up of water, another third of parks and woodland, and it's easy to find a quiet corner to enjoy what's one of Europe's saner and more civilized capitals. Broad boulevards lined with elegant buildings are reflected in the deep blue water of the Baltic, with rows of painted wooden houseboats moored alongside the city's cobbled waterfront, while the world's first urban national park offers a unique opportunity to swim and fish virtually in the city centre.

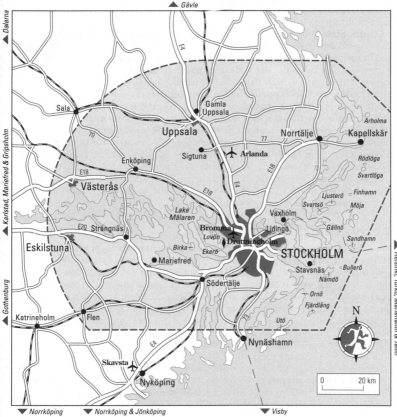

You can appreciate Stockholm's unique geography by taking one of a number of boat trips around the city and through the **Stockholm archipelago** – a staggering 24,000 islands, rocks and skerries, as the Swedish mainland slowly dissolves into the Baltic Sea. A boat trip inland along the serene waters of Lake Mälaren is another easy day-trip, with the target either of seventeenth-century **Drottningholm**, the Swedish royal residence, right on the lakeside or, further along the lake, the castle of **Gripsholm** at Mariefred. Also within day-trip range is the ancient Swedish capital and medieval university town of **Uppsala**, easily reached from Stockholm by frequent trains, as well as the odd boat.

Stockholm

"It is not a city at all", he said with intensity. "It is ridiculous to think of itself as a city. It is simply a rather large village, set in the middle of some forest and some lakes. You wonder what it thinks it is doing there, looking so important."

Ingmar Bergman interviewed by James Baldwin.

STOCKHOLM often feels like two cities. Its self-important status as Sweden's most forward-looking commercial centre can seem at odds with the almost pastoral feel of its wide open spaces and expanses of open water. First impressions can be of a distant and unwelcoming place – provincial Swedes often call it the Ice Queen – but stick around for the weekend and you'll see another side to Stockholm, when the population really lets its hair down.

Gamla Stan (pronounced "Gam-la Starn", meaning Old Town) was the site of the original settlement of Stockholm. Today it's an atmospheric mixture of pomp and history, with ceremonial buildings surrounded by a lattice of medieval lanes and alleyways. Close by to the east is the tiny island of **Skeppsholmen**, with fantastic views of the curving waterfront, while to the north is the modern centre, **Norrmalm**, with its shopping malls, huge department stores and conspicuous wealth, plus the lively Kungsträdgården park and the transport hub of Central Station. East of Norrmalm is the grand residential area of **Östermalm**, southeast of which is the green park island of **Djurgården**, home to two of Stockholm's best-known attractions: the extraordinary seventeenth-century warship, **Vasa**, and **Skansen**, Europe's oldest open-air museum. South of Gamla Stan, the island of **Södermalm** was traditionally Stockholm's working-class area; it's known today for its cool bars and restaurants and lively streetlife. To the west of the centre is **Kungsholmen** island, which is fast coming to rival its southern neighbour with its trendy eateries and drinking establishments.

Arrival and information

Most planes – international and domestic – arrive at **Arlanda airport**, 45km north of Stockholm. A high-speed rail link, the **Arlanda Express**, connects the airport with the city every fifteen minutes (daily from 5.05am to 12.35am; 20min; 140kr), and is the easiest way to get into Stockholm. A cheaper option is to take the **airport buses**, Flygbussarna (daily 6.30am–11.45pm; 35min; 80kr), which run at least once every ten minutes from the airport to the Cityterminalen (Stockholm's long-distance bus station; see below), a journey time of about forty minutes; buy your ticket on the bus. **Taxis** into Stockholm should cost around 350kr, an affordable alternative for a group – choose the ones that have prices displayed in their back windows to avoid being ripped off.

Some domestic flights operated by Braathens Malmö Aviation arrive at the more central **Bromma airport**, to the northwest of the city midway between Brommaplan and Sundbybergs centrum T-bana stations. Bromma is also connected to the Cityterminalen by Flygbussarna – buses run in connection with flight arrivals and departures (20min; 60kr). Ryanair flights arrive at **Skavsta airport**, 100km to the south of the capital close to the town of Nyköping, as well as at **Västerås**, 100km west of Stockholm on Lake Mälaren; buses operate in conjunction with flight arrivals and departures (both 80min; 100kr) and arrive in Stockholm at the Cityterminalen.

By **train**, you'll arrive at and depart from **Central Station**, a cavernous structure on Vasagatan in the Norrmalm district. Inside there's a Forex **money exchange** office and a very useful **room-booking service**, Hotellcentralen (see "Accommodation", p.442).

By **bus**, your arrival point will be the huge glass structure known as the **Cityterminalen**, a high-tech bus terminal adjacent to Central Station and reached by a series of escalators and walkways from the northern end of the main hall. It handles all bus services: airport and ferry shuttle services, and domestic and international buses. There's also an exchange office.

There are two main **ferry** companies connecting Stockholm with Helsinki, Turku and Mariehamn in Finland. **Viking Line** (🖰www.vikingline.se) ferries dock at Vikingterminalen on the island of Södermalm, from where you can catch a bus to Slussen for frequent T-bana trains to T-Centralen. **Silja Line** (🖰www.silja.com) ferries arrive on the northeastern edge of the city at Siljaterminalen; it's a short walk to either Gärdet or Ropsten T-bana stations on the red line, from where you can get a train into town. **Tallink** (🖰www.tallink.se) sailings from Tallinn in Estonia arrive at Frihamnen at the end of the #1 bus route, which will take you all the way into town. If you're heading for Central Station, get off at the junction of Kungsgatan and Vasagatan and walk the short distance from there; the bus goes directly past the Cityterminalen. If you're **leaving Stockholm** by ferry, note the Swedish names for destinations: Helsinki is "Helsingfors"; Turku, confusingly, is "Åbo".

Information

You should be able to pick up a map of the city at most points of arrival, but it's still worth dropping in to Sweden House, the city's **tourist office**; it's in in the Kulturhuset in Sergels Torg (see p.450); (June–Aug Mon–Fri 8am–7pm, Sat & Sun 9am–5pm; Sept–May Mon–Fri 9am–6pm, Sat & Sun 10am–3pm; ☎08/789 24 90, 🖰www.stockholmtown.com). Fistfuls of free information are available, and you'll find a functional (if tiny) **map** in most of the brochures and booklets – though it's probably worth paying 20kr for the larger plan of Stockholm and the surrounding area produced by the Stockholm Information Service. These are on sale at the office, as are Stockholm Cards (see p.440). Look out also for *What's On*, a free listings and entertainment guide. From the tourist office it's a 5–10min walk south along Kungsträdgårdsgatan and over Strömbron bridge to Slottsbacken 10, where the **Sweden Bookshop** (Mon-Fri 10am-6pm, Sat 11am-3pm; ☎08/453 78 00, 🖰www.swedenbookshop.com) run by the Swedish Institute (🖰www.si.se) has an unsurpassed stock of English-language books on Sweden as well as calendars, videos and Sweden-related gifts and souvenirs.

City transport

Stockholm winds its way confusingly across islands, over water and through parkland: the best way to get to grips with it is to equip yourself with a map and walk – it only takes about half an hour to cross central Stockholm on foot. Sooner or later, though, you'll have to use some form of **transport** and, while routes are easy enough to master, there's a bewildering array of passes and **discount cards** available. One thing to try to avoid is paying as you go on the city's transport system – a very expensive business. The city is zoned, a trip within one zone costing 20kr, with single **tickets** valid within that zone for one hour; cross a zone and it's another 10kr. Most journeys worth making cost 30kr.

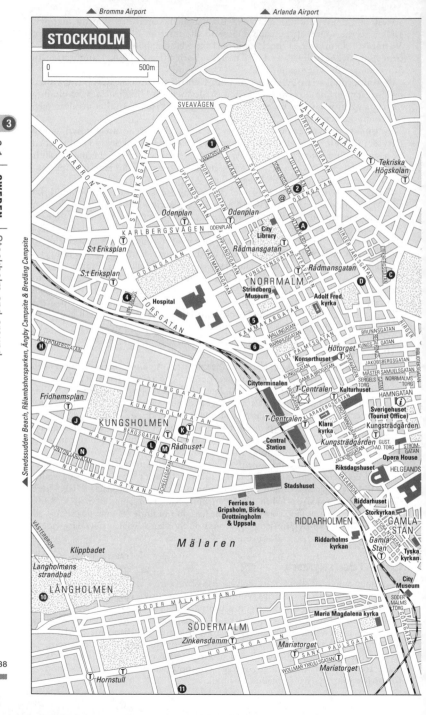

STOCKHOLM

▲ Bromma Airport   ▲ Arlanda Airport

0   500m

SVEAVÄGEN

SOLNABRON

VALLHALLAVÄGEN
BIRGER JARLSGATAN

① Tekriska Högskolan

ODENGATAN

②

Odenplan   Odenplan

KARLBERGSVÄGEN   ODENPLAN

City Library

Ⓐ

S:t Eriksplan

S:t Eriksplan

Rådmansgatan

Rådmansgatan

Ⓒ

NORRMALM   Ⓓ

Strindberg Museum

Adolf Fred. kyrka

④   Hospital

⑤

⑥

Hötorget

Konserthuset

BRUNNSGATAN

H STRÖMERSGATAN

Cityterminalen

Cityterminalen   T-Centralen   Kulturhuset

Fridhemsplan   Ⓙ   T-Centralen

Sverigehuset (Tourist Office)   Kungsträdgården

KUNGSHOLMEN   Klara kyrka

Kungsträdgården

Ⓚ   Ⓣ

Ⓝ   Ⓛ Ⓜ Rådhuset   Central Station   Opera House

Riksdagshuset   HELGEANDS

Stadshuset

Ferries to Gripsholm, Birka, Drottningholm & Uppsala   Riddarhuset

RIDDARHOLMEN   Storkyrkan   GAMLA STAN

Mälaren   Riddarholms kyrkan   Gamla Stan

Klippbadet   Tyska kyrkan

Langholmens strandbad   City Museum

⑩   LÅNGHOLMEN   SÖDER MALMS TORG

SÖDER MÄLARSTRAND   Maria Magdalena kyrka

SÖDERMALM

Zinkensdamm   Mariatorget

Hornstull   Mariatorget

⑪

◀ Smedsudden Beach, Rålambshovsparken, Ängby Campsite & Bredäng Campsite

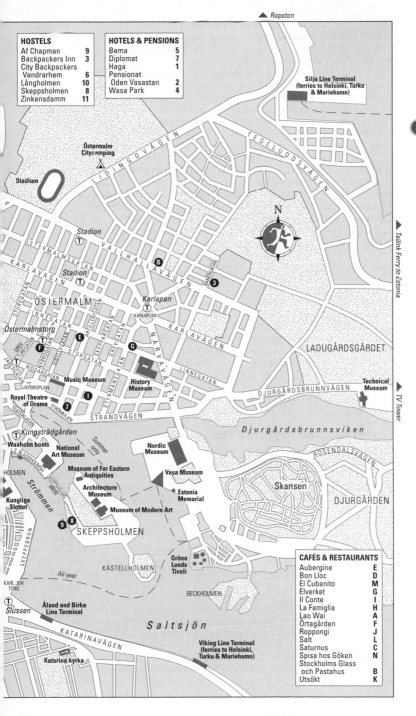

HOSTELS

Af Chapman	9
Backpackers Inn	3
City Backpackers Vandrarhem	6
Långholmen	10
Skeppsholmen	8
Zinkensdamm	11

HOTELS & PENSIONS

Bema	5
Diplomat	7
Haga Pensionat	1
Oden Vasastan	2
Wasa Park	4

Silja Line Terminal
(ferries to Helsinki, Turku
& Mariehamn)

Östermalm
Citycamping

Stadium

Östermalm Citycamping

LIDINGÖVÄGEN

TEGELUDDSVÄGEN

Stadion Ⓣ

VALLHALLAVÄGEN

ÖSTERMALMSGATAN

KARLAVÄGEN

Stadion Ⓣ

Ⓑ

BANÉRGATAN

③

N

ÖSTERMALM

Karlaplan

Ⓣ KARLAPLAN

STURGATAN

LINNÉGATAN

ARTILLERIGATAN

SKEPPARGATAN

GREVGATAN

KARLAVÄGEN

NARVAVÄGEN

LINNÉGATAN

LADUGÅRDSGÄRDET

Östermalmstorg

Ⓣ

Ⓕ

Ⓔ

Ⓖ

STORGATAN

STYRMANSGATAN

GROVGATAN

NYBROGATAN

SIBYLLEGATAN

JAKOBSGATAN

Ⓣ RIDDARGATAN

NYBROPLAN

Music Museum

Ⓘ

History
Museum

Ⓗ

DJURGÅRDSBRUNNVÄGEN

Technical
Museum

Royal Theatre
of Drama

Ⓣ

STRÖMKAJEN

STRANDVÄGEN

Ⓣ Kungsträdgården

Waxholm boats

S. BLASIEHOLMSH.

National
Art Museum

Summer only

Nordic
Museum

Djurgårdsbrunnsviken

ROSENDALSVÄGEN

HOLMEN

Strömmen

SKEPPSHOLMSBRON

Museum of Far Eastern
Antiquities

Vasa Museum

Skansen

Kungliga
Slottet

Architecture
Museum

Estonia
Memorial

DJURGÅRDEN

Museum of Modern Art

SKEPPSBRON

Ⓐ

Ⓑ

SKEPPSHOLMEN

KARL JOH
TORG

Ⓣ

All year

Slussen

Ⓣ

KASTELLHOLMEN

Gröna
Lunds
Tivoli

BECKHOLMEN

Åland and Birka
Line Terminal

KATARINAVÄGEN

Saltsjön

Katarina kyrka

Viking Line Terminal
(ferries to Helsinki,
Turku & Mariehamn)

CAFÉS & RESTAURANTS

Aubergine	E
Bon Lloc	D
El Cubanito	M
Elverket	G
Il Conte	I
La Famiglia	H
Lao Wai	A
Örtagården	F
Roppongi	J
Salt	L
Saturnus	C
Spisa hos Göken	N
Stockholms Glass och Pastahus	B
Utsökt	K

City bus, local train and T-bana **timetables** are easily obtained from the SL-Centers dotted around the city (see below); timetables for main-line trains operated by Swedish Railways can be found at Central Station. For public transport **information**, call ☏08/600 10 00.

Storstockholms Lokaltrafik (SL; ⊛www.sl.se) operate a comprehensive system of buses and trains (underground and regional) that extends well out of the city centre. For information and timetables, the main **SL-Center** (Mon–Fri 7am–6.30pm, Sat & Sun 10am–5pm) is at Sergels Torg just by the entrance to T-Centralen (see "Listings", p.464, for other branches), and has timetables for the city's buses, metro, regional trains and archipelago boats.

The quickest and most useful form of transport both around the centre and out to the suburbs is Stockholm's metro system, the Tunnelbana or **T-bana** (⊛www.tunnelbana.com). There are three main lines (red, green and blue) and a smattering of branches; station entrances are marked with a blue letter "T" on a white background. Trains run from early morning until around midnight (and all through the night on Fridays and Saturdays). All branches of the T-bana meet at **T-Centralen**, the metro station directly below Central Station. The **Pendeltågen** regional trains that run throughout Greater Stockholm leave from the main train platforms on the ground level – not from underground platforms. The T-bana is something of an artistic venture too: T-Centralen is a huge papier-mâché cave, while Kungsträdgården station is littered with statues, spotlights and fountains.

Bus routes can be less direct due to Stockholm's islands and central pedestrianization – consult the route map on the back of the *Stockholms innerstad* bus timetable for help. You board buses at the front, get off at the back or in the middle, and buy tickets from the driver. **Night buses** replace the T-bana after midnight, except on Friday and Saturday nights.

From outside the *Grand Hotel* on Strömkajen, **ferries** provide access to the sprawling archipelago and also link some of the central islands: Djurgården is connected with Skeppsholmen and Nybroplan, the latter a small square behind the *Grand* in Norrmalm (summer only), and with Skeppsbron in Gamla Stan (all year round). **Cruises** on Lake Mälaren leave from outside the Stadshuset at the southeastern tip of Kungsholmen, and city boat tours leave from outside the *Grand Hotel* and from around the corner on Nybroplan.

Travel passes and tickets

If you're planning to do any sightseeing at all, the best pass to have is the **Stockholm Card** (*Stockholmskortet*), which gives unlimited travel on city buses, T-bana and regional trains and the Djurgården ferry, as well as free sightseeing tours, museum entry and parking. Cards last for 24, 48 or 72 hours (220kr/380kr/540kr respectively); each card covers an adult and two children under seven. They're sold undated, then stamped on first use. You can buy the card from the tourist office, from Hotellcentralen (see p.437) in Central Station or from SL Centers.

Among the other options, the **1-day card** is valid for 24 hours (80kr) and the **3-day card** for 72 hours (150kr); these cover unlimited travel by bus, T-bana and regional train, plus travel on ferries to Djurgården and the city's one tram route. These cards were formerly known as tourist cards and you may still find some confusion surrounding the new names. Discounts for under-18s or over-65s bring the cost down to 45kr (1 day) and 90kr (3 days). These cards can be bought from Pressbyrå newsagents or SL travel centres. Alternatively, you can buy a strip of twenty reduced price SL **ticket coupons** (*rabattkuponger*) for 110kr – you'll have to stamp at least two for each journey. Buy them at any T-bana station.

Finally, if you're staying in Stockholm for a week or more it's worth considering a **monthly card** (*Månadskort*), which allows unlimited travel on virtually everything that moves throughout the whole of Greater Stockholm for a mere 500kr. If you're

STOCKHOLM TUNNELBANA

spending several months in the city at a time it's probably worth buying a **season card** (*Säsongskort*) – prices vary depending on the time of year. Both these cards can be bought from any SL-Center.

One-way tickets for the **ferries** to Djurgården cost a basic 20kr – tickets for longer trips into the **archipelago** cost up to 100kr. Tickets can be bought on board or in advance from the offices of the main ferry company, Waxholms Ångfartygs AB (known as *Waxholmsbolaget*), on Strömkajen outside the *Grand Hotel*. If you intend to spend a week or so exploring the islands of the archipelago, it may be worth buying a special pass – see p.468 for details.

Bikes, taxis and parking

Bike rental is available from Skepp O'Hoj at Galärvarvsvägen 2 (☎08/660 57 57), centrally located just over the bridge to Djurgården, or from Cykelstället Servicedepån at Scheelegatan 30 (☎08/651 00 66); at both places, reckon on paying 200kr per day or 800kr per week for the latest mountain bike, less for a bone shaker – the latter also has an outlet on Kungsholmen at Kungsholmsgatan 34.

To get a **taxi**, either try to hail one in the street or, more reliably, call one of the four main operators: Taxi Stockholm (☎08/15 00 00), Taxi Kurir (☎08/30 00 00), Top Cab (☎08/33 33 33) or Taxi 020 (☎020/93 93 93). If you do phone for a cab, the meter will show around 35kr before you even get in and will continue to race upwards at an alarming speed – a trip across the city centre should be in the region of 150–200kr.

If you're driving, be warned that **parking** in Stockholm is a hazardous business. First, it's forbidden to park within ten metres of a road junction, however small; nor can you park within the same distance of a pedestrian crossing; and on one particular night of the week (as specified on the rectangular yellow street signs) no parking is allowed, to permit street cleaning and, in winter, snow clearance. You should never stop in a bus lane or in a loading zone. Also, the closer to the city centre you park the more expensive it will be. For details on **car rental**, see p.463.

Accommodation

Stockholm has **accommodation** to suit all tastes and budgets, from elegant hotels with waterfront views to some unusual youth hostels. Demand is high, however, particularly from mid-June to mid-August, and it's always advisable to book at least your first night's accommodation in advance – this can be done either by calling the hotel or hostel direct or, alternatively, through the excellent **Hotellcentralen**, the room-booking service in the main hall of Central Station (daily: June–Aug 8am–8pm; Sept–May 9am–6pm; ☎08/789 24 90, ✉hotels@stoinfo.se),which has comprehensive hotel and hostel listings, plus information on the latest special offers; if you book in person they charge a fee of 50kr per hotel room (20kr for a hostel room). Between mid-June and mid-August (and at weekends year-round), Hotellcentralen also sells the **Stockholm a la carte Package**, which gives reduced rates on accommodation for each night's stay: deals start at a very economical 450kr per person in a twin room with breakfast, rising to around 870kr in more upmarket hotels. By calling in advance you can choose a particular hotel – on the day, you get whatever's available. Unless otherwise stated, for hotels and pensions in **Södermalm** see the map on p.456; for those in **Gamla Stan and Norrmalm**, see the map on p.445; all other places are on the main Stockholm map, pp.438–439. All hostels are on the main Stockholm map.

Hotels and pensions

In summer, when business trade dwindles, it's a buyer's market in Stockholm, with double rooms going for as little as 580kr. The cheapest **hotels** and **pensions** are generally found to the north of Cityterminalen in the streets to the west of Adolf Fredriks kyrka, but don't rule out the more expensive places either – there are some attractive weekend and summer prices that can make a spot of luxury a little more affordable. All the following places include breakfast in the price unless otherwise stated and, where applicable, we've given the lower summer and non-summer weekend rate followed by the higher weekday rate outside of summer.

Anno 1647 Mariagränd 3, near Slussen, Södermalm ☎08/442 16 80, ⓦwww.swedenhotels.se. A seventeenth-century building handy for the Old Town, with pine floors and period furniture; not recommended for people with disabilities. T-bana Slussen. ❻/❺

Bema Upplandsgatan 13 ☎08/23 26 75, ☎20 53 58. Small pension-style hotel ten minutes' walk north from the station. Twelve en-suite rooms, with modern Swedish decor and beechwood furniture. Summer and weekend deals bring the cost down to the bottom of the ❷ price-code range. Bus #47 or #69 from Central Station. ❸/❷

Central Vasagatan 38, Norrmalm ☎08/566 208 00, ⓦwww.centralhotel.se. Modern hotel that's one of the cheapest of those around the station. T-bana T-Centralen. ❻/❹

Columbus Tjärhovsgatan 11, Södermalm ☎08/503 112 00, ⓦwww.columbus.se. Simple rooms with shared bathrooms in a building that looks like a school. T-bana Medborgarplatsen. ❸/❹

Diplomat Strandvägen 7C ☎08/459 68 00, ⓦwww.diplomathotel.com. Early twentieth-century townhouse with top-of-the-range suites and views out over Stockholm's grandest boulevard and inner harbour. It's not cheap, though much better value than the cheaper rooms at the *Grand* (see opposite). Out of season, rooms start at 2195kr, but there are summer and weekend reductions. T-bana Östermalmstorg or bus #47 or #69. ❻/❺

First Hotel Reisen Skeppsbron 12, Gamla Stan ☎08/22 32 60, ⓦwww.firsthotels.com. Traditional place with heavy wood-panelled interior. All rooms have baths; some also have excellent views over the Stockholm waterfront. T-bana Gamla Stan or Slussen. ❻

Grand Södra Blasieholmshamnen 8, Norrmalm ☎08/679 35 00, ⓦwww.grandhotel.se. Set in a late nineteenth-century harbourside building overlooking Gamla Stan, Stockholm's most refined hotel provides the last word in luxury at world-class prices (even with reductions). Only worth it if you're staying in the best rooms – otherwise, the *Diplomat* has suites with a view for the same price as rooms here. Out-of-season double rooms start at 3295kr, and there are summer and weekend reductions. T-bana Kungsträdgården. ❺

Haga Hagagatan 29 ☎08/545 473 00, ⓦwww.hagahotel.se. Thirty-eight modern, good-value rooms in a quiet road. A little out of the centre, but within striking distance of the top of Sveavägen. T-bana Odenplan. ❹

Mälardrottningen Riddarholmen (see Gamla Stan Map) ☎08/545 187 80, ⓦwww.malardrottningen.se. This elegant white ship moored by the side of the island of Riddarholmen was formerly American millionairess Barbara Hutton's gin palace. Its cabin-style rooms are in need of a lick of paint and a bit of a polish, but still represent good value for such a central location. T-bana Gamla Stan. ❺

Pensionat Oden Söder Hornsgatan 66B, Södermalm ☎08/612 43 49, ⓦwww.pensionat.nu. A good-value choice in the heart of Södermalm, with tastefully decorated rooms at excellent prices. T-bana Mariatorget. ❸

Pensionat Oden Vasastan Odengatan 38 ☎08/612 43 49, ⓦwww.pensionat.nu. Second-floor hotel in a good and central location, with elegant, excellent-value modern rooms. T-bana Rådmansgatan. ❸

Queen's Drottninggatan 71A, Norrmalm ☎08/24 94 60, ⓦwww.queenshotel.se. Shabby mid-range pension-style hotel, with some en-suite rooms and a breakfast buffet. Summer and weekend deals. T-bana Hötorget. ❸

Rica City Gamla Stan Lilla Nygatan 25, Gamla Stan ☎08/723 72 50, ⓦwww.rica.se. Wonderfully situated, elegant building with rooms to match; all 51 are individually decorated. Really the only halfway affordable Gamla Stan option. T-bana Gamla Stan. ❻

Stockholm Norrmalmstorg 1, Norrmalm ☎08/440 57 60, ⓦwww.hotelstockholm.se. Penthouse hotel on the top floor of a central office building, with good views out over Strandvägen and the harbour. Squeaky wooden floors and faded bathrooms. T-bana Östermalmstorg or Kungsträdgården. ❻

Tre Små Rum Högbergsgatan 81, Södermalm ☎08/641 23 71, ⓦwww.tresmarum.se. Despite the name, there are actually seven small rooms (not three) at 695kr. Clean, modern and simple, with a help-yourself breakfast from the kitchen fridge. Very popular and often full. T-bana Mariatorget. ❷

Wasa Park St Eriksplan 1 ☎08/545 453 00, ⓕ545 453 01. A clean, simple hotel; a bit out of the centre but cheap. No en-suite rooms. Summer and weekend deals. T-bana St Eriksplan. ❷

Zinkensdamm Zinkens Väg 20, Södermalm ☎08/616 81 10, ⓦwww.zinkensdamm.com. Pleasant hotel rooms in a separate wing of the youth hostel (see p.444). T-bana Hornstull or Zinkensdamm. ❺

Hostels and private rooms

Stockholm has a wide range of good, well-run **hostel** accommodation, costing from 120kr to 200kr a night per person. There are several official STF youth hostels in the city, two of which – *Af Chapman* and *Långholmen* – are among the best in Sweden. You'll have to plan ahead if you want to stay at most of the hostels listed below, particularly in summer.

For a **private room**, contact Hotelltjänst, Vasagatan 15–17 (☎08/10 44 67), just a few minutes' walk from Central Station. Tell them how much you want to pay, and where you want to stay, and you should land somewhere with a fridge and cooking facilities for around 250kr per person per night.

Af Chapman Flaggmansvägen 8, Skeppsholmen ☎08/463 2266, ⓦwww.stfchapman.com. This square-rigged 1888 ship – a landmark in its own right – has unsurpassed views over Gamla Stan, at least for the price. Without an advance reservation (try a fortnight before you arrive), the chances of a

space in summer are slim. Open all year. Lockout 11am–3pm. T-bana Kungsträdgården or bus #65 from Central Station.

Backpackers Inn Banérgatan 56, Östermalm ☎08/660 75 15, ⓕ665 40 39. Reasonably central former school residence with 300 beds in large

dorms, plus laundry facilities. Open late June to early Aug. T-bana Karlaplan (Valhallavägen exit) or bus #4.
City Backpackers Vandrarhem Upplandsgatan 2A ☎08/20 69 20, ⊛www.citybackpackers.se. Five minutes from the central station, this is a friendly, very central non-HI hostel with 65 beds and some double rooms (❶). The owners and staff have travelled widely, and can provide lots of advice for backpackers; all-day Internet access is available, also cable TV and sauna. Open all year. T-bana T-Centralen.
Långholmen Kronohäktet, Långholmen ☎08/668 05 10, ⊛www.langholmen.com. Stockholm's grandest STF hostel is set on the island of Långholmen inside an old prison building (1724), the cells converted into smart hostel rooms with their original (extremely small) windows. Fantastic views of Stockholm and Lake Mälaren, beaches

nearby, and the whole of Södermalm on the doorstep. T-bana Hornstull and follow the signs.
Skeppsholmen Flaggmansvägen 8, Skeppsholmen ☎08/463 22 66, ⊛www.stfchapman.com. Located at the foot of the gangplank to *Af Chapman*, this is an immensely popular hostel housed in a former craftsman's workshop – you're unlikely to get in without a reservation. There are no kitchen or laundry facilities, but there's no lockout either. T-bana Kungsträdgården or bus #65.
Zinkensdamm Zinkens väg 20, Södermalm ☎08/616 81 00, ⊛www.zinkensdamm.com. Huge hostel with 490 beds and kitchen and laundry facilities. It's in an excellent location for exploring Södermalm, though a 30min walk from the city centre. No lockout. T-bana Hornstull or Zinkensdamm.

Camping

With the nearest year-round sites well out of the city centre, **camping** in Stockholm can prove a bit of a drag. The tourist offices provide free booklets detailing facilities at all Stockholm's campsites, and the sites below represent the best the city has to offer. With the exception of the site in Östermalm, they're all a 45min (or thereabouts) T-bana ride from the city centre. In July and August it costs around 100kr for two people to pitch a tent; half that the rest of the year.

Ängby ☎08/37 04 20, ⊛www.angbycamping.se. West of the city on the lakeshore. Open all year, but phone ahead to book between September and April. T-bana Ängbyplan on the green line towards Hässelby and turn left out of the station.
Bredäng ☎08/97 70 71, ⊛www.camping.se/plats /A04. Southwest of the city with views over Lake Mälaren. Open all year, but phone ahead to book

Nov–April. T-bana Bredäng on the red line towards Norsborg.
Östermalm Citycamping ☎08/10 29 03. The most centrally located of all Stockholm's campsites but only open from late June to mid-Aug. Adjacent to the Östermalm sportsground and walkable from the city centre in around 30min. T-bana Stadion.

The City

Visitors have been responding to Stockholm's charms for 150 years, and today the combination of elegant Old Town architecture, wide tree-lined boulevards and great expanses of open water right in the centre all conspire to offer a city panorama unparalleled anywhere in Europe. Seeing the sights is straightforward: everything is easy to get to, opening hours are long, and the city is a relaxed and spacious place to wander. There's also a bewildering range of museums and galleries, the best of which are described below.

Old Stockholm: Gamla Stan and Riddarholmen

Three islands make up the **oldest part of Stockholm** – Riddarholmen, Staden and Helgeandsholmen – a historic cluster of seventeenth- and eighteenth-century Renaissance buildings backed by narrow medieval alleys. Here, on these three adjoining polyps of land, Birger Jarl erected the first fortification in 1255, and for centuries this was the nucleus of the first city of Stockholm. Rumours abound about the derivation of the name Stockholm, but it's generally thought that the name means "island cleared of trees" – trees on the island that is now home to Gamla Stan were probably felled to make way for settlers. Incidentally, today the words *holm* ("island"), and *stock* ("log"), are still in common use.

Strictly speaking, the **Gamla Stan** (Old Town) area refers only to the streets of the largest island, **Staden**, although in practice the name is usually applied to all three islands. Nowadays Gamla Stan is primarily a tourist city, a rich tableau of cultural history embodied by the royal palace, parliament and cathedral. The central spider's web, especially if you approach it over the bridges of Norrbron or Riksbron, invokes potent images of the past, with sprawling, monumental buildings and airy churches forming a protective girdle around the narrow streets. The tall

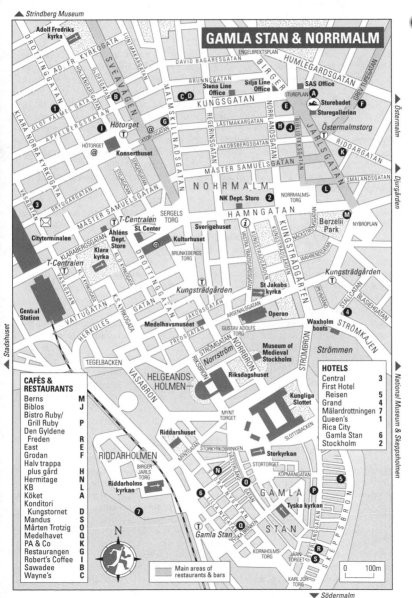

445

dark houses in the centre were mostly those of wealthy merchants, still picked out today by intricate doorways and portals bearing coats of arms. Some of the alleys in between are the skinniest thoroughfares imaginable, steeply stepped between battered walls; others are covered passageways linking leaning buildings. It's easy to spend hours wandering around here, although the atmosphere these days is not so much medieval as mercenary: there's a dense concentration of antique shops, art showrooms and chichi cellar restaurants, though the frontages don't really intrude upon the otherwise light-starved streets. Not surprisingly, this is the most exclusive part of Stockholm in which to live.

The Riksdagshuset and the Museum of Medieval Stockholm

Entering or leaving the Old Town, you're bound to pass the Swedish parliament building, the **Riksdagshuset** (May–Aug Mon–Fri guided tours in English at noon & 1.30pm; free). Despite the assassination of the former Swedish Prime Minister, Olof Palme, in 1986 (see p.451), Swedish politicians still go freely about their business and you'll often see them nipping in and out of the building or lunching in one of the nearby restaurants. The Riksdagshuset itself was completely restored in the 1970s (though only seventy years old even then), and today the grand columned front entrance (seen to best effect from Norrbron) is hardly ever used, the business end being the new glassy bulge at the back – it's round here that the guided tours circulate. This being Sweden, the building contains a crèche, and the seating in the chamber itself is in healthy, non-adversarial rows, with members grouped by constituency rather than party.

In front of the Riksdagshuset, accessible by a set of steps leading down from Norrbron, the **Museum of Medieval Stockholm** (*Medeltidsmuseum*; July–Aug Fri–Mon 11am–4pm, Tues–Thurs 11am–6pm; Sept–June Tues–Sun 11am–4pm, Wed 11am–6pm; ⊛www.medeltidsmuseet.stockholm.se; 40kr) features the medieval ruins, tunnels and walls discovered during excavations under the parliament building. These remains have been incorporated into a fascinating walk-through underground exhibition, with reconstructed houses to poke around in, models and pictures, boats, skeletons and street scenes, all with detailed English labels.

Kungliga Slottet

South across a second section of bridges is the most distinctive monumental building in Stockholm, **Kungliga Slottet** (the Royal Palace; ⊛www.royalcourt.se), a low, yellowy-brown structure whose two front arms stretch down towards the water. Stockholm's old Tre Kronor (Three Crowns) castle burned down at the beginning of King Karl XII's reign, leaving his architect, Tessin the Younger, with a clean slate on which to design his simple but beautiful Renaissance structure. Finished in 1754, the palace is a striking achievement: uniform and sombre from the outside, its magnificent Baroque and Rococo interior is a swirl of state rooms and museums. The sheer size and limited opening hours conspire against seeing everything at once.

The **Apartments** (mid-May to Aug daily 10am–4pm; Sept–April Tues–Sun noon–3pm; 70kr) form a relentlessly linear collection of furniture and tapestries. It's all basically Rent-a-Palace stuff, too sumptuous to take in and inspirational only in terms of its colossal size. The **Treasury** (same times; 70kr), on the other hand, is certainly worthy of the name, with its ranks of jewel-studded crowns: the oldest is that of Karl X (1650); the most charming are intricately worked crowns belonging to princesses Sofia (1771) and Eugëne (1860). Also worth catching is the **Armoury** (June–Aug daily 10am–5pm; Sept–May Tues, Wed & Fri–Sun 11am–5pm, Thurs 11am–8pm; ⊛www.lsh.se/livrustkammaren/Thehela.htm; 65kr), which is less to do with weapons and more to do with ceremony, featuring suits of armour, costumes and horse-drawn carriages from the sixteenth century onwards. It certainly couldn't be accused of skipping over historical detail. King Gustav II Adolf died in the Battle of Lützen in 1632 and the museum displays his horse (stuffed) and the blood- and mud-spattered garments retrieved after the enemy had stripped him down to his underwear on the battlefield. For those with the energy, the **Museum Tre Kronor** (same times as Apartments; 70kr) contains part of the older Tre Kronor castle, whose ruins lie beneath the present building, and exhibitions on the castle's role as a medieval stronghold.

Into Gamla Stan: Stortorget and around

Beyond the Royal Palace, the streets suddenly get narrower and darker and you're into Gamla Stan proper. Here, the highest point of old Stockholm is crowned by **Storkyrkan** (mid-May to mid-Sept daily 9am 6pm; 10kr; rest of the year daily 9am–4pm; free), the "Great Church", consecrated in 1306. Pedantically speaking, Stockholm has no cathedral, but this rectangular brick church fulfils the same role and is the place where the monarchs of Sweden are married and crowned. Storkyrkan gained its present shape at the end of the fifteenth century, with a Baroque remodelling in the 1730s. Inside, twentieth-century restoration has removed the white plaster from the red-brick columns, and although there's no evidence that this was intended in the original, it lends a warm colouring to the rest of the building. Much is made of the fifteenth-century sculpture of St George and the Dragon, though this is easily overshadowed by the golden, throne-like royal pews and the monumental black-and-silver altarpiece. Organ recitals take place here every Saturday at 1pm.

Stretching south from the church is **Stortorget**, Gamla Stan's handsome and elegantly proportioned main square, fringed by eighteenth-century buildings and surrounded by narrow shopping streets. In 1520 Christian II used the square as an execution site during the "Stockholm Bloodbath", dispatching his opposition en masse with gory finality. Now, as then, the streets **Västerlånggatan** and **Österlånggatan**, **Stora Nygatan** and **Lilla Nygatan** run the length of the Old Town on either side of the square, although today their time-worn buildings harbour a succession of art and craft shops and restaurants. Happily, though, the consumerism is largely unobtrusive and in summer buskers and evening strollers clog the narrow alleyways, making it an entertaining area in which to wander and to eat and drink. There are few real targets, though at some stage you'll probably pass the copy of the George and Dragon statues in the small **Köpmantorget** square (off Österlånggatan). Take every opportunity too to scuttle up side streets, where you'll find fading coats of arms, covered alleyways and worn cobbles at every turn.

Just off Västerlånggatan, on Tyska Brinken, is the **Tyska kyrkan** (German Church), originally owned by Stockholm's medieval German merchants, when it served as the meeting place of the Guild of St Gertrude. A copper-topped red-brick building atop a rise, it abandoned its secular role in the seventeenth century when Baroque decorators got hold of it: the result, a richly fashioned interior with the pulpit dominating the nave, is outstanding. Sporting a curious royal gallery in one corner, designed by Tessin the Elder, it comes complete with mini palace roof, angels and the three crowns of Swedish kingship.

Riddarhuset and Riddarholmen

If Stockholm's history has gripped you, it's better to head west from Stortorget towards the handsome Baroque **Riddarhuset** (daily Mon–Fri 11.30am–12.30pm; Ⓦ www.riddarhuset.se; 40kr), the seventeenth-century "House of Nobles". It was in the Great Hall here that the Swedish aristocracy met during the Parliament of the Four Estates (1668–1865) and their coats of arms – around 2500 of them – are splattered across the walls. Some six hundred of the noble families survive; the last ennoblement was in 1974. Take a look downstairs, too, at the Chancery, which stores heraldic bone china by the shelfload and racks full of fancy signet rings – essential accessories for the eighteenth-century noble-about-town.

From Riddarhuset it takes only a matter of seconds to cross the bridge onto **Riddarholmen** (Island of the Knights), to visit the **Riddarholmskyrkan** (May–Aug daily 10am–4pm; Sept Sat & Sun noon–3pm; 30kr), the burial place for Swedish royalty ever since Magnus Ladulås was sealed up here in 1290. Amongst others, you'll find the tombs of Gustav II Adolf (in the green marble sarcophagus), Karl XII, Gustav III and Karl Johan XIV, plus other innumerable and unmemorable descendants. Walk around the back of the church for stunning views of Stadshuset, the City Hall and Lake Mälaren. Incidentally, the island to the left of Västerbron (the bridge in the distance) is Långholmen; in winter people skate and even take their dogs for walks on the ice along here, as the water freezes solid right up to the bridge and beyond.

Skeppsholmen

A ten-minute walk east from Stortorget lie the islands of **Skeppsholmen** and the microscopic **Kastellholmen**, connected by a bridge to the south. Originally settled by the Swedish Navy – some of whose old barracks are still visible – in the nineteenth century, Skeppsholmen is now home to two of the city's youth hostels and an eclectic clutch of museums, the most impressive of them just by the Skeppsholmsbron, the bridge onto the island.

The National Art Museum

As you approach the bridge it's impossible to miss the striking waterfront **National Art Museum** (*Nationalmuseum*; Tues & Thurs 11am–8pm, Wed, Fri–Sun 11am–5pm; ⊛www.nationalmuseum.se; 75kr), looking right out over the Royal Palace. The impressive collection is contained on three floors: the **ground floor** is taken up by changing exhibitions of prints and drawings, and there's a shop and café here too, as well as luggage lockers. So much is packed into the museum that it can quickly become confusing and overwhelming – it's worth splashing out on the guidebook.

The **first floor** is devoted to applied art and if it's curios you're after, this museum has the lot – beds slept in by kings, cabinets leaned on by queens, plates eaten off by nobles – mainly from the centuries when Sweden was a great power. There's modern work alongside the ageing tapestries and furniture, including Art Nouveau coffee pots and vases, and examples demonstrating the intelligent simplicity of Swedish chair design.

It's the **second floor**, however, that's most engaging, featuring a plethora of European and Mediterranean sculpture and some mesmerizing sixteenth- and seventeenth-century Russian icons. The paintings are equally wide ranging and of a similarly high quality, including works by El Greco, Canaletto, Gainsborough and, most notably, Rembrandt's *Conspiracy of Claudius Civilis*, one of his largest monumental works, a bold depiction of well-armed Roman chieftains displayed in room 33. There are also minor paintings by other later masters (most notably Renoir and Gauguin) and some fine sixteenth- to eighteenth-century works by **Swedish artists**.

Skeppsholmen's museums

One of the better collections in Europe, Stockholm's **Museum of Modern Art** (*Moderna Muséet*; Tues–Thurs 11am–8pm, Fri–Sun 11am–6pm; ⊛www .modernamuseet.se; 70kr), is one of the city's must-see museums, with a comprehensive selection of works by some of the leading artists of the twentieth century. Highlights include Dali's monumental *Enigma of William Tell*, showing the artist at his most conventionally unconventional, and Matisse's striking *Apollo*. Look out also for Picasso's *Guitar Player* and a whole host of Warhol, Lichtenstein, Kandinsky, Miró and Magritte. Sharing the same building, the **Architecture Museum** (*Arkitekturmuseet*; same times; 55kr) serves up a taste of Swedish architecture in one of the most inspired buildings in the city – all glass and air. If you plan on taking in either collection during 2003, bear in mind that due to ongoing renovation work to clean up damp and mould damage, the collections are being housed in **temporary accommodation**. Exhibits from the Architecture Museum can be seen in the nearby Skeppholmskyrka church on Skeppsholmen (Tues–Sun 1–5pm) as well as at the Konstakademien at Fredsgatan 12 (Tues–Thurs 11am–8pm, Fri–Sun 1–5pm), close to the Riksdagshuset, while the Modern Art Museum has upped sticks to Klarabergsviadukten 61, near the main train station (Tues–Thurs 10am–8pm, Fri–Sun 10am–6pm). Although both museums expect to be back in their normal premises by the winter of 2003, the date is preliminary and dependent on completion of the renovation work – check the website above for updates. Once they are back in their original homes, both museums will revert to their usual opening hours.

A steep climb up the northern tip of the island brings you to the **Museum of Far Eastern Antiquities** (*Östasiatiska Muséet*; Tues noon–8pm, Wed–Sun noon–5pm; @www.ostasiatiska.se; 50kr), which holds an array of objects displaying incredible craftsmanship – fifth-century Chinese tomb figures, delicate jade amulets, an astounding assembly of sixth-century Buddhas, Indian watercolours and gleaming bronze Krishna figures – and that's just one room.

Norrmalm and Kungsholmen

Modern Stockholm lies immediately to the north and east of Gamla Stan, and is split into two distinct sections. **Norrmalm**, to the north, is the buzzing commercial heart of the city, packed with restaurants, bars, cinemas and shops, while to the east is the more sedate Östermalm, a well-to-do area of classy boulevards. The island of **Kungsholmen**, linked by bridge to the west of Norrmalm, is a mostly residential and administrative district, though with one positive draw in Stockholm's landmark City Hall.

Around Gustav Adolfs Torg

Down on the waterfront, at the foot of Norrbron, is **Gustav Adolfs Torg**, more a traffic island than a square these days, with the nineteenth-century **Operan** (Opera House) its proudest, most notable – and ugliest – building. It was here in an earlier opera house on the same site, at a masked ball in 1792, that King Gustav III was shot by one Captain Ankarström, an admirer of Rousseau and member of the aristocratic opposition. The story is recorded in Verdi's opera *Un ballo in maschera* and you can see Gustav's ball costume, as well as the assassin's pistols and mask, on display in the Palace Armoury in Gamla Stan.

A statues of King Gustav II Adolf marks the centre of the square, between Operan and the Foreign Office opposite. Look out hereabouts for fishermen pulling salmon out of **Strömmen**, the fast-flowing tributary that winds its way through the centre of the city. Stockholmers have had the right to fish this outlet from Lake Mälaren to the Baltic since the seventeenth century; it's not as difficult as it sounds and there's usually a group of hopefuls on one of the bridges around the square trying their luck.

Just off the square, at Fredsgatan 2 in the heart of Swedish government land, is the **Museum of Mediterranean and Near Eastern Antiquities** (*Medelhavsmuséet*; Tues 11am–8pm, Wed–Fri 11am–4pm, Sat & Sun noon–5pm; @www .medelhavsmuseet.se; 50kr), a sparkling museum devoted to ancient Mediterranean cultures, notably Egypt, Cyprus, Greece and Rome. Its enormous Egyptian section covers just about every aspect of life in Egypt up to the Christian era, with several whopping great mummies and some attractive bronze weapons, tools and domestic objects from the time before the pharaohs. The Cyprus collections are also huge, the largest outside Cyprus itself, spanning a period of over six thousand years, and there are also strong displays of Greek, Etruscan and Roman art. A couple of rooms examine Islamic culture through pottery, glass and metalwork, as well as decorative elements of architecture, Arabic calligraphy and Persian miniature painting.

Walk back towards Operan and continue across the main junction onto Arsenalsgatan to reach **St Jakobs kyrka** (daily 11am–3pm), one of the many easily overlooked churches in Stockholm. It's the pulpit that draws the eye, a great, golden affair, while the date of the church's consecration – 1642 – is stamped high up on the ceiling in gold figures. There are weekly classical music recitals here, with organ and choir recitals on Saturday at 3pm.

Kungsträdgården

Just beyond St Jakobs kyrka and Operan, Norrmalm's eastern boundary is marked by **Kungsträdgården**, most fashionable and central of the city's numerous squares, reaching the water northwards at **Hamngatan**. The mouthful of a name literally means "the king's gardens", though if you're expecting neatly trimmed flower beds and rose gardens you'll be sadly disappointed – it's actually a great expanse of concrete with a couple of lines of trees. The area may once have been a royal kitchen garden, but nowadays it serves as Stockholm's main meeting place, especially in summer when there's almost always something happening: free evening gigs, theatre and other performances take place on the central open-air stage. Look out too for the park's cafés, packed out in spring with winter-weary Stockholmers soaking up the sun. In winter the park is equally busy, particularly at the Hamngatan end where there's an open-air ice rink, the **Isbanan** (mid-Nov to March daily 9am–6pm; skate rental 35kr). The main tourist office is close by here, in the Sverigehuset, at the corner of Hamngatan (see p.437).

Hamngatan runs east to **Birger Jarlsgatan**, the main thoroughfare that divides Norrmalm from Östermalm, and now a mecca for eating and drinking.

Sergels Torg to Hötorget

At the western end of Hamngatan, beyond the enormous NK department store, lies **Sergels Torg**, the ugliest part of modern Stockholm. It's an unending free show centred on the five seething floors of **Kulturhuset** (Tues–Fri 11am–7pm, Sat & Sun 11am–5pm, ⓦwww.kulturhuset.stockholm.se), a cultural centre whose windows look down upon the milling concrete square. Inside are temporary art and craft exhibitions together with workshops open to anyone willing to get their hands dirty. Admission to Kulturhuset is free, but you have to pay to get into specific exhibitions or performances; check the information desk as you come in for details of the programme of poetry readings, concerts and theatre performances. The reading room (*läsesalongen*) on the ground level is stuffed with foreign newspapers, books, records and magazines – a good refuge if it's wet and windy outside. Check out the café on the top floor for delicious apple pie and custard and some of the best views of central Stockholm, even if the service often leaves something to be desired. From the café you'll get a bird's-eye view of the tall and singularly ugly wire-like column that dominates the massive open space outside and the surrounding spewing fountain. Down the steps, below Sergels Torg, is **Sergels Arkaden**, a set of grotty underground walkways home to buskers, brass bands and demented lottery ticket vendors; look out for the odd demonstration or ball game, too. There are also entrances down here into **T-Centralen**, the central T-bana station, and Stockholm's other main department store, Åhléns, not quite as posh as NK and easier to find your way around.

A short walk west from Kulturhuset along Klarabergsgatan will bring you to **Central Station** and **Cityterminalen**, hub of virtually all Stockholm's transport. The area around here is given over to unabashed consumerism, but as you explore the streets around the main drag, **Drottninggatan**, you'll find little to get excited about – run-of-the-mill clothing stores and twee gift shops punctuated by *McDonald's* and the odd sausage stand. In summer the occasional busker or jewellery stall livens up what is essentially a soulless grid of pedestrianized shopping streets.

The only point of culture is the **Klara kyrka** (Mon–Fri 10am–6pm, Sat 10am–7pm, Sun 8.30am–6pm), just to the right off Klarabergsgatan, opposite the station. Another of Stockholm's easily missed churches, hemmed in on all sides with only the spires visible from the surrounding streets, it's a particularly delicate example, with a light and flowery eighteenth-century painted interior and an impressive golden pulpit. Out in the churchyard, a memorial stone commemorates eighteenth-century Swedish poet Carl Michael Bellman, whose popular, lengthy ballads are said to have been composed extempore; his unmarked grave is somewhere in the churchyard.

Three blocks further up Drottinggatan, the cobbled square of **Hötorget** hosts an open-air fruit and veg market on weekdays, as well as the wonderful indoor **Hötorgshallen**, an orgy of Middle Eastern smells and sights and a good place to pick up ethnic snacks. Grab something to eat and plonk yourself on the steps of the **Konserthuset** (Concert House), one of the venues for the presentation of the Nobel Prizes, and a good place to hear classical music recitals (often free on Sunday afternoons). The tall building opposite is a former department store where Greta Garbo once worked as a sales assistant in the hat department. Today, though, Hötorget is better known for its superb cinema complex, Filmstaden Sergel, the capital's biggest; to the east, **Kungsgatan**, which runs down to Stureplan and Birger Jarlsgatan, holds most of the city's other cinemas, interspersed with agreeable little cafés (see p.457).

North to the Strindberg Museum

From Hötorget the two main streets of Drottninggatan and Sveavägen run parallel uphill and north as far as Odengatan and the **Stadsbiblioteket** (City Library), in its own little park. Close by, set in secluded gardens between the two roads, sits the eighteenth-century **Adolf Fredriks kyrka**. Although it has a noteworthy past – the French philosopher Descartes was buried here in 1650 before his body was moved to France – the church would be insignificant today were it not the final resting place for the assassinated Swedish Prime Minister, **Olof Palme**: a simple headstone and flowers mark his grave. A plaque now marks the spot on Sveavägen, near the junction with Olof Palmes Gata, where the prime minister was gunned down; the assassin escaped up the nearby flight of steps (see box below).

The assassination of Olof Palme

The shooting of **Prime Minister Olof Palme** in February 1986 sent shockwaves through a society unused to political extremism of any kind. Like most Nordic leaders, Palme's fame was his security, and he died unprotected, gunned down in front of his wife on their way home from the cinema on Sveavägen. Sadly, the murder led to a radical rethink of Sweden's long-established policy of open government: top-ranking ministers no longer walk the streets without bodyguards and security checks now operate in all public buildings. Sweden's biggest ever **murder inquiry** was launched and as the years went by so the allegations of police cover-ups and bungling grew. When **Christer Pettersson** was jailed for the murder in July 1989 (see "History", p.428), most Swedes believed that to be the end of the story, but his release in December of the same year only served to reopen the bitter debate. There have been recriminations and resignations within a derided police force, and although in the past the most popular suspects were immigrant Kurdish extremists, right-wing terror groups or even a hitman from within the police itself. However, more recent theories have suggested that the corrupt regime in South Africa was behind the killing – Palme was an outspoken critic of apartheid, leading calls for an economic blockade against Pretoria.

Continue north along Drottninggatan and you'll come to the "Blue Tower" at no. 85, the last building in which the writer August Strindberg lived, now turned into the **Strindberg Museum** (*Strindbergsmuséet*; Tues–Sun noon–4pm; ⑳www .strindbergsmuseet.se; 40kr). Strindberg lived here between 1908 and 1912, and his house has been preserved to the extent that you must put plastic bags on your feet to protect the floors and furnishings. The study remains as he left it on his death, a dark and gloomy place – he would work with both Venetian blinds and heavy curtains closed against the sunlight. Upstairs is his library, a musty room with all the books firmly behind glass, which is a shame because Strindberg wasn't a passive reader: he underlined heavily and made notes in the margins as he read, though these are rather less erudite than you'd expect: "Lies!", "Crap!", "Idiot!" and "Bloody hell!" seem to have been his favourite comments. Good explanatory notes in English are supplied free.

Kungsholmen: Stadshuset

Take the T-bana back to T-Centralen and it takes only a matter of minutes to cross Stadshusbron to the island of **Kungsholmen** and Stockholm's **Stadshuset** (City Hall; mid-May to Sept daily guided tours at 10am, noon & 2pm; rest of the year daily at 10am and noon; ⑳www2.stockholm.se/stadshuset; 50kr). Finished in 1923, the Stadshuset is a landmark of the modern city and one of the first buildings you'll see when approaching Stockholm from the south by train. Its simple, if somewhat drab, exterior brickwork is no preparation for the intricate decor within. Visiting Heads of State are escorted from their boats up the elegant waterside steps, but for lesser mortals, the only way to view the innards is on one of the guided tours, which reveal the kitschy Viking-style legislative chamber and impressively echoing Golden Hall. The Stadshuset is also the departure point for **boats** to destinations around Lake Mälaren: Birka, Drottningholm, Mariefred (for Gripsholm castle) and Uppsala. Venture further into Kungsholmen and you'll discover a rash of excellent bars and restaurants that have sprung up here – see p.459 – and an excellent **beach** at Smedsudden (buses #54 and #62 to Västerbroplan, then a 5min walk). Another attraction is the popular **Rålambshovsparken**, a large expanse of open grassland gently sloping down to the waters of Lake Mälaren where you can take a swim with fantastic views of the City Hall and Old Town.

Östermalm

East of Birger Jarlsgatan the streets become noticeably broader and grander as you enter the district of **Östermalm**, one of the last areas of central Stockholm to be developed. The first place to head for is the water's-edge square, **Nybroplan**, just east along Hamngatan from Sergels Torg, and marked with the white-stone relief-studded **Royal Theatre of Drama** (*Kungliga Dramatiska Teatern*; ⑳www.dramaten .se), Stockholm's showpiece theatre. The curved harbour in front is the departure point for all kinds of archipelago **ferries** and tours (see p.464), and for a summer shuttle service (May–Aug every 15min; 20kr) via Skeppsholmen to the Nordic and Vasa museums over on Djurgården (see opposite).

Behind the theatre at Sibyllegatan 2 is the innovative **Music Museum** (*Musikmuséet*; Tues–Sun 11am–4pm; ⑳stockholm.music.museum; 30kr), containing a range of instruments that visitors are allowed to experiment with. The collection charts the history of music in Sweden via photographs, instruments and sound recordings. Best are the sections that deal with the late nineteenth century (a time when *folkmusik* was given fresh impetus by the growing labour movement), and the space given over to ABBA.

Just back from the museums, up the hill of Sibyllegatan, **Östermalmstorg** is an absolute find: the square is home to the **Östermalms saluhallen**, an indoor market hall not unlike Norrmalm's Hötorgshallen, but selling more refined delicatessen – reindeer hearts and the like – and attracting a clientele to match. Wander round at lunchtime and you'll spot any number of fur-coated Stockholmers, sipping Chardonnay and munching shrimp sandwiches.

History Museum

As you plod your way around Östermalm's rich streets, you're bound to end up at the circular **Karlaplan** sooner or later: a handy T-bana and bus interchange, full of media types coming off shift from the Swedish Radio and Television buildings at the end of Karlavägen. From here it's a short walk (or #44 bus ride) down Narvavägen to the impressive **History Museum** (*Historiska Muséet*; Tues–Sun 11am–5pm; ⑩ www.historiska.se; 70kr); from Norrmalm, take bus #56 via Stureplan and Linnégatan. The most wide-ranging historical display in Stockholm, it's really two large collections: a museum of National Antiquities and the new underground Gold Room, with its magnificent fifth-century gold collars and other fine jewellery. Ground-floor highlights include a Stone Age ideal home – flaxen-haired youth, stripped pine benches and rows of neatly labelled herbs – and a mass of Viking weapons, coins and boats, much of it labelled in English. Upstairs there's a worthy collection of medieval church art and architecture, with odds and ends turned up from all over the country, evocatively housed in massive vaulted rooms. If you're heading to Gotland, be sure to look out for the reassembled bits of stave churches uncovered on the Baltic island – some of the few examples that survive in Sweden.

Djurgården

When you tire of pounding the streets, there's respite at hand in the form of Stockholm's so-called National City Park, and in particular the section just to the east of the centre, **Djurgården**. Originally royal hunting grounds from the sixteenth to eighteenth centuries, it is actually two distinct park areas separated by the water of **Djurgårdsbrunnsviken** – popular for swimming in summer and skating in winter when the channel freezes over. Also in Djurgården are some of Stockholm's finest **museums**: the massive open-air **Skansen**, an amazing conglomeration of architecture and folk culture from around the country, and the **Vasa Museum**, the home of a marvellously preserved seventeenth-century warship.

You can walk to Djurgården through the centre out along Strandvägen but it's quite a hike; alternatively, take bus #44 from Karlaplan or buses #47 and #69 from Norrmalm to the bridge, Djurgårdsbron, which crosses over onto the island; alternatively, there are ferries from Skeppsbron in Gamla Stan (all year) and Nybroplan (May–Aug only).

The Nordic Museum, Skansen and Gröna Lunds Tivoli

A full day is just about enough to see everything on Djurgården. Starting with the palatial **Nordic Museum** (*Nordiska Muséet*; Tues–Sun 10am–5pm, plus Mon same times late June to Aug; ⑩ www.nordm.se; 60kr), just over Djurgårdsbron from Strandvägen, is the best idea, if only because the same cultural themes pop up repeatedly throughout the rest of the island's exhibitions. The displays are a recent attempt to represent Swedish cultural history (from the past 500 years) in an accessible fashion, and the Sámi section is particularly good. On the ground floor of the cathedral-like interior is Carl Milles's phenomenal statue of Gustav Vasa, the sixteenth-century king who drove out the Danes and whose inspirational qualities summoned the best from the sculptor (for more on Milles, see p.465).

However, it's for **Skansen** (daily: May 10am–8pm; June–Aug 10am–10pm; Sept 10am–5pm; Oct–April 10am–4pm; ⑩ www.skansen.se; 60kr June–Aug, 30kr rest of the year) that most people come here: a great open-air museum with 150 reconstructed buildings, ranging from an entire town to windmills and farms laid out on a region-by-region basis, with each section boasting its own daily activities – traditional handicrafts, games and displays – that anyone can join in. The best of the buildings are the small Sámi dwellings, warm and functional, and the craftsmen's workshops in the old town quarter. You can also potter around a small **zoo** and a bizarre **aquarium**, where fish live cheek by jowl with crocodiles, monkeys and snakes. Partly because of the attention paid to accuracy, partly due to the admirable lack of commercialization (a rarity in Sweden), Skansen manages to avoid the tackiness associated with similar ventures in other countries. Even the snack bars dole out traditional foods and in winter serve up great bowls of warming soup.

Immediately opposite Skansen's main gates (and at the end of the #44 bus route; bus #47 also goes by), **Gröna Lunds Tivoli** (May–Sept daily noon–midnight; Oct–April shorter hours – check at the tourist office; ⓦwww.gronalund.com; 50kr entrance, or 220kr unlimited rides) is not a patch on its more famous namesake, Copenhagen's Tivoli Gardens, though it's worth a visit for some fantastic views back over the water towards the city. It's definitely more of a place to stroll through rather than indulge in the rides which are generally rather tame. One notable exception is the Fritt Fall – a hair-raising vertical drop of 80m in just six seconds; do lunch later. At night the emphasis shifts as the park becomes the stomping ground for Stockholm's youth, with raucous music, cafés and some enterprising chat-up lines to be heard.

Vasa Museum

In a brand new building close to the Nordic Museum, the **Vasa Museum** (*Vasamuséet*; daily: mid-June to mid-Aug 9.30am–7pm; mid-Aug to mid-June 10am–5pm, Wed until 8pm; ⓦwww.vasamuseet.se; 70kr) is without question head and shoulders above anything else that Stockholm has to offer in the way of museums. Built on the orders of King Gustav II Adolf, the *Vasa* warship sank in Stockholm harbour on her maiden voyage in 1628 – built to a design that was both too tall and too narrow, it promptly keeled over and sank as soon as it was put afloat. Preserved in mud for over 300 years, the ship was raised along with 12,000 objects in 1961, and now forms the centrepiece of a startling, purpose-built hall on the water's edge.

Though the building itself is impressive, nothing prepares you for the sheer size of the **ship** itself: 62m long, with a main mast which was originally 50m above the keel, it sits virtually complete in a cradle of supporting mechanical tackle. Surrounding walkways bring you nose to nose with cannon hatches and restored decorative relief, the gilded wooden sculptures on the soaring prow designed to intimidate the enemy and proclaim Swedish might. Faced with its frightening bulk, it's not difficult to understand the terror that such ships must have generated. Adjacent **exhibition halls** and presentations on several levels take care of all the retrieved bits and bobs. There are reconstructions of life on board, detailed models of the *Vasa*, displays relating to contemporary social and political life, films and videos of the rescue operation, excellent English explanations and regular English-language **guided tours** (the latter included in the entrance fee).

Adjacent to the museum, an altogether more frightening reminder of the power of the sea deserves your attention. Located on the Stockholm waterfront, the three-metre-high granite walls of the **Estonia Memorial**, arranged in the form of a tri-angle – not unlike the Vietnam memorial in Washington DC – bear the engraved names of the 852 people who died when the *Estonia* ferry sank in the Baltic Sea in September 1994 whilst crossing from the Estonian capital, Tallinn, to Stockholm.

Thiel Gallery

At the far eastern end of Djurgården (take bus #69 from Norrmalm) is one of Stockholm's major treasures, the **Thiel Gallery** (*Thielska Galleriet*; Mon–Sat noon–4pm, Sun 1–4pm; ⓦwww.thielska-galleriet.a.se; 50kr), a fine example of Swedish architecture and art. The house was built by Fredinand Boberg at the beginning of the twentieth century for a banker, Ernet Thiel, who then sold it to the state in 1924, after which it entered its present incarnation. Thiel, who knew many contemporary Nordic artists, gathered an impressive collection of paintings over the years, including works by Carl Larsson, Anders Zorn, Edvard Munch, Bruno Liljefors and even August Strindberg. The views back towards the city alone are attractive enough to warrant a visit.

The Kaknäs TV Tower

Bus #69 from Norrmalm will take you directly to Stockholm's landmark TV tower, in the northern stretch of parkland known as **Ladugårdsgärdet** (or, more commonly, Gärdet); it's also possible to walk here from Djurgården proper – head northwards across the island on Manillavägen over Djurgårdsbrunnsviken. At 160m, the **Kaknäs TV Tower** (*Kaknästornet*; daily: May–Aug 9am–10pm; Sept–April 10am–9pm; 25kr) is one of the highest buildings in Scandinavia, allowing fabulous views over the city and archipelago; there's also a restaurant about 120m up, should you fancy a vertiginous cup of coffee. If you come here by bus, you'll pass a gaggle of sundry museums – Dance, Maritime, Technical and Ethnographical – while beyond Ladugårdsgärdet, north of the tower, where windmills used to pierce the skyline, lies first Frihamnen, where the Estonia ferry docks, and, just beyond that, Värtahamnen and the Silja Line ferry terminal for Finland.

Södermalm and Långholmen

Whatever you do in Stockholm, don't miss the delights of the city's southern island, **Södermalm**, whose craggy cliffs, turrets and towers rise high above the clogged traffic interchange at Slussen. The perched buildings are vaguely forbidding, but venture beyond the main roads skirting the island and a lively and surprisingly green area unfolds, one that's emphatically working-class at heart, though Swedish-style – there are no slums here. To get here, take bus #46 and get off at Bondegatan, or the #53 to Folkungagatan; alternatively, ride the T-bana to Slussen or, to save an uphill trek, Medborgarplatsen or Mariatorget.

On foot, you reach the island over a double bridge from Gamla Stan into Södermalmstorg – the square around the entrance to the T-bana at Slussen. Just to the south of the square is the rewarding **City Museum** (*Stadsmuséet*; June–Aug daily 11am–7pm; rest of the year Tues–Sun 11am–5pm, Thurs 11am–9pm; ⓦ www.stadsmuseum.stockholm.se; 50kr), hidden in a basement courtyard. The Baroque building, designed by Tessin the Elder and finished by his son in 1685, was once the town hall for this part of Stockholm; it now houses a set of collections relating to the city's history as a seaport and industrial centre. Nearby, the Renaissance-style **Katarina kyrka** on Högbergsgatan stands on the site where the victims of the Stockholm Bloodbath – the betrayed nobility of Sweden who opposed King Christian II's Danish invasion – were buried in 1520. Their bodies were burned as heretics outside the city walls and it proved a vicious and effective coup, Christian disposing of the opposition in one fell swoop.

That's about as far as specific sights go on Södermalm, although it's worth wandering westwards towards **Mariatorget**, a spacious square of Art Nouveau-influenced buildings. This is one of the most desirable places to live in the city, within easy reach of a glut of stylish bars and restaurants where trendy Stockholmers simply have to be seen. The island is also home to one of Stockholm's most popular parks, **Tantolunden**, located close to the Hornstull T-bana at the end of Lignagatan, complete with open-air theatre in summer. It's also the place to come for **swimming pools** – there are three of them – Forgrénskabadet (Medborgarplatsen T-bana), Erikdalsbadet (Skanstull T-bana) and the wonderful little Liljeholmsbadet (Hornstull T-bana) a pool in a boat-like pontoon contraption that floats in Lake Mälaren: there's single-sex nude swimming here on Mondays and Fridays, and the water is never less than 30°C.

You'll probably end up back on Södermalm after dark, since there are some good bars and restaurants in this quarter of town – though it's best to get your bearings during the day, as finding your way around at night can be confusing. The main streets to aim for are **Götgatan, Folkungagatan, Bondegatan** and **Skånegatan** (see the sections on eating and drinking, starting on p.457).

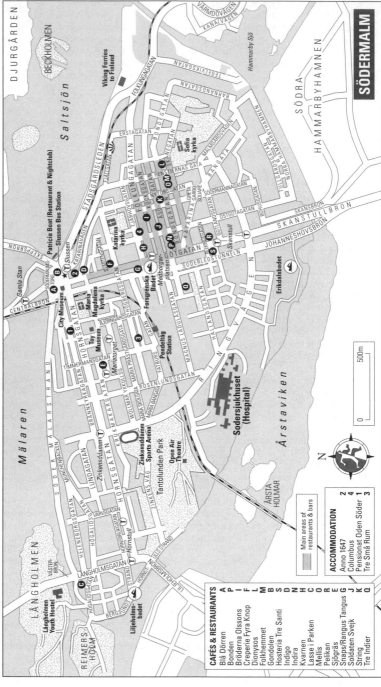

SÖDERMALM

DJURGÅRDEN

BECKHOLMEN

Saltsjön

Viking Ferries to Finland

VÄRMDÖVÄGEN

KANALVÄGEN

Hammarby Sjö

SÖDRA

HAMMARBYHAMNEN

Patricia Boat (Restaurant & Nightclub)
Slussen Bus Station

Sofia kyrka

Katarina kyrka

Gamla Stan

City Museum

Maria Magdalena kyrka

Forsgrenska Badet

Toy Museum

Mariatorget

Pendeltåg Station

Eriksdalsbadet

Medborgar-platsen

Söder sjukhuset (Hospital)

Årstaviken

Mälaren

LÅNGHOLMEN

Långholmen Youth Hostel

Liljeholms-badet

REIMERS HOLM

ÅRSTA HOLMAR

Tantolunden Park

Zinkensdamm Sports Arena

Open Air Theatre

Main areas of restaurants & bars

ACCOMMODATION

Anno 1647	2
Columbus	4
Pensionat Oden Söder	1
Tre Små Rum	3

CAFÉS & RESTAURANTS

Blå Dörren	A
Bonden	P
Bröderna Olssons	I
Creperie Fyra Knop	F
Dionysos	L
Folkhemmet	M
Gondolen	B
Hosteria Tre Santi	S
Indigo	D
Indira	N
Kvarnen	H
Lasse i Parken	C
Melíss	O
Pelikan	R
Sjögräs	E
Snaps/Rangus Tangus	J
Soldaten Svejk	G
String	K
Tre Indier	Q

0   500m

N

▶ Main Line South, also Pendeltåg to Nynäshamn for Ferry to Gotland

Långholmen

The name translates as "long island" and **Långholmen** is just that, a skinny finger of land off the northwestern tip of Södermalm, spanned by the mighty Västerbron bridge which links Södermalm with Kungsholmen. There are a couple of popular **beaches** here: **Långholmens strandbad** to the west of the bridge and rocky **Klippbadet** to the east; if you don't fancy swimming, take a leisurely stroll through the trees instead for some stunning views over the water towards the City Hall and Gamla Stan.

You may well find yourself staying here as the island's large prison building has been converted into one of the better hostels in Sweden (see p.444). There's a café here in the summer, and you can sit outside and have a drink in what used to be the prison's exercise yard – narrow, bricked-up runs with iron gates at one end. Alternatively, you could nip back over to Sodermalm and sample the excellent *Lasse i Parken* café (see p.459).

Långholmen is best reached by taking the T-bana to Hornstull and then following the signs to the youth hostel; bus #4 is also handy as it crosses Västerbron on its way between Södermalm, Kungsholmen, Vasastaden and Östermalm – an excellent way of seeing much of the city for very little cost.

Eating

Eating out in Stockholm needn't be outrageously expensive. If money is tight, switch your main meal of the day to lunchtime, at least on weekdays, when almost every café and restaurant offers an excellent-value set menu, or *dagens rätt*, for 60–70kr. In the evening, look around for the best deals but don't necessarily assume that Italian and Chinese places will be the least expensive; more often than not they're overpriced and the food is tasteless. Having said that, there are plenty of other foreign cuisines on offer, particularly Japanese and Thai, plus, of course, a number of traditional Swedish places.

Breakfast, snacks and shopping for food

Stockholmers don't usually go out for **breakfast**, so there are very few places open in the early morning. Hotels provide help-yourself buffet breakfasts which go a long way to filling you up for the day and are the best place to go early in the morning – most will allow non-guests to have breakfast for 40–50kr. In terms of **snacks**, don't bother with burgers unless you're desperate – you'll pay around 50kr for a large burger and fries at *McDonald's*, only 10–20kr less than the lunchtime *dagens rätt* elsewhere, though coffee is a bargain both here and at *Clockburger*, the Swedish burger chain. If the nibbles strike it's much more economical to pick up a *korv*, a grilled or fried sausage in bread, for 10–15kr from a street vendor.

Of the indoor **markets** (both closed Sun), Hötorgshallen in Hötorget is cheaper and more varied than Östermalmshallen in Östermalmstorg. The former is awash with small cafés and ethnic snacks, but buy your fruit and veg outside where it's less expensive. The latter is posher and pricey – while it's pleasant for a wander, you'll find most things cost less in the city's biggest **supermarket** in the basement of the Åhléns department store on Sergels Torg. In summer, **fruit and veg** stalls spring up outside many of the T-bana stations, especially those out of the centre.

Cafés and restaurants

For decent eating, day or night, head for the city-centre area bounded by Norrmalmstorg, Birger Jarlsgatan and Stureplan; Grev Turegatan in Östermalm; and around Folkungagatan, Skånegatan and Bondegatan on Södermalm. Kungsholmen's restaurants are more spread out, so it's best to have a destination in mind before setting out. Several restaurants in Gamla Stan are also worth checking out, though they tend to be expensive. **Vegetarians** shouldn't have too much difficulty in finding something to eat. Note that in Sweden as a whole there's a fine distinction between cafés, restaurants and bars, with many places offering music and entertainment in the evening as well as serving food throughout the day. Bear in mind, too, that Swedes eat early: lunch is served from 11am to 2pm and dinner from 6pm to around 9pm. Advance booking is generally not required (we've given numbers for places where you do need to book), but as many restaurants don't take bookings at all, it's often a case of just waiting until a table becomes free.

Unless otherwise stated, for places in **Gamla Stan and Norrmalm**, see the map on p.445; for those in **Södermalm** see the map on p.456; those in Östermalm, Kungsholmen and northern Norrmalm appear on the main Stockholm map, pp.438–439. Note also that we list a great gay-friendly restaurant, Mandus, on p.463.

Gamla Stan

Bistro Ruby/Grill Ruby Österlånggatan 14. French bistro in the heart of Gamla Stan, tastefully done out in Parisian style, but pricey. Main dishes go for around 150kr, and there's a wide selection of beers. *Grill Ruby*, next door, serves up reasonably priced American-style grills and weekend brunches.

Den Gyldene Freden Österlånggatan 51. Stockholm's oldest restaurant, "*The Golden Peace*", was opened in 1772, and its vaulted cellars edged with elegant wall paintings remain marvellously atmospheric. Expect to pay around 350kr for just two courses, without drinks.

Hermitage Stora Nygatan 11. Vegetarian restaurant well worth checking out for its hearty, moderately priced food – look out for the spicy Middle Eastern dishes in particular. Closes at 8pm (Sun 7pm).

Mårten Trotzig Västerlånggatan 79. Known throughout Sweden for excellent and stylish food served in a beautiful setting – attracts luvvies and business types from across Stockholm, though it's expense account stuff.

Medelhavet Lilla Nygatan 21. Good, centrally located Mediterranean restaurant with a trendy bar, *Bläckfisken*, next door.

Norrmalm

Berns Berzelii Park, Nybroplan. One of the more chic brasseries in town (prices, though, are moderate), with interior design by Britain's Sir Terence Conran. Originally made famous by writer August Strindberg, who picked up character ideas here for his novel, *The Red Room*.

Biblos Biblioteksgatan 9. Moderately-priced, wonderfully trendy café and restaurant right in the centre of town – a good place to people-watch.

East Stureplan 13. One of the city's finest restaurants. Trendy to a T and excellent food – lots of fish and Asian-style dishes – but expensive: lunch 74–106kr; dinner around 150kr.

Grodan Grev Turegatan 16. Officially called *La Grenouille*, but more usually known by its Swedish name (which means "the frog"). French cuisine at moderate prices.

Halv trappa plus gård Lästmakargatan 3, at junction with Stureplan. Very popular eatery, with moderately-priced modern European dishes, particularly fish, served outside in summer. Bursting with fashion victims.

KB Smålandsgatan 7, Stureplan. Excellent – and very expensive – Swedish food in posh surroundings. A favourite haunt of authors and artists.

Köket Sturegallerian shopping centre, Stureplan. Very popular place for eats when the nightclubs have turned out (it's open till 3am Thurs–Sun), but quite pricey.

Konditori Kungstornet Kungsgatan 28. Popular 1950s-style Swedish coffee house with excellent cakes and sandwiches from 40kr.

PA & Co Riddargatan 8. Fashionable restaurant with moderately priced international dishes, some good old Swedish favourites and a few inventive "crossovers".

Restaurangen Oxtorgsgatan 14. Run by one of Stockholm's top chefs, this is the place for Swedish home cooking with an added international flavour at moderate prices. No starters or main courses – you simply put together a meal from three or five excellent smaller dishes.

Robert's Coffee Kungsgatan 44. Just inside the door of the Kungshallen food hall and a popular place to meet for a good cup of coffee.

Sawadee Olofsgatan 6. Next to Hötorget T-bana. Attractive Thai restaurant with a wonderful 150kr special dinner and reasonably priced drinks.

Wayne's Kungsgatan 14. A popular café for smart city types and trendy young things, who pretend to be reading foreign newspapers whilst sipping cappuccinos.

Södermalm

Blå Dörren Södermalmstorg 6. Beer hall and restaurant with excellent, but expensive, Swedish food.

Bonden Bondegatan 1C. Small and cosy restaurant with rough brick walls and moderate prices; try the delicious fillet of chicken with oyster mushrooms in red wine sauce and potato gratin – a winner every time.

Bröderna Olssons Folkungagatan 84. If you like garlic this is the place for you, with every conceivable dish either laced with the white stuff or washing around in a garliky sauce, all accompanied by shots of ice-cold vodka. Expensive.

Creperie Fyra Knop Svartensgatan 4. A rare treat in Stockholm: excellent crêpes at affordable prices (around 50kr).

Dionysos Bondegatan 56. Tasteful Greek decor gives this place a friendly feel, and the food is excellent, with moussaka for 85kr, or chicken souvlakia for 70kr.

Folkhemmet Renstiernas Gata 30. Very popular place serving reasonably priced Swedish home cooking and international dishes to young trendies and media types. Packed at weekends.

Hosteria Tre Santi Blekingegatan 32. One of Södermalm's better Italian restaurants and excellent value for money – always busy.

Indigo Götgatan 19, near Slussen T-bana exit. The ideal place to stop off for an afternoon cappuccino. Good pastries, too – the carrot cake is a house speciality. There's a small, moderately priced evening menu featuring the likes of lasagne and salad.

Indira Bondegatan 3B. The area's biggest Indian restaurant, with a good, inexpensive tandoori-based menu. Takeaway food, too.

Kvarnen Tjärhovsgatan 4. Small beer hall with simple Swedish food: lunch for around 50kr, and evening fish and meat dishes for 150kr. Open till 3am.

Lasse i Parken Högalidsgatan 56. Daytime café (June–Aug only) housed in an eighteenth-century house with a pleasant garden. Very popular in summer; also handy for the beaches at Långholmen.

Mellis Skånegatan 83–85. Popular place on this busy restaurant street. Greek, French and Swedish dishes at reasonable prices, and good for coffee and cakes, too.

Pelikan Blekingegatan 40. Atmospheric, working-class Swedish beer hall with excellent traditional food, such as *pytt i panna* for 58kr.

Sjögräs Timmermansgatan 24. A modern approach to Swedish cooking, influenced by world cuisines. Moderate prices and always packed.

Snaps/Rangus Tangus Medborgarplatsen. Good, old-fashioned and expensive Swedish food in a 300-year-old building. Very popular.

Soldaten Svejk Östgötagatan 35. Lively Czech-run joint that draws in a lot of students, with a simple menu at around the 100kr mark. Large selection of Czech beers – Staropramen goes for 44kr.

String Nytorgsgatan 38. If you fancy yourself as a brilliant new writer, or if you just fancy yourself, you'll fit in well at this studenty café. Good for moderately priced cakes and snacks. Adopt a ponderous air.

Tre Indier Möregatan 2. Lively, moderately priced Indian restaurant, slightly tucked away in a tiny street off Åsögatan (take bus #55 in the direction of Södra Hammarbyhamnen), but well worth hunting out.

Östermalm

Aubergine Linnégatan 38. Upmarket and expensive place, decked out with lots of wood and glass and located on one of Östermalm's busiest streets. The separate bar menu brings prices within reach – chicken on a skewer for 85kr is good.

Elverket Linnégatan 69. Moderately priced Swedish "crossover" food (international dishes given a Swedish flavour with use of local produce and flavours), served up in a restaurant attached to a theatre. Spacious lounge for drinks before dinner or relaxation afterwards.

Il Conte Grevgatan 9. Easily the best Italian restaurant in town, doling out excellent, good-value pasta dishes.

Örtagården Nybrogatan 31. Expensive, top-notch vegetarian restaurant, with food dished up under a huge chandelier in c.1900 surroundings. Dozens of different salads, warm dishes and soups.

Stockholms Glass och Pastahus Valhallavägen 155. Lunchtime place with excellent, inexpensive fresh pasta and home-made ice cream.

Kungsholmen

El Cubanito Scheelegatan 3. Delicious and reasonably priced Spanish food that deservedly attracts people from across Stockholm. Always packed.

La Famiglia Alströmergatan 45. One of Kungsholmen's better Italian places (even Frank Sinatra once ate here), and a good one for that first date. Expensive.

Roppongi Hantverkargatan 76. The place for sushi and other Japanese delights on Kungsholmen.

Salt Hantverkaregatan 34. On the island's main road, serving inexpensive, stodgy traditional Swedish fare, including elk burgers. *Salt* is no bad name either – drink a lot of water if you're eating the slabs of pork they serve up.

Spisa hos Göken Pontonjärgatan 28. Near Fridhemsplan T-bana and an excellent choice for modern Swedish food served up in a small neighbourhood restaurant. The rack of lamb at 184kr is worth the splurge.

Utsökt Scheelegatan 12. Moderately priced Swedish specialities including salmon, flounder and venison. Wonderful garden at the rear.

Northern Norrmalm

Bon Lloc Regeringsgatan 111 ☎08/660 60 60. Expensive euro-Latino dishes with a hint of Swedish home cooking, prepared by award-winning chefs. Mains from 275kr. Bookings necessary.

Gondolen Stadsgården 6, at the top of the Katarina lift, opposite Slussen T-bana. Breathtaking views over Stockholm from this high-level Place right on the waterfront. Choose

the smaller of the two restaurants here and prices fall dramatically.

Lao Wai Luntmakargatan 74. Sweden's first Thai and Indonesian restaurant. Decidedly good, though not especially cheap.

Peppar Torsgatan 34. Attractive Cajun restaurant with decent-sized, reasonably priced portions. Geared instead towards the rather non-adventurous Swedish palate, however, many dishes lack gusto.

Saturnus Erikbergsgatan 6. Café food during the day, including good, reasonably priced pasta, huge cakes and massive sandwiches, with more substantial dishes on offer in the evening.

Drinking, nightlife and entertainment

There's plenty to keep you entertained in Stockholm, from pubs, gigs and clubs to the cinema and theatre. There's a particularly good **live music** scene in the bars and pubs, but you'll generally have to pay a cover charge of around 60–80kr. Wear something other than jeans and trainers if you don't want to feel very scruffy – many places won't let you in dressed like that anyway – and be prepared to cough up around 20kr to leave your coat in the cloakroom, a requirement at many bars, discos and pubs, particularly in winter. As well as the weekend, Wednesday is a busy night in Stockholm – there's usually plenty going on and queues to get into the more popular places.

Bars, brasseries and pubs

The scourge of Swedish **nightlife** – high alcohol prices – is gradually being neutralized due to increased competition. Over recent years there's been a veritable explosion in the number of bars and pubs in Stockholm, beer prices have dropped considerably, and on Södermalm especially there are some very good deals – you'll pay roughly what you do at home. **Happy hours** also throw up some bargains – look out for signs outside bars and pubs.

Despite the increase in bars, however, it's still the case that many Stockholmers do their drinking over a meal, and several of the places listed below are primarily cafés or restaurants. Almost all are open seven days a week.

Norrmalm and Östermalm

Café Opera Operan, Gustav Adolfs Torg. If your Gucci gear isn't too crushed and you can stand just one more Martini, join the queue outside. Daily till 3am.

Dubliner Smålandsgatan 8. One of the busiest Irish pubs in town, with live music most evenings.

East Bar Stureplan. Loud music, loud dress and loud mouths. Great fun.

Lydmar Sturegatan 10. One of the most popular bars in Stockholm – and very elegant. Dress up a little to get past the beefcakes on the door.

Sturecompagniet Sturegatan 4. Three floors of bars with something for everybody. Worth a look, though the beer's expensive.

Tranan Karlbergsvägen 14. Atmospheric old workers' beer hall.

Gamla Stan

Gråmunken Västerlånggatan 18. Cosy café-pub, usually busy and sometimes with live music to jolly things along.

Kaos Stora Nygatan 21. DJs at weekends and unpretentious people out for a fun time.

Kleins Kornhamnstorg 51. One of the better bars in Gamla Stan and generally full with young professional Stockholmers dying to practise their English.

Magnus Ladulås Österlånggatan 26. Rough brick walls and low ceilings make this bar-cum-restaurant an appealing place for a drink or two.

Södermalm

Bonden Bar Bondegatan 1B. Just along from the Bonden restaurant and down a series of steps. A good choice for an evening beer before strutting your stuff on the adjoining dance floor.

Fenix Götgatan 40. Cheap and nasty American-style bar that's the place to go if you want some bustle and noise.

Folkhemmet Renstiernas Gata 30. Trendy hangout for 20- to 30-somethings. Inordinately popular at weekends.

Gröne Jägaren Götgatan 64. Some of the cheapest beer in Stockholm; *storstark* is just 24kr until 9pm. Perhaps inevitably, the clientele tends to get raucously drunk.

Kvarnen Tjärhovsgatan 4. Busy beer hall popular with southside football fans.

O'Learys Götgatan 11–13. Södermalm's busiest Irish pub – great fun and within stumbling distance of the nearby T-bana at Slussen.

Pelikan Blekingegatan 40. A fantastic old beer hall full of character – and characters.

Sjögräs Timmermansgatan 24. Wonderful little local bar that is always busy and lively.

WC Skånegatan 51. Very busy at weekends with people from across town, and handy for the restaurants around Skånegatan and Blekingegatan.

Clubs

The **club scene** in Stockholm is limited, with several places doubling as bars or restaurants (where you have to eat). Entrance charges aren't too high (around 100kr), but beers sometimes get more expensive as the night goes on, reaching as high as 55kr. For gay venues, see p.462.

Aladdin Barnhusgatan 12–14, Norrmalm ☎08/10 09 32. One of the city's most popular dance restaurants, close to the Central Station, often with live bands. Expensive.

Dailys Kungsträdgården ☎08/21 56 55, ⓦwww.dailys.nu. The *G-Klubben* inside this cheesy nightclub complex, complete with striplights on the stairs, is where you'll find Stockholm's movers and shakers. Be young, beautiful and trendy.

Fasching Kungsgatan 63, Norrmalm ☎08/21 62 67, ⓦwww.fasching.se. Dancing to live jazz from

midnight onwards.

Patricia Stadsgårdskajen, Slussen, Södermalm ☎743 05 70, ⓦwww.patricia.st. Formerly the royal yacht of Britain's Queen Mother, today a restaurant-disco-bar with fantastic views of the city across the harbour. Swedish stand-up comedy nights; and fantastic food. Wed–Sun.

Sturecompagniet Sturegatan 4, Norrmalm (no phone). Strut to house and techno and a fantastic light show or work your way through three floors of bars. Very popular.

Live music: rock and jazz

Apart from the cafés and bars already listed, there's no shortage of specific venues that put on **live music**. Most of the performers will be local bands, for which you'll pay 60–70kr entrance, but nearly all the big names make it to Stockholm, playing at a variety of seated halls and stadiums – naturally, tickets for these are much more expensive. The main venue is the Stockholm Globe Arena (T-bana Globen; ☎08/600 3400, ⓦwww.globen.se), supposedly the largest spherical building in the world – ring for programme details or ask at the tourist offices.

Cirkus Djurgårdsslätten 43 ☎08/587 987 00, ⓦwww.cirkus.se. Occasional rock and R&B performances.

Daily News Kungsträdgården, Norrmalm ☎08/21 56 55, ⓦwww.dailys.nu. Part of the Dagens Nyheter complex, this central rock venue hosts the most consistent range of live music in town – everything from grunge to techno.

Engelen Kornhamnstorg 59, Gamla Stan ☎08/20 10 92, ⓦwww.wallmans.com. Live jazz, rock or blues nightly until 3am, but arrive early to get in; the music starts at 8.30pm (Sun 9pm).

Fasching Kungsgatan 63, Norrmalm ☎08/21 62 67, ⓦwww.fasching.se. Local and foreign

contemporary jazz; a good place to go dancing too. Closed Sunday.

Nalen Regeringsgatan 74 ☎08/566 398 00, ⓦwww.landh-taube.se/gn. Once *the* place to hear music in the city (even the Beatles were booked to play here), now offering jazz, swing and big band.

Södra Teatern Mosebacke torg, Södermalm ☎08/556 972 30. This is one of the best places in the capital for world music, hip hop, rock and pop – if it's happening anywhere, it's happening here. Weekends only.

Stampen Stora Nygatan 5, Gamla Stan ☎08/20 57 93. Long-established and rowdy jazz club, both trad and mainstream; occasional foreign names, too.

Tre Backar Tegnérgatan 12–14, Norrmalm
☎08/673 44 00. Good, cheap pub with a cellar for
live music performances. Rock and blues nightly
Monday to Saturday until midnight.

Classical music, theatre and cinema

For up-to-date **information** about what's on where, check the special Saturday supplement of the *Dagens Nyheter* newspaper, "På Stan". *What's On*, free from the tourist office, is also indispensable for **arts listings**, with day-by-day information about a whole range of events – gigs, theatre, festivals, dance – sponsored by the city, many of which are free and based around Stockholm's many parks. Popular venues in summer are Kungsträdgården and Skansen, where there's always something going on.

Classical music and opera

Classical music is always easy to find. Many museums – particularly the History Museum and Music Museum – have regular programmes, and there's generally something on at one of the following venues: Konserthuset, Hötorget, Norrmalm (☎08/10 21 10); Berwaldhallen, Strandvägen 69, Östermalm (☎08/784 18 00, ⓦwww.sr.se/berwaldhallen); Gamla Musikaliska Akademien, Blasieholmstorg 8, near the National Art Museum (☎08/20 68 18); and Myntet, Hantverkargatan 5 (☎08/652 03 10). Operan (☎08/24 82 40, ⓦwww.operan.se) is Sweden's most famous **operatic** venue; for less rarefied presentations of the classics, check the programme at the Folkoperan, Hornsgatan 72, Södermalm (☎08/658 53 00). If you're after **church music**, you'll find it in Norrmalm at Adolf Fredriks kyrka, Gustav Wasa kyrka in Odenplan, and at St Jakobs kyrka; in Gamla Stan, try Storkyrkan. For more details consult *What's On*.

Theatre and cinema

There are dozens of **theatres** in Stockholm, but only one has regular performances of **English-language productions**: Vasa Teatern, Vasagatan 19 (☎08/24 82 40). If you want tickets for anything else theatrical, it's often worth waiting for reduced-price standby tickets, available from the kiosk in Norrmalmstorg.

    Cinema-going is an incredibly popular pastime in Stockholm, with screenings of new releases nearly always full. The largest venue in the city centre is Filmstaden Sergel in Hötorget (☎08/562 600 00, ⓦwww.sf.se), but there's also a good number of cinemas the entire length of Kungsgatan between Sveavägen and Birger Jarlsgatan, always very lively on Saturday night. Tickets cost around 80kr and films are never dubbed into Swedish.

    Finally, **Kulturhuset** in Sergels Torg (see p.450) has a full range of artistic and cultural events, most of them free; the information desk on the ground floor gives away programmes.

Gay Stockholm

Stockholm's **gay scene** is disappointingly small and closeted. Attitudes in general are tolerant but you won't see gay couples walking hand in hand or kissing in the street – just one of the false perceptions of Sweden. Until just a few years ago, when the country freed itself from restrictive tax rules imposed on bars and restaurants, there was only one specifically gay hangout in the whole of the city. Thankfully today things have changed and bars are springing up all over the place, although a kneejerk reaction by the government in response to AIDS has forced all gay saunas to close. The main bars and clubs to be seen at are listed below but beware that all are male-dominated – lesbians have an extremely low profile in Stockholm.

    Information is available from the **RFSL**, the National Association for Sexual Equality (*Riksförbundet för Sexuellt Likaberättigande*; ☎08/736 02 12, ⓦwww.rfsl.se), the city's main gay centre at Sveavägen 57 (T-bana Rådmansgatan). The centre offers HIV advice (☎08/736 02 11), publishes a free newspaper, *Kom Ut*, and runs a bookstore, a restaurant and radio station. Also look out for the free paper, *QX*, available in bars across the city, and have a look at ⑩www.stockholmtown.com/gay. **Gay Pride Week** (☎08/33 59 55, ⑩www.stockholmpride.org) takes place during the second week of August.

Bars and clubs

Bitch Girl Club Kolingsborg, Slussen ☎070/748 14 24. Scandinavia's biggest lesbian club, held every other Friday in summer and Saturday during the rest of the year.

Häktet Hornsgatan 82 ☎08/84 59 10. A wonderful place with two bars, front and back, as well as a quiet sitting room and a beautiful outdoor courtyard – a real haven in summer. It's only open Wednesday (when there's a mostly female crowd), and on Friday nights.

Mandus Österlånggatan 7 ☎08/20 60 55. The best gay restaurant in Stockholm, serving up tiger prawns, beef and chicken wok dishes and delicious home-made burgers. Deservedly known for its vibrant bar staff, too.

Patricia Stadsgårdskajen ☎08/743 05 70, ⑩www.patricia.st. The Queen Mother's former yacht attracts queens from across Stockholm for fun on Sunday nights (no entrance fee if you eat in the restaurant), often with drag acts or stand-up comedy. A great place for romantic evenings staring out across the harbour.

Regnbågsrummet Sturecompagniet, Stureplan (no phone). Currently Stockholm's hippest club – hence the long queues. Fri & Sat.

Sidetrack Wollmar Yxkullsgatan 7 ☎08/641 16 88, ⑩www.sidetrack.nu. Dark and smoky British-style pub popular with leather and denim boys. Men only.

TipTop Sveavägen 57 ☎08/32 98 00. Stockholm's main gay men's venue – a club, restaurant and bar all rolled into one – and very popular, especially on Friday and Saturday nights. Open daily.

Torget Mälartorget 13, Gamla Stan ☎08/20 55 60, ⑩www.torgetbaren.nu. Opposite Gamla Stan T-bana, this is an elegant place for a drink at any time of the evening. Always busy and full of beauties.

Listings

Airlines American Airlines ☎08/78 03 55; British Airways ☎020/78 11 44; Delta Air Lines ☎08/587 691 01; Finnair ☎020/78 11 00; Icelandair ☎08/690 98 00; KLM and Northwest ☎08/593 624 30; Malmö Aviation, Bromma airport ☎08/597 915 62; Ryanair ☎0911/23 36 88; SAS Stureplan 8 ☎020/72 77 27; United Airlines ☎020/79 54 02.

Airport enquiries Arlanda ☎08/797 61 00; SAS domestic flights to and from Arlanda ☎08/797 50 50; Bromma ☎08/797 68 00; Skavsta ☎0155/28 04 00; Västerås ☎021/80 56 00.

Banks and exchange Banks generally stay open later in central Stockholm than in the rest of the country – usually Mon–Fri 9.30am–3pm, though some stay open until 5.30pm; the bank at Arlanda is open even longer hours. Forex exchange offices offer better value than the banks for changing money; branches can be found in the main hall at Central Station (daily 7am–9pm); Cityterminalen (Mon–Fri 7am–8pm, Sat & Sun 8am–5pm); Vasagatan 14 (Mon–Fri 9am–7pm, Sat 9am–4pm); in the Sverigehuset (Mon–Fri 8am–7pm, Sat & Sun 9am–5pm); and at Arlanda airport Terminal 2 (daily 6am–9pm).

Bookshops Akademibokhandeln, corner of Regeringsgatan & Mäster Samuelsgatan; Aspingtons (secondhand), Västerlånggatan 54; Hedengrens Bokhandel, Sturegallerian, Stureplan 4; Sweden Bookshop, Sverigehuset, Hamngatan 27.

Bus enquiries For SL bus information see "SL travel information" below; for long-distance bus information call Swebus Express on ☎0200/218 218 or visit ⑩www.swebusexpress.se; for Svenska Buss call ☎0771/67 67 67.

Car rental Avis, Vasagatan 10B, and Arlanda and Bromma airports ☎020/78 82 00; Budget, Klarabergsviadukten 92 ☎08/411 15 00; Europcar, Tegelbacken 6 ☎08/611 45 60; Hertz, Vasagatan 26 ☎020/211 211.

Dentist Emergency dental care at St Eriks Hospital, Flemingatan 22; daily 8am–8.30pm. Out of hours ring Stockholm Care on ☎08/672 24 00.

Doctors Tourists can get emergency outpatient care at the hospital for the district they are staying in; check with Stockholm Care ☎08/672 24 00.

Embassies and consulates Australia, Sergels Torg 12 ☎08/613 29 00; Canada, Tegelbacken 4 ☎08/453 30 00; Ireland, Östermalmsgatan 97 ☎08/661 80 05; New Zealand – use the Australian Embassy; UK, Skarpögatan 6–8 ☎08/671 30 00; USA, Dag Hammarskjöldsväg 31 ☎08/783 53 00.

Emergencies Ring ☎112 for police, ambulance or fire services.

Ferries Tickets for Finland from Silja Line at Stureplan or Värtahamnen (☎08/22 21 40, ✆www.silja.com), and from Viking Line at Stadsgårdsterminalen (☎08/452 40 00, ✆www.vikingline.se); tickets for Estonia from Tallink, Frihamnen (☎08/667 00 01, ✆www.tallink.se); for the archipelago from Waxholms Ångfartygs AB, Strömkajen (☎08/679 58 30, ✆www.waxholmsbolaget.se).

Internet access *Internet Café*, 3rd floor, Pub department store, 63 Drottningatan; *Café Access*, Kulturhuset, Sergels torg; *Nine*, Odengatan 44; *Cafe Zenit*, Sveavägen 20. At all these places, you'll pay 40–60kr per hour.

Laundry Self-service launderette at Västmannagatan 61, or try the youth hostels.

Left luggage There are lockers at Central Station, the Cityterminalen bus station and the Silja and Viking ferry terminals. Locker prices start at 30kr per day.

Lost property Östra Kyrkogatan 4, Central Station ☎08/412 69 60.

News in English BBC, NPR, Radio Australia, Radio New Zealand, RTE and CBC programming can be heard on Stockholm International 89.6 FM. Radio Sweden also provide news in English, about Sweden only, on the same frequency several times during the day – for schedules, call ☎08/784 72 88, visit ✆www.sr.se/p6 or look in the *Dagens Nyheter* newspaper.

Newspapers Kiosks at Central Station, Cityterminalen, and at Press Stop shops (branches in the Gallerian shopping centre on Hamngatan and at Sveavägen 52). They can be read for free at the Stadsbiblioteket (City Library), Sveavägen 73, or at the Kulturhuset, Sergels Torg.

Pharmacy 24hr service at C. W. Scheele, Klarabergsgatan 64 ☎08/454 81 30.

Police Stations at Norra Agnegatan 33–37, Kungsholmen ☎08/401 00 00; and at Tulegatan 4 ☎08/401 12 00.

Post office The most useful office is in the Central Station (Mon–Fri 7am–10pm, Sat & Sun 10am–7pm); take your passport if collecting poste restante mail.

SL travel information Bus, T-bana and regional train (*pendeltåg*) information on ☎08/600 10 00. There are SL-Centers at Sergels Torg (Mon–Fri 7am–6.30pm, Sat & Sun 10am–5pm); Slussen (Mon–Fri 7am–6pm, Sat 10am–1pm); Gullmarsplan, Södermalm (Mon–Thurs 7am–6.30pm, Fri 7am–6pm, Sat 10am–5pm); and Fridhemsplan, Kungsholmen (Mon–Fri 7am–6.30pm, Sat 10am–5pm).

Systembolaget Norrmalm: Klarabergsgatan 62; Regeringsgatan 55; Sveavägen 66; Vasgatan 25; Odengatan 58 and 92. Gamla Stan: Lilla Nygatan 18. Södermalm: Folkungagatan 56 & 101; Götgatan 132; and inside the Söderhallarna shopping centre in Medborgarplatsen. Opening hours are generally Mon–Wed 10am–6pm, Thurs & Fri 10am–7pm, Sat 10am–2pm.

Toilets There are central public toilets in the Gallerian shopping centre, Åhléns and NK department stores, T-Centralen and Cityterminalen.

Train information For tickets and information for domestic and international routes with SJ (Swedish State Railways), call ☎0771/75 75 75; from abroad ring ☎00 46 771/ 75 75 75; for Tågkompaniet call ☎020/44 41 11.

Travel agents Kilroy, Kungsgatan 4 (☎0771/54 57 69), for discounted rail and air tickets and ISIC cards. Tickets: branches at Kungsgatan 60 (☎08/24 00 90), Sturegatan 8 (☎08/611 50 20) and Sveavägen 42 (☎08/24 92 20).

Around Stockholm

Such are Stockholm's attractions, it's easy to overlook the city's surroundings; yet only a few kilometres from the centre the countryside becomes noticeably leafier, the islands less congested and the water brighter. As further temptation, some of the country's most fascinating sights are within easy reach, like the spectacular **Millesgården** sculpture museum and **Drottningholm**, Sweden's greatest royal palace. Further out is the little village of **Mariefred**, containing Sweden's other great castle, **Gripsholm** – like Drottningholm, it's accessible by a fine boat ride on the waters of Lake Mälaren. Other trips from Stockholm – out into the stunning **archipelago** or to the university town of **Uppsala** – really merit more time, although if you're pressed it's possible to travel to each and return the same day.

While the Stockholm Card and 1- and 3-day cards are valid on bus, T-bana and regional train services within Greater Stockholm, you can't use them on the more enjoyable boat services to Drottningholm or in the archipelago. The quickest way to get to Uppsala is by SJ train from Central Station, although from July to mid-August there's also a boat service to Uppsala (Wed & Sat only; ☎08/587 140 00, ⓦwww.strommakanalbolaget.com), which leaves Stadshusbron (next to City Hall on Kungsholmen) at 9.30am, arriving at Uppsala at 6.30pm. Boats to Mariefred and Drottningholm also leave from Stadshusbron.

Lidingö and Millesgården

A residential commuter island just northeast of the city centre, **Lidingö** is where the well-to-do of Stockholm live – you'll already have glimpsed it if you arrived from Finland or Estonia on the Silja Line or Estline ferries, as they dock immediately opposite. It's worth a second look, though: eagle eyes may have spotted, across the water, the tallest of the statues in the startling **Millesgården** at Carl Milles Väg 2 (May–Sept daily 10am–5pm; Oct–April Tues–Thurs noon–4pm, Sat & Sun 11am–5pm; ⓦwww.millesgarden.se; 75kr), the outdoor sculpture collection of **Carl Milles** (1875–1955), one of Sweden's greatest sculptors and collectors. To **get there**, take the T-bana to Ropsten, then the rickety Lidingöbanan (a cross between a train and a tram) over the bridge to Torsviks torg, from where it's a short signposted walk down Herserudsvägen.

The statues are placed on terraces carved from the island's steep cliffs, with many of Milles's animated, classical figures perching precariously on soaring pillars, overlooking the distant harbour. A huge *Poseidon* rears over the army of sculptures, the most remarkable of which, *God's Hand*, has a small boy delicately balanced on the outstretched finger of a monumental hand. If you've been elsewhere in Sweden much of the work may seem familiar – copies and casts of the originals adorn countless provincial towns. If this collection inspires, it's worth tracking down three other pieces by Milles in the capital: his statues of *Gustav Vasa* in the Nordic Museum on Djurgården, the *Orpheus Fountain* in Norrmalm's Hötorget and, at Nacka Strand (reached most enjoyably by Waxholmsbolaget boats from Strömkajen), the magnificent *Gud på Himmelsbågen*, a claw-shaped vertical piece of steel topped with the figure of a boy – a stunning marker at the entrance to Stockholm harbour.

Drottningholm and Birka

Even if your time in Stockholm is limited, it's worth saving a day for a visit to the harmonious royal palace of **Drottningholm** (May–Aug daily 10am–4.30pm; Sept daily noon–3.30pm; Oct–April Sat & Sun noon–3.30pm; ⓦwww.royalcourt .se;60kr), beautifully located on the shores of leafy Lovön island, 11km west of the city centre. The fifty-minute boat trip there is part of the experience, with hourly departures from Stadshusbron (May to early Sept daily 9.30am–6pm; 70kr one-way, 100kr return), or take the T-bana to Brommaplan and then any bus numbered between #301 and #323 from there – a less thrilling ride, but one that's covered by the 1- and 3-day cards and Stockholm Card.

Drottningholm is perhaps the greatest achievement of the architects **Tessin**, father and son. Work began in 1662 on the orders of King Karl X's widow, Eleonora, Tessin the Elder modelling the new palace in a thoroughly French style – leading to that tired and overused label of a Swedish Versailles. Apart from anything else it's considerably smaller than its French counterpart, utilizing false perspective and trompe l'oeil to boost the elegant, rather narrow interior. On Tessin the Elder's death in 1681, the palace was completed by his son, already at work on Stockholm's Royal Palace. Inside, good English notes are available to help you sort out each room's detail, a riot of Rococo decoration largely dating from the time when Drottningholm was bestowed as a wedding gift on Princess Louisa Ulrika (a sister of Frederick the Great of Prussia). Since 1981 the Swedish royal family has slummed it out at Drottningholm, using the palace as a permanent home, a move that has accelerated efforts to restore parts of the palace to their original appearance – so that the monumental **Grand Staircase** is now exactly as envisaged by Tessin the Elder.

Nearby in the palace grounds is the **Court Theatre** (*Slottsteater*; May–Sept guided tours only, every 30min; ⓦwww.drottningholmsteatern.dtm.se; 60kr), dating from 1766. Its heyday came a decade later when Gustav III imported French plays and acting troupes, making Drottningholm the centre of Swedish artistic life. Take a guided tour and you'll get a flowery though accurate account of the theatre's decoration: money to complete the building ran out in the eighteenth century, meaning that not everything is quite what it seems, with painted papier-mâché frontages masquerading as the real thing. The original backdrops and stage machinery are still in place, though, and the tour comes complete with a display of eighteenth-century special effects – wind and thunder machines, trapdoors and simulated lighting. If you're in luck you might catch a **performance** of drama, ballet or opera here (usually June–Aug): the cheapest **tickets** cost around 170kr, though decent seats are in the region of 300–600kr – check the schedule at Drottningholm or ask at the tourist offices in the city. With time to spare, the extensive palace grounds also yield the **Chinese Pavilion** (May–Aug daily 11am–4.30pm; 60kr), a sort of eighteenth-century royal summer house.

Birka

Further into Lake Mälaren lies the island of **Björkö**, known for its rich flora and good swimming beaches. Its real draw, though, are the remnants of Sweden's oldest town, **BIRKA**, founded in around 750 AD. A Viking trading centre at its height during the tenth century, a few obvious remains lie scattered about – including the fragments of houses and a vast cemetery. Major excavations were carried out between 1990 and 1995 and a museum, **Birka the Viking Town** (May to mid-Sept daily 10am–5pm; 50kr), now displays rare artefacts recovered during the excavations as well as scale models of the harbour and craftsmen's quarters. You can get there from Stadshusbron in Stockholm on a Strömma Kanalbolaget boat (departures May to late Sept daily 10am, return trip from Birka at 3.30pm); tickets can be bought on board and cost 225k return, which includes admission to the museum.

The Archipelago

If you arrived in Stockholm by ferry from Finland or Estonia you'll already have had a tantalizing glimpse of the **Stockholm archipelago**. This array of hundreds upon hundreds of pine-clad islands and islets is the only one of its kind in the world. The archipelago can be split into three distinct sections: inner, centre and outer. In the inner section there's more land than sea; in the centre it's pretty much fifty-fifty; while in the outer archipelago distances between islands are much greater – out here, sea and sky merge into one and the nearest island is often no more than a dot on the horizon. It's worth knowing that if it's cloudy in Stockholm, chances are that the sun will be shining somewhere out on the islands. Even if your trip to the capital is short, don't miss the chance to come out here.

Practicalities

Getting to the islands is easy and cheap, with Waxholmsbolaget (☏08/679 58 30, ⓦwww.waxholmsbolaget.se) operating the majority of sailings. Most boats leave from Strömkajen in front of the *Grand Hotel*; others leave from just round the corner at Nybrokajen, next to the Royal Theatre of Drama. Buy tickets either on the boats themselves or from the Waxholmsbolaget office on Strömkajen, where you can also pick up free timetables to help you plan your route – timetables are also posted on every jetty. **Departures** to the closest islands are more frequent (often around 4 daily) than those to the outer archipelago; if there's no direct service connections

△ Stockholm skyline

can often be made at the island of Vaxholm. Ticket prices are very reasonable, ranging from 30kr to 95kr depending on the length of the journey, though if you're planning to visit several islands it might be worth buying the **Interskerries Card** (*båtluffarkort*), which gives sixteen days' unlimited travel on all Waxholmsbolaget lines for 385kr. Most boats have a cafeteria or restaurant on board.

Though there are few hotels in the archipelago, **accommodation** is most easily available in a number of several well-equipped and comfortable **youth hostels** – the most useful are at **Finnhamn** (☎08/542 462 12, ⊛www.finnhamn.nu; open all year); **Grinda** (☎08/542 490 72, ☎08/542 493 45; May to late Oct); **Gällnö** (☎08/571 661 17; May–Sept); and **Utö** (☎08/504 203 15, ⊛www.uto-vardshus.se; May to Sept). It's also possible to rent **cottages** on the islands during summer, though you'll need to book way in advance – contact the tourist office in Stockholm. **Campsites** are surprisingly hard to find – you'll be much better off camping rough, as a few nights' stay in most places won't cause any problems. Remember, though, that open fires are prohibited all over the archipelago.

Archipelago highlights

Of the vast number of islands in the archipelago, several are firm favourites with Stockholmers, **Vaxholm** in particular; others offer more secluded beaches and plenty of opportunity for lovely walks. The following are a few of the better islands to make for.

Inner and central archipelago

Lying just an hour's ferry ride northeast of Stockholm, **Vaxholm** is a popular weekend destination. The main settlement on the island, **Vaxholm town**, has an atmospheric wooden harbour with an imposing fortress which once guarded the waterways into the city, successfully staving off attacks from Danes and Russians in the seventeenth and eighteenth centuries; it's now an unremarkable museum of military bits and pieces. Also within easy reach is **Grinda**, two hours or so east, a thickly wooded island typical of the inner archipelago, whose magnificent sandy beaches are much favoured by families.

In the central archipelago, low-lying **Gällnö** is covered with thick pine forest. One of the most beautiful islands, it has been designated a nature reserve, with deer and eider duck the most likely wildlife you'll spot. Ferries take about two hours to get here from Stockholm.

Some two hours by boat from Stockholm, **Svartsö**, near the island of Möja (see below), lies in the most scenic part of the archipelago where dozens of surrounding islands give the impression of giant stepping stones leading to the mainland. Known for its fields of grazing sheep, virgin forest and crystal-clear lakes, the good roads make Svartsö ideal for cycling or walking.

Outer archipelago

If you're heading into the outer archipelago from Stockholm, you can sometimes cut the journey time by taking a bus or train to a further point on the mainland and picking the boat up there – where this is the case, we've given details below.

Three hours from Stockholm, the tiny island of **Finnhamn** lies in the outer reaches of the archipelago, where the islands start to become fewer and where the sea takes over. It's a good place for walking, through forests, meadows and along cliff tops.

Möja (pronounced roughly as "Murr-ya"), three and a half hours from the city, is one of the most popular islands, home to around three hundred people who make their living from fishing and farming. There's a small craft museum in the main town, **Berg**, and even a cinema, though as there are no beaches (private houses line the entire shoreline), it's not the place to come if you want to go swimming.

In the southern stretch of the archipelago, the beautiful island of **Bullerö** is home to a nature reserve with walking trails and an exhibition on the archipelago's plentiful flora and fauna. The journey takes three hours in total: get the train from Slussen to Saltsjöbaden, and from there a boat to the island of Nämdö, where you can take the shuttle service to Bullerö.

Sandhamn has been a destination for seafarers since the 1700s and remains so today, its tiny harbour packed full of sailing yachts of all shapes and sizes. The main village is a haven of narrow alleyways, winding streets and overgrown verandas. It takes three and a half hours to get here from Stockholm by boat, or you can save time by taking bus #434 from Slussen to Stavsnäs – the furthest point on the mainland – and picking up a boat for the hour-long sailing to Sandhamn.

Lying far out in the southern reaches of the archipelago, **Utö** is ideal for cycling, with the sandy beaches at Ålö storsand perfect for a picnic stop. You can also walk along Utö's cliffs at Rävstavik. The journey time from Stockholm is three hours.

Mariefred and Gripsholm

If you've only got time for one boat trip out from Stockholm, make it to **MARIEFRED**, a tiny village to the west of the city whose peaceful attractions are bolstered by the presence of nearby **Gripsholm**, one of Sweden's most enjoyable castles. To get there in summer, take the *S/S Mariefred* steamboat from Klara Mälarstrand near Stadshuset on Kungsholmen (mid-May to mid-June Sat & Sun 10am; mid-June to mid-Aug Tues–Sun 10am; mid-Aug to mid-Sept Sat & Sun 10am; 3hr 30min each way; 120kr one-way, 180kr return); buy your ticket on board. Outside summer, you'll have to travel on an Eskilstuna-bound train as far as **Läggesta**, where connecting buses shuttle passengers to Mariefred, a total journey of around an hour.

Mariefred itself – the name is derived from an old monastery, Pax Mariae (Mary's Peace) – is quiet and quintessentially Swedish. From the quayside, it's a ten-minute stroll through the town's narrow streets, bordered by well-kept wooden houses and little squares that have barely changed in decades, to the main square. This is dominated by the **Rådhus**, a fine eighteenth-century timber building housing the **tourist office** (June–Aug Mon–Sat 10am–6pm, Sun 10am–4pm; Sept–May Mon–Thurs 9am–4pm, Fri 9am–3pm; ☎0159/297 90, ⊛www.mariefred.se). Staff can also arrange **bike rental** (85kr per day; 400kr per week).

Steam train freaks will love the **Railway Museum** (variable hours; free) in the village – you'll probably have noticed the narrow-gauge tracks running to the quayside. There's an exhibition of old rolling stock and workshops, plus the chance to take one of the hourly trips by steam train from Mariefred to Läggesta (see below).

Gripsholm Slott

Lovely though Mariefred village is, it's really only a preface to **Gripsholm Slott** (mid-May to mid-Sept daily 10am–4pm; rest of the year Sat & Sun noon–3pm; ⊛www.royalcourt.se; 60kr), the imposing red-brick castle built on a round island just to the south: walk up the quayside and you'll spot the path to the castle running across the grass by the water's edge.

In the late fourteenth century, Bo Johnsson Grip, the Swedish High Chancellor, began to build a fortified castle at Mariefred, although the present building owes more to two Gustavs – Gustav Vasa, who started rebuilding in the sixteenth century, and Gustav III, who was responsible for major restructuring a couple of centuries later. Rather than the hybrid that might be expected, the result is rather pleasing – a textbook castle, whose turrets, great halls, corridors and battlements provide the material for an engaging **guided tour** (mid-May to mid-Sept 1pm; 10kr in addition to entrance fee). On this you'll be shown a vast portrait collection, which includes recently commissioned works of political and cultural figures as well as assorted royalty and nobility; some fine decorative and architectural work; and, as at Drottningholm, a private theatre, built for Gustav III. It's too delicate to use for performances these days, but in summer plays and events take place out in the castle grounds.

Practicalities

Mariefred warrants a night's stay, if not for the sights – which you can exhaust in half a day – then for the pretty, peaceful surroundings. There's only one **hotel**, *Gripsholms Värdhus*, Kyrkogatan 1 (☎0159/347 50, ⓦwww.gripsholms-vardshus.se; ⓺), a wonderfully luxurious option overlooking the castle and the water. The seasonal **youth hostel** (☎0159/367 00, ⓦwww.redcross.se/gripsholm; mid-June to mid-Aug) is near the ferry jetty in the Red Cross education centre.

As for **eating**, treat yourself to lunch in *Gripsholms Värdhus*, a beautifully restored inn (the oldest in Sweden). The food is excellent and around 200kr will get you a turn at the herring table, a main course, drink and coffee – all enhanced by the terrific views over to Gripsholm. Alternatively, try *Skänken* at the back of the Värdhus, where lunch goes for around 75kr, or the friendly but basic *Mariefreds Bistro*, opposite the castle.

Leaving Mariefred, one option is to take the **narrow-gauge steam train** that leaves roughly hourly from 11am to 5pm (mid-June to mid-Aug daily; May to mid-June & mid-Aug to Sept Sat & Sun; 48kr single, 60kr return) for **Läggesta**, a twenty-minute ride. Here you can pick up the regular SJ train back to Stockholm; check connections on the timetable at the tourist office before you leave. Of course it's also possible to get to Mariefred from Stockholm this way.

Västerås

Around 100km inland from Stockholm, **VÄSTERÅS**, Sweden's sixth biggest city and capital of the county of Västmanland, is an immediately likeable mix of old and new. Today the lakeside city carefully balances its dependence on industrial technology giant, ABB, with a rich history dating back to Viking times.

Arrival, information and accommodation

The **train** and **bus stations** are located together on Södra Ringvägen, a ten-minute walk through Vasaparken from the **tourist office** at Stora Gatan 40 (mid-June to mid-Aug Mon–Fri 9am–7pm, Sat 9am–3pm, Sun 10am–2pm; mid-Aug to mid-June Mon–Fri 9.30am–6pm, Sat 10am–3pm; ☎021/10 38 30, ⓕ10 38 50, ⓦwww.vastmanland.se). The **youth hostel** (☎021/18 52 30, ⓦwww.lovudden.nu) is 5km west of the city on Lake Mälaren at Lövudden; take bus #25 from the bus station.

Hotels

Aaros Metro Vasagatan 22 ☎021/18 03 30, ⓕ18 03 37. The cheapest hotel in town, and very centrally located. ⓷/⓶

Arkad Östermalmsgatan 25 ☎021/12 04 80, ⓦwww.arkad-hotell.se. New building done out in old-fashioned style. Good value for money in summer. ⓹/⓶

Elite Stadshotellet Stora Torget ☎021/10 28 00, ⓦwww.vasteras.elite.se. A Västerås fixture, the hotel has been here as long as anyone can remember. Good-quality modern rooms right in the heart of the city. ⓹/⓷

Klipper Kungsgatan 4 ☎021/41 00 00, ⓕ14 26 70. Centrally located close to the lazy Svartån River in the old town. Charming rooms and good service. ⓸/⓶

Radisson SAS Plaza Karlsgatan 9A ☎021/10 10 10, ⓦwww.radisson.com. Known locally as the "skyscraper", this 25-storey glass and chrome structure is the last word in Scandinavian chic, and is good value in summer. ⓹/⓷

The City

From the tourist office, it's a short stroll up Köpmangatan to the twin cobbled, squares of **Bondtorget** and **Stora Torget**. A narrow lane leads from the southwestern corner of Bondtorget to the narrow **Svartån River**, which runs right through the centre of the city; the bridge across it has great views of the old wooden cottages which nestle eave to eave along the riverside. Although it may not appear so significant, the Svartån was a decisive factor in making Västerås the headquarters of one of the world's largest engineering companies, **Asea-Brown-Boveri** (ABB), which needed a ready source of water for production. North of the thirteenth-century brick **Domkyrkan** (Mon–Fri 8am–5pm, Sat & Sun 9.30am–5pm), last resting place of Erik XIV, who died an unceremonious death in Örbyhus castle in 1577 after eating pea soup laced with arsenic. His tomb lies to the right of the altar; local rumour has it that his feet had to be cut off in order to fit his body into its coffin. Beyond the cathedral is the most charming district of Västerås, **Kyrkbacken**, a hilly area with steep cobblestone alleys winding between well-preserved old wooden houses where the craftsmen and the petit bourgeoisie lived in the 1700s.

A quick walk past the restaurants and shops of Vasagatan will bring you back to Stora Gatan and eventually to the eye-catching modern **Stadshuset**, a far cry from the Dominican monastery which once stood on this spot. Although home to the city's administration, the building is best known for its 47 **bells**, the largest of which (known as "The Monk") can be heard across Västerås at lunchtimes. Across Fiskartorget square, the **Castle** is home to an arrestingly dull collection of local paraphernalia contained within the **county museum** (Tues–Sun noon–4pm; free). The best exhibit lies just inside the entrance: a Viking boat grave from nearby Tuna, Badelunda – the richest female burial yet discovered in Sweden.

Eating and drinking

Västerås has easily the best **restaurants** of any town around Lake Mälaren. Here, you'll find every sort of fare, from Thai to Greek, traditional Swedish to British-style pub food. The city also has a lively **drinking** scene, including one cocktail bar 24 floors up, from where there are unsurpassed views of the lake.

Atrium Corner of Smedjegatan and Sturegatan. Greek favourites from 89kr, and starters from 20kr.

Bill o Bob Stora Torget 5. Handily located in the main square, with all the usual meat and fish dishes for around 100kr. Outdoor seating in summer.

Bishops Arms Östra Kyrkogatan. British-style drinking hole with a large selection of beers, single-malt whisky and pub grub.

Brogården Stora Gatan 42, next to the tourist office. Riverside café with good views of the water and old wooden houses.

Kalle på Spången Kungsgatan 2. Great old-fashioned café with outdoor seating close to the

river. The place for coffee, cakes, grilled baguettes and fresh orange juice.

Karlsson på taket Karlsgatan 9A. Chichi restaurant and café on the 24th floor of the Skrapan skyscraper, which also houses the *Radisson SAS Plaza* hotel. Expensive, but fantastic views.

Kina Thai Gallerian 36. Chinese and Thai dishes for around 140kr, and lunch for 63kr. Handily located next to the Filmstaden cinema.

Piazza di Spagna Vasagatan 26. The best pizzeria in town and a very popular place for lunch (63kr). Pizzas and pasta from around 70kr; meat dishes start at 162kr.

Around Västerås: the Anundshög burial mound

Six kilometres northeast of the city, **Anundshög** is the largest royal burial mound in Sweden. Dating from the sixth century, it's thought to be the resting place of King Bröt-Anund and the stash of gold with which he was buried. Several other smaller burial mounds are located close by, suggesting that the site was an important Viking meeting place for several centuries. Beside the main mound lie a large number of **standing stones** arranged end to end in the shape of two ships. To get here take bus #12 from the centre of town to its final stop, Bjurhovda, from where it's a twenty-minute walk.

Uppsala

First impressions as the train pulls into **UPPSALA**, less than an hour north of Stockholm, are encouraging. The red-washed **castle** looms up behind the railway sidings, while the **cathedral** dominates the foreground. A sort of Swedish Oxford, Uppsala clings to the past through a succession of striking buildings connected with and scattered about its cathedral and **university**. Regarded as the historical and religious centre of the country, it serves as a tranquil daytime alternative to Stockholm – with an active student-oriented nightlife.

Arrival and information

Uppsala's **train** and **bus stations** are adjacent to each other off Kungsgatan, and it's not far to walk down to the **tourist office** at Fyris torg 8 (Mon–Fri 10am–6pm, Sat 10am–3pm, also Sun noon–4pm end June to mid-Aug; ☎018/27 48 00, ⓦwww.res.till.uppland.nu), where you can pick up bundles of leaflets about the city. **Boats** to and from Stockholm use the pier south of the centre, at the end of Bävernsgränd. If you're flying in or out of Sweden, you can bypass Stockholm entirely by using the #801 bus link between Uppsala bus station and **Arlanda airport** (daily 4am–midnight every 15–30min; 40min; 75kr).

Accommodation

Though Uppsala can easily be seen as a day-trip from Stockholm, you may want to stay around a little longer. As well as a fair range of central hotels, there's a **youth hostel** at Sunnerstavägen 24 (☎018/32 42 20), 6km south of the centre (bus #20, #25 or #50 from Nybron by Stora Torget). For **camping**, head a few kilometres north to the open spaces of Gamla Uppsala (see p.474), or use the regular site, *Sunnersta Camping* (☎018/27 60 84), 7km from town by Lake Mälaren and near the youth hostel at Graneberg (bus #20).

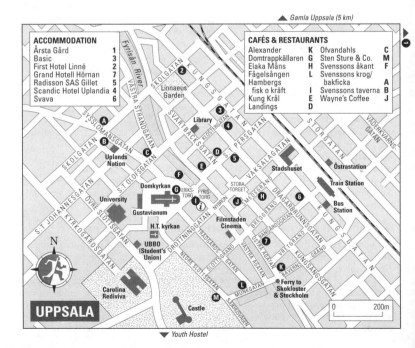

▲ Gamla Uppsala (5 km)

ACCOMMODATION

Årsta Gård	1
Basic	3
First Hotel Linné	2
Grand Hotell Hörnan	7
Radisson SAS Gillet	5
Scandic Hotel Uplandia	4
Svava	6

CAFÉS & RESTAURANTS

Alexander	K	Ofvandahls	C
Domtrappkällaren	G	Sten Sture & Co.	M
Elaka Måns	H	Svenssons åkant	F
Fågelsången	L	Svenssons krog/	
Hambergs		bakficka	A
fisk o kräft	I	Svenssons taverna	B
Kung Krål	E	Wayne's Coffee	J
Landings	D		

UPPSALA

0   200m

▼ Youth Hostel

Årsta Gård Jordgubbsgatan 14 ☎ & ℗ 018/25 35
00. This large cottage-style building in the
outskirts is the cheapest hotel in town; take bus
#7 (daytime) or #56 (evenings) to Södra Årsta
(15min). ❷
Basic Kungsgatan 27 ☎018/480 50 00,
Ⓦwww.basichotel.com. Simple, bright and clean
rooms with en-suite bathrooms and a tiny kitchen.
❸/❷
First Hotel Linné Skolgatan 45 ☎018/10 20 00,
Ⓦwww.firsthotels.com. Tiny and completely
overpriced rooms – a last resort when everything
else is full. ❺/❸
Grand Hotell Hörnan Bangårdsgatan 1 ☎018/13
93 80, Ⓦwww.eklundshof.se. Wonderfully elegant

place with large old-fashioned rooms and a
restaurant. ❺/❹
Radisson SAS Gillet Dragarbrunnsgatan 23
☎018/68 18 00, Ⓦwww.radisson.com. A stone's
throw from the cathedral but with average,
overpriced, shag-piled rooms. Fans of kitsch
should head for the restaurant. ❺/❸
Scandic Hotel Uplandia Dragarbrunnsgatan 32
☎018/495 26 00, Ⓦwww.hotelsvava.com. A
modern hotel that's gone in for a lot of wood – and
small rooms. ❻/❸
Svava Bangårdsgatan 24 ☎018/13 00 30, ℗13
22 30. Modern hotel with all mod-cons, including
specially designed rooms for people with
disabilities.❻/❹

The City

The centre of the medieval town is the great Gothic **Domkyrkan** (daily
8am–6pm; Ⓦwww.uppsaladomkyrka.nu; free), Scandinavia's largest cathedral. Built
to show the people of Trondheim in Norway that even their mighty church could
be overshadowed, it loses out to its competitor by reason of the building material –
local brick rather than imported stone – and only the echoing interior remains
impressive, particularly the French Gothic ambulatory, sided by tiny chapels and
bathed in a golden glow. One chapel contains a lively set of restored fourteenth-
century wall paintings that recount the legend of Saint Erik, Sweden's patron saint:
his coronation, crusade to Finland, eventual defeat and execution at the hands of
the Danes. The Relics of Erik are zealously guarded in a chapel off the nave: poke
around and you'll also find the tombs of Reformation rebel Gustav Vasa and his son
Johan III, and that of Linnaeus, the botanist, who lived in Uppsala. Time and fire
have resulted in the rebuilding of the rest of the cathedral, now scrubbed and painted to the extent that it resembles a historical museum more than a thirteenth-century spiritual centre; even the characteristic twin spires are late nineteenth-century
additions.

The buildings grouped around the Domkyrkan can all claim a purer historical
pedigree. Opposite the towers, the onion-domed **Gustavianum** (May–Sept
daily 11am–5pm; Sept–April Tues–Sun 11am–4pm; 40kr), built in 1625 as part
of the university, is much touted by the tourist office for its **Augsburg Art
Cabinet**, an ebony treasure chest presented to Gustav II Adolf, and for its tidily
preserved anatomical theatre. The same building houses a couple of small collections of Egyptian, classical and Nordic antiquities, with a minimal charge for
each section. The current **University** building (Mon–Fri 8am–4pm) is the
imposing nineteenth-century Renaissance edifice over the way. Originally a
seminary, it's used today for lectures and seminars and hosts the graduation ceremonies each May. The more famous of its alumni include Carl von Linné
(Linnaeus) and Anders Celsius, inventor of the temperature scale. No one will
mind if you stroll into the entrance hall for a quick look, but the rest of the
building is not open to the public.

From the university, Övre Slottsgatan leads to the **Carolina Rediviva** (mid-June
to mid-Aug Mon–Fri 9am–5pm, Sat 10am–5pm, Sun 11am–4pm; 20kr; rest of the
year Mon–Fri 9am–8pm, Sat 10am–4pm; free), the university library. On April 30
each year the students meet here to celebrate the first day of spring (usually in
the snow), all wearing a traditional student cap, which gives them the appearance
of disaffected sailors. This is one of Scandinavia's largest libraries, with around four
million books. Adopt a student pose and you can slip in for a wander round and a
coffee in the common room. It's also worth taking a look in the **manuscript
room**, where there's a collection of rare letters and other paraphernalia. The

beautiful sixth-century Silver Bible is on permanent display, as is Mozart's original manuscript for *The Magic Flute*.

After this, the **Castle** (guided tours June–Aug 1pm & 3pm; 60kr) up on the hill is a disappointment. In 1702 a fire that destroyed three-quarters of the city did away with much of the building, and only one side and two towers remain of what was once an opulent rectangular palace. But the facade still gives a weighty impression of what's missing, like a backless Hollywood set. Inside, admission also includes access to the castle's art museum but, quite frankly, it won't make your postcards home.

Seeing Uppsala, at least the compact older parts, will take up a good half a day. If the weather holds out, use the rest of your time to stroll along the Fyrisån River that runs right through the centre of town. There are several points worth lingering in and enough greenery to make this stretch more than just pleasant. One beautiful spot is the **Linnaeus Garden** (daily: May–Sept 7am–8.30pm; rest of the year 7am–7pm; ⓦ www.linnaeus.uu.se; access to greenhouses 20kr) over the river on Svartbäcksgatan. Sweden's oldest botanical gardens, established in 1655 by Olof Rudbeck the Elder, they were relaid by Linnaeus (Carl von Linné) in 1741, and some of the species he introduced and classified still survive. The adjoining **museum** (same times; 20kr) was once home to Linnaeus and his family, and it attempts to re-create his life through a partially restored library, writing room and a collection of natural-history specimens.

Gamla Uppsala

Five kilometres to the north of the present city, three huge **barrows** – royal burial mounds dating back to the sixth century – mark the original site of Uppsala, **Gamla Uppsala** (ⓦ www.raa.se/gamlauppsala). This was a pagan settlement, and a place of ancient sacrificial rites. Every ninth year the festival of Fröblot demanded the death of nine people, hanged from a nearby tree until their corpses rotted. The pagan temple where this bloody sacrifice took place is now marked by the Christian **Gamla Uppsala kyrka** (daily: April–Sept 9am–6pm; rest of the year 9am–4pm), built over pagan remains when the Swedish kings were first baptized into the new faith. What survives is only a remnant of what was, originally, a cathedral – look inside for the faded wall paintings and the tomb of Celsius, of thermometer fame. An eleventh-century rune stone is set into the wall outside.

Arriving by bus from Uppsala (#2, #24 or #54 from Stora Torget), get off at the terminus – nothing more than a bus stop next to a level crossing – opposite the worthwhile **Historical Centre** (mid-May to mid-Aug daily 10am–5pm; mid-April to mid-May & mid-Aug to Sept Tues–Sun 10am–4pm; Oct–Dec Sat & Sun noon–3pm; 50kr), with exhibitions illustrating the origin of local myths from Roman times as well as Uppsala's era of greatness until the thirteenth century. There's little else to Gamla Uppsala, and perhaps that's why the site remains so mysterious and atmospheric. There's a **restaurant**, *Odinsborg*, if the nibbles strike after an afternoon of pillaging and plundering; it's between the Historical Centre and the church.

Eating, drinking and nightlife

Commensurate with its status as one of Sweden's largest cities and major university centres, Uppsala boasts an impressive range of sophisticated **restaurants** and **bars**. Almost all of them are located in the grid of streets bordered by the Fyrisån River, St Olofsgatan and Bangårdsgatan and, though many places get pretty busy in the summer, it's not necessary to book a table. If you're travelling north from here into the Swedish provinces, it's a good idea to splurge and make the most of the city's eateries, while the bars, often packed with pub-crawling students, are usually pretty lively.

Cafés and restaurants

Alexander Östra Ågatan 59. Completely OTT Greek place with busts of famous personalities from the ancient world at every turn. Mains at 95–165kr.
Domtrappkällaren St Eriks Gränd 15. One of the most chichi places in town – old vaulted roof and great atmosphere. Main courses go for around 200kr, though you can get an excellent lunch upstairs for 110kr.
Elaka Måns Smedsgränd 9. A modern bistro-style restaurant with the usual run of fish and meat dishes. Very popular, not too expensive and definitely worth a look.
Fågelsången Munkgatan 3. Café and lunch place that's full of posey students.
Hambergs fisk o kräft Fyris torg 8. Located next to the tourist office and serving very good fish and seafood. Particularly popular at lunchtime.
Kung Krål St Persgatan 4. Across the river from the tourist office, in a fantastic old stone building with outdoor seating in summer. Swedish home cooking and international dishes for around 120kr.
Landings Kungsängsgatan 5. Busy café in the main pedestrian area.
Ofvandahls Sysslomansgatan 3–5. Near the old part of Uppsala, this lively café (originally opened in 1878) has old wooden tables and sofas – don't leave town without trying the home-made cakes.
Sten Sture & Co Nedre Slottsgatan 3. Trendy and inspired cooking at this large, ramshackle wooden-built restaurant and bar immediately below the castle; there's often live jazz and plenty of young Uppsala folk around. Outdoor tables in summer. A must.
Svenssons åkant St Eriks Torg. Outdoor café right by the river; a delightful place to relax in summer.
Svenssons krog/bakficka Sysslomangatan 15. A wonderful restaurant decked out in wood and glass with everything from Swedish home cooking to top-class salmon. The cheaper *bakficka* ("back pocket") bar serves good pasta dishes.
Svenssons taverna Sysslomangatan 14. One of Uppsala's best eateries, with a large outdoor seating area under the shade of huge beech and oak trees, and an "international" menu with main courses at around 120kr. Recommended.
Wayne's Coffee Smedsgränd 4. The most agreeable café in Uppsala – modern and airy with large windows which open right out onto the street.

Nightlife

At night most of Uppsala's action is generated by the **students** in the "Nations" houses in the grid of streets behind the university, backing onto St Olofsgatan. Not unlike college fraternities, each house organizes dances, gigs and parties of all hues and, most importantly, all boast very cheap bars. The official line is that if you're not a Swedish student you won't get into most of the things; in practice, being foreign and being nice to the people on the door generally yields entrance, while with an ISIC card it's even easier. Since many students stay around during the summer, functions are not strictly limited to term time. A good choice to begin with is *Uplands Nation*, near the river off St Olofsgatan and Sysslomangatan, which has a summer outdoor café open until 3am.

Otherwise, *Sten Sture & Co* (see above) puts on **live bands** in the evenings, while *Katalin and all that jazz* is open late and has jazz nights – it's in the long, low building that was once a goods shed behind the train station at Östra Station.

Listings

Banks and exchange Handelsbanken, Vaksalagatan 8; Nordea, Stora Torget; SEB, Kungsängsgatan 7–9. There's a Forex exchange at Fyris Torg 8, left of the tourist office (Mon–Fri 9am–7pm, Sat 9am–3pm).
Bus enquiries Uppsalabuss ☏018/27 37 00. City buses leave from Stora Torget; long-distance buses from the bus station adjacent to the train station (see Stockholm "Listings", p.463, for phone numbers).
Car rental Avis, Stålgatan 8 ☏018/15 16 80; Europcar, Kungsgatan 103 ☏018/17 17 30; Hertz, Kungsgatan 97 ☏018/16 02 00.
Pharmacy at Bredgränd Mon–Fri 9am–6.30pm, Sat 10am–3pm ☏020/66 77 66.
Police Salagatan 18 ☏018/16 85 00.
Systembolaget at Svavagallerian, Bredgränd (Mon–Wed 10am–6pm, Thurs & Fri 10am–7pm, Sat 10am–2pm).
Taxis Taxi Kurir ☏018/12 34 56; Uppsala Taxi ☏018/10 00 00.
Train enquiries Information on ☏018/65 22 10.

Travel details

Trains

Stockholm to: Boden (2 daily; 14hr); Gällivare (2 daily; 16hr); Gävle (hourly, 1hr 20min); Gothenburg (hourly; 3hr 10min by X2000, 5hr by Inter-City); Helsingborg (hourly; 5hr); Kiruna (2 daily; 17hr); Läggesta (for Mariefred; 8 daily; 40min); Luleå (2 daily; 14hr); Malmö (hourly; 4hr 30min); Mora (4 daily; 4hr); Östersund (3 daily; 6hr); Sundsvall (7 daily; 3hr 30min); Umeå (1 daily; 10hr); Uppsala (hourly; 40min).

Uppsala to: Gällivare (2 daily; 15hr); Gävle (hourly; 40min); Kiruna (2 daily; 16hr); Luleå (2 daily; 13hr); Mora (4 daily; 3hr); Östersund (3 daily; 4hr 30 min); Stockholm (hourly; 40min); Sundsvall (7 daily; 2hr 45 min); Umeå (1 daily; 9hr 30min).

Buses

Stockholm to: Gävle (1 daily; 2hr 20min); Gothenburg (2 daily Mon–Wed, 3 Thurs, 5 Fri & Sun, 1 Sat; 4hr 30min, or 7hr 20min via Kristinehamn or Jönköping); Halmstad (Fri & Sun 1 daily; 7hr 30min); Helsingborg (1–2 Mon–Fri & Sun; 8hr); Jönköping (1–2 Mon–Fri & Sun; 4hr 50min); Kalmar (5 daily; 6hr 30min); Kristianstad (4 weekly; 9hr 30min); Kristinehamn (2–3 daily; 3hr); Malmö (Fri & Sun 1–2 daily; 10hr 20min); Norrköping (2 daily Mon–Wed, 3 Thurs, 5 Fri & Sun, 1 Sat; 2hr); Östersund (1 daily; 8hr 30min); Sollefteå (1 daily; 8hr 15min); Umeå (1 daily; 9hr 20min).

International trains

Stockholm to: Copenhagen (5 daily; 5hr); Narvik (1 daily; 20hr); Oslo (3 daily; 5hr).
Uppsala to: Narvik (1 daily; 18hr 30min).

International ferries

Stockholm to: Eckerö on the Åland Islands (3–5 daily; 3hr); Helsinki (1 Viking Line and 1 Silja Line daily; 17hr); Mariehamn (6 daily; 4hr); Tallinn (1 daily; 13hr); Turku (4 daily; 12–14hr).

3.2

Gothenburg and around

Gothenburg is Sweden's second city and the largest seaport in Scandinavia – facts that have been enough to persuade many travellers arriving here by ferry to move quickly on to the surrounding countryside. But beyond the gargantuan shipyards, Gothenburg's Dutch-designed cityscape of broad avenues, elegant squares, trams and canals is one of the prettiest in Sweden, and with its well-established café society and rich cultural life it's worth a lot more time than most visitors give it. The city's image has also suffered from the inevitable compar-

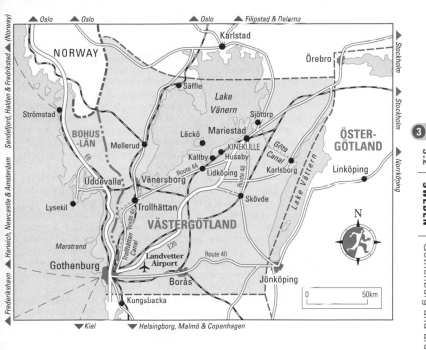

isons with the capital, and while there is a certain resentment on the west coast that Stockholm wins out in the national prestige stakes, many Swedes far prefer Gothenburg's more relaxed atmosphere and its closer proximity to Western Europe, particularly since the Öresunds Bridge has put it within three hours of Copenhagen.

The counties to the north and east of the city are prime targets for domestic tourists. The closest highlight to Gothenburg is the glorious fortress island of **Marstrand**, an easy and enjoyable day-trip away, while heading towards Norway, the uninhabited islands, tiny fishing villages and clean beaches of the craggy **Bohuslän coastline** attract thousands of holidaymakers. To the northeast of the city, the vast and beautiful lakes of **Vänern** and **Vättern** provide the setting for a number of historic towns, fairytale castles and some splendid scenery, all within an hour's train journey from Gothenburg. The lakes are connected to each other (and to the east and west coasts) by the cross-country **Göta Canal**, and if you're inspired by the possibilities of water transport you could always make the complete four-day trip by boat from Gothenburg to Stockholm. The first leg of the journey is from the sea up the Trollhättan Canal to **Trollhättan**, an appealing little town built around the canal and a good place to aim for if you only have time for a short trip out from the city. Beyond here, though, other agreeable lakeside towns vie for your attention, with attractions including the elk safaris on the ancient hills of Halleberg and Hunneberg, near **Vänersborg** at the bottom of Lake Vänern, picturesque medieval **Mariestad**, further up the lake's eastern shore, and the huge military fortress at **Karlsborg** on the western shore of Lake Vättern.

Regular **train** and **bus** services run across most of the region, though the isolated minor attractions along the Bohuslän coast can prove difficult to reach by public transport. **Accommodation** is never a problem, with plenty of hotels, hostels and campsites in each town.

Gothenburg

With its long history as a trading centre, **GOTHENBURG** (Göteborg in Swedish, pronounced "Yur-te-boy") is a truly cosmopolitan city. Founded on its present site in the seventeenth century by Gustav Adolf, it was the last in a long line of attempts to create a trade centre free from Danish influence – Denmark had enjoyed control of Sweden's west coast since the Middle Ages, extracting extortionate tolls from all water traffic travelling into Sweden. An original medieval settlement was sited 40km up the Göta River, but was later moved to a location north of the present city in order to avoid these tolls; a third attempt was built on the island of Hisingen, but this fell to the Danes during the battle of Kalmar. Six years later Gustav Adolf founded a new city on the site of today's main square.

Although Gothenburg's reputation as an industrial and trading centre has been severely eroded in recent years – as evidenced by the stillness of the cranes in the shipyards – the British, Dutch and German traders who settled here during the eighteenth and nineteenth centuries left a rich architectural and cultural inheritance. The city is graced with terraces of grand merchant houses, all carved stone, stucco and painted tiles, while the trade between Sweden and the Far East brought an Oriental influence, still visible in the chinoiserie detail on many buildings. This vital trading route was monopolized for over eighty years by the hugely successful Swedish East India Company, whose auction house, selling exotic spices, tea and fine cloth, attracted merchants from all over the world.

Today the city remains a regular port of call for business travellers, though the flashy central hotels that accommodate them say much less about Gothenburg than the restrained opulence of the older buildings, which reflect not only the city's bygone prosperity but also the understatement of its citizens.

Arrival and information

From **Landvetter airport**, 25km east of the city, Flygbuss buses run every fifteen minutes via Korsvagan, a junction to the south of the centre, to Central Station. The journey takes around 30 minutes (daily 5am–11.15pm; 60kr, Gothenburg Pass not valid). For airline and airport information numbers, see p.494.

All **trains** arrive at Central Station, on Drottningtorget in the centre of the city. There's a Swebus office here too (Mon–Fri 7am–6pm, Sat & Sun 11am–5pm; ☎031/10 32 85, ⓦwww.swebus.se), from where you can buy bus tickets for services to Oslo, which stop outside. Otherwise, buses to and from destinations north of Gothenburg use **Nils Ericsonsplatsen** (ticket office Mon–Fri 7.30am–5.45pm, Sat 8am–2pm), just behind the train station. Buses from the south arrive at the **Heden** terminal, at the junction of Parkgatan and Södravägen, from where there are easy tram connections to all parts of the city.

DFDS Seaways **ferries** from Newcastle (2 weekly) arrive at Frihamnspiren on Hisingen, north of the river (☎031/650 650, ⓦwww.dfdsseaways.se); special buses shuttle from here to Nils Ericsonsplatsen behind the train station in the city centre (40kr, Gothenburg Pass not valid). When leaving, buses return to Frihamnspiren ninety minutes before sailings. Stena Line (031/704 00 00, ⓦwww.stenaline.com) ferries from Frederikshavn in Denmark (tickets from their office in the Nordstan Shopping Centre, see p.485) dock close to Mashuggstorget, twenty minutes' walk or a tram (#3, #4 or #9) ride west of the city centre, while those from Kiel in Germany dock 3km outside Gothenburg – take bus #491 or tram #3 or #9 into the centre. Heading back to Germany, Stena Line runs a special bus from Ericsonsplatsen at 5.50pm in time for the 7pm crossing.

Information

Gothenburg has two **tourist offices**. Handiest for new arrivals is the kiosk in Nordstan, the indoor shopping centre on Östra Hamngatan near Central Station

The Gothenburg Pass

Buying a **Gothenburg Pass** is a good money-saver if you're planning to do a lot of sightseeing. Available from tourist offices, Pressbyrån kiosks and hotels or online at Ⓦ www.goteborg.com, it gives unlimited bus and tram travel within the city, free entry to all city museums except Universeum (see p.488) and the Liseberg Amusement Park (not including rides), free car parking (see p.488) and boat excursions, plus various other reductions. Passes are available for either 24 hours (75kr) or 48 hours (295kr).

(Mon–Fri 9.30am–6pm, Sat 10am–4pm, Sun noon–3pm). The **main office** is on the canalfront at Kungsportsplatsen 2 (May Mon–Fri 9am–6pm, Sat & Sun 10am–2pm; June & mid- to late Aug daily 9am–6pm; July to mid-Aug daily 9am–8pm; Sept–April Mon–Fri 9am–5pm, Sat 10am–2pm; ☎031/61 25 00, Ⓦ www.goteborg.com). From the train station, it's five minutes' walk across Drottningtorget and down Stora Nygatan: the tourist office is on the right, opposite the statue of the so-called *Copper Mare* (see p.487). Both offices provide information, free city and tram maps, and offer a room-booking service, as well as selling the Gothenburg Pass. You can also pick up a copy of the bilingual, annually renewed updated *Guide Göteborg*, which details events, music and nightspots.

City transport

Apart from excursions north of the river or to the islands, almost everywhere of interest in Gothenburg is within easy walking distance of the centre. The wide streets are pedestrian-friendly and the canals and grid layout of the avenues make orientation simple. If you're staying further out, however, some sort of transport may be necessary. A free **transport map** (*Linje Kartan*) is available from either tourist office.

Public transport

The most convenient form of public transport are the **trams**, which clunk around the city and its outskirts on a colour-coded, eight-line system, passing all the central areas every few minutes – you can tell at a glance which line a tram is on as the route colour appears on the front. The main pick-up points are outside Central Station and in Kungsportsplatsen. During summer, there's the chance to ride on **vintage trams**, some dating from 1902, which trundle through the city centre to Liseberg and Slottskogen. Gothenburg also has a fairly extensive **bus** network, using much the same routes as the trams, although central pedestrianization can lead to some odd and lengthy detours. You shouldn't need to use them in the city centre; routes are detailed in the text where necessary.

If you have a Gothenburg Pass, all public transport within the city is free; if not, **tickets** should be bought from tram and bus drivers. There's no zonal system and adult fares cost a flat-rate 16kr. If you're staying for a couple of days, it's cheaper to buy a ticket card from the Tidpunkten (travel information) offices at Brunnsparken, Drottningtorget and Nils Ericsonsplatsen, or from Pressbyrån kiosks – a ten-trip ticket card costs 100kr. Stick these in the machines on a tram or bus, and press twice for an adult, once for a child. Trams run from 5am to midnight, after which there is a night service at double the price. **Fare-dodging** carries an instant fine of 600kr – since all the ticket information is posted in English at bus and tram stops, ignorance is no defence.

Finally, a good way to get to grips with the city is to take a **paddan boat tour**, an hour-long trip around the canals and harbour; tours leave regularly from moorings on the canal by Kungsportsplatsen (daily: late April to mid June & early Aug to mid-Sept 10am–5pm; mid-June to early Aug 10am–9pm; mid-Sept to early Oct noon–3pm; 80kr).

Cars, taxis and bikes

There's no shortage of **car parks** in the city, with a basic tariff of 20kr per hour in the centre. Buying a Gothenburg Pass gets you a free parking card, though this is not valid in privately run or multistorey car parks, or in any car park with attendants. The most useful car parks are the new Ullevigarage at Heden, near the bus terminal, the Lorensbergs near Avenyn, Gamla Ullevi on Alleyn, south

GÖTAÄLVBRON

GÖTAÄLVSGATAN

Frihamnspiren

Utkiken

Gullbergs-kaje

Nordstan Shopping Centre
and Forex (Money Exchange) (i)

0   500m

Maritima Centrum

Packhuskajen

Opera House

Bus Station
(to the harbours)

Forex
(Money
Exchange)

Central Station

Museum of Medical History

NORD-STADS-TORGET

NILS ERICSONS-PLATSEN

ODINS-PLATSEN

Kronhusbodarna & Kronhuset

Börshuset

DROTTNING-TORGET

STAMPGATAN

Stora Hamn Canal

City Museum

Rådhus

G. ADOLFS TORG

NORRA HAMNGATAN

Stora Hamn Canal

HAMNGATAN

Palm House

Gamla Ullevi Stadium

Antikhallarna

LILLA TORGET

BRUNNS-PARK

Trädgårds-föreningen

Museum of Banking

Cathedral

Great Synagogue

Copper Mare

KUNGS-PORTS-PLATSEN

Kungsparken

KUNGS-TORGET

Heden Bus Terminal P

NYA ALLÉN

SÖDRA VÄGEN

VALHALLAGATAN

Museum of Ethnography

Scandinavium

Saluhallen

Rosenlunds Canal

ALLÉGATAN

University Library

Röhsska Museum

University Main Building

VASASTAN

Lorensburg Theatre

ENGELBREKTSGATAN

GÖTA-PLATSEN

Konserthuset

Art Museum

Liseberg Amusement Park

KORSVÄGEN

ÖRGRYTEVÄGEN

Universeum

FÖRENINGSGATAN

▼ *Botanical Gardens &* 21

of Kungsportsplatsen, and two multistorey car parks at Nordstan Shopping Centre near Central Station and Garda-Focus close to Liseberg. The Gothenburg Pass is valid in all of these; if you don't have a Gothenburg Pass, roadside parking areas marked with blue signs are cheaper than meters. Some of the larger hotels offer a discount at the multistorey car parks. For information on **car rental** see p.494.

Taxis can be summoned by calling ⓣ031/65 00 00. There's a 20 percent reduction for women travelling at night, but check with the driver first.

Cycling is a popular and easy way to get around, since Gothenburg boasts a comprehensive series of cycle lanes and plenty of bike racks. The most central place to **rent a bike** (around 150kr per day) is Millennium Cykel at Chalmersgatan 19 (ⓣ031/18 43 00), just south of Avenyn. You can also rent bikes from either Slottskogen or Stigbergssliden youth hostels (see p.483) for just 50kr per day. An excellent *Cykelcarte*, showing all cycle routes through the city and out to the archipelago, is also available from the tourist office.

Accommodation

Gothenburg has plenty of decent accommodation options, with no shortage of comfortable **youth hostels**, a couple of which are very central, along with **private rooms** and a number of big, city-centre **hotels**. Most of these are clustered together around the train station and offer a high standard of service, if with fairly uniform and uninspiring decor. Summer and weekend reductions mean that even the better hotels can prove surprisingly affordable, and most places also take part in the **Gothenburg Package**, which can cut costs further (see below).

Whenever you turn up, you shouldn't have any trouble finding accommodation, though in summer it's a good idea to book ahead if you're aiming to stay in one of the cheaper hotels, or in the most popular youth hostels.

Hotels and pensions

The **Gothenburg Package** scheme, coordinated by the tourist office, is a real bargain, as it bundles together accommodation, breakfast and a 24-hour Gothenburg Pass for 450kr per person in a twin bedroom, with discounts for children sharing. Around thirty good, central hotels take part in the scheme, which operates all week, all year. Unless otherwise stated, note that all the places listed below are part of the Gothenburg Package scheme, and all include breakfast in the price unless otherwise stated. Note that bookings for the Gothenburg Package have to be made through the tourist office; you can't get this offer by contacting the hotels direct.

Alleyn Parkgatan 10 ⓣ031/10 14 50, ⓕ11 91 60, ⓔhotel.allen@telia.com. Very central, sensibly priced hotel close to Avenyn and the old town. Rates include room-service breakfasts and parking. ❸/❷

Barken Viking Gullbergskajen ⓣ031/63 58 00, ⓔbarken.viking@liseberg.se. Moored by the Opera House, this 1906 Danish-built training ship is a charismatic and comfortable choice with dark, cosy rooms and good service. ❷

City Lorensbergsgatan 6 ⓣ031/708 40 00, ⓦwww.cityhotelgbg.se. Not to be confused with *Rica City* (see p.483), this is a cheapish and popular hotel, excellently positioned close to Avenyn. En-suite rooms cost 300kr more than those with shared facilities. ❶

Eggers Drottningtorget ⓣ031/80 60 70, ⓦwww.bestwestern.se. The original station hotel and now part of the Best Western chain, this very characterful establishment has individually furnished bedrooms and a wealth of grand original features. One of the best-value central hotels, especially if you stay here using the Gothenburg Package. ❻/❹

Elite Plaza Västra Hamngatan 3 ⓣ031/720 40 40, ⓔreservations@gbgplaza.elite.se. With its magnificently opulent facade, painted ceilings and mosaic floors, this is the perfect place if money is no concern: a stunning blend of contemporary and classical design. ❻/❺

Europa Köpmansgatan 38 ⓣ031/751 65 00, ⓦwww.scandic-hotels.com. Reputedly the biggest hotel in Sweden, with 460 rooms and a massive facade attached to the Nordstan Shopping Centre. Very plush – all rooms are en suite with bath tubs – and breakfasts are huge. ❻/❸

Excelsior Karl Gustavsgatan 7 ⓣ031/17 54 35, ⓦwww.hotelexcelsior.nu. Stylish yet homely 1880 building in a road of classic Gothenburg houses between Avenyn and Haga. It's been a hotel since 1930 and both Greta Garbo and Ingrid Bergman stayed here, as did, more recently, Sheryl Crow. Classic suites with splendid nineteenth-century features cost no more than plain rooms – Garbo's room was no. 535. ❹/❷.

Hotel 11 Maskingatan 11 ⓣ031/779 11 11, ⓦwww.hotel11.se. At the harbour on the site of an old shipbuilding yard, with views across to Hisingen, this is one of the city's most interesting and stylish options. Take tram #1, #3, #4 or #9 from Järntorget, then the Älv Snabben boat (Mon–Fri 6am–11.30pm every 30min, shorter hours on weekends; 16kr, free with Gothenburg Pass) in the direction of Klippan from in front of the Opera House at Lilla Bommen – get off at Eriksberg. ⑤/❸

Lilton Föreningsgatan 9 ☎031/82 88 08, ⓔhotel.lilton@acrewoodab.se. Close to the Haga district, this is a small, old, ivy-covered place set among trees with very friendly, informal service. 100kr reduction at weekends. ❸

Marla Erikssons Pensionat Chalmersgatan 27A ☎031/20 70 30, Ⓕ16 64 63. Just ten rooms, but well positioned on a road running parallel with Avenyn. Breakfast isn't included, and you can't stay as part of the Gothenburg Package. ❶

Rica City Hotel Burggrevegatan 25 ☎031/771 00 80, ⓦwww.rica.se. Comfortable hotel close to Central Station; en-suite rooms with cable TV, plus a solarium (30kr) and a free sauna. ❸

Robinson Södra Hamngatan 2 ☎031/80 25 21, ⓦwww.hotelrobinson.com. Facing Brunnspark, this mediocre hotel still boasts its original facade – the building was part of the old Furstenburg Palace; etched windows on the lift are some of the few features to have survived decades of architectural meddling. All rooms have cable TV; en-suite rooms cost 160kr more. Not part of the Gothenburg Package scheme. ❸/❷

SAS Radisson Scandinavia Södra Hamngatan 59–65 ☎031/80 60 00, ⓦwww.radissonsas.com. Opposite the train station and exuding all the usual glitz: the atrium foyer is like a shopping mall with glass lifts and fountains; bedrooms are all pastel shades and birch wood. ⑤/❹

Hostels and private rooms

Gothenburg's cheapest accommodation options are either a **private room** (175kr per person in a double, 225kr for a single), bookable through the tourist office (☎031/61 25 00; 60kr booking fee), or a bed in one of the **youth hostels**. All the hostels listed below are run by the STF and are open all year unless otherwise stated. Other than Partille, they all have private double rooms (❶), too.

Göteborgs Minihotel Tredje Långgatan 31 ☎031/24 10 23, ⓦwww.minihotel.se. Open all year, this uninspiring hostel is nevertheless well placed for the alternative scene around the Linné area.

Karralunds Vandrarhem Olbergsgatan 1 ☎031/84 02 00, ⓦwww.liseberg.se. Four kilometres from the centre, close to Liseberg Amusement Park – take tram #5 to Welandergatan, direction Torp. Non-smoking rooms available, plus cabins and a campsite (see below); Breakfast can only be ordered by groups; book ahead in summer.

Kviberg Vandrarhem Kvibergsvägen 5 ☎031/43 50 55, ⓦwww.vandrarhem.com/kviberg. In Gamlestad, ten minutes by tram #6 or #7 from Central Station. Double (❶) rooms and dorms available.

Masthuggsterrassen Masthuggsterrassen 8 ☎031/42 48 20, ⓔmasthuggsterrassen.vandrarhem @telia.com. Up the steps from Masthuggstorget and a couple of minutes' walk from the Stena Line ferry terminal from Denmark. ❶

Partille Landvettervagen, Partille ☎031/44 65 01, ⓦwww.partillevandrarhem.com. Fifteen kilometres east of the city (bus #513 from Heden bus terminal to Astebo; 30min), this hostel has a solarium and day room with TV.

Slottskogen Vegagatan 21 ☎031/42 65 20, ⓔmail@slottskogenvh.se. Superbly appointed and well-designed family-run hostel, just two minutes' walk from Linnegatan and not far from Slottskogen Park. Take tram #1 or #2 to Olivedahlsgatan. ❶

Stigbergssliden Stigbergssliden 10 ☎031/24 16 20, ⓦwww.hostel-gothenburg.com. Excellent hostel, well placed for ferries to Denmark, being just west of the Linné area down Första Långgatan. All rooms have basins, and there's disabled access, laundry facilities (20kr) and pleasant back courtyard. Breakfast is 40kr, and bike rental costs 50kr per day. ❶

Torrekulla Kallered ☎031/795 14 95, ⓦwww.stfturist.se. Pleasantly situated 15km south of the city, with lots of room, a free sauna and a nearby bathing lake. Bus #705 from Heden or a ten-minute train journey from Central Station (direction Kungsbacka), then a fifteen-minute walk. ❶

Campsites and cabins

Two of the following campsites also provide **cabins**, which are worth considering, especially if there are more than two of you. Facilities are invariably squeaky clean and in good working order – there's usually a well-equipped kitchen too – but you'll have to pay extra for bedding. Prices for cabins are given below; if you want to **camp**, you'll pay around 100kr for two people in July or August (50kr the rest of the year).

Askims ☎031/28 62 61, ℗68 13 35, ⓦwww.liseberg.se. Set beside sandy beaches 12km from the centre: take tram #1 or #2 to Linneplatsen, then bus #83, or the Blå Express (Blue Express; direction Saro) from outside Central Station on Drottningtorget. Open early May to late Aug (office daily 9am–noon & 3–6pm, slightly later Thurs–Sat); four-bed cabins cost 615kr in high season, 495kr in low.

Karralunds Vandrarhem Olbergsgatan ☎031/84 02 00, ℗84 05 00, ⓦwww.liseberg.se. Four kilometres from the centre, close to Liseberg Amusement Park – take tram #5 to Welandergatan, direction Torp. Set among forest and lakes, it's open all year; four-bed cabins cost 615kr; 695kr with your own toilet (50kr discount outside June–Aug).

Lilleby Havsbad ☎031/56 50 66, ℗56 16 05. Take bus #21 from Nils Ericsonsplatsen and change to the #23 at Kongshallavagen. It takes an hour to reach, but has a splendid seaside location.

The City

Everything of interest in Gothenburg lies south of the **Göta River**, and there's rarely any need to cross the water. This is a fairly compact city, and easy to get around, so you can cover most of the sights in just a day or two, although to get the most from your stay allow a few more days and slow your pace down to a stroll – which will put you in step with the locals.

At the heart of the city is the historic **old town**, and while Gothenburg's attractions are by no means restricted to this area, its picturesque elegance makes it the best place to start. Tucked between the Göta River to the north and the zigzagging Rosenlunds Canal to the south, old Gothenburg's tightly gridded streets are lined with impressive facades and boast an interesting food market and a couple of worthwhile museums – the **City Museum** and, up by the harbour, the museum of **maritime history**. Just across the canal that skirts the southern edges of the old town is **Trädgårdsföreningen** park, in summer full of picnicking Gothenburgers.

Heading further south into the modern centre, **Avenyn** is Gothenburg's showcase boulevard, alive with showy restaurants and bars. However, it's the roads off Avenyn that hold the area's real interest, with trendy 24-hour café-bars and some of Gothenburg's best museums: in a small area called **Vasastan** to the southwest, you'll find the **Röhsska Museum** of applied arts and, further south in **Götaplatsen**, the city **Art Museum**. For family entertainment day or night, the famous **Liseberg Amusement Park**, just to the southeast of Avenyn, has been pulling in the crowds since the 1920s.

Vasastan stretches west to **Haga**, the city's old working-class district now thoroughly gentrified and fashionable. Haga Nygatan, the main thoroughfare, heads towards Linnegatan, the arterial road through the **Linné** district. The area is home to Gothenburg's most interesting evening haunts, with cafés, bars and restaurants dotted amongst long-established antique emporiums and sex shops. Further out, the rolling **Slottskogen** park holds the **Natural History Museum**, but is perhaps most appealing as a place to relax and enjoy the sun.

The old town and harbour

The **old town** is divided in two by the **Stora Hamn Canal**, to the north of which are most of the main sights and the harbour, where the decaying shipyards make for a dramatic backdrop. The streets south of the Stora Hamn, stretching down to the Rosenlunds Canal, are perfect for an afternoon's leisurely stroll, with some quirky cafés, food markets and junk shops to dip into, as well as Sweden's oldest synagogue. Straddling the Stora Hamn is Gothenburg's main square, **Gustav Adolfs Torg**, the best place to start your explorations.

North of the Stora Hamn

At the centre of stately **Gustav Adolfs Torg**, a copper statue of the city's founder, Gustav Adolf, points ostentatiously at the ground where he reputedly declared "Here I will build my city." The statue is a copy, however: the German-made original was kidnapped on its way to Sweden and Gothenburgers commissioned a new one rather than pay the ransom.

To the east of the square, with the canal behind you, stands the **Rådhus**. Beyond its rather dull classical colonnaded facade, the interior of its extension was designed by the innovative functionalist architect E.G. Asplund in 1936 and retains its original glass lifts, mussel-shaped drinking fountains and huge areas of laminated aspen. Facing the canal, at right angles to the Rådhus, is the white, double-columned 1842 **Börhuset**, the former stock exchange. If you can persuade the attendants to let you in, you'll be rewarded with magnificent banqueting and concert halls, and smaller rooms in a riot of red and blue stucco inspired by the eighteenth-century excavations at Pompeii.

Head north from the square along the filled-in canal of Östra Hamngatan, past the amorphous **Nordstan Shopping Centre**, Sweden's biggest. Despite several attempts to jazz it up, it remains a depressingly bland design; the shopping is good, though, and you might also venture inside to visit the tourist kiosk or one of the ferry company offices. If you have time to spare, it's worth taking a short detour along Burggrevegatan to Drottningtorget to see the city's impressive **Central Station**. The oldest in the country, dating from 1856, it retains its original facade and boasts a grand and marvellously preserved interior. Look out for the wood beam-ends in the ticket hall, each one carved into the likeness of a city council member of the day.

At its far end, Östra Hamngatan runs into **Lilla Bommen**. Here Gothenburg's industrial decline comes together with its artistic regeneration to dramatic visual effect: to the west, the cranes of dormant shipyards loom across the sky, a backdrop to industrial-themed sculptures in bronze and pink granite dotted along the waterfront. The **Opera House** (daily noon–6pm; guided tours July Tues & Wed noon–3pm, book ahead on ☎031/10 82 03; ⊛www.opera.se) to the left was designed with conscious industrial styling. To the right, **Utkiken** ("Look out"; mid-May to early Sept daily 11am–7pm; Jan to mid-May & early Sept to mid-Dec Sat & Sun 11am–4pm; 30kr), designed by the Scottish architect Ralph Erskine in the late 1980s, is an 86-metre-high office block taking the form of a half-used red lipstick. Its top storey offers panoramic views of the city and harbour.

Just west along the quay is the **Maritima Centrum** (May–June daily 10am–6pm, until 8pm July & Aug; ⊛www.gmtc.se; 45kr, free with Gothenburg Pass), which describes itself as "the largest ship museum in the world". An interesting experience, even for non-enthusiasts, it comprises a dozen boats including a 1915 lightship, a submarine and a fire float, each giving a glimpse of how seamen lived and worked on board. The original toilets and washrooms on board, for public use, are an experience in themselves. There's a rather good café and restaurant here, too.

From the maritime museum it's a short walk south to Gothenburg's oldest secular building, the **Kronhuset** on Kronhusgatan (Tues–Fri 11am–4pm, Sat & Sun 11am–5pm; free). Built by the Dutch in 1642 as an artillery depot for the city's garrison, this was where the five-year-old Karl XI was proclaimed king in 1660. Set in the eighteenth-century wings that flank the original building is the **Kronhusbodarna** (Mon–Fri 11am–4pm, Sat 11am–2pm), a cluster of small, pricey shops specializing in gold, silver and glasswork. You can buy a copy of the city's oldest key from the silversmith here, but your money would be better spent at the atmospheric vaulted café.

A couple of blocks further south, the **City Museum** (*Stadsmuseum*; May–Aug daily 11am–4pm; Sept–April Tues & Thurs–Sun 11am–4pm, Wed until 8pm; ⊛www.gbg.stadsmuseum.se; 40kr) is nowadays Gothenburg's primary museum. Located at Norra Hamngatan 12, it's housed in Ostindiska Huset, the offices, store and auction house that were constructed in 1750 for the enormously influential **Swedish East India Company**. Granted sole Swedish rights to trade with China in 1731, the company monopolized Far East commerce for over eighty years, the only condition being that the spices, silk and porcelain it brought back were to be sold in Gothenburg. The museum itself is well worth a browse, not least for its rich interior, a mix of stone pillars, stained glass and frescoes. Head first to the third floor, where there are exhibitions on the East India Company, allowing a look at the renovated auction hall. The section devoted to industry here is also impressive, a well-designed exhibition relating Gothenburg's twentieth-century history with displays on shipping and working conditions in the textile factories at the beginning of the century.

South of the Stora Hamn

Across Stora Hamn just to the west of the City Museum lies **Lilla Torget**, with its statue of Jonas Alstromer, who introduced the potato to Sweden in the eighteenth century. Walk on to the quayside at **Stenpiren**, the spot where hundreds of emigrants said their last goodbyes before sailing off to the United States. The original granite **Delaware Monument** was carted off to America in the early twentieth century, and it wasn't until 1938 that celebrated sculptor Carl Mille cast a replacement in bronze, which stands here looking out to sea.

Today, boats leave Stenpiren for the popular half-hour excursion to the island fortress of **Nya Elfsborg** (early May to Aug hourly 9.30am–5pm; 85kr, free with Gothenburg Pass). Built in the seventeenth century to defend the harbour and the city, the surviving buildings have been turned into a **museum** and café. There are guided tours in English (included in the price of the boat trip) around the square tower, chapel and prison cells.

Back at Lilla Torget, walk down Västra Hamngatan, which leads off the southern side of the square, to the city's cathedral; on the way you'll pass **Antikhallarna** (Mon–Fri 10am–6pm, Sat 10am–2pm), a clutch of pricey antique shops set in a fantastic building with a gilded ceiling and regal marble stairs leading up to a café. A few blocks south of here, to the left off Västra Hamngatan, is the classically styled **Cathedral** (Mon–Fri 8am–5pm, Sat 8am–3pm, Sun 10am–3pm). Built in 1827 (the two previous cathedrals were destroyed by fires at a rate of one a century), four giant sandstone columns stand at the portico, and inside there's an opulent gilded altarpiece. The plain white walls concentrate your eyes on the unusual post-Resurrection cross, devoid of a Jesus, whose gilded grave clothes are strewn below. Another quirky feature are the twin glassed-in verandas that run down either side, designed for the bishop's "private conversations".

Continuing east past the cathedral and north, on Östra Hamngatan, towards Stora Hamn canal, the leafy square known as **Brunnspark** soon comes into view, with Gustav Adolfs Torg just across the canal. The sedate house facing the square (now the snazzy *Palace* restaurant and nightclub) was once home to Pontus and Gothilda Furstenburg, the city's leading arts patrons in the late nineteenth century, who converted the top floor into an art gallery, the first in Gothenburg's to be lit with electric as well as natural light. They later donated their entire collection – the biggest batch of Nordic paintings in the country – to the city Art Museum. As a tribute to the Furstenburgs, the museum has made over the *Palace*'s top floor into an exact replica of the original gallery (see p.488) – you can wander upstairs and see the richly ornate plasterwork and gilding much as it was.

Along the southern canal

Marking the southern perimeter of old Gothenburg, the meandering Rosenlunds Canal (usually referred to as the southern canal) was a moat during the days when the city was fortified, and its banks make for a fine twenty-minute stroll past pretty waterside views and a number of interesting diversions.

Just east of Brunnspark, **Stora Nygatan** wends its way south along the canal's most scenic stretch, with classical buildings stuccoed in cinnamon and cream on one side, and the green expanse of Trädgårdsföreningen park (see below) on the other. Among all the architectural finery sits mainland Sweden's oldest synagogue, the **Great Synagogue**, inaugurated in 1855. This simple domed structure hides one of the most exquisite interiors of any European synagogue: the ceiling and walls are a rich mixture of blues, reds and gold, with Moorish patterns stunningly interwoven with Viking leaf designs. An impressive restoration programme during 2002 has brought the original colours into brilliant relief. Sadly, security concerns mean that it can only be visited by calling ☎031/17 72 45 first.

Heading south from the synagogue, you'll pass **Kungsportsplatsen**, in the centre of which stands a useful landmark, a sculpture known as the *Copper Mare* – though whoever gave it its name obviously didn't see it from below. Also on the square is the main tourist office. A few minutes further on, and a block in from the canal at Kungstorget (the square adjacent to Kungsportsplatsen), is **Saluhallen** (Mon–Fri 9am–6pm, Sat 9am–2pm), a pretty, barrel-roofed indoor market built in the 1880s. Busy and full of atmosphere, it's a great place to wander around; there's a flower market outside.

Five minutes from here is another food market, the neo-Gothic **Feskekörkan**, or "Fish Church" (Tues–Thurs 9am–5pm, Fri 9am–6pm, Sat 9am–1.30pm). Despite its undeniably ecclesiastical appearance, the nearest this 1874 building comes to religion is in the devotion shown by the fish lovers who come to buy and sell here. Inside, every kind of fish lies in gleaming, pungent mounds of silver, pink and black flesh; there's a very small, very good restaurant in a gallery upstairs (see p.490).

Avenyn and around

Across the canal bridge from Kungsportplatsen, the wide cobbled length of Kungsportsavenyn runs all the way southeast to Götaplatsen. Known more simply as **Avenyn**, this is the city's liveliest – if most blandly showy – thoroughfare, lined with nineteenth-century buildings, almost all of their ground floors converted into cafés, bars or restaurants. Gothenburg's young and beautiful strut up and down and sip overpriced drinks at tables that spill onto the street from mid-spring till September. It's enjoyable to sit here and watch life go by, but for all its glamour most of the tourist-oriented shops and brasseries are interchangeable and the grandeur of the city's industrial past is better evoked in the less spoiled mansions along roads like Parkgatan, at right angles to Avenyn over the canal.

The Trädgårdsföreningen

Before you cross over into the crowds of Avenyn, take time out to visit the **Trädgårdsföreningen**, or Garden Society Park (daily: May–Aug 7am–9pm, 10kr; Sept–April 7am–6pm, free), whose main entrance is just over the canal bridge. For once, this park really does lives up to its blurb – "a green oasis in the heart of the city". Among the trees and lawns are a surprising number of experimental sculptures, designed to blend in with their natural surroundings. Within the park, the **Palm House** (daily: June–Aug 10am–6pm; Sept–May 10am–4pm; 20kr, ticket covers entry to Botanical Gardens) of 1878 looks like a huge English-style conservatory and contains a wealth of very un-Swedish plant life. Close by is the **Butterfly House** (June–Aug daily 10am–5pm; April, May & Sept Tues–Fri 10am–4pm, Sat & Sun 10am–4pm; Oct–March Tues–Fri 10am–3pm, Sat & Sun 11am–3pm; 35kr), where you can wander among free-flying butterflies from Asia and the Americas. During summer the place goes into overdrive with lunchtime concerts and a special children's theatre.

Vasastan, Götaplatsen and Liseberg

Once you've had your fill of Avenyn, take one of the roads off to the west and wander into the district of Vasastan, where the streets are lined with fine nineteenth-century and National Romantic architecture, and the cafés are cheaper and more laid-back.

On Vasagatan, the main street through the area, is the excellent **Röhsska Museum** at 37–39, Sweden's only museum of applied arts (May–Aug Mon–Fri noon–4pm, Sat & Sun noon–5pm; Sept–April Tues noon–9pm, Wed–Fri noon–4pm, Sat & Sun noon–5pm; ⓦwww.designmuseum.se; 40kr). Built in 1916, this is an aesthete's Aladdin's cave, each floor concentrating on different areas of decorative and functional art, from early dynasty Chinese ceramics to European arts and crafts of the sixteenth century. The first floor holds an especially interesting section devoted to twentieth-century decor and featuring all manner of familiar designs right up to the present – enough to send anyone over the age of 10 on a nostalgia trip.

At the top of Avenyn, **Götaplatsen** is modern Gothenburg's main square, its focal point Carl Milles' **Poseidon**, a giant bronze nude with the physique of a bodybuilder and a staggeringly ugly face; the size of the figure's penis caused outrage when the sculpture was unveiled in 1930 and it was subsequently dramatically reduced. From the front, Poseidon appears to be squeezing the daylights out of a large fanged fish – a symbol of local trade – but if you climb the steps of the **Concert Hall** to the right, it becomes clear that Milles won the battle over Poseidon's manhood to stupendous effect.

Behind Poseidon looms the impressive **Art Museum** (*Konstmuseum*; May–Aug Mon–Fri 11am–4pm; Sept–April Tues, Thurs & Fri 11am–4pm, Wed 11am–9pm, Sat & Sun 11am–5pm; ⓦwww.konstmuseum.goteborg.se; 35kr), whose massive, symmetrical facade is reminiscent of 1930s Fascist architecture. One of the city's finest museums, it is easy to spend half a day absorbing the diverse and extensive collections. The **Hasselblad Centre** (ⓦwww.hasselbladcenter.se) on the ground floor shows excellent changing photographic exhibitions, while upstairs there's postwar and contemporary Scandinavian paintings, a room full of French Impressionists, and a collection of Italian and Spanish paintings from the sixteenth to eighteenth centuries. Best of all, though, are the **Fürstenburg Galleries** on the sixth floor, which celebrate the work of some of Scandinavia's most prolific and revered artists from the early twentieth century. Well-known paintings by Anders Zorn and Carl Wilhelmson depict the seasons and landscapes of the Nordic countries and evoke a vivid picture of life a hundred years ago. Look out for Ernst Josephson's sensitive portraits and a couple of Hugo Birger paintings depicting the interior of the Fürstenburg Gallery. Also worth a look is the room of Carl Larsson's fantastical and bright wall-sized canvases.

Just a few minutes' walk southeast from Götaplatsen lies Sweden's largest amusement park, **Liseberg** (late April to June & late Aug daily 3–11pm; July to mid-Aug daily noon–11pm; Sept Sat 1–11pm, Sun noon–8pm; 45kr, under-7s free; all-day ride pass 215kr, or limited-ride tickets for 90kr or 150kr). Dating from 1923, it's a league away from today's neon and plastic entertainment complexes, with flowers, trees, fountains and clusters of lights – more Hansel and Gretel than Disneyland. Old and young dance to live bands, and while the young and raucous predominate at night, it's all good-humoured. The newest attraction is an ambitious roller coaster called "Hangover", best avoided if you've got one, while the new "Balder" roller coaster, due to open in 2003, will be built entirely of wood in the traditional manner.

A few steps from Liseberg, **Universeum** (early June to mid Aug daily 10am–8pm, rest of year Tues–Sun 10am–6pm; 110kr; ⓦwww.universeum.se), the city's newest museum, is well worth an hour or so. Contained within a splendidly organic building with soaring glass, wood and concrete walls, it couldn't be more in contrast to the pink paint and fairy lights of the amusement park reflected in its vast windows. A museum of the environment, this isn't as pure-educational as you might think. Water is a main theme (the complex holds the world's largest recirculating water system, processing three million litres a day), and once inside, you can walk some 3km through various different environments – Swedish mountain streams, rainforest, open ocean – all of which feel extremely authentic; expect to emerge dripping. There's also an interactive "inventors' corner" for kids, and a good-value café.

Five minutes' walk north, just over the highway at Avagen 24, lies the well-designed **Museum of Ethnography** (May–Aug Mon–Fri 11am–4pm, Sat & Sun 11am–5pm; 30kr). The best exhibits are those on native North and South American culture, including some dramatically lit textiles up to 2000 years old, and rather grislier finds, such as skulls which have been trepanned to ward off evil spirits.

Haga and Linné

West of Avenyn, and a ten-minute stroll up Vasagatan (or take tram #1 or #2, to Olivedalsgatan), lies the district of **Haga**, the city's oldest working-class area, now transformed into the Greenwich Village of Gothenburg. Centred on **Haga Nygatan**, Haga is one of the city's most picturesque quarters, its cobbled streets lined with pricey alternative-type cafés and antique clothes shops, frequented by right-on and well-off twenty- and thirty-somethings. Although there are a couple of good restaurants along Haga Nygatan, this is really somewhere to come during the day, when tables are put out on the street and the atmosphere is friendly and villagey, if a little self-consciously fashionable. An opportunity for a break in your wanderings is provided by the beautifully renovated **Haga Badet** (Mon 11.30am–2.30pm, Tues–Fri 11.30am–10pm, Sat 11.30am–7pm, Sun 1–4pm, closed July) on Allegatan, a former bathhouse for the working classes that's been glammed up into a very fine health spa, with the prettiest of pools in an Art Nouveau-style setting, as well as a Roman bath, gym and massage area. A one-day card to use the Roman bath complex including sauna and pool costs 95kr (June & Aug), otherwise it's a very steep 320kr per day for access to all facilities.

West of Haga is the cosmopolitan district of **Linné**, named after the botanist Carl von Linné (better known by the Latinized version of his name, Linnaeus), who originated the system of plant classification that's used the world over. Recent years have seen so many new cafés and restaurants spring up along **Linnegatan** – which runs along the western end of Haga Nygatan – that this street of tall, Dutch-style buildings has become a second Avenyn, but without the attitude.

Five minutes' walk south of Linnegatan (or tram #1 or #2 to Linneplatsen) is the huge, tranquil mass of greenery that constitutes the **Slottsskogsparken**. Home to farm animals and many varieties of birds, including pink flamingos in summer, there's plenty here to entertain children. The rather dreary **Natural History Museum** (daily 11am–5pm; 30kr; @www.gnm.se) within the grounds prides itself on being the city's oldest, dating from 1833. Its endless cases of stuffed birds seem particularly depressing after the squawking, living ones outside, and the only worthwhile item is the world's only stuffed blue whale, which was killed in 1865 and now contains a Victorian café complete with original red velvet sofas – unfortunately, it's only opened in election years (the Swedish word for whale also means election). On the South side of Slottsskogsparken are the large **Botanical Gardens** (daily 9am–dusk; greenhouses May–Aug daily 8am–6pm, Sept–April Mon–Fri 10am–3pm, Sat, Sun & holidays noon–4pm; free), which holds some 12,000 species of plants; highlights are the Japanese valley and the rock gardens.

Eating

Gothenburg has a multitude of **eating** places catering for every taste and budget. The foreign restaurants that opened here in the early 1990s are now less prevalent than the host of simpler, pan-European eateries which draw on Swedish staples such as herring and salmon dishes, good breads and, in summer, glorious soft fruits. The emphasis now is much more on casual eating than it was ten years ago: Gothenburgers are as likely to munch on filled ciabattas served with substantial salads as sit down to three-course meals. Naturally, there are great fish restaurants, including some of the most exclusive establishments in town, while for less costly eating there is a growing number of low-priced pasta places, alongside the staple pizza parlours and burger bars.

Café life has really come into its own in Gothenburg, with a profusion of places throughout the city joining the traditional *konditori* (bakeries with tearoom attached). Nowadays, it's easy to stroll from one café to another at any time of day or night, and tuck into enormous sandwiches and gorgeous cakes. Cafés also offer a wide range of light meals, and are the best option for good food at reasonable prices; the most interesting places are concentrated in the fashionable Haga and Linné districts.

Markets and supermarkets

The bustling, historic **Saluhallen** at Kungstorget is a delightful sensory experience, with a huge range of meat, fish, fruit, vegetables and delectable breads; there are also a couple of cheap coffee and snack bars here. **Saluhall Briggen**, on the corner of Tredje Långgatan and Nordhemsgatan in the Linné area, is more continental and much smaller than Saluhallen, specializing in high-quality meats, fish, cheeses and mouthwatering deli delights. Also in Linné at Övra Husargatan 12, Delitalia is a terrific Italian delicatessen selling anything you could want for a picnic. The Konsum supermarket on Avenyn (daily 8am–11pm) has a wide range of the usual staples and a good deli counter.

Cafés and restaurants

If you want to avoid paying over the odds, it's generally a good idea to steer clear of Avenyn itself (where prices are almost double what you'll pay in Haga or Linné), and to eat your main meal at **lunchtime**, when you can fill up on *dagens rätt* deals for 50–70kr. Otherwise, expect to pay 80–120kr for a main dish in most restaurants, a lot higher in the more exclusive places.

It's not usually necessary to **book** tables, but we've given numbers for places where you might need to; things get especially busy between the peak hours of 7pm to 9pm. Restaurants usually open for lunch from 11.30am to 2.30pm, and for dinner from 6pm until 11pm. Again, we have listed opening times which differ from this.

The old town

Ahlstroms Konditori Korsgatan 2. Dating from 1901, this traditional-style café/bakery is very much of the old school, as are many of its patrons. While modernization has watered down the original features, it's still worth a visit for its good selection of cakes, plus lunches for 52kr.

Froken Olssons Kafe Östra Larmgatan 14. Heaps of sandwiches, salads and sumptuous desserts served up in a rural-style atmosphere. Look out for the mountains of giant meringues on tiered, silver cake trays. Sandwiches for 30–50kr, and a good-value lunchtime vegetarian salad buffet for 50kr.

Gabriel at Feskekörka Feskekörkan fish market ℡031/13 90 51. Excellent fish restaurant, though prices seem particularly high when you can see the real cost of the ingredients below. Closed Sun. It's much cheaper to fill up at the tiny eight-seat *Café Feskekorke* at the opposite end of the market.

Grande E.t.c. Kungsgatan 12 ℡031/701 77 84. Big brother to *E.t.c.* at Vasaplatsen (see p.491), serving similar, very fresh pasta dishes from 85kr.

Greta's Drottninggatan 35. Stylish, casual and popular bar-restaurant drawing a mixed gay and straight clientele. The wide-ranging menu has fish, meat and vegetarian options. Small salads start at 50kr, with more substantial meals of meat, fish or shellfish costing 130–160kr.

Mauritz Kaffehus Fredgatan 2. Very small and unassuming café run by the great grandson of its founder, who began importing coffee into Gothenburg in 1888. Come here for espressos and cappuccinos; there's no room to sit down, but the owner will tell you that standing makes the ambience more Italian.

Avenyn and around

Baguetter Södravägen 59. Big, freshly made sandwiches – smoked salmon for just 20kr – in a very small, basic café that's well worth the five-minute walk from Avenyn or Liseberg.

Café Dali Vasagatan 42. Friendly, studenty and stylish basement café with good sandwiches and cakes.

Café Engelen Engelbreksgatan 26. Friendly, studenty 24-hour café serving home-made, excellent-value food such as baked potatoes, lasagne and big sandwiches for 45kr, plus glorious ice cream and a massive range of fruit teas. There's always a vegetarian selection and a good 36kr breakfast.

E.t.c. Vasaplatsen 4. This cool, elegant grey-painted basement is the best place in town for superb home-made pasta. Lunch 55kr; dinner menu also offers meat and fish dishes. Very busy in the evenings.

Family House Café Storgatan 10. With a wacky, cosily designed setting within an old house, this place is an absolute gem and a must for its superbly relaxed atmosphere. Terrific breakfasts, sumptuous and healthy lunches including three home-made pies each day, and wonderful soups and desserts. You name the price for your breakfast, based on what you think it's worth, and on the 18th, 19th and 20th of each month, breakfasts are free.

Java Café Vasagatan 23. Studenty, bookshelf-filled Parisian-style coffee house decorated with such things as a collection of thermos flasks. Serves a wide range of coffees, and breakfasts for 28kr – a good Sunday morning hangout.

Junggrens Café Avenyn 37. One of only a couple of reasonably priced Avenyn cafés, with good snacks and sandwiches. Atmospheric and convivial, it's been run for decades by a charismatic old Polish woman and her sulky staff. Coffee for only 13kr, sandwiches 15–40kr.

Lai Wa Storgatan 11, Vasaplan. One of Gothenburg's better Chinese restaurants with a wide variety of dishes at reasonable prices – try the Peking soup. Good lunches.

Restaurant Frågetecken Södravägen 20. Very popular spot just a minute's walk from Götaplatsen, with a name that translates as "restaurant question mark". Eat out in the conservatory, or inside to watch the chefs at work, carefully preparing Balkan-influenced food. They boast of being "famous for breasts": duck at 230kr is the most expensive thing on the menu, but there's also pasta for under 100kr.

Smaka Vasaplatsen 3, off Vasagatan ℡031/13 22 47. Moderately priced traditional Swedish dishes enjoyed by a lively, young crowd in a striking, modern interior.

Tai Pak Arkivsgatan 4, just off Avenyn near Götaplatsen. Decent Chinese restaurant serving a two-course special for 69kr, and individual courses for 65–75kr.

Teatergatan Café Teatergatan 36. Somewhat posey place where you can sit at one of the black-and-white swivel chairs and try sandwiches at 50kr and salads at 60kr.

Tintin Engelbrektsgatan 22. Very busy 24hr café with mounds of food and coffee at low prices (try

a big plate of chicken salad for 45kr) and a laid-back, student atmosphere.

28+ Götabergsgatan 28 ℡031/20 21 61. Very fine French-style gourmet restaurant, whose name refers to the fat percentage of its renowned cheese, sold in the shop (9am–11pm) near the entrance. Specialities include goose-liver terrine. Service is excellent. Closed Sun.

Haga and Linné

Cyrano Prinsgatan 7 ℡031/14 31 10. A must. Superb, authentic Provençal bistro specializing in wood-fired pizzas and regional French cooking. Laid-back atmosphere and great service.

Hemma Hos Haga Nygatan 12 ℡031/13 40 90. Popular restaurant full of quaint old furniture, serving upmarket and expensive Swedish food including reindeer and fish dishes. Mon–Fri 5pm–midnight, Sat 1pm–midnight.

Hos Pelle Djupedalsgatan 2 ℡031/12 10 31. Sophisticated wine bar off Linnégatan, not cheap, but serving snacks as well as full meals, and decorated with intriguing abstract artwork.

Jacob's Café Haga Nygatan 10. *The* place to sit outside and people-watch; inside, the decor is fabulous, with some fine Jugrend (Swedish Art Nouveau) lamps.

Krakow Karl Gustavsgatan 28 ℡031/20 33 74. Burly staff serving big, basic and very filling Polish food in a large, dark restaurant. Moderate prices.

Café Kringlan Haga Nygatan 13. The best spot in town for wonderful chocolate pies, bagels, strudels and generous open sandwiches. A prime place to people-watch in the summer.

Le Village Tredje Långgatan 13 ℡031/24 20 03. Lovely candlelit restaurant connected to a big antique shop, serving very well-presented if smallish dishes. The main dining area is expensive – sit in the cheaper bar area where meals start at 65kr.

Louice Värmlandsgatan 18, off Andra Långgatan. Justifiably popular and unpretentious neighbourhood restaurant, with occasional live music. Standard main courses are expensive, but look out for the excellent-value specials at 79kr. There's a full children's menu (35kr) in English, too.

Pasta Gambero Övre Husargatan 5 ℡031/13 78 38. The best of a number of good, reasonably priced Italian eateries on this long street at the end of Linnégatan. The servings are generous and the service very obliging.

Plus (+) Corner of Linnégatan and Landsvägsgatan ℡031/24 08 90. Sit at polished tables beneath chandeliers in this beautifully restored wooden house nestling in rough-hewn rock. Fish and meat dishes go for 160–180kr, and there's a wide drinks list and terrace seating.

Publik Andra Långgatan 20. Young, funky and unashamedly retro place where people come to smoke, drink and lounge, with old velvet sofas and scores of LPs to leaf through on a nostalgia trip. Coffee and muffins, or nachos and ciabattas, cost 35–45kr.

Sjöbaren Haga Nygatan 27. Small fish and shellfish restaurant on the ground floor of a traditional Governor's house building. Moderate prices.

Solrosen Kaponjargatan 4A ☎031/711 66 97. The oldest vegetarian restaurant in Gothenburg, this is the place to come for well-prepared veggie and vegan delights: starters such as falafel, Greek salad and fried cheese are 40kr upwards, while mains such as artichoke au gratin and fried aubergine are 90–180kr. The daily special – soups, hot food such as lasagne and salads – is good value at 65kr. There are six beers on tap and smoking Is allowed.

Solsidan Linnegatan. Lovely café with outdoor seating, serving delicious cakes.

Thai Garden Andra Långgatan 18. Nothing special to look at, but big portions and excellent service at good prices.

Drinking

There's an excellent choice of places to **drink** in Gothenburg, but aside from a small number of British- and Irish-style pubs, even the hippest bars also serve food and have more of a restaurant atmosphere. Listed below are some of the most popular pubs and bar-restaurants in the city, but note that many of the cafés and restaurants listed in the previous section are also good places for a beer, especially those around Avenyn and in Linné. Although there are a number of long-established bars in the old town, the atmosphere is generally a bit low-key at night.

The old town

Beefeater Inn Plantagegatan 1. One of the bevy of British-oriented neighbourhood pubs which are very in vogue with Swedes generally. This one really goes overboard, with a stylistic mishmash of red-telephone-box doors, tartan walls and staff in kilts.

Bishops Arms Västra Larmgatan 1. Attached to the glamorous *Elite Plaza* hotel (see p.482), this pub boasts a wide range of beers. It's all faux "olde Englishe" inside, but nicely done and a cut above similarly styled places around the country.

Dubliners Östra Hamngatan 50B. For a while, Swedes have been overtaken with a nostalgia for all things old and Irish – or at least a Swedish interpretation of what's old and Irish. This is the most popular exponent.

Gamle Port Östra Larmgatan 18. The city's oldest watering hole, with British beer in the downstairs pub and an awful disco upstairs.

The Palace Brunnsparken. The rather splendid former home of the Furstenburgs and their art galleries (see p.486) is a very popular spot, with live bands on Thursdays.

Avenyn and around

Avenyn 10 Avenyn 10. Very loud young crowd. Not a place for a drink and a chat, unless you want to stand out on the street.

Brasserie Lipp Avenyn 8. No longer the hippest place on Avenyn, *Lipp* is expensive and so attracts a slightly older crowd – but a crowd it is, especially during summer.

Niva Avenyn 9. Stylish, popular bar with a modern interior heavy on mosaic decor, and a bar and restaurant on different levels.

Scandic Rubinen Avenyn 24. Glitzy hotel-foyer type of bar. Always packed with tourists and right at the heart of Avenyn.

Studs Götabergsgatan 17, off Engelbrecksgatan behind Vasa Church. This is the hub of Gothenburg student life, with a pub, bar and restaurant. The main advantage of the student bar is its prices, with two-for-one beers before 9pm in summer. If you haven't got student ID, friendly bluffing should get you in.

Haga and Linné

Cigarren Järntorget 6, opposite the Folketshus. Looks as if it's been here forever, but has actually only existed since the revamping of this classic old workers' square. Huge range of cigars and lots of coffees and teas alongside the beers and wines.

Gillestugan Järntorget 6. Cosy and panelled without being over the top, this bar has plenty of outdoor seating and offers full meals such as beef fillet at 98kr or seafood burgers at 125kr.

Stars & Stripes Järntorget 4. Though rather unappealing on the outside and slightly rough within, *Stars & Stripes* boasts some remarkable painted ceilings and a very down-to-earth atmosphere.

The Rover Andra Långgatan 12. Run-of-the-mill Anglo-Irish pub selling Boddingtons, with other lagers, ales and cider on tap, plus a wide range of bottled beers. Lamb, steaks and trout dishes for 59–105kr.

Nightlife and entertainment

There's plenty of other things to do in Gothenburg at night besides drink. The city has a brisk **live music scene** – jazz, rock and classical – as well as the usual cinema and theatre opportunities and, despite the fact that Gothenburg has never been particularly noted for its **club** scene, a range of hangouts which make for an appealing and lively night out. The details below should give you some ideas, but it's worth picking up the Friday edition of the *Göteborgs Posten*, which has a weekly listings supplement, *Aveny* – it's in Swedish but not very difficult to decipher.

Clubs

During the past few years, Gothenburg's old, mediocre **clubs** have been usurped in popularity by a cluster of smaller, laid-back joints around Victoriagatan and Storgatan in Vasastan. One to try first is the suave and new *Vasastan* (☎031/13 03 02), at Victoriagatan 2A on the corner of Parkgatan, where confident twenty- to thirty-somethings bask in the mellow atmosphere. Around the corner, *Ici*, Viktoriagatan 3 (☎031/711 02 00), fills to the gills with revellers. Next door, on the corner of Storgatan, *La Bas* (☎031/711 02 05) draws a slightly older crowd, but still not hitting thirty. Best of all, on the other side of Storgatan at Viktoriagatan 1A, is *Klara* (☎031/13 38 54), a long-established and likeable bar with live music and a more catholic mix of people and conversation – when the latter can be heard at all. Mondays are 80s nights, Tuesday has reggae and Wednesday sees jamming sessions with local DJs. With the emphasis on alternative and dance music, *Kompaniet*, Kungsgatan 19 (☎031/711 99 46), has a top-floor pub-bar, while downstairs there's dancing to Euro techno. Drinks are half-price between 8pm and 10pm, and the place stays open until 3am daily in summer (winter Wed–Sat only).

Of the traditional clubs, try *Valand* (☎031/18 30 93), just off Avenyn at Vasagatan 3, which has three bars and a club floor where the clubby crowd strut their stuff. The hip *Trädgårn* (☎031/10 20 90), on Nya Allen near Heden bus terminal, doesn't look too promising outside, but has a stylish pale-wood interior and a restaurant run by the revered Dahlbom brothers. It's also one of the liveliest haunts, with five bars, a casino, disco and live bands. *Rondo* (☎031/40 02 00), at the restaurant in the Liseberg Amusement Park, reputedly has Sweden's biggest dance floor. It's usually packed out with locals of all ages, and blends contemporary bands with foxtrot evenings, the latter usually encouraging the whole place onto the dance floor.

Live music

Gothenburg's large student community means there are plenty of local **live bands**. The best **venue** is *Kompaniet* (see above), while **jazz** enthusiasts should head for the trendy *Nefertiti* club at Hvitfeldtsplatsen 6 (☎031/711 99 46) – you may have to queue. *Jazzhuset*, Eric Dahlbergsgatan 3 (Wed–Sat; ☎031/13 35 44), puts on trad, Dixieland and swing, but is fairly staid and something of an executive pick-up joint.

International bands perform at some sizeable stadium-type venues in the city, notably **Scandinavium** (☎031/81 10 20) and the colossal **Ullevi Stadium** (☎031/61 20 50) – don't confuse this with Gamla Ullevi. Both are off Skånegatan to the east of Avenyn; take tram #1, #3 or #6.

Classical music, cinema and theatre

Classical music concerts are performed regularly in the Konserthuset (Concert House), Götaplatsen (☎031/72 65 300, ⓦwww.gso.se), and the Stora Theatre, Avenyn (ⓦwww.gothenburg.nu/storateatern). Get hold of programme details from the tourist office.

There are plenty of **cinemas** around the city, screening mostly English-language movies with Swedish subtitles. The most unusual is the ten-screen Bio Palatset, on Kungstorget, originally a meat market and then a failed shopping mall. Its interior is now painted in clashing fruity colours, and the foyer has been excavated to reveal floodlit rocks studded with Viking spears. Another multi-screener is Filmstaden, behind the cathedral at Kungsgatan 35. Hagabion on Linnegatan is a fine **arthouse cinema**, showing a wide range of alternative films. If you're around in January or February, look out for the **Gothenburg Film Festival** at Draken cinema on Järntorget, with screenings of a remarkable range of films.

Theatre in Gothenburg is unlikely to appeal to many visitors. Not only are all productions in Swedish, but the city's council-run theatres also put on plays that make Strindberg look like high comedy – the lack of audience is not a big concern. For information on venues and productions, ask at the tourist office.

Gay Gothenburg

Gothenburg's **gay scene** is surprisingly half-hearted. Though things have been looking up in the past couple of years, and there's now something approaching choice, options remain very limited compared to most cities of this size. Sweden's official gay rights group, the **RFSL** (*Riksförbundet för Sexuellt Likaberättigande*; ⓦwww.rfsl.se), have an inconveniently located branch with a café at Karl Johansgatan 31 (☎031/775 40 10, ✉goteborg@rfsl.se); head west towards Klippan, there's a sign when you reach the Karl Johan Church. More appealing is the friendly and well designed *Greta's*, Drottninggatan 35, the city's first gay restaurant and bar. Gothenburg's gay **clubs** emerge and disappear at an alarming rate. One of the longer-standing is *Eros* at *Restaurang Haket*, itself a dull place at Första Långgatan 32 (☎031/14 58 88, ⓦwww.linnestaden.nu/cluberos); take tram #3 or #9 to Masthuggstorget. For more recent entries to the disco scene, head to *Cock Pit* at *Restaurang Pharmacy*, Västra Hamngatan 15 (☎031/701 49 47), or *Club Cosmopolitan* (Sat) at *Restaurang Enter Lounge*, Vasaplatsen, with guest DJs each week, two bars and two dance floors.

Listings

Airlines British Airways, Landvetter airport ☎020/78 11 44; Finnair, Fredsgatan 6 ☎020/78 11 00; KLM, Landvetter airport ☎031/94 16 40; Lufthansa, Fredsgatan 1 ☎031/80 56 40; SAS, Landvetter airport ☎020/91 01 10.

Airport enquiries ☎031/94 10 00.

American Express Local agent is Ticket, Östra Hamngatan 35 ☎031/13 07 12.

Banks and exchange Most banks are open Mon–Fri 9.30am–3pm, and are found on Östra Hamngatan, Södra Hamngatan and Västra Hamngatan. There are four Forex exchange offices, which accept American Express, Diners Club and traveller's cheques: Central Station (daily 8am–9pm), Avenyn 22 (daily 8am–9pm), Nordstan Shopping Centre, Östra Hamngatan (daily 9am–7pm) and Kungsportsplatsen (daily 9am–7pm).

Buses Reservations are obligatory for buses to Stockholm, Helsingborg and Malmö – reserve seats at Bussresebyra, Drottninggatan 50 ☎031/80 55 30.

Car rental Avis, Central Station ☎031/80 57 80, Landvetter airport ☎031/94 60 30; Budget, Kristinelundsgatan 13 ☎031/20 09 30, Landvetter airport ☎031/94 60 55; Europcar, Stampgatan

22D ☎031/80 53 90, Landvetter airport ☎031/94 71 00; Hertz, Stampgatan 16A ☎031/80 37 30, Landvetter airport ☎031/94 60 20.

Dentist Akuttandvården (Dental Emergency Care), Stampgatan 2, near Central Station ☎031/80 78 00.

Doctor Medical Counselling Service and Information ☎031/41 55 00; Sahlgrenska Hospital at Per Dubbsgatan ☎031/60 10 00.

Emergencies For ambulance, police and fire services call ☎112.

Internet access GameOnLine, Magasinsgatan 26 ☎031/13 51 71; IT-Grottan, Chalmersgatan 27 ☎031/778 73 77; IT-Palatset Jaremans, Viktoriagatan 14 ☎031/13 31 13; Globe Internetcenter, Viktoriagatan 7 ☎031/13 98 88.

Laundry Service Centre, in Nordstan Shopping Centre, Östra Hamngatan (daily 9am–10pm; 115kr per load).

Left luggage at Nordstan Service Centre or Central Station.

Newspapers International newspapers from the Press Centre in Nordstan Shopping Centre or Central Station; or read them for free at the City Library, Götaplatsen.

Pharmacy Apoteket Vasen, Nordstan Shopping

Centre (daily 8am–10pm; ☎031/80 44 10).
Police Headquarters at Ernst Fontells Plats
(Mon–Fri 9am–2pm; ☎031/739 20 00).
Post offices The main office for poste restante is
in the Nordstan Shopping Centre (daily
10am–6pm).
Systembolaget Nordstan Shopping Centre, or at
Avenyn 18.

Taxis Taxi Göteborg ☎031/650 000; Flygtaxi
☎031/94 29 90; Miljötaxi ☎031/60 05 00; Taxi
Jurir ☎031/27 27 27.
Train enquiries Central Station ☎020/75 75 75;
international train information ☎031/80 77 10.
Travel agents Kilroy, Berzeliigatan 5 (Mon–Fri
9.30am–5pm; ☎031/20 08 60).

Around Gothenburg

North of Gothenburg, the rugged and picturesque **Bohuslän coast** attracts countless Scandinavian and German tourists each summer. However, the crowds can't
detract from the wealth of natural beauty and the many dinky fishing villages that
make this stretch of country well worth a few days' exploration. The most popular
destination is the island town of **Marstrand**, with its impressive fortress and richly
ornamental ancient buildings, but there are several attractions further up the coast
that are also worthwhile targets, not least the centre for Bronze Age **rock carvings** at **Tanumshede**, near Strömstad.

Northeast of the city, the county of **Västergötland** encompasses the southern
sections of Sweden's two largest lakes, **Vänern** and **Vättern**. Here the scenery is
gentler, and a number of attractive lakeside towns and villages make good bases
from which to venture out into the forested countryside and onto the **Göta
Canal**. The waterway connects the lakes to each other (and, in its entirety, the
North Sea to the Baltic), and there are a number of ways to experience it, from
cross-country cruises to short hops on rented boats. With energy and time to spare,
renting a bike offers a great alternative for exploring Västergötland, using the
canal's towpaths, countless cycling trails and empty roads. Nearly all tourist offices,
youth hostels and campsites in the region rent out bikes for around 80kr a day or
400kr a week.

The Bohuslän coast

A chain of **islands** linked by a thread of bridges and short ferry crossings make up
the county of **Bohuslän** and, despite the summer crowds, it's still easy enough to
find a private spot to swim or bathe. Sailing is a popular pastime among the
Swedes, many of whom have summer cottages here, and you'll see yachts gliding
through the water all the way along the coast. Another feature of the Bohuslän
landscape you can't fail to miss is the large number of **churches** – for long stretches these are the only buildings of note. Dating from the 1840s to 1910, these are
mostly simple white structures with little variation in design; they're usually open
between 10am and 3pm, though the clergyman invariably lives next door and will
be happy to open up outside these hours.

Travelling up the coast by **train** is feasible, with services from Gothenburg
through industrial Uddevalla and on to Strömstad, though there are stops only in
the main towns. **Buses** also cover the coast, but services are sketchy and infrequent
(on some routes, there's only one bus a week). If you really want to explore
Bohuslän's most dramatic scenery, you need a **car**. From Gothenburg, the E6
motorway is the quickest route north, with designated scenic routes leading off it
every few kilometres.

Kungälv

Just under 20km north of Gothenburg on the E6, the quaint old town of
KUNGÄLV, overshadowed by the fourteenth-century ruins of Bohus Fortress, is a
gem of a place to stop for a few hours. Rebuilt after the Swedes razed it in 1676 to

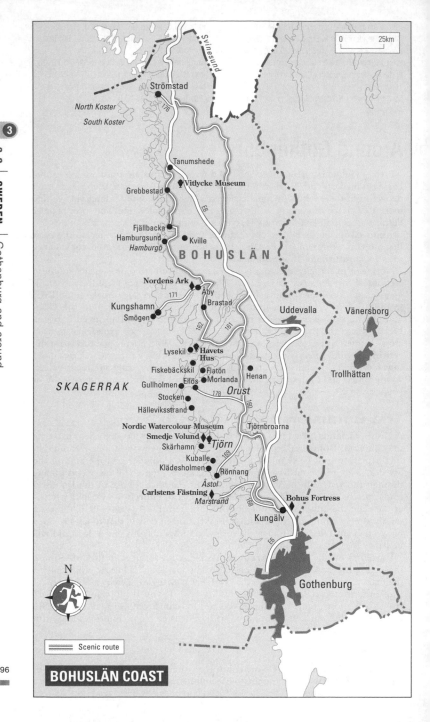

BOHUSLÄN COAST

prevent the Danes finding useful shelter, the town now consists of sprawling cobbled streets with pastel-painted wooden houses, all leaning as if on the verge of collapse. The **tourist office**, in the Fästnungsholmen building (Jan to mid-June Mon–Fri 9.30am–5pm, plus early June Sat & Sun noon–4pm; mid-June to mid-Aug Mon–Fri 9.30am–6pm, Sat 10am–5pm, Sun noon–4pm; mid-Aug to Dec Mon 9.30am–6pm, Tues–Fri 9.30am–5pm; ☎0303/992 00, ⓦwww.kungalv.se), in the square below the fortress, will provide you with a map of a walking tour detailing the history of almost every seventeenth-century property.

The main reason most people visit Kungälv is to see the remains of **Bohus Fortress**. The first wooden fort was built here by the Norwegian king in the fourteenth century, on what was then Norway's southern border. This was replaced by a solid stone building, surrounded by deep natural moats, which managed to withstand six Swedish attacks in the 1560s and, once it became Swedish, a remarkable fourteen sieges by the Danes in the following century. Where attack failed, Swedish weather has succeeded, however, and today the building is very much a ruin. The fortress is open from May to September, with guided tours, concerts and opera performances in July and August – for full details contact the tourist office.

There's little else to do here once you've seen the fortress and wandered round the village, but if you do want to stay, there's an STF **youth hostel** a stone's throw from the fortress at Farjevagen 2 (☎0303/189 00, ⓕ192 95).

Marstrand

About 25km west of Kungälv, the island town of **MARSTRAND** buzzes with summer activity, as holidaymakers flock in to sail, bathe and take tours around the impressive castle. With ornate wooden buildings lining the bustling harbour, Marstrand is a delightful place and is easily visited on a day-trip from Gothenburg.

Founded under Norwegian rule in the thirteenth century, the town achieved remarkable prosperity through herring fishing in the following century; rich herring pickings, however, eventually led to greed and corruption, and Marstrand became known as the most immoral town in Scandinavia. The murder of a cleric in 1586 was seen as an omen: soon after the whole town burned to the ground and the herring mysteriously disappeared. The fish – and Marstrand's prosperity – eventually returned in the 1770s, only to disappear again, for good, forty years later. By the 1820s, the old herring salting houses had been converted into bath houses, and Marstrand had been reborn as a fashionable bathing resort.

From the harbour turn left, then it's a lovely walk up the cobbled lane, past the Renaissance-style *Grand Hotel*, to a small square surrounded by exquisite wooden houses painted in pastel shades. Across the square is the squat, white **St Maria kyrka**; beyond, the streets climb steeply to the castle, **Carlstens Fästning** (mid-June to mid-Aug daily 11am–6pm; early June & late Aug 11am–5pm; rest of the year Sat & Sun noon–4pm; 60kr including guided tour, for English-language tours call ☎0303/602 65), an imposing sweep of stone walls solidly wedged into the rough rock. You could easily spend half a day clambering around the walls, and down the weather-worn rocks to the sea, where there are always plenty of places to bathe in private. The most interesting tales spun by the **tour guides** are related down in the grim prison cells: Carlstens' most noted prisoner was **Lasse Maja**, a thief who got rich by dressing as a woman and seducing rich farmers. A sort of Swedish Robin Hood, Maja was known for giving his spoils to the poor. Once incarcerated here, he ingratiated himself with the officers via his impressive cooking skills, a talent that, after 26 years, won him a pardon from the king.

Some of the tours (depending on the guide; ask in advance) lead up through the castle's hundred-metre towers, built in 1658. The views from the top are stunning, but you'll have to be fit to get there as the steep, spiral climb is quite exhausting. Once a year, around July 20, the fortress hosts a huge **festival**, with an eighteenth-century-style procession and live theatrical performances. It's a colourful occasion and well worth catching.

Practicalities

Gothenburg Pass holders can get a two-for-one ticket deal on the **day-trip by boat** from Gothenburg; boats leave from Lilla Bommen at 9.30am, arriving in Marstrand at 12.30pm (July & Aug daily; May & June selected dates, ask at Gothenburg tourist office, p.478). Otherwise, take **bus** #312 from Nils Ericsonsplatsen; buy a 100kr carnet from Tidpunkten, next to the bus terminal, which also covers the ferry journey from the mainland (2min; 23kr return). By car, take the E6 north out of Gothenburg, then Road 168, which leads west right to the ferry. No cars are allowed on the island, and parking on the mainland costs 25kr per day.

The **tourist office** moves home each year, but is always around the harbour (June Mon–Fri 9.30am–4.30pm, Sat & Sun noon–4pm; late June to early Aug Mon–Fri 9am–6pm, Sat & Sun 11am–5pm; mid-Aug to May Mon–Fri 10am–4pm; ℡0303/600 87, ✉tourist@swipnet.se). It can book **private rooms** in old barracks for a minimum of two people from 370kr per room, and apartments at 600kr for two people. The island's **youth hostel**, *Båtellet* (℡0303/600 10, ✉marstrandsvarmbadhus@telia.com), is situated in an atmospheric old bath house overlooking the sea, and has a sauna, washing facilities, a swimming pool and a restaurant (see below). Of the several very pleasant **hotels** on the island, the finest is the 1892-built *Grand* at Paradis Parken (℡0303/603 22, ⊛www.grandmarstrand.se; ❻), just 50m from the current tourist office location and left through the park. *Nautic*, Långgatan 6 (℡0303/610 30, ℻612 00; ❹), is rather simpler in style, but perfectly adequate.

Eating out is a major sport on Marstrand, but it comes at a price. About the most interesting place to eat on the island is the *American Bar*, opened in 1919, overlooking the harbour, which serves good but pricey meat and fish meals with mains costing 125–225kr. Alternatively, you could try the glamorous, if more formal, *Oscar's*, next door. Another very popular choice is *Lasse Maja's Krog*, in a jolly, yellow-painted house on the harbourfront, whose wide-ranging meat and fish menu has mains at 110–220kr, as well as pizzas at around 100kr. Decent meals are also served in *Drott*, the rather fine restaurant attached to the youth hostel: pasta dishes cost around 50kr; meat and seafood 100–200kr. Alternatively, try one of the three restaurants in the classic old *Societetshuset* (℡0303/606 00), close to the youth hostel by the water. The cheapest places to eat are the excellent *Arvidsons* smoked fish stand at the harbour, or *Skepps Handel*, also at the harbour at the corner of Drottninggatan.

At night, the *American Bar* and *Oscar's* (which doubles as a nightclub) are good **drinking** haunts.

North to Tanumshede

Aside from picturesque scenery and pretty villages, the highlights along this stretch of the coast are the newly established **artists' colony** on **Tjörn**, the exceptional **marine-life museum** at **Lysekil**, several nature reserves, a wildlife sanctuary and, at **Tanumshede**, an extensive array of Bronze Age **rock carvings**. If you have your own transport, you'll be able to follow the designated **scenic routes** which lead off the E6; otherwise, bus connections from Gothenburg are limited to a few of the main towns. If you have a car, it's easy enough to drive to Tanumshede in a day, stopping off at a couple of sights on the way. Although there are plenty of hotels and hostels along the coast, this is one of the most popular parts of the country for **camping** and caravanning, with loads of sites all the way to Tanumshede.

Tjörn to Lysekil

Head north of Marstrand along the E6 for about 25km, then take a left onto the Tjornbroarna, a sequence of three graceful bridges which connect the islands of Tjörn and Orust, affording spectacular views over the fjords. At the village of Skärhamn on the west of Tjörn, the **Nordic Watercolour Museum** (*Nordiska*

Akvarallmuseet; May–Aug daily 11am–6pm; rest of the year Tues–Sun noon–5pm; ☎0304/60 00 80, ⍟www.akvarellmuseet.org; 60kr), opened in 2002, has impressive if sometimes pretentious exhibitions by living Nordic artists, displayed in a striking wood and glass building surrounded by pools of water. More exciting and less publicised, though, is **Smedje Volund**, just beyond the museum (Mon–Fri 10am–4pm, call ☎0304/67 17 55 to arrange a visit at other times; ⍟www.volund.se; free). This stunning house hewn from its pink granite surroundings is the home and studio of Sweden's most celebrated artist-blacksmiths, **Berth Johansson**. You can watch bizarre furniture being made out of salvaged wrecked ships, while upstairs, glass blowers create wonderful designs, selling work far cheaper than elsewhere.

There's nothing else to detain you on Tjörn, so head north to the neighbouring island of **Orust**. A centre for boat-building since Viking times, Orust mirrors mainland Sweden in its physical aspect: westerly winds have stripped its west coast of trees, while forest runs right up to the sea on its eastern shores. The island's STF **youth hostel** (May to mid-Sept; ☎0304/503 80), just outside the village of Stocken, occupies a splendid eighteenth-century wooden manor set in vast grounds.

A few kilometres north of here, via a free car ferry, is the charming village of **FISKEBÄCKSKIL**. Birthplace and home to Carl Wilhelmson, one of Sweden's best-loved artists, his studio stands proud on granite rocks overlooking the sea – the setting for many of his most famous paintings. The glamorous *Gullmarsstrand* **hotel** (summer only; ☎0523/222 60, ℱ228 05; ❹) is just a few metres away. The best place to **eat** is *Kapten Stures Restaurant*, close to the beautiful church on Kaptensgatan, where you can get good fish- or meat-based meals for 100–160kr.

On the mainland just opposite Fiskebäckskil (and connected to it by free ferry) is **LYSEKIL**, the largest coastal town in the Bohuslän region (also reachable by express bus #840 from Gothenburg). Though it's not as immediately attractive as other coastal towns, Lysekil does still have plenty to recommend it. From the **tourist office** (mid-June to mid-Aug Mon–Sat 9am–7pm, Sun 11am–3pm; mid-Aug to mid-June Mon–Fri 9am–5pm; ☎0523/130 50, ⍟www.lysekil.se) at Sodra Hamngatan 6, it's just five minutes' walk to the exceptional museum of marine life, **Havets Hus** (daily: July to mid-Aug 10am–6pm; late Aug to June 10am–4pm; 60kr). Chief attraction here is the underwater glass tunnel, where massive fish swim over and around you; there's also a special "touch pool" for children to experience the texture of slimy algae and spiky starfish. En route to Havets Hus you'll pass a number of intricately carved villas, a reminder of the nineteenth century when Lysekil was a popular and genteel bathing resort. Today, **nude bathing** (segregated) and fishing are popular pastimes and much of the shoreline has been turned into a **nature reserve**, which supports over 250 varieties of plant life – ask at the tourist office about guided botanical and marine walks in summer. Walk up any set of steps from the waterfront and you'll reach the town's **church** (daily 11am–3pm), hacked from the surrounding pink granite. If you want to stay in Lysekil, the *Kust Hotel Strand*, Strandvägen 1 (☎0523/79751,ℱ122 02), has both dorm beds and doubles (❶) and is well placed on the waterfront in a fancy old house, albeit one showing signs of age. The friendliest and most characterful hotel, though, is *Lysekil Havshotell*, Turistgatan 13 (☎0523/797 50, ℱ142 04, ℮info@strandflikorna.se; ❹) in a classic red- and white-painted house with beautifully restored rooms.

A possible diversion after visiting Lysekil is to head north along Route 162 and turn left for Nordens Ark near Åby (about 25km). On the way you'll pass a couple of notable churches, in particular the one at **Brastad**, an 1870s Gothic affair with an oddly haphazard appearance – every farm in the neighbourhood donated a lump of its own granite, none of which matched. Don't be put off by the yeti-sized inflatable puffin at the entrance to **Nordens Ark** (daily: June–Aug 10am–7pm; Sept–May 10am–4pm; ⍟www.nordensark.se; 105kr), a wildlife sanctuary for endangered species where animal welfare is prioritized over human voyeurism. Red pandas, lynx, snow leopards and arctic foxes are among the rare animals being bred and reared at the sanctuary, whose densely forested landscape is kept as close as

△ Gripsholm castle

possible to the animals' natural environment. To improve your changes of multiple animal encounters, ask when the feeding trucks are departing on their rounds – wolves are usually fed between noon and 1pm at weekends.

Smögen, Fjällbacka and Tanumshede

There's no public transport from Nordens Ark to the old fishing village of **SMÖGEN**, 15km west; with a car, you'll have to backtrack on Route 162, then take the road signposted Route 171. It's worth the trouble, though, for you'll find multiple ice-cream parlours, boutiques housed in old wooden houses by the seafront and a quay that runs for several hundred metres. In July and August, Bohuslän's entire teenage population besieges the village for an orgy of drinking – fascinating to watch though hard to sleep through. There's a summer-only **tourist office** at Brunnsgatan (end June to early Aug daily 4–8pm; ☎0523/375 44, ✉info@sotensasturism.se); staff can book private rooms for 400kr per double. There's also the *Makrillvikens* **youth hostel**, Makrillgatan (☎0523/315 65, ⓦwww.makrillviken.se), in a cream wooden house five minutes' walk in from the harbour with open sea views and a sauna (25kr). In terms of **eating**, it's best to forgo Smögen's restaurants in favour of the fantastic and inexpensive smoked fish shops that line the harbour, which dole out breads and salads alongside the fish.

Thirty kilometres north along the coast from Smögen, the picture-perfect settlement of **FJÄLLBACKA** nestles beneath huge granite boulders, its houses painted in fondant shades and boasting a wealth of intricate gingerbreading known in Swedish as *snickargladje* ("carpenter's joy"). As you enter Fjällbacka, it will immediately become apparent that a certain celebrated actress holds sway in this little town. There's a **tourist office** (June–Aug daily 10.30am–12.30pm & 2–7.30pm; ☎0525/321 20, ⓦwww.fjallbacka.com) in a tiny red hut on **Ingrid Bergman's Square**. Here a statue of the big-screen idol looks out to the islands where she had her summer house, and to the sea over which her ashes were scattered. There's not a lot to do, but if you want to stick around there are plenty of **camping** opportunities and a seasonal **youth hostel** (☎0525/312 34; May–Sept); alternatively, the *Badholmen* hostel (☎0525/321 50) is more conveniently located near to the tourist office.

The area around **TANUMSHEDE**, a few kilometres further north on the E6, has the greatest concentration of **Bronze Age rock carvings** in Scandinavia, with four major sites (now listed as UNESCO World Heritage locations) in the surrounding countryside. Between 1500 and 500 BC, Bronze Age man scratched images into the ice-smoothed rock, and at Tanumshede you'll see some fine examples of the most frequent motifs: the simple cup mark (the most frequent design), as well as boats, humans and animals. When you reach town, head for the **tourist office** (July to mid-Aug Mon–Sat 10am–6pm; mid-Aug to June Mon–Thurs 9am–4.30pm, Fri 9am–3pm; ☎0525/204 00, ✉tanum.turist@swipnet.se), oddly sited in a Texaco filling station on the main road; staff can provide you with explanatory booklets (10kr) in English. There's also a **rock-carving museum** at nearby Vitlyckehallen (April–Sept daily 10am–6pm; Oct–Dec Thurs–Sun 11am–5pm; for the rest of the year call ☎0525/209 50 to arrange a visit; ⓦwww.vitlycke.bohusmus.se; 20kr), which explores interpretations of the various images. Tanumshede is reached by five E6 express buses daily from Gothenburg (2hr). There is a smattering of restaurants and a little nightlife at the caravan/camping mecca of **Grebbestad**, a few kilometres southwest of Tanumshede.

Strömstad and the Koster Islands

STRÖMSTAD retains an air of faded grandeur from its days as a fashionable eighteenth-century spa resort. Arriving at the train station, everywhere of interest is easily accessible, and with Color Line (☎0526/620 00) **ferry** connections on to Sandefjord and Halden in Norway, the town makes a good stopover before heading further north. Though its main attraction is its close proximity to the **Koster**

Islands (see below), Strömstad does have a couple of interesting public buildings. Behind its plain exterior, the town's **church**, a few minutes' walk from the train and bus stations at Kyrkogatan 10, is an eclectic mix of decorative features, including busy frescoes, gilt chandeliers and model ships hanging from the roof. More bizarre, however, is the massive, copper-roofed **Stadshus**, the product of a millionaire recluse. Born to a Strömstad jeweller in 1851, Adolf Fritiof Cavalli-Holmgren became a financial whizz-kid, moved to Stockholm and was soon one of Sweden's richest men. When he heard that his poor home town needed a town hall, he offered to finance the building, but only if he had complete control over the project, which was to be situated on the spot where his late parents had lived. By the time the mammoth structure was completed in 1917, he was no longer on speaking terms with the city's politicians, and never returned to see the building he had battled to create, which was topped with a panoramic apartment for his private use. Much later, in 1951, it was discovered that he had designed the entire building around the dates of his parents' birthdays and wedding day – January 27, May 14 and March 7 – with the dimensions of every room, window or flight of stairs a combination of these numbers. Built entirely from rare local apple granite, the town hall is open to the public, but to view the most interesting areas you have to ask for a (free) private tour. You can see Adolf's portrait – dated falsely to include his favourite numbers – in the main council chamber.

Practicalities

Strömstad can be reached by **train** from Gothenburg (8 daily; 3hr), or via the express **bus** between Gothenburg and Oslo (5 daily; 2hr 30min); by **car**, follow Route 176 off the E6 for 12km. Both the train and bus stations are on Södra Hammen, opposite the ferry terminal for services to Sandefjord in Norway; ferries to Halden leave from Norra Hamnen, 100m to the north on the other side of the rocky promontory, Laholmen, as do ferries to the Koster Islands (full details from the tourist office).

The **tourist office** on the quay (mid-June to mid-Aug Mon–Sat 9am–8pm, Sun 10am–8pm; May to mid-June & late Aug Mon–Fri 9am–6pm, Sat & Sun 10am–4pm; Sept–April Mon–Fri 9am–5pm; ☎0526/623 30, ⚛www.stromstadtourist.se) has lots of information about the Koster Islands and surrounds. For **private rooms** (from 150kr per person plus 50kr booking fee), you'll have to head to Västkustbokningen, a few metres away at Västra Klevgatan 3 (daily 10am–1pm & 3.30–4.30pm; ☎0526 109 49). The STF **youth hostel** is at Norra Kyrkogatan 12 (☎0526/101 93), 1km or so from the train station along Uddevallavägen; there's also an independent hostel, *Gastis Roddaren*, at Fredrikshaldsvagen 24 (☎0526/602 01), ten minutes' walk along the road in front of the Stadshus. For a regular, central **hotel** try *Krabban*, Södra Bergsgatan 15 (☎0526/142 00, ⓕ142 04; ❸), or the modern, low-built *Laholmen* (☎0526/197 00, ⚛www.laholmen.se; ❺/❹), which enjoys fine sea views. The nearest **campsite** is 1km from the train station, along Uddevallavägen.

As befits a resort town, there's no shortage of places to eat and drink, most of them around the harbour. The best of the bunch are *Backlund's* (Mon–Fri 8am–7pm, Sat 8am–3pm), a locals' haunt with sandwiches at 18kr; while on Södra Hamngatan, *Kaffe Kompaniet* has a wide range of unusual coffees and an excellent *smörgåsbord*; and, by the station, *Kaff Doppet* is a more characterful konditori. **Nightlife** in Strömstad boils down to *Skagerack*, a very loud, very young music venue in the classic wedding-cake building where the Stockholm elite once partied. It's right in the centre of town, close to the church and harbour.

The Koster Islands

Sweden's most westerly inhabited islands, the **Kosters** enjoy more hours of sunshine than almost anywhere else in the country. **North Koster** (*Nordkoster*) is the more rugged, with a grand nature reserve, and takes a couple of hours to walk around. **South Koster** (*Sydkoster*) is three times as big, but since no vehicles are allowed on the island, **renting a bike** (ask at the Strömstad tourist office) is the best way to explore its undulating landscape. Both islands are rich in wild flowers, and are the starting point for bird- and seal-watching expeditions during the summer; the climate is also gentler here than on the mainland, and the warmer waters here offer great swimming. If you want to visit the south island outside high season it's vital to take an early-morning ferry to North Koster (90kr); if you leave later, the only way of making it across is to hitch a lift in a local's boat. **Taxi boats** to the islands (☎0526/202 85) cost 500kr and can work out economical if there is a group of you; they're the only option if you miss the last ferry back at 9.30pm.

Camping on North Koster is restricted to *Vettnet* (☎0526/204 66), though there are several sites on South Koster. Also on South Koster, there are **cabins** available at *Kostergårdens Stugby* (☎0526/201 23, ⊛www.kostergarden.nu; May–Sept), some 1500m from the ferry stop at Ekenäs; there are also **apartment rentals** for 250–300kr per apartment a night, excellent value if there are three or more of you – ask at Strömstad tourist office. There's just one **hotel** on South Koster, the surprisingly stylish *Skärgårdshotel* at Ekenäs (☎0526/202 50,℮201 94; ❹), with a fine restaurant attached.

The Göta Canal, Trollhättan and Vänersborg

The giant waterway known in its entirety as the **Göta Canal** flows from the mouth of the Göta River to Sweden's largest lake, **Lake Vänern**, via the **Trollhättan Canal**, then cuts across into the formidable **Lake Vättern** and right through southeastern Sweden to the Baltic Sea. If you don't have your own transport then some of the easiest places to see from Gothenburg are the few small towns that lie along the first stretch of the river/canal to Lake Vänern, particularly **Trollhättan**, where the canal's lock system tames the force of the river to dramatic effect. A few kilometres north of Trollhättan, **Vänersborg**, at the southernmost tip of Lake Vänern, provides a useful base for exploring the natural beauty of the nearby hills, the home of Sweden's largest herd of elk. From Gothenburg, regular trains stop at Trollhättan; if you have a car take Route 45.

The Göta Canal

Centuries ago it was realized that lakes Vänern and Vättern, together with the rivers to the east and west, could be used to make inland transport easier. A continuous waterway across the country from Gothenburg to the Baltic would provide a vital trade route, both as a means of shipping iron and timber out of central Sweden and of avoiding Danish customs charges levied on traffic though Öresund. It was not until 1810, however, that Baron Baltzar von Platten's hugely ambitious plans to carve a route to Stockholm were put into practice by the **Göta Canal Company**. Sixty thousand soldiers spent seven million working days over 22 years completing the mammoth task, which was finally opened in 1832, shortly after von Platten's death.

Although the Trollhättan Canal section is still used to transport fuel and timber – the towns on Vänern having their lakeside views blotted by unsightly industrial greyness – this section and the Göta Canal proper, between Vänern and Vättern, are extremely popular tourist destinations, and there's a wide range of **canal trips** on offer. The best way to arrange one of these is to contact the Göta Canal Company, which publishes the ever-bigger list of all possible cost combinations (☎031/80 63 15, ⊛www.gotakanal.se). Many of their trips involve a mixture of **cycling** and relaxing on the boats, though others include **canoeing** and cycling combinations, **Iceland pony riding** and even **ice-skating** trips in winter. Prices vary dramatically, depending on the length of trip and what's included, which could be accommodation, bus transfers, museum entries and guided tours. A trip through sixteen locks in one day between **Sjötorp**, **Lyrestad** and **Töreboda** costs a good-value 250kr

(mid-May to early Sept including a bus back to your starting point). More glamorous is a two-day round trip to and from Motile on the eastern shore of Lake Vättern; 2395kr per person gets you one night on board at Berg, a breakfast, two lunches and a dinner. On a smaller budget, day-trips can be arranged at any tourist office in the region; these can also give information on **renting a boat** or a **bike** to follow the towpaths.

Trollhättan

Seventy kilometres northeast of Gothenburg, **TROLLHÄTTAN** is the kind of place you might end up staying for a couple of days without really meaning to. A small town, it nevertheless manages to pack in plenty of offbeat entertainment along with some peaceful river surroundings. Built around the fast river that for a couple of hundred years powered its flour- and saw-mills, Trollhättan remained fairly isolated until 1800, when the Göta Canal Company successfully installed the first set of locks to bypass the town's furious local waterfalls. River traffic took off and better and bigger locks were installed over the years. The best time to visit is during the **Fallensdagar** (⊛fallensdagar.trollhattan.nu) on the third Friday in July, a three-day festival of dancing and music based around the waterfalls. Summer is the only time when the sluices are opened and you can see the falls in all their crashing splendour (May & June Sat & Sun 3pm; July Fri 11pm; Aug Wed, Sat & Sun 3pm).

The locks and the steep sides of the falls are the main sights in town, and there are paths with orientation maps along the whole system. Strolling south along the riverside path, the network of canal locks is to your left and the beautiful winding river to your right, and you'll pass a grand, English-style church perched on rocks between the waterways. A little further down at the upper lock, the **Canal Museum** (mid-June to mid-Aug daily 11am–7pm; first weekend in April and in Sept Sat & Sun noon–5pm; 10kr) puts the whole thing in perspective, with a history of the canal and locks as well as model ships, old tools and fishing gear. Crossing the canal via the bridge adjacent to the museum and heading into the town's industrial hinterland, you'll soon reach the **Saab Museum** (June–Aug daily 10am–6pm; Sept–May Tues–Fri 11am–4pm; call to arrange a tour on ☎0520/843 44; 30kr), which holds an example of every model built as well as staging themed exhibitions such as rally driving or convertibles.

Practicalities

Trollhättan's **tourist office** (mid-June to mid-Aug daily 10am–6pm; mid-Aug to mid-June Mon–Fri 10am–noon & 1.30–4pm; ☎0520/48 84 72, ⊛www .visittrollhattan.se) is next door to the Saab museum at Åkerssjövägen 10. You can buy the **Sommar Card** here (valid mid-June to mid-Aug; 100kr), which gives free entrance to **Innovatum** (mid-June to mid-Aug daily 10am–6pm; rest of the year Tues–Sun 11am–4pm), a centre dedicated to exhibitions on Swedish inventors – it's in the same building as the tourist office. The card also gives free **cable-car trips** and entry to the Saab and Canal museums. From late June to mid August, there are **boats** (☎0520/321 00) up the canal to Vänersborg; the four-hour round-trip costs 100kr, and there are also evening trips including dinner for 265kr (around four hours). Otherwise, buses #600 and #605 ply the route regularly. The tourist office

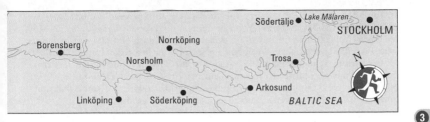

can also book private rooms from 100kr per person (booking fee 26kr). There's an STF **youth hostel** a couple of blocks from the train station at Tingvallavägen 12 (☎0520/129 60, ⓦwww.meravsverige.nu). **Hotels** include the *Albert* (☎0520/129 90, ⓦwww.alberthotell.com; ❹/❸), set in an historic restored house overlooking the river, but on the other side of the water from the rest of town. It's a grand place for dinner, though the annexe bedrooms are not at all in keeping with the original building. There's a campsite ten minutes' walk from the train station by the river (☎0520/306 13; June–Aug), with a heated swimming pool, tennis and golf facilities.

Trollhättan's best **cafés** are mostly along Strandgatan by the canal, notably *Strandgatan* at no. 34, with a terrace and a young crowd, and *Sluss Caféet*, an outdoor summer place overlooking the locks. The cosy *Café Smulan* at Foreningsgatan 6 is a must and serves delicious cakes as well as terrific and good-value vegetarian meals. The best **bar/restaurant** for lively nights out is *M/S Nitlotten*, positioned beneath a spread of huge trees at the water's edge in the centre of town. It's always heaving, with classic and mainstream hits maintaining an energized atmosphere. *The Grand Bar*, at *Hotel Swania* directly opposite, is a fair rival (Mon–Sat). Trollhättan's **gay scene** is organized by **RFSL** Trestad (☎0520/41 17 66), which runs the friendly *Rainbow Café* at Strindbergsgatan 8 (Wed & Thurs 6–10pm); to get there head down Garvaregatan away from the centre.

Vänersborg and around

Dubbed "Little Paris" by the celebrated local poet Birger Sjoberg, **VÄNERSBORG**, on the tip of Lake Vänern 14km north of Trollhättan, doesn't live up to the comparison in any way, but is a pleasant enough little resort town all the same. Its main sites are the nearby twin hills of **Hunneberg** and **Halleberg**, both of which are of archeological interest and support a wide variety of wildlife.

Vänersborg's old town is compact and pleasant to stroll around – though the grand buildings are all overlooked by a bleak old prison at the end of Residensgatan. **Skracklan Park**, just a few minutes from the centre, is a pretty place to relax, with a 1930s coffee house and promenade. Near the coffee house, the bronze statue of Sjoberg's muse, Frida, always has fresh flowers in her hand – even in winter, when the lake is solid ice, locals brave the sub-zero winds to thrust rhododendrons through her fingers.

Vänersborg's **museum**, behind the main market square (June–Aug Tues noon–7pm, Wed, Thurs, Sat & Sun noon–4pm; Sept–May Tues, Sat & Sun noon–4pm; 20kr), is worth viewing not so much for its contents (a superabundance of stuffed birds veiled in a century's worth of dust) but because of the sheer antiquity of the displays, which can hardly have changed since the doors first opened to the public in 1891; a living testimony to nineteenth-century museum culture where nothing was meant to be touched and the pervading darkness meant not much more could be seen either.

The **tourist office** is at the train station (June–Aug Mon–Fri 8am–7pm, Sat & Sun 10am–4pm; Sept–May Mon–Fri 10am–4pm; ☎0521/27 14 00, ⓦwww.vanersborg .se/turist). If you're here with a car, note that two-hour **parking permits** cost 10kr from kiosks and the tourist office. Apart from the **youth hostel** at Hunneberg (see p.506), the cheapest place to **stay** is the friendly and central *Hotel 46* at Kyrkogatan

46 (☎0521/71 15 61; ❷), or try the *Strand* at Hamngatan 7 (☎0521/138 50, ⓦwww.strandhotell.com; ❹/❷). You can camp at the lakeside *Ursands* (☎0521/186 66, ℗686 76); get there on bus #661, which is really more of a taxi – it makes six journeys a day and you'll need to book a place an hour beforehand on ☎020/71 97 17. For **eating**, try the pleasant bakery-café *Konditori Princess* at Sundsgatan 2, or make the two-kilometre journey to the excellent hotel restaurant at Värgon (see below). **Nightlife** is pretty limited, the only options being the town's two somewhat uninspired bars: *Club Roccad*, Kungsgatan 23, or *Oslagbar* at Edsgatan 8.

Halleberg and Hunneberg

The 500-million-year-old twin plateaux of **Halleberg** and **Hunneberg**, just a few kilometres east of Vänersborg, are difficult to get to without your own transport, but well worth the trouble. Crossing the Göta River, you'll first reach **VÄRGON**, home to a renowned, ultra-chic restaurant and hotel, *Ronnums Herrgård* (☎0521/26 00 00, ⓦwww.softwarehotels.se/ronnum; ❺); there's a set two-course lunch daily from 11.30am to 2pm (200kr). Alternatively, you can save your kronor and get a good pizza and salad for 50kr at *Pizzeria Roma* at Nordkroksvagen 1.

Beyond Värgon, the road cuts through the tree-topped hills. Early human remains have been found here, as well as the traces of an old Viking fort, but the area is best known as the home of Sweden's biggest herd of elk. **Elk safaris** run from late June to mid August from Vänersborg's central square (240kr), but disease and continuing royal hunts have reduced the stock to just 100, so don't count on seeing any. Probably the easiest way of spotting the creatures is to drive or walk up the five-kilometre lane around Halleberg at dawn or dusk. Take along some apples: these massive creatures have no qualms about eating from your hand.

Regular **buses** run to Värgon from Vänersborg, replaced in summer by a taxi service that costs the same; there are just three a day and you need to give an hour's notice (☎020/71 97 17). In addition, bus #619 runs from Trollhättan straight to Hunneberg. At the foot of Hunneberg, the excellent **youth hostel**, Bergagårdsvägen 9 (☎0521/22 03 40, ℗684 97; closed mid-Dec to mid-Jan), is housed in a building which dates from 1550 and was used as a base from which Danish soldiers drove the Swedes into the hills. Following the Swedish line of retreat (now a wide path signposted "**Naturskola**") up Hunneberg brings you to the Naturskola Nature Centre (daily: mid-May to late June & early Aug 11am–8pm; mid-Aug to mid-May 11am–4pm; late June to July closed; free), with a café and plenty of information on hand about the wildlife in the hills. A web of nature trails begins here, including some suitable for wheelchair users.

Between the lakes: Vastergötland

The county of **Vastergötland** comprises much of the region between lakes **Vänern** and **Vättern** – a wooded landscape that makes up a large part of the train ride between Gothenburg and Stockholm. The most interesting places lie on the southeastern shore of Lake Vänern, notably the pretty town of **Mariestad**, easily reached from Gothenburg, while with more time you can cut south to the western shore of Lake Vättern, and in particular to the colossal fortress at **Karlsborg**. In between the lakes runs the Göta Canal (see p.503), the main regional target for holidaying Swedes in July and August.

Lidköping and around

Although it flanks a grassy banked reach where the River Lidan meets Lake Vänern, **LIDKÖPING**, around 140km northeast of Gothenburg, won't detain you long, though its layout is pleasant enough due to an age-old decree that the height of a house may not exceed the width of the street on which it stands. The old town square of 1446 on the east bank of the river faces the new town square, founded by Chancellor Magnus de la Gardie in 1671, on the west; both enjoyed a perfect panorama of Vänern until an unsightly concrete screen of coal-storage cylinders and grain silos was plonked just at the water's edge. The town's claim to fame is the **Rörstrand Porcelain Factory** (Mon–Fri 10am–6pm, Sun noon–4pm; guided tours June & Aug; 15kr), Europe's second oldest, situated at the heart of the bleak industrial zone near the lake. The museum here is pretty uninspiring, but there are some pleasant enough designs on sale at supposedly bargain prices.

Trains arrive at the station by the old square. If you're returning to Gothenburg, change trains at Herrljunga; if you're heading back towards Trollhättan, take **bus #5**, while bus #1 runs directly to Karlsborg (see p.508) in just under two hours. The **tourist office** is in the train station building at Bangatan 3 (May to early June & late Aug Mon–Fri 9am–5pm, Sat 9am–1pm; early to late June & early Aug Mon–Fri 9am–7pm, Sat 10am–7pm, Sun 2–7pm; July Mon–Fri 9am–8pm, Sat 10am–8pm, Sun 2–8pm; ☎0510/77 05 00, www.lidkoping.se/turist) staff will book **private rooms** (from 350kr per double room; no booking fee), while the cheapest night's stay is at the **youth hostel**, close by at Nicolaigatan 2 (☎0510/664 30, www.stfturist.se), which has doubles (❶) as well as dorms. *Park Hotell* (☎0510/243 90, www .parkhotell.org; ❸/❷) at 24 Mellbygatan – which runs south from Nya Stadens Torg – is a pink-painted 1920s villa hotel, with huge rooms and original features.

For **cafés** and **konditori**, try the atmospheric *Café Limtorget*, Limtorget, housed in a classic painted wooden cottage in the old town square and a fine place for gorgeous cakes and waffles. For full **meals**, try *Källaregatan 3* at that address for Swedish classics with both fish and meat, plus some pan-European interpretations served up at reasonable cost in pleasant, bright surroundings.

Around Lidköping: north to Läckö castle and east to Kinnekulle

Almost everyone heads for **Läckö castle**, 25km north of Lidköping at the tip of the Kalland peninsula. Surrounded by water on three sides, Läckö is everyone's idea of a fairytale castle – all turrets and towers, rendered in creamy white. The castle dates from 1290, but was last modified and restructured by Lidköping's Chancellor, de la Gardie, when he took it over in 1652. Inside there's a wealth of exquisite decoration, best appreciated on one of the fairly frequent guided tours in English (daily May–Sept 10am–6pm; 70kr May–Aug, 50kr Sept). Be warned, however, that Läckö's charms are no secret, and in summer you should be prepared for the crowds. **Bus #132** from Lidköping travels out here hourly in summer (20kr), via the tiny village of Spiken.

Twelve kilometres east of Lidköping by train, **KÄLLBY** draws visitors for its ancient burial site (turn left at the road junction), where two impressive stones face each other in an Iron Age cemetery, one carved with a comical, goblin-like figure that's said to be the god Thor. Not far beyond, **Husaby** is a tranquil diversion with great religious and cultural significance. It was here in 1008 that Saint Sigfrid, an English missionary, baptized Olof Skötkonung, the first Swedish king to turn his back on the Viking gods and embrace Christianity. Husaby's present three-towered church was built in the twelfth century, just to the west of the well where the baptism is said to have taken place. There's a summer **tourist office** right outside the ancient church (June–Aug daily noon–6pm; ☎0511 34 32 60, husabyturist@telia.com).

Kinnekulle, the "Flowering mountain", is a couple of kilometres further on (get off the train at any of the next few stops), an area of woods and lakes interwoven with paths and boasting hundreds of varieties of flowers, trees, birds and other animals. The strange shape of the plateau is due to its top layer of hard volcanic rock, which even four hundred million years of Swedish weather has not managed to wear down, and which makes for something of a botanical and geological treasure trove. There's an STF **youth hostel** (☎0510/54 06 53, ℱ54 00 85), which has doubles (❶) and dorms, and **campsite** complex nearby in **Hellekis** (Råbäck station).

Mariestad and around

Smaller, prettier and more welcoming than Lidköping, lakeside **MARIESTAD**, with its splendid medieval quarter and harbour area, is just an hour's train ride to the northeast and an excellent base for a day or two's exploration. It's also worth visiting for the extraordinary range of building styles crammed into its centre – Gustavian, Carolean, Classical, Swiss-chalet style and Art Nouveau – like a living museum of architectural design. Have a look, too, at the **cathedral**, on the edge of the centre, which was built by Duke Karl (who named the town after his wife, Maria of Pfalz) in an attempt to compete with his brother King Johan III's Klara kyrka in Stockholm (see p.451). To help you explore the town's compact centre, pick up a copy of the walking-tour map from the tourist office, or join one of the free guided tours which start at the office (mid-June to mid-Aug Mon & Thurs); ask inside for timings.

Mariestad is also an ideal base from which to **cruise** up Lake Vänern to the start of the Göta Canal's main stretch at **Sjötorp**. There are 21 **locks** between Sjötorp and Karlsborg, with the most scenic section up to **Lyrestad**, just a few kilometres east of Sjötorp and 20km north of Mariestad on the E20. Canal cruises cost 250kr for the day, however long you stay on the boat (contact the tourist office for details). There are no lake cruises, since Lake Vänern has been classified as an inland sea, such is its size, and sea-cruising licences are not available.

The **tourist office**, in a ship-shape new building by the harbour on Hamngatan (June–Aug Mon–Fri 8am–7pm, Sat & Sun 9am–6pm; Sept–May Mon–Fri 8am–4pm; ☎0501/100 01, ✆www.turism.mariestad.se), is opposite the hugely popular STF **youth hostel** (☎0501/104 48; book in advance mid-Aug to mid-June). Built after the fire of 1693, the hostel is a former tannery with galleried timber outbuildings and an excellent garden **café**. For a **hotel**, the *Bergs Hotell* of 1698, in the old town at Kyrkogatan 18 (☎ & ☎0501/103 24; ❶), is very plain inside but comfortable enough. Other good-value central options include the mundane but cheap *Hotel Aqua*, Viktoriagatan 15 (☎0501/195 15, ✆187 80; ❶), or the far cosier and more appealing *Hotel Vänerport*, Hamngatan 32 (☎0501/771 11, ✆771 21; ❹/❸). The nearest **campsite** is *Ekuddens*, 2km down the river (☎0501/106 37, ✆186 01; May–Sept).

Mariestad's trendiest **eating** place is *Café Stroget* (Mon–Fri 9am–6pm, Sat 9am–2pm) at Österlånggatan 10, though the *Garden Café* at the youth hostel is more welcoming, serving baguettes for 30kr. One possibility for evening fun is at *Björnes Krog*, Karlsgatan 2 (Mon–Fri 11am–2.30pm, Tues–Thurs 6–11pm, Fri & Sat 6pm–1am, ☎0501 180 50), which serves good food all day and, every third Saturday night, stages an "adults" party – less suggestive than it sounds (just drinking and dancing) – it's an enjoyable place for a 26-plus age group. Reasonable **pub-restaurants** are *Buffalo*, at Österlånggatan 16, and *Hjorten*, Nygatan 21.

Karlsborg and around

Despite the great plans devised for the fortress at **KARLSBORG**, around 70km southeast of Mariestad on the western shores of Lake Vättern, it has survived the years as one of Sweden's greatest follies. By the early nineteenth century, Sweden had lost Finland – after six hundred years of control – and had become jumpy about its own security. In 1818, with the Russian fleet stationed on the Åland Islands and within easy striking distance of Stockholm, Baltzar von Platten persuaded parliament to construct an inland fortress at Karlsborg, capable of sustaining an entire town and protecting the royal family and the treasury – the idea being that enemy forces should be lured into Sweden, then destroyed on home territory. With the town pinched between lakes Vättern and Bottensjön, the Göta Canal – also the brainchild of von Platten and already under construction – was to provide access, but while von Platten had the canal finished by 1832, the fortress was so ambitious a project that it was never completed. It was strategically obsolete long before work was finally abandoned in 1909, and the walls were in any case no longer strong enough to withstand attack from modern weaponry. However, parts are still in use today by the army and air force, and uniformed cadets mill around, lending an air of authenticity.

The complex, which is as large as a town, appears austere and forbidding, but you are free to wander through and to enter the **museum** (daily: mid-May to mid-June & early Aug to end Aug 10am–4pm; mid-June to early Aug 10am–6pm; 35kr) of endless military uniforms; the **guided tour** of the fort (June to late Aug; 70kr), with special sound and smoke effects, is effective enough, though won't be to everyone's taste. For further information contact the tourist office (see below).

There is no train service to Karlsborg, though there are regular **bus** services from both Lidköping and Mariestad; if you're driving, take Route 202 from Mariestad. The **tourist office** (June–Aug daily 9am–6pm; Sept–May Mon–Fri 9am–3pm; ☎0505/173 50, ✆www.karlsborg.se), in a lovely old building at the entrance to the fortress during summer (outside the season it's in the big yellow house close by), can book **private rooms** for around 150kr per person. The **youth hostel** (☎ & ☎0506/446 00) is next door, while the **campsite** (☎0505/449 16, ✆449 12; May–Sept) is located on the banks of Lake Bottensjön, two kilometres north. The loveliest **hotel**, and well worth the price, is the *Kanalhotellet*, Storgatan 94 (☎0505/121 30, ✆127 61, ✆www.kanalhotellet.se; ❷).

Forsvik

As far back as the early 1300s, the Karlsborg area maintained an important flour mill, 8km north at **FORSVIK**, run by the monastery that was founded by Sweden's first female saint, Birgitta. Using the height differential between lakes Viken and Bottensjön, first over water wheels and later through power-generating turbines, a sizeable industry emerged, working all manner of metal and wood products. During the Reformation, Forsvik was burnt down, but the creation of the Göta Canal gave the place new life, and it once again became a busy industrial centre. Its paper mill continued to operate until the 1940s, and its foundry until the Swedish shipyard crises in the 1970s. Today the mill is a **museum** (June–Aug 10am–5pm; 30kr), which has been restored to its 1940s condition and provides a stimulating picture of Forsvik's industrial past. Bus #420 runs from Karlsborg once daily in summer and you can stay in the appealing **youth hostel** at Bruksvägen 11 (☎0505/411 37 in summer, or ☎0505/411 27 in winter). The best **café** around is *Forsvik* (daily 11am–9pm), just beyond the museum at the waterside – the perfect spot to head for on a summer's evening.

Travel details

Trains

Gothenburg to: Kalmar (2–3 daily; 4hr 20min); Karlskrona (1–2 daily; 4hr 40min); Malmö (8–12 daily; 3hr 50min); Stockholm (9–13 daily; 4hr 30min); Strömstad (9 daily; 2hr 40min); Trollhättan (13 daily; 40min); Vänersborg (Mon–Fri 10 daily, Sat & Sun 4 daily; 1hr 5min).

Trollhättan (2–5 daily; 1hr 5min); Varberg/Falkenberg (Fri & Sun 2 daily; 50min/1hr 20min).
Lidköping to: Vänersborg/Trollhättan (Fri & Sun 2 daily; 1hr).
Mariestad to: Gävle (1 daily Mon–Fri; 7hr 30min); Örebro (1–2 daily; 1hr 30min); Skövde/Jönköping (3–4 daily Mon–Fri, 1 Sat; 1hr 30min).
Strömstad to: Svinesund (4–5 daily; 20min).

Buses

Gothenburg to: Borås (Mon–Fri 13 daily, Sat 3 daily, Sun 8 daily; 55min); Falun/Gävle (1–3 daily; 10hr 30min); Halmstad (Fri & Sun 3 daily; 2hr); Karlstad (3–5 daily; 4hr); Linköping/Norrköping (3–4 Daily Mon–Fri & Sun, Sat 1 daily; 4hr 35min); Mariestad (4–5 daily; 3hr); Oskarshamn (Fri & Sun 2 daily; 5hr 20min); Oslo (4–5 daily; 4hr 45min); Tanumshede/Strömstad (4–5 daily; 2hr 30min);

International ferries and catamarans

Gothenburg to: Harwich (2 weekly; 24hr); Frederikshavn (ferries: 4–8 daily; 3hr 15min; catamaran: 3–5 daily; 1hr 45min); Kiel (1 daily; 14hr); Newcastle (2 weekly; 24hr).
Newcastle to: Gothenburg (2 weekly; 24hr).
Strömstad to: Halden (Sat 1 daily; 2hr); Sandefjord (6 daily; 2hr 30min).

3.3

The southwest

There is a real historical interest to the **southwestern** provinces of Halland, Skåne and Blekinge, not least in the towns and cities that line the coast. The flatlands and fishing ports south of Gothenburg were traded almost constantly between Denmark and Sweden from the fourteenth to seventeenth centuries, and several fortresses today bear witness to the region's medieval buffer status.

Halland, facing Denmark, has a coastline of smooth sandy beaches and bare, granite outcrops, punctuated by a number of small towns. Most charismatic is the old society bathing resort of **Varberg**, dominated by its tremendous thirteenth-century fortress. The small, beautifully intact medieval core of **Falkenberg** is also notable, while for beaches and nightlife, regional capital **Halmstad** is a popular base.

Further south in the ancient province of **Skåne**, the coastline softens into curving beaches backed by gently undulating fields. This was one of the first parts of the country to be settled, and the scene of some of the bloodiest battles during the medieval conflict with Denmark. Although Skåne was finally ceded to Sweden in the late seventeenth century, the Danish influence died hard, and is still evident today in the thick Skåne accent, often incomprehensible to other Swedes, and in the province's architecture. The latter has also been strongly influenced by Skåne's agricultural economy, whose centuries of profitable farming have left the countryside dotted with **castles** – though the continued income from the land means that most of these palatial homes are still in private hands and not open to the public.

The popular perception of Skåne is as a fertile but largely flat and uniform landscape; however, it's worth taking a day or two to appreciate the subtle variety of the countryside – blocks of yellow rape, crimson poppy and lush-green fields interspersed with castles, charming white churches and black windmills. One of the best areas for **walking** and **cycling** is the **Bjäre peninsula**, the thumb of land to the west of the glamorous tennis capital of **Båstad**, where forested hill ranges, spectacular rock formations and dramatic cliffs make for some beautiful scenery. To the south, both **Helsingborg**, with its laid-back, cosmopolitan atmosphere, and Sweden's third city, bustling **Malmö**, are only a stone's throw from Denmark. Between these two centres, and in contrast to Malmö's industrial heritage, the university town of **Lund** has some classic architecture and a unique atmosphere – an essential stop for anyone travelling in the south.

Sweeping east towards the pretty medieval town of **Ystad**, the coastline holds some minor resorts with excellent beaches. Beyond here, you enter the splendid countryside of the **Österlen** area, whose pastoral scenery is studded with Viking monuments such as the Swedish Stonehenge at **Ales Stennar**, and whose coast is lined with some brilliant white beaches backed by nature reserves. Edging north, the land becomes green and more hilly, while the coast features a number of interesting little places to stop, such as **Kivik**, with its apple orchards and Bronze Age cairn, and the ancient and picturesque resort of **Åhus**. In the northeast of the county, **Kristianstad**, built as a flagship town by the Danes, retains its fine, Renaissance structure.

Beyond here to the east, the ledge of land running to the Baltic is **Blekinge**. Among the province's small run of not particularly distinguished resorts, **Karlskrona** stands out. Centred on a number of islands forming a small archipelago, Sweden's second city in the eighteenth century still exudes an air of regal and naval grandeur.

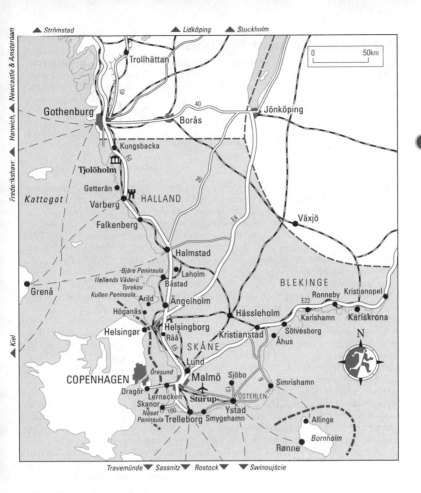

Getting around

The national **train** network follows the coast south from Gothenburg, with frequent trains stopping at all towns as far as Ystad, where the line cuts northeast to Kristianstad. The comfortable Kustpilen Express trains run east and west across the country, linking Malmö, Helsingborg and Lund with Kristianstad and Karlskrona. However, some of the most beautiful and less-frequented areas are not covered by the train network, and the **bus** service is skeletal at best, especially along the south coast. There are also certain transport anomalies to look out for: there are trains but no buses between Malmö and Ystad; between Ystad and Kristianstad the train service is very limited, making buses the more efficient option; and, more generally, some train and bus services stop early in the day – it's a good idea to equip yourself with timetables from the train and bus stations or tourist offices in Gothenburg and Malmö.

With no really steep hills, the southwest is wonderful country for **cycling**, and bike rental outlets are numerous; most tourist offices, youth hostels and campsites also rent out bikes. There are also several recognized **walking trails**, mentioned in the text.

Kungsbacka and Tjolöholm

Just beyond the southernmost suburbs of Gothenburg, the small town of **KUNGS-BACKA** is a residential backwater that's of no particular interest to travellers, unless you time your trip to arrive on the lively market day (first Thurs of month). Although Kungsbacka dates from the thirteenth century, when it was one of a number of prosperous Hanseatic towns along the south coast, the town was razed by fire in 1846, leaving just a couple of houses as testament to its past. It's altogether better to use the town simply as a means of reaching the splendid manor house on the coast at **Tjolöholm**, 15km south.

Tjolöholm

The dream home of Scottish-born merchant and horse-breeder James Dickson, the manor house at **TJOLÖHOLM** (pronounced "Chewla-home") was the result of a grand design competition in the 1890s. Enormously wealthy, Dickson wanted a unique house which would reflect his British ancestry, the then current Swedish fascination for Romanticism, and the latest domestic innovations of the day. The winner of the competition was the 27-year-old Lars Israel Wahlman, who built a stunning Elizabethan-style stately home. Dickson, however, never saw Tjolöholm completed – cutting his finger while opening a champagne bottle, he fatally poisoned himself by wrapping the lead cap around the wound.

In 1901, a village was built around the house, and its little red-and-white wooden cottages have been immaculately preserved. Along the main driveway, the huge stables and indoor riding track have been converted into an airy café, while the next building contains a **carriage museum** (same times as house – see below), worth a peek to see the bizarre horse-drawn vacuum cleaner. The **interior** of the house (mid-June to Aug daily 11am–4pm; Sept Sat & Sun 11am–4pm; Oct Sun 11am–4pm; ☎0300/54 42 00, ⊕www.tjoloholm.se; 60kr) deserves a good hour or so – free pamphlets in English are available (guided tours in English have to be pre-booked on ☎0300/54 42 00). Among the many highlights are the billiard room, whose walls are lined with Belgian marble and punctuated by hot-air vents (part of what was a very new fangled heating system), and the regal study, which was oak-panelled by Liberty's of London. Sweeping through Blanche Dickson's red boudoir and her four fabulous bathrooms, with sunken baths and showers that sprayed from all sides, you're led on to the Charles Rennie Mackintosh-inspired children's nursery, with its simple white motifs. Once you've had your fill of the mansion, you can while away a pleasant few hours in the grounds, which slope down to a grass-fringed beach.

Practicalities

To get to Tjolöholm, take the **local train** to Kungsbacka from Gothenburg's Central Station (journey time 20min). A special bus runs from here to the house at 11am, returning in the afternoon; if you miss that, **bus** #732 goes to within 3km of the manor, from where you'll have to walk or hitch. By car, turn off the E6 highway just south of Kungsbacka at Fjärås, and follow the signs to Åsa for 2km, from where there are signs for Tjolöholm.

Kungsbacka has an STF **youth hostel** (☎0300/194 85; mid-June to mid-Aug), 2km from the train station on the road to Sarö – turn left from the station then right onto the main road. **Private rooms** at 170kr per person can be booked at the **tourist office** opposite the station (mid-May to mid-June Mon–Fri 9am–5pm, Sat 10am–2pm; late June Mon–Fri 9am–6pm, Sat 10am–2pm; July Mon–Sat 9am–6pm, Sun 10am–2pm; Aug Mon–Fri 9am–6pm, Sat & Sun 10am–2pm; Sept to mid-May Mon–Fri 9am–5pm; ☎0300/345 95, ⊕www.kungsbacka.se). The only convenient **hotel** is the reasonable *Halland* at Storgatan 35 (☎0300/775 30, ⊕162 25, ⊕www.hotel-halland.se; ❹/❷), almost next to the tourist office.

Varberg

More atmospheric than any other town in Halland, the fashionable little nineteenth-century bathing resort of **VARBERG** boasts surprisingly varied sights – most obviously its imposing fortress – plus a laid-back atmosphere, opportunities to swim and plenty of good places to eat.

Varberg's sights are concentrated along or near the seafront, with the thirteenth-century moated **fortress**, set on a rocky promontory in the sea, the most prominent attraction. Home to the Swedish king Magnus Eriksson, important peace treaties with Valdemar of Denmark were signed here in 1343. Standing outside, it's easy to imagine how impenetrable the fortress must have appeared to attackers in the past, as the way in is hardly more obvious today: enter on the sea-facing side by climbing the uneven stone steps to a delightful terrace café, or approach through the great archways towards the central courtyard.

Although **tours** in English (July to mid-Aug hourly 11am–4pm; on request at other times; 40kr) take you into the dungeons and among the impressive cocoa-coloured buildings that make up the inner courtyard, it's the **museum** that deserves most of your attention (mid-June to mid-Aug daily 10am–6pm; mid-Aug to mid-June Mon–Fri 10am–4pm, Sat & Sun noon–4pm; mid-June to mid-Aug 50kr, rest of the year 20kr). The most unnerving exhibit is the **Bocksten Man**, a 600-year-old murder victim who was garrotted, drowned, impaled and buried in a local bog until 1936, when a farmer dug him up. His entire outfit preserved by the acid bog, Bocksten Man sports the western world's most complete medieval wardrobe, made up of a cloak, a hood, shoes and stockings. His most shocking feature is the thick, red ringletted hair that cascades around his puny skull, while the three stakes thrust through his body were supposed to ensure that his spirit never escaped to seek out his murderers. Much of the rest of the museum is missable, with sections on farming and fishing in Halland, though the room devoted to the works of the so-called **Varberg School** is worth viewing. This small colony of artists – Richard Bergh, Nils Kreuger and Karl Nordström – who joined together in the last years of the nineteenth century, developed a national painting style reflecting the moods and atmosphere of Halland, Varberg in particular. Night scenes of the fortress beneath the stars show the strong influence of Van Gogh, but in other paintings, the misty colours create a more melancholy effect.

Overlooking the sea, the cream-painted **fortress prison** from 1850 looks incongruously delicate in the shadow of the looming fortress. The first Swedish jail to be built with individual cells, it housed life prisoners until the last one ended his days here in 1931. Today you can stay in a private youth hostel in the fortress, which has been carefully preserved to retain most of its original features (see overleaf).

A minute or so from the fortress lie a couple of fine remnants from Varberg's time as a spa resort. Facing the town just behind the fortress is the grand **Societeshuset**, a confection of cream-and-green carved wood where upper-class ladies took their meals after bathing in the splendid – and now beautifully restored – **Kallbadhuset** (cold bathhouse), just to the north of the fortress and overlooking the harbour. This dainty bathhouse (mid-June to mid-Aug daily 9am–6pm, Wed till 8pm; 40kr for cold bath and sauna) has separate-sex naked-bathing areas and is topped at each corner by Moorish cupolas, lending it an imperial air.

Although the Halland coastline is still a little rocky around here, there are several excellent spots for bathing. Head down Strandpromenaden for about five minutes to get to a couple of well-known **nudist beaches**: Goda Hopp for men, and Kärringhålan for women. Alternatively, a few kilometres further north at Getterön, a fist of land jutting into the sea, there's a nature centre (July & Aug daily 10am–6pm; Sept–June Fri–Sun 10am–4pm; free) and extensive bird reserve, as well as a series of secluded coves, reached by regular buses from town.

Practicalities

Varberg is a handy entry point to southern Sweden, linked by a year-round **ferry** (pedestrians 120kr one-way; car and up to five people 600kr; 3hr 45min) to Grenå in **Denmark**. Regular **trains** run down the coast from Gothenburg, and local **buses** cover the 45-kilometre trip south from Kungsbacka (bus #732, changing to #615 at Frillesås). From the **train and bus stations**, turn right down Vallgatan and the town centre is off to the left, the harbour to the right. The **tourist office** is at Kyrkogatan, just off Västra Vallgatan (April & May Mon–Fri 9am–5pm, Sat 10am–1pm; June–Aug Mon–Sat 9am–7pm, Sun 3–7pm; Sept–March Mon–Fri 9am–5pm; ☎0340/887 70, ⊛www.turist.varberg.se) provides free maps of the town. Varberg is easy to walk around, but to explore the nearby coast it might be worth **renting a bike** from Erlan Cykel och Sport, Västra Vallgatan 41 (☎0340/144 55; 70kr per day, 200kr per week) or from *Getteröns Camping* (see below; 50kr per day).

It's worth booking well in advance for the fortress prison **youth hostel** (☎0340/887 88, ⓔvandrarhem@turist.varberg.se); outside the summer you have to book through the tourist office. Aside from being spotlessly clean, the prison is much as it was, with original cell doors (each has its own key) complete with spyholes. If it's full, try the other very central hostel, *Platsamas Vandrahem* at Villagatan 13 (☎0340/61 16 40). Note that both hostels have some double rooms (❶). Alternatively, a couple of excellent-value and appealing family-run **hotels** are just a few steps away. At Norrgatan 16, *Varberg* (☎0340/161 25, ⊛www.hotellvarberg.nu; ❸) is an excellent choice for its very friendly atmosphere, excellent service and value. Built in 1899, it retains plenty of character and serves a great breakfast. The price includes a ticket worth 100kr in the restaurant next door. *Hotel Gåstis*, Borgmästaregatan 1 (☎0340/180 50, ⊛www.hotellgastis.nu; ❹/❸), includes an evening meal in its rates and offers cycle hire at just 25kr per day for guests; there's also a sauna, spa pool and gym. *Hotel Fregatten* (☎0340/6770 00, ⊛www.fregatten-homehotel.se; ❺/❹), in a former cold-storage warehouse overlooking the harbour, is quite luxurious, boasting a jacuzzi, sauna and spa. There are a number of **camp-sites** in the area, the nearest being *Apelvikens Camping* (☎0340/141 78, ⓕ875 38; April–Oct), 3km south of the fortress along Strandpromenaden. To the north, near the nature reserve, is *Getteröns Camping* (☎0340/168 85, ⓕ104 22). Alternatively, there are plenty of places to put up a tent for free beyond the nudist beaches.

There's no problem finding a good place to **eat** in Varberg, with most of the options north of the main square along Kungsgatan. The best café in town, and great for breakfast, is *Blå Dörren* on the corner of Norrgatan and Västra Vallgatan. The relaxed *Maja's* at Kungsgatan 28 is where the young locals come. Further down the street, *Harry's Pub & Restaurant* serves a range of pastas (85kr), and has a popular happy hour (daily 4–7pm). For lunch, try the *Societen* in Societets Park, directly behind the fortress, where daily specials go for 75kr, or visit on Friday evenings, when it comes alive with foxtrotting Swedes, or Saturday, when there's live bands and a disco.

Falkenberg

It's a twenty-minute train ride south from Varberg to the well-preserved medieval town of **FALKENBERG**, named after the falcons that were once hunted here. With a long beach and a pleasing old quarter, it's a likeable little town, though it only really comes alive in July and August. Sir Humphrey Davy, inventor of the mining safety lamp, visited in the 1820s to go **fly-fishing** in the River Ätran that runs through town, and, as the town's reputation for salmon spread, a succession of wealthy English countrymen followed him here, leaving their mark on the town. Today the waters have been so overfished that it costs relatively little to try your hand in the two-kilometre stretch from the splendid stone **Tullbron** toll bridge of 1756 – permits are available from the tourist office (see overleaf) from March to September, cost 80kr and allow you to catch up to three fish a day.

The **old town**, to the west of the curving river, comprises a dense network of low, wooden cottages and cobbled lanes. Nestling among them is the fine twelfth-century **St Laurentii kyrka**, its interior awash with seventeenth- and eighteenth-century wall and ceiling paintings. When the town acquired a solid new neo-Gothic church in the late nineteenth century, the St Laurentii kyrka was only saved from demolition by being used variously as a shooting range, a cinema and a gymnasium, until being reconsecrated in the 1920s.

Bypassing the pedestrian **Local Museum** on St Lars Kyrkogatan, head straight for the **Falkenberg Museum** (June to early Sept Tues–Fri 10am–4pm, Sat & Sun noon–4pm; mid-Sept to May Tues–Fri & Sun noon–4pm; 20kr) in an old grain store near the main bridge. At the time of writing, most of the museum was devoted to the 1950s, with displays covering Falkenberg's dance bands, alongside original interiors of a shoe repair shop and a stylized café, but plans are afoot to revise the collection sometime soon. The town also boasts a rather unusual **Photography Museum** at Sandgatan 13 (late June to Aug Tues–Thurs 1–7pm, Sun 1-5pm; Sept to late June Tues–Thurs 5–7pm, Sun 2–6pm; ☎0346/879 28, ⓦwww.fotomuseet-olympia.com; 40kr), housed in what was originally Falkenberg's first purpose-built cinema. Among the thousand or so cameras and other cinematic paraphernalia, there are some superb local peasant portraits, taken in 1898 by Axel Aurelius. Less demanding is a tour of the local **Falken Brewery** (July & Aug Mon–Thurs 10am & 1.15pm; 20kr, bookable at the tourist office): Sweden's most popular beer, Falken, has been brewed here since 1896 and is available for sampling at the end of the tour.

Over the river and fifteen minutes' walk south there's a fine, four-kilometre stretch of sandy beach, **Skrea Strand**. At its northern end is the large bathing and tennis complex of **Klitterbadhuset** (mid-June to mid-Aug Mon–Fri 9am–3pm, Tues & Thurs from 6am, Sat 9am–5pm, Sun 9am–4pm; mid-Aug to mid-June Tues & Thurs 6–9am & noon–8pm, Wed noon–8pm, Fri 9am–noon; 35kr plus 15kr for gym), which offers a fifty-metre saltwater pool and shallow children's pool, a vast sauna, jacuzzi and steam rooms. If you walk all the way down past the wooden holiday shacks at the southern end of the beach, you'll come across some secluded coves; in early summer, the marshy grassland around here is full of wild violets and clover and is a great place for birdwatching.

Practicalities

Regular **buses** and **trains** drop you close to the centre on Holgersgatan, just a couple of minutes from the **tourist office** in Stortorget (mid-June to Aug Mon–Sat 9.30am–6pm, Sun 2–6pm; Sept to mid-June Mon–Fri 9am–5pm; ☎0346/861 00, ⓦwww.falkenbergsturist.se). They can book **private rooms** from 160kr per person, plus a steep 65kr booking fee. The comfortable and well-equipped STF **youth hostel** (☎0346/171 11; June to mid-Aug) is in the countryside at Näset, 4km south of town – buses #1 and #2 run there until 7pm. It's just a few minutes' walk through the neighbouring **campsite** (☎0346/171 07) to the south end of the beach. The best-located **hotel** for the beach is the sprawling *Standbaden* (☎0346/71 49 00, ⓦwww.strandbaden.elite.se; ❹/❸); rooms are large and luxurious, and rates include entry to the Klitterbadhuset complex. Rather more interesting is the riverside *Hvitan* (☎0346/820 90, ⓦwww.hwitan.se; ❹), which hosts a very popular **jazz and folk festival** in the first and third weeks of July (get tickets from the tourist office; 255kr for the folk, 150kr for the jazz). The cheapest option is *Hotel Steria*, a ten-minute walk up from the river at Arvidstorpsvägen 28 (☎0346/155 21, ☎101 30; ❶).

About the best place for **lunch** is the atmospheric *Falkmanska Caféet*, Storgatan 42 (closed Sun) in the oldest secular building in town; try the huge baguettes and decadent cakes. For outdoor eating, the *Café Rosengården* enjoys a great location just above the old bridge at Doktorspromenaden, while on the main square, *Harry's Bar* is a busy eating place and pub. The poshest restaurant is *Gustav Bratt*, Brogatan 1, near the main square, though its à la carte menu is nothing special; head instead for the restaurants at the *Hvitan* and *Strandbaden* hotels, both of which offer at least one vegetarian option alongside meat and fish dishes, all of which are priced at 130–150kr.

Halmstad

The principal town in Halland, **HALMSTAD** was once a grand walled city and important Danish stronghold. Today, although most of the original buildings have disappeared, the town boasts a couple of cultural and artistic points of interest, most notably the works of the Halmstad Group, Sweden's first Surrealists, as well as extensive beaches and a wide range of really good places to eat.

In 1619, Halmstad's **castle** was used by Danish King Christian IV to entertain the Swedish king Gustav II Adolf; records show that there were seven days of solid festivities. The bonhomie didn't last much longer than that, and Christian was soon building great stone and earth fortifications around the city, surrounded by a moat with four stone gateways. Soon after, a fire all but destroyed the city; the only buildings to survive were the castle and church. Undeterred, Christian took the opportunity to create a modern Renaissance town with a grid of straight streets – the charming high street, Storgatan, still contains a number of impressive merchants' houses from that time. After the final defeat of the Danes in 1645, Halmstad lost its military significance and the walls were torn down. Today, just one of the great gateways, Norre Port, remains, while Karl XIs Vägen runs directly above the filled-in moat.

The Town

At the centre of the lively market square, **Stora Torg**, is Carl Milles' *Europa and the Bull*, a fountain with mermen twisted around it, all with Milles' characteristically muscular bodies and ugly faces. Flanking one side of the square, the grand fourteenth-century **St Nikolai kyrka** (daily 8.30am–3.30pm) is testimony to the town's former importance, but today, the only signs of its medieval origins are the splodges of bare rock beneath the plain brick columns. Leading north from the square, pedestrianized **Storgatan** holds some creaking old houses built in the years following the 1619 fire, as well as most of the town's restaurants and nightlife venues. The great stone arch of **Norre Port** marks the street's end: through here and to the right is the splendid **Norre Katt Park**, a delightful, shady place, with mature beech and horse chestnut trees sloping down to the river bank.

By the river at the northernmost edge of the park is a fine **museum** (Tues–Sun noon–4pm, Wed till 9pm; 20kr). While the archeological finds on the ground floor are unlikely to set many pulses racing, there are some home interiors from the seventeenth, eighteenth and nineteenth centuries upstairs, including exquisitely furnished dolls' houses and a room of glorious Gustavian harps and square pianos from the 1780s. The top floor contains a decent sample of the work of the Halmstad Group.

A few kilometres north of the town centre, heading out along Karlsrovägen past the tiny airport, **Mellby Arts Centre** (July to mid-Aug Tues–Sun 1–6pm; mid-March to June & mid-Aug to Oct Tues–Sun 1–5pm; Nov to mid-Dec Sat & Sun 1–5pm; 40kr) is home to the largest collection of works by the **Halmstad Group**, a body of six local artists who championed Cubism and Surrealism in 1920s Sweden. Their work caused considerable controversy in the 1930s and 40s, and a quick glance shows how strongly they were influenced by Magritte and Dali. Reputedly the only group of its type to have stayed together in its entirety for fifty years, they sometimes worked together on a single project: you can see a good example at the Halmstad City Library, where an impressive 14-metre-long, six-section work adorns the wall above the shelves. To get to the centre, take bus #350 from the centre of town, which will drop you just after the turnoff. It's also a very enjoyable twenty-minute cycle ride.

Practicalities

From the **train station**, follow Bredgatan to the Nissan River and cross Österbro (East Bridge) to get to the coral-red castle on the opposite bank which contains the **tourist office** (June Mon–Fri 10am–6pm, Sat 10am–3pm, Sun 1–3pm; July to mid-Aug Mon–Sat 9am–7pm, Sun 3–7pm; late Aug & April–May Mon–Fri 9am–6pm, Sat 10am–1pm; Sept–March Mon–Fri 9am–5pm; ☏035/13 23 20, ⓦwww.halmstad.se). Staff can book **private rooms** (from 125kr per person, plus 25kr booking fee in person, 50kr by phone). Renting a **bike** is a good way to get out to the Mellby Arts Centre or the beaches on the coast hereabouts: Arvid Olsson Cykel, Norra Vägen 11 (Mon–Fri 9.30am–6pm, Sat 9.30am–1pm; ☏035/21 22 51), is currently the only outlet in the town centre, and charges 100kr per day for a five-speed bike, or 140kr for two days. A cheaper though less central option is *Kronocampin*, 6km west of the town centre at Tylösand (☏035/305 10).

There's a central **youth hostel** (☏035/12 05 00; mid-June to mid-Aug) at Skepparegatan 23, 500m to the west of St Nicolai kyrka, which has showers and toilets in all rooms, and has some private doubles (❶). The best of the central **hotels** are the very comfortable old *Norre Park*, Norra Vägen 7 (☏035/21 85 55, ⓦwww.norrepark.se; ❸/❷), through the Norre Port Arch north of Storgatan, overlooking the park. The other is the classic *Hotel Continental*, Kungsgatan 5 (☏035/17 63 00, ⓦwww.continental-halmstad.se; ❹/❸), just two minutes' walk from the train station and boasting a free sauna and solarium within its National Romantic-style confines. The nearest **campsite** is *Hägons Camping* (☏035/12 53 63, ⓕ12 43 65), about 3km east of the centre next to a nature reserve bordering a **nudist beach**; the site's few cabins cost 3800–5100kr per week for up to five people.

Eating, drinking and **nightlife** possibilities abound along Storgatan, ranging from casual cafés to glamorous gourmet joints. *Daltons*, at no.35, is a modern bar-restaurant featuring Swedish music and an open-air bar in summer. *Pio & Co* next door is a lovely place with a massive drinks list and a speciality of steak with piles of mashed potato served on wooden planks for 175kr. For a real splurge, *Lilla Helfwetet* ("Little Hell"), on the corner of Hamngatan and Bastiongatan, is the most stylishly contemporary restaurant in town, serving up lamb, turbot and beef dishes in a stunningly designed old turbine engine room overlooking the river. For **cafés**, try the old-fashioned *Skånska Hembageriet*, just off Storgatan at Bankgatan 1; on Storgatan itself, at no.23, head to *Strömbergs Ost & Delikatessen* for great light lunches, and the laid-back, casual and very likeable *Wayne's* at no. 42, which is better for the atmosphere and coffee than the somewhat bland food.

Båstad and the Bjäre peninsula

Although linked together geographically, the town of **Båstad** and the attached **Bjäre peninsula** couldn't be more dissimilar. Båstad is a major Swedish sports

---

Skåne Card

If you're spending a significant amount of time in Skåne, buying a **Skåne Sommarkort** card can be an excellent way to save money. Covering travel on buses and trains throughout the county (including Pågatåg and Österlaren trains, but not Kustpilen trains), it's usable between June 15 and August 15, and costs 395kr for any 25 days within that period. Up to two children under six travel free with one adult holder, and the card gives a 25 percent discount on entry to Dunkers Kulturhus in Helsingborg (see p.523). Before each journey, you simply insert your card into the readers on board trains and buses. Cards are available from the Kund Center at Lund Station on Gustav Adolfs Torg in Malmö (see p.530), and at Knutpunkten in Helsingborg (see p.521); call ☏0771 77 77 77 or visit ⓦwww.skanetrafiken.se for more information.

resort, geared towards the chic pastimes of yachting, golfing and tennis; the peninsula, on the other hand, is a lot less manicured – with both rugged coastlines and lush meadows, it's an area of outstanding natural beauty.

Båstad

The most northerly town in the ancient province of Skåne, **BÅSTAD** has a character markedly distinct from the other towns along the coast. Cradled by the Bjäre peninsula, which bulges westwards into the Kattegat (the water separating Sweden and Jutland), Båstad is Sweden's elite **tennis centre**, home of the annual Swedish Open (℡0431 750 75, ⊛www.swedishopen.org; tickets 150–500kr) at the beginning of July, and boasting sixty tennis courts, five eighteen-hole golf courses and the Drivan Sports Centre. With a horizon of forested hills to the south, Båstad is pretty scenic, too; less pleasant, however, is the fact that ever since King Gustav V chose to take part in the 1930 tennis championships, wealthy retired Stockholmers and social climbers from all over Sweden have flocked here to bask in the social glow, with flocks of well-heeled young men in expensive sports cars overspending and drinking to excess. The down-to-earth and friendly locals grin and bear it for the sake of their local economy.

The **harbour** makes a pretty spot for a picnic or stroll; to get there, follow Tennisvägen off Köpmansgatan through a luxury residential district until you reach Strandpromenaden; to the west, the old bathhouses have been converted into restaurants and bars.

Practicalities

From the **train station**, it's a half-hour walk east along Köpmansgatan to the main square, where the **tourist office** (mid-June to mid-Aug Mon–Fri & Sun 10am–6pm, Sat 10am–4pm; mid-Aug to mid-June Mon–Sat 10am–4pm; ℡0431/750 45, ⊛www.bastad.com) can book **private rooms** for 150kr per person. They can also give information on booking tennis courts and renting out sports equipment. The main **bike rental** place is Svenn's Cykel, Tennisvägen 31 (Mon–Fri 8am–noon & 1–5pm, Sat 8am–noon), which charges 80kr per day or 300kr per week.

The STF **youth hostel** (℡0431/685 00, ℗706 19) is next to the Drivan Sports Centre on Korrödsvagen, signposted off Köpmansgatan. It's open all year, but tends to be reserved for groups in winter, and the sporty young guests can make it noisy. For a really excellent **bed and breakfast**, try *Falken*, Hamngatan 22 (℡0431/36 95 94; ❷), a lovingly maintained 1916-built villa set just above the harbour in delightful gardens, with lots of art on the walls and a welcoming atmosphere. The cheaper **hotels** are mostly around the station end of town; note that prices in Båstad increase dramatically during the summer due to the tennis. Try *Bed & Breakfast Malengården*, Åhusvägen 41 (℡ & ℗0431/36 95 67; ❶) – take the turning off Köpmansgatan towards the youth hostel. For a luxurious and beautifully designed alternative, try the harbourside *Hotel Skansen* (℡0431/55 81 00, ℗55 81 10, ⊛www.hotelskansen.se; ❹/❺). **Camping** is not allowed at the waterside; you're best off heading to the Bjäre peninsula.

Eating and drinking is as much a pastime as tennis in Båstad, and most of the waterside restaurants and hotels both here and on the peninsula offer two-course dinners for around 150kr, with menus changing weekly. *Pepe's Bodega* is a popular pizza place at the harbour, but for value it's hard to beat *Sveas Skafferi*, a wooden hut at the harbour's edge serving smoked salmon and other fish goodies on paper plates for 60kr, as well as home-baked pies and cake. *Caffe & Torta*, opposite the church at the harbour end of Köpmansgatan, is a fine daytime **café** offering freshbaked bread (from 6am daily), gazpacho, big salads and the best coffee and cake in town.

The Bjäre peninsula

The highlight of northern Skåne, the magical **Bjäre peninsula** demands a couple of days' exploration, its varied scenery ranging from open fields of potatoes and strawberries to cliff formations of splintered red rock and remote islands thick with birds and dotted with historical ruins. To help you find your way around, buy a large-scale **map** of the area from Båstad tourist office (40kr). The **Skåneleden walking trail** runs round the entire perimeter of the peninsula, and is equally good for cycling (a few gears help, as the terrain can get quite hilly). **Public transport** around the peninsula is adequate: bus #525 leaves Båstad every other hour on weekdays, running through the centre of the peninsula, via Hov and Karup, to Torekov (20min); at weekends you'll need to call Båstad taxi (☎0431/696 66) an hour before you want to leave – it costs the same as the bus, but be sure to book your return trip. Bus #524 leaves from Förslov, on the peninsula's southern coast, for Hov, which is useful if you've walked this far. If you don't want to head back to Båstad, bus #523 goes regularly from Torekov south to Ängelholm (50min).

Heading north out of Båstad along the coast road, it's just a couple of kilometres to **Norrvikens Gardens** (May to mid-Sept daily 10am–6pm; ⓦwww .norrvikenstradgardar.se; 60kr), a paradise for horticulturists and the site in July of Sweden's biggest annual **classic car show**, at which a remarkable range of gleaming veteran and vintage cars, including early Volvos and Saabs, appears alongside glorious American road monsters, all of which trundle around the surrounding countryside for days before and after the show. By the gardens' car park, you'll find the innovative **glass-blowing studio** of British-born designer Richard Rackham (Mon–Fri 9am–6pm), whose flowing, brilliantly coloured glass bowls and vases are more dramatic than much of what you'll see in the Glass Kingdom (see p.568). Two to three kilometres further on is **KATTVIK**. Once a busy stone-grinding mill village, it's now largely the domain of elderly, wealthy Stockholmers, who snap up the few houses as soon as they appear on the market – it achieved its moment of fame when Richard Gere chose a cottage here for a summer romance. Otherwise, it contains little more than the friendly *Delfin Bed & Breakfast* (☎070/405 15 49; ❶), an idyllic base for exploring the region, with breakfast served on the veranda. In the hills behind here, *Westfield Häst Safari* (☎ & ☎0431/45 13 53) is a base for **horse trekking**, a great way to discover the region. Two-hour trips cost 350kr including lunch, and a two-day trek through the surrounding forests to **Hovs Hallar**, a nature reserve with dramatic red cliffs, is 1300kr including accommodation but not meals.

The sleepy village of **TOREKOV** lies on the peninsula's western coast a few kilometres from Kattvik, and its little harbour is where old fishing boats leave for the nature reserve island of **Hallands Väderö**. Old wooden fishing boats make the fifteen-minute crossing regularly (mid-June to mid-Aug hourly; Sept–May every 2hr; 70kr return), the last one returning at 4.30pm, so it's worth setting off early to give yourself a full day. The island is a glorious mix of trees and sun-warmed bare rocks, with isolated fishing cottages dotted around its edges, while countless birds – gulls, eiders, guillemots and cormorants – fly noisily overhead. If you're lucky, you may be able to make out the **seal colony**, which lies on the farthest rocks at the southern tip of the island – Torekov tourist office (June–Aug daily 10am–6pm; ☎0431/36 31 80, ⓦwww.torekovturism.net), right on Torekov's harbour, has details of organized seal safaris. Check out also the English graveyard, surrounded by mossy dry-stone walls, which contains the remains of English sailors killed in 1809 when stationed here in order to bombard Copenhagen during the Napoleonic Wars. Bizarrely, they were refused burial at Torekov as there was no way of proving they were Christian.

Ängelholm and the Kullen peninsula

The best aspects of peacefully uneventful **ÄNGELHOLM** are its justifiably popular seven kilometres of golden beach and its proximity to everywhere else in the region – Helsingborg is just thirty minutes away by train, and the Bjäre peninsula beckons to the north. With a range of accommodation and some agreeable restaurants, its not a bad base, and there's also a surprisingly lively nightlife scene, too. Ängelholm's efforts to sell itself, however, concentrate not on its beaches but on the town mascot, a musical clay cuckoo (on sale everywhere) and UFOs. The latter have been big business here since 1946, when a railway worker, Gösta Carlsson, convinced the authorities that he had encountered tiny people from another world. Today Ängelholm hosts international UFO conferences, and the tourist board runs tours to the "landing site" of Carlsson's aliens throughout the summer.

From the train station, it's just a few minutes' walk over the Rönneå River to the main square, Stortorget and tourist office. Should you want to see more of the surrounding area, the least strenuous way is on a **boat trip** up the river from the harbour (☎0431/203 00; early June to mid-Aug); there are four daily forty-minute trips (65kr), and a two-hour cruise once a day (85kr). For more freedom of movement, Skåne Marin, the company which runs the tours, also rents out boats and canoes. If none of this appeals, head left from the station for some 4km to get to the **beaches**. A free bus runs there from the market square (late June to mid-Aug hourly 10am–4pm).

Jutting like a stiletto heel into the Kattegatt, the **Kullen peninsula**, west of Ängelholm, is a highlight along this stretch of coast. It's far flatter than the Bjäre peninsula to the north, and so makes for good cycling, but still undulates enough to ensure some great vistas. Head to the picture-perfect village of **Arild**, from where it's just a couple of kilometres northwest to the eighteenth-century farmstead of **Himmelstorp**, with its remarkable and authentic eighteenth century interiors. Between May and September, you can go in and have a look free of charge, though opening hours are variable – check with the owners on ☎042/34 60 06. From Himmelstorp, it's well worth the twenty-minute scramble to the coast to the remarkable "living" sculpture, **Nimis**. Created by Lars Vilks out of driftwood, *Nimis* forms corridors and stairways into the sea, providing a spectacular foreground to the backdrop of the Kattegat and the Bjäre peninsula beyond.

To get to Kullen by car or bike, take Järnvägsgatan from Ängelholm, following directions to Höganäs, then take the scenic northern coastal road at Utvälinge. **Bus** #225 runs from Ängelholm to Höganäsand on to Mölle bus station almost hourly until after midnight.

Practicalities

There are regular **trains** to Ängelholm from Båstad (25min), plus **buses** from Båstad and Torekov. It's a short distance from the train station to the **tourist office** in the main square (June & Aug Mon–Fri 9am–6pm, Sat 9am–2pm; July Mon–Fri 9am–7pm, Sat 9am–3pm, Sun 11am–3pm; Sept–May Mon–Fri 9am–5pm; ☎0431/821 30, ☻www.turist.engelholm.se). For **bike rental**, head to Harry's Cykel, Södra Kyrkogatan 9 (☎0431/143 25; 100kr per day or 450kr per week). The tourist office can also book hotels (30kr booking fee) or **private rooms** (from 110kr, plus 30kr booking fee). There's an STF **youth hostel** (☎0431/45 23 64; booking necessary Nov–March) at the beach at Magnarp Strand, 10km north of the train station and reached by local bus. Of several **campsites**, the most convenient for the beach is *Råbocka*, at the end of Råbockavägen (☎0431/105 43, ☎832 45). For a good-value and friendly **hotel**, try the *Lilton* (☎0431/44 25 50, ☻www.hotel-lilton.se; ❸/❷), a few steps from the square at Järnvägsgatan 29, which has a great garden café in summer. Another stylish option is the *Kitterhus Pensionat* (☎0431/135 30, ☎135 31; ❸/❷), with elegant rooms, big en-suite bathrooms and a gorgeous bar area located in the beautifully renovated premises of the classic old *Klitterhus* restaurant down by the beach.

The best place to look for **food** is the harbour. *Hamn Krogen* doesn't look anything special from the outside, but it serves the best fish dishes in Ängelholm – their speciality is "Toast Skagen", shrimps and red caviar on toast. A few metres up the beach, in a whitewashed wartime bunker, *Bunken* restaurant and bar serves barbecue food alongside more lavish seafood dishes, and puts on regular live music. The most popular **nightclub** is *Bahnhoff Bar* (Thurs–Sat), a cavernous, industrial-looking place occupying old railway buildings just beyond the present train station. If you have your own transport and want a taste of something different, *Ekebo*, in the Ängelholm suburb of Munka-Ljungby around 15km east of town (bus #507), is a popular place to indulge the Swedish obsession with **foxtrots** on Saturday nights. In July it hosts Sweden's biggest foxtrot festival (℡0431/43 22 30, ⊛www.ekebonoje .se) – it's quite an eye-opener.

Helsingborg and around

Long gone are the days when the locals of **HELSINGBORG** joked that the most rewarding sight here was Helsingør, the Danish town whose castle (best known as the "Elsinore" of Shakespeare's *Hamlet*) is clearly visible just 4km away over the Öresund. With its beautifully developed North Harbour area, an explosion of brilliantly styled bars, cafés and restaurants both at the water's edge and among the warren of cobbled old-town streets, and an excellent new museum, Helsingborg is one of the best urban bases Sweden has to offer: bright, pleasing and basking in a tremendous sense of buoyancy.

Past links between Denmark and this likeable city have been less than convivial, though – in fact, Helsingborg has a particularly bloody and tragic history. After the Danes fortified the town in the eleventh century, the Swedes conquered and lost it again on six violent occasions, finally winning out in 1710 under the leadership of Magnus Stenbock. By this time, the Danes had torn down much of the town and on its final recapture, the Swedes razed its twelfth-century castle, except for the five-metre-thick walled keep (*kärnen*) that still dominates the centre. By the early eighteenth century, war and epidemics had reduced the population to just 700, and only with the onset of industrialization in the 1850s did Helsingborg wake up to a new prosperity. Shipping and the railways turned the town's fortunes around, as evidenced by the formidable late nineteenth-century commercial buildings in the centre and some splendid villas to the north overlooking the Öresund. After decades out of the limelight, Helsingborg's fortunes now seem very much on the up.

Arrival, information and city transport

Unless you approach by car on the E6, the chances are that you'll arrive at the harbourside **Knutpunkten**, the vast, glassy expanses of which incorporate all car, train and passenger **ferry** terminals. The **bus station** is on the ground floor behind the main hall, while the ticket and transport information offices are in the front of the complex. Below ground level is the combined **train station** for the national SJ trains and the lilac-coloured local Pågatåg trains, which run south down the coast to Landskrona, Lund and Malmö. One floor up brings you to a Forex **currency exchange** office (daily 8am–9pm). The Sundsbussarna passenger-only ferry to Helsingør uses the quayside at Hamntorget, 100m north. For ferry ticket details, bus and train information, see "Listings", p.525.

The **tourist office** (May Mon–Fri 9am–6pm, Sat & Sun 10am–2pm; June–Aug Mon–Fri 9am–8pm, Sat & Sun 9am–5pm; Sept–April Mon–Fri 9am–6pm, Sat 10am–2pm; ℡042/10 43 50, ⊛www.visit.helsingborg.se) is at the top of the very oblong square, Stortorget, just beneath the steps of the castle keep – from Knutpunkten, turn left along Järnvågsgatan and it's almost immediately on your right. Staff hand out free maps, the listings guide *Helsingborg This Month*, and the excellent English-language *Helsingborg Guide*.

Central Helsingborg is compact enough to explore on foot, although for the youth hostel and outlying sights such as Sofiero and the Pålsjöbaden bathing house on Drottninggatan, 3km north of the centre, you'll need to take a **bus**. Tickets are bought on board, cost 16kr and are valid for two changes within an hour. **Cycling**

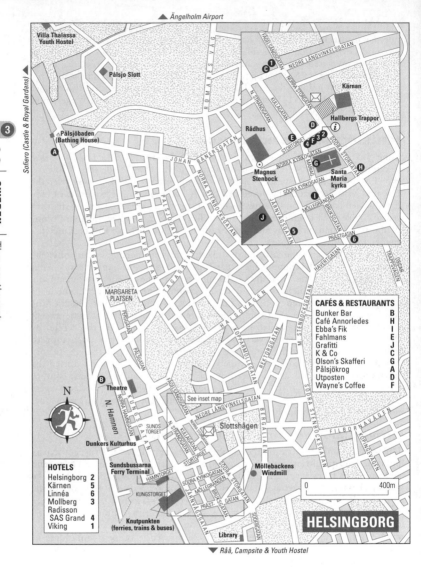

▲ Ängelholm Airport

▼ Råå, Campsite & Youth Hostel

is an enjoyable option – the tourist office has a monopoly on bike rental and charges a steep 125kr per day plus a 50kr returnable deposit, though the bikes are at least new and good.

Accommodation

There are plenty of central **hotel** options in Helsingborg. The tourist office can book **private rooms** from 150kr per person plus a hefty 100kr booking fee (rising to 300kr for three or more nights). The *Villa Thalassa* **youth hostel** at Dag Hammarskjöldsväg (☎042/38 06 60, ⍉www.villathalassa.com), 2.5km north of the town centre, is superbly set around a c.1900 villa – unfortunately the accommodation isn't in the villa itself, but in cabins behind; there are also some holiday cottages (doubles ❶). Bus #219 runs north from Knutpunkten (every 20min) to the Pålsjöbaden bathing house, from where it's a one-kilometre walk through forest. A more central, though less interesting hostel choice, with doubles (❶) as well as dorms, is at Järnvagsgatan 39 (☎042 14 58 50, ⓦwww.hbgturist.com), five minutes' walk from Knutpunkten.

Helsingborg Stortorget 8–12 ☎02/37 18 00, ⓦwww.hkchotels.se. Lovely hotel with marble stairs, comfortable rooms and a perfect location at the foot of the steps up to the castle keep. ❺/❸
Kärnen Järnvägsgatan 17 ☎042/12 08 20, ⓦwww.hotelkarnan.se. Opposite Knutpunkten, this comfortable, recently renovated hotel prides itself on "personal touches", including ominous English-language homilies on each room door (no. 235, for instance, has "He who seeks revenge keeps his wounds open"). There's a small library, cocktail bar and sauna. ❺/❸
Linnéa Prästgatan 4 ☎042/37 24 00, ⓕ37 24 29, ⓦwww.hotell-linnea.se. Very cheap, central and pleasant, with agreeable standard rooms as well as apartments for three people at 5000kr per week. ❹/❸

Mollberg Stortorget 18 ☎042/37 37 00, ⓦwww.elite.se. Every bit a premier hotel, with a grand nineteenth-century facade, elegant rooms and a brasserie. ❺/❸
Radisson SAS Grand Stortorget 8–12 ☎042/38 04 00, ⓦwww.radissonsas.com. No longer quite as exclusive as it once was since it became part of the Radisson chain, but pleasant nonetheless. Big summer reductions make it much more affordable. ❺/❸
Viking Fågelsångsgatan 1 ☎042/14 44 20, ⓦwww.hotellviking.se. This appealing, quiet old hotel in a fine location close to some of the finest old buildings in town is the place to try first. Excellent service, cosy atmosphere and good breakfasts. ❺/❸

The Town

The most obvious place to start exploring is the waterfront, by the copper statue of Magnus Stenbock on his charger. With your back to the Öresund and Denmark, the **Rådhus** (July & Aug Mon–Fri 40min tours at 10am) is to your left, a heavy-handed neo-Gothic pile complete with turrets and towers designed by an architect whose admiration for medieval Italy is perhaps a little too obvious. It's worth a look inside to enjoy the extravagances of nineteenth-century provincial wealth and the fabulous stained-glass windows that tell the entire history of the town. The original wall and ceiling frescoes – deemed too costly to restore and therefore painted over in 1968 – are currently being uncovered.

Crossing the road from the statue and turning right, you can't fail to notice the exceptional city museum **Dunkers Kulturhus** (daily 11am–6pm, Tues & Thurs till 10pm; ⓦwww.dunkerskulturhus.com; 60kr) at the harbour to your left. The collection within this white-brick building, roofed in waves of aluminium and opened in 2002, explores the city's history – via the theme of water – from ice-age to present day with plenty of dramatic lighting and sound effects. It's all great fun, though perhaps more visually stimulating than informative. Henry Dunker, whose foundation funded the museum, was a pioneer of galoshes and his brand, Tretorn, was a world leader till its demise in 1979.

Returning to the Stenbock statue at the bottom of **Stortorget** – the central "square", though it's actually so oblong it's more like a boulevard – you can walk up the slope to meet the steps leading to the remains of the medieval **castle** (June–Aug daily 10am–8pm; Sept–May Mon–Fri & Sun 10am–6pm, Sat 10am–2pm; 5kr). Take the lift to the top, where the massive castellated bulk of the keep, **Kärnen** (daily: April, May & Sept 9am–4pm; June–Aug 10am–7pm; Oct–March 10am–2pm; 15kr) is surrounded by some fine parkland. Shaped simply as a huge upturned brick, it's worth climbing more for its views than the historical exhibitions housed within. The keep and St Maria kyrka (see overleaf) were the sole survivors of the ravages of war, but the former lost its military significance once Sweden finally won the day. In the mid-nineteenth century it was destined for demolition and only survived because seafarers found it a valuable landmark. What cannon fire failed to achieve, neglect and the weather succeeded in bringing about, and the keep fell into ruin before restoration began in 1894.

From the parkland at the keep's base, you can wander down a rhododendron-edged path, Hallbergs Trappor, to the **St Maria kyrka** (Mon–Sat 8am–4pm, Sun 9am–6pm), which squats in its own square by a very French-looking avenue of beech trees. The square is surrounded by a cluster of quaint places to eat and some excellent **shops** for picnic food, notably Maratorgets on the south side of the square, which sells fruit, the adjacent Bengtsons Ost, a cheese shop and, for exquisite indulgence, the Peter Beier Chocalatier, a chocoholic's dream with a molten chocolate fountain in the window behind which you can consume the delicious products with a coffee. The church itself was begun in 1300 and completed a century later; its rather plain facade belies a striking interior, with a clever contrast between the early seventeenth-century Renaissance-style ornamentation of its pulpit and gilded reredos, and jewel-like contemporary stained-glass windows.

Walking back to Stortorget, **Norra** and **Södra Storgatan** (the streets that meet at the foot of the steps to Kärnen) formed Helsingborg's main thoroughfare in medieval times, and are today lined with the town's oldest merchants' houses. Heading south along Södra Storgatan, pass through the gap to the left of the old cream-painted brick building opposite the modern Maria Församling House; from the courtyard here, a flight of 92 steps leads up to the handsome nineteenth-century Möllebackens windmill. Ranged around this are a number of exquisite farm **cottages** with low doorways and eighteenth-century peasant interiors – straw beds, cradles and hand-painted grandmother clocks –you're free to wander in for a closer look (May–Aug daily noon–8pm). A further reward for the climb is to be found at *Möllebackens Våffelbruk* (May–Aug daily noon–8pm), which has been serving home-made waffles here using the same recipe since 1912.

Out from the centre: Sofiero

Four kilometres north of Helsingborg along the coast are the gorgeous **Royal Gardens of Sofiero** (April to mid-Sept 10am–6pm; 60kr), easily reached by bus #219 from Knutpunkten, or by cycling the 4km north along the coast. Built as a summer residence by Oscar II in the 1860s, the house itself looks rather like an elaborate train station (the architect also designed most of Sweden's stations), but the real reason to come here is the gardens, given by Oscar to his grandson, Gustav Adolf, when he married Crown Princess Margareta in 1905. Margareta created a horticultural paradise and, as a granddaughter of the British Queen Victoria, was strongly influenced by English garden design. The rhododendron collection in particular is one of Europe's finest, a stunning array of ten thousand plants, with over five hundred varieties making up a rainbow that stretches down to the Öresund.

Eating, drinking and nightlife

Helsingborg has a range of excellent **restaurants** and some great daytime **cafés** and *konditori*. The harbour restaurants offer some stylish settings overlooking the water, though they're all pretty similar. There are also some superb food shops, useful for picnic fare and mostly clustered on the square containing St Maria kyrka.

In the listings below, we've given telephone numbers only for those places where you are advised to book a table.

Cafés and restaurants

Bunker Bar North Harbour. Very crowded eatery near the far end of the harbour that's good for reasonably priced lunches and dinners.
Café Annorledes Södra Storgatan 15. A friendly atmosphere with pleasant 1950s memorabilia,

though the cakes are not as special as they used to be.
Ebba's Fik Bruksgatan 20. The most fun café in town, with authentic 1950s styling and great music to match. A must.

Fahlmans Stortorget 11. Helsingborg's classic *konditori*, this has been serving elaborate cakes and pastries since 1914. Try the coconut marzipan confections or the sumptuous apple meringue pie.

Grafitti First floor, Knutpunkten. Generously filled baked potatoes or baguettes served up for a mostly young, sometimes rowdy crowd. The ideal place if you're hungry, skint and it's past 9pm.

K & Co Nedre Långvinkelsgatan 9. Very friendly, with great muffins, cakes and filling ciabattas and baguettes.

Olson's Skafferi Mariagatan 6 ☏042/14 07 80. The city's best Italian restaurant, right outside St Maria kyrka. Wonderfully prepared, authentic Italian dishes with fish, meat and pasta options, and zabaglione to drool over.

Pålsjökrog ☏042/14 97 30. Attached to the lovely old Pålasjöbaden bathhouse 2km north of the centre, and run by an architect who has designed it to feel like a Swedish country house. It's a special-occasion place serving traditional, well-presented Swedish food with main courses at around 150kr.

Utposten Stortorget 17. Very stylish decor – a mix of the rustic and industrial – at this great, varied Swedish restaurant beneath the post office at the steps to Kärnen. A two-course meal will cost around 140kr. Try the delicate and filling seafood and salmon stew at 90kr. Open till 1am.

Wayne's Coffee Stortorget 8. One of the hippest cafés in town, with simple modern decor in a grand old building. The cakes, though, can look better than they taste.

Bars and clubs

The glamorous **bars** along the North Harbour have provided a stylish foil to Helsingborg's traditional night-time haunts and music venues. These newer bars overlooking the Öresund are more places for wine- and beer-drinking than restaurants, though they do serve food along new-European lines. They're all located at ground level in the area's upmarket apartment buildings, with views across to Denmark.

You might want to indulge in the classic Helsingborg activity of taking the boat to Helsingør – the entertainment is the boat itself, rather than landing in Denmark. Do what the locals have traditionally done and go back and forth all night, taking advantage of prices cheaper than in any of Helsingborg's bars; nowadays, though, it's not quite as lively a cruise as it once was. Boats are run by Scandlines, Sundbussarna and Tura and leave from Knutpunkten; tickets (50kr) are available from the first-floor office and there are frequent departures.

Helsingborg's **gay scene** is pretty minimal nowadays, but RFSL still runs a café and pub-bar at Pålsgatan 1 (☏042/12 35 32), where there are occasionally parties. The bar is ten minutes' walk from Kuntpunkten.

Jazz Clubben Nedre Långvinkelsgatan 22. Sweden's biggest jazz club and well worth a visit on Wed, Fri and Sat evenings for live jazz, Dixieland, blues, Irish folk and blues jam sessions.

Le Cardinal Södra Kyrkogatan 9. Piano bar and nightclub with a steak-oriented restaurant. The first-floor disco is usually busy, while the second-floor piano bar is quieter, with a roulette table. Cover is 60–70kr and you need to be 25 to get in. Often closed during summer; call ☏042/18 71 71 to check.

Piren Hamn Torget. Opposite Sundsbussarna at the harbour, in the old black wooden building that was once the train station, this is a café by day, but comes alive after dark when it becomes a club with a 1970s student-dive atmosphere. Very popular.

Tivoli Hamn Torget. Lively place occupying the main part of the former train station opposite Knutpunkten, where you'll find lots of concerts and events. There's also a restaurant, *Vinyl Baren*, which is indeed filled with red vinyl bench seats and 1960s pop art.

Listings

Airport The nearest airport for domestic flights is at Ängelholm, 30km north of town; take the bus from Knutpunkten (1hr before flight departure). For international services, you'll need to go to Copenhagen's Kastrup airport. Take the Kustlinjen bus from Knutpunkten (2hr).

Buses The daily bus for Stockholm leaves from Knutpunkten; reservations are essential (☏0625/240 20), but tickets can only be bought on the bus (Mon–Thurs 250kr, Fri–Sun 355kr). Buses for Gothenburg leave daily (Mon–Thurs 140kr, Fri–Sun 200kr); tickets must be bought from the bus information section at the train booking office.

Car rental Avis, Garnisonsgatan 2 ☎042/15 70
80; Budget, Gustav Adolfsgatan 47 ☎042/12 50
40; Europcar, Muskötgatan 1 ☎042/17 01 15;
Hertz, Bergavägen 4 ☎042/17 25 40.
Exchange Forex in Knutpunkten (first floor) or
Järnvägsgatan 13. Both open June–Aug
7am–9pm, and Sept–May 8am–9pm.
Internet There's a Net café at Norra Kyrkogatan
17, by St Maria kyrka (Mon–Thurs 11am–9pm, Fri
& Sat 11am–6pm, Sun noon–9pm).

Pharmacy Björnen, Drottninggatan 14 (Mon–Fri
9am–6pm, Sat 9am–3pm).
Post office Stortorget 17 (Mon–Fri 9am–6pm, Sat
10am–1pm).
Trains The Pågatåg trains from Knutpunkten
require a ticket bought from an automatic machine
on the platform; international rail passes are valid.
It's 50kr one-way to Lund and 60kr one-way to
Malmö. Fare dodging invites a 600kr spot-fine.

Around Helsingborg: Råå

It's just 7km south from Helsingborg to the pretty fishing village of **RÅÅ** (pronounced "Raw-aw"). You can take bus #1 from the Rådhus, or cycle there along
the signposted bike lanes through the industrial mess of Helsingborg's southern
suburbs. Råå's main street, **Rååvägen**, is a subdued place: signs point to the twelfth-
century **Raus kyrka** (left up Lybecksgatan, over the highway and along
Rausvägen), but it's nothing special. Råå's main attraction is rather its **harbour**,
dense with masts and remarkably untouristy. The **Maritime Museum** (variable
hours; free) here is run by a group of Råå residents and shows a comprehensive
collection of seafaring artefacts. A fascinating, if somewhat stomach-churning, sight
at the harbour is that of eel sorting: the giant, spaghetti-like creatures are slopped
into appropriately coffin-shaped boxes to be separated according to size by fishermen using claw-shaped pincers.

There are a couple of good **eating** places at the harbour. Next door to the museum, the long-established *Råå Wärdshus* serves pricey fish dishes at around 150kr,
with lighter snacks and various salads for around 50kr. To the left of the museum,
on the pier, *Råå Hamnservering* is the best bet for a cheap meal, with an excellent
60kr lunch buffet. If you want to **stay** your choice is limited to the *Råå Camping
Site* (☎042/10 76 80, ℗26 10 10), which is advertised as being on the "waterfront".
It is, but the dominant view is of South Helsingborg's industrial smog.

Lund

Some fifty kilometres south of Helsingborg and a few kilometres inland is the celebrated university city of **LUND**. Like England's Oxford, with which it is often and
aptly compared, there's an eccentric and bohemian atmosphere to the place – a
mass of students' bikes will probably be the first image to greet you. Cultural attractions aside, it's the mix of architectural grandeur and the buzz of student life that
lends Lund its unique charm, and with its justly revered twelfth-century
Romanesque cathedral, its medieval streets and numerous museums, Lund could
easily keep you busy for a couple of days.

Arrival, information and getting around

Frequent **trains** from Helsingborg (40min) arrive at the train station on Banegatan
at the western edge of town, which is also the terminus for **buses** and is within
easy walking distance of everything of interest. The **tourist office** (May & Sept
Mon–Fri 10am–5pm, Sat 10am–2pm; June–Aug Mon–Fri 10am–6pm, Sat & Sun
10am–2pm; Oct–April Mon–Fri 10am–5pm; ☎046/35 50 40, ⊛www.lund.se),
opposite the Domkyrkan at Kyrkogatan 11, hands out free maps and copies of *I
Lund*, a monthly diary of events with museum and exhibition listings (the summer
edition is in English and Swedish). There's an **Internet café**, *Studio 9*, at Lilla
Gräbrödersgatan 2 (Mon–Fri 10am–midnight, Sat noon–1am, Sun 1–11pm).

Though none of the sights is more than ten minutes' walk away, you might want
to consider renting a **bike**; ask at the tourist office or try Harry's Cykelaffar,
Banvaktsgatan 2 (Mon–Fri 9am–6pm; ☎046/211 69 46; 90kr per day).

Accommodation

There is a decent range of **accommodation** on offer in Lund, nearly all of it in the centre, and the tourist office can book **private rooms** for 175kr per person, plus a 50kr booking fee. Lund's STF **youth hostel**, *Tåget*, at Vävaregatan 22, through the tunnel behind the train station (℡046/14 28 20, ℻32 05 68), is housed in the carriages of a 1940s train; unfortunately the novelty wears off when you find yourself crammed in three-deep bunks with rope hoists. An alternative is *La Strada*, at Brunnshögsvägen (℡046/32 32 51, ℻30 39 31): take bus #4 from west of Martens Torget 4km to Klosterängsvägen, then follow the bicycle track under the motorway for 1km.

Ahlström Skomakaregatan 3, just south of the Domkyrkan ℡046/211 01 74. Average, very central cheapie with the option of en-suite rooms. Closed June to mid-Aug. ❷

Concordia Stålbrogatan 1 ℡046/13 50 50, ⓦwww.concordia.se. A couple of streets southwest of Stortorget, this former student hostel has been upgraded into a very homely hotel with attentive service, though it's rather plain inside. There's a guest sauna too. ❹/❺

The Grand Bantorget 1 ℡046/280 61 00, ⓦwww.grandilund.se. This imposing nineteenth-century pink-sandstone edifice straddles an entire side of a small, stately and central square. Unpretentious and comfortable, with a fantastic breakfast buffet. ❻/❼

Petri Pumpa Sankt Petri Kyrkogatan 7 ℡046/13 55 19, ℻13 56 71, ⓦwww.petripumpa.se. An exclusive hotel, although its famous restaurant has now moved to the *Savoy* hotel in Malmö (see p.533). ❺/❼

The Town

It's only a short walk east from the train station to the magnificent **Domkyrkan** (Mon, Tues & Fri 8am–6pm, Wed & Thurs 8am–7.15pm, Sat 9.30am–5pm, Sun 9.30am–7.30pm; guided tours 3pm; free), whose storm-cloud charcoal and white

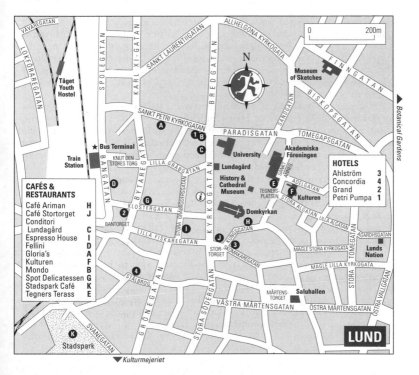

stone gives it an unusual monochrome appearance. Before entering, head around the back, past the grotesque animal and bird gargoyles over the side entrances; at the very back is the most beautiful part of the exterior: the three-storey apse above the crypt, crowned with an exquisite gallery.

Beyond the great carved entrance, the majestic **interior** is surprisingly unadorned, an elegant mass of watery-grey, ribbed stone arches and stone-flagged flooring. One of the world's finest masterpieces of Romanesque architecture, the cathedral was built in the twelfth century when Lund became the first independent archbishopric in Scandinavia, laying the foundation for a period of wealth and eminence that lasted until the advent of Protestantism. There are several interesting features, such as the elaborately carved fourteenth-century choir stalls depicting Old Testament scenes, with grotesque carvings hidden beneath the seats, but most striking is the amazing astronomical clock just to the left of the entrance. Dating from the 1440s, it shows hours, days, weeks and the courses of the sun and moon in the zodiac; if you're here at noon or 3pm, you'll get to see an ecclesiastical Punch and Judy show, as two knights pop out and clash swords as many times as the clock strikes, followed by little mechanical doors opening to trumpet-blowing heralds and the three wise men trundling slowly up to the Virgin Mary.

Don't miss the dimly lit and dramatic **crypt**, which has been left almost untouched since the twelfth century. Most of the tombstones are actually memorial slabs, with just one proper tomb containing the remains of Birger Gunnarsson, Lund's last archbishop. A short man from a poor family, Gunnarsson dictated that his stone effigy should be tall and regal. Two pillars are gripped by stone figures – one of a man, another of a woman and child. Legend has it that Finn the Giant built the cathedral for Saint Lawrence; in return, the saint was to guess the giant's name, or failing that, give him the sun, the moon, or his eyes. Preparing to end his days in blindness, Lawrence heard the giant's wife boasting to her baby, "Soon Father Finn will bring some eyes for you to play with". On hearing Lawrence declare his name, the livid giant and his family rushed to the crypt to pull down the columns and were instantly turned to stone.

Just behind the cathedral on Sandgatan, the **History and Cathedral Museum** (Tues–Fri 11am–1pm; free) is rather dull unless you have a particular interest in the subject, although the statues from Skånian churches in the medieval exhibition deserve a look, mainly because of the way they're arranged – a mass of Jesuses and Marys bunched together in groups, with the crowd of Jesuses on crosses looking ominously Hitchcockian.

A few minutes' walk east of Tegnerplatsen is the town's best museum, the open-air **Kulturen** (daily: May–Sept 11am–5pm, Thurs till 9pm; Oct–April noon–4pm, Thurs till 9pm; 50kr). Despite the lack of labelling in English, it's easy to spend the best part of a day just wandering around this virtual town of perfectly preserved cottages, farms, merchants' houses, gardens and even churches, brought from seven regions around Sweden and from as many centuries.

Head north from the square along Sankt Annegatan, continue up Sandgatan and then take a right on to Finngatan to reach another rather special museum, the **Museum of Sketches** (*Skissernas Museum*; Tues–Sat noon–4pm, Sun 1–5pm; free, though special exhibitions cost 30kr). Closed for extensive renovations at the time of writing, the museum is due to re-open in 2004 (call ☎046/222 72 83 to check), after which its fascinating collection of preliminary sketches and original full-scale models of artworks from around the world should be displayed to full effect. One room is full of work by all the major Swedish artists, while in the international room you'll find sketches by Chagall, Matisse, Léger, Miró and Dufy, and sculptural sketches by Picasso and Henry Moore.

As an antidote to museum fatigue, the **Botanical Gardens** (mid-May to mid-Sept 6am–9.30pm; mid-Sept to mid-May 6am–8pm, greenhouses noon–3pm; free), a few minutes' stroll further southwest down Finngatan (turn left at the end of the street into Pålsjövågen and right into Olshögsvägen), are as much a venue for picnicking and chilling out as a botanical experience.

Eating, drinking and nightlife

There are plenty of appealing places to eat and drink in Lund, most associated with the university. Certain **cafés** are student institutions and a number of the better **restaurants** are attached to student bodies or museums – which serves to keep prices low, especially for beer. If you want to buy your own provisions, the **Saluhallen** market at Mårtenstorget sells a range of fish, cheeses and meats, including Lund's own tasty speciality sausage, *knake*. Opposite the library on Sankt Petri Kyrkogatan, Widerbergs Charkuteri is a long-established foodie shop brimming with all the ingredients for a picnic.

When it comes to **nightlife**, it's worth knowing that the university is divided into "nations", or colleges, named after different geographical areas of Sweden and with strong identities. Each nation has its own bar that's active two nights a week, and there are also regular discos. *Lund Nation* is the biggest, based in the red-brick house on Agardhsgatan, while *Smålands Nation* (☎046/12 06 80) on Kastanjatan, off Mårtenstorget, is the trendiest; both are known for hosting **live bands**. Another lively venue is the bright lilac-painted *Mejeriet*, at the end of Stora Södergatan, off the main square. Converted into a music and cultural centre in the 1970s, this century-old dairy now holds a stylish café, concert hall and arts cinema (concert information on ☎046/12 38 11; cinema details on ☎046/14 38 13). The hippest regular club is the more modern *Basilika* (see below).

Cafés and restaurants

Café Ariman Kungsgatan 2, attached to the Nordic Law Department. A nineteenth-century red-brick building housing a classic, deliberately shabby left-wing coffee house – goatees, pony tails and blond dreadlocks predominate. Cheap snacks and coffee. Closed Sun outside June–Aug.

Café Stortorget Stortorget. Housed in a National Romantic-style former bank, with walls covered in dramatic black-and-white shots of actors, this is a prime meeting spot for Lundites. Try the big, filled focaccia with crab, cheese or meat for 56kr.

Conditori Lundagård Kyrkogatan 17. Classic student *konditori*, with caricatures of professors adorning the walls. Justly famous for its apple meringue pie. Closed July.

Espresso House Stora Grabrodersgatan 4. Part of the popular chain, this stylish café is good for breakfast (8–11am) as well as filled baguettes and cakes. The decor is contemporary, and there are lots of lifestyle magazines (in English) to read while munching muffins and ciabatta.

Feliini Bangatan 6 ☎046/13 80 20. Stylish and popular (book ahead) Italian restaurant that's stood the test of time, decked out in dull chrome and stripped wood. Two-course meals for 135kr. Open late.

Gloria's Sankt Petri Kyrkogata 9. Good-value American food, from burgers to big salads, and very popular with students and tourists. Local bands play Fri & Sat nights, and there's a big, lively garden area at the back. Open till midnight or later.

Kulturen. In front of the Kulturen museum beneath a giant copper beech and facing ancient runestones, this busy café, bar and restaurant is a great place to people-watch, with a youngish crowd drinking cheap beer (28kr). Good lunch with vegetarian choice (59kr), though service can be sluggish.

Mondo Corner Sankt Petri Kyrkogatan and Kyrkogatan. Set in a quaint, beamed house, this café serves bagels, cheesecake, brownies and the like; the large baguettes are good value.

Spot Delicatessen Klostergatan 14. Following from the success of its sister restaurant in Malmö (see p.537), this is a splendid choice: downstairs offers à la carte Italian lunches, while upstairs there's delicious Swedish food. Closed Sun.

Stadspark Café Stadspark. Right at the end of Nygatan in an old wooden pavilion fronted by a sea of white plastic garden furniture, this place is always busy with families munching on snacks. Big baguettes fill you up for 35–40kr.

Tegners Terass Sandgatan 2. Occupying the building next to the student union (*Akademiska Föreningen*), with a main hall resplendent with gilded Ionic columns. Forget any preconceptions about student cafés being tatty, stale sandwich bars. Self-service lunch for 55kr (49kr with student card) allows you as much as you like from a choice of delicious gourmet dishes. There's seating inside or on the terrace. Daily 11.30am–2.30pm.

Bars and clubs

John Bull Pub Bantorget, adjacent to the *Grand Hotel*. Shabby, British-style traditional pub.

Basilika Stora Södergatan 13 ⊕046/211 66 60. Hip and firmly established place, just a few steps south of Stortorget. There's a café, and a bar with a huge drinks list (shots at 39kr, cocktails at 53kr), while events (comedy nights, cabaret) and concerts are also staged; there's a minimum age of 20 for these. Closed Sun.

T- Bar Sandgatan 2 ⊕046 13 13 33, ⓦwww.t-bar.nu. Set in the Tegners Terass building

next to the student union, this student nightclub with restaurant seems to change its name annually. With a student card, people aged eighteen and over can get in to the club, otherwise it's strictly over-23s only. Thurs 7pm–3am; free entry till midnight, then 20kr.

Vespa Karl II Vägen 1. Chic, well-priced bar with Italian styling in Vespa red; more of a post-grad hangout than the usual student haunts. Good pizzas (62–88kr).

Malmö

Founded in the late thirteenth century, **MALMÖ** rose to become Denmark's most important city after Copenhagen. The high density of herring in the sea off the Malmö coast – it was said that the fish could be scooped straight out with a trowel – brought ambitious German merchants flocking to the city, an influence that can be seen in the striking fourteenth-century St Petri kyrka. Eric of Pomerania gave Malmö its most significant medieval boost when, in the fifteenth century, he built the castle and mint, and gave the city its own flag – the gold-and-red griffin of his family crest. It wasn't until the Swedish King Karl X marched his armies across the frozen belt of water to within striking distance of Copenhagen in 1658 that the Danes were forced into handing back the counties of Skåne, Blekinge and Bohuslän to the Swedes. For Malmö this meant a period of stagnation, cut off from nearby Copenhagen and too far from its own uninterested capital. Not until the full thrust of industrialization, triggered by the tobacco merchant Frans Suell's enlargement of the harbour in 1775, did Malmö begin its dramatic commercial recovery, and the city's fortunes remained buoyant over the following two centuries. The 1990s saw a further commercial crisis after the city had invested heavily in the shipping industry which had been in decline since the 1970, but since the turn of the millennium, there's been a heartwarming reversal of Malmö's fortunes, with the new university and the opening of the Öresunds Bridge, which links the city with Copenhagen, attracting an influx of investment which visitors can't fail to notice and creating an upbeat, energetic and thoroughly likeable atmosphere. The attractive medieval centre, delightful parks and the sweeping beach are all major draws, while the plentiful restaurants and bars and a lively nightlife serve as another inducement to stay awhile.

Arrival, information and city transport

If you've driven over from Denmark via the Öresunds Bridge, simply follow the signs north which take you into the centre of Malmö. SJ national trains, the Danish-built (and very comfortable) Kustpilen trains from Denmark, Kristianstad, Karlskrona and Linköping arrive at the central **train station**, bang in the centre of town. The frequent local Pågatåg trains to and from Helsingborg/Lund and Ystad use platforms 9–13 at the back. To get to the square outside, Centralplan, site of the main **bus terminal**, either walk through the station or use the exit marked "Lokal stationen". Frequent buses to and from Lund, Kastrup airport (in Copenhagen), Kristianstad/Kalmar and Ystad all stop here. Buses from Stockholm, Helsingborg and Gothenburg arrive at **Slussplan**, east of the station, just over Slussbron at the end of Norra Vallgatan. From Sturup **airport**, to the east of Malmö, you can take an hourly airport bus (*flygbuss*) into the city centre (Mon–Fri 5.30am–7.30pm, Sat 6.30am–5.30pm; 40min; 80kr). A TT Line bus from the train station heads to Trelleborg to coincide with ferries to **Travemünde** and **Rostock** in Germany, while behind the train station, Polferries make the trip to Poland.

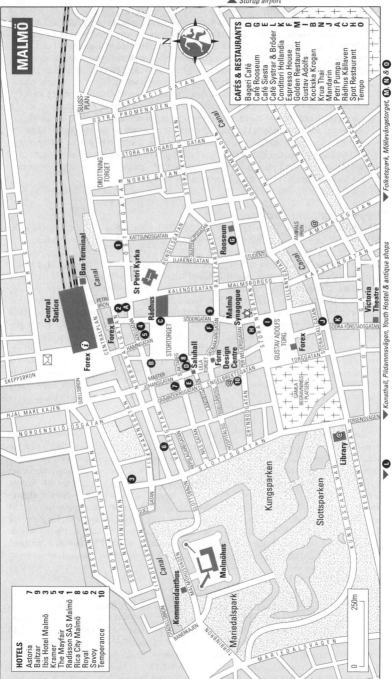

MALMÖ

▲ Sturup airport

▼ Folketspark, Möllevångstorget,

▼ Konsthall, Pildammsvägen, Youth Hostel & antique shops

CAFÉS & RESTAURANTS

Bageri Café	D
Café Rooseum	G
Café Siesta	E
Café Systrar & Bröder	L
Conditori Hollandia	K
Espresso House	F
Golden Restaurant	M
Gustav Adolfs	I
Kockska Krogan	B
Krua Thai	N
Mandarin	J
Petri Pumpa	A
Rådhus Källaren	C
Spot Restaurant	H
Tempo	O

HOTELS

Astoria	7
Baltzar	9
Ibis Hotel Malmö	3
Kramer	5
The Mayfair	4
Radisson SAS Malmö	1
Rica City Malmö	8
Royal	6
Savoy	2
Temperance	10

Central Station

Bus Terminal

Forex

St Petri Kyrka

Rådhus

Rooseum

Malmö Synagogue

Form Design Centre

Saluhall

Victoria Theatre

Forex

Gustav Adolfs Torg

Library

Kungsparken

Slottsparken

Mariedalspark

Kommendanthus

Malmöhus

Riksborg Park & Kallbadhuset ▼

▲ Öresund bridge & Camping Sibbarps

250m

The Öresunds Bridge

Linking Malmö with Copenhagen in Denmark (and thus Sweden with the rest of continental Europe), the **Öresunds Bridge** was finally completed in the summer of 1999 after nearly half a century of debate between those who believed it would have a negative environmental impact and those who felt it would be Sweden's most beneficial and significant construction of the twentieth century. The completion was marked by the symbolic embrace, halfway along the newly finished structure, of Sweden's Crown Princess Victoria and Denmark's Crown Prince Frederick.

From Lernacken, a few kilometres south of Malmö, the bridge runs to a four-kilometre-long artificial island off the Danish coast, from where an immersed tunnel carries traffic and trains across to the mainland – a total distance of 16km. The bridge itself has two levels, the upper for a four-lane highway and the lower for two sets of train tracks, and comprises three sections: a central high bridge, spanning 1km, and approach bridges to either side, each over 3km long.

Information and discount cards

The **tourist office** (June–Aug Mon–Fri 9am–8pm, Sat & Sun 10am–5pm; Sept–May Mon–Fri 9am–5pm, Sat 10am–2pm; ☎040/4 12 00, ⊛www.malmo.se) is inside Central Station. Here you can pick up a wealth of free information, including several good maps and an events and listings brochure, *Malmö This Month*. You can also buy the very useful **Malmö Card** (*Malmökortet*; available for 1, 2 or 3 days for 120kr, 150kr or 180kr respectively), which gives free museum entry, car parking, a guided bus tour and unlimited bus journeys, plus various other discounts on transport, cinemas, concerts and trips around the city. It's also worth considering the two-day **Round the Öresund** ticket (*Öresund Runt*; 199kr), which covers any route (or part of it) by ferry, train and hydrofoil to Lund, Helsingborg, Helsingør and across to Copenhagen. The Öresund ticket is also available at the tourist office, by calling ☎0771 77 77 77, or visiting ⊛www.skanetrafiken.skane.se. There are Forex **money exchanges** just opposite the tourist office in Central Station (daily 8am–9pm), on Norra Vägen 60 (daily 7am–9pm) and Gustav Adolfs Torg (daily 9am–7pm).

City transport

Although the city centre is easy to walk around, you'll need to use **buses** to reach some of the sights and some accommodation. Individual tickets cost 14kr and are valid for an hour; a 200kr magnetic card is also available and can be used by several people at the same time. All tickets are sold on the bus. If you want to use **taxis**, it's worth comparing rates, but for a rough idea of costs: Malmö centre to the airport should be around 260kr. Between May and August, ninety-minute guided **sightseeing tours** (daily; 100kr, free with Malmö Card) leave at noon from the tourist office, but these are pretty slow-going as they're conducted in Swedish, English and German. Alternatively, you can do your own guided tour on city bus #20, which leaves several times an hour from outside the tourist office. The fare is 12kr (free with Malmö Card), and the price includes a brochure pointing out areas of interest.

Accommodation

There are some excellent and surprisingly affordable **hotels** in Malmö. Being a city that attracts business travellers as well as tourists, competition between the hotels can be fierce. Prices also plummet at the weekend, which for the hotel trade means Friday and Saturday nights; it's worth trying to persuade your hotel that it should mean Sunday night as well. Most hotels have good summer rate reductions, too.

Malmö's **youth hostel**, the STF-run *Vandrarhem*, Backavägen 18 (☎040/822 20, ⊛www.meravsverige.nu; closed mid-Dec to mid-Jan), is 5km south of the city centre, pushed up against the E6 motorway, but new owners have made it friendlier than it has been in years. To find it, take bus #21A from Centerplan to Vandrarhemmet, cross over the junction past the traffic lights and take the first right; the hostel is signposted to the left. The nearest **campsite**, *Camping Sibbarps* at Strandgatan 101 in Limhamn (☎040/15 51 65), is in a picturesque spot, very close to the bridge to Copenhagen.

Astoria Gråbrödersgatan 7 ☎040/786 60, ⓦwww.astoria.gs2.com. A few minutes from the train station across the canal, this is a good, plain hotel. ❸

Baltzar Södergatan 20 ☎040/66 57 00, ⓦwww.baltzarhotel.se. Very central (between the two main squares), this is a swanky place done out in swags and flourishes that owe more to British posh hotel design than Swedish style. ❺/❸

Ibis Hotel Malmö City Citadellsvägen 4 ☎040/664 62 50, ⓦwww.ibishotel.com. Five minutes' walk to the right from the train station, towards Malmöhus, this hotel hides a comfortable and pleasant interior behind a 1950s apartment tower facade. Price includes a good breakfast and free parking. ❷

Kramer Stortorget 7 ☎040/693 54 00, ⓦwww.scandic-hotels.com. Beautiful white-stuccoed, turreted hotel from the 1870s, once Malmö's top hotel and still very luxurious. ❻/❹

The Mayfair Adelgatan 4 ☎040/10 16 20, ⓦwww.mayfairtunneln.com. Very central Danish-owned place and one of the finest of Malmö's more intimate hotels. Rooms are well-furnished in cherry or Gustavian pastels. Good breakfasts and weekend discounts. ❺/❸

Radisson SAS Malmö Östergatan 10 ☎040/698 40 00, ⓦwww.radissonsas.com. Just beyond the

Carolina Church, this hotel's blank and unimposing facade opens into a really delightful interior. The rooms are massive and stylish, and breakfast is eaten inside one of Malmö's oldest houses, cunningly incorporated into the 1960s former apartment building. ❻/❸

Rica City Malmö Stortorget 15 ☎040/660 95 50, ⓦwww.rica.se. A grand, c.1900 hotel in a fine position on this central square. Recently renovated and with tasteful rooms. ❺/❷

Royal Norra Vallgatan 94 ☎040/664 25 00, ⓦwww.hotellroyal.com. Small, family-run hotel just up from the train station. Price includes breakfast, which is served in the garden in summer. ❸

Savoy Norra Vallgatan 62 ☎040/664 48 00, ⓦwww.savoy.elite.se. No longer prohibitively priced during summer, this is where the likes of Lenin, Bardot and Dietrich have stayed, with a brass plaque to prove it. Now part of the Best Western chain, it's lost its edge but the rooms are big, very comfortable and breakfast is in the celebrated (though sometimes overrated) *Petri Pumpa* restaurant. It's right by the canal close to the station. ❻/❸

Temperance Engelbrektsgatan 16 ☎040/710 20, ⓕ30 44 06. Pleasant central hotel; price includes sauna, solarium and a big buffet breakfast. ❻/❸

The City

Standing outside the nineteenth-century train station with its ornate red-brick arches and curly-topped pillars, the **canal** in front of you, dug by Russian prisoners, forms a rough rectangle encompassing the **old town** directly to the south and the moated castle, the **Malmöhus**, to the west, surrounded by a series of attractive interconnecting parks. First off, though, head down Hamngatan to the main square, Stortorget. On the way you'll pass the striking sculpture of a twisted revolver, a monument to non-violence, that stands outside the grand former Malmö Exchange building from the 1890s.

The old town

Stortorget, the proud main square, is home to a series of elaborate sixteenth- to nineteenth-century buildings, amongst which the **Rådhus** of 1546 draws the most attention. A pageant of architectural fiddling and statuary, the building's original design was destroyed during remodelling in the nineteenth century, which left the present, finicky Dutch Renaissance exterior. It's impressive nonetheless, and to add to the pomp, the red-and-gold Skånian flag, of which Malmö is so proud, hangs from the eaves. There are occasional tours of the interior; check with the tourist office. The cellars, home to *Rådhus Källaven Restaurant* (see p.537), have been used as a tavern for more than four hundred years.

The crumbling, step-gabled red-brick building on the opposite side of the square was once the home of sixteenth-century mayor and Master of the Danish Mint, Jörgen Kocks. Danish coins were struck in Malmö on the site of the present Malmöhus, until irate local Swedes stormed the building and destroyed it in 1534. In the cellars here you'll find the *Kockska Krogan* restaurant, the only part of the building accessible to visitors. In the centre of the square, a statue of Karl X, high on his charger, presides over the city he liberated from centuries of Danish rule.

Head a block east, behind the Rådhus, to reach the Gothic **St Petri kyrka** on Göran Olsgatan (Mon–Fri 8am–6pm, Sat 9am–6pm, Sun 10am–6pm), dark and forbidding on the outside, but light and airy within. The church has its roots in the fourteenth century and, although Baltic in inspiration, the final style owes much to German influences, for it was beneath its unusually lofty and elegantly vaulted roof that the German community came to pray – probably for the continuation of the "sea silver", the herrings that brought them to Malmö in the first place. The ecclesiastical vandalism of whitewashing over medieval roof murals started early at St Petri – almost the whole interior turned white in 1553 – and consequently your eyes are drawn to the pulpit and four-tiered altarpiece, both of striking workmanship and elaborate embellishment. The only part of the church left with its original artwork was a side chapel, the **Krämare Chapel** (from the entrance, turn left and left again). Added to the church in the late fifteenth century as a Lady Chapel, it was considered redundant at the Reformation and sealed off, thus protecting the paintings from the zealous brushes of the reformers. Best preserved are the paintings on the vaulted ceiling, mainly depicting New Testament figures surrounded by decorative foliage, while underfoot the chapel floor is a chessboard of tombs in black, white and red stone.

Södergatan, Malmö's main pedestrianized shopping street, leads south of Stortorget down towards the southern canal. At the Stortorget end there's a jaunty troupe of sculptured bronze musicians, and a collection of lively cafés and restaurants further down. On the corner of the square, take a peak inside **Apoteket Lejonet**. Gargoyled and balconied on the outside, the pharmacy interior is a busy mix of inlaid wood, carvings and etched glass.

Despite the size of Stortorget, it still proved too small to suffice as the sole city square, so in the sixteenth century **Lilla Torget**, formerly marshland, was sewn on to the southeast corner. Looking like a film set, this little square with its creaky old half-timbered houses, flowerpots and cobbles, is everyone's favourite part of the city. During the day, people congregate here to take a leisurely drink in one of the many bars and wander around the summer jewellery stalls. At night, Lilla Torg explodes in a frenzy of activity, with people from all over the city converging on the square to visit the bars or promenade over the cobbles.

Walk through an arch on Lilla Torg and you'll reach the **Form Design Centre** (Tues, Wed & Fri 11am–5pm, Thurs 11am–6pm, Sat 10am–4pm, Sun noon–4pm; free), housed in a seventeenth-century grain store. Celebrating Swedish design in textiles, ceramics and furniture, its contents are rather less ambitious in quantity than you'd expect. From the beginning of the twentieth century until the 1960s, the whole of Lilla Torg was a covered market, and the sole vestige of those days, **Saluhallen**, is diagonally opposite the Design Centre. Mostly made up of specialist fine food shops, it makes for a pleasant, cool retreat on a hot afternoon.

A few streets away to the east, but well worth a visit if you're interested in contemporary art, is the **Rooseum** (Tues–Sun 11am–5pm, Thurs till 8pm, guided tours Tues–Fri 6.30pm, Sat & Sun 2pm: 30kr, free with Malmö Card) on Stora Nygatan. Space is imaginatively used in this elaborate building from 1900, originally constructed to house the Malmö Electricity Company's steam turbines. The main turbine hall forms the central gallery, displaying experimental installations and interesting photographic works. There's also a fine little café here (see p.536).

Malmöhus and around

Take any of the streets running west from Stortorget or Lilla Torg and you soon come up against the edge of **Kungsparken**, within striking distance of the fifteenth-century castle, **Malmöhus** (daily: June–Aug 10am–4pm; Sept–May noon–4pm; 40kr, includes entry to Kommendanthuset, free with Malmö Card. Free guided tours in English at 3pm). For a more head-on approach, walk west (away from the station) up Citadellsvägen; from here the low castle with its grassy ramparts and two circular keeps is straight ahead over the wide moat.

Originally Denmark's mint, the building was destroyed by the Swedes in 1534. Two years later, a new fortress was built on the site by the Danish King Christian III, only to be of unforeseen benefit to his enemies who, once back in control of Skåne, used it to repel an attacking Danish army in 1677. Serving as a prison for a time (the Earl of Bothwell, Mary Queen of Scots' third husband, was its most notable inmate), the castle's importance waned once back in Swedish hands, and it was used for grain storage until opening as a **museum** in 1937.

Passing swiftly through the natural history section – a taxidermal Noah's ark – the most rewarding part of the museum is upstairs, where an ambitious series of furnished rooms takes you from the mid-sixteenth-century Renaissance through Baroque, Rococo, pastel-pale Gustavian and Neoclassical. A stylish Jugend (Art Nouveau) interior is equally impressive, while other rooms feature Functionalist and post-Functionalist interiors. Just as interesting are the spartan but authentic interiors of the castle itself.

Just beyond the castle to the west along Malmöhusvagen is the **Kommendanthuset** (Governor's House; same hours as Malmöhus, and included in Malmöhus entry fee), containing a strange combination of military and toy museums. The military section is a fairly lifeless collection of neatly presented medals, rifles and swords, along with the usual dummies sporting eighteenth- and nineteenth-century uniforms. The toy museum is more fun – the link between the two being a brigade of toy British soldiers. A little further west, running off Malmöhusvagen, is a tiny walkway, **Banerkajen**, lined with higgledy-piggledy fishing shacks selling fresh and smoked fish.

Once you've had your fill of museums, the castle **grounds** are good for a stroll, peppered with small lakes and an old windmill. The paths lead all the way down to Regementsgatan – the Prime Minister lives at no. 10 – and the City Library in the southeastern corner of the park. You can continue walking through the greenery as far as Gustav Adolfs Torg by crossing Gamla Begravnings Platsen, a rather pretty graveyard.

Out from the centre

Tourists rarely head further south of the city than the canal banks that enclose the old town, yet with a few hours to spare, the areas around Amiralsgatan (which begins south of the canal near the Rooseum) give an interesting insight into Malmö's mix of cultures. A few hundred metres down Amiralsgatan, the splendid copper-domed Moorish building standing out on Föreningsgatan is the restored **Malmö Synagogue**. Designed and built in 1894, the synagogue is decorated with concentric designs in blue and green glazed brick. Strict security measures mean that to see the unrenovated interior you need to telephone the Jewish Community offices (ask at the tourist office).

Back on Amiralsgatan, it's a ten-minute walk to **Folketspark**, Sweden's oldest working people's park, once the pride and joy of the community. Now renovated with an attractive fountain, Folketspark contains a basic amusement park and, at its centre, the **Moriskan**, an odd, low building with Russian-style golden minarets topped with sickles and housing a ballroom. Amusement park and ballroom are both now privately owned, a far cry from the original aims of the park's Social Democratic founders, carved busts of whom are dotted all over the park.

South of the park, the multicultural character of Malmö becomes apparent. Middle Eastern, Asian and Balkan emigré families predominate, and strolling from the park's southern exit down Möllevången to **Möllevångstorget**, you enter an area populated almost entirely by non-Swedes, with Arabic and Urdu the main languages. The vast Möllevångstorget, boasting a poignant and impressive statue at its centre depicting Malmö workers straining under the weight of their toils, is a haven of cafés (see below) and exotic food shops, along with shops selling pure junk.

Along the beach to Limhamn

West of the city centre, and separated from it by the delightful **Ribersborg park**, Malmö's long stretch of sandy **beach** reaches all the way to Limhamn, fringed by the Ribersborgs Recreation Promenade (bus #20 runs along the promenade to Limhamn). At the town end of the beach is the **Ribersborgs kallbadhuset** (mid-April to mid-Sept Mon–Fri 8.30am–7pm, Sat & Sun 8.30am–4pm; mid-Sept to mid-April Mon–Fri noon–7pm, Sat & Sun 9am–4pm; 35kr), a cold-water bathhouse with a sauna and café. All the beaches along this stretch, known as the Golden Coast because of the grand villas overlooking it, boast shallow water.

LIMHAMN (limestone harbour), 3km to the southwest of the city, has an unusual history and one that will become very apparent if you're staying at the *Sibbarps* campsite or arriving at Lernacken, the Swedish terminal for the bridge. Once a quiet limestone-quarrying village, Limhamn was taken by storm by a local man with big ambitions called Fredryk Berg. At the end of the nineteenth century, Berg had a train line built between the village and Malmö and built up the huge cement works known first as Cementa and later as Euroc. Heading down Limhamnsvägen (the road running parallel with the beach) to Limhamn (or take bus #82), the island of **Ön** will come into view. Another of Berg's creations, he had it built out of waste concrete and constructed a couple of churches, and apartment houses on it for factory workers. A strongly religious man, he was fond of saying that the two best things in life were making corporations and attending church, earning him the nickname "Concrete Jesus".

Eating

Most of Malmö's **eating places** are concentrated in and around its central squares, with Lilla Torg attracting the biggest crowds. By day, several cafés serve good lunches and sumptuous cakes; there's also a wide choice of places for dinner, from budget diners to romance-exuding restaurants. If you want a change of scene, head south of the centre to Möllenvångstorget, the heart of Malmö's immigrant community, for cheaper eats and a very un-Swedish atmosphere. Alternatively, to cut costs, stock up at the specialist food shops within Saluhallen, Lilla Torg.

In the listings below, we've given telephone numbers only for places where it's a good idea to book ahead.

Cafés and restaurants

Bageri Café Saluhallen, Lilla Torg. Excellent bagels, baguettes, pies and health foods – with outside seating, too. Closed Sun.

Café Rooseum Gasverksgatan 22. Superb chocolate cake, home-made cheesecakes and brownies dished up in the contemporary art museum. A giant generator takes up most of the room, with seats around the edge.

Café Siesta Corner of Långårdsgatan and Hjorttackegatan. A fun little café specializing in home-made apple cake; turn right at the end of Landbygatan, and it's on the first corner on the left.

Café Systrar och Bröder Östra Ronneholmsvägen 26. With leatherette bench seats and 1960s ambience, this is the haunt of hip Malmöites. Superb breads, cakes and sandwiches, and a great-value breakfast buffet at 45kr.

Conditoria Hollandia Södra Förstadsgatan 8. Traditional, pricey *konditori* south of the canal at Drottninggatan, with a window full of melting chocolate fondants.

Espresso House Skomakaregatan 2. Part of the popular chain, with excellent chocolate cake, muffins, ciabattas and a delicious "Oriental latté"

(24kr) flavoured with cardamom.
Golden Restaurant Corner of Södra Parkgatan and Simrishamnsgatan. South of the city centre in the main immigrant area, this spartan place serves cheap crepes, pizza and kebabs.
Gustav Adolfs Gustav Adolfs Torg 43. Long-established, slightly staid café-restaurant, but still a popular spot in a grand, white-stuccoed building with outside seating. Open late at weekends.
Kockska Krogan Corner of Stortorget and Suellgatan ☎040/703 20. Now also known as *Arstiderna*, this is a very fine – but rather overpriced – old cellar restaurant in the former home of Malmö's sixteenth-century mayor, Jörgen Kock. Daily lunch specials of traditional Swedish fare at 75kr. Closed Sun.
Krua Thai Möllevångtorget 12 ☎ 040/12 22 87. In the big square south of the city centre, this place serves the best Thai food in town with an informal atmosphere that's more domestic than haute cuisine.
Mandarin Södra Vallgatan 3. A welcome addition to Malmö's restaurant scene, serving up Thai food in a really funky atmosphere. Outside tables, and mellow sounds and a well-stocked bar inside. Dishes cost 40–75kr. Closed Sun.

Petri Pumpa *Savoy Hotel*, Norra Vallgatan 62 ☎040/664 48 00. This celebrated restaurant – with prices to match – was Lund's culinary pinnacle before moving here. Attempts to win greater custom with endless special offers detracts from the former exclusivity of this famous place. Summer special of three courses for 265kr.
Rådhus Källaven Stortorget. Gloriously decorative setting beneath the town hall, with dishes at around 200kr, though there's also a well-cooked and beautifully served daily economy meal at 65kr. Outside seating in summer.
Spot Restaurant Stora Nygatan 33 ☎040/12 02 03. Chic Italian daytime restaurant with attached charcuterie (all ingredients imported direct from Italy), serving light meals based on ciabatta and panini breads. All in all, a really great place for lunch. Closed Sun.
Tempo Norra Skolgatan 30 ☎040/12 60 21. Near Möllevångstorget to the south of the city, this is a quirky, hip place where journalists and alternative poseurs come to savour very well prepared and intriguing food from the short but inspired menu. Service is friendly, if agonizingly slow.

Drinking, nightlife and entertainment

Best place to head for an evening **drink** is **Lilla Torg**: the square buzzes with activity, the smell of beer wafts between the old, beamed houses, and music and chatter fill the air. It's a largely young crowd, and the atmosphere is like a summer carnival. It doesn't make a huge difference which of the six or so bars that you go for (and expect to wait for a seat), but as a basic pointer, *Mellow Yellow* is for the 25-plus age group, *Moosehead* for a younger crowd, and *Victors* even younger and more boisterous, although all are fun. On **Möllenvångstorget**, south of the centre in the immigrant quarter, the Danish-style *Nyhavn* at no. 8 is a laid-back place for a beer.

One striking addition to the **nightlife** scene is *The Tunnel*, in the same building as the *Mayfair Hotel* at Adelgatan 4 (first Fri of each month and every Sat; closed July; ⓦwww.tunneln.com; 100kr cover). Designed as a futuristic metallic tunnel by celebrated Argentinian designer Aberlardo Gonzalez, it welcomes a wide age range and boasts a cellar bar with a grand piano, a wild dance floor of silver and mirrors, and a restaurant at street level. For more on Malmö after dark, consult *Malmö This Month*.

Gay nightlife

Though most gay Malmöites head off to Copenhagen for a really good night out, Malmö's own **gay nightlife** is livelier than in any other Swedish city outside Stockholm. The RFSL-run gay centre (☎040/611 99 62, ⓦwww.rfslmalmo.nu) is south of the city centre at Monbijougatan 15 (head down Amiralsgatan and turn off to the right just before the Folketspark). It's home to *Club Indigo* (Fri & Sat from 10pm); first Saturday of each month is women-only and there's a pub night on Wednesdays (9pm–midnight). Entry is 80kr, or 40kr for RFSL members. In September, there's a Rainbow Festival, nine days of non-stop parties, pub nights and a film festival – for more info, contact RFSL. Otherwise, try *Club Wonk*, Adelgatan 2, next to the Tunnel nightclub, on Saturday nights.

Music and festivals

If you know where to look, you'll find are some decent live music venues and discos in Malmö, most of which are cheaper to get into than their southern European counterparts. A good venue is *Matssons Musikpub* (☎040/23 27 56), behind the Rådhus at Göran Olsgatan 1, which puts on a variety of Scandinavian R&B and rock bands every night.

Classical music performances take place at the Concert Hall, Föreningsgatan 35 (☎040/34 35 00), home of the Malmö Symphony Orchestra, and at the Musikhögskolan, Ystadvägen 25 (☎040/19 22 00); check with the tourist office for programme details.

Malmö has two annual **festivals**. The **Folkfesten**, also known as **Västra Hamnen Festen**, is held in Kungsparken near Malmöhus in early June; a sort of mini-Woodstock, it's devoted to progressive and classic rock – for more details, contact the tourist office. A far more all-encompassing event is the **Malmö Festival** (⌨www.malmofestivalen.nu) in August, which takes place mainly in Stortorget. Huge tables are set out and free crayfish tails served, with revellers bringing their own drinks. In Gustav Adolfs Torg, stalls are set up by the immigrant communities, with Pakistani, Somali and Bosnian goodies and dance shows; there are also rowing competitions on the canal.

Listings

Airlines British Airways, Sturup airport ☎020/78 11 44; Finnair, Baltzarsgatan 31 ☎020/78 11 00; KLM, Sturup airport ☎020/50 05 30; Lufthansa, Gustav Adolfs Torg 12 ☎040/717 10; SAS, Baltzarsgatan 18 ☎040/35 72 00.
Buses From Centralplan to Lund (#130), Kristianstad/Kalmar (#805) and Ystad (#330).
Car rental Avis, Skeppsbron 13 ☎040/778 30; Budget, Baltzarsgatan 21 ☎040/775 75; Europcar, Mäster Nilsgatan 22 ☎040/38 02 40; Hertz, Jorgenkocksgatan 1B ☎040/749 55.
Doctor On call daily 7am–10pm, ☎040/33 35 00; at other times, ring ☎040/33 10 00.
Exchange Best rates are at Forex; branches are at Norra Vallgatan 60 (daily 7am–9am), Gustav Adolfs Torg 12 (Mon–Fri 8am–7pm, Sat 9am–3pm), and by the tourist office at Central Station (daily 8am–9pm).

Internet Cyberspace, Engelbrektsgatan 13a (daily 10am–10pm); Surfer's Paradise, Amiralsgatan 14 (Mon–Fri 10am–midnight, Sat & Sun noon–midnight; ⌨www.surfersparadise.se); Twilight Zone, Stora Nygatan 15 (daily noon–3am); City Library, Regementsgatan 3 (Mon–Thurs 10am–2pm, Fri 10am–6pm, Sat & Sun noon–4pm; ⌨www.msb.malmo.se).
Pharmacy 24hr service at Apoteket Gripen, Bergsgatan 48 (☎040/19 21 13) or Lejonet in Stortorget (Mon–Fri 9am–6pm, Sat 10am–2pm; ☎040/712 35).
Post office Skeppsbron 1 (Mon–Fri 8am–6pm, Sat 9.30am–1pm).
Taxis ☎040/97 97 97 or ☎040/23 23 23.
Train enquiries There's a Pågatåg information office inside the Lokalstationen (Mon–Fri 7am–6pm, Sat 8am–3pm, Sun 9am–3pm).

Southeastern Skåne: the coast to Ystad

The local **Pågatåg train** and the E6 and E14 highways cut directly east from Malmö towards Ystad, missing out some picturesque minor resorts and a couple of the region's best beaches along Sweden's most southwesterly tip. If you have time to explore, and particularly if you have your own transport, this quieter part of the south makes for a delightful few days' exploration. Thirty kilometres south of Malmö (by car or bus #150), you cross an expanse of heathland to which birdwatchers flock every autumn to spot nesting plovers and terns, as well as millions of migratory birds fleeing the Arctic for the Stevns peninsula, south of Copenhagen.

Skanör

Some 25km south of Malmö, Route 100 leads west to the fan-shaped southwest tip of the country. Here, at the westernmost reach of the Näset Peninsula, is the seaside resort of **SKANÖR**, a Hanseatic centre founded to take advantage of the abundance of herring off this stretch of the coast. In the first years of the twentieth century, Skanör became a fashionable bathing resort for rich Malmö families and, although it has since gone in and out of vogue, it's currently a desirable destination for much the same set. There's not much to see in Skanör, but its **beaches** are superb, with long ribbons of white sand bordering an extensive bird and nature reserve. From the beach, you can see across the reserve to the town's medieval **church**. Once the herring had moved on to waters new in the sixteenth century, the church never received its intended extensions, making it all the more appealing. From the little harbour, it's a pleasant walk to the town square and the lovely old cottages lining Mellangatan. If you want **to stay** – and the beach is worth it – *Hotell Gässlingen* (⊗040/47 30 35, ⑤47 51 81; ❹) at Rådhustorget 6, is a simple but lovely place. If you're **camping**, there are plenty of places to throw down a tent for free, though be careful to avoid the protected bird reserves. The little harbour at Skanör boasts one of the best **restaurants** in this corner of the country, *Skanör's Fiskroken* (⊗040/47 40 50), where you can sample superb fish dishes in the simple, elegant setting, or choose from a remarkable range of smoked and pickled fish and have them made up into a picnic (around 90kr) – try herring roe marinated in rum or hot smoked salmon with black bread.

Foteviken Viking Museum

Just to the east of Skanör signs point to the **Foteviken Viking Museum** (mid-May to Aug daily 11am–4pm; ⊛www.foteviken.se; 50kr). Foteviken, an ancient coastal village and centre of herring fishing from late Viking times, was the scene of a bloody battle in June 1134 between the Danish king and the would-be king of Skåne. Today, the whole area has been transformed into a working – and remarkably authentic – Viking village which attempts to re-create the way of life here as it existed in 1134. The complex includes houses, workshops, a sacrificial temple and shipbuilding yard, creating a virtually self-sufficient settlement – the atmosphere is like a sort of twelfth-century commune, with unemployed Skånians and others from all over Europe living and working in an 800-year-old time warp. All food, clothes and belongings are cooked, woven and made on site, from curing leather to dying wool, and the houses are built authentically. The most dramatic time to come is the weekend closest to June 10, when the battle is re-enacted, while the last week of June and start of July sees hundreds of people participating in similar Viking-style living projects converge here from all over Northern Europe for an international get-together.

Trelleborg

Heading east along the coast, the rolling fields are punctuated by World War II concrete bunkers, some now converted into unlikely looking summer houses. Approaching **TRELLEBORG** by bus from Malmö (35min), a curtain of low-level industry blocks the sea – although this won't bother you too much if you're taking one of the ferries over to the German towns of Rostock, Sassnitz or Travemünde. Yet behind the graceless factories, this is a busy enough little town, its two attractions an inspired reconstruction of a recently discovered Viking fortress and a beautiful gallery of works by the sculptor Axel Ebbe.

The ferry terminals on the seafront are close to the train station. Walking up Kontinengatan, you'll reach the **Axel Ebbe Gallery** (June to early Sept Tues–Sun 11am–5pm; mid-Sept to May Tues–Sun 1–4pm; 20kr) in a compact, 1930s functionalist building that was once the local bank. Ebbe's superb sculptures make for a powerful collection of sensual nudes, all larger than life and in black or white stone. At the beginning of the twentieth century, Ebbe's gently erotic work was celebrated in Paris, though when his graceful, sprawling *Atlas's Daughter* was unveiled in Copenhagen, it caused an outcry. A few steps into the **Stadsparken**, opposite, is Trelleborg's main square, dominated by Ebbe's *Sea Monster*, a fountain comprising a serpentine fiend intertwined with a characteristically sensuous mermaid.

The main shopping promenade, **Algatan**, runs parallel with the seafront, and walking up from the ferry terminal you'll soon come to **St Nicolai's kyrka**, which has some bright ceiling paintings, elaborate memorial tablets, and monks' chairs from a Franciscan monastery that was destroyed during the Reformation. A couple of minutes' stroll north from here is Trelleborg's most dramatic attraction, the **Trelle Fortress** (open all year; free), an impressive monument to local Viking life. Surrounded by a moat, the original circular fortress, dating from around 980 AD, was built by King Harald Bluetooth around a seventh-century settlement of pit houses and was composed entirely of earth and wood. Archeologists compared the remains with four almost identical forts in Denmark and, using a certain amount of guesswork, have constructed an impressive replica. Despite the authenticity of location, though, if you're interested in Viking culture, you're still better off heading back west to Foteviken (see p.539) for sheer atmosphere.

Practicalities

Three trains a day run from Malmö to the Trelleborg **train station**, and are timed to connect with the Sassnitz ferry; there are also hourly **buses**, stopping at the bus terminal behind the main square. **Ferry** departures to Germany are pretty regular – check "Travel details" at the end of the chapter for details.

The new **tourist office** is by the ferry terminal (mid-June to mid-Aug Mon–Fri 9am–7pm, Sat 9am–6pm, Sun 9–6pm; mid-Aug to mid-June Mon–Fri 9am–5pm; ☎0410/533 22, ◍www.trelleborg.se) and it supplies a good free leaflet entitled *A Couple of Hours in Trelleborg* in recognition of how long most people linger here. If you do want to **stay**, the tourist office can book **private rooms** for 130kr (plus 35kr booking fee), while adjoining the office (and very convenient for ferries), *Hotel Prinz* (☎0410/71 32 39, ☏71 31 44; ❹) is a new place with pleasant rooms. The only really glamorous option is *Hotel Dannegården*, Standgatan 32 (☎0410/481 80, ◍www.dannegarden.se; ❺/❸), a beautiful 1910 villa surrounded by scented bushes, with just five double rooms in original Art Nouveau style. Even if you don't stay here, the **restaurant** (closed July) is the finest place in town for a romantic, though pricey, meal. Otherwise, there are a couple of reasonable **cafés**, *Billings* and *Palmblads*, on Algatan.

Smygehuk and Smygehamn

Around a third of the way from Trelleborg to Ystad along coastal Route 9 (bus #183), the tiny harbour village of **SMYGEHUK** has little to it except a particularly cosy youth hostel (see below), among a group of old wooden houses clustered around a nineteenth-century **lighthouse**. Walk through the flowers and nettles along the coast and you'll soon reach the hamlet of **SMYGEHAMN**, less than a kilometre east, which prides itself on being Sweden's most southerly point – it's not much more than a tiny harbour surrounded by a few summertime restaurants, a café and a smoked-fish shop. The harbour itself is built from stone taken from a nearby limestone quarry, and lime burning was big business here from Smygehamn's heyday in the mid-nineteenth century right up until the 1950s. Lime kilns – odd, igloo-like structures with cupola roofs – are still dotted all around. Back from the harbour, Axel Ebbe's *The Embrace* is a good example of his Romantic style – a female nude rises up from the scrubland, embracing the elements.

Smygehuk's seasonal **tourist office** occupies a fine, early nineteenth-century corn warehouse by the harbour (daily: June & early Aug 10am–6pm; July 10am–7pm; ☎0410/240 53); staff can book **private rooms** from 100kr per person. The **youth hostel** (☎0410/245 83, ☏245 09; mid-May to mid-Sept) is in the lighthouse-keeper's house. The nearest **hotels** are in Trelleborg, 13km away, but *Smygehus Havsbad* (☎0410/243 90, ◍www.smygehus.se), an old bathing house just 500m from the tourist office, has four-bed cabins for 1350kr including breakfast. There's also a rather fine **B&B**, *Hedman's* (☎0410/234 73, ◍www.hedmans.nu; ❷), three kilometres inland in the hamlet of Boste. The best **restaurant** in the area is *Albinslunds Krog*,

ÖstraVemmenhog 7 at Skateholm (☎0411/53 23 10), about four kilometres east of Smygehuk, which serves really good international gourmet dishes.

Ystad

An hour by Pågatåg train from Malmö lies the exquisitely well-preserved medieval market town of **YSTAD**, boasting a core of quaint cobbled lanes lined with half-timbered cottages and a central square oozing rural charm. With the stunningly beautiful coastal region of Österlen stretching northeast from town in the direction of Kristianstad and some excellent walking to the north of town, Ystad is a splendid place to base yourself for a day or so. It's also the departure point for **ferries** to the Danish island of Bornholm, and to Poland.

Arrival and information

From the harbourside **train station**, cross the tracks to St Knuts Torg, where the **tourist office** (May to mid June Mon–Fri 9am–7pm, Sat 11am–2pm, Sun 11am–6pm; mid-June to mid-Aug Mon–Fri 9am–7pm, Sat 10am–7pm, Sun 11am–6pm; mid-Aug to April Mon–Fri 9am–5pm; ☎0411/776 81, ⓦwww.visitystad.com) is next door to the Art Museum. St Knuts Torg is also where **buses** from Lund (#X300), Kristianstad (Skåne Express) and Simrishamn (#572) pull in, and where buses leave for destinations along the coast and into the rest of Skåne. However, there's no bus service from Malmö: either take a Pågatåg train or bus #183 from Trelleborg/Smygehamn to Skateholm and then bus #330 to Ystad; to get to Kristianstad by train, you need to return to Malmö and take the inland train. The **ferry terminal** (signposted "Till Färjorna") is a few hundred metres to the east of the train station – turn left out of the station and walk for ten minutes along the quayside. Tickets **to Poland** cost from 220kr one-way (9hr crossing), or you can buy a four-day return for 420kr. One-way tickets and day returns to Bornholm cost 135kr (2hr 30min). **Cycling** is a great way to see the surrounding landscape and bikes can be rented from Roslins Cykelaffär, Jennygatan 11, just east of the bus and train terminals (☎0411/123 15; 65kr per day or 295kr per week).

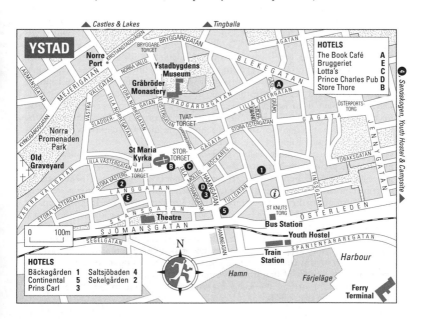

Accommodation

There are several good and reasonably priced **hotels** in Ystad, and one at the beach. There are also two **youth hostels**, one on the beach at Sandskogen (☎0411/665 66), served by buses #572 and #304 – however, from September to May it's open to groups only. The other is much more conveniently situated in the old station building at the train station (☎0708/57 79 95). There's a **campsite** (☎0411/192 70) with four-bed cabins (from 155kr per person) next to the youth hostel at Sandskogen.

Bäckagården Bäckagården 36 ☎0411/198 48, ⓦwww.backagarden.nu. Small-scale guesthouse-type place in a converted home just behind the tourist office. ❷
Continental Hamngatan 13 ☎0411/137 00, ⓦwww.hotelcontinental-ystad.se. Classic hotel touted as Sweden's oldest, with a grand lobby of marble, Corinthian pillars and crystal chandeliers. Rooms are modern Italian-style, and the cold breakfast buffet is a treat. ❹
Prins Carl Hamngatan 8 ☎0411/737 50, ⓔprinscarl.hotell@brevet.nu. A mid-range, non-smoking place with rooms adapted for people with disabilities or allergies. ❷
Saltsjöbaden Saltsjöbadsvägen 6 ☎0411/136 30, ⓦwww.ystadssaltsjobad.se. Renowned for its beachside position, just east of town, this large, 100-year-old hotel (though with endless modern extensions tacked on) has a sauna, pool (summer only), and a restaurant in the original saltwater bathing house. ❹
Sekelgården Stora Västergatan 9 ☎0411/739 00, ⓦwww.sekelgarden.se. The best place to stay in town, this small family-run hotel in a merchant's house of 1793 is friendly and informal, with a new sauna, a cobbled courtyard and flower garden. There are en-suite rooms in both the main house and the old tannery at the back, and excellent breakfasts are served under the trees or in the charming dining room. ❸

The Town

Turning left from the station and ferry terminals then right up Hamngatan brings you to the well-proportioned **Stortorget**, a grand old square encircled by pictur-esque streets. The **St Maria kyrka** is a handsome centrepiece, with additions from nearly every century since it was begun in the thirteenth. In the 1880s, changing tastes saw many of the rich decorative features removed, and only the most interest-ing ones were returned during a restoration programme forty years later. Inside, the early seventeenth-century Baroque pulpit is worth a look for the fearsome face carved beneath it and, opposite, the somewhat chilling medieval crucifix, which was placed here on the orders of Karl XII to remind the preacher of Christ's suffering.

If you stay in Ystad, you'll soon become acquainted with a tradition that harks back to the seventeenth century: from a room in the church's watchtower, a night watchman blows a haunting tune on a bugle every fifteen minutes from 9.15pm to 3am, as a safeguard against the outbreak of fire. The idea was that if one of the thatched cottages went up in flames, the bugle would sound repeatedly for all to go and help extinguish the blaze. The sounding through the night was to assure the town that the watchman was still awake; until the mid-nineteenth century, if he slept on duty he was liable to be executed.

From Stortorget, it's a short stroll up Garevaregränd, past art and craft workshops, and on up Klostergatan to the **Ystadbygdens Museum** (Mon–Fri noon–5pm, Sat & Sun noon–4pm; 20kr). Set in the thirteenth-century Gråbröder ("Greyfriars") Monastery, it contains the usual local history collections, given piquancy here by their preserved medieval surroundings. After the monks were driven out during the Reformation, the monastery was at various times a hospital, a poorhouse, a distillery and finally a dump. A decision to demolish it in 1901 was overturned, and today it's definitely worth a visit.

If you want to explore more of the old town, it's still possible to find your way around using a city map from 1753, copies of which are supplied by the tourist office. Not far from the St Maria kyrka on the western side of town, **Norra Promenaden**, a strip of mature horse chestnut trees and parkland, is good for a stroll. Here you'll find *Café Promenaden*, a white pavilion built in the 1870s to house a genteel café and dance hall.

Walks around Ystad

The forested lake region 20km north of Ystad provides plenty of **hiking** possibilities, either on organized trails or in undeveloped tracts where you can camp rough. Take any bus north in the direction of **Sjöbo** (by car take Route 13), and you'll link with the **Skåneleden** ("Long Trail"), which follows a hundred-kilometre circular route from just outside Ystad. The tourist office (see p.541) can provide route maps as well as details on where to find places to eat and stay along the way. You can also head north on foot from Ystad to Hedeskoga and then follow trails along a chain of forest-fringed lakes – Krageholmsjön, Ellestadssjön and Snogeholmssjön – up to Sövdesjön (a 20km hike).

Eating, drinking and nightlife

There's a fair selection of places to eat in Ystad, including some atmospheric **cafés** and fine **restaurants**, most of the latter around Stortorget. **Nightlife** is pretty minimal – the only clubs are *Starshine* at Österportstorg (☎0411/100 95, ⑩www.starshine.se), east from Stortorget along Stora Östergatan (labelled as Gågatan on some maps, meaning pedestrianized street), while at Stora Östergatan 3 there's the popular *Laura's* disco and casino (☎0411/663 44; same door as the Konsum supermarket). Otherwise, locals tend to take a bus thirty minutes north to **Tingballa**, where there are a couple of dance halls.

Bruggerlet Länggatan 20 ☎0411/699 99. The rough, beamed interior dominated by two copper beer casks creates a welcoming ambience at this fine restaurant. The well-cooked fish and meat dishes, with one vegetarian option, are usually fairly pricey, and it's a good idea to book a table.

The Book Café Gäsegrän. Down a tiny, cobbled street off Stora Östergatan, this precariously leaning wooden house has books – all in English – to read while you feast on the home-baked focaccia or sample one of the varieties of coffee. The gardens are delightful too, and retain their 1778 layout.

Lotta's Stortorget 11. Justifiably the most popular restaurant in town, packed each evening in summer and serving beautifully presented,

scrumptious fish and meat dishes. Closed Sat & Sun. *Lotta's Källare* in the cellars below is a cosy bar with several English beers including the so-called "Manchester United".

Prince Charles Pub Hamngatan 8. Next door to the *Prins Carl Hotel*, this English-style pub and restaurant serves meat and fish dishes in the evenings, with live music on Fri and Sat nights.

Store Thore Stortorget 1. Located in the cellars of the fourteenth-century former Rådhus, and adding a breath of life to Stortorget in summer when tables are brought into the square itself. At weekends, and out of the high season, the more elegant surroundings inside serve as a fitting backdrop to the less touristy Swedish menu.

Österlen and the coast to Åhus

It's easy to see how the landscape of the southeastern corner of Skåne, an area known as **Österlen**, has lured writers and artists to its coastline and plains. Here, yellow fields of rape stand out against a cobalt-blue sky, punctuated by white cottages, blood-red poppy fields and the odd black windmill. Österlen also has a number of engaging sights, notably the Viking ruin **Ales Stennar**, pretty villages and plenty of sandy beaches. Moving further northeast are the orchards of Sweden's apple region, centred on **Kivik**, while **Åhus**, a low-key resort famous for smoked eels, ends this stretch of the coast.

Unfortunately, **getting around** this part of the country isn't easy. The only major road in the area, Route 9 to Kristianstad via Simrishamn, cuts off the main corner of Österlen, the whole area is poorly served by buses and the only train service is the Pågatåg train from Ystad to Simrishamn: if you haven't got a car, you'll need to do some walking and cycling to make the most of this part of Sweden.

△ Visby church

Ales Stennar

Twenty kilometres out of Ystad, near the hamlet of Kåseberga, is the Viking site of **Ales Stennar**. Believed to have been a Viking meeting place, this awe-inspiring monument consists of 56 stones forming a 67-metre-long boat-shaped edifice, the prow and stern denoted by two appreciably larger monoliths. The site was hidden for centuries beneath shifting sands, which only cleared in 1958. Buried several metres into the sand, it's difficult to imagine how these great stones, which aren't native to the region, were transported here. Ales Stennar stands on a windy, flat-topped hill, and despite the inevitable tourists snapping away at the ancient site (most of whom don't bother to climb up), there's a majestic timelessness at the top that more than rewards your climb.

There are two ways to get to Ales Stennar from Ystad: either take the infrequent **bus** #322 (20min) or rent a **bike** and follow the coastal cycle track through pine forests and past white sandy beaches, following the signs to Kåseberga.

Simrishamn

There's not much to the little fishing town of **SIMRISHAMN**, around 40km east of Ystad, although its old quarter of tiny, fondant-coloured cottages and its church, originally built as a twelfth-century fisherman's chapel, are pretty enough. The unexceptional **museum** is full of the usual archeological finds, alongside bits and pieces of farm and fishing equipment. You may want to come here, however, for the summer **catamaran** service to the Danish island of Bornholm (3–4 daily). If you do fancy staying, *Hotell Kockska Garden*, Storgatan 25 (☏0414/41 17 55, ℱ41 19 78; ❷), is a comfortable **accommodation** option, housed in a renovated tavern. For bike rental, ask at the **tourist office**, Tulhusgatan 2 (mid-June to mid-Aug Mon–Fri 9am–8pm, Sat noon–8pm, Sun 2–8pm; mid-Aug to mid-June Mon–Fri 9am–5pm; ☏0414/81 98 00, ℡www.turistbyra.simrishamn.se).

Kivik

Around 20km north from Simrishamn, halfway to Åhus on the coastal road, you'll enter the endless orchards of Sweden's apple-growing region, Kivik. The village of **KIVIK** itself has no real centre, but buses stop outside the *Kivik Vardhus* hotel. The uncommercialized harbour is just a few minutes away down Södergatan; there are a number of sights within a couple of kilometres of here.

Sweden's most notable Bronze Age cairn, **Kungsgraven** (May–Aug daily 10am–6pm; 10kr), is just 500m from the *Kivik Vardhus* hotel. A striking 75-metre upturned saucer of rocks, it lay buried until discovered by a farmer in 1748. At its centre, the burial chamber is entered by a banked entrance passage, and inside are eight floodlit 3000-year-old runic slabs showing pictures of horses, a sleigh and what look like dancing seals. There's a really lovely café, *Sågmöllan* (mid-May to mid-Aug), just a few steps away in the old thatched mill-cottage by a stream.

Two kilometres from the grave, beyond hilly orchards (follow the signs), is the **Kiviksmusteri** cider factory and the entertaining **Apple House** (April & May 10am–5pm; June–Sept 10am–6pm; 20kr), an apple museum each of whose rooms is infused with a different smell: the room devoted to "Great Apples in History" smells of cider, while a room detailing attempts to create an insect-resistant apple summons up apple pie. Other, wackier exhibitions focus on outlandish topics such as the (alleged) "symphonic soul of apples". Just 200m beyond the Apple House, precipitous **Stenshuvuds National Park** is a perfect place to come back to reality. At almost 100m high, the top of the hill that takes up most of the park area is laced with walking trails that afford superb views. Self-guided walking tours lead around remnants of an ancient fortress, while there are special wheelchair-accessible paths through the forested hillsides.

Frequent Skåne Express **buses** to and from Simrishamn (30min) and Kristianstad (55min) stop outside the *Kivik Värdshus* farmhouse **hotel** (☎0414/700 74, ℗710 20; ❸; May–Aug) and restaurant. For cheaper accommodation, the STF **youth hostel** (☎0414/711 95) lies in its own attractive gardens on Tittutvägen, north of the harbour, just five minutes' walk from the bus stop. For exploring the region further, **bikes** can be rented at the harbourside in midsummer for 80kr a day.

Åhus

Once a major trading port, and in medieval times a city of considerable ecclesiastical importance, **ÅHUS**, 55km north of Simrishamn, today relies on holidaying Swedes for its income. The town is famed for its eels, which appear on menus all over the country, smoked and usually served with scrambled eggs. From the tourist office (see below), it's a short walk up Köpmannagatan to the attractive old cobbled main square. The twelfth-century **St Maria kyrka**, behind the old Rådhus that houses the town's unexceptional **museum**, is wonderfully preserved, its sheer size attesting to Åhus's former eminence. However, it's one of the gravestones in the churchyard that really raises the eyebrows: take a look at the headstone of Captain Måns Mauritsson, between the church and the museum. According to the inscription, the captain's wife, Helena Sjöström, was 133 years old when she died, and her daughters were born when she was 82 and 95 respectively. At nearby Västerport (walk to the end of Västergatan from the centre) the **Tobaksmonopolets Lada** (free entry) holds displays of tobacco labels and all the paraphernalia of tobacco processing. For 250 years every garden in Åhus had its own tobacco patch, until the government cancelled its contract with the growers in 1964.

Beyond this, there's little more to do than cut through from the main square down Västra Hamngatan to the waterside, where small pleasure yachts line the harbour, a pretty spot if you avert your eyes from the industrial hinterland to the left. For the popular and lengthy **beach**, head out on Järnvägsgatan, behind the tourist office, past a run of old train carriages – there are no trains running now – and left up Ellegatan following signs for **Åhus Strand**.

Practicalities

Unless you're driving, it's easiest to get to Åhus on bus #551 from Kristianstad (see below), 20km to the northwest; the bus stops outside the **tourist office** at Köpmannagatan 2 (June–Aug Mon–Fri 9am–7pm, Sat 9am–6pm, Sun 2–6pm; Sept, Oct & March–May Mon–Fri 10am–5pm; Nov–Feb Mon–Fri 1–5pm; ☎044/24 01 06, ⓦwww.kristianstad.se/turism) which **rents bikes** at 60kr per day. The STF **youth hostel**, a few metres from the tourist office at Stavgatan 3 (☎044/24 85 35), also owns an appealing bed and breakfast, set in an old cigar factory just behind the hostel with quaint cream brick with pink sills (☎070 606 77 10 or ask at the hostel; ❶). Alternatively, stay on the bus a few minutes longer to get to the beach, where there are plenty of hotels and a **campsite** (☎044/24 89 69) in the nearby forest. *Hotel Åhus Strand* (☎044/28 93 00, ℗24 94 80; ❷) is a reasonable, if plain, choice among the beach **hotels**.

There are some lovely places to **eat** in Åhus. The most charming café in town, *Gallericafeet Fina Fisken* at Västra Hamngatan 4 (June–Aug daily noon–6pm), has a flower-filled garden in which to sample delicious smoked eel omelette or warm smoked salmon and herrings in dill for around 100kr. Down by the harbour, the genteel *Gästgivaregård* specializes in Baltic fish dishes at lunchtime, while the huge white tent you'll see further down the harbour is *Seglis*, which serves buffet suppers at 129kr, and specializes in vodkas from the nearby Åhus Vodka Factory. Just opposite, *Skylight Glassbar* is an old wooden boat serving ice cream on the top deck, and with a cheese and wine restaurant, *Ostkupan*, below.

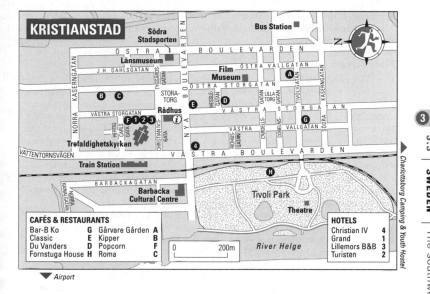

CAFÉS & RESTAURANTS

Bar-B Ko	**G**	Gårvare Gården	**A**
Classic	**E**	Kipper	**B**
Du Vanders	**D**	Popcorn	**F**
Fornstuga House	**H**	Roma	**C**

HOTELS

Christian IV	**4**
Grand	**1**
Lillemors B&B	**3**
Turisten	**2**

River Helge

0   200m

▼ *Airport*

Kristianstad

Twenty kilometres inland of Åhus, quiet **KRISTIANSTAD** (for its correct pronunciation, try a guttural "Krwi-chwan-sta") is eastern Skåne's most substantial historic centre – a Renaissance town created in 1614 by Christian IV, Denmark's seventeenth-century "builder-king". A shining example of the king's architectural preoccupations, with beautifully proportioned central squares and broad gridded streets flanking the wide river, it was only to remain in Danish hands for another 44 years before being permanently ceded to Sweden during the Skånian wars.

Arrival, information and accommodation

Local **buses** from Ystad (1hr 30min), Simrishamn (1hr 30min) and Åhus (30min) all stop outside the central bus station on Östra Boulevarden, although the quickest way here is by **train** (1hr 16min from Malmö) on the ultra-comfortable Kustpilen Express between Copenhagen/Malmö and Karlskrona; onward trains from Karlskrona take about an hour and a half to get to Kristianstad. You might arrive at the sparkling little **airport**, 17km southeast of the city centre, on a domestic service. Buses leave the airport for the city twenty minutes after each flight arrival (20min; 40kr).

The **tourist office** on Nya Boulevarden (mid-June to mid-Aug Mon–Fri 9am–7pm, Sat 9am–3pm, Sun 2–6pm; mid-Aug to mid-June Mon–Fri 10am–5pm and last Sat of each month 11am–3pm; ☏044/12 19 88, ⓦwww.kristianstad.se/turism) books **private rooms** from 150kr (plus 40kr booking fee). There's a **campsite** with attached **youth hostel** at *Charlottsborg Camping* (☏044/21 07 67), 3km west of the town centre (bus #22 or #23).

Three of Kristianstad's **hotels** are side by side, just a few steps from the train station. The cheapest is the very cosy *Lillemors B&B* at Västra Storgatan 19 (☏044/21 95 25, mobile ☏070/521 68 00; ➋), built in the 1790s. Next door at no. 17 is the appealing old *Hotel Turisten* (☏044/12 61 50, ☏10 30 99, ✉info.turisten@swedenhotels .se; ➍/➋); while at no.15 the ironically unassuming *Grand Hotel* (☏044/28 48 00, ☏28 48 10; ➎/➌) offers friendly service and particularly comfortable beds. The most glamorous place to spend the night, though, is *Hotel Christian IV*, Västra

Boulevarden 15 (☎044/12 63 00, ⓕ12 41 40; ⑥/③). A grand, castle-like confection in the old Sparbank building, its beautifully renovated features include original fireplaces and parquet floors.

The Town

The obvious starting point is the **Trefaldighetskyrkan** (Holy Trinity Church; daily 9am–5pm), opposite the train station, which stands as a symbol of all that was glorious about Christian IV's Renaissance ideas. The grandiose exterior has seven magnificent spiralled gables, and the high windows allow light to flood the white interior. Diagonally across from the church, the main square, **Storatorg**, hosts the late nineteenth-century **Rådhus**, itself built in imitation of Christian's Renaissance style. Inside the entrance, a bronze copy of the king's 1643 bust is something of a revelation, with Christian sporting a goatee beard, one earring and a single dreadlock, his one exposed nipple decorated with a flower motif. Back outside in the square, Palle Pernevi's splintered *Icarus* fountain depicts the unfortunate Greek aeronaut falling from heaven into a scaffolded building site.

North of Storatorg on Östra Boulevarden is the **Länsmuseum** (June–Aug Mon–Fri 10am–5pm; Sept–May Tues–Sat noon–5pm; Wed till 6pm year round; free), housed in a building that was begun as a royal palace by Christian in 1616, but soon became an arsenal for Danish partisans during the bloody Skånian wars. Aside from the historical exhibits, there are some interesting textile and art collections on the top floor. If you've time on your hands, it's a pleasant stroll behind the museum to **Södra Stadsporten**, the 1790s southern town gate on Östra Boulevarden, one of the few remaining pieces of fortification.

Walking back through the town centre, a few minutes east of the Storatorg, the **Film Museum**, Östra Storgatan 53 (Tues–Fri & Sun 1–4pm; free), is heralded by a bronze early movie camera outside the door. This was Sweden's first film studio, where the country's earliest movies were recorded between 1909 and 1911; some of these flickering works can now be viewed on videotape inside. From here, wander down any of the roads to the south and you'll reach **Tivoli Park**, where you can stroll beneath avenues of horse chestnuts; at the park's centre is a green-pained Art Nouveau **theatre**, designed by Kristianstad-born Axel Anderberg, who also created the Stockholm Opera House (see p.449). **Sightseeing boats** (*vattenriket*) splash their way up the river on two-hour trips from behind the theatre (May to mid-June & mid-Aug to mid-Sept 3 daily at 11am, 2pm and 6pm; 70kr, book at the tourist office). At the northwestern edge of Tivoli Park, there's an art gallery showing temporary exhibitions and housing the **Barbacka Cultural Centre** (Sept to mid-July Mon–Fri 9am–5pm, Sat & Sun noon–4pm; ☎044/13 56 50), where you can get information on musical events around the town and take in the hands-on science experiment rooms, live snakes in glass columns and mountains of toys – it's an ideal stopoff if you're travelling with children.

Eating, drinking and entertainment

Kristianstad has a number of good **places to eat**. Of the **cafés**, best are *Fornstuga House*, an elaborately carved Hansel-and-Gretel lodge in the middle of Tivoli Park, and the more central *konditori*, *Du Vanders*, Hesslegatan 6. Among the town's **restaurants**, *Restaurant Kipper*, Östra Storgatan 9, is in an atmospheric cellar and specializes in pricey steaks, while the nearby *Restaurant Roma*, Östra Storgatan 15, is an inexpensive Italian serving big pizzas at 65kr. *Bar-B Ko*, Tivoligatan 4, is an inviting place specializing in grilled meats, with main courses for 100kr and a huge range of whiskies, spirits, ale and cider. Authentic **Greek** cuisine can be sampled at *Classic*, Nya Boulevarden 6, with main courses from just 75kr. *Popcorn*, Västra Storgatan 17 next to the *Grand Hotel*, is movie-themed in homage to Sweden's first film studios, with flip-up seats taken from an old cinema. Fish and meat dishes (120–170kr) are served with a surprisingly varied wine list.

For a central **drinking** place, check out the 250 or so beers at *Banken* in the old Riksbank on Storatorg, or try the German-owned-and-themed *Hesslebaren* on Hesslegatan. *Harry's Bar*, Östra Storgatan, is a small but lively place with loud rock music. Best bet, though, is *Garvare Gården*, a lovely old house just up from the park on Tivoligatan, with good food and beers.

The town hosts two annual festivals: **Kristianstadsdagarna**, a huge seven-day cultural festival in the second week of July (during which the tourist office stays open till 10pm; contact them for more information), while the annual **Kristianstad and Åhus Jazz Festival** (ⓣ044/12 68 05, ⓦwww.bluebird.m.se) takes place in both towns throughout June and October. Details of both are available from either tourist office.

East into Blekinge

The county of **Blekinge** is something of a poor relation to Skåne in terms of tourism, though there are some good beaches, plentiful fishing, some fine walking trails and enough cultural diversions to make for an enjoyable few days. The landscape is much the same as in northeastern Skåne: forests and hills with fields fringing the sea, along with a number of islands and a small archipelago south of Karlskrona that make a picturesque destination for short boat trips. If you only have a day or two in the region, it's best to head to the handsome and lively county capital of **Karlskrona**, from where the tiny, fortified hamlet of **Kristianopel** is just 30km away.

Public transport in Blekinge requires some careful timetable studying to avoid being stranded from early evening onwards. Most locals drive, and on weekend evenings there are unlikely to be any trains or buses between towns, while hitching is nigh on impossible – a fact keenly observed by taxi drivers, who charge as much as 250kr to take you between Ronneby and Karlshamn. The Kustpilen Express **train** runs from Malmö/Lund to Karlskrona and stops at all the towns detailed below.

Karlshamn

An hour's train ride from either Kristianstad or Karlskrona (see p.551), **KARLSHAMN** is a rewarding goal for a day's exploration. After a disastrous fire in 1763, wealthy merchants continued to build ever more grand houses for themselves as replacements, and some are still standing. The town saw its heyday in the nineteenth century, when it manufactured goodies such as punch, brandy and tobacco. Today, margarine and ice-cream factories flank the harbour, but don't be put off, as Karlshamn also has some beautiful little streets of pastel-painted houses, a clutch of museums and, within easy reach, some offshore islands that offer a wooded retreat and clean-water swimming.

From the train station, turn left onto Eric Dahlbergsvägen, and right down Kyrkogatan, which is lined with old, painted wooden houses. **Karl Gustav kyrka**, an unusual late seventeenth-century church, squats at the junction with Drottninggatan. Walking down Drottninggatan, you're retracing the steps of nineteenth-century emigrants on their way to the dock for ships sailing to "New Sweden" in America, as related in Wilhem Moberg's book *The Emigrants* (see p.431). A sculpture depicting the book's main characters stands at the small harbour in Karlshamn. The town's **museums** are all close together at the other end of Drottninggatan, at the junction with Vinkelgatan; best of the bunch is **Skottsbergska Gården** (Tues–Sun noon–5pm; 10kr), an amazingly well-preserved eighteenth-century merchant's house. The ground-floor kitchen is furnished in eighteenth-century style, with an enormous open fireplace, while upstairs there's some splendid Gustavian decoration. It's all precisely how Hanna Ljunggren, the final descendant of the original owner, left it when she died here in 1941.

On the corner of Drottninggatan, the **Museum of Local History** (June–Aug
Tues–Sun noon–5pm; Sept–May Sat & Sun noon–5pm; 10kr) contains a run-of-
the-mill collection of domestic and marine exhibits; more interesting are the various buildings out through the old courtyard, where there's a tobacco-processing
works among the authentic interiors. Finally, if you've time on your hands, investigate the intriguing **Punch Museum** (June–Aug Tues–Sun noon–5pm; 10kr or free
with entry to Museum of Local History), which displays the workings of
Karlshamn Flaggpunch, the factory that blended this potent mixture of sugar, arrack
and brandy until forced to close down in 1917.

Practicalities

Ferries leave for Klapeda in Lithuania from Stillerydshamnen, four kilometres west
of town, every other day. You'll need a taxi to bring you into the centre or train
station (100kr) as there are no buses. A good ten-minute walk from the station
along Kyrkogatan or a short hop on bus #310 takes you to the harbourside **tourist
office** on the corner of Ågatan and Ronnebygatan (mid-June to mid-Aug
Mon–Fri 9am–7pm, Sat 10am–6pm, Sun noon–6pm; mid-Aug to mid-June
Mon–Fri 9am–5pm; ☎0454/812 03, ⊛www.karlshamn.se). Staff can book **private
rooms** (150kr per person plus 50kr booking fee) and **cottages** (3000kr per week
for two people) anywhere in the region. The STF **youth hostel** sits next to the
train station at Surbrunnsvägen 1C (☎0454/140 40, ©stfturistkhamn
@hotmail.com). The nearest **campsite** (☎0454/812 10; May–Sept) is by the sea at
Kollevik, 3km out of town, and also has cabins (from 460kr per night for four people) – take bus #312 from the train station or Stortorget. Of the central **hotels**,
cheapest is the *Bode*, just off Drottninggatan along Södra Fogdelyckegatan
(☎0454/315 00; ❶); while *First Hotel Carlshamn*, by the harbour at Varvsgatan 1
(☎0454/890 00, ☎819 50, ©carlshamn@firsthotels.se; ❺/❸), is the luxury option,
with an imposing atrium lobby and a good restaurant.

Karlshamn has an extraordinarily good, principally vegetarian, **restaurant**,
Gourmet Grön, at Drottninggatan 61 (Mon–Sat 11.45am–10pm) serving an
excellent all-you-can-eat buffet for a remarkable 75kr during the day, 125–195kr
in the evening (closed Sun). Bursting with the freshest of flavours, the fragrant
offerings are ample motivation to stay in town long enough to work up an appetite.
For **coffee** and cake, it's just a few steps on to *Christins*, Drottninggatan 65. Though
nothing special to look at, it's a favourite local meeting place and its *konditori* produces rather fine cakes, too.

A laid-back annual two-day **rock festival** (⊛www.swedenrock.com; tickets
300kr), staged in mid-June at the small village of Norje, 15km west of *Karlshamn*,
usually sees the streets littered with half-naked (and more than half-inebriated)
revellers. Even bigger is the **Baltic Festival** in the third week of July (⊛www
.karlshamn.net), an impressive, all-consuming town celebration with lots of eating,
drinking and merry-making to the sounds of live music.

Ronneby

Much of **RONNEBY** has been destroyed by development and, arriving by train,
even the summer sun can't improve the view of banal buildings ahead. There is,
however, a tiny **old town**, a few minutes' walk up the hill to the left, testament to
the fact that in the thirteenth century this was Blekinge's biggest town, and centre
for trade with the Hanseatic League. Only when the county became Swedish four
centuries later did Ronneby fall behind neighbouring Karlskrona. Today, the main
attraction is the beautifully preserved collection of spa houses, a couple of kilometres over the river at **Ronneby Brunnspark**.

In the town itself, walk uphill to the left of the train station, and turn left again
onto the main street, Kungsgatan. There's nothing much of interest here until you
reach **Helga Korskyrkan** (Church of the Holy Cross). With its whitewashed walls,

blocked-in arched windows and red-tiled roof, it's got the distinct look of a Greek chapel presiding over the surrounding modern apartment buildings. Dating originally from the twelfth century, this Romanesque church took quite a bashing during the Seven Years' War (1563–70) against the Danes. On the night of what is known as the **Ronneby Bloodbath** in September 1564, all those who had taken refuge in the church were slaughtered – you can still see the gashes in the heavy oak door in the north wall that were made during the carnage.

In 1775 the waters here were found to be exploitably rich in iron, and Ronneby soon became one of Sweden's principal spa towns, centred on **Ronneby Brunnspark**. Fifteen minutes' walk from the train station up the hill and over the river (or take bus #211), the park's houses stand proudly amid blazing rhododendrons and azaleas. One such property is now a fine STF youth hostel (see below), with the wonderful *Wiener Café* next door. There are pleasant **walks** through the beautifully kept park, past a duck pond, and into the wooded hills behind, picking up part of the Blekingeleden walking trail, the latter a substantial hike through the greater part of Blekinge county. On summer Sunday mornings the park is the site of a giant **flea market**, selling genuine Swedish antiques alongside general tat.

Practicalities

There are frequent **train** and **bus** services from Karlshamn to Ronneby. The **tourist office** (late June & Aug Mon–Fri 9am–6pm, Sat 10am–4pm, Sun noon–4pm; July Mon–Fri 9am–7pm, Sat 10am–4pm, Sun noon–4pm; rest of the year Mon–Fri 10am–5pm; ☎0457/180 90, ⊛www.ronneby.se) is at Västra Torgatan 1 beneath the church in the tiny old town. A pleasant option if you want to stay is the STF **youth hostel** (☎ & ⅌0457/263 00; closed Dec to early Jan) in Ronneby Brunnspark, whose owners also run the inaptly named *Grand Hotel* (☎0457/268 80, ⅌268 84; ❷), in an ugly apartment building opposite the train station at Järnvägsgatan 11. Far more appealing and better placed for Ronneby Brunnspark is the town's best **B&B**, *Villa Vesta*, Nedre Brunnsvägen 25 (☎0457/661 36; ❷), a beautifully conserved 1875-built house with original painted ceilings, Swedish stoves and a peaceful stained-glass conservatory overlooking the river.

For **eating and drinking** in town, *Nya Wienerbageriet*, next to the tourist office at Västra Torgatan 3, is your best bet for fresh salads and sandwiches. Set in a converted old bakery, it also has a stylish **bar** at the back with occasional live music, mostly blues and jazz – there's an occasional cover charge of 70kr. For cakes and baked goods, there's nowhere better than the *Continental Konditori* just off Stortorget; it's also the only place open on a Sunday morning. For evening meals, try the appealing *Garlic House*, in a pistachio- and strawberry-painted old house just up from the train station at Karlskronagatan 29, where meat, chicken and salmon dishes (mains 85–160kr) are served at comfy, leather seats. *Wiener Café* in Ronneby Brunnspark has live music and a disco on Thursdays.

Karlskrona

Blekinge's most appealing destination is the regal county capital **KARLSKRONA**, located on the largest link in a chain of breezy islands. Founded by Karl XI in 1680, who picked it as an ice-free southern harbour for his Baltic fleet, the town today revolves around its maritime heritage. The wide avenues and stately squares were built to accommodate the king's naval parades, and cadets in uniform still career around streets named after Swedish admirals and battleships. However, even if you're not a naval fan, Karlskrona has plenty to offer, particularly the picturesque old quarter around the once-busy fishing port at Fisktorget and some short cruises around the islands in the archipelago; however, due to military restrictions no bathing is allowed on them (there's good swimming off the nearby island of **Dragsö** or at the fine bathhouse in town).

▲ Gdynia (Poland)

Ferry Terminal

HOTELS
Carlskrona 1
Conrad 2
First Hotel Ja 4
First Hotel Statt 3

Borgmästarefjärden

Train Station

JÄRNVAGSTORGET

Dragsö (Island) ▲ Campsite

Stakholmen

Hoglands Park

TROSSÖ

Youth Hostel

N

Björkholmen ▲

FISK-TORGET
SKEPPSGOSSEGATAN

Maritime Museum

Rådhus STOR-TORGET

Fredriks-kyrkan

Båtsmankasern & Art Gallery

Trefaldighets-kyrkan

Stumholmen

Rosenbom Statue

Admiralty Church

KARLSKRONA

0   200m

CAFÉS & RESTAURANTS
Börje Olssons Skafferiet B
Systrarna Lindkvists Café C
Taverna Santorini A

Arriving by **train** or **bus**, you'll pass the island of **Hästö**, once home to Karlskrona's wealthiest residents, before arriving a few minutes later in the town centre on **Trossö**, connected to the mainland by the Österleden main road. Climb uphill past Hoglands Park to the main square, **Stortorget**, at the highest point and geographical centre of the island. It's a vast and beautiful space, spoiled only by some astoundingly inappropriate blocks of faceless apartment buildings, of the type normally relegated to Sweden's suburbs. Nevertheless, the square is dominated by two complementary **churches**, both designed by Tessin the Younger and stuccoed in burnt orange, with dove-grey stone colonnades. **Fredrikskyrkan** (Mon–Fri 11am–3pm, Sat 9.30am–2pm) is elegant enough, but the interior of the circular domed **Trefaldighetskyrkan** (Mon–Fri 11am–3pm, Sat 9.30am–2pm) holds more interest. Built for the town's German merchant community in 1709, the domed ceiling is its most remarkable feature, painted with hundreds of rosettes and brilliantly shaded to look three-dimensional. The altar is also distinctive, with golden angelic faces peering out of a gilded meringue of clouds.

Head between the churches, down the wide, cobbled Södra Kungsgatan, which is divided down the centre by the walls of a tunnel that once carried trains between the station and the harbour. The leafy square ahead is **Amiralitets Torget** and perched at its centre is the huge, apricot and grey wooden bell tower of the **Admiralty Church**. To get to the church itself, head down Vallgatan on the left of the square and the beautifully proportioned wooden church is up on your right. Built in 1685, it's the oldest entirely wooden church in Sweden. Outside the entrance, take a look at one of the city's best-known landmarks: the wooden statue of **Rosenbom**, a local beggar who one night forgot to raise his hat to thank the wealthy German carver, Fritz Kolbe. When admonished for this, Rosenbom retorted, "If you want thanks for your crumbs to the poor, you can take my hat off yourself!" Enraged, Kolbe struck him between the eyes and sent him away, but the beggar froze stiff and died in a snowdrift by the church. Next morning, Kolbe found the beggar's body and, filled with remorse, carved a figure of Rosenbom to stand at the spot where he died, designing it so that you have to raise his hat yourself to give some money.

Karlskrona's best museums are set on the island of Stumholmen, connected to the mainland by road five minutes' walk east of Stortorget down Kyrkogatan. The worthwhile **Maritime Museum** (June–Aug daily 10am–6pm, Sept–May Tues–Sun 11am–5pm; 50kr) to the left has a facade like a futuristic Greek temple, while its exhibits, which thoughtfully and evocatively bring seafaring ways to life, is diverting even for those for whom things nautical usually induce yawns. Close by is Karlskrona's good **art gallery** (Tues–Fri noon–4pm, Wed till 7pm, Sat & Sun noon–5pm; free), set in the splendid old Seamen's Barracks (*båtamanskasern*). The highlight is the poignant work of local artist Erik Langemark, who chronicled the city in his paintings and drawings – modern photographs alongside show how the city has changed since.

For more of a feel of old Karlskrona, wander west past the military hardware towards the **Björkhomen** area. Here a couple of tiny wooden early eighteenth-century houses in little gardens survive, the homes built by the very first craftsmen at the naval yard. Nearby **Fisktorget**, originally the site of a fish market, is pleasant for a stroll, and is also the terminal for boat and river trips.

Practicalities

Karlskrona's **tourist office** (mid-June to mid-Aug Mon–Fri 9am–7pm, Sat & Sun 9am–4pm; Sept–May Mon–Fri 10am–5pm, Sat 10am–1pm; ☎0455/30 34 90, ⊛www.karlskrona.se/tourism) is at Stortorget 2. Staff can book you **private rooms** for around 125kr per person (there's no booking fee), and cheap military **bikes** are available to rent for 30kr a day. The best place for new rental bikes (55kr per day) is the Q8 petrol station near the train station at Järnvägstorget (☎0455/819 93). As usual, the cheapest bed is to be had in the STF **youth hostel**, centrally located at Bredgatan 16 (☎0455/100 20; mid-June to mid-Aug). The nearest **camping** is out on Dragsö island (☎0455/153 54), around 2.5km away: take bus #7 from the bus station to Saltö, from where it's a signposted ten-minute walk. In terms of **hotels**, try the pleasant, modern *Carlskrona*, close to the station at Skeppsbrokajen (☎0455/36 15 00, ⊛www.softwarehotels.se; ❺/❸), while the *First Hotel Ja*, Borgmästaregatan 13 (☎0455/270 00, ⊛www.firsthotels.se; ❸), is another good choice with a very home-ly atmosphere. Within the same chain, the considerably more expensive *First Hotel Statt*, Ronnebygatan 37–39 (☎0455/192 50, ⊛www.firsthotels.se; ❺/❹), is supposed to be its glamorous sister, but in reality it's only a smattering of Empire styling and a bit more gilt to differentiate the two. If more is out of your range, *Hotel Conrad* on Västra Köpmangatan (☎0455/36 32 00, ⊛www.hotelconrad.se; ❸/❶), halfway up the hill towards Stortorget, is plain and reasonable.

Most of the town's **konditori** are indistinguishable, an exception being *Systrarna Lindkvists Café*, Borgmästaregatan 3, across from the tourist office – all fine old gilded tea cups and silver sugar tongs. The majority of Karlskrona's unremarkable **restaurants** are along central Ronnebygatan. The Greek *Taverna Santorini*, Rådhusgatan 11, serves all the usual choices, plus several vegetarian options, with no dish over 100kr. For a real treat, though, try next door at the deli and café *Börje Olssons Skafferiet*, a really fine place for filled baguettes and luscious meats, cheeses and other picnic delights, as well as the fresh cheese and meat-based lunch buffet at 75kr.

Ferries to Gdynia in Poland depart from the ferry terminal at the quays close to the station once daily (10hr 30min); daytime tickets cost from 255kr one-way, 510kr return; night-time 360kr and 575kr.

Kristianopel

Arriving by road at **KRISTIANOPEL**, 30km northeast of Karlskrona, there is not the slightest hint that this idyllic village of some forty inhabitants was once a strategic fortification with a bloody history; if you're here outside July, you'd also be amazed to know that the place bursts with up to two thousand holiday-makers at that time, contributing to a sense of revelry seldom found in the rest of Sweden.

It's only when you've walked past the minute, untouched cottages in their tumbling gardens and all the way to the tiny harbour that you spot the two kilometres of three-metre-thick **fortified walls** that surround the settlement. A 1970s reconstruction, they were built over the original fortifications erected in 1600 by Danish King Christian IV to protect against Swedish aggression. The walls were finally razed by the Swedes after the little town had spent 77 years changing hands with alarming regularity. There is little in the way of specific sights in Kristianopel, the only building worth a brief look being the **church**, near the village shop, a replacement for a medieval church that burnt to the ground in 1605, killing all the village women, children and elderly, who were huddled inside for protection. Today, the original church is just a grassy mound near the campsite.

Practicalities

Getting to Kristianopel by public transport is tricky. **Bus #120** from Karlskrona (to Kalmar) stops at Kristianopel, but only operates during school terms. At other times, bus #500, which runs from Kalmar to Karlskrona along the E22, will drop you at Fågelmara, but it's still a six-kilometre walk from there. Alternatively, **bikes** rented in Karlskrona can be taken on the #120 bus at no extra cost, and **hitching** is easier here than in most places. You can rent a **rowing boat** (10kr per hour, 50kr per day) at the campsite (see below).

For accommodation, you're limited to the **youth hostel** – which has double rooms (●) and dorms – and **campsite** (☎ & ⓕ0455/661 30), tucked inside the low walls overlooking the sea, or the one **hotel**, a simple eighteenth-century farmhouse called *Gästgiferi* (☎ & ⓕ0455/36 60 30; ●; April–Sept), a deliciously mellow old place to the left of the main road into the village.

There are three **restaurants** in the village. The one at *Gästgiferi* serves well-prepared meals, with main courses from 100kr, in an authentic old farmhouse setting. You'll find a younger crowd at the campsite's *Värdshuset Pålsgården* (Fri 6–9pm, Sat noon–9pm, Sun noon–6pm), which serves food from an appealing menu in cosy surroundings and opens late every night in July as a pub. Since 2002, a glorious new **café**, *Sött Och Salt*, has opened up in a white stone house near the harbour, and serves lovely home-made cake. Every July, the two campsite restaurants are the focus for a wide range of **music** and **night-time entertainment**, ranging from Country and Western via blues, jazz and rock'n'roll to Eurovision Song Contest favourites.

Travel details

Express trains

Daily express trains operate throughout the region, in particular Oslo–Copenhagen (via Gothenburg, Varberg, Halmstad and Helsingborg) and Stockholm–Copenhagen (via Helsingborg). Both routes have a branch service through to Malmö. Despite complicated timetabling, the service is frequent and regular north or south between Gothenburg and Helsingborg/Malmö.

Trains

Helsingborg to: Gothenburg (9 daily; 2hr 40min); Lund (13 daily; 40min); Malmö (13 daily; 50min).
Karlskrona to: Emmaboda for connections to Växjö, Stockholm & Kalmar (1–2 hourly; 40min).
Kristianstad to: Karlshamn (hourly; 50min); Karlskrona (hourly; 1hr 45min); Ronneby (hourly; 1hr 20min).
Malmö to: Gothenburg (8–10 daily; 3hr 45min); Karlskrona (hourly; 3hr 15min); Kristianstad (4 daily; 47min); Lund (3 hourly; 13min); Ystad (Mon–Fri hourly, Sat & Sun 5 daily; 50min).

Buses

Ängelholm to: Torekov (5 daily; 45min).
Båstad to: Torekov (5 daily; 30min).
Helsingborg to: Båstad (16 daily; 55min); Halmstad (6 daily; 1hr 50min).
Karlskrona to: Stockholm (Fri & Sun 1 daily; 7hr 30min); Kristianopel (Sat & Sun 2 daily; 25min).
Kristianstad to: Kalmar (1 daily; 3hr); Lund (1 daily; 2hr 30min); Malmö (1 daily; 2hr 45min).
Malmö to: Falkenberg (Fri & Sun 2 daily; 2hr 55min); Gothenburg (Mon–Thurs 1 daily, Fri & Sun 3 daily; 4hr 25min); Halmstad (Fri & Sun 2 daily; 2hr 25min); Helsingborg (Mon–Thurs 1 daily, Fri & Sun 6 daily; 1hr 5min); Jönköping (Mon–Thurs 1 daily, Fri & Sun 3 daily; 4hr 30min); Kalmar (1 daily; 5hr 30min); Kristianstad (1 daily; 2hr); Lund (hourly; 20min); Mellbystrand (Fri & Sun 1 daily; 2hr); Stockholm (Mon–Thurs 1 daily, Fri & Sun 3 daily; 9hr); Trelleborg (hourly; 35min); Varberg (Fri & Sun 2 daily; 3hr 20min).
Ystad to: Kristianstad (Mon–Fri 5–6 daily, Sat & Sun 3 daily; 1hr 55min); Lund (Mon–Fri 3 daily; 1hr 15min); Malmö (3 daily; 1hr); Simrishamn (Mon–Fri 3 daily, 1 on Sat & Sun; 50min); Smygehamn (Mon–Fri 5 daily, Sat & Sun 3 daily; 30min).

International ferries, hydrofoils and catamarans

Halmstad to: Grenå (2 daily; 4hr).
Helsingborg to: Helsingør (3 hourly; 25min).
Karlskrona to: Gdynia (1 daily; 10hr 30min).
Simrishamn to: Allinge (summer only 3–4 daily; 1hr).
Trelleborg to: Rostock (3 daily; 6hr); Sassnitz (5 daily; 3hr 45min); Travemünde (2 daily; 7–9hr).
Varberg to: Grenå (2 daily; 4hr).
Ystad to: Rønne (3–5 daily; 2hr 30min); Swinoujscie, Poland (2 daily; 7–9hr).

3.4

The southeast

Although a less obvious target than the coastal cities and resorts of the southwest, Sweden's **southeast** certainly repays a visit. Impressive castles, ancient lakeside sites and numerous glass-making factories hidden amongst forests are some of the mainland attractions, while off the east coast, Sweden's largest Baltic islands offer beautifully preserved medieval towns and fairytale landscapes. Train transport, especially between Stockholm and the towns close to the eastern shore of Lake Vättern, is good; speedy, regular services mean that you can even visit some places as day-trips from Stockholm.

Småland county in the south encompasses a varied geography and some strikingly varied towns. The glorious historic fortress town of **Kalmar** is an essential stop, and is also the jumping-off point for the island of Öland. Further inland, great swaths of dense forest are rescued from monotony by the many **glass factories** that continue the county's famous tradition of glass production. By the mid-nineteenth century, agricultural reforms and a series of bad harvests in Småland saw mass emigration to America, and in **Växjö**, the largest town in the south, the art of

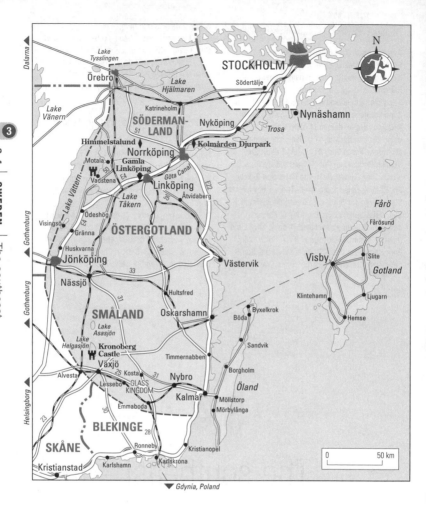

▼ Gdynia, Poland

glass-making and the history of Swedish emigration are the subjects of two superb museums. At the northern edge of the county, **Jönköping** is a great base for exploring the beautiful eastern shore of **Lake Vättern**, particularly the ancient and quaint town of **Gränna** with its unlikely associations with balloons, candy and pears; it's also worth venturing across the water to visit the island of **Visingsö**, rich with remnants of its royal history.

The idyllic pastoral landscape of **Östergotland** stretches from the shores of the lake east to the Baltic. Popular with domestic tourists, the small lakeside town of **Vadstena** is one of the highlights, its medieval streets dwarfed by austere monastic edifices, a Renaissance palace and an imposing abbey. The **Göta Canal** wends its way through the northern part of the county to the Baltic and a number of fine towns line the route, including **Linköping**, with its unusual open-air museum where people live and work in a re-created nineteenth-century environment. Just to the north, bustling **Norrköping** grew up around the textile industry, a background that's preserved in a collection of handsome red-brick and stuccoed factories.

Outside the fragmented archipelagos of the east and west coasts, Sweden's only two true islands are in the Baltic: Öland and Gotland, adjacent slithers of land with unusually temperate climates. Though they've long been targets for domestic tourists, these days an increasing number of foreigners are discovering their charms – sun, beaches and some impressive historic (and prehistoric) sights. **Öland** – the smaller island and closer to the mainland – is less celebrated, but its mix of dark forest and flowering meadows makes it a tranquil spot for a few days' exploration. **Gotland** is known for its medieval Hanseatic capital, **Visby**, a stunning backdrop to the carnival atmosphere that pervades the town in summer, when ferry-loads of young Swedes come here to sunbathe and party – it's also one of the most popular places for Swedes to celebrate **Midsummer's Night**. The rest of the island, however, is little visited by tourists, and all the more worthwhile for that. Both islands are ideal for cycling, and it's easy to rent **bikes**.

Kalmar

Delightful, breezy **KALMAR**, set on a huddle of islands at the southeastern edge of the county of Småland, has treasures enough to make it one of southern Sweden's most delightful towns – a fact sadly missed by most visitors, who have their sights set on the Baltic island of Öland, to which Kalmar is joined by a six-kilometre bridge. Surrounded by fragments of ancient fortified walls, the seventeenth-century **New Town**, set on the Kvarnholmen islet and connected to the mainland by several bridges, is a mass of cobbled streets and lively squares, lined with some lovely old buildings. Close by is the exquisite castle, **Kalmar Slott**, scene of the Kalmar Union which brought Sweden, Norway and Denmark together as a single kingdom in 1397, and now one of Scandinavia's most finely preserved Renaissance palaces. Just a short walk in the other direction, there's the fascinating exhibition on the **Kronan**, one of the world's biggest warships, which sunk off Öland over three hundred years ago. Even now, new finds are being discovered, helping to piece together the world's most complete picture of seventeenth-century maritime life.

Arrival, information and accommodation

Kalmar's **tourist office**, Larmgatan 6 (early June & late Aug Mon–Fri 9am–7pm, Sat & Sun 10am–4pm; mid-June to mid Aug Mon–Fri 9am–8pm, Sat & Sun 10am–5pm; May & Sept Mon–Fri 9am–5pm, Sat 10am–1pm; rest of year Mon–Fri 9am–5pm; ☎0480/153 50, ⊛www.kalmar.se/turism), is within spitting distance of both the **train station** (from where there are several trains daily to Gothenburg and Stockholm) and **bus terminal**, both on Stationsgatan. Tourist office staff hand out maps of Kalmar, the surrounding area and of Öland. Kalmar can be explored easily on foot, but if you want to strike out into the surrounding countryside you can rent a **bike** from Team Sportia, Södravägen 2 (Mon–Fri 10am–6pm, Sat 10am–2pm; 40kr per day).

The tourist office arranges **private rooms** from 200kr per person, 300kr for a double, plus a 50kr booking fee. More popular are the cottages which the tourist office rents out by the week from 3000kr for four people. Other budget options include the **youth hostel**, ten minutes' walk from the tourist office at Rappegatan 1C (☎0480/129 28, ℱ882 93), on the next island to the north, Ängö. The nearest **campsite** is 3km from the centre on Stensö island (☎0480/888 03; ⊛www.camping.se), which also has cheap cabins sleeping up to four people. Local bus #412 heads out this way – check details with the tourist office. Kalmar boasts several very attractive central **hotels**, such as the castle-like *Frimurarehotellet*, Lärmtorget 2 (☎0480/152 30, ⊛www.frimurarehotellet.gs2.com; ❹/❸), or the well-positioned and friendly *Kalmarsund*, Fiskaregatan 5 (☎0480/49 69 00, ⊛www.kalmarsundhotel .se; ❸) which has comfortable, en-suite rooms, and a sauna and roof garden. If you fancy splashing out, the best-located choice is *Slottshotellet*, Slottsvägen 7

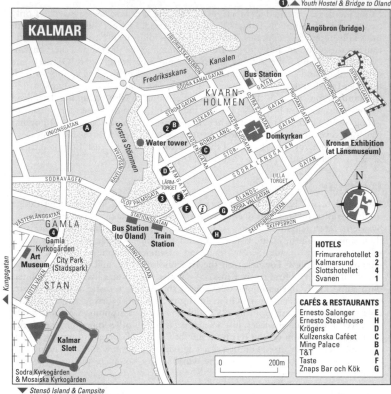

KALMAR

Youth Hostel & Bridge to Öland

Ängöbron (bridge)

Kanalen

Fredriksskans

SÖDRA KANALGATAN

Bus Station

KVARN-
HOLMEN

Domkyrkan

Water tower

Kronan Exhibition
(at Länsmuseum)

UNIONSGATAN

Systra Stömmen

FISKARE

STOR.

SÖDRA LÄNGGATAN

N

SÖDRA VÄGEN

OLOF PALMSGATA

LÄRM-
TORGET

LILLA
TORGET

OLANDS-

SÖDRA VALLGATAN

STATIONSGATAN

SKEPPSBRON

SKEPPSBROGATAN

VÄSTERLÄNGGATAN

GAMLA

Bus Station
(to Öland)

Train
Station

Gamla
Kyrkogården

Art
Museum

City Park
(Stadspark)

STAN

JÄRNVÄGSGATAN

Kungsgatan

Kalmar
Slott

Sodra Kyrkogården
& Mosaiska Kyrkogården

Stensö Island & Campsite

HOTELS	
Frimurarehotellet	3
Kalmarsund	2
Slottshotellet	4
Svanen	1

CAFÉS & RESTAURANTS	
Ernesto Salonger	E
Ernesto Steakhouse	H
Krögers	D
Kullzenska Caféet	C
Ming Palace	B
T&T	A
Taste	F
Znaps Bar och Kök	G

0   200m

(☎0480/882 60, ⊛www.slottshotellet.se; ❺/❹), right opposite the lovely park and
castle, with a grand and very tasteful interior. For something cheaper, try the *Hotel
Svanen* (☎0480/129 28, ℻882 93; ❷), next door to the youth hostel at Rappegatan
1 and run by the same staff.

Kalmar Slott

Beautifully set on its own island, a short way from the train and bus stations, the
first stones of **Kalmar Slott** (daily: April, May & Sept 10am–4pm; June & Aug
10am–5pm, July 10am–6pm; guided tours in English 11.30am & 2.30pm; 70kr)
were probably laid in the twelfth century. A century later, it became the most
impenetrable castle in Sweden under King Magnus Ladulås. The biggest event to
take place within its walls was in 1397, when Erik of Pomerania (under the protection of his aunt, the powerful Danish queen, Margarethe) was crowned king of
Denmark, Sweden and Norway, instigating the **Kalmar Union**, in which the
whole of Scandinavia was united under a single monarch. Subsequently, the castle
passed repeatedly between Sweden and Denmark, but despite eleven sieges
remained almost unscathed. By the time Gustav Vasa became king of Sweden in
1523, Kalmar Slott was beginning to show signs of stress and strain, and the king set
about rebuilding it, while his sons Eric XIV and Johan III continued with the decoration of the interior. The fine Renaissance palace that was the eventual result of
their efforts well illustrates the Vasa family's concern to maintain Sweden's prestige
in the eyes of foreign powers.

Today, if the castle doesn't appear to be defending anything in particular, this is due to a devastating fire in the 1640s, after which the town was moved to its present site on the island of Kvarnholmen – though the Old Town (Gamla Stan) beyond the castle still retains some winding old streets that are worth a look. Unlike many other southern Swedish castles, this one is picture-perfect, with turrets, ramparts, moat, drawbridge, dungeon, and a fully furnished interior that's fascinating to wander through. Among the many highlights is Johan III's bedroom, known as the **Grey Hall**. His bed, which was stolen from Denmark, is decorated with carved faces on the posts, but all their noses have been chopped off – the guilty Johan believed that the nose contained the soul and didn't want the avenging spirits of the rightful owners coming to haunt him. However, it's King Eric's former bedroom, the **King's Chamber**, which is the most intriguing room, with its wall frieze of vividly painted animals and a secret door allowing escape onto the roof – Eric was convinced that his younger brother Johan wanted to kill him. This isn't as paranoid as it sounds: Eric's death in 1569 is widely believed to have been caused by arsenic poisoning.

The rest of the town

Opposite the castle, Kalmar's **Art Museum** (*Konstmuseum*; daily 11am–5pm, Thurs until 8pm; 40kr) displays changing exhibitions of contemporary works, with an emphasis on late 1940s and 1950s Expressionism. The collection is shifted around to make way for temporary exhibitions, but one floor usually contains a gallery of impressive nineteenth- and twentieth-century Swedish nude and landscape paintings.

It's worthwhile to head back into the elegantly laid out Renaissance New Town, centred on the grand **Domkyrkan** (daily 9am–6pm) in Stortorget. Designed in 1660 by Nicodemus Tessin the Elder (as was the nearby Rådhus) after a visit to Rome, this vast and airy church in Italian Renaissance style is today a complete misnomer: Kalmar has no bishop and the church has no dome. Inside, the altar, designed by Tessin the Younger, shimmers with gold, as do the sculptures of *Faith* and *Mercy* around it.

The Kronan Exhibition

Housed in a refurbished steam mill on Skeppsbrongatan, a few minutes' walk from the Domkyrkan, the awe-inspiring **Kronan Exhibition** is the main attraction of the **County Museum** (*Länsmuseum*; mid-June to mid-Aug daily 10am–6pm; mid-Aug to mid-June, Tues–Fri 10am–4pm; 50kr). The royal ship *Kronan*, built by the British naval designer Francis Sheldon, was one of the world's three largest ships, twice the size of the *Vasa*, which sank off Stockholm in 1628 (see p.454). The *Kronan* went down in 1676, blown apart by an explosion in its gunpowder magazine – 800 of its 842 crew were killed, their bodies preserved for more than three hundred years on the Baltic sea bed.

It wasn't until 1980 that super-sensitive scanning equipment detected the whereabouts of the ship, 26m down off the coast of Öland. A salvage operation was led by a descendant of the ship's captain, Admiral Lorentz Creutz, and the amazing finds are displayed in an imaginative walk-through reconstruction of the gun decks and admiral's cabin, accompanied by sound effects of cannon fire and screeching gulls. While the ship's treasure trove of gold coins is displayed at the end of the exhibition, it's the incredibly well-preserved clothing – hats, jackets, buckled leather shoes and even silk bows and cuff links – that brings this exceptional show to life. Other rooms detail the political background to the wars between the Swedes, Danes and Dutch at the time of the sinking. New discoveries are still being made: in 2002, a sealed box containing medical equipment was brought up from the sea bed, and its contents will be on display once conservation work is completed.

Eating and drinking

There's a generous number of good places **to eat** in Kalmar. The liveliest night-time area is **Lärmtorget**, where restaurants, cafés and pubs serve Swedish, Indonesian, Chinese, Greek, Italian and English food.

Cafés and restaurants

Ernesto Salonger Lärmtorget 4. Very popular place serving a huge range of very good pizzas and pastas (60–80kr), as well as traditional Italian salads, antipasti and meat dishes (120kr) in quite upmarket surroundings. Live music at weekends.

Ernesto Steakhouse Larmgatan 2. All hanging Chianti bottles and no sea view, this harbourside restaurant serves substantial and expensive meat and fish meals. The *dagens rätt* is good value at 55kr.

Krögers Lärmtorget 7. Once the most popular pub/restaurant in town, this place isn't what it was now that live music has stopped. Nonetheless, it's still popular, and serves light Swedish meals such as *kottbullesmörgås* (meatball sandwiches, 40kr), as well as less Swedish dishes from fish and chips (6kr) to pastas.

Kullzenska Caféet Kaggensgatan 26. Kalmar's best café by far, this is an exceptional and charming *konditori* occupying the first floor of an eighteenth-century house. Its eight interconnecting rooms are awash with Swedish stoves, Indian carpets, mahogany furnishings and crumbling royal portraits – exactly as they were during the reign of the twin sisters who lived here for the best part of a century before the building was opened as a tea-house.

Ming Palace Fiskaregatan 7. The premier Chinese restaurant in town, with lunch specials for 50–60kr. To find it, head towards the base of the old castellated water tower.

T&T Unionsgatan 20. Kalmar's hippest eatery, and becoming hugely popular, this place serves unusual (and delicious) pizzas with toppings such as banana, onion, curry and pineapple (55–75kr), along with meat dishes (sold by weight). Big range of wines and some great desserts: try the chocolate tart (28kr).

Taste Lärmgatan 5. Fine restaurant with leather and oak decor, though the menu is short and it can be overpriced. Blue mussels followed by lamb, lobster, salmon or ostrich cost around 190kr, though lunch specials are better value at 65kr. The summer bistro menu (99kr) offers four choices of pastas, chicken dishes and salads.

Znaps Bar och Kök Corner Södra Vallgatan and Kaggensgatan. A hip joint with a well designed interior, attracting a youngish crowd. Lots of schnapps and other drinks, and the food isn't bad either – the likes of fish soup, salads, wok dishes and pastas at reasonable prices.

Öland

Linked to mainland Sweden by a six-kilometre bridge, the island of **Öland** is the kind of place a Swedish Famous Five would come on holiday: mysterious forests and flat, pretty meadows to cycle through, miles of mostly unspoilt beaches, wooden cottages with candy-striped canopies, windmills, and ice-cream parlours. Swedes have been coming here in droves for over a century, but since becoming popular with foreign tourists, it's now visited by 55,000 people every July and August. Despite this onslaught, which clogs the road from the bridge north to the main town, Borgholm, this long, splinter-shaped island retains a likeably old-fashioned holiday atmosphere, with a labyrinth of walking trails and bicycle routes and some of the best bathing opportunities in Sweden.

A royal hunting ground from the mid-sixteenth century until 1801, Öland was ruled with scant regard for its native population. Peasants were forbidden from chopping wood or owning dogs or weapons, while Kalmar's tradesmen exploited the trade restrictions to force low prices for the islanders' produce. Danish attacks on Öland saw seven hundred farms destroyed, and following a succession of disastrous harvests in the mid-nineteenth century, a quarter of the population packed their bags for a new life in America. This century, Öland's young are just as likely to migrate to the Swedish mainland.

Today, Öland's attractions include numerous ruined castles, Bronze and Iron Age burial cairns, runic stones and forts, all set amid rich and varied fauna and flora and a striking landscape. To the south is a massive limestone plain known as the Alvaret, whose thin covering of soil is pierced by tiny flowers in summer. In central Öland, the Ice Age left the limestone more hidden and the area is blanketed with forest, while to the north, the coastline is craggy and irregular, with dramatic-looking *rauker* – stone pillars, weathered by the waves into jagged shapes.

Getting to the island

If you're **driving**, take the Ängö link road to Svinö (clearly signposted), just outside Kalmar, which takes you over the bridge to Möllstorp on Öland. **Cycling** over the bridge is forbidden, but there's a free red English bus from Svinö especially for bikes, which drops you off outside the island's main tourist office in Möllstorp. If you're **hitching**, you can try your luck with the free bus, too, as the bridge has no footpath. **Bus** timetables change with the seasons, but buses #101 and #106 are safe bets, running almost hourly from Kalmar bus station to Borgholm (50min), less regularly in the evenings. Buses also run to Färjestaden, hub of the island's bus network, a couple of kilometres south of Möllstorp.

Information and getting around

Öland's main **tourist office** is in a sprawling complex next to the end of the bridge in **Möllstorp** (May, June & late Aug Mon–Fri 9am–6pm, Sat 9am–4pm, Sun 10am–3pm; July to mid-Aug daily 9am–8pm; Sept Mon–Fri 9am–5pm, Sat 10am–3pm; Jan–April & Oct–Dec Mon–Fri 9am–5pm; ☎0485/56 06 00, ⓦwww.olandsturist.se). Pick up a bus timetable and the *Ölands Karten* (75kr), a hugely detailed and excellent, if costly, map which shows hiking routes and coastal treks. While you're at the tourist office complex, pop into the nature centre, **Naturum**, where a twenty-metre model of the island lights up to show all the areas of interest. There's also a very pleasant **café** here with well-priced meals.

It's worth noting the shape and size of Öland before forming ambitious plans to cover it all by bike; although the island is geared for cycling, with endless cycle tracks along the flat roads, you're looking at 130km if you want to

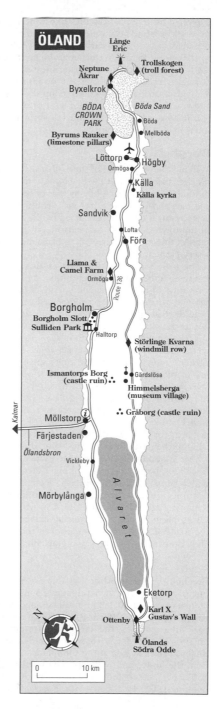

explore it from north to south. **Bike rental** is available in Kalmar, Borgholm and at most of the island's campsites, hostels and the odd farm, for 45–80kr per day, 250kr per week. If you have a **car**, orientation could not be simpler: there is just one main road, Route 136, which runs from the lighthouse at the island's northernmost tip to the lighthouse in the far south; for most of its length it runs close to the west coast. A smaller road runs off the 136 down the east of the island, south from Föra. Though a **bus** network connects most places in Öland, the service is infrequent and you should be prepared for a lot of waiting around, particularly in the south – you need to time trips carefully to avoid being stranded, though **hitching** is not impossible in the far south.

Borgholm

Walking the simple grid of streets that makes up **BORGHOLM**, Öland's "capital", it's clear that tourism is the lifeblood of this villagey town. Although swamped well beyond its capacity each July by tens of thousands of visitors, cramming its pizzerias and bars and injecting a riotous carnival atmosphere, Borgholm is in no way the tacky resort it could be. Encircled by the flaking, turreted villas that were the pride of the town during its first period as a holiday resort in the nineteenth century, most of the centre is a friendly, if bland, network of shops and restaurants leading to a very pleasant harbour.

The only real attraction here is **Borgholms Slotts ruin** (May–Aug daily 10am–6pm; free), just to the southwest of the centre. A colossal stone fortification with rows of huge arches and corridors open to the skies, it can be reached either through a nature reserve, a signposted five-minute walk from the town centre, or from the first exit south off Route 136. When the town was founded in 1816, with just 33 inhabitants, the twelfth-century castle was already a ruin.

A few hundred metres south of the castle is the present royal family's summer residence, **Solliden Park**, an Italian-style villa built to a design specified by Swedish Queen Victoria (the present king's great-grandmother) in 1903. A huge, austere red-granite bust of Victoria rises out of scrubland at the entrance car park. She faces south, away from Sweden which she was reputed to have loathed, and towards Italy which she adored. The villa itself is closed to the public but the **gardens** (daily: mid-May to late June and mid-Aug to Sept 10am–6pm; late June to mid-Aug 11am–6pm, gates close at 5pm; 50kr) make for a pleasant stroll, or you could just head for the delightful thatch-roofed café, *Kaffetorpet*, by the car park.

Just to the north of the town centre, **Blå Rör** is Öland's largest Bronze Age cairn, a huge mound of stones excavated when a coffin was discovered here in 1849. In the 1920s, burnt bones indicating a cremation grave were also discovered, along with bronze swords and tweezers – common items in such tombs. However, there's nothing much to see there now and you're better off visiting **Forngård**, Köpmangatan 23 (mid-June to Aug Mon–Sat 11am–5pm; 20kr), a museum of Öland life whose most interesting exhibits come from the historical sites around the island. The ground-floor displays include bits of ancient skulls, some Viking glass, Bronze Age jewellery and grave finds.

Practicalities

Borgholm's **tourist office** (☎0485/890 00, ⊛www.olandsturist.se) is tucked away out of the hubbub at Sandgatan 25, a couple of streets back from the main Storgatan; expect queues in July. The only place to **rent a bike** is Hallbergs Hojjar, Köpmangatan 10 (☎0485/109 40; 60kr per day or 300kr per week). Set in quiet, park-like gardens, the large and stately STF **youth hostel** at Rosenfors (☎0485/107 56, ☎778 78; May to mid-Aug) is 1km from the town centre – ask the bus driver to stop at the Q8 filling station just before Borgholm proper, 100m from the hostel, and walk east. The tourist office will book **private rooms** from 150kr per person (booking fee 25kr, 50kr for stays of 2–5 days; no telephone bookings). The local **campsite**, *Kapelludden's* (☎0485/101 78, ☎129 44), is on a small peninsula five minutes' walk from the centre, though there's no shortage here, as on the rest of the island, of beautiful spots in which to camp rough.

The best of the **hotels** in the centre of town is *Villa Sol*, at Slottsgatan 30 (☎0485/56 25 52, ⊛www.villasol.just.nu; ❶). A charming old pale-yellow house set in a fruit tree-filled garden, it's beautifully furnished, with stripped floors, old tiled fireplaces and a sun-filled veranda; rooms in the basement are even cheaper, and perfectly comfortable, though less bright. Book early for July, when the place fills up. *Hotel Borgholm*, Trådgårdsgatan 15 (☎0485/770 60, ☎124 66; ❸), has smart en-suite rooms, while facilities at the vast *Strand Hotel*, Villagatan 4 (☎0485/888 88, ⊛www.strand.borgholm.se; ❹), include a shopping mall, nightclub, pool and sauna, though if you're not looking to be awake all night (see below), it's best avoided. Eight kilometres south of Borgholm on Route 136 lies one of the few really fine hotels on the island, *Halltorps Gästgiveri* (☎0485/850 00, ⊛www.halltorpsgast-giveri.nu; ❹), with contemporary, neutrally decorated rooms set in a beautiful eighteenth-century manor house.

There's a pronounced summer-holiday feel to the town's **restaurants** and bars, though standards have dropped in the past few years. Pizza places abound around Stortorget and down to the harbour, all much the same and not cheap at 65–85kr for a pizza. *Mama Rosa*, right at the harbour on Södra Långgatan, is smarter than most and has a more varied menu. On the far side of the harbour, *Skeppet* is a jolly little Italian restaurant open only in summer, hidden behind a group of 1940s industrial silos. For the finest food on the island (with prices to match), head for *Backfickan* at the *Hotel Borgholm*, whose chef is something of a celebrity in Sweden. For good ice cream, head for *Glascafé* on Storgatan, where you can eat the home-made sorbets and ices in the pleasant back garden. For **drinking**, *Pubben*, Storgatan 18, is a cosy pub run by a friendly local who knows his malts, offering 46 varieties of whisky. Otherwise, try *Robinson Crusoe*, jutting into the water at the harbour but with absurdly overpriced food. The atmosphere is much more fun than the depressing, commercial one at *O'Keefe's Bar*, a sprawling, difficult-to-miss place on Storgatan where it's best to stick to drinks only. For night-time drinking, *Znaps*, at the corner of Södralånggatan and Hantverkaregatan, occupies a building which was formerly a hospital for venereal diseases and a church; these days, you'll find R&B, house music and occasional live bands (40kr cover charge on Fri and Sat nights). Otherwise, a raucous young crowd invariably swarms into the *Strand* disco in the *Strand Hotel* every evening, turning it into a sort of Baltic Ibiza throughout the summer nights (cover charge 80kr).

North Öland

The north of the island holds Öland's most varied landscape, with some unexpected diversions to boot. Heading up Route 136, there's no shortage of idyllic villages, dark woods and flowery fields. At **FÖRA**, about 20km north of Borgholm, there's a good example of a typical Öland church, which doubled as a fortress in times of war. About 12km north of here is **KÄLLA**, 2km outside which sits proud, forlorn **Källa kyrka**, empty since 1888 and now sitting in splendid isolation – take care not to confuse it with the present church by the road sign. Surrounded by brightly flowering meadows, this dull-white medieval church is bounded by dry-stone walls, its grounds littered with ancient, weathered tombs. Inside, the lofty interior has seen plenty of action: built of limestone in 1130 to replace an earlier stave church, it was regularly attacked by heathens from over the Baltic seas. Modernized in the fourteenth century, when Källa was a relatively important harbour and trading centre, and stripped of its furnishings in the nineteenth century, six models of the church in various incarnations are the only interior features. One of the most unexpected sights around here is an unsignposted **camel and llama farm**, 14km north of Borgholm at Ormöga, where from 6pm during summer you can try a camel ride in this most unlikely setting (75kr; pre-book on ☎0485/700 27). Even without taking a ride, the animals make an interesting sight in this pastoral, Baltic island setting.

HÖGBY, a few kilometres further along Route 136, has the only remaining tied church houses on the island, relics of the medieval Högby kyrka nearby, but there's not a great deal to stop for. At nearby **LÖTTORP** you can engage in an unusual if expensive dining experience: follow the signs east for 4km down country lanes to the *Lammet & Grisen* restaurant, housed in a Spanish hacienda (daily 5.30pm–midnight). The only dishes on the menu are salmon and spit-roasted lamb and pork (hence the restaurant's name), with baked potatoes, flavoured butters and sauces – you get all you can eat for 250kr.

Continue north and west off Route 136 across the island to the striking **Byrums Rauker**: solitary limestone pillars formed by the sea at the edge of a sandy beach. From here, the north of Öland is shaped like a bird's head, the beak facing east and with a large bite out of its crown. The best **beaches** are along the east coast; the most popular stretch is a couple of kilometres north of Böda Sand at **Kyckesand**; and there's a nudist beach just to the north of here, marked by a large boulder in the sea.

There are some gorgeous areas of natural beauty in the far north. The nature reserve of **Trollskogen** ("Trolls Forest") – exactly the kind of place you would imagine trolls to inhabit, with twisted, gnarled trunks of ancient oaks shrouded in ivy – offers some excellent walking. Around the western edge of the north coast, the waters are of the purest blue, lapping against rocky beaches; on a tiny island at the tip stands **Långe Eric Lighthouse**, a handsome obelisk of 1845 and a good goal for a walk or cycle ride. Three kilometres along the western coast to the south is the ridged land formation of **Neptune Åkrar** ("Neptune's Ploughland"), named by Carl von Linné for its resemblance to ploughed fields and covered with lupin-like flowers during summer, which form a sheet of brilliant blue to rival the sea beyond. The only town in this region is **BYXELKROK**, a quiet place with an attractive harbour.

Practicalities

There's not much in the way of proper hotels north of Borgholm, but high-standard **campsites** abound, mostly beside a beach and marked every couple of kilometres off Route 136. The most extensive site is *Krono Camping* at Böda Sand (℡0485/222 00, ⊛www.kronocamping-oland.se; mid-May to Sept), 50km north of Borgholm and 2km off the main road at the southern end of the beach. Cabins range from 3400kr per week for four people, up to 5000kr with a water supply. Facilities are extensive, with shops, restaurants and a bakery at the site. The STF **youth hostel**, *Vandrarhem Böda* at Mellböda (℡0485/220 38, ℻221 98), just south of *Krono Camping*, is big and well equipped. Just 6km northwest of Mellböda at **Byxelkrok**, *Solö Värdhus* (℡0485/283 70, ℮solo.wardshus@telia.com; ❷) is a pleasant enough **hotel**; the town also has the only decent **nightlife** venue in the north of Öland, the restaurant, pub and disco *Sjöstugan* (℡0485 283 30, ⊛www.sjostugan .nu; closed Sept–March), right by the shore. The food is good and varied, with fish, meat and vegetarian dishes at reasonable prices (light dishes from around 80kr); while troubadours sing every evening in June and Swedish dance bands appear throughout July.

Central Öland

Cutting eastwards from Borgholm (take bus #102) and following signs to Räpplinge brings you to **Störlinge**, where you'll find a row of seven windmills (*kvarna*) by the roadside. A sign tells you this is the island's longest line of postmill-type windmills, and they make an impressive sight. Almost opposite, *Hus och Hem* (closed Jan & Feb) is a very pleasant **café**, at the back of which is a shop selling all the pigments needed to make authentic Swedish paint to restore classic houses. A couple of kilometres south, **GÄRDSLÖSA** has the island's best preserved medieval church. It's the interior that's well worth a look for its 1666 pulpit and thirteenth-century ceiling paintings; these were whitewashed over in 1781, but uncovered in

1950. The present king's sister, Princess Margaretha, married here in 1964, and royalty fanatics have been scooping handfuls of gravel from the churchyard ever since.
A few kilometres further south in a gorgeous setting is the preserved village of **Himmelsberga**, now an **open-air museum** (early May to Aug daily 10am–6pm; 50kr). Following the decline of farming in the middle of the twentieth century, most of Öland's thatched farmhouses were rather brutally modernized; Himmelsberga, however, escaped, and two of its original farms opened as museums in the 1950s. Buildings were subsequently brought from all over the island, and the collection now includes an extensive assortment of crofters' farms, a smithy and a windmill.

East from Himmelsberga, the ancient castle ruin of **Ismantorps Borg** (dating from around 450 AD) only warrants a visit if you fancy a walk along a lovely wooded path. A huge, circular base of stones, you can see the foundations of 88 rooms inside – if you try. **Gråborg**, passed by bus #102, another 10km south of Himmelsberga, is Öland's largest ancient castle ruin, with 640-metre-long walls. Built around 500 AD and occupied throughout the Middle Ages (when the Gothic entrance arch was built), the walls today encircle little more than a handful of hardy sheep.

South Öland

Dominated by **Stora Alvaret**, the giant limestone plain on which no trees can grow, the south of the island is sparsely populated, with its main town the rather dull **Mörbylånga**. You won't see any bare rock, however, only a meadow landscape sprouting rare alpine plant life that has clung on stoically since the Ice Age. **Buses** run so infrequently here that you'll need to check times carefully at Färjestaden, just south of the bridge to the mainland, which is where the few southbound services begin; timings are posted at the bus stop. However, the lack of regular transport means that **hitching** is a feasible option here. There are fewer facilities as a whole than in the north, so it's worth stocking up before you head off. Despite the difficulties of travelling in southern Öland, its great advantage is that summer crowds thin out here, allowing you to explore the most untouched parts of the island in peace.

The prettiest village south along Route 136 is **VICKLEBY**, equidistant between Färjestaden to the north and Mörbylånga to the south, and the site of a remarkable art and design school, **Capella Gården**, the brainchild of furniture designer Carl Malmsten. An idealist, Malmsten's dream was to create a school that stimulated mind, body and soul. In 1959, he bought a range of picturesque farmhouses at Vickleby and opened an art and design school for adults that still runs today. The students' work, including some lovely ceramic and wood pieces, is on sale in a big annual exhibition. If you do want to visit, it's best to call the studios beforehand (☎0485/361 32).

Of all the ruined forts on Öland, the one most worth a visit is at the village of **EKETORP**, reachable by bus from Mörbylånga. The site (May to mid-Sept daily 10am–5pm; guided tours in English 1pm; 50kr) includes an archeological museum containing the finds of a major excavation in the 1970s. Three settlements were discovered, including a marketplace from the fourth century and an agricultural community dating from 1000 AD. The result is a wonderful achievement in speculative archeology, actual physical evidence being thin on the ground. The best of the finds, such as jewellery and weapons, are on show in the museum, and there's a workshop where you can have a go at leatherwork or "authentic" ancient cookery.

If you head south from here, you'll come to a stone wall that cuts straight across the island. Called **Karl X Gustav's Wall**, it was built in 1650 to fence off deer and so improve hunting. A strain of 150 fallow deer still roams about today at **Ottenby**, in the far south of the island. Öland's largest estate, created in 1804, this is now a birdwatcher's paradise, with a huge nature reserve and the Ottenby **bird station**, established in 1946 as a national centre for the study of migrating birds.

Practicalities

The main **tourist office** at Möllstorp (see p.561) will book **private rooms** from 150kr per person per night (plus 25kr booking fee, a few kronor more for longer stays). *Mörby Youth Hostel* (☎ & ⓕ0485/493 93), 15km south of the bridge, is a **hostel and hotel** combined – the price of double hotel rooms (❶) includes sheets and breakfast, while you have to pay separately if you're in a dorm bed. Bus #105 stops right outside. *Haga Park* (☎0485/360 30, ⓦwww.hagaparkcamping.se), 10km south of the bridge at Haga Park, has basic hotel rooms (❶) and a **campsite**; the beach here offers good windsurfing. For a regular **hotel**, try the popular *Hotel Bo Pensionat* at Vickleby (☎0485/360 01; ❸), in a row of traditional village houses – book ahead in high season.

Inland Småland

Thickly forested and studded with lakes, **Småland County** makes up the southeastern wedge of Sweden – a region of appealing if uniform scenery. It's a part of the country which people frequently travel through – from Stockholm to the southwest, or from Gothenburg to the Baltic coast – yet beneath the canopy of greenery, there are a few spots of interest, along with opportunities for hiking, trekking, fishing and cycling.

Historically, Småland has had it tough. The simple, rustic charm of the pretty painted cottages belies the intense misery endured by generations of local peasants; in the nineteenth century, this led to a massive surge of emigration to America. Subsistence farming had failed, the people were starving and ultimately a fifth of Sweden's population left the country – most of them from Småland. Their plight is vividly retold at the **House of Emigrants** exhibition in **Växjö**, a town that makes an excellent base for exploring the region, but the county's most marketed tourist attraction remains the many **glass factories** hidden away in the forest. Further north and perched at the southern tip of Lake Vättern, **Jönköping** has historically been the centre of Swedish match production – the raw materials are readily found in surrounding forests – and is nowadays known as Sweden's Jerusalem due to its multitude of Free Churches.

Växjö and around

Founded by Saint Sigfrid in the eleventh century, **VÄXJÖ** (pronounced "vehquer") is by far the handiest place to base yourself if you are interested in touring the region's glassworks. Deep in the heart of Småland county (110km from Kalmar), the town itself boasts two superb museums: the extensive **Smålands Museum**, notable for being home to the **Swedish Glass Museum**, and the fascinating **House of Emigrants**, which explores the mass emigration from Sweden in the nineteenth and early twentieth centuries. While the town centre doesn't hold much else of appeal, the romantic castle ruin of **Kronoberg** is within easy reach, just 4km to the north of town.

The Town

The **Smålands Museum**, behind the train station (June–Aug Mon–Fri 10am–5pm, Sat & Sun 11am–5pm; Sept–May Tues–Fri 10am–5pm, Sat & Sun 11am–5pm; 40kr), contains two permanent exhibitions: an intelligently displayed history of Småland's manufacturing industries and the rather more appealing "five hundred years of Swedish glass". The latter's exhibits range from sixteenth-century place settings to eighteenth- and nineteenth-century etched and coloured glass, along with stylish Art Nouveau-inspired pieces. Most appealing, though, are the wide-ranging displays of contemporary glass, though with too little light behind the pieces, the newest parts of the collection are not displayed to their full advantage. If you're intending to visit any of the glassworks (see p.568), it's a good idea to come here first to gauge the different styles.

The plain building directly in front of the museum contains the inspired **House of Emigrants** (June–Aug Mon–Fri 9am–6pm, Sat & Sun 11am–4pm; Sept–May Mon–Fri 9am–4pm; ⊛www.svenskaemigrantinstitutet.g.se; 30kr), with its moving "Dream of America" exhibition. The museum presents a living picture of the intense hardship faced by the Småland peasant population from the mid-nineteenth century onwards. Due to agricultural reforms and a series of bad harvests, a million Swedes emigrated to America between 1860 and 1930, most of them from Småland. Most boats left from Gothenburg and, until 1915, sailed to Hull in Britain, where passengers crossed to Liverpool by train to board the transatlantic ships. Conditions on board were usually dire: the steamer *Hero* left Gothenburg in 1866 with 500 emigrants, nearly 400 oxen and 900 pigs, calves and sheep sharing the accommodation.

The attached **Research Centre** (Mon–Fri 9am–4pm; ☎0470/201 20, ⊛info@svenskaemigrantinstitutet.g.se) charges 150kr per half day or 200kr for a full day to help interested parties trace their family roots, using passenger lists from ten harbours, microfilmed church records from every Swedish parish, and records of bodies such as the Swedish New York Society, Swedes in Australia and the Swedish Congo Veterans Association. It's worth booking ahead during the peak season of May to mid-August.

There's not much else to see in Växjö's centre, but take a quick look at the very distinctive **Domkyrkan** (daily 8am–8pm; June–Aug guided tours 9am–5pm), with its unusual twin green towers and apricot-coloured facade. Regular restorations, the most recent in 1995, together with a catalogue of sixteenth-century fires and a lightning strike in 1775, have left nothing of note except a unique 1775 organ and some brilliant modern glass ornaments by Göran Wärff, one of the best known of the contemporary Glass Kingdom designers. Set for installation some time in 2003, the newest addition is a striking triptych altar piece, all in glass, by equally celebrated Bertil Valien. The cathedral is set in the **Linné Park**, named after Carl von Linné, who was educated at the handsome school next door (closed to the public).

Kronoberg Castle

Set on a tiny island in Lake Helgasjön, the ruins of **Kronoberg Castle** lie 4km north of the town centre in a beautiful and unspoilt setting – follow the signs for Evedal, or take the hourly bus #1B from the bus station. The Bishops of Växjö erected a wooden fortress here in the eleventh century, but it was Gustav Vasa who built the present stone version in 1540. Entered over an old wooden bridge set at a narrow spot in the lake, it's a perfect ruin, leaning precariously and complete with rounded tower and deep-set lookouts. Some new brick archways and a couple of reinforced roofs, added in the 1970s, stop the whole thing collapsing. The grass-roofed *Café Ryttmästargården*, set in an eighteenth-century cottage overlooking the castle, is more notable for its quaint old furnishings than its food. The old paddle steamer *Thor* makes regular excursions from here around Lake Helgasjön, the perfect way to appreciate the lakeland scenery. Evening trips tour across to the interconnecting Lake Asasjön and the Asa Herragård country house (five times during the summer leaving at 6pm, ☎0470/ 70 42 00; 400kr including dinner). A less expensive option, at 125kr, are "coffee trips" to the sluice gates between Helgasjön and Asasjön, which leave most Wednesdays at 6pm, and on Saturdays and Sundays at 1pm and 4.30pm; call ☎0470/630 00 to book.

Practicalities

Växjö's **train** and **bus stations** are alongside one another in the middle of town. The **tourist office**, inside the train station building (mid-June to mid-Aug Mon–Fri 9.30am–6pm, Sat & Sun 10am–2pm; mid-Aug to mid-June Mon–Fri 9.30am–5pm; ☎0470/414 10, ⊛www.turism.vaxjo.se), can book **private rooms** from 150kr per person, plus a 50kr booking fee). Of the town's **hotels**, the most striking is the *Teater Park*, in the central Concert Hall building at Västra Esplanaden

10–12 (☎0470/399 00, ⊛www.teaterparken.com; ❺/❸). Otherwise, try the no-frills *Esplanad*, Norra Esplanaden 21A (☎0470/225 80, ℉262 26; ❷/❶), or the good-value *Värend*, Kungsgatan 27 (☎0470/104 85, ℉362 61; ❷). The splendid STF **youth hostel** (☎0470/630 70, ℉632 16) is at Evedal, 5km north of the centre, in an eighteenth-century house set in parkland on tranquil Lake Helgasjön (with its own beach). To get there, head north up Linnegatan, following signs for Evedal, or take bus #1C from the bus terminal to the end of the line (last bus is at 4.15pm, 3.15pm on Sat), or bus #1A, which leaves you with a 1.5km walk, but runs daily till 8.15pm. Next to the hostel is a **campsite**, *Evedal Camping* (☎0470/630 34, ℉631 22), with four-person cabins from 500kr.

Växjö is a good place to eat traditional Småland cuisine, which features lots of berries, potatoes and game. For a **café** with strong gourmet leanings, try *Café Momento* in the Smålands Museum, which serves tasty Italian snacks, plus salads and soups. The best **restaurants** in town are *Spisen*, close to the station at Norra Järnvägsgatan 8 (☎0470/123 00), an expense-account type of place specializing in fine fish and seafood; and *Vibrowski*, Sandgärdsgatan 19 (☎0470/74 04 10), where the excellent lamb, Wienerschnitzel and pepper steak start at 150kr. The waterfront *Evedal Vardhus*, next door to the youth hostel on Lake Helgasjön, is a justifiably pricey place known for its fish fresh from the lake. For a lively and relaxed atmosphere, *PM & Friends*, Storgatan 24, is very popular and stylish – again the emphasis is on fine modern European cuisine using lake-caught fish. It gets packed on Friday and Saturday nights. Note that we've given numbers for places where it's advisable to book a table.

The Glass Kingdom

Within the landscape of dense birch and pine forests, threaded by lakes, that stretches between Kalmar and Växjö, lie the bulk of Småland's celebrated **glassworks**. The area is dubbed **Glasriket**, or the "Glass Kingdom", with each glassworks signposted clearly from the spidery main roads. This seemingly odd and very picturesque setting for the industry is no coincidence. King Gustav Vasa pioneered glass-making in Sweden when he returned from Italy in the mid-sixteenth century and decided to set up a glassworks in Stockholm. However, it was only Småland's forests that could provide the vast amounts of fuel needed to feed the furnaces, and so a glass factory was set up here in 1742, named Kosta after its founders, Koskull and Stael von Hostein – today, under the name Kosta Boda, it's the largest glassworks in Småland.

Visiting the glassworks

All the fifteen or so glassworks still in operation in Småland put on captivating glass-blowing **demonstrations**, usually between Monday and Friday between 9am and 2.30pm, sometimes longer hours; Kosta and Orrefors also have glass blowing on Saturdays (10am–4pm) and Sun (noon–4pm). Several also have permanent **exhibitions** of contemporary work or pieces from the firm's history and, without exception, all have a **shop**. **Bus** services to (or to within walking distance of) the glassworks are extremely limited, and without your own transport it is almost impossible to see more than a couple in a day – although you'll probably find this is enough.

While each glassworks has characteristic individual designs, the Kosta Boda and Orrefors works give the best picture of what is available. **Orrefors** (☎0481/341 95, ⊛www.orrefors.se) is the easiest to reach from Kalmar: take Route 25 to Nybro, then Route 31 or a train from Växjö to Nybro, then bus #138, #139 or #140 to the factory.

The **Kosta Boda** and **Åfors** glassworks (☎0478/345 00, ⊛www.kostaboda.se) are operated by the same team, with the biggest collection at Kosta. The historical exhibition here (Mon–Fri 9am–6pm, Sat 9am–4pm, Sun 11am–4pm, free) contains some delicate c.1900 glassware designed by Karl Lindeberg, while if you're looking for simple modern works, Anna Ehrener's bowls and vases are the most elegant

Glass-making and buying glass

Demonstrations of the **glass-making process** can be mesmerizing to watch. The process involves a plug being fished out of a shimmering lake of molten glass (heated to 1200°C) and then turned and blown into a graphite or steel mould. In the case of wine glasses, a foot is then added, before the piece is annealed (heated and then slowly cooled) for several hours. It all looks deceptively simple and mistakes are rare, but it nevertheless takes years to become a servitor (glass-maker's assistant), working up through the ranks of stem-maker and bowl-gatherer. In smaller works, all these processes are carried out by the same person, but in many of Småland's glassworks, you'll see the bowl-gatherer fetching the glowing gob for the master blower, who then skilfully rolls and shapes the syrupy substance. When the blower is attaching bases to wine glasses, the would-be stem will slide off or sink right through if the glass is too hot; if too cold, it won't stick – and the right temperature lasts a matter of seconds.

If you want to **buy glassware**, which is marketed with a vengeance, don't feel compelled to snap up the first things you see. The same batch of designs appears at most of the glassworks, a testament to the fact that the Kosta Boda and Orrefors outfits are owned by the same umbrella company, and that most of the smaller works have been swallowed up by it too, even though they retain their own names. This makes price comparison easier, but don't expect many bargains; the best pieces go for thousands of kronor.

pieces. Some of the most brilliantly innovative creations are by Göran Wärff – examples of his expressive work are found in Växjö's Cathedral. These can be bought in the adjacent shop, alongside current designs that tend towards colourful high-kitsch. Ulrica Hydman Vallien's name is bandied around all over the place, and the marketing of her work is fierce, though in reality, the painted-on faces and crude flower motifs are far less innovative than the tourist blurbs would have you believe. To get to Kosta from Växjö, take Route 25 to Lessebo then follow signs to the left. By public transport, bus #218 makes the hour-long trip from Växjö bus station to Kosta. Åfors is just ten kilometres south of Kosta on Route 28, but there's no public transport connection.

Studio Glass (formerly Strömbergshyttan; ☎0481/701 05, ⓦwww.glasweb.se), near Hormantorp, is the best bet for a short trip from Växjö. With both Kosta and Orrefors displays, it's more comprehensive than nearby Sandvik, an Orrefors company. To get there, head southeast down Route 25 from Växjö, or take bus #218 (the Kosta bus; 40min). If you're driving, continue on to the small, traditional **Bergdala** works (☎0478/316 50), 6km north of Hormantorp, which produces Sweden's distinctive blue-rimmed glassware. To the north here on Route 31, the 1905-founded **Lindshammar** works (☎0383/210 50) is now Norwegian-owned; the style, previously very plain, has improved and you'll find some really fine vases at 3000kr-plus. To the south, **Johansfors** (☎0471/402 70), set on a lakeside to the south of the region, specializes in stem-ware. One of its chief designers, Astrid Gate, is granddaughter of Simon Gate, one of the biggest names in Swedish glass, a manufacturing and design pioneer during the early twentieth century. To get there by car, take Route 28 from Kosta. Nearby **Skruf** has the most basic, jam jar-style collection. It's run by Ingegerd Råman, who designs the glassware for all overseas Swedish embassies, featuring the distinctive three crowns motif. There's nothing glamorous here, though.

Jönköping

Perched at the southernmost tip of Lake Vättern, **JÖNKÖPING** (pronounced "Yun-shurp-ing") is one of the oldest medieval trading centres in the country, having won its town charter in 1284. Today it's famous for being the home of the matchstick, the nineteenth-century manufacture and worldwide distribution of which made the town wealthy. Matches are no longer made here: in 1932 the town's match magnate, Ivar Kruger, shot himself rather than face bankruptcy, bringing a swift end to the industry in its home town. Despite the town's bland centre, Jönköping's location and ample accommodation and eating possibilities make it a viable base for touring the lake. In 2000, Jönköping's pier was redeveloped to create a lively waterside run of bars and restaurants, and this, coupled with the dramatic expansion of the town's university and the corresponding influx of lively café hangouts, has made the town a very winning one in which to find refreshment and wander. If you can, visit in late August, when Jönköping hosts a five-day **film festival** (Ⓦwww.filmfestival.nu) showing art-house movies from Scandinavia and Europe.

The Town

Jönköping's historic core is an ideal place to start exploring. The biggest of the match factories here, built in 1844, now houses the **Match Museum** (*Tändsticksmuséet*; June–Aug Mon–Fri 10am–5pm, Sat & Sun 10am–3pm; Sept–May Tues–Sat 11am–3pm; 30kr) at Tändsticksgränd 27, a none-too-thrilling collection of matchbox labels, match-making machines and not much else. Opposite, the **Radio Museum** displays every type of radio from early crystal sets to Walkmans. A couple of metres away, and set in another old match factory, is **Kulturhuset**, a trendy centre with a good cheap café and alternative bookshops. Next door is the stylish Bio art-house cinema. From September to May, there's also a bustling early-morning Saturday market on the street outside the Kulturhuset.

The only other museum to bother with is the **County Museum** (*Länsmuseum*; Tues–Sun 11am–5pm, Wed till 8pm; 40kr), on Dag Hammarskjölds Plats, across the canal between lakes Vättern and Munksjön. A mishmash of oddities, with exhibits on garden chairs throughout the ages, bonnets, samovars and doll's houses, it's like wandering around a well-stocked junk shop – and there's no English labelling. The real reason to come here is the well-lit collection of paintings and drawings by **John Bauer**, a local artist who enthralled generations of Swedes with his Tolkienesque representations of gnomes and trolls in the *Bland Tomtar och Troll* books.

Practicalities

The stylish new glass-built **train** and **bus stations** are next to each other on Lake Vättern's edge. Within the complex, the **tourist office** (mid-June to mid-Aug Mon–Fri 9am–7pm, Sat 10am–3pm, Sun 10am–2pm; mid-Aug to mid-June Mon–Fri 11am–4pm, Sat 9am–1pm; ☏036/10 50 50, Ⓦwww.jonkoping.se) can arrange a **private room** for 200–250kr per person. Note that there's no hostel in town. **Hotels** include the *Formula One*, Huskvarnavägen 76 (☏036/30 25 65, ☏30 25 67; ❶) next to the Elmia Exhibition Centre at Rosenlund, 3km from the centre, which has rooms sleeping three people as well as doubles. Several buses head out this way, most frequently bus #1. The *Rosenlund* **campsite** (☏036/12 28 63) is next door. For style, value and atmosphere, the best **hotel** is the classic *Victoria* at F.E. Elmgrensgatan 5 (☏036/71 28 00, Ⓦwww.victoriahome.com; ❺/❸), which includes afternoon tea and a buffet supper in its price and even boasts its own radio and match museums in the corridors. Another good bet is the *Familian Ericsson City Hotel*, just three minutes from the station at Västra Storgatan 25 (☏036/71 92 80, ☏71 88 48; ❹/❷).

Jönköping has plenty of good and lively places to **eat** and **drink**. However, some close for the summer, when many of the townsfolk head off to the coast, while others are closed on Fridays and Sundays. The best **café** is *Mackmakeriet*, five minutes' walk east of the station at Smedjegatan 26. In a lovely eighteenth-century building with an original painted ceiling, this place survived a huge fire in 2000 which devastated much of the area. Photos of the conflagration by local man Andreas

Joakimson adorn the walls and are worth a visit in themselves, though the fresh-filled baguettes (44kr) and cakes are delicious and served in a really friendly atmosphere. On the west side of town, check also the very relaxed *Clara's*, Barnarpsgatan 18, for tasty, well-priced salads, sandwiches and cakes, while next door at no. 16, *Johan 's Coffee & Shop* offers superb salads and home-baked pies as well as excellent-value lunches at 60kr. Among the town's **restaurants**, try *Anna-Gretas Matsal*, in a former market traders' café on Västra Torget, for its eclectic and frequently changing menu, or splash out at the splendid *Svarta Börsen*, Kyrkogatan 4 (☏036/71 22 22) for traditional, though costly, Swedish cuisine. Many of the town's **bars** also serve food: *Hemma*, Smedjegatan 36, is the most popular venue for laid-back live music, with very friendly service and a wide-ranging menu that includes some vegetarian options. *Karlsonn's Salonger*, Västra Storgatan 9, gets very busy and the food is good, while *Rignes*, attached to the *Hotel Savoy* at Brunnsgatan 13–15, is a dark, candlelit pub serving Norwegian beer along with filling Swedish and European dishes, and playing blues and rock'n'roll. On summer evenings, most people head out to the harbour, where you can take your pick of the bars and eateries flanking the pier. *Saltkråkan Restaurant and Pub* at the very end serves great seafood and has a fine whisky bar too.

Along the shore of Lake Vättern

The road heading north along the eastern shore of **Lake Vättern** offers the most spectacular scenery and delightful historical towns in the region. Jönköping can be used as a base for excursions, but there are plenty of other places to eat and stay between here and historic Vadstena (see p.573). It's perfect for **trekking**, too, with several walking paths, the most established being the Södra Vätternleden, John Bauerleden and Holavedsleden.

Six kilometres east of Jönköping on the E4 – initially called Östra Storgatan – is **HUSKVARNA**, originally named "Husqvarna" after its former arms factory (it now manufactures sewing machines and motorbikes). Buses make the trip in around ten minutes. From Huskvarna, buses #120 and #121 make the trip to Gränna in around an hour.

Gränna and Visingsö

An excellent target for a day-trip from Jönköping, **GRÄNNA**, 40km north, is for Swedes irrevocably associated with pears, striped candy and hot-air ballooning. It's easy to while away a whole afternoon in the cafés here, while there are several lovely places to stay should you want to linger. Approaching from the south, the Gränna Valley sweeps down to your left, with the hills to the right, most notably the crest of Grännaberget, which provides a majestic foil to some superb views over Lake Vättern and its island, **Visingsö**.

Per Brahe the Elder, one of Sweden's first counts, built the town, using the symmetry, regularity and spaciousness in planning the settlement that he had learnt in Turku while governor of Finland. He also encouraged the planting of pear orchards – the Gränna pear is still one of the best-known varieties in Sweden today – and if you arrive in late spring, the surrounding hills are a confetti of pear blossom. The main roads were all designed so Brahe could look straight down them as he stood at the windows of his now-ruined castle, **Brahehus**.

A newly designed **Kulturgård** on Brahegatan contains the tourist office, a **local history museum** and a stylish first-floor library which has free Internet access, as well as the fascinating **S.A. Andree Museum** (daily: mid-June to Aug 10am–7pm; late May & Sept–Oct 10am–5pm; Nov & Dec noon–4pm; 40kr), dedicated to Salomon August Andree, the Gränna-born explorer who led a doomed attempt to reach the North Pole by balloon in 1897. Born at Brahegatan 37, Andree was fired by the European obsession of the day to explore and conquer unknown places, and also by the nationalist fervour sweeping through the country, which gained him funding from Alfred Nobel, King Oscar and Baron Oscar Dickson. However, after a flight lasting only three days, the balloon made a forced landing on ice just 470km from its departure point, and after six weeks trekking its crew died either from the cold, starvation or poisoning from trichinosis, after eating the raw meat of a polar bear they had managed to spear. It was 33 years before their preserved, frozen bodies and equipment were discovered by a Norwegian sailing ship. Highlights amongst the poignant displays are the diary of 25-year-old crew member Nils Strindberg, and some film taken by the team, including sequences of them dragging their sledges across the sheets of ice. The most diverting piece in the local history collection, other than a portrait of a miserable looking Per Brahe aged 17, is a silicone model of a courtier, so life-like that visitors are regularly convinced it's a paid actor.

Visingsö

From Gränna a twenty-minute ferry crossing (June–Aug every 30min; Sept–May hourly; pedestrians 40kr return, car and driver 150kr) drops you on the diminutive island of **Visingsö**, just 12km by 3km in size. A lagoon at the harbour makes swimming here less chilly than is usually the case in the deep waters of Vättern. During the twelfth and thirteenth centuries, Swedish kings often lived on the island, and five medieval monarchs died here, including Magnus Ladulås in 1290. It was in the mid-sixteenth century that Erik XIV decided that Sweden should follow the example of continental monarchies, and bestow titles and privileges on deserving noblemen. He created the title of Count of Visingsborg, whose lands included Visingsö, and awarded it to Per Brahe the Elder, who enjoyed a spate of castle building here. However, after Brahe the Younger's death in 1680, the Crown took back much of the land, including the island.

Arriving at the dock, you can **rent a bike** from Visingsö's own little **tourist office** (mid-May to late June & Aug daily 10am–5pm; July daily 10am–7pm; Sept to mid-May Mon–Fri 8am–2pm; ℡0390/401 93, ✉visingsoturist@grm.se). The bikes have no gears and cost 40kr for three hours, or 60kr per day. As Visingsö is entirely flat and there are very few cars around, the whole island can be covered without any strenuous exercise. Even less effort is needed to sit in a horse and trap called a *remmalag*, a tempting way to cover the three-kilometre trip (50–65kr return) to **Kumlaby** church, dating back to the twelfth century, with its beautifully painted ceiling and walls. The church's truncated tower was designed for the astronomy classes organized by Brahe the Younger, whose school was the first in the region to accept girls. Between June and August you can climb the steps of the tower (daily 9am–8pm) for a fine view of the island including the remains of **Näs castle**, at Visingsö's southern tip. This was once a major power centre in Sweden, though there's little sign of its erstwhile glory. **Visingsborg Slott**, near the ferry terminal, is another empty shell of a castle, its roof burned off by Russian prisoners celebrating the death of Karl XII in 1718.

Practicalities

Gränna's **tourist office** is in the Kulturgård on Brahegatan (daily: mid-June to Aug 10am–7pm; late May & Sept–Oct 10am–5pm, Nov & Dec noon–4pm; ℡0390/410 10, ✉turism@grm.se); staff can arrange **private rooms** from 120kr per person (plus 50kr booking fee). Alternatively, two **youth hostels** serve the town: the first (mid-June to early Aug) is close to the tourist office, from where you can make bookings; the second is right on the beach near the ferry (℡0390/107 06; May–Sept). One of the real highlights of this region is staying at the gloriously historic **country house** *Västenås Slott* (℡0390/107 00, ℻418 75; ❸; May–Oct) three kilometres south of Gränna by the hamlet of Röttle. Built in 1590 by Count Sten Bielke, and owned later by Count Per Brahe, this antique-laden mansion is owned and run by the formidable Rolf Von Otter, a descendant of Bielke. Its very reasonable prices reflect the fact that there are no phones or televisions in the rooms, an omission that's quite in tune with the feel of the place. Just above Västenås and built by Von Otter's father, Gränna's other famous **hotel** is the faux-castle *Hotel Gyllene Uttern* ("Golden Otter"; ☎0390/108 00, ✆www.gylleneuttern.se; ❺/❹), glamorous in a somewhat commercialized way and bursting with contrived baronial grandeur.

There are several excellent **cafés** in Gränna, all on Brahegatan, except for *Hembygdsstugan Grännaberget* (May–Aug), reachable via a steep flight of steps from the market square, which specializes in shrimp sandwiches and Swedish cheesecake. Back in town, *Café Amalia*, Brahegatan 47, sells superb lingonberry ice cream, which you can enjoy on a terrace overlooking the rooftops and lake. Best bet, though, is *Café Fiket*, which serves a big range of savoury and sweet pies and some luscious cakes in a 1950s-themed atmosphere. Gränna isn't well endowed with **restaurants** – one really good one, though, and also the place for a **drink**, is *Restaurant Hjörten*, Brahegatan 42, a very pleasant place with a bar, beer garden and well-prepared fish and meat dishes to eat on the terrace or indoors.

Vadstena and Motala

With its beautiful lakeside setting, 60km north of Gränna, **VADSTENA** is the most evocative town in Östergotland county, and a fine place for a day or two's stay. At one time a royal seat and an important monastic centre, the town's main attraction nowadays is its gorgeous moated castle, **Vadstena Slott**, planned in the sixteenth century by Gustav Vasa as part of his defensive ring to protect the Swedish heartland around Stockholm. Vadstena's cobbled, twisting streets, lined with cottages covered in climbing roses, also hold an impressive **abbey**, whose existence is the result of the passionate work of fourteenth-century Saint Birgitta, Sweden's first female saint.

The castle and abbey

Vadstena boasts a number of ancient sites and buildings, notably the Rådhus, which contains Sweden's oldest courthouse, but the town's top attraction is its castle, **Vadstena Slott** (early May Mon–Fri 11am–3pm; late May daily 11am–4pm; June & early Aug daily 10am–6pm; July daily 10am–7pm; late Aug daily 10am–5pm; early Sept Mon–Fri 10am–4pm; mid-Sept to April Mon–Fri 11am–2pm; 50kr). With four seven-metre-thick round towers and a grand moat, it was originally built in 1545 as a fortification to defend against Danish attacks, but was then prettified into a palace to house Gustav Vasa's mentally ill third son, Magnus. His elder brother, Johan III, was responsible for its lavish decorations, but fire destroyed it all just before completion, and to save on costs, the post-fire decor was merely painted on the walls, right down to the swagged curtains that can still be seen today.

From the end of the seventeenth century, the building fell into decay and was used as a grain store; the original hand-painted wooden ceilings were chopped up to make into grain boxes. As a result, there wasn't much to see inside until recently, when the acquisition of period furniture from all over Europe has created more of an atmosphere. Portraits of the Vasa family have also been crammed in, displaying some very unhappy and ugly faces that make for entertaining viewing. English-language **guided tours** of the castle are included in the entrance fee (late May and mid-Aug to early Sept 2 daily; June to early Aug 3 daily).

A few minutes' walk away at the water's edge stands Vadstena's **abbey church** (daily: May 9am–5pm; June & Aug 9am–7pm; July 9am–8pm), the architectural legacy of Saint Birgitta. Birgitta came to Vadstena as a lady-in-waiting to King Magnus Eriksson and his wife, Blanche of Namur, who lived at Bjälbo Palace. After being married at the age of 13, and having given birth to eight children, she began to experience visions and convinced her royal employers to give up their home in order to set up a convent and monastery. Unfortunately, she died abroad before her plans could be completed, and the work was continued by her daughter Katarina, with the church finally being consecrated in 1430. Birgitta's specification that the church should be "of plain construction, humble and strong" is fulfilled from the outside, but the sombre, grey exterior hides a celebrated collection of medieval artwork. More memorable than the crypts of various royals is the statue, now devoid of hands, of Birgitta "in a state of ecstasy". To the right, the rather sad "Door of Grace and Honour" was where each Birgittine nun entered the abbey after being professed – the next time she passed through the doorway would be in a coffin on her funeral day. Birgitta's bones are encased in a red velvet box, decorated with silver and gilt medallions, in a glass case down stone steps in the monks' choir stalls. Although now housing a restaurant and a hotel, the **monastery** and palace-turned-**nunnery** on either side of the abbey are open for tours, though they won't occupy you for long. Two minor but fascinating museums just a few steps from here outside the gates to the abbey graveyard are the **Mental Hospital Museum**, with its alarming contraptions for "curing" the mad, and **Mårten Skinnare's house** next door, an amazingly preserved medieval home to this wealthy furrier, boasting an intact first floor privy overhanging the back wall (both daily: June & Aug 11am–3pm, July 11am–noon & 2–4pm; 40kr).

Practicalities

There are no trains to Vadstena, and the bus system has been rendered lamentably poor after drastic cuts to the services. From Gränna, the only way to reach Vadstena by public transport is by local **bus** to Ödeshög (Mon–Fri three daily at 6.45am, 4.10pm & 6.15pm), then bus #610 (every half hour) into town. By car, it's a straight run along the E4 and Route 50 north from Gränna or southwest on Route 50 from Motala (see below). **Bikes** can be rented from Sport Hörnen, on Storgatan by Rådhustorget (100kr per day or 300kr per week). The **tourist office** is in the castle itself (May daily 9am–5pm; June & Aug daily 9am–7pm; July daily 9am–8pm; Sept Mon–Fri 9am–5pm, Sat 10am–2pm; Oct–April Mon–Fri 9am–5pm; ☎0143/315 70, ⓦwww.vadstena.se).

The tourist office will book **private rooms** (from 165kr per person, plus a 40kr booking fee), while Vadstena's STF **youth hostel** is close to the lake at Skänningegatan 20 (☎0143/103 02, ⓕ104 04); it's advisable to book ahead in summer. The town's **hotels**, most of them housed in converted historic buildings, are fairly expensive. The *Vadstena Kloster*, in the 1369 nunnery next to the abbey (☎0143/315 30, ⓕ136 48; ❺), has very atmospheric public areas including the original Kings Hall, where breakfast (available to non-residents for 50kr) is served, but the bedrooms are surprisingly dated and plain though clean and comfortable enough. A better-value option is the **B&B** *Pensionat Solgården*, Strågatan 3 (☎0143 143 50, ⓦhttp://home9.swipnet.se/~w-94154/solgarden; May–Sept; ❷), a beautifully maintained villa from 1905 in a quiet, central little street.

Eating in Vadstena is equally costly. The pick of the **cafés** is *Mi Casa*, Storgatan 9, where a young, laid-back crowd comes, for the relatively cheap light meals. Also popular is *Gamla Konditori* directly opposite, while the best **restaurant** in town is *Vadstena Valven*, Storgatan 18, which does lunch for 75kr and fish specialities in the evening (closed Sun outside summer). An interesting alternative is *På Hörnet*, Skänningegatan 1, a neighbourhood **pub** serving really well-thought-out dishes, such as marinated mushrooms and herrings. It's a great place for all-day brunch. *Restaurant Rådhus Källeren*, in the cosy cellars of the sixteenth-century courthouse on Rådhustorget, also doubles as a pub, and is particularly busy on Thursday and Saturday evenings, when the locals turn out in force.

Motala and around

At **MOTALA**, 16km north of Vadstena and reached by regular #16 buses, the Göta Canal tumbles into Lake Vättern through a flight of five locks. Designed by the canal's progenitor, Baltzar Von Platen, Motala is one of the most popular spots along the Göta's length – you'll pass Von Platen's grave on the canalside walk. It's worth cruising down a stretch of the canal from here, something that's easiest during the peak summer season (mid-June to mid-Aug), though not impossible at other times of the year. In summer, **boats** run along the canal to Borensburg, 20km east, leaving Motala at 10.30am and taking around five hours for the round trip (200kr; lunch is available on board for 120kr). Alternatively, you could cover the same journey by **bike**; the tourist office can advise about boat tickets and bike rental places. At the harbourside, Motala's **Motor Museum** (daily: June–Aug 10am–8pm; May & Sept 10am–6pm; Oct–April 10am–3pm; 40kr) is the only other inducement to linger in town, and is much more entertaining than it sounds. A museum of style rather than the usual showroom of shiny vehicles, this is great fun even if you've not much interest in cars. Each of the unusual motors is displayed in context, with music appropriate to the era blaring from radio sets.

Just 3km west of the centre, **Varamon Beach**, with its kilometre of golden sand, claims to be Scandinavia's largest inland bathing beach. While that is not strictly true, it does have the warmest waters in Lake Vättern, and on hot summer days the sand is thick with bronzing bodies. It's also a popular windsurfing site.

Practicalities

Trains pull in about a kilometre from the centre of Motala. For the **tourist office**, at Fokets Hus (June to mid-Aug daily 10am–7pm; mid-Aug to May Mon–Fri 10am–5pm; ☎0141/22 52 54, ☒www.motala.se), turn left along Östermalmsgatan, right along Vadstenavägen and left into Repslagaregatan. This brings you past the central Stora Torget and the **bus station**; the tourist office is on the right, close to the harbour. You can **rent a bike** from Velosipede at the harbour (☎0141/521 11) for 95kr per day.

Private rooms from 200kr per person can be booked through the tourist office. The STF **youth hostel** at Varamon (☎ & ☎0141/225 285 June–Aug, ☎22 52 85 rest of year) is right on the beach – take bus #301 from Stora Torget. There's a popular summer café here, too. There's also a well-equipped **campsite** on the beach, *Z-Parkens Camping* (☎0141/21 11 42), next door to *Varamon Chalet Colony*; the latter has some pretty wooden cabins overlooking the lake (book through the tourist office). The main town-centre **hotels** are entirely business-oriented, but are the only option if you want an en-suite bathroom – try *Stadshotellet*, on Stora Torget (☎0141/21 64 00, ☎21 46 05; ❹/❻), which has large, if plain, rooms.

Most of Motala's nondescript **restaurants**, grouped around Stora Torget, offer daily lunches for around 50kr, while the **pubs** here tend to cater for a very young crowd.

Örebro

Ninety kilometres north of Motala and strategically located on the main route from southwest Sweden to Stockholm, the lively and youthful town of **ÖREBRO** lies on the shores of the country's fourth largest lake, Hjälmaren. While its light industrial hinterland promises little, the heart of Örebro comes as a very pleasant surprise, the much-fortified thirteenth-century **castle** forming a magnificent backdrop for the water lily-studded **River Svatån**. Aside from the town's attractions, **Lake Tysslingen**, a few kilometres west, makes for a good afternoon excursion by bike, while in spring the several thousand whooper swans that settle here on their way to Finland provide spectacular viewing.

Arrival, information and accommodation

Örebro is just three hours from Stockholm on the main east–west train line. From the train and bus stations it's a short walk to the helpful **tourist office** in the castle (June–Sept Mon–Fri 9am–7pm, Sat & Sun 10am–5pm; Oct–May Mon–Fri 9am–5pm, Sat & Sun 11am–3pm; ☎019/21 21 21, ☒www2.orebro.se/turism/english); from Östra Bangatan, turn onto Järntorgsgatan, where a crescent of elegant apartments opens out to the left. Follow this around, and the castle is ahead on its own island. The town centre is easy to see on foot, but if you want to get out into the countryside, you can **rent a bike** (☎019/21 19 09; 20kr per hour, 50kr per day) from outside *Harry's Bar* at the riverside Hamnplatsen area on the way to the Stadsparken; there are also tandems at 80kr per day. Another option is take a boat trip around nearby Lake Hjälmaren on *M/S Gustav Lagerbjelke* (2hr, 70kr; day cruises, 275kr).

Private rooms can be booked at the tourist office for 135kr per person. The STF **youth hostel** (☎019/31 02 40, ℱ31 02 56), which has double rooms (❶) as well as dorms, is in a set of very appealing old army barracks just to the north of the centre on Fanjunkarevägen; take bus #31 to Rynninge and get off one stop before the end of the line. If you're **camping**, the nearest site is 2km south of town at **Gustavsvik** (☎019/19 69 50, ℱ19 69 90; May to mid-Sept) – take bus #31.

Of Örebro's **hotels**, the best traditional option is the central *Stora Hotellet*, Drottninggatan l (☎019/15 69 00, ℱ15 69 50; ❺/❸), which is supposedly haunted by the ghost of a young woman and her mother. Örebro's newest hotel, the superbly well-designed *Radisson SAS Örebro*, Kungsgatan 14 (☎019/670 67 00, ⓦwww.radissonsas.com; ❺/❸), with large and sumptuous bedrooms, some with jacuzzis in the bathrooms, offers remarkable summer discounts. *Hotel Continental*, opposite the train station at Järnvägsgatan 2 (☎019/611 95 60, ℱ611 73 10; ❹/❷), is a pleasant mid-range place, while *Hotel Linden*, Köpmangatan 5 (☎019/611 87 11, ℱ13 34 11; ❶), is basic but perfectly adequate.

The Town

A fort has defended Örebro ever since a band of German merchants settled here in the thirteenth century, attracted by the presence of iron ore in the area. Enlarged by King Magnus Eriksson, **Örebro Castle** was further fortified by Gustav Vasa, whose son Karl IX turned it into a splendid Renaissance palace, raising the walls to the height of the medieval towers and plastering them in cream stucco. After the town lost its importance, the castle fell into disuse and was turned into a storehouse and prison.

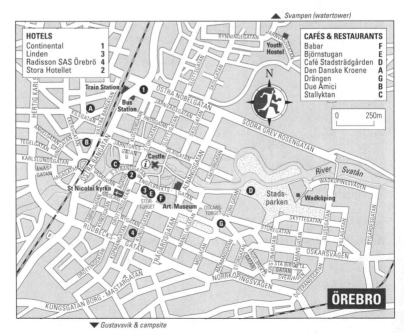

Gustavsvik & campsite

The fairytale exterior you see today is the result of renovation in the 1890s, when the castle was carefully restored to reflect both its medieval and Renaissance grandeur. The same cannot be said for the interior: valiant **tour guides** (June–Aug 5 daily; English tour at noon and 2pm; 45kr) face a real challenge as there is no original furniture, and today many of the rooms are used by the county governor or for conferences. If you do join a tour, the few features of interest are some finely inlaid doors and floors dating from the 1920s, depicting historical events at Örebro, and a large portrait of Karl XII and his family, all their faces painted to look the same – all have popping eyes, the result of using arsenic to whiten their faces. On the top floor there are a few local exhibits moved here from the old county museum.

Nearby, at the top of the very oblong Stortorget, **St Nicolai kyrka** originates from 1260, but lost most of its original medieval character during extensive restoration in the 1860s. Recent renovations have tried to undo the damage, but today it's the contemporary art exhibitions on show here that catch the eye. Historically, however, the church is significant, as it was here in 1810 that Napoleon's unknown marshal, Jean Baptiste Bernadotte, was elected successor to the Swedish throne. The present royal family are descendants of this new king, Karl Johan, who never spoke a word of Swedish.

Following the river eastwards brings you to the **Art Museum** (daily 11am–5pm, Wed till 9pm; free, or entry fee for special exhibitions), a spacious series of galleries housed in what was formerly the county museum. Much of the work on show is mediocre, the best room showing a collection by the late nineteenth-century local artist, Axel Borg. A little further up the river, past the appealing Stadsparken, stands **Wadköping** (daily May–Aug 11am–5pm; Sept–April 11am–4pm; shops and exhibitions closed Mon; free), an entire village of centuries-old wooden cottages and shops brought to the site from the city centre to form a living open-air museum. It's all extremely pretty, but a little staged. Some of the cottages have been reoccupied, and the twee little shops sell pastel-coloured wooden knick-knacks.

Eating and drinking

Örebro boasts plenty of atmospheric places in which to **eat** and, happily, some of the best food is cooked up at the less expensive places. If you're here in July, though, bear in mind that some of the smaller restaurants close for the holidays. We've included telephone numbers only for places where you need to book a table in advance. As for **drinking**, the hippest bar in town is *Babar*, off Stortorget at Kungsgatan 4, where there's also a restaurant serving meat and fish dishes from 120kr. Just opposite, *Björnstugan* is an equally popular place that attracts the same young, hip crowd.

Cafés and restaurants

Babar Kungsgatan 4. The hippest bar in town for some years, and also worth a visit for its restaurant, which serves up meat and fish dishes from 120kr.
Björnstugan Kungsgatan 3. Opposite *Barrbar*, this is almost as popular and attracts the same hip young crowd. There's a restaurant, too.
Café Stadsträdgården Stadsparken. With an unusual setting in the greenhouses at the park entrance, this is a wonderful daytime café offering fine, fresh sandwiches, home-baked cakes and superb pies, all organic.
Den Danske Kroene Kilsgatan 8. Danish bar and restaurant with a lively but relaxed and down-to-earth atmosphere, serving cheap, simple meals

and a wide selection of beers.
Drängen Oskarstorget 9 ⊕019/32 32 96. Consistently superb locals' pub and restaurant of long standing. Book ahead of you want to eat.
Due Amici Ringgatan 30 ⊕019/10 99 96. Fine Italian restaurant with pizzas and pastas at reasonable prices. It's the atmosphere that's the draw here, with very low-voltage lights the only addition to candles.
Stallyktan Södra Strandgatan 3B. This pleasingly rustic pub, just a couple of minutes' walk west of the castle, is perfect for a quiet drink and dinner, with freshly cooked chicken, salmon and steak dishes for around 120kr.

Linköping and around

The range of appealing buildings in **LINKÖPING**, sixty kilometres east of Lake Vättern, stands as testament to the town's 900-year history. Set in a swath of greenery and topped by a soaring 107-metre-high spire, the elegant **Domkyrkan** (June & July Mon–Sat 9am–7pm, Sun 9am–6pm; Aug–May Mon–Sat 9am–6pm, Sun 10am–6pm) dates from 1232 – though the bulk of the present sober building was completed around 1520 – and is built entirely of local hand-carved limestone. Stonemasons from all over Europe worked on the building and, with a belfry and the west facade added as late as 1885, you can make out a number of styles from Romanesque to Gothic. The venerable old buildings around the Domkyrkan include the much-rebuilt thirteenth-century castle, now home to the Bishop's offices; this, like so many others, was fortified by Gustav Vasa and beautified by his son Johan III.

Five minutes down Ågatan in the direction of the Stångån River is the town's most unexpected cultural diversion, housed in the unlikely setting of the **Labourers' Educational Association** (ABF; no set hours; free) at Storgatan 24. On the third floor is a priceless collection of 85 brilliantly executed pictures by the celebrated artist **Peter Dahl**, illustrating all the *Epistles of Bellman*. Carl Michael Bellman was an eighteenth-century poet-songwriter who sought to expose the hypocrisies of contemporary Swedish society, telling of life in pubs, of prostitutes, and of the wild and drunken sexual meanderings of high-society men and women, all set against fear of the Church and final damnation. Officially, the ABF closes for July, but someone will usually let you in nonetheless.

One block back along St Larsgatan, **St Lars kyrka** (Mon–Thurs 11am–4pm, Fri 11am–3pm, Sat 11am–1pm) is frequently overlooked, standing as it does within a few metres of the great Domkyrkan. Consecrated by Bishop Kol in 1170, the present interior has had too many facelifts to show many signs of its age. However, it was a plan to reinforce the floor that led to the discovery of a number of twelfth-century engraved stone and wood coffins. There are no signs to direct you, but beneath the church, in candlelit half-light, complete twelfth-century skeletons reside in glass coffins alongside some remarkably preserved wood coffins and the exposed remains of the original church, rebuilt in the 1730s. To see it all, just ask whoever is selling postcards to unlock the door leading to the basement.

Gamla Linköping

Just 3km west of Linköping proper, **Gamla Linköping** (Mon–Fri 10am–5.30pm, Sat & Sun noon–4pm; ⓦwww.linkoping.se/gamlalinkoping; free) is a remarkable open-air museum, essentially different from the others you may have seen in that it's a true living environment. An entire town of houses, shops and businesses has been brought here from Linköping, along with street lighting, fences, signs and even trees, to re-create an identical copy of Linköping's nineteenth-century incarnation – even the street plan is exactly the same. Look out for Wallenbergsgården, originally home to one of Sweden's biggest financiers, Andre Oscar Wallenberg; the heroics during World War II of his great-grandson Raoul saved tens of thousands of Jews, and his memorial was erected in 2002 in Wallenbergs Platz back in the town. Fifty people live at Gamla Linköping, and there's a massive waiting list for eager new tenants, despite the drawbacks of not being allowed to alter the properties and the fact that tourists trundle through year-round. Craftsmen work at nineteenth-century trades, and most shops are open every day, including a small chocolate factory, gold- and silversmiths, a woodwind workshop and linen shops; there's a cafeteria and an open-air theatre, with performances throughout the summer. Buses #203 and #205 run here from Resecentrum (Sept–May every 20min).

Canal trips

Linköping is riddled with waterways, and a number of trips offer the chance to explore them. The **Göta Canal** (for a map and more information, see p.503) is the most obvious target, wending its way from Motala through Borensberg to the seven-sluice Carl Johan Lock at Berg, just north of Linköping, where it meets Lake Roxen. South of the city, the less well-known **Kinda Canal** has a manually operated triple lock at Tannefors, and you can head south for 35km through a mix of canal and river to Rimforsa.

There are endless combinations of canal and river trips, with mystifying ticket and price permutations, from a basic cruise up and down the Göta Canal for two adults or an adult and two children for 295kr (245kr one-way), to a more glamorous spree on the *M/S Nya Skärgården* to Söderköping (35km east) and back in a steamer from 1915 (bookings for both on ☎070/637 17 00). Another attractive antique steamer, the *M/S Kind* (☎070 638 02 30; ⑩www.kindakanal.se), offers a range of trips down the lesser known Kinda Canal Stångån River to a pleasant outdoor café at Tannefors.

Practicalities

All **trains** and **buses** arrive at and leave from the **Resecentrum** ("travel centre") in the north of the town centre. Linköping is easy to walk around, with the reference point of the Domkyrkan spire rarely out of sight. The **tourist office** (☎013/20 68 35, ⑩www.linkoping.se) is within the *Quality Hotel Ekoxen*, Klostergatan 68, and, uniquely in Sweden, is open 24 hours a day all year. Staff can supply a list of **private rooms** (from around 150kr) and book them for you. Linköping's STF **youth hostel**, Klostergatan 52A (☎013/35 90 00, ⑩www.linkopingsvandrarhem.se), has private doubles (❶) with their own mini-kitchens and en-suite shower and toilets, as well as regular dorm beds. *Glyttinge Camping*, a modern **campsite** with four-bed cabins, is 3km east of town at Berggårdsvägen (☎013/17 49 28; mid-April to Sept); take bus #201. Linköping is not a popular holiday destination with Swedes, and several of the smaller **hotels** close for July – the plus side is that some of those that stay open drop their prices dramatically. Best value and cheapest is the *Hotellet Östergyllen*, Hamngatan 2 (☎013/10 20 75, ⑩12 59 02; ❷), which also operates **cycling and canoeing packages**. For more luxury, try the *Quality Ekoxen*, Klostergatan 68 (☎013/25 26 00, ⑩www.ekoxen.se; ❻/❸), which has every facility including a pool, its own 24-hour delicatessen and large, beautifully renovated rooms with comfortable beds.

Linköping is a likeable spot to spend an evening, and the liveliest and most appealing places to **eat and drink** after dark are mostly on Ågatan, running up to the Domkyrkan. Some of them are open during the day, too. There are several traditional *konditori* around Storatorget: *Lind's*, on the edge of the square, is the best of the bunch. *Chiccolatta*, on the corner of Stortorget and Hantverkaregatan, is a style-conscious, very popular Italian-run place that's perfect for people-watching, and serves good, strong coffee and tasty panini and ciabatta. For bigger meals, try *B.K.* on Ågatan, a fun place with a huge cocktail bar and an elegant though slightly pricey **restaurant** serving mostly meat, plus a couple of fish and vegetarian dishes. For a splash-out dinner, book a table at *Rivå*, Ågatan 43 (☎013/14 45 15), a new, stylish place offering freshly cooked, wholesome meals for 150–250kr and the town's best wood-fired pizzas – a very expensive 129kr, but exceptionally good.

Norrköping and around

It is with good reason that the dynamic, youth-oriented town of **NORRKÖPING** calls itself Sweden's Manchester. Like its British counterpart, Norrköping's wealth came from its textile industry, which thrived in the eighteenth and nineteenth centuries (the Swedish word for corduroy is *manchester*). The legacy from this period is the town's most appealing feature: it's one of Europe's best-preserved industrial urban landscapes, with handsome red-brick and stuccoed mills reflected in the waters of Motala Ström.

NORRKÖPING

Train Station

Turistgården Youth Hostel

NORRA PROMENADEN

Karl Johans Park

Bus Station

Stömsholmen

Theatre

Norrköping Synagogue ✡

City Museum

Concert Hall

Work Museum

CAFÉS & RESTAURANTS

SÖDRA PROMENADEN

Library

SÖDRA PROMENADEN

Art Museum

HOTELS
Centric 3
Elite Grand 2
President 1

Motala Ström

N

0   300m

Kolmården Djurpark

Abborreberg & Youth Hostel

CAFÉS & RESTAURANTS

Café Curiosa	E
Guskelov	C
Källaren Bacchus	D
Pappa Grappa	A
Pub Wasa	B
Tegelvalvet Bar	B

▼ Löfstad Manor

It was this small, rushing river that attracted the Dutch industrialist **Louis De Geer** to the town in the late seventeenth century, and his paper mill, still in operation today, became the biggest factory in the city, to be followed by numerous wool, silk and linen factories. Today, many buildings are painted a strong, tortilla-chip yellow, as are the trams – De Geer's favourite colour has become symbolic of the town. Textiles kept Norrköping booming until the 1950s, when foreign competition began to sap the market, and the last big textile mill closed its doors in 1992.

Like Manchester, Norrköping has also become a nucleus for music-inspired **youth culture** – the city is home to the country's best-known working-class rock band, Eldkvarn, while its charms have been eulogized by Ulf Lundell, one of Sweden's most famous singer-songwriters. In addition, Norrköping has one of the highest immigrant populations in Sweden. The first to come here were the Jews in the mid-eighteenth century; today's immigrant communities are mostly from Asian and Arab countries, though in the past few years there's been a considerable influx from the former Yugoslavia.

Arrival, information and accommodation

The helpful **tourist office**, in an old cotton warehouse opposite the gates of the paper mill at Dalsgatan 16 (June to mid-Aug daily 10am–7pm, Sat 10am–5pm, Sun 10am–2pm; mid-Aug to May Mon–Fri 10am–6pm, Sat 10am–2pm; ☎011/15 50 00, ⊛www.destination.norrkoping.se) is five minutes' walk from the **train** and **bus** terminals. Ask at the tourist office about the 1902 **vintage tram**, which circles around the city on a sightseeing tour during summer. Ordinary yellow trams run on two lines all over the town centre, with tickets costing a flat 15kr, including any tram changes made within the hour.

The tourist office will supply you with a list of **private rooms**, and staff can book **cottages**; in high season, a secluded cottage in the surrounding area sleeping five costs around 1600kr per week, while a central Norrköping one sleeping up to eight costs around 3500kr per week. Among the **hotels**, *Centric*, Gamla Rådstugugatan 18–20 (☎011/12 90 30, ⓦwww.centrichotel.se; ❸/❷), is a cheap, central choice and reasonable enough, but for a more upmarket experience, get a room at the c.1900 *Elite Grand*, bang in the centre at Tyska Torget 2 (☎011/36 41 00, ⓦwww.elite.se; ❺/❸). The *President*, next to the theatre at Vattengränden 11 (☎011/12 95 20, ⓦwww.president.se; ❺/❸), is very pleasant too, with special touches like electrically adjustable beds. There are two STF **youth hostels**. *Turistgården*, Ingelstadsgatan 31 (☎011/10 11 60, ⓕ18 68 63), is just a few hundred metres north of the train station and has double rooms (❶) as well as dorm beds, or there's the more picturesque hostel 5km east of town at Abborreberg (☎011/31 93 44, ⓕ31 79 30; May–Sept); take the Lindo bus (#111) from Repslagaregatan, just off Drottninggatan, and ask the driver to drop you off at the hostel. The closest **campsite**, *City Camp* (☎011/17 11 90, ⓕ17 09 87), is on Campingvägen in Himmelstalund, close to the rock carvings (see p.582) – a forty-minute walk west along the river, and also reachable via bus #118 from the bus station.

The Town

Norrköping's main avenue, **Drottninggatan**, runs north–south from the train station through the city centre. Just a few steps down from the station, the small but pretty **Karl Johans Park** boasts the unusual feature of 25,000 cacti, all formally arranged in thematic patterns. Continuing over the river and following the tram lines up Drottninggatan, a right turn into Repslagaregatan leads into **Gamla Torget**, overlooked by a charismatic sculpture of Louis De Geer by Carl Milles. From here, the steely modern riverside **Concert Hall** is fronted by trees, providing a lovely setting for the *Kråkholmen* café. It's worth stepping inside the Concert Hall for a gander at its strikingly contemporary interior, which belies the fact that this was once one of De Geer's paper factories. You can also pick up information on the symphony orchestra's weekly concerts while you're here.

Go through the impressive, eighteenth-century paper mill gates to the left of the concert hall and cross the wooden bridge behind the hall to reach the **Work Museum** (*Arbetetsmuseum*; daily 11am–5pm, Tues till 8pm Sept–June; free), housed in a triangular, yellow-stuccoed factory from 1917. Known as "The Iron" – though its shape and colour are more reminiscent of a wedge of cheese – the building was considered by Carl Milles to be Europe's most beautiful factory. It's a splendid place, with seven floors of exhibitions on living conditions, workers' rights and daily life in the mills. Take the stairs down, rather than the lift, to see a touching exhibition in the stairwell about the life of Alva, a woman who spent 35 years as a factory worker here. Next door, over another little bridge, is the excellent **City Museum** (*Stadsmuseum*; Tues–Fri 10am–4pm, Thurs till 8pm, Sat & Sun 11am–5pm; free). Set in an interconnecting (and confusing) network of old industrial properties, the most engaging of the permanent exhibitions is a trade street featuring the workplaces of a milliner, confectioner, chimney sweep and, in a backyard, a carriage maker. Three streets north of the Stadsmuseum, on Bråddgatan, stands the beautiful **Norrköping synagogue**, spiritual home to Sweden's oldest Jewish community. The present synagogue, the city's third, was built in 1858. Beautifully restored, highlights of this grand old building include an enormous central chandelier and the pulpit, finely painted in blues, reds and yellows, and with a magnificent ark. To see inside, call the tourist office.

Head back south across the river and follow the bank west for ten minutes into the countryside to reach **Färgargården**, an open-air dyeworks museum (May–Aug Tues–Sun noon–4pm; free), ranged in a huddle of wooden nineteenth-century houses. A better reason to come here than the exhibitions, or the garden of plants used to make dyes, is the outdoor café, open during summer whenever the weather is good.

Retracing your steps back into the town centre, any interest you have in Swedish art can be satisfied at Norrköping's **Art Museum** (*Konstmuseum*; May–Aug Tues–Sun noon–4pm, Wed till 8pm; Sept–April Tues–Sun 11am–5pm, Tues & Thurs till 8pm; 30kr), at the southernmost tip of Drottninggatan, which displays some of the country's best-known modernist works. Founded by a local snuff manufacturer around the beginning of the twentieth century, the galleries offer a fine, well-balanced progression from seventeenth-century Baroque through to up-to-the-minute contemporary paintings. Coming out of the art museum, the bunker-like concrete building to the right is the town **library**, more interesting and user-friendly than most, with a big range of international newspapers and free Internet access.

Eating and drinking

There's a fair selection of eating places in Norrköping, most of them doubling as bars. However, it's the Norrköping custom to have a drink at home before heading out to the pubs, so the city only starts coming alive from 10pm or so.

For an old-fashioned neighbourhood **café**, try *Café Curiosa*, in the centre of town east of Drottninggatan at Hörngatan 6, which serves home-baked cakes, savoury pies and ice cream in an old living room-style environment. The most sensational **restaurant** in town is *Pappa Grappa*, Gamla Rådstugugatan 24 (☎011/18 00 14), a terrific Italian place offering inventive and original combinations of searingly fresh ingredients in a mellow atmosphere; mains start at 120kr. Otherwise, try *Guskelov*, at Dalsgatan 13 by the Concert Hall (☎011/13 44 00; closed Sun), an Art Deco-style restaurant specializing in similarly priced fish dishes. *Pub Wasa* and *Tegelvalvet Bar*, at Gamla Rådstugugatan, along with nearby *Källaren Bacchus* at Gamla Torget 4, provide plenty of scope for **drinking** and dancing. *Källaren Bacchus* has a cellar restaurant, serving traditional Swedish bites from 80kr, and a long cocktail, whisky and beer list, while *Pub Wasa* is in an old, ornate building, serves lots of beers and cheap food and has **live music** every night from 11pm. The *Tegelvalvet Bar* (closed July) is in the basement and also has live singing every Friday and Saturday till 3am and a dance floor. It's a restaurant during the rest of the week.

Around Norrköping

The following are both easy trips from Norrköping; within even closer reach are the rock carvings at **Himmelstalund**, a couple of kilometres west of the centre. These carvings date from around 1500 BC and show, with unusual clarity, ships, weapons, animals and men; burial mounds, though nothing much to look at, attest to Iron Age and Viking settlements in the area. To get there take bus #115 from Norrköping.

Löfstad Manor

Just 10km southwest of town, **Löfstad Manor** (May Sat & Sun noon–4pm; June to mid-Aug daily noon–4pm; late Aug noon–2pm; tours hourly, on the hour; 40kr) dates from the 1650s but was rebuilt a hundred years later after a fire ravaged all but its shell. The same family owned Löfstad until the last, unmarried daughter, Emily Piper, died in 1926. She willed the house, its contents and the whole estate to the Museum of Östergotland, which has kept it untouched since her death. Generations of ancestors before Emily all made their mark, and there's a splendid collection of eighteenth- and nineteenth-century Baroque and Rococo furniture and pictures. Emily's most notable ancestor was Axel Fersen, who, during the French Revolution, tried in vain to save King Louis XVI and Queen Marie-Antoinette. His motives may not have been entirely political – rumoured to have been the queen's lover, it's thought that he fathered the daughter of Marie Antoinette whose portrait hangs in the drawing room. The areas with the most authentic and lived-in feel are the kitchen and servants' quarters; in the latter you

△ Viking Stone Ship, Gotland

can see Miss Piper's bathroom, with her ancient bathrobe still hanging from the door. The tour whisks you round pretty quickly and it's a good idea to ask the guide for English translations before the tour gets underway.

Bus #481 runs from Norrköping bus terminal to Löfstad (ask for Löfstad Slott). Getting back can be a problem, especially on weekend afternoons, but you may be able to get a ride from another visitor. There's a pleasant **restaurant** in one wing of the house, serving traditional Swedish food, plus a cheaper café in the stables.

Kolmården Djurpark

Around 30km northeast of Norrköping, **Komården Djurpark** (ⓦwww.kolmarden .com) is one of the country's biggest tourist attractions. A combined zoo, safari park and dolphinarium, it's understandably popular with children, who have their own zoo, as well as access to a gaggle of other diversions and enclosures. If your views on zoos are negative, it's just about possible to be convinced that this one is different; there are no cages, but instead sunken enclosures, rock barriers and moats to prevent the animals from feasting on their captors. Attractions include a cable-car ride over the safari park, a tropical house, working farm and dolphin shows.

If you're interested in just one or two specific attractions in the park, it might be as well to call first (ⓣ011/24 90 00), as the safari park can be closed in bad weather. Generally, though, most things are open daily from 10am until around 4–6pm. Entrance charges vary according to what you want to see, but a combined ticket for everything runs from 195kr to 235kr, depending on the season. If you don't have your own transport, take bus #432 from Norrköping bus terminal (hourly; 50min). Should you want to stay, there's a **hotel**, the *Vildmarkshotellet* (ⓣ011/15 71 00, ⓦwww.vildmarkshotellet.se; ❹), at the park, or you can **camp** at *Kolmården Camping* (ⓣ011/39 82 50, ⓕ39 70 81), close by at the water's edge.

Nyköping and around

The county of Södermanland – known as Sörmland – cuts diagonally to the northeast of Norrköping above Bråviken bay. Its capital, the very small historic town of **NYKÖPING**, has had a lively past, but today is used by most visitors simply as a springboard for the picturesque coastal islands to the east. This is a pity, as its underrated charms include a fine museum, set in and around the ruins of its thirteenth-century castle, and a harbour that bustles with life in summer.

A late twelfth-century defensive tower, built to protect the trading port at the estuary of the Nyköping River, was converted into a fortress by King Magnus Ladulås, and it was here in 1317 that the infamous **Nyköping Banquet** took place. One of Magnus's three sons, Birger, invited his brothers Erik and Valdemar to celebrate Christmas at Nyköping and provided a grand banquet. Once the meal was complete, and the visiting brothers had retired to bed, Birger had them thrown in the castle's dungeon, threw the key into the river and left them to starve to death (whether the rusting key on display, found by a boy fishing in the river in the nineteenth century, is the genuine item, no one knows). Gustav Vasa fortified the castle with gun towers in the sixteenth century, and his son Karl, Duke of Södermanland, later had it converted into a regal Renaissance palace. The following century all but the King's Tower was devastated by fire, and never rebuilt.

Today, the riverside tower and connected early eighteenth-century house built for the county governor form a **museum complex** (July daily noon–4pm; rest of the year same hours, closed Mon; 20kr). Wandering through the original gatehouse beneath Karl's heraldic shield, you reach the extensively restored **King's Tower**. One the first floor, a stylish job has been done of rebuilding the graceful archways that lead into the Guard Room. One floor further up, the recently revised permanent exhibitions include an interesting display of medieval shoes, but there's no English labelling, and the collection is a lot less inspired than it was before remodelling. Far better is to step outside and into the old **Governor's Residence**. Here you can climb the stairs, lined with menacing portraits, to an exceptional run of magnificently decorated rooms from a variety of periods. Among the highlights is the Jugend room – probably the finest example of this style you'll see in Sweden, boasting some sensuous portraits by the celebrated brothers Bernard and Emil Osterman.

Once you've seen the castle and museum, take the pleasant walk along the river bank, lined with anglers, to the popular harbour and marina, a regular goal for the Stockholm yachting set (the capital being just 100km away by road or train); the flat water inside the 1500-metre-long breakwater is also an important venue for canoe racing.

Practicalities

The **train station**, which is where buses also stop, is at the opposite end of town from the harbour, a good fifteen-minute walk. The central **tourist office**, in the Rådhus, Storatorget (June to mid-Aug Mon–Fri 8am–6pm, Sat & Sun 10am–5pm; mid-Aug to May Mon–Fri 8am–5pm; ☎0155/24 82 00, ⊛www.linkoping.se), rents out **bikes** (40kr per day or 200kr per week) – useful for several excursions to the islands closest to town (see below) The delightful **youth hostel** (no longer part of the STF) is set in the castle grounds at Brunnsgatan 2 (☎0155/21 18 10), and has both double rooms (❶) and dormitory beds. The nearest **camping site** is *Strandstuvikens*, 6km south on the Baltic coast (☎0155/978 10; mid-May to mid-Sept). Among the **hotels**, *Kompaniet*, at Folkungavägen 1 by the harbour (☎0155/28 80 20, ⊛www.choicehotels.se; ❺/❸), is stylishly furnished and excellent value, since breakfast, afternoon tea and a buffet dinner are included in the price. Otherwise, *Hotel Wictoria*, Fruängsgatan 21 (☎0155/21 75 80, ☏21 44 47; ❸/❷), is a passable and inexpensive choice.

Most of the town's **eating and drinking**, unsurprisingly, is done at the harbour, but for the best daytime **café**, head for *Café Hellmans*, just off Storatorget at Västra Trädgårdgatan 24, where you can sit outside in the courtyard in summer. *Tova Stugen*, behind the castle grounds close to the harbour, serves light lunches in low, grass-roofed fifteenth-century cottages brought here from around Södermanland. Of the lively **restaurants** and **bars** set in old wooden warehouses around the harbour, try the fine fish smokery, *Rökeriet*, which has tables outside and a lunch menu of fresh salmon and gravadlax; it's also good for relaxed drinking in the evening. Just beyond, *Hamnmagasinet* has lunch specials at 65kr, plenty of light dishes at 65–100kr and more substantial fish and meat dishes at 150kr and over, together with a wide wine, beer and cider list. *Café Aktersnurran*, just a few buildings up, is more laid-back and cheaper.

If you're **driving** from Nyköping to Stockholm, it's a straight run on the E4; it's also a quick **train** journey (1hr 15min). The **bus** route is convoluted, involving one of five buses to either Trosa or Vagnhärad, then bus #782 to Liljeholmen, followed by a subway trip to the city centre.

Around Nyköping

Hundreds of **islands** are accessible from Nyköping, served by regular boat trips from town. The most popular excursion is to the nature reserve on **Stendörren**, around 30km west of town, from where there's some fine walking between the islands, which are connected by footbridges. From Stendörren boats continue to the idyllic little island settlement of **Trosa** (also reachable by road, 40km northeast along the E4) – ideal for tranquil riverside walks, with forested trails and picture-perfect, red wooden cottages around the old centre.

In summer, *M/S Labrador* leaves the dock at Nyköping for Stendörren and Trosa at 9am (mid-June to mid-Aug Tues & Thurs); it costs 100kr to Stendörren, 140kr to Trosa, and the return boat leaves at 2pm. Alternatively, you can stay on Trosa in the STF **youth hostel** (☎0156/532 00; June to mid-Aug). If you don't want to return to Nyköping, take bus #702 from Trosa bus terminal to Södertälje (1hr), where you can connect with public transport to Stockholm. **Camping** near Trosa is possible at *Nynäs Camping* (℡015/64 10 09; mid-April to mid-Oct). There's only one cabin, so it's worth booking well in advance. A bigger site is *Trosa Havsbaden* (℡015/61 24 94), which also has four-bed cottages bookable through Trosa tourist office (℡015/65 22 22).

Gotland

Rumours about good times on **Gotland** are rife. Wherever you are in Sweden, one mention of this ancient Baltic island will elicit a typically Swedish sigh followed by an anecdote about what a great place it is. You'll hear that the short summer season is an exciting time to visit; that it's hot, fun and lively. Largely, this is all true: the island has a distinctly youthful feel as young, mobile Stockholmers desert the capital for a boisterous summer spent on the beaches. The flower-power era also makes its presence felt with a smattering of elderly VW camper vans lurching off the ferries, but shiny Saabs outnumber them fifty to one. During summer, bars, restaurants and campsites are packed, the streets swarm with revellers, and the sands are awash with bodies. It's not everyone's cup of tea: to avoid the hectic summer altogether, come in late May or September when, depending on your bravado, you can still swim.

Gotland itself, and in particular its capital, **Visby**, has always seen frenetic activity of some kind. A temperate climate and fortuitous geographical position attracted the Vikings as early as the sixth century, and the lucrative trade routes they opened, through to Byzantium and western Asia, guaranteed the island its prosperity. With the ending of Viking domination, a golden age followed, during which Gotland's inhabitants sent ambassadors, maintained trading posts and signed treaties with European and Asian leaders. However, by the late twelfth century the island's autonomy had been undermined by the growing power of the Hanseatic League, under whose influence Visby became one of the great cities of medieval Europe, famed for its wealth and strategic power. A contemporary ballad had it that "The Gotlanders weigh their gold with twenty-pound weights. The pigs eat out of silver troughs and the women spin with golden distaffs."

This romantic notion of prosperity persisted right into the twentieth century, when Gotlanders began relying on tourism to prop up the traditional industries of farming, forestry and fishing. Modern hype makes great play of the sun, and it's true that the flowers that give Gotland its "Island of Roses" tag have been known to bloom at Christmas. It's not all just tourist brochure fodder, however: nowhere else in Scandinavia is there such a concentration of unspoilt medieval country churches, 93 of them still in use and providing the most permanent reminder of Gotland's ancient wealth.

Getting there: ferries and planes

Ferries to Gotland are numerous and, in summer, packed, so try to plan well ahead. Destination Gotland run a range of ferries to the island (reservations on ℡0498/20 10 20 in Visby, ℡08/20 10 20 in Stockholm, ✆www.destinationgotland .se); crossings take five hours from Nynäshamn or four hours from Oskarshamn during the day (on night-time trips you have to stay on the boat until 8am). The newer, daytime-only **high speed ferries** (205–430kr one-way, depending on season) make the crossing in just three hours.

Night-time sailings in summer get packed, so a cabin may be worthwhile. The price list is confusing in the extreme, though during the high season (mid-June to mid-Aug) it roughly divides into three categories: blue (cheapest), green (standard) and yellow (most expensive). Return prices are simply double that of single. Carrying a bike across starts at 35kr. As phone lines to Destination Gotland are notoriously busy it may be quicker to book online. Another option is to try Gotland City (℡08/406 15 00, ✆www.gotlandcity.se), at Kungsgatan 57 in

Stockholm, which can provide plenty of information and sells advance tickets at prices roughly equivalent to Destination Gotland.

The nearest port to Stockholm is **NYNÄSHAMN**, which has a youth hostel (℡09/520 208 34) not far from the train station at Nickstbadsvägen 17 – advance booking is essential. From Gothenburg or the southwest of the country, **OSKAR-SHAMN**, a little over six hours by train from Gothenburg, may well be the more convenient port.

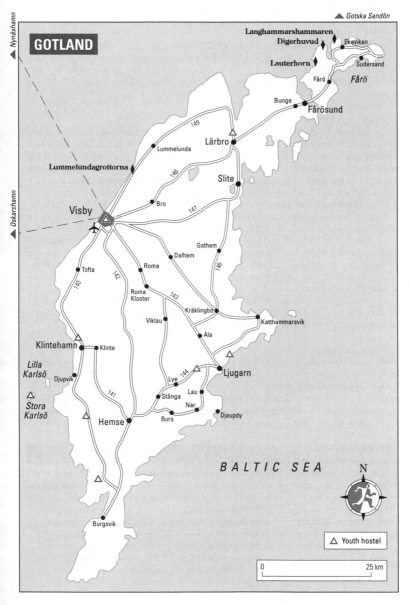

Two airlines **fly** to Gotland; Skyways (☏0498/75 00 00, ⊛www.skyways.se) has services to Visby from Arlanda airport, Stockholm (Mon–Fri 10 daily, Sat 5 daily, Sun 7 daily; 40min) and from Norrköping airport (Mon–Fri 3 daily; 30min). Gotlands Flyg (☏0498/22 22 22, ⊛www.gotlandsflyg.se) has services from Bromma, Stockholm's domestic airport (Mon–Thurs 2–3 daily, Fri 4 daily, Sat 1 daily, Sun 2 daily). Lowest standard flight price for both airlines is around 500kr, though for the under-26 age group it's 300kr which is much more competitive against the ferries.

Visby

Undoubtedly the finest approach to **VISBY** is by ship, when you can take in the old trading centre as it should be seen – from the sea. If you sail on one of the busy summer night-time crossings, try to get out on deck for the early sunrise. By 5am the sun is above the city, silhouetting the towers of the cathedral and the old wall turrets.

Arrival and information

Visby **airport** is 3km from town; a five-minute ride by **taxi** into the centre will cost a maximum of 105kr (airport buses have been discontinued). All the huge **ferries** serving Visby dock at the same terminal, just outside the city walls (and off our map). Just turn left and keep walking for the centre. Alternatively, a short walk to the right along the harbourfront will bring you to **Gotlandsresor** at Färjeleden 3, which has a room-booking service (see "Accommodation", p.590).

The main **tourist office** (May to mid-June & late Aug Mon–Fri 8am–5pm, Sat & Sun 10am–4pm; Sept Mon–Fri 8am–5pm, Sat & Sun 11am–2pm; mid-June to mid-Aug Mon–Fri 8am–7pm, Sat & Sun 8am–6pm; Oct–April Mon–Fri 8am–4pm); ☏0498/20 17 00, ⊛www.gotland.com) is within the city walls at Hamngatan 4, conveniently en route between the ferries and the old city. Here you can buy the excellent *Turistkarta Gotland* (25kr), a map with descriptions of all the island's points of interest. There's also a selection of **tours** available, some of which are worth considering if time is short, the walking tour of Visby (May–Aug 2–3 times weekly; 85kr) in particular. There are no **Internet cafés** in Visby, but the **library** by Almedalen (Mon–Fri 9am–7pm, Sat noon–4pm) provides thirty minutes' connection for free, and will usually oblige if you need longer.

Getting around

Visby itself is best explored on foot. Despite its warren-like appearance, it's a simple matter to find your way around the narrow, cobbled streets. The main square, **Storatorget**, is signposted from almost everywhere, and early arrivals will be rewarded by the smell of freshly baked bread from the bakery here. Modern Visby has spread beyond its old city walls, and today the new town sprawls gently out past **Österport** ("East Gate"), a few minutes' walk up the hill from Storatorget. From

Medieval Week

During the first week of August, Visby becomes the backdrop for a boisterous re-enactment of the conquest of the island by the Danes in 1361. **Medieval Week** sees music in the streets, medieval food on sale in the restaurants (no potatoes – they hadn't yet been brought to Europe) and, on the first Sunday, a procession re-creating Valdemar's triumphant entry through Söderport to Storatorget. Here, modern-day burghers are stripped of their wealth before the procession moves onto the Jungfrutornet. Locals and visitors to Gotland really get into this festival – you'll see crowds on the boats over to Visby already dressed in home-made, specially created medieval garb, and at least half the people on the streets of the town will be dressed up in period costume. It's great fun and a visual feast.

VISBY

Ferry Terminal & Gotlandsresor (Room Booking Service) ▲ ▲ Fängelset Sjömastan

HOTELS
Donnersplats	3
Gute	5
Hamn	7
Solhem	2
Strand	6
Villa Borgen	1
Wisby	4

RESTAURANTS & BARS
Bakfickan	C
Café Boheme	A
Burmeister	K
Clematis Medeltidskrogen	I
Friheten	H
Gutekällaren	E
Munk Källeren	F
Vinäger	G

CAFÉS
Björkstugan	L
Gula Huset	J
Skafferiet	B
Vinäger Café Bar	D

Alleskolan Youth Hostel ▲
Valdemar's Cross ▲
Bus Terminal & Östercentrum ▲
Airport ▲
Noredenstrands Campsite ▲

Söderport
Söderport
Skansporten
Skeppsbron
Slottsterrassen
Färjeleden
Visborgsgatan
Slottsbacken
S.Jots-Baden
Strandgatan
Korsgatan
Slottsgatan
Bredgatan
Kilgränd
Mellangatan
Hamnplan
Hamngatan
Cramergatan
Strandvägen
Strandgatan
Almedalen
Donners Plats
Hästgatan
Art Museum
Gotlands Fornsal Museum
Packhus Plan
Bremergränd
Schweitzergrand
St Karin
St Katrineg
Stora Torget
Lilla Torgränd
Domkyrkan Sankta Maria
Kyrk-Berget
St Hansgatan
St Drottensgatan
Helge And (ruins)
Smedjegatan
St Nikolai (ruins)
St Nikolasgatan
Botanical Gardens
Studentallén
Transhusgatan
Silverhättan
Odalgatan
Norra Kyrkogatan
Norderklint
Nygatan
Norra Murgatan
Backgränd
Norderport
Trapgatan
Södra Kyrkogatan
Nygatan
Hästgatan
Wallersplats
Vårdklockegatan
Adelsgatan
Södra Murgatan
Österport
Hästgatan
Visby Jernvägshotell Hostel
Södertorg

Visby Jernvägshotell Hostel

N

250m

0

here, the **bus terminal**, Östercentrum, serves the rest of Gotland; the tourist office has free timetables.

The best way to get around the island is to **rent a bike**. Most ferry arrivals at Visby are plagued by people hustling bikes, and if you don't have one you might as well succumb here. Bike rental is also available from the kiosks on Korsgatan or just outside the walls at Österport. Most places charge around 60kr per day for three-gear bikes, 70kr per day for seven gears, while tandems, where available, cost around 110kr per day; if you do want to try a tandem, it's best to arrive early as they're extremely popular. If you intend striking out into the countryside beyond Visby – undiscovered by most of the young summer crowd – it's worth knowing that bikes can be rented easily, and more cheaply, at various towns to the south of Visby, though Visby's bike outlets like to play down this possibility. Bikes can be taken on the island's buses for a flat fee of 20kr. Ask at the tourist office for a free map of the **cycle route** that circumnavigates almost the entire island.

Accommodation

Finding **accommodation** in Visby should seldom be a problem; the abandoned-looking souls wrapped in sleeping bags and collapsed in the parks are only there through alcoholic excesses the night before, not homelessness. There are plenty of hotels (though few are particularly cheap), and several campsites and cabins, and three good youth hostels. Both the Gotlandsresor office at Färjeleden 3 (℡0498/20 12 60, ⊛www.gotlandsresor.se) and the tourist office can help with **private rooms** from 285kr per person (425kr for doubles), as well as **cottages** both in or outside Visby. More information is available at the Gotlands Turist Service at Österport (Mon–Fri 9am–6pm; ℡0498/20 33 00, ℱ20 33 90), which has as much access to accommodation information as the tourist office.

Of Visby's several **youth hostels**, all of which have double rooms (❶) as well as regular dorms, the two most central are the *Visby Jernvägshotell*, Adelsgatan 9 (℡0498/27 17 07 or 21 98 19), and the more interesting and well-placed *Fångelset Sjumastam* (℡0498/20 60 50 or 070/426 57 60), situated in a former prison building near the harbour just opposite the ferry terminal. There's a café and sauna here, and it's lively in the evenings. The town's only STF hostel, *Alleskolan*, Fältgatan (June–early Aug; ℡0498/26 98 42, ⊛www.meravsverige.nu), has a café, washing machines, non-smoking rooms and rooms equipped for people with disabilities. It's twenty minutes' walk south from the harbour; go through Söderport (the South Gate) and down Peder Hardingsvägen onto Artillerigatan, and the hostel is off on the right. Chiefly, though, Gotland is a place for **camping**. After the success of Ulf Lundell's youth-culture novel *Jack*, which extolled the simple pleasure of getting wasted on a beach, Gotland became the place to go for wild summer parties: at many campsites, the most exercise you'll get is cycling to and from the *Systembolaget*. The closest campsite, *Nordenstrands* (℡0498/21 21 57, ⊛www.norderstrandscamping.se; late April to mid–Sept), is 1km outside the city walls – follow the cycle path that runs through the Botanical Gardens along the seafront.

Donnersplats Donnersplats 6 ℡0498/21 49 45, ⊛www.donnersplatshotell.nu. A popular, central hotel also offering two- and three-bed apartments for 950kr, and suites for six people for 1800kr. Booking essential in July and Aug. ❸
Gute Mellangatan 29 ℡0498/20 22 60, ⊛www.hotellgute.se. Very central and reasonably comfortable; reductions may be possible if you appear at the last minute. ❹/❸

Hamn Färjeleden 3 ℡0498/20 12 50, ⊛www.gotlandsresor.se/boende/hh.asp?flik=boen de. Opposite the harbour, and convenient for early-morning ferries back to the mainland. All rooms have TV, shower and toilet; breakfast (included) is served from 5am. Open May–Sept. ❸
Solhem Solhemsgatan 3 ℡0498/27 90 90, ⊛www.strandhotel.net/solhem. Just outside the city walls at Skansporten, this large comfortable

hotel has recently been renovated, the better to justify its grand price. It has a basement sauna and is quieter than the more central hotels. ⑤/③ **Strand** Strandgatan 34 ☎0498/25 28 00, ⓦwww.strandhotel.net. A rather glamorous place in the heart of town, with a sauna, steam bath, indoor pool and a stylish atmosphere. ⑥/⑤ **Villa Borgen** Adelsgatan 11 ☎0498/27 99 00,

ⓦwww.gutcinfo.com/villaborgen. Attractive family hotel in the middle of the action, yet with lovely, peaceful gardens. En-suite rooms, sauna and solarium. ④ **Wisby** Strandgatan 6 ☎0498/25 75 00, ⓦwww.wisbyhotell.se. Splendid, central hotel in a building dating back to the Middle Ages. Fine breakfasts (open to non-residents for 65kr). ⑤/⑥

The City

Visby is much older than its medieval remnants suggest – the name derives from its status as a Stone Age sacrificial site: "the settlement" (*by*) at "the sacred place" (*vi*). The magnificent **defensive wall** that encircles Visby is the most obvious manifestation of its previous importance. It was hardly a new idea to fortify trading centres against outside attack, although this land wall, built around the end of the thirteenth century, was actually constructed to separate the city's foreign traders from the island's own locals. Annoyed at seeing all their old trade monopolized, the Gotlanders saw something sinister in the wall's erection. They didn't have to wait long to be vindicated: in 1361, during the power struggle between Denmark and Sweden, the Danish king, Valdemar III, took Gotland by force and advanced on Visby. The burghers and traders, well aware of the wealth of their city, shut the gates and sat through the slaughter outside. Excavations during the twentieth century revealed the remains of two thousand bodies, more than half of them women, children and invalids. **Valdemar's Cross**, a few hundred metres east of Söderport (South Gate), marks their mass grave. Erected by the survivors of the carnage, it reads: "In 1361 on the third day after St James, the Goths fell into the hands of the Danes. Here they lie. Pray for them."

Back inside the city walls, the merchants surrendered, and a section of the wall near Söderport was broken down to allow Valdemar to ride through as conqueror. Valdemar's Breach is recognizable by its thirteen crenellations representing, so the story goes, the thirteen knights who rode through with the Danish king. Valdemar soon left clutching booty and trade agreements, and Visby continued to prosper while the island's countryside around it stagnated, its people and wealth destroyed.

The old **Hanseatic harbour** at Almedalen is now a public park and nothing is much more than a few minutes' walk from here. Pretty **Packhusplan**, the oldest square in the city, is bisected by curving Strandgatan, which runs southwards to the fragmentary ruins of **Visborg Castle**, overlooking the harbour. Built in the fifteenth century by Erik of Pomerania, the castle was blown up by the Danes in the seventeenth century. In the opposite direction, Strandgatan runs northwest towards the sea and the lush **Botanical Gardens** (unrestricted access), just beyond which is the **Jungfrutornet** (Maiden's Tower), where a local goldsmith's daughter was walled up alive – reputedly for betraying the city to the Danes. **Strandgatan** itself is notable for the impressive, step-gabled merchants' houses looming over the narrow street, with storerooms above the living quarters and cellars below – **Burmeisterska house** is particularly impressive. One of the most picturesque buildings is the old pharmacy, **Gamla Apoteket**, a lofty place with gloriously higgledy-piggledy windows.

Next door to the pharmacy at Strandgatan 14, the fine **Gotlands Fornsal Museum** provides comprehensive coverage of Visby's past. Housed in a mid-eighteenth-century distillery, it holds five storeys of exhibition halls covering eight thousand years of history, as well as a good café and bookshop. Among the most impressive sections is the **Hall of Picture Stones** in Room l, a collection of richly carved keyhole-shaped stones dating mostly from the fifth to seventh centuries. The **Hall of Prehistoric Graves** is equally fascinating, its glass cases displaying skeletons dating back six thousand years. Rooms 9 to 13 trace the history of **medieval Visby**, with exhibits including a trading booth, where the burghers of

Visby's churches

At the height of its power, Visby maintained sixteen **churches**, and while only one, the Domkyrkan, is still in use, the ruins of eleven others can be seen. At the centre of Kyrkberget, the **Domkyrkan** (Mon–Fri & Sun 8am–9pm, Sat 8am–6.30pm) was built between 1190 and 1225 and as such dates from just before the great age of Gothic church-building on the island. Used as both warehouse and treasury in the past, it's been heavily restored, and about the only original fixture left is the thirteenth-century sandstone font; have a look, though, beneath the pulpit, decorated with a fringe of unusually hideous angels' faces. The cathedral's most striking feature are its towers, a square one at the western front and two slimmer ones to the east; each was originally topped by a spire, but since an eighteenth-century fire they've been crowned with fancy Baroque cupolas, giving them the appearance of inverted ice-cream cones.

Seventeenth- and eighteenth-century builders and decorators found the smaller churches in the city to be an excellent source of free limestone, tiles and fittings – which accounts for the fact that most are today in ruins. Best of what's left are St Karin's (St Catherine's) on Storatorget (visit after dark, when its fine Gothic interior is floodlit), and the great **St Nikolai** ruin, just down the road from the Domkyrkan, once the largest church in Visby. Destroyed in 1525, its part-Gothic, part-Romanesque shell hosts a week-long **chamber music festival**, starting at the end of July; tickets range from 200kr to 300kr and are available from the tourist office. You can also get a reasonably informative free guide, *The Key to all of Gotland's Churches*, from the tourist office – it has information on churches all around the island.

Visby and foreign merchants dealt in commodities – furs, lime, wax, honey and tar – brought from all over Northern Europe. A series of tableaux brings the exhibition up to 1900, starting with Erik of Pomerania, the first resident of Visborg Castle, and leading on through the years of Danish rule, up to the island's sixteenth-century trading boom. There's a wax model of influential businesswoman Anna Margareta Donner, a member of the eighteenth-century trading dynasty whose name you'll spot all over town. A couple of streets up on St Hansgatan, the **Visby Art Museum** at no. 21 (May to mid-Sept 10am–5pm; 30kr) puts on innovative temporary exhibitions of contemporary painting, sculpture and installations which really tease the eye. The permanent work on the top floor is not so exciting, but does include some twentieth-century Gotlandic art.

Strolling aimlessly around the twisting streets and atmospheric walls is rewarding enough in itself, but if you need a focus, aim for **Norra Murgatan**, above the cathedral, once one of Visby's poorest areas. At the end nearest Norderport (North Gate) you'll be treated to the best view of the walls and city rooftops, along with a rare opportunity to climb onto the ramparts. **Kruttornet**, the dark, atmospheric tower back on Strandgatan (June–Aug daily 10am–6pm; free), affords grander views, while the roof of the **Helge And** church ruin (May–Sept daily 10am–6pm; free), which has been reinforced to allow access to the second floor, provides another central vantage point. Alternatively, head for **Studentallén**, the road along the water's edge, from where the sunsets are magnificent.

Eating, drinking and nightlife

Visby's centre is small enough to wander around and size up the eating options. Near Österport, **Wallersplats** and adjoining **Hästgatan** are both busy at lunchtime, while neighbouring **Adelsgatan** is lined with cafés and snack bars. For good, cheap food all day, try **Saluhallen**, the market opposite the harbour: here you can buy fresh baked bread, fish and fruit and eat it at tables overlooking the water. Visby's restaurants and bars see plenty of life during the day, but at night they positively heave with young bodies – many of them drunk. **Strandgatan** is the focus of the town's evening parade, while **Donnersplats**, midway along it, has lots of take-away food stalls. Alternatively, head down to the **harbour**, where forests of masts make a pretty backdrop to the loud, happy beat of music and revellers grooving away on the dance floors. Note that many of Visby's discos open in the late after-noon, from around 4pm onwards, for "After Beach" sessions where you can get rel-atively cheap beer.

Gotlanders also enjoy a unique licence from the state to brew their own **beer**, the recipe differing from household to household. It's never on sale, but summer parties are awash with the murky stuff – be warned, it is extremely strong. There are central off-licences in Storatorget and at Östervägen 3; the island's other *Systembolagets* are found at Hemse, Slite, Klintehamn, Färösunds and Burgsvik.

Daytime cafés

Björkstugan Speksgränd. In a fabulous, lush garden on Visby's prettiest central cobbled street, this little café serves tasty pies and coffee. Open till 10pm.

Gula Huset Tranhusgatan 2. Close to the Botanical Gardens and a favourite amongst locals: cosy and serving delightful home-baked port-wine cake and concoctions of almonds, chocolate and fruit in an unspoiled garden setting outside a vine-covered cottage.

Skafferiet Adelsgatan. A lovely eighteenth-century house turned into an appealing, characterful café boasting a lush garden at the back. Baked potatoes, great cakes and vast, generously filled baguettes which suffice for a full meal.

Vinäger Café Bar Hästgatan 3. Great place for giant muffins, terrific cakes and pies and a relaxed, mellow atmosphere, all in an anachronistically modern former pharmacy dating from 1896 (note that there's no sign outside). Its bakery, directly opposite, has fresh loaves from 6am, and the café opens till 9pm.

Restaurants and bars

Bakfickan Corner of St Katarinegatan and Storatorget. A quiet, relaxed little restaurant with a tiled interior that specializes in seafood – quite expensive, but some of the best food in town. Also good for a drink.

Burmeister Strandgatan 9. Busy place serving a full à la carte menu with starters around 80kr,

pasta 90kr and main courses at 160kr. Expect long queues.

Café Boheme Hästgatan 9. This mellow but lively candlelit place is a really good bet, serving inexpensive salads, sandwiches and pizzas and lots of cakes, including a rather good *kladdkaka* (gooey chocolate pie).

Clematis Medeltidskrogen Strandgatan 20. Set in the vaulted cellars of a thirteenth-century house, this is Visby's most brilliantly atmospheric and evocative restaurant by far, lit with candles only, with mead served in flagons and food in rough ceramic bowls and on wooden platters. Try the pear cake with lavender cream.

Friheten Donnersplats 6. A lively pub attached to the *Wisby Hotel*. Loud, live bands reverberate on Fri & Sat evenings.

Gutekällaren Lilla Torggränd. Fronting onto Storatorget, this is less frenetic than the other nearby restaurants, cleverly designed with striking primary-colour paintings to complement the vivid harlequin chairs. Excellent food, but quite costly, with mains from 140kr.

Munk Källeren Lilla Torggränd, opposite *Gutekällaren*. Massively fashionable, and subsequently crowded. There's an extensive à la carte menu, entirely in English.

Vinäger Hästgatan 3. Just opposite its sister-café (see above), with a garden, great lighting and comfortable low seating, this is a great place for pasta dishes or a drink. Summer only.

The rest of the island

There's a real charm to the rest of Gotland – rolling green countryside, forest-lined roads, fine beaches and small fishing villages, and everywhere the rural skyline is dominated by churches, the remnants of medieval settlements destroyed in the Danish invasion. Yet perhaps because of the magnetic pull of Visby, very few people bother to go and explore. The **south** of the island, in particular, boasts numerous wonderful and untouched villages and beaches; the **north**, though pretty, can be adequately seen on a day-trip from the capital.

Cycling around the island is immensely enjoyable, since the main roads are free of traffic and minor roads are positively deserted. Gotland's **buses**, though regular, are very few indeed. Outside Visby, they tend to run only twice daily – morning and evening. **Hitching**, however, is an accepted means of transport, and unless you have a specific destination in mind, it's often just as well to go wherever the driver is heading. As you go, keep an eye out for the waymarkers erected in the 1780s to indicate the distance to "Wisby" (the old spelling).

Southern Gotland

The so-called "capital" of the south, **HEMSE**, around 50km from Visby (buses ply the route), is little more than a main street, but there are a couple of banks and a good local café, *Bageri & Conditori Johansson*, on Storgatan – if you're camping or without your own transport, this is the place to stock up with food. You can rent **bikes** from Ondrell's, on Ronevägen, off Storgatan (40kr per day, 20kr each day after or 160kr per week). There's not a lot else to Hemse, except a summer-only **swimming pool** (signposted *simhall*; June–Aug Mon–Thurs 2–8pm, Fri 5–8pm; 45kr), off Storgatan at the north end of town. Hemse **bus station**, parallel with Storgatan (head down Ronevägen for one block and turn left), is oddly sited in a boarded-up and vandalized house.

Along Route 144 towards Burs, the countryside is a glorious mix of meadows, ancient farms and dark, mysterious forest. **BURS** itself, just off Route 144, has a gorgeous thirteenth-century saddle church, so-called because of its low nave and high tower and chancel. Inside there's a fabulously decorated ceiling, medieval stained-glass windows and ornately painted pews. Nearby, *Burs Café* is a friendly locals' joint serving cheap, filling meals. Heading east out of Burs, the scenery is a paradise of wild, flowering meadows and medieval farmholdings with ancient windows and carved wooden portals. The next place you come to is the tranquil and pretty hamlet of **NÄR**, notable for its church, set in an immaculate churchyard. The tower originally served as a defensive fortification in the thirteenth century, but more arresting are the bizarre portraits painted on the pew ends right the way up the left side of the church. All depict women with demented expressions and bare, oddly placed breasts. A couple of kilometres north, just beyond the village of **LAU**, *Garde* **youth hostel** (☎ & ☎0498/49 11 81; pre-booking necessary Nov–April) provides some of Sweden's strangest accommodation: the cluster of buildings is situated right by the local football pitch, and the bathroom facilities are shared with anyone doing football practice. There's a food shop around the corner from the hostel reception and a café-bar in the village.

For beaches, and the nearest thing Gotland has to a resort, the slow-paced and relaxing town of **LJUGARN**, on the coast north of När, makes a good base. The village manages to retain an authentic feel and is famous for its *rauker* – tall limestone pillars rising up from the sea. A delightful cycle or stroll down Strandvägen follows the coastline through woods and clearings carpeted in *blåeld*, the electric-blue flowers for which the area is known. This is one place where it's easy to find a range of eating places to suit most tastes, and accommodation, unlike most of the island, is not restricted to camping or hostels. "*Rums*" (**rooms**) are advertised in appealing-looking cottages all over town, and start at 125kr per person. As Ljugarn's tourist office has been closed down (a strange decision for a place that relies heavily on tourism), you'll need to knock on a few doors to check on vacancies. There's a **youth hostel** (☎0498/49 31 84) on Strandridaregården, as well as Gotland's oldest **B&B**, *Badpensionatet* (☎0498/49 32 05, ✆www.badpensionatet.se; ❷), which first opened its doors in 1921. All rooms are en-suite, there's an attractive outdoor pool with lots of sunbathing space, and a popular restaurant on site – the only one in town that's open all year. Some of the best cakes in Sweden are to be found in Ljugarn at *Café Espegards* on Storvägen, where there's almost always a queue in summer. Finally, *Brunna Dorren* is a pleasant old stuccoed house which is now home to a pizza restaurant, with a big garden where beer is served overlooking the sea.

Heading back west from Ljugarn, Route 144 passes through **LYE**, a charming if sleepy hamlet with an antique shop and café. **STÅNGA**, just a few kilometres on, is worth stopping at for its fourteenth-century church with its unusual wall tablets running down the facade. By the golf course outside is *Gumbalda Golf* (℡0498/48 28 80, ⊚www.golf.se/gumbaldegk; ❶), a stylish **place to stay** at a very reasonable price (breakfast is included); special golf packages are offered here, and the green fee for the eighteen-hole course is 220kr per day.

Stora and Lilla Karlsö

The two **islands** of Stora Karlsö and Lilla Karlsö, lying 6km off the southwest coast, have been declared **nature reserves**, and both have bird sanctuaries where razorbills, guillemots, falcons and eider duck breed relatively undisturbed. **Stora Karlsö** is a 45-minute ferry ride from Klintehamn; tickets are available from the harbour office (200kr return). From May to mid-September, there's one daily service at 10am, returning at 3.30pm; this also runs between late May and early August, when there's an additional service at 11.30am, returning at 5pm. Alternatively, you can take one of the tours which run from Visby (May–Aug daily, 250kr per person; ℡0498/24 05 00, ⊚www.storakarlso.com). The only accommodation on the island is in the tiny, very basic fishermen's huts that comprise the STF **youth hostel** (same number as for ferry bookings, above), a hut sleeping four costs 200–280kr. No camping is allowed on either island.

Lilla Karlsö is reached from Djupvik, 7km south of Klintehamn (no buses). Boat tickets (120kr return) are available from the harbour office, or book on ℡0498/48 52 48. It's possible to stay on the island in hostel-style dorms (℡0498/24 11 39), but you'll have to book all meals in advance.

Northern Gotland

Thirteen kilometres north of Visby are the **Lummelundagrottorna** (daily: late June to mid-Aug 9am–6pm; May to late June & mid- to late Aug daily 9am–4pm; late Aug to mid-Sept 10am–2pm; 45kr), limestone caves, stalagmites and stalactites that make for a disappointingly dull and damp stop. There's a more interesting natural phenomenon 10km to the north, where you'll see the highest of Gotland's **limestone stacks**, the remnants of reefs formed over four hundred million years ago (the fact that they're well above the tide line is taken as proof of earlier, higher sea levels). This stack, 11.5 metres high and known as **Jungfruklint**, is said to look like the Virgin and Child – something you'll need a fair bit of imagination to deduce.

Instead of taking the coastal road from Visby, you could head inland instead along Route 148 towards **BRO**, which has one of the island's most beautiful churches. Several different building stages are evident from the Romanesque and Gothic windows in the tower, but the most unusual aspect is the south wall with its flat-relief picture stones, carved mostly with animals, that were incorporated from a previous church on the site.

On the whole, though, it's far better to press on north, where many of the secluded cottages serve as summer holiday homes for urban Swedes. The peninsula north of **Lärbro** is no longer prohibited to foreign tourists now the army has left. At **BUNGE** it's worth visiting the bright fourteenth-century fortified church and open-air museum (mid-May to mid-Aug daily 10am–6pm; 30kr). **SLITE**, just to the south of Lärbro, is the island's only really ugly place – day-trip buses travel right past its cement factories, quarries and monumentally dull architecture. Beyond this, though, Slite has a sandy beach and good swimming. If you don't mind paying for your camping, then the campsite (℡0498/22 08 30; May–Sept) isn't a bad choice, right on the beach.

Fårö

The tourist office in Visby, has, for the present at least, ceased arranging special day-long bus trips to **Fårö** (Sheep Island), at the northern tip of Gotland, although it's possible to travel to it independently, taking a bus to the town of Fårösund and making the ten-minute ferry crossing (departures every 30min; free) from the quay ten minutes' walk to the south, on the main road. Fårösund has a down-at-heel but surprisingly good working-men's café, *Fårösund Grill*, which serves excellent sandwiches (25kr) and almond tart (10kr), with good, cheap coffee. Just opposite is *Bungehallen*, a very well-stocked supermarket (daily till 10pm).

Most of Fårö island itself is flat limestone heath, with shallow lakes and stunted pines much in evidence. In winter (and sometimes in summer, too) the wind whips off the Baltic, justifying the existence of the local windmills – and of the sheep shelters, with their steeply pitched reed roofs, modelled on traditional Fårö houses. Examples of both line the road as you leave the ferry. The best place to head for (and the target of most of the Swedish holiday-makers who visit) is the five-kilometre white sand arc at **Sundersandsviken**; much of the rest of the swimming is done at **Ekeviken**, on the other side of the isthmus. The remainder of the coastline is rocky, spectacularly so at **Lauterhorn** and, particularly, **Langhammars**, where limestone stacks are grouped together on the beach. At Lauterhorn you can follow the signs for Digerhuvud, a long line of stacks leading to the tiny fishing hamlet of **Helgumannen**, which has no more than a dozen shacks on the beach, now used as holiday homes. Continuing along the same rough track brings you to a junction; right runs back to the township of Fårö; left, a two-kilometre dead-end road leads to Langhammars.

Travel details

Trains

Hallsberg to: Gothenburg (hourly; 2hr 40min); Stockholm (hourly; 1hr 30min).

Jönköping to: Falköping, for Stockholm and Gothenburg (hourly; 45min); Nässjo, for Stockholm and Malmö (hourly; 35min).

Kalmar to: Emmaboda (16 daily; 35min); Gothenburg (5 daily; 4hr 15min); Malmö (8 daily; 3hr 40min); Stockholm (5 daily; 6hr 30min); Växjo (10 daily; 1hr 45min).

Motala to: Hallsberg, for Örebro, Stockholm and Gothenburg (6 daily; 45min); Mjölby, for Malmö and Stockholm (2 daily; 1hr 15min).

Norrköping to: Linköping (1–2 hourly; 25min); Malmö (11 daily; 3hr 15min); Nyköping (5 daily; 40min); Stockholm (hourly; 1hr 40min).

Örebro to: Gävle (6 daily; 3–4hr); Hallsberg, for Stockholm and Gothenburg (1–2 hourly; 20min); Motala (6 daily; 1hr 30min); Stockholm (7 daily; 3hr 10min).

Oskarshamn to: Gothenburg (3 daily; 5hr 30min); Nässjo (3 daily; 2hr 25min); Jönköping (3 daily; 3hr 20min).

Växjö to: Gothenburg (8 daily; 3hr 20min); Kalmar (6 daily; 1hr 40min); Karlskrona (2 daily; 1hr 30min).

Buses

Jönköping to: Gothenburg (Mon–Fri 2–3 daily; 2hr 15min); Gränna (up to 3 daily; 30min); Växjö (Mon–Fri 2 daily, Sat & Sun 1 daily; 1hr 55min).

Kalmar to: Gothenburg (1 daily; 6hr); Lund/Malmö (1 daily; 5hr 30min/5hr 45min); Oskarshamn/Västervik/Stockholm (3 daily; 1hr 25min/2hr 35min/6hr 50min).

Motala to: Norrköping/Stockholm (Fri & Sun 2 daily; 1hr 35min/3hr 25min).

Norrköping to: Linköping/Jönköping/Gothenburg (6 daily; 30min/2hr 40min/4hr 55min); Kalmar (5 daily; 4hr 15min); Stockholm (5 daily; 2hr 10min).

Växjö to: Jönköping/Linköping/Norrköping/Stockholm/Uppsala (Fri & Sun 1 daily; 1hr 20min/3hr 30min/4hr/6hr 30min/7hr 30min).

Ferries

Nynäshamn to: Visby (mid-June to mid-Aug 3 daily; 5hr day, 6hr night; rest of the year night sailings only; 5–6hr).

Oskarshamn to: Visby (mid-June to mid-Aug 1 daily plus one night sailing; rest of the year night sailings only; 4hr day, 6hr night).

Fast ferries

Nynäshamn to: Visby (June–Aug 5 daily; 3hr; rest of year 1 daily; 3hr).

Oskarshamn to: Visby (June–Aug 5 daily; 2hr 30min).

3.5

The Bothnian Coast: Gävle to Haparanda

F acing Finland across the waters of the Gulf of Bothnia, Sweden's **east coast** forms a corridor of land that, with its jumble of erstwhile fishing towns and squeaky-clean modern cities, is quite unlike the rest of the north. The coast is dominated by towns and cities, the endless forest so characteristic of other parts of northern Sweden having been felled here to make room for the settlements that dot almost the entire coastline. Some, like **Gävle** and **Hudiksvall**, still have their share of old wooden houses, offering evocative images of the past, though much was lost during the Russian incursions of the eighteenth century. Others, like **Sundsvall**, **Umeå** and **Luleå**, are more typical – modern, bright and airy, they rank as some of Sweden's liveliest and most likeable northern destinations. Throughout the north you'll also find traces of the religious fervour that swept the region in centuries past: **Skellefteå** and, particularly, **Luleå** boast excellently preserved *kyrkstäder*, or parish villages, clusters of gnarled old wooden cottages dating from the 1700s, where villagers from outlying districts would spend the night after making the lengthy journey to church in the nearest town.

The highlight of the Bothnian Coast, however, is undoubtedly **Höga Kusten**, or the High Coast, between Härnösand and Örnsköldsvik – an indented stretch of shimmering fjords, tall cliffs and a string of pine-clad islands on which it's possible to island-hop up the coast. The weather may not be as reliable as further south but you're guaranteed clean beaches – often all to yourself – crystal-clear waters and some fine walking.

Getting around

The **train** line hugs the coast until Härnösand, where SJ services terminate. From here, **buses** run inland to Långsele to meet Tågkompaniet trains running on the main line north to Swedish Lapland and on to the Norwegian port of Narvik. There are regular trains between Stockholm and Sundsvall, stopping at Gävle and Hudiksvall; from Sundsvall a handful of trains continue on to Härnösand. There's also a handy train connection to Sundsvall from the inland town of Östersund. Beyond Härnösand things get trickier, and it's easier to continue by regular **Norrlandskusten bus** from Härnösand up the High Coast to Örnsköldsvik and further to Umeå, Skellefteå and Luleå. Train connections are available in Umeå, Boden or Luleå. Island-hopping by **ferry** along the High Coast is a wonderful way to make your way north and to take in one of northern Sweden's most beautiful regions.

Over recent years the number of ferry services between the Bothnian coast and **Finland** has shrunk dramatically. The only remaining ferries operate all year between Umeå (4hr) and Härnösand (8hr) across to Vaasa.

NORWAY

Kvikkjokk

Jokkmokk

Adolfström

FINLAND

Ammarnäs

Arjeplog

Tarnaby

Kukkolaforsen

Boden

Haparanda   Tornio

Älsvbyn

Gammelstad   Luleå

Arvidsjaur

NORRBOTTEN

Piteå

Storuman

95

Bastuträsk

Skellefteå

Lycksele

Burträsk

365

E72

VÄSTERBOTTEN

of

Bothnia

Vännäs

Åsele

Umeå

ÅNGERMANLAND

Mellansel

E4

90

Långsele

335

Örnsköldsvik

Sollefteå

Ångerman River

Vaasa

Kramfors

Höga Kusten
(High Coast)

E14

MEDELPAD

Härnösand

Gulf

Sundsvall

HÄLSINGLAND

Hudiksvall

84

FINLAND

301

Bollnäs

E4

Söderhamn

Gävle

Furuvik

30

Åland Islands

N

GÄSTRIKLAND

68

Uppsala

0   100 km

▼ Stockholm & Arlanda airport

Gävle and around

It's only a two-hour train ride north from Stockholm to **GÄVLE** (pronounced "Yev-luh"), capital of the district of Gästrikland and the southernmost city in Norrland, the region that makes up two-thirds of Sweden and covers more or less everything north of Uppsala. Gävle is an old city – its town charter was granted in 1446 – although this is hardly obvious from the modern, sophisticated centre, with its large squares, broad avenues and proud monumental buildings. Almost completely rebuilt after a devastating fire in 1869, the spacious layout of present-day Gävle reflects its industrial success in the late nineteenth century, when it was the export centre for locally produced iron and timber. Today the city is more famous as the home of Gevalia coffee, which you're certain to taste during your time in Sweden.

Arrival, accommodation and information

The city centre is concentrated in the grid of streets that spreads southwest from the **train station** on Stora Esplanadgatan. You'll find left-luggage lockers (15kr) on the main platform. The **bus station**, for both local and long-distance services, is on the east side of the train station – use the subway that runs under the train tracks. A new **resecentrum** (travel centre) is expected to open by 2003 on the site of the current bus and train stations, and will handle arrivals and departures for all services. The **tourist office** is a two-minute walk from the train station at Drottninggatan 37 (June–Aug Mon–Fri 9am–6pm, Sat 9am–2pm, Sun 11am–4pm; Sept–May Mon–Fri 9am–5pm; ☏026/14 74 30, ⓦwww.gavle.se). Staff can book private **apartments** from 400kr per person per night. **Internet** access is available for free from the library near the corner of Södra Strandgatan and Rådmansbron (Mon–Thurs 10am–8pm, Fri 10am–6pm, Sat & Sun 10am–3pm).

Gävle has two **youth hostels**: one is superbly located in the old quarter at Södra Rådmansgatan 1 (☏026/62 17 45, ⓕ61 59 90); the other is on the coast at Bönävägen 118 in Engeltofta, 6km northeast of the city on bus #5 from Rådhuset (☏026/961 60, ⓕ960 55; June–Aug; 140kr). The nearest **campsite** is at Furuvik Amusement Park, a twelve-kilometre ride southeast on bus #821 or #838.

Aveny Södra Kungsgatan 31 ☏026/61 55 90, ⓦwww.aveny.nu. Small and comfortable family-run hotel south of the river. ❸/❷
Boulogne Byggmästargatan 1 ☏ 026/12 63 52, ⓦwww.hotellboulogne.com. Close to Boulognerskogen park, this is a cosy, basic hotel with the feeling of staying in a private home – breakfast is presented on a tray in the room. ❷
Nya Järnvägshotellet Centralplan 3 ☏026/12 09 90, ⓕ10 62 42. The cheapest hotel in Gävle, located on a busy corner close to the station.

Toilets and showers are in the corridor from the rooms. ❷/❶
Scandic Hotel Grand Central Nygatan 45 ☏026/495 8400, ⓦwww.scandic-hotels.com. One of the smartest hotels in town, with old-fashioned en-suite rooms. ❻/❸
Winn Norra Slottsgatan 9 ☏026/64 70 00, ⓦwww.softwarehotels.se/winngavle. Another smart hotel with its own pool, sauna and sunbeds. Rooms are tasteful if styleless, with neutral colours and wooden floors. ❺/❸

The City

Central Gävle is easy to navigate, with the broad, straight streets of the modern city bisected by a stretch of park that runs roughly north–south. To the south, cut off by the river, lies Gamla Gefle, the only part of the city that survived the fire of 1869, and the first place to head for.

Gamla Gefle

The part of the city known as **Gamla Gefle** passes itself off today as the old town, though unfortunately there's not much left of it. If you stay in the youth hostel you'll be right on the edge of the few remaining narrow cobbled streets – notably Övre Bergsgatan, Bergsgränd and Nedre Bergsgränd – with their pastel-coloured

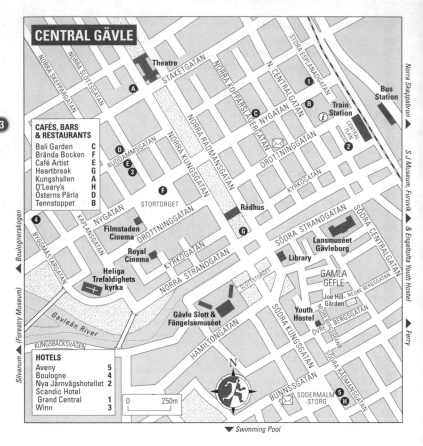

CENTRAL GÄVLE

CAFÉS, BARS & RESTAURANTS

Bali Garden	C
Brända Bocken	F
Café Artist	E
Heartbreak	G
Kungshallen	A
O'Leary's	H
Österns Pärla	D
Tennstoppet	B

HOTELS

Aveny	5
Boulogne	4
Nya Järnvägshotellet	2
Scandic Hotel Grand Central	1
Winn	3

0   250m

▼ *Swimming Pool*

wooden cottages complete with window boxes bursting with summer flowers. For a glimpse of social conditions a century ago, visit the **Joe Hill–Gården** (June–Aug daily 11am–3pm; free; other times by arrangement on ☏026/61 34 25) at Nedre Bergsgatan 28. Joe Hill, born in the house as Johan Emanuel Hägglund in 1879, emigrated to the United States in 1902, where with a new name he went on to become a working-class hero whose songs and speeches served as rallying cries to comrades everywhere. Framed for murder in Salt Lake City, he was executed in 1915. The syndicalist organization to which he belonged runs the museum, a collection of standard memorabilia – pictures and belongings – given piquancy by the telegram announcing his execution.

On the other side of Gamla Gefle, on the canalside at Södra Strandgatan 20, is the county museum, **Länsmuséet Gävleborg** (Tues–Sun noon–4pm, Wed until 9pm; (ⓦ www.lansmuseetgavleborg.se; 30kr). Its extensive displays of artworks by most of the great Swedish artists from the 1600s to the present day, including Nils Kreuger and Carl Larsson, make this a rarity among provincial museums, and attract visitors from across the country. Also on show are displays on the area's ironworks and fisheries, as well as work by local artist Johan-Erik Olsson (popularly known as Lim-Johan), whose vivid imagination and naive technique produced some strangely childlike paintings.

The rest of the city

The modern city lies over the Gavleån River, its broad streets and tree-lined avenues designed to prevent fires from spreading. A central boulevard of parks, trees and fountains runs from the sculpture-spiked **Rådhus** up to the beautiful nineteenth-century **theatre**, neatly dividing the city into two, while the roomy **Stortorget** has the usual all-day open-air market (Mon–Sat), selling good-quality fruit and veg.

Gävle's other main sights – none of them major – are out of the centre but close enough to reach on foot. Back at the river by the main double bridge, **Gävle Slott**, the seventeenth-century residence of the county governor, lost its ramparts and towers years ago and now lurks behind a row of trees like some minor country house. You can't go inside, although you can arrange a visit to the **Fängelsemuséet** (Prison Museum) on the premises by contacting the tourist office. From Gävle Slott a short walk along the river leads to a wooden bridge, across which is Kaplansgatan and the **Heliga Trefaldighets kyrka**, the Church of the Holy Trinity, a seventeenth-century masterpiece of wood-carved decoration. Check out the pulpit, towering altarpiece and screen – each the superb work of a German craftsman, Ewardt Friis. Cross back over the river and take a stroll down **Kungsbäcksvägen**, a narrow street lined with old wooden houses painted yellow, green and orange, with tulips and wild roses growing outside their front doors. Continue and you'll come to the rambling **Boulognerskogen**, which opened in the mid-nineteenth century and still provides an oasis of trees, water and flowers just outside the city centre – a good place for a picnic and a spot of sunbathing.

On a rainy day you may find yourself contemplating the **Sveriges Järnvägsmuséet** (National Railway Museum) at Rälsgatan 1 (June–Aug daily 10am–4pm; Sept–May Tues–Sun 10am–4pm; ⓦmessage.sj.se/museum; 40kr), a fifteen-minute walk south from the station following the train tracks. Now housed in an old engine shed, the fifty or so locomotives, some of them over 100 years old, are of limited appeal to non-enthusiasts. If you walk here from the train station along Muréngatan, you'll pass the old dockside **warehouses** off Norra Skeppsbron, a reminder of the days when ships unloaded coffee and spices in the centre of Gävle. Today, strolling past the red wooden fronts with fading company names, it feels as though you're wandering around an old Hollywood movie set rather than the backstreets of a northern Swedish city.

Eating, drinking and entertainment

There's a fair choice of **eating places** in Gävle, but for the best options stick to the central grid of streets around Stortorget and spots up and down the central esplanade between the Rådhus and the theatre. Nearly all cafés and restaurants double up as bars, and some also mutate into nightclubs, too.

Bali Garden Corner of Nygatan and Norra Kopparslagergatan. Good Indonesian food with dishes from 85kr.

Brända Bocken Stortorget. Young and fashionable eatery, with outdoor seating in summer. Lunch for 63kr, and beef and pork dishes, hamburgers and salmon from around 80kr. Also a popular place for a drink.

Café Artist Norra Slottsgatan 9. Trendy hangout offering fish and meat dishes for around 150kr, as well as inexpensive snacks; in the evenings this is a relaxed place for a beer or two whilst lounging on cosy sofas.

Heartbreak Norra Strandgatan 15. Pub, bistro-style bar and nightclub – worth checking out.

Kungshallen Norra Kungsgatan 17, next to the theatre. Mammoth-sized pizzas for 40–56kr and cheap beer.

O'Leary's Södra Kungsgatan 31. A good 20min walk south from the centre (close to the youth hostel), but still incredibly busy. Catering for a young crowd, this is *the* place to do your boozing and boogying. Closed Mon.

Österns Pärla Ruddammsgatan 23. Fairly standard Chinese restaurant, serving all the usual favourites for 80–90kr.

Tennstoppet Nygatan 38. Cheap and cheerful grill close to the station, with Swedish specialities such as *Jansons frestelse* for 79kr.

Listings

Bank FöreningsSparbanken and Handelsbanken on Nygatan, and Nordea at Norra Kungsgatan 3–5 all have cash machines.

Bus enquiries Local buses are operated by XTrafik ☎020/91 01 09; long-distance buses to Bollnäs, Uppsala and Stockholm are operated by Swebus ☎0200/218 218.

Car rental Europcar Södra Kungsgatan 62 ☎020/78 11 80; Hertz Kryddstegen 19 ☎026/51 18 19; Statoil Krickvägen 4 ☎020/25 25 25.

Pharmacy Drottninggatan 12 ☎020/66 77 66 (Mon–Fri 9am–6pm, Sat 9.30am–3pm, Sun 11am–3pm).

Police Södra Centralgatan 1 ☎026/65 50 00.

Systembolaget Södra Kungsgatan 7, near Gävle Slott, and at Nygatan 13 (both Mon–Wed 10am–6pm, Thurs & Fri 10am–7pm, Sat 10am–2pm).

Taxis Gävle Taxi ☎026/12 90 00.

Around Gävle

If the sun's shining, you'll find locals catching the rays at the nearby beaches of **ENGELTOFTA** (near the youth hostel) or **ENGESBERG**; take bus #5 from the Rådhus. From here the bus continues to **BÖNAN**, where there's more good swimming to be had and an old lighthouse that holds a small museum. There are other enjoyable beaches on the island of **Limön**, which is also a pleasant place for some gentle walks, with paths criss-crossing the island. It can be reached via a summer ferry, *MS Drottning Silvia* (⊛www.swed.net/drottning-silvia; three daily; 30kr), which departs from Norra Skeppsbron – head east along the banks of the Gavleån from behind the train and bus stations, with one departure making a stop in Engeltofta on the way.

In the other direction is the **Furuvik Amusement Park** (daily: mid-May to mid-June & mid-Aug to early Sept noon–4pm; mid-June to mid-Aug noon–6pm; ⊛www.furuvik.se; day-pass for 130kr), featuring a zoo, fairground, parks and playgrounds. Buses #821 and #838 run here roughly every half hour from the bus station.

Hudiksvall

On the first leg of the coastal journey further into Norrland, the railway sticks close to the sea, passing through uneventful Söderhamn en route for **HUDIKSVALL**, which, if you're in no great rush, is worth a leisurely stop for its distinctive wood-panel architecture. One of the oldest settlements in Norrland, the town was originally founded in 1582 around the Lillfjärden bay at the mouth of the River Hornån. At the beginning of the seventeenth century the harbour silted up and Hudiksvall was forced to move to its present location. An important commercial and shipping centre, it bore the brunt of the Russian attacks on the northeast Swedish coast in 1721 and to this day its church is pockmarked with cannon holes; every other building was razed to the ground.

The oldest part of the city is split into two main sections. Turn right out of the train station and cross the narrow canal, Strömmingssundet (Herring Sound), and you'll soon see the small old **harbour** on the right. This area is known as **Möljen**, and is a popular place for locals to while away a couple of hours in the summer sunshine along the wharfside flanked by a line of red wooden fishermen's cottages and storehouses. The backs of the warehouses hide a run of bike and boat repair shops, handicraft studios and the like. More impressive and much larger than Möljen, **Fiskarstan** (Fishermen's Town), down Storgatan beyond the *First Hotel Statt*, contains neat examples of the so-called "Imperial" wood-panel architecture of the late eighteenth and nineteenth centuries. It was in these tightly knit blocks of streets with their fenced-in plots of land that the fishermen used to live during the winter. Take a peek inside some of the little courtyards – all window boxes and cobblestones. The history of these buildings is put into perspective in the excellent

Hälsinglands Museum (late June to mid-Aug Mon & Fri 9am–4pm, Wed & Thurs 9am–7pm, Sat 11am–3pm; rest of the year Mon & Thurs noon–4pm, Wed 9am–7pm, Sat 11am–3pm; ⓦwww.halsinglandsmuseum.se; 20kr), Storgatan 31, which traces the development of Hudiksvall as a harbour town. Have a look at the paintings by **John Sten** on the ground floor: born near Hudiksvall, his work veered strangely from Cubism to a more decorative and fanciful style.

The best time to visit Hudiksvall is the second week in July, when the town hosts the **Musik vid Dellen**, a multifarious cultural festival including folk music and other traditional events; information and tickets from the tourist office.

Practicalities

Conveniently, Hudiksvall's **train** and **bus stations** are adjacent to each other on Stationsgatan, and it's just two minutes' walk along Stationsgatan to the town centre. The **tourist office** (mid-June to mid-Aug Mon–Fri 9am–7pm, Sat & Sun 10am–5pm; mid-Aug to mid-June Mon–Fri 9am–4pm; ☎0650/191 00, ⓦwww.hudiksvall.se) is near the wharf off Hamngatan, behind the old warehouses. For **Net** access, head for the library opposite the *First Hotel Statt* or the Hälsinglands Museum. As for **accommodation**, the *First Hotel Statt* at Storgatan 36 (☎0650/150 60, ⓦwww.firsthotels.com; ❺/❸) is the priciest in town, though good value in summer, or there's the cheaper *Hotell Temperance* near the station at Håstagatan 16 (☎0650/311 07, ⓦhome.swipnet.se/~w-77808; ❸/❷), which also has bunks in a dorm for 150kr per person. The nearest **youth hostel** (☎0650/132 60; ⓦwww.malnbadenscamping.com) is located out at the Malnbaden **campsite**, 3km from town – bus #5 runs there hourly (10am–6pm) in summer; otherwise you'll need to take a taxi from the bus station (100kr each way). Sited on the bay, it has a large sandy beach and offers bike rental.

For a town of this size, Hudiksvall has unusually few **eating and drinking** places. The one and only **bar** in town is the *Pub Tre Bockar* at Bankgränd, opposite the fishermen's warehouses at Möljen, while for food, try the popular *Bruns* at Brunnsgatan 2, with good Swedish home-cooked meals at around 85kr. Alternatively, try the Chinese restaurant, *Ming*, at Bankgränd 1 near the station, which has dishes for around 80kr.

Sundsvall

The capital of the tiny province of Medelpad, **SUNDSVALL**, known as "Stone City", is immediately and obviously different. Once home to a rapidly expanding nineteenth-century sawmill industry, the whole city burned to the ground in June 1888, and nine thousand people lost their homes. Rebuilding began at once, and within ten years a new centre constructed entirely of stone had emerged. The result is a living document of early twentieth-century urban architecture, based around wide esplanades intended to serve as fire breaks and designed and crafted by the same architects who were involved in rebuilding Stockholm's residential areas at the same time. However, the reconstruction was achieved at a price: the workers who had laboured on the new stone buildings were shifted from their homes in the centre and moved south to a poorly serviced suburb, highlighting the glaring difference between the wealth of the new centre and the poverty of the surrounding districts.

Arrival and information

From the **train station** it's a five-minute walk to the city centre: turn left as you come out of the station, walk through the car park then take the underpass beneath Parkgatan. The helpful **tourist office** (Mon–Fri 10am–6pm, Sat 10am–2pm; ☎060/61 04 50, ⓦwww.sundsvallturism.com) is in the main square, Storatorget. The **bus station** is at the bottom of Esplanaden, though if you want information or advance tickets for the express buses south to Stockholm, north to Örnsköldsvik and Umeå or inland to Östersund, visit Y-Bussen at Sjögatan 7 (☎060/17 19 60). For other bus information, including the express bus to Västerås and Gothenburg, contact the tourist office.

Accommodation

There's no shortage of reasonably priced **hotels** in Sundsvall. For budget accommodation, try the recently refurbished **youth hostel** (☎060/61 21 19, ⓦwww.sundsvall.norraberget.se) a thirty-minute walk north of town at Norra Berget, the hill overlooking the city. The nearest **campsite**, *Fläsians Camping* (☎060/55 44 75; mid-May to Aug), also has cabins, which cost 200–400kr per cabin for up to four people; it's 4km outside town – ask at the tourist office for directions.

Baltic Sjögatan 5 ☎060/14 04 40, ⓦwww.baltichotell.com. Centrally located near the Kulturmagasinet and the harbour, with perfectly adequate rooms. ❸

Continental Rådhusgatan 13 ☎060/15 00 60, ⓕ15 75 90. Centrally located and fairly cheap hotel; all rooms are en suite. Sun terrace and cable TV in all rooms. ❸

Grand Nybrogatan 13 ☎060/64 65 60, ⓦwww.grandhotelsundsvall.se. Not a bad choice if you get the summer or weekend reduction, and there's an excellent sauna and Jacuzzi suite in the basement. ❹

Ibis Hotel Sundsvall Trädgårdsgatan 31–33 ☎060/64 17 50, ⓦwww.ibishotel.com. Excellent value for such a central location, though breakfast is an extra 50kr. All rooms are en suite and some have a bath. ❷

Lilla Rådhusgatan 15 ☎060/61 35 87, ⓦhome.swipnet.se/lilla-hotellet. One of the most reasonably priced hotels in town, with just eight rooms, all en suite and with cable TV. ❷

Scandic Hotel Sundsvall City Esplanaden 29 ☎060/785 6200, ⓦwww.scandic-hotels.com. Chain hotel boasting eight cinemas, saunas, sunbeds and a golf simulator, with prices to match the opulence. ❻

Svea Rådhusgatan 11 ☎060/61 16 05. The cheapest hotel in Sundsvall, but its ten rooms soon fill up in summer. ❷

The City

The sheer scale of the rebuilding that followed the fire of 1888 is clear as you walk into town from the train station. The style is simple, uncluttered limestone and brick, the dimensions often overwhelming, with palatial four- and five-storey buildings serving as offices as well as homes. As you stroll the streets you can't help but be amazed by the tremendous amount of space right in the heart of Sundsvall – it's hard to believe that this is the most densely populated city in northern Sweden.

Several of the buildings in the centre are worth a second look, not least the sturdy bourgeois exterior of the **Sundsvall Museum** (Mon–Thurs 10am–7pm, Fri 10am–6pm, Sat & Sun 11am–4pm; June–Aug 20kr, Sept–May free), housed within four nineteenth-century warehouses down by the harbour. The buildings stood empty for twenty years before being turned into what's now the **Kulturmagasinet** ("Culture Warehouse"), comprising the museum, a library and a café. The old street of Magasinsgatan once ran between the warehouses, a reminder of the days when coffee and rice were transported via train to the harbour for export (the railway tracks and the street are long-gone). Inside, the regional museum is worth a quick look, as is the nearby art exhibition. Towards the other end of town, follow the main pedestrian street of Storgatan to its far end, where **Gustav Adolfs kyrka** (daily: June–Aug 11am–4pm; Sept–May 11am–2pm) marks one end of the new town; a soaring red-brick structure, its interior resembles a large Lego set.

Beyond the city's design, the most attractive diversion is the tiring three-kilometre climb to the heights of **Gaffelbyn** on Norra Berget, the hill that overlooks the city to the north; walk up Storgatan, cross over the main bridge and follow the sign to the youth hostel. If you'd prefer to spare your legs, buses for Norra Berget will take you there. The view on a clear day is fantastic, giving a fresh perspective on the

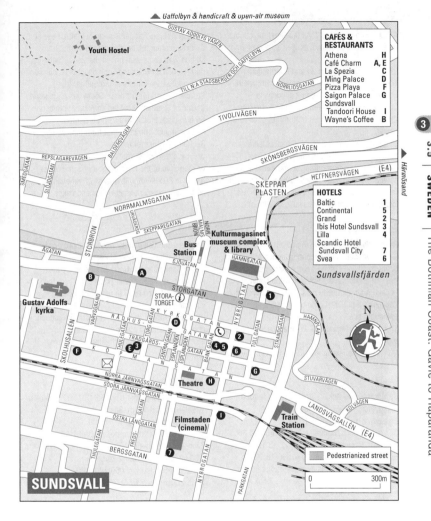

CAFÉS & RESTAURANTS

Athena	H
Café Charm	A, E
La Spezia	C
Ming Palace	D
Pizza Playa	F
Saigon Palace	G
Sundsvall	
Tandoori House	I
Wayne's Coffee	B

HOTELS

Baltic	1
Continental	5
Grand	2
Ibis Hotel Sundsvall	3
Lilla	4
Scandic Hotel	
Sundsvall City	7
Svea	6

SUNDSVALL

city's planned structure and the restrictive nature of its location, hemmed in on three sides by hills and the sea. From here you can see straight across to Södra Berget, the southern hill, with its winter ski slopes. Also here is the **Norra Bergets Hantverksmuseum** (June–Aug Mon–Fri 9am–4pm, Sat & Sun 11am–4pm; Sept–May Mon–Fri 9am–4pm; free), an open-air handicrafts museum with the usual selection of twee wooden huts and assorted activities, though you can try your hand at baking some *tunnbröd*, the thin bread that's typical of northern Sweden.

Eating, drinking and entertainment

Over the last couple of years, **restaurants** have mushroomed in Sundsvall, and there's now a good choice – something you may want to make the most of if you're heading further north. The town's **bars** generally have a good atmosphere, though nightclubs are rather thin on the ground.

Cafés and restaurants

Athena Köpmangatan 7. All the Greek favourites from tzatziki to souvlakia, as well as pizzas, from 100kr.

Café Charm Storgatan 34 and Köpmangatan 34. Good choices for coffee and cakes, with free refills and naughty-but-nice cream concoctions.

Ming Palace Esplanaden 10. A good choice for Chinese, with dishes from 80kr to eat in or take away.

La Spezia Sjögatan 6. Perfectly acceptable bargain-basement pizzas from 35kr.

Pizza Playa Köpmangatan 29. You name it, they have it: pasta, pizzas, salads, kebabs and Chinese food all at reasonable prices; popular amongst locals, though one of Sundsvall's smaller places.

Saigon Palace Trädgårdsgatan 5. Vietnamese and Chinese restaurant, handily placed for the train station with some well-priced dishes, including a buffet lunch for 65kr and such delights as chicken in peanut sauce for dinner (around 80kr).

Sundsvall Tandoori House Södra Järnvägsgatan 9. One of Sweden's best Indian restaurants serving up first-class Indian meals in a basement restaurant just 10min on foot from the centre. Reckon on 145kr for mains.

Wayne's Coffee Storgatan 33. Located at the western end of the main drag, this is *the* coffee house in Sundsvall, with dozens of varieties of coffee and excellent sandwiches and cakes.

Bars and nightlife

Dublin Nybrogatan 16. Irish pub with Irish food and music, darts and a broad selection of different beers, including Caffrey's and Kilkenny's.

Harry's Storgatan 33. Another in the chain of popular American-style bars sweeping Sweden. This one's a pub, restaurant and nightclub all rolled into one.

JOP's Trädgårdsgatan 35. Popular place for a mid-evening tipple.

Mercat Cross Esplanaden 29, in the Filmstaden

complex. Scottish pub serving just about every variety of whisky you can think of.

O'Bar Bankgatan 11. Good, lively bar. Try the excellent cocktails, if your pocket can take the strain – staff are happy to make any concoction you can think of.

O'Leary's Storgatan 40. Sports pub with a good choice of beer, and pub grub with a Tex-Mex flavour. Big screens show football and hockey matches.

Listings

Banks Handelsbanken, Storgatan 23; Nordea, Kyrkogatan 15; SEB, Storgatan 19.

Bus enquiries ☎020/51 15 13.

Car rental Hertz, Bultgatan 1 ☎060/66 90 80; Europcar, Trafikgatan 42 ☎060/12 33 10.

Hospital Lasarettsvägen 19 ☎060/18 10 00.

Internet Free access is available at the library, which is inside the Kulturmagasinet; book a terminal on ☎060/19 18 27.

Pharmacy Storgatan 18 ☎060/18 11 17 (Mon–Fri 10am–6pm, Sat 10am–3pm).

Police Storgatan 37 ☎060/18 00 00.

Systembolaget Storatorget ☎060/61 36 69 (Mon–Wed 10am–6pm, Thurs 10am–7pm, Fri 9.30am–6pm, Sat 10am–2pm).

Taxis Taxi Sundsvall ☎060/19 90 00.

Train enquiries ☎0771/75 75 75.

Härnösand

From Sundsvall it's an hour's train trip north along the coast to **HÄRNÖSAND**, a pleasant little place at the mouth of the River Ångerman. Founded in 1585, the town has had its fair share of disasters – two great fires in 1710 and 1714, followed by a thorough ransacking by invading Russians in 1721 – yet despite this it preserves a host of architectural delights, and is definitely worth a stop on the way north. Härnösand also marks the beginning of the stunningly beautiful province of **Ångermanland**, one of the few areas in Sweden where the countryside resembles that of neighbouring Norway, with its low mountains, craggy coastlines and long fjords reaching far inland. The town is a good base from which to explore the nearby High Coast (see p.608), or from which to head inland to connect with the main train line north at Långsele.

The Town and around

For such a small and provincial place, the proud civic buildings of Härnösand reck of grandeur and self-importance. The town centre is on the island of **Härnön**, and its main square, **Stora Torget**, was once chosen by local worthies as the most beautiful in Sweden. Its western edge is proudly given over to the governor's residence, built in Neoclassical style using local brick by the court architect, Olof Tempelman; this rubs shoulders with the Renaissance former provincial government building on the southwestern edge. From the square's southern edge, take a stroll up Västra Kyrkogatan to the Neoclassical **Domkyrkan** (daily 10am–4pm), which dates from the 1840s, though it incorporates bits and pieces from earlier churches which stood on the site (the Baroque altar is eighteenth-century, as are the VIP boxes in the nave). Trivia lovers will be delighted to learn that this is the smallest cathedral in Sweden, and also the only one which is painted white.

Turn right from here and follow the road round and back down the hill until you come to the narrow old street of **Östanbäcksgatan**, where the painted wooden houses date back to the 1700s. For a taste of the town's architectural splendour, take a walk up the main street, **Nybrogatan**, where the grand building with the yellow ochre facade that houses the Länsstyrelsen (Provincial Administration) at the corner with Brunnhusgatan is particularly beautiful. From the top of the hill here some good views can be had back over the town and the water.

Whilst in town it's worth retracing your steps back down Nybrogatan to the railway station, from where Stationsgatan (later becoming Varvsallén) turns right, passing through the docks and past the terminal for the ferry to Vaasa in Finland on its way to the impressive **open-air museum** at **Murberget** (June–Aug daily 11am–5pm; free), the second biggest in Sweden after Skansen. It's a thirty-minute walk up here from the town centre, or, alternatively, reachable via bus #2, which runs hourly from Nybrogatan in front of the Rådhuset. Around eighty buildings have been transplanted to the site, including traditional Ångermanland farmhouses and the old Murberget church, which is popular for local weddings. The worthy exhibits in the nearby **County Museum** (*Länsmuséet*; daily 11am–5pm; www.ylm.se; free) demonstrate how people settled the area two thousand years ago, alongside desperately dull displays of accordions, silver goblets and wheels from more modern times, and a collection of armoury.

Practicalities

The **tourist office** (June–Aug Mon–Fri 9am–6pm, Sat & Sun 10am–2pm; Sept–May Mon–Fri 9am–4.30pm; ☎0611/881 40, www.turism.harnosand.se) is near the train station at Järnvägsgatan 2, inside the building marked Spiran; the helpful staff can advise on transport and accommodation in the area. Härnösand's **youth hostel** (☎0611/104 46; mid-June to early Aug; ❶), where the only available accommodation are self-contained apartments (no dorms), is a fifteen-minute walk from the centre up Nybrogatan and then left into Kastellgatan. The nearby **Sälstens Camping** (☎0611/181 50) is around 2km from the centre, next to a string of pebble beaches; it also has a small selection of four-bed cabins for 300kr per night per person and rents out bikes to guests. Of the town's three **hotels**, *Hotell Royal*, close to the train station at Strandgatan 12 (☎0611/204 55; ❸/❷), is the cheapest, although *Hotell City* at Storgatan 28 (☎0611/277 00, www.kajutan .com; ❸/❷) is only marginally more expensive when discounted. The *First Hotel Stadt*, Skeppsbron 9 (☎0611/55 44 40, www.firsthotels.com; ❻/❸), is much bigger and a lot plusher, but can be worth it in summer, when a double costs only 200–300kr more than in the other two hotels.

The town's most popular **pub-restaurant** is *Kajutan* on pedestrianized Storgatan, which links Stora Torget and Nybrogatan: meaty main courses cost around 145kr, pasta dishes around 90kr. If you feel like splashing out on some northern Swedish delicacies, *Restaurang Apothequet*, located in an old pharmacy at

Nybrogatan 3, is the place, though count on 200–300kr for dinner. Other eateries include *Östanbäckans Pizzeria* at Östanbäckansgatan 1 for good-value, filling pizzas; the Greek favourite, *Mykonos*, at Storgatan 20, with moussaka for 95kr; and the neighbouring *Rutiga Dukan* café, near the cathedral at Västra Kyrkogatan 1, which does reasonably-priced lunches and delicious home-baked pastries and pies. For **drinking**, try the popular Scottish-theme pub *Highlander*, at Nybrogatan 5 (Tues–Sat evenings only).

North to the Höga Kusten

Between Härnösand and Örnsköldsvik (see p.609) lies the **Höga Kusten** or **High Coast** (ⓦ www.visitmidsweden.com), the beautiful stretch of Bothnian coastline characterized by rolling mountains and verdant valleys that plunge precipitously into the Gulf. The rugged shoreline is composed of sheer cliffs and craggy outcrops of rock, along with some peaceful sandy coves. Offshore are dozens of islands, some no more than a few metres in size, others much larger and covered with dense pine forest – it was on these that the tradition of preparing the foul-smelling *surströmming* (fermented Baltic herring) is thought to have first started. The coastline is best seen from the sea, and a trip out to one of the islands gives a perfect impression of the scale of things; however, it's also possible to walk virtually the entire length of the coast on the **Höga Kusten leden**, a long-distance hiking path that extends 130km from the Golden Gate-style bridge just north of Härnösand to Varvsberget in Örnsköldsvik.

There are two options for seeing the coast from Härnösand: either take one of the Norrlandskusten **buses** from the bus station for Örnsköldsvik – these pass through the tiny villages of Ullånger and Docksta (jumping-off points for the island of Ulvön) and skirt round one of Sweden's smaller national parks, Skuleskogen, though you're better waiting until Lapland for a real taste of the wild. Alternatively, you can take the **Norrlandskusten bus** part of the way up the coast from Härnösand to Bönhamn (see below for details), from where a small boat leaves for the island of Högbonden.

The islands

A trip out to the islands off the High Coast has to rank as the highlight of any trip up the Bothnian coast. Using a combination of buses and boats, you can make your way to three of the most beautiful islands in the chain: **Högbonden**, **Ulvön** and **Trysunda**. Only Högbonden has connections to the mainland, which means doubling back on yourself a little to take the bus up the coast to reach the boat which sails out to Ulvön from Ullånger and Docksta.

Högbonden

After just ten minutes' boat ride from the mainland, the steep sides of the tiny round island of **Högbonden** (ⓦ www.hogbonden.se) rise up in front of you. There are no shops (bring all provisions with you), no hotels, no flush-toilets – in fact the only building on Högbonden is a lighthouse situated at the highest point on a rocky plateau where the pine and spruce trees have been unable to get a foothold. The lighthouse has now been converted into a **youth hostel** (ⓣ0613/230 05, ⓕ420 49; open all year; pre-book between late Sept and late April), with stunning views and just thirty beds. To make the most of it you need to stay a couple of nights, exploring the island's gorge and thick forest by day, and relaxing in the traditional wood-burning **sauna** down by the sea in the evenings.

To **get there**, take the 11am Luleå-bound bus from Härnösand, get off at Ullånger and get the bus to Nordingrå, then change again to get to Bönhamn, from where the *M/F Högbonden* (mid-June to mid-Aug daily 10am, noon, 3pm & 6pm; 70kr return) makes the trip out to the island.

Ulvön

The largest island in the chain, **Ulvön** (⊛www.ulvon.com) is really two islands: Norra Ulvön and, across a narrow channel, the uninhabited Södra Ulvön. Before the last war Ulvön boasted the biggest fishing community along the High Coast, but many islanders have since moved to the mainland, leaving around forty permanent residents.

All boats to the island dock at the main village, **Ulvöhamn**, a picturesque one-street affair with red-and-white cottages and tiny boathouses on stilts. The island's only **hotel**, *Ulvö Skärgårdshotell* (☎0660/22 40 09, ℗22 40 78; ❸; June to Aug), is at one end of the street, just to the right of where the *M/S Kusttrafik* from Ullånger and Docksta puts in. Walk a short distance to the left of the quay and you'll come to a tiny wooden hut that functions as a summer **tourist office** (mid-June to mid-Aug daily 11am–3.30pm; ☎0660/23 40 93) – you can also rent bikes here at 30kr for four hours. Continue and you'll soon reach a seventeenth-century fishermen's chapel, decorated with flamboyant murals; the road leading uphill to the right just beyond here leads to the **youth hostel** (☎0660/22 41 90; late May to mid-Aug). At the other end of the main street is the village shop; *M/F Ulvön* to Trysunda and Köpmanholmen leaves from the quay just in front, while *M/S Otilia II*, for Örnsköldsvik, docks just on the other side of the jetty.

To **get to Ulvön**, make your way to **Docksta** on the Norrlandskusten bus, from where *M/S Kusttrafik* (☎0613/105 50, ⊛www.hkship.se; 145kr same-day return) leaves daily from June to August at 10.15am, arriving in Ulvöhamn at 11.30am, and returning at 3pm. A year-round boat, the *M/F Ulvön*, runs to Trysunda and Ulvön from Köpmanholmen, fifteen minutes south of Örnsköldsvik: out of summer there's generally one departure daily, depending on ice – check at the tourist office. To get to Docksta from Högbonden, take the bus from Bönhamn via Nordingrå to Gallsäter, where you can connect with the frequent Norrlandskusten buses that stop there on their way between Sundsvall and Umeå (for bus information, ring Din Tur on ☎0771/51 15 13 or visit ⊛www.dintur.se). There are frequent bus services to Docksta **from Härnösand**. From late June to early August it's also possible to reach Ulvön from Örnsköldsvik on the *M/S Otilia II* (☎0660/22 34 31; 110kr single; 1 daily at 9.30am, returning 3pm).

Trysunda

Boats from Ulvön, just an hour away, dock in **Trysunda**'s narrow U-shaped harbour, around which curves the island's tiny village. This is the best-preserved fishing village in Ångermanland: a charming little spot with forty or so red-and-white houses right on the waterfront and a seventeenth-century chapel with wonderful murals. The island's gently shelving rocks make it ideal for bathing and there's no shortage of secluded spots. Trysunda is also criss-crossed with walking paths leading through the gnarled and twisted dwarf pines. You can stay on the island in one of seven simple **rooms** (☎0660/430 29 or 430 38; ❶; June–Sept) at the service building of the small marina at the harbour entrance. **Getting here** from Ulvöhamn is simple: the *M/F Ulvön* (☎020/51 15 13; 45k one-way) makes the trip at least once a day year round, before continuing on to **Köpmanholmen** back on the mainland (35kr), where there's a youth hostel (☎0660/22 34 96) and regular buses to Örnsköldsvik.

Örnsköldsvik

About 120km north of Härnösand beyond the High Coast lies the port of **Örnsköldsvik**, an ugly modern town stacked behind a superbly sheltered harbour. The only saving grace is the **museum** at Läroverksgatan 1 (Tues–Sun noon–4pm; 20kr); to get there from the long-distance bus station, walk up the steps on the other side of Strandgatan, which will bring you out on Storgatan, then continue east along either Läroverksgatan or Hamnagatan. Ignore the typical collections of prehistoric finds and dreadful nineteenth-century furniture and ask to be let into the adjacent workshop, which conceals an interesting account of the work of locally born artist, **Bror Marklund**. Most of his art was commissioned by public bodies: his *Thalia*, the goddess of the theatre, rests outside the City Theatre in Malmö, and his figures adorn the facade of the Historical Museum in Stockholm. Inside the workshop, look for the brilliantly executed jester plaster casts, one of Marklund's most easily identifiable motifs. The only other vaguely interesting thing to do in town is to take a stroll along the harbourside past the old warehouses and the impressive culture and business centre known as Arken.

Practicalities

Approaching Örnsköldsvik by **train**, you'll have to alight at Mellansel on the main line from Stockholm to Swedish Lapland, about 30km to the northwest; to get into town from here take one of the frequent buses. The Norrlandskusten **buses** that run along the coast between Sundsvall and Luleå arrive at the long-distance bus station in the town centre, which is also the arrival point for services from Östersund (℡020/51 15 13, ⑨www.dintur.se). **Boats** to and from Ulvön and Trysunda dock at the Arken quay in front of the bus station along Strandgatan.

The **tourist office**, at Nygatan 18 (mid-June to mid-Aug Mon–Fri 9am–7pm, Sat 10am–3pm, Sun 10am–3pm; mid-Aug to mid-June Mon–Fri 10am–5pm; ℡0660/881 00, ⑨www.ornskoldsvik.se), can provide information on the High Coast islands. If you need **Internet** access, head for the free terminals at the library, at the corner of Lasarettsgatan and Torggatan. Budget **accommodation** options include the *Strand City Hotell*, right in the centre at Nygatan 2 (℡0660/106 10, ℻21 13 05; ❸/❷), a cheap and cheerful hostel-like establishment. Best, however, is the plain and functional *Hotell Focus* up the hill at Lasarettsgatan 9 (℡0660/821 00, ⑨www.norrhotell.se; ❺/❷). The **youth hostel** (℡0660/702 44) is 7km southwest of town in **Överhörnäs** – take the bus marked Köpmanholmen and ask the driver to let you off.

For daytime **eating**, sandwiches and cakes are available from *Café Brittas II* in the pedestrianized Storgatan. For more substantial fare, head for the lively harbourside, where many restaurants have outside tables overlooking the waters of the Örnsköldsviksfjärden: try the brasserie-style *Harry's*, next to the harbour, where pub food costs around 95kr and a strong beer goes for 48kr. Also on the harbourside, and serving up a terrific fish buffet (June to mid-Aug only) for around 100kr, *Fina Fisken* is definitely worth investigating, as is the neighbouring *Church Street Saloon*, renowned for its huge, inexpensive portions of something-and-chips. Of the pizzerias, the best is *Mamma Mia* on Storgatan.

Umeå

UMEÅ is the biggest city in northern Sweden, with a population of around 105,000. Demographically it's probably Sweden's most youthful city, with an average age of just 36, no doubt influenced by the presence of Norrland University and its 25,000 students. Strolling around the centre, you'll notice that those who aren't in pushchairs are pushing them, while the cafés and city parks are full of teenagers. With its fast-flowing river and wide, stylish boulevards, Umeå is a distinctly likeable city, and it's no bad idea to spend a couple of days here sampling some of the bars and restaurants – the variety of which you won't find anywhere else in Norrland.

Arrival, information and accommodation

It's a ten-minute walk from either the **train station** or **long-distance bus station** on Järnvägsallén to the centre, down one of the many parallel streets that lead in the general direction of the river. **Ferries** from Vaasa in Finland dock at nearby Holmsund, from where buses run into Umeå city centre. A good first stop is the

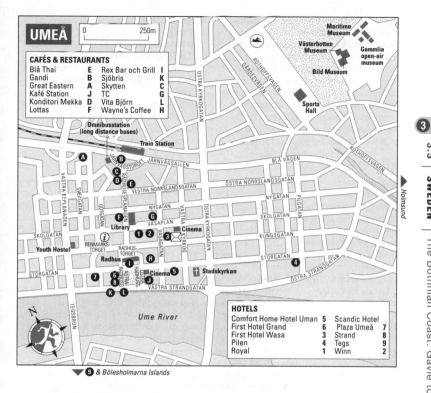

CAFÉS & RESTAURANTS

Blå Thai	E	Rex Bar och Grill	I
Gandi	B	Sjöbris	K
Great Eastern	A	Skytten	C
Kafé Station	J	TC	G
Konditori Mekka	D	Vita Björn	L
Lottas	F	Wayne's Coffee	H

HOTELS

Comfort Home Hotel Uman	5	Scandic Hotel	
First Hotel Grand	6	Plaza Umeå	7
First Hotel Wasa	3	Strand	8
Pilen	4	Tegs	9
Royal	1	Winn	2

tourist office (May to mid-June & mid-Aug to late Sept Mon–Fri 10am–6pm, Sat 10am–2pm; mid-June to mid-Aug Mon–Fri 8am–7pm, Sat 10am–5pm, Sun 11am–5pm; Oct to April Mon–Fri 10am–5pm; ℡090/16 16 16 ＠www.umea.se) in the ugly concrete square of Renmarkstorget. The staff here are very helpful and dish out, among other things, a free newspaper with detailed listings; they also have a supply of **private rooms** from 170kr per night (booking fee 25kr). Umeå's bright and modern **youth hostel** (℡090/77 16 50, ℻70 16 95) is in the centre at Västra Esplanaden 10. The nearest **campsite** is the lakeside *Umeå camping stugby* (℡090/70 26 00, ℻70 26 10), 5km out of town on the E4 at Nydala; it also has **cabins** for four people for 685kr, individual double rooms (❶) in other cabins and tiny two-bed huts called *trätält* (❶); facilities include washing machines and bike rental. Take bus #67 or #69, get off at Nydala and the campsite is about a five-minute walk towards Nydalabadet.

Hotels

Comfort Home Hotel Uman Storgatan 52 ℡090/12 72 20, ＠www.choicehotels.se. Home-from-home, with evening coffee and newspapers for all guests, and comfortable, modern rooms. ❺

First Hotel Grand Storgatan 46 ℡090/77 88 70, ＠www.firsthotels.com. Newly renovated and rather chic, right in the heart of town. ❺

First Hotel Wasa Vasagatan 12 ℡090/77 85 40,

＠www.firsthotels.com. A comfortable hotel in a lively, central location, though its rooms have a chain-hotel feel. ❺

Pilen Pilgatan 5 ℡090/14 14 60, ℻13 42 58. One of the cheaper smaller hotels with clean and basic rooms, and weekend and summer doubles for 500kr. ❷

Royal Skolgatan 62 ℡090/10 07 30, ＠www.royalhotelumea.com. Pleasant, centrally located hotel with sauna, whirlpool and solarium. Good summer deals. ⑤/❸

Scandic Hotel Plaza Umeå Storgatan 40 ⓣ090/205 6300, ⓦwww.scandic-hotels.com. Voted one of the best hotels in Sweden, this is very smart, with marble washbasins in the bathrooms and superb views from the sauna suite on the fourteenth floor. Weekend and summer discounts make it worth the indulgence. ⑥/❹

Strand Västra Strandgatan 11 ⓣ090/70 40 00, ⓕ70 40 90. Another low-budget but perfectly adequate hotel. Ask for a room with views of the river. ❹/❷

Tegs Verkstadsgatan 5 ⓣ090/12 27 00, ⓕ13 49 90. The cheapest hotel in town – in summer, the dingy doubles are as little as 460kr – though it's south of the river and some way from the action. ❷/❶

Winn Skolgatan 64 ⓣ090/71 11 00, ⓕ71 11 50. Close to the bus station and good for nearby restaurants and bars, though the modern rooms lack inspiration and style. ⑤/❸

The City

Umeå is known as the "City of Birch" for the trees that were planted along every street following a devastating fire in 1888. Most of the city was wiped out in the blaze, but rebuilding began apace, and two wide esplanades, together forming Rådhusesplanaden, were constructed to act as firebreaks should a similar disaster occur again. You'll be hard pushed to find any of the original wooden buildings, but around the little park in front of the former **Rådhus**, lingering bits of c.1900 timber architecture still look out over the river responsible for the town's name: *uma* means "roar" and refers to the sound of the rapids along the River Ume, now put to use by the hydroelectric power station further upstream.

Umeå also offers one terrific museum complex, **Gammlia**, which merits a good half-day. The original attraction around which everything else developed is the **Open-Air Museum** (*Friluftsmuseum*; mid-June to mid-Aug daily 10am–5pm; ⓦwww.vasterbottensmuseum.se; free), a group of twenty regional buildings, the oldest being the seventeenth-century gatehouse on the way in. As usual, the complex is brought to life by people dressed in period costume – you can watch them preparing traditional unleavened *tunnbröd* in the bakery – while cows, pigs, goats, sheep and geese are kept in the yards and farm buildings. The main collection is housed in the indoor **Västerbotten Museum** (mid-June to mid-Aug daily 10am–5pm, rest of the year Tues–Fri 10am–4pm, Sat noon–4pm, Sun noon–5pm; 20kr): a number of exhibitions canter through the county's development, from pre-history (including the oldest ski in the world, dated at 5200 years old) to the Industrial Revolution. It's all good stuff, well laid out and complemented by an array of videos and recordings, with a useful English leaflet available. Housed in the same building as Västerbotten Museum but run by Umeå University is the **Bildmuséet** (mid-June to mid-Aug noon–5pm; rest of the year Tues–Sun noon–4pm, Sun noon–5pm; ⓦwww.umu.se/bildmuseet; free), which houses interesting displays of contemporary Swedish and international art, photo-journalism and visual design. Back outside, county history continues in the separate **Fish and Maritime Museum** (*Fiske och Sjöfartsmuseum*; same times as Friluftsmuséet; free), an attempt at a maritime museum which is really no more than a small hall clogged with fishing boats.

Eating and drinking

Umeå's **eating and drinking** possibilities are enhanced by the number of students in the city. Most of the restaurants can be found around the central pedestrianized Kungsgatan and Rådhusesplanaden; for a quick bite, the best **café** in town is *Konditori Mekka*, close to the train station at Rådhusesplanaden 17, serving heavenly pastries and free coffee refills. Otherwise, there's a branch of the highly successful *Wayne's Coffee* chain at Storgatan 50; or try *Kafé Station*, Östra Rådhusgatan 2L, next to the Filmstaden cinema, with its rough brick walls and wooden floors; or the *Vita Björn*, the white boat moored down from the Rådhus.

Restaurants

Blå Thai Corner of Rådhusesplanaden and Västra Norrlandsgatan. Genuinely tasty Thai food in the basement of the pretentious street-level bar of the same name. Look out for the eat-until-you-drop buffet deal for just 99kr.

Gandi Järnvägstorget. Despite its dingy basement location (it's opposite the railway station), Gandi offers excellent Indian food and is good value, too, with dishes for around 140kr.

Great Eastern Magasinsgatan 17. Close to the railway and bus stations, this is the best Chinese restaurant north of Stockholm. With a 60kr deal, it's busy at lunchtime, while in the evening there's chicken and beef dinners from 86kr, as well as a Mongolian barbecue.

Lottas Nygatan 22. This British-style pub is currently *the* place to go drinking. The adjoining restaurant has fish and chips for 99kr, salmon pasta for 112kr and good-value lunches for just 73kr.

Rex Bar och Grill Rådhustorget. Probably the most popular – and stylish – place to eat in Umeå. Avoid the fussy à la carte menu of northern Swedish specialities at sky-high prices and choose instead from the bar meals, which start at 85kr.

Sjöbris Kajplats 10. Excellent fish restaurant on board an old white fishing boat moored off Västra Strandgatan, with dishes from 100kr.

Skytten Järnvägstorge. Two restaurants – an upmarket place and a cheaper brasserie – in one building. Both offer a good range of imaginative modern Swedish dishes at reasonable prices.

TC Vasaplan. A firm Umeå favourite and an excellent choice for Swedish home cooking – always busy and good value. Reckon on 120kr for mains.

Listings

Banks Handelsbanken, Storgatan 48; Nordea, Rådhusesplanaden 3; SEB, Kungsgatan 52; FöreningsSparbanken, Rådhustorget.

Bus enquiries Long-distance buses leave from the station at Järnvägstorget 2 (☎020/91 00 19, ⓦwww.lanstrafikeniac.se); city buses from Vasaplan (☎090/16 22 50).

Newspapers in English English-language newspapers can be read at the library (*stadsbiblioteket*) at Rådhusesplanaden 6.

Pharmacy Renmarkstorget 6 ☎090/77 05 41(Mon–Fri 9.30am–6pm, Sat 9.30am–2pm).

Police Ridvägen 10 ☎090/15 20 00.

Post office Vasaplan (Mon–Fri 8am–6pm, Sat 10am–2pm).

Systembolaget Kungsgatan 50A and Vasagatan 11 (both Mon–Wed & Fri 10am–6pm, Thurs 10am–7pm, Sat 10am–2pm).

Taxis City Taxi ☎090/14 14 14; Taxi Direkt ☎090/10 00 00; Umeå Taxi ☎090/77 00 00.

Train enquiries ☎020/44 41 11.

Skellefteå

"In the centre of the plain was Skellefteå church, the largest and most beautiful building in the entire north of Sweden, rising like a Palmyra's temple out of the desert." So enthused the nineteenth-century traveller Leopold von Buch, for there used to be a real religious fervour about **SKELLEFTEÅ**. In 1324 an edict in the name of King Magnus Eriksson invited "all those who believed in Jesus Christ or

Ferries to Finland

RG Line (☎090/18 52 00, ⓦwww.rgline.com) operate a year-round service between Umeå and **Vaasa in Finland**, with a crossing time of around 4 hours. Boats sail from the port of **Holmsund**, southeast of Umeå; buses for Holmsund leave from Skolgatan one hour before boat departures. Generally, during the summer months, there's one boat daily (not Tues) in each direction. The one-way foot passenger fare is 360kr (students 270kr). For more information call in at the tourist office in Renmarkstorget in Umeå. A second service, run by Botnialink (☎0611/55 05 55, ⓦwww.botnialink.se), leaves from Umeå for Vaasa (Mon, Tues, Thurs, Sat & Sun). It's a cargo ship with limited passenger space but fares are generally cheaper than on the RG Line – 310kr one-way. Botnialink also sails from the centre of Härnösand to Vaasa (Tues–Fri & Sun; 490kr).

wanted to turn to Him" to settle between the Skellefte and Ume rivers. Many heeded the call and parishes mushroomed on the banks of the Skellefte. By the end of the eighteenth century a devout township was centred on the monumental church, which stood out in stark contrast to the surrounding plains and wide river. Nowadays more material occupations support the town, and the tourist office makes the most of modern Skellefteå's gold and silver refineries, while admitting that the town centre doesn't have much to offer: concentrate instead on the church and its nearby *kyrkstad*, or parish village.

Skellefteå's church and parish village, **Bonnstan**, are within easy striking distance of the centre: head west along Nygatan and keep going for about fifteen minutes. On the way you'll pass the **Nordanå Kulturcentrum**, a large and baffling assortment of buildings that's home to a theatre, a twee period grocer's shop (*lanthandel*) and a dire **museum** (Mon & Fri–Sun noon–4pm, Tues–Thurs 9am–5pm; 20kr) containing three floors of mind-numbing exhibitions on everything from the region's first settlers to swords. Tucked away to the side of the *lanthandel* is *Nordanå Gårdens Värdshus*, a pleasant restaurant serving lunches for around 70kr.

Bonnstan's **kyrkstad** consists of five long rows of weatherbeaten log houses with battered wooden shutters (the houses are protected by law and any modernization is forbidden, including the installation of electricity). Take a peek inside, but bear in mind that they're privately owned by local people who use them as summer cottages. Beyond the parish village you'll find the **kyrka** (daily 10am–4pm), a proud white Neoclassical building with four mighty pillars supporting the domed roof. Inside there's an outstanding series of medieval sculptures including the 800-year-old *Virgin of Skellefteå*, a walnut carving on the reverse side of the altar and one of the few remaining Romanesque images of the Virgin in the world.

Practicalities

Skellefteå's small centre is based around a modern paved square flanked by Kanalgatan and Nygatan; at the top of the square is the **bus station**, at the bottom the **tourist office** (end–June to early Aug Mon–Fri 9am–6pm, Sat 10am–4pm, Sun 10am–3pm; rest of the year Mon–Fri 9am–5pm, Sat 10am–4pm; ☎0910/73 60 20, ⊛www.skelleftea.se), at Trädgårdsgatan 7, which can provide all the usual information and help with accommodation. The library at Kanalgatan 73 has plenty of **Internet** terminals which you can use for free.

There are four central **hotels** to choose from: cheapest is the *Hotell Victoria* at Trädgårdsgatan 8 (☎0910/174 70, ℱ894 58; ❸/❷), a family-run establishment on the top floor of a block on the south side of the main square; virtually next door at Torget 2, *Rica Hotel Skellefteå* (☎0910/73 25 00, ⊛www.rica.cityhotels.se; ❹/❸) has perfectly adequate rooms and is also the centre of Skellefteå's nightlife. The smartest

---

Parish villages

Consisting of rows of simple wooden houses grouped tightly around a church, **parish villages** are common throughout the provinces of Västerbotten and Norrbotten. After the break with the Catholic Church in 1527, the Swedish clergy were determined to teach their parishioners the Lutheran fundamentals. Church services became compulsory: in 1681 it was decreed that those living within 10km of the church should attend every Sunday, those between 10km and 20km every fortnight and those between 20km and 30km every three weeks. Within a decade parish villages had appeared throughout the region to provide the travelling faithful with somewhere to spend the night after attending church. The biggest and most impressive is at Gammelstad near Luleå (see p.617), and another good example can be seen at Bonnstan in Skellefteå (see above). Today they're no longer used in their traditional way, but many people still live in the old houses, especially in summer, and sometimes even rent them out to tourists.

hotel is the *Scandic* (☎0910/75 24 00, ⑩www.scandic-hotels.com; ❻/❸) at Kanalgatan 75, across Viktoriagatan. The **youth hostel**, at Brännavägen 25 (☎0910/72 57 00, ⑩www.stiftsgardenskelleftea.com) – a rustic red two-storey building by the banks of the Skellefte river, half an hour's walk from the centre – is well worth seeking out. Head west along Nygatan (which later becomes Brännavägen) until the junction with Kyrkvägen and the hostel is on the corner. For **campers**, *Skellefteå campingplats* (☎0910/188 55, ⑩www.skelleftea.se/skellefteacamping) is 1500m north of the centre on Mossgatan, just off the E4; it also has **cabins** for up to four people costing 270kr per cabin per night.

The best spot for **lunch** (70kr) is *Carl Viktor*, Nygatan 40, or the twee *Lilla Mari* at Köpmangatan 13. Skellefteå's **restaurants** aren't exactly impressive, though the *M/S Norway* at Kanalgatan 58 has gorgeous, if somewhat pricey, Nordic specialities from 270kr such as fillets of ptarmigan or reindeer. Among the usual cluster of pizzerias, the best and most popular is *Monaco*, Nygatan 31, which also does take-aways. *Pizzeria Pompeii* at Kanalgatan 43, where pizzas cost 60kr and a strong beer is 45kr, is reasonable value but the pizzas are on the dry side. **Drinking** is best done at *O'Leary's* at Kanalgatan 31 or at *Old Williams Pub* in the main square.

Luleå

Last stop on the Norrlandskusten bus line, **LULEÅ** lies at one end of the Malmbanan, the iron-ore railway that connects the ice-locked Gulf of Bothnia with the ice-free Norwegian port of Narvik in the Norwegian Sea. The town's wide streets and lively atmosphere have an immediate appeal, making this a much better stopoff than nearby Boden (see p.618), 25 minutes down the train line. If you're heading north for the wilds of Gällivare and Kiruna, or indeed to the sparsely pop-ulated regions inland, it's a good idea to spend a day or so here enjoying the sights and the impressive range of bars and restaurants: Luleå is the last oasis in a frighten-ingly vast area of forest and wilderness spreading north and west.

Luleå was founded in 1621 around the medieval church and parish village of nearby Gammelstad (meaning Old Town; see p.617). Even in those days trade with Stockholm was important, and Gammelstad's tiny harbour soon proved inadequate to the task. In 1649, by royal command, the city was moved lock, stock and barrel to its present site – only the church and parish village remained. Shipping is still an important part of the local economy, but over recent years Luleå has become the high-tech centre of northern Sweden, specializing in metallurgy, research and edu-cation.

Arrival and information

The **train** and **bus** stations are about five minutes' walk apart at one end of the grid of parallel streets that make up the city centre. Luleå's **tourist office** is a good ten minutes away in the Kulturcentrum Ebeneser at Storgatan 43B (mid-June to mid-Aug Mon–Fri 9am–7pm, Sat & Sun 10am–4pm; mid-Aug to mid-June Mon–Fri 10am–6pm, Sat 10am–2pm; ☎0920/29 35 00, ⑩www.lulea.se). Ask here about boat trips to some of the hundreds of mostly uninhabited islands in the archi-pelago off the coast. For free **Internet** access head for the library on Kyrkogatan.

Accommodation

The tourist office has a very small number of **private rooms** for about 300kr per person per night. The non-STF **youth hostel** (☎0920/22 26 60), fifteen minutes' walk from the centre at Sandviksgatan 26, is open all year round.

Amber Stationsgatan 67 ☎0920/102 00, ⑩www.amber-hotell.nu. Small and cosy family-run place in an old wooden building near the train station. ❹/❷

Aveny Hermelinsgatan 10 ☎ 0920/22 18 20, ⑩www.hotellaveny.com. Small, modern and comfortable hotel, with reasonable prices in summer. ❹/❷

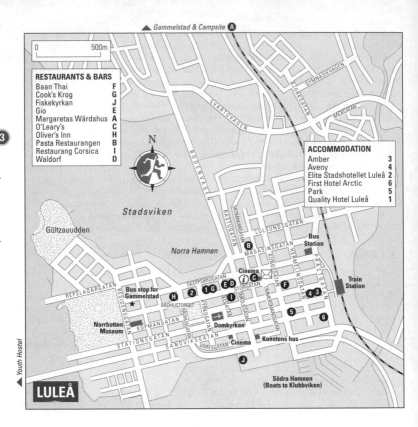

Elite Stadshotellet Luleå Storgatan 15
☎0920/670 00, ⓦwww.elite.se. The oldest and
smartest of the city's hotels, right in the centre of
town, with tasteful, old-fashioned rooms and a
huge breakfast buffet. ⑤/③
First Hotel Arctic Sandviksgatan 80 ☎0920/109
80, ⓦwww.arctichotel.se. Very handy for the train
station, this is a smart little hotel with en-suite
rooms. ⑤/③

Park Kungsgatan 10 ☎0920/21 11 49,
ⓦwww.parkhotell.se. The least expensive of
Luleå's hotels, basic but perfectly adequate, with
doubles (not en suite) in summer for just 400kr.
③/②
Quality Hotel Luleå Storgatan 17 ☎0920/20 10
00, ⓦwww.choicehotels.se. A modern hotel with
heavy colours and gloomy wooden interiors. Not
worth the money, though it might have rooms if
the city's other options are full. ⑤/②

The City

Luleå only really has one main street, the long **Storgatan**, south of which, past the
main square, Rådhustorget, is the **Domkyrkan**. The medieval original disappeared
centuries ago and the current edifice, built in 1893, contains a modern barrage of
copper chandeliers hanging like Christmas decorations. Walking west up
Köpmangatan from the Domkyrkan you'll find the **Norrbotten Museum**
(Mon–Fri 10am–4pm, Sat & Sun noon–4pm; closed Mon in winter; ⓦwww
.norrbottensmuseum.nu; free) at Storgatan 2. Among the humdrum resumé of
county history are some good displays on the Sámi culture that begins to predominate northwest of Luleå. Just south of the Domkyrkan, **Konstens hus**, at
Smedjegatan 2 (Tues, Thurs & Fri 11am–6pm, Wed 11am–8pm, Sat & Sun

noon–4pm; free), is worth a look for some interesting works by local and not-so-local artists and sculptors.

If the weather's good, the next stop should be the **Gültzauudden** – a wooden promontory with a sandy beach that's easily reached on foot from the centre: from the cathedral head north on Rådstugatan, which later becomes Norra Strandgatan and veers northwest past the Norrbotten theatre to the junction with Fagerlindsvägen. Turn right into this road for the beach. Gültzauudden's odd name derives from the German shipbuilder, Christian Gültzau, who helped to make Luleå a shipbuilding centre. For more room to stretch out, you're better off taking the *M/S Stella Marina* out to the island of **Klubbviken**, the prettiest of the score of tiny islets that lie in the archipelago offshore. Here you'll find an enormous sandy beach and enough privacy to satisfy even the most solipsistic of souls. Boats leave from the southern harbour (Södra Hamnen) from late June to early August; information from the tourist office or on ☎0920/22 38 90 or 010/565 07 61 (mobile).

Gammelstad

The original settlement of Luleå, **GAMMELSTAD** is 10km northwest of the city centre. When the town moved to the coast a handful of the more religious stayed behind to tend the church, and the attached **parish village** remained in use. One of the most important places of historical interest north of Uppsala, the site now proudly boasts inclusion on the UNESCO World Heritage List. The **church** itself (daily 9am–6pm) was completed at the end of the fifteenth century and adorned with the work of church artists from far and wide: both the decorated choir stalls and the ornate triptych are medieval originals, while the sumptuous pulpit is a splendid example of Bothnian Baroque, trimmed with gilt cherubs and red and gold bunches of grapes. Look out for the opening above the south door, through which boiling oil was generously poured over unwelcome visitors.

Around 450 cottages are gathered around the church, making this the biggest parish village in Sweden, though nowadays they're unoccupied except during important religious festivals. Free guided walks can be arranged with Gammelstad's **tourist office** (mid-June to mid-Aug daily 9am–6pm; mid-Aug to mid-June Mon–Fri 11am–4pm; ☎0920/29 35 81, ⓦwww.lulea.se/gammelstad), located in one of the cottages. Down the hill from the tourist office is the **Hägnan Open-Air Museum** (*Friluftsmuséet Hägnan*; June to mid-Aug daily 11am–5pm; ⓦwww.lulea.se/hagnan; free), an open-air heritage park whose main exhibits are two old farmstead buildings from the eighteenth century. During the summer there are demonstrations of rural skills such as sheep husbandry, the crafting of traditional wooden roof slates and the baking of *tunnbröd*, northern Sweden's unleavened bread.

Getting to Gammelstad from Luleå is straightforward. **Buses** #9 and #32 run twice-hourly from Hermelinsparken, at the west end of Skeppsbrogatan.

Eating and drinking

Storgatan is stuffed with **restaurants** and **bars**, and you'll find that during the light summer evenings many young people simply drink their way from one end of the street to the other. As usual, you can happily order a beer in any of the restaurants listed below, with no obligation to eat there, too.

Baan Thai Corner of Storgatan and Kungsgatan. Authentic and extensive Thai menu with all meat dishes at 89kr. Vegetarian and noodle dishes are 79kr; a strong beer is just 38kr. Don't miss it.
Cook's Krog *Quality Hotel Luleå* hotel, Storgatan 17. An intimate and cosy place to enjoy the best steak in Luleå, cooked over a charcoal grill for around 200kr.

Fiskekyrkan Södra Hamnen. Housed in the orange warehouse building by the sea (walk down Nygatan and cross Sandviksgatan), this is one of the cheaper restaurants in town, and a popular drinking hole in the evenings. Pasta and other simple dishes for around 100kr.
Gio Storgatan 27. One of Luleå's trendsetting bars. Wear your sharpest clothes, darkest shades and

sip a chilled foreign beer before going clubbing. There's a predictably stylish – yet surprisingly good-value – menu of modern Swedish dishes for around 120kr.

Margaretas Wärdshus Lulevägen 2, Gammelstad. Fine food, including Norrbotten delicacies at around 160kr, served in a beautiful old wooden house close to the old church.

O'Leary's Skomakargatan 22. Tex-Mex mains for around 130kr and a good choice of beer. Definitely *the* place to watch the summer sun set over the northern harbour from the adjoining terrace.

Oliver's Inn Storgatan 11. Pub grub and a good selection of beer. Known for its 1970s and 1980s music, which attracts a large crowd at weekends.

Pasta Restaurangen Magasinsgatan 5. Hefty pizzas from around 70kr, pasta dishes for 80kr, but reckon on the place being pretty empty due to its backstreet location.

Restaurang Corsica Nygatan 14. Dark and dingy interior but worth seeking out for its traditional Corsican dishes (which you won't find anywhere else in Norrland), along with lots of steak and pizzas all at 100–150kr. Lunch is popular at 58kr.

Waldorf Wasa City Shopping Centre, Storgatan 33. Renowned for its pizzas (from 60kr), and also serving Chinese and Japanese food.

Listings

Banks Handelsbanken, Storgatan 27, between the *Elite Stadshotellet* and the tourist office; Nordea, Köpmangatan 38.

Bus enquiries City bus times on ☎0920/24 11 00; long-distance bus information on ☎020/47 00 47, or visit ⊛www.ltnbd.se.

Car rental Avis, Banvägen 6 ☎0920/183 50; Budget, Stationsgatan 26 ☎0920/881 88; Hertz, Gammelstadsvägen 23 ☎0920/873 44; Statoil, Stationsgatan 30 ☎0920/186 22.

Hospital Repslagaregatan 2 ☎0920/714 00.

Pharmacy Köpmangatan 36C (Mon–Fri 9am–6pm, Sat 9am–2pm, Sun 1–4pm).

Police Skeppsbrogatan 37 ☎0920/29 50 00.

Post office Storgatan 53 ☎020/23 22 21.

Systembolaget Storgatan 25 (Mon–Wed 10am–6pm, Thurs & Fri 10am–7pm, Sat 10am–2pm).

Taxis Taxi Luleå ☎0920/100 00; 6:ans Taxi ☎0920/666 66.

Train station Prästgatan. For train times call ☎020/44 41 11.

Boden

Twenty-five minutes by train from Luleå, **BODEN** is a major transport junction for the entire north of the country; from here trains run northwest to Gällivare and Kiruna and eventually on to Narvik in Norway, and south to Stockholm and Gothenburg. **Buses** also run east to Haparanda (change at Luleå) for connections to Finland. Boden's strategic location means that in summer, the tiny train station can be filled with backpackers; if you've got time, it's well worth stepping out into the town.

Boden's position, roughly halfway along the coast of Norrbotten at the narrowest bridging point along the Lule River, was no doubt one of the reasons that the **Överluleå kyrka** (late June to early Aug daily 10am–7pm; rest of the year Mon–Fri 9am–3pm) and its **parish village** were founded here in 1826. A twenty-minute walk from the train station, down the modest main street, **Kungsgatan**, over the bridge towards the pedestrianized centre and right along Strandplan, the church impresses most by its location, perched on a hillock overlooking the water and surrounded by whispering birch trees. The surrounding cottages of the parish village once spread down the hill to the lake, Bodträsket, complete with their stables and narrow little alleyways. Nowadays they're rented out as superior **hostel accommodation** during the summer (see opposite).

Today Boden is Sweden's largest military town – the first garrison was established in 1901 and a fortress completed in 1907 – and everywhere you look you'll see spotty-faced young men kitted out in camouflage gear and black boots strutting purposefully (if somewhat ridiculously) up and down the streets; there are infantry, tank, artillery and air corps here. For an insight into the region's military history, visit the **Garrison Museum** (*Garnisonsmuséet*; June–Aug daily 11am–4pm; ⊛www.boden.mil.se; free) on the southwestern edge of town, which proudly displays the largest collection of military uniforms north of Stockholm amongst the other paraphernalia.

Practicalities

Ask at the **tourist office**, in the town centre at Kungsgatan 40 (June–Aug Mon–Fri 9am–7pm, Sat 9am–4pm, Sun noon–4pm; Sept–May Mon–Fri 10am–5.30pm, Sat 10am–1pm; ℡0921/624 10, ❼www.turistbyran.com), about staying in the **parish cottages** close to the church. Although these usually book up months in advance, particularly for July, it's always worth checking availability on ℡0921/198 70). Cottages for two people cost 350kr in June and August, and there are also a few sleeping three for around 500kr – and you'll pay a bit more in July whatever the cottage size. The **youth hostel** (℡0921/133 35 or ℡070/681 3335) is just 100m from the train station at Fabriksgatan 6. There are also rather extortionately priced dormitory beds at the *Standard Hotell*, Stationsgatan 5 (℡0921/160 55, ℡175 58;), which is the first thing you'll see when coming out of the station building. For more comfort and style, there's *Hotell Bodensia* in the centre of town at Kungsgatan 47 (℡0921/177 10, ❼www.bodensia.se; ❹/❸). The **campsite** (℡0921/624 07, ❼www.boden.se/camping), a few minutes' walk from the church following the path along the lakeside to Björknäs, also has six-bed **cabins** (750kr per cabin per night), four-bed cottages (550kr per cottage per night) and rents **canoes** (40kr per hour, 150kr per day) and **bikes** (50kr per day).

Don't expect to be overwhelmed by choice when it comes to **eating** in Boden. For a solid meal (80–90kr), try *Panelen* at the station end of Kungsgatan, whilst finer food is served up across the road at the excellent and unexpectedly chic *Pär och Mickes Kök* at Kungsgatan 20 – three courses here are just 195kr. For pizza or pasta you're best off at *Restaurang Romeo* in the pedestrianized centre at Drottninggatan 9, with pizzas from 62kr. Opposite, *Café Ollé* at Drottninggatan 4 does a 59kr lunch deal and tasty open sandwiches. Boden's best **drinking** spots are *Oliver's Inn*, just before the bridge on Kungsgatan, and the oddly-named *Puben med stort P* ("Pub with a capital P") closer to the station at Kungsgatan 23.

Haparanda and around

Hard by the Finnish border and at the very north of the Gulf of Bothnia, **HAPARANDA** is hard to like. The train station sets the tone of the place – an austere and rather grand-looking building reflecting Haparanda's aspirations to be a major trading centre. That never happened, and walking up and down the streets around the main square, Torget, can be a pretty depressing experience. The signpost near the bus station doesn't help matters either, reinforcing the feeling that you're a very long way from anywhere: Stockholm is 1100km, the North Cape 800km, and Timbuktu 8386km.

To fully understand why Haparanda is so grim, you need to know a little history: the key is the neighbouring Finnish town of **Tornio** (Torneå in Swedish). From 1105 until 1809 Finland was part of Sweden and Tornio was an important trading centre, serving markets across northern Scandinavia. But things began to unravel when Russia attacked and occupied Finland in 1807; the Treaty of Hamina then forced Sweden to cede Finland to Russia in 1809 – thereby losing Tornio. It was decided that Tornio had to be replaced, and so in 1821 the trading centre of Haparanda was founded, on the Swedish side of the new border along the River Torne. However, it proved to be little more than an upstart compared to its neighbour across the water. Nearly two hundred years on, with Sweden and Finland both now members of the European Union, Haparanda and Tornio have declared themselves a "Eurocity" – one city made up of two towns from different countries.

There are only a couple of sights in town: the train station building from 1918 and the peculiar **Haparanda kyrka**, a monstrous modern construction that looks like a cross between an aircraft hangar and a block of flats topped off in dark-coloured copper. When the church was finished in 1963 it caused a public scandal and has even been awarded a prize for being the ugliest church in Sweden.

Practicalities

There are no **border formalities** and you can simply walk over the bridge to Finland and wander back whenever you like; it's worth remembering that Finland is an hour ahead of Sweden.

Haparanda's **tourist office** (June to mid-Aug Mon–Fri 9am–7pm, Sat & Sun 11am–7pm; rest of the year Mon–Fri 9am–5pm; ☎0922/120 10, ⊛www.haparanda.se) is actually in Finland, hence the above times are in Finnish time. The building is just over the bridge to Tornio in the Green Line Welcome Center. From June to August it's also possible to get basic information from the *Stadshotel* in Haparanda's main square. Haparanda's **youth hostel** (☎0922/611 71; ⊛www.haparandavandrarhem .com) is a smart riverside place at Strandgatan 26 and has the cheapest beds in town, with good views across to Finland. Alternatively, there's the cheap-and-cheerful pension, *Resandehem*, in the centre of Haparanda at Storgatan 65B (☎0922/120 68; ❶). *Haparanda Stadshotel*, at Torget 7 (☎0922/614 90, ☏102 23; ❺/❸), is the only **hotel** in town, an elegant and sumptuous place, dating from 1900, full of squeaky parquet floors and chandeliers.

Tornio (see p.766) has many more **bars** and **restaurants** than its Swedish neighbour, so you may want to do what the locals do and nip over into Finland for a bit of high life, especially at the weekend. In Haparanda, however, the plastic-looking *Prix Restaurant*, at Norra Esplanaden 8, is an adequate place for **lunch**, with mains for 50kr; the food is OK, if not particularly inspiring. Otherwise *dagens rätt* is available from the restaurant at the youth hostel for 55kr, but your best bet is *Hasans Pizzeria* at Storgatan 88, close to Torget, which has lunch for 50kr. Lunch and pizzas are also served at the Chinese restaurant *Leilani*, Köpmangatan 15, as well as a range of Chinese and Thai dishes in the 80–100kr bracket. *Nya Konditoriet* on Storgatan is good for coffee and cakes; for open sandwiches try *Café Rosa* in the Gallerian shopping centre on Storgatan. For **drinking** in Haparanda head for the pub *Ponderosa* at Storgatan 82, or try the *Gulasch Baronen* pub attached to the *Stadshotel*.

Around Haparanda: Kukkolaforsen

If you're stuck in Haparanda for a day or two, it's worth making the trip 15km north to the impressive **KUKKOLAFORSEN** (⊛www.kukkolaforsen.se). Although there's little other than a cluster of houses and a campsite here, it's a good place to soak up the pastoral beauty of the Torne Valley, which marks the border between Sweden and Finland, without journeying too far into it. On the last weekend in July the rapids here are the scene of the **Sikfesten** or Whitefish Festival. This local delicacy is caught in nets at the end of long poles, fishermen dredging the fast, white water and scooping the whitefish out onto the bank, then grilling them on large open fires. Originally a centuries-old fishermen's harvest festival, it's now largely an excuse to get plastered, with a beer tent, evening gigs and dancing the order of the day. It costs 100kr to get in on the Saturday, 60kr on the Sunday, although if you're staying in the adjacent **campsite** (☎0922/310 00, ☏310 30), which also has cabins (from 450kr per cabin), you should be able to sneak in for free.

Moving on to Finland from Haparanda

It's perfectly feasible to **walk over to Finland**; indeed, many local people do this several times daily without batting an eyelid. However, with luggage, you may want to make use of the Finnish **buses** that connect Haparanda with Tornio and Kemi roughly every hour – times are displayed at the bus station in Haparanda. There are also two direct afternoon buses from Haparanda to Rovaniemi (1 only Sat & Sun; 3hr), and a twice-daily bus connection to Oulu (Uleåborg in Swedish) via Kemi. Remember that Finland is one hour ahead of Sweden.

River rafting down the rapids can also be arranged here, either through the campsite or at the tourist office in Haparanda – 200kr gets you the gear, helmet and life jacket, and pays for a short trip downriver plus a certificate at the end. Finally, the **saunas** at Kukkolaforsen have been declared some of the best in the country by the Swedish Sauna Academy; after boiling yourself in temperatures of over 100°C, step out onto the veranda with a cool beer, breathe the crisp air heavy with the scent of pine, and listen to the roar of the rapids. And don't forget to wave to Finland across the river.

Travel details

Trains

Boden to: Gällivare (3 daily; 2hr); Gävle (2 daily; 11hr); Gothenburg (1 daily; 16hr); Kiruna (3 daily; 3hr); Luleå (6 daily; 25min); Stockholm (2 daily; 13hr); Uppsala (2 daily; 12hr).

Gävle to: Boden (2 daily; 11hr); Falun (8 daily; 1hr); Gällivare (2 daily; 13hr 30min); Härnösand (1 daily; 3hr); Hudiksvall (8 daily; 1hr 15min); Kiruna (2 daily; 15hr); Luleå (2 daily; 12hr); Östersund (4 daily; 4hr); Stockholm (hourly; 1hr 30min); Sundsvall (8 daily; 2hr); Umeå (1 daily; 9hr); Uppsala (hourly; 45min).

Härnösand to: Gävle (1 daily; 3hr); Hudiksvall (1 daily; 2hr); Stockholm (1 daily; 4hr 30min); Sundsvall (1 daily; 1hr).

Hudiksvall to: Gävle (8 daily; 1hr 15min); Härnösand (1 daily; 2hr); Stockholm (8 daily; 2hr 30min); Sundsvall (8 daily; 45min); Uppsala (8 daily; 2hr).

Luleå to: Boden (5 daily; 25min); Gällivare (3 daily; 2hr 30min); Gävle (2 daily; 12hr); Gothenburg (1 daily; 16hr 45min); Kiruna (3 daily; 3hr 30min); Stockholm (2 daily; 14hr); Umeå (2 daily; 4hr 15min); Uppsala (2 daily; 13hr).

Sundsvall to: Gävle (8 daily; 2hr); Härnösand (1 daily; 1hr); Hudiksvall (8 daily; 45min); Östersund (5 daily; 2hr 20min); Stockholm (8 daily; 3hr 30min).

Umeå to: Gävle (1 daily; 9hr); Gothenburg (1 daily; 13hr 30min); Luleå (2 daily; 4hr 15min); Stockholm (1 daily; 11hr 15min); Uppsala (1 daily; 10hr 30min).

Buses

Boden to: Luleå (Mon–Fri every 30min, Sat & Sun 9 daily; 50min).

Haparanda to: Boden (4–6 daily; 3hr); Kiruna (1–2 daily; 6hr); Luleå (Mon–Fri 12 daily, Sat & Sun 5 daily; 2hr 30min); Pajala (Mon–Fri 3–4 daily, 1 on Sun; 3hr 30min).

Luleå to: Arvidsjaur (1–2 daily; 3hr); Boden (Mon–Fri 43 daily, Sat & Sun 9 daily; 50min); Gällivare (1–3 daily; 3hr 15min); Haparanda (Mon–Fri 11 daily, Sat & Sun 5 daily; 4hr); Jokkmokk (1–3 daily; 2hr 45min); Kiruna (1–3 daily; 5hr); Pajala (1–2 daily; 3hr 30min).

Örnsköldsvik to: Östersund (1–2 daily; 4hr 30min).

Skellefteå to: Arvidsjaur (1 daily except Sat; 2hr).

Umeå to: Storuman (Mon–Sat 3–4 daily, 1 on Sun; 3hr 40min); Tärnaby/Hemavan (Mon–Sat 3–4 daily, 1 on Sun; 6hr).

Norrlandskusten buses

Norrlandskusten buses run four times daily between Sundsvall and Luleå, generally connecting with trains to and from Sundsvall. Buy your tickets from the bus driver before boarding. From Sundsvall, buses call at Härnösand (45min); Gallsäter (1hr 35min); Docksta (1hr 50min); Örnsköldsvik (2hr 30min); Umeå (4hr); Skellefteå (6hr 15min) and Luleå (8hr 30min).

International trains

Boden to: Narvik (1 daily; 6hr).
Luleå to: Narvik (1 daily; 6hr 30min).

International buses

Haparanda to: Rovaniemi (Mon–Fri 2 daily; 3hr).
Skellefteå to: Bodø (Mon–Fri & Sun 1 daily; 9hr); Fauske (Mon–Fri & Sun 1 daily; 7hr 30min).
Umeå to: Mo-i-Rana (1 daily; 8hr).

International ferries

Härnösand to: Vaasa (3–4 weekly; 10hr).
Umeå to: Vaasa (1 daily; 4hr).

3.6

Central and northern Sweden

I
n many ways the long wedge of land that comprises **central and northern Sweden** – from the shores of **Lake Vänern** up to the Finnish border north of the Arctic Circle – encompasses all that is most typical of the country. Rural and underpopulated, it fulfils the image most people have of Sweden: lakes, pine forests, wooden cabins and reindeer – a vast area of land which is really one great forest broken only by the odd village or town.

Folklorish **Dalarna** province is the most intensely picturesque region. Even a quick tour around one or two of the more accessible places gives an impression of the whole: red cottages with white doors and window frames, sweeping green countryside and water which is bluer than blue. Dalarna's inhabitants maintain a cultural heritage (echoed in contemporary handicrafts and traditions) that goes back to the Middle Ages. And the province is *the* place to spend midsummer, particularly Midsummer's Eve, when the whole region erupts in a frenzy of celebration featuring the age-old tradition of dancing around the maypole (an ancient fertility symbol), countless impromptu musical gatherings and much beer drinking.

The privately owned **Inlandsbanan**, the great inland railway, cuts right through central and northern Sweden and links virtually all the towns and villages covered in this chapter. Running from **Mora** to **Gällivare**, above the Arctic Circle, it ranks with the best European train journeys, an enthralling two-day, 1100km adventure. It's certainly a much livelier approach to the north than the east-coast run up from Stockholm. Buses connect the rail line with the **mountain villages** that snuggle alongside the Norwegian border – the Swedish *fjäll*, or fells, not only offer some of the most spectacular scenery in the country but also some of the best, and least spoilt, hiking in Europe. North of Mora, **Östersund** is the only town of any size, situated by the side of Storsjön, the "Great Lake", reputed to be home to Sweden's very own Loch Ness Monster. From here trains head in all directions: west to Norway through the country's premier ski resort, **Åre**, south to Dalarna and Stockholm, east to Sundsvall on the Bothnian coast and north to Swedish Lapland.

The wild lands of the **Sámi** people make for the most fascinating trip in northern Sweden. Omnipresent reindeer are a constant reminder of how far north you are, but the enduring Sámi culture, which once defined much of this land, is now under threat. The problems posed by tourism are escalating, principally the erosion of grazing land under the pounding feet of hikers, making the Sámi increasingly economically dependent on selling souvenirs and handicrafts. Further north, around industrial **Gällivare** and **Kiruna**, and as far as the Norwegian border at **Riksgränsen**, the rugged **national parks** offer a chance to hike and commune with nature in the last great wilderness in Europe.

Karlstad

Capital of the province of Värmland (ⓦwww.varmland.org), **KARLSTAD** is named after King Karl IX, who granted the place its town charter in 1584. The

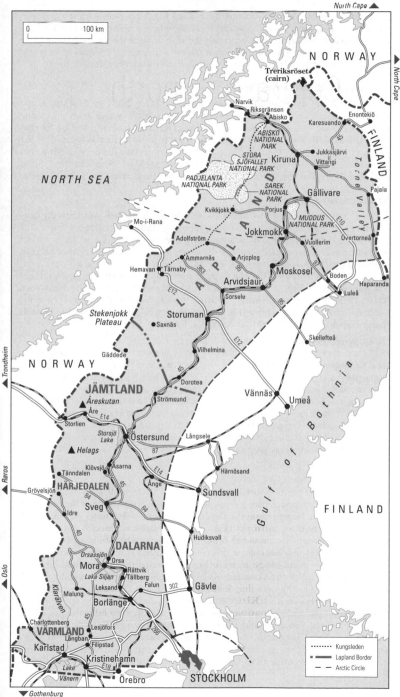

North Cape ▲

North Cape ▶

0   100 km

NORWAY

Treriksröset
(cairn)

Narvik
Riksgränsen
Abisko
Karesuando
Enontekiö

ABISKO
NATIONAL
PARK

STORA
SJÖFALLET
NATIONAL PARK

PADJELANTA
NATIONAL PARK

Kiruna

Jukkasjärvi
Vittangi

Pajala

NORTH SEA

SAREK
NATIONAL
PARK

Gällivare

Torne Valley

FINLAND

Kvikkjokk
Porjus

MUDDUS
NATIONAL PARK

Mo-i-Rana

Adolfström
Jokkmokk
Vuollerim
Övertorneå

Ammarnäs
Arjeplog

Hemavan Tärnaby

Moskosel
Boden
Haparanda

Arvidsjaur

LAPLAND

Sorsele
Luleå

E12

Stekenjokk
Plateau

Storuman

Saxnäs

Skellefteå

Vilhelmina

E12

Gäddede

Dorotea

NORWAY

Strömsund

Vännäs
Umeå

Trondheim

JÄMTLAND

Åreskutan
Åre
E14

Storlien

Storsjö
Lake

Östersund

Långsele

Helags

87

Gulf of Bothnia

Klövsjö Åsarna

Härnösand

Tänndalen

HÄRJEDALEN

Ånge
E14

Grövelsjön

84

Sundsvall

FINLAND

Idre

Sveg

84

Roros

Hudiksvall

DALARNA

Orsasjön Orsa

Mora Rättvik
Lake Siljan Tällberg

Leksand Falun

Oslo

Malung

302

Gävle

Borlänge

Klarälven

Charlottenberg

Lesjöfors

VÄRMLAND

Långban Filipstad

Karlstad

Kristinehamn

Lake
Vänern

E18

STOCKHOLM

Örebro

Gothenburg

·········	Kungsleden
▪–▪–▪	Lapland Border
– – –	Arctic Circle

623

town has had its fair share of disasters: devastating fires ripped through the centre in 1616, 1729 and, most catastrophically, in 1865, when a blaze started in a bakery burnt virtually the entire town, including the cathedral, to the ground. Rebuilding began apace, with an emphasis on wide streets and large open squares to guard against another tragedy. The result is an elegant and thoroughly likeable town.

Arrival and information

Draped along the shores of Lake Vänern roughly halfway between Stockholm and Oslo, Karlstad is served by **trains** between the two capitals as well as services along the western side of the lake from Gothenburg. Karlstad is also linked by Swebus Express **bus** with Gothenburg and Gävle. The **tourist office** is located in the Carlstad Conference Centre, Tage Erlandergatan 10 (June–Aug Mon–Fri 9am–7pm, Sat 10am–6pm, Sun 11am–4pm; Sept–May Mon–Fri 9am–5pm; ☎054/14 90 55, ⊛www.karlstad.se). Ask here about **boat trips on Lake Vänern**.

Accommodation

Karlstad's **youth hostel** (☎054/56 68 40, ℗56 60 42) is located 3km from the centre in a rambling old three-storey house, Ulleberg, and is reachable on buses #11 and #32 towards Bellevue. The nearest **campsites** are a nine-kilometre drive out of town west along the E18: *Skutbergets Camping* (☎054/53 51 39) is open all year, whereas *Bomstad Badens Camping* (☎054/53 50 68, ⊛www.camping.se) next door, and beautifully situated on the lakeshore, is only open from June to August. From mid-June to mid-August the campsites can be reached on the daily Badbussen (#18; 10.30am–5.30pm hourly; 25min) which runs from Stora Torget via Drottninggatan to the beaches at Bomstad. Note that in summer, all Karlstad **hotels** charge 550kr for a double room if booked at least one day in advance.

Carlton Järnvägsgatan 8 ☎054/21 55 40, ℗18 95 20. Located in the pedestrianized centre, this is one of the cheaper hotels in Karlstad. ❷

Comfort Hotel Drott Järnvägsgatan 1 ☎054/10 10 10, ⊛www.choicehotels.se. Smart, elegant place dating from 1908; it's next to a busy main road just 50m from the railway station. ❺

First Hotel Plaza Västra Torggatan 2 ☎054/10 02 00, ⊛www.plaza-karlstad.nu. Large, modern and plush with fantastic views over the city from its panoramic sauna. ❻

Freden Fredsgatan 1A ☎054/21 65 82, ⊛www.fredenhotel.com. Cheap-and-cheerful place close to the bus and train stations. ❷

Ibis Hotel Karlstad City Västra Torggatan 20 ☎054/17 28 30, ⊛www.ibishotel.com. Good-value hotel in the centre of town with a large breakfast buffet and free evening parking. ❷

Solsta Drottninggatan 13 ☎054/15 68 45, ⊛www.solstahotell.se. Inexpensive and central, with cable TV and some rooms adapted for the disabled. ❸

The Town

It's best to start your wanderings around town from the airy main square, Stora Torget, one of the largest market squares in the country. The rather austere **Peace Monument** in front of the Town Hall commemorates the peaceful dissolution of the union between Sweden and Norway in 1905, which was negotiated in Karlstad. Unveiled fifty years after this event, it portrays an angry woman madly waving a broken sword whilst planting her right foot firmly atop a dismembered soldier's head: "feuds feed folk hatred, peace promotes people's understanding" reads the inscription. The Neoclassical **Rådhuset** itself was the cause of much local admiration upon its completion in 1867, just two years after the great fire – town worthies were particularly pleased with the two fearsome Värmland eagles which adorn the building's roof, no doubt hoping they would ward off another devastating blaze. Across Östra Torggatan, the nearby **Domkyrkan** was consecrated in 1730, although only its arches and walls survived the flames of 1865. Its most interesting features are the altar, made from Gotland limestone with an Orrefors crystal cross, and the crystal font.

Continuing east along Kungsgatan and over the narrow Pråmkanalen, the road swings left and changes its name to Nygatan ahead of the longest arched stone bridge in Sweden, **Östra Bron**. Completed in 1811, this massive construction spans 168m across the eastern branch of the Klarälven river. It's claimed that the builder, Anders Jacobsson, threw himself off the bridge and drowned, afraid his life's work would collapse – his name is engraved on a memorial stone tablet in the centre of the bridge. On sunny days (and Karlstad is statistically one of the sunniest places in Sweden) the nearby wooded island of **Gubbholmen**, reached by crossing the stone bridge and turning right, is a popular place for catching the rays; take a picnic and dip your toes in the refreshing waters of the river.

Back in town, at the junction of Norra Standgatan and Västra Torggatan, the two-storey yellow wooden building with the mansard roof dates from 1781, one of the handful of dwellings which weren't destroyed in the great fire. This building, the **Bishop's Residence** (*Biskopsgården*), owes its survival to the massive elm trees on its south side, which formed a natural firebreak, as well as to the sterling firefighting efforts of the bishop of the time. The only other houses which survived are located in the **Almen district**, next to the river at Älvgatan; the oldest parts of these wooden buildings date from the 1700s, but their facades are all nineteenth-century.

A half-hour walk along Jungmansgatan, Hööksgatan and then Rosenborgsgatan will bring you to **Mariebergsskogen** (June–Aug daily 7am–10pm; ℗www .mariebergsskogen.karlstad.se; free). Originally modelled on the Skansen open-air museum in Stockholm, this contains a number of old wooden buildings from across Värmland. There's also a **leisure park** (May–Aug daily 11am–6pm) here with a funfair and children's animal park.

Eating and drinking

Eating and **drinking** in Karlstad is a joy, with a good selection of restaurants specializing in everything from Spanish to vegetarian dishes. For a Swedish provincial town, **bars** are also thick on the ground – the *Bishop's Arms* and the *Woolpack Inn* are particularly popular.

Bishop's Arms Kungsgatan 22. Classic British-style pub with a wide range of beers. A great location overlooking the river, with outdoor seating in summer.
Casa Antonio Drottninggatan 7. Good Spanish restaurant with tapas from 35kr and paella for two for 260kr.
Glada Ankan Kungsgatan 12. Lively first-floor restaurant and bar with a balcony overlooking the main square. It serves mostly Swedish dishes (from 130kr) and is a nice place for coffee.
Gröna Trädgården Västra Torggatan 9. First-floor, lunch-only vegetarian restaurant with a small balcony overlooking the pedestrianized street below. Large salad buffet and home-made bread included with all meals; reckon on 60–80kr.
Harrys Kungsgatan 16. American-style bar, café

and restaurant in the main square, popular with drinkers in the evening, and with open-air seating in summer. The small menu has pub grub from 75kr.
Jäger Västra Torggatan 8. Buzzing evening restaurant open till 2am, with mains such as salmon, chicken or pork fillet from 95kr.
Kebab House Västra Torggatan 7. Small but pleasant pizza and kebab place with outdoor seating in summer; pizzas from 40kr.
Rådhuscafeet, Tingvallagatan 8. Elegant café in the town hall; enter from the left side of the building.
Woolpack Inn, Järnvägsgatan 1. Just across the road from the station, this is another pub doing its best to create a traditional British drinking atmosphere in central Sweden. Very popular.

Listings

Banks FöreningsSparbanken, Kungsgatan 10; Handelsbanken, Tingvallagatan 17; Nordea, Tingvallagatan 11–13; S-E Banken, Drottninggatan 24.
Beaches Sundstatjärnet, in the centre of town by the swimming pool on Drottning Krisitinas väg; Mariebergsviken, take bus #20 and #31; Bomstad,

take bus #18.
Bus station Drottninggatan. Information on buses in Värmland on ℗020/22 55 80 or at ℗www.kollplatsen.com.
Car rental Avis, Hamngatan 24 ℗054/15 26 60; Europcar, Hagalundsvägen 29 ℗054/18 23 20.

Police Drottninggatan 4 ☎054/14 50 00.
Systembolaget Drottninggatan 26 (Mon–Wed
10am–6pm, Thurs & Fri 10am–7pm, Sat
10am–2pm).

Taxi Taxi Kurir ☎054/101 101.
Train station Hamngatan. For information call
☎054/14 33 50 or 0771/75 75 75.

Around Lake Siljan

Swedes consider the area around **Lake Siljan** (🌐www.siljan.se) to be the heartland of the sizeable **Dalarna** province, itself perhaps the most typically "Swedish" area of the country. The idyllic landscape here is one of verdant cow pastures, gentle rolling meadows sweet in summer with the smell of flowers, and tiny rural villages nestling on the lakeshore. The lush vegetation of the Siljan region, enriched by the waters of the lake and benefiting from the relative lack of forest, has produced what the Swedes call *öppna landskap* (literally, open landscapes). Indeed, the temperate surroundings of Lake Siljan, coupled with age-old traditions and local handicrafts, weave a subtle spell on many visitors, too, and it certainly all adds a pleasing dimension to the small, low-profile towns and villages of this part of Dalarna. **Leksand** and **Mora** are the best of the lakeside towns, though **Rättvik** is also worth a visit if time allows. **Orsa**, on the other hand, with its massive bear park, is a must for all animal lovers and makes a perfect stop on any journey north from Dalarna.

Trains operated by the national rail company, SJ, call at all the towns around the lake and terminate in Mora. Privately run Inlandsbanan trains (see opposite) call at Orsa on their way north from Mora, but it's easier to reach the town by bus. Another good way to get around Lake Siljan is to rent a **bike** from one of the tourist offices, which also dole out the handy, free *Siljanskartan* cycling map of the region. Since Lake Siljan and its surrounding districts are popular Swedish holiday destinations, there's no shortage of **accommodation** – though it can be a good idea to book ahead in the peak season of mid-June to mid-August.

Mora

If you've only got time to see part of the lake, then **MORA** is the place to head for, especially if you're travelling further north, as it's the starting point of the Inlandsbanan (see box opposite). The largest of the lakeside settlements, Mora's main draw is the work of Sweden's best-known artist, **Anders Zorn** (1860–1920), who moved here in 1896 and whose paintings are exhibited in the excellent **Zorn Museum** at Vasagatan 36 (mid-May to mid-Sept Mon–Sat 9am–5pm, Sun 11am–5pm; mid-Sept to mid-May Mon–Sat noon–5pm, Sun 1–5pm; 🌐www.zorn.se; 35kr) – look out for the self-portrait and the especially pleasing *Midnatt* (Midnight) from 1891, which depicts a woman rowing on Lake Siljan, her hands blue from the cold night air. You might also want to wander across the lawn and take in his home, **Zorngården** (mid-May to mid-Sept Mon–Sat 10am–4pm, Sun 11am–4pm; mid-Sept to mid-May Mon–Sat noon–3pm, Sun 1–4pm; 45kr), where he lived with his wife, Emma, during the early 1900s. However, what really makes this place unusual is the cavernous 10-metre-high hall where the couple lived out their roles as darlings of local society, with its steeply V-shaped roof, entirely constructed from wood and decked out in traditional Dalarna designs and patterns. Also on Vasagatan, but on the other side of the church, is the **Vasaloppet Museum** (*Vasaloppsmuséet*; mid-June to mid-Aug daily 10am–5pm; mid-Aug to mid-June Mon–Fri 10am–5pm; 🌐www.vasaloppet.se; 30kr). Here you'll find an exhibition on the history of the Vasaloppet, a ski race that started 500 years ago with the attempts of two Mora men to catch up with King Gustav Vasa, who was fleeing from the Danes.

Once you've covered the town's sights, you might want to take a **cruise** (mid-June to mid-Aug only) on the lake aboard the lovely old steamship *M/S Gustaf Wasa* (timetables vary; info on ☎010/252 32 92, 070/542 10 25 or 🌐www.wasanet.nu); it costs 120kr for a round-trip to Leksand or 80kr for a two-hour lunch cruise.

Practicalities

Mora's **tourist office** (mid-June to mid-Aug Mon–Fri 9am–7pm, Sat & Sun 10am–5pm; mid-Aug to mid-June Mon–Fri 10am–5pm, Sat 10am–1pm; ☎0250/56 76 00, ⊛www.siljan.se) is at Stationsvägen 3 in the same building as Mora train station (not Mora Strand station). SJ trains terminate at the latter; buses (⊛www.dalatrafik.se) use the bus station opposite, actually on Moragatan, but just off the main Strandgatan.

The cheapest place to stay is the **youth hostel** (☎0250/381 96, ⊛www.maalkullann.se), at Vasagatan 19; get off the train at Mora station, turn left, and keep walking for about five minutes along the main street, Vasagatan. Mora's **campsite**, *Mora Camping* (☎0250/276 00, ⊛www.moraparken.se), is a ten-minute walk from the centre along Hantverkaregatan, which begins near the bus station: there's a good beach here, as well as a small lake. Among the **hotels**, the biggest and best is the *First Hotel Mora* at Strandgatan 12 (☎0250/59 26 50, ⊛www.firsthotelmora.com; ❻/❸), opposite Mora Strand train station, with a choice of modern and old-fashioned rooms. *Hotel St Mikael*, Fridhemsgatan 15 (☎0250/150 70, ⊛www.stab.se/fi/trehotell; ❺/❷), is small with tasteful rooms, while *Hotell Kung Gösta*, Kristinebergsgatan 1, is handy for Mora train station (☎0250/150 70, ⊛www.stab.se/fi/trehotell; ❹/❷).

As for **eating and drinking**, all the hotels serve up a decent *dagens rätt* for around 55kr – there's little to choose between them. *Wasastugan*, a huge log building at Tingnäsvägen between the main train station and the Vasaloppsmuséet, is particularly lively in the evenings, with TexMex-style meat and fish dishes from 80kr. Alternatively, *Pizzeria Prima* in Fridhemplan or *Pizzeria Torino* in Älvgatan serve up virtually any pizza you can imagine, all at reasonable prices. In summer, coffee and cakes can be enjoyed outside at *Helmers Konditori* and at *Mora Kaffestugan*, virtually next door to each other on Kyrkogatan. Alongside *Wasastugan*, *Jérnet*, Moragatan 1, is one of the liveliest places in the evening.

Orsa and the bear park

North of Mora, the Dalarna landscape becomes more mountainous and less populous, and the only place of any note, **ORSA**, is also the last town of any significance for miles around. Sitting aside Lake Orsasjön, a northerly adjunct of Lake Siljan, Orsa is right in the heart of Sweden's bear country: it's reckoned that there are a good few hundred **brown bears** roaming the dense forests around town, though few sightings are made, except by the hunters who cull the steadily increasing

Inlandsbanan practicalities

The **Inlandsbanan** – the great inland railway that links Dalarna with Swedish Lapland – is a mere shadow of its former self today. In 1992, spiralling costs and low passenger numbers forced Swedish Railways to sell the line to the fifteen municipalities the route passes through, and a private company, Inlandsbanan AB, was launched. It now operates only as a tourist venture in summer – generally from late June to early August. Under-26 InterRail passes give free travel; see p.21 for details of other discounts. Timetables are approximate and the train is likely to stop whenever the driver feels like it; maybe for a spot of wild strawberry picking or to watch a beaver damming a stream. It's certainly a fascinating way to reach the far north of the country, but isn't recommended if you're in a rush. If you decide to travel the line in one go, the distances are such that it'll take two days, with an overnight stop in Östersund. However, you'll get much more out of it if you make a couple of stops along the route and take in some of the stunning scenery passing by your train window first-hand – special guides available on board contain commentaries and information about places along the route. For **timetables** and other **information** ask at any tourist office around the lake, call ☎020/53 53 53, or visit ⊛www.inlandsbanan.se.

numbers. Your best chance of seeing one is to visit the bear park, **Orsa Grönklitt björnpark** (mid-May to mid-June & mid-Aug to mid-Sept daily 10am–3pm, mid-Sept to mid-Oct Sat & Sun 10am–3pm; mid-June to mid-Aug daily 10am–6pm; ⓦwww.orsa-gronklitt.se; 75kr), 13km outside town and reachable via twice-daily bus #118 from Mora, which stops at Orsa train station. The bears here are not tamed or caged, but wander around the 900 square kilometres of the forested park at will; instead, it's the humans who are restricted, having to clamber up viewing towers and along covered-in walkways. Funny, gentle and vegetarian for the most part, the bears are occasionally fed the odd dead reindeer or elk that's been killed on the roads. Out of season they hibernate in specially constructed lairs that are monitored by closed circuit television cameras.

From the train station on Järnvägsgatan it's a short walk to the Orsa's **tourist office** at Dalagatan 1 (mid-June to mid-Aug Mon–Fri 9am–7pm, Sat & Sun 10am–5pm; mid-Aug to mid-June Mon–Fri 10am–5pm, Sat 10am–1pm; ⓣ0250/55 25 50, ⓦwww.siljan.se). If you need to stay over, the best bet is the **youth hostel** (ⓣ0250/421 70, ⓕ423 65), beautifully located at Gillevägen 3 close to the side of Lake Orsasjön, 1km west of the centre. There's also a second, well-equipped hostel at the bear park (ⓣ0250/462 00; ⓦwww.orsa-gronklitt.se).

Rättvik

Situated at the eastern bulge of Lake Siljan, 37km from Mora, **RÄTTVIK** is altogether much smaller and quieter: one tiny shopping street, a massive jetty out into the lake (reputed to be the longest in the world) and an outdoor swimming pool are about the sum of it. While there's not much in the way of sights, what Rättvik does have is access to plenty of gorgeous countryside. Get out of the village as soon as you can and head up for the viewing point at **Vidablick** – about an hour's walk and a stiff climb, but the view is worth it – you can see virtually all of Lake Siljan and the surrounding hillsides, covered in forests broken only by the odd farm. You can get to the viewing point by walking on marked trails through the forests above Rättvik: pick up a free map of town from the tourist office. In the forest itself there are a couple of information boards showing different walking trails, while Vidablick has a small café and a shop to reward your efforts. The quickest way back down to Rättvik is to take one of the steep roads down the hill (ask the staff in the shop to point out the correct one); go left at the end onto Wallenkampfvägen and then right along Mårsåkervägen towards Lerdal, and you'll see some of the most beautifully located residential houses in Dalarna – all wood logs and flowers and with a view out over the lake.

Rättvik's **tourist office** (mid-June to mid-Aug Mon–Fri 9am–7pm, Sat & Sun 10am–5pm; mid-Aug to mid-June Mon–Fri 10am–5pm, Sat 10am–1pm; ⓣ0248/79 72 10, ⓦwww.siljan.se) is handily situated in the train station. The best and cheapest place to stay is the **youth hostel** on Centralgatan (ⓣ0248/105 66, ⓕ561 13), surrounded by trees and built in traditional Dalarna style out of large pine logs; to get there, follow Domarbacksvägen 1km from the train station. There are two **campsites** in town, one opposite the youth hostel (ⓣ0248/561 10), the other right on the lakeside behind the railway tracks (ⓣ0248/516 91). In terms of **hotels** there's not much choice: the best in town is the average *Hotell Lerdalshöjden* (ⓣ0248/511 50, ⓕ511 77; ❸) on Bockgatan, or there are some comfortable pine cabins at *Hotell Vidablick* (ⓣ0248/302 50, ⓦwww.hantverksbyn.se; ❸), about 3km out of Rättvik at Faluvägen.

There's a dearth of good places to **eat and drink** in Rättvik and most people head off to Leksand or Mora for a night out. A decent bet is *Restaurant Anna* on Vasagatan – a cosy place with local specialities in the evening from 100kr; otherwise you're looking at *Krögar'n* on pedestrianized Storgatan, which serves burgers for around 50kr and meat dishes from 90kr; or *Bella Pizza* at Ågatan 11, where pizzas go for around 45kr.

Leksand

Located at the southernmost point of Lake Siljan, fifteen minutes down the train line from Rättvik, **LEKSAND** is perhaps the most popular and traditional of Dalarna's lakeside villages and is certainly worth making the effort to reach at Midsummer, when **festivals** recall age-old dances performed around the maypole (Sweden's maypoles, incidentally, aren't erected until June: spring comes late here, and in May there are few leaves on the trees and often some lingering snow). Celebrations culminate in the **church boat races**, an aquatic procession of sleek wooden longboats that the locals once rowed to church every Sunday. The race starts on Midsummer's Day in nearby Siljansnäs and continues for ten days around the lake, reaching Leksand on the first Saturday in July. Between twenty and twenty-five teams take part, all cheered on by villagers at the water's edge. Another event worth coming here for is **Music by Lake Siljan** (*Musik vid Siljan*; ☏0248/102 90, ⓦwww.musikvidsiljan.se) in the first week of July: nine days of nonstop classical, jazz and dance-band music performed in churches, on the lakeside and at various locations in the surrounding forest – check with the tourist office for the latest details on this and the boat races.

At other times there's little to do in Leksand other than take it easy for a while. Stroll along the riverside down to **Leksands kyrka**, which enjoys a magnificent setting overlooking the river and the lake. One of the biggest churches in the country, it has existed in its present form since 1715, although the oldest parts date back to the thirteenth century.

All trains to Mora stop in Leksand; the **tourist office** (mid-June to mid-Aug Mon–Fri 9am–7pm, Sat & Sun 10am–5pm; mid-Aug to mid-June Mon–Fri 10am–5pm, Sat 10am–1pm; ☏0247/79 61 30, ⓦwww.siljan.se) is at the train station. Leksand's comfortable **youth hostel**, one of the oldest in Sweden, is over the river, around 2.5km from the train station in Parkgården (☏0247/152 50, ☏101 86). Otherwise, there are two **hotels** to choose between: *Moskogen*, at Insjövägen 50 (☏0247/146 00, ⓦwww.moskogen.com; ❸), a modern place that nonetheless manages to use traditional wooden wall panelling and woven textiles in Dalarna colours; and the beautiful *Korstäppen* at Hjortnäsvägen 33 (☏0247/123 10, ⓦwww.korstappan.se; ❹), also tastefully done out in traditional colours and styles. The nearest **campsite**, *Leksands Camping*, is a twenty-minute walk from the tourist office along Tällbergsvägen (☏0247/803 13, ⓦwww.leksand.se/camping_stugby). The best place **to eat** is at *Siljans Konditori & Bageri*, in the main square, with excellent open sandwiches, light snacks and salads for 40–50kr – in summer there are a couple of tables on the front terrace. Alternatively, try *Bosporen*, just opposite, a passable place serving pizzas and meat and fish dishes, which does lunch for 60kr and is also a good spot for a **drink**.

Falun

If you're in Dalarna for more than a couple of days, the copper-mining town of **FALUN** can be a relief after the folksiness of the lakeside and the visiting hordes that dominate the area in summer. Getting to Falun by train from any of the towns around Lake Siljan, or indeed directly from Stockholm, involves passing through the eminently missable Borlänge, Dalarna's biggest – and dullest – town. Just 20min northeast of Borlänge, Falun is essentially an industrial settlement, though a surprisingly pleasant one at that. At their peak in the seventeenth and eighteenth centuries the mines here produced two-thirds of the world's copper ore, and Falun acquired buildings and a layout commensurate with its status as Sweden's second largest town. In 1761, however, two devastating fires wiped out virtually all of central Falun – the few old wooden houses to survive can be found in the areas of Elsborg (southwest of the centre), Gamla Herrgården and Östanfors (north of the centre), which are worth seeking out for an idea of the cramped conditions the mineworkers had to live in.

The **mines** themselves, out of town at the end of Gruvgatan, were said by the botanist Carl von Linné to be as dreadful as hell itself. An unnerving element of eighteenth-century mining was the omnipresence of copper vitriol gases, a strong preservative: one case is recorded of a young man known as Fat Mats whose body was found in the mines in 1719. He'd died 49 years previously in an accident, but the corpse was so well preserved that his erstwhile fiancée, by then an old woman, recognized him immediately. Hour-long **guided tours** (May–Sept daily 10am–5pm; rest of the year Mon–Fri same hours; ⓦwww.kopparberget.com; 80kr), begin with a lift ride that takes you down 55m to a network of old mine roads and drifts – be warned that the temperature drops to 6–7°C. Make sure you also peer into the "Great Pit", **Stora Stöten**, which appeared on Midsummer's Day in 1687 – the result of a huge underground collapse caused by extensive mining and the unplanned driving of galleries and shafts.

Apart from the mines, Falun's attractions boil down to **Dalarnas Museum** at Stigaregatan 2–4 (Mon–Fri 10am–5pm, Sat & Sun noon–5pm; ⓦwww .dalarnasmuseum.se; 40kr), which includes sections on the county's folk art, and, on the hill overlooking town, Sweden's **National Ski Stadium** (*Riksskidsstadion*; ask for directions from the tourist office), where you can take a **lift** (mid-May to mid-Aug daily 10am–6pm; 20kr) up to the top of the ninety-metre ski jump for a terrifying peer down.

Practicalities

From the **train** and **bus stations**, east of the centre, take the underpass beneath the main road and head towards the shops in the distance and Falun's **tourist office** (mid-June to mid-Aug Mon–Fri 9am–7pm, Sat 9am–6pm, Sun 11am–5pm; mid-Aug to mid-June Mon–Fri 9am–6pm, Sat 10am–2pm; ☏023/830 50 ⓦwww.visitfalun.se) is opposite the *First Hotel Grand* in Trotzgatan. The nearest **youth hostel** (☏023/105 60, ℱ141 02), a modern affair, is about 3km from the train station at Vandrarvägen 3 in Haraldsbo – take bus #701 or #712 from the centre. The **campsite** (☏023/835 63) is up at Lungnet by the National Ski Stadium, about fifteen minutes' walk from town. Central **hotels** include the swanky *First Hotel Grand* at Trotzgatan 9–11 (☏023/79 48 80, ⓦwww.firsthotels.com; ⑤/❸), and the more homely *Hotell Winn*, near the train station at Bergskolegränd 7 (☏023/70 17 00, ⓦwww.softwarehotels.se/winnfalun; ⑤/❷).

In terms of **eating and drinking** places, Falun far outstrips the towns around Lake Siljan in quality as well as choice. Most popular is the trendy *Banken Bar & Brasserie* at Åsgatan 41, housed in an old bank building and serving burgers, baked potatoes and fish from around 80kr. Next door is the posh but cosy *Två rum och kök*, where meat and fish dishes start at 150kr. Another popular spot is *Rådhuskällaren*, a cellar under the town hall in Stora Torget serving delicious, if somewhat pricey, food – reckon on 200kr upwards. The *Bakfickan* **bar** next door is the place to hang out among Falun's trendy young things. Other drinking establishments include the excellent *Pub Engelbrekt*, at Stigaregatan 1, and the average English-themed *King's Arms* at Falugatan 3. For entertainment value, the best time to be in Falun is mid-July, when musicians from all over the world take over the town for a four-day **International Folk Music Festival** – check latest dates with the tourist office or visit ⓦwww.falufolk.com.

Sveg and around

From Mora and Orsa, the Inlandsbanan trundles through the northern reaches of Dalarna, offering breathtaking vistas of the vast forested hillsides that comprise some of the emptiest tracts of land in the whole of Sweden. Indeed, it's a good three hours before the train finally reaches the first place of any significance: **SVEG**, the uneventful provincial town of Härjedalen (ⓦwww.harjedalen.se), a sparsely populated fell region which belonged to Norway until 1645, something that has left its mark in the local dialect. The area offers excellent terrain for walking, as well as some of Sweden's most magnificent scenery – more than thirty mountains exceed the 1000-metre mark, the highest peak being **Helagssfjället** (1797m), whose icy slopes support Sweden's southernmost glacier. Härjedalen is also home to the largest single population of bears in the country, as well as a handful of shaggy musk oxen, ferocious creatures that have wandered over the border from Norway.

In 1273 Sveg was the site of a parliament called to hammer out a border treaty between Sweden and Norway. Since then, things have quietened down considerably and even on a Friday night in midsummer you're likely to find yourself alone in the wide streets lined with grand old wooden houses. A graceful river runs right through the centre of town and there are some delightful meadows and swimming spots just a few minutes' walk from the centre.

Sveg's **tourist office** (mid-June to mid-Aug Mon–Fri 9am–4pm; rest of the year Mon–Fri 1–5pm; ☎0680/107 75, ✆www.harjedalen.se) is in the centre of town at Kyrkogränd 1 next to the campsite. If you're keen to **stay overnight**, try the ramshackle **youth hostel**, a fifteen-minute walk from the station at Vallarvägen 11 (☎0680/103 38; advance booking required Oct–May). In the same building is the rather shabby *Hotell Härjedalen* (same phone number; ❷); or try the more upmarket *Hotell Mysoxen* (☎0680/170 00, ✆100 62; ❸/❷), the other side of Torget on the corner of Fjällvägen and Dalagatan. The **campsite** (☎0680/130 25) is located right on the riverside. Your best chances of not **eating** alone are at the greasy-spoon *Inlandskrogen* café next to the bus and train stations on Järnvägsgatan, or at the *Knuten* pizzeria in the main square, Torget.

Klövsjö

From Sveg the Inlandsbanan veers northeast to skirt a large area of marshland separating northern Härjedalen from neighbouring Jämtland, a province known, amongst Swedes at least, as the location of one of the country's most beautiful villages, **KLÖVSJÖ**. There's some justification to this – it's a thoroughly charming place of log cabins set amid rolling pastures, while the distant lake and forested hills that enclose the settlement on all sides create the feeling that it's in a world of its own. Ten farms continue to work the land much as in days gone by – ancient grazing rights still in force mean that horses and cows are free to roam through the village at will – while flowering meadows, trickling streams, wooden barns and the smell of freshly mown hay drying on frames in the afternoon sun cast a wonderful spell. Once you've taken a look at the old wooden buildings of the seventeenth-century farm estate, **Tomtangården** (July to mid-Aug daily; free), there's not much else to do except breathe the bitingly clean air and admire the view – you won't find anywhere as picturesque as this. Unfortunately there are no rooms to let in the village itself, but the **tourist office** on the main road (Mon–Fri noon–3.30pm; ☎0682/41 36 60) has cabins to rent in the vicinity (around 500kr per cabin for up to four people).

To **reach Klövsjö**, get off the train at **Åsarna**, a low-key cross-country skiing centre, from where buses make the twenty-minute trip to the village four times a day. In summer at least it's fairly easy to find accommodation in Åsarna. There's a well-equipped **campsite** (☎0687/302 30, ✆www.asarnaskicenter.se) and **youth hostel** (same phone and website) behind the ski centre on the one and only main road – turn left out of the train station. There's a **tourist office** in the same ski centre (daily: June–Aug 8am–8pm; Sept–May 8am–7pm; ☎0687/301 93). Opposite the train station, rooms at the *Åsarna Hotell* (☎0687/300 04; ❷) are a little on the shabby side; there's a restaurant and bar on site.

Östersund

North of Åsarna, the Inlandsbanan hugs the shores of the enormous Lake Storsjön before pulling into one of central Sweden's most agreeable towns, **ÖSTERSUND**. It's well worth spending a couple of days in what is the last large town until

Gällivare, inside the Arctic Circle – if you're heading north this is your final chance to indulge in a bit of high life, since the small towns and villages beyond have few of the entertainment or culinary possibilities available here. Östersund is also a major **transport hub**: the E14 highway cuts through town, offering good links to Sundsvall and Trondheim in Norway, while as well as the summer Inlandsbanan service there are trains west to Åre and Storlien (the latter with connections to Trondheim in Norway), east to Sundsvall and south to Stockholm and Gothenburg, plus express buses north to Gällivare, which run all year and are a better option than the Inlandsbanan if you're in a hurry.

Arrival and information

From the **train station** on Strandgatan it's a five-minute walk north to the town centre; the **bus station**, off Rådhusgatan, is more central. A couple of blocks to the north, the helpful **tourist office** (June Mon–Fri 9am–7pm, Sat & Sun 9am–3pm;

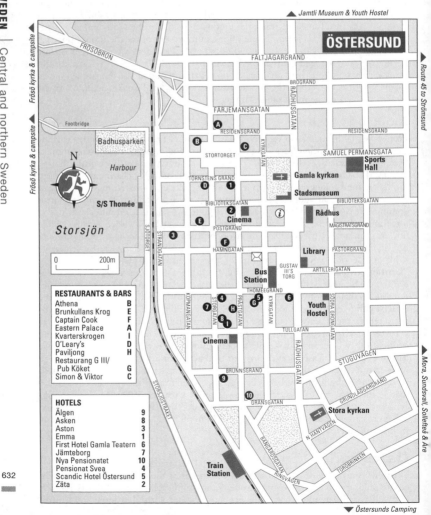

▲ Jamtli Museum & Youth Hostel

ÖSTERSUND

RESTAURANTS & BARS

Athena	B
Brunkullans Krog	E
Captain Cook	F
Eastern Palace	A
Kvarterskrogen	I
O'Leary's	D
Paviljong	H
Restaurang G III/ Pub Köket	G
Simon & Viktor	C

HOTELS

Ålgen	9
Asken	8
Aston	3
Emma	1
First Hotel Gamla Teatern	6
Jämteborg	7
Nya Pensionatet	10
Pensionat Svea	4
Scandic Hotel Östersund	5
Zäta	2

▼ Östersunds Camping

late June to early Aug Mon–Sat 9am–9pm, Sun 9am–7pm; Aug Mon–Fri 9am–5pm, Sat & Sun 9am–3pm; rest of the year Mon–Fri 9am–5pm; ☏063/14 40 01, ⊛www.turist.ostersund.se) is opposite the minaret-topped Rådhus at Rådhusgatan 44.

Accommodation

For accommodation, the modern STF **youth hostel** (☏063/341 30, ℗13 91 00; late June to early Aug) is ten minutes' walk north of the train station at Södra Gröngatan 32. More atmospheric, though, is a night spent inside *Jamtli* (☏063/12 20 60, ⊛www.jamtli.com), another STF hostel set amid the old buildings in the open-air museum grounds. **Campers** can stay either at *Ostersunds Camping* (☏063/14 46 15, ⊛www.camping.se/z11), a couple of kilometres south down Rådhusgatan; or over on Frösön at *Frösö Camping* (☏063/432 54; mid-June to mid-Aug) – take bus #3 or #4 from the centre.

Älgen Storgatan 61 ☏063/51 75 25, ⊛www.hotelalgen.se. Small, central and handy for the train station, with plain yet comfortable en-suite rooms. ❹/❷

Asken Storgatan 53 ☏063/51 74 50. Only eight rooms, all en suite but rather plain and simple; one is specially equipped for people with allergies. ❸/❷

Aston Köpmangatan 40 ☏063/51 08 51. The cheapest in town, this is a small place with plain rooms – some en suite. Entrance in Postgränd. ❸/❷

Emma Prästgatan 26 ☏063/51 78 40, ⊛www.hotelemma.com. Nineteen tiny, garishly decorated rooms, mostly en suite. ❹/❷

First Hotel Gamla Teatern Thoméegränd 20 ☏063/51 16 00, ⊛www.gamlateatern.se. Without doubt the best hotel in town, in an atmospheric early twentieth-century theatre with sweeping wooden staircases, tall doorways and wide corridors, but disappointingly plain rooms. ❺/❸

Jämteborg Storgatan 54 ☏063/51 01 01. Tasteless, drab and miserable – but cheap and central. ❸/❷

Nya Pensionatet Prästgatan 65 ☏063/51 24 98. Near the train station, this tastefully decorated house, dating from around 1900, has just six rooms, with a shared toilet and shower in the corridor. ❷/❶

Pensionat Svea Storgatan 49 ☏063/51 29 01. Seven tweely decorated rooms with shared toilet and shower. Discounted rates for long-term stays. ❷

Scandic Hotel Östersund Kyrkgatan 70 ☏063/57 57 00, ⊛www.scandic-hotels.com. A massive modern hotel with 126 rooms; high on quality, but low on charm. ❺/❸

Zäta Prästgatan 32 ☏063/51 78 60, ⊛www.hotel-z.com. Simple, plain but comfortable rooms, with cable TV and sauna. ❹/❷

The Town

Östersund's position on the eastern shore of the mighty **Storsjön** (Great Lake) lends the town a seaside holiday atmosphere, unusual this far inland. An instantly likeable place, it's made up of the familiar grid of parallel streets lined with modern quadruple-glazed apartment blocks designed to keep the winter freeze at bay (temperatures regularly plummet as low as -20°C). Strolling through the pedestrianized centre is a relaxed experience; take time out and sip a coffee around the wide open space of Stortorget and watch Swedish provincial life go by, or amble down one of the many side streets that slope down to the still, deep waters of the lake. Here you may be lucky enough to spot Sweden's own Loch Ness monster, **Storsjöodjuret** (⊛www.storsjoodjuret.jamtland.se), a vast dog-headed creature of which sightings are numerous if unsubstantiated.

The main attraction in town is **Jamtli** (late June to mid-Aug daily 11am–5pm; rest of the year Tues–Fri 10am–4pm, Sat & Sun 11am–5pm; ⊛www.jamtli.com; 90kr late June to mid-Aug, otherwise 60kr), an impressive open-air museum a quarter of an hour's walk north of the centre along Rådhusgatan. For the first few minutes it's a bit bewildering, full of people milling around in traditional country costume, farming and milking much as their ancestors did. They live here throughout the summer and everyone is encouraged to join in – baking, tree-felling, grasscutting. Kids, naturally, love it, and you'd have to be pretty cynical not to enjoy the enthusiastic atmosphere. Some intensive work has been done on getting the settings right: the restored and working interiors are gloomy and dirty, with no hint of the usual pristine historical travesty. In the woodman's cottage, presided over by a bearded lumberjack who makes pancakes for visitors, shoeless and scruffy children snooze contentedly in the wooden cots. Outside, even the planted crops and roaming cattle are historically accurate, while an old-fashioned local store, Lanthandel, has been set up among the wooden buildings around the square near the entrance. The indoor **museum** on the same site shows off the county collections: a rambling houseful of local exhibits that includes monster-catching gear devised by nineteenth-century lakeside worthies. The museum's prize exhibits are the awe-inspiring Viking **Överhogdal tapestries**, which date from the ninth or tenth centuries – discovered in an outhouse in 1910, the tapestries are crowded with brightly coloured animals and buildings.

Back in the centre, apart from the **City Museum** (*Stadsmuseum*; Mon–Fri 10am–4pm, Sat & Sun 1–4pm; 30kr) – a crowded two hundred years of history in a building the size of a shoebox – on Rådhusgatan, and the neighbouring **Gamla kyrkan** (June–Aug 8am–8pm; Sept–May Mon–Fri 1–3pm), there's not a vast amount in the way of sights. Take a look though, at the **harbour**, with its fleet of tiny boats and the occasional seaplane bobbing about on the clean water. Immediately to the right of the harbour is the tiny **Badhusparken** – an inordinately popular spot in summer for catching a few rays.

Finally, it's possible to go monster-spotting on a **lake cruise** on board *S/S Thomée* – a creaking old wooden steamship built in 1875. Routes and timetables vary but always include a two-hour trip around the lake (75kr), amongst other destinations; for more information contact the tourist office.

Frösön

Take the foot- or road-bridge across the lake from Badhusparken and you'll come to the island of **Frösön**. People have lived here since prehistoric times – Frösön's name derives from the Viking settlement on the island and its association with the pagan god of fertility, Frö. There's plenty of good walking here, as well as a couple of historical stops. Just over the bridge in front of a red-brick office block, look out for the eleventh-century **rune stone** that tells of a man called Östmadur (East Man), son of Gudfast, who brought Christianity to the people of Jämtland – presumably from some point to the east. From here you can clamber up the nearby hill of Öneberget, where you'll find the fourth-century settlement of Mjälleborgen – the most extensive in Norrland.

Follow the main road west and up the hill for about 5km (or take bus #3 from the centre of Östersund) to the beautiful **Frösö kyrka**, an eleventh-century church with a detached bell tower. In 1984 archeologists digging under the church's altar came across a bit of birch stump surrounded by the bones of bears, pigs, deer and squirrels – evidence of the cult of ancient gods, the *Aesir*, and an indication that the site has been a place of worship for almost two thousand years. Today the church is one of the most popular in Sweden for marriages – especially at Midsummer, for which you have to book years in advance.

Eating, drinking and nightlife

Gastronomically, Östersund has more to offer than any other town further north. For **breakfast**, the train station café is good value and always busy, while **coffee** and cakes are best had at *Wedemarks Konditori*, Prästgatan 27, where you can also make up your own sandwiches.

Athena Stortorget 3. Pompously decorated place tucked away in one corner of Stortorget, offering tasty pizzas from 55kr.
Brunkullans Krog Postgränd 5. This old-fashioned, home-from-home restaurant, with polished lanterns

and a heavy wooden interior, is Östersund's premier eating place, offering traditional Swedish fare as well as more international fish and meat dishes. It's expensive, although in summer there are tables in the garden at the rear with a cheaper menu.

Captain Cook Hamngatan 9. A selection of delicious, moderately-priced Australian-style grilled delights (around 100kr) that really draw in the crowds – also one of the most popular places for a drink, with an extensive beer and whisky selection.

Eastern Palace Storgatan 15. The town's best Chinese food, with all the usual dishes at moderate prices.

Kvarterskrogen Storgatan 54. Upmarket restaurant, with tables decked out in fresh linen and high prices to match. Lamb, entrecôte, beef and sole dishes, as well as northern Swedish delicacies, start at 170kr.

O'Leary's Storgatan 28. Popular Irish-style pub offering a large selection of beer and a TexMex-inspired menu with mains around 120kr.

Paviljong Prästgatan 50B. The best Thai and Indonesian restaurant in central northern Sweden – make the most of it. Main courses go for around 119kr (try the excellent chicken with garlic chilli and Thai basil), or there's a lunch for 60kr.

Restaurang G III/Pub Köket *Hotel Östersund*, Kyrkgatan 70. The first is a standard, fairly expensive à la carte restaurant; the second (right beside it) is one of the town's popular drinking holes.

Simon & Viktor Prästgatan 19. An English-style watering hole at the top end of Stortorget serving upmarket pub grub. If you're longing for fish and chips (75kr), you're in luck.

Listings

Banks Handelsbanken, Sparbanken and FöreningsSparbanken are all on Prästgatan.

Bike rental Cykelogen, Kyrkogatan 45 (☏063/12 20 80), rents mountain bikes from about 100kr per day.

Bus enquiries For information on all buses call ☏020/61 62 63 or visit ⌨www.lanstrafiken-z.se. The express bus, Inlandsexpressen (#45), leaves from the bus station south to Mora (2 daily) and north to Gällivare (1 daily). You can't book seats, just pay on board, but there is usually enough room – though it's always wise to get there early. For information on the Y-Bussen express service to Stockholm, call ☏063/15 55 65.

Car rental Avis, Bangårdsgatan 9 ☏063/10 12

50; Europcar, Hofvallsgränd 1 ☏063/57 47 50; Hertz, Kyrkgatan 32 ☏063/57 50 30.

Left luggage Lockers at the train station for 15kr.

Pharmacy Prästgatan 51 (Mon–Wed & Fri 9am–6pm, Thurs 10am–7pm, Sat 9am–4pm, Sun 11am–4pm).

Police Köpmangatan 24 ☏063/15 25 00.

Systembolaget Prästgatan 18 (Mon–Wed & Fri 10am–6pm); Kyrkgatan 82 (Mon–Wed & Fri 10am–6pm, Thurs 10am–7pm, Sat 10am–2pm).

Taxi Taxi Östersund ☏063/51 72 00.

Trains For SJ information, call ☏0771/75 75 75. The Inlandsbanan leaves daily (late June to early Aug) heading south for Mora at 3pm and north to Gällivare at 7.05am.

West to Åre

The E14 highway and the train line from Östersund follow the route trudged by medieval pilgrims on their way to Nidaros (now Trondheim) over the border in Norway, a twisting course that threads its way through sharp–edged mountains rising high above a bevy of fast-flowing streams and deep, cold lakes. Time and again the eastern Vikings assembled their armies beside the holy Storsjön lake to begin the long march west, most famously in 1030 when King Olaf of Norway collected his mercenaries for the campaign that led to his death at the Battle of Stiklestad. The Vikings always crossed the mountains as quickly as possible and so today – although the scenery is splendid – there's nothing much to stop for en route, other than the winter-skiing and summer-walking centres of **Åre** and **Storlien**.

Åre

The Alpine village of **ÅRE**, two hours by train from Östersund, is Sweden's most prestigious ski resort, with 44 lifts and snow guaranteed between December and May. During the snowbound season rooms are like gold dust and prices sky-high: if you do come to ski, book accommodation well in advance through the tourist office or, better still, come on a package tour. Equipment rental isn't too expensive: downhill and cross-country gear starts at 180kr per day – contact the tourist office.

In summer the village is a haven for ramblers, sandwiched as it is between Åresjön lake and a range of craggy hills overshadowed by the mighty 1420-metre-high

Åreskutan mountain. A network of **walking tracks** criss-crosses the hills or, for a more energetic scramble, take the **Kabinbanan**, Sweden's only cable-car (100kr return), up to a viewing platform from where it's a thirty-minute clamber to the summit. The view is stunning – on a clear day you can see over to the border with Norway and a good way back to Östersund. Bear in mind, though, that even the shortest walk back to Åre takes two hours and requires some stamina.

The **tourist office** (mid June to Aug & early Dec to April daily 9am–6pm; May to mid-June & Sept to early Dec Mon–Fri 9am–5pm, Sat & Sun 10am–3pm; ☏0647/177 20) is in the square, 100m up the steps opposite the train station. It has detailed mountain maps and endless information on hiking in the nearby mountains and further afield – ask for the excellent *Hiking in Årefjällen* booklet. They can also help with mountain biking in the area.

The tourist office can help fix up a **private room** from around 125kr per person in summer, almost all of them with kitchen, shower and TV. Otherwise, the cheapest option is the unofficial **youth hostel** known as *Parkvillan* (☏0647/177 33; groups only in summer), in the park below the square; the **campsite** (☏0647/136 00; closed Sept–Nov) is five minutes' walk from the station – head to the right. There are a few private double rooms (❶) here, as well as dorms.

Åre's **eating** possibilities aren't up to much, but there are several cheap places around the square: try the cheerful *Café Bubblan*, which does reasonable lunches of pies and sandwiches, or the more substantial dishes and pizzas served at nearby *Werséns*. At the cable-car terminus, *Bykrogen* serves decent main meals from 100kr.

Storlien

Just 6km from the Norwegian border and a favourite feasting spot for the region's mosquitoes, **STORLIEN** is the place to stop if you plan to do some hiking, which is good and rugged around here. The countryside hereabouts is also prime berry-picking territory (the rare cloudberry grows here), while mushrooms, in particular chanterelles, can be found in great number. There's not much else here though, apart from a **tourist office** inside the train station (Mon–Fri 9.30am–2.30pm; ☏0647/705 70, ☏703 51), a supermarket and a couple of **hotels**, the best of which is *Storliens Högfjällshotell* (☏0647/701 70, ❻), ten minutes' walk from the tourist office, a luxury affair with nearly two hundred well-appointed rooms and its own swimming pool.

Storlien's **youth hostel** (☏0647/700 50, ☢www.scout.se/km/storvallen) is a four-kilometre walk across the railway tracks to the E14 and then left down the main road towards Storvallen. **Eating and drinking** is not easy, with just two options, the better of which is the *Le Ski* restaurant, nightclub and bar at the train station; otherwise, coffee, pizzas and burgers are available at *Sylvias Kanonbar* in the main square in front of the station.

Moving on from Storlien, trains operated by Norwegian Railways leave for Trondheim in Norway (2 daily). In the opposite direction there are also services to Stockholm and Gothenburg via Östersund.

North to Swedish Lapland

Beyond Östersund the **Inlandsbanan** slowly snakes its way across the remote Swedish hinterland heading for **Swedish Lapland** (known in Swedish as the province of Lappland), a truly enormous region stretching from just south of the town of Vilhelmina (see opposite) to the Finnish and Norwegian borders in the north and east towards (but not including) the Bothnian Coast. This is a vast and scarcely populated region where the train often has to stop for elk and reindeer – and occasionally bears – to be cleared from the tracks. On the other occasions that the train comes to a halt with no station in sight, it's usually for a reason – a spot of berry-picking, perhaps – while at the Arctic Circle everyone jumps off for photos.

Route 45, the **Inlandsvägen**, sticks close to the train line on its way north to Gällivare – if you're not bound to the train this should be your preferred road north. It's easy to drive and well surfaced for the most part, though watch out for suicidal reindeer – once they spot a car hurtling towards them they'll do their utmost to throw themselves underneath it. **Bus** travellers on the daily Inlandsexpressen from Östersund to Gällivare will also take this route.

Vilhelmina and Storuman

Four hours up the Inlandsbanan from Östersund, **VILHELMINA** is a pretty little town that was formerly an important forestry centre. The timber business moved out of town some ten years ago, however, and the main source of employment nowadays is a telephone-booking centre for Swedish Railways. Despite the grandeur hinted at by the town's name (from Fredrika Dorotea Vilhelmina, the wife of King Gustav IV Adolf), Vilhelmina remains a quiet little place with just one main street. The principal attraction is the **parish village**, nestling between Storgatan and Ljusminnesgatan, whose thirty-odd wooden cottages date back to 1792 when the first church was consecrated. It's since been restored and today the cottages can be rented out via the **tourist office** (mid-June to mid-Aug Mon–Fri 8am–8pm, Sat & Sun noon–6pm; mid-Aug to mid-June Mon–Fri 9am–5.30pm; ☎0940/152 70, ⓦwww.vilhelmina.se) on the main street, Volgsjövägen, a five-minute walk up Postgatan from the **train station**, which also serves as the **bus station**.

Vilhelmina's **campsite**, *Rasten Saiva Camping* (☎0940/107 60), is about ten minutes' walk from the centre and has four-berth cabins for rent for 250–525kr, as well as a great sandy **beach**; head down Volgsjövägen from the centre and take the first left. There are two central **hotels** in town: the ostentatious *Wilhelmina* (☎0940/554 20, ⓦwww.hotell.vilhelmina.com; ❹/❸), at Volgsjövägen 16, and the friendly *Lilla* (☎0940/150 59, ⓦwww.lillahotellet.vilhelmina.com; ❸/❷) at Granvägen 1.

There isn't exactly a multitude of **eating and drinking** options: try the à la carte restaurant at the *Hotell Wilhelmina* for traditional northern Swedish dishes and 65kr lunches, or the plain *Pizzeria Lascité*, Volgsjövägen 27. In the evenings locals gravitate towards *Krogen Besk* opposite *Lilla Hotellet* for a drink or two.

Storuman

STORUMAN, an hour up the line from Vilhelmina, is a transport hub for this part of southern Lapland. **Buses** run northwest up the E12, skirting the Tärnafjällen mountains, to Tärnaby and Hemavan, before wiggling through to Mo-i-Rana in Norway and, in the opposite direction, down to Umeå via Lycksele, where there are connections on to Vindeln and Vännäs on the main coastal rail line. A direct bus, the Lapplandspilen, also links Storuman with Stockholm.

There's not much to Storuman itself – the centre consists of one tiny street supporting a couple of shops and banks. The **tourist office** (late June to mid-Aug Mon–Fri 9am–8pm, Sat & Sun 10am–5pm; rest of the year Mon–Fri 9am–5pm; ☎0951/333 70, ⓦwww.storuman.se) is 50m right of the **train station** on Järnvägsgatan. While it's possible to stay here – the **youth hostel** (☎0951/333 80) and the luxurious *Hotell Toppen* (☎0951/777 00, ⓦwww.hotelltoppen.com; ❹/❷) are both only a ten-minute walk up the hill at Blå Vägen 238 – it's much better to head off into the mountains for some good **hiking** and **fishing**.

If you do stay, try the **restaurant** at *Hotell Toppen*, which has a lunch buffet for 65kr, or alternatively there's the basic, reasonably priced *Blå Stjärnan* behind the Konsum supermarket in the main square. Better is *Restaurang Storuman*, opposite the train station, which does Chinese food, pizzas and lunch deals.

Tärnaby and Hemavan

Four **buses** daily make the two-hour drive northwest from Storuman to the tiny mountain village of **TÄRNABY**, birthplace of Ingemar Stenmark, double Olympic gold medallist and Sweden's greatest skier. It's a pretty place, with flower-decked meadows running to the edge of the mountain forests, and great swaths of world-class ski slopes. At the eastern edge of the village as you approach from Storuman, the **Samegården** (late June to mid-Aug daily 9am–5pm; 20kr) offers a pleasant introduction to Sámi history, culture and customs. The museum recalls older times when, after a kill in a bear hunt, the gall bladder was cut open and the fluid drunk by the hunters. The **tourist office** (mid-June to mid-Aug daily 9am–8pm; mid-Aug to mid-June Mon–Fri 8.30am–5pm; ☎0954/104 50, ⊛www.tarnaby.se) on the main street can provide information on fishing and hiking in the area. One popular walk is across the nearby Laxfjället mountain, with its fantastic views down over the village – it can be reached by chair lift from either of the two hotels mentioned below. If it's sunny, head for the **beach** at Lake Laisan, where the water is often warm enough to swim – take the footpath which branches off right from Sandviksvägen past the **campsite**. There are several inexpensive places **to stay** – try the *Tärnaby Fjällhotell*, Östra Strandvägen 16 (☎0954/301 50, ℗106 27; Dec–April; ❶), which also has four-bed apartments for 445kr per day; or the *Tärnaby Skilodge* (☎0954/104 25, ℗106 80; Dec–April; ❷) on Skyttevägen, which also rents out two- to six-berth cabins during the summer for 545kr per day.

Buses continue on from Tärnaby to **HEMAVAN**, which marks the beginning and the end of the 500-kilometre Kungsleden trail – see p.647. If you need to stay, head for the *FBU-Gården* **youth hostel** (☎0954/300 02, ⊛www.fbu.to; mid-June to Sept) on Blå Vägen, the main road into the village from Tärnaby. If you have your own transport, you could continue along the E12 towards Norway to the friendly *Sånninggården* guesthouse (☎0954/330 00, ℗330 06; ❶), dramatically located next to a range of craggy mountains and renowned for its excellent food – the all-day lunch buffet is just 99kr. It's also the last stop for the Lapplandspilen bus from Stockholm and Hemavan.

Arvidsjaur and the Arctic Circle

Four hours north of Storuman on the Inlandsbanan, **ARVIDSJAUR** is by far the largest town you'll have passed since Östersund – though that's not saying much. Streets of drab houses spread out either side of a nondescript and indeterminate main street, Storgatan. For centuries this was where the region's Sámi gathered to trade and debate, until their agenda was hijacked by the Protestant missionaries who established their first church here in 1606. Arvidsjaur's success was secured when silver was discovered in the nearby mountains and the town flourished as a staging point and supply depot. Despite these developments, the Sámi continued to assemble here on market days and during religious festivals, building their own parish village, the **Lappstaden** (daily tours in July at 6pm, 25kr; at other times you can walk in for free), of simple wooden huts at the end of the eighteenth century. About eighty of these have survived, clumped unceremoniously towards the north end of town next to a modern yellow apartment block; they're still used today for the Storstämningshelgen festival over the last weekend in August, as well as for auctions and other events throughout the year. There are still around twenty Sámi families in Arvisdjaur, making their living from reindeer husbandry.

There's no real reason to tarry, but if you want to stay, head for the **tourist office** (mid-June to mid-Aug daily 8.30am–6.30pm; mid-Aug to mid-June Mon–Fri 9am–5pm; ☎0960/175 00, ⊛www.arvidsjaurturism.se) at Östra Skolgatan 18C, just off Storgatan and five minutes' walk from the station up Lundavägen. They'll fix you up with a **private room** for around 130kr per person, plus a booking fee of 20kr. The best place to stay, however, is *Rallaren* (☎070/682 32 84; late June–Aug), a wonderful old wooden house, tastefully restored by a local artist, that operates as a luxury **youth hostel**. There's also the cosy private hostel, *Lappugglan*, conveniently situated at Västra Skolgatan 9 (☎0960/124 13); or you could try *Camp Gielas* (☎0960/556 00), which also has **cabins** from 450kr for up to four people set beside Tvättjärn, one of the town's dozen or so lakes, a few minutes' walk along Strandvägen and Järnvägsgatan from the tourist office. The only **hotel** in town is *Hotell Laponia* at Storgatan 45 (☎0960/555 00, ⊛www.laponia-gielas.se; ❹/❸), with comfortable, modern en-suite rooms and a swimming pool. Be warned that in winter much of the town's accommodation is full of test drivers from Europe's leading car companies, who come to the area to experience driving on the frozen lakes – book well in advance to secure a room.

For **snacks** and **coffee** try *Kaffestugan* at Storgatan 21, which has sandwiches and salads for around 50kr. There's a small choice of **restaurants**: for pizzas and Italian food try *Athena* at Storgatan 10, which has a 65kr lunch deal. Next door at Storgatan 8, *Cazba* serves up pizzas for the same price but has less atmosphere. For finer food, head for the restaurant at the *Hotell Laponia*, where delicious à la carte meals, including local reindeer, go for 120–150kr. The **bar** here is the place to be seen of an evening, but be prepared to shell out around 55kr for a beer.

The Arctic Circle

A couple of hours north of Arvidsjaur the Inlandsbanan finally crosses the **Arctic Circle** (⊛www.turism.jokkmokk.se/arcticcircle.shtml). This is occasion enough for a bout of whistle-blowing as the train pulls up to allow everyone to take photos of the hoardings announcing the crossing: due to the earth's uneven orbit the line is creeping northwards at a rate of up to 15m a year and the circle is now around 1km north, but for argument's sake this spot is as good as any. Painted white rocks curve away over the hilly ground, a crude but popular representation of the Circle: one foot on each side is the standard photographic pose.

Jokkmokk

During his journey in Lapland, the botanist Carl von Linné said "If not for the mosquitoes, this would be earth's paradise"; his comments were made after journeying along the river valley of the Lilla Luleälven during the short summer weeks when the mosquitoes are at their most active. **JOKKMOKK**'s Sámi name comes from one particular bend (*mokk*) in the river (*jokk*), which runs through a densely forested municipality the size of Wales with a minuscule population of just 6500; needless to say, the town is a welcome oasis, though not an immediately appealing one. Once wintertime Sámi quarters, a market and church heralded a permanent settlement by the beginning of the seventeenth century. Today, as well as being a well-known handicrafts centre, the town functions as the Sámi capital and is home to the Samernas Folkhögskola, the only further education college teaching handicrafts, reindeer husbandry and ecology in the Sámi language.

Jokkmokk's fantastic **Ájtte Museum** (*ájtte* means storage hut in Sámi), a brief walk east of the centre on Kyrkogatan, off the main Storgatan (mid-June to mid-Aug daily 9am–6pm; rest of the year Mon–Fri 10am–4pm, Sat & Sun noon–4pm, closed Sat Oct–April; ⊛www.ajtte.com; 50kr), is the place to really mug up on the Sámi. Displays and exhibitions recount the tough existence of the original settlers of northern Scandinavia and show how things have slowly improved over time – today's Sámi are more dependent on snow scooters and helicopters to herd their reindeer than on the age-old methods employed by their ancestors. There are some imaginative temporary exhibitions on Sámi culture and local flora and fauna, and the museum staff can also arrange day-trips into the surrounding marshes for a spot of mushroom-picking (and mosquito-swatting). Close to the museum on Lappstavägen, the **alpine garden** (late June to early Aug Mon–Fri 10am–4pm, Sat & Sun 10am–3pm; other times by arrangement on ☎0971/101 00; 25kr) is home to moor-king, mountain avens, glacier crowfoot and other vegetation to be found on the fells around Jokkmokk.

The Jokkmokk winter market

Now nearly 400 years old, the great **Jokkmokk winter market** (*Jokkmokks marknad*; ⓦwww.jokkmokksmarknad.com) is held in the first week of February (Thurs–Sun), and sees 30,000 people force their way into town, increasing the population almost tenfold. It's the best and coldest time of the year to be in Jokkmokk – there's a Wild West feeling in the air – with lots of drunken stall holders trying to flog reindeer hides and other unwanted knick-knacks to even more drunken passers-by – and all in, literally, Arctic temperatures. The **reindeer races** can be a real spectacle: held on the frozen Talvatissjön lake behind the *Hotell Jokkmokk*, man and beast battle it out on a specially marked track on the ice; however, the reindeer often have other ideas and frequently veer off with great alacrity into the crowd, sending spectators fleeing for cover. Staying in town at this time of year means booking accommodation a good year in advance (although some private rooms become available in the autumn before the market). A smaller and less traditional autumn fair is held at the end of August (around the 25th) – an easier though poorer option.

Have a look, too, at the **Lapp kyrka**, off Stortorget, a recent copy of the eighteenth-century church that stood on this site. The octagonal design and curiously shaped tower betray a Sámi influence, but the surrounding graveyard wall is all improvisation: the space in between the coarsely hewn timbers was used to store coffins during winter until the thaw in May, when the Sámi could go out and dig graves again – temperatures in this part of Sweden regularly plunge to -30°C and below in winter.

Practicalities

Arriving by Inlandsbanan, it's a short walk south up Stationsgatan to the two main parallel streets, Storgatan and Åsgatan. If you're here for the winter market (when the Inlandsbanan isn't running), get off the train at Murjek (between Boden and Gällivare), from where buses run west to Jokkmokk four times a day. Jokkmokk's **tourist office**, at Stortorget 4 (mid-June to mid-Aug daily 9am–7pm; mid-Aug to mid-June Mon–Fri 8.30am–4pm; ☎0971/121 40, ⓦwww.turism.jokkmokk.se), is a five-minute walk from the train station along Stationsgatan. The **youth hostel** (☎0971/559 77, ⓦwww.jokkmokkhostel.com) is located in a wonderful old house with a garden at Åsgatan 20, behind the tourist office. The *Jokkmokk-Camping-Center* **campsite** (☎0971/123 70, ⓦwww.jokkmokkcampingcenter.com) is a 3km walk southeast of town on Lule River, off the main E97 to Luleå and Boden. Of the town's two **hotels**, *Jokkmokk* has a convenient and attractive lakeside setting at Solgatan 45 (☎0971/777 00, ⓦwww.hoteljokkmokk.se; ❺/❸), though its en-suite rooms are very ordinary and the restaurant a 1970s throwback; *Hotell Gästis* at Herrevägen 1 (☎0971/100 12, ⓦwww.hotell-gastis.com; ❹/❸) is nothing to write home about either, with simple, modern en-suite rooms.

Jokkmokk has a limited number of **eating** and **drinking** possibilities. The cheap and cheerful *Restaurang Kowloon* at Berggatan has lunch for 62kr and Chinese meals for around 90kr at other times, while pizzas from 60kr and simple fry-ups are available at *Restaurang Opera* at Storgatan 36. For traditional Sámi dishes such as reindeer, head for the restaurant at the Ájtte Museum, where lunch costs 60kr – the cloudberries and ice cream here are simply divine. The best place to drink is the *Restaurang Opera*; failing that, the bar inside the *Hotell Jokkmokk* – if you've drunk your way round Jokkmokk this far you won't mind the inebriated late-night company here.

Gällivare

Last stop on the Inlandsbanan and by far the biggest town since Östersund, **GÄLLIVARE** is far more pleasant than you'd imagine from its industrial surroundings. Strolling around its open centre, heavily glazed and insulated against the biting cold of winter, is a great antidote to the small inland villages along the train route. There's a gritty ugliness to Gällivare that gives the place a certain charm: a steely grey mesh of modern streets that has all the hallmarks of a city, although on a scale that's far too modest for the title to be applied with any justification. It's also an excellent base for hiking in the nearby national parks (see p.643).

Arrival, information and accommodation

Gällivare's **train station**, on Lasarettsgatan, is five minutes' walk from the **tourist office** at Storgatan 16 (late June to late Aug Mon–Fri 9am–8pm, Sat & Sun 10am–5pm; rest of the year Mon–Fri 9am–4pm; ℡0970/166 60, ⓦwww.gellivare.se), where you can get hiking information and good free maps; upstairs in the same building there's a simple **museum** dealing with Sámi history and forestry.

The tourist office can fix you up with a **private room** for around 150kr per person, plus a booking fee of 25kr, or you could sample the town's **youth hostel**

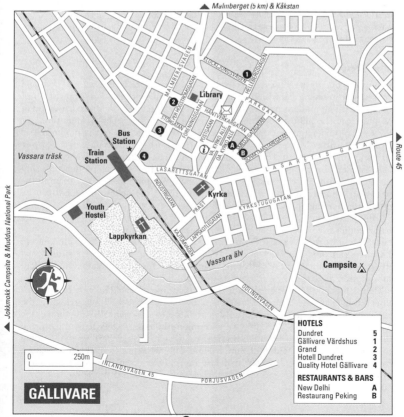

▲ *Malmberget (5 km) & Kåkstan*

◄ *Jokkmokk Campsite & Muddus National Park*

Vassara träsk

Bus Station

Train Station

Library

Kyrka

Youth Hostel

Lappkyrkan

N

Vassara älv

Campsite ⚊

► *Route 45*

0   250m

INLANDSVÄGEN 45

PORJUSVÄGEN

GÄLLIVARE

HOTELS
Dundret	5
Gällivare Värdshus	1
Grand	2
Hotell Dundret	3
Quality Hotel Gällivare	4

RESTAURANTS & BARS
New Delhi	A
Restaurang Peking	B

▼ ⑤ *(1 km) & Sámi Camp at Repisvare*

(☎0970/143 80, ℗165 86; open all year but bookings required Sept–May), behind the train station – cross the tracks by the metal bridge; because of the town's position on routes north to Kiruna and Narvik (and south to Stockholm and Gothenburg), booking ahead in summer is advised. This is a wonderful place to stay in winter when the Vassara träsk lake is frozen – snow scooters whizz up and down its length under the eerie Northern Lights, clearly visible in Gällivare. There's also a **campsite** (☎0970/100 10; mid-May to mid-Sept) by the river and off the main E45 between Porjusvägen and Jokkmokk. If you've your own transport, undoubtedly the most interesting place to stay is in the simple wooden huts at the reconstructed shantytown, **Kåkstan**, up at Malmberget, the hill 1km to the north of the town (☎0970/183 96 or book through the tourist office). A four-berth hut costs 360kr; cheaper dormitory accommodation in an eight-bed room goes for just 90kr.

Dundret ☎0970/145 60, ⊛www.dundret.se. The most luxurious hotel, but it's at the top of the Dundret mountain south of the town, so you'll need your own transport to get here. Not to be confused with the *Hotell Dundret* in town. ❺/❹

Hotell Dundret Per Högströmsgatan 1 ☎0970/550 40. Actually a small pension, with just seven rooms and shared shower and toilet. ❸/❷

Gällivare Värdshus Klockljungsvägen 2 ☎0970/162 00, ℗155 45. A German-run cheapie which is an excellent central choice and a good place to meet other backpackers. ❸/❷

Grand Per Högströmsgatan 9 ☎0970/164 20, ⊛www.grand-hotel.nu. The second-best hotel in town, with decent en-suite rooms. Handily situated for the *Kilkenny Inn*, which shares the same building. ❸/❷

Quality Hotel Gällivare Lasarettsgatan 1 ☎0970/550 20, ℗154 75. The best in town, with smart, tastefully decorated rooms and a good restaurant (see opposite), and handy for the station. ❹/❸

The Town

Gällivare is one of the most important sources of **iron ore** in Europe, and if you've any interest in seeing a working mine, don't wait until Kiruna's tame "tourist tour" (see p.645). The modern mines and works are distant, dark blots, tucked away up at Malmberget, the hill overlooking Gällivare. There are two separate tours (book at the tourist office), both running from June to August: one is of the underground **iron-ore mine** (Mon–Fri 1.30pm; 200kr); the other of the opencast **copper mine** (Mon–Fri 1.30pm; 160kr), which is the biggest in Europe (and also, incidentally, Sweden's biggest gold mine – gold is recovered from the slag produced during the extraction of the copper). The ear-splitting noise produced by the mammoth-sized trucks in the iron-ore mine (they're five times the height of a man) can be quite disconcerting in the confined darkness.

Gällivare occupies the site of a Sámi village and one theory has it that the town's name comes from the Sámi language – *djelli* (a crack or gorge) *vare* (in the mountain). Down by the river near the train station, you'll come across the Sámi church, **Lappkyrkan** (mid-June to late Aug 10am–3pm), a mid-eighteenth-century construction. It's known as the "Ettöreskyrkan" (One Öre Church) after the one öre subscription drive throughout Sweden that paid for it.

There's precious little else to see or do in Gällivare and you'd be wise to use your time strolling up the **Dundret** mountain, overshadowing the town, which is the target of Midnight Sun spotters. You can walk up to the *Björnfällan* restaurant (the name means "bear trap"), about a four-kilometre hike on a well-marked path, and the views are magnificent, though this isn't the very top. Buses head up the winding road specially for the Midnight Sun, leaving daily at 11pm from the train station (mid-June to mid-July), and returning at 1am. Tickets, available from the tourist office, cost 200kr return and include the ubiquitous Swedish waffle covered with cloudberries and cream.

Eating and drinking

If you're arriving from one of the tiny villages on the Inlandsbanan, the wealth of **eating and drinking** possibilities in Gällivare will make you quite dizzy; if you're coming from Luleå, grit your teeth and bear it. A good place for lunch is the *Restaurang Peking* at Storgatan 21B, which has pizzas and reasonable Chinese food from 60kr. The *New Delhi*, Storgatan 19, offers Indian dishes for around 120k, but the food can be a little on the bland side. As for **drinking**, the place to be seen is the Irish-theme pub, *Kilkenny Inn* at Per Högströmsgatan 9, or the *Vassara Pub* inside the *Quality Hotel Gällivare* opposite the train station.

Around Gällivare: the national parks

Gällivare is surrounded by some of Sweden's remotest and most beautiful terrain, and the town is within easy striking distance of no less than four **national parks**, which provide a ready taste of the wild side of Swedish Lapland – Europe's last wilderness.

Hemmed in by the Inlandsbanan on one side and the train line from Boden to Gällivare on the other, **Muddus** (⊚www.fjallen.nu/parker/muddus.htm) is the ideal national park for beginners, a pine forest and marshland park between Jokkmokk and Gällivare that's home to bears, lynx, martens, weasels, hares, elk and, in summer, reindeer; the whooper swan is one of the most commonly sighted birds. Muddus is easy to reach with your own car. The park's western edges are skirted by Route 45 and the easiest approach is to leave the highway at Liggadammen and

Hiking in the National Parks

It's not a good idea to go **hiking in the national parks** of northern Sweden on a whim. Even for experienced walkers, the going can be tough and uncomfortable in parts, downright treacherous in others. Mosquitoes are a real problem: it's difficult to imagine the utter misery of being covered in a blanket of insects; your eyes, ears and nose full of the creatures. Yet this is one of the last wilderness areas left in Europe: the map of this part of the country shows little more than vast areas of forest and mountains; roads and human habitation are the exception rather than the norm. Reindeer are a common sight since the parks are breeding grounds and summer pasture, and Sámi settlements are dotted throughout the region – at Ritsem and Vaisaluokta, for example. Although there are some good short trails in the national parks, suitable for beginners, the goal for more ambitious hikers is the northern section of the **Kungsleden** trail (see p.647), which crosses several of the parks.

The best **time** to go hiking in the Swedish mountains is from late June to September. During May and early June the ground is very wet and boggy due to the rapid snow melt. Once the snow has gone, wild flowers burst into bloom to make the most of the short summer months. The **weather** is very changeable – one moment it can be hot and sunny, the next it can be cold and rainy – snow showers are by no means uncommon even in summer. It goes without saying that you'll need to be **well equipped** with hiking gear, a sleeping bag, decent boots and of course a map.

then follow the small road to Skaite. You can also reach the park from the southeast via Nattavaara and Messaure. An easy hiking trail of 50km starts at Skaite, with cabins along the route and a campsite by the Muddus falls. There's no public transport right to the start of the trail: take the bus to Liggadammen and then walk 12km to Skaite and the beginning of the network of trails.

Beginning about 120km northwest of Gällivare, the tract of wilderness edging Norway contains no fewer than three national parks, with the low fells, large lakes and moors of Padjelanta and Stora Sjöfallet parks framing the sheer face of the mountainous and inhospitable Sarek park. **Padjelanta** (Wwww.fjallen .nu/parker/padje.htm) is the largest national park in Sweden; the Sámi name means "the higher country", an apt description for an elevated tableland almost exclusively above the treeline and home to thousands of reindeer. A 150-kilometre hiking route, the **Padjelanta Trail**, runs from Kvikkjokk (reached by bus from Jokkmokk) north through Stora Sjöfallet to Vaisaluokta, from where a boat (late Feb to mid-May and late June to late Sept; ☎0973/420 30) crosses the Akkajaure lake to and from Ritsem. Padjelanta is a good option for inexperienced walkers, but allow at least a week. From Ritsem there are buses back to Gällivare.

The real baddie of the parks is **Sarek** (Wwww.fjallen.nu/parker/sarek.htm), the terrain being officially classed as "extremely difficult". There are no tourist facilities, trails, cabins or bridges; the rivers are dangerous and the weather rotten – definitely not for anyone without Chris Bonington-type experience.

Kiruna and around

KIRUNA was at the hub of the battle for the control of the iron-ore supply during World War II. Ore was transported north from Kiruna by train to the great harbour at Narvik over the border in Norway, and much German fire power was expended in an attempt to interrupt the supply to the Allies and wrest control for the Axis. In the process, Narvik suffered grievously, whilst Kiruna – benefiting from supposed Swedish neutrality – made a packet selling to both sides.

Today the train ride to Kiruna rattles through sidings, slag heaps and ore works, a bitter contrast to the surrounding wilderness. Brooding reminders of Kiruna's prosperity, the **mines** still dominate the town, and much more depressingly than in neighbouring Gällivare, two hours back down the train line: despite the new central buildings and open parks, Kiruna retains a gritty industrial air. **Guided tours** of the mines are arranged by the tourist office (July to mid-Aug 3 daily; late June and late Aug 2 daily; 140kr); times are variable. A coach takes visitors through the underground road network and then stops off at a "tourist mine", a closed-off section of a leviathan structure containing service stations, restaurants, computer centres, trains and crushing mills. All the other sights in town are firmly wedded to the all-important metal in one way or another. The tower of the **Stadshus** on Hjalmar Lundbohmsvägen (June–Aug daily 9am–6pm; Sept–May Mon–Fri 8am–5pm) is obvious even from the train station, a strident metal pillar harbouring an intricate latticework clock face and sundry bells that chime raucously at noon. It was designed by Bror Marklund and the whole hall unbelievably won the 1964 award for the most beautiful Swedish public building. Inside there's a tolerable art collection and Sámi handicraft displays in summer.

Only a few minutes up the road, **Kiruna kyrka** (daily 11am–4.45pm; July till 10pm) causes a few raised eyebrows. Built in the style of a Sámi hut, it's a massive origami creation of oak beams and rafters the size of a small aircraft hangar. LKAB, the iron-ore company that to all intents and purposes *is* Kiruna, and which paid for its construction, was also responsible for the nearby **Hjalmar Lundbohmsgården** (June–Aug daily 10am–5pm; Sept–May Mon–Fri 10am–4pm; 30kr), a country house once used by the managing director of the company and "founder" of Kiruna. Displays inside mostly consist of early twentieth-century photographs featuring the man himself and assorted Sámi in their winter gear. Visit before going

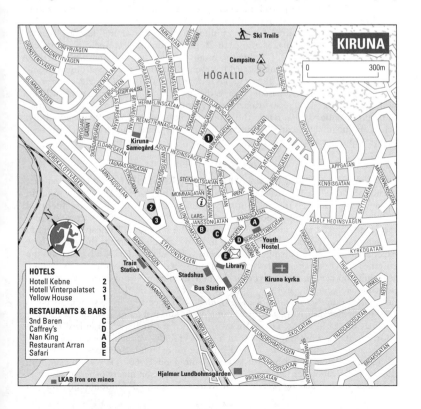

KIRUNA

HÖGALID

Ski Trails

Campsite

0   300m

Kiruna Samegård

Youth Hostel

Train Station

Stadshus

Library

Kiruna kyrka

Bus Station

HOTELS
Hotell Kebne — 2
Hotell Vinterpalatset — 3
Yellow House — 1

RESTAURANTS & BARS
3nd Baren — C
Caffrey's — D
Nan King — A
Restaurant Arran — B
Safari — E

LKAB Iron ore mines

Hjalmar Lundbohmsgården

3

3.6 | SWEDEN | Central and northern Sweden

down the mine and everything will take on an added perspective – without the mine, Kiruna would be a one-reindeer town instead of the thriving place it is today.

The **Kiruna Samegård**, at Brytaregatan 14 (mid-June to Sept daily 10am–6pm; Oct to mid-June Mon–Fri 10am–4pm; 20kr), is the most rewarding exhibition of Sámi culture in town. The handicrafts may be familiar but what won't be is the small display of really very good Sámi art featuring scenes from everyday life. There's a souvenir shop where you can buy a piece of antler bone or reindeer skin to take home.

Practicalities

Arriving by **train**, it's a brisk ten-minute walk from the station, first through the car park, then under the road bridge and up the steep hill, Konduktörsgatan, to the **tourist office** within Folkets Hus, in the central square off Mommagatan (mid-June to Aug Mon–Fri 8.30am–8pm, Sat & Sun 8.30am–6pm; Sept to mid-June Mon–Fri 9am–5pm, Sat 10am–4pm; ☎0980/188 80, ⓦwww.lappland.se). Kiruna's **youth hostel** (☎0980/171 95) is 900m from the train station at Bergmästaregatan 7. It fills quickly in summer, as does the **campsite** (☎0980/630 00, ⓦwww.ripan.se), a twenty-minute walk north on Campingvägen, in the Högalid part of town; two-person cabins (❸) are available here too. Kiruna also has a number of central **hotels** – try *Hotell Vinterpalatset* at Järnvägsgatan 18 (☎0980/677 70, ⓦwww.kiruna.se/~vinterp; ❺/❸), which has a superb sauna and Jacuzzi suite on the top floor. Round the corner at Konduktörsgatan 7, *Hotell Kebne* (☎0980/681 80, ⓦwww.hotellkebne.com; ❹/❷) is also handy for the train station and has good-quality rooms. A cheap alternative is *Yellow House* (☎0980/137 50, ⓦwww.yellowhouse.nu) at Hantverkaregatan 25, which has hostel-style rooms sleeping up to four with shared bathrooms for 140kr per person.

Kiruna is hardly a centre of haute cuisine, but there are several decent places to **eat**: the best is *Nan King*, Mangigatan 26, an inexpensive Chinese place where lunch is 60kr. Alternatively, *3nd Baren*, in an old wooden building with coarsely hewn floorboards at Föreningsgatan 11, serves up decent lunches and dinners: reindeer is 99kr, salmon 133kr and lasagne 69kr. *Cafferys*, at the corner of Föreningsgatan and Bergmästaregatan, is the place to find pizzas and pasta dishes – both around 90kr. Coffee and cakes are served up at *Safari*, Geologgatan 4. Kiruna's most popular **bar** is *3nd Baren*; the grotty drinking den that is *Restaurang Arran*, across the main square at Föreningsgatan 9, often serves staggeringly cheap beer before 11pm but attracts a corresponding clientele – go in with a friend.

Around Kiruna: Jukkasjärvi

Just 17km east of Kiruna, the tiny village of **JUKKASJÄRVI** is a mecca – albeit a disproportionately expensive one for the dubious pleasure of spending a night in subzero temperatures – for any tourist travelling in Lapland in winter: the **Icehotel** (☎0980/668 00, ⓦwww.icehotel.com) that is built here late every October is also the world's biggest igloo and stands proudly by the side of the Torneälven river until it melts in May. Thousands of tons of ice and snow are used to make the igloo, whose exact shape and design changes from year to year. There is usually a bar beyond the entrance hall, bedrooms with compacted snow beds covered with reindeer hides, an exhibition hall, cinema and a chapel where local couples can marry. Winter temperatures are generally around -20 to -30°C, which means that inside the igloo it's normally around -5°C. Guests are provided with specially made sleeping bags as used by the Swedish army, who have done Arctic survival training here – don't wear pyjamas or you'll sweat. There are two types of room here: a standard **double room** containing nothing more than a reindeer-hide-swathed block of snow and ice for a bed costing a pricey 1960kr, and the more stylish **decorated suites** featuring ice carvings and a bed for a totally outrageous 2960kr. If you chicken out, there are also cabins for rent on the site (850kr per person in a two-berth cabin); all bookings are handled by *Jukkas AB* at Marknadsvägen 63. Undoubtedly the best way to arrive at the *Icehotel* is by **dog sled** from the airport; for a hefty 4350kr you and three friends can be met from your plane and pulled to your room. You can **eat** across the road at *Jukkasjärvi Wärdhus*, where lunch goes for around 105kr.

In **summer** Jukkasjärvi is a good place for river-rafting, fishing and hiking – ring the *Icehotel* number for details. In the *Icehotel*'s all-year Art Center, you can also see the massive blocks of ice cut from the river in March in readiness for the next season's construction, and, should you wish to escape the summer mosquitoes, it's even possible to spend a night inside specially constructed igloos in the Art Center – once again the hotel staff on site have details.

From Kiruna to the Norwegian border

Quite amazingly, it's only since 1984 that there's been a choice of ways to continue your journey towards Norway: until then, only the train covered the last leg of the long run from Stockholm or Luleå towards Narvik. Today, though, there's the **Nordkalottvägen** road which runs parallel to the railway, threading its way across the barren plateaux (the lakes up here are still frozen in mid-June) before slicing through the mighty Norwegian mountains. It's an exhilarating run that passes the start of the **Kungsleden** trail at Abisko: get off the train at Abisko Turiststation (not Abisko Ö, which is the village) and the adjoining fell station offers all sorts of useful advice for hikes from half a day upwards. The **cable car** (*linbanan*; 95kr return) offers fantastic views of the surrounding wilderness, including the spectacular U-shaped peaks of Lapporten (used as a landmark by the Sámi for guiding reindeer between their summer and winter grazing lands), the 70km-long Torneträsk lake and the vast wooded expanses of Abisko National Park. Both train line and road continue on to **RIKSGRÄNSEN**, the last settlement in Sweden, where it's possible to ski right up to late June. There's a **hotel** here, the *Hotell Riksgränsen* (☎0980/400 80, ⓦwww.riksgransen.nu; ⑤/③), opposite the train station, which has information about **hiking**, **mountain biking** and **canoeing** in the area. Remember though that this is the wettest spot in Sweden.

The Torne Valley

The gently sloping sides of the lush **Tornedalen** (Torne Valley) are one of the most welcoming sights in northern Sweden. Stretching over 500km from the mouth of the Gulf of Bothnia to Sweden's remote northern tip, the three rivers, Torne, Muonio and Könkämä mark out the long border between Sweden and Finland in the far north of Scandinavia. The valley is refreshingly different from the coast; the villages here are small and rural, often no more than a couple of wooden cottages surrounded by open flower meadows running down to the river's edge; and different too from the heavily wooded inland regions of the country, the

---

The Kungsleden

The **Kungsleden** is the most famous and popular of Sweden's hiking trails, a 500-kilometre route from **Abisko** in the north to **Hemavan**, near Tärnaby (see p.638), in the south. From Abisko to Kvikkjokk, north of the Arctic Circle, and in the south between Ammarnäs and Hemavan there are STF cabins and fell stations. Huts are placed at intervals of 15–20km, a distance that can be covered in one day, while shelter from the wind is provided at various places along the route. The Kungsleden is an easy trail to walk: it's well-marked; all the streams en route are crossed by bridges and patches of marshy ground overlaid with wooden planks; and there are also boat services or rowing boats for crossing the several large lakes on the way.

If you're looking for total isolation this is not the trail for you – it's the busiest in the country. One handy tip is to go against the flow: most people start from Abisko, but if you walk the route in reverse you'll find it easier going – or avoid July.

open plains here providing much needed grazing land for the farmers' livestock. **Buses** run from Haparanda (see p.619) up the valley and you can break the journey whenever you feel like it to take in one of the many lakes swirling in mist.

Pajala

The valley's main village is pretty **PAJALA** – a place which has earned itself something of a reputation in Sweden. To celebrate the village's 400th anniversary in 1987, the local council placed ads in Swedish newspapers inviting women from the south of the country up to Lapland to take part in the birthday festivities; the predominance of heavy-labouring jobs in the north of Sweden has produced a population imbalance (around three men to every woman) and explains the ridiculously macho behaviour that prevails in these parts. Journalists outside Sweden soon heard about the ads and before long busloads of women from across Europe were heading north to take part in a drunken, debauched bash. The plan worked, however, with dozens of east European women losing their hearts to gruff Swedish lumberjacks and beginning new lives north of the Arctic Circle. However, it remains to be seen whether the effects of several winters of 24-hour darkness, coupled with temperatures of -25°C, will tip the balance back; however, some thirty women have stayed on.

The last week of September, the **Römpäviiko** (@www.pajala.se/welcome/culture/festivals.shtml#Romp%20) or "romp week", as this ongoing cultural festival is called, is undoubtedly the liveliest time to be in the village. At any other time Pajala is a great place to rest up for a day or so, take a walk along the riverside or head off in search of the great grey owl (*strix nebulosa*) that sweeps through the nearby forests; the huge wooden model in the bus station will give you an idea of what the bird looks like: lichen grey with long slender tail feathers and a white crescent between its black and yellow eyes.

Pajala's **tourist office** (May–Aug Mon–Fri 9am–5pm, mid-June to mid-Aug also Sat & Sun 9am–5pm; Sept–April Mon–Fri 9am–5pm; ☎0978/100 15, @www .pajalaturism.bd.se) is located in the bus station and can provide information on the surrounding area. Close by at Soukolovägen 2, *Bykrogen Hotell* (☎0978/712 00, @www.bykrogen.se; ❹/❸) has cosy little **rooms**, or there's the similar *Hotell Smedjan* at Fridhemsvägen 1 (☎0978/108 15, @www.fa-hotell-rest.se/se/index .html; ❹/❷). But the best place to stay is right at the other end of the village: *Pajala Camping* (☎0978/741 80; May–Sept) offers stunning views over the lazy Torne river, plus some **cabins**: no.17 and no.18 are fully equipped with a kitchen and cost 485kr per night, while the others have only cold water and cost 285kr per night.

For **eating and drinking**, head for the *Bykrogen Hotell* at lunchtime for the cheapest meals – *dagens rätt* goes for 66kr, traditional northern Swedish delicacies start at 120kr. For pizzas, head for the *Tre Kronor* pizzeria in the centre of town on Tornedalsvägen – reckon on around 60kr.

Heading north: Karesuando and Treriksröset

Two buses leaves Pajala once daily (except Sun) for Sweden's northernmost village, **KARESUANDO** (change in Vittangi), a surprisingly likeable place where the land is in the grip of permafrost all year round and life is pretty tough. Karesuando is 250km north of the Arctic Circle and deep in Sámi country – here national borders carry little significance, people cross them without so much as a bat of an eyelid as they go about their everyday business.

If you're heading for **Treriksröset** – a cairn where Sweden, Norway and Finland meet – you can spend the night here and travel on the next day; *Karesuando Camping* (☎0981/201 39; June to mid-Sept) has **cabins** from 275kr per cabin for up to four people. However, the lakeside **youth hostel** (☎0980/200 00 or 203 70; mid-May to mid-Sept), situated along the road to Pajala, is a better and more comfortable bet. For **eating**, you're limited to self-catering or the greasy-spoon grill restaurant between the OK and Statoil filling stations.

The **tourist office** (mid-June to mid-Aug daily 8am–8pm; rest of the year

Mon–Fri 8am–3pm; ☎0981/202 05, ✺www.karesuando.com) is in the customs house on the bridge across to Finland. The only sight to speak of in Karesuando is the wooden cabin beyond the tourist office which was once home to revivalist preacher, **Lars Levi Laestadius**. The rectory, complete with simple wooden pews, was used as a meeting place whilst Laestadius was rector in Karesuando. Also worth a quick look is the **Sámiid Viessu** (July to mid-Aug daily 10am–7pm; free), a photography and handicraft exhibition along the road to the campsite which has some atmospheric black-and-white shots of local Sámi.

To continue to Treriksröset, cross the River Könkämä to **Kaaresuvanto** in Finland (remember Finnish time is an hour ahead), from where buses leave in summer for Kilpisjärvi, the settlement closest to the border junction. From Kilpisjärvi there are two choices: an eleven-kilometre hike down a track to the Treriksröset cairn or a twenty-minute **boat** ride (July to mid-Aug 9am, 1pm and 5pm; 80kr return) across the lake which shortens the hike to just 3km.

Travel details

Trains

Falun to: Gävle (4 daily; 1hr); Örebro (4 daily; 2hr 30min); Stockholm (10 daily; 2hr 40min); Uppsala (10 daily; 2hr 20min).
Gällivare to: Boden (3 daily; 2hr); Gävle (2 daily; 14hr); Gothenburg (1 daily; 19hr 30min); Kiruna (3 daily; 1hr); Luleå (3 daily; 2hr 20min); Stockholm (2 daily; 16hr 30min); Umeå (1 daily; 7hr); Uppsala (2 daily; 15hr 30min).
Karlstad to: Stockholm (5 daily; 2hr 40min).
Kiruna to: Boden (3 daily; 3hr); Gothenburg (1 daily; 20hr 30min); Luleå (3 daily; 3hr 20min); Narvik (3 daily; 3hr); Stockholm (2 daily; 17hr 30min); Uppsala (2 daily; 16hr 30min).
Mora to: Leksand (5 daily; 40min); Rättvik (5 daily; 20min); Stockholm (6 daily; 4hr); Uppsala (8 daily; 3hr 40min).
Östersund to: Åre (4 daily; 1hr 45min); Gothenburg (1 daily; 11hr); Stockholm (6 daily; 6hr); Storlien (2 daily; 3hr); Sundsvall (5 daily; 2hr 15min); Uppsala (6 daily; 5hr 40min).

The Inlandsbanan

Timetables change slightly from year to year, but the following is a rough idea of Inlandsbanan services and times. The Inlandsbanan runs from Mora to Gällivare via Östersund from late June to early August. Northbound trains leave Mora daily at 6.35am, calling at Orsa and Sveg and many other wayside halts en route for Östersund. From Östersund, trains leave daily for Gällivare at 7.05am, calling at Vilhelmina, Storuman, Arvidsjaur, the Arctic Circle, Jokkmokk and Gällivare. Southbound trains leave Gällivare daily at 6.45am for stations to Östersund. From Östersund a train leaves at 3pm daily for Mora.

Buses

The Inlandsexpressen (#45) runs north from Mora to Gällivare via Orsa, Sveg, Östersund, Vilhelmina, Storuman, Arvidsjaur and Jokkmokk. It operates daily all year, leaving Mora at 8am and 2pm for Östersund, from Östersund at 7am for Gällivare, at 1.40pm for Arvidsjaur and at 4.55pm for Storuman. Heading south, a bus leaves Gällivare at 9.30am for Östersund, from Arvidsjaur at 8.35am for Östersund and from Storuman for Östersund at 7.10am. From Östersund two buses leave for Mora at 6.50am and 12.30pm.
Åsarna to: Klövsjö (3 daily; 15min); Östersund (5 daily; 1hr 20min).
Gällivare to: Jokkmokk (5 daily; 1hr 30min); Kiruna (4 daily; 2hr); Luleå (4 daily; 3hr 15min); Pajala (3 daily; 2hr 20min); Ritsem (3 daily; 3hr 30min).
Jokkmokk to: Gällivare (5 daily; 1hr 30min); Kvikkjokk (2 daily; 1hr 50min).
Kiruna to: Gällivare (3 daily; 2hr); Karesuando (2 daily; 3hr); Luleå (2 daily; 4hr 45min); Pajala (2 daily; 3hr 15min).
Kvikkjokk to: Jokkmokk (2 daily; 1hr 50min).
Mora to: Orsa (26 daily; 20min).
Östersund to: Arvidsjaur (1 daily; 7hr); Gällivare (1 daily; 11hr); Mora (2 daily; 5hr); Storuman (1 daily; 4hr 30min); Umeå (2 daily; 6hr).
Storuman to: Hemavan (3 daily; 2hr 20min); Tärnaby (4 daily; 2hr).

International trains

Karlstad to: Oslo (3 daily; 2hr).

Finland

Map: 0 — 250 km

NORWAY

Arctic Circle

SWEDEN

RUSSIA

Gulf of Bothnia

Finland highlights

* **Travel by tram, Helsinki**
The best way to see the capital's centre. See p.692

* **Pihlajasaari island, Helsinki** A great day-trip and the perfect place to work on your all-over tan. See p.704

* **Turku Castle, Turku** Delve into Finland's often uneasy relationship with neighbouring Sweden at this former seat of power. See p.723

* **Åland Islands** A summer paradise of verdant flower meadows, sheltered swimmable creeks and rolling countryside perfect for biking. See p.728

* **Sauna, Kuopio** Experience the real thing and get tips from the locals on technique. See p.754

* **Wife-carrying competition, Sonkajärvi** Witness one of the country's most bizarre – and enjoyable – competitions. See p.757

* **Hiking the Karhunkierros trail** A must for serious hikers, traversing some of Lapland's most beautiful stretches. See p.771

* **Rovaniemi, Lapland** No matter what time of year, visit Santa Claus and place your order for Christmas. See p.771

* **Inari, Lapland** Get to grips with Sámi culture at the excellent village museum. See p.778

Introduction and basics

Mainland Scandinavia's most culturally isolated and least understood country, Finland has been independent only since 1917, having been ruled for hundreds of years by imperial powers: first the Swedes and then the tsarist Russians. Much of its history involves a struggle simply for recognition and survival.

Today, though, the battle has been won and the Finns are the proudest of all the Nordic nations, trumpeting the fact that this little known country on the very edge of Europe is truly one of the continent's best kept secrets. Finland is without a doubt the most welcoming of all of the Scandinavian countries; Finns of all ages are inordinately proud of their nation's achievements (it is, after all, only by a quirk of history that Finland was not invaded by the Soviet Union and well and truly taken in to Moscow's sphere of influence) and are anxious that visitors learn more about their country, where a joy in all things Finnish goes hand in hand with eager participation in the European Union. Forget any lingering perceptions that Finland is mundane, grey or even Communist – today it's a welcoming, honest and prosperous society keen to make up for years of living on the sidelines.

During the Swedish period, the Finnish language (one of Europe's least familiar and most difficult) was regarded as fit only for

peasants – which the majority of Finns were – and attempts were later made to forcibly impose Russian. All publications were in Swedish until the *Kalevala* appeared in the early nineteenth century. A written collection of previously orally transmitted folk tales telling of a people close to nature, living by hunting and fishing, the *Kalevala* instantly became regarded as a truly Finnish history, and formed the basis of the **National Romantic** movement in the arts that flourished from the mid-nineteenth century, stimulating political initiatives towards Finnish nationalism.

It's not surprising, therefore, that modern-day Finns have a well-developed sense of their own culture, and that the legacy of the past is strongly felt – in the still widely popular Golden Age paintings of Gallen-Kallela, Edelfelt and others; the music of Sibelius; and the National Romantic architecture which paved the way for modern greats like Alvar Aalto. Equally in evidence, even among city dwellers, are the deeply ingrained, down-to-earth values of rural life, along with a sense of spirituality epitomized by the **sauna**, which for Finns is a meaningful ritual rather than an exercise in health.

Some elderly rural dwellers are prone to suspicion of anything foreign, but in general the Finnish population is much less staid than its Nordic neighbours, and the disintegration of its once powerful neighbour, the Soviet Union, has allowed it to form closer ties with Europe through membership of the European Union. By the end of the 1990s Finland's **economy** was buoyant enough to allow it to join the first wave of countries in the European Monetary Union. It's currently the only one of the three Nordic EU members to have introduced the euro, and with

the success of Finnish telecommunications giant Nokia and a flourishing IT sector, the country reached the millennium with renewed confidence and self-belief. However, unemployment is still high in some places, particularly in rural areas, and some sections of the country's society are being left behind in Finland's drive to become a technological world leader.

Where to go

Finland is mainly flat, and filled by huge forests and lakes – you'll need to travel around a lot to appreciate the country's wide regional variations. The **south** contains the least dramatic scenery, but the capital, **Helsinki**, more than compensates, with its brilliant architecture and superb museum collections. Stretching from the Russian border in the east to the industrial city of **Tampere**, the water systems of the **Lake Region** provide a natural means of transport for the timber industry – indeed, water here is a more common sight than land.

Ostrobothnia, the upper portion of the west coast, is characterized by near-featureless farmlands and long sandy beaches which are – to Finns at least – the region's main draw. Here, too, you'll find the clearest Swedish influence: in parts up to a third of the population are Swedish-speaking – known as "Finland-Swedes" – and there's a rich heritage from the days of Swedish trading supremacy. **Kainuu** is the thickly forested heart of the country, much of its small population spread among scattered villages. The land begins to rise as you head north from here, folding into a series of fells and gorges that are ripe for spectacular hiking. **Lapland,**

Finland on the net

ⓦ **www.finland-tourism.com** The official tourist board site, with bundles of info in a functional layout.

ⓦ **www.finland.org** General facts about Finland.

ⓦ **www.sauna.fi** Home of the Finnish Sauna Society, with indispensible practical advice on sauna do's and don'ts.

ⓦ **www.srmnet.org** Finnish Youth Hostels Association website, with an online booking facility.

ⓦ **virtual.finland.fi** News and views from the Finnish Foreign Ministry.

completely devoid of large towns, contains the most alluring terrain of all, its stark and haunting landscapes able to absorb any number of visitors on numerous hiking routes. This region is home to the Sámi people, semi-nomadic reindeer herders whose traditional way of life remains relatively untainted by modern culture.

When to go

The official Finnish **holiday season** is early July to mid-August, and during these weeks there's an exodus from the towns to the country. The best time to visit the rural regions is either side of these dates, when things will be less crowded and hectic – though no cheaper.

In **summer**, regarded as being from June to early September, Helsinki, the south and the Lake Region enjoy mild and sunny weather. Temperatures are usually 18–24°C (65–75°F), sometimes reaching 32°C (90°F) in the daytime, but they drop swiftly in the evening, when you'll need a light jacket. The north is always a few degrees cooler and often quite cold at night, so carry a thick jumper at least. The Midnight Sun can be seen from Rovaniemi northwards for two months over midsummer; the rest of the country experiences a night-long twilight from mid-June to mid-July.

Winter, roughly from late October to early April in the south, plus a few weeks more on either side in the north, is painfully cold. Helsinki generally fluctuates between 0°C and -20°C (32°F and -4°F), the harshest months being January and February; in the north it's even colder, with just a few hours of daylight; and in the extreme north the sun doesn't rise at all. The snow cover generally lasts from November to March in the south, a few weeks longer in the north. On the plus side, Finland copes easily with low temperatures and transport is rarely disrupted.

Thanks to its relatively flat terrain, Finland is one of the most enjoyable countries in Scandinavia to go **hiking**, one of the Finns' favourite pastimes. The best time for hiking is from May to September in the south and from June to September in the north. You'll need a good-quality tent, a warm sleeping bag, rainwear, spare warm clothing, thick-soled waterproof boots, a compass and detailed maps, all of which can be bought in tourist centres close to the hiking routes. See p.40 for more on hiking.

Getting there from the rest of Scandinavia

Finland's geographical position – effectively separated from the rest of Scandinavia by the Gulf of Bothnia – means that except in the extreme north of the country the easiest approaches are usually by ferry or plane. Crossing from the east coast of Sweden is easy, with regular **ferry** services from a number of points and usually good onward links once you've arrived. Further north, Sweden and Norway both have land borders with Finland and these are no fuss to cross by **bus**, although in a few spots you may have to wait several days between connections. From Denmark, it's impossible to get to Finland without passing through Sweden unless you **fly**, although there's a direct bus–ferry service and fairly frequent trains.

By train

There are no direct **train** connections between Finland and other Scandinavian countries. The nearest railhead is at **Boden** in Sweden, at the northern end of the Gulf of Bothnia, around 100km before the Finnish border at Haparanda–Tornio (rail passes are valid on buses from Boden to Haparanda). Other train connections, such as those between Helsinki and **Stockholm** or **Copenhagen** (1–2 daily; 25hr), make use of ferry crossings for part of their route.

By bus

In the Arctic North, **buses** connect the Norwegian–Finnish border towns of **Karasjok–Karigasniemi** and **Skibotn–Kilpisjärvi**, as well as the Finnish border villages of **Utsjoki**, **Polmak** and **Nuorgam**; fares and schedules, beyond what we've included under the "Travel Details" at the end of the relevant chapters, can be checked at any tourist office or bus station. There are also regular services from points in northern Sweden via the twin border towns of **Haparanda–Tornio**, at the northern end of the Gulf of Bothnia.

Long-distance bus-and-ferry connections to Finland are also fairly frequent. The service **from Copenhagen** to Finland runs four times a week to Helsinki, via **Stockholm** and **Turku**. Naturally, it's a fairly exhausting journey, taking 25 hours.

By ferry

The most frequent **ferries** from Sweden to Finland run between **Stockholm** and Helsinki and are operated by Silja (ⓦwww.silja.com; 16hr; €100 foot passenger, car €55) and Viking Line (ⓦwww.vikingline.fi; 16hr; €70 foot passenger, car €60). Each company has a year-round overnight service, leaving at 5pm and arriving at 9.30am. Both lines also run a twice-daily service from Stockholm to **Turku**, which takes ten or eleven hours (Silja foot passenger €65, car €55; Viking Line €55, car €50). Quicker still (4hr) are the daily services between Stockholm and **Mariehamn**, run by Viking (passengers €12, car €13) and Silja Line (€12, car €21). There are no ferries from Denmark to Finland.

For current details on timetables and the numerous discounts available – ranging from 50 percent reductions for holders of InterRail or Eurail cards to other generous concessions for children and senior citizens – check with a travel agent or the relevant ferry office.

By plane

Finnair (ⓦwww.finnair.com) have nonstop flights to Helsinki from **Copenhagen** (3 daily; 1hr 30min), **Stockholm** (hourly; 1hr) and **Oslo** (4 daily; 2hr). There are also daily flights from Stockholm with SAS (ⓦwww.scandinavian.net) or Finnair to a number of Finnish regional cities including **Tampere** (6 daily; 1hr), **Oulu** (3 daily; 1hr 20min), **Vaasa** (4 daily; 1hr 15min) and **Turku** (3 daily; 1hr). Getting to these cities though from Copenhagen or Oslo involves going via Stockholm or Helsinki. Check with a travel agent for occasional bargain fares between Scandinavian cities.

Costs, money and banks

Though the cost of a meal or the bill for an evening's drinks can occasionally come as a shock, for the most part prices in Finland are comparable with those in most European capitals, and there is no shortage of places catering for those on tighter budgets. Bargain lunchtime "specials" are common and travelling costs, in particular, can come as a pleasant surprise – travel by train, for example, is cheaper in Finland than in the other Scandinavian countries.

There are ways to cut **costs**, which we've detailed where relevant, but as a general rule you'll need £20–30/$30–45 a day even to live fairly modestly – staying mostly at youth hostels or campsites, eating out every other day and supplementing your diet with food from supermarkets, visiting only a few selected museums and socializing fairly rarely. To live well and see more, you'll be spending closer to £50/$75.

Finnish **currency** is the **euro** (€), which comes in coins of 1 to 50 cents, €1 and €2, and notes of €5 to €500. The **exchange rate** at the time of writing was €1.48 to £1, €1 to US$1.

As usual, one of the best ways to carry money is as traveller's cheques. These can be changed at most **banks** (Mon–Fri 9.15am–4.15pm), the charge for which is usually €2 (though several people changing money together need only pay the commission once). You can also change money at hotels, though normally at a much worse rate than at the banks. In a country where every cent counts, it's worth looking around for a better deal: in rural areas some banks and hotels are known not to charge any commission at all. Outside normal banking hours, the best bet for changing money are the **currency exchange desks** at transport terminals which open to meet international arrivals, where commission is likely to be €3–5, roughly the same as at banks, though airport exchange rates are often a little more generous.

Major **credit** and **charge cards** – Amex, MasterCard, Visa, Diner's Club – are usually accepted by hotels, car rental offices, department stores, restaurants and sometimes even by taxis. However, it's still advisable to check beforehand.

There are no restrictions on the amount of money you can take into or out of Finland.

Mail and telecommunications

In general, **communications** in Finland are dependable and quick, although in the far north, and in some sections of the east, minor delays arise due simply to geographical remoteness.

Unless you're on a hiking trek through the back of beyond, you can rest assured your letter or postcard will arrive at its destination fairly speedily. The cost of mailing anything weighing under 20g to other parts of Europe is 60 cents priority class; or 70 cents to the rest of the world. You can buy **stamps** from **post offices** (Mon–Fri 9am–5pm; longer hours at the main post office in Helsinki), street stands or R-Kiosks, and at some hotels. **Poste restante** is available at the main post office in every large town.

An out-of-order **public phone** is virtually unheard of in Finland. Most, however, only take **phonecards**, which you can buy in denominations of €5–15 from the R-Kiosk chain and some other outlets. If you intend to use the phone frequently, it may be worth stocking up on phonecards, since it can sometimes be impossible to buy them late at night or in out-of-the-way places. Also note that each municipality runs its own phonecard system – which may or may not be compatible with systems in other areas. Your best bet is probably to invest in a Sonera phonecard, since their telephones can be found pretty much everywhere. The minimum cost of a **local call** is €1. **International calls** are cheapest between 10pm and 8am. The bill for using a hotel phone is often dramatically more expensive.

International dialling codes for calling **from and to Finland** are given on p.27. Operator numbers are ☎118 for domestic calls and ☎92020 for reverse-charge international calls.

Finland comes second only to the USA in terms of per-person Internet use, a fact borne out by the amount of free public **Internet and email** access that is available in even the most remote places. The first point of call should be any public library – in the busier ones you may need to book a slot the day before, although most have short-use walk-up terminals. You may need to show some kind of ID when booking a terminal, which you may also have to leave as a deposit while using it. Another source of free Internet access is tourist offices, a number of which have terminals, while some towns also have cafés with free Internet access; otherwise, you'll pay €3–5 per hour.

The media

The biggest-selling **Finnish newspaper**, and the only one to be distributed all over the country, is the daily *Helsingin Sanomat* (€2). Most of the others are locally based and sponsored by a political party; however, all carry entertainment listings – only the cinema listings (where the film titles are translated into Finnish) present problems for non-Finnish speakers. A better bet may be the Swedish language tongue-twister, *Hufvudstadsbladet*, a quality daily that can be found in Helsinki. A better source of information about **what's on**, if you're in Helsinki, Tampere or Turku, is the free *City* (appearing fortnightly in Helsinki, monthly in Turku and Tampere), which carries regional news, features and entertainment details in Finnish and English; it's available at tourist offices.

Overseas newspapers, including most British and some US titles, can be found, often on the day of issue, at the Academic Bookstore, Pohjoisesplanadi 39, in Helsinki. Elsewhere, foreign papers are harder to find and less up-to-date, though they often turn up at the bigger newsagents and train stations in Helsinki, Turku, Tampere and, to a lesser extent, Oulu.

Finnish **television**, despite its three channels (one of which is called MTV, but is unrelated to the round-the-clock music station), isn't exactly inspiring and certainly won't keep you off the streets for long. Moderately more interesting is the fact that, depending on where you are, you might be able to watch Swedish, Norwegian, Estonian and Russian programmes. A few youth hostels have TV rooms, and most hotel-room TVs have the regular channels plus a feast of cable and satellite alternatives. As with films shown in the cinema, all TV programmes are broadcast in their original language with Finnish subtitles.

The only **radio station** that non-Finnish speakers are likely to find interesting and useful is Capital FM (Ⓦwww.yle.fi), a multi-language channel which relays programmes from foreign broadcasters including the BBC, ABC, CBC and NPR; a large part of the day's programming is given over to English material, and generally between 3.30pm and 6.30pm, and 9pm to 11pm, there'll be a series of news broadcasts in English. Broadcast on 97.5FM in Helsinki, the channel also transmits a short English-language news summary (Mon–Fri 7.30am) put together by the Finnish national broadcaster YLE. This bulletin can also be heard at the same time in Lahti on 90.3FM, Kuopio 88.1FM, Tampere 88.3FM and in Turku on 96.7FM.

Getting around

Save for the fact that traffic tends to follow a north–south pattern, you'll have few headaches **getting around** the more populated parts of Finland. The chief form of public transport is the train, backed up, particularly on east–west journeys, by long-distance coaches. For the most part trains and buses integrate well, and you'll only need to plan with care when travelling through sparsely inhabited areas such as the far north and east. Feasible and often affordable variations come in the form of boats, planes, bikes, and even hitching – though car rental is strictly for the wealthy.

The complete **timetable** (*Suomen Kulkuneuvot*) for train, bus, ferry and air travel within the country is published every two months; it's sold at stations and kiosks for €23. This is essential for plotting complex routes; for simplified details of the major train services, pick up the free *Rail Pocket Guide* booklet, available at most train stations.

Trains

The swiftest land link between Finland's major cities is invariably the reliable **train service**, operated by the national company, VR. Large, comfortable express trains, super-smooth IC (inter-city trains) and an increasing number of state-of-the-art tilting *pendolino* trains serve the principal **north–south** routes several times a day, reaching as far north as Rovaniemi on the Arctic Circle, although occasional services penetrate as far north as Kemijärvi and Kolari. Elsewhere, especially on east–west hauls through sparsely populated regions, rail services tend to be skeletal and trains are often tiny two-carriage affairs. The Arctic North has a very limited network of services. More details on Finnish Railways can be found at Ⓦwww.vr.fi.

InterRail, BIJ and ScanRail **passes** are valid on all trains; if you don't have one of these and are planning a lot of travelling, get a **Finnrail Pass** before arriving in Finland (the pass cannot be purchased in Finland itself) from a travel agent or Finnish Tourist Office (for addresses, see p.22). This costs around €114 for three days' unlimited travel within a month, €154 for five days, or €208 for ten days.

Otherwise, train **fares** are surprisingly reasonable. As a guide, a one-way, second-class ticket from Helsinki to Turku (a trip of around 200km) costs between €20.80 and €24.80 depending on the speed of the train; Helsinki to Kuopio (465km) costs around €45.20, and Helsinki to Rovaniemi (900km) around €65.20. If you've brought a car with you, car sleeper services are a convenient way of covering long distances. A one-way trip from Helsinki to Rovaniemi for a car and up to four passengers costs around €380, including sleeping berths.

All tickets are valid for a month, and some allow you to break your journey en route – check when you purchase. You should **buy tickets** from station ticket offices (*lippumyymälä*), although you can also pay the inspector on the train. If there are three or more of you travelling together, **group tickets**, available from a train station or travel agent, can cut the regular fares on journeys over 80km by at least 20 percent (25 percent for parties of 11 or more). **Senior citizens** with Rail Europ cards are entitled to a

30 percent discount on regular tickets, or 50 percent if they are over 65 and buy a Finnish Senior Citizens railcard (€8.40). The cost of **seat reservations** depends on the distance travelled but is generally around €5 – remember that although they are not necessary on express trains, they can be a good idea if you're travelling over a holiday period or on a Friday or Sunday evening.

Buses

Run by local private companies but with a common ticket system, **buses** cover the whole country, and are often quicker and more frequent than trains over the shorter east–west hops, and essential for getting around the remoter regions. In the Arctic North there is a very limited railway network, so almost all public transport is by road; hence it's here that you'll find buses most useful. The main operators are Gold Line (☎016/334 5500, ✆www.goldline.ti), Lapin Bussivuorot (☎0200/4000 ✆www.lapinbussivuorot.com) and Lapin Linjat (only ☎016/342 2160). The free bus **timetable**, *Suomen Pikavuorot*, lists all the routes in the country and can be picked up at most long-distance bus stations but is not very user-friendly. Information on travel in Finland by coach and bus can also be found at ✆www.matkahuolto.fi. To be frank, though, you're more likely to use Finland's excellent network of rail services (much more complete than in neighbouring Sweden where regional services have been cut to a bare minimum) than hassle with buses.

All **fares** are calculated according to the distance travelled: Helsinki to Lahti (100km) costs around €17, Helsinki to Kuopio (400km) around €44. Express buses charge a supplement of €2.40 per journey and are worth it for the correspondingly faster journey times. All types of ticket can be purchased at bus stations or at most travel agents; only ordinary one-way tickets can be bought on board the bus, though on journeys of 80km or less there's no saving in buying a return anyway. On return trips of over 80km, expect a reduction of 10 percent.

Ferries

Lake travel is aimed more at holidaying families than the budget-conscious traveller. **Prices** are high considering the distances, and progress is slow as the vessels chug along the great lake chains. If you have the time, money and inclination, though, it can be worth taking one of the shorter trips simply for the experience. There are numerous routings and details can be checked at any tourist office in the country and at Finnish Tourist Offices abroad.

Planes

With their range of discounts, domestic **flights** can be comparatively cheap as well as time-saving if you want to cover long distances, such as from Helsinki to the Arctic North. That said, travelling by air means you'll miss many interesting parts of the country; another point to bear in mind is that flights from smaller towns to the bigger centres – Helsinki, Tampere and Oulu – tend to depart at around 6am. Finnair run a variety of off-peak summer reductions which can be checked at travel agents and airline or tourist offices in Finland. Youth **fares** are available for 17–24-year-olds and offer a fifty percent discount on the normal fare, though it's usually cheaper to look for special offers or to buy a weekend ticket which is always cheaper than the standard fare.

Driving and hitching

Renting a car is extremely expensive (as is petrol), and with such a good public-transport network, it's only worth considering if you're travelling as a group of four or five. The big international companies such as Avis (✆www.avis.com), Budget (✆www.budgetrentacar.com), Europcar (✆www.europcar.co.uk) and Hertz (✆www.hertz.com) have offices in most Finnish towns and at international arrival points. If you're in Helsinki it's also worth checking the local company Transvell (☎08000/7000, ✆www.transwell.fi). They all accept major credit cards; if paying by cash, you'll need to leave a substantial deposit. You'll also need a valid driving licence, at least a year's driving experience, and to be a minimum of 19–23 years old, depending on the company you rent from.

Rates for a medium-sized car are €30–50 per day, with reductions for longer periods – you'll pay around €400 for a fortnight's use.

On top of this, there can be a surcharge of up to 75 cents per kilometre (which may be waived on long-term loans) and a drop-off fee of around €50 if you leave the car somewhere other than the place from which it was rented. For more details on car rental before arriving in Finland, visit the website of one of the international companies mentioned above, or ask at a Finnish Tourist Board office.

If you **bring your own car** to Finland, it's advisable (though not compulsory) to have a Green Card as proof that you are comprehensively insured in the event of an accident. Some insurers in EU countries will offer you a Green Card for free as part of your insurance package, whilst others will charge a premium. Further **information** about driving in Finland can be obtained from Autoliitto, the Automobile and Touring Club of Finland, Hämeentie 105A, 00550 Helsinki (☎09/7258 4400, ✪www.autoliitto.fi).

Once underway, you'll find the next financial drain is **fuel**, which costs around €1.1 a litre (unleaded), though bear in mind that in rural areas, especially in Lapland, fuel is much more expensive than in Helsinki. Except in the far north, **service stations** are plentiful and usually open from 7am to 9pm between Monday and Saturday, and are often closed on Sunday – although in busy holiday areas many stay open round the clock during the summer. Though **roads** are generally in good condition there can be problems with melting snows, usually during April and May in the south and June in the far north. Finnish **road signs** are similar to those throughout Europe, but be aware of bilingual place names; one useful sign to watch for is *Keskusta*, which means "town centre". **Speed limits** vary between 40kph and 60kph in built-up areas to 100kph – if it's not signposted, the basic limit is always 80kph. On motorways the maximum speed is 120kph in summer, 100kph in winter.

Other **rules of the road** include using headlights all the time when driving outside built-up areas, as well as in fog and in poor light, and the compulsory wearing of seatbelts by drivers and all passengers. As elsewhere in Scandinavia, penalties for drunk driving are severe – the police may stop and breathalyze you if they think you've been driving erratically. In some areas in the north of the country, reindeer and elk are liable to take a stroll across a road, especially around dusk. These are sizeable creatures and damage (to the car) is likely to be serious; all such collisions should be reported at the nearest police station and the Finnish Motor Insurers' Centre (*Liikennevakuutuskeskus*), Bulevardi 28, 00120 Helsinki (☎09/680 401) which can also help with local breakdown companies.

Hitching is generally easy, and sometimes the quickest means of transport between two spots. Finland's large student population has helped accustom drivers to the practice, and you shouldn't have to wait too long for a ride on the busy main roads between large towns. Make sure you have a decent road map and emergency provisions/shelter if you're passing through isolated regions. While many Finns speak English, it's still handy to memorize the Finnish equivalent of "let me out here" (*"jään pois tässä"*).

Cycling

Cycling can be an enjoyable way to see the country at close quarters, particularly because the only appreciable hills are in the far north and extreme east. Villages and towns may be separated by several hours' pedalling, however, and the scenery can get monotonous. Finnish **roads** are of high quality in the south and around the large towns, but are much rougher in the north and in isolated areas; beware the springtime thaw when the winter snows melt and sometimes cover roads with water and mud. All major towns have bike shops selling spares – Finland is one of the few places in the world where you can buy bicycle snow tyres with tungsten steel studs. Most youth hostels, campsites and some hotels and tourist offices offer **bike rental** from €9 per day, €45 per week; there may also be a deposit of around €30.

Accommodation

Whether you're at the end of one of Finland's long-distance hiking trails or in the centre of a city, you'll find some kind of **accommoda-**

tion to suit your needs. You will, however, have to pay dearly for it: prices are high, and only by making use of special offers and travelling during low season will you be able to sleep well on a budget.

Hotels

Finnish **hotels** (*hotelli*) are rarely other than polished and pampering: TV, phone and private bathroom are standard fixtures, breakfast is invariably included in the price, and there's often free use of the sauna and swimming pool, too. Costs can be formidable – frequently in excess of €90 for a double – but planning ahead and taking advantage of various discount schemes and seasonal reductions can cut prices, often to as little as €50.

In major cities, particularly Helsinki, there can be bargains in business-oriented hotels during July and August, and on Fridays, Saturdays and Sundays throughout the year. Exact details of these change frequently, but it's worth checking the current situation at a local tourist office. Reductions are also available to holders of Helsinki Cards and the similar card issued for Tampere. Otherwise, between July and August you're unlikely to find anything under €50 by turning up on spec. Hotels in country areas are no less comfortable than those in cities, and often a touch less costly, typically €40–50. However, space is again limited during summer.

Expense can be trimmed a little by using the **Finncheque** system: you buy an unlimited number of €34 vouchers, each valid for a night's accommodation for one person in any of the 200 participating hotels from mid-May to September. There are three price categories, depending on the quality of room. You can only buy the Finncheque outside Finland at a Finnish Tourist Board office (see p. 000) or a specialist travel agent, who will also supply addresses of the hotels involved. Don't worry about buying more vouchers than you might need – they are refundable at the place of purchase. Another discount is offered by the Scanhotel chain's "Scandic Holiday Cheque" vouchers. They're valid at all Scandic hotels (⊛ www.scandic-hotels.com) in Finland throughout the year and cost from €95 per double room including breakfast, though beware that some hotels add on a "quality surcharge". The cheques are widely available from travel agents outside Finland.

In many towns you'll also find **tourist hotels** (*matkustajakoti*), a more basic type of family-run hotel. They charge €30–45 per double room, but may well be full throughout the summer. The facilities of **summer hotels** (*kesähotelli*), too, are more basic than regular hotels, since the accommodation is in student blocks which are vacated from June to the end of August: there are universities in all the major cities and in an impressive number of the larger towns. Reservable with any Finnish travel agent, summer hotel prices are around €35 per person. Bear in mind that identical accommodation – minus the bed linen and breakfast – comes a lot cheaper in the guise of a youth hostel.

Youth hostels

Often the easiest and cheapest place to rest your head is a **youth hostel** (*retkeilymaja*). These exist throughout the country, in major cities (which will have at least one) and isolated country areas, and are run by the Finnish Youth Hostel Association, *Suomen Retkeilymajajärjestö* (SRM). It's always a

Accommodation price codes

The hotels and guesthouses listed in the Finland chapters of this Guide have been graded according to the following price bands, based on the cost of the **least expensive double room in summer**, usually mid-June to mid-August. However, many hotels offer summer and/or weekend discounts, and in these instances we've given two grades, covering both the regular and the discounted rate.

❶ Under €30
❷ €31–50
❸ €51–70

❹ €71–90
❺ €91–110
❻ Over €111

good idea to phone ahead and reserve a place, which many hostel wardens will do for you, or book online at the address below. If you're arriving on a late bus or train, say so when phoning and your bed will be kept for you; otherwise bookings are only held until 6pm. Hostels are busiest during the peak Finnish holiday period which runs roughly from mid-June to mid-August. Things are quieter after mid-August, although a large number of hostels close soon after this date – check that the one you're aiming for doesn't. Similarly, many hostels don't open until June.

Overnight **charges** are generally around €17 per person, depending on the type of accommodation, with hostels ranging from the basic dormitory type to those with two- and four-bed rooms and at least one bathroom for every three rooms. Bed linen, if not already included, can be rented for an extra €3–5. With a Hostelling International Card (not obligatory) you can get a €2.50 reduction per person per night. The SRM publishes a useful free guide, *SRM hostels in Finland*, available directly from them at Suomen Retkeilymajajärjestö, Yrjönkatu 38B, 00100 Helsinki (℡09/565 7150, ⓦwww.srmnet.org), listing all Finnish hostels, and the very helpful staff there can also provide a free Finland map showing locations.

All youth hostels have wardens to provide general assistance and arrange **meals**: most hostels offer breakfast, usually for €3–4, and some serve dinner as well (around €7.50). Hostel breakfasts, especially those in busy city hostels, can be rationed affairs and – hunger permitting – you'll generally be better off waiting until you can find a cheapish lunch somewhere else (see "Food and Drink", p.665). The only hostel breakfasts really worth taking advantage of are those offered at summer hotels, where hostellers can mingle with the hotel guests and, for €5–7, partake of the help-yourself spread.

Campsites and camping cottages

There are some 200 official **campsites** (*leirintäalue*) in Finland, and around 150 more operating on a less formal basis. Most open from May to September, although around seventy stay open all year. The approved sites, marked with a blue and white tent sign in a letter C, are classified by a star system: one-star sites are in rural areas and usually pretty basic, while on a five-star site you can expect excellent cooking and laundry facilities and sometimes a well-stocked shop. The cost for two people sharing is €5–15 per pitch, depending on the site's star rating. Campsites outside major towns are frequently very big (a 2000-tent capacity isn't uncommon), and they're very busy at weekends during July and August. Smaller and more remote sites (except those serving popular hiking routes) are, as you'd imagine, much less crowded.

Holiday villages have been sprouting up throughout Finland in the last few years and there are now around 200 of them. Standards vary considerably, with accommodation ranging from basic cabins to luxurious bungalows. All provide fuel, cooking facilities, bed linen and often a sauna – but you'll need to bring your own towels. Costs range from €100 to €450 per week for a cabin sleeping up to four people, though for a luxury bungalow you might be paying up to €900. Camping cottage cheques, valid between May and September and available from travel agents for €33.65 per cabin per night, can be used at some ninety campsites and holiday villages throughout the country from May 15 to September 15 – an economical option if there are enough of you.

If you don't have an International Camping Card (see p.35) you'll need a National Camping Card, available at every site for €5 and valid for a year. If you're considering **camping rough**, remember it's illegal without the landowner's permission – though in practice, provided you're out of sight of local communities, there shouldn't be any problems.

Hiking accommodation

Hiking routes invariably start and finish close to a campsite or a youth hostel, and along the way there will usually be several types of basic accommodation. Of these, a *päivätupa* is a cabin with cooking facilities which is opened during the day for free use; an *autiotupa* is an unlocked hut which can be used by hikers to sleep in for one night only – there's no fee but often no space either during the busiest months. A *varaustupa* is a locked hut for which you can obtain a key at the Tourist Centre at the start of the hike – there's a smallish fee and you'll almost certainly be sharing. Some routes have a few *kämppä* – cabins originally erected for forest workers but now used mainly by hikers; check their exact location with the nearest tourist centre. On most hikes there are also marked spots for pitching your own tent and building fires.

Food and drink

Finnish **food** is full of surprises and demands investigation. It's pricey, but you can keep a grip on the expenses by indulging most often at markets and at the many down-to-earth dining places, saving restaurant blowouts for special occasions. Though tempered by many regulations, alcohol is more widely available here than in much of Scandinavia: there are many places to **drink** but also many people drinking, most of them indulging moderately but some doing it to excess on a regular basis.

Food

Though it may at first seem a stodgy, rather unsophisticated cuisine, **Finnish food** is an interesting mix of western and eastern influences. Many dishes resemble those you might find elsewhere in Scandinavia – an enticing array of delicately prepared fish (herring, whitefish, salmon and crayfish), together with some exotic meats like reindeer and elk – while others bear the stamp of Russian cooking: solid pastries and casseroles, strong on cabbage, pork and mutton.

All Finnish restaurants will leave a severe dent in your budget, as will the foreign places, although the country's innumerable pizzerias are relatively cheap by comparison. The golden money-saving rule is to treat **lunch** (*lounas*, usually served 11am–2pm) rather than the much dearer **dinner** (*päivällinen*, usually from 6pm) as your main meal. Also, eke out your funds with stand-up snacks and by selective buying in supermarkets. If you're

staying in a hotel, don't forget to load up on the inclusive **breakfast** (*aamiainen*) – often an open table laden with herring, eggs, cereals, porridge, cheese, salami and bread.

Snacks, fast food and self-catering

Economical **snacks** are best found in market halls (*kauppahalli*), where you can get basic foodstuffs along with local and national specialities. Adjoining these halls are cafeterias, where you're charged by the weight of food on your plate. Look out for *karjalan piirakka* – oval-shaped Karelian pastries containing rice and mashed potato, served hot with a mixture of finely chopped hard-boiled egg and butter for around €2. Also worth trying is *kalakukko*, a chunk of bread with pork and whitefish baked inside it – legendary around Kuopio but available almost everywhere. Expect to spend around €3 for a chunk big enough for two. Slightly cheaper but just as filling, *lihapiirakka* are envelopes of pastry filled with rice and meat – ask for them with mustard (*sinappi*) and/or ketchup (*ketsuppi*). Most train stations and the larger bus stations and supermarkets also have cafeterias proffering a selection of the above and other greasier nibbles.

Less exotically, the big **burger** franchises are widely found, as are the Grilli and Nakkikioski roadside fast-food stands turning out burgers, frankfurters and hot dogs for €2–3; they're always busiest when the pubs shut.

Finnish **supermarkets** – Sokos, K-Kaupat, Pukeva and Centrum are widespread names – are fairly standard affairs. In general, a substantial oval loaf of dark rye bread (*ruisleipä*) costs €1–1.50, ten *karjalan piirakkas* €2, a litre of milk €1, and a packet of biscuits around €1.30. A usually flavoursome option containing hunks of meat and vegetables, Finnish tinned **soup** (*keitto*) can be an excellent investment if you're self-catering.

Coffee (*kahvi*) is widely drunk and costs €1–1.50 per cup; in a *baari* or *kahvila* (bar or coffee shop) it's sometimes consumed with a *pulla* – a kind of doughy bun. It's normally drunk black, although milk is always available if you want it; you'll also commonly find espresso and cappuccino, although these are more expensive. **Tea** (*tee*) costs around €1, depending on where you are and

Basics

Juusto	Cheese
Kakku	Cake
Keitto	Soup
Keksit	Biscuits
Leipä	Bread
Maito	Milk
Makeiset	Sweets
Perunat	Potatoes
Piimä	Buttermilk
Piirakka	Pie
Riisi	Rice
Voi	Butter
Voileipä	Sandwich

Meat (lihaa)

Häränfilee	Fillet of beef
Hirvenliha	Elk
Jauheliha	Minced beef
Kana	Chicken
Kinkku	Ham
Lihapyörykat	Meatballs
Nauta	Beef
Paisti	Steak
Sianliha	Pork
Poro	Reindeer
Vasikanliha	Veal

Seafood (äyriäisiä) and fish (kala)

Ankerias	Eel
Graavilohi	Salted salmon
Hauki	Pike
Hummeri	Lobster
Katkaravut	Shrimp
Lohi	Salmon
Makrilli	Mackerel
Muikku	Small whitefish
Rapu	Crayfish
Sardiini	Sardine
Savustettu lohi	Smoked salmon
Savustettut silakat	Smoked Baltic herring
Siika	Large, slightly oily, whitefish
Silakat	Baltic herring
Silli	Herring
Suolattu	Pickled herring
Taimen or forelli	Trout
Tonnikala	Tuna
Turska	Cod

Egg dishes (munaruoat)

Hillomunakas	Jam omelette
Hyydytetty muna	Poached egg
Juustomunakas	Cheese omelette
Keitetty muna	Boiled eggs
Kinkkumunakas	Ham omelette
Munakas	Omelette
Munakokkeli	Scrambled eggs
Paistettu muna	Fried egg
Pekonimunakas	Bacon omelette
Perunamunakas	Potato omelette
Sienimunakas	Mushroom omelette

Vegetables (vihannekset)

Herneet	Peas
Kaali	Cabbage
Kurkku	Cucumber
Maissintähkät	Corn on the cob
Paprika	Green pepper
Pavut	Beans
Peruna	Potato
Pinaatti	Spinach
Porkkana	Carrot
Sieni	Mushroom
Sipuli	Onion
Tilli	Dill
Tomaatti	Tomato

Fruit (hedelmä)

Appelsiini	Orange
Aprikoosi	Apricot
Banaani	Banana
Greippi	Grapefruit
Kirsikka	Cherries
Luumu	Plums
Mansikka	Strawberry
Meloni	Melon
Omena	Apple
Päärynä	Pear
Pähkinä	Nuts

whether you want to indulge in some exotic brew. In rural areas, though, drinking it is considered a bit effete. When ordering tea, it's a good idea to insist that the water is boiling before the teabag is added – and that the bag is left in for more than two seconds.

Lunch and dinner

If you're in a university town, the campus cafeteria or **student mensa** is the cheapest place to get a hot dish. Theoretically you have to be a student, but you are unlikely to

| Persikka | Peach | Sitruuna | Lemon |
| Raparperi | Rhubarb | Viinirypäle | Grapes |

Sandwiches (voileipä)

Kappelivoileipä	Fried French bread with bacon and topped by a fried egg
Muna-anjovisleipä	Dark bread with slices of hard-boiled egg, anchovy fillets and tomato
Oopperavoileipä	Fried French bread with hamburger and egg
Sillivoileipä	Herring on dark bread, usually with egg and tomato

Finnish specialities

Kaalikääryleet	Cabbage rolls: cabbage leaves stuffed with minced meat and rice
Kaalipiirakka	Cabbage and minced meat
Karjalanpaisti	Karelian stew: beef and pork with onions
Kurpitsasalaatti	Pickled pumpkin served with meat dishes
Lammaskaali	Mutton and cabbage stew or soup
Lasimestarin silli	Pickled herring with spices, vinegar, carrot and onion
Lihakeitto	Soup made from meat, potatoes, carrots and onions
Lindströmin plhvi	Beefburger made with beetroot and served with a cream sauce
Lohilaatikko	Potato and salmon casserole
Lohipiirakka	Salmon pie
Makaroonilaatikko	Macaroni casserole with milk and egg sauce
Maksalaatikko	Baked liver purée with rice and raisins
Merimiespihvi	Casserole of potato slices and meat patties or minced meat
Piparjuuriliha	Boiled beef with horseradish sauce
Porkkanalaatikko	Carrot casserole; mashed carrots and rice
Poronkäristys	Sautéed reindeer stew
Sianlihakastike	Gravy with slivers of pork
Silakkalaatikko	Casserole with alternating layers of potato, onion and Baltic herring, with an egg and milk sauce
Stroganoff	Beef with gherkins and onions, browned in a casserole, braised in stock with tomato juice and sour cream
Suutarinlohi	Marinated Baltic herring with onion and peppers
Tilliliha	Boiled veal flavoured with dill sauce
Venäläinen silli	Herring fillets with mayonnaise, mustard, vinegar, beetroot, gherkins and onion
Wieninleike	Fried veal cutlet

Drinks

Appelsiinimehu	Orange juice	Olut	Beer
Gini	Gin	Tee	Tea
Kahvi	Coffee	Tonic vesi	Tonic water
Kivennäisvesi	Mineral water	Vesi	Water
Konjakki	Cognac	Viini	Wine
Limonaati	Lemonade	Viski	Whisky

be asked for ID. There's a choice of three meals: *Kevytlounas* (KL), the "light menu", which usually comprises soup and bread; *Lounas* (L), the "ordinary menu", which consists of a smallish fish or meat dish with dessert; and *Herkkulounas* (HL), the "delicious menu" – a substantial and usually meat-based plateful. All three come with bread and coffee, and each one costs €2–3. Prices can be cut by half if you borrow a Finnish student ID card from a friendly diner. The busiest period is lunchtime

(11.30am–12.30pm); later in the day (usually 4–6pm) many *mensas* offer price reductions. Most universities also have cafeterias where a small cup of coffee can cost as little as 45 cents.

If funds stretch to it, you should sample at least once a **ravintola**, or restaurant, offering a lunchtime buffet table (*voileipäpöytä* or *seisova pöytä*), which will be stacked with tasty traditional goodies that you can feast on to your heart's content for a set price of around €12. Less costly Finnish food can be found in a **baari**. These are designed for working people, generally close at 5pm or 6pm, and serve a range of Finnish dishes and snacks (and often the weaker beers; see "Drink", below). A good day for traditional Finnish food is Thursday, when every *baari* in the country dishes up *hernekeitto ja pannukakut*, thick pea soup with black rye bread, followed by oven-baked pancakes with strawberry jam, with buttermilk to wash it down – all for around €5.50. You'll get much the same fare from a *kahvila*, though a few of these, especially in the big cities, fancy themselves as being fashionable and may charge a few euro extra.

Although *ravintola* and *baaris* are plentiful, they're often outnumbered by **pizzerias**. They're as varied in quality here as they are in any other country, but especially worthwhile for their lunch specials, when a set price (€6–8) buys a pizza, coffee and everything you can carry from the bread and salad bar. Many of the bigger pizza chains offer discounts for super-indulgence – such as a second pizza for half-price and a third for free if you can polish off the first two. **Vegetarians** are likely to become well acquainted with pizzerias – specific vegetarian restaurants are thin on the ground, even in major cities.

Drink

Finland's **alcohol** laws are as bizarre and almost as repressive as those of Norway and Sweden, although unlike those countries, boozing is tackled enthusiastically, and is even regarded by some as an integral part of the national character. Some Finns, men in particular, often drink with the sole intention of getting paralytic; younger people are more inclined to regard the practice simply as an enjoyable social activity.

What to drink

Finnish spirits are much the same as you'd find in any country. **Beer** (*olut*), on the other hand, falls into three categories: "light beer" (*I-Olut*) – more like a soft drink; "medium-strength beer" (*Keskiolut*, *III-Olut*) – more perceptibly alcoholic and sold in many food shops and cafés; and "strong beer" (*A-Olut* or *IV-Olut*), which is on a par with the stronger international beers, and can only be bought at the ALKO shops and fully licensed (Grade A) restaurants and nightclubs.

The main – and cheapest – outlet for alcohol of any kind are **ALKO** shops (Mon–Thurs 10am–5pm, Fri 10am–6pm, Sat 9am–2pm). Even the smallest town will have one of these, and prices don't vary. In an ALKO shop, strong beers like Lapin Kulta Export – an Arctic-originated mind blower – and the equally potent Karjala, Lahden A, Olvi Export, and Koff porter, cost around €1.20 for a 300ml bottle. Imported beers such as Heineken, Carlsberg and Becks go for €1.50 a bottle. As for **spirits**, Finlandia vodka and Jameson's Irish Whiskey are €24 and €30 respectively per 75cl bottle. There's also a very popular rough form of vodka called Koskenkorva, ideal for assessing the strength of your stomach lining, which costs €20 for 75cl. The best **wine** bargains are usually Hungarian or Bulgarian, which cost around around €15 per bottle in a restaurant, though you can buy bottles in ALKO for under €5.50. French wines range from €7.50 to €50 a bottle at ALKO.

Where to drink

Continental-style **brasseries** or British-influenced **pubs** are the most pleasant places to have a drink. Frequented by both men and women of all ages, you're most likely to feel more at home in these familiar environments than in the smoky, generally all-male bars which proliferate in many of the small towns away from Helsinki, especially in the north – these charmless drinking dens are nothing more than places to get seriously drunk.

Most **restaurants** have a full licence, and some are actually frequented more for drinking than eating; it's these that we've listed under "Drinking" throughout the text. They're often also called bars or pubs by Finns simply for convenience. Just to add to the confusion, some so-called "pubs" are not licensed; neither are *baari*.

Along with ordinary restaurants, there are also **dance restaurants** (*tanssiravintola*). As the name suggests, these are places to dance rather than dine, although most do serve food as well as drink. They're popular with the over-40s, and before the advent of discos were the main places for people of opposite sex to meet. Even if you're under 40, dropping into one during the (usually early) evening sessions can be quite an eye-opener. Expect to pay a €2–5 admission charge.

Once you've found somewhere to drink, there's a fairly rigid set of **customs** to contend with. Sometimes you have to queue outside the most popular bars since entry is permitted only if a seat is free – there's no standing. Only one drink per person is allowed on the table at any one time except in the case of porter – a stout which most Finns mix with regular beer. There's always either a doorman (*portsari*) – whom you must tip (around €1) on leaving – or a cloakroom into which you must check your coat on arrival (again around €1). Bars are usually open until midnight or 1am and service stops half an hour before the place shuts. This is announced by a winking of the lights – the *valomerkki*.

Some bars and clubs have **waitress/waiter service**, whereby you order, and pay when your drinks are brought to you. A common order is *iso tuoppi* – a half-litre glass of draught beer, which costs €3–4 (up to €6 in some nightclubs). This might come slightly cheaper in **self-service** bars, where you select your tipple and queue up to pay at the till.

Wherever you buy alcohol, you'll have to be of **legal age**: at least 18 to buy beer and wine, and 20 or over to have a go at the spirits. ID will be checked if you look too young – or if the doorman's in a bad mood.

Directory

Canoeing With many lakes and rivers, Finland offers challenges to every type of canoe enthusiast, expert or beginner. There's plenty of easy-going paddling on the long lake systems, innumerable thrashing rapids to be shot, and abundant sea canoeing around the archipelagos of the south and southwest coast. Canoe rental (available wherever there are suitable waters) costs around €3 per hour, €8–20 per day, or €60 per week, with prices dependent on the type of canoe. Many tourist offices have plans of local canoeing routes, and you can get general information from the Finnish Canoe Federation, Olympiastadion, Eteläkaarre, 00250 Helsinki (0☎09/494 965, ⊛www .kanoottiliitto.fi).

Customs There are few, if any, border formalities when entering Finland from another Scandinavian country by land (although the crossing from Norway at Näätämö is – at least in theory – closed to non-Scandinavians from 10pm to 7am). The same applies when crossing by sea; only by air do you usually need to show your passport.

Dentists Seeing a dentist can be very expensive: expect to spend a minimum of €15. Look under *Hammaslääkari* in the phone book, or ask at a tourist office.

Doctors Provided you're insured, you'll save time by seeing a doctor at a private health centre (*lääkäriasema*) rather than queueing at a national health centre (*terveyskeskus*). You are required to present a doctor's referral and a written statement confirming that you will pay the bill in order to stay in hospital.

Emergencies For police, ambulance and fire service, dial ☎112.

Fishing Non-Scandinavians need a General Fishing Licence if they intend to fish in Finland's waterways; this costs €3 for a seven-day period from post offices. In certain parts of the Arctic North you'll need an additional licence costing €5 and obtainable locally. Throughout the country you'll also need the permission of the owner of the particular stretch of water, usually obtained by buying a permit on the spot. The nearest campsite or tourist office will have details of this, and advise on the regional variations on national fishing laws.

Markets In larger towns, these usually take place every day except Sunday from 7am to 2pm. There'll also be a market hall (*kauppahalli*) open weekdays 8am–5pm. Smaller places have a market once or twice a week, usually including Saturday.

Nude bathing Finns are uptight and very un-Scandinavian in their attitude to public nudity. Hence, sections of some Finnish beaches are designated nude bathing areas, more often than not sex-segregated and occasionally with an admission charge of around €1.50. The local tourist office or campsite will part with the facts – albeit rather reluctantly. However, you should encounter no problem sunbathing naked by a secluded lake or in the forest.

Pharmacies *Kemikaalikauppa* sell only cosmetics; for medicines you need to go to an *apteekki*, generally open daily 9am–6pm.

Public holidays January 1, May 1, December 6, December 24, 25 and 26. Variable dates: Epiphany (between Jan 6 and 12), Good Friday and Easter Weekend, the Saturday before Whit Sunday, Midsummer's Eve, All Saint's Day (the Saturday between Oct 31 and Nov 6). Shops and banks close on these days and most public transport will operate a Sunday schedule; museum opening hours may also be affected.

Saunas These are cheapest at a public swimming pool, where you'll pay €2–3 for a session. Hotel saunas, which are sometimes better equipped than public ones, are more expensive (€5–7) but free to guests. Many Finnish people have saunas built into their homes and it's common for visitors to be invited to share one.

Shops Supermarkets are usually open Mon–Fri 9am–8pm, Sat 9am–6pm. Some in cities keep longer hours, for example 8am–10pm. In Helsinki the shops in Tunneli are open until 10pm. In the weeks leading up to Christmas some stores and markets are open on Sunday, too.

History

Inextricably bound with the medieval superpowers, Sweden and Russia, and later with the Soviet Union, Finland's history is a stirring tale of a small people's survival – and eventual triumph – over what have often seemed impossible odds. It's also a story that's been full of powerful contemporary resonances – the Finns' battle to regain their independence has not gone unnoticed on the other side of the Baltic Sea, and served as an exemplary case for the three Baltic States who fought for independence from the Soviet Union in the late 1980s.

First settlements

As the ice sheets of the last Ice Age retreated, parts of the Finnish Arctic coast were settled by tribes from eastern Europe. They hunted bear and reindeer, and fished the well-stocked rivers and lakes: relics of their existence have been found and dated to around 8000 BC. Pottery skills were introduced around 3000 BC, and trade with Russia and the east flourished. At the same time, other peoples were arriving and merging with the established population. The

Finnish and Swedish place names

On most maps and many transport timetables cities and towns are given their **Finnish names** followed by their **Swedish names** in parentheses. Both Swedes and Finland-Swedes will frequently use the Swedish rather than the Finnish names. The main places in question are listed below, with the Finnish name first.

Helsinki (Helsingfors)
Porvoo (Borgå)
Turku (Åbo)
Pori (Björneborg)
Hamina (Fredrikshamn)
Lappeenranta (Villmanstrand)
Kajaani (Kajana)

Iisalmi (Idensalmi)
Tampere (Tammerfors)
Mikkeli (St Michel)
Savonlinna (Nyslott)
Vaasa (Vasa)
Kokkola (Gamla Karleby)
Oulu (Uleåborg)

Boat Axe culture (1800–1600 BC), which originated in central Europe, spread as Indo-Europeans migrated into Finland. The seafaring knowledge they possessed enabled them to begin trading with Sweden from the Finnish west coast, as indicated by **Bronze Age** findings (around 1300 BC) concentrated in a narrow strip along the seaboard. The previous settlers withdrew eastwards and the advent of severe weather brought this period of occupation to an end.

The arrival of the Finns

The antecedents of the Finns were a race from central Russia, from where they moved outwards in two directions. One tribe went south, eventually to Hungary; and the other westwards to the Baltic, where it mixed with Latgals, Lithuanians and Germans. The latter, the "**Baltic Finns**", were migrants who crossed the Baltic around 400 AD to form an independent society in Finland. In 100 AD the Roman historian Tacitus described a wild and primitive people called "the Fenni". This is thought to have been a reference to the earliest **Sámi**, who occupied Finland before this. With their more advanced culture, the Baltic Finns absorbed this indigenous population, although some of their customs were maintained. The new Finns worked the land, utilized the vast forests and made lengthy fishing expeditions on the lakes.

The pagan era

The main Finnish settlements were along the west coast facing Sweden, with whom trade was established, until the Vikings' opening up of routes further to the east forced these communities into decline. Meanwhile, the Finnish south coast was exposed to seaborne raiding parties and most Finns moved inland and eastwards, a large number settling around the huge Lake Ladoga in **Karelia**. Eventually the people of Karelia were able to enjoy trade in two directions – with the Varangians to the east and the Swedes to the west. Groups from Karelia and the more northern territory of Kainuu regularly ventured into Lapland to fish and hunt. At the end of the pagan era Finland was split into three regions: Varsinais-Suomi ("Finland proper") in the southwest, Häme in the western part of the lake region, and Karelia in the east. Although they often helped one another, there was no formal cooperation between the inhabitants of these areas.

The Swedish era (1155–1809)

At the start of the tenth century, pagan Finland was caught between two opposing religions: Catholicism in Sweden on one side and the Orthodox Church of Russia on the other. The Russians wielded great influence in Karelia, but the west of Finland began to gravitate towards Catholicism on account of its high level of contact with Sweden. In 1155 King Erik of Sweden launched a "crusade" into Finland – although its real purpose was to strengthen trade routes – which swept through the southwest and established Swedish control, leaving the English **Bishop Henry** at **Turku** to establish a parish. Henry was killed by a Finnish yeoman, but became the patron saint of the Turku diocese and the region became the administrative base of the whole country. Western Finland generally acquiesced to the Swedes, but Karelia didn't, becoming a territory much sought after by both the Swedes and the Russians. In 1323, under the **Treaty of Pähkinäsaari**, an official border was drawn up, giving the western part of Karelia to Sweden while the Russian principality of Novgorod retained the eastern section around Lake Ladoga. To emphasize their claim, the Russians founded the Orthodox **Valamo Monastery** on an island in the lake.

Under the Swedish crown, Finns still worked and controlled their own land, often living side by side with Swedes, who came to the west coast to safeguard sea trade. Finnish provincial leaders were given places among the nobility and in 1362 King Håkon gave Finland the right to vote in Swedish royal elections. When the Swedish throne was given to the German Albrecht of Mecklenburg, in 1364, there was little support for the new monarch in Finland, and much violent opposition to his forces who arrived to occupy the Swedish-built castles. Once established, the Mecklenburgians imposed forced labour and the Finnish standard of living swiftly declined. There was even a proposal that the country should be sold to the Teutonic Order of Knights.

In a campaign to wrest control of the Swedish realm, a Swedish noble, **Grip**, acquired control of one Finnish province after another, and by 1374 was in charge of the whole country. In doing this he was obliged to consider the welfare of the Finns and consequently living conditions improved. Another effect of Grip's actions was to underline Finland's position as an individual country – under the Swedish sovereign but distanced from Sweden's political offices.

Grip had intended to ensure that Finnish affairs would be managed by the Swedish nobility irrespective of the wishes of the monarch. The nobility, however, found themselves forced to look for assistance to Margrethe, Queen of Denmark and Norway. She agreed to come to the Swedes' aid provided they recognized her as sovereign over all the Swedish realm including Finland. This resulted in the **Kalmar Union** of 1397.

While the Finns were barely affected by the constitution of the Union, there was a hope that it would guarantee their safety against the Russians, whose expansionist policies were an increasing threat. Throughout the fifteenth century there were repeated skirmishes between Russians and Finns in the border lands and around the important Finnish Baltic trading centre of Viipuri (now Russian Vyborg).

The election of King Charles VIII in 1438 caused a rift in the Union and serious strife between Sweden and Denmark. He was forced to abdicate in 1458 but his support in Finland was strong, and his successor, Christian I, sent an armed column to subdue Finnish unrest. While Turku Castle was under siege, the Danish noble **Erik Axelsson Tott**, already known and respected in the country, called a meeting of representatives from every Finnish estate where it was agreed that Christian I would be acknowledged as king of the Union.

Tott went on to take command of Viipuri Castle and was able to function almost independently of central government. Although he planned to make Viipuri the major centre for east–west trade, resources had to be diverted to strengthen the eastern defences. During the 1460s Novgorod was sucked into

Moscow's sphere of influence and finally absorbed altogether. This left Finland's eastern edge more exposed than ever before. Novgorod had long held claims on large sections of Karelia, and the border situation was further confused by the Finnish peasants who had drifted eastwards and settled in the disputed territories. Part of Tott's response to the dangers was to erect the fortress of **Olavinlinna** (in the present town of Savonlinna) in 1475, actually inside the land claimed by Russia.

Tott died in 1481 and **Sten Sture**, a Swedish regent, forced the remaining Axelssons to relinquish their family's domination of Finland. By 1487 Sture had control of the whole country, and appointed bailiffs of humble birth – instead of established aristocrats – to the Finnish castles in return for their surplus revenue. These monies were used to finance Sture's ascent through the Swedish nobility. As a result nothing was spent on maintaining the eastern defences.

Strengthened by an alliance with Denmark signed in 1493, Russia attacked Viipuri on November 30, 1495. The troops were repulsed by the technically inferior Finns, an achievement perceived as a miracle. After further battles it was agreed that the borders of the Treaty of Pähkinäsaari would remain. However, the Swedes drew up a bogus version of the treaty in which the border retained its fifteenth-century position, and it was this forgery which they used in negotiations with the Russians over the next hundred years.

Within Finland a largely Swedish-born nobility became established. Church services were conducted in Finnish, although Swedish remained the language of commerce and officialdom. Because the bulk of the population was illiterate, any important deed had to be read to them. In the thirteenth and fourteenth centuries, any Finn who felt oppressed simply moved into the wild lands of the interior – out of earshot of church bells.

By the time **Gustav Vasa** took the Swedish throne in 1523, many villages were established in the disputed border regions. Almost every inhabitant spoke Finnish, but there was a roughly equal division between those communities who paid taxes to the Swedish king and those who paid them to the Russian tsar. In the winter of 1555, a Russian advance into Karelia was quashed at Joutselkä by Finns using skis to travel speedily over the icy roads, a victory that made the Finnish nobility confident of success in a full-scale war. While hesitant, Vasa finally agreed to their wishes: 12,000 troops from Sweden were dispatched to eastern Finland, and an offensive launched in the autumn of 1556. It failed, with the Russians reaching the gates of Viipuri, and Vasa retreating to the Åland Islands, asking for peace.

In 1556 Gustav Vasa made Finland a Swedish Grand Duchy and gave his son, Johan, the title Duke of Finland. It was rumoured that **Duke Johan** not only spoke Finnish but was an advocate of Finnish nationalism. These claims were exaggerated, but the duke was certainly pro-Finnish, surrounding himself with Finnish nobles and founding a chancery and an exchequer. He moved into Turku Castle and furnished it in splendour. However, the powers of his office, as defined by the Articles of Arboga, were breached by a subsequent invasion of Livonia and he was sentenced to death by the Swedish Diet in 1563, although the king's power of pardon was exercised. Finland was divided between loyalty towards the friendly duke and the need to keep on good terms with the Swedish crown, now held by Erik XIV. The Swedish forces sent to collect Johan laid siege to Turku castle for three weeks, executing thirty nobles before capturing the duke and imprisoning him.

The war between Sweden and Denmark over control of the Baltic took its toll on Erik. He became mentally unbalanced, slaying several prisoners who were being held for trial, and, in a moment of complete madness, releasing Johan from detention. The Swedish nobles were incensed by Erik's actions and rebelled against him – with the result that Johan became king in 1568.

In 1570 Swedish resources were stretched when hostilities again erupted with Russia, now ruled by the aggressive Tsar Ivan ("the Terrible") IV. The conflict was to last 25 years, a period known in Finland as "**The Long Wrath**". It saw the introduction of a form of conscription instead of the reliance on mercenary soldiers, which had been the norm in other Swedish wars. Able-bodied men aged between fifteen and fifty were rounded up by the local bailiff and about one in ten selected for military service. Russia occupied almost all of Estonia and made deep thrusts into southern Finland. Finally the Swedish–Finnish troops regained Estonia and made significant advances through Karelia, capturing an important Eastern European trading route. The war was formally concluded in 1595 by the **Treaty of Täyssinä**. Under its terms, Russia recognized the lands gained by Sweden and the eastern border was altered to reach up to the Arctic coast, enabling Finns to settle in the far north.

Sweden was established as the dominant force in the Baltic, but under Gustav II, who became king in 1611, Finland began to lose the special status it had previously enjoyed. Its administration was streamlined and centralized, causing many Finnish nobles to move to Stockholm. Civic orders had to be written rather than passed on orally, and many ambitious Finns gave themselves Swedish surnames. Finnish manpower supported Swedish efforts overseas – the soldiers gaining a reputation as wild and fearless fighters – but brought no direct benefit to Finland itself. Furthermore, the peasants were increasingly burdened by the taxes needed to support the Swedish wars with Poland, Prussia and Germany.

Conditions continued to decline until 1637, when **Per Brahe** was appointed governor-general. Against the prevailing mood of the time, he insisted that all officers should study Finnish, founded Turku University – the country's first – and instigated a successful programme to spread literacy among the Finnish people. After concluding his second term of office in 1654 he parted with the terse but accurate summary: "I was highly satisfied with this country and the country highly satisfied with me."

A terrible harvest in 1696 caused a **famine** that killed a third of the Finnish population. The fact that no aid came from Sweden intensified feelings of neglect and stirred up a minor bout of Finnish nationalism led by **Daniel Juslenius**. His book, *Aboa Vetus Et Nova*, published in 1700, claimed Finnish to be a founding language of the world, and Finns to be descendants of the tribes of Israel.

In 1711 Viipuri fell to the Russians. Under their new tsar, Peter ("the Great"), the Russians quickly spread across the country, causing the nobility to flee to Stockholm and Swedish commanders to be more concerned with salvaging their army than saving Finland. In 1714, eight years of Russian occupation – "**The Great Wrath**" – began. Descriptions of the horrors of these times have been exaggerated, but nonetheless the events confirmed the Finns' longtime dread of their eastern neighbour. The Russians saw Finland simply as a springboard to attack Sweden, and laid waste to anything in it which the Swedes might attempt to regain.

Under the **Treaty of Uusikaupunki**, in 1721, the tsar gave back much of Finland but retained Viipuri, east Karelia, Estonia and Latvia, and thus control of the Baltic. Finland now had a new eastern border that was totally unprotected; Russian occupation was inevitable but would be less disastrous if entered into voluntarily. The Finnish peasants, with Swedish soldiers forcibly billeted on them, remained loyal to the king but with little faith in what he could do to protect them.

The aggressive policies of the Hats in the Swedish Diet led to the 1741 declaration of war on Russia. With barely an arm raised against them, Russian troops again occupied Finland – the start of "**The Lesser Wrath**" – until the **Treaty of Turku** in 1743. Under this, the Russians withdrew, ceded a section of Finland back to Sweden but moved their border west.

The Russian era (1809–1917)

In an attempt to force Sweden to join Napoleon's economic blockade, Russia, under Tsar Alexander I, attacked and occupied Finland in 1807. The **Treaty of Hamina**, signed in September of that year, legally ceded all of the country to Russia. The tsar had needed a friendly country close to Napoleon's territory as a reliable ally in case of future hostilities between the two leaders. To gain Finnish favour, he had guaranteed beneficial terms at the Diet (based in Porvoo) in 1809, and subsequently Finland became an **autonomous Russian Grand Duchy**. There was no conscription and taxation was frozen, while realignment of the northern section of the Finnish–Russian border gave additional land to Finland. Finns could freely occupy positions in the Russian empire, although Russians were denied equal opportunities within Finland. The long period of peace that ensued saw a great improvement in Finnish wealth and well-being.

After returning Viipuri to Finland, the tsar declared Helsinki the **capital** in 1812, regarding Turku as too close to Sweden for safety. The "Guards of Finland" helped crush the Polish rebellion and fought in the Russo-Turkish conflict. This, along with the French and English attacks on Finnish harbours during the Crimean War, accentuated the bond between the two countries. Many Finns came to regard the tsar as their own monarch.

There was, however, an increasingly active **Finnish-language movement**. A student leader, the future statesman **Johan Vilhelm Snellman**, had met the tsar and demanded that Finnish replace Swedish as the country's official language. Snellman's slogan "Swedes we are no longer, Russians we cannot become, we must be Finns" became the rallying cry of the **Fennomen**. The Swedish-speaking ruling class, feeling threatened, had Snellman removed from his university post and he retreated to Kuopio to publish newspapers espousing his beliefs. His opponents cited Finnish as the language of peasants, unfit for cultured use – a claim undermined by the efforts of a playwright, **Aleksis Kivi**, whose works marked the beginning of Finnish-language theatre. In 1835, the collection of Karelian folk tales published in Finnish by **Elias Lönnrot** as the **Kalevala** became the first written record of Finnish folklore, and a focal point for Finnish nationalism.

The liberal tsar Alexander II appointed Snellman to Turku University, from where he went on to become minister of finance. In 1858 Finnish was declared the official language of local government in areas where the majority of the population were Finnish speaking, and the Diet, convened in 1863 for the first time since the Russian takeover, finally gave native-tongued Finns equal status with Swedish speakers. The only opposition was from the so-called **Svecomen**, who sought not only the maintenance of the Swedish language but unification with Finland's westerly neighbour.

The increasingly powerful Pan-Slavist contingent in Russia was horrified by the growth of the Finnish timber industry and the rise of trade with the west. They were also unhappy with the special status of the Grand Duchy, considering the Finns an alien race who would contaminate the eastern empire by their links with the west. Tsar Alexander III was not swayed by these opinions but, after his assassination in

1894, Nicholas I came to power and instigated a **Russification process**. Russian was declared the official language, Finnish money was abolished and plans were laid to merge the Finnish army into the Russian army. To pass these measures the tsar drew up the unconstitutional **February Manifesto**. Opposition came in varying forms. In 1899, a young composer called **Jean Sibelius** wrote *Finlandia*. The Russians banned all performances of it "under any name that indicates its patriotic character", causing Sibelius to publish it as Opus 26 No. 7. The painter **Akseli Gallen-Kallela** ignored international art trends and depicted scenes from the *Kalevala*, as did the poet **Eino Leino**. Students skied to farms all over the country and collected half a million signatures against the manifesto. Over a thousand of Europe's foremost intellectuals signed a document called "Pro-Finlandia".

But these had no effect, and in 1901 the **Conscription Law** was introduced, forcing Finns to serve directly under the tsar in the Russian army. A programme of civil disobedience began, the leaders of which were soon obliged to go underground, where they titled themselves the Kagel – borrowing a name used by persecuted Russian Jews. The Finnish population became divided between the "compliants" (acquiescent to the Manifesto) and the "constitutionalists" (against the Manifesto), causing the rival sides to do their shopping in different stores and even splitting families.

The stand against conscription was enough to make the Russians drop the scheme, but their grip was tightened in other ways. A peaceful demonstration in Helsinki was broken up by cossacks on horseback, and in April 1903 the tsar installed the tough **Nicolai Bobrikov** as governor-general, giving him new and sweeping powers. The culmination of sporadic acts of violence came on June 16, 1904, when the Finnish civil servant **Eugen Schauman** climbed the Senate staircase and shot Bobrikov three times before turning the gun on himself. After staggering to his usual Senate seat, Bobrikov collapsed and died – and his assassin became a national hero.

In 1905 the Russians suffered defeat in their war with Japan and the general strike that broke out in their country spread to Finland, the Finnish labour movement being represented by the Social Democratic Party. The revolutionary spirit that was moving through Russia encouraged the conservative Finnish Senate to reach a compromise with the demands of the Social Democrats, and the result was a gigantic upheaval in the Finnish parliamentary system. In 1906, the country adopted a single-chamber parliament (the Eduskunta) elected by national suffrage – Finnish women being the first in Europe to get the vote. In the first election under the new system the Social Democrats won eighty seats out of the total of two hundred, making it the most left-wing legislature seen so far in Europe.

Any laws passed in Finland, however, still needed the ratification of the tsar, who now viewed Finland as a dangerous forum for leftist debate (the exiled Lenin met Stalin for the first time in Tampere). In 1910 Nicholas II removed the new parliament's powers and reinstated the Russification programme. Two years later the **Parity Act** gave Russians in Finland status equal to Finns, enabling them to hold seats in the Senate and posts in the civil service. The outspoken anti-tsarist parliamentary speaker **P.E. Svinhufvud** was exiled to Siberia for a second time.

As World War I commenced, Finland was obviously allied with Russia and endured a commercial blockade, food shortages and restrictions on civil liberties, but did not actually fight on the tsar's behalf. Germany promised Finland total autonomy in the event of victory for the Kaiser and provided clandestine military training to about two thousand Finnish students – the Jäger movement who reached Germany through

Sweden and later fought against the Russians as a light infantry battalion on the Baltic front.

Towards independence

When the tsar was overthrown in 1917, the Russian provisional government under Kerensky declared the measures taken against Finland null and void and restored the previous level of autonomy. Within Finland there was uncertainty over the country's constitutional bonds with Russia. The conservative view was that prerogative powers should be passed from the deposed ruler to the provisional government, while socialists held that the provisional government had no right to exercise power in Finland and that supreme authority should be passed to the Eduskunta.

Under the **Power Act**, the Eduskunta vested in itself supreme authority within Finland, leaving only control of foreign and military matters residing with the Russians. Kerensky refused to recognize the Power Act and dissolved the Finnish parliament, forcing a fresh election. This time a bigger poll returned a conservative majority.

The loss of their parliamentary majority and the bitterness felt towards the bourgeois-dominated Senate, who happily complied with Kerensky's demands, made the Social Democrats adopt a more militant line. Around the country there had been widespread labour disputes and violent confrontations between strikers and strike-breaking mobs hired by landowners. The Social Democrats sanctioned the formation of an armed workers' guard, soon to be called the **Red Guard**, in response to the growing **White Guard** – a right-wing private army operating in the virtual absence of a regular police force. A general strike was called on November 13, which forced the Eduskunta into reforms after just a few days. The strike was called off, but a group of dissident Red Guards threatened to break from the Social Democrats and continue the action.

After the Bolsheviks took power in Russia, the conservative Finnish government became fearful of Soviet involvement in Finnish affairs and a de facto **statement of independence** was made. The socialists, by now totally excluded from government, declared their support for independence but insisted that it should be reached through negotiation with the Soviet Union. Instead, on December 6, a draft of an independent constitution drawn up by **K.J. Ståhlberg** was approved by the Eduskunta. After a delay of three weeks it was formally recognized by the Soviet leader, Lenin.

The civil war

In asserting its new authority, the government repeatedly clashed with the labour movement. The Red Guard, who had reached an uneasy truce with the Social Democratic leadership, were involved in gun-running between Viipuri and Petrograd, and efforts by the White Guard to halt it led to full-scale fighting. A vote passed by the Eduskunta on January 12, 1918, empowered the government to create a police force to restore law and order. On January 25 the White Guard was legitimized as the Civil Guard.

In Helsinki, a special committee of the Social Democrats took the decision to resist the Civil Guard and seize power, effectively pledging themselves to **civil war**. On January 27 and 28, a series of occupations enabled leftist committees to take control of the capital and the major towns of the south. Three government ministers who evaded capture fled to Vaasa and formed a rump administration. Meanwhile, a Finnish-born aristocrat, **C.G.E. Mannerheim**, who had served as a cavalry officer in the Russian army, arrived at the request of the government in Ostrobothnia, a region dominated by right-wing farmers, to train a force to fight the Reds.

Mannerheim, who had secured a 15 million markkaa loan from a Helsinki bank to finance his army, drew on the German-trained Jäger for officers, while the Ostrobothnian farmers – seeking to protect their landowning privileges – along with a small number of Swedish volunteers, made up the troops. Their initial task was to mop up the Russian battalions remaining in western Finland, which had been posted there by the tsar to prevent German advancement in World War I, and which by now were politicized into Soviets. Mannerheim had achieved this by the beginning of February, and his attention then turned to the Reds.

The Whites were in control of Ostrobothnia, northern Finland and parts of Karelia, and were connected by a railway from Vaasa to Käkisalmi on Lake Ladoga. Although the Reds were numerically superior they were poorly equipped and poorly trained, and failed to break the enemy's line of communication. Tampere fell to the Whites in March. At the same time, a German force landed on the south coast, their assistance requested by White Finns in Berlin (although Mannerheim opposed their involvement). Surrounded, the leftists' resistance collapsed in April.

Throughout the conflict, the Social Democratic Party maintained a high level of unity. While containing revolutionary elements, it was led mainly by socialists seeking to retain parliamentary democracy and believing their fight was against a bourgeois force seeking to impose right-wing values on the newly independent state. Their arms, however, were supplied by the Soviet Union, causing the White taunt that the Reds were "aided by foreign bayonets". Many of the revolutionary socialists within the party fled to Russia after the civil war, where they formed the Finnish Communist Party. The harsh treatment of the Reds who were captured – 8000 were executed and 80,000 were imprisoned in camps where more than 9000 died from hunger or disease – fired a resentment that would last for generations. The Whites regarded the war as

one of liberation, ridding the country of Russians and the Bolshevik influence, and setting the course for an anti-Russian Finnish nationalism. Mannerheim and the strongly pro-German Jäger contingent were keen to continue east, to gain the whole of Karelia from the Russians, but the possibility of direct Finnish assistance to the Russian White Army – who were seeking to overthrow the Bolshevik government – came to nothing thanks to the Russian Whites' refusal to guarantee recognition of Finland's independent status.

Later that year, a **provisional government of independent Karelia** was set up in Uhtua. Its formation was masterminded by Red Finns, who ensured that its claims to make Karelia a totally independent region did not accord with the desires of the Finnish government. The provisional government's congress, held the following year, also confirmed a wish for separation from the Soviet Union and requested the removal of the Soviet troops, which was agreed, with a proviso that Soviet troops retained a right to be based in eastern Karelia. The eventual collapse of the talks caused the provisional government and its supporters to flee to Finland as a Finnish battalion of the Soviet Red Army moved in and occupied the area. Subsequently the Karelian Workers' Commune, motivated by the Finnish Communists and backed by Soviet decree, was formed.

A few days later, the state of war which existed between Finland and Russia was formally ended by the **Treaty of Tartu**. The existence of the Karelian Workers' Commune gave the Soviet negotiators a pretext for refusing Finnish demands for Karelian self-determination, claiming the new set-up to be an expression of the Karelian people's wishes. The treaty was signed in an air of animosity. A bald settlement of border issues, it gave Finland the Petsamo area, a shoulder of land extending to the Arctic coast.

The republic

The White success in the civil war led to a right-wing government with a pro-German majority, which wanted to establish Finland as a monarchy rather than the republic allowed for under the 1917 declaration of independence. Although twice defeated in the Eduskunta, Prime Minister **J.K. Paasikivi** evoked a clause in the Swedish Form of Government from 1772, making legal the election of a king. As a result, the Finnish crown was offered to a German, Friedrich Karl, Prince of Hessen. Immediately prior to German defeat in World War I, the prince declined the invitation. The victorious Allies insisted on a new Finnish government and a fresh general election if they were to recognize the nation's independent status. Since the country was now compelled to look to the Allies for future assistance, the request was complied with, sealing Finland's future as a republic. The first president was the liberal **Ståhlberg**.

The termination of the monarchists' aims upset the unity of the right and paved the way for a succession of centrist governments. These were dominated by two parties, the **National Progressives** and the **Agrarians**. Through a period of rapidly increasing prosperity, numerous reforms were enacted. Farmers who rented land were given the opportunity to buy it with state aid, compulsory schooling was introduced, laws regarding religious freedom were passed and the provision of social services strengthened. As more farmers became independent producers, the Agrarians, claiming to represent the rural interests, drew away much of the Social Democrats' traditional support.

Finnish economic development halted abruptly following the world slump of the late 1920s. A series of strikes culminated in a dock workers' dispute which began in May 1928 and continued for almost a year. It was settled by the intervention of the Minister for Social Affairs on terms perceived as a defeat for the strikers. The dispute was seen by the right as a communist-inspired attempt to ruin the Finnish export trade at a time when the Soviet Union had re-entered the world timber trade. It was also a symbolic ideological clash – a pointer to future events.

Moves to outlaw communist activity had been deemed an infringement of civil rights, but in 1929 the Suomen Lukko was formed to legally combat Communism. It was swiftly succeeded by the more extreme and violent **Lapua Movement** (the name coming from the Ostrobothnian town, where a parade of Communist youth had been brought to a bloody end by "White" farmers). The Lapuans rounded up suspected Communists and Communist sympathizers, and drove them to the Russian border, insisting that they walk across. Even the former president, Ståhlberg, was kidnapped and dumped at the eastern town of Joensuu. The Lapuans' actions were only half-heartedly condemned by the non-socialist parties, and in private they were supported. But when the Lapuans began advocating a complete overthrow of the political system, much of this tacit approval dried up.

The government obtained a two-thirds majority in the elections of October 1930 and amended the constitution to make communist activity illegal. This was expected to placate the Lapuans but instead they issued even more extreme demands, including the abolition of the Social Democrats. In 1932, a coup d'état was attempted by a Lapuan group who prevented a socialist member of parliament from addressing a meeting in Mäntsälä, 50km north of Helsinki. They refused to disperse, despite shots being fired by police, and sent for assistance from Lapuan bases around the country. The Lapuan leadership took up the cause and broadcast demands for a new government. They were unsuccessful because of the loyalty of the troops who surrounded the town on the orders of the then prime minister, Svinhufvud. Following this, the

Lapuans were outlawed, although their leaders received only minor punishments for their deeds. Several of them regrouped as the Nazi-style Patriotic People's Movement. But unlike the parallel movements in Europe, there was little in Finland on which Nazism could focus mass hatred, and, despite winning a few parliamentary seats, it quickly declined into insignificance.

The Finnish **economy** recovered swiftly, and much international goodwill was generated when the country became the only nation to fully pay its war reparations to the USA after World War I. Finland joined the League of Nations hoping for a guarantee of its eastern border, but by 1935 the League's weakness was apparent and the Finns looked to traditionally neutral **Scandinavia** for protection as Europe moved towards war.

World War II

The Nazi–Soviet Non-Aggression Pact of August 1939 put Finland firmly into the Soviet sphere. Stalin had compelled Estonia, Latvia and Lithuania to allow Russian bases on their land, and in October was demanding a chunk of the Karelian isthmus from Finland to protect Leningrad, as well as a leasing of the Hanko peninsula on the Finnish Baltic coast. Russian troops were heading towards the Finnish border from Murmansk, and on November 30 the Karelian isthmus was attacked – an act that triggered the **Winter War**.

Stalin had had the tsarist military commanders executed, and his troops were led by young Communists well versed in ideology but ignorant of war strategy. Informed that the Finnish people would welcome them as liberators, the Soviet soldiers anticipated little resistance to their invasion. They expected to reach the Finnish west coast within ten days and therefore carried no overcoats, had little food, and camped each night in open fields. The Finns, although vastly outnumbered, were defending their homes and farms as well as their hard-won independence.

Familiarity with the terrain enabled them to conceal themselves in the forests and attack through stealth – and they were prepared for the winter temperatures, which plunged to -30°C (-18°F). The Russians were slowly picked off and their camps frequently surrounded and destroyed.

While Finland gained the world's admiration, no practical help was forthcoming and it became simply a matter of time before Stalin launched a better-supplied, unstoppable advance. It came during February 1940 and the Finnish government was forced to ask for peace. This was granted under the **Treaty of Moscow**, signed in March by President **Kyösti Kallio**, who cursed "let the hand wither that signs such a paper" as his hand put pen to paper. The treaty ceded 11 percent of Finnish territory to the Soviet Union. There was a mass exodus from these areas, with nearly half a million people travelling west to the new boundaries of Finland. Kyösti Kallio was later paralyzed on his right side.

The period immediately following the Winter War left Finland in a difficult position. Before the war, Finland had produced all its own food but was dependent on imported fertilizers. Supplies of grain, which had been coming from Russia, were halted as part of Soviet pressure for increased transit rights and access to the important nickel-producing mines in Petsamo. Finland became reliant on grain from Germany and British shipments to the Petsamo coast, which were interrupted when Germany invaded Norway. In return for providing arms, Germany was given transit rights through Finland. Legally, this required the troops to be constantly moving, but a permanent force became stationed at Rovaniemi.

The Finnish leadership knew that Germany was secretly preparing to attack the Soviet Union, and a broadcast from Berlin had spoken of a "united front" from Norway to Poland at a time when Finland was officially outside the Nazi sphere. Within Finland there was little support for the Nazis, but there was a fear of Soviet occupation. While Finland clung to its neutrality, refusing to fight unless attacked, it was drawn closer and closer to Germany. Soviet air raids on several Finnish towns in June 1941 finally led Finland into the war on the side of the Nazis. The ensuing conflict with the Russians, fought with the primary purpose of regaining territory lost in the Winter War, became known as the **Continuation War**. The bulk of the land ceded under the Treaty of Moscow was recovered by the end of August. After this, Mannerheim, who commanded the Finnish troops, ignored Nazi encouragement to assist in their attack on Leningrad. A request from the British prime minister, Winston Churchill, that the Finns cease their advance, was also refused, although Mannerheim didn't cut the Murmansk railway which was moving Allied supplies. Even so, Britain was forced to acknowledge the predicament of its ally, the Soviet Union, and declared war on Finland in December 1941.

In 1943, the German defeat at Stalingrad, which made Allied victory almost inevitable, had a profound impact in Finland. Mannerheim called a meeting of inner-cabinet ministers and decided to seek a truce with the Soviet Union. The USA stepped forward as mediators but announced that the peace terms set by Moscow were too severe to be worthy of negotiation. Germany, meanwhile, had learned of the Finnish initiative and demanded an undertaking that Finland would not seek peace with Russia, threatening to withdraw supplies if it was not given. (The Germans were also unhappy with Finnish sympathy for Jews – several hundred who had escaped from central Europe were saved from the concentration camps by being granted Finnish citizenship.) Simultaneously, a Russian advance into Karelia made Finland dependent on German arms to launch a counterattack. An agreement with the Germans was signed by President **Risto**

Ryti in June 1944 without the consent of the Eduskunta, thereby making the deed invalid when he ceased to be president.

Ryti resigned the presidency at the beginning of August and Mannerheim informed Germany that the agreement was no longer binding. A peace with the Soviet Union was signed in Moscow two weeks later. Under its terms, Finland was forced to give up the Pestamo region and the border was restored to its 1940 position. The Hanko peninsula was returned but instead the Porkkala peninsula, nearer to Helsinki, was to be leased to the Soviet Union for fifty years. There were stinging reparations. The Finns also had to drive the remaining Germans out of the country within two weeks. This was easily done in the south, but the bitter fighting that took place in Lapland caused the total destruction of many towns. It was further agreed that organizations disseminating anti-Soviet views within Finland would be dissolved and that Finland would accept an Allied Control Commission to oversee war trials.

The postwar period

After the war, the Communist Party was legalized and, along with militant socialists expelled from the Social Democratic Party, formed a broad leftist umbrella organization – the **Finnish People's Democratic League**. Their efforts to absorb the Social Democrats were resisted by that party's moderate leadership, who regarded Communism as "poison to the Finnish people". In the first peace-time poll, the Democratic League went to the electorate with a populist rather than revolutionary manifesto – something that was to characterize future Finnish Communism. Both they and the Social Democrats attained approximately a quarter of the vote. Bolstered by two Social Democratic defections, the Democratic League narrowly became the largest party in the Eduskunta. The two of them, along with the Agrarian Party, formed an alliance ("The Big Three Agreement") that held the balance of power in a coalition government under the premiership of Paasikivi.

Strikes instigated by Communist-controlled trade unions allowed the Social Democrats to accuse the Democratic League of seeking to undermine the production of machinery and other goods destined for the Soviet Union under the terms of the war reparation agreement, thereby creating a scenario for Soviet invasion. Charges of communist vote-rigging in trade union ballots helped the Social Democrats to gain control of the unions. The Democratic League won only 38 seats in the general election of 1948, and rejected the token offer of four posts in the new government, opting instead to stay in opposition. Their electoral campaign wasn't helped by the rumour – almost certainly groundless – that they were planning a Soviet-backed coup.

To ensure that the terms of the peace agreement were adhered to, the Soviet-dominated Allied Control Commission stayed in Finland until 1947. Its presence engendered a tense atmosphere both on the streets of Helsinki – there were several incidents of violence against Soviet officers – and in the numerous clashes with the Finnish government over the war trials. Unlike the Eastern European countries under full Soviet occupation, Finland was able to carry out its own trials, but had to satisfy the Commission that they were conducted properly. Delicate manoeuvring by the Chief of Justice, **Urho Kekkonen**, resulted in comparatively short prison sentences for the accused, the longest being ten years for Risto Ryti.

The uncertain relationship between Finland and the Soviet Union was resolved, to some extent, by the signing of the **Treaty of Friendship, Cooperation and Mutual Assistance** (FCMA) in 1948. It confirmed Finnish responsibility for its own defence and pledged the country not to join any alliance hostile to the Soviet Union. In the suspicious atmosphere of the Cold War, the treaty was perceived by the Western powers to place Finland firmly under Soviet influence. The Soviet insistence that the treaty was a guarantee of neutrality was viewed as hypocritical while they were still leasing the Porkkala peninsula. When it became clear that Finland was not becoming a Soviet satellite and had full control over its internal affairs, the USA reinstated credit facilities – carefully structured to avoid financing anything that would be of help to the Soviets – and Finland was admitted to Western financial institutions such as the IMF and World Bank.

The postwar **economy** was dominated by the reparations demand. Much of the bill was paid off in ships and machinery, which established engineering as a major industry. The escalating world demand for timber products boosted exports, but inflation soared and led to frequent wage disputes. In 1949 an attempt to enforce a piece-work rate in a pulp factory in Kemi culminated in two workers being shot by police, a state of emergency being declared in the town, and the arrest of Communist leaders. Economic conflicts reached a climax in 1956 after right-wingers in the Eduskunta had blocked an annual extension of government controls on wages and prices. This caused a sharp rise in the cost of living and the trade unions demanded appropriate pay increases. A general strike followed, lasting for three weeks until the strikers' demands were met. Any benefit, however, was quickly cancelled out by further price rises.

In 1957 a split occurred in the Social Democrats between urban and rural factions, the former seeking increased industrialization and the streamlining of unprofitable farms, the latter pursuing high agricultural subsidies. By 1959 a group of breakaway ruralists had set up the Small Farmers' Social Democratic Union, causing a rift within the country's internal politics that was to have important repercussions in Finland's dealings with the Soviet Union. Although the government had no intention of changing its foreign policy, the Social Democrat's chairman, **Väinö Tanner**, had a well-known antipathy to the Soviet Union. Coupled with a growing number of anti-Soviet newspaper editorials, this precipitated the "**night frost**" of 1958. The Soviet leader, Khruschev, suspended imports and deliveries of machinery, causing a rise in Finnish unemployment. **Kekkonen**, elected president in 1956, personally intervened in the crisis by meeting with Khruschev, angering the Social Democrats, who accused Kekkonen of behaving undemocratically; meanwhile, the Agrarians were lambasted for failing to stand up to Soviet pressure.

In 1960 Tanner was re-elected as chairman and the Social Democrats continued to attack Kekkonen. The Agrarians refused to enter government with the Social Democrats unless they changed their policies. As global relations worsened during 1961, the Soviet Union sent a note to Kekkonen requesting a meeting to discuss the section of the 1948 treaty dealing with defence of the Finnish–Soviet border. This was the precursor to the "**note crisis**". The original note went unanswered, but the Finnish foreign secretary went to Moscow for exploratory talks with his opposite number. Assurances of Soviet confidence in Finnish foreign policy were given, but fears were expressed about the anti-Kekkonen alliance of conservatives and Social Democrats formed to contest the 1962 presidential election. Kekkonen again tried to defuse the crisis himself: using his constitutional powers he dissolved parliament early, forcing the election forward by several months and in so doing weakened the alliance. Kekkonen was re-elected and foreign policy remained unchanged. This was widely regarded as a personal victory for Kekkonen and a major turning point in relations with the Soviet Union.

Through all subsequent administrations, the maintenance of the **Paasikivi-Kekkonen line** on foreign policy became a symbol of national unity.

Following Tanner's retirement from politics in 1963, the Social Democrats ended their stand against the established form of foreign policy, making possible their re-entry to government.

Throughout the early 1960s there was mounting dissatisfaction within the People's Democratic League towards the old pro-Moscow leadership. In 1965, a moderate non-Communist was elected as the League's general secretary, and two years later he became chairman; a similar change took place in the Communist leadership of the trade unions. The new-look Communists pledged their desire for a share in government. The election of May 1966 resulted in a "popular front" government dominated by the Social Democrats and the People's Democratic League, under the prime ministership of **Rafael Paasio**.

This brought to an end a twenty-year spell of centre-right governments in which the crucial pivot had been the Agrarian Party. In 1965, the Agrarians changed their name to the Centre Party, aiming to modernize their image and become more attractive to the urban electorate. A challenge to this new direction was mounted by the **Finnish Rural Party**, founded by a breakaway group of Agrarians in the late 1950s, who mounted an increasingly influential campaign on behalf of "the forgotten people" – farmers and smallholders in declining rural areas. In the election of 1970 they gained ten percent of the vote, but in subsequent years lost support through internal divisions.

The Communists retained governmental posts until 1971, when they too were split – between the young "reformists" who advocated continued participation in government, and the older, hard-line "purists" who were frustrated by the failure to implement socialist economic policies, and preferred to stay in opposition.

Modern Finland

Throughout the postwar years Finland promoted itself vigorously as a **neutral country**. It joined the United Nations in 1955 and Finnish soldiers became an integral part of the UN Peace-Keeping Force. In 1969 preparations were started for the European Security Conference in Helsinki, and in 1972 the city was the venue for the **Strategic Arms Limitation Talks** (SALT), underlining a Finnish role in mediation between the superpowers. But an attempt to have a clause stating Finland's neutrality inserted into the 1970 extension-signing of the FCMA Treaty was opposed by the Soviet Union, whose foreign secretary, Andrei Gromyko, had a year earlier defined Finland not as neutral but as a "peace-loving neighbour of the Soviet Union".

In 1971 the revelations of a Czech defector, General Sejna, suggesting that the Soviet army was equipped to take over Finland within 24 hours should Soviet defences be compromised, brought a fresh wave of uncertainty to relations with its eastern neighbour; as did the sudden withdrawal of the Soviet ambassador, allegedly for illicit scheming with the People's Democratic League.

The stature of Kekkonen as a world leader guaranteed continued support for his presidency. But his commitment to the Paasikivi-Kekkonen line ensured that nothing potentially upsetting to the Soviet Union was allowed to surface in Finnish politics, giving – as some thought – the Soviet Union a covert influence on Finland's internal affairs. Opposition to Kekkonen was simply perceived as an attempt to undermine the Paasikivi-Kekkonen line. Equally, the unchallengeable nature of Kekkonen's presidency was considered to be beyond his proper constitutional powers. A move in 1974 by an alliance of right-wingers and Social Democrats within the Eduskunta to transfer some of the presidential powers to parliament received a very hostile reaction, emphasizing the almost inviolate position that Kekkonen enjoyed. Kekkonen was re-elected in 1978, although forced to stand down through illness in 1981.

Because Finland is heavily dependent on foreign trade, its well-being has closely mirrored world trends. The international financial boom of the 1960s enabled a range of social legislation to be passed and created a comparatively high standard of living for most Finns – albeit not on the same scale as the rest of Scandinavia. The global **recession** of the 1970s and early 1980s was most dramatically felt when a fall in the world market for pulp coincided with a steep increase in the price of oil. Although the country tackled the immediate problems of the recession, industry remained heavily concentrated in the south, causing rural areas further north to experience high rates of unemployment and few prospects for economic growth – save through rising levels of tourism.

The election of 1987 saw a break with the pattern of recent decades. Non-socialist parties made large gains, mainly at the expense of the Rural Party and Communists. The new government of **Harri Holkeri**, however, appeared inept – particularly in its hesitant reaction to events in the Soviet Union and continued deference to Moscow, whether real or apparent. Public disillusionment resulted in large gains for the Centre Party in the election of March 1991. The Centre Party chairman, 47-year-old **Esko Aho**, subsequently became prime minister, leading a new coalition in which many of the members reflected the comparative youth and fresh ideas of its leader.

In 1992 celebrations to mark 75 years of Finnish independence were muted by the realization that the country was entering a highly critical period, facing more problems (few of its own making) than it had for many decades. The end of the Cold War had diminished the value of Finland's hard-won neutrality, the economic and ethnic difficulties in Russia were being watched with trepidation, while another global **recession** hit Finland just as the nation lost its major trading partner – the Soviet Union – of the last fifty years.

Throughout the early 1990s Finland's economic depression was among the worst in the industrial west, with its banking system in crisis and unemployment figures almost the highest in Europe. Such events forced Finland to pin its hopes on closer links with Western Europe. On January 1, 1995, Finland became a full member of the **European Union**, and, in the same year the Social Democratic Party's **Martti Ahtisaari** was elected as president, with the general election resulting in a coalition win for the Social Democrats, their Chairman Paavo Lipponen forming a majority government that includes conservatives, socialists, the Swedish Folk Party and the Green Party.

By the Millennium, as Russia descended into farce, Finland had become more firmly linked to the European Union and its economy had recovered sufficiently for it to be accepted into the first wave of countries to join European Monetary Union. In 1999, for the first time, it assumed the presidency of the European Union, while President Ahtisaari established himself as an important international statesman through his interventions in the war in Kosovo. Economically, the country's highly educated populace and technological expertise made it a powerful

player in the world IT market, while EU membership provided a new sense of security and confidence. However, the contemporary picture is not entirely rosy: high unemployment and the chaos of Russia's gangster economy on the doorstep provide major worries, as do continuing debates around membership of NATO and the role of the welfare state. Other pressing issues include the need to diversify an economy that is over-reliant on the Nokia phone company and how to continue development in rural areas without the support of big government subsidies. How these problems are addressed will be the major concerns of Finland in the first years of the new millennium. The adoption of the **euro** as Finland's new currency on January 1, 2002 brought a new pride to the Finnish nation after years of living in the shadow of the Soviet Union; political and economic freedom had finally, and most importantly tangibly, been won. However, although financial concerns about the stability of the new currency abound, it's the role of the **environment** that's likely to grab the headlines in the coming years. In early 2002, the Finnish parliament gave permission for a new nuclear power station to be built at a time when the rest of Europe – and neighbouring Sweden – is winding down nuclear power because of excessive cost and increasing fears of pollution. A heated public debate on this very sensitive issue now looks set to take the established practice of Finnish consensus politics to new extremes.

Books

Due to Finland's relative obscurity in terms of English-language audiences, there's a real dearth of decent publications about anything Finnish. Although some of the books listed below are out of print, it should still be possible to get hold of many of them in public libraries. It's a sign of the times that you will always find much more written information about Finland on the Internet than in any reasonably priced book.

History

Eloise Engel and Lauri Paananen *The Soviet Attack on Finland 1939–1940.* An excellent and popular account of the Finns' resistance and final defeat by overwhelming numbers of Soviet troops during the Winter War.

D.G. Kirby *Finland in the Twentieth Century – A History and Interpretation.* By far the best insight into contemporary Finland and the reshaping of the nation after independence.

⭐ **Fred Singleton** *A Short History of Finland.* A very readable and informative account of Finland's past. It lacks the detail of most academic accounts, but is an excellent starting point for general readers.

Miscellaneous

F. Valentine Hooren *Tom of Finland.* The definitive life story of Finland's most famous gay erotic artist. Although it contains few drawings, the book is an excellent biography of one of the gay world's most famous names.

Tove Jansson The *Moomin* books. Enduring children's tales, with evocative descriptions of Finnish nature.

⭐ **Matti Joensuu** *Harjunpää and the Stone Murders* (o/p). The only one of the Harjunpää series, involving the Helsinki detective, Timo Harjunpää, to have been translated into English. It's set in contemporary Helsinki during a bout of teenage gang warfare.

Christer Kihlman *The Rise and Fall of Gerdt Bladh* (o/p). Supremely evocative study of personal anguish set against a background of Finland's ascent from rural backwater to prosperous modern nation.

Väinö Linna *The Unknown Soldier* (o/p). Using his experiences fighting in the Winter War, Linna triggered immense controversy with this book, depicting for the first time Finnish soldiers not as "heroes in white" but as drunks and womanizers.

Elias Lönnrot *Kalevala.* The classic tome of Finnish literature, this collection of folk tales was transcribed over twenty years by Lönnrot, a rural doctor. Set in an unspecified point in the past, the plot centres on a state of war between the mythical region of Kalevala (probably northern Karelia) and Pohjola (possibly Lapland) over possession of a talisman called the Sampo. The story is regarded as quintessentially Finnish, but it's not an easy read, due mainly to its length (some 22,750 lines), and the non-linear course of the plot. Its influence on Finnish literature is huge, though, and it was a linchpin of the Finnish nationalist and language movements.

Beatrice Ojakangas *Finnish Cookbook.* These excellent all-round recipes shed light on one of Scandinavia's least known cuisines – everything from fish stew to prune tarts, as well as short stories about the Finnish way of life.

★ **Oscar Parland** *The Year of the Bull*. Absorbing look at the civil war-torn Finland of 1918 through the eyes of a young boy.

Kenneth D. McRae *Conflict and Compromise in Multilingual Societies: Finland*. Although academic in tone, this is an excellent account of the unique problems faced by Finland's Swedish-speaking minority, explaining how the language of Finland's former colonial masters came to fall into minority use.

Kirsti Simonsuuri (ed) *Enchanting Beasts*. A slender but captivating tome, and one of the few English translations of the best of Finland's modern female poets.

A brief guide to Finnish

Finnish is going to pose a problem to anyone whose mother tongue is an Indo-European language such as English. There's very little common ground between Finnish and any other mainstream western European language, and this can frustrate basic understanding and communication – simple tasks like deciphering a menu are fraught with difficulty.

Finnish also has nothing in common with the other Scandinavian languages – something that has led to considerable misunderstanding of the Finns, particularly in neighbouring Sweden. Part of the **Finno-Ugric** group of languages, Finnish is closely related to Estonian and much more distantly to Hungarian, and its grammatical structure is complex: with fifteen cases alone to grapple with, it's initially a tricky language to learn, although once a basic vocabulary is attained things become less impenetrable. Unlike Indo-European German, for example, which uses prepositions to determine the case of a noun, Finnish employs a set of complex suffixes, which, although straightforward to learn, can complicate the grammar due to a process of obligatory vowel harmony. For instance, *autossa* means "in the car", *autolla* "at the car"; whereas *autosta* is "out of the car". Surprisingly, English is not widely spoken, although most people in the main towns can speak it a

bit, as can almost all young people. **Swedish** is a common second language, although many Finns are reluctant to use the language of their former colonial masters – it is, of course, the first of the Finland-Swedes, who live mainly in the western parts of the country, and the only language spoken on Åland. If the idea of learning Finnish makes you weak at the knees, at least memorize the longest palindrome in the world, Finnish *saippuakivikauppias* – the extremely useful "soapstone salesman".

Of the few available phrasebooks, *Finnish For Travellers* (Berlitz) is the most useful for practical purposes; the best Finnish–English dictionary is *The Standard Finnish Dictionary* (Holt, Rinehart and Winston).

Pronunciation

In Finnish, words are pronounced exactly as they are written, with the stress always on the first syllable: in a compound word the stress is on the first syllable of each part of the word. Each letter is pronounced individually, and doubling a letter lengthens the sound: double "kk"s are pronounced with two "k" sounds and the double "aa" pronounced as long as the English "a" in "car". The letters b, c, f, q, w, x, z and å are only found in words derived from foreign languages, and are pronounced as in the language of origin.

a as in father but shorter
d as in riding but sometimes soft as to be barely heard
e between the e in pen and the i in pin.
g (only after "n") as in singer
h as in hot
i as in pin
j like the y in yellow
np like the m in mother
o like the aw in law
r is rolled
s as in said but with the tongue a little further back from the teeth
u as in bull
y like the French u in "sur"
ä like the a in hat
ö like the ur in Fur but without any "r" sound.

Basics

Do you speak English? - **Puhutteko englantia?**
Yes - **kyllä/joo**
No - **ei**
I don't understand - **En ymmärrä**
I understand - **Ymmärrän**
Please - **olkaa hyvä**
Thank you - **kiitos**
Excuse me - **anteeksi**
Good morning - **hyvää huomenta**
Good afternoon - **hyvää päivää**
Good evening - **hyvää iltaa**
Good day - **hyvää päivää** (usually shortened to **päivä**)
Goodnight - **hyvää yötä**
Goodbye - **näkemiin**
Yesterday - **eilen**
Today - **tänään**
Tomorrow - **huomenna**
Day after tomorrow - **ylihuomenna**
In the morning - **aamulla/aamupäivällä**
In the afternoon - **iltapäivällä**
In the evening - **illalla**

Some signs

Entrance - **Sisään**
Exit - **Ulos**
Gentlemen - **Miehille/Miehet/Herrat**
Ladies - **Naisille/Naiset/Rouvat**
Hot - **Kuuma**
Cold - **Kylmä**
Open - **Avoinna**
Closed - **Suljettu**
Push - **Työnnä**
Pull - **Vedä**
Arrival - **Saapuvat**
Departure - **Lähtevät**
Police - **Poliisi**
Hospital - **Sairaala**
No Smoking - **Tupakointi kielletty**
No Entry - **Pääsy kielletty**
No Trespassing - **Läpikulku kielletty**
No Camping - **Leiriytyminen kielletty**

Questions and directions

Where's ... ? - **Missä on ... ?**
When? - **Koska/milloin?**
What? - **Mikä/mitä?**
Why? - **Miksi?**
How far is it to ...? - **Kuinka pitkä matka on ... n?**
Where is the railway station? - **Missä on rautatieasema?**
Train/bus/boat/ship - **Juna/bussi** (or) **linja auto/vene/laiva**
Where is the youth hostel? - **Missä on retkeilymaja?**
Can we camp here? - **Voimmeko leiriytyä tähän?**
Do you have anything better/bigger /cheaper? - **Onko teillä mitään parempaa/isompaa/halvempaa?**
It's too expensive - **Se on liian kallis**
How much? - **Kuinka paljon?**
How much is that? - **Paljonko se maksaa?**
I'd like - **Haluaisin**
Cheap - **Halpa**
Expensive - **Kallis**
Good - **Hyvä**
Bad - **Paha/Huono**
Here - **Täällä**
There - **Siellä**
Left - **Vasen**
Right - **Oikea**
Go straight ahead - **Ajakaa suoraan eteenpäin**

Is it near/far? - Onko se lähellä/kaukana?
Ticket/ticket office - Lipputoimisto
Train/bus station/Bus stop - Rautatieasema/
linjaautoasema/bussipysäkki

0 - nolla
1 - yksi
2 - kaksi
3 - kolme
4 - neljä
5 - viisi
6 - kuusi
7 - seitsemän
8 - kahdeksan
9 - yhdeksän
10 - kymmenen
11 - yksitoista
12 - kaksitoista
13 - kolmetoista
14 - neljätoista
15 - viisitoista
16 - kuusitoista
17 - seitsemäntoista
18 - kahdeksantoista
19 - yhdeksäntoista
20 - kaksikymmentä
21 - kaksikymmentäyksi
30 - kolmekymmentä
40 - neljäkymmentä
50 - viisikymmentä

60 - kuusikymmentä
70 - seitsemänkymmentä
80 - kahdeksankymmentä
90 - yhdeksänkymmentä
100 - sata
101 - satayksi
151 - sataviisikymmentäyksi
200 - kaksisataa
1000 - tuhat

Days and months

Monday - maanantai
Tuesday - tiistai
Wednesday - keskiviikko
Thursday - torstai
Friday - perjantai
Saturday - lauantai
Sunday - sunnuntai
January - tammikuu
February - helmikuu
March - maalisku
April - huhtikuu
May - toukokuu
June - kesäkuu
July - heinäkuu
August - elokuu
September - syyskuu
October - lokakuu
November - marraskuu
December - joulukuu

FINLAND | Basics

Glossary of Finnish terms and phrases

Järvi - Lake
Joki - River
Katu - Street
Kauppahalli - Market hall
Kauppatori - Market square
Kaupungintalo - Town hall
Keskusta - Town centre
Kirkko - Church
Kylä - Village
Linja-autoasema - Bus station
Linna - Castle
Lipputoimisto - Ticket office
Matkailutoimisto - Tourist office

Museo - Museum
Pankki - Bank
Posti - Post office
Puisto - Park
Rautatieasema - Train station
Sairaala - Hospital
Taidemuseo - Art museum
Tie - Road
Tori - Square
Torni - Tower
Tuomiokirkko - Cathedral
Yliopisto - University

4.1

Helsinki and the south

The southern coast of Finland is the most populated, industrialized and richest part of the country, centred around the capital, **Helsinki**, a city of half a million people with the friendliness of a peasant village on market day. Helsinki's innovative architecture and batch of fine museums and galleries collectively expose the roots of the national character, while at night the pubs and clubs strip it bare. It may seem the perfect prelude to exploring the rest of Finland, and in the practical sense it is, being the hub of the country's road, rail and air traffic routes. However, if you can, try to arrive in Helsinki *after* seeing the rest of the country. Only with some prior knowledge of Finland does the significance of the city as a symbol of Finnish self-determination become clear.

A couple of towns **around Helsinki** evince the change from ruralism to modernism even further. **Porvoo** sits placidly locked in the nineteenth century, while the suburban area of **Espoo** forms a showpiece of twentieth-century design. Further away, in the country's southeastern extremity, the only community of significant size and importance between Helsinki and the Russian border is the shipping port of **Kotka** – not wildly appealing in itself, but at the heart of a historically intriguing coastal region.

Helsinki only became the capital in 1812, after Finland had been made a Russian Grand Duchy and Tsar Alexander I had deemed the previous capital, **Turku**, too close to Sweden for comfort. Today Turku, facing Stockholm across the Gulf of Bothnia, handles its demotion well. Both historically and visually it's one of Finland's most enticing cities; indeed, the snootier elements of its Swedish-speaking contingent still consider Åbo (its Swedish name) the real capital, and Helsinki just an uncouth upstart.

Between Helsinki and Turku, along the entire southern coast, only small villages and a few slightly larger towns break the continuity of the forests. Beyond Turku, though, things are more interesting, with the two most southerly of the Finland-Swedish

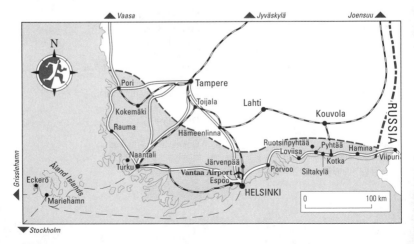

communities: **Rauma,** with its unique dialect and well-preserved town centre; and the likeably downbeat **Pori,** famous for its annual jazz festival.

Where this corner of Finland meets the sea it splinters into an enormous archipelago, which includes the curious **Åland Islands** – a grouping of thousands of fragments of land, only about half a dozen of which are inhabited, connected by small roadways skirting the sea. There's a tiny self-governing population here, Swedish-speaking but with a history that's distinct from both Sweden and Finland.

Much of the region is most easily reached from Helsinki, from where there are frequent bus and rail services to Turku. Rauma and Pori are best reached by bus from Turku, and from Pori there are easy rail connections to Tampere and the Lake Region (covered in the following chapter). Daily ferries also connect Turku to the Åland Islands.

Helsinki and around

HELSINKI has a character quite different from the other Scandinavian capitals, and in many ways is closer in mood (and certainly in looks) to the major cities of Eastern Europe. For years an outpost of the Russian empire, its very shape and style was originally modelled on its powerful neighbour's former capital, St Petersburg. Yet throughout the twentieth century the city was also a showcase for independent Finland, much of its impressive **architecture** drawing inspiration from the dawning of Finnish nationalism and the rise of the republic. Equally the **museums,** especially the National Museum and the Art Museum of the Atheneum, reveal the country's growing awareness of its own folklore and culture.

Much of central Helsinki is a succession of compact granite blocks, interspersed with more characterful buildings, alongside waterways, green spaces and the glass-fronted office blocks and shopping centres you'll find in any European capital. The city is hemmed in on three sides by water, and all the things you might want to see are within walking distance of one another – and certainly no more than a few minutes apart by tram or bus. The streets have a youthful buzz, and the short summer is acknowledged by crowds strolling the boulevards, cruising the shopping arcades and socializing in the outdoor cafés and restaurants; everywhere there's prolific **street entertainment**. At night the pace picks up, with a great selection of pubs and clubs, free rock concerts in the numerous parks, and an impressive quota of fringe events. It's a pleasure just to be around, merging with the multitude and witnessing the activity.

Arrival, information and city transport

However you arrive you'll be deposited somewhere close to the heart of town. Helsinki's **airport,** Vantaa, 20km to the north, is served by frequent airport buses (30min; €4.90 or €3.40 with a tourist ticket, see p.692). These stop at the Finnair terminal behind the *Scandic Hotel Continental,* halfway between the city centre and the Olympic Stadium, before continuing to the train station. A cheaper, if slightly slower, airport connection is city bus #615; this costs €3 and runs roughly every fifteen minutes from the airport to the bus terminal beside the train station. City bus #617 (also €3) runs from the airport via the Olympic Stadium to Elielinaukio square at the railway station once or twice an hour.

The Viking and Silja **ferry** lines have their terminals on opposite sides of the South Harbour (at docks known respectively as Katajanokka and Olympia), and disembarking passengers from either have a walk of less than 1km to the centre. The **train station,** equipped with luggage lockers, is right in the heart of the city on Kaivokatu, next door to the **city-bus terminal**. All trams stop immediately outside or around the corner along Mannerheimintie. Just across Mannerheimintie, behind the Lasipalatsi, and a short way up Simonkatu, is the **long-distance bus station**.

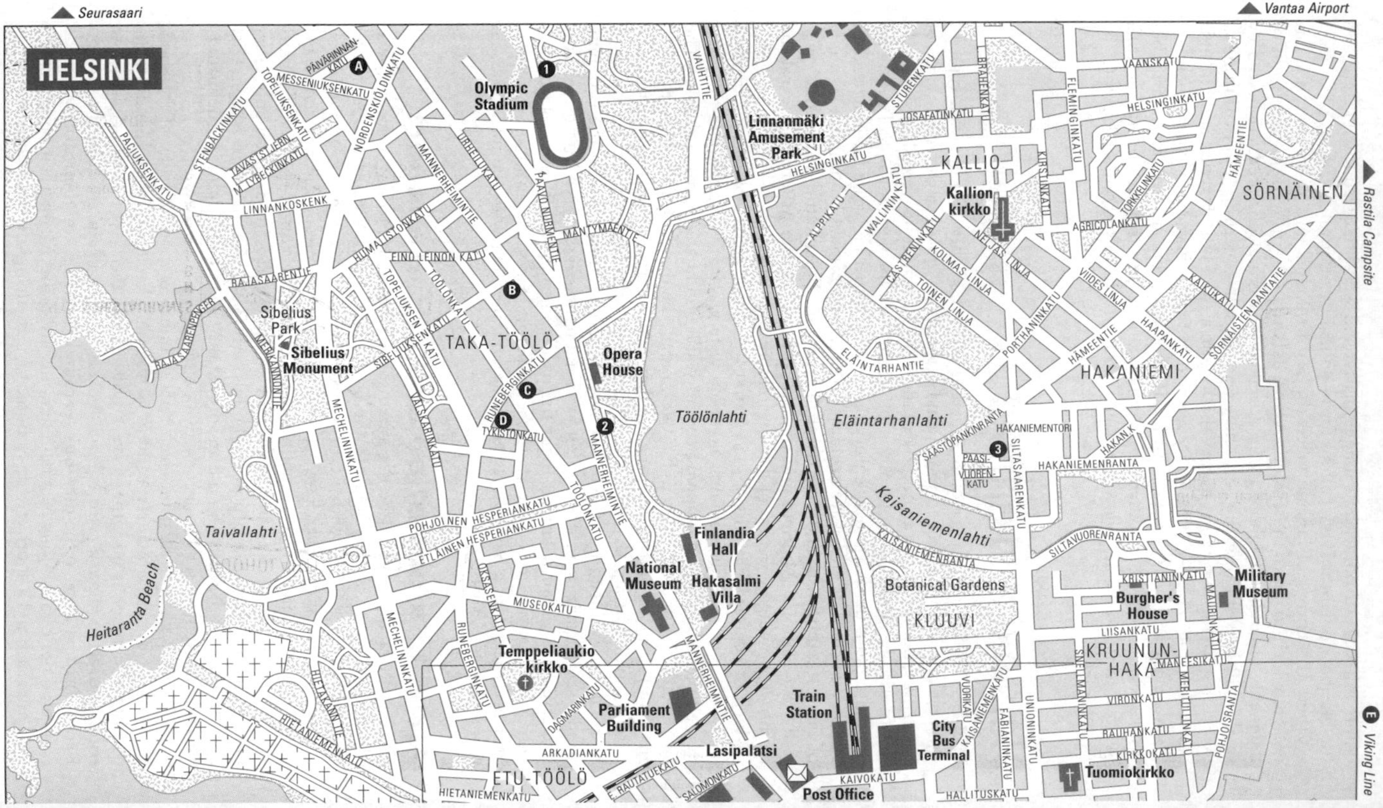
HELSINKI
Seurasaari
Vantaa Airport
Rastila Campsite
E, Viking Line
Olympic Stadium
Linnanmäki Amusement Park
Kallion kirkko
KALLIO
SÖRNÄINEN
HAKANIEMI
TAKA-TÖÖLÖ
ETU-TÖÖLÖ
KLUUVI
KRUUNUN-HAKA
Opera House
Töölönlahti
Eläintarhanlahti
Kaisaniemenlahti
Finlandia Hall
National Museum
Hakasalmi Villa
Botanical Gardens
Burgher's House
Military Museum
Temppeliaukio kirkko
Parliament Building
Train Station
City Bus Terminal
Lasipalatsi
Post Office
Tuomiokirkko
Sibelius Park
Sibelius Monument
Taivallahti
Heitaranta Beach
MANNERHEIMINTIE
HELSINGINKATU
HÄMEENTIE
MECHELININKATU
RUNEBERGINKATU
TÖÖLÖNKATU
PAAVO NURMENTIE
UNIONINKATU
FABIANINKATU
SNELLMANINKATU
KAIVOKATU
ARKADIANKATU
HIETANIEMENKATU
PACIUKSENKATU
STENBÄCKINKATU
TOPELIUKSENKATU
NORDENSKIÖLDINKATU
MESSENIUKSENKATU
PÄIVÄRINNANKATU
VAUHTITIE
STURENKATU
BRAHENKATU
FLEMINGINKATU
VAANSKATU
SILTASAARENKATU
HAKANIEMENRANTA
SILTAVUORENRANTA
KAISANIEMENRANTA
ELÄINTARHANTIE
LIISANKATU
MARIANKATU
MERITULLINKATU
POHJOISRANTA
VIRONKATU
RAUHANKATU
KIRKKOKATU
HALLITUSKATU
VUORIKATU
KAISANIEMENKATU
SALOMONKATU
DAGMARINKATU
MUSEOKATU
OKSASENKATU
POHJOINEN HESPERIANKATU
ETELÄINEN HESPERIANKATU
TYKISTÖNKATU
VALSKARINKATU
SIBELIUKSENKATU
TOPELIUKSEN KATU
FINO LEINON KATU
HUMALISTONKATU
MÄNTYMÄENTIE
URHEILUKATU
LINNANKOSKENK
RAJASAARENTIE
MERIKANNONTIE
HIETAKANNTIE
WALLININKATU
ALPPIKATU
CASTRENINKATU
TOINEN LINJA
KOLMAS LINJA
NELJÄS LINJA
VIIDES LINJA
PORTHANINKATU
HAAPANKATU
KAIKUKATU
SÖRNÄISTEN RANTATIE
AGRICOLANKATU
TORKKELINKATU
KIRSTINKATU
JOSAFATINKATU
HAKANIEMENTORI
SÄÄSTÖPANKINRANTA
PAASIVUORENKATU

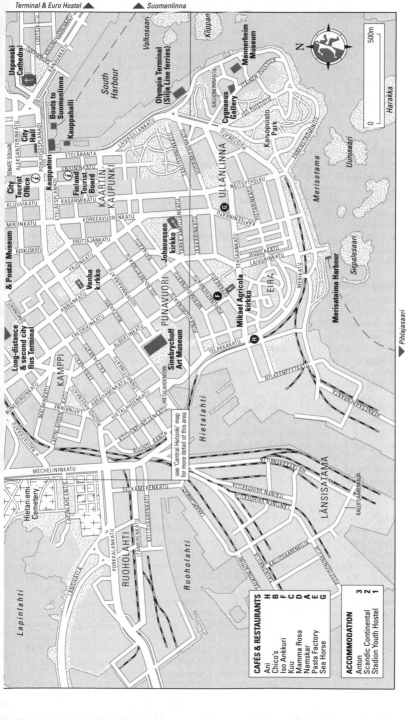

Uspenski
Cathedral

Boats to
Suomenlinna

Kauppahalli

South
Harbour

Valkosaari

Klippan

Olympia Terminal
(Silja Line ferries)

Mannerheim
Museum

Cygnaeus
Gallery

Kaivopuisto
Park

N

500m

0

City
Tourist
Office

City
Hall

SENATE SQUARE

ALEKSANTERINKATU

POHJOISESPLANADI

Kauppatori

ETELÄRANTA

Finland
Tourist
Board

KAARTIN-
KAUPUNKI

KLUUVIKATU

MIKONKATU

KESKUSKATU

& Postal Museum

UILANLINNA

Johannesen
kirkko

Vanha
kirkko

PUNAVUORI

Sinebrychoff
Art Museum

Long-distance
& second city
Bus Terminal

KAMPPI

Mikael Agricola
kirkko

EIRA

Merisataima Harbour

Merisatama

Sirpalesaari

Uunisaari

Harakka

Hietalahti

Hietaniemi
Cemetery

MECHELININKATU

RUOHOLAHTI

see 'Central Helsinki' map
for more detail of this area

LÄNSISATAMA

Ruoholahti

Lapinlahti

Pihlajasaari

CAFÉS & RESTAURANTS	
Ani	H
Chico's	B
Iso Ankkuri	F
Kuu	C
Mamma Rosa	D
Namskar	A
Pasta Factory	E
Sea Horse	G

ACCOMMODATION	
Anton	3
Scandic Continental	2
Stadion Youth Hostel	1

Information

The **City Tourist Office**, at Pohjoisesplanadi 19 (May–Sept Mon–Fri 9am–8pm, Sat & Sun 9am–6pm; Oct–April Mon–Fri 9am–6pm, Sat & Sun 10am–4pm; ☎09/169 3757, ⓦwww.hel.fi/tourism), supplies free street and transport maps, along with the useful free tourist magazine *Helsinki This Week*, which contains masses of listings for forthcoming events in the capital as well as a couple of decent maps on the back pages. While here, try to get hold of another worthy free brochure, *See Helsinki On Foot*, useful even though it uses both Finnish and Swedish street names on its maps; since Finland is officially bilingual you will find this dual-naming practice in use throughout the city and on all street maps. If you're staying for a while and plan to see as much of the city and its museums as possible, consider purchasing a **Helsinki Card** (available from the tourist office), which gives unlimited travel on public transport, including the ferry to Suomenlinna, and entry to around fifty museums. The three-day card (€38) is the best value, although there are also two-day (€32) and one-day (€24) versions.

For information on the rest of the country, visit the **Finnish Tourist Board**, just south of the City Tourist Office at Eteläesplanadi 4 (May–Sept Mon–Fri 9am–5pm, Sat & Sun 11am–3pm; Oct–April Mon–Fri 9am–5pm; ☎09/4176 9300, ⓦwww.mek.fi). Next door is Edita, the best place for **maps** of Finland, the Baltic and Scandinavia generally; there's a second branch at Annankatu 44 (both open Mon–Fri 9am–5pm).

City transport

The central area and its immediate surrounds are covered by an integrated transport network of buses, trams and a small metro system. A single-journey **ticket** for the system costs €2 when bought from the conductor or driver, €1.40 if purchased in advance from an R-Kiosk or other outlet, with unlimited transfers allowed within one hour, while a **multi-trip** ticket gives ten rides for €12.80. A **tram** ticket entitling you to one single journey without changing costs €1.50 or €1 if bought in advance. You can also buy a **tourist ticket** covering the city and surrounding areas such as Espoo and Vantaa for one (€7.50), three (€15) or five days (€22.50), which permits travel on buses and trams displaying double arrows (effectively all of them); obviously, this is only a cost-cutter if used frequently. If you don't intend to leave the city proper, you're better off with a **Helsinki-only tourist ticket**, again available in one- (€4.20), three- (€8.40) and five-day (€12.60) versions. All these tickets can be bought from R-Kiosk stands, the long-distance bus station or the City Tourist Office.

On **buses** you enter at the front, where you must either buy or show your ticket. On **trams**, get on at the front or back, and stamp your ticket in the machine. **Metro** tickets can be bought from the machines in the stations. If you're tempted to fare-dodge in Helsinki, note that there's a €42 on-the-spot fine plus the cost of a single ticket. **Taxis** can either be hailed in the street (a vehicle is free if the yellow "taxi" sign is illuminated) or pre-booked: call the *Taxi Centre* on ☎0100/0700 for immediate travel, or ☎0100/0600 for trips more than an hour or so away. There's a basic charge of €3.87, with a further €1.20 per kilometre, plus a €2.18 surcharge between 8pm and 6am weekdays and from 4pm Saturday to 6am Monday.

Tram **#3T** follows a figure-of-eight route around the city, and if you're pushed for time will take you past the most obvious attractions. For a more leisurely exploration, join one of the two-hour guided **walking tours** (€11) run by Helsinki Expert, Lönrotinkatu 7B (☎09/2288 1200, ⓦwww.helsinkiexpert.fi); you'll finish up knowing more about the city than most of its residents do. For details, phone the above number or visit them at the City Tourist Office. There are also numerous **boat sightseeing tours** from the south harbour, Eteläsatama, costing around €14 for an hour and a half. These run daily from around 11am to 7pm, and brochures are available at the tourist office, or from touts at the harbour itself.

Accommodation

There's plenty of **accommodation** in Helsinki, although the bulk of it is in mid-range hotels. Various discounts (see p.661) can reduce costs in these places, or alternatively there are a couple of cheaper summer hotels, several tourist hotels and a few hostels. If you arrive without a reservation, the very helpful **Hotel Booking Centre** in the train station, to the left of the platforms near the left-luggage office (June–Aug Mon–Sat 9am–7pm, Sun 10am–6pm; Sept–May Mon–Fri 9am–5pm; ☎09/2288 1400, ⌨www.helsinkiexpert.fi), will book you a hotel room for €5, or hostel accommodation for €4.

Hotels and tourist hotels

Although the cost of a room in one of Helsinki's top-flight **hotels** can be high, the better hotels aren't necessarily completely out of reach: many drop their rates dramatically in the summer tourist season, while nearly everywhere offers reductions at weekends. To take advantage of any bargains, it's essential to book as early as possible – either by phoning the hotel directly or by making a reservation through a travel agent. However much you pay, it's unlikely that you'll leave any Helsinki hotel feeling ripped off: service and amenities – such as the inclusive help-yourself breakfast which is generally included in the price of the room – are usually excellent.

Though they lack the luxury of regular hotels, the city's **tourist hotels** can be a good-value alternative, especially for three or four people sharing. All provide basic accommodation in private rooms without bathrooms, and usually offer inexpensive meals as well.

Note that hotels are marked on both the Helsinki (p.690–691) and Central Helsinki (p.695) maps.

Hotels

Academica Hietaniemenkatu 14 ☎09/1311 4334, ⌨www.hostelacademica.fi. A well-placed summer hotel (June–Aug only) with morning sauna and pool; see also "Hostels", p.694. ❸

Anna Annankatu 1 ☎09/616 621, ⌨www.hotelanna.com. Small, central place with a cosy atmosphere, set in a former Christian mission. ❻/❺

Anton Paasivuorenkatu 1 ☎09/774 900, ⌨www.hotelanton.fi. A bit out of the way, just north of the centre close to Hakaniementori, but good value at weekends. ❺

Arthur Vuorikatu 19 ☎09/173 441, ⌨www.hotelarthur.fi. You can save money in this good-quality hotel by getting a room with a shared bathroom – but book ahead as there's only a few. ❺/❹

Cumulus Kaisaniemi Kaisaniemenkatu 7 ☎09/172 881, ⌨www.cumulus.fi. Adequate, clean rooms that are good value at weekends, though the chain-hotel feel is very much in evidence. ❻/❺

Cumulus Seurahuone Kaivokatu 12 ☎09/69 141, ⌨www.cumulus.fi. A stylish, classic hotel opposite the train station, with the historic *Café Bellman* attached. Big, splendid rooms with original features. ❻

Finn Kalevankatu 3B ☎09/684 4360, ⌨www.hotellifinn.fi. Compact and rather down-at-heel hotel, though the rooms (the cheapest have shared bathrooms) are good value considering the city-centre location. ❸

Helka Pohjoinen Rautatiekatu 23 ☎09/613 580, ⌨www.helka.fi. Rather plain-looking exterior but very welcoming on the inside, and within easy reach of everything. Some weekend reductions. ❺

Palace Eteläranta 10 ☎09/1345 6656, ⌨www.palacehotel.fi. Luxurious place overlooking the Olympic Harbour. A quiet day in summer can bring substantial reductions, although it's difficult to get discounts on rooms with a sea view unless you're really pushy. ❻

Radisson SAS Royal Runeberginkatu 2 ☎09/69 580, ⌨www.radisson.com. Five-star, white-tiled and glamorous, resembling buildings like the Opera House and Finlandia Hall, this is not surprisingly expensive; visit in summer, when rates are cut by half. ❻

Scandic Continental Mannerheimintie 46 ☎09/40 551, ⌨www.scandic-hotels.com. Close to the parliament building, this is very good value at weekends and in summer. Excellent service. ❻/❺

Scandic Grand Marina Katajanokanlaituri 7 ☎09/16 661, ⌨www.scandic-hotels.com. The vast former harbour customs house from the 1930s, now transformed into an elegant, very Scandinavian-looking hotel just a few strides from the arrival

point of Viking Line boats from Sweden. ⑥/⑤
Scandic Hotel Marski Mannerheimintie 10
℡09/68 061, ⓦwww.scandic-hotels.com.
Opposite the Stockmann department store and
named after Marski (Marshal) Mannerheim, this is
one of the best hotels in the city, though less
atmospheric than the *Palace*, above. ⑥/⑤
Sokos Helsinki Kluuvikatu 8 ℡09/43 320,
ⓦwww.sokoshotels.fi. The best aspect of this
place is its location, a stone's throw from Senate
Square in one of the city's prime central streets,
though its modern rooms are characterless and
typical of the homogenized chain-hotel feel. ⑥/④

Sokos Torni Yrjönkatu 26 ℡09/43 360,
ⓦwww.sokoshotels.fi. Next door to the classic
sauna and pools on Yrjönkatu. On a clear day, the
thirteenth-floor bar gives views, so the locals
claim, all the way to Estonia, but the drinks are
pricey, as are the rooms – though weekend rates
can drop dramatically. ⑥/⑤
Sokos Vaakuna Asema-Aukio 2 ℡09/43 370,
ⓦwww.sokoshotels.fi. In the heart of the city
facing the train station, built for the 1952 Olympic
Games, this smartly refurbished hotel still contains
many of its original, quintessentially Finnish
architectural features. ⑥/⑤

Tourist hotels

Erottajanpuisto Uudenmaankatu 9 ℡09/642
169, ⓦwww.erottajanpuisto.com. Usefully
positioned, and especially good value for two
people sharing. ③
Matkakoti Margarita Itäinen Teatterikuja 3 ℡ &
℗09/622 4261. Fairly basic place set in a quiet
street close to the train and bus stations, and quite

adequate for a night's rest. It also rents rooms
cheaply by the day for those arriving in the city
early and leaving later the same day. ②
Omapohja Gasthaus Itäinen Teatterikuja 3
℡09/666 211, ℗09/6228 0053. Downstairs from
Matkakoti Margarita, this tourist hotel has en-suite
rooms with colour TVs and other mod cons. ③

Hostels

Though the staple accommodation option of budget travellers, Helsinki's **hostels**
are not without drawbacks: curfews are common in dormitories, and there is sometimes a limit imposed on the length of stay during the peak summer period.

Academica Hietaniemenkatu 14 ℡09/1311 4334,
ⓦwww.hostelacademica.fi. Dormitory
accommodation is available in this summer hotel
(see p.693) on production of an IYHF or student
card. June–Aug only.
Euro Linnankatu 9 ℡09/622 0470,
ⓦwww.eurohostel.fi. Comfortable place in a clean
modern building with free morning sauna. It's in
the up-and-coming but quiet Katajanokka area,
close to the Viking Line arrival point; take tram #4.

Stadion Olympic Stadium ℡09/477 8480,
ⓦwww.stadionhostel.com. A three-kilometre hike
from the city centre up Mannerheimintie; the
hostel entrance is on the far side of the stadium
complex. A great venue, with sizeable dormitories
sleeping up to twenty, and large and well-
equipped shower rooms. You'll be asked to vacate
the premises from 10am to 4pm and there is a
2am curfew. Trams #3T, #4, #7A and #10 from
Mannerheimintie stop outside.

Campsites

Of Helsinki's **campsites**, only one makes a reasonable base if you're planning to
spend time in the city. This is *Rastila* (℡09/321 6551, ℗344 1578), 13km to the
east in Itäkeskus, on the metro line (Itäkeskus station) and also served by buses #90,
#90A, #965 and #98 from Mannerheimintie. It's open all year and there's always
plenty of space.

The City

Following a devastating fire in 1808, and the city's elevation to capital in 1812,
Helsinki was totally rebuilt in a style commensurate with its status: a grid of wide
streets and Neoclassical, Empire-style brick buildings, modelled on the then
Russian capital, St Petersburg. This grid forms the basis of the modern city, and it's a
tribute to the vision of planner Johan Ehrenström and architect Carl Engel that in
and around **Senate Square** the grandeur has endured, often quite dramatically. The
square itself, overlooked by the gleaming Lutheran cathedral, is still the city's single
most eye-catching feature; and, just a few blocks away, past the South Harbour and

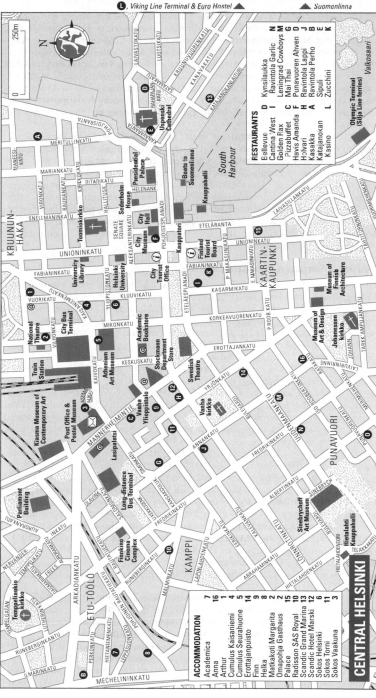

CENTRAL HELSINKI

L Viking Line Terminal & Euro Hostel ▲

▲ Suomenlinna

South Harbour

Valkosaari

RESTAURANTS

Eellevue	D	Kynsilaukka	N
Cantina 'West	I	Ravintola Garlic	M
Golden Pax		Leningrad Cowboys	O
Pizzabuffet	C	Mai Thai	J
Havis Amanda	F	Punavuoren Ahven	G
Holvari	H	Ravintola Lappi	B
Kasakka	A	Ravintola Perho	E
Katajanocan		Sipuli	K
Kasino	L	Zucchini	

ACCOMMODATION

Academica	7
Anna	16
Arthur	1
Cumulus Kaisaniemi	4
Cumulus Seurahuone	5
Erottajanpuisto	14
Finn	9
Helka	8
Matkakoti Margarita	2
Omapohja Gasthaus	15
Palace	
Radisson SAS Royal	10
Scandic Grand Marina	13
Scandic Hotel Marski	12
Sokos Helsinki	6
Sokos Torni	11
Sokos Vaakuna	3

the waterside market, **Esplanadi** remains a handsome tree-lined avenue with a narrow strip of greenery along its centre. Meeting the western end of Esplanadi, the great artery of **Mannerheimintie** – the main route into the centre from the suburbs – carries traffic and trams past Finlandia Hall and the Olympic Stadium on one side, and the National Museum and the streets leading to Sibelius Park and the vast Hietaniemi Cemetery on the other. The bulge of land that extends **south of Esplanadi** has long been one of the most affluent sections of town. Dotted by palatial embassies and wealthy dwellings, it rises into the rocky **Kaivopuisto** park, where the peace is disturbed only by the rumble of the trams and the summer rock concerts.

West of Kaivopuisto are the narrow streets of the equally exclusive **Eira** quarter, while to the north of the city centre and divided by the waters of Kaisaniemenlahti, the districts of **Kruununhaka** and **Hakaniemi** contain what little is left of pre-seventeenth-century Helsinki, in the small area up the hill behind the cathedral, compressed between the botanical gardens and the bay; over the bridge is a large marketplace and the hill leading past the formidable **Kallion kirkko** towards the modern housing districts further north. Helsinki also has innumerable offshore islands, the biggest of which are **Suomenlinna** and **Seurasaari**. Both of these, despite their location close to the city centre, offer untrammelled nature and a rewarding crop of museums.

Senate Square and Esplanadi

The heart of Helsinki lies in and around **Senate Square**, a compact area of broad bustling streets, grand buildings, famous (to Finns) shops, and, in Esplanadi, the most popular promenading spot in the entire country. Most of the streets leading into Senate Square are fairly narrow and unremarkable, however, a fact that simply serves to increase the impact as the square comes into view and you're struck by the sudden burst of space, the graceful symmetry of the buildings, and most of all by the exquisite form of the **Tuomiokirkko**, or Lutheran Cathedral (Mon–Sat 9am–6pm, Sun noon–6pm), raised on granite steps that support it like a pedestal. Designed, like most of the other buildings on the square, by Engel, its construction was overseen by him until his death in 1840, before being finally completed, with a few variations, in 1852. Among the post-Engel additions are the statues of the twelve apostles that line the roof, which may seem familiar if you've visited Copenhagen: they're copies of Thorvaldsen's sculptures for Vor Frue Kirke. After the Neoclassical extravagances of the exterior, the spartan Lutheran interior comes as a disappointment; better is the gloomily atmospheric **crypt**, which is now used as a café (June–Aug daily 10am–4pm; entrance on Kirkkokatu).

The buildings around the square contribute to the pervading sense of harmony, and although none is open to the public, some are of great historical significance. The **Government Palace** (*Valtioneuvosto*), known as the Senate House until independence and seating the Senate from 1822, consumes the entire eastern side. It was here that an angry Finnish civil servant, Eugen Schauman, became a national hero by assassinating the much-hated Russian governor-general Bobrikov in 1904. Opposite are the Ionic columns of **Helsinki University** (*Helsingin Yliopisto*), next door to which is the **University Library** (*Yliopiston Kirjasto*), considered by many to be Engel's finest single building, although only students and bona fide researchers are allowed in.

Just north of the square between Kirkkokatu and Rauhankatu is **The House of Scientific Estates** (*Säätytalo*), the seat of the Diet that governed the country until 1906, when it was abolished in favour of a single-chamber parliament elected by universal suffrage (at the time, Europe's most radical parliamentary reform). In the small park behind the Government Palace is the **House of Nobility** (*Ritarihuone*), where the upper crust of Helsinki society rubbed shoulders a hundred years ago.

Directly opposite the cathedral at Aleksanterinkatu 18 is Helsinki's oldest stone building, **Sederholm House** (June–Aug daily 11am–5pm; Sept–May Wed–Sun

11am–5pm; €3), dating from 1757. It now houses a small museum concentrating on aspects of eighteenth-century life in the city, with particular reference to industrialist Johan Sederholm. There are exhibitions on trade, education and construction, but what makes it perhaps most enjoyable is the eighteenth-century music collection – you can ask to hear a range of classical CDs while you wander around. A more high-tech record of Helsinki life can be found one block south from Sederholm House at the new **City Museum**, Sofiankatu 4 (Mon–Fri 9am–5pm, Sat & Sun 11am–5pm; €3), where a permanent exhibition entitled "Time" gives glimpses of Helsinki from its origins as a country village right up to the present day. It's an impressive show, beautifully lit with fibre optics and halogen lamps, though the chronology jumps around disconcertingly.

The square at the eastern end of Aleksanterinkatu is overlooked by the red-and-green onion-shaped domes of the Russian Orthodox **Uspenski Cathedral** (Mon & Wed–Sat 9.30am–4pm, Tues 9.30am–6pm, Sun noon–3pm, closed Mon Oct–April; ⊛www.ort.fi; tram #4) on Katajanokka, a wedge of land extending out to sea between the North and South harbours and currently the scene of a dockland development programme, converting the area's old warehouses into pricey new restaurants and apartments. In contrast to its Lutheran counterpart, the cathedral is drab outside, but inside has a rich display of icons and other sumptuous adornments, including an impressive array of chandeliers dangling from the vaulted ceiling.

Esplanadi and around

Walking from the Uspenski Cathedral towards the South Harbour along Aleksanterinkatu takes you past the **President's Palace**, noticeable only for its conspicuous uniformed guard, and the equally bland **City Hall**, used solely for administrative purposes. There's more colour and liveliness along the waterfront among the stalls of the **kauppatori**, or market square (Mon–Thurs 8am–5.30pm, Fri 8am–6pm, Sat 8am–3pm), laden with fresh fruit and vegetables; you can buy fresh fish directly from the boats moored around the edge of the harbour and, if your principles allow it, the market is also the best place to buy fur – mink and fox hats and coats are cheaper here than in the city's many fur salons. A bit further along, the **kauppahalli** or market hall (Mon–Fri 8am–5pm, Sat 8am–2pm), with its interior of original carved mahogany and carved pediments, is a good place for snacks such as reindeer kebab and Russian caviar.

Across a mishmash of tram lines from here lie the **twin thoroughfares of** Pohjoisesplanadi and Eteläesplanadi, known collectively as **Esplanadi**. At the height of the Swedish/Finnish language conflict that divided the nation during the mid-nineteenth century, this neat boulevard was where opposing factions demonstrated their allegiance – the Finns walking on the south side and the Swedes on the north. Nowadays it's dominated at lunchtime by office workers, later in the afternoon by buskers, and at night by strolling couples. Musical accompaniment is provided free on summer evenings from the hut in the middle of the walk – expect anything from a Salvation Army band to rock groups. Entertainment of a more costly type lies at the far end of Esplanadi in the dreary off-white horseshoe of the **Swedish Theatre** building – its main entrance is on Mannerheimintie.

Around the Stockmann Department Store

If you think Esplanadi is crowded, wait until you step inside the brick Constructivist **Stockmann Department Store**, at the junction of Mannerheimintie and Aleksanterinkatu. Europe's largest department store, this is the place to buy everything from bubble gum to a Persian rug. Also part of Stockmann's (though it has its own entrance on Aleksanterinkatu), the **Academic Bookstore** complete with **Internet café** allegedly holds more titles than any other bookstore in Europe, including many English-language paperbacks and a sizeable stock of foreign newspapers and magazines. Directly across Mannerheimintie is the massive **Forum shopping mall**, which has been cutting into the Stockmann profits in recent years.

Opposite Stockmann's main entrance is the eye-catching *Three Smiths* statue by Felix Nylund; a trio of naked men swinging hammers in unison around a centrally positioned anvil, it commemorates the workers of Finland who raised money to erect a building for the country's students. This building is the **Vanha Ylioppistalo** – the old Students' House – its main doors facing the statue. The Finnish Students' Union is based here, owning what is now some of the most expensive square metres of land in Finland and renting them out at considerable profit. In the Vanha, as it's usually known, is the **Vanhan Galleria** (during exhibitions usually 10am–6pm; free), a small gallery with frequent displays of modern art. It's worth becoming acquainted with the building's layout, as it contains a couple of lively bars which are worthy of an evening visit. Taking a few strides further along Mannerheimintie brings you to the Bio cinema; beside it, steps lead down into a little modern courtyard framed by burger joints and pizzerias, off which runs the entrance to **Tunneli**, an underground complex containing shops, the central metro station and a pedestrian subway to one of the city's most striking structures – the train station.

The train station and National Theatre

Erected in 1914, **Helsinki train station** ranks among architect Eliel Saarinen's greatest achievements. In response to criticism of his initial design, Saarinen jettisoned the original National Romantic features and opted for a style more akin to late Art Nouveau. Standing in front of the huge doors (so sturdy they always give the impression of being locked), it's hard to deny the sense of strength and solidity the building exudes. Yet this power is tempered by gentleness, a feeling symbolized by four muscular figures on the facade, each clasping a spherical glass lamp above the heads of passers-by. The interior details can be admired at leisure from either one of the station's two restaurants. Later, Saarinen was to emigrate to America; his son in turn became one of the best-known postwar American architects, whose most famous creation is the TWA terminal building in New York.

Just northeast of the station is the imposing granite form of the **National Theatre**, home of Finnish drama since 1872. Under the country's then governing Swedish-speaking elite, "Finnish culture" was considered simply a contradiction in terms, while later under the tsars it was felt (quite rightly) to pose a nationalist, anti-Russian threat – Finnish theatre during the Russification process became so politically charged that it had to be staged away from the capital in the southwest coastal town of Pori. At the forefront of Finnish drama during its early years was Aleksis Kivi, who died insane and impoverished before being acknowledged as Finland's greatest playwright. He's remembered here by Wäinö Aaltonen's bronze sculpture. Interestingly, nobody knows for sure what Kivi actually looked like, and this imagined likeness, finished in 1939, has come to be regarded as a true one.

Just across from the train station inside the city's main post office is the surprisingly enjoyable **Postal Museum** (*Posti Museo*; Mon–Fri 10am–7pm, Sat & Sun 11am–4pm; ⓦ www.posti.fi/postimuseo; free), a remarkably innovative collection displaying the unlikely-looking implements connected with more than 350 years of Finnish postal history, along with interactive computer games, multiscreen displays and a special crayoning area for toddlers.

The Atheneum Art Museum

Just southeast of the train station is the **Atheneum Art Museum** (Tues & Fri 9am–6pm, Wed & Thurs 9am–8pm, Sat & Sun 11am–5pm; €5.50, €7.50 for special exhibitions). Chief among the museum's large collection of Finnish paintings is the stirring selection of works from the late nineteenth century, the so-called Golden Age of Finnish painting, when the spirit of nationalism was surging through the country and the movement towards independence gaining strength;

indeed, the art of the period was a contributing factor in the growing awareness of Finnish culture, both inside and outside the country. Among the prime names of this era were **Akseli Gallen-Kallela** and **Albert Edelfelt**, particularly the former, who translated onto canvas many of the mythic scenes of the *Kalevala* (all but one of Gallen-Kallela's works, however, the unrepresentative *Kallervo Goes To War*, have been moved to Turku – see p.719). Slightly later came **Juho Rissanen** with his moody and evocative studies of peasant life, and **Hugo Simberg**, responsible for the eerie *Death and the Peasant* and the powerful triptych *Boy Carrying a Garland*. Cast an eye, too, over the works of **Helene Schjerfbeck**, for a long time one of the country's most underrated artists but now enjoying an upsurge in popularity – and collectability. Among the best examples of pure Finnish landscape are the works of **Pekka Halonen**: *Pioneers in Karelia* is typical, with soft curves expressively denoting natural scenes.

This cream of Finnish art is assembled on the first floor, appropriately placed directly off the main landing of the grand staircase that leads up from the entrance. Continue to the second floor and you'll find the provocative expressionism of **Tyko Sallinen** and the November Group, most active around 1917, some token **foreign** masters – a couple of large Munchs, a Van Gogh, a Chagall and a few Cézannes – and several much more recent installations by innovative contemporary Finnish artists. Before you leave, check out the excellent art bookshop on the ground floor.

North along Mannerheimintie

Mannerheimintie is the logical route for exploring north of the city centre. The wide thoroughfare is named after the military commander and statesman C.G.E. Mannerheim, who wielded considerable influence on Finnish affairs in the first half of the twentieth century. He's commemorated by a statue near the busy junction with Arkadiankatu, a structure on which the city's bird population has left its mark.

The Lasipalatsi
Opposite the Postal Museum is the recently renovated **Lasipalatsi** (ⓦwww .lasipalatsi.fi), the old Olympic transit and entertainment building. Reopened in 1998, the functional two-storey building is typical of late 1930s Finnish Art Nouveau design, and now contains some 25 shops, galleries, exhibition sites, cafés and a media centre embodying the Finns' faith in publicly accessible new technology – enough to feed mind and body for a few hours at least. On the glass-fronted lower level check out the **mbar** (Mon–Fri 8.30am–1am, Sat 10am–1am, Sun 11.30am–9pm), with Internet terminals inset into glasstop tables, and the glass-fronted studio of **MTV3**, one of the main Finnish TV companies – it overlooks the street and is often surrounded by hordes of teenagers anxious to catch a glimpse of the stars at work inside. Also on the ground floor is **Bio Rex**, a cinema that specializes in screening independent films that you probably won't find anywhere else in the city. Upstairs, the **Cable Book Library** (Mon–Thurs 10am–midnight, Sat & Sun noon–6pm) has magazines and a couple of dozen more free Internet terminals.

Museum of Contemporary Art: Kiasma
Just beyond the Lasipalatsi at Mannerheiminaukio 2 is the new **Museum of Contemporary Art: Kiasma** (Tues 9am–5pm, Wed–Sun 10am–8.30pm; ⓦwww.kiasma.fi; €5.50), a slightly forbidding, steel-clad and tube-like structure that looks from the side like a mix of the Sydney Opera House and the Guggenheim in Bilbao – a rather pretentious building for the usually functionalist Finns. Inside the catacomb-like interior are sweeping curves and well-lit hallways. On the ground floor natural light pours in from a variety of angles onto a brilliant-white interior that looks like it gets a new coat of paint on a weekly basis. Entry to this floor is free, and there's a decent café, Internet access, one of the best art bookshops in Finland and an interactive children's playroom.

The Kiasma draws its exhibition material from an archive of four thousand pieces of contemporary art, as well as works by visiting artists. Nothing is permanently on display, although as you explore you begin to feel that it's the building itself – with its play on space, light and technology – that is the principal exhibit. Some rooms are blacked out completely; others have high overhanging arches through which the light spills into the display area, giving the place an almost religious feel. Various touchscreen terminals built into the wall at strategic points tell you all you need to know about the works on display, and there's also a room in which about ten state-of-the-art computers are set up with numerous CD-ROMs on art and culture; one about the Kiasma itself is projected continuously onto the wall. Exhibitions change every two to three months – check the museum's website for details.

The Parliament Building and National Museum

The section of Mannerheimintie north from the Kiasma passes a number of outstanding buildings, the first of which is the **Parliament Building** on the left (guided tours July & Aug Mon–Fri 2pm, Sat 11am & noon, Sun noon & 1pm; Sept–June Sat & Sun only, same times; when in session, access is to the public galleries only; ⊛www.nba.fi/natmus/kmeng.html; free). The work of J.S. Sirén, the porridge-coloured building, with its pompous columns and choking air of solemnity, was completed in 1931. Intended to celebrate the new republic, its style was drawn from the revolutionary Neoclassicism that dominated public buildings from Fascist Italy to Nazi Germany, and its authoritarian features can appear wildly out of place in Helsinki, though it's worth a look nonetheless.

North of here things improve with the **National Museum** (Tues & Wed 11am–8pm, Thurs–Sun 11am–6pm; €4), whose design was the result of an early twentieth-century competition won by the three Young Turks of Finnish architecture – Armas Lindgren, Herman Gesellius and Eliel Saarinen. With National Romanticism at its zenith, they steeped their plan in Finnish history, drawing on the country's legacy of medieval churches and granite castles (even though many of these were built under Swedish domination), culminating in a weighty but slender tower that gives the place a cathedral-like profile. The entrance is guarded by Emil Wikström's sculptured bear and the interior ceilings are decorated by Gallen-Kallela with scenes from the *Kalevala*.

The museum may seem the obvious place to discover what Finland is all about but, especially if you've spent hours exploring the copiously stocked national museums of Denmark and Sweden, you might well find the collections disappointing. Being dominated by other nations for many centuries, Finland had little more than the prerequisites of peasant life to call its own up until the mid-1800s (when moves towards Finnish nationalism got off the ground), and the rows of farming and hunting tools alongside endless displays of bowls and spoons from the early times do little to fire the imagination. The most interesting sections are those relating to the rise of Finnish self-determination and the early years of the republic. Large photographs show the enormous crowds that massed in Helsinki's streets to sing the Finnish anthem in defiance of their (then) Russian rulers, and cabinets packed with small but intriguing objects outline the left–right struggles that marked the early decades of independence and the immediate postwar years – periods when Finland's political future teetered precariously in the balance, a long way from the stability and prosperity enjoyed in more recent times.

Finlandia Hall to the Olympic Stadium

Stylistically a far cry from the National Museum building but equally affecting, **Finlandia Hall** (guided tours when not in use; ring ☎09/40 241 or check at the City Tourist Office) stands directly across Mannerheimintie, partially hidden by the roadside foliage. Designed by the country's premier architect, **Alvar Aalto**, a few years before his death in 1976, Finlandia Hall was conceived as part of a grand plan to rearrange the entire centre of Helsinki. Previously, Eliel Saarinen had planned a

△ Cathedral/Senate Square, Helsinki

traffic route from the northern suburbs into a new square in the city centre, to be called Vapaudenkatu ("Freedom Street") in celebration of Finnish independence. Aalto plotted a continuation of this scheme, envisaging the removal of the rail-freight yards, which would enable arrivals to be greeted with a fan-like terrace of new buildings reflected in the waters of Töölönlahti. Finlandia was to be the first of these, and only by looking across from the other side of Töölönlahti do you perceive the building's soft sensuality and the potential beauty of the greater concept. Inside the hall, Aalto's characteristic wave pattern (the architect's surname, as it happens, means "wave" in Finnish) and asymmetry are in evidence. From the walls and ceilings through to the lamps and vases, the place has a quiet and graceful air. But the view from the foyer is still of the rail-freight yards, and the great plan for a future Helsinki remains under discussion.

Next door is **Hakasalmi Villa** (Wed–Sun 11am–5pm; €3), one of four satellite museums belonging to the new City Art Museum (see p.706). An Italian-style Neoclassical villa built in the 1840s by a councillor and patron of the arts whose collection inspired the founding of the museum, it houses long-term temporary exhibitions, often strikingly designed and worth a peek. Finland's **Opera House** (Mon–Fri 9am–6pm, Sat 3–6pm, Sun open 2hr before performances; ◉www .operafin.fi), a little way beyond Finlandia, is, like so many contemporary Finnish buildings, a Lego-like expanse of white-tiled facade. Its light-flooded interior is enlivened by displays of colourful costumes though, and its grounds and entrance spiked with minimalist black-granite sculptures.

From this point on, the decisive outline of the **Olympic Stadium** becomes visible. Originally intended for the 1940 Olympic Games, the stadium eventually staged the second postwar games in 1952. From the **Stadium Tower** (Mon–Fri 9am–8pm, Sat & Sun 9am–6pm; €2) there's an unsurpassed view over the city and a chunk of the southern coast. If you're a stopwatch-and-spikes freak, ask at the tower's ticket office for directions to the **Sport Museum** (Mon–Fri 11am–5pm, Sat & Sun noon–4pm; €3.50), whose mind-numbing collection of track officials' shoes and swimming caps overshadows a worthy attempt to present sport as an integral part of Finnish culture. The nation's heroes, among them Keke Rosberg and Lasse Virén, are lauded to the skies. Outside, Wäinö Aaltonen's sculpture of Paavo Nurmi captures the champion runner of the 1920s in full stride, and full nudity – something that caused a stir when the sculpture was unveiled in 1952.

West of Mannerheimintie

As there's little of note north of the stadium, it's best to cross Mannerheimintie and follow the streets off it leading to **Sibelius Park** and Eila Hiltunen's monument to the composer, made from 24 tons of steel tubes, like a big silver surrealist organ, and, next to it, an irrefutably horrid sculpture of Sibelius's dismembered head. The shady and pleasant park is rudely cut by a main road called Mechelininkatu. Following this back towards the city centre brings you first to the small Islamic and Jewish cemeteries, and then to the expanse of tombs comprising **Hietaniemi Cemetery** (usually open until 10pm). A prowl among these is like a stroll through a "Who was Who" of Finland's last 150 years: Mannerheim, Engel and a host of former presidents are buried here, while just inside the main entrance lies Alvar Aalto, his witty little tombstone consisting partly of a chopped Neoclassical column; behind it is the larger marker of Gallen-Kallela, his initials woven around a painter's palette. It's to the cemetery that local schoolkids head when skipping off lessons during warm weather, not for a smoke behind the gravestones but to reach the **beaches** that line the bay just beyond its western walls. From these you can enjoy the best sunset in the city.

On the way back towards Mannerheimintie, at Lutherinkatu 3, just off Runeberginkatu, is the breathtaking **Temppeliaukio kirkko** (Mon–Fri 10am–8pm, Sat 10am–6pm, Sun noon–1.45pm & 3.15–5.45pm; closed Tues 1–2pm and during services; tram #3B). Brilliantly conceived by Timo and Tuomo

Suomalainen and finished in 1969, the underground church is built inside a massive block of natural granite in the middle of an otherwise ordinary residential square. Whilst here, try and see it from above if you can (even if you have to shin up a drainpipe), when the copper dome that pokes through the rock makes the thing look like a ditched flying saucer. The odd combination of man-made and natural materials has made it a fixture on the tourist circuit, but even when crowded it's a thrill to be inside. Classical concerts frequently take place here, the raw rock walls making for excellent acoustics – check the noticeboard at the entrance for details.

South of Esplanadi: Kaivopuisto, Eira and Pihlajasaari island

From the South Harbour it's a straightforward walk past the Silja terminal to Kaivopuisto, but it's more interesting to leave Esplanadi along Kasarmikatu and take in some small, offbeat museums along the way. First of these is the **Museum of Finnish Architecture** (Tues & Thurs–Sun 10am–4pm, Wed until 7pm; ⓦwww.mfa.fi; €3.50–5, depending upon exhibitions) at no. 24, which is aimed at the serious fan: architectural tours of less accessible buildings both in Helsinki and around the country can be arranged here. Combined with an extensive archive, it's a useful resource for a nation with an important architectural heritage.

A block from Kasarmikatu is Korkeavuorenkatu, with the excellent **Museum of Art and Design** at no. 23 (Tues & Thurs–Sun 11am–6pm, Wed until 8pm; ⓦwww.designmuseum.fi; €6.50), which traces the relationship between art and industry in Finnish history. There are full explanatory texts and period exhibits, from Karelianism – the representations of nature and peasant life from the Karelia region in eastern Finland that dominated Finnish art and design in the years just before and after independence – to the modern movements, along with the post-war shift towards the more familiar, and less interesting, pan-Scandinavian styles.

Kaivopuisto park

Kasarmikatu ends close to the base of a hill, from where footpaths lead up to the Engel-designed **Astronomical Observatory**. Down on the other side and a few streets on is the large and rocky **Kaivopuisto** park. In the 1830s this was developed as a health resort, with a spa house that drew Russian nobility from St Petersburg to sample its waters. The building, another of Engel's works (although greatly modified), can be found in the middle of the park's central avenue, today pulling in the crowds as a restaurant.

Off a smaller avenue, Itäinen Puistotie, runs the circular Kallionlinnantie, which contains the house where Gustaf Mannerheim spent the later years of his life, now maintained as the **Mannerheim Museum** (Fri–Sun 11am–4pm, other times by appointment, call ☎09/635 443; ⓦwww.mannerheim-museo.fi; €7 including guided tour). A Finnish-born, Russian-trained military commander, Mannerheim was pro-Finnish but had a middle-class suspicion of the working classes: he led the right-wing Whites during the Civil War of 1918 and two decades later the Finnish campaigns in the Winter and Continuation wars (for more on which, see the "Military Museum", p.705). His influence in the political sphere was also considerable, and included a brief spell as president. While acknowledging his importance, the regard that Finns have for him these days, naturally enough, depends on their own political viewpoint.

Ideology aside, the house is intriguing. The interior is left much as it was when the man died in 1951, and the clutter is astounding. During his travels Mannerheim raided flea markets at every opportunity, collecting a remarkable array of plunder – assorted furniture, antiques, ornaments and books from all over the globe. Upstairs is the camp-bed which Mannerheim found too comfortable ever to change, and in the wall is the vent inserted to keep the bedroom as airy as a field-tent.

If he had lived a few decades earlier, one of Mannerheim's Kallionlinnantie neighbours would have been Frederik Cygnaeus, art patron and Professor of Aesthetics at

Helsinki University. In 1860 Cygnaeus built a summer house at no. 8, a lovely yellow-turreted affair, and filled it with an outstanding collection of art. Later he donated the lot to the nation and today it's displayed as the **Cygnaeus Gallery** (Wed 11am–7pm, Thurs–Sun 11am–4pm; ⊛www.nba.fi; €2.50). Everything is beautifully laid out in the tiny rooms of the house, with whole walls of work by the most influential of his contemporaries. The von Wright brothers (Ferdinand, Magnus and Wilhelm) are responsible for the most touching pieces – the bird and nature studies. Look out, too, for a strange portrait of Cygnaeus by Ekman, showing the man sprouting sinister wings from under his chin.

The edge of Kaivopuisto looks out across a sprinkling of little islands and the Suomenlinna fortress. You can follow one of the pathways down into **Merikatu**, along which lie several of the Art Nouveau villas lived in by the big cheeses of Finnish industry during the early part of the twentieth century. Easily the most extreme is no. 25, the Enso-Gutzeit villa, now portioned off into offices and with a lingering air of decay hanging over its decorative facade.

Eira

Inland from Merikatu, the curving alleys and tall, elegant buildings of the **Eira** district are landmarked by the needle-like spire rising from the roof of **Mikael Agricola kirkko**, named after the translator of the first Finnish Bible but making no demands on your time. A few blocks northeast, the twin-towered Johanessen kirkko is again not worth a call in itself but functions as a handy navigation aid. Following Yrjönkatu northwards from here takes you past the partly pedestrianized Iso Roobertinkatu, before reaching Bulevardi and the square containing **Vanha kirkko**, or Old Church. A humble wooden structure, and another example of Engel's work, this was the first Lutheran church to be erected after Helsinki became the Finnish capital, predating that in Senate Square by some years but occupying a far less glamorous plot – a plague victim's burial ground dating from 1710.

Heading left along Bulevardi for a couple of hundred metres brings you to the Sinebrychoff brewery which, besides bestowing a distinctive aroma of hops to the locality, also finances the **Sinebrychoff Foreign Art Museum** at no. 40 (Mon, Thurs & Fri 9am–6pm, Wed 9am–8pm, Sat & Sun 11am–5pm; ⊛www.fng.fi; €1.50, €5 for special exhibitions). This rather precious museum houses mostly seventeenth-century Flemish and Dutch paintings, along with some excellent miniatures, delicately illustrated porcelain and refined period furniture. Continuing east along Bulevardi to the waterfront brings you to the wide **Hietalahdentori**, a concrete square that perks up with a daily morning flea market and, in summer, an evening market between 3.30pm and 8pm.

Pihlajasaari island

One of Helsinki's most enjoyable islands, ideal for a day-trip from the capital, **Pihlajasaari island** is barely a fifteen-minute boat ride from the Merisatama small-boat harbour on Merisatamanranta, opposite the junction of Merikatu and Laivurinkatu. Creaking thirty-year-old wooden pleasure boats leave once or twice hourly from here (mid-May to Aug; €4.50 return) for the short trip across to the island, which also goes by its Swedish name of Rönnskär. Actually two small islands linked by a narrow isthmus and footbridge, Pihlajasaari is a summer haven of wild flowers, long grasses and swaying pine and rowan trees vying for space between the outcrops of smooth bare rock that are perfect for catching a few rays. In fact, on the smaller of the two islands, reached by turning left from the boat jetty and crossing the small footbridge, is Helsinki's best **nudist beach** – follow the signs for the *naturistiranta* and note that the outer limits of the area are obsessively marked by signposts so as not to offend the Finns' very un-Scandinavian unease with public nudity. Back on the main island, itself no more than one or two kilometres in length, a network of walking paths leads through the forest to a series of rocky beaches and a **café** near the southwestern tip, a pleasant place to sit and watch the enormous superferries glide towards their destinations in Helsinki en route from Sweden.

Kruununhaka and Hakaniemi

North of Senate Square is the little district of **Kruununhaka**. Away from the city hubbub, its closely built blocks shield the narrow streets from the sunlight, evoking a forlorn and forgotten mood. At Kristianinkatu 12, the single-storey wooden **Burgher's House** (Wed–Sun 11am–5pm; ❀www.hel.fi/kaumuseo; €3) stands in vivid contrast to the tall granite dwellings around it – and gives an indication of how Helsinki looked when wood was still the predominant building material. The interior has been kitted out with mid-nineteenth-century furnishings, the period when a city burgher did indeed reside here.

Kristianinkatu meets at right-angles with Maurinkatu, a short way along which is the **Military Museum** (Tues–Thurs 11am–6pm, Fri–Sun 11am–4pm; €3.50), a rather formless selection of weapons, medals and glorifications of armed-forces life, but with some excellent documentary photos of the Winter and Continuation wars of 1939–44. Finland was drawn into World War II through necessity rather than choice. When Soviet troops invaded eastern Finnish territories in November 1939, under the guise of protecting Leningrad, they were repelled by technically inferior but far more committed Finns. The legends of the "heroes in white" were born then, alluding to the Finnish soldiers and the camouflage used in the winter snows. Soon after, however, faced with possible starvation and a fresh Soviet advance, Finland joined the war on the Nazi side, mainly in order to continue resisting the threat from the east. For this reason, it's rare to find World War II spoken of as such in Finland: much more commonly it's divided into these separate conflicts.

Hakaniemi

The western edge of Kruununhaka is defined by the busy Unioninkatu (if it's a sunny day, take a stroll around the neat **botanical gardens**, just off Unioninkatu), which continues northwards across a slender body of water into **Hakaniemi**, a district chiefly visited for its **kauppahalli** indoor market (Mon–Fri 8am–5pm, Sat 8am–2pm), where you'll find an excellent array of fresh fruit, vegetables, meats and fish. Although the square of Hakaniementori is surrounded by drab storefronts and office blocks, the kauppahalli is about the liveliest in the city – mainly due to its position near a major junction for city buses and trams, as well as a metro station. From the square you can see right up the hill to the impressive Art Deco brickwork of the **Kallion kirkko**, beyond which is the busy Sturenkatu and the open green area partly consumed by **Linnanmäki amusement park**. After crossing Sturenkatu, head for the nearby **Museum of Workers' Housing** at Kirstinkuja 4 (May–Sept Wed–Sun 11am–5pm; €3), for some fascinating social history. The series of wooden buildings that now hold the museum were constructed during the early 1900s to provide housing for the impoverished country folk who moved to the growing, increasingly industrialized city to work as street cleaners and refuse collectors. Six of the one-room homes where the new arrivals settled have been re-created with period furnishings, and a biography on the door describes each flat's occupants – woeful tales of overcrowding, overwork, and sons who left for America and never returned.

Suomenlinna

Located in the southeast of the Kaivopuisto district and built by the Swedes in 1748 to protect Helsinki from seaborne attack, the fortress of **Suomenlinna** stands on five interconnected islands, reached by half-hourly ferry from the South Harbour, which make a rewarding break from the city centre – even if you only want to laze around on the dunes. (These were created by the Russians with sand shipped in from Estonia to strengthen the new capital's defences after they'd wrested control of

Finland.) For information, head to the **Inventory Chambers Visitors Centre** (March, April & Oct Mon–Fri 11am–4pm, Sat & Sun 11am–5pm; May–Aug daily 10am–6pm; Sept daily 11am–5pm, Sat & Sun 10am–5pm; Nov–Feb Tues–Sun 11am–4pm), housed in a former naval stores. Here you'll also find the **Suomenlinna Museum and Experience** (March & April Sat & Sun 11am–5pm; May–Aug daily 10am–6pm; Sept daily 11am–5pm; Oct Tues–Fri 11am–4pm, Sat & Sun 11am–5pm; Nov & Dec Tues–Sun 11am–4pm; ⓦwww.suomenlinna.fi; €5), which charts the history of the fortress. Suomenlinna has a few museums, none particularly riveting, although the **Ehrensvärd Museum** (March, April & Oct Sat & Sun 11am–5pm; May–Aug daily 10am–5pm; Sept daily 11am–5pm; €3) is worth a look, occupying the residence used by the first commander of the fortress, Augustin Ehrensvärd. He oversaw the building of Suomenlinna and now lies in the elaborate tomb in the grounds; his personal effects remain inside the house alongside displays on the fort's construction. Finally, the **Coastal Artillery Museum** (March & April Sat & Sun 11am–3pm; May–Aug daily 10am–5pm; Sept daily 11am–3pm; €3.50) records Suomenlinna's defensive actions and allows the opportunity to clamber around the darkly claustrophobic World War II submarine *Vesikko*.

Seurasaari and around

A fifteen-minute tram (#4) or bus (#24) ride northwest of the city centre (get off one stop after the big hospital on the left, from where it's a one-kilometre walk) lies **Seurasaari**, a small wooded island delightfully set in a sheltered bay. The three contrasting museums on or close by the island make for a well-spent day. Access to the island proper is by a bridge at the southern end of Tamminiementie, conveniently close to the **Helsinki City Art Museum** (Wed–Sun 11am–6.30pm; ⓦwww.hel.fi/artmuseum; €4.20). Though one of the best collections of modern Finnish art, with some eerily striking work, the museum is hardly a triumph of layout, with great clumps of stuff of differing styles scattered about the walls. But the good pieces shine through. Be warned, though, that during temporary exhibitions the permanent stock is locked away.

A few minutes' walk from the art museum, towards the Seurasaari bridge, is the long driveway leading to the **Urho Kekkonen Museum** (mid-May to mid-Aug daily 11am–5pm, Wed until 7pm; mid-Aug to mid-May Wed–Sun 11am–5pm, Wed until 7pm; ⓦwww.nba.fi; €3.50, includes guided tour), the villa where the esteemed president lived until his death in 1986. Whether they love him or loathe him, few Finns would deny the vital role Kekkonen played in Finnish history, most significantly by continuing the work of his predecessor, Paasikivi, in the establishment of Finnish neutrality. He accomplished this largely through delicate negotiations with Soviet leaders – whose favour he would gain, so legend has it, by taking them to a sauna – narrowly averting major crises and seeing off the threat of a Soviet invasion on two separate occasions. Kekkonen often conducted official business here rather than at the Presidential Palace in the city – yet the feel of the place is far from institutional, with a light and very Finnish character, filled with birchwood furniture, its large windows giving peaceful views of surrounding trees, water and wildlife.

Close by, in another calm setting across the bridge on Seurasaari itself, is the **Open-Air Museum** (late May Mon–Fri 9am–3pm, Sat & Sun 11am–5pm; June–Aug daily 11am–5pm; early Sept Mon–Fri 9am–3pm, Sat & Sun 11am–5pm; mid-Sept to mid-Nov Sat & Sun 11am–5pm; €4), a collection of vernacular buildings assembled from all over Finland, connected by the various pathways that extend around the island. There are better examples of traditional Finnish life elsewhere in the country, but if you're only visiting Helsinki this will give a good insight into how the country folk lived until surprisingly recently. The old-style church is a popular spot for city couples' weddings.

Aside from the museums and the scenery, people also come to Seurasaari to strip off. Sex-segregated **nudist beaches** line part of the western edge – also a popular offshore stop for the city's weekend yachtsmen, armed with binoculars; however, Pihlajasaari island (see p.704) is an altogether more pleasing location for nude sunbathing.

Outlying museums

Helsinki has a few other **museums** outside the centre that don't fit into any walking tour. All are within fairly easy reach with public transport, and sometimes a little legwork.

Gallen-Kallela Museum

On the Tarvaspää peninsula, the **Gallen-Kallela Museum**, Gallen-Kallelantie 27 (mid-May to Aug daily 10am–6pm; Sept to mid-May Tues–Sat 10am–4pm, Sun 10am–5pm; €8), is housed inside the Art Nouveau studio of the influential painter Akseli Gallen-Kallela (1865–1931), who lived and worked here from 1913. Sadly, it's a bit of an anticlimax, lacking either atmosphere or a decent display of the artist's work. There are a few old paints and brushes under dirty glass coverings in the studio, while in an upstairs room are the pickled remains of reptiles and frog-like animals collected by Gallen-Kallela's family. Inscribed into the floor is a declaration by Gallen-Kallela: "I Shall Return". Unless you're a huge fan, it's probably not worth the bother. To get there, take tram #4 from the city centre to the end of its route (on Saunalahdentie), then walk 2km along Munkkiniemi on the bay's edge to a footbridge which leads over the water and towards the poorly signposted museum. Alternatively, bus #33 runs from the tram stop to the footbridge about every twenty minutes.

The Cable Factory museums (Kaapelitehdas)

The former cable factory to the west of the city centre at Tallberginkatu 1F is now home to a clutch of museums (ⓦ www.kaapelitehdas.fi), accessible on tram #8. The **Hotel and Restaurant Museum** (Tues–Sun noon–7pm; €2) is specifically designed for aficionados of the catering trade, although the photos on the walls of its two rooms reveal a fascinating social history of Helsinki, showing hotel and restaurant life from both sides of the table, alongside a staggering selection of matchboxes, beer mats emblazoned with the emblems of their establishments, and menus signed by the rich and infamous.

Despite its grand title, the **Photographic Museum of Finland** (Tues–Sun noon–7pm; €4) comprises a shabby herd of old cameras that suggest Finnish photography never progressed beyond the watch-the-birdie stage. Amends are made by the innovative temporary collections of photos that regularly adorn the walls. The third museum in the complex is the city's **Theatre Museum** (Tues–Sun noon–7pm; €5.50), displaying a permanent collection of costumes, stage sets and lights. Frequent temporary exhibitions focus on different aspects behind the scenes in Finnish theatre.

Eating and drinking

As in the rest of the country, **eating** in Helsinki isn't cheap, but there is plenty of choice and, with careful planning, plenty of ways to stretch out funds. Other than all-you-can-eat **breakfast** tables in hotels (hostel breakfasts in the city tend to be rationed), it's best to hold out until **lunch**, when many restaurants offer a reduced fixed-price menu or a help-yourself table, and in almost every pizzeria you'll get a pizza, coffee, and all you can manage from the bread and salad bar for under €10. **Picnic food**, too, is a viable option. Use the markets and market halls at the South Harbour or Hakaniementori for fresh vegetables, meat and fish. Several supermarkets in Tunneli, by the train station, stay open until 10pm. The popular **Forum** shopping centre (see p.698), directly opposite the Stockmann, has a number of popular, inexpensive eateries on two floors, while the **precinct** opposite the train station contains a range of mid-standard, filling eateries open till late.

Throughout the day, up until 5pm or 6pm, you can also get a coffee and pastry or a fuller snack for around €5 at one of the numerous **cafés**. The best cafés are stylish, atmospheric affairs dating from the beginning of the twentieth century. Alternatives include myriad multinational hamburger joints and the slightly more unusual *grilli* roadside stands, which sell hot dogs and the like; if you're tempted, experts claim the *Jaskan Grilli*, in Töölönkatu behind the National Museum, to be the best of its kind. If you're hungry and impoverished (and are, in theory at least, a student), you can get a full meal for €5 from one of the **student mensas**, two of which are centrally located in the main university buildings at Aleksanterinkatu 5, and at Hallituskatu 11–13. One or the other will be open during the summer; both are open during term time. The *mensas* can be cheaper still in the late afternoon, from 4pm to 6pm, and are also usually open on Saturdays from 9am to 1pm. As for **evening eating**, there are plenty of restaurants serving reasonably priced ethnic foods, as well as a number of Finnish *haute cuisine* places.

Cafés

Aalto Academic Bookstore, Pohjoisesplanadi 39. Designed by the world-famous Finnish architect whose name it bears, and well worth a visit after a morning's book-browsing.

Bellman Kaivokatu 12. Big, cosmopolitan and very beautiful – though also very expensive.

Caramelle by Hakasalmi Villa, Karamzininkatu 2. Small, intimate and serving gorgeous gooey cakes.

Ekberg Bulevardi 9. Nineteenth-century fixtures and a deliberately *fin de siècle* atmosphere, with starched waitresses bringing the most delicate of open sandwiches and pastries to green-marble tables.

Eliel Helsinki train station. On the station's ground floor, this has an airy, vaulted Art Nouveau interior, good-value self-service breakfasts (Mon–Sat 7–10am, Sun 8–10am) – and a roulette table.

Engel Aleksanterinkatu 26. Named after the Berlin-born designer of all the buildings you can see from its window, this is a haven of fine coffee, pastries, cakes and intellectual chitchat, just across from Senate Square. Try the smoked-fish salad.

Esplanad Pohjoisesplanadi 37. The best place in town for inexpensive eating. Filled baguettes, a choice of fresh soups daily and always a queue.

Fazer Kluuvikatu 3. Helsinki's best-known bakery, justly celebrated for its lighter-than-air pastries; there's another branch in the Forum Shopping Centre. At either, try the speciality, "Bebe", a praline cream-filled pastry for €1.70.

Kappeli Esplanadi Park, Esplanadi. An elegant glasshouse with massive wrought-iron decorated windows overlooking Esplanadi and the harbour, with lots of live entertainment outside and in during the summer. The cellar is also a great spot for an evening drink – see *Kappelin Olutkellari*, p.710.

Pariisin Villa Pohjoisesplanadi 21. Elegant place for good cakes and tarts. There's courtyard eating at the back, near the entrance to a beautiful interior design shop.

Strindberg Pohjoisesplandi 33. Stylish outdoor coffee sipping – though it's expensive if you want to eat, with a menu listing such items as smoked reindeer with Lapland cheese followed by glow-fried grayling and arctic cloudberry.

Tamminiementie Tamminiementie 8. A good stopoff when visiting the nearby City Art Museum or Seurasaari Island, for high-quality tea or coffee served in elegant surroundings, with Chopin playing in the background.

Tomtebon Kahvila Tamminiemi, opposite the Kekkonen Museum at Seurasaari. Coffee served with home-made cookies and cakes in a lovely old wooden villa set in a lush garden.

Ursula Ehrenströmintie 3. On the beach at the edge of the Kaivopuisto park, with a wonderful sea view from the outdoor terrace. Decent sandwiches, light lunches and cakes.

Victor Bulevardi 32. Enticing selection of reasonably priced lunch dishes that attract a regular local clientele; large windows for watching the world go by.

Restaurants

Foreign restaurants are reasonably plentiful in Helsinki, and in a typical **pizzeria** you can expect to pay €12–24 per person for dinner, provided you don't drink anything stronger than mineral water. There are also a few **vegetarian** restaurants, which charge about the same. **Finnish** restaurants, on the other hand, and those serving **Russian** specialities, can be terrifyingly expensive; expect to spend around €30 each for a night of upmarket overindulgence. Restaurants are usually open daily until around 1am, though the kitchens close at about 11pm.

Note that restaurants are marked on both the Helsinki (p.690–691) and Central Helsinki (p.695) maps.

Finnish and Russian

Alexander Nevski Pohjoisesplanadi 17. A very fine, classic Russian restaurant with live music. The food is fairly expensive at €14–20 per dish. Closed Sun lunchtime.

Bellevue Rahapajankatu 3, behind the Uspenski Cathedral. A superb Russian restaurant opened, ironically, in 1917, the year Finland won independence from Russia. Expensive, gourmet Russian food: try Marshal Mannerheim's favourite of minced lamb flavoured with herring for €25. Closed Sat & Sun lunchtime.

Havis Amanda Unioninkatu 23. An excellent fish restaurant, albeit pricey and somewhat staid. Main dishes start at €20.

Holvari Yrjönkatu 15. Specializes in mushrooms, personally picked by the owner and providing the basis of tasty soups and stews. Dishes start €12.

Hullu Kukko Simonkatu 8. Nothing special to look at, but great fish soup, excellent pizzas and one of the best wine lists in town.

Iso-Ankkuri Pursimiehenkatu 16. Fairly downbeat, and favoured mostly by locals for its filling, unextravagant menu. Buffet lunch for €7.50.

Kasakka Meritullinkatu 13. Old-style Russian restaurant with a deliciously over-the-top spirit-of-the-tsars atmosphere and great, if expensive, food.

Katajanokan Kasino Laivastokatu 1. Just east of the Uspenski Cathedral, this theme restaurant offers the chance to feast on à la carte gourmet dishes such as elk or reindeer in anything from a mock wartime bunker to the "Cabinet Room", decorated with markers to Finnish independence. A great place if someone else is paying – mains are around €20.

Kuu Töölönkatu 27. Between the Opera House and Sibelius Park, this is an unpretentious place to consume filling, down-to-earth Finnish food. Dishes from €15.

Kynsilaukka Ravintola Garlic Fredrikinkatu 22. Pricey, but the ultimate pleasure if you like garlic, as its name suggests.

Punavuoren Ahven Punavuorenkatu 12. Much of the original interior, designed by Alvar Aalto, remains in this locals' haunt, where the staff dish up stodgy, inexpensive Finnish food for €7–10 per dish.

Ravintola Lappi Annankatu 22. A fine, though not cheap Finnish restaurant specializing in real Finnish foods like pea soup and oven pancakes, as well as Lappish specialities of smoked reindeer and warm cloudberries.

Ravintola Perho Mechelininkatu 7 (near corner of Hietaniemenkatu). The restaurant of the Finnish Culinary College and an excellent choice for lunch, which is normally a three-course buffet for around €17. Prices are much lower than normal and service impeccable.

Sea Horse Kapteeninkatu 11. This cavernous and smoky restaurant is frequented by locals and makes an excellent place to people-watch. Serves a range of fairly inexpensive Finnish dishes, though it's especially renowned for its various fish dishes, which start at €12.

Sipuli Kanavaranta 3. A tastebud-thrilling, formal and glamorous – though financially ruinous – choice of gourmet dishes, several based on traditional Sámi fare. Just west of the Uspenski Cathedral.

Terrace Bar Stockmann Department Store. Situated on the top floor – bright and relaxed, with Lloyd loom-style seating. Specialities are salads, soups and grills such as potato and anchovy bake or grilled chicken; reckon on €8 for a main dish.

Italian, ethnic and vegetarian

Ani Telakkakatu 2. Turkish food at its best; go for the €7.10 buffet table laid out at lunchtime.

Cantina West Kasarmikatu 23. Fiery, reasonably priced TexMex food in a lively, western-themed restaurant spread over several floors. Gets loud late at night.

Chico's Mannerheimintie 68. Very friendly, inexpensive all-American eatery with pizzas and burgers starting at around €7.50, alongside specialities from the Deep South and Mexico.

Golden Rax Pizzabuffet Mannerheimintie 18, second floor of the Forum Shopping Centre. Bargain-basement unlimited pizza and pasta buffet for €7.49.

Mai Thai Annankatu 32. The least expensive and quite possibly the best of the city's crop of Thai restaurants. Mains from €11.

Mamma Rosa Runeberginkatu 55. A classic pizzeria also serving fish, steaks and pasta. One of the best mid-priced restaurants in the city with dishes from €9 – not surprisingly, it's generally full.

Namaskar Mannerheimintie 100. Currently the most expensive Asian restaurant in Helsinki, and the pick of a slowly growing band of Indian restaurants struggling to make an impression on local eating habits.

Pasta Factory Mastokatu 6. Intimate, discreetly stylish and quite affordable Italian place.

Zucchini Fabianinkatu 4. A friendly and stylish vegetarian restaurant big on aubergines, courgettes and salads – a filling meal here will cost around €15.

Drinking

Although never cheap, alcohol is not a dirty word in Finland, and **drinking**, especially beer, can be enjoyed in the city's many café-like pubs, which are where most Helsinki folk go to socialize. You'll find one on virtually every corner, but the pick of the bunch are listed below. Only the really swanky places have a dress code, and they are usually too elitist – and expensive – to be worth bothering with anyway. Sundays to Thursdays are normally quiet; on Fridays and Saturdays on the other hand, it's best to arrive as early as possible to get a seat without having to queue. Most drinking dives also serve food, although the grub is seldom at its best in the evening (where it's good earlier in the day, we've included it under "Restaurants"). If you want a drink but are feeling antisocial, or just very hard-up, the cheapest method, as ever, is to buy from the appropriately named ALKO shop: there are self-service ones at Fabiankatu 7 and Vuorikatu 7.

Angleterre Fredrikinkatu 47. Utterly Finnish despite the flock wallpaper and Dickensian fixtures – good for a laugh and cultural disorientation.

Aseman Yläravintola second floor of the train station. Socially much more interesting than the *Eliel* downstairs (see "Cafés", p.708), this is a lively and diverse place for a drink, surrounded by architect Saarinen's fabulous features. Don't risk it if you've a train to catch.

Ateljeebaari *Hotel Torni*, Yrjönkatu 26. On the thirteenth floor of a plush hotel: great views, great posing – but be warned that the women's toilet has bizarre ceiling-to-floor windows. Drinks are pricey.

Baker's Mannerheimintie 12. A good place to initiate yourself into drinking Helsinki-style; open until 3am, it has a reputation as a last-chance pick-up spot.

Bulevardia Bulevardi 34. Many customers are technicians or singers from the neighbouring Opera House who swoop in after a concert. Join them for the Art Deco decor – matt-black furniture designed by 1930s architect Pauli Blomstedt, and burr-birch walls.

Corona Eerikinkatu 11. Famous pool hall-cum-bar, very popular with Helsinki's alternative set. It's owned by the Kaurismaki brothers, creators of the Leningrad Cowboys.

Elite Etläinen Hesperiankatu 22. Northwest of the National Museum, this was once the haunt of the city's artists, many of whom would settle the bill not with money but with paintings – a selection of which lines the walls. Especially good in summer, when you can drink on the terrace.

Juttutupa Säästöpankinranta 6. Once the HQ of the Social Democrats, who built it with a tower to allow their red flag to fly above the neighbouring church spires. The decision to take up arms, which

culminated in the 1918 civil war, was made here, and photos commemorate the fact. Apolitical entertainment is provided on Wed, Fri and Sat by an accordion and/or violin player, encouraging enjoyable singalongs.

Kaarle XII Kasarmikatu 40. Fine Art Nouveau features hewn into the red-granite walls make this the most traditional-looking of the city's bars; not that the customers allow the surroundings to inhibit their merrymaking.

Kappelin Olutkellari Esplanadi Park, Esplanadi. The entrance is to the side of this distinctive multipurpose building of glass and fancy ironwork (see also *Kappeli*, p.708). A garrulous and gloriously eclectic clientele.

Kosmos Kalevankatu 3. This is where the big media cats – TV producers, PR people, the glitzier authors – hang out and engage in loud arguments as the night wears on. The wonderful interior is unchanged since the 1920s, but you'll only see it if you get past the officious doorman.

Leningrad Cowboys Uudenmaankatu 16–20. Tribute restaurant to the eponymous Finnish rock band. This American-style diner complete with stylish chandeliers has all manner of meat and vegetarian dishes around €15 and not surprisingly is often packed out.

Merimakasiini Hietalahdenranta 4. Slightly out-of-the-way, on a street running off Hietalahdentori towards the waterfront, but worth sampling on a Friday or Saturday night when the customers spill onto the terrace to drink while gazing at the cranes of the city's cargo harbour.

Moskva Eerikinkatu 11. An anonymous looking entrance gives way to the Kaurismaki brothers' quirky Soviet-themed bar.

Salve Hietalahdenranta 11. Filled with nautical paraphernalia but no longer the seedy sailors' haunt that it was. Worth a call, to eat or drink, although the recently hiked-up prices suggest the place has ideas above its station. On same street as *Merimakasiini* (see above).

St Urho's Pub Museokatu 10. Close to the National Museum, this is one of the most popular student pubs – which accounts for the lengthy queue that forms from about 9pm on Fri and Sat.

Teatteri Pohjoisesplanadi 2. Spend a few hours in this sometimes rowdy bar and you'll encounter a cross-section of Helsinki characters – some coming, some going, others falling over.

Vanhan Kahvila Mannerheimintie 3. A self-service and hence comparatively cheap bar. It fills quickly, so try to arrive early for a seat on the balcony overlooking the bustle of the streets below.

Vanhan Kellari Mannerheimintie 3. Downstairs from the *Vanhan Kahvila*, with underground setting and bench-style seating helping to promote a cosy and smoky atmosphere. Rumour has it that this is where the Helsinki Beat poets of the early 1960s drank, and where they now bring their children.

Vastarannan Kiiski Runeberginkatu 26. A crowded pub with a wide selection of beers both on tap and bottled.

William K Mannerheimintie 72. A cosy, locals' pub with old Indian carpets for tablecloths and every beer you could want, though the imported ones are expensive.

Zetor Kaivopiha, near the train station. A loud, country-themed bar designed by the people behind the Leningrad Cowboys rock group.

Nightlife and entertainment

Helsinki probably has a greater number of ways to spend the evening than any other Scandinavian city; there is, for example, a steady diet of **live music**. Finnish rock bands, not helped by the awkward metre of their native language, often sound absurd on first hearing, but at least seeing them is relatively cheap at €5–15 – around half the price of seeing a British or American band – and sometimes even free. The best gigs tend to be during term-time, but in summer there are dozens of free events in the city parks, the biggest of which take place almost every Sunday in Kaivopuisto. Many bands also play on selected nights in one of the growing number of surprisingly hip **clubs and discos**, in which you can gyrate, pose or just drink into the small hours – admission is usually around €5.

For up-to-the-minute details of **what's on**, read the entertainment page of *Helsingin Sanomat* or the free fortnightly paper *City* (found in record shops, bookshops and department stores), which has listings in English covering rock and classical music, clubs, cinema, theatre and opera. The Lasipalatsi (see p.699) has a youth service centre with information on festivals, concerts and events, or else simply watch out for posters on the streets. **Tickets** for most events can be bought at the venue or, for a small commission, at Tiketti, Yrjönkatu 29c (Mon–Fri 9am–5pm; ☎0600/11 616).

Clubs and music venues

Clubs in Helsinki change ownership, style and format with baffling rapidity and the listings below are only a pointer to what may be on offer. For up-to-the-moment information, check out the city's listings magazines.

Botta Museokatu 10. Joined to *St Urho's Pub* (see "Drinking", above). Vibrant dance music of various hues most nights.

Helmi Eerikinkatu 14. The only non-gay venue on this street – very crowded and loud, with a good bar selection.

Kaivohuone Kaivopuisto Park. One of the city's longest established late-night party spots; come here to dance, drink and join the very long taxi queues for home.

KY-Exit Pohjoinen Rautatiekatu 21. Sometimes has visiting foreign bands, more often lively disco nights for clubbers in their early twenties.

Manala Dagmarinkatu 2. Two floors and long queues for anything from ballroom dancing to grinding to MTV's latest offerings.

Soda Uudenmaankatu 16–20. One of the hippest places in town – at least for the time being. All varieties of dance music downstairs; standard bar with guest DJs upstairs.

Storyville Museokatu 8. Buzzing jazz joint, with live Dixieland, swing or bebop on stage every night. Open till the small hours.

Tavastia Urho Kekkosenkatu 4–6. A major showcase for Finnish and Swedish bands. Downstairs has the stage and self-service bar; the balcony is waitress service.

Vanha Maestro Fredrikinkatu 51–53. Legendary venue among the country's enthusiasts of *humpa* – a truly Finnish dance, distantly related to the waltz and tango. Afternoon and evening sessions most days (entry €2–5).

Vanha Ylioppilastalo Mannerheimintie 3. The main venue for leading indie bands from around the world; see also the *Vanhan* bars under "Drinking", p.710.

Gay Helsinki

Always the slowest of the Scandinavian countries to reform sexuality laws, Finland finally decriminalized homosexuality in 1971 and introduced partnership laws in 2001. In recent years, though, the **gay scene** in Helsinki has flourished and today there's an impressive number of exclusively gay and gay-friendly establishments within a couple of minutes' walk of each other around **Eerikinkatu** and the southern end of **Mannerheimintie**. For the latest details, pick up a copy of the monthly *Z* **magazine** – in Finnish only but with a useful listings section; it's widely available in larger newsagents, or from the state-supported gay organization SETA, Hietalahdenkatu 2B 16 (☎09/612 3233, ⊛www.seta.fi).

Con Hombres Eerikinkatu 14. The most popular gay bar in Helsinki and one of the oldest in the country. If it's quiet elsewhere, the chances are there'll be people here. Very cruisy at weekends.
DTM (Don't Tell Mamma) Annankatu 32 ⊛www.dtm.fi. The capital's legendary nightclub and *the* place to go, with occasional drag shows and house music most nights.
Hercules Lönnrotinkatu 4b. Not quite as trendy as *DTM*, but still attracting a mixed crowd, this club plays varied music including some of Finland's best home-grown offerings.

Lost and Found & Hideaway Annankatu 6. Two bars on two floors, with a small dance floor downstairs. Very popular at weekends with a mixed crowd.
Mann's Street Mannerheimintie 12 (upstairs). If you're looking for karaoke, Finnish music and older gay men, you'll find generous helpings here.
Room Erottajankatu. Next to *Lost and Found* and one of Helsinki's better neighbourhood bars; attracts the young and beautiful.

Cinema

Both the latest blockbusters and a good selection of fringe **films** are normally showing somewhere in Helsinki. A seat is usually €7.50–8.50, although some places offer a €6 matinee show. Check the listings in *City* (see p.711) or pick up a copy of *Elokuva-Viikko*, a free weekly leaflet that lists the cinemas and their programmes; it's available at the cinemas themselves. English-language films are shown with Finnish subtitles – there's no overdubbing. The cinema to head for is *Tennispalatsi* opposite the long distance bus station at Salomonkatu 15 – Finland's biggest with a dozen or so screens.

Listings

Airlines British Airways, Aleksanterinkatu 21a ☎09/650 677; Finnair, Töölönkatu 21 ☎09/818 800; SAS, Keskuskatu 7a ☎09/228 021.
Airport Enquiries ☎09/600 1800; Finnair terminal for airport buses ☎09/818 7750.
American Express Kanavaranta 9 (Mon–Fri 9am–4pm; ☎09/6132 0400).
Banks and exchange Outside banking hours at the airport 6.30am–11pm, and slightly more cheaply at Katajanokka harbour (where Viking and Finnjet dock) daily 9–11.30am & 3.45–6pm. Also Forex in the central train station (daily 8am–9pm), though it doesn't accept Visa; and Otto, opposite the station (Mon–Fri 8am–8pm, Sat 10am–6pm), which handles cash advances on all major cards.

Bus enquiries Long-distance buses ☎0200/4010; city buses ☎0100/111.
Car rental Avis, Pohjoinen Rautatiekatu ☎09/441 155; Budget, Malminkatu 24 ☎09/686 6500; Europcar, Mannerheimintie 50 ☎09/4780 2220.
Dentist Dentarium (24hr), 6th floor, 7A Mikonkatu ☎09/622 1533. Expect to pay €75 for a consultation.
Doctor ☎10023.
Embassies Canada, Pohjoisesplanadi 25B ☎09/171 141; UK, Itäinen Puistotie 17 ☎09/2286 5100; USA, Itäinen Puistotie 14A ☎09/171 931. Citizens of Australia and New Zealand should contact the Australian Embassy in Stockholm (see p.25).

Ferries from Helsinki to Estonia

Following Estonia's regaining of its independence, a growing number of passenger vessels are plying the 85-kilometre route across the Baltic between Helsinki and the Estonian capital, Tallinn. EU citizens no longer need a visa but other nationalities should check the latest situation at the tourist office in Helsinki.

Estonia and Finland have similar languages, a common ancestry, and histories which had largely run parallel up until the Soviet Union's annexation of Estonia in 1940. Despite the decades of Soviet occupation, **Tallinn**, within its medieval walls, is a beautifully maintained Hanseatic city with many museums and some fine old churches just a few minutes' walk from the harbour. If you have time, take a look, too, at the enormous Song Festival Grounds just outside the old centre, scene of the much-publicized pro-independence rallies of the late 1980s.

While independence has brought Estonians many new freedoms, it hasn't brought them any money. The introduction of the kroon (rhymes with "prawn", not "prune"), a new version of the pre-Soviet currency, did little to ease the uphill struggle faced by the country's economy – however, with the prospect of future EU membership, Estonia's fortunes look set to improve.

Crossings (1hr 40min–3hr) are offered by Tallink (tickets from South Harbour booking office; ☎09/228 311, ⊛www.tallink.fi); Linda Line, Makasiini Terminal (☎9/668 9700, ⊛www.lindaline.fi); Nordic Jet Line, Kanavaterminaali, Katajanokanlaituri (☎09/681 771 99, ⊛www.njl.fi) and Silja Line, Olympiaterminaali (☎09/180 4422, ⊛www.silja.fi). Expect to pay €40–65 for a one-way ticket; cars cost €70–100.

Emergencies Ambulance ☎112; Police ☎10022.
Ferries Reservations and information: Silja Line ☎09/18 041, ⊛www.silja.fi; Tallink ☎09/228 211, ⊛www.tallink.fi; Viking Line ☎09/123 577, ⊛www.vikingline.fi.
Hospital Marian Hospital, Lapinlahdenkatu 16 ☎4711.
Internet cafés *Café Aalto*, 2nd floor Akateeminen kirjapauppa, Keskuskatu 1; *Wave Bar*, Vuorikatu 16; *Netcup*, Aleksanterinkatu 52; *mbar* in the Lasipalatsi, Mannerheimintie 22–24. Reckon on €2–4 per hour.
Late shopping The shops in Tunneli, the underground complex by the train station, are open Mon–Sat 10am–10pm, Sun noon–10pm.
Laundry Punavuorenkatu 3.
Left luggage There are lockers (around €2) in the long-distance bus station (Mon–Thurs & Sat 9am–6pm, Fri 8am–6pm), or in the train station (Mon–Fri 7am–10pm).
Libraries (*kirjasto*) Central branches at Topeliuksenkatu 6 in Töölö, at Rikhardinkatu 3 near Esplanadi, and at Viides linja 11, close to Kallio kirkko (all Mon–Fri 9.30am–8pm, Sat 9.30am–3pm).
Lost property (*löytötavaratoimisto*) 3rd floor,

Päijänteentie 12A (Mon–Fri 8am–4.15pm and Wed until 5.30pm; ☎09/189 3180).
Newspapers Almost every central Helsinki newsstand stocks some UK or US papers. Try at the train station, the airport, or inside Stockmann Department Store.
Pharmacy Yliopiston Apteeki, Mannerheimintie 96 (☎09/4178 0300), is open 24hr; its branch at Mannerheimintie 5 is open daily 7am–midnight.
Police Pieni Roobertinkatu 1–3 ☎1891.
Post office The main office is at Mannerheiminaukio 1A (Mon–Fri 9am–6pm); poste restante at the rear door (Mon–Fri 9am–9pm, Sat & Sun 10am–6pm). Stamps are available from post offices or the yellow machines in shops.
Train enquiries ☎0307 10.
Travel agents Kilroy Travels, Kaivokatu 10D (☎09/680 7811), is the Scandinavian youth travel agent, specializing in discounted tickets for students and young people. Suomen Matkatoimisto (SMT), the Finland Travel Bureau, Kaivokatu 10A (☎09/18 261), organizes trips to Russia and the necessary visas.
What's on Listings in *Helsinki This Week* (monthly), and *City*, from the City Tourist Office, hotels and hostels.

Around Helsinki

To be honest, there's little in Helsinki's outlying area that's worth venturing out for. But three places, all an easy day-trip from the city, merit a visit: the visionary suburbs of **Espoo**; the home of the composer Sibelius at **Järvenpää**; and the evocative old town of **Porvoo**, which also serves as an obvious access point to the underrated southeastern corner of the country.

The Espoo area

Lying west of Helsinki, the suburban area of **Espoo** (Esbo in Swedish) comprises several separate districts. The one nearest to Helsinki, directly across the bay, is the "garden city" of TAPIOLA. In the 1950s Finnish urban planners attempted to blend new housing schemes with the surrounding forests and hills, frequently only to be left with a compromise that turned ugly as expansion occurred. Tapiola was the exception to this rule, built as a self-contained living area rather than a dormitory town, with alternating high and low buildings, abundant open areas, parks, fountains and swimming pools. Much praised on its completion by the architectural world, it's still refreshing to wander through and admire the idea and its execution. The **tourist office** at Pohjantie 3 (☎09/8164 7230, ⊛www.espoo.fi) handles enquiries about the whole Espoo area.

About 3km north of Tapiola, past the traffic-bearing Hagalundintie, brings you to the little peninsula of **Otaniemi** and a couple more notable architectural sites. One of these is the Alvar Aalto-designed campus of Helsinki University's technology faculty; the other – far more dramatic – is the Dipoli student union building on the same campus. Ever keen to harmonize the artificial with the natural, architects Reimi and Raili Pietilä here created a building which seems fused with the rocky crags above, the front of the structure daringly edging forward from the cliff face.

Though the town of Espoo itself has little to delay you, just beyond lies the hugely absorbing **Hvitträsk** (daily: June–Aug 10am–6pm; rest of the year 11am–6pm; €4), the studio-home built and shared by Eliel Saarinen, Armas Lindgren and Herman Gesellius until 1904, when their partnership dissolved amid the acrimony caused by Saarinen's independent (and winning) design for Helsinki's train station. Externally, this is an extended and romanticized version of the traditional Finnish log cabin, the leafy branches that creep around making the structure look like a mutant growth emerging from the forest. Inside are frescoes by Gallen-Kallela and changing exhibitions of Finnish art and handicrafts. Eliel Saarinen and his wife are buried in the grounds.

Buses run throughout the day from Helsinki **to Tapiola**, but you usually need to request them to stop there; check details and times at the bus station or the City Tourist Office. To get from central Helsinki **to Hvitträsk**, take the local (line L) train to Louma (10 daily; 37min) and follow the signs for 3km, or take bus #166 from Helsinki (3 daily; 55min).

Järvenpää: Ainola

Around 40km north of Helsinki in **JÄRVENPÄÄ**, easily reached by either bus or train, is **Ainola** (May–Sept Tues–Sun 10am–5pm; €5) – the house where Jean Sibelius lived from 1904 with his wife, Aino (sister of the artist Eero Järnefelt), after whom the place is named.

Though now regarded as one of the twentieth century's greatest composers, **Jean Sibelius**, born in Hämeenlinna in 1865, had no musical background, and by the age of nineteen was enrolled on a law course at Helsinki University. He had, however, developed a youthful passion for the violin and took a class at the capital's Institute of Music. Law was soon forgotten as Sibelius's real talents were recognized, and his musical studies took him to the cultural hotbeds of the day, Berlin and Vienna. Returning to Finland to teach at the Institute, Sibelius soon gained a government grant, which enabled him to begin composing full time, the first concert of his works taking place in 1892. His early pieces were inspired by the Finnish folk epic, the *Kalevala*, and by the nationalist movement of the times; in 1899 the country's Russian rulers banned performances of Sibelius's rousing *Finlandia* under any name that suggested its patriotic sentiment – it was instead published simply as "Opus 26 No. 7".

While the overtly nationalistic elements in Sibelius's work mellowed in later years, his music continued to reflect a very Finnish obsession with nature: "Other composers offer their public a cocktail," he said, "I offer mine pure spring water". He is still revered in his own land, although he was also notorious for his bouts of heavy drinking, and a destructive quest for perfection which fuelled suspicion that he had completed, and destroyed, two symphonies during his final thirty years. This was an angst-ridden period when no new work appeared, which became known as "the silence from Järvenpää". Sibelius died in 1957, his best-known symphonies setting a standard younger Finnish composers have yet to live up to.

The house is just the kind of home you'd expect for a man who included representations of flapping swans' wings in his music: a tranquil place, close to lakes and forests. The wood-filled grounds are as atmospheric as the building, which is a place of pilgrimage for devotees, although books, furnishings and a few paintings are all there is to see. His grave is in the grounds, marked by a marble stone inscribed simply with his name. For more tangible Sibelius memories, and more of his music, visit the Sibelius Museum in Turku (see p.722).

While in Järvenpää, it would be a pity to miss out on a visit to the **Halosenniemi Museum** (Tues–Sun: May–Aug 11am–7pm; Sept–April 11am–5pm; €5). On the Tuusula Lakeside road, just a few minutes' walk from Ainola, this is the rustic home of Pekka Halonen, one of Finland's most renowned artists. A beautifully serene place, its National Romantic decor has been painstakingly restored and now houses some of Halonen's pictures and painting materials in their original setting.

Porvoo

One of the oldest towns on the south coast, **PORVOO** (Borgå in Swedish), 50km northeast of Helsinki, with its narrow cobbled streets lined by small wooden buildings, gives a sense of the Finnish life that predated the capital's bold squares and Neoclassical geometry. This, coupled with its elegant riverside setting and unhurried mood, means you're unlikely to be alone. Word of Porvoo's peaceful time-locked qualities has spread.

First stop should be the newly built **tourist office** at Rihkamakatu 4 (July & Aug Mon–Fri 10am–6pm, Sat & Sun 10am–4pm; Sept–June Mon–Fri 10am–4.30pm, Sat 10am–2pm; ☎019/520 2316, ⊛www.porvoo.fi), for a free map of the town. For something more historic, look in at the preserved **Johan Ludwig Runeberg House**, at Aleksanterinkatu 3 (May–Aug Mon–Sat 10am–4pm, Sun 11am–5pm; Sept–April Wed–Sat 10am–4pm, Sun 11am–5pm; €4), where the man regarded as Finland's national poet lived from 1852 while a teacher at the town school. Despite writing in Swedish, Runeberg greatly aided the nation's sense of self-esteem, especially with *Tales of Vänrikki Ståhl*, which told of the people's struggles with Russia in the 1808–09 conflict. The first poem in his collection *Our Land* later provided the lyrics for the national anthem. Across the road, the **Walter Runeberg Gallery** (due to reopen in 2004 with same times as above; €4) displays a collection of works by Runeberg's third son, one of Finland's more celebrated sculptors. Among many acclaimed pieces, he's responsible for the statue of his father that stands in the centre of Helsinki's Esplanadi.

The old town (follow the signs for "Vanha Porvoo") is built around the hill on the other side of Mannerheimkatu. Near the top, its outline partially obscured by vegetation, is the fifteenth-century **Tuomiokirkko** (May–Sept Mon–Fri 10am–6pm, Sat 10am–2pm, Sun 2–5pm; Oct–April Tues–Sat 10am–2pm, Sun 2–4pm). It was here in 1809 that Alexander I proclaimed Finland a Russian Grand Duchy, himself Grand Duke, and convened the first Finnish Diet. This, and other aspects of the town's past, can be explored in the **Porvoo Museum** (May–Aug daily 10am–4pm; Sept–April Wed–Sun noon–4pm; €5) at the foot of the hill in the old town's main square. There are no singularly outstanding exhibits here, just a diverting selection of furnishings, musical instruments and general oddities, largely dating from the years of Russian rule.

Practicalities

Buses run all day from Helsinki to Porvoo from the long-distance bus station; a one-way trip costs around €7. Idling around the town is especially pleasant late in the day as the evening stillness descends; the last bus back to the city conveniently departs around midnight. There are also a couple of **boats** from Helsinki in summer: the *J.L. Runeberg* (May–June & Aug Wed, Sat & Sun; July daily; €29 day-trip) departs at 10am, arrives at 1.20pm, and returns to Helsinki at 4pm; and the quicker *M.S. King* (late June to mid-Aug daily 10.20am; €20 single), which arrives at 1.20pm and leaves Porvoo at 3.30pm. Tickets for both boats can be bought from their respective ticket offices in the kauppatori in Helsinki.

If you've exhausted Helsinki, **spending a night** in Porvoo leaves you well placed to continue into Finland's southeastern corner. If possible, try to arrange accommodation while in Helsinki, particularly if you're after hotel bargains – rates in Porvoo are steep. There is, however, a **youth hostel**, open all year, at Linnankoskenkatu 1 (☎019/523 0012, ⊛www.porvoohostel.cjb.net), and a **campsite** (☎019/581 967; June–Aug) 2km from the town centre.

The Southeast

As it's some way from the major centres, foreign tourists tend to neglect the extreme **southeastern corner** of Finland; Finns, however, rate it highly, flocking here to make boat trips around the islands and to explore the many small communities, which combine a genuine rustic flavour with sufficient places of minor interest to keep boredom at bay. For Finns, the region also stirs memories: its position on the Soviet border means it saw many battles during the Winter and Continuation wars, and throughout medieval times it was variously under the control of Sweden and Russia. It's an intriguing area, worth two or three days of travel – most of it will be by bus, since rail lines are almost nonexistent.

East to Kotka

If Porvoo seems too tourist-infested, make the 40km journey east to **LOVIISA**, an eighteenth-century fishing village pleasantly free from Helsinki day-trippers. The village, whose 8000-strong population divides into equal numbers of Finnish- and Swedish-speakers, is overlooked by the two old **fortresses** of Rosen and Ungern, both worth exploring. The **tourist office** (Mon–Fri 8.30am–4pm; ☎019/555 234, ⊛www.loviisa.fi), at Tullisilta 5, can supply details of how to get to them; off the square, a row of prettily preserved houses points the way to the **Municipal Museum** (June–Aug Tues–Sun 11am–4pm; Sept–May Sun noon–4pm; €2), containing, besides the usual local hotchpotch of bits and pieces, a fine stock of romantic postcards. Later on, if you have the cash, spend it on a slap-up meal at *Degerby Gille*, Sepänkuja 4, a restaurant set in a seventeenth-century house that's one of the town's most important historical sights; if you don't, poke your head around the door anyway to marvel at the wonderfully maintained interior.

In the bay off Loviisa there's a less welcome modern sight – one of the country's two **nuclear power stations**. Finland's Cold War balancing act between East and West led to the country buying its nuclear hardware from both power blocs; this one has spent the past thirty years producing plutonium for (allegedly) Soviet nuclear weapons. The other, Western-backed, at Olkiluoti (near Rauma), is newer and still the subject of much argument. The Finnish public is divided over the merits of nuclear power in general: the country takes about forty percent of its energy from nuclear sources, but the growing anti-nuclear movement is calling for a switch to hydroelectric power. Whatever the outcome of the debate, mindful of the design flaws in Soviet-built reactors, the view is an unnerving one.

If you have the time, a couple of smaller settlements between Loviisa and Kotka can comfortably consume half a day. In 1809 the Swedish–Russian border was drawn up in this area, splitting the region of Pyhtää in two. Some 20km from Loviissa is **RUOTSINPYHTÄÄ (Strömfors** in Swedish), whose local **tourist office** (June–Aug daily 10am–6pm; Sept–May Mon–Fri 8am–4pm; ☎019/618 474, ⓕ618 475) is diplomatically positioned on the bridge over the inlet that once divided the two feuding empires. Historical quirks aside, the main attraction here is the seventeenth-century **ironworks**, now turned into craft studios, with demonstrations of carpet-weaving, jewellery-making and painting – all quite enjoyable to stroll around on a sunny day. You should also visit the oddly octagonal-shaped **wooden church** (June–Sept Mon–Fri 10am–6pm, Sat & Sun 8am–4pm; Oct–May, book with tourist office) to admire Helene Schjerfbeck's beautiful altarpiece. It was here, incidentally, that a Finnish TV company filmed a very popular soap opera, *Vihreän Kullanmaa* ("The Land of the Green Gold"), making good use of the contrast between the spacious mill-owners' houses and the cramped workers' cottages.

The village of **PYHTÄÄ** is a twenty-minute bus ride further east. There's a **stone church** here (June–Sept daily noon–3pm; Oct–May Sun noon–3pm); dated at around 1300, it's one of the oldest in the country. The interior frescoes are primitive and strangely moving, and were discovered only recently when the Reformation-era whitewash was removed. From the quay on the other side of the village's sole street there's a ferry service to the nearby islands, including Kaunissaari ("Beautiful Island"), where you can connect with an evening motorboat straight on to Kotka (see below).

The land route to Kotka takes you through **SILTAKYLÄ**, a small town significant only for the hills around it and its **tourist information** counter (Mon–Fri 8am–3.45pm; ☎05/758 3202) at the town hall, beside the main road, which has information on walks in the district. The hills afford great views over a dramatic legacy of the Ice Age: spooky Tolkienesque forests and many miles of a red-granite stone known as *rapakivi* that's unique to southeast Finland, covered by a white moss. A number of waymarked hiking trails lead through the landscape, strewn with giant boulders, some as big as four-storey buildings and supporting their own little ecosystem of plant and tree life. After a day's trek, you can reward yourself with food and drink – or even a swim – at the not too pricey *Pyhtään Motelli* (☎05/343 1661), which despite its name is situated on the edge of Siltakylä.

Kotka to the Russian border

After the scattering of little communities east of Porvoo, **KOTKA**, a few kilometres on from Siltakylä, seems immense. Built on an island in the Gulf of Finland, Kotka's past reflects its proximity to the sea. Numerous battles have been fought off its shores, among them the Sweden–Russia confrontation of 1790, the largest battle ever seen in Nordic waters: almost 10,000 people lost their lives. Sixty-odd years later, the British fleet reduced Kotka virtually to rubble during the Crimean War. In modern times the sea has been the basis of the town's prosperity: sitting at the end of the Kymi river and boasting a deep-water harbour, the town makes a perfect cargo transit point – causing most locals to live in fear of a major accident occurring in the industrial section, or in the freight yards. Only two roads link Kotka to the mainland and a speedy evacuation of its inhabitants would be almost impossible.

The town itself has little to delay you; it's more a place to eat and sleep than anything else. Only the eighteenth-century Orthodox **St Nicolai kirkko** (June–Aug Tues–Fri noon–3pm, Sat & Sun noon–6pm) survived the British bombardment,

Overland from Helsinki

Two trains – one Finnish and one Russian – leave Helsinki every morning (Finnish train; 7am) and afternoon (Russian train; 3.30pm) for the six-hour trip to St Petersburg; there's also an overnight Russian train to Moscow which departs Helsinki around 5.30pm. All border formalities are carried out on the train, but you must have a Russian visa before you leave – the tourist office has a list of travel agencies that can arrange these, though be warned that they take a week to process. A one-way second-class ticket to St Petersburg on both the Finnish and Russian trains costs €49.10 including seat reservation; a sleeping compartment to Moscow costs €83.

Day cruises

If sailing to St Petersburg for a short visit sounds more attractive, you could book a place on one of the seven cruises operated each year by Kristina Cruises: there's one in late May, one in June, two in July and three in August. All leave Helsinki's Makasiiniterminaali, off Laivasillankatu, at 5.30pm, arrive in St Petersburg at 8.30am the following morning and return at 10.30pm the next day, arriving Helsinki 11.20am; all-inclusive packages with cabin start at €250. You don't strictly need a visa for one of these excursions, although if you want to come and go as you please once the boat docks in Russia, you'll need to get one a week in advance from the tour operator. If you don't have a visa, you'll have to either see the city with a guided tour or pay €10 for a transfer ticket. Irregular visa-free overnight cruises also leave from Kotka and Lappeenranta for the Russian city of Vyborg, allowing three hours ashore before returning to Finland. For more information, contact Kristina Cruises, Kirkkokatu 16, Kotka (℡05/21 144, ⍟www.kristinacruises.com).

and even that is not particularly interesting, although it's worth visiting the **Langinkoski Imperial Fishing Lodge** (May–Aug daily 10am–7pm; Sept & Oct Sat & Sun 10am–7pm; €4), off the main island, about 5km north of the town centre (take bus #12). It was here that Tsar Alexander III would relax in transit between Helsinki and St Petersburg; the wooden building, a gift to him from the Finnish government, is most striking for its simplicity and the attractive setting in the woods near the fast-flowing Kymi river.

Practicalities

Rail and road connections bring you right into the compact centre, where the **tourist office** at Kirkkokatu 3 (June to mid-Aug daily 9am–7pm; rest of the year Mon–Fri 9am–5pm; ℡05/234 4424, ⍟www.kotka.fi) will fill you in on local bus details – essential for continuing around the southeast.

Grumbling stomachs can be quietened in *Canttiini*, Kaivokatu 15, an excellent TexMex **restaurant** that also serves up Finnish dishes, pastas and steaks. Alternatively, try *Fenix*, Kapteeninkatu 14, which has a very similar menu and equally reasonable prices. Although Kotka is no longer popular with Eastern European sailors due to shorter onshore times, there is still a lively bar scene – the best pub in town is *Jack Up* at Kirkkokatu 10, although the Irish bar *Karoliina*, at Puutarhakatu 1, puts up strong competition. A good-value **hotel** is the pleasant *Merikotka*, Satamakatu 9 (℡05/215 222, ⨎215 414; ❸), or there's the more upmarket *Seurahuone*, Keskuskatu 21 (℡05/35 035, ⍟www.sokoshotels.fi; ❺/❹). The nearest guesthouse, *Kärkisaari*, is 6km north of Kotka in Mussalo (bus #13 and #27), overlooking a spectacular bay (℡05/260 4804, ⨎260 4805; mid-May to mid-Sept; ❷). There's also a holiday village in Mussalo (℡05/260 5055 or 0400/415 815; May–Sept) which has cabins for four people from €49 per night depending on the season.

Hamina and east to the Russian border

Twenty-six kilometres east of Kotka is **HAMINA**, founded in 1653 and sporting a magnificently bizarre town plan, the main streets forming concentric circles around the centre. It was built this way to allow the incumbent Swedish forces to withstand attack – the town being the site of many Swedish–Russian battles. Besides the layout, however, there's not an awful lot to amuse, although you can pick up suggestions and local information from the **tourist office** at Puistokatu 2B (Mon–Fri 9am–4pm; ℡05/749 5251, ⊛www.hamina.fi).

The tourist office can also give you the latest schedule of the bus that runs to Virolahti, 31km east, and within a few kilometres of the **Salpalinjan Bunkkerit**, or Salpa Line Bunkers – massive hunks of granite stretching from here to Lapland, which acted as fortifications and were intended to protect Finland from Soviet attack during the run-up to the Winter War of 1939. These days Finnish war veterans are eager to show off the bunker's details and lead visitors to the seats (and controls) of ageing anti-tank guns. Buses from Helsinki to Viipuri, the formerly Finnish town now on the Russian side of the border (see p.744), pass through Hamina; again, details are best checked at the tourist office.

The Southwest

The area between Helsinki and Finland's **southwestern** extremity is probably the blandest section of the whole country. By road or rail the view is much the same, endless forests interrupted only by modest-sized patches of water and virtually identical villages and small towns. Once at the southwestern corner, however, things change considerably, with islands and inlets around a jagged shoreline, and the distinctive Finnish-Swedish coastal communities.

Turku

There is very little in Åbo which has entertained me in the survey, or can amuse you by the description. It is a wretched capital of a barbarous province. The houses are almost all of wood; and the archiepiscopal palace, which has not even a single storey, but may be called a sort of barrack, is composed of no better materials, except that it is painted red. I inquired if there was not any object in the university, meriting attention; but they assured me that it would be regarded as a piece of ridicule, to visit it on such an errand, there being nothing within its walls except a very small library, and a few philosophical instruments.

A Tour Round The Baltic, Sir N.W. Wraxall, 1775.

TURKU (or **Åbo** as it's known in Swedish) was the principal town in Finland when the country was a province of Sweden, losing its status in 1812, along with most of its buildings in a ferocious fire soon after – occurrences that clearly improved the place, if the above quotation is to be believed. These days Turku is small and highly sociable – thanks to the boom years under Swedish rule and the number of students from its two universities – bristling with history and culture, and with a sparkling nightlife to boot.

Arrival and information

The River Aura splits the city, its tree-lined banks forming a natural promenade as well as a useful landmark. The cathedral and castle stand at opposite ends of the river, while the main museums are found along its edge. There are gleaming department stores, banks and offices on the northern side of the river in Turku's central grid, where you'll also find the **tourist office** at Aurakatu 4 (Mon–Fri

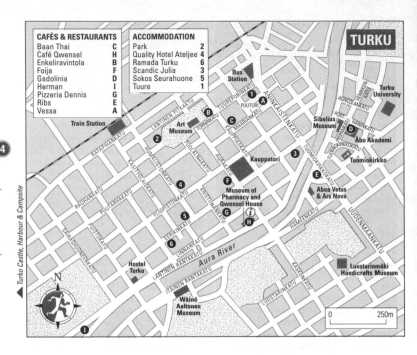

CAFÉS & RESTAURANTS		ACCOMMODATION	
Baan Thai	C	Park	2
Café Qwensel	H	Quality Hotel Ateljee	4
Enkeliravintola	B	Ramada Turku	6
Foija	F	Scandic Julia	3
Gadolinia	D	Sokos Seurahuone	5
Herman	I	Tuure	1
Pizzeria Dennis	G		
Ribs	E		
Vessa	A		

TURKU

8.30am–6pm, Sat & Sun 9am–4pm; ☎02/262 7444, ☏262 7674, ⓦwww.turkutouring.fi). Outside banking hours you can **change money** at Forex, Eerikinkatu 12 (Mon–Sat 8am–7pm, Sun 10am–4pm). Both the **train station** and **bus station** are within easy walking distance of the river, just north of the centre.

Accommodation

Finding **accommodation** in Turku is rarely a problem – even in the height of summer. The town has a fair array of comfortable – if expensive – hotels, the pick of which we've listed below. However, if you're on a tighter budget, the excellent official **youth hostel**, *Hostel Turku* (☎02/262 7680, ☏262 7675), open all year and beautifully situated by the river in the city centre at Linnankatu 39, is a sound choice. To get here take bus #30 from the train station or #1 from the airport and bus station. Alternatively, there's a decent **bed and breakfast**, *Tuure*, near the bus and train stations at Tuureporinkatu 17C (☎02/233 0230; ②). The nearest **campsite** (☎050/559 0139) is on the small island of Ruissalo, overlooking Turku harbour. It's open from June to mid-August and takes about fifteen minutes to reach on bus #8. Ruissalo is a good place to visit anyway, for its two sandy beaches, a botanical garden sporting a host of rare and spectacular plants, and fine views to the archipelago.

Scandic Julia Eerikinkatu 4 ☎02/336 311, ⓦwww.scandic-hotels.com. Smart, elegant and full of Scandinavian design features such as tasteful glassware and lighting. Summer and weekend bargains make this a good choice out of season. ⑤/❸

Ramada Turku Eerikinkatu 28 ☎02/338 211, ⓦwww.restel.fi. Chain hotel which does its best to shake off the *Ramada* feel, but doesn't quite

succeed. Comfortable rooms and an excellent buffet breakfast though overall nothing special. ⑤/❹

Sokos Seurahuone Eerikinkatu 23 ☎02/337 301, ⓦwww.sokoshotels.fi. Suffering from a bad case of chain-hotel anonymity, this place has all you'd expect from a top-notch hotel but lacks individuality. Rooms though are spacious and well-equipped. ⑤/❹

Park Rauhankatu 1 ☏02/273 2555, ⓦwww.parkhotelturku.fi. A five-minute walk from the train station, this hotel was built in 1902 and oozes turn-of-the-century Art Nouveau charm. It's the hotel of choice in Turku though the stylish rooms are not cheap. ⑥/⑤

Quality Ateljee Humalistonkatu 7 ☏02/336 111, ⓦwww.choicehotels.fi. Housed in a rather drab building designed by Alvar Aalto, the themed rooms copy the style of Finnish designers – including a nice Aalto-style room among them. ⑤/④

The City

Arriving in Turku by train, you'll quickly make the pleasing discovery that the town's major places of interest unintentionally arrange themselves into a very logical pattern. By beginning at the Art Museum, a few strides from the station, and from there moving south through the town centre and heading westwards along the river's edge, you'll be able to take in everything worth seeing in a day – although allowing two days might be more sensible if you want to have energy left for the Turku nightlife. During the 1970s and 80s parts of Turku were subjected to some thoughtless redevelopment, resulting in a number of really hideous buildings, and a new national byword, the "Turku Disease". However, streets of intricately carved wooden houses still survive around the Port Arthur area, a lovely part of town for simply strolling around.

The Art Museum

Though it's not much of a taster for the actual city, **Turku Art Museum** (Tues–Thurs 11am–6pm, Fri–Sun 10am–4pm; ⓦwww.turuntaidemuseo.fi; €5.50; or €7 for special exhibitions), housed in a purpose-built Art Nouveau granite structure close to the train station, is one of the better collections of Finnish art, with works by all the great names of the country's Golden Age – Gallen-Kallela, Edelfelt, Pekka Halonen, Simberg and others – plus a commendable stock of moderns. Not least among these are the wood sculptures of Kain Tapper and Mauno Hartman, which stirred up heated debate on the merits of carefully shaped bits of wood being presented as art when they were first shown during the 1970s.

The Cathedral and around

To get to grips with Turku itself, and its pivotal place in Finnish history, cut through the centre to the river, and the tree-framed space that, before the great fire of 1879, was the bustling heart of the community, and which is still overlooked by the **Tuomiokirkko** (daily: mid-April to mid-Sept 9am–8pm; rest of the year until 7pm). The cathedral, erected in the thirteenth century on the "Knoll of Sheep", a pre-Christian place of worship, was at the centre of the Christianization process inflicted by the crusading Swedes on the pagan Finns, and grew larger over the centuries as the new religion became stronger and Swedish involvement in Finland escalated. The building, still the centre of the Finnish Church, has been repeatedly ravaged by fire, although the thickness of the walls enabled many of its medieval features to survive. Of these, it's the tombs that catch the eye: Torsten Stålhandske, commander of the Finnish cavalry during the seventeenth-century Thirty Years' War, in which Sweden sought to protect its domination of the Baltic and the Finns confirmed their reputation as wild and fearless fighters, lies in a deliriously ornate coffin (to the right as you enter) opposite Samuel Cockburn and Patrick Ogilvie, a couple of Scots who fought alongside him. On the left-hand side, Catharine Månsdotter, the commoner wife of the Swedish king Erik XIV, with whom, in the mid-sixteenth century, she was imprisoned in Turku Castle, is as popular in death as she reputedly was in life, judging by the numbers who file past her simple black-marble sarcophagus. The window behind it carries her stained-glass image – and if you crane your neck to the left, you can see a wall plaque bearing the only known true likeness of her. You can also visit the **cathedral museum** upstairs (same times as cathedral; €2), which gives a stronger insight into the cathedral's past. There's an assortment of ancient jugs, goblets, plates and spoons, though more absorbing are the collections of church textiles.

Immediately outside the cathedral is a statue to **Per Brahe**, governor-general of Finland from 1637 and the first Swedish officer to devote much attention to the welfare of the Finns, encouraging a literacy programme and founding the country's first university. The site of this is within the nearby yellow Empire-style buildings, although the actual seat of learning was moved to Helsinki during the era of Russian rule. Next to these are the oldest portions of the **Åbo Akademi** – Finland's only remaining Swedish-language university – while the modern, Finnish-language **Turku University** is at the other end of Henrikinkatu: these days both are more notable as places for eating rather than sightseeing.

Turku's newest and most splendid museum is the combined **Aboa Vetus** and **Ars Nova** (May to mid-Sept daily 11am–7pm; rest of the year closed Mon; ⊛www.aboavetusarsnova.fi; €7 for either museum) on the bank of the Aurajoki river just a few steps from the university. Translating as "Old Turku, New Art", the place was intended to be simply a modern art gallery, but when the building's foundations were dug a warren of medieval lanes and cellars came to light, an unmissable opportunity to present the history and archeology of the city. Glass flooring allows a near-perfect view of the remains. The New Art part comprises a striking collection of 350 works, alongside frequent temporary exhibitions. There's a great café, too: prepare yourself here by browsing through the museum's English-language brochure, since the guided tours are in Finnish only.

Back past the cathedral and across Piispankatu is the sleek low form of the **Sibelius Museum** (Tues–Sun 11am–4pm, Wed also 6–8pm; ⊛www.sibeliusmuseum .com; €3). Although Sibelius had no direct connection with Turku, this museum is a fitting tribute to him and his contribution to the emergence of an independent Finland. Chances are that the recorded strains of *Finlandia* will greet you as you enter: when not the venue for live concerts (which usually take place during the winter), the small but acoustically perfect concert area pumps out recorded requests from the great man's oeuvre; take your place beside dewy-eyed Finns for a lunch hour of Scandinavia's finest composer. Elsewhere, the Sibelius collection gathers family photo albums and original manuscripts along with the great man's hat, walking stick and even a final half-smoked cigar. Other exhibits cover the musical history of the country, from intricate musical boxes and the frail wooden *kantele* – the instrument strummed by peasants in the *Kalevala* – to the weighty keyboard instruments downstairs.

The Luostarinmäki, Aaltonen and pharmacy museums

On the other side of the cathedral from the Sibelius museum, you'll see a small hill topped by the wooden dome of the **Observatory**, designed – rather poorly – by Carl Engel, who had arrived in Turku seeking work in the days before his great plan for Helsinki made him famous. Originally the building was intended to serve the first Turku University as an observatory, but disputes between Engel and his assistants and a misunderstanding of scientific requirements rendered the place useless for its intended purpose. To make things worse, the university moved to Helsinki, and the building was then turned into a navigational school. From the observatory, head directly down the side of the hill to the far more engrossing **Luostarinmäki Handicrafts Museum** on Luostarinkatu (mid-April to Sept daily 10am–6pm; Oct to mid-April Tues–Sun 10am–3pm; ⊛www.turku.fi/ museo/english/handcraf.htm; €3.40), one of the best – and certainly the most authentic – open-air museums in Finland. Following a severe fire in 1775, rigorous restrictions were imposed on the town's new buildings, but due to a legal technicality they didn't apply in this district. The wooden houses here were built by local working people in traditional style and evolved naturally into a museum as descendants of the original owners died and bequeathed their inherited homes to the municipality. The unpaved streets run between tiny wooden houses, which once had goats tethered to their chimneys to keep the turfed roofs cropped. The chief inhabitants now are the museum volunteers who dress up in period attire and demonstrate the old handicrafts.

A short walk from the handicrafts museum, on the southern bank of the river, is another worthwhile indoor collection: the **Wäinö Aaltonen Museum** (daily 11am–7pm, closed Mon in winter; ⊛www.wam.fi; entry fee varies according to exhibition). Unquestionably the best-known modern Finnish sculptor, Wäinö Aaltonen was born in 1894, grew up close to Turku and studied for a time at the local art school. His first public show, in 1916, marked a turning point in the development of Finnish sculpture, introducing a freer, more individual style to a genre struggling to break from the restraints of the Neoclassical tradition and French realism. Aaltonen went on to dominate his field totally throughout the 1920s and 30s and his influence is still felt today; the man's work turns up in every major town throughout the country, and even the parliament building in Helsinki was designed with special niches to hold some of his pieces. Much of his output celebrates the individuals who contributed to the growth of the Finnish republic, typically remembering them with enormous heads, or as immense statues that resemble massive social-realist chunks. But Aaltonen, who died in 1966, really was an original, imaginative and sensitive sculptor, as the exhibits here demonstrate. There's also a roomful of his paintings, some of which show perhaps why he concentrated on sculpture.

Across the river from the Aaltonen museum, there's a sign in the grass which spells out TURKU:ÅBO; immediately behind this is a wooden staircase running up to the front door of the **Museum of Pharmacy and Qwensel House** (mid-April to mid-Sept daily 10am–6pm; mid-Sept to mid-April Tues–Sun 10am–3pm; ⊛www.turku.fi/museo/english/pharmacy.htm; €3.40). Qwensel was a court judge who moved to the house in 1694, and it later became the home of Professor Josef Gustaf Pipping – the "father of Finnish medicine" – in 1785. Period furnishings remain, proving just how wealthy and stylish the life of the eighteenth-century bourgeoisie actually was. Many chemists' implements from around the country are on show, among them some memorable devices for drawing blood.

Turku Castle

The town's museums, and its cathedral and universities, are all symbols of Turku's elevated position in Finnish life, though by far the major marker to its many years of importance stands at the western end of Linnankatu. Follow the signs for "Turun Linna", or take bus #1 from the harbour, and you'll eventually see, oddly set among the present-day ferry terminals, the relatively featureless and unappetizing exterior of **Turku Castle** (mid-April to mid-Sept daily 10am–6pm; mid-Sept to mid-April Tues–Sun 10am–3pm; ⊛www.turku.fi/museo/english/castle.htm; €5). Fight any dismay though, since the compact cobbled courtyards, maze-like corridors and darkened staircases of the interior provide a good place to wander – and to dwell on the fact that this was the seat of the government of the country for centuries, as well as that much of Finland's (and a significant portion of Sweden's) medieval history took shape within these walls. Unless you're an expert on the period, you'll get a migraine trying to figure out the importance of everything that's here, and it's a sensible idea to buy one of the guide leaflets on sale at the entrance.

The castle probably went up sometime around 1280, when the first bishop arrived from Sweden; gradual expansion through the following years accounts for the patchwork effect of its architecture – and the bewildering array of finds, rooms and displays. The majority of the fortification took place during the turbulent sixteenth century, instigated by Swedish ruler Gustavus Vasa for the protection of his son, whom he made Duke Johan, the first Duke of Finland. Johan pursued a lavish court life but exceeded his powers in attacking Livonia and was sentenced to death by the Stockholm Diet. Swedish efforts to seize Johan were successful only after a three-week siege, and he was removed to Stockholm. The subsequent decision by the unbalanced Erik XIV to release Johan resulted not only in Johan becoming king himself, but also in poor Erik being imprisoned here – albeit with a full quota of servants and the best food and wine. The bare cell he occupied for a few weeks contrasts strongly with the splendour from Johan's time, offering a cool reminder of shifting fortunes. There's a gloomy nineteenth-century painting here, by Erik Johan Löfgren, of Erik with his head on the lap of his queen (Catharine Månsdotter), while the lady's eyes look askance to heaven.

Eating, drinking and entertainment

You'd need to be very fussy not to find somewhere to **eat** in Turku that's to your liking. Walking around checking the lunchtime offers can turn up many bargains, plus there's the usual selection of economical pizzerias. Floating restaurants are popular among tourists, if not with too many locals, and the boats change each summer, though the names *Papa Joe*, *Svarte Rudolf* and *Lulu* reappear year after year: all have decent enough restaurants, and often put on live music.

Cafés and restaurants

Baan Thai Kauppiaskatu 15. Right in the heart of town, and offering an excellent range of tasty Thai dishes from €7.60. Always popular.

Café Qwensel Auransilta. In a courtyard behind the Museum of Pharmacy, offering fabulous cakes in atmospheric eighteenth-century surroundings.

Enkeliravintola Kauppiaskatu 16. A stylishly old-fashioned café serving up wonderful cakes and coffee, although a little out of the centre up a steep hill.

Foija Aurakatu 10. Busy restaurant on the main square, with good-value and delicious pizzas from €7.90. Always popular with the city's young crowd.

Gadolinia Henrikenkatu. This student *mensa* is part of Åbo Akademi – look in the courtyard near the junction of Piispankatu and Porthaninkatu. Easily the cheapest option in town.

Herman Läntinen Rantakatu 37 ☎02/230 3333. Set in a bright and airy storehouse dating from 1849, and right on the riverside in an area that was renovated when Turku hosted the Tall Ships Race in 1996 – ask to reserve the table for two overlooking the river. Fantastic food that comes at a price, with main courses running from €16.50 to €23. Lunch is tremendous value at €7.

Pinella Porhaninpuisto. Café in an antique wooden pavilion in a park, serving decadent chocolate brownies and ice cream (€2), as well as main dishes such as cold smoked reindeer pancakes (€10).

Pizzeria Dennis Linnankatu 17. Although this place looks a bit tatty on the outside, don't be put off. It's known in Turku for its range of decent, well-priced pizzas.

Ribs Suutorin Square. Popular steakhouse with outdoor seating right on the riverside in summer. Young, trendy and expensive.

Vessa Puutori. Bizarre restaurant housed in a former public toilet, and worth a visit if only for its location. The excellent Finnish home cooking here is reasonably priced – reckon on €10–20 per dish.

Bars and entertainment

The riverside restaurant *Samppalinna*, on Itäinen Rantakatu, is a good night-time **drinking** venue, and has a wonderful restaurant. Other popular bars are *Olavinkrouvi*, Hämeenkatu 30, which draws a studenty crowd, and *Erik*, Eerikinkatu 6, which also serves decent food. Consider also the "English-style" pub, *Hunter's Inn*, part of *Hotel Julia* but with its own entrance at Brahenkatu 3. One drinking hole which attracts a young crowd is *Uusi Apteeki*, Kaskenkatu 1, housed in an old chemist's shop, with drug and pill bottles scattered about the place. It allegedly predates Damien Hirst's famous London bar-restaurant of the same name by a year. The floating restaurants mentioned above are also good for a beer.

If you want to fill your nights with something more energetic than boozing, there are several **discos**, most of them within the bigger hotels. *Börs Night Club* in the *Hotel Hamburger Börs*, Kauppiaskatu 6, is one of the best known. *Puuteri*, Eerikinkatu 12 is one of the trendiest in town, while not far behind are *Metropol*, Aurakatu 8, and *Forte* on Kristiinankatu. More sedate, and with a slightly older clientele, are *Kilta*, Humalistonkatu 8, and *Quality Hotel Ateljee*, Humalistonkatu 7, which sometimes holds Finnish tango nights.

During August, the **Turku Music Festival** packs thousands into a number of venues for performances in a wide range of musical genres (information on ☎02/251 1162, ⓦwww.turkumusicfestival.fi). If your tastes are for classical music, try and get a ticket for the **Turku Philharmonic Orchestra**, founded in 1790 and thus one of the oldest orchestras in Europe. It's now based in the Concert Hall at Aninkaistenkatu 9, which hosts symphonic and chamber-music concerts. The box office telephone line (☎02/262 0800) opens in mid-August, one month before concerts begin. Alternatively, check with the tourist office for a rundown of the week's films: Turku has five **cinemas**, the largest, with five screens, being the Julia, Eerikinkatu 4.

Around Turku – and moving on

NAANTALI, 16km from Turku, is famous as the home of **Moominworld** (mid-June to mid-Aug daily 10am–7pm; ⓦwww.muumimaailma.fi; adults and children from €13), a theme park set on an island and based on Tove Jansson's famous creations. It's a must-see if you have kids in tow, and many tour operators run buses to the park from Turku. Naantali itself is pleasant enough, with its wooden buildings and slight passageways, but hardly worth hanging around for more than a few hours, and with regular buses there's no need to stay, though there's a tourist office at Kaivotori 2 should you need further information (☎02/4350 850, ⓦwww .naantalinmatkailu.fi).

Moving on from Turku

Continuing from Turku **north along the coast**, there are direct bus services to the nearest main towns, Rauma and Pori. It's also possible to reach Pori by train, although this takes virtually a whole day and involves going via Tampere and changing at least once, possibly three times. From **Turku harbour** ferries sail through the vast archipelago to the Åland Islands, and on to Sweden. The harbour is 3km from the city centre and bus #1 covers the route frequently.

Rauma and Pori

RAUMA, 90km north of Turku, is one of the few places in Finland where you can't help but stop at every street corner to admire the elegance and understated charm of a town whose appearance has barely changed since the Middle Ages. Although Finns know Rauma as the most complete and best preserved wooden town in Scandinavia, with its historic importance reflected by its designation as a UNESCO World Heritage Site, relatively few foreigners have yet realized that a couple of days spent exploring the cobbled eighteenth- and nineteenth-century streets are likely to be some of the most enjoyable spent in Finland. True, Rauma is becoming increasingly touristy, but the town still retains plenty of quiet lanes and alleyways where you can explore undisturbed.

Until the early 1900s, **Old Rauma** was entirely contained within a narrow triangle of land (bordered on two sides by the small Raumanjoki river), which had been established as a toll-free zone three hundred years before. Although modern Rauma gracelessly encircles this medieval core completely today, it's this undisturbed medieval centre that makes the town so appealing – the layout of the narrow winding streets, alleys and curiously shaped gardens and allotments has barely changed since the last great fire in 1682, a remarkable achievement for a wooden town. Rauma's architectural delights are best explored by simply strolling along the two main streets, **Kauppakatu** and **Kuninkaankatu**, and heading off down whichever lane takes your fancy. Although most houses are now clad in the decorative Neo-Renaissance style and painted in a riot of pastel shades, you can still see a few dressed with the vertical boarding of the 1700s, or the wider empire cladding of the 1820s. The town's rich past is expertly documented via the **Rauma Museum**, in the eighteenth-century town hall at Kauppakatu 13 (mid-May to Aug daily

10am–5pm; Sept to mid-May Tues–Fri 10am–5pm, Sat 11am–2pm, Sun 11am–5pm; €4), where you'll find a couple of scale models of the sailing ships that once brought vast wealth into the town. Further evidence is on show at **Marela**, Kauppakatu 24 (same times as History Museum; €4), a house preserved in the style of a rich shipowner's home from the beginning of the twentieth century. Combined entry to Marela and the History Museum costs €4 (€2 Sept to mid-May) with a day pass available from either museum. If you want to plunge even further into local history, the **Old Rauma Renovation Centre** at Vähäkirkkokatu 8 (June–Aug Mon–Sat 10am–6pm, Sun noon–6pm; free) runs evening classes (unfortunately, all in Finnish) covering activities such as Rauma-style community singing, lessons in how to tie seafarers' knots and instruction in the local dialect – strangely for the west coast, this is a mainly Finnish-speaking community, although with an archaic dialect that many other Finns find hard to understand.

Practicalities

Unfortunately there are no longer train services to Rauma, and coming from Turku, the easiest solution is to take one of the frequent buses (#372 or #810) which run along the West Coast. From the bus station it's a two-minute walk to the **tourist office** at Valtakatu 2 (June–Aug Mon–Fri 8am–6pm, Sat 10am–3pm, Sun 11am–2pm; Sept–May Mon–Fri 8am–4pm; ☎02/834 4551, ⊛www.rauma.fi), where you can pick up leaflets on local history and walking tours. Free Internet access is available at Rauma public library, Ankkurikatu 1 (Mon–Fri 10am–7pm, Sat 10am–2pm). If you want to stay, it's just 1km along Poroholmantie from the old town centre to *Poroholma*, the combined **youth hostel** and **campsite** (☎02/8388 2500, ☏8388 2400; mid-May to Aug); otherwise, **hotel** accommodation is available at the *Cumulus*, Aittakarinkatu 9 (☎02/837 821, ⊛www.cumulus.fi; ❺/❹), which boasts two saunas, a pool and summer terrace. There is also the *Kesähotelli Rauma*, Satamakatu 20 (☎02/824 0130; June–Aug; ❸), which offers more basic hostel-style accommodation in double rooms, and allows free use of its sauna.

Rauma doesn't throw up a multitude of **eating** options, but filling lunches (around €10) are served at *Villa Tallbo*, in a shipowner's restored *fin-de-siècle* summer villa at Petäjäksentie 178 (☎02/8220 733). The best evening choice is *La Bamba*, at Kappakatu 16 in the Old Town, with an extensive choice of pizzas and pasta dishes from around €7.

Pori

Due to its yearly jazz **festival** – increasingly rock- and pop-oriented in recent years – **PORI** has become one of the best-known towns in Finland. For one week each July, its streets are full of music and the 150,000 people who come to hear it for more on the event, see opposite. Throughout the rest of the year Pori reverts to being a small, quiet industrial town with a worthy regional museum and a handful of architectural and historical oddities. The central section, despite its spacious grid-style streets, can be crossed on foot in about fifteen minutes.

In the centre of Pori at Hallituskatu 14, just across the road from the tourist office (see opposite), stands the recently renovated **Pori Theatre** (Mon–Fri 11am–6pm; free), the temporary home of Finnish-language theatre during the period of Russification when Finnish drama was considered too provocative to appear in a larger centre like Turku or Helsinki. Built in 1884, it has a striking Renaissance facade, and the tiny interior – seating just 300 – is heavy with opulent frescoes and sculptured chandeliers. To see inside, ask at the tourist office. A few steps away, at Hallituskatu 11, the **Satakunta Museum** (Tues–Sun 11am–5pm; €4) has three well-stocked floors which trace the life of both Pori and the surrounding Satakunta region through medieval findings, late nineteenth-century photos and shop signs, and typical house interiors, alongside interesting memorabilia from the powerful labour movement of the 1930s.

Pori's strangest sight, however, is in the big Käppärä cemetery, a twenty-minute walk along Maantiekatu. In the cemetery's centre is the Gothic-arched **Juselius Mausoleum** (May–Aug daily noon–3pm; Sept–April Sun noon–2pm; free), erected in 1898 by local businessman F.A. Juselius as a memorial to his daughter, Sigrid, who died aged 11. The leading Finnish church architect of the time, Josef Steinbäck, was called on to design the thing, while Gallen-Kallela decorated the interior with some of his best large-scale paintings. The artwork was adversely affected by both fire and the local sea air, but has been restored by Gallen-Kallela's son from the original sketches, enabling the structure to fulfil its purpose as powerfully, and as solemnly, as ever.

Practicalities

It's a short walk from either the **bus station** – into Isolinnankatu and straight on – or the **train station** – follow Rautatienpuistokatu – into the centre of town, where the **tourist office** is opposite the theatre in the opulent old town hall at Hallituskatu 9A (June to mid-Aug Mon–Fri 8am–6pm, Sat 10am–3pm; mid-Aug to May Mon–Fri 8am–4pm; ☎02/621 1273, ⓦwww.pori.fi). There's free Internet access at the library, Gallen-Kallenkatu 12 (Mon–Fri 10am–7pm, Sat 10am–3pm). The city's **campsite**, *Isomäki* (☎02/641 0620), is 2km from the centre in the Isomäki Sports Centre, next to the outdoor swimming pool, but it's only open during the jazz festival; buses #7 and #8 run from the centre to the hospital (*sairaala*) close by. During the festival the Porin Linjojen Jazzliikenne bus links the main festival sites, the town square and campsite (10am–4am, every 20min). At other times of year, the nearest campsite is the *Yyteri*, 20km distant (☎02/634 5700), though it does have a shop, café, sauna and many cabins; the #32 bus heads that way. Among the **hotels**, you could try the *Cumulus*, Itsenäisyydenkatu 37 (☎02/550 900, ⓦwww.cumulus.fi; ❹), one of the larger places and with its own restaurant. A smarter option is the *Vaakuna*, Gallen-Kallankatu 7 (☎02/528 100, ⓦwww.sokoshotels.fi; ❺), a business-oriented hotel with good weekend discounts.

In the **evening** most people gravitate to the town centre and watch a procession of highly polished cars heading aimlessly up and down the main streets. Cafés and bars fall in and out of favour quite rapidly, although one of the most consistently popular is *Café Anton* at Antinkatu 11, where a €2 cup of coffee comes with a cloudberry liqueur chocolate. *Café Anton* also offers a decent lunch, though in the evening it's primarily a place to drink beer. Otherwise, for eating there are numerous fast-food outlets – particularly *grillis*, which tend to serve a local speciality called the *porilainen*, a large, thick slice of grilled onion sausage that is served hamburger style in a roll with pickles, ketchup and some chopped onion. Of the town's pizza places, the best are *Pizza Mestarit*, Länsipuisto 16, where pizzas and pasta dishes go for around €12; and the ubiquitous *Rax Pizza Buffet* at Itäpuisto 3, where €7.49 gets you all the pizza you want. If you fancy something more substantial, try the excellent *Raatihuoneen Kellari* in the cellar of the old town hall, the same building as the tourist office, where lunchtime spreads of various Finnish-style meat and fish dishes cost a bargain €12–15. Check out also the all-year spin-off from the jazz festival, the *Jazz-Café*, at Eteläranta 6 on the banks of the Kokemäenjoki, or for Finnish food, just a few doors down, there's the excellent, reasonably priced *Suomalainen Klubbi* at no. 10.

If you're planning to come here for the **jazz festival**, it's best to have accommodation fixed up at least six months in advance – hotels, hostel and campsite fill very quickly, although the tourist office endeavours to house as much of the overspill as possible in private homes (€22 per person in a double room, €31 single) or on mattresses in local schools (€15 per person). It's easiest to purchase festival **tickets** online at ⓦwww.porijazz.com, the main festival website; alternatively, contact the Pori tourist office. A third of the festival's 150-odd concerts are free, in any case. If you plan to stay the whole week it's best to buy a pass (costing up to €140; on sale from mid-April). Individual tickets range from €36 to €55 for the bigger acts (in

2002 these included Paul Simon, Joe Cocker, Elvis Costello, Herbie Hancock and Chaka Khan). During the festival there's a Festival Centre at Pohjoisranta 11, in an old cotton mill on the left-hand side just after you cross the main Pori bridge heading away from the town centre. Here you can buy any tickets that haven't already been sold and pick up festival programmes and information.

The Åland Islands

The flat and thickly forested **Åland Islands**, all 6000-plus of them, lie scattered between Finland's southwest coast and Sweden. Politically Finnish but culturally Swedish, the islands cling to a weird form of independence, with their own parliament and flag (a red and yellow cross on a blue background). The currency is the euro but the language is Swedish – which explains why the main and only sizeable town is more commonly known by its Swedish name of **MARIEHAMN** than by the Finnish **Maarianhamina** – and as Swedish is mercifully closer to English, a visit here can make a welcome break from the perpetual battle with the Finnish language. Although Mariehamn – known locally as the "town of a thousand linden trees" after the elegant specimens that line virtually every street – is a peacefully uneventful seaside resort and a pleasant place to rest up for a couple of days, the real appeal here is sea, sun and beckoning terrain in unlimited quantities. There are plenty of secluded spots perfect for nude bathing, and you can hire a boat and sail out to your very own island.

The Åland islands (**Ahvenanmaa** in Finnish) were in Swedish hands through the Middle Ages, but, coveted by the Russians on account of their strategic location on the Baltic, they became part of the Russian Grand Duchy of Finland in 1807. When Finland gained independence, the future of the Ålands was referred to the League of Nations (though not before several Åland leaders had been imprisoned in Helsinki on a charge of high treason). As a result, Finnish sovereignty was established, in return for autonomy and complete demilitarization: the Ålanders now regard themselves as a shining example of Nordic cooperation, and living proof that a small state can run its own affairs while being part of a larger one.

The islands' ancient history is as interesting as the modern: many Roman coins have been found and there are scores of Viking burial mounds, plus the remains of some of the oldest Finnish churches. The excellent **Åland Museum** (May–Oct daily 10am–4pm, Tues until 8pm; Sept–April Tues–Sun 10am–4pm; €2.50) in Mariehamn's Stadshusparken tells the full story, and is complemented by the ship-shaped **Åland Maritime Museum** on Hamngatan (May, June & Aug daily 9am–5pm; July daily 9am–7pm; rest of the year Tues–Sun 10am–4pm; €4.50), 1km away at the other end of Storagatan, which celebrates the fact that, despite their insignificant size, the Åland islands once had the world's largest fleet of wooden sailing ships.

Smaller local history museums in the islands' other communities reflect the surprisingly strong regional differences among the islands; it seems the only thing that's shared are the ubiquitous Åland maypoles – which stand most of the year round – and the fact that specific sights generally take a back seat to the various forms of nature. There are, however, several things worth making for. To the northeast of Mariehamn, in Tosarby Sund, are the remains of **Kastelholm**, a fourteenth-century fortress built to consolidate Swedish domination of the Baltic. Strutted through by numerous Swedish monarchs, it was mostly destroyed by fire in the mid-nineteenth century and is now being restored. In summer guided tours run several times a day (€5) from the gate to the nearby open-air **Jan Karlsgården Museum** (May–Sept daily 10am–5pm; free). The Russians also set about building a fortress, **Bomarsund**, but before it could be completed the Crimean War broke out and an Anglo–French force stormed the infant castle, reducing it to rubble; just the scattered ramparts remain. Both would-be castles are on the same bus route from Mariehamn.

Elsewhere, you can trace the route of the old **post road**, the only mail link from Stockholm to what was then tsarist St Petersburg. To their long-lasting chagrin, the

Åland people were charged with seeing the safe passage of the mail, including taking it across the frozen winter sea – and quite a few died in the process. The major remnant of these times is the nineteenth-century Carl Engel-designed **Post House** in **ECKERÖ**, at the islands' western extremity. Standing on the coast facing Sweden, the building was intended to instil fresh arrivals with awe at their first sight of the mighty Russian empire. Despite retaining its grandeur, it now looks highly incongruous amid the tiny local community.

Practicalities

Ferries from Finland and Sweden (see "Travel Details", below) stop in Mariehamn's West Harbour and there's a **tourist office** fifteen minutes' walk away at Storagatan 8 (March to mid-June & mid-Aug to Oct Mon–Fri 9am–4pm, Sat 10am–3pm; mid-June to mid-Aug daily 9am–6pm; rest of the year Mon–Fri 9am–4pm; ☎018/24 0000, ⍟www.mariehamn.aland.fi), which can provide the latest details regarding travel and accommodation. The library at Strandgatan 29 has several **Internet** terminals for use free of charge, though you may have to book a slot if you need to do more than check your mail.

You're going to have a hard time finding **accommodation** if you turn up in summer on spec and without a tent: there are no official youth hostels on the islands and, although there are a number of cheapish guesthouses, some of which offer hostel-type facilities, these fill quickly. If you're at a loose end in Mariehamn, try *Kronan* at Neptunigatan 52 (☎018/12 617; ❷), or *Kvarnberget*, Parkgatan 28 (same phone number; ❷). For more luxury, there's the *Scandic Savoy* at Nygatan 12 (☎018/15 400, ⍟www.scandic-hotels.com; ❻/❺) with well-appointed rooms, though a little on the small size. The wise option, though, is to camp: there are plentiful **campsites** (in isolated areas you should be able to camp rough with no problems) and a fairly thorough **bus service** covering the main islands.

Cycling is a sound alternative to the buses, offering not only more freedom but also slightly cheaper rental rates than on the mainland; reckon on €9 per day for a bike with gears. In Mariehamn, RO NO is the best bet, with outlets at Hamngatan (☎018/12821) right opposite the ferry terminal, and on the waterside at Österhamn (☎018/12820) in the town proper; both open 9am to 6pm daily from June to mid-August. They also have **boats for hire** with outboard motors at €71 for five hours and will provide advice and tips on some of the best islands to visit in the archipelago just outside Mariehamn harbour.

Eating in Åland is not cheap and many restaurants simply hike up their prices during the summer months to make a killing from the Swedish tourist traffic. However, the best and most atmospheric place to eat is onboard the ship, *F.P. von Knorring*, moored in the Österhamn near RO NO – don't even think about the expense-account à la carte meals, but head straight out on deck where there's a cheaper selection of bar meals such as good-quality burgers, kebabs and salads for around €15 – the rear deck catches the evening sun and, after a day's hard cycling or archipelago exploration, is the ideal place to sip a beer or two and watch the sun sink (very) slowly towards the horizon. Alternatively, there's the less evocative *Cha Shao Tropical* at Torggatan 10, serving up pizzas and traditional Finnish food at reasonable prices.

Travel details

Trains

Helsinki to: Espoo (half-hourly; 30min); Järvenpää (half-hourly; 30min); Jyväskylä (9 daily; 3hr); Kajaani (4 daily; 7hr 30min); Kuopio (7 daily; 5hr); Lahti (hourly; 1hr 20min); Mikkeli (6 daily; 3hr 30min); Oulu (7 daily; 6hr); Rovaniemi (4 daily; 10hr); Tampere (hourly; 1hr 40min); Turku (hourly; 2hr).

Pori to: Tampere (6 daily; 1hr 30min).

Turku to: Helsinki (hourly; 2hr); Tampere (8 daily; 1hr 50min).

Buses

Helsinki to: Joensuu (4 daily; 8hr 55min); Jyväskylä (8 daily; 5hr); Kotka (7–9 daily; 1hr 30min–2hr 10min); Mikkeli (8 daily; 4hr); Porvoo (18 daily; 1hr); Tampere (16 daily; 3hr); Turku (21 daily; 2hr 30min).
Kotka to: Hamina (4 daily; 35min); Kouvola (4 daily; 1hr 10min).
Mariehamn to: Bomarsund (5 daily; 30min); Eckerö (5 daily; 45min); Kastelholm (5 daily; 30min).
Pori to: Rauma (4 daily; 45min); Turku (every two hours; 2hr).
Porvoo to: Helsinki (18 daily; 1hr); Kotka (8–10 daily; 40min); Loviisa (8–10 daily; 1hr); Pyhtää (8–10 daily; 1hr 40min).
Rauma to: Pori (4 daily; 45min); Turku (12 daily; 1hr 30min).
Turku to: Helsinki (21 daily; 2hr 30min); Pori (every two hours; 2hr); Rauma (12 daily; 1hr 30min).

Ferries

Helsinki to: Mariehamn (2 daily; 10hr 30min).
Mariehamn to: Helsinki (2 daily; 10hr 30min); Turku (4 daily; 5hr 20min).

Turku to: Mariehamn (4 daily; 5hr 30min).

International trains

Helsinki to: Moscow (1 daily; 14hr); St Petersburg (2 daily; 5hr 30min).

International buses

Hamina to: St Petersburg (2 daily; 6hr); Viipuri/Vyborg (2 daily; 2hr 30min).
Helsinki to: St Petersburg (2 daily; 8hr 30min); Viipuri/Vyborg (2 daily; 5hr).
Loviisa to: St Petersberg (2 daily; 7hr); Viipuri/Vyborg (2 daily; 3hr 30min).
Porvoo to: St Petersberg (2 daily; 7hr 30min); Viipuri/Vyborg (2 daily; 4hr).

International ferries

Eckerö to Grisslehamn: (2–3 daily; 2hr).
Helsinki to: Stockholm (2 daily; 15hr); Tallinn (every two hours; 1hr 45min–3hr 30min).
Mariehamn to: Kappelskär (2 daily; 3hr); Stockholm (6 daily; 5hr 30min).
Turku to: Stockholm (4 daily; 11hr).

4.2

The Lake Region

With extensive lake chains – chiefly the Päijanne and Saimaa systems – taking up a third of its area, the **Lake Region** is unique in Finland, and indeed in Scandinavia. Each of the chains features countless bays, inlets and islands, interspersed with dense forests, and the settlements that flourished around the waters grew up around the paper mills which used natural waterways and purpose-built canals to transport timber to pulping factories powered by gushing rapids.

Wherever you go here, water is never far away, further pacifying an already tranquil and verdant landscape. Even **Tampere**, Finland's major industrial city, is likeable as much for its lakeside setting as for its cultural delights. It's also the most

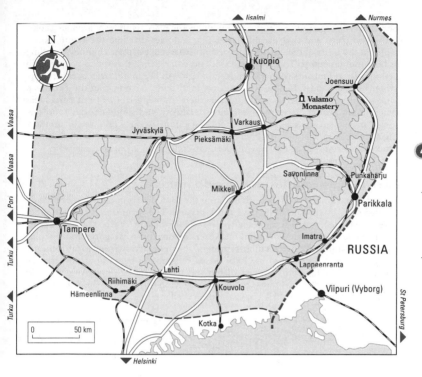

accessible of the region's centres, being on the railway line between Helsinki and the north. Also reachable by train from Helsinki, **Lahti** comes into its own as a winter sports resort; during summer the town is comparatively lifeless. Diminutive **Mikkeli** has more character, and makes a good stopover en route to the atmospheric eastern part of the Lake Region, where slender ridges furred with conifers link the few sizeable areas of land. Its regional centre, **Savonlinna**, stretches delectably across several islands, and boasts a superbly preserved medieval castle. To get a sense of Karelian culture (for more on which, see p.669) visit **Joensuu**, or **Lappeenranta** or the city of **Kuopio**, three towns where many displaced Karelians settled after World War II. In the heart of the region lies **Jyväskylä**, whose wealth of buildings by Alvar Aalto draws modern architecture buffs to what is otherwise a typically sleepy town. Down-to-earth **Iisalmi** is effectively a bridge between the Lake Region and the rougher, less watery terrain further north.

Unless you want total solitude (which is easily attained), it's best to spend a few days in the larger towns and make shorter forays into the more thinly populated areas. Although the western Lake Region is mostly well served by **trains**, rail connections to – and within – the eastern part are awkward and infrequent. With daily services between the main towns and less frequent ones to the villages, **buses** are handier for getting around. Slow, expensive **ferries** also link the main lakeside towns, while practically every community runs short pleasure cruises, but to really explore the countryside, you'll need to rent a **car** or **bicycle**.

Tampere and around

"Here it was as natural to approve of the factories as in Mecca one would the mosques," wrote John Sykes of **TAMPERE** in the 1960s – and you soon see what he meant. Although Tampere is Finland's biggest manufacturing centre and

Scandinavia's largest inland city, it's a highly scenic place, with leafy avenues, sculpture-filled parks and two sizeable lakes. The factories that line the Tammerkoski rapids in the heart of the city actually accentuate its appeal, their chimneys standing as bold monuments to Tampere's past – it's no coincidence that the town is known colloquially as Finland's Manchester. Its rapid growth began just over a century ago, when Tsar Alexander I abolished taxes on local trade, encouraging the Scotsman James Finlayson to open a textile factory here, drawing labour from rural areas where traditional crafts were in decline. Metalwork and shoe factories soon followed, their owners paternalistically supplying culture to the workforce by promoting a vigorous local arts scene. Free outdoor rock and jazz concerts, lavish theatrical productions and one of the best modern art collections in Finland maintain such traditions to this day.

Arrival, information and accommodation

Almost everything of consequence is within the central section of the city, bordered on two sides by the lakes Näsijärvi and Pyhäjärvi. The main streets run off either side of Hämeenkatu, which leads directly from the **train station** across Hämeensilta – the bridge over Tammerkoski, famous for its weighty bronze sculptures by Wäino Aaltonen, which represent four characters from local folklore. Although there's little call to use local **buses**, most routes begin from the terminal on Hämeenkatu. Tampere's **tourist office**, Verkatehtaankatu 2 (June–Aug Mon–Fri 8.30am–8pm, Sat & Sun 11am–3pm; Sept–May Mon–Fri 8.30am–5pm; ☎03/3146 6800, ⊛www.tampere.fi), has copies of the excellent, free *Tampere* guide and also

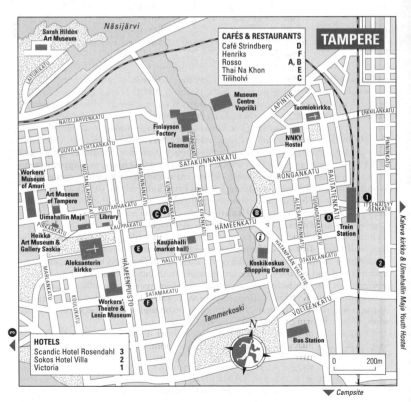

▼ Campsite

▶ Kaleva kirkko & Uimahallin Maja Youth Hostel

offers free Internet access. From June to August they also organize two-hour sight-seeing tours (daily at 2pm; €9).

Accommodation
Budget travellers are catered for best during the summer, when both the main **youth hostels** are open. *NNKY Hostel* (the Finnish YWCA, open to both sexes) stands opposite the cathedral at Tuomiokirkkokatu 12A (☎03/254 4020, ⦿yritys.soon.fi/tnnky/hostel-e.htm; June to late Aug); *Uimahallin Maja*, centrally located in the same building as the swimming pool at Pirkankatu 10–12 (☎03/222 9460, ⦿www.hosteltampere.com), 1km from the train station, is a superb, cheap official hostel open all year, with rooms sleeping one to six people, plus dorm beds. Of Tampere's regular **hotels**, the *Victoria*, Itsenäisyydenkatu 1 (☎03/242 5111, ⦿www.hotellivictoria.fi; ❺/❹), and *Sokos Hotel Villa*, Sumeliuksenkatu 14 (☎03/262 6267, ⦿www.sokoshotels.fi; ❻), are both handily placed though a little expensive, or an early booking might get you some luxury beside the lake at the *Scandic Hotel Rosendahl*, Pyynikintie 13 (☎03/244 1111, ⦿www.scandic-hotels.com; ❻), a couple of kilometres from the city centre. As usual, however, the least expensive lakeside option is a **campsite** – *Härmälä* (mid-May to late Aug ☎03/265 1355, rest of the year ☎09/6138 3210, ⦿www.lomaliitto.fi/english/kohteet/camping/harmalac.htm), 5km to the south and accessible by bus #1 – cabins for three people cost €27, those sleeping five €60.

The City
Short, broad streets make central Tampere very easy to explore. From the train station, Hämeenkatu runs across the Tammerkoski into the heart of the city, and almost everything of interest lies within a few minutes' walk of this busy thoroughfare. You'll need to cross back over the river (most easily done by following Satakunnankatu), however, to reach Tampere's historic cathedral – and to get the best view of the Finlayson factory, on which the city's fortunes were founded – it's now home to the editorial offices of the region's main newspaper, a cinema and several upmarket restaurants.

Hämeenkatu and around
Walking the length of Hämeenkatu from the train station leaves you in front of the upwardly thrusting neo-Gothic **Aleksanterin kirkko** (daily: May–Aug 10am–5pm; Sept–April 11am–3pm). With its riot of knobbly ceiling decorations, the effect inside is something like an ecclesiastical train station, with an unusually unpleasant artexed altar. To the left, following the line of greenery south down Hämeenpuisto, is the Tampere Workers' Theatre and, in the same building, the excellent **Lenin Museum** (Mon–Fri 9am–6pm, Sat & Sun 11am–4pm; €4), which, oddly, is the only permanent museum dedicated to Lenin anywhere in the world. After the abortive 1905 revolution in Russia, Lenin lived in Finland for two years and attended the Tampere conferences, held in what is now the museum. It was here that he first encountered Stalin, although this is barely mentioned in the displays, one of which concentrates on Lenin himself, the other on his relationship with Finland and on his visits to numerous Finnish cities. For a detailed explanation, borrow the English-language brochure from reception. If you want more Lenin, head to Kyttälänkatu, one block north of the railway station off Rautatienkatu, where a plaque marks the otherwise undistinguished house (no. 11) where he lived during his stint in Tampere.

Several blocks north of Hämeenkatu, the Amuri district was built during the 1880s to house Finlayson's workers. Some thirty homes have been preserved as the **Workers' Museum of Amuri** at Makasiininkatu 12 (early May to mid-Sept Tues–Sun 10am–6pm; €4; during the rest of the year only the museum shop is open, same times), a simple but affecting place that records the family life of working people over a hundred-year period. In each home is a description of the inhabitants and their jobs, and authentic articles from the relevant periods – from beds and tables to family photos, newspapers and biscuit packets.

Just around the corner at Puutarhakatu 34 is the **Art Museum of Tampere** (Tues–Sun 10am–6pm; €4; guided tours by arrangement on ☎03/3146 6580), whose first floor holds powerful if staid temporary exhibitions featuring Finnish and international artists; the large basement galleries are filled with contemporary local work. If you're looking for older Finnish art, head instead for the far superior **Heikka Art Museum**, a few minutes' walk away at Pirkankatu 6 (Tues–Thurs 3–6pm, Sun noon–3pm; other times by arrangement ☎03/212 3973; €4). Kustaa Heikka was a gold- and silversmith whose professional skills and business acumen made him a local big shot around 1900. The art collection he bequeathed to Tampere reflects his interest in traditional lifestyles; borrow a catalogue from reception, since most pieces are identified only by numbers. Amongst the most notable work (including sketches by Gallen-Kallela and Helene Schjerfbeck) are two of Heikka's own creations: a delicately wrought brooch marking the completion of his apprenticeship, and a finely detailed bracelet with which he celebrated becoming a master craftsman. Well worth the diversion, and free too, is the next-door **Gallery Saskia** (daily noon–6pm), showing intriguing and unusual new work.

Nearby, at Pirkankatu 2, stands the **Tampere Library** (June–Aug Mon–Sat 9.30am–7pm; Sept–May Mon–Fri 9.30am–8pm, Sat 9.30am–3pm), an astounding feat of user-friendly modern architecture. The work of Reimi and Raili Pietilä (who also designed the epic Kalevala kirkko – see opposite), and finished in 1986, the library's curving walls give it a warm, cosy feel; believe it or not, the building's shape was inspired by a certain type of grouse (a stuffed specimen of which sits in the reception area). Strolling around is the best way to take in the many small, intriguing features, and will eventually lead you up to the top-floor café, which gives a good view of the cupola, deliberately set eleven degrees off the vertical – to match the off-centre pivot of the earth. In the basement of the library, with its own entrance at Hämeenpuisto 20, **Moomin Valley** (June–Aug Mon–Fri 9am–5pm, Sat & Sun 10am–6pm; Sept–April Tues–Fri 9am–5pm, Sat & Sun 10am–6pm; €4) recreates with dolls and 3-D displays scenes from the incredibly popular children's books by Finnish author Tove Jansson.

The Näsijärvi lakeside

Just north of Tampere's central grid-plan streets, the tremendous **Sara Hildén Art Museum** (daily 11am–6pm, closed Mon Sept–May; €4), built on the shores of Näsijärvi, displays Tampere's premier modern art collection by means of changing exhibitions. The museum is on the other side of Paasikventie from Amuri (take bus #16, or the summer-only #4 bus from the town centre or train station).

Occupying the same waterside strip as the Hildén collection is **Särkänniemi** (@www.sarkanniemi.fi), a tourist complex incorporating a dolphinarium, aquarium, planetarium and observation tower. Seen from the **tower** – an unmistakeable element of Tampere's skyline – the city seems insignificant compared to the trees and lakes that stretch to the horizon. The rapids that cut through them can be identified from afar by the factory chimneys alongside. The tower is open from 11am to midnight during summer, and there's a €3.50 admission charge, waived if you're using the tower restaurant; the other diversions cost €3.50 apiece and are usually crowded with families. To make a day of it, buy the €27 Särkänniemi Key, valid for all parts of the complex except parasailing. There's a café here, too, serving uninspired pizza, quiche and the like.

The Tuomiokirkko and around

Cross to the eastern side of the Tammer River along Satakunnankatu and you'll not only see – foaming below the bridge – the rapids that powered the **Finlayson Factory**, but also the factory building itself, still standing to the north and well worth a wander for its crafts shops.

Immediately ahead in a grassy square, the **Tuomiokirkko** (daily: May–Aug 9am–6pm; Sept–April 11am–3pm) is a picturesque cathedral in the National Romantic style, designed by Lars Sonck and finished in 1907. It is most remarkable for the gorily symbolic frescoes by Hugo Simberg – particularly the *Garden of Death*, where skeletons happily water plants, and *The Wounded Angel*, showing two boys carrying a bleeding angel through a Tampere landscape – which caused an ecclesiastical outcry when unveiled. So did the viper (a totem of evil) which he placed amongst the angel wings on the ceiling; Simberg retorted that evil could lurk anywhere – including a church.

Out from the centre

To learn more about Tampere's origins, visit the **Museum Centre Vapriiki** (Tues–Sun 10am–6pm; €4–7), housed in a former mill just across the river from the great Finlayson factory. Though the museum covers everything from archeology to handicrafts, its most interesting section deals with the impact of the early twentieth century – a turbulent time for both Tampere and Finland. As an industrial town with militant workers, Tampere instigated a general strike against the Russification of Finland, filling the streets with demonstrators and painting over the Cyrillic names on trilingual street signs. After independence the city became a Social Democratic stronghold, and one ruthlessly dealt with by the right-wing government following the civil war of 1918 – yet the municipal administration remains amongst the most left-leaning in Finland. Vapriiki also contains the **Finnish Ice Hockey Museum** (same times and entrance fee), which accords due honour to local teams Ilves and Tappora, which have won more national championships than all of Finland's other teams combined.

Away to the east of the centre, Itsenäisyydenkatu runs uphill behind the train station to meet the vast concrete folds of the **Kaleva kirkko** (daily: May–Aug 9am–6pm; Sept–April 11am–3pm). Built in 1966, it was a belated addition to the neighbouring **Kaleva estate**, which was heralded in the 1950s as an outstanding example of high-density housing. Though initially stunning, the church's interior lacks the subtlety of the city library, despite being designed by the same team of Reimi and Raili Pietilä – who this time based their plan on a fish.

Eating

Tampere boasts an eclectic range of restaurants and cafés to suit most pockets. Several places in the *Koskikeskus* shopping mall, Hatanpään valtatie 1, offer cheap lunchtime specials, but, as usual, the cheapest **places to eat** are the student mensas – in the university at the end of Yliopistonkatu, just over the railway line from the city centre – where full meals can cost as little as €5. There are all the usual pizza places in town: *Rosso* has two outlets, one just by the bridge on Hämeenkatu and another on the pedestrianized Kuninkaankatu. For quiet posing, *Café Strindberg* opposite the train station serves fine cakes as well as breakfasts and more lunches. For something more substantial, *Tiiliholvi*, Kauppakatu 10, is known for its good meat dishes – grilled fillet of lamb for €17 or breast of guinea fowl for €18. *Henriks*, Satamakatu 7, serves up French cuisine in a more intimate atmosphere – try the delicious poached salmon in bouillabaisse sauce for €15. For enormous Thai portions head for the unbeatable *Thai Na Khon*, Hämeenkatu 29. If you want to try a Tampere speciality, head for the Laukontori open-air market, by the rapids, where the local black sausage, *mustamakkara*, is sold.

There are numerous **supermarkets** at which to stock up on provisions. Two central options are the big Sokos store at Hämeenkatu 21 or Anttila, Puutarhakatu 10. Slightly further out, and cheaper, are City Market, Sotilaankatu 11, and Prisma at Sammonkatu 73. There's also a large **kauppahalli** (market hall) at Hämeenkatu 19 (Mon–Fri 8am–6pm, Sat 8am–4pm), and the open-air markets at Laukontori (Mon–Fri 6am–2pm, Sat 6am–1pm), Keskustori (first Mon of month 6am–6pm) and Tammelantori (Mon–Fri 6am–2pm, Sat 6am–1pm).

Drinking and entertainment

Tampere at night is very much alive and buzzing, with numerous late-night bars, cafés and clubs. One of the most popular **pubs** is the Irish *Dublinin Ovet* ("Doors of Dublin") at Kauppakatu 16. Another summertime favourite is *Falls*, down by the rapids. For live music, try the laid-back *Klubbi*, a nightclub set in an old customs house behind the train station on Itsenäisyydenkatu, or, almost opposite the tourist office, *Paapankapakka*, a swing-style jazz club with up-and-coming bands. Despite its name, *Café Europa* on Aleksanterinkatu is more of a bar and restaurant than café, and a good place to meet some of Tampere's trendy young things who gravitate here for the occasional live music, while on the same street, the extremely popular rock disco *Doris*, in the basement of *Restaurant Katupoika*, is the place where locals go to drink and dance till morning. On warm nights the crowds head out to the Pyynikki area, a natural ridge on the edge of Tampere, beside Pyhäjärvi. Tickets for the **Pyynikki Summer Theatre** cost around €18.50, but it's worth trekking out just to look at the revolving auditorium which slowly rotates the audience around during performances, blending the surrounding woods, rocks and water into the show's scenery – though remember that all performances here are in Finnish only.

Finland's one and only **gay bar** outside Helsinki, the friendly and laid-back *Mixei* (closed Mon) on Otavalankatu 3, is worth seeking out to gain an insight into what it's like to be gay in the Finnish provinces – sadly, not an immediately appealing prospect, which perhaps explains the lack of other gay establishments outside the capital.

Around Tampere – and moving on

Half an hour from Tampere on the busy rail line to Helsinki, **HÄMEENLINNA** (Tavastehus in Swedish) is revered both as the birthplace of Sibelius and as Finland's oldest inland town. The major attraction is **Häme Castle** (daily May to mid-Aug 10am–6pm; mid-Aug to April 10am–4pm; €4), the sturdy thirteenth-century fortress from which the town takes its name. Next comes the **Sibelius Childhood Home** (daily: May–Aug 10am–4pm; Sept–April noon–4pm; €3) at Hallituskatu 11, where the great composer was born, now reverentially restored to how it was during the first years of his life. A few blocks away at Viipuriintie 2, the **Art Museum** (Tues–Sun noon–6pm, Thurs until 8pm; €5) musters a mundane collection of minor works by major Finnish names, among them Järnefelt, Gallen-Kalella and Halonen.

Seeing all this won't take long, and any spare hours are better spent in the outlying area of **Hattula**, roughly 5km from the centre of Hämeenlinna. The local **Hattulan kirkko** (daily mid-May to mid-Aug 11am–5pm; other times by appointment on ☎03/631 1540) is probably the finest medieval church in Finland – outwardly plain, with an interior totally covered by 180 sixteenth-century frescoes of biblical scenes. En route to the church, a combined **youth hostel** (☎03/682 8560; May to mid-Aug) and **campsite** (same number; June–Aug) face Hämeenlinna across the river, 4km from the town centre.

Moving on from Tampere

Tampere has excellent **train links** to the rest of Finland. To reach the rest of the Lake Region, however, there are two main choices. Aiming for Jyväskylä also puts you within comparatively easy reach of Varkaus, Joensuu and Kuopio. Alternatively, heading for Lahti (change at Riihimäki) makes more sense if you want to press on to Mikkeli or Lappeenranta, or see more of the eastern Lake Region. For Savonlinna, there are two alternative routes: either take a train to Pieksämäki, from where there are direct buses (which accept train passes and tickets) to the town, or head east through Riihimäki and Lappeenranta to Parikkala for the branch line to Savonlinna.

Jyväskylä

JYVÄSKYLÄ is the most low-key and provincial of the main Lake Region towns, despite the industrial section that takes up one end and a big university which consumes the other – though the latter does provide something of a youthful feel. The town also has more than its fair share of buildings by **Alvar Aalto**. The legendary architect grew up here and opened his first office in the town in 1923, and his handiwork – a collection of buildings spanning his entire career – litters the place.

After some minor projects, Aalto left Jyväskylä in 1927 for fame, fortune and Helsinki, but returned in the 1950s to work on the teacher-training college. By the 1970s this had grown into the **Jyväskylä University**, whose large campus halts traffic where the main road gives way to a series of public footpaths, leading to a park and sports ground. Although Aalto died before his ambitious plan for an Administration and Cultural Centre was complete, the scheme is still under construction along Vapaudenkatu. Across the road from the (perhaps intentionally) uninspiring police station – unveiled in 1970 – stands a **city theatre** resembling a scaled-down version of Helsinki's Finlandia.

Two of the town's most important museums are situated close together on the hill running down from the university towards the edge of the lake, Jyväsjärvi. At the request of the town authorities rather than through vanity, Aalto built the **Alvar Aalto Museum** at Alvar Aallon Katu 7 (Tues–Sun 11am–6pm, Aug until 8pm; ⓦwww.alvaraalto.fi; €6). The architect's best works are obviously out on the streets, making this collection of plans, photos and models seem rather superfluous. But the Aalto-designed furniture makes partial amends. The first floor hosts temporary art exhibitions and the ground floor has a pleasant if unexciting café. Aalto also contributed to the exterior of the nearby **Museum of Central Finland** (*Keski-Suomen Museo*; Tues–Sun 11am–6pm, Aug until 8pm; ⓦwww.jkl.fi/ksmuseo; €4, free on Fri), which contains two separate exhibitions: one devoted to Middle Finland – well designed but with no English translations – and the other representing each decade of the twentieth century through the car number plates, music and kitchen gadgetry of the day. The collection of room interiors is worth the visit alone.

Jyväskylä also hosts an impressive **Art Museum** (Tues–Sun 11am–6pm, Aug until 8pm; ⓦwww.jkl.fi/taidemuseo; €5, free on Fri) at Kauppakatu 25 which is split into two exhibition sites. The main site houses the permanent collection of the Ester and Jalo Sihtola Fine Arts Foundation, plus that of the Association of Finnish

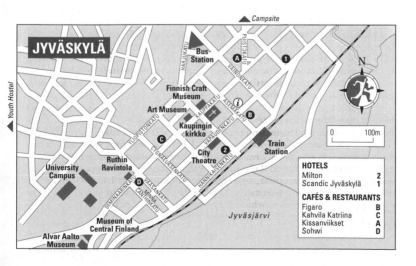

Printmakers. The site next door houses temporary exhibitions reflecting the latest trends in modern art from Finland and the rest of the world. Also at Kauppakatu 25, the **Finnish Craft Museum**, with displays ranging from bell-making to spectrolite jewellery, and the **National Costume Centre**, which holds the Finnish National Costume Council's collection, are worth a quick look. Don't leave Jyväskylä though without seeing the nineteenth-century **Kaupungin kirkko** (June–Aug Mon–Fri 11am–6pm; Sept–May Wed–Fri 11am–2pm), in the small park one block west of the tourist office. The church was the centrepiece of town life a century ago, but declined in importance as Jyväskylä gained new suburbs and other churches. Despite recent restoration – when the interior was repainted in its original pale yellow and green – the church looks authentically dingy.

Practicalities

From the train and bus stations, right in the centre, it's a short walk to the **tourist office**, in a beautiful wooden building at Asemakatu 6 (mid-June to Aug Mon–Fri 9am–6pm, Sat & Sun 10am–3pm; Sept to mid-June Mon–Fri 9am–5pm, Sat 10am–3pm; ☎014/624 903, ⓦwww.jyvaskyla.fi/touristinfo), which can supply a useful free leaflet on the local buildings designed by Aalto and has Internet access. There's free Net access in the public library at Vapaudenkatu 39–41 (June to mid-Aug Mon–Fri 11am–7pm, Sat 11am–3pm; rest of the year Mon–Fri 11am–8pm, Sat 11am–3pm), though you'll need to book in advance. For **accommodation**, the central, family-run *Hotel Milton*, Hannikaisenkatu 27–29 (☎014/337 7900, ⓦwww.kolumbus.fi/hotelli.milton; ❹), is a good choice, right by the train station, while for a bit more luxury, try the *Scandic Jyväskylä* at Vapaudenkatu 73 (☎014/330 3000, ⓦwww.scandic-hotels.com; ❻/❹) – some rooms have their own private saunas. The local **youth hostel**, *Laajari* (☎014/624 885, ⓦwww.laajavuori.com), is a state-of-the-art affair, 4km from the centre, at Laajavuorentie 15 – take bus #25 from Vapaudenkatu. The nearest **campsite**, *Tuomiojärvi* (☎014/624 895, ℻624 888; June–Aug), is 2km north off the E4 – take Puistokatu and then continue along to Taulumäentie 47, or take bus #22 – here there are **cabins** sleeping four people for €38.

Eating options veer from the pizza establishments along the main streets to the more upscale *Kissanviikset* ("The Cat's Whiskers") at Puistokatu 3, which serves some sizeable fish dishes at lunchtime, while *Figaro*, in the centre of town at Asemakatu 14, serves up fair-priced salads, pasta dishes, steaks and fish dishes and is justifiably busy. However, the most popular place is the light and airy *Sohwi* at Vaasankatu 21, which doubles as a tapas bar. Among the cafés, *Kahvila Katriina* at Kauppakatu 11 serves deliciously calorific cakes and some excellent vegetarian dishes.

The university hosts events in and out of term-time, so it's always worth looking out for posters. The neighbourhood around the university is also a focus for the town's **nightlife**, such as it is. Two notable haunts are *Ilokivi*, Keskussairaalantie 2, often featuring art exhibitions and live bands; and the smoky *Ruthin Ravintola*, Seminaarinkatu 19, where members of the philosophy and politics departments get down to chess and/or hard drinking. *Memphis*, at Kauppakatu 30, is a more central hangout, while there's less expensive beer downstairs at the *Ale Pub*; the relaxed bar *Freetime* is just a couple of doors away, too. However, on sunny evenings, it's the outdoor seating at *Old Bricks Inn*, Kauppakatu 41, that really pulls the crowds.

Thanks to the university, there is quite a strong **gay** scene in town; for information on local gay events, call in at SETA, Yliopistonkatu 26 (☎014/310 0660).

Lahti

LAHTI doesn't know if it's a Lake Region town or a Helsinki suburb, and it's perhaps this confusion that conspires to make the place so dull. Its entire growth took place in the twentieth century (mostly since Alvar Aalto opened several furniture factories, which kept him going between architectural commissions), and although it's now the major transport junction between the Lake Region and the south, it lacks any lake-area atmosphere, while local cultural life is diminished by the relative proximity of Helsinki. Lahti's one compensation is its status as a **winter sports** centre of international renown: three enormous ski jumps hang over the town, and there's a feeling of biding time when summer grass, rather than winter snow, covers their slopes.

Unless you're here to ski, Lahti isn't a place you'll need or want to linger in – the town can easily be covered in half a day. Head first for the **observation platform** on the highest ski jump (June–Aug daily 10am–5pm; Sept–May Sat & Sun 11am–3pm; €4 including the chairlift to the top), whose location is unmistakeable. From such a dizzying altitude the lakes and forests around Lahti stretch dreamily into the distance, and the large swimming pool below the jump resembles a puddle (when frozen in winter it's used as a landing zone).

The only structures matching the ski jumps for height are the twin radio masts atop Radiomäki hill, between the train station (a 15min walk away) and the town centre. Steep pathways wind uphill towards the **Radio and Television Museum** (*Radio Ja TV Museo*; Mon–Fri 10am–5pm, Sat & Sun 11am–5pm; €4.30), inside the original transmitting station at the base of one of the masts. Here, two big rooms are packed with bulky Marconi valves, crystal sets, antiquated sound-effect discs, room-sized amplifiers and intriguing curios. Look out for the Pikku Hitler – the German-made "little Hitler", a wartime portable radio that forms an uncanny facsimile of the dictator's face.

At Radiomäki's foot, the distinctive red brickwork of Eliel Saarinen's **Town Hall** injects some style into the concrete blocks that make central Lahti so dull and uniform. Built in 1912, many of its Art Nouveau features were considered immensely daring at the time, and although most of the originals were destroyed in World War II, careful refurbishment has re-created much of Saarinen's design. Viewable during office hours, the interior is definitely worth seeing. Lahti's other notable building is at the far end of Mariankatu, which cuts through the town centre from the town hall: the **Ristinkirkko** (daily 10am–6pm), whose white roof slopes down from the

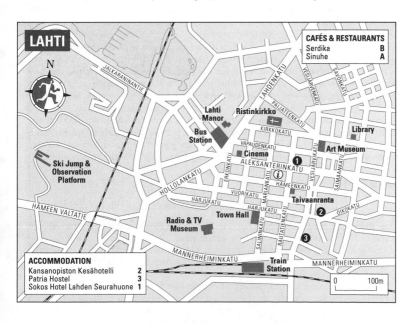

bell tower in imaginative imitation of the local ski jumps. Interestingly, this was the last church to be designed by Alvar Aalto: he died during its construction and the final work was overseen by his wife. Outside, Wäinö Aaltonen's discreetly emotive sculpture marks the war graves in the cemetery.

By now you've more or less exhausted Lahti, although Hämeenkatu, running parallel to the far more hectic Aleksanterinkatu, contains a number of little art galleries owned by local artists, and a few secondhand bookshops. The **Art Museum** (Mon–Fri 10am–5pm, Sat & Sun 11am–5pm; €4.30), just around the corner at Vesijärvenkatu 11, exhibits nineteenth- and twentieth-century works, most notably by Gallen-Kallela and Edelfelt.

Finally, near the hazardous web-like junction by the bus station, is the wooden nineteenth-century **Lahti Manor**, hidden behind a line of trees. Now a historical museum (Mon–Fri 10am–5pm, Sat & Sun 11am–5pm; €4.30), it contains regional paraphernalia, numerous Finnish medals and coins, plus an unexpected hoard of French and Italian paintings and furniture.

Practicalities

The **tourist office** is at Aleksanterinkatu 16 (June–Aug Mon–Fri 9am–6pm, Sat 10am–2pm; Sept–May Mon–Fri 9am–5pm, Sat 10am–2pm; ☎03/877 67, ⊛www.lahtitravel.fi). Both the tourist office and the library at Kirkkokatu 31 (Mon–Fri 10am–6pm, Sat 10am–3pm) provide free Internet access. There are some good budget **accommodation** options in Lahti. A decent choice is the *Patria* hostel at Vesijärvenkatu 3 (☎03/782 3783, ℱ782 3793), near the train station, which has double rooms (②) as well as dorms. In summer, try the excellent *Kansanopiston Kesähotelli* (☎03/878 1181, ℱ878 1234; June to mid-Aug; ②) in a very central position in the town's folk high school at Harjukatu 46. For more luxury the *Sokos Hotel Lahden Seurahuone*, Aleksanterinkatu 14, boasts a sauna and pool, and TV and video in all rooms (☎03/851 11, ⊛www.sokoshotels.fi; ⑥/④). About 4km to the north of Lahti at **Mukkula**, reached directly by bus #30 from the bus station at the end of Aleksanterinkatu, is a lakeside **campsite** (☎03/874 1442; June–Aug) with cottages (③).

Low-priced **eating** options include *Serdika* at Hämeenkatu 21, which not only claims to be the cheapest steakhouse in Lahti but also serves up some tasty and otherwise hard-to-find Bulgarian food, while the best place for cakes and pastries is the central *Sinuhe*, Mariankatu 21. You'll find the larger **supermarkets** clustered along Savonkatu. Though hardly remarkable for its nightlife, Lahti holds its own compared to smaller towns in the Lake Region. For an evening **drink**, the best place is undoubtedly *Restaurant Taivaanranta*, Rautatienkatu 13, which makes its own beer, blueberry cider and whisky. Otherwise try the lively *Memphis* in the *Sokos Hotel Lahden Seurahuone* (see above), or *Diva*, at Hämeenkatu 16.

Train and bus connections onwards from Lahti are good. Mikkeli, to the north, is the sensible target if you're ultimately making for Kuopio, while Lappeenranta is a better destination if you're keen to discover the small towns and glorious scenery of the eastern Lake Region, and makes an enjoyable stop en route to Savonlinna.

Mikkeli

In 1986 a Helsinki bank robber chose the market square in **MIKKELI** as the place in which to blow up himself, his car and his hostage. This, the most violent event seen in Finland for decades, was perhaps an echo of Mikkeli's blood-spattered past. In prehistoric times the surrounding plains were battlegrounds for feuding tribes from east and west, the Finnish Infantry has a long association with the town, and it was from Mikkeli that General Mannerheim conducted the campaign against the Soviet Union in the Winter War.

Military matters are a strong local feature, but you don't need to be a bloodthirsty warmonger to find interest in the town's military collections – the insights they

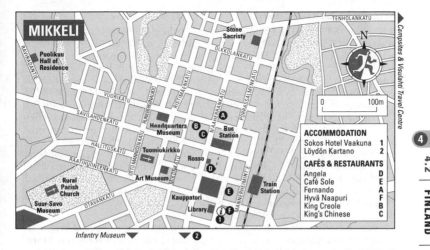

ACCOMMODATION
Sokos Hotel Vaakuna 1
Löydön Kartano 2

CAFÉS & RESTAURANTS
Angela D
Café Sole E
Fernando A
Hyvä Naapuri F
King Creole B
King's Chinese C

provide into Finland's recent history can be fascinating. More generally, Mikkeli lacks the heavy industry you'll find in some Lake Region communities, functioning instead as a district market town (the daily crowds and activity within its market hall – *kauppatori* – seem out of all proportion to its size), while sporting a handsome cathedral and a noteworthy art collection.

The military museums

Older Finns visiting Mikkeli tend to make a beeline for Ristimäenkatu, where the office used by Mannerheim is preserved as the **Headquarters Museum** (May–Aug daily 10am–5pm; rest of the year Fri–Sun 10am–5pm; €4). It's not so much the exhibits that give the museum its significance – the centrepiece is Mannerheim's desk, holding his spectacles and favourite cigars – but the fact that the Winter War, which effectively prevented a Soviet invasion of Finland in 1939 (see p.678), was waged and won from this very room. An adjoining room on the ground floor has photo displays and a not-to-be-missed English-language video which offers a first-class account of the predicament Finland found itself in during the Winter War. For more Mannerheim, check out his **saloon car** at the railway station, which clocked up an impressive 78,000km during the war years when the General used it to travel around Finland – sadly, the carriage interior is only open for viewing on Mannerheim's birthday (June 4).

When not travelling, Mannerheim spent much of his time at the **Mikkeli Club**, a cross between a speakeasy and a Masonic lodge, which still exists, occupying what is now part of the Sokos department store on Hallituskatu, facing the *kauppatori*. The club's walls are lined with photos of Mannerheim and his staff, although less prominence is given to the snaps of the Marshal riding with Hitler during the Führer's birthday visit (these are in an unmarked folder usually lying on a side table). The club is not strictly open to the public but *Sokos Hotel Vaakuna* (see p.742) can arrange for interested individuals to be shown around.

A few minutes' walk south from the town centre is the **Infantry Museum**, Jääkärinkatu 6–8 (May–Aug daily 10am–5pm; Sept–Dec Fri–Sun noon–4pm; €3.50), which records the key armed struggles that marked Finland's formative years as an independent nation. Assorted rifles, artillery pieces and maps of troops' movements provide the factual context, but it's the scores of frontline photos and display cases of troops' letters and lucky charms that reveal the human story. A second, substantially less interesting section of the museum concentrates chiefly on the Finnish role in the United Nations Peace-Keeping Force.

The rest of the town

Raised in 1897, Mikkeli's Gothic Revival **Tuomiokirkko** (daily: June–Aug 10am–6pm; Sept–May 10–11am) sits primly on a small hill in the middle of Hallituskatu. Inside, Pekka Halonen's 1899 altarpiece attracts the eye, a radiant Christ against a dark, brooding background. Take a close look, too, at Antii Salmenlinna's stained-glass windows and you'll spot depictions of three Finnish towns (Viipuri, Sortavala and Käkisalmi) ceded to Russia after World War II.

Opposite the cathedral, the excellent **Art Museum**, at Ristimäenkatu 5A (Tues–Sun 10am–5pm, Sat 10am–1pm; €3), stages some engaging temporary exhibitions of the latest Finnish art and has two permanent displays of artworks bequeathed to the town. The Martti Airio Collection is a forceful selection of early twentieth-century Finnish Impressionism and Expressionism – Tyko Saalinen's *Young American Woman* and *On the Visit* are particularly striking. The museum's other benefactor was the Mikkeli-born sculptor Johannes Haapasalo, who bequeathed nearly three hundred finished works and over a thousand sketches. One of Haapasalo's better works can be seen beside the cathedral: called *Despair*, it marks the graves of Mikkeli's Civil War dead.

If you've ever wondered how vergers in eighteenth-century Finland kept their church congregations awake, the answer (a big stick) can be seen at the tiny **Stone Sacristy**, to the north at Porrassalmenkatu 32A (July daily 11am–5pm; other times by appointment on ☎015/194 2424; free); the church which the sacristy served was demolished in 1776. Several other historic items from the Mikkeli diocese sit in the room, a wooden pulpit, a "shame bench" (for women deemed unvirtuous) and a wood-framed Bible among them.

A fifteen-minute walk from the town centre along Otavankatu (easily combined with a visit to the Infantry Museum) leads to the **Rural Parish Church** (mid-June to mid-Aug daily 11am–5pm), believably claimed to be one of the largest wooden churches in Finland. Size aside, the church is a modest sight, but is a more satisfying time-filler than the small stone building in its grounds which houses the **Suur-Savo Museum** (May–Aug Tues–Fri 10am–5pm, Sat 2–5pm; Sept–April Wed 10am–5pm, Sat 2–5pm; €2), a hotchpotch of broken clocks, cracked crockery, and even a bent-wheeled penny-farthing bicycle, which purports to be a record of regional life.

Practicalities

The **train and bus stations** are both within a few minutes' walk of Mikkeli's centre, where the **tourist office** faces the southern corner of the *kauppatori* at Porrassalmenkatu 15 (June to mid-Aug Mon–Fri 9am–5.30pm, Sat 9am–2pm; mid-Aug to May Mon 9am–5pm, Tues–Fri 9am–4.30pm; ☎015/194 3900, ⓦwww.travel.fi/mikkeli). Free Internet access is available at the library (Mon–Fri 10am–8pm, Sat 9am–2pm), opposite the tourist office at Raatihuoneenkatu 6.

Of Mikkeli's **hotels**, the top-notch *Sokos Hotel Vaakuna*, Porrassalmenkatu 9 (☎015/202 01, ⓦwww.sokoshotels.fi; ❻/❹), is a good bet, or if that's too pricey, try a room at the *Puolikuu* hall of residence, Raviradantie 8 (☎2041 441; ❶; look for the sign "Aikviskoulutuskeskus asuntola") – rooms must be booked ahead as the hall is not staffed and the key is left with the *Kahvila Pauliina* café at the corner of Savilahdenkatu and Raviradantie. The nearest official **youth hostel**, one of the most beautiful in the country, at *Löydön kartano* (☎015/664 101, ⓔloydonkartano @co.inet.fi), lies 20km to the south at Kartanontie 151 in **Ristiina** (5 or 6 Kouvola-bound buses a day stop there). This family-run hostel occupies a large, atmospheric pink-painted wooden house, for two hundred years home to an aristocratic Russian general and his descendants, who bought it in 1752. Beds are €10 and a generous breakfast costs €4.50. Mikkeli also has a couple of **campsites** within striking distance: *Visulahti* (☎015/18 281; mid-May to mid-Aug), 5km from the centre, ask the tourist office about how to get there by bus, and *Mäntyniemi*, Ihastjärventie 40B (☎015/174 220), 7km from the centre (no public transport).

When it comes to **eating**, a tasty range of pizzas, fish and pasta dishes are served up by the mid-priced *Hyvä Naapuri*, Raatihuoneenkatu 4, and *Café Sole* on Porrassalmenkatu, opposite the *kauppatori*, serves filling, cheap lunches. You'll sacrifice atmosphere but save a few euro by eating at *Rosso*, Maaherrankatu 13, but if you want excellent pizza try *Angela*, a Turkish-run place between the bus station and the *kauppatori*. Excellent Mexican food can be found at *Fernando*, Maaherrankatu 17, whilst a few doors down at no. 24, *King's Chinese Restaurant* is no more than average. Of an evening, locals gravitate towards *King Creole* at Vuorikatu 11 which also serves simple burger meals. The main square hosts a particularly good daily market selling fresh breads, fish, fruit and snacks.

Lappeenranta

Likeable **LAPPEENRANTA** (Villmanstrand in Swedish) provides an excellent first taste of the eastern Lake Region, conveniently sited on the main rail line between Helsinki and Joensuu and along all the eastern bus routes. It's a small, slow-paced town where summer evenings find most of the population strolling around the linden tree-lined harbour. Once holding a key position on the Russian border, Lappeenranta boasts historical features that its neighbouring towns don't share and provides an eye-opening introduction to political conflicts that not only affected medieval Finland but also had an impact on recent generations.

It's a twenty-minute walk from the train station, ten minutes from the bus station, through the town centre to the harbour, where the main activity is strolling and snacking from the numerous stands selling the local specialities – spicy meat pastries called *vetyjä* and *atomeja*. If you're feeling more energetic, climb the steep path on the harbour's western side, which brings you to the top of the town's old earthen ramparts and into the Russian-built fortress area, where Lappeenranta's past soon becomes apparent. Its **origins** as a trading centre reach back to the mid-seventeenth century, but it was with the westward shift of the Russian border in 1721 that the town found itself in the front line of Russian–Swedish conflicts. After the Peace of Turku in 1743, the border was again moved, this time leaving Lappeenranta inside Russian territory. Subsequently, a garrison of the Tsar's army arrived and, by 1775, had erected most of the stone buildings of the **fortress** on the short headland that forms the western wall of the harbour. You can buy a joint ticket for both the South Karelian museums (€5; see below) inside the fortress.

Several of these structures still line the cobblestoned Kristiinankatu, which leads across the headland before descending to the shores of the lake, three of them housing museums. Unless you've a particular interest in the military role of horses and the uniforms worn by their riders, however, the collections of the **Cavalry Museum** (June–Aug Mon–Fri 10am–6pm, Sat & Sun 11am–5pm; rest of the year by appointment on ☏05/616 2257; €2.50) can safely be ignored. A better quick stop is the **Orthodox Church** (June to mid-Aug Tues–Sun 10am–6pm; rest of the year by appointment on ☏05/451 5511), just opposite, where the glow of beeswax candles helps illuminate the icons of what is Finland's oldest Orthodox church, founded in 1785.

Step back across Kristiinankatu and you're outside the **South Karelian Art Museum** (June–Aug Mon–Fri 10am–6pm, Sat & Sun 11am–5pm; Sept–May Tues–Sun 11am–5pm; €2.50), which rotates its permanent stock of paintings with south Karelian connections – mostly a mundane bunch of landscapes and portraits, although some important Finnish artists are represented – and stages exhibitions of emerging regional artists in an adjoining building. More rewarding, however, is the **South Karelian Museum** (same hours; €2.50) at the end of Kristiinankatu. Surprisingly, it isn't collections from Lappeenranta that form the main displays here, but ceramics, souvenirs and sporting trophies from Viipuri, the major Finnish town 60km from Lappeenranta that was ceded to the Soviet Union after World War II (see the box on p.744). Many of those who left Viipuri to stay on the Finnish side of the border began their new lives in Lappeenranta, and it's mostly they who shed a tear when looking at these reminders (including a large-scale model) of their home town. Elsewhere in the museum are numerous Karelian costumes, subtle differences in which revealed the wearer's religion and (for women) marital status, and worthy displays on hunting, farming and traditional handicrafts.

Practicalities

The **tourist office**, looking out over the *kauppatori*, is at Kievarinkatu 1 (℡05/667 788, ℗www.lappeenranta.fi). There's also a small tourist booth open by the harbour in summer (℡05/411 8853, daily June to mid-Aug 9am–8/9pm). There's free Internet access at the town library, Valtakatu 47 (June to mid-Aug Mon–Fri 10am–6pm; rest of the year Mon–Fri 10am–8pm).

Reward yourself after a tour of the fortress area with coffee and a home-baked pie or cake at *Café Majurska*, close to the Orthodox Church on Linnoitus. Sour rye bread and the softer *rieska* bread are easily found in Lappeenranta's marketplace or by the harbour, where you'll also find stuffed waffles as well as *atomeja* and *vetyjä* pastries, both local favourites. For more substantial **eating**, try the fair-priced pizzas at *Suvan Kebab Pizzeria*, Kirkkokatu 8, or the tasty fish dishes at *Majakka*, Satamatie 4, facing the harbour. A good choice for affordable pizzas, meat, fish and vegetarian dishes is *Huviretki* at the *Cumulus* hotel, Valtakatu 31; or there's excellent Finnish food on offer at around €10 per dish (lunch for €7–8) at *Grammari*, Kauppakatu 41. For **drinking**, the best chance of finding a full pub is the Irish-style *Old Park*, Valtakatu 36, although during long summer evenings, locals head instead to the harbour where you can catch the last rays and enjoy a beer on the deck of the *Prinsessa Armada*.

Lappeenranta is easily covered in a day, though you may well need to stay overnight between transport links. The pick of several high-standard **hotels** is *Sokos Lappee*, Brahenkatu 1 (℡05/678 61, ℗www.sokoshotels.fi; ❻/❹), and the *Cumulus*, Valtakatu 31 (℡05/677 811, ℗www.cumulus.fi; ❻/❹). There are also some cheaper

---

Viipuri

Before it was ceded to the Soviet Union in 1944, **VIIPURI** (Vyborg in Russian and Swedish) was one of Finland's most prosperous and cosmopolitan towns. Once a major port, being the Saimaa waterway's main link to the Baltic Sea, with a mixed population of Finns, Swedes, Russians and Germans, the town's fortunes declined under Soviet administration. Lack of investment (Viipuri was never allowed to challenge Leningrad's place as the USSR's major western seaport) resulted in a dearth of new construction, and allowed many of the town's once elegant structures to reach advanced states of dilapidation.

Viipuri today has a strange, time-locked quality – a crumbling reminder both of the conflicts that have enveloped the region and of the fading power of the Soviet Union. There's still a host of medieval buildings, the magnificent Alvar Aalto public library, and an enthralling covered market, while Lenin's statue continues to stand in the town's Red Square. But the depths to which the great Russian Bear has fallen are self-evident, with the town's entire infrastructure seemingly in danger of imminent collapse and aggressive-looking moneychangers clutching wads of hard currency on street corners.

From Lappeenranta, there's a **daily bus** to Viipuri (€24 return), which continues to St Petersburg (€62 return). Russian visas, which can take up to ten days to acquire, are needed for this journey. An alternative is a **visa-free day-trip by boat** from Lappeenranta (€50), with (usually) one daily sailing between June and August (Karelia Lines; ℡05/453 0380, ℗411 9096). It's best to reserve as far in advance as possible (at least one week) as these trips get booked up early; if you do call with the hope of a last-minute booking, try asking if there have been any cancellations, but remember all bookings must be finalized the night before the cruise. Boats leave from the main harbour.

guesthouses, such as *Gasthaus Turistilappee*, Kauppakatu 52 (☎05/415 0800, ☏415 0804; ❷). The town's two **youth hostels** are 2km west of the centre: *Karelia Park*, Korpraalinkuja 1 (☎05/675 211, ☏452 8454; June–Aug), and *Huhtiniemi*, Kuusimäenkatu 18 (☎05/453 1888, ⊛www.huhtiniemi.com; June–Aug), which is also where you'll find the local **campsite** (same phone number). Both hostels have double rooms (❶/❷) as well as dorms.

Savonlinna and around

Draped across a series of tightly connected islands, **SAVONLINNA** is one of the most relaxed towns in Finland. Formerly sustained by its woodworking industries and position at a major junction on the Saimaa route, the town nowadays prospers on the income generated from tourism and the cultural kudos derived from its annual international opera festival. It's packed throughout July (when the opera festival takes place) and early August, but on either side of the peak season the town's streets and numerous small beaches are uncluttered. The easy-going mood, enhanced by the slow glide of pleasure craft in and out of the harbour, makes Savonlinna a superb base for a two- or three-day stay, giving ample time to soak up the mellow atmosphere, discover the local sights and curiosities – such as a remarkable modern art centre and a huge nineteenth-century church – that lie within the town's idyllic surrounds.

The Town

Savonlinna's centrally placed passenger harbour and *kauppatori* are pleasant spots to mingle with the crowds and enjoy a snack from one of the numerous food stalls – ask for a *lörtsy*, a local pie which comes in two varieties: savoury with meat and rice, or sweet with apple jam and sugar. Within a few strides, you might poke your head inside the **Savonlinna Art Gallery**, Olavinkatu 40 (Tues–Sun 11am–5pm, July also Mon same hours; €2), which provides a spacious home for temporary shows usually mounted in tandem with those at the Savonlinna Regional Museum (see below); or the smartly restored **Pikkukirkko** (June to mid-Aug daily 11am–5pm), a Lutheran church which began life serving the Greek Orthodox faithful.

Fine as these places may be, however, none of them holds a candle to Savonlinna's greatest possession: the engrossing **Olavinlinna Castle** (daily: June to mid-Aug 10am–5pm; mid-Aug to May 10am–3pm; €5), a fifteen-minute walk from the harbour, at the end of Linnankatu. Perched on a small island and looking like some

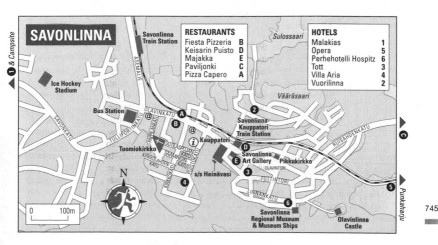

SAVONLINNA

❶ & Campsite

RESTAURANTS
Fiesta Pizzeria   B
Keisarin Puisto   D
Majakka   E
Paviljonki   C
Pizza Capero   A

HOTELS
Malakias   1
Opera   5
Perhehotelli Hospitz   6
Tott   3
Villa Aria   4
Vuorilinna   2

Savonlinna Train Station

Sulossaari

Ice Hockey Stadium

Vääräsaari

Bus Station

Savonlinna-Kauppatori Train Station

Kauppatori

Tuomiokirkko

Savonlinna Art Gallery

Pikkukirkko

s/s Heinävesi

N

Savonlinna Regional Museum & Museum Ships

Olavinlinna Castle

Punkaharju

0   100m

The Savonlinna Opera Festival

Begun in 1912, and an annual event since 1967, Savonlinna's **Opera Festival** lasts the whole of July. The major performances take place in the courtyard of the castle and there are numerous spin-off events all over the town. **Tickets**, priced €35–170, go on sale the preceding November and sell out rapidly, although the tourist office keeps some back to sell during the festival. For further details contact the **Opera Office**, Olavinkatu 27 (☎015/476 750, ⊛www.operafestival.fi).

great, grey sea monster surfacing from the deep, the castle was founded in 1475 to guard this important lake-transport junction at the eastern extremity of what was then the Swedish empire – a region being eyed by an expansionistic Russia. The Swedes built walls 5m thick to resist attack on the eastern side, but the castle was to switch hands fairly frequently in later years; the last change saw the Russians moving in after the westward shift of the border that followed the 1743 Peace of Turku. They added the incongruous Adjutant's Apartment which, with its bright yellow walls and curved windows, resembles a large piece of Emmenthal cheese. With military importance lost when Finland became a Russian Grand Duchy in 1809, the castle ended its pre-restoration days rather ignominiously as the town jail.

The castle can only be visited on guided **tours** (in English), included in the admission fee, which begin on the hour from the entrance. The guides' commentary is a vital aid to comprehending the complex historical twists and turns that the castle endured, and for pointing out the numerous oddities, such as the sole original indoor toilet in the maiden's chamber, through which there's a sheer drop to the lake below.

Occupying an 1852 granary a stone's throw from the castle, the **Savonlinna Regional Museum** (July to mid-Aug daily 11am–8pm; rest of the year Tues–Sun 11am–5pm; €3, ticket also covers the art gallery – see above) is among the Lake Region's better accounts of the evolution of local life, beginning with an intriguing display on the prehistoric rock paintings found near Savonlinna. The bulk of the museum charts hunting and farming techniques, and the birth of the area's tar and logging industries, although the upper level holds temporary art exhibitions, often culled from the country's most interesting private collections.

Outside, docked at the end of a jetty, are three c.1900 steamers known as the **Museum Ships** (June–Aug only, same times as Regional Museum; admission with same ticket), which earned their keep plying the Saimaa waterways, sometimes travelling as far as St Petersburg and Lübeck.

Practicalities

While there are very few trains to Savonlinna, there is a choice of **train stations**: Savonlinna-Kauppatori is by far the most central, although if you're making straight for the *Malakias* youth hostel (see below), get off at Savonlinna, 1km to the west. The **bus station**, served by six buses a day from Mikkeli and Helsinki, is also a short distance west of the centre, just off Olavinkatu. The **tourist office**, Puistokatu 1 (June & Aug daily 8am–6pm; July daily 8am–8pm; rest of the year Mon–Fri 9am–5pm; ☎015/517 510, ⊛www.travel.fi/savonlinna), faces the passenger harbour. Staff can point you in the right direction to rent out bicycles and also supply useful route maps for cycling in the area; there's free Internet access, too. Unusually for a provincial Finnish town, Savonlinna has two **Internet cafés**: *Knut Posse*, Olavinkatu 44, and *Kastelli*, Olavinkatu 53.

Savonlinna has several budget accommodation possibilities and some good **hotels**, but don't expect the big discounts you might find elsewhere, as there's no shortage of summer business, and prices shoot up for the Opera Festival in July. The bland summer-only *Hotel Tott*, Satamakatu 1 (☎015/573 673, ℗514 504; ❺, ❻ during festival), is a sound if uninspiring choice, with apartments on offer (€128 without a sauna, €218 with) as well as rooms. Other **summer hotels** include *Villa Aria* (☎015/476 7515; advance bookings when closed ☎015/515 555; ❻), a recently renovated c.1900 building on Puistokatu 15, just down the street from the tourist office; and *Hotel Opera* (☎015/521 116; advance bookings when closed on ☎015/476 7515, ℱ476 7540; ❹), just past the castle near the road to Punkaharju at Kyrönniemenkuja 9. Two of Savonlinna's other summer hotels have **dormitory** accommodation as well as rooms: *Malakias*, Pihlajavedenkatu 6 (☎015/533 283, ℱ533 283; ❸/❹ during festival), 2km west of the centre, and the handier *Vuorilinna* (☎015/739 5430, ℱ272 524; ❸/❹ during festival) on Vääräsaari, the island linked by a short bridge to the *kauppatori*. *Perhehotelli Hospitz*, Linnankatu 20 (☎015/515 661, ℱ515 120; ❸/❺ during festival), also has good-value rooms, but you'll need to book ahead as it's very popular. For an atmospheric night's accommodation it's hard to beat the superior **hostel** accommodation of the steamboat cabins (❶; no cabins are en-suite) on board the *S/S Heinävesi* – the vessel is moored in the harbour overnight once it returns from its day-trips to Punkaharju (see below). There's a marked absence of **campsites** in Savonlinna: the nearest is *Vuohimäki* (☎09/613 832 10, ℱ09/713 713; June to late Aug), 7km west of the centre and served by bus #3.

When it comes to **eating**, the usual pizza joints line Olavinkatu – *Pizza Capero*, at no. 51, is as good as any of them – but if you really want to sate your appetite, cross the road and head into the courtyard at Olavinkatu 46 where *Fiesta Pizzeria* has huge pizzas for just €5. With a bit more to spend you might try the Chinese restaurant, *Keisarin Puisto*, at Olavinkatu 33 (main courses €8.50–10.50, lunch €6). For **Finnish food**, sample the extensive menu at *Majakka*, Satamakatu 11, though mains here start at around €12. The most adventurous place to dine, however, is *Paviljonki*, Rajalahendenkatu 4, where Finland's top trainee chefs serve up their latest creations. The service is excellent, the food imaginative and well prepared. Lunch here costs around €10. **Drinking** your way round diminutive Savonlinna won't take long, but sooner or later you're bound to find yourself at *Sillansuu*, Verkkosaarenkatu 1, close to the *kauppatori* and railway station, which is known for its wide selection of beers, while *Happy Time*, nearby at Olavinkatu 36, is the most popular place to imbibe.

North of Savonlinna: Villa Rauhalinna

Completed in 1900 in the village of Lehtiniemi, 17km north of Savonlinna, **Villa Rauhalinna** was built by a high-ranking officer in the Russian army as a silver-wedding present to his wife. The villa is a phenomenal example of intricate and ornate carpentry, and is decorated throughout with many of its original fixtures and fittings. It's not a museum, however, and while visitors are free to explore most of the villa, and the tree-filled grounds that extend to the lakeside, most people make the day-trip from Savonlinna to partake of the slap-up Russian lunch buffet (July daily, €23; June & Aug Sun only, €12) served in the dining room.

If eating in the villa is beyond your means, bring a picnic to consume beside the lake and take the opportunity to discover something of the privileged lifestyles of well-heeled Russians in early twentieth-century Finland. Regular **buses** run from Savonlinna to Lehtiniemi, but it's more in keeping with the spirit of the place to arrive by **boat** (at €6 return, only slightly pricier than the bus) from the passenger harbour. If you can't face leaving the villa, a few double rooms are available (☎015/517 640, ✉casino.myynti@svlkylpylaitos.fi; ❸).

East of Savonlinna: Punkaharju Ridge and beyond

According to local belief, the **Punkaharju Ridge** is the healthiest place to breathe in the world, thanks to an abundance of conifers that super-oxygenate the air. This narrow, seven-kilometre-long thread of land between lakes Puruvesi and Pihlavesi begins 27km east of Savonlinna, and three roads and a railway line are squeezed onto it. With the water never more than a few metres away on either side, this is the

Lake Region at its most beautiful, and is easily reached on any train heading this way from Savonlinna. However, it's also the most hyped destination in Finland, and, although you should make an effort to see the ridge, don't rule out other places further north.

Along the ridge, at the centre of things, you'll find **Lusto**, the national forest museum (May & Sept daily 10am–5pm, June–Aug daily 10am–7pm; Oct–April Tues–Sun 10am–5pm; €7). Designed, predictably, from wood, its permanent exhibits examine how forests function and survive; there's also a shop stocked with wooden items, though perhaps the best part is the restaurant-café, where you can fill up on sautéed reindeer, fillet of elk and *kuusenkerkkä*, a gloriously rich cake of *smetana*, pine kernels and Lappish berries. For exploring the area further, you can rent bikes here for €5 a day.

Should you want to stay, the most atmospheric **hotel** is *Punkaharjun Valtionhotelli*, Punkaharju 2 (☎015/739 611, ☞441 784; July ❻/❹, rest of year ❺), an ornate wooden house on the ridge that still summons up the tsarist era, despite an insipid restoration. Only a little cheaper in season but decidedly ugly is *Gasthaus Punkaharju*, Palomäentie 18 (☎015/473 123, ☞441 771; ❸). To be honest though, there's more reason to spend the night in Savonlinna than to be stuck out on the ridge dependent on skeletal public transport to continue your journey.

Retretti Arts Centre

About 25km southeast from Savonlinna, just before reaching the village of Punkaharju, the main road passes the extraordinary **Retretti Arts Centre** (daily: June & Aug 10am–5pm; July 10am–6pm; €15), a place devoted to the visual and performing arts. The unique element is the setting – man-made caves gouged into three-billion-year-old rock by the same machines which dug the Helsinki metro – it cost so much to build that the project bankrupted the original owner. Outside, in the large sculpture park, fibreglass human figures by Finnish artist Olavi Lanu entwine cunningly with the forms of nature; tree branches suddenly become human limbs and plain-looking boulders slowly mutate under your gaze into a pile of male and female torsos. Inside the caves, the exhibitions are changed every year, with artists developing site-specific projects to complement the dramatic setting. The interior also features underground streams, whose gushings and bubblings underpin the music piped into the air. There are also several above-ground sites that show work from well-known European masters – the last few years have seen major displays by Cézanne, Monet, Repin and Munch.

The few daily **trains** between Savonlinna and Parikkala call at Retretti train station; their timings can be very inconvenient, however, and buses provide a more reliable alternative. Another option, though an expensive one (€24 return), is to travel by *boat* from Savonlinna's passenger harbour via the *S/S Heinävesi*, which departs at 11am, and returning from Punkaharju at 3.40pm (mid-June to mid-Aug only). All these transport details should be checked at the tourist office as they fluctuate frequently. One way to enjoy the art without keeping an eye on your watch is to stay virtually next door at *Punkaharjun Lomakeskus* (☎015/739 611, ❻ 441 784), an extensive camping area with simple cabins (❷) and fully equipped cottages (❻) as well.

Kerimäki church

Though, like Retretti, it lies to the east of Savonlinna (23km distant), the village of **Kerimäki** is nearly impossible to reach by public transport without first returning to Savonlinna, from where there are several daily buses (check the latest details at the tourist office). The reason to come to this otherwise unremarkable village on the shores of Lake Puruvesi is to see the **Kerimäki kirkko** (mid-May to late Aug daily 10am–6/7pm; closed rest of year), an immense wooden construction built in 1848 to hold 3000 people, and claimed to be the largest wooden church in the world. Complete with double-tiered balconies, and a yellow- and white-painted exterior beaming through the surrounding greenery, it's a truly astonishing sight. Kerimäki can be a pleasant place to spend a quiet couple of days: there's a nice little place to swim and a decent guesthouse, the *Kerihovi* (☎015/541 225; ❸), which has a traditional bar/restaurant that offers home-cooking and alcoholic beverages.

Varkaus, Valamo Monastery and Joensuu

Due to the preponderance of water in the vicinity, **train connections** around Savonlinna are extremely limited, only running east to Parikkala to link with Helsinki and Joensuu-bound express trains. However, **buses** (accepting train tickets and passes) operate from Savonlinna to **Pieksämäki**, the major rail junction in central Finland from where there are good connections north to Kuopio, Kajaani and Oulu, west to Jyväskylä, Vaasa, Tampere and Turku and east to the industrial town of **Varkaus**, which lies on the Turku–Joensuu line. In all cases, the latest timetables should be carefully checked before making plans. **Valamo Monastery**, situated off the railway line between Varkaus and Joensuu, makes for an intriguing stop, but one fraught with difficulties unless you have your own transport.

Varkaus

The sawmills and engineering factories that dominate diminutive but commercially important **VARKAUS** sit amid gentle hills and dense forests. On a good day, the billowing chimneys and steel pipes are artily mirrored in the placid waters of the town's lakes; on a bad day, unwelcome smells fill the air and there can be few Finnish towns where nature seems so obviously to be losing the battle against heavy industry. Even if you hate Varkaus on arrival, stick around long enough to see the canal and mechanical music museums: both, in their very different ways, are unique.

The Town

In such a place, it seems appropriate that **Varkaus kirkko**, on Savontie (early June to late Aug daily 9am–7pm; rest of the year by appointment only on ☎017/578 5205), should be designed in a severe functional style. Inside, the church is notable less for its architecture than an immense altar fresco. Measuring almost 300 square metres, it's the largest in the Nordic countries, painted – with the aid of several helpers and a large amount of scaffolding – by revered Finnish artist Lennart Stegerstråle.

A short walk from the church at Savontie 7, a group of yellow wooden buildings from 1916 holds the **Museum of Workers' Housing** (*Työväenasuntomuseo*; early June to late Aug Tues, Thurs & Sun 11am–4pm, Wed 2–7pm; other times by appointment only on ☎017/579 4440; €3), comprising a briefly interesting succession of single rooms furnished to show typical living conditions from the 1920s (when Varkaus factory labourers kept pigs and cows to remind them of their country origins) to the 1960s. The **Museum of Esa Pakarinen**, also in the workers' housing complex (same times as above; same ticket valid), remembers a tremendously popular Finnish comic actor of the postwar years who was a Varkaus resident. Pakarinen's forte was playing the fool (he rejoiced in the on-screen nickname "wood head") and singing with his false teeth removed. Besides assorted mementos of his glittering career, a TV runs videos of Pakarinen's finest films – though the subtleties are well and truly lost on non-Finnish speakers.

A fifteen-minute walk from Savontie along factory-dominated Ahlströminkatu brings you to the **Varkaus Museum**, Wredenkatu 5A (Tues & Thurs 10am–4pm, Wed noon–7pm, Sun 11am–5pm; €2), which provides some proof – with displays on the beginnings of local settlements and early agricultural life – that Varkaus did exist before the discovery of iron ore in local river beds set the town on course to becoming an engineering powerhouse. Much of the museum, however, charts the rise and rise of the local firm founded in 1909 by Walter Ahlström (after whom most things in the town appear to be named); by the 1950s, the company was – and continues to be – among the world's leading innovators in industrial machinery.

The canal and mechanical music museums

Leaving the town centre on Taipaleentie takes you over the rapids that made lake transport around Varkaus difficult until 1835, when a rough canal was built a kilometre east of the ferocious waters (look for the tower above the locks of the modern-day Taipale Canal). Following successive poor harvests, emergency labour was used to build a second, wider canal in 1867. Before this task was completed, 227 labourers had died from hunger or disease and been buried in mass graves; their final resting places can still be seen at the end of a rough track on Varkausmäki hill, some 7km from Varkaus. Rather than make the long and morbid trek to the grave sites, however, a visit to the **National Central Canal Museum**, inside a former warehouse beside the modern canal (June–Aug daily 10am–6pm; Sept–May by appointment on ☎017/579 4440; €2), provides all the background you'll need on the building of the Varkaus canals and the growth of canals generally in Finland. It's less drab than you might expect: the early canals not only opened up important new transport routes in the pre-motorized days, but had strategic importance in the border disputes between Finland and Russia.

Close to the canal museum, the bizarre and superb **Museum of Mechanical Music**, Pelimanninkatu 8 (July daily 10am–6pm; Aug to mid-Dec & March–June Tues–Sat 11am–6pm, Sun 11am–5pm; €7.50), is really more of a personal show than a museum, with the eccentric German curator and his family singing along with his extraordinary collection of music-making devices – from an ancient pianola to a prototype stereo gramophone – gathered from all over Europe and restored to working order.

Practicalities

From the **bus and train terminals** on Relanderinkatu, it's a walk of just a few minutes to Kauppakatu, Varkaus's main street. To reach the **tourist office** at Kauppatori 6 (Mon–Fri 9am–4.30pm; ☎017/579 4944, ⓦwww.varkaus.fi/matkailu), however, you'll need to walk for a further ten minutes along Taipaleentie – note that there's no sign outside. The well-stocked library (Mon–Thurs 10am–7pm, Fri 10am–6pm) on Osmajoentie has free Internet access.

There's little incentive to spend longer than you have to in Varkaus, but if you do need to **stay overnight**, try the adequate but old-fashioned (and receptionless) *Keskus-Hotelli*, Ahlströminkatu 18 (❹/❸), which has a wonderful mirrored entrance hall. If you want to get in touch with the *Keskus* then you need to contact the more modern *Oscar*, around the corner at Kauppatori 4 (☎017/579 011, ℻579 0500; ❻/❺), which handles reservations for both hotels. A more basic alternative is *Joutsenkulma*, Käämeniementie 20 (☎017/366 9797, ℻366 9798; ❸). The only truly budget accommodation in town is the *Taipale* **campsite** (☎017/552 6644; June–Aug), on Leiritie.

Varkaus isn't the nation's culinary hot spot, and **eating** cheaply is limited to the *Dahong* Chinese restaurant at Ahlströminkatu 10 or the local branch of *Rosso*, Ahlströminkatu 21, plying the usual pizzas.

Valamo Monastery

The original **Valamo Monastery**, on an island in Lake Ladoga, was the spiritual headquarters of Orthodox Karelia from the thirteenth century onwards. In 1940, however, with Soviet attack imminent, the place was abandoned and rebuilt well inside the Finnish border, roughly halfway between Varkaus and Joensuu.

Volunteer workers arrive each summer to assist the monks in their daily tasks, and shorter-term visitors are welcome to imbibe the spiritual atmosphere and enjoy the tranquillity of the setting, though the somewhat austere regime won't suit everyone. Without transport of your own, **getting to the monastery** is not easy. There's a once-daily bus from Varkaus in the summer leaving at 1.45pm for the fifty-minute journey. Annoyingly, outside the summer months there's also a later evening bus to the monastery from Varkaus. Both these services operate from Helsinki to Joensuu,

751

△ Porvoo

calling at Lahti, Mikkeli, Varkaus and the monastery. To get there from other destinations try contacting the monastery direct. There are both dormitories and private rooms (**①**) if you want **to stay** overnight (☎017/570 1504, ✆www.valamo.fi).

Joensuu

JOENSUU, the capital of what was left of Finnish Karelia after the eastern half was ceded to the Soviet Union in 1944, has attracted attention for all the wrong reasons in recent years due to several well-documented racist attacks on refugees. However, things have quietened down of late and the town appears to be making a considered effort to welcome all visitors. Whether you arrive by bus or train (the terminals are adjacent to one another), the kilometre-long walk into the centre of Joensuu is one of the most enjoyable introductions to any Lake Region town: the route crosses the broad Pielisjoki River and then the narrow Joensuu Canal before reaching Eliel Saarinen's epic Art Nouveau town hall and the wide *kauppatori*. Pleasing first impressions apart, compact and modestly sized Joensuu doesn't have too much beyond the usual round of local museums and churches to fill your time – a day will cover it with ease.

The culture and tourist centre, **Carelicum** (Mon–Fri 10am–5pm, Sat & Sun 11am–4pm; €4.20), in the centre of town at Koskikatu 5, houses the **tourist office** (Mon–Fri 9am–5pm, Sat & Sun 11am–4pm; ☎013/267 5223, ✆www.jns.fi), an excellent source of information (plus free Internet access), a **box office** (☎013/267 5222) selling tickets for all the town's theatrical and musical performances, and a decent café and a gift shop. Also housed in the centre is the **North Karelian Museum** (same times and ticket as Carelicum), focusing on Karelia's historical position in the middle of an East–West power struggle.

Considering the devastation caused by World War II, Joensuu has a surprising number of nineteenth-century buildings intact. These include the wood-framed structure that used to house the tourist office at Koskikatu, and the red-brick former schoolhouse which holds the **Art Museum**, at Kirkkokatu 23 (Tues–Sun noon–6pm; €3). The museum's minor pieces and an unexpected crop of Far Eastern and Greek antiquities fail to divert attention from Edelfelt's finely realized portrait, *The Parisienne* – worth the admission fee alone. Some of Finland's more radical new artists get a showing a hundred metres down the road at the **Avant Art Gallery**, Koskikatu 7 (Mon–Fri 10am–4pm, Sat 11am–2pm; free).

Leaving the art museum and glancing either way along the aptly named Kirkkokatu, you'll spot Joensuu's major churches standing at opposite ends. To the right, the neo-Gothic **Lutheran Church** (June to mid-Aug Mon 11am–4pm; other times by arrangement through the tourist office) can seat a thousand worshippers but, aside from Antti Salmenlinna's impressive stained-glass windows, it's not wildly different from its counterparts in other towns. A few years older, the icon-rich **Orthodox Church** of Saint Nikolaos (mid-June to mid-Aug Mon–Fri 10am–4pm; other times by arrangement on ☎013/127 925) is more deserving of a swift peek inside.

If you find yourself with time to spare, take a trip through the cactus-filled greenhouses of Joensuu University's **Botanical Gardens**, Heinäpurontie 70 (April–Aug Mon & Wed–Fri 10am–6pm, Sat & Sun 11am–4pm; Sept–March Mon & Wed–Fri 10am–4pm, Sat & Sun 11am–4pm; €4.20). In summer the greenhouses are also home to flocks of tropical butterflies which are flown in weekly from Malaysia. Afterwards, you could explore the gardens themselves, which are claimed to hold a specimen of every plant native to northern Karelia – there are many more of these than you might expect.

Practicalities

For an overnight stay, you'll find some very good summer rates at the central and comfortable *Sokos Hotel Vaakuna*, Torikatu 20 (☎013/277 511, ✆www.sokoshotels.fi; **⑤/④**). Elsewhere, there are **dorm beds** as well as regular double rooms (**③**) at the

Crossing the Russian border; Sortavala

If you've visited the Carelicum in Joensuu, you'll have seen a scale model of **Sortavala**, one of the many Finnish towns to come under Soviet control following the postwar realignment of the border. Since the collapse of the Soviet Union, it's been possible for Finns (and indeed any other Westerners equipped with Russian visas) to visit the town with comparative ease. Despite occupying a scenic position on the shores of Lake Ladoga, Sortavala itself has no intrinsic appeal whatsoever. **The journey from Joensuu to Sortavala** takes nearly four hours and several local tour companies go there in the summer; get the latest details from the Joensuu tourist office.

central summer hotel *Elli*, Länsikatu 18 (☎013/225 927, ☯www.kolumbus.fi/hotel .elli). The *Partiotalo*, a **youth hostel** run by the Scouts organization (☎013/123 381; June–Aug), is located 1km north of the town centre, at Vanamokatu 25; the town **campsite** is beside the Pyhäselkä lake at Linnunlahdentie 1 (☎013/126 272, ℻223 337; June–Aug) and also has **cabins** from €35.

Besides the tasty morsels which can be picked up for a few euro inside the *kauppahalli* (beside the *kauppatori*), Joensuu's bargain **eating** options include the usual pizza joints – *Rosso*, Siltakatu 8, is the most dependable. For something more extravagant, try the French and Finnish cuisine and subdued atmosphere provided by an old-fashioned live orchestra at the *Hotel Kimmel* restaurant, Itäranta 1. For good Hungarian food, head for the *Astoria*, overlooking the river at Rantakatu 32, where you can eat outside in warm weather; this is the most enjoyable restaurant in town by a long chalk.

Two major festivals enliven the town's entertainment calendar. The last weekend of July sees the **Gospel Festival** (☯www.suomigospel.net), when thousands of singers turn up from all around Europe. Even bigger, however, is the annual **Ilosaari Rock Festival** (middle weekend of July; ☯www.ilosaarirock.fi), attracting top Finnish and international acts as well as hordes of thrill-seeking Finnish youths. If you're in any doubt as to the sheer scale of these events, take a look at the huge **Song Bowl**, which sits beside the Pyhäselkä lake, just southwest of Joensuu's centre. Tickets to both festivals can be booked via the box office in the Carelicum.

North from Joensuu: Nurmes

Should Joensuu be as rural as you want to get, swing inland (change trains at Pieksämäki) to the more metropolitan Kuopio (see p.754). Otherwise, continue north from Joensuu into some of the eastern Lake Region's least populated but scenically most spectacular sections, where there are hilltop views out above the tips of fir trees across watery expanses that stretch far into Russia. The small town of **NURMES**, 120km from Joensuu and linked to it by twice-daily train, is the obvious base for exploration, though you'll need private transport – or a lot of careful juggling with bus local timetables – to find the best of the forested and lake-studded landscape. There's a useful **tourist office** on Lomatie (June–Aug daily 8am–4pm; rest of the year Mon–Fri 8am–4pm; ☎013/481 770, ☯www.nurmes.fi). Budget **accommodation** in Nurmes can be found at two hostels, *Pompannappi* (☎049/806 725), Koulukatu 16, and *Hyvärilä* (☎013/481 770, ℻481 775), on Lomatie, which is also the location of the town's **campsite**. There's also an exceedingly ordinary, central **hotel**, *Nurmeshovi*, Kirkkokatu 21 (☎013/480 750; ❸). **Moving on** from Nurmes is surprisingly easy for such a relatively remote location – **buses** (accepting train tickets and passes) run to **Kajaani** or Kontiomäki (one stop further north), both of which are on the Kuopio–Oulu train line.

Kuopio

Sited on a major inland north–south rail route and the hub of local long-distance bus services, **KUOPIO** has the feel – and, by day, much of the hustle and bustle – of a large city, although it is in fact only marginally bigger than most of the other Lake Region communities. Nonetheless, it's an important Finnish town and, especially if you're speeding north to Lapland, provides both a break in the journey and an enjoyable taste of the region.

Arrival, information and accommodation

Adjacent to one another at the northern end of Puijonkatu, Kuopio's **train and long-distance bus stations** are an easy walk from the town centre. There are good bus and train connections north from Kuopio to Iisalmi (see p.757) and on to Kajaani and Oulu (see the following chapter), as well as with Helsinki and all the main southern towns. The **tourist office** faces the *kauppatori* at Haapaniemenkatu 17 (June to mid-Aug Mon–Fri 9.30am–5pm, Sat 10am–3pm; mid-Aug to May Mon–Fri 9.30am–4.30pm; ☎017/182 584, ⓦwww.kuopioinfo.fi).

The rock-bottom budget **accommodation** options are both some distance from the centre of town: the *Hostelli Rauhalahti* **youth hostel** is a four-kilometre trek to the south at Katiskaniementie 8 (☎017/473 473, ⓕ473 470), while the **campsite** (☎017/312 244; May–Aug) is 500m further south from the hostel; to get there take bus #7. Staying centrally costs more, although there are no-frills double rooms (and a few dorm beds) at *Guesthouse Rautatie*, Vuorikatu 35 (☎017/580 0569; ❶). More luxurious accommodation, with lake views and private saunas, can be found at the *Sokos Hotel Puijonsarvi*, Minna Canthinkatu 16 (☎017/170 111, ⓦwww.sokoshotels.fi;

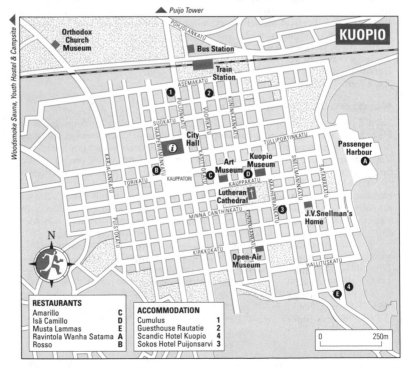

RESTAURANTS

Amarillo	C
Isä Camillo	D
Musta Lammas	E
Ravintola Wanha Satama	A
Rosso	B

ACCOMMODATION

Cumulus	1
Guesthouse Rautatie	2
Scandic Hotel Kuopio	4
Sokos Hotel Puijonsarvi	3

❺/❹). Otherwise, try the *Cumulus*, Puijonkatu 32 (☎017/617 711,🌑www.cumulus
.fi; ❺/❸), which has a pool, or the glitzier *Scandic Hotel Kuopio*, Satamakatu 1
(☎017/195 111, 🌑www.scandic-hotels.com; ❺) which has unsurpassed views of
the Kallavesi lake as well as a superb ground-floor sauna and pool.

The Town

Kuopio's broad *kauppatori*, overlooked by the nineteenth-century city hall, is very
much the heart of the town, with live jazz and rock music issuing from its large
stage in summer. Walk the kilometre eastwards from here along Kauppakatu,
towards the busy passenger harbour on the Kallavesi lake, and you'll pass most
things worth seeing in town – with the exception of the extraordinary Orthodox
Church Museum (see p.756).

At Kauppakatu 35, the **Kuopio Art Museum** (Tues–Fri 10am–5pm, Wed until
7pm, Sat & Sun 11am–4pm; €2.50; for guided tours call ☎017/182 633) fills a
sturdy granite building with an enterprising assortment of contemporary exhibitions, and, on the upper floor, keeps a less stimulating stock of twentieth-century
Finnish painting with local connections. Further along the same street at no. 23, the
Kuopio Museum (May–Aug Mon–Sat 9am–4pm, Wed until 8pm, Sun
11am–6pm; Sept–April closed Sun; €4) charts the evolution of local settlements,
from motley Stone Age findings to the thousand-and-one uses that tree bark was
put to in pre-industrial Finland. The switch from rural to urban life caused great
changes in Finnish society, but one thing that remained constant was a dependency
on coffee: using the original fittings, the museum re-creates a Kuopio institution:
Alli Karvonen's coffee shop, which dispensed the beverage from 1933 to 1969 in
cups etched with Finnish landscapes. Unless stuffed reindeer munching plastic
lichen and a bleak collection of painted wooden insects set your pulse racing, the
rest of the museum can be ignored, but keep an eye out for Juho Rissanen's *The
Builders*, a study of eleven naked Nordic men constructing a wall, on the staircase –
a fresco that turns many heads. Also within the Kuopio Museum, and included in
the entrance fee, the **Museum of Natural History** houses a spectacular, full-size
reconstruction of a woolly mammoth, one of only four in the world. Musk oxen
hides have been used to recreate the beast's shaggy appearance, based on a real
mammoth found in Siberia two hundred years ago. Satisfy yourself instead, however, with the knowledge that there once were mammoths in this part of Finland and
that a molar tooth was discovered near Kuopio in 1873 – hence all the museum
excitement.

Leave the museum and cross the road to the **Lutheran Cathedral** (Mon–Thurs
10am–3pm, Fri 10am–midnight), a handsome creation erected in 1815 using local
stone. Although spacious, the cathedral's interior could hardly be described as opulent, but years ago it did contrast dramatically with the cramped living quarters of
most Kuopio folk. Walk south along Kuninkaankatu until you reach Kirkkokatu
and the **Open-Air Museum** (mid-May to mid-Sept daily 10am–5pm, Wed until
7pm; mid-Sept to mid-May Tues–Sun 10am–3pm; €2.50), where the stock of
mostly wooden dwellings reveals the up-against-it domestic conditions that prevailed, at least for Kuopio's poorer inhabitants, from the 1840s to the 1930s.

Another old house, interesting for a quite different reason, stands at
Snellmaninkatu 19, preserved as **J.V. Snellman's Home** (mid-May to Sept daily
10am–5pm, Wed until 7pm; rest of the year by appointment on ☎017/182 624, in
winter ☎017/182 625; €1.50). From 1844, when the 39-year-old Snellman (for
more on whom, see p.673) married his 17-year-old bride, the couple spent several
years in this large but far from grand home. At the time, Snellman was earning a living as head of Kuopio's elementary school after the country's Swedish-speaking
ruling class had booted him out of his university post, angry at his efforts to have
Finnish made an official language. Aided by a few original furnishings and a colour
scheme devised by Snellman, the house may be fairly authentic, but there isn't

actually a lot to see – though that shouldn't deter anyone with an interest in Finnish history from paying their respects.

Set on the brow of the hill at Kuopio's northwest corner, the enormously impressive **Orthodox Church Museum**, Karjalankatu 1 (May–Aug Tues–Sun 10am–4pm; Sept–April Mon–Fri noon–3pm, Sat & Sun noon–5pm; €5), draws the Orthodox faithful from many parts of the world. Even if the workings of the Orthodox religion are a complete mystery to you, there's much to be enjoyed: elaborate Russian-made icons, gold-embossed Bibles, gowns and prayer books, and lots more. The placing of the museum in Kuopio is no accident. This part of Finland has a large Orthodox congregation, many of them (or their parents) from the parts of eastern Finland that became Soviet territory after World War II. Many objects from the original Valamo Monastery (see p.751), likewise caught on the wrong side of the border, are also on display here.

One of the highlights of Kuopio is a visit to the world's biggest **woodsmoke sauna** (€10) at the *Rauhalahti* hostel (see p.754), an enormous unisex affair which can hold up to sixty people. Its size is such that it takes 24 hours just to heat up – consequently, it's only open on Tuesdays and Fridays. For €27 you can avail yourself of an inclusive deal combining sauna and a traditional Finnish feast – visit the tourist office or call the hostel for more details.

Situated about 2km behind the train station on a ridge is the 75-metre-high **Puijo Tower** (June–Aug daily 9am–10pm, May & Sept Mon–Sat 9am–8pm, Sun 9am–5pm; Oct–April Mon–Sat noon–8pm, Sun noon–5pm; €3), with fantastic views over the surrounding countryside, a revolving restaurant (closed during winter) and a small goblin theme park for the kids.

Eating, drinking and nightlife

While you're in Kuopio, look out for *kalakukko* – a kind of bread pie, baked with fish and pork inside it. While it's found all around the country, Kuopio is *kalakukko*'s traditional home and the town's bakeries generally sell it warm and wrapped in silver foil; a fist-sized piece costs about €2.50. You can also buy *kalakukko* hot from the oven at the *Hanna Partanen*, in a backyard on Kasamikatu (daily 5am–9pm); it's reckoned to be the best place in town, if not the whole of Finland, to sample it. A kilo loaf costs about €12.

Despite Kuopio's expertise in fish pies, it's the pizza joints that provide nourishment at the most reasonable prices: *Rosso*, on Haapaniemenkatu at the side of the *kauppatori*, is the best bet. The town's finest restaurant is undoubtedly the *Musta Lammas*, down in the cellar vaults at Satamakatu 4, opposite the *Scandic Hotel Kuopio* (☎017/581 0458), which has been in business since 1862 – try the goose breast in honey vinegar sauce with parsnip purée for €16.20. Another excellent and popular choice is *Isä Camillo*, Kauppakatu 25–27 (☎017/581 0450), which serves a range of Mediterranean cooking. Several of the pubs mentioned below also offer good-value **lunches**; for something more exotic, try the Mexican food at *Amarillo*, Kirjastokatu 10, where lunches cost around €6.40. On sunny summer evenings though, you'll find most people down by the harbourside eating and drinking in the former customs house that is now the excellent *Ravintola Wanha Satama*, which serves up modern Finnish cuisine.

Kuopio has a reputation for being the stamping ground of some of Finland's best rock musicians, and the town has a number of **pubs** where you can hear live music. *Apteekkari*, Kauppakatu 18, sees jam sessions and some live bands; *O'Connel's* (adjacent to *Amarillo*) at Käsityökatu 23, and *Emigrant*, Kauppakatu 16, are less music-oriented but are usually enjoyable drinking spots. For a more mellow evening out, try the upmarket *Sampo*, Kauppakatu 13, noted for its fine fish restaurant with dishes around €10. Out of central Kuopio (but close to the campsite), the *Yölintu* bar at the *Rauhalahti* hostel stages some wild bashes on Friday nights. Find out what's happening there by asking at the tourist office, or try phoning the hotel itself on ☎017/473 473.

Iisalmi and around

The farmland around **IISALMI**, an hour north of Kuopio by bus, makes a welcome break from pine forests and marks the centre of northern Savolax, a district that, in public opinion polls, is regularly voted the least desirable place to live in Finland. The reason for this is slightly mysterious – the modestly sized town looks nice enough – but might be due to the locals' reputation for geniality mixed with low cunning. Whether this is innate, or a defensive reaction by country folk who've been pitchforked into urban life, is debatable.

Whatever the truth, two museums give a very good insight into local life. The **District Museum** (June to mid-Aug Mon–Fri 9am–6pm; rest of the year Mon–Fri 9am–5pm; free), at Kivirannantie 5 on the shores of the Paloisvirta river – cross the river from the centre of town and turn right – reveals the down-at-heel life of the peasantry via a number of wooden farmhouses once occupied by local farmers and fishermen; while the **Juhani Aho Museum** (May–Aug daily 10am–6pm; €2) in Mansikkaniemi, 5km along the main road, Pohjolankatu, by local bus, shows how the other half lived. Juhani Aho was a major influence on Finnish literature as it emerged around the beginning of the twentieth century, and the simple buildings filled with the author's possessions manage to convey the commitment of the artists who came together in the last years of Russian rule. However, it's the **Brewery Museum**, Luuniemenkatu 4 (Mon–Fri 10am–5pm; free) which is Iisalmi's greatest draw – from the tourist office head west one block on Satamakatu before turning left into Riistakatu and walking another block; Luuniemenkatu begins at the junction with Veikonkatu. Finns flock here to see the brewing process that has created one of the nation's favourite tipples, *Olvi*, and although there's no tasting as part of the tour, there is a beer hall, *Holvi Oluthalli*, attached to the site where it's possible to lay your hands – against hard cash – on some of the hard stuff. Don't think of coming here in the evening for a drink – it's closed.

Practicalities

Aside from the *Artos* **hotel** at Kyllikinkatu 8 (℡017/812 244, ℻814 941; ❸), and the *Iisalmi Seurahuone*, Savonkatu 2 (℡838 31, ℻823 565; ❺, ❹) budget accommodation in the town is limited. However, if you're here in July and August head for the *NMKY* hostel, Sarvikatu 4 (℡823 940; ❶), whose seven rooms fill up fast. Otherwise, the **tourist office** at Kauppakatu 22 (June to mid-Aug Mon–Fri 9am–6pm; Sept–May Mon–Fri 9am–5pm; ℡017/8303 391, ⊛www.iisalmenseutu .info), on the corner with the main street, Pohjolankatu, can point you towards summertime budget options on the outskirts, and to **campsites** with cabins (❶), such as *Koljonvirta Camping*, Ylemmäisentie (℡017/825 252; May–Sept). **Eating and drinking** in Iisalmi won't set your heart racing: the choice is between *Rosso* at Savonkatu 18 or the stodgy Finnish dishes at *Olutmestari* down at the harbour (May–Aug only). For an evening drink, head for *Nelly's*, Savonkatu 20.

Around Iisalmi: Sonkajärvi

The reputation that the village of **Sonkajärvi** (⊛www.sonkajarvi.fi), 20km east of Iisalmi, has gained over recent years is quite out of proportion with its tiny size. Throughout Finland, and increasingly abroad, too, this otherwise undistinguished forest village is becoming known for that quintessentially northern Finnish event: the **world championships in wife carrying**. During the first Saturday in July (occasionally the second; check with the tourist office in Iisalmi for the latest details) hundreds of people from across the world crowd into Sonkajärvi to gawp at dozens of burly men negotiating obstacles as they stagger round the 250m course bearing a wife in their arms or on their backs. Confusingly, the borne female need not be the man's wife; however, she must be over seventeen years of age, weigh at least 49kg and must not touch the ground during the race otherwise penalty seconds are incurred – the winner, clearly, is the first man to cross the finishing line. Although cheesy in the extreme, it's actually quite a fun time to be in this part of Finland and once the event is over the entire village degenerates into one mass drunken party. Unfortunately there's no **accommodation** in Sonkajärvi, so you'll be dependent on the daily **bus** which makes the journey out here from the bus station in Iisalmi. Other than a few snack bars on the day of the event there are no **eating** opportunities in the village either.

Travel details

Trains

Iisalmi to: Kajaani (4 daily; 1hr); Oulu (3 daily; 3hr 30min).
Joensuu to: Helsinki (6 daily; 5hr 15min).
Jyväskylä to: Tampere (11 daily; 1hr 40min).
Kuopio to: Iisalmi (7 daily; 1hr); Jyväskylä (6 daily; 2hr); Kajaani (5 daily; 2hr); Mikkeli (6 daily; 1hr 45min).
Lahti to: Helsinki (hourly; 1hr 30min); Mikkeli (6 daily; 2hr).
Lappeenranta to: Helsinki (6 daily; 2hr 40min); Lahti (6 daily; 1hr 15min).
Mikkeli to: Kuopio (6 daily; 1hr 45min); Lahti (6 daily; 2hr).
Savonlinna to: Parikkala (2 daily; 55min).
Tampere to: Hämeenlinna (hourly; 40min); Helsinki (hourly; 2hr); Jyväskylä (11 daily; 1hr 40min); Oulu (8 daily; 5hr); Pori (6 daily; 1hr 25min); Turku (9 daily; 2hr).
Varkaus to: Joensuu (4 daily; 1hr 30min).

Buses

Joensuu to: Kuopio (5 daily; 2hr 30min); Valamo Monastery (1 daily; 1hr 10min).
Kuopio to: Jyväskylä (3 daily; 2hr 15min).
Lahti to: Mikkeli (6 daily; 2hr 15min); Savonlinna (2 daily; 3hr 45min).
Mikkeli to: Savonlinna (4 daily; 1hr 45min).
Savonlinna to: Kuopio (4 daily; 3hr 40min); Parikkala (2 daily; 1hr 20min); Punkaharju (2 daily; 50min); Varkaus (4 daily; 2hr 20min).
Tampere to: Helsinki (5 daily; 2hr); Pori (5 daily; 1hr 45min); Turku (5 daily; 2hr 30min).
Varkaus to: Joensuu (2 daily; 2hr); Kuopio (8 daily; 1hr 15min).

International buses

Joensuu to: Sortavala (1 daily in summer; 3hr 45min).
Lappeenranta to: St Petersburg (1 daily; 5hr); Viipuri (1 daily; 1hr 30min).

4.3

Ostrobothnia, Kainuu and Lapland

etween them, these three regions take up nearly two-thirds of Finland, but unlike the populous south or the more industrialized sections of the Lake Region, they're predominantly rural, with small and widely separated communities. Despite this – or perhaps because of it – each region has a very individual flavour. Living along the coast of **Ostrobothnia** are most of the country's Swedish-speaking Finland-Swedes, a small subsection of the national population whose culture differs from that of both Swedes and Finns. Towns hereabouts are known as often by their Swedish names as by their Finnish, while their distance from the ravages of World War II enabled them to retain some of their old wooden architecture. Much of the region's affluence stems from its flat and fertile farmlands, although the coastal area's fortunes are changing as the once-numerous ferry connections from Sweden – the "booze cruises" – have all but gone now that European law has done away with duty-free alcohol, the main reason for the ferries' existence – today, **Vaasa** is the region's only maritime entry point. Overall, though, given the lack of exciting scenery – save for a few fishing settlements scattered along the jagged shoreline – and the region's social insularity, you'd be generous to devote more than a couple of days to it. Even busy and expanding **Oulu**, the major city, has a surprisingly anodyne quality, although you could always join the Swedes drinking their way into oblivion slightly further north at the border town of **Tornio**.

Kainuu is the thickly forested, thinly populated heart of Finland. It's traditionally peasant land – something perhaps felt more strongly here than anywhere else in the country – and over recent decades has suffered a severe economic decline as wealth has become concentrated in the south. There's still a surprising level of poverty in some parts, although tourism is beginning to help alleviate this. The only sizeable town, **Kajaani** is a good base for wider explorations by foot, bike or canoe, and, since no railways serve the area, it's also the hub of a bus network which connects

Ostrobothnia, Österbotten and Pohjanmaa

The curious and little encountered Latin word, **Ostrobothnia**, is allied to the Swedish name *Österbotten*, meaning "east of the Gulf of Bothnia", and confusingly refers to the western Finnish coast. To understand this apparent contradiction, it's necessary to go back to the centuries of Swedish rule when this Finnish province, on the east of the Gulf as seen from Sweden, was administered from Stockholm. *Österbotten* looked out across the sea towards the Swedish province of *Västerbotten*, "west of the Gulf of Bothnia", two Swedish provinces separated by a physical divide. Today the name *Österbotten* is still in use by the many Swedish-speaking communities in this part of Finland and stretches roughly from Vaasa to Oulu. Thankfully in Finnish there is no such confusion, since *Pohjanmaa*, the Finnish name for Ostrobothnia, simply means "northern land".

the region's far-flung settlements. **Kuhmo**, east of Kajaani, is at the centre of a notable web of nature trails and hiking routes, while heading north through **Suomussalmi** and on past **Kuusamo**, the landscapes become wilder, with great gorges, river rapids and fells on which reindeer are as common as people. Hikers here are well catered for by a number of marked tracks, in addition to totally unin-

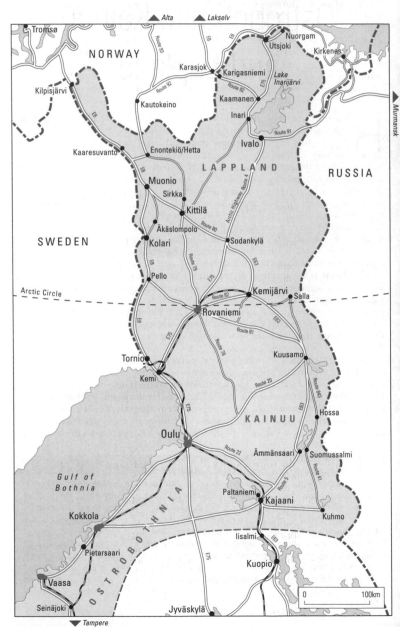

habited regions traversable only with map, compass and self-confidence. The villages have little to offer beyond accommodation and transport to and from the endpoints of the hikes, so stay away if you're not the hiking type.

Much the same applies to **Lapland**, one of the most thrilling places to hike in the world. **Rovaniemi**, the main stopover en route, is useful mainly for its transport connections and information on the area beyond. Beyond Rovaniemi, two roads lead into the **Arctic North**. Here you'll find wide open spaces that are great for guided treks through gold-panning country and along the edges of mountain chains which continue far into Sweden and Norway. Elsewhere you can be totally isolated, gazing from barren fell-tops into Russia. But while the Arctic settlements are small, and few and far between, the whole region is home to several thousand **Sámi** (for more on whom, see p.761), who've lived in harmony with this special, often harsh environment for millennia. Discovering their culture and way of life can be as exciting as experiencing the Arctic North itself.

Vaasa and around

There's little reason to visit **VAASA**, although it's a useful stopover if you're travelling along the coast and has good travel connections with Oulu to the north and Pori to the south; there's also a little advertised but very useful cross-country rail line connecting Vaasa directly with Jyväskylä. The lifeblood of the town is its harbour, through which the produce of southern Ostrobothnia's wheat fields is exported and the lucrative tourist traffic from Sweden arrives. Years of steady income have given the town a staid, commercial countenance, and its wide avenues (the old centre was obliterated by fire a century ago) are lined with shipping offices, consulates and a plethora of boozing venues aimed at Swedes from Umeå, who come here to get smashed.

Eighty-odd years ago, Vaasa was briefly the seat of the provisional government after the Reds (an alliance of Communists and Social Democrats who had taken up arms against Finland's repressive Civil Guard) had taken control of Helsinki and much of the south at the start of the Civil War in 1918; it was among Ostrobothnia's right-wing farmers that the bourgeois-dominated government drew most of its support. This barely endearing fact is recalled by the reliefs of the then president Svinhufvud and Mannerheim, who commanded the Civil Guard, on the front of the town hall and by the monument outside it.

Since then, it seems, little besides drunkenness has broken the peace. The pinnacle of local cultural activity is represented by the **Ostrobothnia Museum** (daily 10am–5pm, Wed until 8pm; €2) at Museokatu 3, which recounts the history of the town and boasts an enjoyable collection of sixteenth- and seventeenth-century Dutch, Italian and Flemish art.

Practicalities

The **bus** and **train** stations are at the northern end of the town centre, within walking distance of the **tourist office**, which is located in part of the town hall at Raastuvankatu (June–Aug Mon–Fri 8am–8pm, Sat & Sun 10am–6pm; Sept–May Mon–Fri 8am–4pm; ☎06/325 1145, ⊛www.vaasa.fi). There's free **Internet** access close by at the town library, Kirjastonkatu 13 (Mon–Fri 11am–8pm, Sat 10am–3pm). If you have to stay overnight before moving on, **hostels** are your best bet. The official hostel (open all year) is part of the summer hotel *Tekla* at Palosaarentie 58 (☎06/327 6411, ☎321 3989), about 3km from the town centre; take bus #3. Slightly more central but also pricier is the *Olo* hostel, Asemakatu 12 (☎06/317 4558), whilst further out is the better-value *EFÖ*, Rantakatu 21–22 (☎06/317 4913, ⊛www.efo.fi; mid-June to mid-Aug). Just up the road from *EFÖ* at Korsholmanpuistikko 6–8 is the *Kenraali Wasa Hostel* (☎0400/668 521, ⊛www.nic.fi/~mjerohin), situated in an old army barracks. In the summer months, there's the further option of the **campsite**, *Wasa Camping* (☎06/211 1255, winter bookings ☎06/211 1200), which is 2km from the town centre but close to the ferry harbour. The most pleasant central **hotel** is the small *Astor*, Asemakatu 4 (☎06/326 9111, ⓦwww.astorvaasa.com; ❻/❺), where for €18 extra you can get a room with its own sauna; the newest is the *Best Western Hotel Silveria*, Ruutikellarintie 4 (☎06/326 7611, ⓦwww.bestwestern.com/prop_91074; ❺/❹), where there's a pool, and morning sauna and breakfast are included in the room price.

Oddly for such a comparatively large place, **eating** and **drinking** establishments are thin on the ground in Vaasa. The best deals are to be found at the *Golden Rax Pizzabuffet*, at the top end of the main square at Kauppapuistikko 13, where the all-you-can-eat buffet is just €7.49. For more pleasant surrounds, head for *Fondis*, Hovioikeudenpuistikko 15, which specializes in Mediterranean food – the beef casserole with garlic and red pepper stuffed with vegetable couscous is especially good value. A night's drinking in a multilingual town like Vaasa (one in four people here speak Swedish as their mother tongue), is divided on linguistic lines: Finnish speakers tend to be found at *Hullu Pullo*, Kauppapuistikko 15 or *Birra* at no. 16, whereas the Finland-Swedes prefer *Oliver's Inn* at no. 8.

Onward from Vaasa

Ferries currently run from Vaasa to **Umeå** in Sweden (RG Line; ☎06/3200 300, ⓦwww.rgline.com), generally once-daily all year round; remember that Umeå is Uumaja in Finnish. A second ferry, run by Botnialink (☎06/322 6610, ⓦwww.botnialink.se) leaves for Umeå and Härnösand – this is essentially a cargo service and accommodation on board is limited.

Heading **south from Vaasa** usually involves changing trains at Seinäjoki, from where there are direct services to Tampere, Turku and Helsinki. There's also a direct service **east** to Jyväskylä where connections can be made for Kuopio and Joensuu. There are numerous buses to Pori and Turku. About 70km south of Vaasa, these pass through Kaskinen (in Swedish, Kaskö) and neighbouring Kristiinankaupunki (Kristinestad), notable for its surviving seventeenth-century layout.

Travelling **north from Vaasa** by road to the major coastal city of Oulu involves a mildly scenic journey passing fishing hamlets along the archipelago, and the small and still largely wooden towns of Uusikaarlepyy (Nykarleby) and Pietarsaari (Jakobstad). Northbound **trains** (once again changing in Seinäjoki) swing inland before meeting up with the coastal road north in the uninspiring port of **KOKKOLA**. If you feel like hanging around, the **tourist office** on Kauppatori (June–Aug Mon–Fri 8am–5pm, Sat 9am–1pm; Sept–May Mon–Fri 8am–4pm; ☎06/831 1902, ⓦwww.tourism.kokkola.fi) can help sort out accommodation and point you towards the only remotely interesting local sight: the **English Park**, at one end of Isokatu, which contains a boat captured when the British fleet tried to land here during the Crimean campaign in 1854. A much more welcome sight, though, is the **train station** at Isokatu's other end. **Travelling on** from Kokkola is straightforward since the town is on the main rail line between Oulu and Helsinki.

Oulu

Despite **OULU**'s role as national leader in the computing and microchip industries, the city still has sufficient remnants from the past to remind visitors of its nine-teenth-century status as a world centre for tar. The black stuff was brought by river from the forests of Kainuu, and the international demand for its use in ship- and road-building helped line the pockets of Oulu's merchants. Their affluence and quest for cultural refinement made the town a vibrant centre, not only for business, but also for education and the arts. Today, a handsome series of islands, a couple of highly conspicuous old buildings, and a nightlife fuelled by the university's fun-hungry students bring colour into an otherwise pallid city. Though it has its share of faceless office blocks, there's an ancient feel to Oulu, too, as seen in tumbledown wooden shacks around the intricately carved *kauppahalli*.

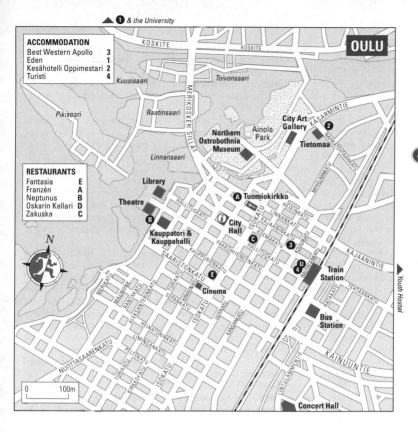

On the map:

ACCOMMODATION
Best Western Apollo	3
Eden	1
Kesähotelli Oppimestari	2
Turisti	4

RESTAURANTS
Fantasia	E
Franzén	A
Neptunus	B
Oskarin Kellari	D
Zakuska	C

OULU

0   100m

Arrival and accommodation

Oulu is handy for **trains** in various directions, most usefully the direct services to and from Helsinki, Kajaani in the east (see p.767) and Rovaniemi in the north (see p.771). Arriving here, you'll find the platforms of the **train station** feed conveniently into an underground walkway with two exits: one runs to the nearby **bus station** (with regular services to and from Kuusamo), while the other leads towards the compact city centre, where the **tourist office** (mid-June to mid-Aug Mon–Fri 9am–6pm, Sat 10am–3pm; rest of the year Mon–Fri 9am–4pm; ☎08/5584 1330, ⓦwww.oulutourism.fi) is close to the City Hall at Torikatu 10.

Low-cost **accommodation** is, unfortunately, limited. The **youth hostel** is at Kajaanintie 36 (☎08/880 3311, ⓕ880 3754; June–Aug), a fifteen-minute walk east from the train and bus stations. The very central *Turisti*, Rautatienkatu 9 (☎08/375 233, ⓕ311 0755; ❹), has the cheapest year-round **hotel** beds. If you arrive in June or July the *Kesähotelli Oppimestari*, Nahkatehtaankatu 3 (☎08/884 8527, ⓦwww.merikoski.fi; ❷), can provide well-kept rooms, while the best summer discounts can be found at the *Best Western Apollo*, Asemakatu 31–33 (☎08/374 344, ⓦwww.bestwestern.fi; ❺/❹). If you're looking for luxury, the *Eden*, on the island of Nallikari (☎08/8842 000, ⓦwww.holidayclub.fi; ❻), won't disappoint – it's got a superb pool and offers spa treatments and steam rooms, as well as a fine restaurant. Bus #5 runs there, as well as to the cabin-equipped **campsite** (☎08/558 61351), 4km from town on Hietasaari Island; nearby is the sliver of sand that locals call a beach.

Leaving either the bus or train station, it's just a few minutes' walk straight ahead to the **harbour** and the neighbouring **kauppatori** and **kauppahalli** (Mon–Thurs 8am–4pm, Fri 8am–5pm, Sat 8am–3pm), an appealing and ornate place, good for cheap eats. Nearby, the sleekly modern **library** and **theatre** rise on stilts from the waters of Rommakonselkä. The library frequently stages art and craft exhibitions, which are usually worth a look.

Built as a luxury hotel symbolizing the affluent and cosmopolitan tar-rich town, the **City Hall**, a few minutes away on Kirkkokatu, retains some of its late nineteenth-century grandeur. A local newspaper called it "a model for the whole world. A Russian is building the floor, an Austrian is doing the painting, a German is making the bricks, an Englishman is preparing the electric lighting, the Swede is doing the masonry, the Norwegian is carving the relief and the Finn is doing all the drudgery." Nowadays, the drudgery is performed by local government officials, who've become accustomed to visitors stepping in to gawp at the wall paintings and enclosed gardens that remain from the old days. While inside, venture up to the second floor, where the Great Hall still has its intricate Viennese ceiling paintings and voluminous chandeliers.

Further along Kirkkokatu, the copper-domed, yellow-stuccoed **Tuomiokirkko** (summer daily 11am–8pm; winter Mon–Fri noon–1pm; free) was built in the 1770s following a great fire that more or less destroyed the city, and underwent a full and successful restoration in 1996. Within the cathedral is a portrait of Swedish historian Johannes Messinius, supposedly painted by **Cornelius Arenditz** in 1612. Restored and slightly faded, it's believed to be the oldest surviving oil painting in Finland, despite the efforts of the Russian Cossacks, who lacerated the canvas with their sabres in 1714. The small park outside the cathedral is part of a former cemetery, and bits of clothing and bone found nearby beneath the floor of the seventeenth-century cellar in the pleasant *Franzen Café*, on the corner of Kirkkokatu and Keyaaninkatu, have been reburied beneath the cafe's tiled floor – the barman can point out the spot.

Cross the small canal just north of the cathedral to reach **Ainola Park**, a pleasantly wooded space which makes a nice spot for a picnic or a late evening stroll. In the park, the **Northern Ostrobothnia Museum** (Mon–Thurs 8am–4pm, Sat & Sun 11am–5pm; €1.70) is packed with tar-stained remnants from Oulu's past and an interesting Sámi section. There's no English labelling, but the displays are mostly self-explanatory.

If the future does more to excite your imagination than the past, head for **Tietomaa**, the Science Museum, a few minutes' walk away at Nahkatehtaankatu 6 (May, June & Aug daily 10am–6pm; July daily 10am–8pm; Sept–April Mon–Fri 10am–4pm, Sat & Sun 10am–6pm; ⍟www.tietomaa.fi; €10). Housed in an old power station, this is a great place if you like exploring the bounds of technological possibility, with several floors of gadgets to test mental and physical abilities as well as video games, holograms, a ski jump simulator, a giant-screen IMAX cinema and a glass elevator that takes you to the top of a tower from which you can get unparalleled views of Oulu.

Just around the corner, the **City Art Gallery** (Tues & Thurs–Sun 11am–6pm, Wed 11am–8pm; ⍟www.ouka.fi/taidemuseo/english; €3, free on Fri), Kasarmintie 7, is located in a renovated glue factory. One of the largest galleries in Finland, it houses permanent and visiting international and Finnish contemporary art collections, plus a pleasant café – a good place to kill a few hours on a cold day.

Koskikeskus, the University and Botanical Gardens

A pleasant way to pass a few hours is to set off for the four small islands across the mouth of Rommakonselkä, collectively known as **Koskikeskus**. The first island, Linnansaari, has the inconsequential remains of Oulu's sixteenth-century castle; next comes Raatinsaari, followed by Toivonsaari, and the rapids that drive a power station designed by Alvar Aalto, with twelve fountains added by the architect to prettify the plant. Pikisaari, the fourth island, is much the best to visit, reached by a short road bridge from Raatinsaari. A number of tiny seventeenth-century wooden houses here have survived Oulu's many fires, and Pikisaari has become the stamping ground of local artists and trendies, with several **art galleries** and **craft shops**.

The islands can also be glimpsed through the windows of buses #4, 6, 7 and 19, which pass them during the twenty-minute ride to the **University**. It's not a bad destination if you're at a loose end, if only for the opportunity to gorge in the student mensa. To work up an appetite, try finding the **Geological Museum** (Mon–Fri & Sun 11am–3pm, free) or the **Zoological Museum** (Mon–Fri 8.30am–3.30pm, Sun 11am–3pm; free), both secreted within the university's miles of corridors. The former is much as you'd expect, with a large collection of rare gems; the latter's best feature is the painstakingly hand-painted habitats created for each of the numerous specimens of stuffed Finnish wildlife.

Once you've ventured onto the campus you may as well take a look at the tropical and Mediterranean flora inside the two glass pyramidal structures that make up the **Botanical Gardens** (June–Aug Tues–Fri 8am–3pm, Sat & Sun 11am–3pm; Sept–May Tues–Fri 8am–3pm, Sat & Sun noon–3pm; €0.90).

Eating, drinking and nightlife

Oulu boasts some delightful **cafés** for lunch or the odd snack, the best of which include *Sokeri Jussi*, set in an old salt warehouse on Pikisaari, and, just over the bridge from the mainland, the *Café Pilvikirsikka*, in an old greenhouse in Hupisaari park; *Café Koivuraranta*, a wooden café on the riverside, is also popular, while *Café Saara* is a peaceful place to stop off for a coffee, right in the centre at Kirkkokatu 2. For **cakes**, the finest outlet in Oulu is *Katri Antell* on Rotuaari, while the more basic *Bisketti* is just opposite. If you're stuck for somewhere to go on a Sunday, NUKU, the youth cultural centre, has a laid-back café in an atrium courtyard at Hallituskatu 7. Finally, for a little more class, venture into the Concert Hall on Lintulammentie, a short walk south of the bus station. A coffee in the hall's café isn't cheap, but it does allow you to admire the gleaming Italian marble interior.

For a waterside **meal**, try the central *Neptunus*, which serves good fish and meat dishes in a boat moored by the *kauppatori*. In the centre of town, *Zakuska*, Hallituskatu 20, is a long-established, authentic mid-priced Russian restaurant, while *Fantasia*, Isokatu 23, is the best of Oulu's pizzerias, with a stuff-your-face evening buffet for €8. Another place to fill up with good food is *Franzén*, in a charismatic old building diagonally opposite the Tuomiokirkko at Kirkkokatu 2 (☎08/311 3224); as well as the ultra-swish street-level restaurant, there's a cellar bar serving German beers and sausages. *Oskarin Kellari*, at Rautatienkatu 9 opposite the train station, and in the same block as the *Hotel Turisti*, is a good choice for a reasonably priced Finnish meal and is usually busy with locals.

Nightlife and entertainment

Oulu's **nightlife** revolves around its numerous **cafés** and **pubs**, the best of the bunch being the friendly *Panimo*, Kauppurienkatu 13, and the busy *Leskinen*, at Isokatu 30 near the Suomalainen Kirjakauppa bookshop. *Kaarenholvi* at Kauppurienkatu 6 is a popular bar and nightclub rolled into one. For dancing, though, you're better off at *Giggling Marlin* at the corner of Torikatu and Saaristonkatu.

Towards Tornio: Kemi icebreaker tours

If you want to cross overland into Sweden, the place to make for is Tornio, 130km northwest of Oulu – reached by bus from **KEMI**, a small town on the Oulu–Rovaniemi train route around 110km northwest of Oulu. Although undistinguished during the summer months, bar the stench of wood pulp issuing from the nearby sawmills, it's during the dark winter months that Kemi really comes to life. From January to April, hundreds of people pour through this small town to experience one of Finland's most alluring winter attractions: a tour on the only private **icebreaker** in the world. The *Sampo* departs once daily for a four-hour "cruise" through the icefields at the very top of the Gulf of Bothnia, breaking ice several metres thick (the ice is at its thickest in February and March). During the tour there's also an unmissable opportunity to don a bright orange rubber survival suit and float in the icy waters off the ship's stern – all this costs a pricey €156, but is undoubtedly worth the expense. The icing on the cake, however, is to depart by snowmobile from the centre of Kemi, travelling out over the ice to join the ship at its parking position out in the icefield – this 7hr tour doesn't come cheap at €280 per person but, if you can afford it, is an experience not to be missed; for more information, contact Sampo Tours at Torikatu 2 in Kemi (☎016/256 458, ☻www.sampotours.com). Prices come down if these tours are booked via a travel agent such as Norvista Travel (see p.19). In winter or summer, however, try not to get stuck in uninspiring Kemi – eating, drinking and accommodation are all far better in Oulu or Tornio.

Tornio

Situated on the extreme northern tip of the Gulf of Bothnia, **TORNIO** makes a living by selling booze to fugitives from Sweden's harsh alcohol laws, and catering to the Finns who come here to enjoy the beach, to fish, or shoot the Tornionjoki Rapids. After the Swedish–Russian conflict of 1808–09, the border between Sweden and Finland was drawn around **Suensaari**, an oval piece of land jutting from the Swedish side into the river, on which central Tornio now sits. With no formalities at the customs post on the bridge linking the two countries, the traffic in liver-damaged Swedes from nearby Haaparanta (in Swedish, Haparanda) is substantial. If you're **arriving by bus** the journey will terminate in Suensaari.

The dominant features of the town are its bars and restaurants, so numerous that it's pointless to list them. Simply stroll around Hallituskatu and Kauppakatu and drop into the ones with the most promising noises. Always lively are the waterside *Umpitunneli*, by the second road bridge over to mainland Tornio, *Wanha Mestari*, Hallituskatu 5, and *Café Nina*, Laivurinkatu 5, while everyone who sets foot in Tornio seems to visit *Dal Laziale*, Kauppakatu 12, one of the cheapest spots for solid nourishment. For coffee and fresh bread and cakes, it's hard to beat *Karkiaisen Leipomo*, Länsiranta 9. Alternatively, you can buy a bag of salted and smoked whitefish along the banks of the rapids (roughly €2 for a meal's worth).

If you find the boozy atmosphere unappealing, try visiting the seventeenth-century **Tornionkirkko** (late May to mid-Aug Mon–Fri 9am–5pm; mid-June to early Aug Mon–Fri 9am–7pm, Sat & Sun 11.30am–5pm) on the edge of the town park, or climbing the **observation tower** (June to mid-Aug daily 11am–8pm). Otherwise, there's only the **Tornio River Valley Historical Museum** (Mon–Fri noon–5pm, Sun noon–3pm; July to mid-Aug also Sat noon–3pm; €2), near the corner of Torikatu and Keskikatu, or the possibility of some diversion suggested by the **tourist office**, in the Green Line Centre at the Swedish border (June to mid-Aug Mon–Fri 9am–7pm, Sat & Sun 11am–7pm; mid-Aug to May Mon–Fri 9am–5pm; ☎016/432 733, ☻www.tornio.fi/tourism).

With far more choice in Tornio, don't even consider joining the drunken legions staggering back across the border to sleep in Haparanta (see p.619). The town has a decent enough summer hotel, *Joentalo* (☎016/2119 244, ☻www.ppopisto.fi; late May to mid-Aug; ❸), about 2.5km out from the centre at Kivirannantie 13; plus a **campsite** on Matkailijantie (☎016/445 945, ☻www.lapland.fi/campingtornio), which has two-bed cottages (❷). Among the town's **hotels**, *Kaupunginhotelli*, Itäranta 4 (☎016/433 11, ☻icom.kemi.fi/pressvisual2; ❺/❹), boasts a trio of restaurants, a nightclub and five saunas.

Into Kainuu: Kajaani and around

KAJAANI, 178km southeast of Oulu by bus, could hardly be more of a contrast to the communities of the Bothnian coast. Though small and pastoral, the town is by far the biggest settlement the Kainuu province, a very rural part of Finland, has to offer; trains and buses are rare here and the pleasures of nature take precedence over everything else. Obviously there's little bustle or nightlife, but the place offers some insight into Finnish life in one of its less prosperous regions. Fittingly, it was in Kajaani that Elias Lönnrot completed his version of the *Kalevala*, the nineteenth-century collection of Finnish folk tales that extolled the virtues of traditional peasant life. During the first week of July Kajaani also hosts Finland's biggest annual **poetry festival**, during which the main street, Kauppakatu, turns into a bustling market.

From the gloriously Art Nouveau **train station**, Kauppakatu leads directly into Kajaani's minuscule centre, but first turn left into Asemakatu and you'll spot the decorative exterior of the **Kainuun Museum** at no. 4 (Mon–Fri noon–4pm, Wed until 8pm, Sun noon–5pm; €2). Inside, the engrossingly ramshackle collection of local art and history says a lot about the down-to-earth qualities of the area. Heading for the centre along Pohjolankatu, you'll pass the dramatic **Kajaani kirkko** (summer daily 10am–6pm; winter Mon–Sat 5–7pm), whose wooden frame, weird turrets and angular arches were heralded as the epitome of the neo-Gothic style when the church was completed in 1896. Resembling a leftover from a *Munsters* set, its spectral qualities are most intense by moonlight. At the far end of Kauppakatu, at the junction with Linnankatu, is the **Old Town Hall**, designed by Carl Engel.

More historically significant, perhaps, but far less thrilling, is the ruined **Kajaani Castle**. Built in the seventeenth century to forestall a Russian attack, it later served as a prison where, among others, Johannes Messenius, the troublesome Swede, was incarcerated. Although there's constant talk of schemes to rebuild it, the castle was ruined so long ago that nobody's sure what it actually looked like, and the present heap of stones is only worth seeing if you're already idling along the riverside beside it.

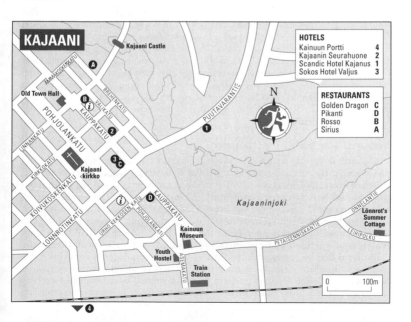

Given the lack of other evening activities, idling is what you're likely to be doing if you stay here overnight. The problem of complete boredom is no less severe for the local youth, who've taken to lining the pavements of Kauppakatu in their hundreds, waiting for something to happen. About the only other way to pass the sunset hours is to take a quiet walk along the riverside footpath, from the corner of Ämmäkoskenkatu and Brehenkatu. Heading west, the path passes the **open-air theatre**, and also provides a chance to gaze at logs sliding blissfully towards destruction at the pulp mill ahead. Following the river eastwards leads to **Lönnrot's summer cottage**. Built by Elias Lönnrot for his wife, the small wooden structure now stands totally empty, isolated and seemingly insignificant; the only acknowledgement of its existence is in the name of the neighbouring *Elias Restaurant* inside the neighbouring *Hotel Kajaani* – an odd neglect for a man whose life's work was so influential, and revered.

Practicalities

The official **youth hostel**, at Pohjolankatu 4 (℡ & ℡08/622 254), is open all year, and though the town's only campsite recently closed there are plans to open a new one – check with the **tourist office** at Pohjolankatu 16 (June–Aug Mon–Fri 9am–6pm, Sat 9am–1pm; Sept–May Mon–Fri 9am–5pm; ℡08/615 5555, ✉www .kajaani.fi). There are a number of adequate choices in the town centre, and rates drop during the summer and at weekends. Two of these, *Sokos Hotel Valjus*, Kauppakatu 20 (℡08/615 0200, ✉www.sokoshotels.fi; ➏/➍), and *Hotel Kajaanin Seurahuone* (℡08/623 076, ✉personal.inet.fi/yritys/kajaanin.seurahuone; ➎/➌), Kauppakatu 11, have cheaper rooms in so-called "traditional" sections, though tradition here amounts simply to a less recent lick of paint. If you can afford it, the best hotel in town is the *Scandic Hotel Kajanus* (℡08/616 41, ✉www.scandic-hotels .com; ➏/➎) across the main bridge in pleasant riverside surroundings at Koskikatu 3. *Hotel Kainuun Portti*, 4km south of town on Route 5 (℡08/613 3000, ℡613 3010; ➌) has regular singles and doubles, as well as rooms for five with kitchen; to get there, take bus #7 from the bus station – Kajaani's tent-only **campsite** is also located here.

There's not a huge number of decent places to **eat** in Kajaani, the most reliable option being the *Golden Dragon* at Kauppakatu 18. Other options lined up along Kauppakatu include the *Pikanti*, at no. 10–12, where an all-you-can-eat lunch costs €8.60; and the ubiquitous *Rosso* at no. 21. The most atmospheric place to dine is *Sirius*, just off the main drag at Brahenkatu 5, in a building originally constructed as a residence for the Kajaani paper company and later used to accommodate visiting dignitaries including Soviet and Finnish Presidents Leonid Brezhnev and Urho Kekkonen. The Finnish food here is not cheap but is certainly tasty. *Parnell's Irish Bar* at Kauppakatu 30 and *Brahe*, immediately opposite at no. 21, are the only decent places to **drink**.

Around Kajaani: Paltaniemi

The hourly #4 bus from Kajaani winds its way to the well-preserved village of **PALTANIEMI**, 9km away on the shores of Oulujärvi – an attractive place but, since the closure of its campsite, one without anywhere to stay. In contrast to down-at-heel Kajaani, eighteenth-century Paltaniemi was home to Swedish-speaking aesthetes lured here by the importance of Kajaani Castle during the halcyon days of the Swedish empire. Their transformation of Paltaniemi into something of a cultural hotbed seems incredible given the place's tiny size and placid setting, but evidence of a refined pedigree isn't hard to find. Most obviously there's the **Paltaniemi kirkko** (summer daily 10am–6pm; winter guided tours only, bookable in the tourist office in Kajaani), built in 1726, a large church whose interior is deliberately chilled in order to preserve **frescoes** painted by Emmanuel Granberg between 1778 and 1781, which include a steamy vision of hell in a gruesome *Last Judgement*.

It's also fun to ferret around behind the pews, trying to decipher centuries-old graffiti. Even Tsar Alexander I paid a visit to Paltaniemi after Finland had become a Russian Grand Duchy, and his impromptu meal in a stable is reverentially commemorated in the **Tsar's Stable** by the church. **Hövelö**, the old cottage across the road, was the birthplace of **Eino Leino**, whose poems captured the increasingly assertive mood of Finland at the beginning of the twentieth century: his life and the history of Kajaani Castle form the subject of a rather dull exhibition.

Moving on from Kajaani

Buses provide the easiest way of **moving on** from Kajaani. The only rail links are west to Oulu (4 daily via Kontiomäki), plus the six daily connections for Iisalmi, Kuopio and beyond, including a useful sleeper service direct to both Helsinki and Turku. The best direction to head for more rural delights is east towards Kuhmo, where the scenery becomes increasingly spectacular, especially around the town of Sotkamo (39km from Kajaani) and the acclaimed beauty spot of **Vuokatti** – a high, pine-clad ridge commanding views all the way to Russia. The rolling hills make this Finland's premier ski-training area.

Kuhmo

With belts of forests, hills and lakes, and numerous nature walks and hikes within easy reach, **KUHMO** makes a fine base for exploring the countryside. The terrain is in some ways less dramatic than that further north, but then again it's also far less crowded.

You can get details of hiking routes, maps and other practical information from the **tourist office**, Kainuuntie 126 (June–Aug Mon–Fri 8am–6pm, Sat 10am–4pm; Sept–May Mon–Fri 8am–5pm; ☎08/655 6382, ⓦwww.kuhmonet.fi /matkailu). The tourist office can also explain how best to reach the **Kalevala Village** on the outskirts of the town. This re-creation of a wooded Karelian village provides an illuminating account of traditional building methods, plus it's a good excuse to indulge in some pricey souvenirs – and interesting handicrafts – which are sold to the many genuine Karelians who visit. It's also the only thing close to Kuhmo of appeal to non-hikers.

Low-budget **accommodation** options in Kuhmo include the **youth hostel** *Piilolan Koulu* (☎08/655 6245, ⓕ655 6384), which has rooms (❶) as well as dorms, though it's only open July. *Hotel Kalevala*, 3km from the centre (☎08/655 4100, ⓦwww.hotellikalevala.fi; ❺), is a fair bet for a clean, modern room and also rents out **canoes** and **bikes**. The town **campsite** (☎08/655 6388, ⓕ655 6384; June–Aug) is 4km from the centre along Koulukatu.

Continuing northwards from Kuhmo leads only to more hiking lands, and if you need urbanity, nightlife and easy living, now's the time to own up and duck out. If not, and your feet are itching to be tested over hundreds of kilometres of untamed land, simply clamber on the bus for Suomussalmi.

Hiking routes around Kuhmo

The local section of the several hundred kilometres of track that make up the **UKK hiking route** starts from the Kuhmo Sports Centre and winds 70km through forests and the Hiidenportti canyon. Several other hikes begin further out from Kuhmo and can be reached by bus from the town. **Elimyssalo**, to the east, is a fifteen-kilometre track through a conservation area, and also to the east is **Kilpelän-kankaan**, where a cycle path runs 3.5km across heathland, passing a number of Winter War memorials. To the north, **Sininenpolku** is a hike of more than 20km over a ridge, past small lakes and rivers. In the northwest, **Iso-Palosenpolku** has two paths through a thickly forested area, where there are overnight shelters. Additionally, several **canoeing routes** trace the course of the old tar-shipping routes between Kuhmo and Oulu.

Suomussalmi and around

Divided by a lake, Kiantajärvi, **SUOMUSSALMI** falls into two distinct parts: one the older, more traditional village of Suomussalmi proper; the other, Ämmänsaari, a newer administrative centre. Ämmänsaari is on the main road, Route 5, about 100km from Kajaani, while the smaller Route 41 covers the similar distance from Kuhmo to Suomussalmi. The villages themselves are connected by a more or less hourly bus service. Ämmänsaari, which serves as the administrative centre of the whole of northern Kainuu, is a good place to gather details on hiking and accommodation: contact the **tourist office**, Jalloniemi, by Route 5 (mid-June to mid-Aug Mon–Fri 8am–8pm, Sat 10am–6pm, Sun 11am–7pm; rest of the year Mon–Fri 8am–4pm; ☎08/6176 2243, ⓦwww.suomussalmi.fi). There's also a handy **campsite** here (☎08/711 209 or 050/566 4252; June–Aug) and an expensive hotel, *Scandic Hotel Kiannon Kuohut* (☎08/710 770, ⓦwww.scandic-hotels.com; ❻/❺), at Jalonkatu 1. Buses from both parts of Suomussalmi run to the main hiking areas in the province, usually on a daily basis.

To the east, something of the old Karelian culture can still be felt in the tiny villages of Kuivajärvi and Hietajärvi, close to the Russian border. Near Kuivajärvi is the **Saarisuo Nature Reserve**, where an eight-kilometre hiking trail traverses a protected forest and marshy areas that are home to a wide variety of bird life. Adjacent to the reserve is the *Hostelli Domnan Pirtti* (☎08/723 179, ⓕ711 189; April–Sept), which serves breakfast (€5.90) and other meals to order.

A few kilometres north of Suomussalmi, in the Ruhtinansalmi area, is the **Martinselkonen Nature Reserve**, known locally as the "last wilderness". A solitary marked path passes through the reserve, and there are some open cabins and *laavu* shelters – crude slope-roofed huts open to the elements on one side, which were used by early lumber workers and based on the design of peasant hunters. It's best to contact the Martinselkonen Wilds Centre in the reserve (☎08/736 160, ⓦwww.martinselkosenerakeskus.com) before you venture forth, which as well as offering the usual information on the local area can also provide accommodation and meals.

Heading north from Suomussalmi along Route 843 to Kuusamo brings you to **HOSSA**, situated close to a network of hiking paths graded according to difficulty and ranging in length from 1km to 25km, which pass through pine forests and over ridges between limpid lakes. Dotted about are old tar pits, lumber camps and a few traditional *laavu* shelters. Various cabins are also available on the trails, some with open access, others which have to be booked in advance. Hossa also offers about 100km of excellent canoeing routes and some great fishing. All the hikes begin 8km from the village, which has an all-year **campsite** (☎ & ⓕ08/732 310) and a **holiday village** (☎08/732 322, ⓕ732 307), both with affordable cabins. If you travel 5km north of Hossa you'll find the Hossa Visitor Centre (daily: March–May 10am–4.30pm; June–Aug 9am–10pm; Sept & Oct 10am–4.30pm; ☎08/205 646 041, ⓦwww.metsa.fi), which has a café, an activity service to help you get the most out of the local area and an adjacent campsite.

Kuusamo and around

KUUSAMO, 120km north of Suomussalmi, is reached by daily express buses from Oulu, plus regular services from Rovaniemi. For full details of local hiking and accommodation, and the many summer events that bring some life to the town, call in at the **Karhuntassu Tourist & Nature Centre** at Torangintaival 2 (☎08/850 2910, ⓦwwww.kuusamo.fi) and pick up the excellent *Kuusamo Service Guide*. For accommodation, try the **youth hostel**, across the street from the bus station at Kitkantie 35 (☎08/852 2132, ⓕ852 1134; late June–Aug; ❶), or alternatively the soulless *Sokos Hotel Kuusamo* (☎08/859 20, ⓦwww.sokoshotels.fi; ❻/❺) at Kirkkotie 23, a ten-minute walk from the centre of town at the junction with Oulumtie; the hotel overlooks the Toranki lake, and has an exceptionally large indoor swimming pool. Before setting out hiking, the best place in town to **eat and drink** is the adjoining *Martina* and *Parnell's Irish Bar* at Ouluntie 3 – fried chicken, fries, salad and a beer will cost around €15.

Kuusamo is the starting point for the **Karhunkierros Trail** (also known as the Kuusamo Bear Circuit); one of the most popular hiking routes in Finland, it's a seventy-kilometre trek weaving over the summit of Rukatunturi, dipping into canyons and across slender log suspension bridges over thrashing rapids. Herds of hikers are a far more common sight than bears, but the hike is still a good one and there are several interesting shorter routes off the main track. From Kuusamo, take the bus to **Ristikallio** for the start of the hike. Wilderness huts are placed roughly at ten-kilometre intervals along the route, though during peak months these are certain to be full. Fortunately there's no shortage of places to pitch your own tent, and about halfway along the route are three **campsites**, *Juuma* (☎08/863 212; late May to Sept), *Jyrävä* (☎050/361 4631; June-Aug) and *Retki-Etappi* (☎08/863 218; June–Sept).

Heading north again, the tougher and little known **Six Fells Hiking Route** (more commonly known by its tongue-twisting Finnish name *kuudentunturinkevelyreitti*) starts at **Salla**. A bus runs here from Kuusamo two times a day from Monday to Friday, pulling up at *Hotel Revontuli* (☎016/879 711, ☎837 760; ⑥); nearby, there are also some **cabins** with showers costing (☎016/831 931, ☎837 765; ❷). The 35-kilometre hike, actually part of the UKK trail, begins a couple of kilometres north of Salla at the *Sallan Maja* roadside café, and includes some stiff climbs up the sides of spruce-covered fells, with spectacular views from their bare summits. **Niemelä**, close to the road between Kuusamo and Salla, marks the other end of the trail. From Salla you can continue by bus into the Arctic North (see p.775), or to Kemijärvi to meet the train for Rovaniemi and all points south.

Rovaniemi and around

Easily accessible by train or bus, **ROVANIEMI** is touted as the capital of Lapland. Just south of the Arctic Circle it may be, but anyone arriving with an expectation of sleighs and tents will be disappointed by a place whose administrative buildings, busy shopping streets and *McDonald's* (the most northerly in the world) make it a far cry from the surrounding rural hinterland. The elegant wooden houses of old Rovaniemi were razed to the ground by departing Germans at the close of World War II, and the town was completely rebuilt during the late 1940s. Alvar Aalto's bold but impractical design has the roads forming the shape of reindeer antlers – though the centre of town is based on a familiar grid pattern. Although the town can be quite dismal in summer, with its uniform greyish-white buildings and an unnerving newness to everything – even the smattering of antique shops contains nothing older than 1970s junk – it's during the **winter** that Rovaniemi really comes into its own, with the neutral colour of the buildings working in perfect harmony with the snow and ice that covers the city's streets for almost six months of the year. During the cold months, the town plays host to busloads of nervous southern Europeans swathed from head to toe in the latest designer cold weather gear, heading out on snowmobile safaris (see below) or simply stumbling around the icy streets as proof that they have endured an Arctic winter. The best idea is to use Rovaniemi only as a short-term stopover, or as a base for studies in Sámi culture, before heading off to one of the north's smaller villages for a more genuine taste of Finnish Lapland.

Arrival, information and accommodation

Rovaniemi's bus and train stations are just a couple of minutes' walk from each other, located on the western edge of the city centre. From either terminus, the best route into town is to take the subway under Valtatie (the E4 highway) and to walk down Hallituskatu turning left into Rovakatu, where the friendly **tourist office** is

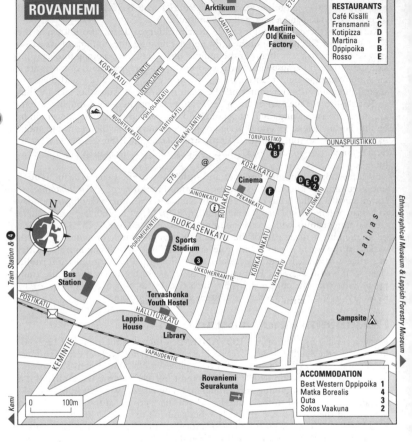

at no. 21 (June–Aug Mon–Fri 8am–6pm, Sat & Sun 10am–4pm; rest of the year Mon–Fri 8am–4pm; ☎016/346 270, ⊛www.rovaniemi.fi).

Budget accommodation in Rovaniemi is not hard to find as the city has several good **hostels** – but booking ahead, especially around midsummer, is recommended. A few minutes from the tourist office at Hallituskatu 16, the friendly all-year *Tervashonka* hostel (☎ & ☎016/344 644) is always crowded in summer. Other options include the weirdly decorated *Outa* guesthouse, Ukkoherrantie 16 (☎016/312 474; ❶), whose elderly owner only speaks Finnish, or the excellent value *Matka Borealis*, Asemieskatu 1 (☎016/3420 130, ⊛personal.inet.fi/business /matkaborealis; ❷), close to the railway station and accordingly very popular with Interrailers – rooms here are all en-suite and the price includes breakfast. With a little more money to spend, try one or two of the city's **hotels**: the *Best Western Oppipoika*, Korkalonkatu 33 (☎016/3388 111, ⊛www.bestwestern.com/prop _91082; ❹), is in the same building as a hotel and catering school and boasts a pool and two saunas, as well as good food. Swankier still is the *Sokos Vaakuna*, Koskikatu 4 (☎016/332 211, ⊛www.sokoshotels.fi; ❺/❹), close to the Ounaskoski river. Rovaniemi's **campsite** is at Jäämerentie 1 (☎016/345 304), on the other bank of the river, and equipped with a café and sauna.

The City

If you have any interest in Sámi culture, make a beeline for the fascinating **Arktikum**, in the northern part of town at Pohjoisranta 4 (mid-June to Aug daily 10am–6pm; Sept–April same hours, closed Mon; ⊛www.arktikum.fi; €10). Its great arched atrium emerges from the ground like a U-boat, with almost all the exhibition areas submerged beneath banks of stone. The complex contains both the **Provincial Museum of Lappland** and the **Arctic Centre**, which together provide a varied insight into the history and present-day lives of the peoples of the Arctic North. Taking an intelligent, unsentimental approach, the museum superbly evokes the remarkable Sámi culture and is well worth a couple of hours. Displays range from raincoats made of seal intestine, polar bear trousers, arctic fox and caribou hide to superb photographic displays on reindeer husbandry today – modern technology has made its mark, with cellular phones, snowmobiles and four-wheel-drive buggies now the norm. There are also pictures of the horrific devastation caused by German soldiers in 1944, when they were forced to retreat, burning every building in sight – look out for the two scale models showing the city before and after the retreat, and be sure to take in the poignant video footage that compares the heady life in Rovaniemi before the war, when loggers and lumberjacks would pour into the city's hotels and bars at weekends creating one big party atmosphere, with the sharply contrasting scenes of total devastation just a couple of years later – the people of Lapland have still not forgiven the Germans for what happened.

Back in the town centre, **Lappia House**, an Aalto-designed building a short distance from the bus and train stations at Hallituskatu 11, contains a theatre and concert hall, plus an excellent **library** (Mon–Thurs 11am–8pm, Fri 11am–5pm, Sat 11am–4pm) with several free Internet terminals (bookable in advance). There's also a **Lappland Department** (turn immediately left as you enter the building), housing a staggering hoard of books, magazines and newspaper articles in many languages covering every conceivable Sámi-related subject. This constantly growing collection is already the largest of its kind in the world, and probably the best place anywhere for undertaking Lapland-related research.

Other points of interest in Rovaniemi are few. At Rauhankatu 70, **Rovaniemi Seurakunta** (daily 9am–4pm), the parish church, repays a peek on account of its jumbo-sized altar fresco, *Fountain of Life* by Lennart Segerstråle, an odd work that pitches the struggle between good and evil into a Lapland setting. If you're here in winter, ask about the concerts that are staged here. About the only other thing meriting a look is the **Marttiini Old Knife Factory** (Mon–Fri 10am–6pm, Sat 10am–1pm; ⊛www.marttiini.fi) at Vartiokatu 32 (adjacent to the Arktikum). In the kingdom of the sharp edge the Marttiini multipurpose knife reigns supreme, and if you're looking for one the prices in the factory shop are cheaper than anywhere else – plus you can have your name inscribed on the blade. Prices range from a few euro up to €60–70 for the latest model.

If you have more time to kill and the weather isn't too cold (Rovaniemi is prone to chilly snaps even in summer), visit one of the two outdoor museums that lie near each other just outside town, accessible by bus #6. The **Ethnographical Museum** in Pöykkölä, 3km southeast of town (June–Aug Tues–Sun noon–4pm; €2), is a collection of farm buildings that belonged to the Pöykkölä family between 1640 and 1910, and forms part of a potpourri of objects pertaining to reindeer husbandry, salmon fishing and rural life in general. About 500m up the road is the **Lappish Forestry Museum** (June–Aug Tues–Sun noon–6pm; €2), where the reality of unglamorous forestry life is remembered by a reconstructed lumber camp.

Around Rovaniemi: the Arctic Circle and Santa Claus Village

Most people are lured to Rovaniemi solely for the dubious thrill of crossing the **Arctic Circle**. While the "circle" itself doesn't remain constant (it's defined as the area where the midnight sun can be seen, which shifts a few hundred metres every year), its man-made markers do – 8km north of town along Route 4 – and it's generally heralded by a crowd of visitors taking photographs of each other with one foot either side of the line. Bus #8 goes to the circle from the train station around every hour (€4.80 return; more frequent in summer), and also calls at several stops in town.

Near the circle and served by the same bus is the **Santa Claus Village** (daily: June–Aug 9am–7pm; rest of the year 10am–5pm; free). Considering its tourist pitch, the place – inside a very large log cabin – is quite within the bounds of decency: you can meet Father Christmas all year round, contemplate the reindeer grazing in the adjoining farm and leave your name for a Christmas card from Santa. Within the village is the ticket office for **Santa Park** (mid-June to mid-Aug daily 10am–6pm, Dec–March Fri 1–5pm; ☻www.santapark.fi; €20) from which a train connects to the park itself. A collection of themed fairground rides within a cavern inside a granite hill, Santa Park is predominantly aimed at those who believe the big guy with the white beard is real. For those without children, it's most definitely worth missing, unless you want to pretend you're four again.

Eating, drinking and entertainment

There are a few pleasant **cafés** in town, the best being the small *Antinkaapo*, just a few buildings up from *Walentina*, Rovakatu 21, another good spot for sticky buns. For filling food at very reasonable prices, *Café Kisälli*, Korkalonkatu 35 (closed Sat & Sun), and the neighbouring *Oppipoika Restaurant* are both run by the local hotel and catering school. Another decent choice is *Martina*, Koskikatu 11, where pizzas and pasta dishes cost €8–9 and steaks around €15. Italian food can also be found at *Rosso*, Koskikatu 4, but the best takeaway pizzas are to be had at *Kotipizza* (☎310 303), Koskikatu 5. If you haven't yet tried reindeer or any other **Lappish specialities**, the place to head for is the *Fransmanni* inside the *Sokos Vaakuna* at Koskikatu 4 – while prices here are not especially low, the quality of the food is excellent and you're likely to find everything from reindeer heart to cloudberry liqueur on the menu.

In the **evening** the most popular places for a drink are the chrome and glass-fronted *Zoomit*, generally stuffed with trendy young things from the Lapland University, and *Panimo*, a more traditional-style bar – both opposite each other at the corner of Koskikatu and Korkolankatu. Other favourite local hangouts are *Tupsu* at Hallituskatu 24, *Tivoli*, Valtakatu 19, or the dark and dingy *Paha Kurki*, Koskikatu 5 opposite *Rosso*. A more relaxed atmosphere prevails at the *Roy Club*, Maakuntakatu 24. The hotels tend to host the limited **nightlife**: *Scandic Rovaniemi*, Koskikatu 23, is popular, while *Doris*, at the *Hotel Vaakuna*, attracts an older crowd. The town wakes up a bit in the summer when ROPS, the Rovaniemi **football team** – one of the best in the country – are playing at home. You'll hear the cheering all over town, and can see the game for free through gaps in the fencing of the stadium, on Pohjolankatu. Rovaniemi also boasts a decent public **sauna** and **swimming pool** at Nuortenkatu 11, a fifteen-minute walk from the town centre west along Koskikatu and then left into Kokintie.

Listings

Airport ☎016/363 6700.
Bus information ☎0200/4060; national enquiries ☎0200/4000.
Car hire Avis, Valtakatu 26 ☎016/310 524; Budget, Koskikatu 9 ☎016/312 266; Hertz, Pohjanpuistikko 2 ☎016/332 332; Europcar, Koskikatu 6 ☎016/315 645.
Cinema Finnkino, inside the Sampokeskus shopping centre on Pekankatu.

Hospital Lapin Keskussairaala, Ounasrinteentie 22 ☎016/3282 100.
Railway station ☎0307/47579.
Safari companies Arctic Safaris, Koskikatu 6 ☎016/3400 400, ☻www.arcticsafaris.com; Lapland Safaris, Koskikatu 1 ☎016/362 811, ☻www.laplandsafaris.com.
Sauna Vesihiisi swimming hall, Nuortenkatu 11 ☎016/322 2592.
Train information VR ☎0307 10.

Moving on from Rovaniemi – cross-border bus routes in northern Scandinavia

With the exception of the once-daily train from Rovaniemi to Kemijärvi, all public transport north of the Arctic Circle is by **bus**. From Rovaniemi buses follow two main routes: northeast to Sodankylä, Ivalo, Inari and Utsjoki or northwest to Kittilä, Muonio, Karesuvanto and Kilpisjärvi – it's not possible to travel between these two routes without first backtracking to Rovaniemi. However, from the far north, cross-border services operate into Norway. From June to August a daily bus leaves Rovaniemi around 11am for the North Cape via Inari (5pm), crossing into Norway at **Karasjok** – a total journey of twelve hours. The bus waits at the North Cape for three and a half hours before returning overnight via the same route to Rovaniemi. Connections can be made in Karasjok east towards Kirkenes and west ultimately for Tromsö. During the rest of the year this service terminates in Karasjok.

It's also possible to reach Norway and the Nord-Norgeekpressen services from **Utsjoki**: from June to September there is a direct daily bus from Rovaniemi departing at 5pm via Inari and Utsjoki to Vadsö (March–May daily except Sat; Oct–Feb Thurs, Fri & Sun). Alternatively, you can reach Norway by simply walking across the bridge in Utsjoki yourself (remember the hour's time difference between Finland and Norway); Norwegian buses do not drive over the bridge into Finland.

From June to mid-September a daily service leaves Rovaniemi at 11.30am for **Tromsö** via Muonio, Karesuvanto (walk on foot over the bridge here to connect with Swedish bus services in Karesuvanto for Kiruna) and Kilpisjärvi. Be sure to check timetables carefully and plan several days ahead: get the *Pikavuorot*, available at the bigger bus stations, and ask any tourist office to help decipher the Finnish key.

The Arctic North

Squeezed inland by the northern tip of Norway, Finland's **Arctic North** mixes forests, lakes and rivers with tracts of desolate upland that rise high above the treeline. In these uncompromising latitudes, some of the indigenous Sámi population still herd their reindeer and maintain their traditions despite serious threats from a number of sources – most dramatically, in recent years, the fallout from Chernobyl. The Sámi tend to remain far from the prying eyes of the tourist, though their angular *tipis* (tents), wreathed in reindeer antlers, skins, and all sorts of Arctic trinkets, are to be found along the region's main roads during the summer, in what can seem a rather crass and commercially inspired conformity. This racial stereotyping is intended to appeal to the wallets of the thousands of motorists who use the **Arctic Highway**, the E75/4, the fastest approach to the Nordkapp (see p.393). But don't let this put you off: the Arctic wilderness is a ready escape, its stark and often haunting landscapes easily accessible.

Two main roads lead north from Rovaniemi: the Arctic Highway, which services the **northeast**, linking the communities of Sodankylä, Ivalo, Inari and Utsjoki; and Route 79/E8, which crosses the **northwest**, connecting Muonio and Kilpisjärvi. Inari and Sodankylä are the only settlements worth a second look, but the landscape which surrounds the Arctic North's minuscule communities will hold your gaze for much longer – provided you take the trouble to do at least some **hiking**. If you're planning to travel north from Rovaniemi on one route then back on the other, be warned that there are no roads in between, only rough tracks – with no facilities – traversing some desolate landscape. For safety, you need either to retrace your steps to Rovaniemi before taking the other route, or travel in an arc into Norway and over the other side, a journey by car of around four hours.

The northeast: Sodankylä and the national parks

North of Rovaniemi, it's an uneventful 130-kilometre drive along the Arctic Highway to **SODANKYLÄ**, a modest, comfortable town, whose modern appearance belies its ancient foundation. From the late seventeenth century, Finnish settlers and Christian Sámi gathered here on high days and holidays to trade and to celebrate religious festivals. Unusually, their wooden **church** (summer daily 10am–6pm) of 1689 has survived intact, its rough-hewn timbers crowding in upon the narrowest of naves with the pulpit pressing intrusively into the pews. The old church nestles beside the Kitinen River in the shadow of its uninspiring nineteenth-century replacement and a stone's throw from the **Alariesto Art Gallery** (June to mid-Sept Mon–Fri 10am–5pm, Sat 10am–5pm, Sun noon–6pm; rest of year Sat 10am–4pm, Sun noon–6pm; €5). The gallery features the work of Andreas Alariesto, a twentieth-century Sámi artist of some renown. Each canvas is an invigorating representation of traditional native life and custom, notably a crystalline *View from the Arctic Ocean* embellished with chaotic boulders, predatory fish jaws and busy Sámi. A useful catalogue available at reception explains the background to the exhibits.

Sodankylä is little more than an elongated main street: Jäämerentie. The bus station, post office and petrol stations are within a few metres of each other, while the **tourist office** (☎016/618 168, ⊛www.sodankyla.fi) is in the centre of the village, a ten-minute walk from the bus station. In winter it's a good idea to book

Hiking in the Arctic North

The best way to experience the Arctic North is to get off the bus and explore slowly, which means on foot. The rewards for making the physical effort are manifold. There's a tremendous feeling of space here, and the wild and inhospitable terrain acquires a near-magical quality when illuminated by the constant daylight of the summer months (the only time of year when hiking is feasible).

Many graded **hiking routes** cover the more interesting areas; most of the more exhilarating are distributed among the region's four national parks: **Pyhätunturi**, southeast of Sodankylä; **Urho Kekkonen** and **Lemmenjoki**, further north off the Arctic Highway; and **Pallas-Ounastunturi**, near Muonio in the northwest. There are challenges aplenty for experienced hikers, though novices need have nothing to fear provided basic common sense is employed. The more popular hikes can become very busy and many people find this an intrusion into their contemplation of the natural spectacle – others enjoy the camaraderie. If you are seeking solitude you'll find it, but you'll need at least the company of a reliable compass, a good-quality tent, and emergency supplies.

We've assembled a broad introduction to the major hikes and described the type of terrain that you'll find on them. Bear in mind that these aren't definitive accounts as conditions and details often change at short notice; always gather the latest information from the nearest tourist centre or park information office.

Hiking rules and tips

Obviously you should observe the **basic rules** of hiking, and be aware of the delicate ecology of the region: don't start fires in any old place (most hikes have marked spots for this), and don't pitch your tent out of specified areas on marked routes. You should always check that you have maps and adequate supplies before setting out, and never aim to cover more ground than is comfortable. Bathe your feet daily to prevent blisters, and carry some form of mosquito repellent – the pesky creatures infest the region.

Hiking accommodation

To be on the safe side, you shouldn't go anywhere without a good-quality **tent**, although the majority of marked hikes have some form of basic shelter (see p.662), and most have a **youth hostel** and **campsite** (plus comfy hotels for those who can afford them) at some point on the trail. These fill quickly, however, and few things are worse than having nowhere to relax after a long day's trek – so make an advance reservation whenever possible.

accommodation in advance, since Sodankylä is used by test drivers from *Peugeot* who come here for several months to test new models in Arctic conditions. There are just two **hotels** in the village, the down at heel *Hotelli Kultaisen Karhun Majatalo* (ⓣ016/613 801, ⓕ613 810; ❸), a five-minute walk from the bus station at Sodankyläntie 10, and the smarter *Hotelli Sodankylä*, Lapintie 21 (ⓣ016/617 121, ⓕ617 177; ❺/❹), both of which are open year round. The *Kolme Veljestä* guesthouse, north of the bus station, at Ivalontie 1 (ⓣ016/611 216; ❸), has comfortable rooms; breakfast and use of the kitchen and sauna are included. There's also a **campsite** (ⓣ016/612 181; early June to mid-Aug) and a **youth hostel** (ⓣ016/612 218, ⓕ611 503; same dates), a ten- to fifteen-minute walk from the centre: cross the bridge, veer left along Savukoskentie and follow the signs. As for **meals**, the pizzas served up at *Pizza Pirkko*, Jäämerentie 25, are the best in town, while for a wider choice of local meat and fish dishes try *Ravintola Revontuli*, Jäämerentie 9, which is also a popular place for a drink. The central *Seita-baari* serves up the best local food, however, earning its reputation from its excellent reindeer stew, but the orange plastic chairs and tacky feel are off-putting.

Around Sodankylä: Pyhätunturi National Park

Off the Arctic Highway some 65km southeast of Sodankylä lies **Pyhätunturi National Park**, and the steep slopes and deep ravines of the most southerly of Finland's fells. Here, the 45-kilometre **Pyhätunturi hiking trail** rises from marshlands and pine woods and rounds five fell summits. Five kilometres from the start is the impressive waterfall of the Uhrikuru gorge, after which the track circles back for a short stretch, eventually continuing to Karhunjuomalampi ("The Bear's Pool"). There's a *päivätupa* (cabin) here, but the only other hut on the route is by the pool at Pyhälampi.

Near the hike's starting point are a **nature centre** (ⓣ016/882 773, ⓕ882 824), a **campsite** (ⓣ016/852 103, ⓕ852 140), and two reasonably priced hotels: the *Pyhätunturi* (ⓣ016/856 111, ⓕ882 740; ❸) and *Pyhän Asteli* (ⓣ016/852 141, ⓕ852 149; ❸). The hike ends at Luostotunturi, where accommodation includes the *Scandic Hotel Luosto* (ⓣ016/624 400, ⓦwww.scandic-hotels.com; ❺/❹) and the more basic *Luostonhovi* (ⓣ016/624 420, ⓕ624 297; ❷). The daily **bus** between Sodankylä and Kemijärvi (on the rail line from Rovaniemi) stops close to both ends of the trail.

Continuing north: Urho Kekkonen National Park

Travel north by car from Sodankylä on the Arctic Highway for 110km and just after the village of **Vuotso** you'll arrive at **Koilliskaira Visitor Centre** (June–Sept daily 9am–6pm; Oct–May Mon–Fri 9am–4pm; ⓣ016/205 64 7251, ⓦwww .metsa.fi/customerservice/koilliskaira/first.htm), where you can reserve cabin beds, get information on dozens of hikes and watch a film about the local terrain. Just 100m from the centre lurks a gaggle of tourist establishments: the **Tankavaara Gold Museum and Panning Centre** (same hours; €5), the *Nugget* restaurant, serving Lapland specialities for around €15, and a guesthouse, the *Korundi* (ⓣ016/626 158, ⓕ626 261; ❸), with **cabins** (❷).

Twenty kilometres further north (130km from Sodankylä), at the hamlet of Kakslauttanen, is the turning for **Fell Centre Kiilopää** (ⓣ016/6700 700, ⓕ667 121), a popular and well-equipped fell-walking centre on the edge of the **Urho**

Kekkonen National Park. The park is one of the country's largest, incorporating the uninhabited wilderness that extends to the Russian border – pine moors and innumerable fells scored by gleaming streams and rivers. With regular bus connections to north and south, the Fell Centre (also known by its Finnish name, Tunturikeskus) is easily the most convenient base for exploring the park. It's at the head of several walking trails, from the simplest of excursions to exhausting expeditions using the park's chain of wilderness cabins. As well as providing park information, selling detailed trail maps, renting mountain bikes and organizing guided walks, staff can arrange accommodation in the adjoining year-round **youth hostel** (same phone number); the Centre also has some en-suite rooms (❺/❹), a good restaurant and a smoke sauna.

Ivalo, Inari and around

Try not to get stuck in **IVALO**, a town of singular ugliness on the Arctic Highway 40km north of the Fell Centre Kiilopää. If you do have to stay, however, the riverside *Hotel Kultahippu*, Petsamontie 1 (☎016/661 825, ℱ662 510; ❹/❸), is the most palatable option, with breakfast and sauna included in the price. There's no longer an official **tourist office** here, the nearest being in Inari (see below), though the *Kultahippu* does have limited information. **Eating** options amount to the *Anjan Pizza* on the main road near the *Shell* filling station, and the *Lauran Grilli*, opposite, which also has pizzas and kebabs. Whilst Ivalo lacks any obvious charm, it does offer a rare direct **bus to Russia**: a once-daily (Mon–Fri) service leaves the village at 3.30pm for the 300-kilometre trip to **Murmansk** via the border at Raja-Jooseppi – however, you'll need advance planning if you want to use the service, as you'll need to be equipped with a Russian visa to get on, which can only be obtained in Helsinki.

The road heading north to Inari winds around numerous lakes dotted with islands – it's a spectacular route if you can time your trip with the glorious Lapland **Ruska**, a season that takes in late summer and autumn when the trees take on brilliant citrus colours that reflect in the still waters. **INARI** itself, 35km away, is slightly more amenable than Ivalo, straggling along the bony banks of the Juutuanjoki River as it tumbles into the freezing-cold, islet-studded waters of Lake Inarijärvi. There's nothing remarkable about the village itself, but it's a pretty little place with several appealing diversions. The bus stops outside the **tourist office** on the one and only main road (June–Aug Mon–Fri 10am–6pm, Sat & Sun 10am–3pm; Sept–May Mon–Fri 9am–5pm; ☎016/661 666, ❂www.inarilapland.org), where staff can advise on accommodation and organize a fishing licence (from €20). Across the road is the Sámi handicraft store, *Sámi Duodji* (daily: July to early Sept 9am–8pm; rest of the year 10am–5pm), whose exhibits show a marked contrast in quality with the tourist souvenirs that pop up everywhere here. Close by lies the recently renovated Sámi museum and nature centre **Siida** (June–Sept daily 9am–8pm; Oct–May Tues–Sun 10am–5pm; €7), one of the best museums in Lapland. An excellent outdoor section features a re-sited nineteenth-century village and various reconstructions illustrating aspects of Sámi life – principally handicrafts and hunting and fishing techniques – while the indoor section has a well-laid-out and easy-to-understand exhibition on all aspects of life in the Arctic. Beginning about 2.5km from the museum, the four-kilometre **Pielpajärvi Wilderness Church hiking trail** leads to the isolated remains of a 1752 church – this trail, though, can be very slippery when wet. If you don't fancy expending any energy to see some scenery, though, head for the bridge over the Juutuanjoki, from where, in summer, you can take a two-hour **lake cruise** (June to mid-Sept 1–2 daily; ☎016/663 562; €12), as well as fishing trips (all year); a twelve-seat boat and a guide for two and a half hours for three to eleven people costs €30.

Many travellers pass through Inari during the summer, so it's best to reserve accommodation during this period. There's a **campsite**, *Uruniemi Camping* (☎016/671 331; June to Sept), 3km away on the southern outskirts of the village,

779

△ Husky, Lapland

with cottages (●); nearby, the *Lomakylä Inari* (☎016/671 108) has better-quality cabins (④). Back in the village, the *Inarin Kultahovi* **hotel** (☎016/671 221, ℗671 250; ④) offers comfortable rooms with river views, plus an excellent, reasonably priced **restaurant**. If money's tight, stick to the popular *Ranta-Mari* restaurant and café, beside the bus stop, though be prepared to share the place with drunken locals at weekends.

Around Inari: Lemmenjoki National Park
A vast tract of birch and pinewood forest interrupted by austere, craggy fells, marshland and a handful of bubbling rivers, **Lemmenjoki National Park**, about 40km southwest of Inari, witnessed a short-lived gold rush in the 1940s. A few panners remain, eking out a meagre living.

The park's most breathtaking scenery is to be found on its southeastern side along the Lemmenjoki river valley. To get there, take the daily bus from Inari to **Njurgalahti**, a tiny settlement on the edge of the park about 12km off Route E75 to Kittilä (the district's main road), which is where the 55-kilometre, two-day hike down the river valley begins; taking the twice-daily boat (June–Aug) from Njurgalahti to Kultasatama cuts 20km off the hike's full distance.

At **Härkäkoski**, hikers cross the river by a small boat, pulled by rope from bank to bank; the track then ascends through a pine forest to **Morgamoja Kultala**, the old gold-panning centre, where there's a big unlocked hut. There are a couple of other huts set aside for those walking the trail, but the nearest **campsite** (☎ & ℗016/673 001), with cottages, is back on the main road at **Menesjärvi**. The holiday village, *Ahkun Tupa* (☎ & ℗016/673 435), in the hamlet of **Lemmenjoki**, is far closer, with four-berth **cabins** from around €40 per cabin per day. For more information on the park ask at the Lemmenjoki nature hut (June–Sept varying hours, ☎0205/64 7793) at the park entrance.

North from Inari: crossing into Norway
Travelling north from Inari is rather pointless unless you're aiming for Norway. The Finnish section of the Arctic Highway continues to dreary **KAAMANEN**, though on the way, just past a sign for the *Jokitörmä Hostel*, is a bold, stark and deeply evocative memorial in rusty red metal to World War II in Finland. In simple words, it states "the battles of the light infantrymen in the wilds of Lapland were brought to an end in Kaamanen, Inari at the end of October 1944. 774 killed, 262 missing, 2904 wounded". In Kaamanen there's an all-year **campsite** with cottages (☎016/672 713). The route then swings westwards on its way to the Nordkapp, exiting Finland at **KARIGASNIEMI**, an unprepossessing hamlet that has a restaurant (*Soarve Stohpu*) and pleasant rooms in the small and basic *Kalastajan Majatalo* hotel next door (☎ & ℗016/676 171; ②). There are also two **campsites**: *Lomakylä* (☎016/676 160; June–Sept), and the *Tenorinne* (☎016/676 113; early June to mid-Sept).

From Kaamanen, a minor road branches due north to **UTSJOKI**, a small border village beside the Tenojoki River. The nearest **campsite** (☎016/678 803; mid-June to Aug) is a few kilometres away, by the river's edge in Vetsikko. The road on from Utsjoki runs parallel to the Norwegian border, then crosses it just beyond the hamlet of **Nuorgam**, where there's a guesthouse, the *Matkakoti Suomenrinne* (☎016/678 620; mid-June to mid-Aug), and a year-round **campsite** (☎016/678 312). Once across the border, it's a 160-kilometre journey to Kirkenes in Norway (see p.395).

The northwest
Heading northwest from Rovaniemi, Route 79 sticks close to the banks of the Ounasjoki River before it reaches the straggling settlement of **KITTILÄ**, a distance of 150km. There's little to detain you here – the departing German army burnt the place to the ground in 1944 and the rebuilding has been uninspired – though both the **youth hostel**, Valtatie 5 (☎016/648 508; mid-June to early Aug), and neighbouring **campsite** are conveniently located beside the main road.

It's a further 20km to the dishevelled ski resort of **SIRKKA**, whose surrounding hills boast seven hiking (or, in winter, cross-country skiing) routes, including the enjoyable river and fell walking of the eighteen-kilometre Levi Fell trail. All seven tracks begin in or near the centre of Sirkka, where you should find a whole range of places to stay, though nearly all are open only during the winter.

Muonio and around

Modest **MUONIO** lies 60km northwest of Sirkka beside the murky river that separates Finland from Sweden. What passes for the town centre falls beside the junction of the E8, the main north–south highway, and Route 79 from Kittilä; the ESSO filling station at the crossroads here functions as the bus station. The **tourist office** (mid-Dec to mid-April, June & mid-Aug to mid-Sept daily 10am–6pm; July to mid-Aug daily 10am–8pm; rest of the year Mon–Fri 11am–5pm; ☎016/532 280, ⓦwww.muonio.fi) lies beside this junction in the newly constructed *Kiela Naturum* nature centre (same hours), whose star attraction is its **northern lights planetarium** (€10), a worthy film show which explains how the phenomenon occurs. Incidentally, if you're in Muonio during the winter months there's a 55 percent chance of seeing the northern lights; however, it must be a clear night. For accommodation, head for the superbly located year-round **youth hostel** *Lomamaja Pekonen*(☎016/532 237, ☎532 236; ❶), on a small hill overlooking a lake at Lahenrannantie 10. There are also excellently equipped **cabins** here costing just €45; the ones at the top of the hill have their own saunas and cost €58. **Canoes** can also be hired here for €25 per day.

South of Muonio: the Harriniva holiday centre

Some 3km south of Muonio towards Tornio lies the well organized and well equipped *Harriniva Holiday Centre* (☎016/530 0300, ⓦwww.harriniva.fi), where you can pitch a tent, hook up your camper van or stay in a range of accommodation that runs from basic cabins (❷) to fully equipped apartments (❹). However, what makes this place special is the range of summer and winter **activities** on offer. Harriniva has 250 huskies – making it the biggest husky centre in Finland – and if you're here in winter and thinking of a **husky safari**, this is *the* place to do it. Although safaris are quite pricey – a week-long round-trip safari from Muonio up towards Enontekiö, covering a daily distance of around 40km and including overnight accommodation in log cabins, costs around €1100 – you can cut costs by booking via a travel agent such as Norvista (see p.19) rather than at the centre itself; Norvista also have good deals on air fares to Finland. The final price will include all food, your huskies and sledge plus overnight accommodation – and, of course, the experience of riding across frozen lakes, winding through Lapland's silent snow-covered forests and ending the day with a roll in the snow after a genuine smoke sauna. The centre's other winter activities include a week-long **snowmobile safari** (€1580), a four-hour **reindeer safari** (€118), and seven days of **cross-country skiing with huskies** (€665). In summer, the centre offers such things as **white-water rafting** (€150), **salmon fishing/reindeer farm** tours (€165) and **canoe trips** (€42).

Pallas-Ounastunturi National Park

From Muonio, buses leave for Kilpisjärvi (see p.783) and (once-daily) to Enontekiö/Hetta, skirting the **Pallas-Ounastunturi National Park**, a rectangular slab of mountain plateau whose bare peaks and coniferous forests begin about 30km northeast of Muonio. A bus leaves Muonio at 9.30am Monday to Friday for the National Park, stopping outside the **visitor centre**, Pallastunturi (mid-June to Sept daily 9am–5pm; rest of the year Mon–Fri 9am–4pm; ☎0205/64 7930, ⓦwww.metsa.fi/customerservice/pallastunturi/index.htm). Pallastunturi marks the start of the **Pallas-Hetta hiking route**, an arduous 55-kilometre trail that crosses a line of fell summits with several *autiotupa* and *varaustupa* (locked and unlocked huts)

Hikes in the Pallas-Ounastunturi park: the Pallas-Olos-Ylläs trail

Although the Pallas-Hetta trail is the Pallas-Ounastunturi National Park's most impressive walk, and the one with the best transport links, there are several other options. Of these, the most notable is the 87-kilometre **Pallas-Olos-Ylläs trail**, which also begins from Pallastunturi visitor centre. With several unlocked huts on route, this track twists south past fells and lakes until it leaves the park and reaches the Muonio–Sirkka road close to the swanky *Hotel Olostunturi* (☎016/536 111, ⟨w⟩www.pallas-hotel.com; ❻). The hotel is open only for winter skiing between September and April but the hills that surround it are crisscrossed by a number of shorter walking trails.

From the hotel, the Pallas-Olos-Ylläs trail continues south, soon reaching the dam on the Särkijoki river before proceeding down to Lake Äkäsjärvi, where there's a café in a former grain mill. From here, the track heads onto the eastern slopes of Äkäskero, passing the remarkably good-value *Äkäskero Wilderness Lodge* (☎016/533 077, ⟨w⟩www .akaskero.com; ❸) and continuing for 4km to the tiny settlement of **ÄKÄSLOMPOLO**, on the upper slopes of Yllästunturi.

The **bus service** on from Äkäslompolo is dreadful: there's a once-weekly (Sat) summer service to Kolari at 4pm, eventually reaching Tornio, Kemi and Oulu, but to reach Muonio, 76km north of Kolari, you'll have to hitch or change in Kolari.

and camping areas en route, as well as a sauna about halfway along in the hut at **Hannukuru**. The highest point is the summit of Taivaskero, near the start. The track ends at Lake Ounasjärvi, which you'll need to cross by **ferry** (7am–11pm); if the boat isn't there, raise the flag to indicate that you want to cross.

On the other side of the lake is the unremarkable village of **HETTA** (known administratively as **ENONTEKIÖ**; ⟨w⟩www.enontekio.fi) – hardly an inspiring place, although the thrice-weekly flights to and from Helsinki can make it an accessible starting point for exploring Lapland. The services on offer are also excellent, including Enontekiö Flights (☎016/521 230), whose air taxis can take you quickly (and expensively) into the depths of Lapland. There's also the **Fell Lapland Nature Centre** (mid-June to Sept daily 9am–5pm; rest of the year Mon–Fri 9am–4pm; ☎0205/64 7959, ⟨w⟩www.metsa.fi/customerservice/fell-lapland/), where you can buy maps and get help with reservations for a host of cottages in the Pallas-Ounastunturi National Park. There is some reasonable accommodation in and around the village, including a **youth hostel** (☎016/521 361, ⓕ521 049; mid-Feb to April & June to mid-Sept) and a trio of **campsites**: *Hetan Lomakylä* (☎016/521 521, ⓕ521 293; June–Sept), which also has some cabins (❸), *Kotatieva* (☎016/521 062; June to mid-Aug) and *Ounasloma* (all year, but call ahead on ☎016/521 55, ⓕ521 004). Among the settlement's **hotels**, a good choice is the *Hetan Majatalo* (☎016/5540 400, ⓕ521 362; ❸), which offers excellent en-suite rooms as well as cheaper and more basic accommodation. In winter they organize a whole host of activities, from winter ice-fishing, reindeer safaris and dog-sleigh tours to summer fishing trips, and boat and bike rental, while the hotel restaurant cooks up highly recommended traditional Lappish dinners. The *Hotelli Hetta* (☎016/521 361, ⟨w⟩www.hetta-hotel.com; ❸) offers a plush alternative, with several rooms overlooking the lake.

If you're driving north through Hetta towards Norway, 6km before you get to the border on the Alta road is **PALOJÄRVI**, where the log cabins of *Galdotieva* (☎016/528 630; ❷), some with their own sauna, offer a reasonable, if somewhat isolated, overnight spot.

North from Muonio: Kilpisjärvi and around

The thumb-shaped chunk of Finland that sticks out above the northern edge of Sweden is almost entirely uninhabited, a hostile arctic wilderness whose tiny settlements are strung along the only road, the E8. For the most part this seems a gloomy route of desolate landscapes and untidy villages, comparing poorly with the splendour of the parallel road to the south that connects Sweden's Kiruna and Norway's Narvik. However, the E8 does have its moments as it approaches the Norwegian frontier, with the bumpy uplands left behind for dramatic snow-covered peaks.

From the E8, you might cross into Sweden via **KAARESUVANTO**, a dreary village 95km north of Muonio, to reach the Kiruna–Narvik road. Otherwise there's little reason to cross the border here or stay longer than you need to in Kaaresuvanto – if you do, use the all-year **campsite** (☏016/522 079), which has some smart cabins (❶ for a twin-bed cabin). Otherwise, try the *Hotelli Davvi* (☏016/522 101, ⓦwww.davvihotel.com; ❸), which has fully equipped cabins (❷) as well as regular rooms, and a good restaurant.

There's more to be said for continuing for 110km on the E8 to the hamlet of **KILPISJÄRVI** on the Norwegian frontier. On the way, about 25km south of Kilpisjärvi, you'll pass the welcoming *Peeran Retkeilykeskus* **youth hostel** (☏016/259 492), which also serves good food. At Kilpisjärvi itself, perched beside the coldest of lakes in the shadow of a string of stark tundra summits, the *Hotelli Kilpis* (☏016/537 761, ⓦwww.pallas-hotel.com; ❸) has a gorgeous location which means it gets booked up months ahead for the March to mid-June period; however, 5km further down the road, the tourist hotel *Kilpisjärven Retkeiltkeskus* (☏016/537 771, ☏537 772; ❷) offers rooms and cottages in just as fine a setting. Both places sell maps covering a number of **local hikes**, the most popular of which are the brace of ten-kilometre trails running to the top of the neighbouring Saanatunturi, 1029m high. The main way up (and down) is the track on the steep north side, although another route runs behind the fell to the northern shore of Saanijärvi, where there's a *päivätupa* (cabin).

Another option is the 24-kilometre loop trail, beginning and ending at Kilpisjärvi, that runs north through the **Malla Nature Reserve** to the **Three Countries Frontier** where Finland, Norway and Sweden meet. The track crosses the rapids of Siilajärvi by footbridge, after which a secondary track ascends to the summit of Pikku Malla. The main route continues to Iso Malla. There's a steep and stony section immediately before the waterfalls of Kihtsekordsi, and then a reindeer fence marking the way down to an *autiotupa* cabin beside the Kuokimajärvi lake. From the tourist office, a stone path leads to the cairn marking the three national borders. There's a **campsite** at the tourist centre (June–Sept) and, nearby, a **guesthouse**, *Saananmajat* (☏016/537 746; ❷).

Travel details

Trains

Oulu to: Kajaani (6 daily; 2hr 20min); Kemi (7 daily; 1hr 20min); Rovaniemi (7 daily; 3hr).
Rovaniemi to: Kemijärvi (1 daily; 1hr 15min); Oulu (7 daily; 3hr).
Vaasa to: Helsinki (7 daily via Seinäjöki; 4hr 30min); Oulu (10 daily; 5hr 30min); Tampere (7 daily; 2hr 30min).

Buses

Inari to: Kaamanen (6 daily; 1hr 45min); Kargasneimi (2 daily; 1hr 45min); Utsjoki (2 daily; 3hr 45min).
Kajaani to: Ämmänsaari (1 daily; 2hr 30min direct, longer by slower, indirect routes); Kuusamo

(1 daily; 4hr 10min direct, also slower, indirect routes).
Kemi to: Tornio (8 daily; 40min).
Kolari to: Äkäslompolo (1 weekly; 55min).
Kuusamo to: Ristikallio (1 daily; 1hr 15min); Salla (2 daily; 3hr).
Muonio to: Kilpisjärvi (3 daily; 3hr 45min).
Oulu to: Kuusamo (6 daily; 4hr).
Pallastunturi to: Enontekiö (1 daily; 2hr 30min); Muonio (1 daily; 40min).
Pietarsaari to: Kokkola (6 daily; 40min).
Rovaniemi to: Enontekiö/Hetta (2 daily; 5hr 15min); Inari (2 daily; 6hr); Ivalo (3 daily; 5hr); Kiilopää (1 daily; 4hr); Kilpisjärvi (2 daily; 7hr 45min); Kittilä (4 daily; 2hr 30min–2hr 50min); Muonio (2 daily; 4hr); Pallastunturi (1 daily; 4hr 45min); Sodankylä (4 daily; 1hr 40min).

Sodankylä to: Kemijäarvi (5 daily; 2hr).
Suomussalmi to: Kuusamo (3 daily; 2hr 45min).
Tornio to: Äkäslompolo (1 weekly; 3hr 45min).
Utsjoki to: Nuorgam (2 daily; 55min).
Vaasa to: Pori (5 daily; 2hr 45min); Turku (6 daily; 5hr).

International ferries

Vaasa to: Umeå (1 daily; 4hr); Härnösand (1 daily; 7–8hr).

4

4.3 | FINLAND | Ostrobothnia, Kainuu and Lapland

Index

and small print

Index

Map entries are in **colour**

K

Twenty Years of Rough Guides

In the summer of 1981, Mark Ellingham, Rough Guides' founder, knocked out the first guide on a typewriter, with a group of friends. Mark had been travelling in Greece after university, and couldn't find a guidebook that really answered his needs.There were heavyweight cultural guides on the one hand – good on museums and classical sites but not on beaches and tavernas – and on the other hand student manuals that were so caught up with how to save money that they lost sight of the country's significance beyond its role as a place for a cool vacation. None of the guides began to address Greece as a country, with its natural and human environment, its politics and its contemporary life.

Having no urgent reason to return home, Mark decided to write his own guide. It was a guide to Greece that tried to combine some erudition and insight with a thoroughly practical approach to travellers' needs. Scrupulously researched listings of places to stay, eat and drink were matched by careful attention to detail on everything from Homer to Greek music, from classical sites to national parks and from nude beaches to monasteries. Back in London, Mark and his friends got their Rough Guide accepted by a farsighted commissioning editor at the publisher Routledge and it came out in 1982.

The Rough Guide to Greece was a student scheme that became a publishing phenomenon. The immediate success of the book – shortlisted for the Thomas Cook award – spawned a series that rapidly covered dozens of countries. The Rough Guides found a ready market among backpackers and budget travellers, but soon acquired a much broader readership that included older and less impecunious visitors. Readers relished the guides' wit and inquisitiveness as much as the enthusiastic, critical approach that acknowledges everyone wants value for money – but not at any price.

Rough Guides soon began supplementing the "rougher" information – the hostel and low-budget listings – with the kind of detail that independent-minded travellers on any budget might expect. These days, the guides – distributed worldwide by the Penguin group – include recommendations spanning the range from shoestring to luxury, and cover more than 200 destinations around the globe. Our growing team of authors, many of whom come to Rough Guides initially as outstandingly good letter-writers telling us about their travels, are spread all over the world, particularly in Europe, the USA and Australia. As well as the travel guides, Rough Guides publishes a series of dictionary phrasebooks covering two dozen major languages, an acclaimed series of music guides running the gamut from Classical to World Music, a series of music CDs in association with World Music Network, and a range of reference books on topics as diverse as the Internet, Pregnancy and Unexplained Phenomena. Visit **www.roughguides.com** to see what's cooking.

Rough Guide Credits

Text editor: Polly Thomas
Series editor: Mark Ellingham
Editorial: Martin Dunford, Jonathan Buckley,
Kate Berens, Ann-Marie Shaw, Helena Smith,
Olivia Swift, Ruth Blackmore, Geoff Howard,
Claire Saunders, Gavin Thomas, Alexander
Mark Rogers, Joe Staines, Richard Lim,
Duncan Clark, Peter Buckley, Lucy Ratcliffe,
Clifton Wilkinson, Alison Murchie, Matthew
Teller, Andrew Dickson, Fran Sandham, Sally
Schafer, Matthew Milton (UK); Andrew
Rosenberg, Yuki Takagaki, Richard Koss,
Hunter Slaton (USA)
Production: Link Hall, Helen Prior, Julia
Bovis, Katie Pringle, Rachel Holmes, Andy
Turner, Dan May, Tanya Hall, John McKay,
Sophie Hewat

Cartography: Maxine Repath, Melissa Baker,
Ed Wright, Katie Lloyd-Jones
Cover art direction: Louise Boulton
Picture research: Sharon Martins,
Mark Thomas
Online: Kelly Martinez, Anja Mutic-Blessing,
Jennifer Gold, Audra Epstein,
Suzanne Welles, Cree Lawson (USA)
Finance: John Fisher, Gary Singh,
Edward Downey, Mark Hall, Tim Bill
Marketing & Publicity: Richard Trillo, Niki
Smith, David Wearn, Chloë Roberts, Demelza
Dallow, Claire Southern (UK); Simon Carloss,
David Wechsler, Megan Kennedy (USA)
Administration: Julie Sanderson, Karoline
Densley

Publishing Information

This sixth edition published April 2003 by
Rough Guides Ltd,
80 Strand, London WC2R 0RL.
345 Hudson St, 4th Floor,
New York, NY 10014, USA.
Distributed by the Penguin Group
Penguin Books Ltd,
80 Strand, London WC2R 0RL
Penguin Putnam, Inc.
375 Hudson Street, NY 10014, USA
Penguin Books Australia Ltd,
487 Maroondah Highway, PO Box 257,
Ringwood, Victoria 3134, Australia
Penguin Books Canada Ltd,
10 Alcorn Avenue, Toronto, Ontario,
Canada M4V 1E4
Penguin Books (NZ) Ltd,
182–190 Wairau Road, Auckland 10,
New Zealand
Typeset in Bembo and Helvetica to an
original design by Henry Iles.

Printed in Italy by LegoPrint S.p.A

824pp includes index
A catalogue record for this book is available
from the British Library

ISBN 1-84353-053-8

The publishers and authors have done their
best to ensure the accuracy and currency of
all the information in **The Rough Guide to
Scandinavia**, however, they can accept no
responsibility for any loss, injury, or
inconvenience sustained by any traveller as a
result of information or advice contained in
the guide.

Help us update

We've gone to a lot of effort to ensure that
the sixth edition of **The Rough Guide to
Scandinavia** is accurate and up-to-date.
However, things change – places get
"discovered", opening hours are notoriously
fickle, restaurants and rooms raise prices or
lower standards. If you feel we've got it
wrong or left something out, we'd like to
know, and if you can remember the address,
the price, the time, the phone number, so
much the better.

We'll credit all contributions, and send a
copy of the next edition (or any other Rough
Guide if you prefer) for the best letters.
Everyone who writes to us and isn't already a
subscriber will receive a copy of our full-
colour thrice-yearly newsletter. Please mark
letters: "**Rough Guide Scandinavia Update**"
and send to: Rough Guides, 80 Strand,
London WC2R 0RL, or Rough Guides, 4th
Floor, 345 Hudson St, New York, NY 10014.
Or send an email to **mail@roughguides.com**

Have your questions answered and tell
others about your trip at
www.roughguides.atinfopop.com

SMALL PRINT

Acknowledgements

Polly Thomas would like to thank the authors for all their hard toil; Helena Smith for stepping in and finishing up; Ed Wright for patient, marvellous mapping beyond the call of duty; Andy Turner and Daniel May for slick layout; Michelle Draycott for fab pictures; Jan Wiltshire for proofreading; and Andrew Spooner for updating parts of the Jutland chapter.

Lone Mouritsen: Tina Schneider for housing me during the entire update; Bettina Lemtorp and Lars Ringgaard for sharing their knowledge of Copenhagen cafés and nightlife; Knud (Lars) Funch for helping out with Bornholm; Merete, Pauline and Emma Sørensen for exploring Bornholm Danish campsites; Jan and Mads Fgelund and Marlis, Nanna and Rhea Dall for providing me with facts on Århus and Copenhagen nightlife; Elisabeth Jensen for checking out southern Funen; Mette and Nina Mouritsen for Northern Jutland, yet again; Natalie and Helene for in-depth research into gay Copenhagen; and Henrik Theirlein of Wonderful Copenhagen.

James Proctor: James would like to extend grateful thanks to Leena Yli-Piipari, Matti Linnoila and especially Mia Luostarinen of the Finnish Tourist Board in London for their enthusiasm and devotion to duty – and detail. Also to the voice of Finnish Railways, Eija Kare, whose dulcet tones brought a wry smile to every journey. Kaarina Delafosse-Guiramond of the City of Helsinki Tourist and Convention Bureau not only excelled in tracking down lost passports, but also in luggage storage and computer access. Thanks also to Nan Holmström and family for renewed contact and shared knowledge of all things Finland-Swedish – and Yorkshire. In Sweden, a big thankyou to Emelie Klein and Ann-Charlotte Carlsson of the Swedish Travel and Tourism Council in London. Finally to Marc Davidson of Norvista, who didn't believe anyone was man, or mad, enough at $-17°C$.

Neil Roland: I would like to thank Kalle & Janis Sundin of Kalmar, Ingvar Grimberg and Stigake Berkin of Gothenburg for their much appreciated friendship. I am also very grateful for all the enthusiasm and help shown by Lena Larsson at Gothenburg & Co, Stefanie Feldmann in Lund, a special thanks to Lena Birgersson at Skane Tourist Board, to Torgney Andersson at Destination Gotland, to Cecilia Theisen in Visby, Kerstin Hallberg at Kronoberg and Sylva Schaefer at Örebro.

Readers' letters

Thanks to all the readers who took the trouble to write in with their comments and suggestions (and apologies to anyone whose name we've misspelt or omitted):
Karen Aplin, R. Blakeway-Phillips, John Brandham, I. Brett, Fiona Brooks-Wood, Chris Burin, Pauline Cutts, John Dobson, Chris Ewels and Florence, Claudia Froldi, Gideon Greenspan, Nicky Griffin, Helena Gustafsson, Thomas Hakewill, Andy Hall, Tissa Hami, Henrik Harr, Patricia Harrison, C. Haynes, Stuart Hicks, Jason Hsu, Maija Hurme, S. Hussain, Malcolm Jackson, Alf and Roberta Jacobson, Anu Johansson, James Jolly, Michael Jubb, Hanna Leicht, Jeffrey Mahn, Rosemary Marley, Jane Monaghan, Jette Norre, P.L. Pounds, J.F.C. Reeves, Sharon and Steve Rhys-Davies, Antonio D. Ribeiro, Liam Rigby, Sue Stanbury, Anna Taranko, Ulrik, Lee Walker.

Photo credits

Cover credits

Main front picture – Sweden ©Photonica
Top small front picture – Tjörnbro, Bohuslän coast, Sweden, ©Robert Harding
Lower small front picture – Stave church, Norway ©Pictor
Top back picture – Farm near Turku, Finland ©Pictor
Lower back picture – Glacial Lake, Olden, ©Norway

Colour introduction

Birch trees, Finland ©Jim Holmes/AXIOM
Gierangerfjord, Norway ©R. Westlake/TRIP
Viking carving, Urnes stave church, Norway ©Phil Lee
Midnight sun, Norway ©A. Ghazzal/TRIP
Sauna at edge of forest ©Layne Kennedy/CORBIS
Reindeer running, Finland ©James Proctor
Aurlandsfjord, Norway ©Gavin Hellier/Robert Harding

Briksdalsbreen Glacier, Norway ©Gavin
Hellier/Robert Harding
Stockholm archipelago, Sweden ©Luke
White/AXIOM
Abba ©Swedish Tourist Board

Things not to miss
01. Skagen, Denmark ©Bob Krist/CORBIS
02. Holmenkollen ski jump, Norway ©S.H &
D.H. Cavanaugh/Robert Harding
03. *The Scream* by Edvard Munch ©Burstein
Collection/CORBIS/DACS
04. Skåne, Sweden ©Neil Roland
05. Savonlinna Castle, Finland ©Ken
Gillham/Robert Harding
6. Sauna ©Robert Harding
07. Viking Ships Museum, Norway ©Michael
Jenner
08. Danish pastry ©DK Images
09. Ice hotel, Jukkasjarvi, Sweden ©Ian
Cook/AXIOM
10. Fürstenburg Gallery, Sweden
©Gotesborgs Konstmuseum
11. Århus old town, Denmark ©R. Powers/
TRIP
12. Mandal beach, Norway ©Phil Lee
13. Husky safari ©Finnish Tourist Board
14. Nimis, Sweden ©James Proctor
15. Vox Hall, Århus, Denmark ©Rikki Madsen
16. Jotunheimen National Park, Norway ©D.
Saunders/TRIP
17. Nyhavn, Denmark ©ML Sinibaldi/CORBIS
18. Santas for sale, Finland ©Michael Jenner
19. Flåmsbana railway, Norway ©R. Belbin/
TRIP
20. Grenen, Denmark ©Danish Tourist Board
21. Pickled herring and beer, Denmark
©K. Gillham/Robert Harding
22. Svalbard, Norway ©N. Price/TRIP
23. Aurora borealis ©Finnish Tourist Board
24. Tivoli Gardens fireworks, Copenhagen,
Denmark ©Neil Egerton/Travel Ink
25. Nordkapp, Norway ©Royalty-
Free/CORBIS

26. Kalmar castle, Sweden ©James Proctor
27. Alta rock carving, Norway ©Phil Lee
28. Vigeland Sculpture Park, Oslo, Sweden
©Michael Jenner
29. Gamla Stan at dusk, Stockholm, Sweden
©E. Simanor/Robert Harding
30. Inlandsbanan Railway ©Swedish Tourist
Board
31. Whale-watching, Norway ©Staffan
Widstrand/Nature Picture Library
32. Louisiana Museum of Modern Art,
Denmark ©Martin Llado

Black and white photos
Ny Carlsberg Glyptotek ©Martin Llado (p.50)
Sand dunes ©Danish Tourist Board (p.97)
Odense ©Adam Woolfitt/Robert Harding
(p.137)
Viking Ship Museum, Roskilde ©M. Feeney/
Robert Harding (p.180)
Trondheim Cathedral, Norway ©Rolf
Richardson/Robert Harding (p.186)
Stave church, Bygdoy, Norway ©Rolf
Richardson/Robert Harding (p.269)
Stavanger, Norway ©Gavin Hellier/Robert
Harding (p.305)
Viking carving, Urnes stave church, Norway
©Phil Lee (p.358)
Nimis, Kullen peninsula ©James Proctor
(p.402)
Stockholm skyline ©Ellen Rooney/Robert
Harding (p.467)
Gripsholm Castle ©Robert Harding (p.500)
Visby church ©Robert Harding (p.544)
Viking stone ship, Gotland ©Michael Jenner
(p.583)
Turku Castle, Finland ©G. Spenceley/TRIP
(p.652)
Cathedral, Senate Square, Finland ©Paul van
Riel/Robert Harding (p.701)
Porvoo, Finland ©K. Gillham/Robert Harding
(p.751)
Husky ©James Proctor (p.779)

Visit us online
roughguides.com

Information on over 25,000 destinations around the world

- **Read** Rough Guides' trusted travel info
- **Share** journals, photos and travel advice with other readers
- Get exclusive Rough Guide **discounts** and travel **deals**
- Earn membership points every time you contribute to the
  Rough Guide **community** and get **free** books, flights and trips
- Browse thousands of CD reviews and artists in our **music** area